GOVERNMENT ASSISTANCE ALMANAC
★2017★

GOVERNMENT ASSISTANCE ALMANAC
★2017★

The Guide to Federal Domestic Financial and Other Programs

Covering Grants, Loans, Insurance, Personal Payments and Benefits, Subsidies, Fellowships, Scholarships, Traineeships, Technical Information, Advisory Services, Investigation of Complaints, Sales and Donations of Federal Property — with Funding Summaries, over 4,000 Program Headquarters and Field Office Addresses and Phone Numbers, an Agency Index, and a Comprehensive Master Index

★24th EDITION★

OMNIGRAPHICS

155 W. Congress, Suite 200, Detroit, MI 48226
Phone (800) 234-1340 • www.omnigraphics.com

GOVERNMENT ASSISTANCE ALMANAC 2017:
The Guide to Federal Domestic Financial and Other Programs Covering Grants, Loans, Insurance, Personal Payments and Benefits, Subsidies, Fellowships, Scholarships, Traineeships, Technical Information, Advisory Services, Investigation of Complaints, Sales and Donations of Federal Property — with Funding Summaries, Over 4,000 Program Headquarters and Field Office Addresses and Phone Numbers, and a Comprehensive Master Index.

Co-published by:

Omnigraphics, Inc.
155 W. Congress St.
Suite 200
Detroit, Michigan 48226

Co-published by:

Foggy Bottom Publications
P.O. Box N-7776
Nassau, Bahamas

The Library of Congress has assigned the following International Standard Serial Number:

ISSN 0883-8690

International Standard Book Number:

ISBN 978-0-7808-1540-7

CONTENTS

DISCLAIMER/INVITATION

We have attempted to compile and present the information in this book accurately and in the most helpful form possible. The information is intended to provide basic guidance concerning programs and benefits available from the federal agencies cited.

Federal program policies, regulations, funding levels, addresses, and phone numbers tend to change. There could be unintentional errors in the information, caused by changes in government programs or organization, inaccuracies in the source material, omissions, or typographical or other inadvertent mistakes. A great deal of care was taken to avoid such errors.

The information in this publication was compiled from the sources cited and from other sources considered reliable. While every possible effort has been made to ensure reliability, the publisher and the editor will not assume liability for damages caused by inaccuracies in the data, and make no warranty, express or implied, on the accuracy of the information contained herein.

Users of *GOVERNMENT ASSISTANCE ALMANAC* are invited to send their observations about the book, its form, and their experience in referring to the information, to the editor at the address below. Suggestions for improvements in any aspect of the book will be especially appreciated.

Editor
GOVERNMENT ASSISTANCE ALMANAC
c/o Omnigraphics, Inc
155 W. Congress St.
Suite 200
Detroit, MI 48226

Abbreviations Used in This Book

ACF	Administration for Children and Families (HHS)
ADA	Americans with Disabilities Act
ADAA	Anti-Drug Abuse Act of 1988
AFDC	Aid to Families with Dependent Children
AIDS	acquired immunodeficiency syndrome
AMS	Agricultural Marketing Service (USDA)
AOA	Administration on Aging (HHS)
ARDA	Appalachian Regional Development Act of 1965
ARDRA	Appalachian Regional Development Reform Act of 1998
ARRA	American Recovery and Reinvestment Act of 2009
ARS	Agricultural Research Service (USDA)
ATEDPA	Anti-Terrorism and Effective Death Penalty Act of 1996
ATELS	Apprenticeship, Training, Employer and Labor Service (DOL)
ATF	Bureau of Alcohol, Tobacco and Firearms (DOJ)
AREERA	Agricultural Research, Extension, and Education Reform Act of 1998
BAT	Bureau of Apprenticeship and Training (DOL) *(Note: BAT functions now are in OATELS)*
BEA	Bureau of Export Administration (USDC) *(Note: BEA is now Bureau of Industry and Security*
BECA	Bureau of Educational and Cultural Affairs (Department of State)
BIA	Bureau of Indian Affairs (DOI)
BJA	Bureau of Justice Assistance (DOJ)
BLM	Bureau of Land Management (DOI)
BLS	Bureau of Labor Statistics (DOI)
BPRM	Bureau of Population, Refugees, and Migration (Department of State)
C of C	chamber of commerce
CAA	Clean Air Act
CARE	Comprehensive AIDS Resources Emergency
CBRNE	chemical, biological, radiological, nuclear, and explosive (devices)
CCC	Commodity Credit Corporation (USDA)
CDAPCA	Comprehensive Drug Abuse Prevention and Control Act of 1970
CDBG	Community Development Block Grant
CDCP	Centers for Disease Control and Prevention (HHS)

CDCU	Community Development Credit Union
CDPVTEA	Carl D. Perkins Vocational and Technical Education Act of 1998
CEPP	Chemical Emergency Preparedness and Prevention
CERCLA	Comprehensive Environmental Response, Compensation and Liability Act ("Superfund")
CERT	Council of Energy Resource Tribes
CFDA	Catalog of Federal Domestic Assistance
CFRDA	Consolidated Farm and Rural Development Act
CJAA	Childrens Justice and Assistance Act of 1986
CMHS	Center for Mental Health Services (SAMHSA-DHS)
CMS	Centers for Medicare and Medicaid Services (HHS) *(formerly, HCFA)*
CNCS	Corporation for National and Community Service
COATES	Community Opportunities, Accountability, Training, and Educational Services Act of 1998
CODIS	Combined DNA Index System
COPS	Community Oriented Policing Services
CPD	Community Planning and Development (HUD)
CRA	Civil Rights Act of 1964
CRIPA	Civil Rights of Institutionalized Persons Act
CRP	Conservation Reserve Program
CRS	Community Relations Service (DOJ)
CSAP	Center for Substance Abuse Prevention (SAHMSA-HHS)
CSAT	Center for Substance Abuse Treatment (SAHMSA-HHS)
CSBG	Community Services Block Grant
CSREES	Cooperative State Research, Education and Extension Service (USDA)
CWA	Clean Water Act
DC	District of Columbia
DEA	Drug Enforcement Administration (DOJ)
DHS	Department of Homeland Security
DIC	dependency and indemnity compensation
DOD	Department of Defense
DOE	Department of Energy
DOED	Department of Education
DOI	Department of the Interior
DOJ	Department of Justice
DOL	Department of Labor

DOT	Department of Transportation
DVA	Department of Veterans Affairs
EBS	Emergency Broadcast System
EBSA	Employee Benefits Security Administration (DOL)
ECOA	Equal Credit Opportunity Act
EDA	Economic Development Administration (USDC)
EEOC	Equal Employment Opportunity Commission
EFN	exceptional financial need
EHS	environmental health center
EIS	environmental impact statement
ELOA	Early Learning Opportunities Act of 2001
EMI	Emergency Management Institute (FEMA-DHS)
EMS	emergency medical services
EOC	emergency operating center
EPA	Environmental Protection Agency
ERDDIA	Educational Research, Development, Dissemination, and Improvement Act of 1994
ESA	Economics and Statistics Administration (USDA)
ESEA	Elementary and Secondary Education Act of 1965
ESL	English as a second language
EST	estimate
ETA	Employment and Training Administration (DOL)
FAA	Federal Aviation Administration (DOT)
FACE	Freedom of Access to Clinic Entrances Act
FACTA	Food, Agriculture, Conservation, and Trade Act of 1990
FAIRA	Federal Agriculture Improvement and Reform Act of 1996
FAS	Foreign Agricultural Service (USDA)
FCA	Flood Control Act
FCC	Federal Communications Commission
FCIC	Federal Crop Insurance Corporation (USDA)
FDA	Food and Drug Administration (HHS)
FEMA	Federal Emergency Management Agency (DHS)
FFB	Federal Financing Bank
FFP	federal financial participation
FHA	Federal Housing Administration (HUD)
FHAP	Fair Housing Assistance Program
FHIP	Fair Housing Initiatives Program
FHWA	Federal Highway Administration (DOT)
FIFRA	Federal Insecticide, Fungicide, and Rodenticide Act
FIP	Forestry Incentives Program

FLAS	foreign language and area studies
FMCS	Federal Mediation and Conciliation Service
FMCSA	Federal Motor Carrier Safety Administration (DOT)
FmHA	Farmers Home Administration (USDA) *(Note: FmHA functions now are within FSA and RHS)*
FNS	Food and Nutrition Service (USDA)
FRA	Fund for Rural America
FS	Forest Service (USDA)
FSRIA	Farm Security and Rural Investment Act of 2002
FSA	Farm Service Agency (USDA)
FTA	Federal Transit Administration (DOT)
FTC	Federal Trade Commission
FTZ	foreign trade zone
FY	Fiscal Year *(Federal fiscal year: October 1 through September 30)*
FWS	U.S. Fish and Wildlife Service (DOI)
GAA	Government Assistance Almanac
GPO	U.S. Government Printing Office
GSA	General Services Administration
HBCU	Historically Black College and University
HCFA	Health Care Financing Administration (HHS) *(Note: HCFA functions now are within CMS)*
HEA	Higher Education Act of 1965
HEAL	Health Education Assistance Loan
HHS	Department of Health and Human Services
HIP	Housing Improvement Program (BIA)
HIV	human immunodeficiency virus
HMO	health maintenance organization
HOPE	Housing Opportunities for People Everywhere
HPEPA	Health Professions Education Partnership Act of 1998
HQ	headquarters
HRSA	Health Resources and Services Administration (HHS)
HSA	health system agency
HUD	Department of Housing and Urban Development
IBDC	Indian business development center
ICE	Immigration and Customs Enforcement (DHS) *(formerly,)* INS)
IDEA	Individuals with Disabilities Education Act
IHE	institution of higher education
IHS	Indian Health Service (DHS)
IMLS	Institute of Museum and Library Services

INS	Immigration and Naturalization Service (DHS) (*Now, ICE*)
IRS	Internal Revenue Service
ISDEAA	Indian Self-Determination and Education Assistance Act
ITA	International Trade Administration (USDC)
JJDPA	Juvenile Justice and Delinquency Prevention Act
JTPA	Job Training Partnership Act of 1982
LC	Library of Congress
LEA	local education agency
LSCA	Library Services and Construction Act
MARC	minority access to research careers
MB&IA	minority business and industry association
MBDA	Minority Business Development Agency (USDC)
MBDC	minority business development center
MBE	minority business enterprise
MECEA	Mutual Educational and Cultural Exchange Act of 1961
MFB	marine and freshwater biology
MIA	missing in action
MIP	mortgage insurance premium
MMA	Medicare Modernization Act (i.e. , Medicare Prescription Drug, Improvement and Modernization Act of 2003)
MMA	Merchant Marine Act
MPRSA	Marine Protection, Research, and Sanctuaries Act
MRA	Migration and Refugee Assistance Act of 1962
MSA	Metropolitan Statistical Area
MSLA	Museum and Library Services Act of 1996
MVHAA	McKinney-Vento Homeless Assistance Act
N.A.	not available, or not applicable
NAFSA	National Association of Foreign Student Advising Associations
NAHASDA	Native American Housing Assistance and Self-Determination Act of 1996
NARETPA	National Agricultural Research, Extension, and Teaching Policy Act of 1977
NASA	National Aeronautics and Space Administration
NASS	National Agricultural Statistics Service (USDA)
NBS	National Bureau of Standards (USDC) (*Note: as of 1988, NBS became NIST*)
NBSOA	National Bureau of Standards Organic Act

NCIC	National Crime Information Center
NCRR	National Center for Research Resources(HHS)
NCSA	National Community Service Act
NCSCI	National Center for Standards and Certification Information
NCUA	National Credit Union Administration
NEA	National Endowment for the Arts
NEH	National Endowment for the Humanities
NEIC	National Energy Information Center
NESDIS	National Environmental Satellite, Data, and Information Service
NFAHA	National Foundation on the Arts and Humanities Act of 1965
NFIP	National Flood Insurance Program
NHA	National Housing Act of 1934
NHSC	National Health Service Corps (HHS)
NIAAA	National Institute on Alcohol and Abuse and Alcoholism (HHS)
NIDA	National Institute on Drug Abuse (HHS)
NIEHS	National Institute of Environmental Health Sciences (HHS)
NIH	National Institutes of Health (HHS)
NIMH	National Institute of Mental Health (HHS)
NINDS	National Institute of Neurological Disorders and Stroke (HHS)
NIOSH	National Institute for Occupational Safety and Health (HHS)
NIS	New Independent States (of the former Soviet Union)
NIST	National Institute for Standards and Technology (USDC)
NLRB	National Labor Relations Board
NMFS	National Marine Fisheries Service (USDC)
NOAA	National Oceanic and Atmospheric Administration (USDC)
NOS	National Ocean Service (USDC)
NPS	National Park Service (DOI)
NRC	Nuclear Regulatory Commission
NRCS	Natural Resources Conservation Service (USDA)
NRSA	National Research Service Award
NSA	National Security Agency (DOD)
NSEP	National Security Education Program

NSF	National Science Foundation
NSFA	National Science Foundation Act of 1950
NSRDS	National Standard Reference Data System
NTIA	National Telecommunications and Information Administration (USDC)
NTIS	National Technical Information Service (USDC)
NWS	National Weather Service (NOAA-USDC)
OAA	Older Americans Act of 1965
OAR	Office of Air and Radiation (EPA)
OATELS	Office of Apprenticeship, Training, Employer and Labor Service (DOL)
OCCSSA	Omnibus Crime Control and Safe Streets Act
OCSE	Office of Child Support Enforcement
OEA	Office of Export Administration (USDC)
OECA	Office of Enforcement and Compliance Assurance (EPA)
OEERE	Office of Energy Efficiency and Renewable Energy (DOE)
OERI	Office of Educational Research and Improvement (DOED)
OESE	Office of Elementary and Secondary Education (DOED)
OFCCP	Office of Federal Contract Compliance Programs
OFHEO	Office of Fair Housing and Equal Opportunity (HUD)
OFSA	Office of Federal Student Aid (DOED)
OJJDP	Office of Juvenile Justice and Delinquency Prevention (DOJ)
OJP	Office of Justice Programs (DOJ)
OMB	Office of Management and Budget
OPDR	Office of Policy Development and Research (HUD)
OPE	Office of Postsecondary Education (DOED)
OPIC	Overseas Private Investment Corporation
OPM	Office of Personnel Management
OPPPTS	Office of Pollution Prevention, Pesticides, and Toxic Substances (EPA)
OS	Office of the Secretary
OSERS	Office of Special Education and Rehabilitative Services (DOED)
OSHA	Occupational Safety and Health Administration (DOL)
OSTI	Office of Scientific and Technical Information (USDC)
OSWER	Office of Solid Waste and Emergency Response (EPA)

OTAA	Office of Trade Adjustment Assistance
OVAE	Office of Vocational and Adult Education (DOED)
OW	Office of Water (EPA)
OWOW	Office of Wetlands, Oceans, and Watersheds (EPA)
PACA	Perishable Agricultural Commodities Act
PD&R	Office of Policy Development and Research (HUD)
PHPEPA	Public Health Professions Education Partnership Act of 1998
PHS	Public Health Service (HHS)
PHSA	Public Health Service Act
PIK	payment-in-kind
PL	Public Law
PPACA	Patient Protection and Affordable Care Act
PR	Puerto Rico
PRM	Population, Refugees, and Migration *(Bureau of)* (Department of State)
PRNS	projects of regional and national significance
PRWORA	Personal Responsibility and Work Opportunity Reconciliation Act of 1996
PWBA	Pension and Welfare Benefits Administration (DOL) *(Note: PWBA is now EBSA)*
PWEDA	Public Works and Economic Development Act of 1965
R&D	research and development
RBCS	Rural Business-Cooperative Service (USDA)
RC&D	resource conservation and development
RCRA	Resource Conservation and Recovery Act
REA	Rural Electrification Act of 1936
REA	Rural Electrification Administration (USDA) *(Note: REA functions now are within RUS)*
REACH	Racial and Ethnic Approaches to Community Health
RHA	River and Harbor Act
RHS	Rural Housing Service (USDA)
RLUIPA	Religious Land Use and Institutionalized Persons Act
RMA	Research and Marketing Act of 1946
RMA	Risk Management Agency (USDA)
RSVP	Retired and Senior Volunteer Program
RUS	Rural Utilities Service (USDA)
SAMHSA	Substance Abuse and Mental Health Services Administration (HHS)
SARA	Superfund Amendments and Reauthorization Act
SBA	Small Business Administration

SBIC	Small Business Investment Center
SBIR	small business innovation research
SBIRPRA	Small Business Innovation Research Program Reauthorization Act of 1992
SBMHAA	Stewart B. McKinney Homeless Assistance Act of 1987
SBRDEA	Small Business Research and Development Enhancement Act of 1992
SCORE	Service Corps of Retired Executives (SBA)
SCS	Soil Conservation Service (USDA) *(Note: SCS functions now are within NRCS)*
SDWA	Safe Drinking Water Act
SEA	state education agency
SEOG	supplemental educational opportunity grant
SEPA	Science Education Partnership Award
SERCA	Special Emphasis Research Center Award
SESA	state employment security agency
SIG	shared instrumentation grant
SMSA	Standard Metropolitan Statistical Area
SPRANS	special projects of regional and national significance
SRM	Standard Reference Materials
SRO	single room occupancy
SSA	Social Security Act of 1935
SSA	Social Security Administration
SSBG	Social Services Block Grant
SSBIC	Specialized Small Business Investment Center
SSI	Supplemental Security Income
STORET	storage and retrieval
STTR	Small Business Technology Transfer
SWDA	Solid Waste Disposal Act
TANF	Temporary Assistance to Needy Families
TDD	telecommunications devices for the deaf
TDHE	Tribally-Designated Housing Authority
TERO	Tribal Employment Rights Office
TRIO	three—i.e. , not an abbreviation *(Per DOED, when the "TRIO" programs began in the Division of Student Services, Office of Postsecondary Education, three programs were established; the original nomenclature has remained.)*
TSA	Transportation Security Administration (DHS)
TSCA	Toxic Substances Control Act

TVA	Tennessee Valley Authority *(Note: TVA programs were deleted from the CFDA in 2001)*
USAID	United States Agency for International Development
USAPA	U.S.A. Patriot Act of 2001 *(officially,* Uniting and Strengthening America by Providing Appropriate Tools Required to Intercept and Obstruct Terrorism Act of 2001)
U.S.C.	United States Code
USCG	U.S. Coast Guard (DHS)
USDA	U.S. Department of Agriculture
USDC	U.S. Department of Commerce
USDOD	U.S. Department of Defense
USFS	U.S. Forest Service (USDA)
USGPO	U.S. Government Printing Office
USGS	U.S. Geological Survey (DOI)
USIA	U.S. Information Agency *(Note: USIA no longer exists; its functions now are in BECA)*
USIP	U.S. Institute of Peace
USIS	U.S. Information Service
VA	Veterans Administration *(Note: as of 1989, VA became DVA)*
VAWA	Violence Against Women Act of 2000
VCCLEA	Violent Crime Control and Law Enforcement Act
VI	Virgin Islands (U.S.)
VISTA	Volunteers in Service to America
VOCA	Victims of Crime Act
VTVPA	Victims of Trafficking and Violence Prevention Act of 2000
WIA	Workforce Investment Act of 1998
WIC	Women, Infants, and Children
WIN	Work Incentive Program
WMD	weapons of mass destruction *(including nuclear, biological, chemical, and explosive)*

PART I

Obtaining
Federal Assistance

What This Book Gives You

GOVERNMENT ASSISTANCE ALMANAC has two purposes: (1) to provide information enabling users to identify *all domestic programs offering financial or nonfinancial assistance available from federal agencies*; (2) to help users reach the point of obtaining assistance.

This twenty-fourth edition describes 2,013 federal programs. The information presented is based on data in the *Catalog of Federal Domestic Assistance* ("CFDA"), maintained by the General Services Administration pursuant to federal statute.

The *ALMANAC* reduces the information in the CFDA's over 3,200 pages to the essentials needed by most persons seeking federal assistance. Modifications in the presentation of the information, especially the *ALMANAC*'s indexes, enable users to identify available programs and their features more efficiently.

PART I provides *basic guidance on using this book* to identify and obtain available assistance. The guidelines are intended for newcomers to federal programs; more experienced users of similar information may find some helpful reminders.

PART II outlines *domestic financial and other assistance programs available per the CFDA as of July, 2016*. When available the following is provided for each program:

*   federal program number and title; popular title when applicable;
*   types of assistance available;
*   description of objectives, permitted uses of funds, and project examples when they clarify program purposes; enacting legislation is noted to help define program purposes;
*   eligibility factors concerning both applicants and beneficiaries;

- range and average amounts awarded through programs providing financial assistance;
- summary of recent activity;
- mailing address, phone number, and web site for program headquarters, and other referrals when applicable.

PART III provides tables showing *funding levels for all programs and administering agencies* for the last *four fiscal years*. To our knowledge such comprehensive tables showing allocations specifically for federal domestic programs are exclusive to the *ALMANAC*. Table 1 also serves as a *listing of the programs in the numerical sequence* in which they appear in PART II.

PART IV provides *addresses and phone numbers for more than 3,000 field offices*, organized to correspond with the program numbers within their purview. This system was established specifically for users of the *ALMANAC*; like the tables, this system exists nowhere else.

The **AGENCY INDEX** provides an *alphabetical listing of federal administrative units and sub-units*, including the program numbers within their purview. (The CFDA does not provide an alphabetical listing.) While administrative units also are incorporated within the MASTER INDEX, the AGENCY INDEX may expedite user searches specifically for these entities.

ALMANAC users will find the **MASTER INDEX** unique and exhaustive, particularly its subject headings, references, and cross-references. This index identifies all available federal domestic assistance programs. It also includes: administrative units and cross-references to sub-units; official and popular program titles; abbreviated program, agency, and other titles and terms; many enabling laws and their section and title numbers; and, general program references not found in other indexes of government assistance. The format enables users to distinguish programs providing financial assistance from those that do not, through the use of italicized program numbers. The copyright for *GOVERNMENT ASSISTANCE ALMANAC* makes its index an exclusive feature.

The list of **Abbreviations Used in This Book** preceding this section does not appear in the CFDA.

By definition, "domestic programs" do not necessarily include assistance available through ongoing government activities—e.g., operation of federal facilities and services, public information activities, enforcement of many federal laws and regulations, or products or services obtained through contractors, etc. The section entitled "Types of Federal Assistance Available," beginning below, explains what assistance is and is not covered.

Encountering the information in this book for the first time, some will be surprised by the scope of available federal assistance, which may seem very broad or rather meager in many areas. The assistance is available subject to program eligibility criteria, discussed under "Who May Obtain Federal Assistance?"

Timeliness of the Information

The twenty-thid edition of the *ALMANAC* identified 1,981 federal programs. Since the publication of that edition 71 programs were added and 39 were deleted, producing the present total of 2,013 as of July, 2016; this twenty-fourth edition incorporates the new programs, as well as many program changes.

Federal programs rarely are terminated unless similar assistance is available through another program; this book helps identify those other programs. There has been an almost steady increase in the total number of domestic programs since the mid-1980s, from 989 programs in 1984 to 2,013 programs in 2016.

Currently some 65 departments, commissions, agencies, bureaus, and other federal entities administer the assistance programs. They manage the programs either through their main offices, through 170 "administrative sub-units," or through approximately 3,000 field offices.

Regarding the reliability of addresses and phone numbers, generally, ten to twelve percent of phone numbers and five to seven percent of office addresses change in the course of a year, based on federal directories studied. It can reasonably be expected that few changes in program contact information will be encountered.

Changes are inevitable in program application requirements, governmental organization, and addresses and phone numbers. Keeping abreast of all changes would require a daily compilation, such as is provided in the *Federal Register*. However, most substantive program changes affect the details of regulations, seldom affecting the factors included in the *ALMANAC*'s program entries; in pursuing programs with federal officials, inquirers will be advised of major changes.

Types of Federal Assistance Available

Fifteen types of federal domestic assistance are available through existing programs, providing financial or nonfinancial resources. Programs that provide *financial assistance* are classified as:

- *Direct loans*—offering the loan of federal funds for a specific term, with or without interest, with repayment expected. Example: FSA's

"Emergency Loans" program provides USDA loans directly to farmers and others (see **10.404**).

- *Direct payments/specified use*—providing funds for a specified purpose, with no repayment expected. Example: "Payments for Essential Air Services" to air carriers by DOT (see **20.901**).

- *Direct payments/unrestricted use*—providing federal funds for use at will by the recipient, with no repayment expected. Example: "Social Security—Retirement Insurance," administered by SSA (see **96.002**). Programs in this classification may be known as "entitlements."

- *Formula grants*—through which federal funds are distributed to states or other recipients according to a formula (often based on population), for continuing activities not confined to a specific project. No repayment is expected. Example: DOED's "Adult Education—State Grant Program" (see **84.002**). Programs in this classification also may be known as "entitlements."

- *Guaranteed/insured loans*—offering private or public lending institutions a guarantee or insurance against loan defaults, covering all or a portion of the amount borrowed. Example: HUD's "Mortgage Insurance—Homes" program (see **14.117**).

- *Insurance*—assuring reimbursement for losses under specified conditions. Insurance coverage may be provided directly by a federal agency or through a private company, depending on specific program provisions. Example: "Foreign Investment Insurance," administered by OPIC (see **70.003**). Some programs also provide for federal payment of a portion of insurance premiums. Example: USDA's "Crop Insurance" program (see **10.450**).

- *Project grants*—awarding federal funds for specific projects, services, products, or other activities such as scholarships, construction, research, planning, technical assistance. Some project grants cover cooperative agreement arrangements with state governments or other organizations to assist the federal granting agency in the performance of a certain function. No repayment is expected. Project grants do not necessarily cover 100 percent of project costs. Example: NSF's "Geosciences" program (see **47.050**).

The classifications of programs providing *nonfinancial assistance* are:

- *Advisory services/counseling*—through which federal specialists provide consultation, advice, or other assistance—delivered through conferences, workshops, personal contacts, or published information. Example: USDA-NRCS's "Soil and Water Conservation" program (see **10.902**).

- *Federal employment*—offering jobs with the federal government through the activities of OPM in recruiting and hiring civilian personnel. Example: "Federal Summer Employment" (see **27.006**). Note that only OPM programs provide federal employment as structured programs; the ongoing recruitment activities of other federal agencies are not classified as "domestic programs."

- *Investigation of complaints*—through which federal agencies examine or investigate claims of violations of federal laws, policies, or regulatory procedures. The claim must originate outside the federal government. Example: "Shipping—Dispute Resolution and Investigation of Complaints," conducted by the Federal Maritime Commission (see **33.001**).

- *Sale, exchange, or donation of property and goods*—featuring the transfer of federally-owned real estate or personal property, commodities, and other goods including equipment, food, drugs, or supplies. Example: "Disposal of Federal Surplus Real Property," administered by GSA (**39.002**).

- *Specialized services*—providing federal personnel to perform certain services for communities, individuals, or others. Example: "Planning Assistance to States," administered by the DOD-Corps of Engineers (**12.110**). *(Note that several Corps of Engineers programs provide specialized services involving construction activities; however, these programs are not classified as providing financial assistance, and a portion of total costs for such projects usually must be matched locally.)*

- *Technical information*—through which technical information is prepared, published, and distributed—often through clearinghouses, libraries, centers, or through electronic media. Example: USDC-NIST's "Standard Reference Materials" (see **11.604**).

- *Training*—offering federal agency instruction to persons not employed by the federal government. Example: DHS-FEMA's "Emergency Management Institute (EMI)—Resident Educational Program" (see **97.028**).

- *Use of property, facilities, and equipment*—providing for the temporary use of or access to federally-owned resources, with or without charge to the user. Example: "National Gallery of Art Extension Service" (see **68.001**).

Not included as a classification, but reflected in the list and included, are "block grants" which may be used for a range of related activities. Block grants usually are awarded as "formula grants" or "project grants." Their permitted uses generally are more flexible than other types of programs. Such programs are cited in the index under the subject heading "Block grant programs."

Many programs offer more than one type of assistance; for example, the second program listed in PART II, **10.025**, offers project grants as well as specialized services, advisory services/counseling, technical information, and training.

The following types of government activities are not defined as domestic programs; they are *not included*:

- *Procurement contracts* for the purchase of goods and services by the federal government. For instance, basic DOD contracting activities do not meet the definition of domestic programs; however, DOD administers several programs classified as providing "domestic assistance." Programs offering assistance to firms wanting to do business with the federal government through its procurement contracts *are included*.

- *U.S. government foreign activities* without a direct benefit in the domestic economy. For instance, most Department of State activities are not classified as domestic programs; however, the state department also administers several domestic programs; and, the federal government sponsors several programs pertaining to importing and exporting—which *are included*.

- *Employee recruitment programs* of individual federal departments and agencies.

- *Programs benefiting only current or retired military personnel or federal employees*. However, all DVA benefit programs *are included*— although many DVA programs are not classified as providing financial assistance.

- *Ongoing public information services* of federal entities.

- *Basic domestic functions of the federal government* such as operation and maintenance of services and facilities, collection of taxes, enforcement of federal laws and regulations, judicial processes, etc.

Also not included are various tax incentives offered through the Internal Revenue Code, which are not classified as federal programs. These include so-called tax shelters, tax credits, writeoffs, and the like. Such government benefits to private taxpayers have stimulated activity in the domestic economy in recent years. Their features are the subject of other books dealing with taxes, finance, investment, etc.

Frequently, however, such "non-programs" relate directly to certain structured domestic programs which *are included* in this book. Examples: program **15.904**, "Historic Preservation Fund Grants-in-Aid," can be used to obtain accelerated depreciation of the value of improvements for tax purposes; program **20.812**, "Construction Reserve Fund," relating to merchant vessels, offers tax incentives to participants.

Resources for the Resourceful

GOVERNMENT ASSISTANCE ALMANAC may reveal previously unknown resources available to various types of users—farmers, students, small businesses, investors, entrepreneurs, homemakers, scientists, the elderly, parents, journalists, civic and social organizations, health professionals, guidance counselors, scholars, state and municipal governments, educators, artists and arts sponsors, members of minority groups, veterans and their dependents, community improvement groups, researchers, and others including those interested in the needs of the foregoing groups, as well as persons planning to enter those fields. They may find programs that offer technical information, services, training, or other types of assistance that they did not know existed.

The simplest assistance programs are those meeting a single purpose. For instance, someone seeking resources for an elderly person whose home needs repairs will find that the index cites a number of programs that could provide help. Selecting the most appropriate of the available programs is a matter of finding the programs in the index, carefully reading the program entries in PART II, and pursuing the most promising. The section entitled "Obtaining Federal Assistance: How to Use PART II,", provides guidance along these lines.

Frequently, assistance will be found for elderly persons with several needs. For instance, in addition to programs providing loan or grant funds to repair property, subsidies are available to help pay fuel bills—even the cost of air conditioning under certain conditions. Also available are programs through which older persons might obtain part-time employment, or meals, or help with home management tasks; dependents of deceased veterans may be entitled to pensions, health care, and burial expenses and grave markers for the deceased veteran.

Seeking federal assistance becomes more challenging when two or more programs are combined to meet more complex needs. For instance, someone interested in obtaining mortgage insurance on a loan covering a multi-unit housing structure in an older declining area through **14.123** may decide to also pursue the rental subsidies available to tenants through **14.871**.

Resourcefulness often is the key to obtaining federal assistance. The successful outcome of use of available assistance is illustrated across the country, in virtually all fields—from child care to environmental enhancement to job creation to the performing arts to scientific research.

Often, those who have successfully applied for public resources are eager to show what they did and how they went about it. Their experience could save prospective applicants countless hours of trial and error. Federal officials also may provide guidance in learning how to use federal programs effectively; their perspective can be unique, an important resource to tap.

The challenge may increase when federal assistance is channeled through a state, municipal, or private organization. The next section, "Who May Obtain Federal Assistance?" addresses the situation. In such instances, the application *process* is usually similar to making federal office contacts. However, the competition for funds help could be stiffer. The award process could be more complicated, requiring a good deal of groundwork at the community level to obtain the assistance. An applicant's resourcefulness usually pays off, just as with federal contacts.

Who May Obtain Federal Assistance?

Eligibility depends on the specific program.

Assistance through many programs is available to the general public—e.g., use of the national libraries, technical information, and similar facilities and services.

Some programs, because of laws or regulations governing their administration, offer assistance only to certain categories of *applicants*—e.g., farmers, states, small businesses, native Americans. Only specified categories of prospective recipients may *apply*.

Other programs may directly *benefit* only certain industries—e.g., shipbuilding or agriculture, or certain population groups such as the elderly, or teenagers, or immigrants from specific countries.

Under still other federal programs, eligible applicants and beneficiaries are the same. Examples include certain veterans, small business, and student programs.

The distinction between programs offering assistance specifically to eligible applicants, eligible beneficiaries, and eligible applicants/beneficiaries is clear in the program entries presented in PART II.

The point to be understood is that the distinction between eligible applicants and eligible beneficiaries is very important to those seeking assistance. Many deserving persons have not obtained assistance to which they were entitled because this distinction was not understood. Being ineligible to *apply* to a federal agency for assistance under certain programs does not necessarily mean that one cannot *benefit* from those programs. The following actual example illustrates the point.

"The Case of the Muffin Machine"

Some years ago, a baker in a small city used his savings to establish a franchised doughnut business. The city was economically depressed; it managed to obtain relatively large sums of federal money for economic development from several federal agencies.

In a relatively short time after starting, the business did well enough for the owner to meet expenses while employing eleven persons, mostly waiters and waitresses for its 24-hour operation.

The owner was notified by the franchise company of a new product, muffins, that was boosting other franchise owners' sales and profits substantially in market test areas. The franchise company offered an $11,000 package that would include the necessary equipment to begin making and selling muffins. The owner's assets were tied up in the business and in keeping it solvent. So, he applied to a bank for an $11,000 loan to finance purchase of the package. The bank told the owner that it would lend him only $5,500 toward the purchase. The owner did not have the $5,500 balance that he needed, nor would any other bank lend him more because his assets were heavily mortgaged.

Meanwhile, the city's success in obtaining federal funds to help in the creation of new jobs was publicized in the local media. The owner phoned the Department of Housing and Urban Development's nearest office for information about obtaining the funds, because he had heard that HUD was the source of much of the money received by the city. Unfortunately, whoever answered the phone at HUD told the owner that only the city could receive that type of funds from HUD.

Several weeks passed before the owner "badmouthed" the HUD program to the right customer. The customer happened to be another small business owner who had obtained some of the HUD funds to finance the expansion of his business. The customer told the owner whom to contact *locally* to apply for funds. Following a short meeting with an official in the city's economic development organization, the baker-owner had an entirely different attitude toward the program he had been complaining about.

Three weeks later, financing had been arranged to purchase the "muffin machine." The bank loaned the small businessman $5,500 at its commercial interest rate. From the city's funds received from HUD, he obtained $4,400 at 5 percent interest. And, he scraped up the remaining $1,100, or 10 percent of the total investment, on his own. One full-time job and two part-time jobs resulted from this loan.

In this particular program (**14.228**) only small cities may *apply* for the available project grants, which may be used for quite a broad range of activities, including revolving loan funds with interest rates established locally. However, as an *eligible beneficiary* of the program the small business owner was able to obtain the assistance; the city accomplished its objectives of creating jobs and "leveraging" private funds through its economic development efforts; and, most important perhaps, three persons received jobs generated by the program.

The importance of this example to persons seeking federal assistance is the distinction between eligible *applicants* and eligible *beneficiaries*. If only certain types of applicants may apply for a program and you are not eligible, but you are eligible to *benefit*—say, under a training program— find out who has obtained funds and apply there for the training. If it cannot be established who has received funds by contacting organizations at the community level, contact the appropriate federal field office listed in PART IV of this book; if there is no field office, contact the program headquarters listed in PART II.

Organization of the Federal Programs in This Book

PART II of *GOVERNMENT ASSISTANCE ALMANAC* uses the same numerical system of listing federal programs followed in the CFDA. The system is not totally logical, in that the programs are not listed alphabetically, functionally, or by type of assistance. They are organized according to their administering department or agency; this makes this book's MASTER INDEX especially useful in identifying available assistance.

Each program is identified by a five-digit number. The first two digits identify the administrative entity responsible for the program. The last three digits identify the administrative sub-unit, if any, and the program. For example, the programs described in PART II, illustrate the numerical system:

DEPARTMENT OF COMMERCE

This administrative entity has responsibility for all programs that begin with the digits "**11**."

BUREAU OF THE CENSUS

This administrative sub-unit of the Department of Commerce has management responsibility for the programs outlined. **11.001** through **11.006** are the numbers identifying programs managed by the U.S. Census Bureau.

All programs with "**12**" as their first two digits, are administered by the Department of Defense. The system continues throughout PART II and PART III, as well as PART IV which provides field contact information.

PART III. Program Funding Levels—Summary Tables lists the departments, agencies, commissions, and other governmental entities in the order in which they are presented in PART II.

Note, however, that PARTS II and III provide headings for administrative sub-units only when the sub-unit's program series is uninterrupted in the CFDA. The *ALMANAC*'s AGENCY INDEX lists all administrative units and sub-units alphabetically, and it includes the program numbers within their respective purviews.

(The numerical system originated in the 1960s when the first edition of the *Catalog of Federal Domestic Assistance* was published. It was organized alphabetically by the name of the administering agency. Many numbers were not used, to allow for inclusion of new programs. Through the years, new agencies and programs were established and existing ones were terminated. The new agencies were added to the end of the list, to avoid changing the numerical sequence within the numbering system. Program numbers for terminated agencies or programs were removed altogether, and reserved in case they are reinstated eventually.)

Red Tape—Should You Hire a Consultant?

Federal laws, regulations, statutory provisions, policies, forms, criteria, procedures, processes, standards, deadlines, audits, certifications, documentation, appeals, authorizations, records, credentials, formulas, obligations, guidelines—these terms and many others signify the "red tape" of federal programs.

The terms form an important part of the language used in administering federal programs. Expect to encounter the language in seeking federal assistance. Depending on the program pursued, none, some, or all of the terms may be encountered.

The following general principles concerning "red tape" are understood by persons experienced in applying for federal assistance.

1. *Programs involving financial benefits in any form involve more red tape than other types of assistance.*

2. *The more persons served by a given program, the less red tape to the beneficiaries.* For example, applicants for basic Social Security benefits must produce certain information to enable federal officials to verify their eligibility and to calculate their benefits. Because millions of persons participate in the Social Security program, red tape has been minimized and usually is simple enough to overcome.

3. *Programs providing for one-on-one contacts between federal officials and applicants usually involve less red tape.* Examples: persons applying for some types of farming assistance or fellowships, training, veterans benefits, and similar assistance. In such cases, the applicant/ beneficiary usually can easily arrange to provide the required information.

4. *Programs with relatively few participants nationwide and with large benefit amounts involve extensive lengths of red tape.* Examples: programs addressing the problem of toxic waste; multi-year intensive research projects; financial assistance programs based on the recipient's promise to perform certain tasks, such as construction projects involving federal mortgage insurance.

5. *Programs with several parties to an application for assistance involve increased red tape.* For example, a housing developer applying for a mortgage guaranty on apartments to receive rental subsidies will be required to produce documents from a lender, attorneys, architects, housing management experts, local housing officials, and others—with each party needing to satisfy various requirements. Such applications must be "packaged" into a single application. Moreover, the approval process requires "sign-off" (i.e., approval) by several officials both outside and within the administering federal agency.

6. *Programs that provide federal assistance to beneficiaries through non-federal offices may or may not have added red tape.* The five preceding principles apply. Examples: information about drug abuse might be obtained easily through a federally-funded state agency, but obtaining federal funds through the same state agency to establish a local drug

abuse program could be more difficult than dealing with a federal office because of complex state requirements *in addition to* federal requirements; a student applying to a college financial aid office for federal educational assistance could have to meet federal, state, *and* the institution's requirements.

For most programs, paid consultants are not needed to apply for federal assistance. Generally, the official receiving the application will guide applicants in meeting requirements. Many programs require that applications be submitted through public administering agencies, private organizations, banks, or similar entities. Personnel in these organizations might well be considered the "consultant" or advocate for the application.

Programs involving complicated applications may require expert assistance to assure favorable action by the funding agency. Applicants without the time or patience to learn about and fulfill all requirements may find it advantageous to hire an experienced consultant.

In selecting a consultant, verify his or her credentials, experience, and record in obtaining federal assistance *of the type to be sought*. Check with the consultant's other clients and with federal offices to confirm that the qualifications are pertinent to the specific program. A consultant's impressive background in one field or with one federal agency is not necessarily a recommendation in another field or with a different federal agency. Most federal offices will provide advice about the need for a consultant's help in applying for given programs.

Keep the red tape in perspective. Try to understand its necessity. Federal requirements are intended to assure the proper use of federal funds. Virtually everyone agrees that many federal programs involve excessive red tape. Separate complaints and constructive recommendations about program requirements from the application process.

Obtaining Federal Assistance: How to Use PART II

Identifying and obtaining federal assistance is a reasonably straightforward process when one proceeds carefully and resourcefully. The previous section commented generally on the most complicated part of the process: the requirements that must be met to obtain assistance from the federal government. Complications can be minimal if a few basic steps are followed.

STEP ONE: USE THE MASTER INDEX

Thumb through the MASTER INDEX at the end of this book. Each program appears in the index an average of ten times. Together with the cross-references, the index assures that users will be able to identify *all* available assistance programs. Become familiar with the types of headings, sub-headings, and cross references. The index presents:

- subjects (shown in bold face);
- official program titles (in capital letters); bracketed agency identifiers are added to program titles to clarify the federal agency involved in cases where the program title alone is indistinct;
- popular titles of programs;
- miscellaneous (abbreviations, agency names, names of Acts, etc.).

The numbers following the headings refer to the program numbers in PART II where they appear in the left column. *Indexed programs that offer financial assistance are italicized, distinguishing them from programs that do not,* to further assist users in quickly identifying programs most pertinent to their needs.

Finding programs by title, popular name, abbreviation, or administrative entity is a simple procedure of looking in the index alphabetically, and then turning to PART II where the program descriptions are presented in numerical order. The introductory notes preceding the MASTER INDEX may prove useful.

Finding programs by subject involves looking for a main term and then scanning the indented entries under it. Generally, programs *intended* for the benefit of certain groups of people, such as women, youth, Indians, the disadvantaged, the disabled or handicapped, etc., are indexed directly under the common name of the group. Many programs are available to group members even though not targeted primarily for them. For example, programs relating to housing for Indians will be found under "Indian housing;" however, programs listed under the more general headings beginning with "Housing"—such as "Housing, rental" or "Housing, construction"— may also be applicable. To ascertain that every possible available program has been identified, both approaches should be followed.

The MASTER INDEX also includes section and title numbers of certain Acts, as well as the names of the Acts themselves. So if an *ALMANAC* user is interested in "section 109," for example, but does not know or cannot remember the exact name of the Act, in looking under "Section" numerous section numbers will be found with their corresponding program numbers.

Finding programs by administrative entity, such as "Department of Labor," can be done through the MASTER INDEX for all agencies. Or, the AGENCY INDEX might be consulted instead. The AGENCY INDEX also shows programs administered by sub-units. "PART III. Program

Funding Levels—Summary Tables" gives the names of all the agencies, arranged by government department, in the order in which the programs are presented in PARTS II and IV.

For other programs, the recommended procedure is to check first under the specific term, and then under more general terms. "*See*" and "*see also*" references have been used liberally to direct searches. For example, under "Aquaculture" a "*see also*" reference suggests looking under such other headings as "Farm, nonfarm enterprises," "Fish," and "Fisheries industry" for more entries of possible interest.

Or, if a scholarship to attend podiatry school is sought, users should look first under "Podiatry" where one or more programs will be found; but the *see also* reference directs users to "Health professions" where more general programs will be found that may be of interest; users also will be referred to "Fellowships, scholarships, traineeships" for still other related programs.

The index includes some terms indicating permitted uses of programs, which may not be mentioned in the program entry. These terms are included in the index for programs where it is known that program funds possibly may be used for activities embodied in the indexed term. "Block grant" programs frequently are indexed in this manner.

Often, more than one program will be found providing assistance under a given heading. Read all program entries in PART II carefully, and pursue the most pertinent.

After perusing the index, if no reference is found to a program providing assistance for a specific purpose, it is almost certain that such federal assistance is unavailable. There is one more step that might be taken: contact the federal office most apt to know about assistance available for specific purposes. Many programs can be "stretched" to cover activities that are not found in the program entry or in the index.

STEP TWO: "READ" A FEDERAL PROGRAM

PART II provides outlines of all available domestic programs. Properly "reading" the information on a given program—that is, understanding the program entry—will facilitate decisions on whether to pursue the available assistance. The following explanation of the program entries explains how to "read" the entries to greatest advantage. Program **14.239** serves as the example.

① *Administrative sub-unit* with management responsibility for all programs under the heading.

② *Program number,* and *official program title.*

① **COMMUNITY PLANNING AND DEVELOPMENT**

② **14.239 HOME INVESTMENT PARTNERSHIPS PROGRAM**
③ **("HOME Program")**

④ **Assistance:** formula grants. (67-75 percent/2-5 years).

⑤ **Purposes:** pursuant to the National Affordable Housing Act as amended, to support partnerships among all levels of government and the private sector, including profit and nonprofit organizations, in the production and operation of affordable housing, particularly rental housing for low- and very-low-income families. Funds may be used for: planning; development of model projects; technical assistance; housing rehabilitation; tenant-based rental assistance; assistance to homebuyers; new construction of housing; site acquisition and improvements including improved energy efficiency, demolition, relocation. As of FY 03, the American Dream Downpayment Initiative (ADDI) may provide funds for low-income families to make down payments on or to rehabilitate suitable housing. Ineligible funds uses include: public housing modernization; matching funds for other federal programs; rental housing operating subsidies; activities under the Low Income Housing Preservation Act, except for priority purchasers.

⑥ **Eligible applicants:** formula allocations—states, cities, urban counties, or consortia of general local government units; Insular Areas. Technical Assistance—nonprofit and profit firms; public purpose organizations; nonprofit national and regional HOME organizations; community development organizations (CHDOs).

⑦ **Eligible beneficiaries:** rental housing—90 percent of funds for families with incomes at 60 percent of area median, and the remainder for families below 80 percent. Homeownership assistance—families with incomes below 80 percent of the area median.

⑧ **Range:** $123,660 to $58,228,225. **Average:** $1,575,176.

⑨ **Activity:** anticipate completing 38,665 units and providing rental assistance for 8,813 tenants in FY 2016.

⑩ **HQ:** Director, Office of Affordable Housing Programs, CPD-HUD, 451 7th St., SW, Rm. 7164, Washington, DC 20410. Phone: (202) 708-2685.

---

③ *Popular title.*

Many program titles in PART II are followed by one or more *popular titles*, shown within parentheses and quotation marks as in this illustration. Field office officials and others may refer to programs only by their popular titles.

④ *Classification of assistance* available through the program. (The fifteen "Types of Federal Assistance Available" are defined beginning on page 3.)

Many programs provide more than one type of assistance. When financial assistance is provided this line indicates the percentage of assistance provided by the federal agency, as well as the usual project term *when the term is other than for one year*. For some programs, the percentage and project term are clarified under "**Purposes**."

Project grants usually are awarded either through competitions or solicitations of proposals by the sponsoring federal agency; however, authorizing statutes for some programs allocate funds on the basis of a formula, as in the "HOME Program," in which case the federal administrative agency notifies eligible applicants of the availability of funds. It is necessary for prospective applicants for competitive, solicited, or unsolicited proposals to remain aware of available programs.

Although the percentage of federal assistance may say "100 percent," most programs have maintenance of effort ("MOE") or "non-supplementation" requirements—meaning that federal funds may not supplant existing non-federal funding allocated to the effort for which federal funds are sought. Also, some level of cost sharing by the applicant almost always is required, if only through the provision of administrative space and services supporting project activities; such contributions by applicants are known as "in-kind" contributions. *Frequently, the level of "MOE" or of cost sharing by applicants will influence the approval of applications.*

⑤　Description of the *basic objectives* and *permitted uses* of the program, as well as *restrictions* on the use of funds. Examples of funded projects also are included when they help to explain the types of activities that are eligible.

The information on the purposes of program **14.239** should be sufficient to permit a decision on whether to pursue it. Note that many programs include more than a single program purpose. Other program features also are included in program descriptions.

⑥　*Who may apply* for the available assistance.

⑦　*Who may benefit* from the program.

Thus, the headings setting forth the eligibility for program **14.239** indicate that only states, cities, urban counties, or consortia or general local government units, and Insular Areas may apply directly for available formula grants; however, other types of applicants are eligible to apply for technical assistance funding. And, when program assistance is sought for rental housing, 90 percent of approved funds must benefit families with incomes at 60 percent of area median, and the remainder for families below 80 percent; when assistance is approved for homeownership projects, families with incomes below 80 percent of the area median may benefit.

It follows that someone interested in participating in this program, if not an eligible applicant, should contact appropriate state or local officials to learn more about it. Contact the state or city public information office to find out whom to contact for details; if that fails, contact the nearest HUD Community Planning and Development field office listed in PART IV.

Frequently, there is no distinction between eligible applicants and eligible beneficiaries, because they are one and the same. Many program descriptions name the intended beneficiaries; those beneficiaries need not apply because services will (or should) be provided to them by the applicants— for instance, programs intended to benefit elderly persons, children and youth, substance abusers, and other general categories of beneficiaries. Such programs have the following eligibility heading:

Eligible applicants/beneficiaries:

Review the section beginning on page 8 entitled "Who May Obtain Federal Assistance?" for a discussion and example of the significance of eligible applicants vs. eligible beneficiaries.

⑧   Indicates the *range and average amounts* provided to applicants or, sometimes, to beneficiaries for programs that provide financial assistance.

Knowing range and average amounts helps in assessing the chances of obtaining a certain sum. Often, applying for a sum that is outside the range shown is pointless, whether the sum sought is below or above the range.

Complementing the "Range" heading are the tables in PART III. *Used together*, the amounts provide a perspective of the funding available nationally for a given activity, and how much an applicant or a beneficiary might expect to obtain through that program.

In "reading" the tables, remember that the U.S. government's fiscal year begins on October 1 and ends on September 30. Fiscal years are expressed in the ending date; thus, FY 16 ends September 30, 2016. Table 1 shows the following funding available for program **14.239**:

(FY 13) $919,045,000; (FY 14) $1,023,768,000; (FY 15) $848,108,000; (FY 16) $1,032,320,000 e

Note that amounts are rounded to the nearest $1,000 in Tables 1 and 2 (but not in the example above).

The information on funding for the four years: (1) indicates the amount available nationally; (2) shows whether, from year to year, a program's funding level remains relatively consistent or if it is increasing or decreasing.

"*" following an amount indicates that the amount is a "credit" rather than an actual outlay of funds. For purposes of the tables, amounts loaned or insured by the government were classified as credits. Program **14.239** provides formula grants and, therefore, is classified as an outlay.

"e" next to an amount indicates that it is *estimated*. In the example, the amounts shown are actual for FY 13, FY 14, and FY 15; the FY 16 amount is estimated.

Estimated amounts could mean that Congress had not approved a specific amount when the information was compiled, or that the amount obligated for a program fluctuates depending on demands for the funds.

Estimates of "$0" also may indicate that the program has been proposed for termination.

Amounts shown in the tables must meet demands nationwide. The total often is allocated geographically by government agencies to regions, states, districts, or areas, according to legislative or administrative policy. Therefore, it could be useful to learn the amount available in a given geographical area, from the officials contacted concerning a specific program—for an indication of the extent of competition to be expected.

The tables offer a perspective of government support for agencies and programs, in relation to one another and to other federal domestic activities. The introduction to the tables further discusses their usefulness in "reading" federal programs.

⑨ *Activity within the program* in the most recent period reported by the administering entity, including such information as the number of assistance awards or of persons benefiting. It is also noted when the program is new, with or without reported activity.

In combination with the information provided under *Range/Average* and in the Tables, "reading" the level of activity provides an indication of the participation nationally in given programs.

⑩ *Program headquarters address, phone number, and web sites* of the administering agency. FAX numbers are included when provided in the source material.

THE FIRST CONTACT WITH A FEDERAL AGENCY ABOUT A PRO-
GRAM SHOULD ALWAYS BE WITH THE FIELD OFFICE IF ONE
EXISTS. The "HQ" entry always indicates when there are no field offices
for a given program with "(Note: no field offices for this program.)" following the HQ address. If the notation does not appear, field office contact
information is provided in PART IV.

Contacting field offices has advantages for both applicants and federal
officials: the nearer a federal office is to applicants, the more probable it is
that the officials will be able to provide pertinent information; field office
personnel usually are more aware of needs in the area they serve; contacts
with them add to this awareness.

Also, they are more apt to know who else in a given area has similar interests; they could provide leads to others experienced with the program. It is
important for the field offices to know the extent of interest in the programs that they manage. Generally, headquarters personnel are more
involved with "big picture" matters than with handling individual contacts
from throughout the country.

PART IV provides contact information for regional, state, and area or district offices. The hierarchy should be followed upwards when deciding
which office to contact—that is, if there is a district, branch, or area office,
it should be contacted before state or regional offices; state offices should
be contacted before regional offices.

When contacting a field office, address the "Director" unless the entry in
PART IV suggests otherwise. Include the full name of the agency. For
example, correspondence with HUD's Chicago state office, concerning
program **14.239**, should be addressed as follows:

> Director
> Community Planning and Development
> Department of Housing and Urban Development
> 451 7th St., SW, Rm. 7164
> Washington, DC 20410

PART IV also provides contact information for specialized field service
offices such as research centers, laboratories, and testing stations.

STEP THREE: ASK THE RIGHT QUESTIONS

"STEP ONE" and "STEP TWO" involve the selection of programs to pursue. The process of obtaining federal assistance begins when those steps are completed. Hundreds of programs involve very little red tape. They require little or no additional "homework", especially those involving non-financial assistance. For nonfinancial programs, one or two contacts with the right federal official usually will bring the desired assistance.

This "step" is meant for newcomers to federal programs, deciding to pursue the more complicated programs involving awards of funds. All the points discussed will not be pertinent to all the programs, obviously.

Before formally applying for financial assistance under all but the least complicated programs, a preliminary contact with the responsible federal office is always advisable; indeed, some programs require a preap-plication conference. An appointment with the responsible official should be requested; when making this request, the eligibility criteria for the pro-gram being pursued should be discussed generally. At this first meeting at least the following should be accomplished:

1. *Verify the eligibility of the applicant*—whether as an individual or as an organization. This should have been done verbally when the appointment was made. If the official mentioned credentials required to document eligibility, these should be shown at the meeting. The required credentials could include documents such as a birth certifi-cate, academic certificates, a financial statement, endorsements, a copy of the organization's charter or license, etc. If the required cre-dentials are not ready, evidence that they can be produced should be shown—e.g., publications, sample products, leaflets describing the organization, a good resume.

2. *Explain the applicant's specific need for the assistance in very basic terms*. Prior to the meeting an outline for using the assistance should be prepared, and it should be shown to the official. This will open a discussion of the program, its objectives, the permitted uses of funds, program restrictions, etc. All possible questions about the program should be posed, including the availability of funding. The official should be allowed to do most of the talking—the purpose of the meet-ing is for the applicant to obtain information, not give it. On the other hand, prospective applicants should answer all questions honestly to reveal potential problems early in the process; if problems do surface, the official's advice should be sought on how to resolve them. *Written* notes should be made, both during and immediately after the meeting.

3. *Obtain all available written information pertaining to the program.* The following could be useful in preparing a thorough application:

- a copy of the law establishing the program;
- policy statements;
- procedural guidelines and instructions to applicants;
- regulations governing the program, including those published in the *Federal Register* and those pertaining mainly to the processing requirements that federal agencies themselves must fulfill—the latter often provide instructions for "scoring" the merits of applications, giving insights into what those reviewing an application will look for;
- statements of application deadlines, if any;
- general literature describing the program and the experiences of others that have obtained funds under the same or similar programs;
- a copy of a sample successful application;
- most important, copies of any pertinent circulars governing the program issued by the Office of Management and Budget, as well as Executive Orders or other regulations issued by federal or state agencies that will coordinate or review applications—e.g., the Environmental Protection Agency;
- lists of requirements for records to be kept and reports to be filed if the application is approved—including copies of pertinent accounting procedures;
- a description of the "appeal process," in case the application is not approved and the decision is appealed.

4. *If the program requires cost sharing or a matching contribution* by the applicant, it should be determined whether any portion of this sum can be provided through "in-kind" services, use of facilities or equipment, or other noncash contributions. Review the explanation of the program description entry heading "Assistance" for insights on cost sharing.

5. *Ask to be placed on the office's mailing list* to receive announcements, news releases, notifications of invitations to apply or of awards, changes in regulations or deadlines, and the like.

6. *Keep the meeting as brief as possible.*

STEP FOUR: COMPLETE YOUR HOMEWORK

Examine carefully all the material obtained in "STEP THREE." Make a list of the most important points. Note especially items that are not readily understood, and follow through on each of them. Follow all instructions carefully. In your application, projecting an ability to adhere carefully and fully to instructions and regulations is all-important. "Dot every i, cross every t."

At this point, the "grantsmanship" process begins. Grantsmanship is a term often used inaccurately to describe *obtaining* federal assistance. Successful grantsmanship necessitates thorough familiarity with program and project planning, development, and operations. A good application will reflect complete understanding of program purposes and requirements, *as well as sound project management capability.* The grantsmanship process is both an art and a science; its productive outcome requires extensive research, discipline, precise work, sound psychology, effective presentation, a good sense of business, and persistence.

The *ALMANAC*'s author/editor and publisher wish users success in their quest, trusting that this book points them in the right direction.

Finding More Information

Several sources might be checked for more information on obtaining federal assistance.

1. The principal source providing additional details about the programs outlined in the *ALMANAC* is the *Catalog of Federal Domestic Assistance* ("CFDA"), subscriptions to which may be ordered from:

   Superintendent of Documents
   U.S. Government Printing Office
   Washington, DC 20402

The "Catalog" is published every year, pursuant to federal statute; it contains some 3,200 pages and is mailed unbound for filing in a loose-leaf binder. Subscriptions no longer include the "Update to the Catalog of Federal Domestic Assistance," formerly published in December and numbering several hundred additional pages; the General Services Administration, which maintains the database for the CFDA, discontinued preparation of a printed version of the Update in 2001.

GSA recommends now that interested parties use its "on-line version" of the CFDA to obtain updated information, which may be accessed through the following web site: "https://www.cfda.gov".

It should be noted that the CFDA web site provides most of the information presented in the ALMANAC only in printer definition file ("PDF") format, including the CFDA's several indexes; the CFDA on-line version provides ongoing updates only for individual programs—i.e., the version in PDF format has been updated only annually in recent years.

The catalog contains a brief section with "Suggestions for Proposal Writing and Following Grant Application Procedures," which could be helpful to newcomers to federal programs.

Until 2003 GSA distributed free copies of the CFDA to the entities listed below; however, this policy was changed, requiring the recipients to purchase subscriptions; presumably, many of them did so and would have copies available for examination:

> Members of Congress
> Congressional staff
> All federal Depository Libraries (see program **40.002**)
> Federal offices
> Governors
> State coordinators of federal-state relations
> Directors of state departments of administration
> Directors of state agricultural extension services
> Directors of state departments of community affairs
> Directors of state planning agencies
> State budget offices
> State municipal leagues
> State associations of counties
> Chief state school officers
> State employment security agencies
> Mayors
> County chairmen
> Chairmen of boards of commissioners
> City planners

Some other state and local government agencies and officials *Federal Information Centers* and *Federal Regional Councils* also may have copies available for examination.

2. *The United States Government Manual* is a useful reference source for persons wanting to better understand the federal government. The manual describes the basic functions and operations of all government agencies, including the judicial, legislative, and executive branches.

Most libraries have copies available for reference. The current manual may be purchased from the Government Printing Office.

3. *The Federal Register,* published daily, provides the public with federal agency regulations and other legal documents covering government activities, including *proposed* changes in regulations. Newly authorized programs and the availability of funding also are announced in *The Federal Register.*

The Federal Register Index, published monthly, consolidates entries appearing in the basic publication, with broad references to the contents.

Additional *Federal Register* resources include "Weekly Compilation of Presidential Documents" and "The Federal Register: What It Is and How to Use It."

The *Code of Federal Regulations* ("CFR") codifies the general and permanent rules published in the *The Federal Register* by federal executive departments and agencies. The CFR includes all statutory regulations; it is updated by *The Federal Register.*

The foregoing publications are available for examination in federal depository libraries and major libraries, or for purchase from the Government Printing Office.

4. *Libraries* are obvious places to look for additional information about government programs, "grantsmanship," proposal writing, and similar topics. Larger or more specialized libraries also will have available directories of trade or professional associations and of commercial publishers specializing in information on various government activities, which might provide assistance or guidance concerning certain federal assistance programs. Directories of consultants and consulting organizations also are available.

5. *Congressional offices* may or may not be able to provide help in obtaining additional information or actual assistance. Some senators and representatives are more anxious to do so than others, depending on the capacity, interest, and capabilities of their staffs.

Many elected officials respond more quickly to requests for assistance from other elected officials, or from campaign supporters. Keep this in mind when deciding to seek a congressman's intercession. The first contact should be with district or state offices. The Washington addresses for offices of Members of Congress are:

United States Senate   House of Representatives
Washington, DC 20510   Washington, DC 20515

The best source of more information about given programs and obtaining the assistance they provide usually is someone experienced in those programs or similar ones.

PART II

Program Information

DEPARTMENT OF AGRICULTURE

10.001 AGRICULTURAL RESEARCH—BASIC AND APPLIED RESEARCH ("Extramural Research")

Assistance: project grants (100 percent).

Purposes: for agricultural discovery research; to provide scientific technical information. Most projects are conducted with in-house staff; limited discretionary research funds are available.

Eligible applicants/beneficiaries: nonprofit IHEs and other research organizations.

Range: $1,000 to $25,000. **Average:** $15,000.

Activity: N.A.

HQ: Administrator, Agriculture Research Service (ARS) USDA, 5601 Sunnyside Ave., MS-5110, Beltsville, MD 20705. Phone: (301) 504-1702.

Internet: www.ars.usda.gov.

10.025 PLANT AND ANIMAL DISEASE, PEST CONTROL, AND ANIMAL CARE

Assistance: project grants (cost sharing).

Purposes: pursuant to the Plant Protection Act, Farm Security and Rural Investment Act of 2002 (FSRIA), and Animal Welfare Act as amended, for surveys, demonstration projects, and inspections to detect, appraise, eradicate, and control plant and animal diseases and pests injurious to agriculture, including brucellosis and tuberculosis; to ensure the safety and potency of veterinary biologics. Emphasis is on prevention of interstate spread of infestations and diseases.

Eligible applicants: foreign, state, local, and territorial government agencies; nonprofit IHEs and other organizations.

Eligible beneficiaries: in addition to applicants: farmers, ranchers, agricultural producers.

Range/Average: N.A.

Activity: estimate 50 states and 3 territories brucellosis-free, and a 96% success rate of tracking tuberculosis-positive signal animals back to their origin in FY 2016.

HQ: Agreement Services Center, Marketing and Regulatory Programs, Animal and Plant Health Inspection Service-USDA, USDA Center, 4700 River Rd. - Unit 55, Riverdale, MD 20737. Phone: (301) 851-2856.

Internet: www.aphis.usda.gov.

10.028 WILDLIFE SERVICES

Assistance: project grants (cost sharing).

Purposes: pursuant to the Animal Damage Control Act of 1931 as amended, to reduce damage caused by nuisance mammals and birds, including those carrying zoonotic diseases. Project examples: predator control programs in the western states, including coyote, mountain lion, and bear; aerial blackbird hazing program protecting the sunflower crop; control of beaver, deer, and cormorants against damage to aquaculture in the eastern and southern states. Most direct technical assistance is provided through state fish and game, agriculture, and health departments.

Eligible applicants/beneficiaries: state, local, territorial, and tribal governments; public or private nonprofit organizations; nonprofit IHEs; individuals.

Range/Average: N.A.

Activity: N.A.

HQ: Agreement Services Center, Marketing and Regulatory Programs, Animal and Plant Health Inspection Service-USDA, USDA Center, 4700 River Rd. - Unit 55, Riverdale, MD 20737. Phone: (301) 851-2856.

Internet: www.aphis.usda.gov.

10.030 INDEMNITY PROGRAM

Assistance: direct payments/unrestricted use (100 percent).

Purposes: as authorized by The Animal and Plant Health Inspection Service, payment will be made for a wide variety of indemnity situations ranging from large livestock depopulations to small fowl depopulations based upon an emergency declared by the Secretary of Agriculture. Payment for the destroyed animals is based on fair market value. As authorized by Section 415 (e) of the Plant Protection Act, in the event of a declaration of extraordinary emergency due to the presence of a plant pest or noxious weed that is new to or not known to be widely prevalent in the United States, the Secretary may pay compensation for eligible economic losses.

Eligible applicants/beneficiaries: N.A.

Range/Average: N.A.

Activity: N.A.

HQ: Director, Animal and Plant Health Inspection Service, USDA, 4700 River Rd., Suite 3D04.15, Riverdale, Maryland 20737. Phone: (301) 851-2859.

Internet: N.A.

10.051 COMMODITY LOANS AND LOAN DEFICIENCY PAYMENTS ("Price Supports")

Assistance: direct payments/unrestricted use; direct loans (to 9 months).

Purposes: pursuant to the Agricultural Adjustment Act of 1938, Commodity Credit Corporation Charter Act, Food, Agriculture, Conservation, and Trade Act of 1990 (FACTA), Federal Agriculture Improvement and Reform Act of 1996 (FAIRA), Agricultural Risk Protection Act of 2000, amendments, and other acts, to help growers stabilize their income from commodities through a system of price supports involving loans and purchases by the CCC. Producers may receive nonrecourse loans against the support price established for crops serving as loan collateral; if market prices exceed the support price, farmers may market the commodity and repay the loan principal plus interest; if market prices are low, the loan is repaid through forfeiture of the collateral to the CCC in return for a loan deficiency payment (LDP) for the difference between the support and the market prices. Commodities eligible for loans include feed grains, wheat, rice, peanuts, tobacco, upland cotton, extra-long staple cotton, sugar, soybeans, canola, flaxseed, mustard seed, rapeseed, safflower, and sunflower seed. LDPs are offered for feed grains, wheat, upland cotton, rice, soybeans, canola, flaxseed, mustard seed, rapeseed, safflower, and sunflower seed. If the loan repayment rates are less than the established loan levels, producers may forego the loan and elect to receive LDPs which are equal to the amount by which the loan rate exceeds the loan repayment rate in effect on the delivery date. Recourse loans may be made for low quality grain or unginned seed cotton; such loans require repayment at maturity.

Eligible applicants/beneficiaries: owners, landlords, tenants, or sharecroppers on farms producing eligible commodities; for sugar, processors or refiners meeting USDA program requirements.

Range/Average: N.A.

Activity: N.A.

HQ: Price Support Division, FSA-USDA, 1400 Independence Ave., SW, Stop 0510, Washington, DC 20250-0512. Phone: (202) 690-3307.

Internet: www.fsa.usda.gov/programs-and-services/price-support/Index.

10.053 DAIRY INDEMNITY PROGRAM ("DIPP")

Assistance: direct payments/unrestricted use (100 percent).

Purposes: pursuant to the Agricultural Act of 1970, Agriculture and Consumer Protection Act of 1973, FACTA, amendments, and other acts, to indemnify dairy farmers and dairy product manufacturers against losses when their milk or dairy products are contaminated by pesticides, chemicals, toxic substances, or nuclear radiation or fallout, if the cause was outside their control; in such cases CCC pays the fair market value of the product.

Eligible applicants/beneficiaries: dairy farmers and manufacturers with products removed from the market by a public agency. Available also in PR.

Range/Average: N.A.

Activity: N.A.

HQ: FSA-USDA, 1400 Independence Ave., SW, Washington, DC 20250-0512. Phone: (202) 720-1919.

Internet: www.fsa.usda.gov/programs-and-services/price-support/Index.

10.054 EMERGENCY CONSERVATION PROGRAM (ECP)

Assistance: direct payments/specified use.

Purposes: pursuant to the Agricultural Credit Act of 1978 as amended, for emergency conservation measures to control wind erosion; to rehabilitate farmlands damaged by wind, floods, or other natural disasters; to take water enhancing or conservation measures during drought. Assistance is limited basically to new conservation problems created by natural disasters. Cost-sharing payment rates vary.

Eligible applicants/beneficiaries: owners, landlords, tenants, or sharecroppers on farms or ranches, including associated groups. Available also in Guam, Northern Marianas, PR, and VI.

Range/Average: N.A.

Activity: N.A.

HQ: Director, Disaster Relief Appropriations Act EFRP, FSA-USDA, 1400 Independence Ave., SW, Washington, DC 20250. Phone: (202) 205-4537; FAX: (202) 720-4619.

Internet: www.fsa.usda.gov/programs-and-services/conservation-programs/emergency-conservation/index.

10.055   DIRECT AND COUNTER-CYCLICAL PAYMENTS PROGRAM (DCP)

Assistance: direct payments/specified use.

Purposes: pursuant to the FSRIA, to provide CCC income support to producers of covered commodities. Contract payments equal the contract payment rate, times 85 percent of the contract acreage, times the farm program payment yield. Participants must: share the risk of producing a crop on base acres and be entitled to share in the crop available for marketing from the base acres; comply with conservation, wetland, and similar requirements; comply with planting flexibility requirements; use the base acres for agricultural or related activities.

Eligible applicants/beneficiaries: owners, operators, landlords, tenants, or sharecroppers on producing farms enrolled in DCP for the 2002-2007 crop years. FSA offices should be consulted for specifics.

Range/Average: N.A.

Activity: N.A.

HQ: Compliance Branch, Production Emergencies and Compliance Division, FSA-USDA, 1400 Independence Ave., SW, Washington, DC 20250-0514. Phone: (202) 720-7641.

Internet: www.fsa.usda.gov/programs-and-services/dccp-acre/index.

10.056   FARM STORAGE FACILITY LOANS

Assistance: direct loans. (85 percent/7 years).

Purposes: for new, remodeled, or refinanced farm grain storage structures and drying equipment; to meet handling requirements for genetically enhanced production.

Eligible applicants/beneficiaries: owner, landlord, tenant, or sharecropper producing one or more of the CCC-approved commodities, participating in the Federal Crop Insurance program, and producing proof of flood insurance.

Range/Average: N.A.

Activity: N.A.

HQ: FSA, Director, Price Support Division, 1400 Independence Ave., SW, Washington, DC 20250. Phone: (202) 720-2270.

Internet: www.fsa.usda.gov/FSA/webapp?area=home&subject=prsu&topic =flp.

10.069 CONSERVATION RESERVE PROGRAM (CRP)

Assistance: direct payments/specified use (10-15 years).

Purposes: pursuant to the Food Security Act of 1985 as amended, FACTA, and FAIRA, to convert highly erodible or environmentally sensitive cropland to less intensive uses such as grasses, legumes, shrubs, trees. Basic program objectives include reducing soil erosion or sedimentation, and improving water quality and wildlife habitat. Participants must institute approved conservation plans and reduce the aggregate total of acreage bases, allotments, and quotas for the contract period.

Eligible applicants/beneficiaries: individuals, partnerships, associations, tribal ventures corporations, estates, trusts, other businesses and legal entities; states and their political subdivisions.

Range/Average: N.A.

Activity: N.A.

HQ: FSA-USDA (CEPD), 1400 Independence Ave., SW, Washington, DC 20250. Phone: (202) 720-9563; FAX (202) 720-4169.

Internet: www.fsa.usda.gov/programs-and-services/conservation-programs/ conservation-reserve-program/index.

10.072 WETLANDS RESERVE PROGRAM (WRP)

Assistance: direct payments/specified use. (to 100 percent/5-30 years).

Purposes: pursuant to the Food Security Act of 1985 as amended, FACTA, FAIRA, and other acts, to install restoration practices needed to protect farmed or converted wetlands, certain riparian areas, and buffer areas. Landowners must: place the wetlands under permanent or long-term easement with USDA; provide an access road to the land to enable easement management and monitoring. Landowners receive payments based on the fair agricultural market value of the land or 75 percent of such value. Permitted land uses after installing restoration or protective practices include haying, grazing, and buffer areas.

Eligible applicants/beneficiaries: individual landowners, partnerships, associations, corporations, estates, trusts; other businesses or legal entities; states and their political subdivisions.

Range/Average: N.A.

Activity: N.A.

HQ: Watersheds and Wetlands Division, NRCS-USDA, 14th and Independence Ave., SW, Washington, DC 20250. Phone: (202) 720-1882.

Internet: www.nrcs.usda.gov/wps/portal/nrcs/main/national/programs/ease ments/wetlands.

10.080 MILK INCOME LOSS CONTRACT PROGRAM ("MILC")

Assistance: direct payments/unrestricted use.

Purposes: pursuant to FSRIA, to provide payments to milk producers for milk produced and marketed between 1 December 2001 and 30 September 2005—when the prices under milk marketing orders fall below $16.94 per cwt.

Eligible applicants/beneficiaries: U.S. dairy producers with MIL contracts; foreign producers with a working U.S. visa or other valid taxpayer identification number.

Range/Average: N.A.

Activity: N.A.

HQ: FSA-USDA, 1400 Independence Ave., SW, Washington, DC 20250-0512. Phone: (202) 720-1919; FAX: (202) 690-3307.

Internet: www.fsa.usda.gov.

10.085 TOBACCO TRANSITION PAYMENT PROGRAM (TTPP)

Assistance: direct payments/unrestricted use (years beginning 2005, ending 2014).

Purposes: pursuant to the Fair and Equitable Tobacco Reform Act of 2004 (FETRA) which repeals the federal tobacco price support control program, to compensate tobacco quota owners for the elimination of their government-created asset—i.e., quota—through a system of transition payments by the CCC.

Eligible applicants/beneficiaries: tobacco producers owning, controlling, or growing eligible tobacco on farms with an established marketing quota or allotment for the 2004 marketing year, or their assignees.

Range/Average: N.A.

Activity: N.A.

HQ: Tobacco Branch, FSA-USDA, 1400 Independence Ave., SW, Washington, DC 20250-0512. Phone: (202) 720-0448.

Internet: www.fsa.usda.gov.

10.090 SUPPLEMENTAL REVENUE ASSISTANCE PROGRAM ("SURE")

Assistance: direct payments/specified use (100 percent).

Purposes: pursuant to the American Recovery and Reinvestment Act of 2009 (ARRA), to make crop disaster assistance payments to eligible producers on farms in disaster counties whose actual production is less than 50 percent of their normal production with at least one crop of economic significance reduced by at least 10 percent due to disaster, adverse weather, or disaster-related conditions. A disaster county must be within the geographic area covered by the Secretary of Agriculture's qualifying natural disaster declaration.

Eligible applicants/beneficiaries: individuals or entities who are U.S. citizens, resident aliens, or belong to a partnership of U.S. citizens and a producer on a farm that is an individual or entity who assumes the production and market risks associated with the agricultural production of crops or livestock.

Range/Average: N.A.

Activity: N.A.

HQ: Deputy Administrator for Farm Programs, Production, Emergencies, and Compliance Division, Disaster Assistance Branch, USDA, 14th and Independence Ave., SW, Stop 0517, Washington, DC 20250. Phone: (202) 720-5172; FAX: (202) 720-0051.

Internet: www.fsa.gov.

10.098   REIMBURSEMENT TRANSPORTATION COST PAYMENT PROGRAM FOR GEOGRAPHICALLY DISADVANTAGED FARMERS AND RANCHERS (RTCP)

Assistance: direct payments for unrestricted use (100 percent).

Purposes: pursuant to The Food, Conservation, and Energy Act of 2008, provides direct payments to geographically disadvantaged farmers and ranchers to reimburse them for a portion of the costs of transporting inputs used to produce an agricultural commodity and transporting products to markets. Input transportation costs include, but are not limited to, air, ocean, and land freight of chemicals, feed, fertilizer, fuel, seeds, plants, supplies, equipment parts, and other inputs. To be eligible, a geographically disadvantaged farmer or rancher must be a producer of an eligible agricultural commodity in substantial commercial quantities. Eligible commodities include any agricultural commodity (including horticulture, aquaculture, and floriculture) food, feed, fiber, livestock (including elk, reindeer, bison, horses, and deer), insects or products thereof. Farmers and ranchers located outside the continental U.S. (the 48 contiguous U.S.), receive the ultimate benefit from the program because they operate at a competitive disadvantage relative to farmers and ranchers in the continental U.S. due to the high cost of transporting agricultural commodities from those areas to markets in the continental U.S. and in other countries, and the high cost of transporting agricultural inputs to those areas.

Eligible applicants/beneficiaries: farmers, ranchers, agricultural producers.

Range/Average: N.A.

Activity: N.A.

HQ: Director, Reimbursement Transportation Cost Payment Program for Geographically Disadvantaged Farmers and Ranchers, FSA-USDA, 1400 Independence Ave., SW, Washington, DC 20250-0512. (202) 720-1919.

Internet: www.fsa.usda.gov/programs-and-services/price-support/RTCP-Program/index.

10.099   CONSERVATION LOANS

Assistance: direct loans; guaranteed/insured loans (to 20 years).

Purposes: pursuant to the Consolidated Farm and Rural Development Act, to provide access to credit for farmers who need and want to implement conservation measures on their land but do not have the "up front" funds available to implement these practices. Some conservation practices might include: reducing soil erosion, improving water quality, promoting sustainable and organic agricultural practices, establishment of forest cover, and adaptation of other emerging or existing conservation practices, techniques or technologies.

Eligible applicants/beneficiaries: qualified families, individuals, and entities who are farmers.

Range: to $1,392,000. **Average:** N.A.

Activity: 1 loan made in FY 2015.

HQ: Director, FSA-USDA, 1400 Independence Ave., SW, Washington, DC 20250. Phone: (202) 690-0756.

Internet: www.fsa.usda.gov/programs-and-services/farm-loan-programs/ind ex. (Note: no field offices for this program.)

10.102 EMERGENCY FOREST RESTORATION PROGRAM (EFRP)

Assistance: direct payments/unrestricted use.

Purposes: pursuant to the Food, Conservation, and Energy Act of 2008, to make financial assistance available to eligible participants to restore non-industrial private forest land that has been damaged by a natural disaster on or after January 1, 2010, as determined by FSA. The land must have existing tree cover or have had tree cover immediately before the natural disaster and, if not treated, would impair or endanger the natural resources on the land and would materially affect future use of the land.

Eligible applicants/beneficiaries: person or legal entity (including Indian tribes) who owns nonindustrial private forest land affected by a natural disaster, with full decision-making authority over the land, and liable for the expense that is the subject of the financial assistance.

Range/Average: N.A.

Activity: N.A.

HQ: Director, FSA-USDA, 1400 Independence Ave., SW, Washington, DC 20250. Phone: (202) 690-0794; FAX: (202) 720-4619.

Internet: www.fsa.usda.gov/programs-and-services/disaster-assistance-pro gram/emergency-forest-restoration/index.

10.105 DISASTER RELIEF APPROPRIATIONS ACT—EMERGENCY CONSERVATION PROGRAM

Assistance: direct payments for specified use (100 percent/to 6 months).

Purposes: pursuant to the Disaster Relief Appropriations Act, Public Law 113-2, financial assistance is available for farmland losses occurring as a result of Hurricane Sandy. The purpose of the program is to enable farmers to perform emergency conservation measures to control wind erosion on farmlands, and to rehabilitate farmlands damaged by Hurricane Sandy. Emergency cost-sharing is limited to new conservation problems created by Hurricane Sandy which, if not treated, will impair or endanger the land, materially affect the productive capacity of the land, represent damage that is unusual in character and, except for wind erosion, is not the type that would recur frequently in the same area and will be so costly to rehabilitate that Federal assistance is or will be required to return the land to productive agricultural use. Once applicants are approved for rehabilitation cost-share assistance, producers have up to six months to perform the farmland rehabilitation practice and report completion.

Eligible applicants/beneficiaries: an agricultural producer who as owner, landlord, tenant, or sharecropper on a farm or ranch, including associated groups, bears part of the cost of an approved conservation practice affected by Hurricane Sandy.

Range/Average: N.A.

Activity: N.A.

HQ: Director, Disaster Relief Appropriations Act ECP, FSA-USDA, 1400 Independence Ave., SW, Washington, DC 20250. Phone: (202) 205-4537; FAX: (202) 720-4619.

Internet: www.fsa.usda.gov/programs-and-services/conservation-programs/emergency-conservation/index.

10.106 DISASTER RELIEF APPROPRIATIONS ACT—EMERGENCY FOREST RESTORATION PROGRAM

Assistance: direct payments for specified use, direct payments for unrestricted use.

Purposes: pursuant to the Disaster Relief Appropriations Act, Public Law 113-2, funds to provide cost share payments to assist owners of nonindustrial private forest land who carry out emergency measures to restore land damaged by Hurricane Sandy. To be eligible the land must have existing tree cover or have had tree cover immediately before Hurricane Sandy, be suitable for growing trees, have damage to natural resources caused by Hurricane Sandy that, if not treated, would impair or endanger the natural resources on the land and would materially affect future use of the land.

Eligible applicants/beneficiaries: owners of nonindustrial private forest land damaged by Hurricane Sandy who have full decision making authority over the land, or with required waivers, to undertake program commitments. Land is ineligible for the program if it is owned or controlled by the US government, a state, an agency or political subdivision of a state.

Range/Average: N.A.

Activity: N.A.

HQ: Director, Disaster Relief Appropriations Act EFRP, FSA-USDA,1400 Independence Ave., SW, Washington, DC 20250. Phone: (202) 205-4537; FAX: (202) 720-4619.

Internet: www.fsa.usda.gov/programs-and-services/disaster-assistance-program/emergency-forest-restoration/index.

10.108 LIVESTOCK INDEMNITY PROGRAM—2014 FARM BILL

Assistance: direct payments/unrestricted use. (100 percent).

Purposes: pursuant to the Agricultural Act of 2014, to provide benefits to eligible livestock owners or livestock contract growers for livestock deaths in excess of normal mortality caused by adverse weather, and to cover attacks by animals reintroduced into the wild by the federal government or protected by federal law, including wolves and avian predators.

Eligible applicants/beneficiaries: farmers, ranchers, and agricultural producers.

Range/Average: N.A.

Activity: N.A.

HQ: Production, Emergencies, & Compliance Division, FSA-USDA, 1400 Independence Ave., SW, Stop 0517, Washington, DC 20250. Phone: (202) 720-8954; FAX: (202) 690-2130.

Internet: www.fsa.usda.gov/programs-and-services/disaster-assistance-program/livestock-indemnity/index.

10.109 LIVESTOCK FORAGE PROGRAM—2014 FARM BILL

Assistance: direct payments/unrestricted use. (100 percent).

Purposes: pursuant to the Agricultural Act of 2014, to provide compensation to eligible livestock producers that have suffered grazing losses for covered livestock on land that is native or improved pastureland with permanent vegetative cover or is planted specifically for grazing. The program also provides compensation to eligible livestock producers that have suffered grazing losses on rangeland managed by a federal agency if the eligible livestock producer is prohibited by the federal agency from grazing the normal permitted livestock on the managed rangeland due to a qualifying fire.

Eligible applicants/beneficiaries: farmers, ranchers, and agricultural producers.

Range/Average: N.A.

Activity: N.A.

HQ: Deputy Administrator for Farm Programs, FSA-USDA, 14th and Independence Ave., SW, Stop 0517, Washington, DC 20250. Phone: (202) 720-7997; FAX: (202) 720-0051.

Internet: www.fsa.usda.gov/programs-and-services/disaster-assistance-program/livestock-forage/index.

10.110 EMERGENCY ASSISTANCE FOR LIVESTOCK, HONEYBEES AND FARM-RAISED FISH PROGRAM

Assistance: direct payments/specified use. (100 percent).

Purposes: pursuant to the Agricultural Act of 2014, to provide emergency assistance to eligible producers of livestock, honeybees and farm-raised fish who have losses due to an eligible adverse weather or eligible loss condition, including blizzards, disease (including cattle tick fever), water shortages and wildfires, as determined by the Secretary, that occurs on or after October 1, 2011. This program covers losses that are not covered under the Livestock Forage Program (LFP), and Livestock Indemnity Program (LIP).

Eligible applicants/beneficiaries: eligible producers of livestock, honeybees, and farm-raised fish.

Range/Average: N.A.

Activity: N.A.

HQ: Production, Emergencies, & Compliance Division, FSA-USDA, 1400 Independence Ave., SW, Stop 0517, Washington, DC 20250. Phone: (202) 720-8954; FAX: (202) 690-2130.

Internet: www.fsa.usda.gov/programs-and-services/disaster-assistance-program/emergency-assist-for-livestock-honey-bees-fish/index.

10.111 TREE ASSISTANCE PROGRAM—2014 FARM BILL

Assistance: direct payments/unrestricted use. (100 percent).

Purposes: pursuant to the Agricultural Act of 2014, to cover eligible losses back to October 1, 2011. Eligible orchardists and nursery tree growers will be compensated for eligible tree, bush, and vine losses that occurred in the calendar year (or loss period in the case of plant disease) for which benefits are requested and as a direct result of a natural disaster.

Eligible applicants/beneficiaries: orchardists and nursery tree growers.

Range/Average: N.A.

Activity: N.A.

HQ: Deputy Administrator for Farm Programs, FSA-USDA, 14th and Independence Ave., SW, Stop 0517, Washington, DC 20250. Phone: (202) 720-5172; FAX: (202) 720-0051.

Internet: www.fsa.usda.gov/programs-and-services/disaster-assistance-program/tree-assistance-program/index.

10.112 PRICE LOSS COVERAGE

Assistance: direct payments/specified use. (100 percent).

Purposes: pursuant to the Agricultural Act of 2014 to provide revenue and price loss payments to eligible (PLC) producers. The price-loss coverage yield for covered commodities on a farm is equal to the counter-cyclical payment yield established for each covered commodity on the farm that was effective on September 13, 2013, unless the PLC yield is updated.

Eligible applicants/beneficiaries: farmers, ranchers, and producers in the US and its territories.

Range/Average: N.A.

Activity: N.A.

HQ: Farm Service Agency, Department of Agriculture, 1400 Independence Ave., SW, Rm. 4759-S, Washington, DC 20024. Phone: (202) 720-7641; FAX: (202) 690-2130.

Internet: www.fsa.usda.gov.

10.113 AGRICULTURE RISK COVERAGE PROGRAM

Assistance: direct payments/specified use. (100 percent).

Purposes: pursuant to the Agricultural Act of 2014, to cover a portion of a farmer's out-of-pocket loss when crop revenues fall below benchmark revenue levels, with the benchmark revenue based on either county level historic revenue or the individual farm's historic revenue.

Eligible applicants/beneficiaries: eligible producers on farms enrolled for the 2014 through 2018 crop year.

Range/Average: N.A.

Activity: N.A.

HQ: FSA-USDA, 1400 Independence Ave., SW, Rm. 4759-S, Washington, DC 20024. Phone: (202) 720-7641; FAX: (202) 690-2130.

Internet: www.fsa.usda.gov/programs-and-services/arcplc_program/index.

10.116   THE MARGIN PROTECTION PROGRAM

Assistance: direct payments/specified use. (100 percent).

Purposes: pursuant to the Agricultural Act of 2014, to provide payments to dairy operations when the difference between the all-milk price and the average feed cost falls below a certain, producer selected, dollar amount. Producers will be eligible for a basic level of margin protection for a small administrative fee, and be able to purchase greater coverage for a premium.

Eligible applicants/beneficiaries: participating dairy operations.

Range/Average: N.A.

Activity: N.A.

HQ: FSA-USDA, 1400 Independence Ave., SW, Washington, DC 20250-0512. Phone: (202) 720-1919.

Internet: www.fsa.usda.gov/programs-and-services/Dairy-MPP/index.

10.117   BIOFUEL INFRASTRUCTURE PARTNERSHIP

Assistance: project grants. (100 percent).

Purposes: pursuant to the Commodity Credit Corporation Charter Act, to expand the infrastructure for renewable fuels in order to increase the demand for ethanol by offering competitive grants. Funds may be used to pay a portion of the costs related to the installation of fuel pumps and related infrastructure dedicated to the distribution of higher ethanol blends at fueling stations or fleet facilities.

Eligible applicants: states, IHEs, and hospitals.

Eligible beneficiaries: anyone/general public.

Range/Average: N.A.

Activity: N.A.

HQ: FSA-USDA, 1400 Independence Ave., SW, Washington, DC 20250. Phone: (202) 720-3175.

Internet: origin2.www.fsa.usda.gov/programs-and-services/energy-programs/index. (Note: no field offices for this program.)

10.153   MARKET NEWS

Assistance: technical information.

Purposes: pursuant to the Agricultural Marketing Act of 1946, Food Security Act of 1985, amendments, and other acts, to provide reports on prices, demand, movement, volume, and quality of all major U.S. agricultural commodities. Information is disseminated through news media and through printed reports, bulletin boards, phone, facsimile machines, data networks, and telegraph.

Eligible applicants/beneficiaries: anyone may subscribe.

Range/Average: N.A.

Activity: N.A.

HQ: Associate Administrator, AMS-USDA, 1400 Independence Ave., SW, Washington, DC 20250. Phone: (202) 720-5115.

Internet: www.ams.usda.gov.

10.155 MARKETING AGREEMENTS AND ORDERS

Assistance: specialized services; advisory services/counseling.

Purposes: pursuant to the Agricultural Marketing Agreement Act of 1937 as amended, Agriculture and Food Act of 1981, and other acts, to help maintain adequate prices to producers of agricultural products by issuing federal marketing orders or agreements relating to marketing and economic problems of the commodity or area covered by the federal actions. Marketing orders are issued by USDA only after a public hearing where milk, fruit, and vegetable producers, marketers, and consumers testify, and after farmers vote approval through a referendum.

Eligible applicants/beneficiaries: generally, growers of certain fruits, vegetables, and specialty crops (e.g., nuts, raisins, olives, hops); dairy farmers.

Range/Average: N.A.

Activity: N.A.

HQ: Associate Administrator, AMS-USDA, 1400 Independence Ave., SW, Washington, DC 20250. Phone: (202) 720-5115.

Internet: www.ams.usda.gov. (Note: no field offices for this program.)

10.156 FEDERAL-STATE MARKETING IMPROVEMENT PROGRAM

Assistance: project grants (50 percent).

Purposes: pursuant to the Agricultural Marketing Act of 1946, for state pilot marketing service projects to improve the marketability of agricultural products, expand export markets, and improve economic and physical marketing efficiency and competitive trading.

Eligible applicants: state agencies.

Eligible beneficiaries: producers, processors, marketing agencies, and general public.

Range: $25,000 to $135,000. **Average:** $65,000.

Activity: N.A.

HQ: Staff Officer, Federal-State Marketing Improvement Program, AMS-USDA, 1400 Independence Ave., SW, Rm. 4543, Stop 0234, Washington, DC 20250. Phone: (202) 720-5024.

Internet: www.ams.usda.gov/FSMIP. (Note: no field offices for this program.)

10.162 INSPECTION GRADING AND STANDARDIZATION ("Agricultural Fair Practices Act")

Assistance: specialized services.

Purposes: pursuant to the Agricultural Marketing Act of 1946, Food Security Act of 1985, amendments, and other acts, to develop and apply standards of quality and condition for agricultural commodities, for use by owners and dealers; to help develop international standards; to conduct quarterly inspections of egg handlers and hatcheries.

Eligible applicants: agricultural commodity owners or dealers with a financial interest in the commodity to be graded; egg hatcheries and shell egg handlers with an annual production from 3,000 or more hens, packing for the retail consumer—located within the U.S. or its territories.

Eligible beneficiaries: buyers and sellers of agricultural commodities, shell handlers with annual production of 3,000 or more hens, and located in the U.S. or its Territories.

Range/Average: N.A.

Activity: N.A.

HQ: Associate Administrator, AMS-USDA, 1400 Independence Ave., SW, Washington, DC 20250. Phone: (202) 720-5115.

Internet: www.ams.usda.gov.

10.163 MARKET PROTECTION AND PROMOTION

Assistance: specialized services; advisory services/counseling; training.

Purposes: pursuant to the Agricultural Marketing Act of 1946, Agricultural Fair Practices Act, amendments, and other acts, to assure a fair and open marketing distribution system for agricultural products, through the prevention and elimination of deceptive, unfair, or fraudulent trade practices. Various activities fall under the national dairy promotion research and nutrition education program, the Federal Seed Program, the Plant Variety Protection Program, the Research and Promotion Program, and the Pesticide Data Program.

Eligible applicants/beneficiaries: any state government, public or private organization, business, or individual.

Range/Average: N.A.

Activity: N.A.

HQ: Associate Administrator, AMS-USDA, 1400 Independence Ave., SW, Washington, DC 20250. Phone: (202) 720-5115.

Internet: www.ams.usda.gov.

10.164 WHOLESALE FARMERS AND ALTERNATIVE MARKET DEVELOPMENT

Assistance: advisory services/counseling; training.

Purposes: pursuant to the Agricultural Marketing Act of 1946, to provide marketing assistance to food producers through studies on wholesaling, conducted in cooperation with other government agencies and private industry. Project examples: central refrigeration systems in modern food centers; wholesale and farmers markets for distributing produce.

Eligible applicants: government agencies and private industry. Cooperative agreements—states, trade associations, universities, and other nonprofit organizations.

Eligible beneficiaries: producers, processors, marketing agencies, and consumers.

Range/Average: N.A.

Activity: N.A.

HQ: Associate Administrator, AMS-USDA, 1400 Independence Ave., SW, Washington, DC 20250. Phone: (202) 690-1300.

Internet: www.ams.usda.gov. (Note: no field offices for this program.)

10.165   PERISHABLE AGRICULTURAL COMMODITIES ACT

Assistance: investigation of complaints.

Purposes: pursuant to the Act of 1930 as amended and Produce Agency Act, to suppress unfair and fraudulent practices in the marketing of perishable agricultural commodities in interstate and foreign commerce, such as dumping or destruction of farm produce.

Eligible applicants/beneficiaries: businesses or individuals may apply for a PACA license.

Range/Average: N.A.

Activity: N.A.

HQ: Associate Administrator, AMS-USDA, 1400 Independence Ave., SW, Washington, DC 20250. Phone: (202) 720-5115.

Internet: www.ams.usda.gov.

10.167   TRANSPORTATION SERVICES

Assistance: advisory services/counseling; training.

Purposes: pursuant to the Agricultural Adjustment Act of 1938, Agricultural Marketing Act of 1946, Rural Development Act of 1972, and other acts, for the development and promotion of efficient agricultural transportation policies and systems, toward improved farm income and expanded exports. Assistance is provided in cases of significant regional impact or with broad policy implications.

Eligible applicants/beneficiaries: any state government, public or private organization, business or industry, individual.

Range/Average: N.A.

Activity: N.A.

HQ: Associate Administrator, AMS-USDA, 1400 Independence Ave., SW, Washington, DC 20250. Phone: (202) 690-1300.

Internet: www.ams.usda.gov. (Note: no field offices for this program.)

10.168 FARMERS' MARKET AND LOCAL FOOD PROMOTION PROGRAM (FMPP)

Assistance: project grants. (100 percent/to 18 months).

Purposes: pursuant to FSRIA, to improve or expand existing or develop new domestic farmers markets, roadside stands, community-supported agriculture programs, and other direct producer-to-consumer market opportunities—through innovative approaches to market operations and management, improving access to pertinent marketing and financial opportunities, and consumer-based education and market access. Funds may not be used for routine operational expenses such as salaries, utility charges, insurance premiums, nor for any real estate-related costs.

Eligible applicants: agricultural cooperatives; local and tribal governments; nonprofit, public benefit, and economic development corporations; regional farmers market authorities; projects located within 50 states or District of Columbia.

Eligible beneficiaries: direct marketing operations that include two or more farm vendors; consumers.

Range/Average: N.A.

Activity: N.A.

HQ: FMPP, Marketing Services Branch, AMS-USDA, 1400 Independence Ave., SW, Washington, DC 20250. Phone: (202) 720-8317.

Internet: www.ams.usda.gov/FMPP. (Note: no field offices for this program.)

10.170 SPECIALTY CROP BLOCK GRANT PROGRAM—FARM BILL

Assistance: project grants (100 percent/to 3 years).

Purposes: pursuant to Specialty Crops Competitiveness Act of 2004, to increase fruit, vegetable, and nut consumption—enhancing the competitiveness of crop producers. Funds may be also be used for horticulture.

Eligible applicants/beneficiaries: state agriculture departments, agencies, or commissions (including Guam, American Samoa, U.S. Virgin Islands, and Northern Marianas).

Range/Average: N.A.

Activity: N.A.

HQ: Project Manager, Specialty Crop Block Grant Program, AMS-USDA, 1400 Independence Ave., SW, Rm. 4543, Stop 0264, Washington, DC 20250. Phone: (202) 720-1403.

Internet: www.ams.usda.gov/scbgp. (Note: no field offices for this program.)

10.171 ORGANIC CERTIFICATION COST SHARE PROGRAMS ("AMA, NOCCSP")

Assistance: direct payments for specified use/cooperative agreements.

Purposes: pursuant to the Food, Conservation and Energy Act of 2008 and the Federal Crop Insurance Act, financial assistance to reimburse eligible certified organic producers and handlers for a portion of the costs of organic certification. Applicants may receive reimbursements of up to 75% of the costs of certification, with an annual maximum of $750. State agencies (typically departments of agriculture) process applications for cost share funds from certified organic producers and handlers, and the USDA reimburses them. Funds may only be used to provide reimbursements to certified organic producers and handlers. A 10% indirect cost recovery is allowed. Allocations are awarded to state departments of agriculture or their equivalents based on the number of certified organic operations in the state, as well as the history of participation in the cost share program by certified organic operations in that state.

Eligible applicants: state departments of agriculture.

Eligible beneficiaries: certified organic producers and handlers.

Range: $2,500 to $3,000,000. **Average:** N.A.

Activity: N.A.

HQ: Director, AMA-NOCCSP, USDA, 100 Riverside Pkwy., Suite 101, Fredericksburg, Virginia 22406. Phone: (540) 361-1126.

Internet: www.ams.usda.gov. (Note: no field offices for this program.)

10.172 LOCAL FOOD PROMOTION PROGRAM

Assistance: project grants. (75 percent).

Purposes: pursuant to the Farmer-to-Consumer Direct Marketing Act of 1976, as amended by the Agricultural Act of 2014, to increase domestic consumption of and access to locally and regionally produced agricultural products, and to develop new market opportunities for farm and ranch operations serving local markets, by developing, improving, expanding, and providing outreach, training, and technical assistance to, or assisting in the development, improvement, and expansion of local and regional food business enterprises.

Eligible applicants/beneficiaries: anyone/general public.

Range: $25,000 to $100,000. **Average:** N.A.

Activity: 191 awards in FY 2014.

HQ: Agricultural Marketing Service, USDA, 1400 Independence Ave., SW, Rm. 4543, Stop 0234, Washington, DC 20250. Phone: (202) 720-2731.

Internet: www.ams.usda.gov/lfpp. (Note: no field offices for this program.)

10.200 GRANTS FOR AGRICULTURAL RESEARCH—SPECIAL RESEARCH GRANTS
("Special Research Grants")

Assistance: project grants (1-3 years).

Purposes: for applied research, extension, and education projects toward breakthroughs in the food and agricultural sciences, and for ongoing state-federal programs. Current priority areas include integrated pest management and pest management alternatives. Project examples: small fruit crops research; arid rangelands.

Eligible applicants/beneficiaries: state agricultural experiment stations; U.S. IHEs, federal agencies, private organizations and corporations, individuals.

Range/Average: N.A.

Activity: N.A.

HQ: Proposal Services Unit, Competitive Programs, CSREES-USDA, 1400 Independence Ave., SW, Stop 2240, Washington, DC 20250-2240. Phone: (202) 401-4939.

Internet: nifa.usda.gov/grants. (Note: no field offices for this program.)

10.202   COOPERATIVE FORESTRY RESEARCH ("McIntire-Stennis Act")

Assistance: formula grants.

Purposes: pursuant to the Cooperative Forestry Research Act of 1962 and other acts, for forestry research and research training at state forestry schools, in such categories as reforestation, forest and watershed management, rangeland management, production of wildlife and domestic livestock forage, forest pest control, outdoor recreation, wood products development, and protection against fire, insects, and diseases.

Eligible applicants/beneficiaries: governor-designated state institutions; territories and possessions.

Range/Average: N.A.

Activity: N.A.

HQ: Deputy Administrator/Natural Resources and Environment, CSREES-USDA, 1400 Independence Ave., SW, Stop 2210, Washington, DC. 20250. Phone: (202) 720-5229.

Internet: nifa.usda.gov/program/mcintire-stennis-capacity-grant. (Note: no field offices for this program.)

10.203   PAYMENTS TO AGRICULTURAL EXPERIMENT STATIONS UNDER THE HATCH ACT ("Hatch Act")

Assistance: formula grants (50 percent).

Purposes: pursuant to the Hatch Act of 1887 as amended and other acts, for basic and applied research in broad subject areas at state agricultural experiment stations—to promote efficient production, marketing, distribution, and use of farm products. Funds also may be used to pay for administrative planning and direction, and for such purposes as purchasing or renting land and acquiring or constructing or repairing buildings used for research. The stations may contract with agencies and individuals for research projects.

Eligible applicants/beneficiaries: state agricultural experiment stations; territories and possessions.

Range/Average: N.A.

Activity: N.A.

HQ: National Program Leader, Institute of Food Production and Sustainability, Division of Plant Systems-Production, NIFA-USDA, 1400 Independence

Ave., SW, Stop 2240, Washington, DC 20250-2240. Phone: (202) 401-4202; FAX: (202) 401-1782.

Internet: www.nifa.usda.gov. (Note: no field offices for this program.)

10.205 PAYMENTS TO 1890 LAND-GRANT COLLEGES AND TUSKEGEE UNIVERSITY

Assistance: formula grants (50 percent).

Purposes: pursuant to the National Agricultural Research, Extension, and Teaching Policy Act of 1977 as amended (NARETPA) and other acts, for continuing agricultural research and research training, toward the promotion of efficient production, marketing, distribution, and utilization of farm products, and toward sound agriculture and rural life. Funds may be used to pay for developmental costs, retirement programs, administrative planning and direction, and for such purposes as purchasing or renting land and acquiring or constructing or repairing buildings used for research. Recipients may contract with agencies and individuals.

Eligible applicants/beneficiaries: Tuskegee University and the "1890" land grant colleges in Alabama, Arkansas, Delaware, Florida, Georgia, Kentucky, Louisiana, Maryland, Mississippi, Missouri, North Carolina, Oklahoma, South Carolina, Tennessee, Texas, Virginia, and West Virginia.

Range/Average: N.A.

Activity: anticipate awarding funds to 19 institutions in FY 2016.

HQ: National Program Leader, Institute of Youth, Family, and Community, CSREES-USDA, 1400 Independence Ave., SW, Stop 2250, Washington, DC 20250-2250. Phone: (202) 720-9278.

Internet: nifa.usda.gov/program/agricultural-research-1890-land-grant-insti tutions. (Note: no field offices for this program.)

10.206 GRANTS FOR AGRICULTURAL RESEARCH—COMPETITIVE RESEARCH GRANTS
("National Research Initiative Competitive Grants Program")

Assistance: project grants. (100 percent/to 4 years).

Purposes: for research, education and extension grants in food, agriculture, and related areas. Priority areas for funding include agricultural security, plant science and plant pathology, animal science, entomology and nematology, nanotechnology, nutrition/obesity, food quality and health, natural resources and environment, nutrition, rural development, and new products and processes.

Eligible applicants/beneficiaries: state agricultural experiment stations; U.S. IHEs, federal agencies, private organizations and corporations, individuals.

Range/Average: N.A.

Activity: N.A.

HQ: Chief Scientist, National Research Initiative Competitive Grants Program, CSREES-USDA, 1400 Independence Ave., SW, Washington, DC 20250-2240. Phone: (202) 401-1782.

Internet: nifa.usda.gov. (Note: no field offices for this program.)

10.207 ANIMAL HEALTH AND DISEASE RESEARCH (AHDR)

Assistance: formula grants (50 percent matching above base amount).

Purposes: pursuant to NARETPA, amendments, and other acts, for research on health and disease of food animals and horses. Focus is on: infectious diseases; internal and external parasites; noninfectious diseases, toxins, poisons, transportation losses, predators, and other hazards; diseases and parasites of wildlife and other animals transmissible to food animals, horses, or humans.

Eligible applicants/beneficiaries: public nonprofit schools and colleges of veterinary medicine; state agricultural experiment stations.

Range/Average: N.A.

Activity: anticipate 65 capacity block grants to be awarded in FY 2016.

HQ: National Program Leader, Economic and Community Systems or Competitive Programs, CSREES-USDA, 1400 Independence Ave., SW, Stop 2240 or 2215, Washington, DC 20250. Phone: (202) 401-4952.

Internet: nifa.usda.gov/program/animal-health-research-and-disease-program. (Note: no field offices for this program.)

10.210 HIGHER EDUCATION—GRADUATE FELLOWSHIPS GRANT PROGRAM

Assistance: project grants. (100 percent/to five years).

Purposes: pursuant to NARETPA as amended, to support graduate degree candidates and professionals in the food and agricultural sciences. Fellowships are awarded to outstanding students pursuing graduate degrees in fields for which there is a national need for the development of scientific expertise. Doctoral and masters fellows may receive three and two years of support, respectively. The targeted national need areas include: animal, plant biotechnology; food science; human nutrition; food, forest product, or agricultural engineering; water science; agribusiness marketing or management.

Eligible applicants: U.S. public and private nonprofit IHEs.

Eligible beneficiaries: graduate students.

Range/Average: N.A.

Activity: anticipate 13 awards in FY 2016.

HQ: National Program Leader, Institute of Youth, Family, and Community, CSREES-USDA, 1400 Independence Ave., SW, Stop 2250, Washington, DC 20250-2250. Phone: (202) 720-2030.

Internet: nifa.usda.gov/program/national-needs-graduate-and-postgraduate-fellowship-grants-program-funding-opportunity-nnf. (Note: no field offices for this program.)

10.212 SMALL BUSINESS INNOVATION RESEARCH ("SBIR Program")

Assistance: project grants. (100 percent/phase I, to 6 months; phase II, to 2 years).

Purposes: pursuant to the Small Business Innovation Development Act of 1982 as amended, for research by small businesses to stimulate technological innovation, mainly in the areas of: forests and related resources; plant, animal production and protection; air, water, and soils; food science and nutrition; rural and community development; industrial applications; aquaculture; industrial applications; marketing and trade. Previous phase I grants have ranged up to $65,000 for six months of activity; phase II, to $300,000 for up to two years; phase III covers pursuit of commercialization of research products, and receives no federal funding. An objective of SBIR programs is to foster and encourage participation by women-owned and socially disadvantaged firms.

Eligible applicants/beneficiaries: small, U.S. for-profit businesses.

Range/Average: N.A.

Activity: SBIR Phase I: 60 to 80 awards; SBIR Phase II: 50 to 65 awards in FY 2016.

HQ: SBIR Director, CSREES-USDA, 1400 Independence Ave., SW, Stop 2210, Washington, DC 20250-2210. Phone: (202) 720-5229.

Internet: nifa.usda.gov/grants. (Note: no field offices for this program.)

10.215 SUSTAINABLE AGRICULTURE RESEARCH AND EDUCATION (SARE)

Assistance: project grants. (100 percent/1-5 years).

Purposes: pursuant to NARETPA and FACTA, for scientific investigations and education to: reduce the use of chemical pesticides, fertilizers, and toxic materials; improve management of farm resources to enhance productivity and competitiveness; promote crop, livestock, and enterprise diversification; facilitate research projects designed to study agricultural production systems located in areas with various soil, climatic, and physical characteristics; study farms that are managed using production practices optimizing on-farm resources and conservation practices. Funds may not be used to pay indirect costs or tuition.

Eligible applicants/beneficiaries: land grant colleges or universities, other universities, state agricultural experiment and cooperative extension stations, nonprofit organizations, individuals, federal or state government entities.

Range/Average: N.A.

Activity: N.A.

HQ: National Program Leader, Economic and Community Systems or Competitive Programs, CSREES-USDA, 1400 Independence Ave., SW, Stop 2240 or 2215, Washington, DC 20250. Phone: (202) 401-0151.

Internet: nifa.usda.gov/program/sustainable-agriculture-program. (Note: no field offices for this program.)

10.216 1890 INSTITUTION CAPACITY BUILDING GRANTS

Assistance: project grants. (100 percent/1-5 years).

Purposes: pursuant to NARETPA as amended, to build research and teaching capacities at "1890" land grants institutions and Tuskegee University. Teaching grants may support: curricula design and materials development;

faculty development; instruction delivery systems; scientific instrumentation; student recruitment and retention; student experiential learning. Research grants may support studies and experimentation in food and agricultural sciences, centralized research support systems, and technology delivery systems. CSREES encourages cost-sharing by grant recipients.

Eligible applicants/beneficiaries: "1890" land grant institutions, Tuskegee University.

Range/Average: N.A.

Activity: N.A.

HQ: National Program Leader, Institute of Youth, Family, and Community, CSREES-USDA, 1400 Independence Ave., SW, Stop 2250, Washington, DC 20250-2250. Phone: (202) 720-2030.

Internet: nifa.usda.gov/program/1890-land-grant-institutions-programs. (Note: no field offices for this program.)

10.217 HIGHER EDUCATION—INSTITUTION CHALLENGE GRANTS PROGRAM

Assistance: project grants. (50 percent/1-5 years).

Purposes: pursuant to NARETPA as amended, to increase institutional capacity to respond to state, regional, national, or international educational needs in food and agricultural sciences. Funds may be used for curriculum design and materials development, faculty development, instruction delivery systems, scientific instrumentation, student recruitment and retention.

Eligible applicants/beneficiaries: U.S. colleges and universities.

Range/Average: N.A.

Activity: N.A.

HQ: National Program Leader/Higher Education Challenge Grants, Higher Education Programs, CSREES-USDA, 1400 Independence Ave., SW, Stop 2250, Washington, DC 20250-2250. Phone: (202) 720-2324; FAX: (202) 720-2030.

Internet: nifa.usda.gov/program/higher-education-challenge-grants-program. (Note: no field offices for this program.)

10.219 BIOTECHNOLOGY RISK ASSESSMENT RESEARCH (BRAG)

Assistance: project grant. (100 percent/1-5 years).

Purposes: for research focusing on environmental effects of agricultural biotechnology. Project examples: gene crop flow and introgression into natural populations; hazard of pest evolution.

Eligible applicants/beneficiaries: any public or private research or educational institution or organization.

Range/Average: N.A.

Activity: N.A.

HQ: National Program Leader, Institute of Food Production and Sustainability, Division of Plant Systems-Production, NIFA-USDA, 1400 Independence

Ave., SW, Stop 2240, Washington, DC 20250-2240. Phone: (202) 401-4202; FAX: (202) 401-1782.

Internet: www.nifa.usda.gov. (Note: no field offices for this program.)

10.220 HIGHER EDUCATION MULTICULTURAL SCHOLARS PROGRAM ("Minority Scholars Program")

Assistance: project grants. (75 percent/5 years).

Purposes: pursuant to NARETPA as amended and the Food and Agriculture Act of 1977, for four-year undergraduate scholarships supporting minority students pursuing baccalaureate degrees in the food and agricultural sciences, including natural resources, forestry, veterinary medicine, home economics, and closely allied disciplines.

Eligible applicants: all U.S. colleges and universities with appropriate baccalaureate or higher degree programs and with significant minority enrollments.

Eligible beneficiaries: full-time students from groups traditionally under-represented in the fields of study in which funds are awarded.

Range/Average: N.A.

Activity: N.A.

HQ: National Program Leader, Institute of Youth, Family, and Community, CSREES-USDA, 1400 Independence Ave., SW, Stop 2250, Washington, DC 20250-2250. Phone: (202) 720-2030.

Internet: nifa.usda.gov/program/higher-education-multicultural-scholars-program-msp. (Note: no field offices for this program.)

10.221 TRIBAL COLLEGES EDUCATION EQUITY GRANTS

Assistance: formula grants (1-2 years).

Purposes: pursuant to the Equity in Educational Land-Grant Status Act of 1994 as amended, to enhance educational opportunities at the 30 tribal colleges designated as the "1994 Land-Grant Institutions" by strengthening their teaching programs in the food and agricultural sciences in targeted need areas. Funds may support: curricula design and instructional materials development; faculty development; instruction delivery systems; scientific instrumentation; student experiential learning; student recruitment and retention.

Eligible applicants/beneficiaries: the 30 tribal colleges designated as 1994 Land-Grant Institutions.

Range/Average: N.A.

Activity: 34 schools funded in FY 2014.

HQ: National Program Leader, Institute of Youth, Family, and Community, CSREES-USDA, 1400 Independence Ave., SW, Stop 2250, Washington, DC 20250-2250. Phone: (202) 720-2030.

Internet: nifa.usda.gov/program/tribal-equity-grants-program. (Note: no field offices for this program.)

10.222 TRIBAL COLLEGES ENDOWMENT PROGRAM
("1994 Institutions Endowment Interest Program")

Assistance: formula grants (100 percent).

Purposes: pursuant to the Equity in Educational Land-Grant Status Act of 1994, to enhance educational opportunities at the 30 tribal colleges designated as the "1994 Land-Grant Institutions" by strengthening their teaching programs in the food and agricultural sciences in targeted need areas. Funds may be used to establish an endowment supporting activities described in **10.221**.

Eligible applicants/beneficiaries: the 30 tribal colleges designated as 1994 Land-Grant Institutions.

Range/Average: N.A.

Activity: N.A.

HQ: National Program Leader, Institute of Youth, Family, and Community, CSREES-USDA, 1400 Independence Ave., SW, Stop 2250, Washington, DC 20250-2250. Phone: (202) 720-2030.

Internet: nifa.usda.gov/program/tribal-college-endowment-program. (Note: no field offices for this program.)

10.223 HISPANIC SERVING INSTITUTIONS EDUCATION GRANTS
("HSI Grants")

Assistance: project grants. (some matching/1-3 years).

Purposes: pursuant to NARETPA as amended, to support activities by a consortium of Hispanic serving institutions to enhance educational equity for under-represented students, by strengthening their capacities to respond to identified state, regional, national, or international needs in the food and agricultural sciences.

Funds may support cooperative initiatives between two or more institutions and units of state government or the private sector, for activities such as: student mentoring beginning at the high school level and continuing with the provision of financial support for students through graduate training; library resources; curricula design and materials development; faculty development; instruction delivery systems; scientific instrumentation; student experiential learning; student recruitment and retention.

Eligible applicants/beneficiaries: Hispanic-serving IHEs with an enrollment of at least 25 percent Hispanic students, and providing postsecondary programs for which a two-year associate, baccalaureate, or higher degree is awarded.

Range/Average: N.A.

Activity: 30 awards in FY 2015.

HQ: National Program Leader, Institute of Youth, Family, and Community, CSREES-USDA, 1400 Independence Ave., SW, Stop 2250, Washington, DC 20250-2250. Phone: (202) 720-2030.

Internet: nifa.usda.gov/program/hispanic-serving-institutions-education-grants-program. (Note: no field offices for this program.)

10.225 COMMUNITY FOOD PROJECTS
("Community Foods")

Assistance: project grants. (50 percent/1-3 years).

Purposes: pursuant to the Food Stamp Act of 1977 as amended and FAIRA, for community food projects designed to provide food to low-income persons; to increase self-reliance in communities; to promote comprehensive responses to local food, farm, and nutrition issues. Funds may support: improving access to affordable food by low-income households; local food systems such as urban gardening and obtaining food from local farms; expanding economic opportunities for community residents through local businesses or other economic development, job training, youth apprenticeships, school-to-work transitions. Projects should link the food sector to community development, economic opportunity, and environmental enhancement.

Eligible applicants: experienced private nonprofit entities and partnerships thereof.

Eligible beneficiaries: low income people.

Range/Average: N.A.

Activity: 6 planning projects and 21 community food projects were recommended for funding in FY 2015.

HQ: National Program Leader, Institute of Food Safety and Nutrition, NIFA-USDA, 1400 Independence Ave., SW, Stop 2225, Washington, DC 20250-2225. Phone: (202) 401-2138; FAX: (202) 401-6488.

Internet: nifa.usda.gov/program/community-food-projects-competitive-grant-program-cfpcgp. (Note: no field offices for this program.)

10.226 SECONDARY AND TWO-YEAR POSTSECONDARY AGRICULTURE EDUCATION CHALLENGE GRANTS
("SPECA Grants Program")

Assistance: project grants. (50 percent/1-5 years).

Purposes: pursuant to FAIRA as amended, to promote excellence in agriscience and agribusiness education, and to encourage increased pursuit of undergraduate and higher degrees in the food and agricultural sciences. Funds may be used for such targeted areas as curricula design and materials development, promotion of teaching competency, student experiential learning, increasing the diversity of students enrolling.

Eligible applicants/beneficiaries: public secondary schools; public or private nonprofit junior and community colleges.

Range/Average: N.A.

Activity: 9 awards in FY 2014.

HQ: National Program Leader, Institute of Youth, Family, and Community, CSREES-USDA, 1400 Independence Ave., SW, Stop 2250, Washington, DC 20250-2250. Phone: (202) 720-2030.

Internet: nifa.usda.gov/program/secondary-education-two-year-postsecondary-education-and-agriculture-k-12-classroom. (Note: no field offices for this program.)

10.227 TRIBAL COLLEGES RESEARCH GRANTS PROGRAM ("1994 Institutions Research Program")

Assistance: project grants. (100 percent/to 3 years).

Purposes: pursuant to the Equity in Educational Land-Grant Status Act of 1994 as amended, for competitive research grants to the 30 institutions designated as "1994 Institutions," to conduct agricultural research addressing high priority concerns of tribal, national, or multi-state significance.

Eligible applicants/beneficiaries: the 30 institutions designated as "1994 Institutions" (i.e., specified Indian colleges and institutions).

Range/Average: N.A.

Activity: N.A.

HQ: National Program Leader, Institute of Youth, Family, and Community, CSREES-USDA, 1400 Independence Ave., SW, Stop 2250, Washington, DC 20250-2250. Phone: (202) 720-2030.

Internet: www.nifa.usda.gov. (Note: no field offices for this program.)

10.228 ALASKA NATIVE SERVING AND NATIVE HAWAIIAN SERVING INSTITUTIONS EDUCATION GRANTS ("ANNH Grants Program")

Assistance: project grants. (100 percent/1-3 years).

Purposes: to recruit, support, and educate under-represented scientists and professionals, and to advance the educational capacity of Alaska native- and Hawaii native-serving institutions in the food, agricultural, and natural resource systems and careers. Funds may support: curriculum, faculty and library development; scientific instrumentation; instruction delivery systems; student recruitment and retention; and, cooperative initiatives between institutions, state governments, the private sector.

Eligible applicants/beneficiaries: Alaska native- and Hawaii native-serving IHEs.

Range/Average: N.A.

Activity: anticipate 2 awards in FY 2016.

HQ: National Program Leader, Institute of Youth, Family, and Community, CSREES-USDA, 1400 Independence Ave., SW, Stop 2250, Washington, DC 20250-2250. Phone: (202) 720-2030.

Internet: nifa.usda.gov/program/alaska-native-serving-and-native-hawaiian-serving-institutions-education-competitive-grants. (Note: no field offices for this program.)

10.250 AGRICULTURAL AND RURAL ECONOMIC RESEARCH, COOPERATIVE AGREEMENTS AND COLLABORATIONS

Assistance: technical information.

Purposes: to provide economic and other social science information and analysis related to U.S. and world agriculture, food, natural resources, and rural America. Reports are prepared by USDA staff, and are available in printed or electronic form. Fees may be charged.

Eligible applicants/beneficiaries: anyone in the U.S. and territories.

Range/Average: N.A.

Activity: N.A.

HQ: Director, Extramural Agreement Division, Economic Research Service-USDA, 355 E St. SW, Rm. 5-254, Washington, DC 20024-3231. Phone: (202) 694-5008.

Internet: www.ers.usda.gov. (Note: no field offices for this program.)

10.253 CONSUMER DATA AND NUTRITION RESEARCH

Assistance: technical information.

Purposes: pursuant to FY 2006 Agricultural, Rural Development, Food and Drug Administration, and Related Agencies Appropriation Act, to provide economic and other social science information and analysis related to U.S. and world agriculture, food, natural resources, and rural America. Reports are available in printed or in electronic form on the ERS web site. There are no restrictions on use of ERS- produced information, although a fee may be charged.

Eligible applicants/beneficiaries: anyone in the U.S. and territories.

Range/Average: N.A.

Activity: N.A.

HQ: Director, Extramural Agreement Division, Economic Research Service-USDA, 355 E St. SW, Rm. 5-254, Washington, DC 20024-3231. Phone: (202) 694-5008.

Internet: www.ers.usda.gov. (Note: no field offices for this program.)

10.255 RESEARCH INNOVATION AND DEVELOPMENT GRANTS IN ECONOMICS (RIDGE)

Assistance: technical information.

Purposes: pursuant to FY 2006 Agricultural, Rural Development, Food and Drug Administration, and Related Agencies Appropriation Act, to provide economic and other social science information and analysis related to U.S. and world agriculture, food, natural resources, and rural America. Reports are available in printed or in electronic form on the ERS web site. There are no restrictions on use of ERS- produced information, although a fee may be charged.

Eligible applicants/beneficiaries: anyone in the U.S. and territories.

Range/Average: N.A.

Activity: N.A.

HQ: Director, Extramural Agreement Division, Economic Research Service-USDA, 355 E St. SW, Rm. 5-254, Washington, DC 20024-3231. Phone: (202) 694-5008.

Internet: www.ers.usda.gov. (Note: no field offices for this program.)

10.290 AGRICULTURAL MARKET AND ECONOMIC RESEARCH

Assistance: project grants.

Purposes: to conduct research in cooperation with the Office of the Chief Economist's in-house research and analysis programs. Projects may cover such areas as: nation's agricultural commodity markets; risk and cost-benefit analyses related to international food and agriculture; sustainable development; energy issues related to agricultural economy; agricultural labor and global climate change.

Eligible applicants/beneficiaries: nonprofit institutions of higher education; nonprofit scientific or economic research organizations.

Range: $10,000 to $230,000. **Average:** $80,985.

Activity: N.A.

HQ: Chief Economist, Department of Agriculture, 12th & Jefferson Dr., SW, Whitten Bldg., Rm. 11, Washington, DC 20250. Phone: (202) 720-4164.

Internet: www.usda.gov/oce. (Note: no field offices for this program.)

10.303 INTEGRATED PROGRAMS

Assistance: project grants. (100 percent/to 3 years).

Purposes: pursuant to the Food Stamp Act of 1977, for competitive integrated and multi-functional research, education, and extension projects addressing priorities in U.S. agriculture.

Eligible applicants/beneficiaries: state agricultural experiment stations; U.S. IHEs, federal agencies, private organizations and corporations, individuals.

Range/Average: N.A.

Activity: N.A.

HQ: Administrator, CSREES-USDA, 1400 Independence Ave., SW, Stop 2210, Washington, DC. 20250-2210. Phone: (202) 720-5229.

Internet: nifa.usda.gov/grants. (Note: no field offices for this program.)

10.304 HOMELAND SECURITY—AGRICULTURAL ("Homeland Security Program")

Assistance: project grants (100 percent/1-3 years).

Purposes: pursuant to NARETPA as amended, to protect the food supply and agricultural production; to protect USDA facilities and other agricultural infrastructure; and to protect USDA staff and manage emergency preparedness. Project examples: establishment of two diagnostic networks-one each for plant and animal diseases and pests. Research projects may not be funded.

Eligible applicants/beneficiaries: recipients eligible under Section 1472(c) of NARETPA.

Range: $250,000 to $1,000,000. **Average:** N.A.

Activity: anticipate 30 awards FY 2016.

HQ: Office of the Administrator, CSREES-USDA, 1400 Independence Ave., SW, Stop 2201, Washington, DC. 20250-2201. Phone: (202) 401-1112.

Internet: nifa.usda.gov/grants. (Note: no field offices for this program.)

10.305 INTERNATIONAL SCIENCE AND EDUCATION GRANTS (ISE)

Assistance: project grants (1-4 years).

Purposes: pursuant to NARETPA as amended, to strengthen the global competence of students, faculty, and staff in agriculture and related areas, and to enhance business performance in international agriculture and related sectors—through extension, research, and teaching programs. Projects should be designed to: enhance the international content of curricula; enable U.S. faculty to work beyond the U.S. and bring back lessons learned; promote international partnerships; enhance the use of foreign technologies in the U.S.; strengthen the role of IHEs in maintaining U.S. competitiveness.

Eligible applicants/beneficiaries: accredited public or other nonprofit U.S. IHEs that award bachelor's or higher degrees.

Range/Average: N.A.

Activity: N.A.

HQ: International Programs, CSREES-USDA, 1400 Independence Ave., SW, Stop 2203, Washington, DC. 20250-2203. Phone: (202) 720-3801.

Internet: nifa.usda.gov. (Note: no field offices for this program.)

10.306 BIODIESEL FUEL EDUCATION PROGRAM

Assistance: project grants. (100 percent/5 years).

Purposes: to educate governmental and private entities that operate vehicle fleets, as well as the general public, about the benefits of biodiesel fuel use—through education and outreach activities.

Eligible applicants/beneficiaries: nonprofit organizations or IHEs.

Range/Average: N.A.

Activity: 2 proposals selected for funding in FY 2015

HQ: Deputy Administrator/Natural Resources and Environment, CSREES-USDA, 1400 Independence Ave., SW, Stop 2210, Washington, DC. 20250. Phone: (202) 401-5244.

Internet: nifa.usda.gov/funding-opportunity/biodiesel-fuel-education. (Note: no field offices for this program.)

10.307 ORGANIC AGRICULTURE RESEARCH AND EXTENSION INITIATIVE (OREI)

Assistance: project grants (50-100 percent).

Purposes: pursuant to FSRIA as amended and FACTA, for projects emphasizing research and outreach activities that assist farmers and ranchers with whole farm planning and ecosystem integration. Field work for both program areas must be done on certified organic land or land in transition to certification. Projects should: facilitate the development of organic agriculture production, breeding, and processing methods; explore both barriers to and opportunities for marketing, both domestically and abroad; be designed to study and apply most related aspects of organic agriculture.

Eligible applicants/beneficiaries: state agricultural experiment stations, IHEs, other research institutions and organizations, federal agencies, national laboratories, private organizations and corporations, individuals.

Range/Average: N.A.

Activity: anticipate 20 new awards in FY 2015.

HQ: National Program Leader, Economic and Community Systems or Competitive Programs, CSREES-USDA, 1400 Independence Ave., SW, Stop 2240 or 2215, Washington, DC 20250. Phone: (202) 401-6134.

Internet: nifa.usda.gov/program/organic-agriculture-program. (Note: no field offices for this program.)

10.308 RESIDENT INSTRUCTION GRANTS FOR INSULAR AREA ACTIVITIES

Assistance: project grants (100 percent).

Purposes: pursuant to FSRIA, to enhance teaching programs in extension programs in U.S. insular areas, including PR, VI, Guam, Samoa, Northern Marianas, Micronesia, Marshall Islands, and Palau. Funded activities should be similar to those funded under **10.228**, and they facilitate cooperative initiatives between two or more insular area institutions and organizations.

Eligible applicants/beneficiaries: institutions with demonstrated commitment to higher education in the food and agricultural sciences.

Range/Average: N.A.

Activity: N.A.

HQ: National Program Leader, Institute of Youth, Family, and Community, CSREES-USDA, 1400 Independence Ave., SW, Stop 2250, Washington, DC 20250-2250. Phone: (202) 720-2030.

Internet: nifa.usda.gov/program/resident-instruction-grants-riia-and-distance-education-grants-deg-institutions-higher. (Note: no field offices for this program.)

10.309 SPECIALTY CROP RESEARCH INITIATIVE (SCRI)

Assistance: project grants (matching/to 10 years).

Purposes: pursuant to the Agricultural Research, Extension, and Education Reform Act of 1998, as amended to address the critical needs of the specialty crop industry by developing and disseminating science-based tools. Funds shall not be used for the construction of a new building or facility or the acquisition, expansion, remodeling, or alteration of an existing building or facility (including site grading and improvement, and architect fees).

Eligible applicants/beneficiaries: federal agencies, national laboratories, colleges and universities, research and private institutions or organizations, state agricultural experiment stations, individuals, or groups consisting of two or more of these entities.

Range/Average: N.A.

Activity: anticipate 15 to 30 new awards in FY 2016.

HQ: National Program Leader, Plant and Animal Systems, CSREES-USDA, 1400 Independence Ave., SW, Stop 2240, Washington, DC 20250-2240. Phone: (202) 401-4202.

Internet: nifa.usda.gov/program/specialty-crop-research-initiative. (Note: no field offices for this program.)

10.310   AGRICULTURE AND FOOD RESEARCH INITIATIVE (AFRI)

Assistance: project grants (to 50 percent/10 years).

Purposes: pursuant to Competitive, Special and Facilities Research Grant Act, to provide funding for fundamental and applied research, extension, and education to address food and agricultural sciences.

Eligible applicants/beneficiaries: federal agencies, states (includes DC, public IHEs and hospitals), public and quasi-public institutions/organizations, and individuals/families.

Range/Average: N.A.

Activity: N.A.

HQ: Competitive Programs, CSREES-USDA, 1400 Independence Ave., SW, Stop 2240, Washington, DC 20250. Phone: (202) 401-6134.

Internet: nifa.usda.gov/grants. (Note: no field offices for this program.)

10.311   BEGINNING FARMER AND RANCHER DEVELOPMENT PROGRAM (BFRDP)

Assistance: project grants (75 percent/to 3 years).

Purposes: pursuant to FSRIA of 2002, to support the nation's beginning farmers and ranchers by making competitive grants for new and established local/regional training, education, outreach, and technical assistance initiatives. Not less than 25 percent of funds must be set aside to support programs and services that address the needs of limited resource or disadvantaged beginning farmers or ranchers and/or farm workers desiring to become farmers or ranchers. Grant funds may not be used for planning, repair, rehabilitation, acquisition, or construction of a building or facility.

Eligible applicants: state (includes DC, public IHEs and hospitals) and local governments, Indian tribes and organizations, and sponsored institutions/organizations.

Eligible beneficiaries: beginning farmers and ranchers.

Range: to $250,000. **Average:** N.A.

Activity: anticipate funding 25 to 30 new projects in FY 2016.

HQ: National Program Leader, Economic and Community Systems or Competitive Programs, CSREES-USDA, 1400 Independence Ave., SW, Stop 2240 or 2215, Washington, DC 20250. Phone: (202) 401-0151.

Internet: nifa.usda.gov/program/beginning-farmer-and-rancher-development-program. (Note: no field offices for this program.)

10.312   BIOMASS RESEARCH AND DEVELOPMENT INITIATIVE COMPETITIVE GRANTS PROGRAM (BRDI)

Assistance: project grants (50 to 80 percent/to 5 years).

Purposes: pursuant to Food, Conservation, and Energy Act of 2008 and Energy Policy Act of 2005, as a collaboration between DOE and USDA, to carry out R&D and demonstration of biofuels and biobased products and methods, practices, and technologies for the production of biofuels and biobased products. Grant recipient matching funds required: 20 percent for R&D projects; 50 percent for Demonstration and Commercial Projects.

Eligible applicants/beneficiaries: federal government, states (includes DC, public IHEs and hospitals), public and private institutions/organizations.

Range/Average: N.A.

Activity: anticipate funding 6 to 9 projects in FY 2015.

HQ: National Program Leader, Plant and Animal Systems, CSREES-USDA, 1400 Independence Ave., SW, Stop 2210, Washington, DC 20250-2210. Phone: (202) 401-5244.

Internet: nifa.usda.gov/program/biobased-products-processing-programs. (Note: no field offices for this program.)

10.313 VETERINARY MEDICINE LOAN REPAYMENT PROGRAM (VMLRP)

Assistance: direct payments/specified use (100 percent/to 3 years).

Purposes: pursuant to the National Agricultural Research, Extension, and Teaching Policy Act of 1977 (NAREPTA), to encourage large animal veterinarians through loan repayment, to provide veterinary service in designated rural shortage areas. The veterinarian shall not be required to serve more than 60 working days per year of the agreement and shall receive a salary commensurate with the duties and be reimbursed for travel and per diem expenses.

Eligible applicants/beneficiaries: veterinarians.

Range/Average: N.A.

Activity: 40 to 50 loan repayment agreements anticipated for FY 2016.

HQ: National Program Leader, Economic and Community Systems or Competitive Programs, CSREES-USDA, 1400 Independence Ave., SW, Stop 2240 or 2215, Washington, DC 20250. Phone: (202) 401-6134.

Internet: nifa.usda.gov/program/veterinary-medicine-loan-repayment-program. (Note: no field offices for this program.)

10.314 NEW ERA RURAL TECHNOLOGY COMPETITIVE GRANTS PROGRAM ("Rural Technology Program")

Assistance: project grants (100 percent/to 3 years).

Purposes: pursuant to Subtitle K of the National Agricultural Research, Extension, and Teaching Policy Act of 1977, to establish a competitive grants program to provide funding for technology development, applied research, and training to aid in the development of an agriculture-based renewable energy workforce, especially in the areas of: bioenergy; pulp and paper manufacturing; and agricultural- based renewable energy. Preference shall be given to entities working in partnership to improve information-sharing capacity.

Eligible applicants/beneficiaries: public and quasi-public nonprofit institutions/organizations (includes IHEs and hospitals); other public institutions/organizations, including higher education and research.

Range/Average: N.A.

Activity: N.A.

HQ: National Program Leader, Institute of Youth, Family, and Community, CSREES-USDA, 1400 Independence Ave., SW, Stop 2250, Washington, DC 20250-2250. Phone: (202) 720-2030.

Internet: N.A. (Note: no field offices for this program.)

10.315 TRADE ADJUSTMENT ASSISTANCE FOR FARMERS TRAINING COORDINATION PROGRAM (TAAF)

Assistance: project grants/cooperative agreements (100 percent/3 years).

Purposes: pursuant to Subtitle C of Title 1 of the Trade Adjustment Assistance Reform Act of 2002, amended the Trade Act of 1974, establishing the Trade Adjustment Assistance for Farmers (TAAF) program and ARRA 2009, to provide U.S. agricultural producers whose commodities have been certified as affected by imports, and who have been approved through individual application, with knowledge, skills and tools needed to make adjustments to their operations, business plans, marketing plans for their operations, with the goal of enhancing farm profitability and ability to adjust to imports. Producers of commodities certified by the USDA-FAS and who meet the eligibility requirements by USDA-FSA are eligible for TAAF program participation.

Eligible applicants/beneficiaries: states (includes DC, IHEs and hospitals), and public institutions/organizations.

Range/Average: N.A.

Activity: N.A.

HQ: National Program Leader, Institute of Youth, Family, and Community, CSREES-USDA, 1400 Independence Ave., SW, Stop 2250, Washington, DC 20250-2250. Phone: (202) 720-2030.

Internet: N.A. (Note: no field offices for this program.)

10.317 FOOD AID NUTRITION ENHANCEMENT PROGRAM (FANEP)

Assistance: project grants/discretionary (100 percent/to 5 years).

Purposes: pursuant to Subtitle K of the National Agricultural Research, Extension, and Teaching Policy Act of 1977, to develop and field test new food products designed to improve the nutritional delivery of humanitarian food assistance provided through the McGovern-Dole and the Food for Peace programs. Competitive grants awarded for collaborative projects that are mutually beneficial to the U.S. and other countries and encourage private sector involvement.

Eligible applicants/beneficiaries: non-foreign and international organizations, including: state agricultural experiment stations, colleges and universities, university research foundations, other research institutions and organizations, Federal agencies, national laboratories, private organizations/corporations, individuals who are U.S. citizens or permanent residents, and any group consisting of two or more eligible entities.

Range/Average: N.A.

Activity: N.A.

HQ: National Program Leader, Competitive Programs, NIFA-USDA, 1400 Independence Ave., SW, Stop 2251, Washington, DC 20024. Phone: (202) 720-1973.

Internet: nifa.usda.gov. (Note: no field offices for this program.)

10.322 DISTANCE EDUCATION GRANTS FOR INSTITUTIONS OF HIGHER EDUCATION IN INSULAR AREAS

Assistance: project grants (100 percent/to 5 years).

Purposes: pursuant to 7 U.S.C. 3362, funds to strengthen the capacity of institutions of higher education in insular areas to carry out resident instruction, curriculum, and teaching programs in the food and agricultural sciences through distance education technology. Grant funds must be used for allowable costs necessary to conduct approved fundamental and applied research, extension and education objectives to address food and agricultural sciences. Use of grant funds to plan, acquire, or construct a building or facility is not allowed. With prior approval, some grant funds may be used for minor alterations, renovations, or repairs deemed necessary to retrofit existing teaching or research spaces in order to carry out a funded project. Grant funds may not be used for endowment investing. Recovery of indirect costs is limited to 30 percent of total federal funds awarded.

Eligible applicants/beneficiaries: land-grant colleges and universities, and other IHEs that have secured land-grant status through Federal legislation located in insular areas are automatically eligible for awards, either as direct applicants or as parties to a consortium agreement.

Range/Average: N.A.

Activity: N.A.

HQ: National Program Leader, Institute of Youth, Family, and Community, CSREES-USDA, 1400 Independence Ave., SW, Stop 2250, Washington, DC 20250-2250. Phone: (202) 720-2030.

Internet: www.nifa.usda.gov. (Note: no field offices for this program.)

10.325 PEOPLE'S GARDEN GRANT PROGRAM (PGGP)

Assistance: cooperative agreements (100 percent but 10 percent cost sharing encouraged/to 2 years).

Purposes: pursuant to National Agricultural Research, Extension, and Teaching Policy Act, to create gardens that will improve food access and serve as science-based educational sites for the community. Establish new gardens, revitalize and repurpose moribund local community gardens and develop locally-sponsored, self-sufficient gardens nationwide. The purchase of equipment is limited to that which is required for training, teaching, extension demonstration, and other relevant project activities.

Eligible applicants/beneficiaries: state agricultural experiment stations and cooperative extension services, all colleges and universities, other research or education institutions and organizations, federal and private agencies/organizations, non-profit organizations and individuals.

Range/Average: N.A.

Activity: N.A.

HQ: National Program Leader, Institute of Food Production and Sustainability, Division of Plant Systems-Production, NIFA-USDA, 1400 Independence Ave., SW, Stop 2240, Washington, DC 20250-2240. Phone: (202) 401-4202; FAX: (202) 401-1782.

Internet: nifa.usda.gov/grants. (Note: no field offices for this program.)

10.328 NATIONAL FOOD SAFETY TRAINING, EDUCATION, EXTENSION, OUTREACH, AND TECHNICAL ASSISTANCE COMPETITIVE GRANTS PROGRAM

Assistance: project grants/discretionary. (100 percent/1 to 5 years).

Purposes: pursuant to the Federal Food, Drug, and Cosmetic Act of 2002, to increase the understanding and adoption of established food safety standards, guidance, and protocols. Grants awarded through this program will facilitate the integration of food safety standards and guidance with a variety of agricultural production and processing systems, including conventional, sustainable, organic, and conservation and environmental practices carried out by the eligible entities.

Eligible applicants/beneficiaries: federal, state, local, tribal, and territorial agencies, nonprofits, and IHEs.

Range/Average: N.A.

Activity: N.A.

HQ: National Program Leader, Institute of Food Safety and Nutrition, NIFA-USDA, 1400 Independence Ave., SW, Stop 2225, Washington, DC 20024. Phone: (202) 205-0250; FAX: (202) 401-4888.

Internet: nifa.usda.gov/program/food-safety. (Note: no field offices for this program.)

10.331 FOOD INSECURITY NUTRITION INCENTIVE GRANTS PROGRAM

Assistance: project grants. (50 percent/1 to 4 years).

Purposes: pursuant to the Agricultural Act of 2014, and the Food, Conservation, and Energy Act of 2008, to provide incentives to low-income consumers participating in the supplemental nutrition assistance program (SNAP) to purchase fruits and vegetables at the point of sale.

Eligible applicants/beneficiaries: federal, state, local, tribal, and territorial organizations/institutions, and public and private nonprofits.

Range/Average: N.A.

Activity: N.A.

HQ: National Program Leader, Institute of Food Safety and Nutrition, USDA, 1400 Independence Ave., SW, Stop 2255, Washington, DC 20024. Phone: (202) 720-0740; FAX: (202) 401-4888.

Internet: nifa.usda.gov/program/food-insecurity-nutrition-incentive-fini-grant-program. (Note: no field offices for this program.)

10.350 TECHNICAL ASSISTANCE TO COOPERATIVES (TA)

Assistance: specialized services; advisory services/counseling; training; technical information.

Purposes: pursuant to the Cooperative Marketing Act of 1926 and Agricultural Marketing Act of 1946, to develop and administer research, technical assistance, and educational programs on the financial, organization, management, legal, social, and economic aspects of rural cooperatives. Assistance may include publications, workshops, audiovisual materials, computer systems.

Eligible applicants/beneficiaries: farmer cooperatives and groups of rural residents, Native Americans, farmers, ranchers, agricultural producers, including in the territories.

Range/Average: N.A.

Activity: N.A.

HQ: Deputy Administrator/Cooperative Services, RBCS-USDA, 1400 Independence Ave., SW, Washington, DC 20250-3250. Phone: (202) 720-3350.

Internet: www.rurdev.usda.gov/rbs/coops/csdir.htm.

10.352 VALUE-ADDED PRODUCER GRANTS

Assistance: project grants (50 percent).

Purposes: pursuant to Agricultural Risk Protection Act of 2000 as amended and FSRIA, to refine agricultural commodity product values and enhance returns to producers. Grants may cover either: planning activities to prepare feasibility studies, and business plans; or, working capital for operating expenses of ventures.

Eligible applicants/beneficiaries: independent agricultural commodity producers and producer groups, farmer and rancher cooperatives, and majority-controlled, producer-based business ventures.

Range: $5,000 to $250,000. **Average:** $120,000.

Activity: N.A.

HQ: Deputy Administrator/Cooperative Services, RBCS-USDA, 1400 Independence Ave., SW, Stop 3253, Rm. 4208-S, Washington, DC 20250. Phone: (202) 690-1374.

Internet: www.rd.usda.gov/programs-services/value-added-producer-grants.

10.404 EMERGENCY LOANS

Assistance: direct loans. (80-100 percent/15-40 years).

Purposes: pursuant to the Consolidated Farm and Rural Development Act of 1987 (CFRDA) and other acts, to repair, restore, or replace damaged or destroyed farm property, required as a result of declared natural disasters; for farm operating expenses and other costs necessary to return disaster victims' farming operations to financially sound condition, including debt refinancing. Loans at 3.75 percent interest may cover: 100 percent of the cost of physical loss for up to 40 years; 80 percent of actual production loss for up to 15 years.

Eligible applicants/beneficiaries: established family farmers, ranchers, or aquaculture operators (tenant-or owner-operator) conducting a farming operation at the time of the disaster, as proprietors, partnerships, cooperatives, corporations, or joint operations—and that: are U.S. citizens or legal resident aliens, or entities operated by citizens owning over a 50 percent interest; are unable to obtain necessary credit from other sources to qualify for subsidized loss loans; are capable of managing the operation; have county committee eligibility certification; provide suitable collateral to secure the loan; have crop insurance if available for affected crops; have not caused a loss to FSA, nor received FSA debt forgiveness on more than one occasion, after 4 April 1996. Available also in most territories when those areas are designated. Prospective applicants should contact FSA county offices immediately after sustaining the loss.

Range: to $500,000. **Average:** N.A.

Activity: anticipate 357 emergency loans FY 2016.

HQ: Director, FSA-USDA, 1400 Independence Ave., SW, Washington, DC 20250. Phone: (202) 690-0756.

Internet: www.fsa.usda.gov.

10.405   FARM LABOR HOUSING LOANS AND GRANTS ("Labor Housing - Sections 514 and 516")

Assistance: project grants; guaranteed/insured loans. (to 90 percent/1 percent/ to 33 years).

Purposes: pursuant to the Housing Act of 1949 as amended, to construct, repair, or purchase basic year-round or seasonal housing and related support facilities for domestic farm laborers. Funds may be used for land acquisition, recreation areas, central cooking and dining facilities, small infirmaries, laundry facilities, day care centers. Grants are available only when there is a pressing need and when facilities could not be developed otherwise.

Eligible applicants: loans—farmers, family farm partnerships or corporations, associations of farmers. Loans and grants—states and their political subdivisions, PR, VI, broad-based public or private nonprofit organizations, tribes, and nonprofit corporations of farm workers.

Eligible beneficiaries: domestic farm laborers that are U.S. citizens or legal permanent residents.

Range/Average: N.A.

Activity: repaired 317 units and constructed 1,076 units in FY 2014.

HQ: Preservation and Direct Loan Division, RHS-USDA, 1400 Independence Ave., SW, Stop 0782, Washington, DC 20250-0781. Phone: (202) 720-1604.

Internet: www.rurdev.usda.gov.

10.406   FARM OPERATING LOANS

Assistance: direct loans; guaranteed/insured loans (7-22 years).

Purposes: pursuant to CFRDA and other acts, to enable family farm operators to: purchase livestock, poultry, fur-bearing and other farm animals, fish, and bees; purchase farm, forestry, recreation, or nonfarm enterprise equipment and provide operating funds for such enterprises; meet family subsistence needs; purchase essential home equipment; refinance certain secured and unsecured debts; pay property taxes and property insurance premiums; finance youth projects. The interest rate on guaranteed loans may be subsidized at 4 percent; direct loans are awarded at one percent interest above the federal borrowing rate.

Eligible applicants/beneficiaries: U.S. citizens or permanent residents with: experience or training to operate a farm; an acceptable credit history; legal capacity to incur a loan obligation; inability to obtain a reasonable loan elsewhere; and, who will become owners or tenants operating family farms through the program; except for youth projects, no history of causing a loss to FSA, nor of receiving FSA debt forgiveness more than three times after 4 April 1996. Certain corporations, cooperatives, partnerships, and joint operations conducting family farms. Available also in most territories.

Range: to $300,000 for direct farm operating loans; to $1,392,000 for guaranteed farm operating loans. **Average:** $52,848 for direct farm operating loans; $242,104 for guaranteed farm operating loans.

Activity: anticipate 22,764 direct loans and 64,848 guaranteed loans in FY 2016.

HQ: Director, FSA-USDA, 1400 Independence Ave., SW, Washington, DC 20250. Phone: (202) 690-0756.

Internet: www.fsa.usda.gov.

10.407 FARM OWNERSHIP LOANS

Assistance: direct loans; guaranteed/insured loans (to 40 years).

Purposes: pursuant to CFRDA and other acts, to: purchase, enlarge, and improve family farms; provide necessary water and water facilities; take necessary basic soil treatment and land conservation measures; construct, repair, or improve buildings needed in farm operations; provide facilities to produce fish under controlled conditions.

Eligible applicants/beneficiaries: U.S. citizens or permanent residents with: experience or training to operate a farm; an acceptable credit history; legal capacity to incur a loan obligation; inability to obtain a reasonable loan elsewhere; and, who will become owners or tenants operating family farms through the program; except for youth projects, no history of causing a loss to FSA, nor of receiving FSA debt forgiveness more than three times after 4 April 1996. Certain corporations, cooperatives, partnerships, and joint operations conducting family farms. Available also in most territories. If an individual, not have a combined farm ownership loan, soil and water loan, and recreation loan indebtedness to FSA of more than $200,000 for direct loans, and $717,000 for guaranteed loans, or a total indebtedness against the property securing the loan of more than the market value of the security, whichever is the lesser amount.

Range: N.A. **Average:** $181,034 for direct farm ownership loans; $439,089 for guaranteed farm ownership loans.

Activity: anticipate 8,876 direct loans and 4,785 guaranteed loans in FY 2016.

HQ: Director, FSA-USDA, 1400 Independence Ave., SW, Washington, DC 20250. Phone: (202) 690-0756.

Internet: www.fsa.usda.gov.

10.410   VERY LOW TO MODERATE INCOME HOUSING LOANS ("Section 502 Rural Housing Loans")

Assistance: direct loans; guaranteed/insured loans (guaranteed, to 30 years; direct, to 38 years).

Purposes: pursuant to the Housing Act of 1949 and CFRDA as amended and other acts, for below-market-rate loan financing to lower-income rural families to: purchase, construct, improve, or repair housing to be used as a permanent residence; to finance the cost of sewage disposal, water supply facilities, weatherization, and essential household equipment; and, under certain conditions, to refinance housing debts, finance the purchase of manufactured homes and sites for their location. Loans can be subsidized through interest credits to as low as an effective rate of one percent, depending on the loan amount and applicant income and family size; interest subsidies are subject to recapture if property is liquidated.

Eligible applicants/beneficiaries: applicants determined to be very low income (below 50 percent of area median), low income (between 50 and 80 percent or area median), or moderate income (below 115 percent of area median)—with adequate and dependable available income to meet operating and family living expenses, including taxes, insurance, maintenance, and repayments on debts including the proposed loan, and without sufficient resources to obtain the necessary housing or related facilities. For direct loans, applicants must be eligabile for interest credit, with income not above established limits. Available in territories and possessions.

Range: N.A. **Average:** $125,348 estimated for direct loans; $136,986 estimated for guaranteed loans.

Activity: N.A.

HQ: Director, Single-Family Housing Processing Division, RHS-USDA, 1400 Independence Ave., SW, Washington, DC 20250. Phone (804) 287-1559.

Internet: www.rurdev.usda.gov.

10.415   RURAL RENTAL HOUSING LOANS

Assistance: direct loans; project grants (loans, 30 years).

Purposes: pursuant to the Housing Act of 1949 as amended, for the purchase, construction, or substantial rehabilitation of rural rental or cooperative housing with two or more family units, including manufactured housing, and certain related uses including recreational and service facilities. Loans may be made in communities with up to 10,000 population, and up to 20,000 under certain conditions. Tenants pay basic rent or 30 percent of adjusted income, whichever is greater; RHS rental assistance subsidies can be used to limit rental payments to 30 percent of income (see **10.427**). Loans may not cover nursing, special care, or institutional homes.

Eligible applicants: individuals, cooperatives, nonprofit organizations, state or local public agencies, profit corporations, trusts, partnerships, limited partnerships and, except for state or local public agencies, unable to finance the housing either with their own resources or with credit obtained from private sources. Available also in territories.

Eligible beneficiaries: very-low-, low-, and moderate-income households, elderly, and handicapped or disabled persons.

Range/Average: N.A.

Activity: N.A.

HQ: Director, Multifamily Housing Processing Division, RHS-USDA, 1400 Independence Ave., SW, Washington, DC 20250. Phone: (202) 720-1604.

Internet: www.rd.usda.gov.

10.417 VERY LOW-INCOME HOUSING REPAIR LOANS AND GRANTS ("Section 504 Rural Housing Loans and Grants")

Assistance: direct loans; project grants (direct, 1 percent interest/direct, to 20 years).

Purposes: pursuant to the Housing Act of 1949 as amended, to provide loans of up to $20,000 to very low-income rural owner-occupants and/or grants of up to $7,500 to eligible elderly persons—to repair or modernize their existing homes, including weatherization, and to upgrade water and waste disposal systems.

Eligible applicants/beneficiaries: owner-occupants of rural homes, with sufficient income to repay loans, and that are U.S. citizens or legal residents or on indefinite parole. Applicant's income may not exceed very-low-income limits set forth in USDA instructions. Grant recipients must be at least age 62 and unable to repay the part of the assistance received as a grant. Available also in territories.

Range: N.A. **Average:** $5,820 for loans; $6,133 for grants.

Activity: N.A.

HQ: Director, Single-Family Housing Processing Division, RHS-USDA, 1400 Independence Ave., SW, Washington, DC 20250. Phone (804) 287-1559.

Internet: www.rurdev.usda.gov.

10.420 RURAL SELF-HELP HOUSING TECHNICAL ASSISTANCE ("Section 523 Technical Assistance")

Assistance: project grants. (100 percent/2 years).

Purposes: pursuant to the Housing Act of 1949 as amended, for the organizational, administrative, and basic costs of carrying out mutual self-help housing programs in rural areas. Grant funds may be used to pay the costs of training self-help group members and of purchasing tools and equipment—but not to hire construction personnel, nor to buy real estate or building materials.

Eligible applicants: states or political subdivisions, public or private nonprofit corporations. Available also in PR, VI, Guam, Northern Marianas.

Eligible beneficiaries: very-low- and low-income rural families, usually in groups of 6 to 10 families.

Range: N.A. **Average:** $561,948.

Activity: N.A.

HQ: Director, Single-Family Housing Processing Division, RHS-USDA, 1400 Independence Ave., SW, Washington, DC 20250. Phone (804) 287-1559.

Internet: www.rurdev.usda.gov.

10.421   INDIAN TRIBES AND TRIBAL CORPORATION LOANS

Assistance: direct loans. (100 percent/to 40 years).

Purposes: pursuant to the Loans to Indian Tribes and Tribal Corporations Act, to buy land within tribal reservations and Alaskan communities. Loan funds may be used to acquire land and for related costs, for such purposes as rounding out farming or ranching units or to eliminate fractional heir ships. Loan funds may not be used for development, improvements, or operating costs.

Eligible applicants/beneficiaries: recognized tribes and tribal corporations or Alaska communities.

Range/Average: N.A.

Activity: N.A.

HQ: Director, Loan Servicing and Property Management Division, FSA-USDA, 1400 Independence Ave., Washington, DC 20250. Phone: (202) 690-0756.

Internet: www.fsa.usda.gov. (Note: no field offices for this program.)

10.427   RURAL RENTAL ASSISTANCE PAYMENTS
("Rental Assistance - Section 521")

Assistance: direct payments/specified use (5 years).

Purposes: pursuant to the Housing Act of 1949 as amended, to subsidize rents paid by low-income senior citizens, families, and domestic farm laborers occupying eligible RHS-assisted units, and whose rents exceed 30 percent of an adjusted annual income figure established for each state.

Eligible applicants: basically, state and local agencies and nonprofit or limited-profit sponsors of certain rural rental housing projects financed by RHS. (New construction and rehabilitation projects receiving Section 8 assistance from HUD are ineligible.)

Eligible beneficiaries: low- or very-low-income families and handicapped or senior citizens occupying eligible rural rental, cooperative, or farm labor housing.

Range/Average: N.A.

Activity: N.A.

HQ: Director, Multifamily Housing Portfolio Management Division, RHS-USDA, Washington, DC 20250. Phone: (202) 720-1615.

Internet: www.rd.usda.gov.

10.433   RURAL HOUSING PRESERVATION GRANTS

Assistance: project grants.

Purposes: pursuant to the Housing Act of 1949 as amended, to assist low- and very-low-income rural homeowners, rental property owners, and cooperatives to repair or rehabilitate their housing. Generally, assistance is used in conjunction with other federal funding, such as HUD's CDBG or HHS's weatherization programs, or with programs sponsored by states. Revolving loan funds may be established. Applicants may use up 20 percent of funds for project operating costs, including training of project personnel; the remaining 80 percent must be used as loans or grants for housing improvements.

Eligible applicants/beneficiaries: authorized public or private nonprofit organizations; city and county agencies, state governments; tribes; consortia of eligabible entities—in communities with up to 10,000 population, or up to 20,000 under certain conditions. Available also in territories and possessions.

Range/Average: N.A.

Activity: assisted 1,231 housing units in FY 2014.

HQ: Multifamily Housing Processing Division, RHS-USDA, 1400 Independence Ave SW, Washington, DC 20250-0788. Phone: (202) 720-1604.

Internet: www.rd.usda.gov.

10.435 STATE MEDIATION GRANTS

Assistance: project grants (70 percent).

Purposes: pursuant to the Agricultural Credit Act of 1987, FACTA, Agricultural Credit Improvement Act of 1992, Federal Crop Insurance Reform and Department of Agriculture Reorganization Act of 1994, and United States Grain Standards Act of 2000, to cover state operating and administrative costs in connection with certified agricultural loan mediation programs for producers, creditors, and others affected by USDA actions.

Eligible applicants: state governments.

Eligible beneficiaries: agricultural producers and their creditors; others directly affected by USDA actions.

Range/Average: N.A.

Activity: N.A.

HQ: FSA-USDA, 1400 Independence Ave. SW, Stop 0523, Washington, DC 20250-0523. Phone: (202) 720-1360.

Internet: www.fsa.usda.gov.

10.438 SECTION 538 RURAL RENTAL HOUSING GUARANTEED LOANS

Assistance: guaranteed/insured loans.

Purposes: pursuant to the Housing Act of 1949 as amended, for partnerships between RHS and major lenders including state and local housing finance agencies and bond insurers, resulting in an increased supply of new, affordable, multifamily, rural housing consisting of two or more family units. Projects must provide new forms of credit enhancements for housing development. Nursing, special care, and industrial type housing are ineligible.

Eligible applicants: lenders approved by the Federal National Mortgage Association, Federal Home Loan Mortgage Corporation, HUD, or state housing finance agencies.

Eligible beneficiaries: rural households with income not exceeding 115 percent of the median.

Range/Average: N.A.

Activity: N.A.

HQ: Director, Multifamily Housing Processing Division, RHS-USDA, 1400 Independence Ave., SW, Washington, DC 20250. Phone: (202) 720-1604.

Internet: www.rurdev.usda.gov.

10.443 OUTREACH AND ASSISTANCE FOR SOCIALLY DISADVANTAGED AND VETERAN FARMERS AND RANCHERS

Assistance: project grants. (100 percent/1-5 years).

Purposes: pursuant to FACTA, to provide outreach, training, and technical assistance socially disadvantaged farmers and ranchers—toward their ownership and operation of farms and their participation in farm programs.

Eligible applicants: experienced "1890" land-grant colleges and Tuskegee University; tribal community colleges and Alaska native cooperative colleges, Hispanic-serving and other postsecondary educational institutions, and community-based organizations.

Eligible beneficiaries: socially disadvantaged farmers or ranchers including Blacks, women, American Indians, Alaska natives, Hispanics, Asians, and Pacific Islanders.

Range: to $400,000. **Average:** N.A.

Activity: N.A.

HQ: Office of Outreach (1710), USDA, 1400 Independence Ave., SW, Washington, DC 20250. Phone: (202) 720-6350.

Internet: www.outreach.usda.gov/oasdfr. (Note: no field offices for this program.)

10.446 RURAL COMMUNITY DEVELOPMENT INITIATIVE (RCDI)

Assistance: project grants. (50 percent/3 years).

Purposes: for capacity building toward the improvement of rural housing, community facilities, and community and economic development projects. Grant funds may be used to train and provide technical assistance to subgrantees in such areas as: conducting homeownership education and minority entrepreneurial programs, and developing child care facilities; strategic planning, obtaining alternative funding, fundraising, board training. Funds may also be used to develop training tools including videos, workbooks, and reference guides.

Eligible applicants/beneficiaries: private, public, or tribal organizations with three years of pertinent rural experience, including in territories and possessions.

Range: $50,000 to $152,000. **Average:** N.A.

Activity: N.A.

HQ: Deputy Administrator/Community Programs, RHS-USDA, 1400 Independence Ave., Washington, DC 20250. Phone: (202) 720-1498.

Internet: www.rd.usda.gov/had-rcdi_grants.html.

10.447   THE RURAL DEVELOPMENT (RD) MULTI-FAMILY HOUSING REVITALIZATION DEMONSTRATION PROGRAM ("Restructuring Program")

Assistance: debt deferral; grants; loans (to 50 years).

Purposes: pursuant to the Housing Act of 1949, as amended, Section 515, and The Agriculture, Rural Development, Food and Drug Administration, and Related Agencies Appropriation Act of 2007, to preserve and revitalize existing rural rental projects financed by RHS under Section 515 of the Housing Act of 1949 and to ensure continued safe and affordable housing for low-income residents.

Eligible applicants: owners or buyers of financially viable Section 515 financed rental properties.

Eligible beneficiaries: low-income rural renters.

Range: to $20,000. **Average:** N.A.

Activity: N.A.

HQ: Director, Office of Rental Housing Preservation, Rural Development, Department of Agriculture, 1400 Independence Ave., SW, Stop 0782, Washington, DC 20250-0781. Phone: (202) 720-1604.

Internet: www.rurdev.usda.gov.

10.448   RURAL DEVELOPMENT MULTI-FAMILY HOUSING RURAL HOUSING VOUCHER DEMONSTRATION PROGRAM

Assistance: direct payments for specified use.

Purposes: to provide rental housing assistance vouchers to tenants in properties that prepay their Rural Development mortgage. The amount of this subsidy is the difference between the comparable market rent for the familys former Section 515 unit and the amount of rent being paid by the tenant when prepayment occurs. Prepaying properties may be located anywhere in the 50 states, Puerto Rico, the U.S. Virgin Islands and Guam. The rental unit must pass a Rural Development health and safety inspection. The owner must be willing to accept a Rural Development voucher.

Eligible applicants/beneficiaries: a tenant residing in a Section 515 project on the date of the prepayment of the Section 515 loan or upon foreclosure by Rural Development. Must be a citizen, U.S. non-citizen national, or qualified alien, and have an adjusted household income at or below 80 percent of area median income as determined annually by the U.S. Department of Housing and Urban Development.

Range/Average: N.A.

Activity: N.A.

HQ: Director, Rural Development Voucher Demonstration Program, Portfolio Management Division, Rural Development-USDA, 1400 Independence Ave., SW, Stop 0782, Washington, DC 20250-0782. Phone: (202) 720-1615.

Internet: www.rd.usda.gov.

10.449   BOLL WEEVIL ERADICATION LOAN PROGRAM

Assistance: direct loans. (100 percent/1-7 years).

Purposes: to eradicate boll weevils from the U.S. Loan funds may be used to: purchase or lease supplies and equipment; pay operating expenses, salaries, and benefits—but not for lobbying, public relations, or similar activities.

Eligible applicants/beneficiaries: nonprofit entities authorized under appropriate state law.

Range/Average: N.A.

Activity: N.A.

HQ: Director, FSA-USDA, 1400 Independence Ave., SW, Washington, DC 20250. Phone: (202) 690-0756.

Internet: www.fsa.usda.gov. (Note: no field offices for this program.)

10.450 CROP INSURANCE

Assistance: insurance.

Purposes: pursuant to the Federal Crop Insurance Act, Agricultural Adjustment Act of 1938, Federal Crop Insurance Reform Act of 1994, FAIRA, AREERA, Agriculture Risk Protection Act of 2000, amendments, and other acts, to insure farmers against losses resulting from unavoidable causes and uncontrollable events. Producers must obtain at least the catastrophic level of coverage to be eligible under the price support or production adjustment programs, the Conservation Reserve Program, or farm credit programs. The premium is fully subsidized on catastrophic crop insurance, except for a processing fee. Coverage compensates producers for yield losses exceeding 50 percent, at a price equal to 55 percent of maximum price. Additional protection at higher levels of coverage is also offered. The program provides for ongoing research to devise and establish crop insurance protection programs, as well as risk management education for producers including futures and options trading. Pilot insurance programs currently are being tested for various crops. Various insurance programs in certain areas cover specific crops; regulations concerning crops and insurance coverage may be obtained from USDA regional offices or private industry crop insurance agents.

Eligible applicants/beneficiaries: owners or operators of farmland, with an insurable interest in a crop in a county where insurance is offered on that crop. The Noninsured Assistance Program is available in other areas (see **10.451**). Note: applications are to be submitted to companies reinsured by FCIC.

Range/Average: N.A.

Activity: provided risk protection with over 2.1 million policies in FY 2014.

HQ: Administrator, RMA-USDA, SW Wanamaker Rd., Suite 201, Topeka, KS 66614. Phone: (785) 228-5531.

Internet: www.rma.usda.gov.

10.451 NONINSURED ASSISTANCE ("NAP")

Assistance: direct payments/unrestricted use.

Purposes: pursuant to FAIRA as amended, to provide producers with protection comparable to the catastrophic risk protection plan of crop insurance (see **10.450**) and to help reduce production risks faced by crop producers for which federal insurance is not available under the Federal Crop Insurance Act; to reduce financial losses that occur when natural disasters cause catastrophic loss of production or prevent planting of an eligible crop. Payment eligibility is based on an expected yield for the area and the producer's approved yield based on actual production history, or a transitional yield if sufficient records are unavailable. Yields must fall below specified percentages to be eligible for payment. Eligible areas may be located within or outside the continental U.S., as determined by USDA; generally, areas within the continental U.S. are eligible if they have suffered a greater than 35 percent loss of eligible production because of damaging weather or of an adverse natural occurrence. Eligible crops include any commercial agricultural crop (excluding livestock and their by-products, tobacco, and trees grown for wood, paper, or pulp), commodity, or acreage of a commodity grown for food or fiber for which catastrophic coverage is unavailable; included also are floriculture, ornamental nursery, Christmas tree crops, turfgrass sod, seed crops, aquaculture including ornamental fish, and industrial crops.

Eligible applicants/beneficiaries: producers including owners, landlords, tenants, or sharecroppers with total annual gross revenue less than $2,000,000 for the preceding tax year.

Range/Average: N.A.

Activity: N.A.

HQ: Deputy Administrator for Farm Programs, Production, Emergencies, and Compliance Division, Disaster Assistance Branch, USDA, 14th and Independence Ave., SW, Stop 0517, Washington, DC 20250. Phone: (202) 720-5172; FAX: (202) 720-0051.

Internet: www.fsa.usda.gov/programs-and-services/disaster-assistance-program/noninsured-crop-disaster-assistance/index.

10.456 PARTNERSHIP AGREEMENTS TO DEVELOP NON-INSURANCE RISK MANAGEMENT TOOLS FOR PRODUCERS (FARMERS)

Assistance: project grants (100 percent/to 3 years).

Purposes: pursuant to the Federal Crop Insurance Act and Agricultural Market Transition Act, for research partnerships to develop noninsurance risk management tools for agricultural producers, emphasizing producers of specialty crops, livestock, rangeland, and underserved commodities.

Eligible applicants/beneficiaries: public and private entities including: IHEs; federal, state, and local government agencies; tribal organizations; nonprofit and profit organizations or corporations; other qualified entities.

Range/Average: N.A.

Activity: N.A.

HQ: Risk Management Education Division, RMA-USDA, 1400 Independence Ave., SW, South Bldg., Rm. 6717-S, Washington, DC 20250-0808. Phone: (202) 720-1416.

Internet: www.rma.usda.gov.

10.458   CROP INSURANCE EDUCATION IN TARGETED STATES ("Targeted States")

Assistance: project grants.

Purposes: pursuant to the Federal Crop Insurance Act as amended, to deliver crop insurance education and information to agricultural producers in designated states historically underserved by crop insurance—including specifically Connecticut, Delaware, Maine, Maryland, Massachusetts, Nevada, New Hampshire, New Jersey, New York, Pennsylvania, Rhode Island, Utah, Vermont, West Virginia, and Wyoming.

Eligible applicants/beneficiaries: state departments of agriculture, universities, nonprofit agricultural organizations, other public and private organizations, agricultural producers, individuals.

Range: $195,379 to $700,000. **Average:** N.A.

Activity: N.A.

HQ: Risk Management Education Division, RMA-USDA, 1400 Independence Ave., SW, South Bldg., Rm. 6717-S, Washington, DC 20250-0808. Phone: (202) 720-1416.

Internet: www.rma.usda.gov.

10.475   COOPERATIVE AGREEMENTS WITH STATES FOR INTRASTATE MEAT AND POULTRY INSPECTION ("Meat and Poultry Inspection State Programs")

Assistance: project grants (to 50 percent).

Purposes: pursuant to the Federal Meat Inspection Act, Federal-State Cooperative Act (Talmadge-Aiken), and Poultry Products Inspection Act, to cover cooperating states' costs of meat and poultry inspection programs.

Eligible applicants/beneficiaries: state or territorial agencies administering meat or poultry inspection programs under applicable laws equivalent to federal acts.

Range: $245,000 to $6,188,000. **Average:** 1,853,000.

Activity: N.A.

HQ: Director, Federal-State Relations Staff, Field Operations, FSIS-USDA, Patriot Plaza III Bldg., Stop 3778, Rm. 9-258, 355 E St., Washington, DC 20024. Phone: (202) 690-6522.

Internet: www.fsis.usda.gov.

10.477   MEAT, POULTRY, AND EGG PRODUCTS INSPECTION

Assistance: specialized services.

Purposes: pursuant to the Federal Meat Inspection Act, Poultry Products Inspection Act, and other acts, to provide inspection by USDA personnel of the slaughtering, processing, and labeling of meat, poultry, and egg products shipped in commerce. All U.S. plants are required to be under continuous USDA inspection, including in the territories.

Eligible applicants/beneficiaries: any meat or poultry plant engaging in slaughtering or processing meat, poultry, and all egg products processing—for shipment in commerce.

Range/Average: N.A.

Activity: N.A.

HQ: Assistant Administrator/Field Operations, FSIS-USDA, Washington, DC 20250-3700. Phone: (202) 720-8803.

Internet: www.fsis.usda.gov.

10.479 FOOD SAFETY COOPERATIVE AGREEMENTS

Assistance: project grants (100 percent).

Purposes: to reduce the incidence of foodborne illnesses associated with meat, poultry, and egg products. Funds are available for educational programs or special studies, and to further develop the Food Emergency Response Network, consisting of federal, state, and, local laboratories that provide the analytic capabilities and capacity to cope with agents threatening the national food supply.

Eligible applicants/beneficiaries: state, local, and tribal government agencies; academic institutions; nonprofit organizations.

Range: $100,812 to $355,404. **Average:** $139,286.

Activity: N.A.

HQ: Strategic Initiatives, Partnerships and Outreach Staff, FSIS-USDA, 950 College Station Rd., Athens, GA 30605. Phone: (706) 546-2349.

Internet: www.fsis.usda.gov. (Note: no field offices for this program.)

10.500 COOPERATIVE EXTENSION SERVICE (CES)

Assistance: formula grants; project grants (50 percent).

Purposes: pursuant to the Smith-Lever Act, Food and Agriculture Act of 1977, FACTA, FAIRA, AREERA, FSRIA, amendments, and other acts, for land grant institutions to operate state and county agricultural extension service programs providing educational and technical assistance to: farmers, producers, and marketing firms in applying technical developments ensuing from research; community organizations to develop natural, economic, and human resources; homemakers and youth regarding food and nutrition, home economics, child development, and parent education; 4-H youth programs. "1890" institutions may receive funds to construct, renovate, plan, and develop new facilities and to purchase equipment.

Eligible applicants/beneficiaries: designated state land grant institutions including in the territories; "1890" and "1994" institutions, and Tuskegee extension programs.

Range/Average: N.A.

Activity: N.A.

HQ: Deputy Administrator/Planning and Accountability, CSREES-USDA, 1400 Independence Ave., SW, Stop 2240, Washington DC 20250. Phone: (202) 401-4939.

Internet: N.A. (Note: no field offices for this program.)

10.543 HEALTHIER US SCHOOL CHALLENGE: SMARTER LUNCHROOMS

Assistance: direct payments/specified use. (100 percent/4 years).

Purposes: pursuant to the Healthy, Hunger-Free Kids Act of 2010, to certify and award monies to those schools participating in the National School Lunch Program (NSLP) and School Breakfast Program (SBP) that have created healthier school environments through the promotion of smarter lunchrooms, nutrition education, and physical activity. All award monies must be deposited into the nonprofit school food service account and used for allowable expenses under that account.

Eligible applicants/beneficiaries: NSLP and SBP participating schools.

Range: $500 to $2,000. **Average:** N.A.

Activity: more than 7,000 certified schools in FY 2015.

HQ: Food and Nutrition Service, USDA, 3101 Park Center Dr., Rm. 640, Alexandria, VA 22302. Phone: (703) 305-2590.

Internet: www.fns.usda.gov/hussc/healthierus-school-challenge-smarter-lunchrooms.

10.551 SUPPLEMENTAL NUTRITION ASSISTANCE PROGRAM

Assistance: direct payments/specified use (100 percent).

Purposes: pursuant to the Food Stamp Act of 1977 as amended, to enable low-income households to purchase food. Eligible recipients receive a coupon allotment, varying according to household size and income, to be used to buy food or seeds and plants to produce food for their personal consumption. Coupons may also be used to purchase meals by special categories of recipients, including the elderly, handicapped, homeless persons living in authorized shelters, alcoholics and drug addicts participating in rehabilitation programs, disabled or blind, specific categories of noncitizens, and residents of shelters for battered women and children.

Eligible applicants: state or territorial agencies.

Eligible beneficiaries: households receiving welfare assistance in some form, or unemployed, part-time employed, working for low wages, receiving limited pensions. Able-bodied adults must meet a work requirement.

Range: N.A. **Average:** $275 for household of 4.

Activity: N.A.

HQ: Deputy Administrator/Food Stamp Program, FNS-USDA, 3101 Park Center Dr., Alexandria, VA 22302. Phone: (703) 305-2026.

Internet: www.fns.usda.gov/snap.

10.553 SCHOOL BREAKFAST PROGRAM (SBP)

Assistance: formula grants.

Purposes: pursuant to the Child Nutrition Act of 1966 as amended, to reimburse participating entities for the cost of providing breakfasts to eligible public and private nonprofit school children through the high school grades, through cash grants and food donations. Breakfasts are served free or at a reduced price to children determined by local school authorities to be unable to pay the full price, based on income eligibility guidelines. Reimbursements rates are based on the "Food Away From Home" series of the Consumer Price Index. The maximum reduced price charged for breakfast is 30 cents.

Eligible applicants: state and territorial agencies; public and nonprofit private schools and residential child care institutions except Job Corps Centers; residential summer camps that participate in the Summer Food Service Program.

Eligible beneficiaries: all children attending schools where the breakfast program is operating may participate.

Range/Average: N.A.

Activity: approximately 2.25 billion breakfasts were served in FY 2014.

HQ: Director, Child Nutrition Division, FNS-USDA, 3101 Park Center Dr., Rm. 628, Alexandria, VA 22302. Phone: (703) 305-2590.

Internet: www.fns.usda.gov.

10.555   NATIONAL SCHOOL LUNCH PROGRAM ("School Lunch Program")

Assistance: formula grants (70 percent).

Purposes: pursuant to the National School Lunch Act as amended, to reimburse participating entities for the cost of providing school lunches to public and private nonprofit school children through the high school grades, through cash grants and food donations. Eligible schools also may be reimbursed for snacks served to children in after-school-hour care programs. Meals are served free or at a reduced price to children determined by local school authorities to be unable to pay the full price, based on income eligibility guidelines. Reimbursement rates are based on the "Food Away from Home" series of the Consumer Price Index. The maximum reduced price charge for lunch is 40 cents.

Eligible applicants: state and territorial agencies; public and nonprofit private schools and residential child care institutions except Job Corps Centers; residential summer camps that participate in the Summer Food Service Program.

Eligible beneficiaries: All children attending schools where the breakfast program is operating may participate.

Range/Average: N.A.

Activity: approximately 71.5% of lunches served were provided free or at reduced price in FY 2014.

HQ: Director, Child Nutrition Division, FNS-USDA, 3101 Park Center Dr., Rm. 628, Alexandria, VA 22302. Phone: (703) 305-2590.

Internet: www.fns.usda.gov.

10.556   SPECIAL MILK PROGRAM FOR CHILDREN

Assistance: formula grants.

Purposes: pursuant to the Child Nutrition Act of 1966 as amended, to reimburse the cost of milk served to primary and secondary pupils in public and private nonprofit schools and institutions. A portion of the cost of the milk is subsidized for non-needy children; milk is free to students meeting certain income guidelines. Nonprofit schools with split-session kindergartens and pre-kindergartens that do not have access to the meal service program operating in the school may receive milk subsidies. States bear the costs in excess of the federal reimbursement.

Eligible applicants: state or territorial agencies; public or private nonprofit schools or child care institutions of high school grade or under, including nursery schools, child-care centers, settlement houses, summer camps, and similar institutions devoted to the care and training of children, except Job Core Centers—provided they do not participate in a meal service program authorized under the National School Lunch Act or Child Nutrition Act of 1966.

Eligible beneficiaries: All children attending schools where the Special Milk Program is in operation may participate.

Range/Average: N.A.

Activity: 9% of half pints served free in FY 2014.

HQ: Director, Child Nutrition Division, FNS-USDA, 3101 Park Center Dr., Rm. 628, Alexandria, VA 22302. Phone: (703) 305-2590.

Internet: www.fns.usda.gov.

10.557 SPECIAL SUPPLEMENTAL NUTRITION PROGRAM FOR WOMEN, INFANTS, AND CHILDREN ("WIC Program")

Assistance: formula grants (100 percent).

Purposes: pursuant to the Child Nutrition Act of 1966 as amended, to supply supplemental foods, nutrition education, and health care referrals at no cost to low-income pregnant, postpartum, and breast-feeding women, infants, and children under age five, identified as at nutritional risk. Grants are awarded to state health or comparable agencies and certain tribes or Indian groups; in turn, funds and food are distributed through local public or nonprofit agencies.

Eligible applicants: local public or private nonprofit health or human service agencies. Applications must be submitted to the responsible state or territorial agency.

Eligible beneficiaries: pregnant, postpartum, or breast-feeding women, infants and children to age five—determined to be in need of supplemental foods, meeting an income standard or receiving benefits under the Food Stamp, Medicaid, or Temporary Assistance for Needy Families Programs. Must also reside in the state in which benefits are received.

Range/Average: N.A.

Activity: 1,972,833 women, 1,964,393 infants, and 4,321,250 children received services in FY 2014.

HQ: Director, Supplemental Food Programs Division, FNS-USDA, 3101 Park Center Dr., Alexandria, VA 22302. Phone: (703) 305-2746; FAX: (703) 305-2196.

Internet: www.fns.usda.gov/wic.

10.558 CHILD AND ADULT CARE FOOD PROGRAM (CACFP)

Assistance: formula grants.

Purposes: pursuant to the National School Lunch Act as amended, to provide funding and commodity foods to institutional food service programs that serve meals to eligible children, including in emergency shelters, or to elderly or impaired adults receiving care in nonresidential day care facilities.

Eligible applicants: state and territorial agencies. In Virginia where the state does not administer the program, institutions may receive funds directly from USDA.

Eligible beneficiaries: public and private nonprofit organizations, including day care centers, outside-school-hour centers, settlement houses, recreation centers, family and group day care home programs, Head Start programs, institutions providing day care services to children with disabilities; certain licensed private for-profit centers that receive compensation under Title XX for at least 25 percent of the children, or under Title XIX or XX for at least 25 percent of the adults, enrolled in nonresidential day care services.

Range/Average: N.A.

Activity: 1.98 billion meals were served in FY 2014.

HQ: Director, Child Nutrition Division, FNS-USDA, 3101 Park Center Dr., Rm. 628, Alexandria, VA 22302. Phone: (703) 305-2590.

Internet: fns.usda.gov.

10.559 SUMMER FOOD SERVICE PROGRAM FOR CHILDREN (SFSP)

Assistance: formula grants.

Purposes: pursuant to the National School Lunch Act as amended, to provide funding and other donations to nonprofit food service programs for needy children age 18 and under and for disabled persons, when schools are closed for summer vacation or for periods of 15 days or more during the regular school year. Funds are available to institutions conducting regularly scheduled programs for children in areas where at least 50 percent of the children meet the family income eligibility criteria for free and reduced-price lunches. Disbursements equal the full cost of food service operations, but cannot exceed per meal rates.

Eligible applicants: state and territorial agencies. Where states do not administer the program, beneficiary agencies may apply directly.

Eligible beneficiaries: public and private nonprofit school food authorities, residential summer camps serving eligible children, and IHEs operating the National Youth Sports Program; units of local, municipal, county, or state government. Other organizations may participate under certain conditions.

Range/Average: N.A.

Activity: 160.1 million meals provided to needy children in FY 2014.

HQ: Director, Child Nutrition Division, FNS-USDA, 3101 Park Center Dr., Rm. 628, Alexandria, VA 22302. Phone: (703) 305-2590.

Internet: fns.usda.gov.

10.560 STATE ADMINISTRATIVE EXPENSES FOR CHILD NUTRITION (SAE)

Assistance: formula grants.

Purposes: pursuant to the Child Nutrition Act of 1966 as amended, for the costs of administering various child nutrition programs, including technical assistance to operating agencies. Program funds may be used to purchase supplies, equipment, and services.

Eligible applicants/beneficiaries: state and territorial agencies administering child nutrition programs, and agencies distributing USDA donated commodities to schools.

Range: $44,720 to $30,584,612. **Average:** $3,092,923.

Activity: N.A.

HQ: Director, Child Nutrition Division, FNS-USDA, 3101 Park Center Dr., Rm. 628, Alexandria, VA 22302. Phone: (703) 305-2590.

Internet: www.fns.usda.gov.

10.561 STATE ADMINISTRATIVE MATCHING GRANTS FOR THE SUPPLEMENTAL NUTRITION ASSISTANCE PROGRAM

Assistance: formula grants (from 50-60 percent).

Purposes: pursuant to the Food Stamp Act of 1977 as amended, for the administrative costs of operating the food stamp program, including for fraud investigations and for developing computer systems. States also conduct an employment and training program requiring no state matching funds. Reimbursements are made to participants for up to 50 percent their dependent care costs, not exceeding $25 monthly per participant; states also receive 50 percent of case management costs.

Eligible applicants/beneficiaries: state and territorial cooperators.

Range/Average: N.A.

Activity: 46 million recipients served in FY 2014.

HQ: Deputy Administrator/Food Stamp Program, FNS-USDA, 3101 Park Center Dr., Alexandria, VA 22302. Phone: (703) 305-2026.

Internet: www.fns.usda.gov/fsp.

10.565 COMMODITY SUPPLEMENTAL FOOD PROGRAM

Assistance: sale, exchange, or donation of property and goods; formula grants.

Purposes: pursuant to the Agriculture and Consumer Protection Act of 1973 and Food and Agriculture Act of 1977 as amended, for the donation of supplemental foods to low-income persons. Grant funds may be used only for administrative costs incurred in making the donated goods and nutrition education services available to beneficiaries.

Eligible applicants: state agencies; recognized tribes, bands, or groups—which distribute funds to local public or nonprofit agencies.

Eligible beneficiaries: infants or children to age 6; pregnant, postpartum, or breast-feeding women; or, elderly persons age 60 or older—certified as income-eligible for benefits under existing federal, state, or local food, health, or welfare program.

Range: $6,271 to $5,670,700 per state. **Average:** $903,424 per state.

Activity: average of 573,703 individuals participated monthly in FY 2014.

HQ: Director, Food Distribution Division, FNS-USDA, 3101 Park Center Dr., Alexandria, VA 22302. Phone: (703) 305-2662.

Internet: www.fns.usda.gov/csfp/commodity-supplemental-food-program-csfp.

10.566   NUTRITION ASSISTANCE FOR PUERTO RICO (NAP)

Assistance: direct payments/specified use (benefits, 100 percent; administrative, 50 percent).

Purposes: for low-income Puerto Ricans to purchase food—as an alternative to Food Stamps.

Eligible applicants: only the Commonwealth of PR.

Eligible beneficiaries: low-income Puerto Rican individuals and families.

Range/Average: N.A.

Activity: average of 1.35 million served during FY 2014.

HQ: Deputy Administrator/Food Stamp Program, FNS-USDA, 300 Corporate Blvd., Robbinsville, NJ 08691. Phone: 609-259-5025.

Internet: www.fns.usda.gov.

10.567   FOOD DISTRIBUTION PROGRAM ON INDIAN RESERVATIONS (FDPIR)

Assistance: project grants; sale, exchange, or donation of property and goods (75 percent).

Purposes: pursuant to the Agricultural Act of 1949, Food and Agriculture Act of 1963, Food Stamp Act of 1977, amendments, and other legislation, to provide food to needy persons living on or near Indian reservations, and funds for the administrative costs incurred by organizations operating the program. Donated foods may be acquired under USDA's surplus removal or price support operations.

Eligible applicants: state agencies; tribal organizations.

Eligible beneficiaries: households living on Indian reservations; Indian households living near an Indian reservation (or, for Oklahoma, living in Indian country)—certified by local authorities as having inadequate income and resources. Upper limits of allowable income vary with family size.

Range/Average: N.A.

Activity: N.A.

HQ: Director, Food Distribution Division, FNS-USDA, 3101 Park Center Dr., Alexandria, VA 22302. Phone: (703) 305-2662.

Internet: www.fns.usda.gov/fdpir/food-distribution-program-indian-reservations-fdpir.

10.568   EMERGENCY FOOD ASSISTANCE PROGRAM (ADMINISTRATIVE COSTS)
("TEFAP Administrative Costs")

Assistance: formula grants.

Purposes: pursuant to the Emergency Food Assistance Act of 1983 as amended and other acts, to cover state and local costs of processing, storage, and distribution of food used to feed needy persons.

Eligible applicants: state agencies.

Eligible beneficiaries: public or private non-profit organizations that operate USDA food programs.

Range: $21,596 to $10,157,915. **Average:** $1,256,222.

Activity: provided 384,457,787 pounds of food in FY 2014.

HQ: Director, Food Distribution Division, FNS-USDA, 3101 Park Center Dr., Alexandria, VA 22302. Phone: (703) 305-2662.

Internet: www.fns.usda.gov/tefap/emergency-food-assistance-program-tefap.

10.569 EMERGENCY FOOD ASSISTANCE PROGRAM (FOOD COMMODITIES) ("TEFAP Commodities, USDA Foods")

Assistance: formula grants (100 percent).

Purposes: pursuant to the Emergency Food Assistance Act of 1983 and Hunger Prevention Act of 1988, to make food commodities available to needy persons, including for meals served at congregate meal sites.

Eligible applicants: designated state food commodity distributing agencies.

Eligible beneficiaries: needy persons including the unemployed, homeless, welfare recipients, and the low-income.

Range: $115,538 to $31,670,610. **Average:** $4,467,926.

Activity: provided 384,457,787 pounds of food in FY 2014.

HQ: Director, Food Distribution Division, FNS-USDA, 3101 Park Center Dr., Alexandria, VA 22302. Phone: (703) 305-2662.

Internet: www.fns.usda.gov/tefap/emergency-food-assistance-program-tefap.

10.572 WIC FARMERS' MARKET NUTRITION PROGRAM (FMNP)

Assistance: formula grants (70 percent; tribal organizations, 70- 90 percent).

Purposes: pursuant to the WIC Farmers' Market Nutrition Act of 1992 and Child Nutrition Act of 1966 as amended, to provide fresh and nutritious unprepared foods (such as fruits and vegetables) from farmers' markets to low-income women, infants, and children at nutritional risk—through the use of FMNP coupons; to expand awareness and use of farmers' markets. States may meet matching fund requirements through state contributions to similar programs.

Eligible applicants: state health, agriculture, and other agencies; recognized Indian organizations.

Eligible beneficiaries: WIC program participants (i.e., pregnant, postpartum, or breast-feeding women, infants over age 4 months, children to age 5). At the discretion of the states, WIC program applicants may also participate.

Range: $6,337 to $3,238,995. **Average:** N.A.

Activity: N.A.

HQ: Director, Supplemental Food Programs Division, FNS-USDA, 3101 Park Center Dr., Alexandria, VA 22302. Phone: (703) 305-2746; FAX: (703) 305-2196.

Internet: www.fns.usda.gov/fmnp/wic-farmers-market-nutrition-program-fmnp.

10.574 TEAM NUTRITION GRANTS ("TN Training Grants")

Assistance: project grants. (100 percent/2 years).

Purposes: pursuant to the National School Lunch Act and amendments, to establish and enhance nutrition training and technical assistance programs to school food service professionals, as well as to children and parents. The program provides start-up money for projects, and may include a cafeteria-classroom link to support nutrition education and healthy food choices. States may use funds to provide comprehensive, action-oriented delivery of training programs for schools.

Eligible applicants: state agencies—applying individually or as coalitions.

Eligible beneficiaries: school and child care decision makers, service staff, and caregivers; children, parents, and teachers/educators.

Range: $178,787 to $349,812 for competitive awards; $19,993 to $50,000 for non-competitive awards. **Average:** $298,533 for competitive awards.

Activity: N.A.

HQ: Director, Child Nutrition Division, FNS-USDA, 3101 Park Center Dr., Rm. 628, Alexandria, VA 22302. Phone: (703) 305-2590.

Internet: www.fns.usda.gov/tn/team-nutrition-training-grants.

10.576 SENIOR FARMERS MARKET NUTRITION PROGRAM (SFMNP)

Assistance: project grants.

Purposes: pursuant to FSRIA, to expand, develop, or aid domestic farmers markets, roadside stands, and community-supported agriculture programs serving low-income seniors. Grants are competitive, and may support costs of food only.

Eligible applicants: states, territories, and tribal governments, which may make subgrants to local governments and nonprofit organizations.

Eligible beneficiaries: low-income seniors, generally defined as individuals at least age 60 with household income not exceeding 185 percent of federal poverty guidelines.

Range: $9,925 to $1,793,037. **Average:** N.A.

Activity: N.A.

HQ: Director, Supplemental Food Programs Division, FNS-USDA, 3101 Park Center Dr., Alexandria, VA 22302. Phone: (703) 305-2746; FAX: (703) 305-2196.

Internet: www.fns.usda.gov/sfmnp/senior-farmers-market-nutrition-program-sfmnp. (Note: no field offices for this program.)

10.578   WIC GRANTS TO STATES (WGS)

Assistance: project grants. (100 percent/ 1-3 years).

Purposes: pursuant to the Child Nutrition Act of 1966 as amended, to provide funding to WIC state agencies for Electronic Benefit Transfer Projects (EBT) and pilots exploring the technical and financial feasibility of providing WIC benefits electronically; for WIC state agencies and tribal governments to fund, implement, and evaluate innovative projects that improve WIC services provisions and impact the nutrition and health of WIC participants. Grants are competitive. Special projects examples: motivational interviewing in nutrition education; increasing breastfeeding among Indians.

Eligible applicants/beneficiaries: state WIC program agencies; state coalitions.

Range/Average: N.A.

Activity: 19 awards in FY 2014.

HQ: Director, Supplemental Food Programs Division, FNS-USDA, 3101 Park Center Dr., Alexandria, VA 22302. Phone: (703) 305-2746; FAX: (703) 305-2196.

Internet: www.fns.usda.gov/wic/women-infants-and-children-wic.

10.579   CHILD NUTRITION DISCRETIONARY GRANTS—LIMITED AVAILABILITY

Assistance: project grants (100 percent).

Purposes: pursuant to the Food, Conservation and Energy Act, to make pre-development planning grants for feasibility studies, design assistance, and technical assistance to financially distressed communities in rural areas with populations of 2,500 or fewer inhabitants for water and waste disposal projects.

Eligible applicants/beneficiaries: public bodies or governmental entities such as states, municipalities, counties, districts, authorities, and other political subdivisions of a State; nonprofit organizations such as associations, cooperatives, private nonprofit corporations, and institutions of higher education and hospitals; Native American Indian tribes on Federal and State reservations, other federally recognized Indian tribes, and Native American Organizations (includes Indian groups, cooperatives, corporations, partnerships, and associations.

Range: $50,000 to $35,000,000. **Average:** N.A.

Activity: 7 awards in FY 2014.

HQ: Director, Child Nutrition Division, FNS-USDA, 3101 Park Center Dr., Rm. 628, Alexandria, VA 22302. Phone: (703) 305-2590.

Internet: www.fns.usda.gov.

10.580   SUPPLEMENTAL NUTRITION ASSISTANCE PROGRAM, PROCESS AND TECHNOLOGY IMPROVEMENT GRANTS

Assistance: project grants (100 percent).

Purposes: pursuant to the Food Stamp Act of 1977, for research into food stamp outreach activities, methods, or technologies, directed to targeted groups that are eligible but that traditionally under-use food stamp benefits—involving new technology and partnerships to educate eligible beneficiaries about the nutrition benefits of the program and about how to apply.

Eligible applicants: non-food stamp governmental authorities, nonprofit organizations.

Eligible beneficiaries: persons potentially eligible for food stamps (low-income individuals or families).

Range/Average: N.A.

Activity: 6 awards in FY 2015

HQ: Grants Management Division, FNS-USDA, 3101 Park Center Dr., 8th fl., Alexandria, VA 22302. Phone: (703) 305-2803.

Internet: www.fns.usda.gov. (Note: no field offices for this program.)

10.582 FRESH FRUIT AND VEGETABLE PROGRAM (FFVP)

Assistance: project grants (100 percent).

Purposes: pursuant to the National School Lunch Act as amended, to reimburse states providing free fresh fruits and vegetables to school children of high school grade and under in designated public and private schools.

Eligible applicants: state agencies specified in Section 18(g) of the National School Lunch Act or selected by USDA, including Indian tribal organizations and public and private schools participating in the National School Lunch Program or School Breakfast Program and selected by their State agencies to participate in the FFVP. States must ensure that the majority of schools have 50 percent or more students eligible for free or reduced price meals, with priority to schools with partnerships with nonfederal resources, except for schools previously participating in the Fresh Fruit and Vegetable Pilot Program prior to 1 May 2004.

Eligible beneficiaries: All children enrolled in schools participating in the Fresh Fruit and Vegetable Program.

Range/Average: N.A.

Activity: N.A.

HQ: Director, Child Nutrition Division, FNS-USDA, 3101 Park Center Dr., Rm. 628, Alexandria, VA 22302. Phone: (703) 305-2590.

Internet: www.fns.usda.gov.

10.585 FNS FOOD SAFETY GRANTS

Assistance: cooperative agreements/discretionary grants (100 percent).

Purposes: pursuant to the National Agriculture Research, Extension, and Teaching Policy Act of 1977, to increase awareness, visibility, and impact of food safety on USDA nutrition assistance programs. Funding is provided to a university or organization to achieve the objectives of the grant. The university or organization may award sub-grants to obtain the expertise and skills needed to accomplish the objectives of the Center. Guidance on restrictions are set forth in the grant document.

Eligible applicants/beneficiaries: FNS nutrition assistance program decision makers, FNS nutrition assistance program providers, and children and teachers.

Range/Average: N.A.

Activity: N.A.

HQ: Director, Office of Food Safety Food and Nutrition Service, 3101 Park Center Dr., Alexandria, Virginia 22302. Phone: (703) 305-2608; FAX: (703) 305-2420.

Internet: www.fns.usda.gov/fns/food_safety.htm. (Note: no field offices for this program.)

10.586 SPECIAL SUPPLEMENTAL NUTRITION PROGRAM FOR WOMEN, INFANTS AND CHILDREN; NUTRITION EDUCATION INNOVATIONS ("WIC Nutrition Education Innovations Grant, WIC Periconceptional Grant")

Assistance: cooperative agreements (100 percent/60 months).

Purposes: pursuant to the National Agriculture Research, Extension, and Teaching Policy Act of 1977, to enable Food and Nutrition Service (FNS) to enter into grants and cooperative agreements with states and local governments, universities, hospitals, and non-profit organizations to identify, develop and undertake projects to meet FNS program needs and the food, nutrition, and health of program eligible participants.

This project shall support a university-based grant series for researcher-initiated projects to demonstrate creative approaches to evaluate WIC impacts on periconceptional nutrition, coordinate activities among researchers, and widely disseminate findings from current research.

Eligible applicants/beneficiaries: state and local governments, hospitals, non-profit organizations and accredited colleges/universities offering advanced degrees at the PhD level in biological and social sciences such as sociology, psychology, education, nutrition, public health and economics.

Range: $997,759 to $1,999,980. **Average:** $1,498,870.

Activity: N.A.

HQ: Director, 3101 Park Center Dr. Alexandria, Virginia 22302. Phone: (703) 305-2732.

Internet: N.A. (Note: no field offices for this program.)

10.587 NATIONAL FOOD SERVICE MANAGEMENT INSTITUTE ADMINISTRATION AND STAFFING GRANT ("ICN")

Assistance: cooperative agreements/project grants (100 percent/3-5 years).

Purposes: pursuant to the Richard B. Russell National School Lunch Act, dedicated to applied research, education and training, and technical assistance for child nutrition programs, supports the Child Nutrition Programs through training and technical assistance for foodservice, nutrition education for children and their caregivers, and school and community support for healthy eating and physical activity. Funding is provided to a university or organization to achieve the objectives of the grant. The university or organization may award sub-grants to obtain the expertise and skills needed to accomplish the objectives.

Eligible applicants: University of Mississippi.

Eligible beneficiaries: FNS nutrition assistance program decision makers, FNS program providers, children and teachers.

Range/Average: N.A.

Activity: N.A.

HQ: Director, Child Nutrition Division, FNS-USDA, 3101 Park Center Dr., Rm. 628, Alexandria, VA 22302. Phone: (703) 305-2590.

Internet: www.fns.usda.gov. (Note: no field offices for this program.)

10.589   CHILD NUTRITION DIRECT CERTIFICATION PERFORMANCE AWARDS

Assistance: direct payments/specified use (100 percent).

Purposes: pursuant to the Healthy, Hunger-Free Kids Act of 2010,designs awards to encourage States to ensure that all eligible children living in households receiving benefits under the Supplemental Nutrition Assistance Program (SNAP) are directly certified for free school meals. Each year for three years, USDA may award a total of up to 15 States for exemplary performance in their direct certification efforts with SNAP. These funds are only available to the State agencies administering the NSLP and to the SFAs to which the States may choose to transfer funds. The amounts of the awards and the number of awards given (up to a total of 15) are at the discretion of USDA.

Eligible applicants/beneficiaries: state agencies that administer the NSLP.

Range/Average: N.A.

Activity: N.A.

HQ: Director, Child Nutrition Division, FNS-USDA, 3101 Park Center Dr., Rm. 628, Alexandria, VA 22302. Phone: (703) 305-2590.

Internet: www.fns.usda.gov. (Note: no field offices for this program.)

10.594   FOOD DISTRIBUTION PROGRAM ON INDIAN RESERVATIONS NUTRITION EDUCATION GRANTS

Assistance: project grants (75 percent).

Purposes: pursuant to the Food and Nutrition Act of 2008, the Food Distribution Program Nutrition Education (FDPNE) provides project grants for administrative funding to a Tribe or Indian Tribal Organization (ITO) operating a Food Distribution Program on Indian Reservations (FDPIR), or a nutrition assistance program. The goal of the FDPNE is to provide nutrition education and enhance the nutrition knowledge of FDPIR participants underserved by the Supplemental Nutrition Assistance Program Nutrition Education (SNAP-Ed) SNAP-Ed. ITOs and State Distributing Agencies (SDA) that administer FDPIR may apply individually or as a consortium of ITOs or SDAs. The program has a 25% match requirement, which may be waived for a compelling justification.

Eligible applicants: an entity that has a direct agreement with the Food and Nutrition Service to administer a Food Distribution Program on Indian Reservations (FDPIR).

Eligible beneficiaries: Food Distribution Program on Indian Reservations (FDPIR) participants.

Range: $3,000 to $215,000. **Average:** N.A.

Activity: anticipate 20 tribal organization awards in FY 2016.

HQ: Director, Food Distribution Program Nutrition Education Grants, FNS-USDA, 3101 Park Center Dr., Alexandria, VA 22302. Phone: (703) 305-1126. FAX: (703) 305-2964.

Internet: www.fns.usda.gov/fdpir/fdpir-nutrition-education-grant-awards.

10.595 FARM TO SCHOOL TRAINING AND TECHNICAL ASSISTANCE

Assistance: provision of specialized services/training (100 percent).

Purposes: pursuant to the Healthy, Hunger-Free Kids Act of 2010, funds to assist eligible entities, through grants and technical assistance, in implementing farm to school programs that improve access to local foods in eligible schools. This program allows cooperative agreements to be established for the development and review of training and technical assistance materials, and the delivery of training and technical assistance. The purpose of the Farm to School Programs technical assistance activities is to facilitate the coordination and sharing of information and resources that may be applicable to the farm to school program; to collect and share information on best practices; and to disseminate research and data on existing farm to school programs and the potential for programs in underserved areas.

Eligible applicants/beneficiaries: schools, Indian Tribal Organizations, non-profit organizations, producer and producer groups, state and local agencies.

Range/Average: N.A.

Activity: N.A.

HQ: Director, Farm to School Training and Technical Assistance, FNS-USDA, 1400 Independence Ave., Washington, DC 29815. Phone: (303) 844-0356.

Internet: www.fns.usda.gov/farmtoschool/farm-school. (Note: no field offices for this program.)

10.600 FOREIGN MARKET DEVELOPMENT COOPERATOR PROGRAM

Assistance: direct payments/specified use. (50 percent/ 1-3 years).

Purposes: pursuant to the Agricultural Trade Act of 1978, for CCC projects abroad to develop, expand, and maintain long-term export markets for U.S. agricultural products, usually conducted by U.S. nonprofit trade associations (Cooperats). Funded activities may include trade servicing, market research, and technical assistance to actual or potential foreign purchasers. (FAS administers the program for the CCC).

Eligible applicants/beneficiaries: U.S. nonprofit nationwide or industry-wide agricultural trade groups.

Range: $11,000 to $7,000,000. **Average:** $1,243,000.

Activity: N.A.

HQ: Deputy Administrator, Commodity and Marketing Programs, FAS-USDA, 1400 Independence Ave., SW, Washington, DC 20250. Phone: (202) 205-9432.

Internet: www.fas.usda.gov/programs/foreign-market-development-program-fmd. (Note: no field offices for this program.)

10.601 MARKET ACCESS PROGRAM (MAP)

Assistance: direct payments/specified use. (50-90 percent/ 1-3 years).

Purposes: pursuant to the Agricultural Trade Act of 1978 as amended, to develop, expand, and maintain export markets for U.S. agricultural commodities. Projects may involve generic (90 percent funding) or brand-specific (50 percent) promotions. Activities may include consumer advertising, point-of-sale demonstrations, public relations, trade fairs, exhibits, market research, or technical assistance. Funding is through CCC reimbursements for authorized activities.

Eligible applicants/beneficiaries: U.S. nonprofit agricultural trade organizations, state regional trade groups, agricultural cooperatives, state agencies, small private entities.

Range: $22,000 to $9,611,000. **Average:** $1,375,000.

Activity: N.A.

HQ: Deputy Administrator, Commodity and Marketing Programs, FAS-USDA, 1400 Independence Ave., SW, Washington, DC 20250. Phone: (202) 720-4327.

Internet: www.fas.usda.gov/programs/market-access-program-map. (Note: no field offices for this program.)

10.602 CCC'S DAIRY EXPORT INCENTIVE PROGRAM (DEIP)

Assistance: direct payments/specified use (100 percent).

Purposes: pursuant to the Food, Agriculture, Conservation and Trade Act of 1990, to develop export markets for dairy products where U.S. products are not price competitive and thereby, make sales in targeted overseas markets for the purpose of market development or where competitor countries are making subsidized sales.

Eligible applicants/beneficiaries: agricultural producers, processors, and exporters.

Range/Average: N.A.

Activity: N.A.

HQ: Office of Trade Programs 1400 Independence Ave., SW, Washington, DC 20250. Phone: (202) 720-2949.

Internet: N.A. (Note: no field offices for this program.)

10.603 EMERGING MARKETS PROGRAM (EMP)

Assistance: direct payments/specified use.

Purposes: pursuant to FACTA as amended and FAIRA, to promote, enhance, or expand U.S. agricultural commodity exports to emerging markets abroad. Project funds may finance feasibility studies, market research, sector assessments, orientation visits, specialized training, business workshops, and similar activities. Funding is provided through the Commodity Credit Corporation. Implementers contribute a share of project costs.

Eligible applicants/beneficiaries: U.S. agricultural or agribusiness organizations, nonprofit trade associations, universities, state departments of agriculture, certain consultant groups.

Range/Average: N.A.

Activity: N.A.

HQ: Deputy Administrator, Commodity and Marketing Programs, FAS-USDA, 1400 Independence Ave., SW, Washington, DC 20250. Phone: (202) 720-4327.

Internet: www.fas.usda.gov/programs/emerging-markets-program-emp. (Note: no field offices for this program.)

10.604 TECHNICAL ASSISTANCE FOR SPECIALTY CROPS PROGRAM (TASC)

Assistance: direct payments/specified use.

Purposes: pursuant to FSRIA, for projects addressing sanitary, phytosanitary, and technical barriers that prohibit or threaten the export of U.S. specialty crops. Activities eligible for funding include initial preclearance programs, export protocol and work plan support, seminars and workshops, study tours, field surveys, pest lists development, pest and disease research, data base development, logistical and administrative support, and travel costs. Costs are reimbursed by CCC.

Eligible applicants/beneficiaries: federal and state government agencies; U.S. nonprofit trade associations, universities, agricultural cooperatives, private companies, and other organizations.

Range: to $250,000 per year. **Average:** N.A.

Activity: N.A.

HQ: Deputy Administrator, Commodity and Marketing Programs, FAS-USDA, 1400 Independence Ave., SW, Washington, DC 20250. Phone: (202) 720-4327.

Internet: www.fas.usda.gov/programs/technical-assistance-specialty-crops-tasc. (Note: no field offices for this program.)

10.605 QUALITY SAMPLES PROGRAM (QSP)

Assistance: direct payments/specified use.

Purposes: pursuant to the CCC Charter Act, to develop and expand export markets for U.S. agricultural commodities by assisting U.S. entities in providing commodity samples to potential foreign importers. Costs of purchasing and transporting the samples may be reimbursed by the CCC; technical assistance costs may not.

Eligible applicants/beneficiaries: U.S. entities.

Range: $5,000 to $75,000. **Average:** $31,131.

Activity: N.A.

HQ: Deputy Administrator, Commodity and Marketing Programs, FAS-USDA, 1400 Independence Ave., SW, Washington, DC 20250. Phone: (202) 720-4327.

Internet: www.fas.usda.gov/programs/quality-samples-program-qsp. (Note: no field offices for this program.)

10.606   FOOD FOR PROGRESS

Assistance: project grants/sale, exchange, or donation of property or goods (100 percent/3-5 years).

Purposes: pursuant to the Food for Progress Act of 1985, the Food for Progress program provides for the donation of U.S. agricultural commodities to developing countries and emerging democracies that are committed to introducing or expanding free enterprise in their agricultural economies. Donated commodities are typically "monetized," and the proceeds are used to fund agricultural development activities. Food for Progress strategic objectives are to increase agricultural productivity and expand trade of agricultural products (domestically, regionally, and internationally).

Eligible applicants: private organizations, cooperatives, intergovernmental organizations, and foreign governments.

Eligible beneficiaries: developing countries and emerging democracies that are committed to introducing or expanding free enterprise in their agricultural economies.

Range: $20,000,000 to $30,000,000. **Average:** N.A.

Activity: N.A.

HQ: Director, FAS-USDA, 1400 Independence Ave., SW, Stop 1030, Washington, DC 20706. Phone: (202) 720-4221.

Internet: WWW.FAS.USDA.GOV. (Note: no field offices for this program.)

10.608   FOOD FOR EDUCATION (FFE)

Assistance: project grants. (100 percent/3-5 years).

Purposes: pursuant to the FSRIA, to reduce hunger and improve literacy and primary education, especially for girls, with a focus on developing countries. Projects may provide for such activities as school meals, teacher training, and related support including nutrition programs for pregnant women, nursing mothers, and pre-school youngsters.

Eligible applicants/beneficiaries: "Cooperating Sponsors" including: foreign governments; entities registered with USAID; entities demonstrating satisfactory experience and other qualifications to the CCC.

Range: $20,000,000 to $35,000,000. **Average:** N.A.

Activity: N.A.

HQ: Director, FAS-USDA, 1400 Independence Ave., SW, Stop 1030, Washington, DC 20706. Phone: (202) 720-4221.

Internet: www.fas.usda.gov. (Note: no field offices for this program.)

10.609   TRADE ADJUSTMENT ASSISTANCE (TAA)

Assistance: direct payments/unrestricted use.

Purposes: pursuant to the Trade Act of 1974 as amended by the Trade Act of 2002, to provide technical assistance and cash benefits to farmers, ranchers, fish farmers, and fishermen competing with imported aquaculture products, if increased imports have contributed to a price decline of at least 20 percent. Technical assistance may be provided by CSREES in cooperation with county Extension Services, in helping producers respond proactively to import competition through training, cash benefits, and employment services.

Eligible applicants/beneficiaries: producers of raw commodities that: are owners, operators, landlords, tenants, or sharecroppers—sharing in production risk and entitled to share in the crop availability; have been adversely affected by import competition; are covered by a certification of eligibility.

Range: to $12,000 per year. **Average:** N.A.

Activity: N.A.

HQ: Trade Adjustment Assistance, FAS-USDA, 1400 Independence Ave., SW, Rm. 6539C, Washington, DC 20250. Phone: (202) 690-0633.

Internet: www.fas.usda.gov/itp/taa/taa.asp.

10.610   EXPORT GUARANTEE PROGRAM
("The GSM-102 Program")

Assistance: guaranteed/insured loans (100 percent).

Purposes: pursuant to, the Agricultural Trade Act of 1978, to provide credit guarantees to encourage financing of commercial exports of U.S. agricultural products, while providing competitive credit terms to buyers; encourage exports to buyers in countries that have sufficient financial strength to have foreign exchange available for scheduled payments; guarantee credit extended by the private banking sector in the U.S. to approved foreign banks using dollar-denominated, irrevocable letters of credit for purchases of U.S. food and agricultural products by foreign buyers.

Eligible applicants: Export Credit guarantee Program (GSM-102) provides credit guarantees to encourage financing of commercial exports of U.S. agricultural products, while providing competitive credit terms to buyers. By reducing financial risk to lenders, credit guarantees encourage exports to buyers in countires-mailnly developing countries- that have sufficient financial strength to have foreign exchange available for scheduled payments. This Program provides guarantees to lenders.

Eligible beneficiaries: Exporters or the exporters assignee are the direct beneficiaries and must meet the applicant eligibility requirements. Interested parties, including U.S. exporters, foreign buyers, banks, may request that the CCC establish a GSM-102 program for a country or region. Prior to announcing the availability of guarantees, the CCC evaluates the ability of each country and foreign bank to service CCC guaranteed debt.

Range/Average: N.A.

Activity: N.A.

HQ: Office of Trade Programs 1400 Independence Ave., SW, Washington, DC 20250. Phone: (202) 720-2949.

Internet: www.fas.usda.gov/programs/export-credit-guarantee-program-gsm-102.

10.612   USDA LOCAL AND REGIONAL FOOD AID PROCUREMENT PROGRAM ("USDA LRP Project")

Assistance: project grants (100 percent).

Purposes: pursuant to the Food, Conservation, and Energy Act of 2008, to examine the timeliness, cost and market impact of using local and regional procurement as a tool to respond to food crises and disasters in developing countries around the world. Resources may only be used in accordance with the terms and conditions specified in the Interim Guidelines for the Local and Regional Food Aid Procurement Pilot Project.

Eligible applicants: Private Voluntary Organizations (PVOs), Intergovernmental Organizations (IGOs), and Cooperatives.

Eligible beneficiaries: food-insecure populations in developing countries.

Range/Average: N.A.

Activity: N.A.

HQ: Director, FAS-USDA, 1400 Independence Ave., SW, Stop 1030, Washington, DC 20706. Phone: (202) 720-4221.

Internet: www.fas.usda.gov/excredits/foodaid/lrp/lrp.asp. (Note: no field offices for this program.)

10.613   FACULTY EXCHANGE PROGRAM

Assistance: direct payments/specified use; project grants (100 percent).

Purposes: pursuant to the National Agricultural Research, Extension, and Teaching Act of 1977, to assist developing countries in improving their university agricultural education, research and extension programs by providing a one semester training program at U.S. Land Grant Agricultural Universities. No funding is available for unsolicited proposal. Faculty Exchange Program funds are used to provide participant training at Land Grant Universities in the U.S.

Eligible applicants: U.S. Land Grant Universities.

Eligible beneficiaries: foreign governments and related agricultural institutions in their countries.

Range: $10,000 to $45,000. **Average:** N.A.

Activity: anticipate 10 participants will be trained in FY 2016.

HQ: Director, 1400 Independence Ave., SW, Stop 1030, Washington, DC 20250. Phone: (202) 720-6888.

Internet: www.fas.usda.gov. (Note: no field offices for this program.)

10.614   SCIENTIFIC COOPERATION EXCHANGE PROGRAM WITH CHINA (SCEP)

Assistance: direct payments/specified use; project grants (100 percent).

Purposes: pursuant to the National Agricultural Research, Extension, and Teaching Policy Act of 1977, to facilitate mutual cooperation in agricultural research, education, and extension between the United States and China. Funds may be used for direct costs of conducting approved agricultural exchanges. Allowable expenses include travel for research, extension, training, and indirect costs associated with hosting Chinese exchange teams.

Eligible applicants: U.S. Institutions of higher learning, and public and private nonprofit organizations whose primary purpose is agriculture, natural resources management and/or rural development (including those located in U.S. territories).

Eligible beneficiaries: U.S. institutions from the public, private, and academia sectors.

Range: N.A. **Average:** $6,500.

Activity: expect to host 8 exchange teams from China and deploy 8 U.S. teams to China in FY 2016.

HQ: Director, 1400 Independence Ave., SW, Stop 1030, Washington, DC 20250. Phone: (202) 720-6888.

Internet: www.fas.usda.gov. (Note: no field offices for this program.)

10.615 PIMA AGRICULTURE COTTON TRUST FUND

Assistance: direct payments/unrestricted use. (100 percent).

Purposes: pursuant to the Agricultural Act of 2014, to reduce the injury to domestic manufacturers resulting from tariffs on cotton fabric that are higher than tariffs on certain apparel articles made of cotton fabric.

Eligible applicants: for-profit businesses, private nonprofits, and IHEs.

Eligible beneficiaries: nationally recognized associations established for the promotion of pima cotton in apparel; yarn spinners of pima cotton that produce ring spun cotton yarns in the United States, and manufacturers who cut and sew cotton shirts in the United States who certify that they used imported cotton fabric during calendar year 2013.

Range: $500,000 to $4,500,000. **Average:** $2,200,000.

Activity: N.A.

HQ: FSA-USDA, 1400 Independence Ave., SW, Washington, DC 20250. Phone: (202) 720-8877.

Internet: www.fas.usda.gov. (Note: no field offices for this program.)

10.652 FORESTRY RESEARCH

Assistance: project grants (1-5 years).

Purposes: pursuant to the Forest and Rangeland Renewable Resources Research Act of 1978, for fundamental research in: management of forests, watersheds, forest ranges, wildlife habitat; recreation; fire protection; insect and disease protection and control; forest products utilization; forest engineering; forest production economics and marketing; forest surveying; urban forestry; and social/cultural influences.

Eligible applicants/beneficiaries: state agricultural experiment stations, IHEs, state and local governments, territories; profit, nonprofit, and international organizations; individuals.

Range: $2,000 to $300,000. **Average:** $35,000.

Activity: N.A.

HQ: Deputy Chief/Research and Development, Forest Service-USDA, 201 14th St., SW, 2NW, Washington, DC 20024. Phone: (202) 205-1665.

Internet: www.fs.fed.us/links/research.html.

10.664   COOPERATIVE FORESTRY ASSISTANCE

Assistance: formula grants; project grants (50-80 percent).

Purposes: pursuant to the Cooperative Forestry Assistance Act of 1978 and FACTA as amended, for state forest stewardship programs on private, local, state, and other nonfederal forest and rural lands. Programs may include: timber production: insect and disease control; processing of wood products; producing and distributing tree seeds and seedlings, urban forestry; conversion of wood to energy; improvement and maintenance of fish and wildlife habitat; financial and technical assistance for rural firefighting; organizational improvement; technology transfer; acquisition and loan of federal surplus property.

Eligible applicants: states, tribes, municipalities, territories and possessions, nonprofit organizations.

Eligible beneficiaries: owners of nonfederal lands; rural community firefighting forces; urban and municipal governmental and other state, local, and private agencies acting through state foresters or equivalent state officials.

Range: $25,000 to $6,000,000. **Average:** $1,000,000.

Activity: N.A.

HQ: Deputy Chief, State and Private Forestry, Forest Service - USDA, 1400 Independence Ave., SW, Stop 1109, Washington, DC 20250. Phone: (202) 205-1657.

Internet: www.fs.fed.us/spf.

10.665   SCHOOLS AND ROADS—GRANTS TO STATES

Assistance: formula grants (25 Percent Payments to States).

Purposes: to return 25 percent of revenues from the national forests to states and U.S. territories, for the benefit of public schools and public roads of the counties in which the forests are located.

Eligible applicants/beneficiaries: states or territories with national forest land.

Range: Title I: to $9,587,418; Title II: $1,922 to $1,294,931; Title III: $1,682 to $789,552. **Average:** Title I: $366,907; Title II: $98,145; Title III; $54,134.

Activity: N.A.

HQ: Acquisitions Management, Grants and Agreements, Forest Service-USDA, 201 14th St., SW, Suite 4 NW, Washington, DC 20024. Phone: (202) 205-1468.

Internet: www.fs.usda.gov/main/pts/home.

10.666 SCHOOLS AND ROADS—GRANTS TO COUNTIES

Assistance: formula grants.

Purposes: to return 25 percent of revenues from national grasslands and land utilization projects, for the benefit of public schools and roads of the counties in which they are located.

Eligible applicants/beneficiaries: U.S. counties with national grasslands or land utilization projects.

Range/Average: N.A.

Activity: N.A.

HQ: Acquisitions Management, Grants and Agreements, Forest Service-USDA, 201 14th St., SW, Suite 4 NW, Washington, DC 20024. Phone: (202) 205-1468.

Internet: www.fs.fed.us/srs. (Note: no field offices for this program.)

10.672 RURAL DEVELOPMENT, FORESTRY, AND COMMUNITIES ("Rural Development Through Forestry")

Assistance: project grants (the Federal contribution to the overall implementation of a planned project may have a matching requirement, but that match is negotiated).

Purposes: pursuant to the Annual Department of the Interior, Environment, and Related Agencies Appropriations, to help rural areas analyze and assess forest resource opportunities, maximize local economic potential through market development and expansion, and diversify communities' economic base. Funding may be allocated for such things as technical assistance, training and education, equipment, marketing, and all costs associated with making these services available to tribal nations, State and Federal agencies, State Foresters, local governments, not-for-profit organizations, and others extending services to rural communities.

Eligible applicants/beneficiaries: tribal nations, State and Federal agencies, State Foresters, local governments, not-for-profit organizations, and others. Forest Service Regions/Areas/Institutes are encouraged to further define program policies that focus resources to meet the regional, State and local needs of communities.

Range/Average: N.A.

Activity: N.A.

HQ: Director, 201 14th St. SW, Washington, DC 20024. Phone: (202) 205-1380.

Internet: N.A. (Note: no field offices for this program.)

10.674 WOOD UTILIZATION ASSISTANCE

Assistance: project grants. (80 percent/to 3 years).

Purposes: to turn small diameter and under-utilized wood species into marketable forest products, including biomass energy. Programs may include: technical assistance for processing and manufacturing; prototype development of potential new products; demonstration projects showcasing innovative uses; economic feasibility and market assessments. Land treatment must be adjacent to national forest system lands, and may include other lands as part of treatment activities.

Eligible applicants/beneficiaries: nonprofit organizations; local, state, and tribal, governments; special purpose districts; profit businesses.

Range: $50,000 to $500,000. **Average:** N.A.

Activity: 43 grants and agreements funded in FY 2015.

HQ: Director, 1400 Independence Ave. SW, Washington, DC 20250. Phone: (202) 253-6483.

Internet: www.na.fs.fed.us/werc.

10.675 URBAN AND COMMUNITY FORESTRY PROGRAM (UCF)

Assistance: project grants (50 percent).

Purposes: pursuant to the Cooperative Forestry Assistance Act of 1978 as amended, to improve urban livability through projects to: plan, establish, and protect trees, forests, green spaces, and related resources in and adjacent to cities and towns; link governmental, private, and grass-roots organizations and resources to address environmental issues at the local, regional, and national levels; engage people in citizen-based, grass-roots volunteer efforts to assist in retaining and protecting their natural environment to provide a balance between quality of life and land consumption associated with urban sprawl; improve the ecological function and social and economic stability of cities and communities.

Eligible applicants/beneficiaries: state forestry or equivalent state agencies; interested members of the public; private nonprofit organizations, tribes and others. Available also in territories and possessions.

Range/Average: N.A.

Activity: N.A.

HQ: Deputy Chief, State and Private Forestry, Forest Service - USDA, 1400 Independence Ave., SW, Stop 1151, Washington, DC 20090. Phone:(202) 401-4416.

Internet: www.fs.fed.us/ucf/contact_regional.shtml.

10.676 FOREST LEGACY PROGRAM (FLP)

Assistance: project grants. (75 percent/2 years).

Purposes: pursuant to Cooperative Forestry Assistance Act of 1978 FACTA. FAIRA, and amendments, to protect and conserve environmentally important forest areas threatened by conversion to nonforest uses, through conservation easements and other mechanisms. Projects must be conducted on a strictly voluntary basis—i.e., without eminent domain or other legal compulsions.

Eligible applicants: state lead agencies in consultation with state forest stewardship coordinating committees, including in territories and possessions.

Eligible beneficiaries: state agencies, private forest landowners and land trust organizations.

Range/Average: N.A.

Activity: 78,823 acres protected in FY 2015.

HQ: Cooperative Forestry, State and Private Forestry, Forest Service-USDA, 1400 Independence Ave., SW, Stop 1123, Washington, DC 20850. Phone: (202) 205-1618.

Internet: www.fs.fed.us/spf/coop/programs/loa/flp.shtml.

10.678 FOREST STEWARDSHIP PROGRAM (FSP)

Assistance: project grants (12-18 months).

Purposes: pursuant to the Cooperative Forestry Assistance Act of 1978 and FACTA as amended, to provide financial, technical, educational, and related assistance to promote and enable the long-term active management of nonindustrial private and other nonfederal forest land.

Eligible applicants: state forestry or equivalent agencies in the states, territories, and possessions; municipalities; nonprofits; tribes.

Eligible beneficiaries: owners of nonfederal lands, nonprofit organizations, tribes, other state and local private organizations and agencies acting through states.

Range: $50,000 to $400,000. **Average:** N.A.

Activity: 27,500,000 acres covered by Forest Stewardship Plans in FY 2015.

HQ: Forest Stewardship Program Manager, State & Private/Cooperative Forestry, Forest Service-USDA, 1400 Independence Ave., Washington, DC 20250. Phone: (202) 401-4489.

Internet: www.fs.fed.us/spf/coop/programs/loa/fsp.shtml.

10.679 COLLABORATIVE FOREST RESTORATION Program (CFRP)

Assistance: project grants. (80 percent/to 4 years).

Purposes: pursuant to Secure Rural Schools and Community Self- Determination Act of 2000, to promote healthy watersheds and to reduce high intensity wildfires, insect infestation, and diseases in federal, tribal, state, county, and municipal forest lands in New Mexico; to improve the forests' ecosystems functioning and enhance plant and wildlife biodiversity by reducing the high number and density of small diameter trees; to improve communication and joint problem-solving among interested groups. Funds may support costs of technical assistance, training and education, equipment, marketing, and related services.

Eligible applicants/beneficiaries: local and tribal governments, educational institutions, landowners, conservation associations, and other public and private entities that include a diverse and balanced group of stakeholders, including public officials.

Range: $66,361 to $360,000. **Average:** N.A.

Activity: recommended funding 9 projects in FY 2015.

HQ: Cooperative and International Forestry Staff, Southwestern Region, Forest Service-USDA, 333 Broadway SE, Albuquerque, NM 87102. Phone: (505) 842-3425.

Internet: www.fs.usda.gov/goto/r3/cfrp.

10.680 FOREST HEALTH PROTECTION (FHP)

Assistance: formula grants; project grants (50-100 percent).

Purposes: pursuant to the Cooperative Forestry Assistance Act of 1978 and FACTA as amended, to protect nonfederal forest and tree resources from damaging insects, disease-causing agents, and invasive plants; to develop or improve forest health protection technologies. Project funds may be used for project planning, surveys, assessments, monitoring, technical assistance, technology and applied methods development.

Eligible applicants/beneficiaries: state forestry, agriculture, and equivalent agencies, including in territories; municipalities; profit and nonprofit organizations in all states, possessions and territories; Alaska native corporations, tribal governments.

Range/Average: N.A.

Activity: N.A.

HQ: Director, Forest Health Protection - USDA, 1400 Independence Ave., SW, Stop 1110, Washington, DC 20090-6090. Phone: (703) 605-53407.

Internet: www.fs.fed.us/spf/foresthealth.

10.681 WOOD EDUCATION AND RESOURCE CENTER (WERC)

Assistance: project grants (50 percent/18 months).

Purposes: pursuant to the Cooperative Forestry Assistance Act of 1978 and the Forest and Rangeland Renewable Resources Act of 1978, as amended, to provide funds, on a cost-share basis, for projects that focus on enhancing opportunities for sustained forest products production for primary and secondary hardwood industries located in the eastern hardwood forest region. Projects should compliment existing activities and/or focus on niches that are not being met by either industry or service providers and to clearly document industry support and involvement.

Eligible applicants: non-federal agencies, including public, private, state, local and tribal agencies or governments; institutions of higher education; non-profit and for-profit organizations; corporations, businesses and others.

Eligible beneficiaries: non-federal agencies, including public, private, state, local and tribal agencies or governments; institutions of higher education; non-profit and for-profit organizations; corporations, businesses and others located in the 35 states of the eastern hardwood forest region (AL, AR, CT, DE, FL, GA, IL, IN, IA, KS, KY, LA, ME, MD, MA, MI, MN, MS, MO, NE, NH, NJ, NY, NC, OH, OK, PA, RI, SC TN, TX, VT, VA, WV, WI).

Range: $10,000 to $80,000. **Average:** $50,000.

Activity: N.A.

HQ: USDA Forest Service, Wood Education and Resource Center, 1400 Independence Ave., SW, Washington, DC 24740. Phone: (202) 205-1380.

Internet: www.na.fs.fed.us/werc.

10.682 NATIONAL FOREST FOUNDATION

Assistance: direct payments/specified use (the Federal contribution to the overall implementation of a planned project may have a matching requirement, but that match is negotiated).

Purposes: pursuant to the National Forest Foundation Act, to encourage, accept, and administer private gifts of money, and of real and personal property for the benefit of, or in connection with, the activities and services of the Forest Service of the Department of Agriculture; undertake and conduct activities that further the purposes for which units of the NFS are established that are consistent with approved forest plans; and undertake, conduct and encourage educational, technical and other assistance, and other activities that support the multiple use, research, cooperative forestry and other programs administered by the Forest Service. Shall obtain, by the end of the period of Federal financial assistance, private contributions to match on at least one-for-one basis funds made available by the Forest Service.

Eligible applicants: National Forest Foundation under National Forest Foundation Act, Public Law 101-593 as amended by Public Law 103-106.

Eligible beneficiaries: non-governmental, nonprofit 501(c)(3) organizations and Native American tribes working on or adjacent to National Forests and Grasslands.

Range/Average: N.A.

Activity: N.A.

HQ: Director, 201 14th St. NW, Suite 4NW, Washington, DC 20250-1158. Phone: (202) 205-8336.

Internet: www.nationalforests.org. (Note: no field offices for this program.)

10.683   NATIONAL FISH AND WILDLIFE FOUNDATION (NFWF)

Assistance: direct payments/specified use (the Federal contribution to the overall implementation of a planned project may have a matching requirement, but that match is negotiated).

Purposes: pursuant to Section 2(b)(2) of Public Law 98-244, to direct public conservation dollars to the most pressing environmental needs and matches those investments with private funds. To work with a full complement of individuals, foundations, government agencies, nonprofits, and corporations to identify and fund the nation's most intractable conservation challenges. To aid cost-share conservation projects, without regard to when expenses are incurred, on or benefitting National Forest System lands or related to Forest Service programs.

Eligible applicants/beneficiaries: program authorized for the National Fish and Wildlife Foundation (NFWF).

Range/Average: N.A.

Activity: N.A.

HQ: Director, 201 14th St., NW, 3SE, Washington, DC 20024. Phone: (202) 205-1671.

Internet: www.nfwf.org. (Note: no field offices for this program.)

10.684   INTERNATIONAL FORESTRY PROGRAMS

Assistance: project grants (to 5 years).

Purposes: pursuant to the International Forestry Cooperation Act of 1990, to extend Forest Service efforts to improve forest policies and practices internationally, conserve and protect critical global forest environments and resources, and improve the lives of forest-dependent peoples by awarding grants to and entering into cooperative agreements with nonprofit organizations, multilateral organizations, and other individuals, organizations, institutions, and governments engaged in forest conservation and management. Eligible applicant cost share may consist of: funds, donations, in-kind contributions, direct costs, indirect costs, and other as determined by the Forest Service.

Eligible applicants: U.S. and international organizations sanctioned by the State Department, educational institutions, government entities, and individuals.

Eligible beneficiaries: host-country forest management agencies, non-profit organizations, forest landowners, forest-dependent communities and peoples in target countries, and U.S. landowners and organizations.

Range/Average: N.A.

Activity: N.A.

HQ: Outreach & Partnerships Unit, International Programs, FS-USDA, 1 Thomas Circle, NW, Suite 400, Washington DC, 20005. Phone: (202) 644-4613.

Internet: www.fs.fed.us/global.

10.685 COMMUNITY WOOD ENERGY PROGRAM
("Farm Bill, Title IX Energy, Section 9013")

Assistance: project grants/discretionary (50 percent).

Purposes: pursuant to the Food, Conservation and Energy Act of 2008, to encourage the development of community wood energy plans and/or acquire or upgrade community wood energy systems. A community wood energy system acquired with grant funds or receiving technical assistance shall not exceed an output of 50 million Btu per hour for heating and/or 2 megawatts for electric power production, and shall not exceed an output of 50 million Btu per hour for heating and/or 2 megawatts for electric power production.

Eligible applicants: state, Tribal, and local governments (or designees).

Eligible beneficiaries: public facilities owned or operated by State or local governments, including schools, town halls, libraries, hospitals and other public buildings which use woody biomass as the primary fuel. Tribal governments are eligible.

Range/Average: N.A.

Activity: N.A.

HQ: Director, 1400 Independence Ave. SW, Washington, DC 20250. Phone: (202) 253-6483.

Internet: www.fpl.fs.fed.us. (Note: no field offices for this program.)

10.689   COMMUNITY FOREST AND OPEN SPACE CONSERVATION PROGRAM (CFP)

Assistance: project grants/discretionary (50 percent).

Purposes: pursuant to the Food, Conservation, and Energy Act of 2008, to achieve community benefits by establishing community forests through 50/50 financial assistance competitive grant awards to local governments, Indian tribes, and nonprofit organizations. Landowner participation in the program is voluntary and consists of conveying land to achieve conservation objectives.

Eligible applicants/beneficiaries: local governments, Indian tribes, or nonprofit organizations qualified to acquire land and with the authority to manage land.

Range: to $400,000. **Average:** N.A.

Activity: N.A.

HQ: Director, 1400 Independence Ave SW, MS-1123, Washington, DC 20850. Phone: (202) 205-1376.

Internet: www.fs.fed.us/spf/coop/programs/loa/cfp.shtml. (Note: no field offices for this program.)

10.690   LAKE TAHOE EROSION CONTROL GRANT PROGRAM

Assistance: project grants (50 percent/5 years).

Purposes: pursuant to the Lake Tahoe Restoration Act, to make annual payments to the governing bodies of each of the political subdivisions (including public utilities) located in the Lake Tahoe Basin to be used primarily for erosion control and water quality projects; to address urban stormwater runoff pollution, the primary source of pollutants (fine sediment and nutrients) affecting the clarity of Lake Tahoe.

Eligible applicants/beneficiaries: governing bodies of each of the political subdivisions (including public utilities) located in the Lake Tahoe Basin.

Range/Average: N.A.

Activity: N.A.

HQ: Director, 35 College Dr., South Lake Tahoe, California 96150. Phone: (530) 543-2657.

Internet: www.fs.fed.us/r5/ltbmu/ecgp/index.shtml.

10.691   GOOD NEIGHBOR AUTHORITY

Assistance: cooperative agreements/discretionary grants (100 percent/to 5 years).

Purposes: pursuant to the Omnibus Appropriations Act of 2009, to permit the State Forester of Colorado and Utah to perform forest, rangeland, and watershed restoration services on national forest system lands in those two states. Projects may be completed by Colorado and Utah or subcontracts utilizing state contract procedures. Grants are based on available appropriated funding and awarded on a project-by-project basis.

Eligible applicants/beneficiaries: 35 IHEs selected by the CDC as Prevention Research Centers (PRCs).

Range: $5,000 to $1,000,000. **Average:** N.A.

Activity: N.A.

HQ: Director, Forest Service, USDA, 1400 Independence Ave., SW, Washington, DC 20706. Phone: (202) 649-1713.

Internet: N.A.

10.692   DISASTER RELIEF APPROPRIATIONS ACT FOR EMERGENCY FOREST RESTORATION PROGRAM (EFRP)

Assistance: project grants (100 percent, to 24 months).

Purposes: pursuant to the Disaster Relief Appropriations Act of 2013, funds to reimburse state forester or equivalent state agency for technical support provided to private forest landowners suffering damage from Hurricane Sandy in support of USDA Farm Service Agency and the delivery of the Emergency Forest Restoration Program. Damaged forest must be located in areas that were also named in a major disaster declaration. Eligible states include: VA, WV, MD, DE, PA, NJ, NY, CT, RI, MA, NH and OH, but not all counties in these states are eligible. Reimbursement can be for services provided which may include determination of needs, plan development for each practice, supervising the installation of the practice, certification of compliance as prerequisite for payment, furnishing technical assistance to applicant as needed, and checking on practice maintenance during the practices lifespan.

Eligible applicants: state foresters or equivalent state officials of states with producers and landowners suffering forest damage from Hurricane Sandy.

Eligible beneficiaries: private landowners suffering forest damage from Hurricane Sandy.

Range/Average: N.A.

Activity: N.A.

HQ: Director, Emergency Forest Restoration Program EFRP for Hurricane Sandy Relief, FS-USDA, 1400 Independence Ave., Washington, DC 20250. Phone: (202) 401-4489.

Internet: www.na.fs.fed.us.

10.694   SOUTHWEST FOREST HEALTH AND WILDFIRE PREVENTION

Assistance: direct payments/specified use (100 percent).

Purposes: to require the Institutes established under the Southwest Forest Health and Wildfire Prevention Act to collaborate with Federal agencies to use ecological restoration treatments to reverse declining forest health, reduce the risk of severe wildfires across the forest landscape and to design, implement, monitor, and regularly revise representative wildfire treatments based on the use of adaptive ecosystem management. Funds cannot be used to pay costs of constructing any facilities.

Eligible applicants: N.A.

Eligible beneficiaries: one Institute in each of Northern Arizona University, New Mexico Highlands University, and Colorado State University, engaging the full resources of the consortium of universities represented in the Institute of Natural Resource Analysis and Management (INRAM).

Range: $150,000 to $1,500,000. **Average:** N.A.

Activity: N.A.

HQ: Cooperative and International Forestry Staff, Southwestern Region, Forest Service-USDA, 333 Broadway SE, Albuquerque, NM 87102. Phone: (505) 842-3425.

Internet: www.fs.usda.gov/goto/r3/sweri. (Note: no field offices for this program.)

10.700 NATIONAL AGRICULTURAL LIBRARY

Assistance: technical information.

Purposes: to provide agricultural information products and services through traditional library functions and through electronic distribution. Publications are available through interlibrary loan or photo-reproduction.

Eligible applicants/beneficiaries: general public.

Range/Average: N.A.

Activity: N.A.

HQ: Administrator, Agriculture Research Service (ARS) USDA, 5601 Sunnyside Ave., MS-5110, Beltsville, MD 20705. Phone: (301) 504-1702.

Internet: www.nal.usda.gov.

10.759 PART 1774—SPECIAL EVALUATION ASSISTANCE FOR RURAL COMMUNITIES AND HOUSEHOLDS PROGRAM ("SEARCH Grant Program")

Assistance: project grants (100 percent).

Purposes: pursuant to the Food, Conservation and Energy Act, amended by the Consolidated Farm and Rural Development Act (CONACT), to make predevelopment planning grants for feasibility studies, design assistance, and technical assistance to financially distressed communities in rural areas with populations of 2,500 or fewer inhabitants for water and waste disposal projects.

Eligible applicants/beneficiaries: states, municipalities, counties, districts, authorities, public/private nonprofit organizations, IHEs, hospitals, eligible Indian tribes and Native American organizations.

Range: to $30,000. **Average:** N.A.

Activity: N.A.

HQ: Director, RUS, USDA, 1400 Independence Ave., SW, Stop 1570, Washington, DD 20005. Phone: (202) 690-3789.

Internet: www.rd.usda.gov/programs-services/all-programs/water-environmental-programs. (Note: no field offices for this program.)

10.760 WATER AND WASTE DISPOSAL SYSTEMS FOR RURAL COMMUNITIES

Assistance: project grants; direct loans, guaranteed/insured loans. (grants, 45-75 percent/loans, 40 years).

Purposes: pursuant to CFRDA as amended, to install, repair, improve, or expand rural water facilities and waste disposal systems including the collection and treatment of sanitary, storm, and solid wastes. Funds may be used to pay for distribution lines, well-pumping facilities, and their related costs. Loans have varying interest rates beginning as low as 4.5 percent, depending on area median income. Grants are made only when necessary to reduce the average annual benefited user charges to a reasonable level, with the matching percentage based on the applicant area's median income. Grant funds may not be used to pay loan interest, operation and maintenance costs, nor to acquire or refinance existing systems. Grants funding for this program includes **10.761** and **10.770.**

Eligible applicants: municipalities, counties, state political subdivisions such as districts and authorities; associations, cooperatives, and nonprofit corporations; tribes on federal and state reservations and other federally recognized tribes; also authorized in territories.

Eligible beneficiaries: farmers, ranchers, rural residents and businesses; other users in eligible applicant areas.

Range: direct loans, $6,000 to $15,000,000; grants, $500,000 to $16,000,000; guaranteed loans, $500,000 to $2,500,000. **Average:** direct loans, $1,520,968; grants, $1,071,233; guaranteed loans, $1.449,768.

Activity: N.A.

HQ: Assistant Administrator, Water and Environmental Programs, RUS, USDA, 1400 Independence Ave., SW, Stop 1548, Washington, DC 20250. Phone: (202) 690-2670.

Internet: www.rd.usda.gov/programs-services/all-programs/water-environ mental-programs.

10.761   TECHNICAL ASSISTANCE AND TRAINING GRANTS ("TAT Grants")

Assistance: project grants (100 percent).

Purposes: pursuant to CFRDA as amended, to identify and evaluate solutions to rural water problems relating to source, storage, treatment, and waste disposal; to provide training to improve the management, operation, and maintenance of water and waste disposal facilities. Funding for this program is included in **10.760.**

Eligible applicants: tax-exempt nonprofit organizations.

Eligible beneficiaries: state political subdivisions such as counties, municipalities, districts, and authorities; tribes; cooperatives; nonprofit corporations.

Range: $17,500 to $9,000,000. **Average:** N.A.

Activity: N.A.

HQ: Assistant Administrator, Water and Environmental Programs, RUS, USDA, 1400 Independence Ave., SW, Stop 1548, Washington, DC 20250. Phone: (202) 690-2670.

Internet: www.rd.usda.gov/programs-services/water-waste-disposal-technic al-assistance-training-grants.

10.762   SOLID WASTE MANAGEMENT GRANTS

Assistance: project grants (100 percent).

Purposes: pursuant to CFRDA as amended, to evaluate landfill conditions to determine threats to water resources in rural areas; to provide technical assistance and training in the operation of landfills, and to reduce the solid waste stream; to provide planning assistance for closing landfill sites and for future uses of such sites. Funds may not be used to pay for capital assets.

Eligible applicants/beneficiaries: tax-exempt nonprofit organizations; public bodies including local government-based multijurisdictional organizations.

Range: $15,300 to $852,700. **Average:** $133,333.

Activity: N.A.

HQ: Assistant Administrator, Water and Environmental Programs, RUS, USDA, 1400 Independence Ave., SW, Stop 1548, Washington, DC 20250. Phone: (202) 690-2670.

Internet: www.rd.usda.gov/programs-services/all-programs/water-environmental-programs.

10.763   EMERGENCY COMMUNITY WATER ASSISTANCE GRANTS

Assistance: project grants (100 percent).

Purposes: pursuant to Consolidated Farm and Rural Development Act, pursuant to Consolidated Farm and Rural Development Act, to assist rural residents who have experienced a significant decline in quantity or quality of water to obtain adequate quantities of water that meet the standards of the Safe Drinking Water Act. Funds may support: new wells, reservoirs, transmission lines, or treatment plants, repairs of distribution waterlines or breaks, or payment for operation and maintenance items that remedy an acute shortage or significant decline in the quality or quantity of portable water. Projects must serve rural areas, excluding any city or town having a population greater than 10,000.

Eligible applicants/beneficiaries: states, municipalities, counties, districts, authorities, public/private nonprofit organizations, IHEs, hospitals, eligible Indian tribes and Native American organizations.

Range: $100,000 to $500,000. **Average:** $294,220.

Activity: N.A.

HQ: Assistant Administrator, Water and Environmental Programs, RUS, USDA, 1400 Independence Ave., SW, Stop 1548, Washington, DC 20250. Phone: (202) 690-2670.

Internet: www.rd.usda.gov/programs-services/all-programs/water-environmental-programs.

10.766   COMMUNITY FACILITIES LOANS AND GRANTS

Assistance: direct loans; guaranteed loans; project grants.

Purposes: pursuant to CFRDA as amended, to construct, enlarge, extend, or improve public facilities serving rural residents, including child care, food recovery and distribution, assisted living, group homes, mental health clinics, shelters, fire and rescue services, industrial park sites, transportation, access ways, utility extensions, educational facilities.

Eligible applicants: state agencies, counties, cities, state political and quasi-political subdivisions, tribes, associations including nonprofit corporations—in communities with populations under 20,000. Available also in territories.

Eligible beneficiaries: farmers, ranchers, rural residents, rural businesses, and other users of such public facilities in eligible applicant areas.

Range: direct loans, $3,500 to $55,000,000; guaranteed loans, $108,000 to $27,000,000; grants, to $50,000. **Average:** direct loans, $1,878,621; guaranteed loans, $4,602,786; grants, $25,419.

Activity: anticipate servicing 8,000,000 rural residents in FY 2015.

HQ: Deputy Administrator/Community Programs, RHS-USDA, 1400 Independence Ave., Washington, DC 20250. Phone: (202) 720-1498.

Internet: www.rd.usda.gov.

10.767 INTERMEDIARY RELENDING PROGRAM (IRP)

Assistance: direct loans. (75 percent at 1 percent interest/to 30 years).

Purposes: pursuant to the Health and Human Services Act of 1986, Food Security Act of 1985, and Community Economic Development Act of 1981, and amendments, for business facilities and community development in rural areas with under 25,000 population. Successful applicants become intermediary lenders that may make loans to ultimate recipients to finance up to 75 percent of project costs, but not more than $250,000 to any one ultimate recipient.

Eligible applicants: private nonprofit organizations, state or local governments, recognized tribes, cooperatives.

Eligible beneficiaries: individuals, public and private profit or nonprofit organizations.

Range/Average: N.A.

Activity: N.A.

HQ: RBCS-USDA, 1400 Independence Ave., SW Rm. 4204, Stop 3226, Washington, DC 20250. Phone: (202) 720-4100.

Internet: www.rd.usda.gov/programs-services/intermediary-relending-program.

10.768 BUSINESS AND INDUSTRY LOANS

Assistance: guaranteed/insured loans (to 80-90 percent).

Purposes: pursuant to CFRDA as amended, for the development or improvement of rural businesses, industry, and employment. Loan funds may cover such costs as business and industrial acquisition, construction, conversion, enlargement, repair, modernization, equipment, machinery, supplies, pollution control and abatement—for 30 years for real estate, up to 15 years for machinery and equipment, and 7 years for working capital. Assistance is unavailable for community antenna TV services or facilities, charitable and educational institutions, hotels and tourist facilities, large businesses, or uses other than those that will protect or create jobs, improve existing business and industry, and provide economic stability to rural areas. Project examples: agri-business expansion; radio station start-up; catfish farm operating loan; printing company expansion.

Eligible applicants/beneficiaries: cooperatives, corporations, partnerships, trusts, or other for-profit enterprises; certain nonprofit entities; tribes, municipalities, counties, or other state political subdivisions; individuals. Applicants must be U.S. citizens or legal permanent residents; if corporations, 51 percent ownership must be held by U.S. citizens. Available also in some territories. Projects must be in rural jurisdiction under 50,000 population, with preference to those under 25,000.

Range/Average: N.A.

Activity: N.A.

HQ: Administrator, B&I Processing Branch-USDA, 1400 Independence Ave., SW, Stop 3224, Washington, DC 20250-3224. Phone: (202) 690-4103.

Internet: www.rd.usda.gov/programs-services/business-industry-loan-guarantees.

10.769 RURAL BUSINESS ENTERPRISE GRANTS (RBEG)

Assistance: project grants.

Purposes: pursuant to CFRDA as amended, to facilitate the development of small and emerging private business, industry, and related employment—toward economic improvement of rural areas. Grants may be used to: create, expand, or operate distance learning networks or programs providing educational or job training instruction; to establish revolving loan funds, provide operating capital, and finance industrial sites—including land acquisition; construction, conversion, enlargement, repair, or modernization of buildings, plants, machinery, equipment; access streets and roads, parking areas, transportation serving the site; utility extensions; water supply and waste disposal facilities, pollution control and abatement; technical assistance, fees, and refinancing. Television demonstration grants (TDG) may be used for programming demonstrating the effectiveness of providing information on agriculture and other issues of importance to farmers and other rural residents.

Eligible applicants: RBEG—public bodies and nonprofit corporations serving rural areas, such as states, counties, cities, townships, and incorporated towns and villages, boroughs, authorities, districts, and tribes on federal and state reservations serving rural areas. TDG—statewide nonprofit public television systems whose coverage is predominantly rural. For this program, "rural area" is defined as city, town, or unincorporated area with a population of 50,000 or less. Priority is accorded to projects: in areas with a large number of low-income persons; designed to save existing or to create new jobs; in areas with high unemployment.

Eligible beneficiaries: private businesses that will employ 50 or fewer new employees, and with under $1,000,000 in projected revenue.

Range: $25,000 to $500,000. **Average:** less than $100,000.

Activity: N.A.

HQ: Director, Specialty Programs Division, RBCS-USDA, 1400 Independence Ave., SW, Rm. 4204, Stop 3226, Washington, DC 20250-3222. Phone: (202) 720-1400.

Internet: www.rd.usda.gov/programs-services/rural-business-development-grants.

10.770 WATER AND WASTE DISPOSAL LOANS AND GRANTS ("Section 306C")

Assistance: project grants; direct loans (100 percent).

Purposes: pursuant to CFRDA as amended and FACTA, to develop water and waste disposal facilities and services for rural low- income communities facing significant health risks. Funds may be used to: construct, enlarge, extend, or improve community water or sewer systems; connect residences to community systems; enable individuals to install plumbing and related fixtures and to construct bathrooms within their dwellings. Funded projects must primarily serve residents of counties with per capita incomes not more than 70 percent of the national average, and with unemployment not less than 125 percent of the national average rate. Grant funds for this program are included in **10.760**, and may be used only in colonias.

Eligible applicants/beneficiaries: local governments, tribes, nonprofit associations, cooperatives—including territories and possessions.

Range: $119,407 to $6,356,474 for Colonias grants; $300,000 to $3,984,860 for Native American Tribe grants. **Average:** $2,620,137 for Colonias grants; $1,347,593 for Native American Tribe grants.

Activity: N.A.

HQ: Assistant Administrator, Water and Environmental Programs, RUS, USDA, 1400 Independence Ave., SW, Stop 1548, Washington, DC 20250. Phone: (202) 690-2670.

Internet: www.rd.usda.gov/programs-services/all-programs/water-environ mental-programs.

10.771 RURAL COOPERATIVE DEVELOPMENT GRANTS

Assistance: project grants (75 percent).

Purposes: pursuant to the FACTA, CFRDA, and FAIRA, to establish and operate centers for rural cooperative development to improve economic conditions by promoting development of new cooperatives, or to improve existing cooperatives. Funds may be used for basic feasibility studies, technical assistance, advisory services, and research or technical support for individuals, small businesses, cooperatives, or rural industries.

Eligible applicants: nonprofit corporations and IHEs serving rural areas not within the outer boundary of any city having a population of 50,000 or more according to latest U.S. decennial census.

Eligible beneficiaries: rural residents.

Range: $70,000 to $200,000. **Average:** $180,000.

Activity: N.A.

HQ: Assistant Deputy Administrator/Cooperative Services, RBCS-USDA, 1400 Independence Ave., SW, Stop 3253, Rm. 4208-S, Washington, DC 20250-3253. Phone: (202) 690-1374.

Internet: www.rd.usda.gov/programs-services/rural-cooperative-development-grant-program.

10.773 RURAL BUSINESS OPPORTUNITY GRANTS (RBOG)

Assistance: project grants (2 years).

Purposes: pursuant to FAIRA, to promote sustainable economic development in rural communities with exceptional needs. Grants may support technical assistance, training, and planning costs.

Eligible applicants/beneficiaries: public bodies, nonprofit corporations, tribes, cooperatives.

Range/Average: N.A.

Activity: N.A.

HQ: Specialty Lenders Division, RBCS-USDA, 1400 Independence Ave., SW, Rm. 4016, Washington, DC 20250. Phone: (202) 720-7558.

Internet: www.rd.usda.gov/programs-services/rural-business-development-grants.

10.777 NORMAN E. BORLAUG INTERNATIONAL AGRICULTURAL SCIENCE AND TECHNOLOGY FELLOWSHIP ("Borlaug Fellowship Program")

Assistance: direct payments/specified use; project grants (100 percent/to 5 years).

Purposes: Borlaug fellowships help developing countries strengthen sustainable agricultural practices by providing U.S. based scientific training and collaborative research opportunities for entry- to mid-career agricultural research scientists and policymakers from developing and middle income countries. No funding available for unsolicited proposals.

Eligible applicants: U.S. land grant universities, USDA agencies, U.S. government agency research facilities, not-for-profit institutions, international agricultural research centers.

Eligible beneficiaries: foreign governments and related agricultural institutions in their countries.

Range: $35,000 to $37,000 per fellow. **Average:** N.A.

Activity: 50 fellowships in FY 2016.

HQ: Director, 1400 Independence Ave., SW, Stop 1030, Washington, DC 20250. Phone: (202) 720-6888.

Internet: www.fas.usda.gov. (Note: no field offices for this program.)

10.850 RURAL ELECTRIFICATION LOANS AND LOAN GUARANTEES

Assistance: direct loans. (70-90 percent/to 35 years).

Purposes: pursuant to the Rural Electrification Act of 1936 (REA) as amended, to supply or improve central station electric services in rural areas—i.e., any farm or nonfarm area not within the boundaries of an urban area. RUS also guarantees loans used primarily for generation and transmission projects.

Eligible applicants/beneficiaries: rural electric cooperatives, public utility districts, power companies, municipalities, and other qualified power suppliers, including in territories.

Range: N.A. **Average:** $32,668,948.

Activity: N.A.

HQ: Assistant Administrator, Electric Program, RUS-USDA, 1400 Independence Ave., SW, Stop 1560, Washington, DC 20250. Phone: (202) 720-9540.

Internet: www.rd.usda.gov/programs-services/all-programs/electric-programs. (Note: no field offices for this program.)

10.851 RURAL TELEPHONE LOANS AND LOAN GUARANTEES ("Telecommunications Infrastructure Loan Program")

Assistance: direct loans; guaranteed/insured loans.

Purposes: pursuant to REA as amended, to improve, expand, construct, acquire, and operate telecommunications systems in rural areas—i.e., any area of the U.S. not within the boundaries of a city, village, or borough with over 5,000 population. Average loan term, 18 years.

Eligible applicants/beneficiaries: telephone companies or cooperatives; non-profit, limited dividend, or mutual associations; public bodies—including in territories.

Range: $4,668,000 to $29,753,000 for direct loans; $7,695,000 to $24,483,000 for loan guarantees. **Average:** $15,028,8080 for direct loans; $16,225,333 for loan guarantees.

Activity: awarded 16 loans in FY 2015.

HQ: Assistant Administrator, Telecommunications Program, RUS-USDA, 1400 Independence Ave., SW, Stop 1590, Rm. 5151, Washington, DC 20250. Phone: (202) 720-9564; FAX: (202) 720-0810.

Internet: www.rurdev.usda.gov/utp_infrastructure.html. (Note: no field offices for this program.)

10.854 RURAL ECONOMIC DEVELOPMENT LOANS AND GRANTS (REDLG)

Assistance: direct loans; project grants. (loans, 80 percent; grants, 80 percent/loans, no interest/10 years).

Purposes: pursuant to REA as amended, for rural economic and job development projects, including the costs of feasibility studies, project start-up, and other reasonable expenses. Project examples: business incubators; establishment or expansion of factories or businesses; revolving loan funds.

Eligible applicants: electric and telephone utilities with current RUS loans.

Eligible beneficiaries: rural/general public.

Range/Average: N.A.

Activity: N.A.

HQ: Specialty Lenders Division, RBCS-USDA, 1400 Independence Ave., SW, Stop 3226, Washington, DC 20250. Phone: (202) 720-1400.

Internet: www.rd.usda.gov/programs-services/rural-economic-development-loan-grant-program.

10.855 DISTANCE LEARNING AND TELEMEDICINE LOANS AND GRANTS

Assistance: project grants; direct loans. (grants, 85 percent; loans, 100 percent/grants and loans, 3 years).

Purposes: pursuant to FAIRA, for telecommunications, computer networks, and related technologies in rural areas, providing educational and/or medical benefits to students, teachers, medical professionals, and rural residents—through distance learning and telemedicine projects.

Eligible applicants/beneficiaries: legally organized corporations, partnerships; tribes and tribal organizations; state and local governments; schools, libraries, hospitals, medical centers, and similar organizations.

Range: from $50,000. **Average:** $313,789

Activity: 65 awards in FY 2014.

HQ: Assistant Administrator, Telecommunications Program, RUS-USDA, 1400 Independence Ave., SW, Stop 1590, Rm. 5151, Washington, DC 20250. Phone: (202) 720-9564; FAX: (202) 720-0810.

Internet: www.rd.usda.gov/programs-services/distance-learning-telemedi cine-grants. (Note: no field offices for this program.)

10.857 STATE BULK FUEL REVOLVING FUND GRANTS

Assistance: project grants. (100 percent/3 years).

Purposes: pursuant to REA as amended, for states to establish revolving funds to enable cost-effective fuel purchases for communities where fuel cannot be shipped by surface transportation.

Eligible applicants/beneficiaries: state entities in existence as of 9 November 2000, including in territories and possessions.

Range/Average: N.A.

Activity: N.A.

HQ: Assistant Administrator, Electric Program, RUS-USDA, 1400 Independence Ave., SW, Stop 1560, Washington, DC 20250. Phone: (202) 720-9540.

Internet: www.rd.usda.gov/programs-services/state-bulk-fuel-revolving-loan-fund. (Note: no field offices for this program.)

10.858 DENALI COMMISSION GRANTS AND LOANS

Assistance: project grants; direct loans (project grants, from 3 years).

Purposes: pursuant to REA as amended, for the Denali Commission to finance facilities serving several rural communities in Alaska where average residential energy expenditures are at least 275 percent of the national average—in coordination with state rural development initiatives. Project examples: improvements in bulk fuel storage and handling facilities; electric distribution system improvements.

Eligible applicants: Denali Commission only.

Eligible beneficiaries: Alaska rural residents.

Range: $2,310,686 to $18,500,000. **Average:** N.A.

Activity: N.A.

HQ: Assistant Administrator, Electric Program, RUS-USDA, 1400 Independence Ave., SW, Stop 1560, Washington, DC 20250. Phone: (202) 720-9540.

Internet: www.denali.gov. (Note: no field offices for this program.)

10.859   ASSISTANCE TO HIGH ENERGY COST—RURAL COMMUNITIES ("High Energy Cost Grants")

Assistance: project grants; direct loans.

Purposes: pursuant to REA as amended, for projects in rural communities with high energy costs to acquire, construct, extend, upgrade, and improve energy generation, transmission, or distribution facilities—where the average residential home energy expenditure is at least 275 percent of the national average.

Eligible applicants/beneficiaries: states, state political subdivisions, and state entities including profit and nonprofit businesses, partnerships, associations, cooperatives, public bodies, tribal entities, and individuals—including in territories and possessions.

Range: $50,000 to $3,000,000. **Average:** N.A.

Activity: N.A.

HQ: Assistant Administrator, Electric Program, RUS-USDA, 1400 Independence Ave., SW, Stop 1560, Washington, DC 20250. Phone: (202) 720-9545.

Internet: www.rd.usda.gov/programs-services/high-energy-cost-grants. (Note: no field offices for this program.)

10.862   HOUSEHOLD WATER WELL SYSTEM GRANT PROGRAM ("HWWS Program")

Assistance: project grants.

Purposes: pursuant to CFRDA as amended, to establish and maintain revolving loan funds to make loans, in turn, to eligible rural homeowners to construct, refurbish, and service individually owned household water well systems.

Eligible applicants: experienced private nonprofit corporations.

Eligible beneficiaries: households with a combined income not exceeding 100 percent of the nonmetropolitan median for the area.

Range: $50,000 to $300,000. **Average:** N.A.

Activity: N.A.

HQ: Assistant Administrator, Water and Environmental Programs, RUS, USDA, 1400 Independence Ave., SW, Stop 1548, Washington, DC 20250. Phone: (202) 690-2670.

Internet: www.rd.usda.gov/programs-services/all-programs/water-environmental-programs.

10.863   COMMUNITY CONNECT GRANT PROGRAM

Assistance: project grants. (to 85 percent/3 years).

Purposes: to deploy broadband transmission services to critical rural community facilities such as schools, education centers, libraries, hospitals, health care providers, law enforcement agencies, public safety organizations, fire and rescue services, and residents and businesses that will operate a community center providing free and open access to area residents. Funds may cover costs of construction, acquisition, expansion, and operation of centers for at least 2 years.

Eligible applicants/beneficiaries: incorporated profit or nonprofit organizations; tribes and tribal organizations, state or local governments.

Range: $470,000 to $3,000,000. **Average:** $1,710,701.

Activity: N.A.

HQ: Assistant Administrator, Telecommunications Program, RUS-USDA, 1400 Independence Ave., SW, Stop 5151, Washington, DC 20250. Phone: (202) 720-9554; FAX: (202) 720-9564.

Internet: www.rd.usda.gov/programs-services/community-connect-grants. (Note: no field offices for this program.)

10.864 GRANT PROGRAM TO ESTABLISH A FUND FOR FINANCING WATER AND WASTEWATER PROJECTS ("RFP Program")

Assistance: project grants (80 percent).

Purposes: pursuant to CFRDA as amended, to establish and maintain a revolving loan fund to finance small and short-term predevelopment costs of proposed or existing water and wastewater projects or systems, including costs of replacement equipment and small-scale extension of services—in rural communities with populations not higher 10,000.

Eligible applicants: private nonprofit organization.

Eligible beneficiaries: municipalities, counties, other state political subdivisions including districts and authorities; associations, cooperatives, nonprofit corporations; tribes.

Range: $250,000 to $500,000. **Average:** $333,333.

Activity: N.A.

HQ: Assistant Administrator, Water and Environmental Programs, RUS, USDA, 1400 Independence Ave., SW, Stop 1548, Washington, DC 20250. Phone: (202) 690-2670.

Internet: www.rd.usda.gov/programs-services/all-programs/water-environmental-programs.

10.866 REPOWERING ASSISTANCE ("Section 9004 Repowering Assistance")

Assistance: direct payments/specified use.

Purposes: pursuant to the Food, Conservation, and Energy Act of 2008, to provide payments to eligible biorefineries (in existence on or before June 18, 2008) in order to facilitate replacement of fossil fuels used to produce heat or power at their facilities by installing new systems that utilize renewable biomass or produce new energy from renewable biomass.

Eligible applicants/beneficiaries: eligible producers (whose primary production is biofuels) and biorefineries that have been in existence on or before June 18, 2008.

Range/Average: N.A.

Activity: N.A.

HQ: Director, Rural Development, Energy Division, USDA, 1400 Independence Ave., SW, Stop 3225, Washington, DC 20250-3225. Phone: (202) 690-0784.

Internet: www.rd.usda.gov/programs-services/repowering-assistance-program.

10.867   BIOENERGY PROGRAM FOR ADVANCED BIOFUELS ("Advanced Biofuel Payments Program")

Assistance: direct payments/unrestricted use.

Purposes: pursuant to the Food, Conservation, and Energy Act of 2008, to support and ensure an expanding production of advanced biofuels (other than corn kernel starch) and promote sustainable economic development in rural America. Funds will be provided to eligible advanced biofuel producers, including biodiesel facilities producing advanced biofuel from canola oil, greases, and soybean oil. Other examples of eligible producers are ethanol facilities that use milo or sorghum, farms that use an anaerobic digester to use animal waste to produce electricity, and manufacturing facilities that produce wood pellets.

Eligible applicants/beneficiaries: eligible individuals, corporations, companies, foundations, associations, labor organizations, firms, partnerships, societies, joint stock companies, groups of organizations, or non-profit entities that produce and sell an advanced biofuel.

Range/Average: N.A.

Activity: N.A.

HQ: Director, 511 W. 7th St., Atlantic, Iowa 50022. Phone: (712) 243-2107.

Internet: www.rd.usda.gov/programs-services/repowering-assistance-program.

10.868   RURAL ENERGY FOR AMERICA PROGRAM (REAP)

Assistance: loan guarantees; grants (25 to 75 percent/2 years).

Purposes: pursuant to the Food, Conservation, and Energy Act of 2008, to promote energy efficiency improvements and renewable energy systems development in rural areas by providing grants and loan guarantees, primarily to farmers, ranchers (agricultural producers) and rural small businesses. Grants fund a portion of project costs and/or loan guarantees to purchase and install energy efficiency improvements and renewable energy systems. Grants fund agricultural producers and rural small businesses for a portion of the cost of a feasibility study for a renewable energy system. Government entities, educational institutions, rural electric cooperatives, and public power entities are eligible for energy audits or renewable energy development assistance with 25 percent cost sharing.

Eligible applicants/beneficiaries: farmers, ranchers, rural small businesses, states, tribal and local governments, land-grant colleges and other IHEs, rural electric cooperatives and public power entities.

Range: grants, $2,500 to $500,000; guaranteed loans, $5,000 to $25,000,000. **Average:** grants, $45,000; guaranteed loans, $85,000.

Activity: N.A.

HQ: Director, Rural Business-Cooperative Service, USDA, 1400 Independence Ave., SW, Washington, DC 20250. Phone: (515) 720-6819.

Internet: N.A.

10.870   RURAL MICROENTREPRENEUR ASSISTANCE PROGRAM (RMAP)

Assistance: direct loans; project grants (75 percent).

Purposes: pursuant to the Food, Conservation, and Energy Act of 2008, to provide rural microentrepreneurs with the skills necessary to establish new rural microenterprises and to provide continuing technical and financial assistance related to the successful operation of rural microenterprises. Loans to Microenterprise Development Organizations (MDO) for the purpose of capitalizing microloan revolving funds to provide fixed interest rate business loans of $50,000 for startup and growing rural microenterprises. Technical assistance grant awards require a 25 percent match (10 percent non-federal cash; 15 percent in the form of non-federal cash, in-kind goods, services, or indirect costs).

Eligible applicants: eligible microlenders must be a non-profit entity, an Indian tribe, or a public IHE and at least 51 percent controlled by persons who are either citizens of the U.S., the Republic of Palau, the Federated States of Micronesia, the Republic of the Marshall Islands, American Samoa or legally admitted permanent residents residing in the U.S.

Eligible beneficiaries: current or prospective owners/operators of a rural microenterprise who need training and technical assistance.

Range: $131,250 to $500,000. **Average:** N.A.

Activity: N.A.

HQ: Director, USDA, 1400 Independence Ave., SW, Washington, DC 20250. Phone: (202) 720-1400.

Internet: www.rd.usda.gov/programs-services/rural-microentrepreneur-assistance-program.

10.874   DELTA HEALTH CARE SERVICES GRANT PROGRAM

Assistance: project grants/discretionary (100 percent/to 3 years).

Purposes: pursuant to the Consolidated Farm and Rural Development Act of 1972, to provide financial assistance to address the continued unmet health needs in the Delta Region through cooperation among health care professionals, institutions of higher education, research institutions, and other individuals/entities in the Delta Region. Grant funds may be utilized for the development of health care services, education programs, and job training programs and for the development and expansion of public health-related facilities. Delta Region means the 252 counties and parishes within the states of Alabama, Arkansas, Illinois, Kentucky, Louisiana, Mississippi, Missouri, and Tennessee that are served by the Delta Regional Authority.

Eligible applicants/beneficiaries: consortiums (combination/group of regional IHEs, academic health and research institutes, and economic development entities) located in the Delta Region having experience addressing health care issues in the region and have at least one member with the legal authority to contract with the government.

Range: $50,000 to $3,000,000. **Average:** N.A.

Activity: N.A.

HQ: Director, Rural Business-Cooperative Service, USDA, 1400 Independence Ave., SW, Stop 3253, Washington, DC 20250-1550. Phone: (202) 690-1374.

Internet: www.rd.usda.gov/programs-services/delta-health-care-services-grants.

10.886 RURAL BROADBAND ACCESS LOANS AND LOAN GUARANTEES ("Farm Bill Broadband Loans")

Assistance: direct loans; guaranteed/insured loans. (direct loans, 4 percent/guaranteed/insured loans, 5 years).

Purposes: pursuant to REA as amended, for rural communities to finance the construction, improvement, and acquisition of telecommunications facilities and equipment to provide broadband service comparable in reliability and quality to the rest of the nation.

Eligible applicants/beneficiaries: cooperative, nonprofit, limited dividend, or mutual associations; limited liability companies; commercial organizations; tribes and tribal organizations; state and local governments; territories and possessions—serving communities with population not exceeding more than 20,000.

Range/Average: N.A.

Activity: N.A.

HQ: Assistant Administrator, Telecommunications Program, RUS-USDA, 1400 Independence Ave., SW, Stop 1590, Rm. 5151, Washington, DC 20250. Phone: (202) 720-9564; FAX: (202) 720-0810.

Internet: www.rd.usda.gov/programs-services/farm-bill-broadband-loans-loan-guarantees. (Note: no field offices for this program.)

10.902 SOIL AND WATER CONSERVATION

Assistance: advisory services/counseling.

Purposes: pursuant to the Soil Conservation and Domestic Allotment Act of 1936 as amended, to assist in planning and applying soil and water conservation practices, systems, and treatment; to provide technical natural resource conservation information.

Eligible applicants/beneficiaries: land users and owners, community organizations, state and local governments. Available also in PR, VI, and Western Pacific Trust Territories.

Range/Average: N.A.

Activity: N.A.

HQ: Deputy Chief/Programs, Resource Conservation and Community Development Division, NRCS-USDA, PO Box 2890, Washington, DC 20013. Phone: (202) 720-1510.

Internet: www.nrcs.usda.gov.

10.903   SOIL SURVEY

Assistance: technical information.

Purposes: to produce and maintain current published soil surveys and related data bases of counties and areas of comparable size for use by environmentalists, engineers, planners, zoning and tax commissions, homeowners, farmers, ranchers, land developers, and others—in selecting and implementing appropriate use and treatment of the soils surveyed.

Eligible applicants/beneficiaries: anyone needing soil surveys.

Range/Average: N.A.

Activity: N.A.

HQ: Deputy Chief/Soil Survey and Resource Assessment, NRCS-USDA, 1400 Independence Ave., Washington, DC 20013. Phone: (202) 720-5493.

Internet: www.nrcs.usda.gov.

10.904   WATERSHED PROTECTION AND FLOOD PREVENTION ("Small Watershed Program")

Assistance: project grants; advisory services/counseling (project grants, 50-100 percent).

Purposes: pursuant to the Watershed Protection and Flood Prevention Act as amended and other acts, to plan and execute projects to protect, develop, and utilize land and water resources in small watersheds (250,000 acres or less). Funds may support watershed protection measures, flood prevention, irrigation, drainage, agricultural water management, sedimentation control, and public water-based fish, wildlife, and recreation resources; also, to extend long-term credit to help local interests with their share of costs. Single structure capacity is limited to 25,000 acre-feet of total capacity and 12,500 acre-feet of flood-water detention capacity.

Eligible applicants/beneficiaries: any authorized state agency, county or groups of counties, municipality, town or township, soil and water conservation district, flood prevention or flood control district, tribe or tribal organization, or nonprofit agency. Available also in territories.

Range: to $2,164,000. Average: $650,000.

Activity: N.A.

HQ: Watersheds and Wetlands Division, NRCS-USDA, 1400 Independence Ave., SW, Washington, DC 20013. Phone: (202) 720-3413.

Internet: www.nrcs.usda.gov.

10.905   PLANT MATERIALS FOR CONSERVATION

Assistance: specialized services.

Purposes: pursuant to the Soil Conservation and Domestic Allotment Act of 1936 as amended, to assemble, evaluate, select, release, and introduce into commerce the use of new and improved plant materials such as grasses, legumes, forbs, shrubs, and trees for soil, water, and related resource conservation and environmental improvement programs—including erosion control, roadside and stream bank protection, surface-mined land reclamation, and wildlife food and cover. Plant materials are produced only for field testing and to provide commercial producers with breeder and foundation quality seed or propagules. Free plants or seed are not provided to the general public under this program.

Eligible applicants/beneficiaries: cooperating state and federal agencies and cooperators of conservation districts; commercial seed growers and nurseries interested in the production of selected plant materials, including in PR and VI.

Range/Average: N.A.

Activity: N.A.

HQ: Deputy Chief/Science and Technology, NRCS-USDA, 1400 Independence Ave., SW, PO Box 2890, Washington, DC 20013. Phone: (202) 720-0536.

Internet: www.nrcs.usda.gov.

10.907 SNOW SURVEY AND WATER SUPPLY FORECASTING ("Snow Surveys")

Assistance: technical information.

Purposes: pursuant to the Soil Conservation and Domestic Allotment Act of 1936 as amended, to provide information on forthcoming seasonal water supplies from streams that derive most of their runoff from snowmelt in the mountain states and the far west—assisting farm operators, rural communities, municipalities, and others in planning for and managing water resources. Data are used in the regulation of small and large reservoirs for irrigation, flood control, power generation, recreation, industry, and municipal supplies.

Eligible applicants/beneficiaries: general public, including in the territories.

Range/Average: N.A.

Activity: N.A.

HQ: Deputy Chief/Science and Technology, NRCS-USDA, PO Box 2890, Washington, DC 20013. Phone: (503) 414-3055.

Internet: www.nrcs.usda.gov.

10.912 ENVIRONMENTAL QUALITY INCENTIVES PROGRAM (EQIP)

Assistance: direct payments/specified use. (to 75 percent/5-10 years).

Purposes: pursuant to FSRIA, FAIRA, and Food Security Act of 1985, to assist farmers and ranchers in complying with environmental laws and to encourage environmental enhancement by providing technical, educational, and financial assistance to implement structural, vegetative, and land management practices that address soil, water, and related natural resource concerns. Program is funded through the CCC. Fifty percent of available funding must be targeted at practices relating to livestock production.

Eligible applicants/beneficiaries: agricultural producers including owners, landlords, operators, or tenants of eligabible lands—with special encouragement to apply to limited resource producers, small-scale producers, and minority groups, tribal governments, Alaskan natives and Pacific Islanders.

Range: to $450,000. **Average:** $23,000.

Activity: N.A.

HQ: Deputy Chief/Programs, NRCS-USDA, PO Box 2890, Washington, DC 20013. Phone: (202) 690-2621.

Internet: www.nrcs.usda.gov.

10.913   FARM AND RANCH LANDS PROTECTION PROGRAM (FRPP)

Assistance: direct payments/specified use (50 percent).

Purposes: pursuant to Food Security Act of 1985, to purchase conservation easements or other interests in lands to limit nonagricultural uses of farm land with prime, unique, or other productive soils—with a minimum 30-year duration.

Eligible applicants/beneficiaries: local or state agencies, counties, municipalities, towns, local government units, tribes, soil and water conservation districts—with a farmland protection program. Available also in territories.

Range: $2,700 to $1,000,000 per landowner. **Average:** $97,000.

Activity: N.A.

HQ: Farmland Protection and Community Planning Staff, NRCS-USDA, 14th and Independence Ave., SW, Washington, DC 20250. Phone: (202) 720-9476; FAX: (202) 720-4265.

Internet: www.nrcs.usda.gov.

10.914   WILDLIFE HABITAT INCENTIVE PROGRAM (WHIP)

Assistance: direct payments/specified use. (to 75 percent/ 5-10 years minimum).

Purposes: pursuant to FAIRA, to develop habitats for upland and wetland wildlife, threatened and endangered species, and fish. Technical assistance is provided to prepare a Wildlife Habitat Development Plan.

Eligible applicants/beneficiaries: owners, landlords, operators, tenants of eligible lands. Limited resource producers, small-scale producers, and minority groups, tribal governments, Alaska natives, and Pacific Islanders are encouraged to apply.

Range: N.A. **Average:** $4,500.

Activity: N.A.

HQ: Deputy Chief/Programs, NRCS-USDA, PO Box 2890, Washington, DC 20013. Phone: (202) 690-2621.

Internet: www.nrcs.usda.gov.

10.916   WATERSHED REHABILITATION PROGRAM
("PL-566 Watershed Program")

Assistance: project grants; advisory services/counseling (grants, 65-100 percent).

Purposes: pursuant to the Watershed Protection and Flood Prevention Act and other acts, to plan, design, and implement watershed rehabilitation and improvement projects involving dams originally constructed with USDA assistance. Projects may include reconstruction or decommissioning of dams and relocation or flood proofing of downstream property.

Eligible applicants/beneficiaries: state agencies, counties or groups of counties, towns or townships, soil and water conservation districts, flood prevention or flood control districts, tribes or tribal organizations, other state-authorized nonprofit organizations.

Range: to $6,451,000. **Average:** $770,000.

Activity: N.A.

HQ: Watersheds and Wetlands Division, NRCS-USDA, PO Box 2890, Washington, DC 20013. Phone: (202) 720-3414.

Internet: www.nrcs.usda.gov/wps/portal/nrcs/main/national/programs/land scape/wr.

10.917 AGRICULTURAL MANAGEMENT ASSISTANCE

Assistance: direct payments/specified use. (75 percent/3-10 years).

Purposes: pursuant to the Agricultural Risk Protection Act of 2000, for producers on private lands to: construct or improve water management or irrigation structures; plant trees for windbreaks or to improve water quality; mitigate financial risk through production or marketing diversification or resource conservation practices including soil erosion control, integrated pest management, or transition to organic farming.

Eligible applicants/beneficiaries: applicants with control of the land during the contract period—i.e., 3-10 years—only in Connecticut, Delaware, Maine, Maryland, Massachusetts, Nevada, New Hampshire, New Jersey, New York, Pennsylvania, Rhode Island, Utah, Vermont, West Virginia, and Wyoming.

Range: to $50,000 per participant. **Average:** N.A.

Activity: N.A.

HQ: Conservation Operations Division, NRCS-USDA, PO Box 2890, Washington, DC 20013. Phone: (202) 720-1873; FAX: (202) 260-9232.

Internet: www.nrcs.usda.gov.

10.920 GRASSLAND RESERVE PROGRAM (GRP)

Assistance: project grants.

Purposes: to restore and protect eligible grasslands and certain other lands through rental agreements and easements that: permit controlled grazing; permit controlled haying, mowing, or harvesting for seed production; allow for fire rehabilitation and construction of firebreaks, fencing, water facilities; prohibit production of row crops, fruit trees, vineyards, and the like.

Eligible applicants/beneficiaries: easements—owners of eligible lands; rental agreements—entities with sufficient control of land.

Range: easements: $65 per acre to over $30,000 per acre. **Average:** easements: $400 per acre; rental agreements: $134 per acre.

Activity: N.A.

HQ: Deputy Chief/Programs, NRCS-USDA, 1400 Independence Ave., SW, Washington, DC 20250. Phone: (202) 260-9111.

Internet: www.nrcs.usda.gov.

10.921 CONSERVATION SECURITY PROGRAM (CSP)

Assistance: direct payments/specified use (5-10 years).

Purposes: pursuant to the Food Security Act of 1985 and FSRIA, for the conservation and improvement through approved appropriate stewardship of soil, water, air, energy, and plant and animal life on tribal and working lands—including cropland, grassland, prairie land, improved pasture, and rangeland, as well as forested land incidental to an agricultural operation. Funding is provided through the CCC.

Eligible applicants/beneficiaries: individual producers, partnerships, associations, corporations, estates, trusts, and other business entities enrolling eligible lands.

Range/Average: N.A.

Activity: N.A.

HQ: Financial Assistance Programs Division, NRCS-USDA, 1400 Independence Ave., SW, Washington, DC 20013. Phone: (202) 720-6700.

Internet: www.nrcs.usda.gov.

10.922 HEALTHY FORESTS RESERVE PROGRAM (HFRP)

Assistance: direct payments/specified use; technical assistance (restoration, 10 years; easement, 30 or 99 years).

Purposes: pursuant to Title V of the Healthy Forest Restoration Act of 2003, to assist landowners in restoring and enhancing forest ecosystems in order to promote the recovery of threatened and endangered species, improve biodiversity, and enhance carbon sequestration. Restoration agreements and easements are designed for working agricultural lands and landowners, their heirs, successors and assigns shall enter into contract with the United States through the NRCS. Lump sum or annual easement payments made in no more than 10 annual payments of equal or unequal size to landowner in agreement with NRCS.

Eligible applicants/beneficiaries: landowners of eligible private land as determined by the NRCS.

Range/Average: N.A.

Activity: N.A.

HQ: Deputy Chief for Programs, NRCS-USDA, 1400 Independence Ave., SW, Rm. 5236-S, Washington, DC 20250. Phone: (202) 720-1511.

Internet: www.nrcs.usda.gov.

10.923 EMERGENCY WATERSHED PROTECTION PROGRAM (EWP)

Assistance: project grants (75-90 percent/until all recovery measures installed).

Purposes: pursuant to FCA of 1950, FAIRA, and the Agricultural Credit Act of 1978, as amended, to assist in the implementation of emergency recovery measures to a watershed impaired as the result of a natural disaster. All work must reduce threats to life and property and be environmentally, economically, socially, and technically sound.

Eligible applicants/beneficiaries: public and private landowners represented by state, local, or tribal government or agency with a legal interest or responsibility for values threatened by a watershed emergency and capable of carrying out operation and maintenance responsibilities and furnishing local cost share. Work can be done through federal or local contracts and is authorized in all U.S. states and territories.

Range/Average: N.A.

Activity: N.A.

HQ: Conservation Engineering Division, USDA, 14th and Independence Ave., SW, Rm. 6036-S, Washington, DC 20013. Phone: (202) 690-0793.

Internet: www.nrcs.usda.gov/programs/ewp.

10.924 CONSERVATION STEWARDSHIP PROGRAM (CSP)

Assistance: cooperative agreements (100 percent/to 5 years).

Purposes: pursuant to the Food Security Act of 1985, NRCS will provide financial and technical assistance to eligible producers to conserve and enhance soil, water, air, and related natural resources on their land. Eligible lands include cropland, grassland, prairie land, improved pastureland, rangeland, nonindustrial private forest lands, agricultural land under the jurisdiction of an Indian tribe, and other private agricultural land. The NRCS will make CSP available nationwide on a continuous application basis.

Eligible applicants/beneficiaries: 35 IHEs selected by the CDC as Prevention Research Centers (PRCs).

Range: $40,000 to $200,000. **Average:** N.A.

Activity: N.A.

HQ: Director, Financial Assistance Programs Division, NRCS, USDA, 1400 Independence Ave., SW, Rm. 5247-S, Washington, DC 20250. Phone: (202) 720-6700.

Internet: www.nrcs.usda.gov/wps/portal/nrcs/main/national/programs/finan cial/csp.

10.925 AGRICULTURAL WATER ENHANCEMENT PROGRAM (AWEP)

Assistance: direct payments/specified use (75 to 90 percent).

Purposes: pursuant to the Food Security Act of 1985, as amended by the Food, Conservation, and Energy Act of 2008, this program seeks to enable eligible partners to enter into multi-year agreements with Natural Resources Conservation Service (NRCS) to promote ground and surface water conservation or improve water quality on eligible agricultural lands.

High priority areas are located in the following regions: Eastern Snake Plain Aquifer, Everglades, Ogallala Aquifer, Puget Sound, Red River, Sacramento River Basin, and Upper Mississippi River Basin.

Eligible applicants: agricultural producers include: owners, landlords, operators, or tenants of eligible agricultural lands or non-industrial forestlands. Limited resource producers, small-scale producers, socially disadvantaged individuals, federally recognized Indian tribes, Alaska natives, and Pacific Islanders are encouraged to apply.

Eligible beneficiaries: eligible partners include: federally-recognized Indian tribes, states, units of local government, agricultural or silvicultural associations, irrigation associations, agricultural land trusts, or other non-governmental organizations experienced working with agricultural producers.

Range: to $300,000 per producer. **Average:** $40,841.

Activity: N.A.

HQ: Deputy Chief/Programs, NRCS-USDA, PO Box 2890, Washington, DC 20013. Phone: (202) 690-2621.

Internet: www.nrcs.usda.gov/wps/portal/nrcs/main/national/programs/finan cial/awep.

10.926   CHESAPEAKE BAY WATERSHED PROGRAM (CBWP)

Assistance: direct payments/specified use (75 to 90 percent).

Purposes: pursuant to the Food Security Act of 1985, as amended by The Food, Conservation, and Energy Act of 2008, to help agricultural producers improve water quality and quantity, and restore, enhance, and preserve soil, air, and related resources in the Chesapeake Bay Watershed through the implementation of conservation practices. This program encompasses all tributaries, backwaters, and side channels (including their watersheds) draining into the Chesapeake Bay.

Eligible applicants/beneficiaries: eligible agricultural producers owning or operating lands within the Chesapeake Bay Watershed. Limited resource, socially-disadvantaged, and small-scale producers, beginning farmers and ranchers, and federally-recognized Indian tribes are encouraged to apply.

Range/Average: N.A.

Activity: N.A.

HQ: Director, Natural Resources Conservation Service, USDA, 1400 Independence Ave., SW, South Bldg., Rm. 6238, Washington, DC 20013. Phone: (202) 690-2621.

Internet: N.A.

10.927   EMERGENCY WATERSHED PROTECTION PROGRAM—DISASTER RELIEF APPROPRIATIONS ACT
("EWP—Disaster Relief Hurricane Sandy")

Assistance: project grants/cooperative agreements (75-90 percent).

Purposes: pursuant to the Disaster Relicf Appropriations Act, Public Law 113-2, funds to implement emergency recovery measures for runoff retardation and erosion prevention to relieve imminent hazards to life and property created by Hurricane Sandy. All emergency watershed protection (EWP) work must reduce threats to life and property and must be economically, environmentally, and socially defensible and technically sound.

EWP funds cannot be used to solve problems that existed before the disaster or to improve the level of protection above that which existed before the disaster. EWP funds cannot be used for operation and maintenance work or to repair private or public transportation facilities or utilities. The work cannot adversely affect downstream water rights and funds cannot be used to install measures not essential to the reduction of hazards. In addition, funds cannot be used to perform work on measures installed by another federal agency.

Eligible applicants: Public and private landowners affected by Hurricane Sandy and in a geographic area declared as a major disaster. Applicants must have a project sponsor (state or local government or agency, Native American tribe or organization), that will be responsible for furnishing the local cost share and for accomplishing the installation of work.

Eligible beneficiaries: anyone/general public.

Range/Average: N.A.

Activity: N.A.

HQ: Director, EWP—Disaster Relief Hurricane Sandy, NRCS-USDA, 1400 Independence Ave., PO Box 2890, Washington, DC 20013. Phone: (202) 690-0793.

Internet: N.A.

10.928 EMERGENCY WATERSHED PROTECTION PROGRAM—FLOODPLAIN EASEMENTS—DISASTER RELIEF APPROPRIATIONS ACT ("EWP-FPE Hurricane Sandy")

Assistance: direct payments for specified use (100 percent).

Purposes: pursuant to the Disaster Relief Appropriations Act of 2013, direct payments to acquire, restore, and enhance floodplain easements in areas that suffered damage from Hurricane Sandy, but only those located within an area declared as a major disaster. An easement acquired under the EWP-Floodplain Easement regulations shall provide Natural Resources Conservation Service (NRCS) with the full authority to restore, protect, manage, maintain, and enhance the functions and values of the floodplain. NRCS may bear up to 100 percent of costs related to easement acquisition. NRCS will determine easement compensation in accordance with applicable regulation and other law, and will not acquire any easement unless the landowner accepts the amount of the easement payment that is offered. NRCS may also provide up to 100 percent of the restoration and enhancement costs of the easement, and may enter into an agreement with the landowner or another third party to ensure that identified practices are implemented. Restoration and enhancement efforts may include both structural and nonstructural practices to restore the flood storage and flow, erosion control, and improve the practical management of the easement. Structures, including buildings, within the floodplain easement must be demolished and removed, or relocated outside the 100-year floodplain or dam breach inundation area.

Eligible applicants: state, local governments, private non-profit institutions and organizations, Indian tribal governments, general public affected by Hurricane Sandy and only in those areas declared as a major disaster.

Eligible beneficiaries: Private and non-federal landowners affected by Hurricane Sandy and only in those areas declared as a major disaster.

Range/Average: N.A.

Activity: N.A.

HQ: Director, Easement Programs Division, NRCS-USDA, 14th and Independence Ave., SW, Rm. 5243-S, Washington, DC 20250. Phone: (202) 720-1067.

Internet: www.nrcs.usda.gov/programs/ewp.

10.929 WATER BANK PROGRAM

Assistance: direct payments for specified use/cooperative agreements (100 percent/10 years).

Purposes: pursuant to the Water Bank Act, Public Law 91-559, funds to provide annual payments to eligible landowners of specified types of wetlands in designated important migratory waterfowl nesting, breeding and feeding areas. Agreements under the program are for 10 years, during which time the participants agree in return for annual payments not to drain, burn, fill, or otherwise destroy the wetland character of important nesting, breeding, and feeding areas of migratory waterfowl, and to not to use areas for agricultural purposes. The purpose of the program is to conserve surface waters, preserve and improve the nations wetlands, and increase migratory waterfowl habitat in nesting, breeding and feeding areas in the U.S.

Eligible applicants/beneficiaries: Landowners and operators of specified types of wetlands in designated important migratory waterfowl nesting, breeding and feeding areas.

Range: $20 to $50 per acre. **Average:** $35 per acre.

Activity: N.A.

HQ: Director, Water Bank Program, NRCS-USDA,1400 Independence Ave., SW, South Bldg, Rm. 5235, Washington, DC 20013. Phone: (202) 206-9232.

Internet: www.nrcs.usda.gov/wps/portal/nrcs/detail/national/programs/financial/?cid=stelprdb1047790.

10.933 WETLANDS MITIGATION BANKING PROGRAM

Assistance: cooperative agreements/project grants. (100 percent).

Purposes: pursuant to the Food Security Act of 1985, as amended by section 2609 of the Agricultural Act of 2014, to help establish wetland mitigation banks to help producers meet their wetland conservation compliance responsibilities, and to maintain eligibility for the federal crop insurance premium subsidy administered by the Risk Management Agency.

Eligible applicants/beneficiaries: state, local, tribal, and territorial institutions/organizations, and nonprofit andfor-profit NGOs.

Range/Average: N.A.

Activity: N.A.

HQ: Natural Resources Conservation Service, USDA, 8000 South 15th St., Lincoln, NE 68508. Phone: (402) 560-1309.

Internet: N.A. (Note: no field offices for this program.)

10.950   AGRICULTURAL STATISTICS REPORTS ("Agricultural Estimates")

Assistance: technical information.

Purposes: to collect and publish statistics related to agriculture, resources, and rural communities. Reports cover crops, agricultural chemical usage, livestock and poultry estimates, prices received by farmers, prices for commodities and services, data on farm employment and wage rates.

Eligible applicants/beneficiaries: farmers and agricultural producers, marketing and processing groups, transportation and handler groups, consumers, state governments, educational institutions, and the general public, including in the territories.

Range/Average: N.A.

Activity: N.A.

HQ: Administrator, NASS-USDA, 1400 Independence Ave SW, South Agriculture Bldg., Rm. 5041A, Washington, DC 20250. Phone: (202) 720-4415.

Internet: www.nass.usda.gov.

10.960   TECHNICAL AGRICULTURAL ASSISTANCE

Assistance: project grants (100 percent).

Purposes: pursuant to NARETPA and Food Security Act of 1985 as amended, for technical research and assistance projects dealing with international agricultural problems in developing countries. Program is conducted in cooperation with the State Department's Agency for International Development.

Eligible applicants/beneficiaries: U.S. IHEs, public and private nonprofit scientific research organizations—including in territories.

Range: $10,000 to $2,000,000. **Average:** N.A.

Activity: anticipate 89 awards in FY 2016.

HQ: Development Resources Division, Office of International Cooperation and Development, FAS-USDA, 1400 Independence Ave., SW, Washington, DC 20250. Phone: (202) 690-1941.

Internet: www.fas.usda.gov. (Note: no field offices for this program.)

10.961   SCIENTIFIC COOPERATION AND RESEARCH

Assistance: project grants (cost sharing); direct payments/specified use.

Purposes: pursuant to NARETPA and Food Security Act of 1985 as amended, for research on international agriculture and the environment in collaboration with foreign scientists—through short- (2-4 weeks) and long-term (1-3 years) exchanges.

Eligible applicants/beneficiaries: U.S. IHEs, public and private nonprofit scientific research organizations—including in territories—and federal or state agencies; designated international agricultural research centers.

Range: N.A. **Average:** $40,000.

Activity: anticipate funding 6 projects in FY 2016.

HQ: Director, 1400 Independence Ave., SW, Stop 1030, Washington, DC 20250. Phone: (202) 720-6888.

Internet: www.fas.usda.gov. (Note: no field offices for this program.)

10.962 COCHRAN FELLOWSHIP PROGRAM—INTERNATIONAL TRAINING— FOREIGN PARTICIPANT ("Cochran Fellowship Program")

Assistance: project grants (100 percent).

Purposes: pursuant to NARETPA and Food Security Act of 1985 as amended, for international research training and extension in food, agricultural, and related subjects, including in the areas of course development and evaluation. Funding currently supports projects involving short-term agricultural and trade-related training and orientation for senior and mid-level officials, including marketing and production of forestry and wood products, soybean utilization, rice processing, food safety, and dairy production and livestock management.

Eligible applicants/beneficiaries: U.S. IHEs or nonprofit organizations.

Range: N.A. **Average:** $52,500.

Activity: anticipate training 650 Cochran Fellows in FY 2016.

HQ: Food Industries Division, Office of International Cooperation and Development, FAS-USDA, 1400 Independence Ave., SW, Rm. 3239 S, Washington, DC 20250. Phone: (202) 690-0032.

Internet: www.fas.usda.gov. (Note: no field offices for this program.)

10.999 LONG TERM STANDING AGREEMENTS FOR STORAGE, TRANSPORTATION AND LEASE

Assistance: direct payment/specified use.

Purposes: to provide payments for the storage, transportation, and leasing for wheat, grain and other commodities during the designated CCC price support period of activity. Payments may go to private entities in addition to State and local government's for STO/CTY lease agreements.

Eligible applicants: approved, certified crop storage facilities, transportation companies, state and local governments, and private entities that participate in STO/CTY lease agreements.

Eligible beneficiaries: farmers and producers whose crops meet CCC price support eligibility requirements. For storage and lease agreements: state, county and local governments.

Range/Average: N.A.

Activity: N.A.

HQ: Director, Supplemental Food Programs Division, FNS-USDA, 3101 Park Center Dr., Alexandria, VA 22302. Phone: (703) 305-2746; FAX: (703) 305-2196.

Internet: www.fsa.usda.gov.

DEPARTMENT OF COMMERCE

11.001   CENSUS BUREAU DATA PRODUCTS

Assistance: technical information.

Purposes: pursuant to the Act of August 31, 1954, to provide statistical results of censuses, surveys, and other programs. Data cover population, housing, American Community Survey, retail and wholesale trade, service and construction industries, transportation, communications, utilities, manufacturing, mineral industries, governments, foreign trade statistics, and financial, insurance, real estate industries. Certain estimates, projections, and boundary and code maps covering various types of geographic areas also are available. Reports include statistical compendia, directories, indexes, catalogues, and guides—distributed both in print form and on computer disks and tapes, CD-ROMs, DVDs, online, and other media.

Eligible applicants/beneficiaries: anyone may purchase Census products.

Range/Average: N.A.

Activity: N.A.

HQ: Customer Services Center, Marketing Services Office, Bureau of the Census-USDC, Washington, DC 20233. Phone: (301) 763-4636.

Internet: www.census.gov.

11.002   CENSUS CUSTOMER SERVICES

Assistance: advisory services/counseling; technical information; training.

Purposes: pursuant to the Act of August 31, 1954, to assist census data users in the access to and use of census data—through newsletters, on-line catalogues, conferences, training courses, and related activities including development of informational and data products to meet specific user needs. Staff are available to participate in conferences and workshops on the censuses and other Census Bureau programs.

Eligible applicants/beneficiaries: materials and consultation at the Census Bureau—anyone. User training—officials of federal, state, and local governments, universities, community organizations, the private sector; nominal fees may be charged.

Range/Average: N.A.

Activity: N.A.

HQ: Customer Services Center, Marketing Services Office, Bureau of the Census-USDC, Washington, DC 20233. Phone: (301) 763-4636; (*training opportunities,* Phone: (301) 763-4094.

Internet: www.census.gov.

11.003   CENSUS GEOGRAPHY
("Census Mapping and Statistical Areas")

Assistance: specialized services; technical information.

Purposes: pursuant to the Act of August 31, 1954, to prepare computer-generated maps for use in conducting censuses and surveys, and to show their results geographically; to determine names and current boundaries of selected statistical areas; to develop geographic code systems; to provide maps and area reports for states and local areas throughout the U.S. including territories and possessions; to develop computer files of area measurements, geographic boundaries, and map features with address ranges. The "TIGER" (Topologically Integrated Geographic Encoding and Referencing) system, an automated cartographic data base developed in cooperation with the U.S. Geological Survey, covers the entire U.S. and its possessions; the system generates maps and other geographic products; geographic base files, called TIGER/Line files, are available on computer tape, CD-ROM, and online. Published maps are sold by GPO; unpublished maps are sold directly by the Census Bureau.

Eligible applicants/beneficiaries: anyone.

Range/Average: N.A.

Activity: N.A.

HQ: Geography Division, Bureau of the Census-USDC, Washington, DC 20233-7400. Phone: (301) 457-1128. *Customer Service,* Phone: (301) 763-3646.

Internet: www.census.gov.

11.004 CENSUS INTERGOVERNMENTAL SERVICES ("Intergovernmental Services Program")

Assistance: advisory services/counseling; technical information; training.

Purposes: pursuant to the Act of August 31, 1954, to provide technical assistance and information on methods of making population estimates and projections. Consultation services are available to local officials to plan and conduct special surveys. Special surveys are taken on a cost reimbursement basis. Assistance is provided to states in establishing and operating State Data Centers and Business and Industry Data Centers (BIDC).

Eligible applicants/beneficiaries: federal, state, local government officials; community organizations.

Range/Average: N.A.

Activity: N.A.

HQ: Bureau of the Census-USDC, Washington, DC 20233. Phone: (*special censuses,* Office of Special Censuses, (301) 763-1429; *population estimates and projections,* Population Division, (301) 763-2422; *State Data Center and BIDC Programs,* Customer Liaison Office Staff, (301) 763-1305.

Internet: www.cenus.gov.

11.005 CENSUS SPECIAL TABULATIONS AND SERVICES

Assistance: technical information; specialized services.

Purposes: pursuant to the Act of August 31, 1954, to provide customized census tabulations in a variety of output forms to meet user needs and to conduct statistical surveys, on a reimbursable basis.

Eligible applicants/beneficiaries: federal, state, local government officials; community and private organizations; individuals.

Range/Average: N.A.

Activity: N.A.

HQ: Director, Bureau of the Census-USDC, Washington, DC 20233. Phone: (*demographic and household special surveys*, Chief, Demographic Surveys Division, (301) 763-3773; Office of Special Censuses, (301) 763-1429; *special economic surveys*, Chief, Economic Planning and Coordination Division, (301) 763-2558; *special tabulations-demographic*, Population Division, (301) 763-2429; *special tabulations-housing*, Chief, Survey Processing Branch, (310) 763-3204.

Internet: www.census.gov.

11.006 PERSONAL CENSUS SEARCH ("Age Search")

Assistance: specialized services.

Purposes: pursuant to the Act of August 31, 1954, to provide data for proof of age, family relationship, or citizenship, for such purposes as qualifying for: government program benefits (e.g., Medicare, Social Security, pensions); certain types of employment; inheritances, annuities, and other rights or benefits. A $65 fee is charged for searches, whether or not the applicant's record is found.

Eligible applicants/beneficiaries: personal information from census records is confidential and may be furnished only upon written request by the person to whom it relates, or, for a proper purpose, to a legal representative of an estate. Information regarding a child not of legal age may be obtained upon written request by either parent. For records of a deceased person, application must be signed by either: (1) a blood relative in the immediate family; (2) the surviving spouse; (3) a beneficiary; or, (4) the administrator or executor of the estate. Appropriate certifications are required.

Range/Average: N.A.

Activity: N.A.

HQ: none provided, see listing of field offices.

Internet: www.census.gov/genealogy. (Note: no field offices for this program.)

11.008 NOAA MISSION-RELATED EDUCATION AWARDS

Assistance: project grants/cooperative agreements (to 5 years).

Purposes: pursuant to Navigation and Navigable Waters, to provide funds to support educational activities and studies related to NOAA's mission. Funds may not be used for construction of facilities. Grant recipient cost-sharing may be required for this USDC/NOAA collaborative program.

Eligible applicants: non-profit organizations.

Eligible beneficiaries: anyone/general public.

Range: $100,000 to $1,500,000. **Average:** $500,000.

Activity: N.A.

HQ: Office of Education-NOAA, 1401 Constitution Ave., NW, Washington, DC 20230. Phone: (202) 482-3384.

Internet: www.oesd.noaa.gov. (Note: no field offices for this program.)

11.011 OCEAN EXPLORATION

Assistance: project grants/cooperative agreements (100 percent/to 3 years).

Purposes: pursuant to the Omnibus Public Lands Management Act of 2009, to explore the oceans for the purpose of discovery and the advancement of knowledge, using state of the art technologies in evolutionary and revolutionary ways within Oceanic and Atmospheric Research (OAR). Cooperative agreements/grants includes funds for research and development, education and training, and advisory services.

Eligible applicants: IHEs, other nonprofits, commercial organizations, state, local and Indian tribal governments.

Eligible beneficiaries: organizations, researchers and individuals supporting effective management of the nation's ocean exploration resources.

Range/Average: N.A.

Activity: N.A.

HQ: Director, NOAA, 1315 East-West Hwy., Rm. 10210, Silver Spring, MD 20910. Phone: (301) 734-1010.

Internet: www.explorer.noaa.gov.

11.012 INTEGRATED OCEAN OBSERVING SYSTEM (IOOS)

Assistance: project grants (100 percent/to 5 years).

Purposes: pursuant to the Integrated Coastal and Ocean Observation System Act of 2009, to support projects for the development and sustainability of a national/international integrated ocean-observing system designed to collect, monitor and disseminate marine environment data in an interoperable, reliable, timely, and user-specified manner by leveraging federal, regional and private-sector partnerships. Assistance available for deliverance of data and information to increase understanding of our oceans, coasts, and great lakes, enabling decision makers to improve safety, enhance the economy, and protect the environment.

Eligible applicants/beneficiaries: organizations/individuals with professional expertise in the sciences, engineering, and economics.

Range/Average: N.A.

Activity: N.A.

HQ: Director, NOAA Integrated Ocean Observing System Program, NOAA, 1315 East-West Highway, Silver Spring, MD 20910. Phone: (301) 427-2420.

Internet: www.ioos.noaa.gov.

11.013 EDUCATION QUALITY AWARD AMBASSADORSHIP

Assistance: cooperative agreements (75 percent/ to 3 years).

Purposes: pursuant to Stevenson-Wydler Technology Innovation Act, to support Baldrige National Quality Program (BNQP) award winners in conducting outreach, serving as role models, and encouraging other organizations to practice effective quality control in the provision of their services. Non-commercial award recipients will share information about their successful performance and quality strategies with other U.S. organizations at the Quest for Excellence Conference, regional conferences, workshops and meetings.

Eligible applicants/beneficiaries: anyone/general public.

Range/Average: N.A.

Activity: N.A.

HQ: Director, NIST, 100 Bureau Dr., Bldg. TRF A143-Stop 1650, Gaithersburg, MD 20899-1650. Phone: (301) 975-8942.

Internet: www.nist.gov/baldrige. (Note: no field offices for this program.)

11.014 BAND 14 INCUMBENT SPECTRUM RELOCATION

Assistance: project grants/discretionary. (100 percent/1 year).

Purposes: pursuant to the Middle Class Tax Relief and Job Creation Act of 2012, to establish a grants program to assist eligible state, county and municipal public safety entities in relocating their currently active communication operations from frequencies 758.00 to 769.00 MHz and 788.00 to 799.00 MHz (ÙBand 14^) to other frequency assignments allocated by the Federal Communications Commission.

Eligible applicants/beneficiaries: state, county and municipal government public safety entities and agencies that are currently FCC-licensed and operating on Band 14 for the express purposes of public safety communications.

Range/Average: N.A.

Activity: N.A.

HQ: National Telecommunications and Information Administration, DOC, 12201 Sunrise Valley Dr., Stop 243, Reston, VA 22201. Phone: (571) 665-6147.

Internet: www.firstnet.gov. (Note: no field offices for this program.)

11.016 STATISTICAL, RESEARCH, AND METHODOLOGY ASSISTANCE

Assistance: cooperative agreements. (100 percent).

Purposes: pursuant to the Department of Commerce Appropriation Act 2016, to aid and promote statistical, research, and methodology activities related to the Census Bureau mission under Title 13 of the United States Code. Awards provided under this notice support the Census Bureau and the Dept. of Commerce by developing and analyzing information for program and policy considerations, and undertaking special research.

Eligible applicants/beneficiaries: federal state, and local institutions/organizations, public and private nonprofits, and IHEs.

Range: $300,000 to $1,000,000. **Average:** N.A.

Activity: N.A.

HQ: USCB-DOC, 4600 Silver Hill Rd., Suitland, MD 20746. Phone: (301) 763-4628.

Internet: www.census.gov.

11.025 MEASURES AND ANALYSES OF THE U.S. ECONOMY

Assistance: technical information.

Purposes: to produce measures and analyses of national economic accounts statistics, as well as a series of related economic data analyses, used to formulate and execute fiscal, financial, international, and other policies. The principal analyses include: gross domestic product; corporate profits; personal income by state and region; U.S. balance of payments; international trade; gross domestic product by industry. Regular and special reports are produced, including the monthly "Survey of Current Business," available by subscription through GPO. On-line services and CD-ROMs are available.

Eligible applicants/beneficiaries: general public.

Range/Average: N.A.

Activity: N.A.

HQ: Public Information Office, Bureau of Economic Analysis (BE-53), Economics and Statistics Administration-USDC, 1441 L St., NW, Washington, DC 20230. Phone: (202) 606-9900; TDD (202) 606-5335.

Internet: www.bea.gov. (Note: no field offices for this program.)

11.026 STAT-USA: KEY BUSINESS, ECONOMIC, AND INTERNATIONAL TRADE INFORMATION

Assistance: technical information.

Purposes: pursuant to the Omnibus Trade and Competitiveness Act of 1988, to provide the public with access to key business, economic, and international trade information in an easy to use "one-stop shop" format. STAT-USA/Internet offers a single point of access and consists of two main databases: 1) State of the Nation (SOTN), which tracks the direction of the U.S. economy and provides a repository for statistical releases of economic indicators from a number of federal agencies; and 2) Global Business Opportunities (GLOBUS) and the National Trade Data Bank (NTDB), offering daily trade leads, exchange rates, extensive market and country research, and contact databases. STAT-USA publishes over 100,000 documents, which are updated daily, weekly, monthly, quarterly, and annually. Funding for this program is derived from revolving fund proceeds from product sales.

Eligible applicants/beneficiaries: subscriptions available to the general public.

Range/Average: N.A.

Activity: N.A.

HQ: Director, STAT-USA, ESA-USDC, HCHB, Rm. 4885, Washington, DC 20230. Phone: (202) 482-3429; *subscriptions,* (202) 482-3429, Toll Free (800) STAT-USA; FAX: (202) 482-2164.

Internet: www.stat-usa.gov. (Note: no field offices for this program.)

11.106 REMEDIES FOR UNFAIR FOREIGN TRADE PRACTICES—ANTIDUMPING AND COUNTERVAILING DUTY INVESTIGATIONS

Assistance: specialized services; investigation of complaints.

Purposes: pursuant to the Tariff Act of 1930 as amended, Trade Agreements Act of 1979, Trade and Tariff Act of 1984, and Uruguay Round Agreements Act, to protect U.S. industries against economic injury from the sale of foreign merchandise at less than fair value and by unfair subsidies provided by foreign governments. Import duties are assessed against such merchandise if "dumping" or countervailing subsidies are found to occur, which may be revoked five years after violations of the act have ceased.

Eligible applicants/beneficiaries: any interested party may file a complaint on behalf of an affected U.S. industry.

Range/Average: N.A.

Activity: N.A.

HQ: Office of Policy, Import Administration, ITA-USDC, 14th & Constitution Ave., NW, Washington, DC 20230. Phone: (202) 482-1255.

Internet: ia.ita.doc.gov. (Note: no field offices for this program.)

11.108 COMMERCIAL SERVICE

Assistance: advisory services/counseling.

Purposes: pursuant to the Omnibus Trade and Competitiveness Act of 1988, to expand export markets by providing information and guidance on overseas trade markets and opportunities to U.S. firms, through: nonfinancial assistance in export promotion with displays, trade and industrial exhibits, trade missions, catalog shows, and foreign buyer shows; information on trade statistics, foreign tariffs, customs regulations and procedures; overseas government-to-government advocacy and representation; assistance on sources of export finance available from the U.S. Export- Import Bank, SBA, and USAID—in U.S. Export Assistance Centers.

Eligible applicants/beneficiaries: any U.S. citizen, firm, organization or branch of government.

Range/Average: N.A.

Activity: N.A.

HQ: none provided, see listing of field offices.

Internet: ita.doc.gov.

11.110 MANUFACTURING AND SERVICES

Assistance: advisory services/counseling.

Purposes: to provide a central federal source of industry- specific expertise, negotiation and enforcement of bilateral and multilateral trade agreements, and industry and trade competitiveness analysis. Principal services include regular statistical reports, forecasts of industry/sector outputs and cost trends, information on technological developments, and other foreign market information.

Eligible applicants/beneficiaries: anyone.

Range/Average: N.A.

Activity: N.A.

HQ: ITA-USDC, 14th & Constitution Ave., NW, Washington, DC 20230. *manufacturing*, Phone: (202) 482-1872; *aerospace, automotive affairs,* (202) 482-0554; *energy, environment, materials*, (202) 482-5225; *health, consumer goods,* (202) 482-1176.

Internet: www.export.gov.

11.111 FOREIGN-TRADE ZONES IN THE UNITED STATES

Assistance: specialized services.

Purposes: pursuant to the Foreign Trade Zones Act of 1934 as amended, to stimulate domestic production of export goods by encouraging domestic warehousing, manufacturing, and processing activity in foreign trade zones (FTZs). States and local communities establish FTZs that are operated by local public or quasi-public corporations. The FTZs function like public utilities, subject to U.S. Customs and other requirements, providing access to businesses and manufacturers.

Eligible applicants/beneficiaries: public and private corporations in states with enabling legislation.

Range/Average: N.A.

Activity: 60 to 80 applications processed annually.

HQ: Executive Secretary, Foreign-Trade Zones Board, ITA-USDC, 1401 Constitution Ave., NW, Rm. FCB-4100W, Washington, DC 20230. Phone: (202) 482-2862.

Internet: www.trade.gov.

11.112 MARKET DEVELOPMENT COOPERATOR PROGRAM (MDCP)

Assistance: project grants (33 percent/to 3 years).

Purposes: pursuant to the Omnibus Trade and Competitiveness Act of 1988, to develop, maintain, and expand foreign markets for nonagricultural goods and services produced in the U.S. "Cooperators" conduct activities abroad to promote certain industries, including outreach campaigns, conferences, consultative services, exhibitions, training, market research. Project funds support direct costs only.

Eligible applicants/beneficiaries: nonprofit industry organizations, trade associations, state departments of trade and their regional associations, and, if approved, private industry firms or groups of firms.

Range: to $300,000. **Average:** N.A.

Activity: N.A.

HQ: MDCP Manager, Trade Development, Management and Planning Division, Office of Planning, Coordination and Management, 14th St. & Constitution Ave., NW, Rm. 4324, Washington, DC 20230. Phone: (202) 482-2969; FAX: (202) 482-44628.

Internet: www.export.gov/mdcp.

11.113 ITA SPECIAL PROJECTS

Assistance: project grants (100 percent).

Purposes: to assist organizations identified by Congress to provide information and conduct research and development activities assisting small- and medium-sized businesses in expanding exports.

Eligible applicants/beneficiaries: organizations or individuals specifically identified by Congress.

Range/Average: N.A.

Activity: N.A.

HQ: Trade Development, Management and Planning Division, Office of Planning, Coordination and Management, 14th St. & Constitution Ave., NW, Washington, DC 20230. Phone: (202) 482-3587.

Internet: N.A. (Note: no field offices for this program.)

11.150 EXPORT LICENSING SERVICE AND INFORMATION ("Export Control - Exporter Assistance Program")

Assistance: advisory services/counseling.

Purposes: pursuant to the Export Administration Act of 1979 as amended and extended under the International Emergency Economic Powers Act, to provide information, training, seminars, and other assistance on export licensing requirements, regulations, and policies; to expedite export applications when priority action is warranted.

Eligible applicants/beneficiaries: anyone.

Range/Average: N.A.

Activity: N.A.

HQ: Outreach and Educational Services Division, Office of Exporter Services, Bureau of Industry and Security-USDC, Rm. 1099, PO Box 273, Washington, DC 20044. Phone: (202) 482-4811.

Internet: www.bis.doc.gov.

11.300 INVESTMENTS FOR PUBLIC WORKS AND ECONOMIC DEVELOPMENT FACILITIES

Assistance: project grants (50-100 percent).

Purposes: pursuant to the Public Works and Economic Development Act of 1965 (PWEDA) as amended, to construct or improve public works and economic development facilities to create or retain permanent jobs in the private sector in areas experiencing substantial economic distress. Projects may involve water and sewer systems, railroad spurs, industrial parks, access roads, other business infrastructure, port facilities, tourism facilities, vocational schools, renovation and recycling of old industrial buildings, business incubator facilities, technology infrastructure, projects enabling telecommunications, redevelopment of brownfields. Projects must be consistent with approved Comprehensive Economic Development Strategies. Grants cover 50 percent of costs; severely depressed areas may receive 80 percent; designated tribes receive 100 percent; projects in redevelopment areas supporting Economic Development Districts may receive 80 percent and a 10 percent bonus for public works projects.

Eligible applicants/beneficiaries: states, cities, counties, other political subdivisions; IHEs; consortia; tribes; private or public nonprofit organizations or associations; territories and possessions.

Range: $200,000 to $3,000,000. **Average:** N.A.

Activity: N.A.

HQ: Construction Coordinator, Economic Development Administration, 1401 Constitution Ave., NW, Rm. 71030, Washington, DC 20230. Phone: (202) 400-0662.

Internet: www.eda.gov.

11.302 ECONOMIC DEVELOPMENT—SUPPORT FOR PLANNING ORGANIZATIONS
("Section 203 Grants for Planning and Administrative Expenses")

Assistance: project grants. (grants, from 50 percent; tribes, to 100 percent/to 3 years).

Purposes: pursuant to PWEDA as amended, for economic development planning and to formulate and establish comprehensive economic development, process, and strategies to reduce unemployment and increase incomes. Funds may be used to pay administrative expenses.

Eligible applicants/beneficiaries: economic development districts, tribes, states, cities, IHEs, public or private nonprofit organizations.

Range: $40,000 to $200,000. **Average:** $70,000.

Activity: N.A.

HQ: Office of External Affairs and Communication, EDA-USDC, HCHB, Rm. 71030, 1401 Constitution Ave., NW, Washington, DC 20230. Phone: (202) 482-0529.

Internet: www.eda.gov.

11.303 ECONOMIC DEVELOPMENT—TECHNICAL ASSISTANCE
("National, University Center and Local Technical Assistance")

Assistance: project grants (from 50 percent/to 3 years).

Purposes: pursuant to PWEDA as amended, to provide technical assistance in developing data and expertise in evaluating and planning specific economic development projects and programs in depressed areas. Technical assistance is provided through: university economic development centers; innovative projects; information dissemination and studies of issues of national significance; feasibility studies and other projects leading to local economic development.

Eligible applicants/beneficiaries: public or private nonprofit organizations, educational institutions; tribal, state, municipal, county, and territorial governments.

Range: $50,000 to $300,000. **Average:** $64,000.

Activity: N.A.

HQ: Office of External Affairs and Communication, EDA-USDC, HCHB, Rm. 71030, 1401 Constitution Ave., NW, Washington, DC 20230. Phone: (202) 482-0529.

Internet: www.eda.gov.

11.307 ECONOMIC ADJUSTMENT ASSISTANCE

Assistance: project grants (50-100 percent).

Purposes: pursuant to PWEDA as amended, to design and implement strategies to address problems stemming from serious structural deterioration of local economies, such as result from corporate or industrial restructuring, new requirements in federal laws, reduction in defense expenditures, natural disasters, or depletion of natural resources. Strategy Investments may be used for plan development resulting in a Comprehensive Economic Development Strategy. Implementation Investments may be used for development of organizational capacity, business development and financing including through the capitalization of revolving loan funds, infrastructure improvement, and market or industry research and analysis.

Eligible applicants/beneficiaries: economic development districts, tribes, states, cities, IHEs, public or private nonprofit organizations.

Range: $100,000 to $1,250,000. **Average:** $820,000.

Activity: N.A.

HQ: Construction Coordinator, Economic Development Administration, 1401 Constitution Ave., NW, Rm. 71030, Washington, DC 20230. Phone: (202) 400-0662.

Internet: www.eda.gov.

11.312 RESEARCH AND EVALUATION PROGRAM

Assistance: project grants (50-100 percent).

Purposes: pursuant to PWEDA as amended, for research, evaluative and otherwise, and technical assistance programs to promote competitiveness and innovation in urban and rural regions throughout the U.S. and territories.

Eligible applicants/beneficiaries: economic development districts, tribes, states, cities, IHEs, public or private nonprofit organizations.

Range: $100,000 to $400,000. **Average:** N.A.

Activity: N.A.

HQ: Office of External Affairs and Communication, EDA-USDC, 1401 Constitution Ave., NW, Rm. 71030, Washington, DC 20230. Phone: (202) 482-0951.

Internet: www.eda.gov.

11.313 TRADE ADJUSTMENT ASSISTANCE FOR FIRMS (TAA)

Assistance: project grants (50-100 percent).

Purposes: pursuant to the Trade Act of 1974 as amended, for trade adjustment assistance to firms and industries adversely affected by increased imports, in the form of technical assistance for which participants must share the expense. Assistance may consist of such detailed aid as industrial engineering, marketing studies, product diversification, and the like. To receive Trade Act certification, firms must demonstrate that increased imports of articles like or directly competitive with those that they produce contribute significantly to declines in sales or production, and to separation or threat of separation of their workers. Firms must submit an acceptable adjustment proposal to be eligible to apply. Industry associations or other organizations must submit evidence demonstrating import competition, and that the industry includes a substantial number of Trade Act-certified firms or workers.

Eligible applicants: intermediary organizations including Trade Adjustment Assistance Centers or industry groups that can demonstrate injury from imports.

Eligible beneficiaries: private firms with Trade Act certification.

Range: $1,000,000 to $1,600,000. **Average:** N.A.

Activity: N.A.

HQ: Office of Strategic Initiatives, EDA-USDC, 1401 Constitution Ave., NW, Washington, DC 20230. Phone: (202) 482-0556.

Internet: www.eda.gov.

11.400   GEODETIC SURVEYS AND SERVICES

Assistance: project grants. (cost sharing/1-5 years).

Purposes: pursuant to the Coast and Geodetic Survey Act, to assist in the development and implementation of Multipurpose Land Information Systems/Geographic Information Systems (MPLIS/GIS) into areas inadequately covered by the national networks. The networks consist of horizontal and vertical geodetic reference monuments at various specified intervals, providing scale, orientation, coordinated positions, and elevations of specific points—for use in surveying, boundary delineation and demarcation, mapping, planning, and development. The system provides the standards of reference which provide the basis for state plane coordinate systems, land and public utility records, and boundary delineations—and from which restricted coastal and other boundaries are marked. This program also provides funding to the University of New Hampshire for research and other programs at the Joint Hydrographic Center (JHC).

Eligible applicants/beneficiaries: state, local, municipal, or regional agencies and universities. JHC funding, University of New Hampshire only.

Range/Average: N.A.

Activity: N.A.

HQ: Grant Program Office, Geodetic Service Division, National Ocean Service, NOAA-USDC, 1315 East West Highway, SSMC3, Station 8657, Silver Spring, MD 20910. Phone: (301) 713-3228.

Internet: www.ngs.noaa.gov/www.nauticalcharts.gov. (Note: no field offices for this program.)

11.407   INTERJURISDICTIONAL FISHERIES ACT OF 1986

Assistance: formula grants (75-90 percent).

Purposes: pursuant to the act of 1986 as amended, to manage interjurisdictional fisheries resources. Permissible uses of funds include research, management planning, enforcement, restoration of resources damaged by natural disasters.

Eligible applicants/beneficiaries: state agencies; the Pacific, Atlantic, and Gulf Interstate Marine Fisheries Commissions.

Range/Average: N.A.

Activity: N.A.

HQ: Director, Office of Sustainable Fisheries, NMFS-NOAA-USDC, 1315 East-West Hwy., Silver Spring, MD 20910. Phone: (301) 713-2334; FAX: (301) 713-0596.

Internet: N.A.

11.408 FISHERMEN'S CONTINGENCY FUND ("Title IV")

Assistance: direct payments/unrestricted use.

Purposes: pursuant to the Outer Continental Shelf Lands Act Amendments of 1978, to compensate U.S. commercial fishermen for damage to or loss of fishing gear, and 50 percent of resulting financial loss caused by oil- and gas-related activities in Outer Continental Shelf areas.

Eligible applicants/beneficiaries: U.S. commercial fishermen.

Range/Average: N.A.

Activity: N.A.

HQ: Chief, Financial Services Division, NMFS-NOAA-USDC, 1315 East-West Hwy., Silver Spring, MD 20910. Phone: (301) 713-2396; FAX: (301) 713-1306.

Internet: www.nmfs.noaa.gov/mb/financial_services/fcf.htm.

11.413 FISHERY PRODUCTS INSPECTION AND CERTIFICATION ("Inspection and Grading of Fishery Products")

Assistance: specialized services.

Purposes: pursuant to the Agricultural Marketing Act of 1946 and Fish and Wildlife Act of 1956 as amended, to provide voluntary inspection, grading, and certification of seafood harvesting and processing operations to ensure adherence to minimum public health requirements, as well as product identity, condition, quality, and quantity. Fees are charged for the service, in support of program costs.

Eligible applicants/beneficiaries: individuals; federal, state, county, or municipal agencies; carriers with a financial interest in the commodity.

Range/Average: N.A.

Activity: N.A.

HQ: Inspection Services Division, NMFS-NOAA-USDC, 1315 East-West Hwy., Silver Spring, MD 20910. Phone: (301) 713-2355.

Internet: seafood.nmfs.noaa.gov.

11.415 FISHERIES FINANCE PROGRAM

Assistance: direct loans. (to 80 percent/to 25 years).

Purposes: for certain fisheries costs including: purchase or reconstruction of used vessels; refinancing of existing debt; financing or refinancing of shoreside fishery and aquaculture facilities; financing of Individual Fishing Quota (IFQ) for first-time purchasers and small vessel operators in the

Halibut Sablefish industries and to Community Development Quota (CDQ) groups fisheries investments in the Bering Sea Aleutian Islands Pollock fishery; long-term fishery buyback financing to retire fishing permits or fishing vessels in overcapitalized fisheries. Funds may not be used for loans that add to fishing capacity or that over-capitalize the industry.

Eligible applicants/beneficiaries: commercial fishermen, fishery products processors or distributors.

Range/Average: N.A.

Activity: N.A.

HQ: Chief, Financial Services Division, NMFS-NOAA-USDC, 1315 East-West Hwy., Silver Spring, MD 20910. Phone: (301) 713-2390. FAX: (301713-1306).

Internet: www.nmfs.noaa.gov/mb/financial_services/ffp.htm.

11.417   SEA GRANT SUPPORT

Assistance: project grants (67-100 percent).

Purposes: pursuant to the Sea Grant College Program Improvement Act of 1976 as amended, for marine resources research, education, training, and advisory services. Some institutions may obtain coherent area, institutional, or Sea Grant College support. Project examples: cardiovascular, anticancer, and central nervous system drugs from marine organisms; marine fouling and corrosion in seawater; marine finfish and shellfish aquaculture; seafood quality and safety; coastal erosion. Funds may not be used to purchase or construct ships or facilities.

Eligible applicants/beneficiaries: IHEs, junior colleges, technical schools, institutes, laboratories; public or private corporations, partnerships, or other associations or entities; states or political subdivisions or agencies; individuals.

Range/Average: N.A.

Activity: N.A.

HQ: Director, National Sea Grant College Program, NOAA-USDC, 1315 East-West Hwy., Silver Spring, MD 20910. Phone: (301) 713-2448.

Internet: www.noaa.gov. (Note: no field offices for this program.)

11.419   COASTAL ZONE MANAGEMENT ADMINISTRATION AWARDS

Assistance: formula grants; project grants (cost sharing/18 months).

Purposes: pursuant to the Coastal Zone Management Act of 1972 and amendments, to administer various elements of approved Coastal Zone Management programs, including such activities as management and protection of coastal wetlands, natural hazards management, public access improvements, reduction of marine debris, ocean resource planning, siting of coastal energy facilities.

Eligible applicants/beneficiaries: coastal states including those bordering the Great Lakes; territories and possessions.

Range/Average: N.A.

Activity: N.A.

HQ: Chief, Coastal Programs Division, Office of Ocean and Coastal Resource Management, NOS-NOAA-USDC, 1305 East-West Hwy. - 11th floor, Silver Spring, MD 20910. Phone: (301) 713-3155.

Internet: coastalmanagement.noaa.gov/programs/czm.html. (Note: no field offices for this program.)

11.420   COASTAL ZONE MANAGEMENT ESTUARINE RESEARCH RESERVES

Assistance: project grants (to 50 percent/from 18 months).

Purposes: pursuant to the Coastal Zone Management Act of 1972 and amendments, to acquire, monitor, develop, and operate national estuarine research reserves; for data gathering, research, and educational purposes.

Eligible applicants/beneficiaries: acquisition, development, construction operating grants—coastal states including those bordering the Great Lakes; territories. Research or monitoring grants—qualified scientists, educators, students, and entities.

Range/Average: N.A.

Activity: N.A.

HQ: Chief, Estuarine Reserves Division, Office of Ocean and Coastal Resource Management, NOS-NOAA-USDC, 1305 East-West Hwy., N/ORM5, 10th floor, Silver Spring, MD 20910. Phone: (301) 713-3155.

Internet: www.nerrs.noaa.gov. (Note: no field offices for this program.)

11.426   FINANCIAL ASSISTANCE FOR NATIONAL CENTERS FOR COASTAL OCEAN SCIENCE

Assistance: project grants (100 percent/to 5 years).

Purposes: pursuant to the Marine Protection, Research, and Sanctuaries Act of 1972 and National Ocean Pollution Planning Act of 1978, for research to determine the long-term consequences of human activities affecting the coastal and marine environment; to assess the ecological, economic, and social impacts of these activities upon human, physical, and biotic environments; to define and evaluate management alternatives that minimize adverse consequences of human use of marine environments and resources. Project examples: analyses of estuarine and marine contaminants, habitats, and natural resources; data set of characteristics of coasts and oceans including erosion rates, coastal vulnerability indices, and coastal hazards for incorporation into a geographic information system.

Eligible applicants/beneficiaries: IHEs, junior colleges, technical schools, institutes, laboratories, public or private profit or nonprofit entities, state and local government agencies, individuals.

Range: $20,000 to $550,000. Average: $250,000.

Activity: N.A.

HQ: National Centers for Coastal Ocean Science (N/SCI), NOS-NOAA-USDC, 1305 East-West Hwy., SSMC4, Station 8211, Silver Spring, MD 20910. Phone: (301) 713-3020.

Internet: coastalscience.noaa.gov.

11.427 FISHERIES DEVELOPMENT AND UTILIZATION RESEARCH AND DEVELOPMENT GRANTS AND COOPERATIVE AGREEMENTS PROGRAM

Assistance: project grants. (50-90 percent/2 years).

Purposes: pursuant to the Saltonstall-Kennedy Act as amended, for research to develop and strengthen the U.S. fishing industry. Project examples: risk management of a new oyster disease threat; engineering design and analysis for more secure salmon net pen systems.

Eligible applicants/beneficiaries: U.S. citizens or nationals including in the territories and possessions; state and local governments. Federal and Regional Fishery Management Council employees are ineligible.

Range/Average: N.A.

Activity: N.A.

HQ: Financial Services Division, State/Federal Liaison Branch, NMFS-NOAA-USDC, 1315 East-West Highway, Rm. 14358, Silver Spring, MD 20910. Phone: (301) 713-2259; FAX: (301) 713-1306.

Internet: www.nmfs.noaa.gov/mb/financial_services/skhome.htm.

11.429 MARINE SANCTUARY PROGRAM

Assistance: project grants (100 percent).

Purposes: pursuant to the Marine Protection, Research, and Sanctuaries Act of 1972 and amendments, for research and educational programs in the marine sanctuary system; for enforcement activities at sanctuary sites; for projects enhancing public awareness, appreciation, and wise use of the marine environment. Scholarships are available for masters and doctorate level studies, particularly by women and minorities pursuing degrees in marine biology, maritime archaeology, and oceanography.

Eligible applicants/beneficiaries: project grants—states, local, and tribal governments; regional and interstate agencies, K-12 public and independent schools and school systems; IHEs; commercial and nonprofit organizations; other persons. Agreements to solicit private donation—nonprofit organizations. Scholarships—U.S. citizens, particularly women and minorities with financial needs.

Range/Average: N.A.

Activity: N.A.

HQ: Director, National Marine Sanctuary Program, NOS-NOAA-USDC, 1305 East-West Hwy., SSMC4, Station 11523, Silver Spring, MD 20910. Phone: (301) 713-7235.

Internet: sanctuaries.noaa.gov/fosterscholars.noaa.gov.

11.430 UNDERSEA RESEARCH

Assistance: project grants (100 percent).

Purposes: pursuant to the Coast and Geodetic Act, for undersea research and development projects. Funds may be used to acquire necessary technology. Examples: Nutrient Cycling and Primary Productivity of Marine

Ecosystems; diving safety and physiology research; submarine venting of liquids and gases.

Eligible applicants/beneficiaries: IHEs, junior colleges, technical schools, institutes, laboratories; states, political subdivisions, agencies; individuals.

Range/Average: N.A.

Activity: N.A.

HQ: Director, Office of Undersea Research, NOAA-USDC, 1315 East-West Hwy., Silver Spring, MD 20910. Phone: (301) 713-2427.

Internet: www.nurp.noaa.gov.

11.431 CLIMATE AND ATMOSPHERIC RESEARCH

Assistance: project grants. (95-100 percent/1-5 years).

Purposes: pursuant to the Federal Aviation Act and National Climate Program Act as amended, and Weather Service Organic Act, for research and development, advisory services, and operational systems designed to establish a predictive capability for short- and long-term climate fluctuations and trends. Projects funded to date have ranged from some with a global scope to specific activities in the Indian Ocean and the S.W. Tropical Pacific Ocean.

Eligible applicants/beneficiaries: IHEs and other nonprofits, commercial and international organizations; state, local, tribal governments.

Range/Average: N.A.

Activity: N.A.

HQ: Director, Climate Program Office, NOAA-USDC, 1315 East-West Hwy., Suite 12860, Silver Spring, MD 20910. Phone: (301) 427-2089.

Internet: cpo.noaa.gov. (Note: no field offices for this program.)

11.432 NATIONAL OCEANIC AND ATMOSPHERIC ADMINISTRATION (NOAA) COOPERATIVE INSTITUTES

Assistance: project grants (cost sharing/5 years).

Purposes: for research and development, education, training, advisory services, and operational systems as they relate to specific programs in the environmental sciences. Projects involve research in oceanography, atmospherics, limnology, and the solar, Arctic, near-space environments.

Eligible applicants/beneficiaries: universities or nonprofit research institutions, usually located near NOAA environmental research laboratories or facilities.

Range: $1,300,000 to $30,000,000. **Average:** $10,000,000.

Activity: N.A.

HQ: Program Manager, OAR (R/OSSX5), NOAA-USDC, 1315 East-West Hwy., Rm. 11230, Silver Spring, MD 20910. Phone: (301) 734-1156.

Internet: www.nrc.noaa.gov/ci. (Note: no field offices for this program.)

11.433 MARINE FISHERIES INITIATIVE ("MARFIN")

Assistance: project grants (cooperative grants). (100 percent/to 3 years).

Purposes: pursuant to the Fish and Wildlife Act of 1956, Magnuson Fishery Conservation and Management Act, and Saltonstall-Kennedy Act, for fisheries research and development projects involving harvest methods, economic analyses, processing methods, and fish stock assessment and enhancement in the Gulf of Mexico, South Atlantic, and New England fisheries.

Eligible applicants/beneficiaries: state or local governments, IHEs, profit and nonprofit entities, U.S. citizens.

Range/Average: N.A.

Activity: N.A.

HQ: none provided, see listing of field offices.

Internet: N.A.

11.434 COOPERATIVE FISHERY STATISTICS

Assistance: project grants (100 percent/to 5 years).

Purposes: pursuant to the Fish and Wildlife Act of 1956, for cooperative state-federal programs to collect, analyze, and distribute statistics on commercial and recreational fishing in the States' Territorial Sea and the U.S. Exclusive Economic Zone—supporting the Magnuson-Stevens Fishery Conservation and Management Act.

Eligible applicants/beneficiaries: fisheries conservation agencies in the southeast and Gulf states, and PR and VI; Gulf States Marine Fisheries Commission.

Range/Average: N.A.

Activity: N.A.

HQ: none provided, see listing of field offices.

Internet: sero.nmfs.noaa.gov/grants/csp.htm.

11.435 SOUTHEAST AREA MONITORING AND ASSESSMENT PROGRAM (SEAMAP)

Assistance: project grants (100 percent/to 5 years).

Purposes: pursuant to the Fish and Wildlife Act of 1956, to collect, manage, and disseminate independent information on marine fisheries, and to participate in inter-jurisdictional fisheries management programs, exclusively in the Gulf of Mexico, South Atlantic, and U.S. Caribbean—supporting the Magnuson- Stevens Fishery Conservation and Management Act.

Eligible applicants/beneficiaries: fisheries conservation agencies in the southeast and Gulf states, and PR and VI; Gulf States Marine Fisheries Commission.

Range: $71,500 to $1,372,023. **Average:** $337,845.

Activity: N.A.

HQ: none provided, see listing of field offices.

Internet: caldera.sero.nmfs.gov/grants/programs/seamap.htm.

11.436 COLUMBIA RIVER FISHERIES DEVELOPMENT PROGRAM

Assistance: project grants (100 percent).

Purposes: pursuant to the Mitchell Act, to develop measures to protect and enhance salmon and steelhead resources in the Columbia River Basin, using the facilities and personnel of state fisheries agencies.

Eligible applicants/beneficiaries: state governments, quasi- public nonprofit organizations.

Range/Average: N.A.

Activity: N.A.

HQ: none provided, see listing of field offices.

Internet: www.noaa.gov.

11.437 PACIFIC FISHERIES DATA PROGRAM

Assistance: project grants (100 percent).

Purposes: pursuant to the Magnuson-Stevens Fishery Conservation and Management Act as amended, to enhance state fishery data collection and analysis systems to respond to Pacific coastwide and insular fisheries management needs, including projects providing catch, effort, and economic and biological data on federally managed species.

Eligible applicants/beneficiaries: state governments, quasi- public nonprofit organizations, and Guam, Samoa, and Northern Marianas.

Range/Average: N.A.

Activity: N.A.

HQ: none provided, see listing of field offices.

Internet: www.st.nmfs.gov/st1.

11.438 PACIFIC COAST SALMON RECOVERY—PACIFIC SALMON TREATY PROGRAM

Assistance: project grants (75-100 percent).

Purposes: pursuant to the Pacific Coast Salmon Treaty Act, to fund state fishery agencies assisting the U.S. in fulfilling its administrative and management responsibilities for salmon recovery.

Eligible applicants/beneficiaries: state governments, treaty tribes.

Range: salmon recovery, $30,000 to $30,000,000; salmon treaty, $25,000 to $985,000. **Average:** N.A.

Activity: N.A.

HQ: none provided, see listing of field offices.

Internet: www.fakr.noaa.gov.

11.439 MARINE MAMMAL DATA PROGRAM

Assistance: project grants. (75-100 percent/to 3 years).

Purposes: pursuant to the Marine Mammal Act of 1972 and Marine Mammal Rescue Assistance Act of 2000, to collect and analyze information on the abundance and distribution of marine mammals and their interactions with fisheries and other marine resources, toward the conservation of such mammals. Funds may be available for related research projects.

Eligible applicants/beneficiaries: state governments, quasi-public nonprofit organizations; U.S. Marine Mammal Stranding Network participants including state and local governments, academia, aquaria, nonprofits, individuals, and organizations.

Range/Average: N.A.

Activity: N.A.

HQ: Office of Protected Resources, NMFS-NOAA-USDC, 1315 East-West Hwy., Silver Spring, MD 20910. Phone: (301) 713-2322, ext. 178.

Internet: www.nmfs.noaa.gov/prot_res/PR2.

11.440 ENVIRONMENTAL SCIENCES, APPLICATIONS, DATA, AND EDUCATION

Assistance: project grants (100 percent/1-5 years).

Purposes: for applied research, data assimilation and management, technology development, and education in environmental science. Funds also may support advisory services and long-term partnerships between the federal government and research institutions and IHEs for cooperative science and education.

Eligible applicants/beneficiaries: any state IHE, institute, laboratory; any public or private nonprofit institution or consortium.

Range/Average: N.A.

Activity: N.A.

HQ: Office of Research and Applications, NESDIS-NOAA-USDC, 5830 University Research Court, College Park, MD 20740. Phone: (301) 683-3510; FAX: (301) 683-3526.

Internet: www.noaa.gov. (Note: no field offices for this program.)

11.441 REGIONAL FISHERY MANAGEMENT COUNCILS

Assistance: project grants (100 percent/to 5 years).

Purposes: pursuant to the Magnuson-Stevens Fishery Conservation and Management Act as amended, for the eight regional fishery management councils to prepare, monitor, and revise fishery management plans and data collection programs for domestic and foreign fishing within the 200-mile U.S. Exclusive Economic Zone.

Eligible applicants/beneficiaries: Regional Fishery Management Councils (New England, Mid-Atlantic, South Atlantic, Gulf of Mexico, Caribbean, Pacific, North Pacific, and Western Pacific).

Range: $890,400 to $2,451,000. **Average:** N.A.

Activity: N.A.

HQ: none provided, see listing of field offices.

Internet: www.nmfs.noaa.gov/sfa/domes_fish/index.htm.

11.452 UNALLIED INDUSTRY PROJECTS

Assistance: project grants (to 100 percent).

Purposes: pursuant to the Fish and Wildlife Coordination Act of 1956 and the Saltonstall-Kennedy Act, for biological, economic, sociological, public policy, and other research and administration projects benefiting the U.S. fisheries; to develop innovative approaches and methods to ensure the safety, quality, and integrity of fishery products; to develop, test, and apply new technology in molecular biology for use in the management of commercial and recreational marine fisheries, emphasizing the development of molecular genetics techniques. Project funds may support research and management activities for high-priority marine and estuarine resources, especially for species and habitats currently under or proposed for federal or interjurisdictional management.

Eligible applicants/beneficiaries: state and local governments, IHEs, territorial agencies, tribal governments, private profit and nonprofit research and conservation organizations, individuals.

Range: $50,000 to $1,361,000. **Average:** N.A.

Activity: N.A.

HQ: Management and Administration Division, NMFS-NOAA-USDC, 1315 East-West Hwy., Silver Spring, MD 20910. Phone: (301) 713-1364; FAX: (301) 713-2258.

Internet: sero.nmfs.noaa.gov/grants/uip.htm.

11.454   UNALLIED MANAGEMENT PROJECTS

Assistance: project grants (to 100 percent).

Purposes: pursuant to the Fish and Wildlife Coordination Act of 1956 and the Magnuson Fishery Conservation and Management Act, for fisheries management and conservation activities by providing economic, sociological, public policy, and other information relating to fishery resources and protected species and their environments—in federal, state, and territorial waters. Activities are intended to benefit high-priority marine and estuarine resources, especially for species and habitats currently under or proposed for federal or interjurisdictional management.

Eligible applicants/beneficiaries: state and local governments, IHEs, territorial agencies, tribal governments, private profit and nonprofit research and conservation organizations, individuals.

Range: $146,500 to $1,270,000. **Average:** N.A.

Activity: N.A.

HQ: Management and Administration Division, NMFS-NOAA-USDC, 1315 East-West Hwy., Silver Spring, MD 20910. Phone: (301) 713-1364; FAX: (301) 713-2258.

Internet: www.fakr.noaa.gov.

11.457   CHESAPEAKE BAY STUDIES

Assistance: project grants (to 100 percent/to 3 years).

Purposes: pursuant to the Fish and Wildlife Act of 1956 and NOAA Authorization Act of 1992, for research and development projects providing information for the living marine resources of Chesapeake Bay; for the

Chesapeake Bay Watershed Education and Training Initiative, providing environment-based education to students, teachers, and communities.

Eligible applicants/beneficiaries: IHEs, hospitals, other nonprofits, commercial organizations; state, local, and tribal governments; international organizations; foreign governments and their jurisdictional entities.

Range/Average: N.A.

Activity: N.A.

HQ: none provided, see listing of field offices.

Internet: noaa.chesapeakebay.net.

11.459 WEATHER AND AIR QUALITY RESEARCH

Assistance: project grants (100 percent).

Purposes: pursuant to the Federal Aviation Act, Weather Service Organic Act, and National Climate Program Act as amended, and Clean Air Act Amendments of 1990, for research and development, science assessments, advisory services, and operational systems to establish a predictive capability for short- and long-term climate and air quality fluctuations and trends.

Eligible applicants/beneficiaries: IHEs, technical schools, institutions, laboratories; states, political subdivisions, agencies; individuals.

Range/Average: N.A.

Activity: N.A.

HQ: Director, Office of Weather and Air Quality, Office of Oceanic and Atmospheric Research, NOAA-USDC, 1315 East-West Hwy., Silver Spring, MD 20910. Phone: (301) 713-9397.

Internet: owaq.noaa.gov. (Note: no field offices for this program.)

11.460 SPECIAL OCEANIC AND ATMOSPHERIC PROJECTS ("Ocean Exploration")

Assistance: project grants (100 percent).

Purposes: pursuant to the National Weather Service and Related Agencies Authorization Act of 1999 as amended, for research and development, education and training, advisory services, and operational systems relating to oceanic and atmospheric resources.

Eligible applicants/beneficiaries: organizations and individuals specified in NOAA special announcements.

Range/Average: N.A.

Activity: N.A.

HQ: Director, Planning and Evaluation, OAR-NOAA-USDC, 1315 East-West Hwy., Silver Spring, MD 20910. Phone: (301) 713-1010.

Internet: www.explorer.noaa.gov.

11.462 HYDROLOGIC RESEARCH

Assistance: project grants (to 100 percent).

Purposes: pursuant to the Weather Service Organic Act, for research and development on issues relating to the forecasting of surface hydrologic conditions. Project examples: automated calibration of hydrologic models; flash flood guidance procedures and models.

Eligible applicants/beneficiaries: IHEs, state and local government agencies, quasi-public institutions such as water supply or power companies, and hydrologic consultants and companies.

Range: $80,162 to $124,999. **Average:** $105,789.

Activity: N.A.

HQ: Chief, Hydrology Laboratory, National Weather Service (W/OHD-1), NOAA-USDC, 1325 East-West Hwy., Silver Spring, MD 20910. Phone: (301) 713-0640.

Internet: www.noaa.gov. (Note: no field offices for this program.)

11.463   HABITAT CONSERVATION

Assistance: project grants (50-100 percent/to 2 years).

Purposes: pursuant to ARRA 2009, Fish and Wildlife Coordination Act of 1956 and Coral Reef Conservation Act, for biological, economic, sociological, public policy, and other research, and for administration, public education, and construction activities relating to marine and estuarine habitats, especially for species currently under or proposed for federal or interjurisdictional management.

Eligible applicants/beneficiaries: state and local governments, IHEs, territorial agencies, tribal governments, private profit and nonprofit research and conservation organizations, individuals.

Range: $15,000 to $36,000,000. **Average:** N.A.

Activity: N.A.

HQ: Office of Habitat Conservation, NMFS-NOAA-USDC, 1315 East-West Hwy., Silver Spring, MD 20910. Phone: (Community-based Restoration Program, (301) 713-0174; FAX: (301) 713-0184; General Coral Reef Conservation Grant Program, (301) 713-4300; FAX: (301) 713-1043.

Internet: www.nmfs.noaa.gov/habitat/ecosystem/index.htm.

11.467   METEOROLOGIC AND HYDROLOGIC MODERNIZATION DEVELOPMENT

Assistance: project grants; direct payments/specified use; direct payments/unrestricted use; technical information; training (grants, to 100 percent).

Purposes: pursuant to the Weather Service Organic Act, to maintain a cooperative university-federal partnership to conduct meteorological training, education, professional development, and research and development on hydrometeorological issues. Funding supports the Cooperative Program for Operational Meteorology, Education and Training (COMET) and outreach.

Eligible applicants/beneficiaries: IHEs and consortia; state or local government agencies including school systems, quasi-public institutions; consultants, companies.

Range: $6,000 to $2,783,042. **Average:** $409,810.

Activity: N.A.

HQ: Chief, Training Division, National Weather Service (OS6), NOAA-USDC, 1325 East-West Hwy., Silver Spring, MD 20910. Phone: (301) 713-0280; FAX: (301) 713-1598.

Internet: www.noaa.gov. (Note: no field offices for this program.)

11.468 APPLIED METEOROLOGICAL RESEARCH

Assistance: project grants (to 100 percent/1-3 years).

Purposes: for the Collaborative Science, Technology, and Applied Research (CSTAR) program, designed to create a cost-effective transition from basic and applied research to operations and services. Project examples include: operational system for probalistic quantitative precipitation forecasts to improve prediction of warm- and cold-season heavy precipitation events; forecasts of topographically-forced weather systems; improving operational radar algorithms.

Eligible applicants/beneficiaries: U.S. IHEs.

Range: $10,000 to $5,084,742. **Average:** $409,267.

Activity: N.A.

HQ: CSTAR Program Manager (SSMC2 - W/OST12), National Weather Service, NOAA-USDC, 1325 East-West Hwy., Rm. 15326, Silver Spring, MD 20910. Phone: (301) 713-5570, ext. 150.

Internet: www.noaa.nws.gov. (Note: no field offices for this program.)

11.469 CONGRESSIONALLY IDENTIFIED AWARDS AND PROJECTS

Assistance: project grants (to 100 percent).

Purposes: to facilitate education, research, and development in the atmospheric and marine sciences; for related construction of facilities.

Eligible applicants/beneficiaries: state and local governments, IHEs, tribal governments, private profit and nonprofit research and conservation organizations, individuals.

Range/Average: N.A.

Activity: N.A.

HQ: Chief, Grants Management Division, (OFA62 - SSMC2), NOAA-USDC, 1325 East-West Hwy., Silver Spring, MD 20910. Phone: (301) 713-0926.

Internet: www.noaa.gov. (Note: no field offices for this program.)

11.472 UNALLIED SCIENCE PROGRAM

Assistance: project grants (to 100 percent).

Purposes: pursuant to the Fish and Wildlife Coordination Act of 1956 and Fish and Wildlife Act, for biological, socio-economic, and physical science research on the stocks of U.S. fishery and protected resources and their environment, contributing to their optimal management; to develop innovative approaches and methods for marine and estuarine science.

Eligible applicants/beneficiaries: state and local governments, U.S. territories, IHEs, tribal governments, private profit and nonprofit research and conservation organizations, individuals.

Range/Average: N.A.

Activity: N.A.

HQ: Management and Administration Division, NMFS-NOAA-USDC, 1315 East-West Hwy., Silver Spring, MD 20910. Phone: (301) 713-1364; FAX: (301) 713-2258.

Internet: www.fakr.noaa.gov.

11.473 OFFICE FOR COASTAL MANAGEMENT

Assistance: project grants (100 percent/1-3 years).

Purposes: to develop a science-based, multi-dimensional approach allowing for the maintenance or improvement of environmental quality while allowing for economic growth. Funds may be used for such activities as: outreach; coastal fellowships and apprenticeships; training materials development and information dissemination; development of geographic information system and tabular and spatial data bases; to generate, archive, interpret, and validate aircraft, satellite, and other remotely sensed data and derived products; related purposes.

Eligible applicants/beneficiaries: IHEs, hospitals, other nonprofits, commercial organizations; state, local, and tribal governments; international organizations; foreign governments and their jurisdictional entities.

Range/Average: N.A.

Activity: N.A.

HQ: Assistant Administrator, Coastal Services Center, NOS-NOAA-USDC, 1305 East-West Hwy., Silver Spring, MD 20910. Phone: (301) 713-3074.

Internet: coast.noaa.gov.

11.474 ATLANTIC COASTAL FISHERIES COOPERATIVE MANAGEMENT ACT

Assistance: project grants (to 100 percent).

Purposes: pursuant to the act, to develop, implement, and enforce interstate conservation and management plans pertaining to Atlantic Coastal fishery resources, and for activities required by such plans including: collection, management, and analysis of fishery data; law enforcement; habitat conservation; fishery research and management planning.

Eligible applicants/beneficiaries: Atlantic States Marine Fisheries Commission; Atlantic Coast state governments; Potomac River Fisheries Commission; DC.

Range: $38,000 to $1,900,000. **Average:** $330,000.

Activity: N.A.

HQ: Director, Office of Sustainable Fisheries, NMFS-NOAA-USDC, 1315 East-West Hwy., Silver Spring, MD 20910. Phone: (301) 713-2334. FAX: (301) 713-0596.

Internet: N.A.

11.478 CENTER FOR SPONSORED COASTAL OCEAN RESEARCH—COASTAL OCEAN PROGRAM (CSCOR/COP)

Assistance: project grants (100 percent/1-5 years).

Purposes: to provide a predictive capability for managing coastal ecosystems, including in Great Lakes areas. Funds support research and interagency initiatives in coastal ecosystem oceanography, cumulative coastal impacts, and forecasting coastal and natural hazards.

Eligible applicants/beneficiaries: IHEs; nonprofit institutions; state, local, and tribal governments; federal agencies.

Range/Average: N.A.

Activity: N.A.

HQ: Coastal Ocean Program, Center for Sponsored Coastal Ocean Research, NOAA, 1305 East-West Hwy., SSMC4, Station 8307, Silver Spring, MD 20910. Phone: (301) 713-3338.

Internet: coastalscience.noaa.gov/about/centers/cscor. (Note: no field offices for this program.)

11.481 EDUCATIONAL PARTNERSHIP PROGRAM

Assistance: project grants (100 percent/1-5 years).

Purposes: to develop programs to increase research and educational partnerships between NOAA and minority-serving institutions, by establishing: new cooperative science centers in atmospheric, oceanic, environmental sciences, and remote sensing (AOES); an environmental entrepreneurship program supporting restoration projects in environmentally depleted zones and program development in AOES. Funds may support a distinguished professor, research and development programs, and students undertaking NOAA-related sciences course work and/or research.

Eligible applicants/beneficiaries: DOED-approved minority serving institutions with AOES graduate programs; non-minority institutions in partnerships with minority-serving institutions.

Range: $2,400,000 to $3,000,000 to cooperative science centers. **Average:** $36,000 for undergraduate scholarship awards.

Activity: N.A.

HQ: Education Partnership Program (SSMC 3), Office of Oceanic and Atmospheric Research, NOAA-USDC, 1315 East-West Hwy., Silver Spring, MD 20910. Phone: (301) 628-2905.

Internet: www.epp.noaa.gov. (Note: no field offices for this program.)

11.483 NOAA PROGRAMS FOR DISASTER RELIEF APPROPRIATIONS ACT—NON-CONSTRUCTION AND CONSTRUCTION

Assistance: project grants/cooperative agreements (100 percent/2 years).

Purposes: pursuant to the Disaster Relief Appropriations Act of 2013, funds for activities including: mapping, charting, geodesy services marine debris surveys for coastal States impacted by Hurricane Sandy; repair and replacement of ocean observing and coastal monitoring assets damaged by Hurricane Sandy; technical assistance to support State assessments of coastal impacts of Hurricane Sandy; improve weather forecasting and hurricane intensity forecasting capabilities, to include data assimilation from ocean observing platforms and satellites; laboratories and cooperative institutes research activities associated with sustained observations weather research programs, and ocean and coastal research; necessary expenses related to fishery disasters during calendar year 2012 that were declared by the Secretary of Commerce as a direct result of impacts from Hurricane Sandy.

Eligible applicants: public or private profit or not-for-profit organizations, IHEs, state, local and Indian tribal governments.

Eligible beneficiaries: entities impacted by Hurricane Sandy in 2012; entities benefitting from other activities funded through Disaster Relief Appropriations Act of 2013.

Range/Average: N.A.

Activity: N.A.

HQ: Director, National Ocean Service, N/MB3, 1305 East-West Hwy, SSMC4, #13267, Silver Spring, MD 20910. Phone: (301) 713-3050.

Internet: www.noaa.gov. (Note: no field offices for this program.)

11.549   STATE AND LOCAL IMPLEMENTATION GRANT PROGRAM (SLIGP)

Assistance: project grants (80 percent/3 years).

Purposes: pursuant to the Middle Class Tax Relief and Job Creation Act of 2012, Public Law 112-96, project grants to states to assist them, in collaboration with regional, tribal, and local jurisdictions, with activities related to planning for the establishment of a nationwide public safety broadband network. Project funds are intended to assist states to identify, plan, and implement the most efficient and effective way for such jurisdictions to utilize and integrate the infrastructure, equipment, and other architecture associated with the nationwide public safety broadband network to satisfy the wireless communications and data services needs of that jurisdiction, including with regards to coverage, siting, and other needs. Grants will not be used for activities related to broadband deployment, construction, or the acquisition of equipment used to provision wireless broadband services, including for long-term evolution (LTE) related activities. 20% cost share is required unless waived by the Secretary for good cause shown upon determining that such a waiver is in the public interest.

Eligible applicants: states and territories.

Eligible beneficiaries: police officers, fire fighters, emergency medical professionals and other public safety officials, and general public.

Range/Average: N.A.

Activity: 1 award in FY 2014.

HQ: Director, SLIGP, NTIA-U.S. Department of Commerce, 1401 Constitution Ave., NW, Rm. 7324, Washington, DC 20230. Phone: (202) 482-1181.

Internet: www.ntia.doc.gov. (Note: no field offices for this program.)

11.550   PUBLIC TELECOMMUNICATIONS FACILITIES PLANNING AND CONSTRUCTION (PTFP)

Assistance: project grants. (75-100 percent/to 2 years).

Purposes: pursuant to the Communications Act of 1934 as amended, to plan, acquire, install, or modernize public telecommunications facilities including conversion to digital broadcasting. Planning grants may cover 100 percent of costs. Construction grant funds, requiring a 25 percent match, may be applied against costs of apparatus needed for production, dissemination, interconnection, and reception of noncommercial educational and cultural radio and television programs. Real estate, operating, or indirect expenses are ineligible.

Eligible applicants/beneficiaries: public or noncommercial educational broadcast stations, entities, or systems; nonprofit foundations, corporations, institutions, or associations organized primarily for educational or cultural purposes; state, local, tribal governmental agencies. Applications for facilities involving ownership, operation, and participation by minorities and women receive special consideration.

Range: $5,122 to $731,924. **Average:** $177,889.

Activity: N.A.

HQ: Director, Public Telecommunications Facilities Program, Office of Telecommunications and Information Applications, NTIA-USDC, 1401 Constitution Ave., NW, Rm. 4827, Washington, DC 20230. Phone: (202) 482-1949.

Internet: www.ntia.doc.gov/ptfp. (Note: no field offices for this program.)

11.557   BROADBAND TECHNOLOGY OPPORTUNITIES PROGRAM (BTOP)

Assistance: project grants (80 percent/to 2 years).

Purposes: pursuant to ARRA 2009, to provide access to broadband service to U.S. consumers in unserved and underserved areas and strategic institutions; improve access to public safety agencies and stimulate broadband demand, economic growth, and job creation.

Eligible applicants: IHEs; nonprofit institutions, including hospitals; state (including U.S. territories and possessions), local, and tribal governments and organizations, minority organizations; federal agencies.

Eligible beneficiaries: anyone/general public.

Range: $176,400 to $126,323,296. **Average:** N.A.

Activity: N.A.

HQ: Office of Telecommunications Applications, Office of Telecommunications Applications-BTOP, 1401 Constitution Ave., NW-Rm. 4812, Washington, DC 20230. Phone: (202) 482-2048.

Internet: www.ntia.doc.gov/broadbandgrants. (Note: no field offices for this program.)

11.558   STATE BROADBAND DATA AND DEVELOPMENT GRANT PROGRAM

Assistance: project grants (80 percent).

Purposes: pursuant to Broadband Data Services Improvement Act of 2008 and ARRA 2009, to identify and track the availability and adoption of broadband services within each state in order to promote the development and maintenance of a comprehensive nationwide inventory map of existing broadband service capability and availability in the United States.

Eligible applicants/beneficiaries: state (includes District of Columbia, public IHEs and hospitals).

Range/Average: N.A.

Activity: N.A.

HQ: NTIA, Department of Commerce, 1401 Constitution Ave., NW, Washington, DC 20230. Phone: (202) 482-5802.

Internet: www.ntia.doc.gov/broadbandgrants. (Note: no field offices for this program.)

11.601 CALIBRATION PROGRAM

Assistance: specialized services.

Purposes: pursuant to the National Bureau of Standards Organic Act (NBSOA) as amended, to provide a national consistent system of physical measurements used for assurance of interchangeability and uniformity of manufactured items, for process control, for informational and scientific purposes, and for fairness and objectivity in commerce and regulation. Fees are charged for tests and calibrations.

Eligible applicants/beneficiaries: state and local governments, academic institutions, laboratories, industrial firms, corporations, individuals.

Range/Average: N.A.

Activity: N.A.

HQ: Calibration Program, NIST-USDC, 100 Bureau Drive, Gaithersburg, MD 20899-2330. Phone: (301) 975-2684.

Internet: www.nist.gov/calibrations. (Note: no field offices for this program.)

11.603 NATIONAL STANDARD REFERENCE DATA SYSTEM (SRD)

Assistance: sale, exchange, or donation of property and goods.

Purposes: pursuant to the Standard Reference Data Act and NBSOA as amended, to provide evaluated scientific and technical data on the chemical, physical, and other properties of substances and systems. Publications, data bases, and online services may be purchased, subject to copyright restrictions.

Eligible applicants/beneficiaries: federal agencies, firms, corporations, universities, industrial laboratories, research establishments, general public.

Range/Average: N.A.

Activity: N.A.

HQ: Standard Reference Data Group, NIST-USDC, 100 Bureau Drive, Gaithersburg, MD 20899-2330. Phone: (301) 975-2684.

Internet: www.nist.gov/srd. (Note: no field offices for this program.)

11.604 STANDARD REFERENCE MATERIALS (SRM)

Assistance: sale, exchange, or donation of property and goods.

Purposes: pursuant to NBSOA as amended, to develop accurate methods of analysis and to calibrate measurement systems, through the certification and dissemination of reference materials used to: facilitate the exchange of goods; institute quality control; determine material performance characteristics; measure materials at state-of-the-art limits; assure the long-term adequacy and integrity of measurement quality assurance programs. SRMs are used as primary reference measurement standards for such purposes as: clinical laboratories testing; monitoring of air, water, and low-level radioactive pollution; quality control in the production of basic materials such as steel, rubber, cement, and plastics. Materials may be purchased from NIST.

Eligible applicants/beneficiaries: federal agencies, state and local governments, societies, institutions, firms, corporations, individuals.

Range/Average: N.A.

Activity: N.A.

HQ: SRM Program, NIST-USDC, 100 Bureau Drive, Gaithersburg, MD 20899-2330. Phone: (301) 975-2684.

Internet: www.nist.gov/srm. (Note: no field offices for this program.)

11.606 WEIGHTS AND MEASURES SERVICE

Assistance: advisory services/counseling; specialized services; technical information; training.

Purposes: pursuant to NBSOA as amended, to provide education, technical and other assistance, and training to states, users and manufacturers of weights and measures devices, and other devices users—concerning: weights and measures operations development of model laws and regulations; upgrading of state laboratories; administration of device evaluation; promotion of a uniform national weights and measures system; harmonization of national and international legal metrology standards; transition to the metric system.

Eligible applicants/beneficiaries: states, political subdivisions, private industry, general public.

Range/Average: N.A.

Activity: N.A.

HQ: Chief, Weights and Measures Division, NIST-USDC, 100 Bureau Drive, Gaithersburg, MD 20899-2330. Phone: (301) 975-2684.

Internet: www.nist.gov/pml/wmd/index.cfm. (Note: no field offices for this program.)

11.609 MEASUREMENT AND ENGINEERING RESEARCH AND STANDARDS

Assistance: project grants (100 percent/1-3 years).

Purposes: pursuant to NBSOA as amended, for scientific research and technology transfer for measurement and engineering research and standards, in such areas as fire prevention, building construction, precision measurement, automation manufacturing, materials science, chemistry, physics, biotechnology, electronics, optical technologies, mathematics, communications and information.

Eligible applicants/beneficiaries: IHEs, professional institutes and associations, nonprofit and commercial organizations, state and local governments.

Range/Average: N.A.

Activity: N.A.

HQ: NIST-USDC, 100 Bureau Dr., Stop 1650, Gaithersburg, MD 20899. Phone: (301) 975-3086.

Internet: www.nist.gov. (Note: no field offices for this program.)

11.610 NATIONAL CENTER FOR STANDARDS AND CERTIFICATION INFORMATION (NCSCI)

Assistance: technical information.

Purposes: pursuant to NBSOA as amended and the Trade Agreements Act of 1979, to serve as an information center and referral service—maintaining a reference collection of standards and specifications, regulations, certification rules, directories, reference books, special publications, copyrights, lending restrictions, and similar data; information relating to foreign trade. NCSCI does not analyze, evaluate, translate, or interpret standards. Published directories, indexes, and bibliographies are available from GPO, NTIS, and NCSCI.

Eligible applicants/beneficiaries: state and local governments; private, public, profit and nonprofit organizations; individuals.

Range/Average: N.A.

Activity: N.A.

HQ: Global Standards and Information Group, NIST-USDC, 100 Bureau Dr., Gaithersburg, MD 20899-2100. Phone: (301) 975-4040; FAX: (301) 926-1559.

Internet: ts.nist.gov/ncsci. (Note: no field offices for this program.)

11.611 MANUFACTURING EXTENSION PARTNERSHIP

Assistance: project grants; technical information. (project grants, 50 percent/project grants, to 2 years).

Purposes: pursuant to the Omnibus Trade and Competitiveness Act of 1988, American Technology Preeminence Act of 1991, and Technology Administration Act of 1998, to establish and maintain extension centers and services for the transfer of appropriate manufacturing technology to smaller U.S. manufacturing firms. Funding may support: demonstrations and technology deployment especially to firms with fewer than 500 employees; statewide planning and pilot testing projects.

Eligible applicants/beneficiaries: extension services—U.S. nonprofit organizations. Planning and pilot services grants—state and local governments, state-affiliated nonprofit organizations, consortia.

Range: extension planning and testing, $25,000 to $100,000; extension centers, $200,000 to $6,500,000. **Average:** N.A.

Activity: N.A.

HQ: Director, Manufacturing Extension Partnership, NIST-USDC, 100 Bureau Drive, Gaithersburg, MD 20899-4800. Phone: (301) 975-4676.

Internet: www.mep.nist.gov. (Note: no field offices for this program.)

11.616 TECHNOLOGY INNOVATION PROGRAM (TIP)

Assistance: project grants (50 percent/3-5 years).

Purposes: pursuant to Section 3012 of the America Creating Opportunities to Meaningfully Promote Excellence in Technology, Education, and Science (COMPETES) Act, to support, promote and accelerate innovation in the U.S. through high- risk, high-reward research in areas of critical national need. Only small or medium-sized companies may apply for funding and TIP funds may only be used to pay direct costs.

Eligible applicants/beneficiaries: U.S. businesses or a joint venture (of which IHEs, nonprofit research institutions, national and government laboratories, excluding NIST, may be a member) doing most of their business in the United States may apply. In addition, companies incorporated in the U.S. with a parent company incorporated in another country are eligible to apply for TIP funding.

Range/Average: N.A.

Activity: N.A.

HQ: Technology Program, NIST-USDC, 100 Bureau Drive, Gaithersburg, MD 20899-4701. Phone: (301) 975-4429.

Internet: www.nist.gov/tip. (Note: no field offices for this program.)

11.620 SCIENCE, TECHNOLOGY, BUSINESS AND/OR EDUCATION OUTREACH

Assistance: project grants/cooperative agreements (100 percent/to 5 years).

Purposes: project grants to evaluate the benefits and impacts of National Institute of Standards and Technology (NIST) research and develop efforts and/or evaluate and/or stimulate technological innovation in the private sector, strengthen the role of small businesses in meeting Federal research and development needs, and/or increase private sector commercialization of innovations derived from NIST research and development efforts and/or NISTs Small Business Innovation Research Program; also, to support innovative approaches and methods for science and/or technology education.

Eligible applicants/beneficiaries: public and private non-profit organizations (including IHEs and hospitals), and other quasi-public and private non-profit organizations such as, but not limited to, community action agencies, research institutes, educational associations, and health centers. The term may include commercial organizations, and foreign or international organizations, which are recipients, subrecipients, contractors, or subcontractors of recipients or subrecipients at the discretion of the Department of Commerce.

Range/Average: N.A.

Activity: N.A.

HQ: Director, Science, Technology, Business, and Education Outreach, NIST-Commerce, 100 Bureau Dr., Stop 6000, Gaithersburg, MD 20899. Phone: (301) 975-2684.

Internet: www.nist.gov. (Note: no field offices for this program.)

11.801 NATIVE AMERICAN BUSINESS ENTERPRISE CENTERS (NABEC)

Assistance: project grants (100 percent/1-3 years).

Purposes: for eight designated Native American Business Development Centers (NABDCs) to provide electronic and one-on-one business development and technical assistance of all types to new or existing American Indian businesses. No loans or grants are awarded to individual businesses under this program; however, businesses may be helped in obtaining financial assistance for their operations.

Eligible applicants/beneficiaries: state and local governments, tribes, educational institutions, nonprofit and profit organizations, individuals.

Range: $155,000 to $287,500. **Average:** N.A.

Activity: N.A.

HQ: Office of Business Development, MBDA-USDC, 14th & Constitution Ave., NW, Washington, DC 20230. Phone: (202) 482-1940.

Internet: www.mbda.gov.

11.900   PATENT AND TRADEMARK TECHNICAL INFORMATION DISSEMINATION

Assistance: technical information.

Purposes: to support the growth of American commerce and technology through the utilization and dissemination of technical information available through patents and trademarks, and for the maintenance of public search centers. The office examines patent and trademark applications, and grants patents and approves trademarks when legal requirements are met. Fees are charged for services.

Eligible applicants/beneficiaries: general public.

Range/Average: N.A.

Activity: N.A.

HQ: General Information Services, U.S. Patent and Trademark Office-USDC, Alexandria, VA 20313-1450. Phone: (General Information Services, (703) 308-4357, (800) 786-9199.

Internet: www.uspto.gov. (Note: no field offices for this program.)

11.999   MARINE DEBRIS PROGRAM

Assistance: cooperative agreements. (50 percent/1 to 2 years).

Purposes: pursuant to the Marine Debris Research, Prevention, and Reduction Act, as amended by the Marine Debris Act, to help identify, determine sources of, assess, reduce, and prevent marine debris and its adverse impacts on the marine environment and navigation safety within the coastal United States and territories.

Eligible applicants/beneficiaries: state, local, tribal, and territorial governments, nonprofit and for-profit organizations/institutions, and IHEs.

Range: $15,000 to $250,000. **Average:** $90,000.

Activity: anticipate 16 to 30 awards in FY 2016.

HQ: NOAA, 1305 East West Hwy., SSMC 4, Rm. 13267, Silver Spring, MD 20910. Phone: (301) 713-3050; FAX: (301) 713-4292.

Internet: www.marinedebris.noaa.gov. (Note: no field offices for this program.)

DEPARTMENT OF DEFENSE

12.002 PROCUREMENT TECHNICAL ASSISTANCE FOR BUSINESS FIRMS ("PTA Cooperative Agreement Program")

Assistance: project grants (50-75 percent).

Purposes: to establish and operate new or existing procurement technical assistance programs to assist business firms in selling their goods and services to DOD, other federal agencies, and state and local governments.

Eligible applicants/beneficiaries: state and local governments, private non-profit organizations, tribal organizations, profit or nonprofit Indian economic enterprises.

Range: $30,000 to $300,000. **Average:** $160,185.

Activity: N.A.

HQ: Office of Small and Disadvantaged Business Utilization (DDAS), Defense Logistics Agency-DOD, 8725 John J. Kingman Rd. - Ste. 2533, Ft. Belvoir, VA 22060-6221. Phone: (703) 767-1650.

Internet: www.d/a.mil/ddas. (Note: no field offices for this program.)

12.100 AQUATIC PLANT CONTROL

Assistance: specialized services; technical information.

Purposes: pursuant to the River and Harbor Act of 1958 as amended, to assist in controlling and eradicating obnoxious aquatic plants in rivers, harbors, and allied waters. Localities must provide 50 percent matching funds.

Eligible applicants/beneficiaries: states, political subdivisions, instrumentalities.

Range/Average: N.A.

Activity: N.A.

HQ: Commander, U.S. Army Corps of Engineers - Attn: CECW-ON, DOD, Washington, DC 20314-1000. Phone: (202) 272-0247.

Internet: www.usace.army.mil/business.html.

12.101 BEACH EROSION CONTROL PROJECTS ("Small Beach Erosion Control Projects")

Assistance: specialized services; technical information.

Purposes: pursuant to the River and Harbor Act of 1962 as amended, to design and construct beach and shore erosion control projects not specifically authorized by Congress. The Corps funds the first $100,000 in planning costs, and 50 percent of additional study costs; localities must provide the balance. Cost-sharing is required for construction, with a $2,000,000 maximum federal share.

Eligible applicants/beneficiaries: states, political subdivisions, other authorized local agencies.

Range/Average: N.A.

Activity: N.A.

HQ: Headquarters - Attn: CERM-FC, U.S. Army Corps of Engineers, DOD, 441 G. St., NW, Washington, DC 20314. Phone: (202) 761-1504.

Internet: www.usace.army.mil/business.html.

12.102 EMERGENCY REHABILITATION OF FLOOD CONTROL WORKS OR FEDERALLY AUTHORIZED COASTAL PROTECTION WORKS ("Public Law 84-99, Code 300 Program")

Assistance: specialized services.

Purposes: pursuant to the Flood Control Act of 1941 as amended, to assist in the emergency repair or rehabilitation of flood control works damaged by flood, or federally authorized hurricane flood and shore protection works damaged by extraordinary wind, wave, or water action. Nonfederal sources must provide 20 percent of project costs.

Eligible applicants/beneficiaries: owners of damaged flood protective works, or state and local public entities responsible for their maintenance, repair, and operation.

Range/Average: N.A.

Activity: N.A.

HQ: Commander, U.S. Army Corps of Engineers - Attn: CECW-OE, DOD, Washington, DC 20314-1000. Phone: (202) 272-0251.

Internet: www.usace.army.mil/business.html.

12.103 EMERGENCY OPERATIONS FLOOD RESPONSE AND POST FLOOD RESPONSE ("Public Law 84-99, Code 200 Program")

Assistance: specialized services.

Purposes: pursuant to the Flood Control Act of 1941 as amended, to provide emergency assistance in all phases of flood fighting, and post-flood response and rescue operations in times of flood or coastal storm.

Eligible applicants/beneficiaries: state or local public agencies.

Range/Average: N.A.

Activity: 50 to 250 flood emergency operations annually.

HQ: Commander, U.S. Army Corps of Engineers - Attn: CECW-OE, DOD, Washington, DC 20314-1000. Phone: (202) 272-0251.

Internet: www.usace.army.mil/business.html.

12.104 FLOOD PLAIN MANAGEMENT SERVICES (FPMS)

Assistance: advisory services/counseling; technical information.

Purposes: pursuant to the Flood Control Act of 1960 as amended, to promote recognition of flood hazards in land and water use planning and development, by providing and interpreting historical data maintained by the Corps on floods and flood plains areas subject to flooding and flood losses from streams, lakes, and oceans. Services are available to states and local governments on a reimbursable basis; fees are charged to private parties.

Eligible applicants/beneficiaries: states, political subdivisions, general public.

Range/Average: N.A.

Activity: N.A.

HQ: U.S. Army Corps of Engineers - Attn: CECW-PF, DOD, Washington, DC 20314-1000. Phone: (202) 761-0169.

Internet: www.usace.army.mil/business.html.

12.105 PROTECTION OF ESSENTIAL HIGHWAYS, HIGHWAY BRIDGE APPROACHES, AND PUBLIC WORKS ("Emergency Bank Protection")

Assistance: specialized services.

Purposes: pursuant to the Flood Control Act of 1946 as amended, to design and construct projects protecting highways, highway bridges, essential public works, churches, hospitals, schools, and other nonprofit public services endangered by flood-caused erosion. Federal costs are limited to $1,000,000 per project; localities are responsible for costs in excess.

Eligible applicants/beneficiaries: states, political subdivisions, other authorized local agencies.

Range/Average: N.A.

Activity: N.A.

HQ: Headquarters - Attn: CERM-FC, U.S. Army Corps of Engineers, DOD, 441 G. St., NW, Washington, DC 20314. Phone: (202) 761-1504.

Internet: www.usace.army.mil/business.html.

12.106 FLOOD CONTROL PROJECTS ("Small Flood Control Projects")

Assistance: specialized services.

Purposes: pursuant to the Flood Control Act of 1948 as amended, to design and construct flood control projects not specifically authorized by Congress. The Corps funds the first $100,000 in planning costs, and 50 percent of additional study costs; localities must provide the balance. Cost-sharing is required for construction, with a $7,000,000 maximum federal share.

Eligible applicants/beneficiaries: states, political subdivisions, other authorized local agencies.

Range/Average: N.A.

Activity: N.A.

HQ: Headquarters - Attn: CERM-FC, U.S. Army Corps of Engineers, DOD, 441 G. St., NW, Washington, DC 20314. Phone: (202) 761-1504.

Internet: www.usace.army.mil/business.html.

12.107 NAVIGATION PROJECTS ("Small Navigation Projects")

Assistance: specialized services.

Purposes: pursuant to the River and Harbor Act of 1960 as amended, to design and construct small general navigation projects not specifically authorized by Congress. The federal cost limit is $4,000,000 per project; localities must provide a share of study costs, and pay construction costs exceeding the federal maximum.

Eligible applicants/beneficiaries: states, political subdivisions, other authorized local agencies.

Range/Average: N.A.

Activity: N.A.

HQ: Headquarters - Attn: CERM-FC, U.S. Army Corps of Engineers, DOD, 441 G. St., NW, Washington, DC 20314. Phone: (202) 761-1504.

Internet: www.usace.army.mil/business.html.

12.108 SNAGGING AND CLEARING FOR FLOOD CONTROL ("Section 208")

Assistance: specialized services.

Purposes: pursuant to the Flood Control Act of 1937 as amended, to design and construct snagging and clearing projects for flood control. The federal cost limit is $500,000 per project; localities must share in construction costs.

Eligible applicants/beneficiaries: states, political subdivisions, other authorized local agencies.

Range/Average: N.A.

Activity: N.A.

HQ: Headquarters - Attn: CERM-FC, U.S. Army Corps of Engineers, DOD, 441 G. St., NW, Washington, DC 20314. Phone: (202) 761-1504.

Internet: www.usace.army.mil/business.html.

12.109 PROTECTION, CLEARING AND STRAIGHTENING CHANNELS ("Section 3 Emergency Dredging Projects")

Assistance: specialized services.

Purposes: pursuant to the River and Harbor Act of 1945 as amended, for the emergency protection, clearing, and straightening of navigation channels in rivers, harbors, and other waterways, including for flood control purposes. Localities must provide maintenance.

Eligible applicants/beneficiaries: states, political subdivisions, other authorized local agencies.

Range/Average: N.A.

Activity: N.A.

HQ: Commander, U.S. Army Corps of Engineers - Attn: CECW-OD, DOD, Washington, DC 20314-1000. Phone: (202) 272-8835.

Internet: www.usace.army.mil/business.html.

12.110 PLANNING ASSISTANCE TO STATES ("Section 22")

Assistance: specialized services.

Purposes: pursuant to the Water Resources Development Act of 1974 as amended, to assist states in preparing comprehensive plans for the development, utilization, or conservation of water and related land resources of drainage basins. No state may receive more than $500,000 in assistance in any one year; 50 percent cost sharing is required.

Eligible applicants/beneficiaries: states, tribes, territories.

Range/Average: N.A.

Activity: N.A.

HQ: Headquarters - Attn: CERM-FC, U.S. Army Corps of Engineers, DOD, 441 G. St., NW, Washington, DC 20314. Phone: (202) 761-1504.

Internet: www.usace.army.mil/business.html.

12.111 EMERGENCY ADVANCE MEASURES FOR FLOOD PREVENTION ("Public Law 84-99, Code 500 Program")

Assistance: specialized services.

Purposes: pursuant to the Flood Control Act of 1941 as amended, to provide assistance when there is an immediate threat of unusual flooding, including such work as removal of waterway obstructions, dam failure prevention, and work necessary to prepare for abnormal snowmelt.

Eligible applicants/beneficiaries: state governors.

Range/Average: N.A.

Activity: N.A.

HQ: Commander, U.S. Army Corps of Engineers - Attn: CECW-OE, DOD, Washington, DC 20314. Phone: (202) 272-0251.

Internet: www.usace.army.mil/business.html.

12.112 PAYMENTS TO STATES IN LIEU OF REAL ESTATE TAXES

Assistance: formula grants (100 percent).

Purposes: pursuant to the Flood Control Acts of 1941, 1946, and 1954 as amended, to compensate local taxing units for loss of real estate taxes lost as the result of federal acquisition of land for flood control, navigation, hydroelectric power projects, and allied purposes. Funds are derived from federal receipts from leases covering such lands, 75 percent of which are distributed through this program.

Eligible applicants: state governments.

Eligible beneficiaries: state, county governments.

Range/Average: N.A.

Activity: N.A.

HQ: Headquarters - Attn: CERM-FC, U.S. Army Corps of Engineers, DOD, 441 G. St., NW, Washington, DC 20314. Phone: (202) 761-1504.

Internet: www.usace.army.mil/business.html. (Note: no field offices for this program.)

12.113 STATE MEMORANDUM OF AGREEMENT PROGRAM FOR THE REIMBURSEMENT OF TECHNICAL SERVICES (DSMOA)

Assistance: project grants (100 percent/2 years).

Purposes: pursuant to CERCLA as amended and Superfund amendments, to reimburse states for costs incurred to provide technical services in support of the DOD Environmental Restoration Program, in cleaning up DOD hazardous wastes sites.

Eligible applicants: state, territorial governments.

Eligible beneficiaries: state, local, territorial governments; public, private, nonprofit and profit organizations.

Range: $104,000 to $11,400,000. **Average:** N.A.

Activity: N.A.

HQ: Corps of Engineers, CEMP-RI, DOD, 20 Massachusetts Ave., NW, Washington, DC 20314. Phone: (202) 504-4950.

Internet: www.usace.army.mil/business.html. (Note: no field offices for this program.)

12.114 COLLABORATIVE RESEARCH AND DEVELOPMENT ("CPAR")

Assistance: project grants (50 percent).

Purposes: pursuant to the Water Resources Development Act of 1988, to improve construction productivity through research and development and application of advanced technologies involving collaborative projects, field demonstrations, licensing agreements, and other means of commercialization and technology transfer. Corps laboratories must perform a significant portion of projects.

Eligible applicants/beneficiaries: U.S. private firms including corporations, partnerships, and industrial development organizations; public and private foundations; nonprofit organizations; units of state or local government; academic institutions; other.

Range: $200,000 to $900,000. **Average:** $400,000.

Activity: 76 projects to date.

HQ: Headquarters - Attn: CERD-C, U.S. Army Corps of Engineers, DOD, 20 Massachusetts Ave., NW, Washington, DC 20314-1000. Phone: (202) 272-1846.

Internet: www.usace.army.mil/business.html.

12.116 DEPARTMENT OF DEFENSE APPROPRIATION ACT OF 2003 ("Section 8044")

Assistance: specialized services.

Purposes: pursuant to the Act, to develop a system for prioritization of environmental impacts mitigation and costs to complete estimates for mitigation on Indian lands resulting from DOD activities, including: training and technical assistance to tribes; related administrative support; information gathering; documenting environmental damage.

Eligible applicants/beneficiaries: states, tribes, territories and possessions.

Range/Average: N.A.

Activity: N.A.

HQ: Headquarters - Attn: CERM-FC, U.S. Army Corps of Engineers, DOD, 441 G. St., NW, Washington, DC 20314. Phone: (202) 761-1504.

Internet: N.A.

12.217 ELECTRONIC ABSENTEE SYSTEMS FOR ELECTIONS ("EASE Grants")

Assistance: project grants.

Purposes: Project grants to state, local, and territorial governments to develop innovative electronic election systems tools that will reduce impediments faced by the Uniformed and Overseas Citizens Absentee Voting Act (UOCAVA) voters. The specific objectives of these activities will be to establish and ensure successful, sustainable and affordable electronic tools that will improve voting systems for voters protected by the UOCAVA; increase the percentage of ballots successfully returned by UOCAVA voters to be either equal to, or greater than the percentage of ballots returned by the general voting population; collect and analyze data to increase effectiveness of absentee voting procedures and systems; and establish and maintain a pipeline of ideas, techniques and best practices of election officials and their services for UOCAVA voters.

Eligible applicants/beneficiaries: state, local governments, U.S. territories.

Range/Average: N.A.

Activity: N.A.

HQ: Director, EASE Grants, FVAP-DOD, 4040 N Fairfax Dr., Arlington, VA 22203-1613. Phone: (703) 696-8785; FAX: (703) 588-1489.

Internet: www.fvap.gov. (Note: no field offices for this program.)

12.218 FVAP POLICY CLEARINGHOUSE ("Overseas Voting Policy Clearinghouse")

Assistance: cooperative agreements (100 percent/3 years).

Purposes: to collaborate and participate with state officials to enable the Federal Voting Assistance Program (FVAP) to provide electronic absentee voting systems for a statistically relevant number of military voters so that they may cast votes for Federal elections.

Eligible applicants: qualified coordinating agents that work closely with FVAP and the states to facilitate and support FVAPS's electronic voting assistance research efforts.

Eligible beneficiaries: elected and appointed state and territorial officials.

Range: N.A. **Average:** $2,800,000.

Activity: N.A.

HQ: Grants Officer, Defense Human Resources Activity (DHRA), 4800 Mark Center Dr., Alexandria, VA 22350. Phone: (571) 372-0722.

Internet: www.fvap.gov. (Note: no field offices for this program.)

12.219 EFFECTIVE ABSENTEE SYSTEMS FOR ELECTIONS 2.0 ("EASE 2.0")

Assistance: project grants (100 percent/to 5 years).

Purposes: Funds to support research on the effectiveness of online ballot delivery systems as well as other related methods to streamline the absentee voting process for voters covered by the Uniformed and Overseas Citizens Absentee Voting Act (UOCAVA). Program objectives are to establish and ensure successful, sustainable, and effective methods to improve voting systems for voters protected by UOCAVA; increase the percentage of ballots successfully returned by UOCAVA voters to be either equal to, or greater to that of the general population; and collect and analyze data to increase the effectiveness of absentee voting procedures and systems for voters protected by UOCAV.

Eligible applicants/beneficiaries: state and local governments (including state-designated Indian tribes), U.S. territories and possessions.

Range/Average: N.A.

Activity: N.A.

HQ: Director, EASE 2.0, FVAP-DOD, 4800 Mark Center Drive, Alexandria, VA 22032. Phone: (571) 372-2614.

Internet: N.A. (Note: no field offices for this program.)

12.225   COMMERCIAL TECHNOLOGIES FOR MAINTENANCE ACTIVITIES PROGRAM (CTMA)

Assistance: project grants/cooperative agreements.

Purposes: pursuant to Research and Development Projects under Section 2358 of Title 10 U.S.C., cooperative agreements with industry to advance the development, integration, and use of sustainment technologies and processes that: improve weapon systems readiness and reliability; improve weapon systems capability with lowered overall sustainment costs; reduce cycle time for sustainment; improve business practices and data collection/management.

Eligible applicants/beneficiaries: local, state, territorial government entities.

Range: $10,000,000 to 25,000,000. **Average:** $15,000,000.

Activity: N.A.

HQ: Director, Commercial Technologies for Maintenance Activities Program, 1225 S. Clark St., CG2, Ste. 910, Arlington, VA 22202. Phone: (703) 545-1417.

Internet: N.A. (Note: no field offices for this program.)

12.300   BASIC AND APPLIED SCIENTIFIC RESEARCH

Assistance: project grants (100 percent).

Purposes: for basic and applied research and training in the physical, mathematical, environmental, engineering, and life sciences, leading to the improvement of naval operations; for programs encouraging careers in those disciplines by supporting outstanding graduate, undergraduate, and high school students; to increase the number of graduates from under-represented minority groups; to assist universities in buying major high-cost research equipment; for symposia.

Eligible applicants/beneficiaries: nonprofit private and public IHEs and other research organizations.

Range: $5,000 to $20,000,000. **Average:** $500,000.

Activity: anticipate 5,070 awards in FY 2016.

HQ: Office of Naval Research (ONR 22), Department of the Navy-DOD, 875 North Randolph St., Arlington, VA 22203. Phone: (703) 696-4601.

Internet: www.onr.navy.mil. (Note: no field offices for this program.)

12.350   DEPARTMENT OF DEFENSE HIV/AIDS PREVENTION PROGRAM

Assistance: project grants.

Purposes: to train and assist select foreign militaries with establishing and implementing HIV/AIDS prevention, care and treatment programs for their military personnel and dependents.

Eligible applicants/beneficiaries: anyone, especially U.S. non-governmental organizations and educational institutions. Individuals may not apply.

Range: $50,000 to $2,000,000. **Average:** N.A.

Activity: N.A.

HQ: Department of Defense HIV/AIDS Prevention Program, Naval Health Research Center, 140 Sylvester Rd., San Diego, CA 92106. Phone: (619) 553-8528.

Internet: N.A. (Note: no field offices for this program.)

12.351   BASIC SCIENTIFIC RESEARCH—COMBATING WEAPONS OF MASS DESTRUCTION

Assistance: project grants.

Purposes: to support and stimulate basic, applied, and advanced scientific research and technology at accredited educational or research institutions, nonprofit organizations, and commercial firms with an emphasis on innovative methods for combating or countering WMDs.

Eligible applicants/beneficiaries: in general, private and public nonprofit accredited institutions of higher learning that carry out research or education in science and/or engineering. Some awards are available for nonprofit, commercial or federal laboratories for basic research. No awards made to individuals.

Range: N.A. **Average:** $450,000.

Activity: N.A.

HQ: Defense Threat Reduction Agency BE-BC, 8725 John J. Kingman Rd., MS 6201, Ft. Belvoir, VA 22060-6201. Phone: (703) 767-5870; FAX: (703) 767-4450, Toll-free: (800) 701-5096.

Internet: www.dtra.mil/be/business_opp/procurement/acq_procopp.cfm. (Note: no field offices for this program.)

12.352   SCIENTIFIC RESEARCH—COMBATING WEAPONS OF MASS DESTRUCTION

Assistance: project grants (50-100 percent).

Purposes: to support and stimulate basic, applied, and advanced scientific research and technology at accredited educational or research institutions, nonprofit organizations, and commercial firms with an emphasis on innovative methods for combating or countering WMDs.

Eligible applicants/beneficiaries: any domestic or foreign industrial/commercial concerns including small business; accredited degree-granting institutions of higher learning; nonprofit organizations; and certain DoD and DOE-sponsored Federally Funded Research and Development Centers (FFRDCs). No awards are made to U.S. government agencies and organizations, individuals and federal academic institutions or laboratories not specifically identified in DFARS 235-071-1.

Range/Average: N.A.

Activity: N.A.

HQ: Defense Threat Reduction Agency, 8725 John J. Kingman Rd., MS 6201, Ft. Belvoir, VA 22060-6201. Phone: (703) 767-5870; FAX: (703) 767-4450, Toll-free: (800) 701-5096.

Internet: See Broad Agency Announcement for specific website information. (Note: no field offices for this program.)

12.355 PEST MANAGEMENT AND VECTOR CONTROL RESEARCH

Assistance: cooperative agreements/project grants. (100 percent).

Purposes: pursuant to the Federal Grant and Cooperative Agreement Act, to develop new interventions for protection of deployed military personnel from diseases caused by arthropod-borne pathogens and to improve control of filth flies. Recipients are required to conform to their accepted research protocol and are usually required to submit some form of annual or project report.

Eligible applicants/beneficiaries: nonprofit and for-profit institutions/organizations, and IHEs.

Range: $100,000 to $250,000. **Average:** N.A.

Activity: N.A.

HQ: Office of the Secretary of Defense, DOD, 110 Thomas Johnson Dr., Frederick, MD 21702. Phone: (301) 619-2895.

Internet: www.3.natick.army.mil/.

12.357 ROTC LANGUAGE AND CULTURE TRAINING GRANTS ("ROTC Project GO Global Officers")

Assistance: project grants (100 percent/2 years).

Purposes: pursuant to the National Defense Authorization Act of 2006, Project GO (Global Officers), a DoD-funded initiative, promotes critical language education, study abroad, and intercultural dialogue opportunities within the ROTC student population in order to develop future military officers who possess the cross-cultural communication skills required for effective leadership in the 21st Century operational environment. Applicant cost-sharing not required, but encouraged.

Eligible applicants: accredited 2- and 4-year IHEs with an on-campus ROTC unit. Federal government schools are not eligible.

Eligible beneficiaries: accredited U.S. IHEs and their ROTC students.

Range: $50,000 to $350,000. **Average:** N.A.

Activity: N.A.

HQ: Director, Office of the Secretary of Defense, DOD, 1101 Wilson Blvd., Suite 1210, Arlington, VA 22209-2248. Phone: (703) 696-6516; FAX: (703) 696-5667.

Internet: N.A. (Note: no field offices for this program.)

12.360 RESEARCH ON CHEMICAL AND BIOLOGICAL DEFENSE

Assistance: project grants (100 percent/to 5 years).

Purposes: to further the capability to prevent, detect, diagnose, and treat the effects of chemical, radiological, and biological warfare agents.

Eligible applicants: public or private educational institutions, nonprofit organizations operated for public interest, and commercial firms.

Eligible beneficiaries: independent investigators associated with an applicant organization.

Range/Average: N.A.

Activity: N.A.

HQ: Chemical and Biological Medical Systems, 64 Thomas Johnson Dr., Frederick, MD 21702. Phone: (302) 619-2895.

Internet: www.jpeocbd.osd.mil. (Note: no field offices for this program.)

12.369 MARINE CORPS SYSTEMS COMMAND FEDERAL ASSISTANCE PROGRAM

Assistance: project grants (100 percent/to 3 years).

Purposes: pursuant to FY2008 DoD Appropriations Act, to provide federal assistance in support of families of active duty Marines and for the betterment of the general public.

Eligible applicants/beneficiaries: private/public nonprofit organizations, IHEs, commercial concerns.

Range/Average: N.A.

Activity: N.A.

HQ: Director, Marine Corps Systems Command Federal Assistance Program, DoD, 2200 Lester St., Quantico, VA 22134. Phone: (703) 432-5590.

Internet: N.A. (Note: no field offices for this program.)

12.400 MILITARY CONSTRUCTION, NATIONAL GUARD

Assistance: project grants (75-100 percent).

Purposes: to provide facilities for training and administering Army and Air Force National Guard units. Funds may be used for armories or to provide offices, storage, assembly areas, rifle ranges, and classrooms. For non-armories, funds may provide for maintenance, supply, training, and other logistical and administrative expenses.

Eligible applicants/beneficiaries: states, DC, territories and possessions.

Range: from $300,000. **Average:** N.A.

Activity: N.A.

HQ: Chief of Installations (NGB-ARI), National Guard Bureau, Department of the Army-DOD, ARNG Readiness Center, DOD, 111 S. George Mason Drive, Arlington, VA 22204-1382. Phone: (703) 601-7941.

Internet: www.ngb.dtic.mil/indexshtm.

12.401 NATIONAL GUARD MILITARY OPERATIONS AND MAINTENANCE (O&M) PROJECTS

Assistance: project grants (75-100 percent).

Purposes: for services provided by states for such National Guard activities as real property maintenance and repair, environmental resources management and services, security guard services, electronic security systems, telecommunications services, air traffic control, automated target systems, recruitment, fire protection, and related activities.

Eligible applicants/beneficiaries: states, DC, PR, VI, Guam.

Range: from $100,000. Average: N.A.

Activity: N.A.

HQ: *National Guard Bureaus*—Army National Guard Bureau, Department of the Army-DOD, ARNG Readiness Center, 1411 Jefferson Davis Hwy, NGB-PARC-A Suite 8200, Arlington, VA 22202-3231. Phone: (Real Property O&M Projects, (703) 607-1002.

Internet: www.ngb.army.mil.

12.404 NATIONAL GUARD CHALLENGE PROGRAM

Assistance: formula grants (60 percent).

Purposes: to use the National Guard to provide military-based training to civilian youth that have graduated from secondary school, including supervised work experience in community service and conservation projects—to improve their life skills and employment potential. Funds may support civilian personnel hired to conduct the program.

Eligible applicants/beneficiaries: states and territories.

Range/Average: N.A.

Activity: 25 states participating; 22,000 graduates to date.

HQ: Youth Programs Division (NGB/NGB-YP), National Guard Bureau, Department of the Army-DOD, 1411 Jefferson Davis Hwy (JP1), Arlington, VA 22202-3221. Phone: (703) 607-5975.

Internet: www.ngb.dtic.mil/indexstm. (Note: no field offices for this program.)

12.420 MILITARY MEDICAL RESEARCH AND DEVELOPMENT

Assistance: project grants. (100 percent/to 5 years).

Purposes: for fundamental basic and applied medical research projects that expand the technology base or understanding of biological-medical processes. Project examples: analysis of investigational drugs in biological fluids; altered response to infection induced by severe injury; conferences and symposia.

Eligible applicants/beneficiaries: public, quasi-public, or private nonprofit institutions and organizations; specialized groups.

Range: $100,000 to $5,000,000. **Average:** $650,000.

Activity: N.A.

HQ: U.S. Army Medical Research and Material Command-DOD (ATTN: MCMR-ACQ-BA), Fort Detrick, Frederick, MD 21702-5012. Phone: (301) 619-7216.

Internet: www.mrmc.army.mil; cdmrp.army.mil. (Note: no field offices for this program.)

12.431 BASIC SCIENTIFIC RESEARCH

Assistance: project grants (100 percent/3-5 years).

Purposes: for basic research in the mathematical, physical, engineering, biological, and geosciences related to the improvement of Army programs or operations. Funds may support: programs encouraging careers for outstanding graduate, undergraduate, and high school students; increases in the number of graduates from under-represented minority groups; symposia; purchases of major high-cost research equipment.

Eligible applicants/beneficiaries: educational institutions, nonprofit scientific research organizations.

Range: $1,374,000 to $1,500,000. **Average:** $1,457,744.

Activity: N.A.

HQ: U.S. Army Research Office, 4300 S. Miami Blvd., Durham, NC 27703. Phone: (919) 549-4270.

Internet: N.A. (Note: no field offices for this program.)

12.440 DISSERTATION YEAR FELLOWSHIP
("CMH Dissertation Fellowship")

Assistance: project grants (100 percent).

Purposes: pursuant to the National Defense Authorization Act for Fiscal Year 1993, fellowships to support scholarly research and writing among qualified civilian graduate students preparing dissertations in the history of land warfare. The area of study is broadly defined, and includes military campaigns, biography, military organization and administration, policy, strategy, tactics, weaponry, technology, training, logistics, and the evolution of civil-military relations. Topics focusing on the history of the U.S. Army are preferred but not required. The fellowships can be used to cover any costs related to dissertation research, required visits to the Center of Military History, or as supplemental income during the writing/editing phase of the dissertation. The program offers between two and three fellowships per year depending upon funding availability.

Eligible applicants/beneficiaries: civilian U.S. citizens, unaffiliated with the federal government, pursuing a doctoral degree in history. Military personnel, civilian federal service employees, and contractors with the U.S. government are ineligibable.

Range/Average: $10,000 per fellowship.

Activity: N.A.

HQ: Director, Dissertation Year Fellowship, Army Center of Military History-DOD, Bldg 35, 102 Fourth Ave., SW, Fort McNair, DC 20319. Phone: (202) 685-2252.

Internet: www.history.army.mil/html/about/fellowship.html. (Note: no field offices for this program.)

12.550   LANGUAGE FLAGSHIP GRANTS TO INSTITUTIONS OF HIGHER EDUCATION
("Language Flagship")

Assistance: project grants. (to 75 percent/1-2 years).

Purposes: to develop and strengthen IHE capabilities in critical language education, area studies, and international fields. International exchanges are ineligible for funding. The National Security Education Trust Fund supports this program.

Eligible applicants/beneficiaries: U.S. IHEs. Others may be included in proposals, but may not receive direct grants.

Range: $200,000 to $500,000. **Average:** $325,000.

Activity: N.A.

HQ: NSEP, Under Secretary of Defense/Policy, Assistant Secretary/Strategy and Requirements, DOD, 1101 Wilson Blvd. - Ste. 1210, Arlington, VA 22209. Phone: (571) 256-0756.

Internet: www.thelanguageflagship.org. (Note: no field offices for this program.)

12.551   NATIONAL SECURITY EDUCATION PROGRAM DAVID L. BOREN SCHOLARSHIPS

Assistance: project grants. (100 percent/2 academic terms per year).

Purposes: for undergraduate scholarships in critical languages and world area studies. Recipients must agree to work in a federal organization or in higher education for a time equal to the award period. Studies may be conducted abroad. International exchanges are ineligible for funding. The National Security Education Trust Fund supports this program.

Eligible applicants/beneficiaries: U.S. citizens enrolled in public or private two- or four-year IHEs. Students in federal government schools are ineligible.

Range: to $20,000. **Average:** $18,000.

Activity: N.A.

HQ: NSEP, Under Secretary of Defense/Policy, Assistant Secretary/Strategy and Requirements, DOD, PO Box 20010, Arlington, VA 22209. Phone: (571) 256-0771.

Internet: www.borenawards.org. (Note: no field offices for this program.)

12.552   NATIONAL SECURITY EDUCATION PROGRAM DAVID L. BOREN FELLOWSHIPS
("Boren Fellowships Program")

Assistance: project grants (100 percent/one semester to 2 years).

Purposes: for graduate fellowships in critical languages and world area studies. All Boren Fellowship recipients must agree to work in a federal organization for a time equal to the award period but not less than one year. Studies may be conducted abroad.

Eligible applicants/beneficiaries: U.S. citizens enrolled in graduate programs in public or private U.S. IHEs. Students in federal government schools are ineligible.

Range: to $30,000. **Average:** $23,000.

Activity: N.A.

HQ: NSEP, Under Secretary of Defense/Policy, Assistant Secretary/Strategy and Requirements, DOD, PO Box 20010, Arlington, VA 22209. Phone: (571) 256-0771.

Internet: www.borenawards.org. (Note: no field offices for this program.)

12.553 LANGUAGE FLAGSHIP FELLOWSHIPS

Assistance: project grants (100 percent/to 2 years).

Purposes: for fellowships to address the urgent and growing need for Americans with professional levels of competency in languages critical to national security. All Flagship Fellowship recipients must agree to work in a federal organization for a time equal to the award period but not less than one year. Studies may be conducted abroad.

Eligible applicants/beneficiaries: U.S. citizens with superior level proficiency in English and minimum proficiency in the appropriate foreign language, possessing an undergraduate degree at the time of beginning NFLP Fellowship, and not currently employed by U.S. government. Past recipients of NSEP Boren scholarships or fellowships are eligible and encouraged to apply.

Range: $19,000 to $86,000. **Average:** $45,880.

Activity: N.A.

HQ: NSEP, DOD, PO Box 20010, Arlington, VA 22219. Phone: (703) 696-5670.

Internet: thelanguageflagship.org. (Note: no field offices for this program.)

12.554 ENGLISH FOR HERITAGE LANGUAGE SPEAKERS GRANTS TO U.S. INSTITUTIONS OF HIGHER EDUCATION ("National Security Education Program")

Assistance: project grants (100 percent).

Purposes: to provide intensive English language instruction for U.S. citizens who are native speakers of critical languages, with the goal of enabling participants to reach professional working proficiency in English in order to build a critical base of future leaders in government service and the broader professional community.

Eligible applicants/beneficiaries: U.S. private and public 2 and 4 year colleges and universities. Other organizations, agencies, associations, and foreign institutions may be included in proposals, but may not be direct recipients of a grant.

Range: $250,000 to $400,000. **Average:** $300,000.

Activity: N.A.

HQ: National Security Education Department, National Defense University, DOD, 1101 Wilson Blvd. - Ste. 1210, Arlington, VA 22209-2248. Phone: (703) 696-1991 Or: Center for Applied Linguistics, 4646 40th St NW, Washington, DC 20016. Phone: (202) 355-1572.

Internet: www.cal.org/ehls. (Note: no field offices for this program.)

12.555 ENGLISH FOR HERITAGE LANGUAGE SPEAKERS SCHOLARSHIPS ("EHLS Program")

Assistance: project grants. (100 percent/6 months).

Purposes: to provide intensive English language instruction for U.S. citizens who are native speakers of critical languages, with the goal of enabling participants to reach professional working proficiency in English in order to build a critical base of future leaders in government service and the broader professional community.

Eligible applicants/beneficiaries: U.S. citizens with superior level proficiency in their native language and a minimum proficiency in English, possessing an undergraduate degree at the time of application, and not currently employed by U.S. government. Eligible native languages of interest are updated annually and available on the program web site.

Range/Average: N.A.

Activity: N.A.

HQ: National Security Education Department, PO Box 20010, Arlington, VA 22219. Phone: (703) 696-5672.

Internet: www.cal.org/ehls. (Note: no field offices for this program.)

12.556 COMPETITIVE GRANTS: PROMOTING K-12 STUDENT ACHIEVEMENT AT MILITARY-CONNECTED SCHOOLS ("DoDEA Grant—Military K-12")

Assistance: project grants/discretionary (100 percent).

Purposes: pursuant to Section 574 (d) of P.L. 109-364, to enhance student learning opportunities, student achievement, and educator professional development at military-connected schools significantly impacted by military force structure changes. These grants may be used to address student achievement in science, technology, mathematics, or English language arts/reading.

Eligible applicants: military-connected school districts that have been significantly impacted by force structure changes.

Eligible beneficiaries: K-12 students and teachers.

Range/Average: N.A.

Activity: N.A.

HQ: Director, 4040 North Fairfax Drive, 9th Floor, Arlington, VA 22203. Phone: (703) 588-3345.

Internet: militaryk12partners.dodea.edu. (Note: no field offices for this program.)

12.557   INVITATIONAL GRANTS FOR MILITARY-CONNECTED SCHOOLS ("DoDEA Grant—Military")

Assistance: project grants/discretionary (100 percent/3 years).

Purposes: to enhance student learning opportunities, student achievement, and educator professional development and to ease the challenges students who are military dependents face due to their parents' military station transfers or deployments. Grants may be used to address student achievement in science, technology, mathematics, or English language arts/ reading and students' transitional needs, such as additional guidance counselor support.

Eligible applicants: military-connected local educational agencies (LEAs) by invitation only.

Eligible beneficiaries: K-12 students, teachers.

Range/Average: N.A.

Activity: N.A.

HQ: Director, DoDEA, 4040 North Fairfax Dr. 9th Fl., Arlington, VA 22203. Phone: (703) 588-3345; FAX: (703) 588-3702.

Internet: militaryk12partners.dodea.edu. (Note: no field offices for this program.)

12.560   DOD, NDEP, DOTC-STEM EDUCATION OUTREACH IMPLEMENTATION

Assistance: project grants (100 percent).

Purposes: to obtain support for the management, development, and furthering of new and existing partnerships between the Department of Defense, National Defense Education Program, and Defense Ordnance Technology Consortium for Science, Technology, Engineering, and Mathematics education and other outreach organizations, professional societies, and local education activities.

Eligible applicants: eligible education outreach organizations, professional societies, local education groups.

Eligible beneficiaries: K-12 students and public in all 50 states, U.S. territories, and DoDEA schools.

Range/Average: N.A.

Activity: N.A.

HQ: Director, Office of the Secretary of Defense, DoD, Bldg. 322, Picatinny Arsenal, NJ 07806. Phone: (973) 724-8115.

Internet: N.A. (Note: no field offices for this program.)

12.579   LANGUAGE TRAINING CENTER

Assistance: project grants (100 percent/1 year).

Purposes: pursuant to the National Defense Authorization Act of 2010, to accelerate the development of foundational or higher-level expertise in critical and strategic languages and regional studies for DOD personnel (both military and civilian) by leveraging U.S. institutions of higher education to meet the existing and demonstrated training needs of DOD units, offices, or agencies.

Eligible applicants/beneficiaries: accredited U.S. IHEs.

Range: $150,000 to $2,000,000. **Average:** N.A.

Activity: N.A.

HQ: Director, 1101 Wilson Blvd, Suite 1210, Arlington, VA 22209. Phone: (571) 256-0716; FAX: (703) 588-5667.

Internet: N.A. (Note: no field offices for this program.)

12.598 CENTERS FOR ACADEMIC EXCELLENCE

Assistance: project grants (100 percent/1 year4 option years).

Purposes: pursuant to the National Security Act, to enhance the recruitment and retention of an ethnically and culturally diverse intelligence community workforce with capabilities critical to the national security interests of the United States. Uses include Curriculum or program development, Faculty Development, Laboratory equipment or improvements, Faculty and student research, Pre-collegiate outreach, and Language and cultural studies including foreign travel to attain same.

Eligible applicants: public nonprofit institutions/organizations.

Eligible beneficiaries: education professionals, student/trainees, graduate Students, scientist/researchers.

Range: $100,000 to $600,000. **Average:** N.A.

Activity: N.A.

HQ: Director, Defense Intelligence Agency, HCL5E, 200 MacDill Blvd. Joint Base Bolling Anacostia, Washington, DC 20340. Phone: (202) 231-6041; FAX: (202) 231-4172.

Internet: N.A. (Note: no field offices for this program.)

12.600 DEPARTMENT OF DEFENSE COMMUNITY INVESTMENT

Assistance: cooperative agreements; dissemination of technical information; project grants.

Purposes: to provide special assistance directed by the Department of Defense and/or statute. Uses may include, or be restricted to, construction, planning, technical assistance or other forms of financial assistance, and program restrictions may include matching share requirements or limit eligibility to certain types of applicants.

Eligible applicants/beneficiaries: 35 IHEs selected by the CDC as Prevention Research Centers (PRCs).

Range: $1,000,000 to $40,000,000. **Average:** $17,000,000.

Activity: N.A.

HQ: Program Director, Office of Economic Adjustment, DOD, 2231 Crystal Dr., Suite 520, Arlington, VA 22202-3711. Phone: (703) 697-2130; FAX: (703) 607-0170.

Internet: www.oea.gov.

12.604 COMMUNITY ECONOMIC ADJUSTMENT ASSISTANCE FOR REDUCTIONS IN DEFENSE SPENDING

Assistance: cooperative agreements; dissemination of technical information; project grants (75 to 90 percent).

Purposes: to provide technical and financial assistance to states and local governments to: assess the impact of a Defense spending reduction, operate and maintain a community-based organization to represent an impacted area and its workers, businesses, and communities; prepare cost effective strategies and action plans for sustainable economic recovery; conduct research and/or carry out a community adjustment and economic diversification program.

Eligible applicants/beneficiaries: 35 IHEs selected by the CDC as Prevention Research Centers (PRCs).

Range: $300,000 to $400,000. **Average:** N.A.

Activity: N.A.

HQ: Program Director, Office of Economic Adjustment, DOD, 2231 Crystal Dr., Suite 520, Arlington, VA 22202-3711. Phone: (703) 697-2130; FAX: (703) 607-0170.

Internet: www.oea.gov.

12.607 COMMUNITY ECONOMIC ADJUSTMENT ASSISTANCE FOR ESTABLISHMENT, EXPANSION, REALIGNMENT, OR CLOSURE OF A MILITARY INSTALLATION

Assistance: project grants (75 percent).

Purposes: for community economic adjustment planning activities in coordination with communities, concerning military installation closures or realignment. Funds may be used for staffing, operating and administrative costs, studies.

Eligible applicants/beneficiaries: in DOD-approved areas—local governments or states on their behalf; regional organizations; tribes, DC, PR, Guam.

Range: $60,000 to $1,612,367. **Average:** $528,915.

Activity: N.A.

HQ: Program Director, Office of Economic Adjustment, DOD, 2231 Crystal Dr., Suite 520, Arlington, VA 22202-3711. Phone: (703) 697-2130; FAX: (703) 607-0170.

Internet: www.oea.gov.

12.610 COMMUNITY ECONOMIC ADJUSTMENT ASSISTANCE FOR COMPATIBLE USE AND JOINT LAND USE STUDIES

Assistance: project grants (75 percent).

Purposes: pursuant to the Defense Authorization Act, to prepare joint military/community comprehensive land use plans concerning public or private land development around military installation, to assure that land uses are compatible with both military operations and plans of nonmilitary jurisdictions; in certain cases, to carry out the recommendations of such a study.

Eligible applicants/beneficiaries: in DOD-approved areas—local governments or states on their behalf; regional organizations; tribes, DC, PR, Guam.

Range: $50,000 to $750,000. **Average:** $250,000.

Activity: anticipate funding 24 new studies in FY 2015.

HQ: Program Director, Office of Economic Adjustment, DOD, 2231 Crystal Dr., Suite 520, Arlington, VA 22202-3711. Phone: (703) 697-2130; FAX: (703) 607-0170.

Internet: www.oea.gov.

12.611 COMMUNITY ECONOMIC ADJUSTMENT ASSISTANCE FOR REDUCTIONS IN DEFENSE INDUSTRY EMPLOYMENT

Assistance: project grants (75 percent).

Purposes: for communities to undertake economic adjustment planning activities to respond to major reductions in defense industry employment resulting from the cancellation, termination, or failure to proceed with DOD spending under a previously approved program. Funds may be used for planning expenses including staffing, operating and administrative costs, studies.

Eligible applicants/beneficiaries: states on behalf of local governments, local governments, tribes, DC, PR, Guam—if the spending reduction involves the loss of at least: 2,500 full-time contractor employee jobs in a metropolitan statistical area; or1,000 jobs outside a metropolitan statistical area; or one percent of the total number of jobs in that area.

Range: $500,000 to $1,500,000. **Average:** $500,000.

Activity: N.A.

HQ: Program Director, Office of Economic Adjustment, DOD, 2231 Crystal Dr., Suite 520, Arlington, VA 22202-3711. Phone: (703) 697-2130; FAX: (703) 607-0170.

Internet: www.oea.gov.

12.614 COMMUNITY ECONOMIC ADJUSTMENT ASSISTANCE FOR ADVANCE PLANNING AND ECONOMIC DIVERSIFICATION

Assistance: project grants (90 percent).

Purposes: for community economic adjustment planning activities to lessen dependence on military base-related defense spending; to prepare strategies and schematic plans for the potential reuse of redevelopment of active bases.

Eligible applicants/beneficiaries: states; local governments or states on their behalf; regional governmental organizations.

Range: $1,000,000 to $4,000,000. **Average:** $2,000,000.

Activity: N.A.

HQ: Program Director, Office of Economic Adjustment, DOD, 2231 Crystal Dr., Suite 520, Arlington, VA 22202-3711. Phone: (703) 697-2130; FAX: (703) 607-0170.

Internet: www.oea.gov.

12.615   RESEARCH AND TECHNICAL ASSISTANCE

Assistance: project grants (to 100 percent).

Purposes: pursuant to 10 U.S.C. Section 2391(c), or Executive Order 12788, as amended to conduct research and provide technical assistance related to community economic adjustment needs, including assisting state and local governments with planning and/or execution of community adjustments and economic diversification required by closure of military installations, reduced military spending, or cancellation of DoD contracts or major weapon system programs. Funding may not be used for direct hard- or soft-construction activities.

Eligible applicants/beneficiaries: any governmental or private entity.

Range: $300,000 to $1,000,000. **Average:** $600,000.

Activity: anticipate 2 cooperative agreements in FY 2015.

HQ: Program Director, Office of Economic Adjustment, DOD, 2231 Crystal Dr., Suite 520, Arlington, VA 22202-3711. Phone: (703) 697-2130; FAX: (703) 607-0170.

Internet: www.oea.gov.

12.630   BASIC, APPLIED, AND ADVANCED RESEARCH IN SCIENCE AND ENGINEERING

Assistance: project grants.

Purposes: for research in areas that cut across traditional academic disciplines, in mathematical, physical, engineering, environmental, life sciences, and other fields—with long-term potential for contributing to technology for DOD missions; for fellowships and research traineeships for graduate education.

Eligible applicants: private and public educational institutions.

Eligible beneficiaries: graduate and undergraduate students in science and engineering disciplines important to DOD.

Range: $50,000 to $3,000,000. **Average:** N.A.

Activity: N.A.

HQ: U.S. Army Research Office, 4300 S. Miami Blvd., Durham, NC 27703. Phone: (919) 549-4270.

Internet: www.aro.army.mil. (Note: no field offices for this program.)

12.631   SCIENCE, TECHNOLOGY, ENGINEERING AND MATHEMATICS (STEM) EDUCATIONAL PROGRAM: SCIENCE, MATHEMATICS AND RESEARCH FOR TRANSFORMATION (SMART) ("SMART Scholarship-for-Service Program")

Assistance: projects grants (100 percent/1 to 5 years).

Purposes: pursuant to SMART Defense Education Program, to increase: the intellectual capacity and proficiency of future scientists and engineers in disciplines critical to defense and the number of science, technology, engineering and mathematics (STEM) qualified individuals in the DoD workforce. Participants will be required to obtain and/or maintain a security clearance and upon completion of their degree, applicants will be expected to work full-time for the DoD.

Eligible applicants/beneficiaries: eligible undergraduate or graduate students enrolled in an eligible IHE, at least 18 years old and U.S. citizens who are majoring in a DoD-relevant STEM field.

Range: N.A. **Average:** $70,000.

Activity: N.A.

HQ: Director, SMART Program, 1 University Circle, Hermann Hall, Rm. 061, American Society for Engineering Education, 1818 N St., NW, Ste. 600, Washington, DC 20036-2479. Phone: (202) 331-3544.

Internet: smart.asee.org.

12.632   LEGACY RESOURCE MANAGEMENT PROGRAM

Assistance: cooperative agreements/project grants. (100 percent/to 5 years).

Purposes: pursuant to the National Defense Authorization Act for Fiscal Year 1991 and the National Defense Authorization Act for Fiscal Year 1997, to provide funding to help manage and sustain Department of Defense (DOD) land in the United States. The program is tasked with funding high priority national and regional natural and cultural resources projects that support military readiness; enhance conservation objectives; and help the DOD fulfill the guiding principles of stewardship, leadership, and partnership.

Eligible applicants/beneficiaries: federal, state, local, tribal, nonprofit, and for-profit institutions/organizations.

Range: $40,000 to $150,000. **Average:** N.A.

Activity: N.A.

HQ: Office of the Deputy Under Secretary of Defense, Installations and Environment, DOD, 4800 Mark Center Dr., Ste. 16G14, Alexandria, VA 22352. Phone: (571) 372-6905.

Internet: www.dodlegacy.org. (Note: no field offices for this program.)

12.700   DONATIONS/LOANS OF OBSOLETE DOD PROPERTY

Assistance: use of property, facilities, and equipment.

Purposes: to donate or lend obsolete combat material and other specified items for historical, ceremonial, or display purposes—including books, manuscripts, models, vessels. Recipients must pay packing and handling costs.

Eligible applicants/beneficiaries: veterans' organizations recognized by the Office of the Deputy Under Secretary of Defense (LIMDM); libraries, historical societies, educational institutions, and tax-exempt museums operated and maintained only for education purposes; municipalities, states, territories, and possessions.

Range/Average: N.A.

Activity: N.A.

HQ: appropriate military department, DOD, Pentagon, Washington, DC 20301.

Internet: www.usace.army.mil/business.html.

12.750   UNIFORMED SERVICES UNIVERSITY MEDICAL RESEARCH PROJECTS
("Uniformed Services University USU")

Assistance: projects grants (100 percent).

Purposes: Uniformed Services University (USU) enters into grant agreements on a sole-source basis with the Henry M. Jackson Foundation to carry out cooperative enterprises in medical research, medical consultation and medical education in order to prepare outstanding scientists and health care practitioners for careers in service to our nation.

Eligible applicants: Uniformed Services University in partnership with Henry M. Jackson Foundation.

Eligible beneficiaries: USU scientists/researchers.

Range: $50,000 to $80,000,000. **Average:** $1,500,000.

Activity: N.A.

HQ: Director, Uniformed Services University of the Health Sciences, DoD, 4301 Jones Bridge Rd., Bethesda, MD 20814. Phone: (301) 295-3861; FAX: (301) 295-9536.

Internet: www.usuhs.mil. (Note: no field offices for this program.)

12.800   AIR FORCE DEFENSE RESEARCH SCIENCES PROGRAM

Assistance: project grants (1-3 years).

Purposes: for research to maintain technological superiority in scientific areas relevant to Air Force needs; to prevent technology surprise to the nation and to create it for adversaries; to maintain a strong research infrastructure composed of Air Force laboratories, industry, and universities; to complement the national research effort. Projects may be in such areas as the aerospace, engineering, chemistry and materials, and life, environmental, mathematical, and computer sciences.

Eligible applicants/beneficiaries: private and public educational institutions; private and public nonprofit organizations; commercial concerns.

Range/Average: N.A.

Activity: N.A.

HQ: HQ-Air Force Materiel Command/PKT, DOD, 1060 Air Force Pentagon, Washington, DC 20330. Phone: (571) 256-2048.

Internet: ww3.safaq.hq.af.mil/contracting.

12.900   LANGUAGE GRANT PROGRAM

Assistance: project grants (100 percent).

Purposes: to foster foreign language training of Americans. Funded projects have included documentation of low density languages, foreign language reference works, and research in training methods and computer-assisted instruction technologies.

Eligible applicants/beneficiaries: employees of U.S. private or public IHEs and nonprofit organizations operated primarily for language training.

Range: $5,000 to $500,000. **Average:** N.A.

Activity: N.A.

HQ: Chief, Language Training, National Security Agency (ATTN: E41), DOD, Fort George Meade, MD 20755-6000. Phone: (410) 859-6087.

Internet: www.darpa.mil/cmo. (Note: no field offices for this program.)

12.901   MATHEMATICAL SCIENCES GRANTS PROGRAM

Assistance: project grants. (100 percent/to 2 years).

Purposes: pursuant to the National Security Act of 1959, to stimulate developments and promote careers in areas of mathematics identified with cryptography, including number theory, discrete mathematics, statistics, probability. Funds may support summer salary (one month maximum), professional travel, publishing costs, graduate or postgraduate student support, conferences.

Eligible applicants/beneficiaries: employees and graduate students at U.S. IHEs, that are U.S. citizens, permanent residents, or intending to apply for citizenship.

Range: research grants, $5,000 to $60,000; conferences, $5,000. to $195,000; undergraduates, $20,000 to $300,000. **Average:** research grants, $26,000; conferences, $32,000; undergraduates, $110,000.

Activity: N.A.

HQ: National Security Agency (ATTN: R51A), DOD, 9800 Savage Rd., Fort George Meade, MD 20755. Phone: (443) 479-7660.

Internet: www.nsa.gov. (Note: no field offices for this program.)

12.902   INFORMATION ASSURANCE SCHOLARSHIP PROGRAM ("INFORMATION SECURITY GRANTS")

Assistance: project grants. (100 percent/1-2 years).

Purposes: for research to design, build, and maintain secure computing systems involving unclassified information; to develop and train computer science graduates to be recruited by NSA. Project examples: "Multilevel Secure Distributed Systems Security;" "Computer Misuse and Anomaly Detection." Funds may support summer salary (two months maximum), professional travel, publishing costs, graduate and postdoctoral student support, conferences.

Eligible applicants/beneficiaries: employees and graduate students at U.S. IHEs, that are U.S. citizens, permanent residents, or intending to apply for citizenship.

Range: $40,000 to $312,000. **Average:** $67,000.

Activity: N.A.

HQ: Program Director, INFOSEC University Research Program, National Security Agency (ATTN: R23), DOD, 9840 O'Brien Rd., Fort George Meade, MD 20755-6000. Phone: (301) 688-0847; FAX: (301) 688-0255.

Internet: www.darpa.mil/cmo. (Note: no field offices for this program.)

12.910   RESEARCH AND TECHNOLOGY DEVELOPMENT

Assistance: project grants (50 percent/3-5 years).

Purposes: for basic and applied research and development in science and technology; for projects advancing the state of the art or resulting in fundamental changes in technology—in areas that may have military or dual-use applications. Funds may also support: symposia and conferences; programs encouraging careers in science, technology, and engineering, and an increase in the number of graduates from under-represented minority groups; university research instrumentation.

Eligible applicants/beneficiaries: grants—public and private educational institutions and nonprofit organizations. Cooperative agreements—educational institutions, nonprofit organizations, commercial firms.

Range: $100,000 to $100,000,000. **Average:** $1,150,000.

Activity: N.A.

HQ: Director, Contract Management Office (CMO), Defense Advanced Research Projects Agency, DOD, 3701 N. Fairfax Dr., Arlington, VA 22203. Phone: (703) 696-2399.

Internet: www.darpa.mil/cmo. (Note: no field offices for this program.)

DEPARTMENT OF HOUSING AND URBAN DEVELOPMENT

14.008 TRANSFORMATION INITIATIVE: CHOICE NEIGHBORHOODS DEMONSTRATION SMALL RESEARCH GRANT PROGRAM

Assistance: cooperative agreements (100 percent/to 3 years).

Purposes: pursuant to the Consolidated and Further Continuing Appropriations Act of 2012, to develop and implement small scale research projects that build upon the larger Choice Neighborhood Demonstration research project, solicit research ideas that are not already apparent to HUD, and to broaden the community of researchers working on Choice Neighborhoods. Proposals should identify research questions that will help to demonstrate the impacts of Choice Neighborhoods or to help improve the program.

Eligible applicants/beneficiaries: 35 IHEs selected by the CDC as Prevention Research Centers (PRCs).

Range: to $200,000. **Average:** N.A.

Activity: N.A.

HQ: Director, Office of Policy Development and Research, HUD, 451 7th St., SW, Rm. 8226, Washington, DC 20410. Phone: (202) 402-3852.

Internet: N.A.

14.103 INTEREST REDUCTION PAYMENTS—RENTAL AND COOPERATIVE HOUSING FOR LOWER INCOME FAMILIES
("Section 236 Cooperative Housing")

Assistance: direct payments/specified use; guaranteed/insured loans (loans, 40 years).

Purposes: pursuant to the National Housing Act (NHA) as amended, to subsidize interest costs for mortgages on rental or cooperative housing developed for the low- and moderate-income. Subsidies are paid directly to lenders during the term of the mortgage; payments are adjusted to equal the difference between market rate interest costs and as low as one percent, depending on the incomes of tenants who must pay at least 30 percent of their adjusted gross incomes toward rent. The program now is inactive except for commitments to existing projects; no new projects have been insured since 1992.

Eligible applicants: nonprofit, cooperative, builder-seller, investor-sponsor, and limited-distribution sponsors. Public bodies were ineligible.

Eligible beneficiaries: within certain locally determined income limits, families and individuals including the elderly or handicapped or those displaced by government action or natural disaster. Families with incomes exceeding eligibility for subsidies may occupy apartments, but with no benefit from subsidy payments.

Range/Average: N.A.

Activity: N.A.

HQ: Director, Office of Multifamily Housing Management, Housing-HUD, 451 7th St., SW, Washington, DC 20410. Phone: (202) 708-2495.

Internet: www.hud.gov/offices/hsg/mfh/progdesc/progdesc.cfm.

14.108   REHABILITATION MORTGAGE INSURANCE ("Section 203(k)")

Assistance: guaranteed/insured loans (30 years).

Purposes: pursuant to NHA as amended, to insure loans for rehabilitation, acquisition and rehabilitation, acquisition and relocation from another site, and rehabilitation, or rehabilitation and debt refinancing—for existing one- to four-unit residential buildings. Rehabilitation cost must be at least $5,000. Certain application fees must be paid by purchasers.

Eligible applicants/beneficiaries: individual purchasers.

Range/Average: N.A.

Activity: N.A.

HQ: Asset Management and Disposition Division, Housing-HUD, 451 7th St., SW, Washington, DC 20410. Phone: (800) 225-5342.

Internet: portal.hud.gov/hudportal/HUD?src=/program_offices/housing/sfh /203k/203kmenu. (Note: no field offices for this program.)

14.110   MANUFACTURED HOME LOAN INSURANCE—FINANCING PURCHASE OF MANUFACTURED HOMES AS PRINCIPAL RESIDENCES OF BORROWERS ("Title I Manufactured Homes")

Assistance: guaranteed/insured loans. (to 90 percent/15-25 years).

Purposes: pursuant to NHA as amended, to insure loans to manufactured home purchasers when the unit will be used as the principal residence. 5 percent down payments and fees must be provided by purchasers. Funding for this program includes **14.162.**

Eligible applicants/beneficiaries: anyone.

Range: to $69,678. **Average:** $47,146.

Activity: N.A.

HQ: Asset Management and Disposition Division, Housing-HUD, 451 7th St., SW, Washington, DC 20410. Phone: (800) 225-5342.

Internet: portal.hud.gov/hudportal/HUD?src=/program_offices/housing/sfh /title/manuf1414.117. (Note: no field offices for this program.)

14.117   MORTGAGE INSURANCE—HOMES ("Section 203(b)")

Assistance: guaranteed/insured loans (to 30 years).

Purposes: pursuant to NHA as amended, to insure loans to purchasers acquiring existing or newly constructed one- to four- unit housing. Mortgage indebtedness on existing housing owned by applicants may also be refinanced. Small down payments, certain closing costs, and other expenses must be covered by purchasers. Funding for this program includes **14.119**, **14.126**, **14.159**, **14.163**, **14.172**, and **14.175**.

Eligible applicants/beneficiaries: purchasers that will occupy insured units.

Range/Average: N.A.

Activity: N.A.

HQ: Asset Management and Disposition Division, Housing-HUD, 451 7th St., SW, Washington, DC 20410. Phone: (800) 225-5342.

Internet: portal.hud.gov/hudportal/HUD?src=/program_offices/housing/sfh /ins/sfh203b. (Note: no field offices for this program.)

14.119   MORTGAGE INSURANCE—HOMES FOR DISASTER VICTIMS ("Section 203(h)")

Assistance: guaranteed/insured loans. (100 percent/to 30-35 years).

Purposes: pursuant to NHA as amended, to insure loans to enable disaster victims to acquire new or reconstructed existing single- family housing. Certain fees must be paid by purchasers. Funding for this program is included in **14.117**.

Eligible applicants/beneficiaries: victims of major disasters that will occupy acquired housing as their principal residence.

Range/Average: N.A.

Activity: N.A.

HQ: Asset Management and Disposition Division, Housing-HUD, 451 7th St., SW, Washington, DC 20410. Phone: (800) 225-5342.

Internet: portal.hud.gov/hudportal/HUD?src=/program_offices/housing/sfh /ins/203h-dft. (Note: no field offices for this program.)

14.122   MORTGAGE INSURANCE—HOMES IN URBAN RENEWAL AREAS ("Section 220 Homes")

Assistance: guaranteed/insured loans (to 30-35 years).

Purposes: pursuant to the Housing Act of 1954, to insure loans for new, existing, or rehabilitated, owner-occupied one- to 11- unit housing acquired or rehabilitated in approved urban renewal or code enforcement areas. Small down payments and fees must be paid by purchasers. Funding for this program is included in **14.133**.

Eligible applicants/beneficiaries: all families.

Range/Average: N.A.

Activity: N.A.

HQ: none provided, see listing of field offices.

Internet: www.hud.gov.

14.123   MORTGAGE INSURANCE—HOUSING IN OLDER, DECLINING AREAS ("Section 223(e)")

Assistance: guaranteed/insured loans.

Purposes: pursuant to NHA as amended, for purchasers of existing, new, or rehabilitated single-family or multifamily housing in older declining areas where conditions are such that certain normal eligibility requirements for mortgage insurance cannot be met. HUD insures loans made under other programs (e.g., **14.135**); claims are paid from the Special Risk Insurance Fund. Small down payments and insurance fees may be required of beneficiaries. Funding for this program is included in **14.133**.

Eligible applicants: HUD-approved mortgagees.

Eligible beneficiaries: single-family houses—individuals or families. Multi-family sponsorship eligibility is determined by applicable program requirements.

Range/Average: N.A.

Activity: N.A.

HQ: Asset Management and Disposition Division, Housing-HUD, 451 7th St., SW, Washington, DC 20410. Phone: (800) 225-5342.

Internet: portal.hud.gov/hudportal/HUD?src=/program_offices/housing/sfh/ins/sfh203b. (Note: no field offices for this program.)

14.126   MORTGAGE INSURANCE—COOPERATIVE PROJECTS ("Section 213 Cooperatives")

Assistance: guaranteed/insured loans. (90-98 percent/to 40 years).

Purposes: pursuant to NHA as amended, Housing Acts of 1950 and 1956, and other acts, to insure loans for existing, new, or rehabilitated cooperative housing consisting of detached, semi- detached, row, walk-up, or elevator structures, with five units minimum. Certain fees must be paid by purchasers. Maximum mortgage term: "management-type" projects, 40 years; "sales-type," 35 years. Funding for this program is included in **14.117**.

Eligible applicants: nonprofit cooperatives, ownership housing corporations, or trusts that may sponsor projects directly, sell individual units to cooperative members, or purchase projects from investor-sponsors.

Eligible beneficiaries: members of cooperatives.

Range/Average: N.A.

Activity: N.A.

HQ: Office of Multifamily Development, Housing-HUD, 451 7th St. SW, Washington, DC 20410. Phone: (202) 402-2579.

Internet: www.hud.gov/offices/hsg/hsgmulti.cfm.

14.127 MORTGAGE INSURANCE—MANUFACTURED HOME PARKS ("Section 207 Manufactured Home Parks")

Assistance: guaranteed/insured loans. (90 percent/to 40 years).

Purposes: pursuant to NHA as amended, to insure loans for manufactured home park development, new or rehabilitated, with five or more spaces. Funding for this program is included in **14.135**.

Eligible applicants: investors, builders, developers, others.

Eligible beneficiaries: families or individuals owning manufactured houses and leasing spaces.

Range/Average: N.A.

Activity: N.A.

HQ: Office of Multifamily Development, Housing-HUD, 451 7th St. SW, Washington, DC 20410. Phone: (202) 402-2579.

Internet: www.hud.gov/offices/hsg/hsgmulti.cfm.

14.128 MORTGAGE INSURANCE—HOSPITALS ("Section 242 Hospitals")

Assistance: guaranteed/insured loans. (to 90 percent/to 25 years).

Purposes: pursuant to NHA as amended, to insure loans for acute care hospital construction, rehabilitation, or refinancing, including the costs of major movable equipment—including facilities designated as "Critical Access Hospitals."

Eligible applicants/beneficiaries: profit or nonprofit hospitals licensed or regulated by the state, municipality, or other political subdivision.

Range/Average: N.A.

Activity: N.A.

HQ: Office of Insured Health Care Facilities, Housing-HUD, 451 7th St., SW, Rm. 6264, Washington, DC 20410. Phone: (202) 402-2333.

Internet: www.fha.gov/healthcare. (Note: no field offices for this program.)

14.129 MORTGAGE INSURANCE—NURSING HOMES, INTERMEDIATE CARE FACILITIES, BOARD AND CARE HOMES AND ASSISTED LIVING FACILITIES ("Section 232 Nursing Homes")

Assistance: guaranteed/insured loans.

Purposes: pursuant to NHA and Housing Act of 1959 as amended, and Housing and Urban Development Act of 1969, to insure loans for the purchase, construction, rehabilitation, or refinancing of nursing homes providing skilled nursing care or intermediate care facilities accommodating 20 or more patients, or board and care homes and assisted living facilities with five or more accommodations or units, or a combination of the foregoing types of facilities. Loans also may cover the cost of fire safety equipment and major equipment.

Eligible applicants/beneficiaries: investors, builders, developers, public entities, nursing homes, and private nonprofit corporations or associations.

Range/Average: N.A.

Activity: N.A.

HQ: Office of Insured Health Care Facilities, Housing-HUD, 451 7th St., SW, Rm. 6264, Washington, DC 20410. Phone: (202) 402-2333.

Internet: www.hud.gov/healthcare. (Note: no field offices for this program.)

14.133 MORTGAGE INSURANCE—PURCHASE OF UNITS IN CONDOMINIUMS
("Section 203(b) Condominiums")

Assistance: guaranteed/insured loans (to 30-35 years).

Purposes: pursuant to NHA as amended, to insure loans to purchase new or existing individual units in condominium projects containing four or more dwellings. Units converted from rental to condominiums are insurable, provided: the conversion occurred more than one year prior to the application for insurance; mortgagor occupied the rental housing; conversion was sponsored by an approved tenants organization. Small down payments and fees must be paid by purchasers. Funding for this program includes **14.122**, **14.123**, **14.165**, **14.183**, and **14.184**.

Eligible applicants/beneficiaries: condominium purchasers.

Range/Average: N.A.

Activity: N.A.

HQ: Asset Management and Disposition Division, Housing-HUD, 451 7th St., SW, Washington, DC 20410. Phone: (800) 225-5342.

Internet: portal.hud.gov/hudportal/HUD?src=/program_offices/housing/sfh /condo. (Note: no field offices for this program.)

14.134 MORTGAGE INSURANCE—RENTAL HOUSING
("Section 207 Rentals")

Assistance: guaranteed/insured loans. (90 percent/to 40 years).

Purposes: pursuant to NHA as amended, to insure loans for the construction or rehabilitation of middle-income rental housing in detached, semi-detached, row, walk-up, or elevator structures, with five units minimum. Funding for this program is included in **14.135**.

Eligible applicants/beneficiaries: investors, builders, developers, others.

Range/Average: N.A.

Activity: N.A.

HQ: Office of Multifamily Development, Housing-HUD, 451 7th St. SW, Washington, DC 20410. Phone: (202) 402-2579.

Internet: www.hud.gov/offices/hsg/hsgmulti.cfm.

14.135 MORTGAGE INSURANCE—RENTAL AND COOPERATIVE HOUSING FOR MODERATE INCOME FAMILIES AND ELDERLY, MARKET INTEREST RATE
("(221(d)(3) and (4) Multifamily—Market Rate")

Assistance: guaranteed/insured loans. (90-100 percent/to 40 years).

Purposes: pursuant to NHA as amended, to insure loans to sponsors of new or rehabilitated market-rate rental or cooperative housing developed for moderate-income families, the elderly, and the handicapped, including for "single-room occupancy" (**14.184**). Units may be in detached, semi-detached, row, walk-up, or elevator structures containing five units minimum. Funding for this program includes **14.112, 14.127, 14.132, 14.134, 14.138,** and **14.139**.

Eligible applicants: public, profit-motivated, limited- distribution, nonprofit, cooperative, builder-seller, investor, and general sponsors.

Eligible beneficiaries: all households regardless of income.

Range/Average: N.A.

Activity: N.A.

HQ: Office of Multifamily Development, Housing-HUD, 451 7th St. SW, Washington, DC 20410. Phone: (202) 402-2579.

Internet: www.hud.gov/offices/hsg/hsgmulti.cfm.

14.138 MORTGAGE INSURANCE—RENTAL HOUSING FOR THE ELDERLY
("Section 207 Rental Housing—Elderly")

Assistance: guaranteed/insured loans. (90-100 percent/to 40 years).

Purposes: pursuant to NHA as amended, to insure loans for rental housing for elderly or handicapped persons—in new or rehabilitated detached, semi-detached, walk-up, or elevator structures with a minimum of five units. Funding for this program is included in **14.135**.

Eligible applicants/beneficiaries: private profit-motivated investors, nonprofit sponsors.

Range/Average: N.A.

Activity: N.A.

HQ: Office of Multifamily Development, Housing-HUD, 451 7th St. SW, Washington, DC 20410. Phone: (202) 402-2579.

Internet: www.hud.gov/offices/hsg/hsgmulti.cfm.

14.139 MORTGAGE INSURANCE—RENTAL HOUSING IN URBAN RENEWAL AREAS
("Section 220 Multifamily")

Assistance: guaranteed/insured loans. (90 percent/40 years).

Purposes: pursuant to NHA as amended, to insure loans for new or rehabilitated rental housing located in urban renewal, code enforcement, or other approved public program areas including disaster areas; loans may also cover existing properties rehabilitated by a local public agency. Projects must include a minimum of two units, and may involve detached, semi-detached, walk-up, or elevator structures. Funding for this program is included in **14.135**.

Eligible applicants: private profit entities, public bodies, others.

Eligible beneficiaries: all families.

Range/Average: N.A.

Activity: N.A.

HQ: Office of Multifamily Development, Housing-HUD, 451 7th St. SW, Washington, DC 20410. Phone: (202) 402-2579.

Internet: www.hud.gov/offices/hsg/hsgmulti.cfm.

14.142 PROPERTY IMPROVEMENT LOAN INSURANCE FOR IMPROVING ALL EXISTING STRUCTURES AND BUILDING OF NEW NONRESIDENTIAL STRUCTURES

Assistance: guaranteed/insured loans. (90 percent/20-30 years).

Purposes: pursuant to NHA as amended, to insure loans for property improvement for existing housing, including the cost of erecting new non-residential structures that substantially protect or improve the livability or utility of the properties.

Eligible applicants/beneficiaries: owners of properties to be improved; lessees with a lease extending at least six months beyond loan maturity; purchasers under a land installment contract.

Range/Average: N.A.

Activity: N.A.

HQ: Asset Management and Disposition Division, Housing-HUD, 451 7th St., SW, Washington, DC 20410. Phone: (800) 225-5342.

Internet: portal.hud.gov/hudportal/HUD?src=/program_offices/housing/sfh /title/ti_home. (Note: no field offices for this program.)

14.149 RENT SUPPLEMENTS—RENTAL HOUSING FOR LOWER INCOME FAMILIES
("Rent Supplement Program")

Assistance: direct payments/specified use (to 40 years).

Purposes: pursuant to the Housing and Urban Development Act of 1965, to subsidize rents paid by lower-income tenants of certain HUD-insured and other housing. Assistance covers the difference between the rent paid by the tenant and up to 70 percent of the market rent, with the tenant paying between 25 and 30 percent of monthly adjusted income. This program is inactive except for commitments to existing projects.

Eligible applicants: eligible sponsors included nonprofit, cooperative, builder-seller, investor-sponsor, and limited- distribution mortgagors.

Eligible beneficiaries: families with income within the limits for admission to Section 8 housing (see **14.856**). Families may continue in occupancy if 30 percent of adjusted monthly income exceeds market rents, but subsidy may be adjusted downward or eliminated.

Range/Average: N.A.

Activity: N.A.

HQ: Director, Office of Multifamily Housing Management, Housing-HUD, 451 7th St., SW, Washington, DC 20410. Phone: (202) 402-2614.

Internet: www.hud.gov/offices/hsg/mfh/progdesc/progdesc.cfm.

14.151 SUPPLEMENTAL LOAN INSURANCE—MULTIFAMILY RENTAL HOUSING
("Section 241(a)")

Assistance: guaranteed/insured loans. (90 percent/varying term).

Purposes: pursuant to NHA as amended, to insure loans for expansion or improvement of existing multifamily housing and health care facilities, including hospitals, group practice facilities, or nursing homes, already covered by HUD mortgage insurance—including energy conservation and purchase of major movable equipment for health facilities.

Eligible applicants/beneficiaries: owners of multifamily projects or facilities subject to a HUD-insured mortgage.

Range/Average: N.A.

Activity: N.A.

HQ: Office of Multifamily Development, Housing-HUD, 451 7th St. SW, Washington, DC 20410. Phone: (202) 402-2579.

Internet: www.hud.gov/offices/hsg/hsgmulti.cfm.

14.155 MORTGAGE INSURANCE FOR THE PURCHASE OR REFINANCING OF EXISTING MULTIFAMILY HOUSING PROJECTS
("Sections 223(f) and 207")

Assistance: guaranteed/insured loans. (85 percent/10-35 years).

Purposes: pursuant to NHA and Housing and Community Development Act of 1974 as amended, to insure loans for the purchase or refinancing existing rental multifamily housing not requiring substantial rehabilitation. The property must have five or more living units; three years must have elapsed from the later of completion of project construction or substantial rehabilitation, or beginning of occupancy to date of application for mortgage insurance; the remaining economic life must be long enough to permit at least a ten-year mortgage term.

Eligible applicants/beneficiaries: private or public mortgagors.

Range/Average: N.A.

Activity: N.A.

HQ: Office of Multifamily Development, Housing-HUD, 451 7th St. SW, Washington, DC 20410. Phone: (202) 402-2579.

Internet: www.hud.gov/offices/hsg/hsgmulti.cfm.

14.157 SUPPORTIVE HOUSING FOR THE ELDERLY
("Section 202")

Assistance: direct payments/specified use.

Purposes: pursuant to the Housing Act of 1959 as amended, Housing and Community Development Act of 1992, and American Homeownership and Economic Opportunity Act of 2000, for the acquisition, construction, or substantial rehabilitation of rental or cooperative housing with supportive services and related facilities (e.g., central dining) for the very low-income elderly. Capital advances are provided by HUD to meet development costs; these advances need not be repaid, provided the project is available to the very-low-income elderly for 40 years. HUD project rental assistance payments may cover the difference between per-unit operating cost and the rent amount paid by tenants, under five-year contracts with project sponsors. Funding for this program includes **14.191**, **14.314**, and **14.315**.

Eligible applicants/beneficiaries: private nonprofit organizations and consumer cooperatives. Also, profit-motivated limited partnerships may participate in projects with mixed financing.

Range/Average: N.A.

Activity: N.A.

HQ: Office of Housing Assistance and Grants Administration, Housing-HUD, 451 7th St., SW, Rm. 6152, Washington, DC 20410. Phone: (202) 708-3000.

Internet: portal.hud.gov/hudportal/HUD?src=/program_offices/housing/mfh/progdesc/eld202.

14.159 SECTION 245 GRADUATED PAYMENT MORTGAGE PROGRAM

Assistance: guaranteed/insured loans (30 years).

Purposes: pursuant to NHA, Housing and Community Development Acts of 1974 and 1979, and amendments, to insure loans for existing or new single-family housing, and condominiums financed with graduated payment mortgages—allowing smaller monthly payments initially, and with increased amounts over time as the borrower's income increases. Small down payments are required, and mortgagors must pay certain closing costs. Funding for this program is included in **14.117**.

Eligible applicants/beneficiaries: prospective owner-occupants.

Range/Average: N.A.

Activity: N.A.

HQ: Asset Management and Disposition Division, Housing-HUD, 451 7th St., SW, Washington, DC 20410. Phone: (800) 225-5342.

Internet: portal.hud.gov/hudportal/HUD?src=/hudprograms/gpm. (Note: no field offices for this program.)

14.162 MORTGAGE INSURANCE—COMBINATION AND MANUFACTURED HOME LOT LOANS
("Title I Manufactured Home Lot")

Assistance: guaranteed/insured loans. (90 percent/15-25 years).

Purposes: pursuant to NHA as amended, to insure loans to purchase manufactured homes and lots. The maximum term is 20 years for a single module and lot, 25 years for a double module, and 15 years for a lot only. Funding for this program is included in **14.110**.

Eligible applicants/beneficiaries: purchasers intending to use property as their principal place of residence.

Range: manufactured home on lot: to $92,904; developed lot only: to $23,226. **Average:** N.A.

Activity: N.A.

HQ: Asset Management and Disposition Division, Housing-HUD, 451 7th St., SW, Washington, DC 20410. Phone: (800) 225-5342.

Internet: portal.hud.gov/hudportal/HUD?src=/program_offices/housing/sfh /title/manuf146. (Note: no field offices for this program.)

14.163 MORTGAGE INSURANCE—SINGLE FAMILY COOPERATIVE HOUSING ("Section 203(n)")

Assistance: guaranteed/insured loans (to 30 years).

Purposes: pursuant to NHA as amended and the Emergency Home Purchase Assistance Act of 1974, to insure loans to purchase the Corporate Certificate and Occupancy Certificate for a unit in a HUD-insured cooperative housing project covered by a blanket mortgage, giving purchasers the right to occupy the unit. Funding for this program is included in **14.117.**

Eligible applicants/beneficiaries: potential owner-occupant mortgagors.

Range/Average: N.A.

Activity: N.A.

HQ: Asset Management and Disposition Division, Housing-HUD, 451 7th St., SW, Washington, DC 20410. Phone: (800) 225-5342.

Internet: portal.hud.gov/hudportal/HUD?src=/programdescription/203n. (Note: no field offices for this program.)

14.168 LAND SALES—CERTAIN SUBDIVIDED LAND ("Interstate Land Sales Registration Program")

Assistance: technical information; investigation of complaints.

Purposes: pursuant to the Interstate Land Sales Full Disclosure Act as amended, to provide consumer protection in subdivision lot sales through enforcement of fraud prohibitions and full disclosure requirements. The law requires developers that engage in interstate land sales consisting of 100 or more nonexempt lots to register with HUD; prospective purchasers must be given a property report with pertinent facts about the development and the developer. Anti-fraud provisions of the act apply to subdivisions of 25 lots or more. Affected land developers are required to submit a filing in compliance with registration requirements. Lot purchasers are entitled to certain rights and remedies.

Eligible applicants/beneficiaries: lot purchasers.

Range/Average: N.A.

Activity: N.A.

HQ: Office of RESPA and Interstate Land Sales, Housing-HUD, 451 7th St., SW, Rm. 9154, Washington, DC 20410. Phone: (202) 402-3006.

Internet: www.hud.gov/offices/hsg/ramh/ils/ilshome.cfm. (Note: no field offices for this program.)

14.169 HOUSING COUNSELING ASSISTANCE PROGRAM

Assistance: project grants.

Purposes: pursuant to the Housing and Urban Development Act of 1968 as amended, to provide counseling services to homeowners, homebuyers, and prospective tenants in HUD-assisted or -insured housing and other housing—toward the prevention and reduction of mortgage or rental delinquencies, defaults, and foreclosures.

Eligible applicants/beneficiaries: HUD-approved national, regional, multi-state, or state agencies.

Range/Average: N.A.

Activity: N.A.

HQ: Asset Management and Disposition Division, Housing-HUD, 451 7th St., SW, Washington, DC 20410. Phone: (800) 225-5342.

Internet: portal.hud.gov/hudportal/HUD?src=/program_offices/housing/sfh /hcc/hcc_home. (Note: no field offices for this program.)

14.171 MANUFACTURED HOME DISPUTE RESOLUTION

Assistance: technical information; investigation of complaints.

Purposes: pursuant to the National Manufactured Housing Construction and Safety Standards Act as amended, to provide consumer protection for manufactured homes purchasers and residents, by enforcing standards covering safety, quality, durability, and installation—through certifications, testing, in-plant inspections, design review, and investigations of complaints against manufacturers or dealers. Siting and other local activity are considered to be under state or local jurisdiction, and are not covered by the program; however, model siting standards are under development; in the interim such work must meet at least minimum standards established by HUD.

Eligible applicants/beneficiaries: purchasers of manufactured homes built since June 15, 1976.

Range/Average: N.A.

Activity: N.A.

HQ: Office Manufactured Housing Programs, Office of Regulatory Affairs and Manufactured Housing, Housing-HUD, 451 7th St., SW, Washington, DC 20410-8000. Phone: (202) 402-7112.

Internet: portal.hud.gov/hudportal/HUD?src=/program_offices/housing/rmr a/mhs/mhdrp. (Note: no field offices for this program.)

14.172 MORTGAGE INSURANCE—GROWING EQUITY MORTGAGES ("GEMs - Section 245(a)")

Assistance: guaranteed/insured loans (varying term).

Purposes: pursuant to NHA as amended, to insure loans to purchase existing, new, or refinanced single-family housing including condominiums, with growing equity mortgages providing for a rapid principal reduction and shorter mortgage terms, by gradually increasing monthly payments over a 10-year period. Small down payments are required, and mortgagors must pay certain closing costs. Funding for this program is included in **14.117**.

Eligible applicants/beneficiaries: prospective purchasers.

Range/Average: N.A.

Activity: N.A.

HQ: Asset Management and Disposition Division, Housing-HUD, 451 7th St., SW, Washington, DC 20410. Phone: (800) 225-5342.

Internet: portal.hud.gov/hudportal/HUD?src=/programdescription/245a. (Note: no field offices for this program.)

14.175 ADJUSTABLE RATE MORTGAGES ("ARMS")

Assistance: guaranteed/insured loans (30 years).

Purposes: pursuant to NHA as amended and Housing and Urban-Rural Recovery Act of 1983, to insure loans with adjustable rate mortgages financing the purchase of new, existing, or refinanced one- to four-family housing including condominiums—offering lenders more assurance of long-term profitability than fixed rate mortgages. Interest rates may not increase more than one percent per year or five percent over the mortgage term. Small down payments are required, and mortgagors must pay certain closing costs. Funding for this program is included in **14.117**.

Eligible applicants/beneficiaries: prospective owner-occupants.

Range/Average: N.A.

Activity: N.A.

HQ: Asset Management and Disposition Division, Housing-HUD, 451 7th St., SW, Washington, DC 20410. Phone: (800) 225-5342.

Internet: portal.hud.gov/hudportal/HUD?src=/program_offices/housing/sfh /ins/203armt. (Note: no field offices for this program.)

14.181 SUPPORTIVE HOUSING FOR PERSONS WITH DISABILITIES ("Section 811")

Assistance: direct payments/specified use (100 percent).

Purposes: pursuant to the National Affordable Housing Act and American Homeownership and Economic Opportunity Act of 2000, to provide capital advances to construct, acquire, or rehabilitate supportive housing for persons with disabilities, including group homes, for 40-year projects. Project Rental Assistance Contract payments may be obtained for 5-year periods (renewable), and may cover operating costs not met from project income; payments cover the difference between approved operating costs and tenant rental contributions of 30 percent of adjusted income.

Eligible applicants: 501(c)(3) nonprofit corporations. Also, profit-motivated limited dividend organizations may participate in projects with mixed financing.

Eligible beneficiaries: very-low-income physically or developmentally disabled or chronically mentally ill persons, age 18 or older.

Range/Average: N.A.

Activity: N.A.

HQ: Office of Housing Assistance and Grants Administration, Housing-HUD, 451 7th St., SW, Rm. 6142, Washington, DC 20410. Phone: (202) 708-3000.

Internet: portal.hud.gov/hudportal/HUD?src=/program_offices/housing/mfh /progdesc/disab811.

14.183 HOME EQUITY CONVERSION MORTGAGES ("Section 255")

Assistance: guaranteed/insured loans.

Purposes: pursuant to NHA as amended and Housing and Community Development Act of 1987, to insure "reverse mortgage" loans obtained by elderly homeowners to convert equity in their homes to monthly streams of income or (except in Texas) lines of credit. Eligible properties are one- to four-unit dwellings including condominiums and manufactured homes. Borrowers must pay loan origination charges and other fees. Funding for this program is included in **14.133**.

Eligible applicants/beneficiaries: homeowners at least age 62.

Range/Average: N.A.

Activity: N.A.

HQ: Asset Management and Disposition Division, Housing-HUD, 451 7th St., SW, Washington, DC 20410. Phone: (800) 225-5342.

Internet: portal.hud.gov/hudportal/HUD?src=/program_offices/housing/sfh /hecm/hecmhome. (Note: no field offices for this program.)

14.184 MORTGAGE INSURANCE FOR SINGLE ROOM OCCUPANCY (SRO) PROJECTS ("Section 221(d) Single Room Occupancy")

Assistance: guaranteed/insured loans. (90-100 percent/to 40 years).

Purposes: pursuant to NHA as amended, to insure loans for the construction or substantial rehabilitation of multifamily properties with at least five single-room occupancy residential units—intended to provide housing for tenants with income insufficient to enable them to rent a standard apartment. Projects may have no more than 10 percent of total gross floor space dedicated to commercial use (20 percent for substantial rehabilitation). Funding for this program is included in **14.133**.

Eligible applicants: nonprofit entities; builder-sellers with a nonprofit purchaser; limited-distribution, private profit, or public sponsors.

Eligible beneficiaries: anyone, subject to normal tenant selection procedures.

Range/Average: N.A.

Activity: N.A.

HQ: Office of Multifamily Development, Housing-HUD, 451 7th St. SW, Washington, DC 20410. Phone: (202) 402-2579.

Internet: www.hud.gov/offices/hsg/hsgmulti.cfm.

14.188 HOUSING FINANCE AGENCIES (HFA) RISK SHARING ("Section 542(c) Risk Sharing Program")

Assistance: guaranteed/insured loans.

Purposes: pursuant to the Housing and Community Development Act of 1992 as amended, to provide HUD mortgage insurance to state and local housing finance agencies on affordable multifamily projects for which they share in the insurance risk. The program provides for HUD and HFAs to share between 10 and 90 percent of the financial risk.

Eligible applicants: state and local housing finance agencies.

Eligible beneficiaries: investors, builders, developers, public entities, private nonprofit corporations or associations. Applications are submitted to qualified housing finance agencies.

Range/Average: N.A.

Activity: N.A.

HQ: Office of Multifamily Development, Housing-HUD, 451 7th St. SW, Washington, DC 20410. Phone: (202) 402-2579.

Internet: www.hud.gov/offices/hsg/mfh/progdesc/progdesc.cfm.

14.189   QUALIFIED PARTICIPATING ENTITIES (QPE) RISK SHARING ("Section 542(b) Risk Sharing Program")

Assistance: guaranteed/insured loans (50 percent).

Purposes: pursuant to the Housing and Community Development Act of 1992 as amended, for projects in which HUD provides reinsurance on multifamily housing projects whose loans covering affordable housing are originated, underwritten, serviced, and disposed of by QPEs or approved lenders. In the event of default, the QPE will pay all costs associated with loan disposition, 50 percent of which may be reimbursed by HUD.

Eligible applicants/beneficiaries: HUD-approved lenders and QPEs. Investors, builders, developers, public entities, private nonprofit corporations or associations submit applications to the lender.

Range/Average: N.A.

Activity: N.A.

HQ: Office of Multifamily Development, Housing-HUD, 451 7th St. SW, Washington, DC 20410. Phone: (202) 402-2579.

Internet: www.hud.gov/offices/hsg/hsgmulti.cfm.

14.191   MULTIFAMILY HOUSING SERVICE COORDINATORS

Assistance: project grants (100 percent).

Purposes: pursuant to the National Affordable Housing Act and Housing and Community Development Act of 1992 as amended and American Homeownership and Economic Opportunity Act of 2000, to hire multifamily housing service coordinators—to link elderly, especially the frail and disabled, or disabled non- elderly, assisted-housing residents to community supportive or medical services; to prevent premature and unnecessary institutionalization; and, to assess individual service needs, determine eligibility for public services, and make resource allocation decisions enabling residents to remain in the community longer. Coordinators are social service staff persons providing such services as: formal case management; resident and management education; monitoring of services;

and, resident advocacy. Project funds may not be used to pay coordinators to serve as recreational or activities director, nor to provide supportive services directly or perform administrative duties. Funding for this program is included in **14.157**.

Eligible applicants: owners of HUD-assisted housing projects, including in rural areas, that are under management and current in mortgage payments. Congregate Housing Service Programs, Section 202 Capital Advance, or Section 811 projects are ineligible.

Eligible beneficiaries: residents of approved projects, at least age 62 and frail (unable to perform at least three activities of daily living), disabled, or *at risk* (i.e., deficient in one or two activities of daily living).

Range: $88,825 to $402,196. **Average:** $171,064.

Activity: N.A.

HQ: Office of Housing Assistance and Grants Administration, Housing-HUD, 451 7th St., SW, Rm. 6146, Washington, DC 20410. Phone: (202) 708-3000.

Internet: portal.hud.gov/hudportal/HUD?src=/program_offices/housing/mfh /scp/scphome.

14.195   SECTION 8 HOUSING ASSISTANCE PAYMENTS PROGRAM ("Project-based Section 8")

Assistance: direct payments/specified use (to 20 years).

Purposes: pursuant to the U.S. Housing Act of 1937, to reduce claims on HUD's insurance fund by aiding insured or Secretary- held projects mortgages with immediate or potentially serious financial difficulties. HUD makes payments to owners of assisted housing on behalf of tenants, representing the difference between the contract and tenant rent. Assistance is available only on a renewable basis; current projects receive a one-year renewal upon expiration of a Section 8 contract.

Eligible applicants/beneficiaries: only Section 8 project owners of record, with an expiring Section 8 contract. No funding is available to new applicants.

Range/Average: N.A.

Activity: N.A.

HQ: Office of Housing Assistance and Grants Administration, Housing-HUD, 451 7th St., SW, Washington, DC 20410. Phone: (202) 708-3000.

Internet: portal.hud.gov/hudportal/HUD?src=/program_offices/housing/mfh /mfhsec8.

14.198   GOOD NEIGHBOR NEXT DOOR SALES PROGRAM

Assistance: sale, exchange, donation of property and goods.

Purposes: to improve security in HUD-designated revitalization areas, by providing 50 percent discounts to law enforcement officers purchasing homes in those neighborhoods. Officers must agree to occupy the homes as their sole residence for at least 3 years; if they do not, a proportion of the discount must be returned to HUD. Available homes are listed on the Internet; purchasers are selected by lottery when more than one officer indicates an interest in a property.

Eligible applicants/beneficiaries: federal, state, county, municipal, and academic institution law enforcement officers possessing general arrest powers.

Range/Average: N.A.

Activity: N.A.

HQ: Asset Management and Disposition Division, Housing-HUD, 451 7th St., SW, Washington, DC 20410. Phone: (800) 225-5342.

Internet: portal.hud.gov/hudportal/HUD?src=/program_offices/housing/sfh /reo/goodn/gnndabot.

14.218 COMMUNITY DEVELOPMENT BLOCK GRANTS—ENTITLEMENT GRANTS (CDBG)

Assistance: formula grants (100 percent).

Purposes: pursuant to the Housing and Community Development Act of 1974 as amended, for a broad range of activities designed to result in decent housing and suitable living environments, neighborhood revitalization, economic development, and improved community facilities and services. Program policy requires that the "principal benefit" of projects be to low- and moderate-income persons—i.e., at least 70 percent of the grant allocation. Projects may be operated by the locality or through subgrantees, including public or nonprofit agencies, neighborhood-based organizations, local development corporations, small business investment companies, and other groups. Permitted uses of funds include: virtually any aspect of residential or nonresidential rehabilitation, including historic preservation and energy conservation; energy development; grants or loans to businesses; revolving loan funds for rehabilitation or for economic development purposes; real property acquisition; relocation of households or businesses; demolition; redevelopment site clearance and preparation for re-use; improvement or installation of public works; certain public service programs; housing code enforcement; meeting urgent community needs that present an immediate threat to health or welfare; city planning and related studies. Ineligible uses include: facilities for the general conduct of government; community-wide facilities; new housing construction; housing subsidies paid directly to occupants; income maintenance payments. Cities must: include citizen participation in program planning; have an approved comprehensive housing assistance plan. For "entitlement" communities CDBG grant amounts are based on a statutory formula.

Eligible applicants: cities in metropolitan areas with populations over 50,000; qualified urban counties of at least 200,000 (excluding the population in entitlement cities); and cities with populations under 50,000 that are central cities in Metropolitan Statistical Areas. NOTE: small cities obtain CDBG funds under **14.228**.

Eligible beneficiaries: low- and moderate-income residents, including those benefiting from projects sponsored by CDBG subgrantees or others awarded CDBG funds.

Range: $72,231 to $178,008,585. **Average:** $2,956,494.

Activity: N.A.

HQ: Entitlement Communities Division, Office of Block Grant Assistance, CPD-HUD, 451 7th St., SW, Rm. 7282, Washington, DC 20410. Phone: (202) 402-3416.

Internet: www.hud.gov/offices/cpd/index.cfm.

14.225 COMMUNITY DEVELOPMENT BLOCK GRANTS—SPECIAL PURPOSE GRANTS—INSULAR AREAS ("Insular CDBG")

Assistance: project grants (formula based, 100 percent).

Purposes: pursuant to the Housing and Community Development Act of 1974 as amended, to provide community development assistance to the Pacific Islands of American Samoa, Guam, the Northern Marianas and the Virgin Islands in the Caribbean. Basically the same as for program **14.218**.

Eligible applicants/beneficiaries: Samoa, Guam, Northern Marianas, VI.

Range/Average: N.A.

Activity: N.A.

HQ: Office of Block Grant Assistance, CPD-HUD, 451 7th St., SW, Rm. 7184, Washington, DC 20410. Phone: (202) 402-3461.

Internet: www.hudexchange.info/cdbg-insular-areas.

14.228 COMMUNITY DEVELOPMENT BLOCK GRANTS—STATE'S PROGRAM AND NON-ENTITLEMENT GRANTS IN HAWAII ("State CDBG")

Assistance: formula grants (100 percent).

Purposes: pursuant to the Housing and Community Development Act of 1974 as amended, to provide funding to states—to be granted, in turn, to small cities for uses permitted in program **14.218**.

Eligible applicants: forty-nine state governments and the Commonwealth of Puerto Rico receive funds from HUD under this program. The state of Hawaii does not participate and HUD allocates the state's share of funds to the three Hawaii non-entitled counties. Funds are allocated to each state based on a statutory formula and states must distribute the funds to units of general local government in nonentitlement areas.

Eligible beneficiaries: residents with low- and moderate-income, generally defined as 80 percent of state, county or metropolitan-area median income, adjusted for family size.

Range: $1,923,531 to $59,833,115. **Average:** $17,632,984.

Activity: N.A.

HQ: Office of Block Grant Assistance, CPD-HUD, 451 7th St., SW, Rm. 7184, Washington, DC 20410. Phone: (202) 402-3461.

Internet: www.hudexchange.info/cdbg-state.

14.231 EMERGENCY SHELTER GRANTS PROGRAM

Assistance: formula grants. (50 percent/to 2 years).

Purposes: pursuant to the McKinney-Vento Homeless Assistance Act of 1987 (MVHAA) as amended, to improve existing or to develop additional emergency shelters, transitional housing, and homeless assistance programs. Funds may be used for: renovation, major rehabilitation, or conversion of existing buildings; essential social services; certain maintenance and operating costs; activities to prevent homelessness.

Eligible applicants/beneficiaries: states, metropolitan cities, urban counties, territories. Other local government units and nonprofit organizations apply to states for funds rather than to HUD. Grantees may, in turn, subcontract with nonprofit entities to conduct program activities.

Range: $74,478 to $13,600,063. **Average:** N.A.

Activity: N.A.

HQ: Office of Special Needs Assistance Programs, CPD-HUD, 451 7th St., SW, Rm. 7262, Washington, DC 20410. Phone: (202) 402-4482.

Internet: www.hudexchange.info.

14.239 HOME INVESTMENT PARTNERSHIPS PROGRAM ("HOME Program")

Assistance: formula grants. (67-75 percent/2-5 years).

Purposes: pursuant to the National Affordable Housing Act as amended, to support partnerships among all levels of government and the private sector, including profit and nonprofit organizations, in the production and operation of affordable housing, particularly rental housing for low- and very-low-income families. Funds may be used for: planning; development of model projects; technical assistance; housing rehabilitation; tenant-based rental assistance; assistance to homebuyers; new construction of housing; site acquisition and improvements including improved energy efficiency, demolition, relocation. As of FY 03, the American Dream Downpayment Initiative (ADDI) may provide funds for low-income families to make down payments on or to rehabilitate suitable housing. Ineligible funds uses include: public housing modernization; matching funds for other federal programs; rental housing operating subsidies; activities under the Low Income Housing Preservation Act, except for priority purchasers.

Eligible applicants: formula allocations—states, cities, urban counties, or consortia of general local government units; Insular Areas. Technical Assistance—nonprofit and profit firms; public purpose organizations; nonprofit national and regional HOME organizations; community development organizations (CHDOs).

Eligible beneficiaries: rental housing—90 percent of funds for families with incomes at 60 percent of area median, and the remainder for families below 80 percent. Homeownership assistance—families with incomes below 80 percent of the area median.

Range: $123,660 to $58,228,225. **Average:** $1,575,176.

Activity: anticipate completing 38,665 units and providing rental assistance for 8,813 tenants in FY 2016.

HQ: Director, Office of Affordable Housing Programs, CPD-HUD, 451 7th St., SW, Rm. 7164, Washington, DC 20410. Phone: (202) 708-2685.

Internet: www.hud.gov/homeprogram.

14.241   HOUSING OPPORTUNITIES FOR PERSONS WITH AIDS (HOPWA)

Assistance: formula grants; project grants (to 3 years).

Purposes: pursuant to the AIDS Housing Opportunity Act, to develop long-term comprehensive strategies to meet the housing needs of low-income persons with AIDS or related diseases, and their families. Eligible funds uses include: resource identification to establish, coordinate, and develop housing assistance; information services including counseling and referral; acquisition, rehabilitation, conversion, lease, and repair of facilities to provide housing and services; new construction of single-room occupancy and community residences; project- or tenant-based rental assistance including for shared housing arrangements; short-term rent, mortgage, and utility payments to prevent the homelessness of a tenant or mortgagor; supportive services including health, mental health, assessment, permanent housing placement, alcohol and drug abuse treatment and counseling, nutritional services, day care, intensive care; housing operating costs; training; technical assistance. Resident rent payments are required.

Eligible applicants/beneficiaries: entitlement (formula) grants—states and eligible metropolitan areas with the largest number of AIDS cases; communities in metropolitan areas must designate one unit of local government to serve as the applicant/grantee for the area. Competitive project grants—states, local governments, and nonprofit organizations for projects of national significance; states and localities not qualifying for formula grants.

Range: N.A. **Average:** $2,167,883 for formula grants; $1,170,818 for competitive grants.

Activity: estimated 52,600 low-income households will receive housing assistance in FY 2015.

HQ: Director, Office of HIV/AIDS Housing, CPD-HUD, 451 7th St., SW, Rm. 7248, Washington, D.C. 20410. Phone: (202) 402-1934.

Internet: www.hudexchange.info/programs/hopwa.

14.247   SELF-HELP HOMEOWNERSHIP OPPORTUNITY PROGRAM (SHOP)

Assistance: project grants (2-3 years).

Purposes: pursuant to the Housing Opportunity Extension Act of 1996 as amended, for innovative projects enabling low-income families to become homeowners under the self-help concept, by contributing "sweat equity" toward the construction of dwellings. Program funds may be used for land acquisition and infrastructure improvements, with a maximum of 20 percent of grants for administrative costs.

Eligible applicants/beneficiaries: nonprofit national or regional organizations or consortia.

Range: $562,500 to $6,211,368. **Average:** $1,693,342.

Activity: anticipate 533 homeownership units in FY 2016.

HQ: Office of Affordable Housing Programs, CPD-HUD, 451 7th St., SW, Washington, DC 20410. Phone: (202) 708-1744.

Internet: www.hud.gov/offices/cpd/affordablehousing/programs/shop/index .cfm. (Note: no field offices for this program.)

14.248   COMMUNITY DEVELOPMENT BLOCK GRANTS—SECTION 108 LOAN GUARANTEES ("Section 108")

Assistance: guaranteed/insured loans (to 20 years).

Purposes: pursuant to the Housing and Community Development Act of 1974 as amended, to provide communities with a source of financing for economic development, housing rehabilitation, public facilities, and large-scale physical development projects—provided the "principal benefit" of such projects: is to low- or moderate-income persons; aids in the elimination or prevention of slums and blight; or, meets urgent community needs. Maximum approvable loan amounts generally are five times the latest CDBG amount received by the public entity, minus any outstanding Section 108 commitment or principal balances.

Eligible applicants/beneficiaries: CDBG recipients. The public entity may be the borrower, or it may designate a public agency.

Range: $575,000 to $50,000,000. **Average:** N.A.

Activity: N.A.

HQ: Financial Management Division, CPD-HUD, 451 7th St., SW, Rm. 7180, Washington, DC 20410. Phone: (202) 708-1871.

Internet: portal.hud.gov/hudportal/HUD?src=/program_offices/comm_plan ning/communitydevelopment/programs/108.

14.252   SECTION 4 CAPACITY BUILDING FOR COMMUNITY DEVELOPMENT AND AFFORDABLE HOUSING

Assistance: project grants. (25 percent/to 5 years).

Purposes: pursuant to Section 4, HUD Demonstration Act of 1993, as amended, to improve the capacity of community organizations to develop affordable housing and other community development projects. Grants may used to assist community development corporations (CDCs) and community housing development organizations (CHDOs) to carry out community development and affordable housing activities that benefit low-income families and persons, including: training, education, support, advice, loans, grants, development assistance, predevelopment assistance, or other financial assistance.

Eligible applicants: per authorizing legislation, only four organizations are eligible: Enterprise Community Partners, Inc. (formerly The Enterprise Foundation), Local Initiatives Support Corporation, Habitat for Humanity, and YouthBuild USA.

Eligible beneficiaries: CDCs, CHDOs and other nonprofit community based organizations that develop affordable housing and community development projects and programs.

Range: $4,400,000 to $14,500,000. **Average:** N.A.

Activity: N.A.

HQ: Office of Policy Development and Coordination, Community Planning and Development, HUD, 451 7th St., SW, Rm. 7143, Washington, DC 20410. Phone: (202) 402-4885.

Internet: www.onecpd.info/section-4-capacity-building. (Note: no field offices for this program.)

14.259 COMMUNITY COMPASS TECHNICAL ASSISTANCE AND CAPACITY BUILDING

Assistance: cooperative agreements (100 percent/3 years).

Purposes: pursuant to the HUD Appropriations Act of 2010, to provide grantees with a single cross-program, results-focused demand-response delivery system (OneCPD) driven by local needs and administered directly from HUD headquarters. HUD will identify technical assistance and capacity building needs and prioritize them based on departmental, programmatic and jurisdictional priorities and is solely responsible for determining the entities to be assisted, the location, and the nature of the assistance to be provided.

Eligible applicants/beneficiaries: 35 IHEs selected by the CDC as Prevention Research Centers (PRCs).

Range: $500,000 to $51,000,000. **Average:** $3,000,000.

Activity: N.A.

HQ: Program Director, Office of Community Planning and Development, HUD, 451 7th St., SW, Washington, DC 20410. Phone: (202) 402-4496.

Internet: www.hud.gov/offices/cpd/affordablehousing/programs/home.

14.261 HOMELESS MANAGEMENT INFORMATION SYSTEMS TECHNICAL ASSISTANCE (HMIS-TA)

Assistance: cooperative agreements (100 percent/2 to 3 years).

Purposes: pursuant to the Omnibus Appropriations Act, to provide technical assistance for homeless programs in the Office of Special Needs Assistance Programs (SNAPS). An organization may not provide assistance to itself. An organization may not provide assistance to another organization with which it contracts or sub-awards funds to carry out activities under the TA award.

Eligible applicants: states, units of local government, public housing authorities and public, private and for-profit organizations, including IHEs and area-wide planning organizations. Applicants may partner with other organizations.

Eligible beneficiaries: McKinney-Vento Homeless Assistance Program grantees, project sponsors, and applicants for the implementation of local Homeless Management Information Systems (HMIS).

Range: from $750,000. **Average:** N.A.

Activity: N.A.

HQ: Program Director, Office of Special Needs Assistance Programs, Office of Community Planning and Development, HUD, 451 7th St., SW, Rm. 7262, Washington, DC 20410. Phone: (202) 708-1226.

Internet: www.onecpd.info.

14.267 CONTINUUM OF CARE PROGRAM

Assistance: direct payments/specified use; project grants (25 percent/2, 3, 5, 15 years).

Purposes: pursuant to McKinney-Vento Homeless Assistance Act, promotes community-wide commitment to the goal of ending homelessness; provide funding for efforts by nonprofit providers, States, and local governments to quickly re-house homeless individuals and families while minimizing the trauma and dislocation caused to homeless individuals, families, and communities by homelessness; promote access to and effective utilization of mainstream programs by homeless individuals and families; and optimize self-sufficiency among individuals and families experiencing homelessness. No assistance provided under program (or any State or local government funds used to supplement this assistance) may be used to replace State or local funds previously used, or designated for use, to assist homeless persons or persons at-risk of homelessness.

Eligible applicants: states, local governments, other governmental entities, private nonprofit organizations, and community mental health associations that are public nonprofit organizations.

Eligible beneficiaries: homeless individuals and families with children; homeless persons with disabilities and their families.

Range/Average: N.A.

Activity: 410 CoCs funded in FY 2014.

HQ: Director, Office of Special Needs Assistance Programs, Community Planning and Development, Department of Housing and Urban Development, 451 7th St., SW, Rm. 7262, Washington, DC 20410. Phone: (202) 708-4300.

Internet: www.hudexchange.info/coc.

14.268   RURAL HOUSING STABILITY ASSISTANCE PROGRAM

Assistance: direct payments/specified use; project grants (25 percent/3 years).

Purposes: pursuant to the McKinney-Vento Homeless Assistance Act, provide assistance for rural counties to re-house or improve the housing situations of individuals and families who are homeless, at risk of homelessness, or in the worst housing situations, stabilize the housing of individuals and families who are at risk of becoming homeless, and improve the ability of the lowest-income residents to afford stable housing.

Eligible applicants: Counties, that meet the definition of a rural county, local units of government authorized by the county and private non-profit organizations authorized by the county.

Eligible beneficiaries: individuals and families who are homeless, at risk of homelessness or are in a worst housing situation. Worst housing situation is defined as housing that has serious health and safety defects and at least one major system that has failed or is failing.

Range/Average: N.A.

Activity: N.A.

HQ: Director, Office of Special Needs Assistance Programs, Community Planning and Development, Department of Housing and Urban Development, Rm. 7262, 451 7th St., SW, Washington, DC 20410. Phone: (202) 402-4080.

Internet: www.hudexchange.info.

14.269 HURRICANE SANDY COMMUNITY DEVELOPMENT BLOCK GRANT DISASTER RECOVERY GRANTS (CDBG-DR)

Assistance: formula grants (100 percent/to 2 years).

Purposes: pursuant to the Disaster Relief Appropriations Act of 2013, funds for necessary expenses related to disaster relief, long-term recovery, restoration of infrastructure and housing, and economic revitalization in the most impacted and distressed areas resulting from a major disaster declared due to Hurricane Sandy and other eligible events in calendar years 2011, 2012, and 2013. Funds may not be used for activities reimbursable by or for which funds are made available by the Federal Emergency Management Agency or the Army Corps of Engineers.

Eligible applicants: state and local governments in areas designated as major disaster areas.

Eligible beneficiaries: low or moderate income persons in communities that have experienced a disaster event.

Range: 1,200,000 to $2,901,736,000. **Average:** N.A.

Activity: N.A.

HQ: Director, Hurricane Sandy Community Development Block Grant Disaster Recovery Grants, OCPD-HUD, 451 7th St., SW, Rm. 7272, Washington, DC 20410. Phone: (202) 402-3217; FAX: (202) 401-2044.

Internet: portal.hud.gov/hudportal/HUD?src=/program_offices/comm_plan ning/communitydevelopment/programs/drsi.

14.270 APPALACHIA ECONOMIC DEVELOPMENT INITIATIVE

Assistance: project grants (100 percent/3 years).

Purposes: The objective of the Appalachia Economic Development Initiative (AEDI) is to increase access to capital for business lending and development in the Appalachian region. The AEDI project grants will provide direct investment and technical assistance to community development lending and investing institutions in areas of the Appalachian Region that will increase the capital and support available to businesses in underserved communities and enhance the effectiveness of economic development programs for these areas. Program funds may be used for innovative economic development uses, including but not limited to loan or investment capital, loan loss reserves, program staff costs, information systems, market studies, portfolio analyses, business planning, and other activities supporting the program goals. Award must be used to support the eligible activities. Applicants may serve markets other than Appalachia residents and communities, using other sources of financing.

Eligible applicants: state community and/or economic development agencies that apply on behalf of local rural nonprofit organizations in the 420 counties in 13 states that make up the Appalachia Region, as defined by the Appalachian Regional Commission: Alabama, Georgia, Kentucky, Maryland, Mississippi, New York, North Carolina, Ohio, Pennsylvania, South Carolina, Tennessee, West Virginia, and Virginia.

Eligible beneficiaries: eligible target markets for use of AEDI funds include geographic areas and/or populations in the Appalachia Region.

Range: to $1,000,000. **Average:** N.A.

Activity: N.A.

HQ: Director, Appalachia Economic Development Initiative, Office of Rural Housing and Economic Development-HUD, 451 7th St., SW, Rm. 7137, Washington DC, 20410. Phone: (877) 787-2526.

Internet: N.A. (Note: no field offices for this program.)

14.271   DELTA COMMUNITY CAPITAL INITIATIVE

Assistance: project grants (100 percent/3 years).

Purposes: The objective of the Delta Community Capital Initiative (DCCI) is to increase access to capital for business lending and development in the Lower Mississippi Delta Region. The DCCI project grants will provide direct investment and technical assistance to community development lending and investing institutions to improve their capacity to raise capital, and to lend and invest in local communities so that funding opportunities will be more effective and economic development services will expand to the under-served residents of Lower Mississippi Delta Region. Program funds may be used for innovative economic development uses, including but not limited to loan or investment capital, loan loss reserves, program staff costs, information systems, market studies, portfolio analyses, business planning, and other activities supporting the program goals. Award must be used to support the eligible activities. Applicants may serve other markets than Delta residents and communities, using other sources of financing.

Eligible applicants: community development lenders and investors, including local rural non-profit organizations or federally recognized tribes, serving low income residents of the 252 counties and parishes in eight states that make up the Lower Mississippi Delta Region, as defined by the Delta Regional Authority. The eight states that are included in the region are: Alabama, Arkansas, Illinois, Kentucky, Louisiana, Mississippi, Missouri, and Tennessee.

Eligible beneficiaries: eligible target markets for use of DCCI funds include businesses owned by or serving low income residents of the Lower Mississippi Delta Region.

Range: N.A. **Average:** $1,478,040.

Activity: N.A.

HQ: Director, Appalachia Economic Development Initiative, Office of Rural Housing and Economic Development-HUD, 451 7th St., SW, Rm. 7137, Washington DC, 20410. Phone: (877) 787-2526.

Internet: N.A. (Note: no field offices for this program.)

14.273   PAY FOR SUCCESS PERMANENT SUPPORTIVE HOUSING DEMONSTRATION

Assistance: project grants. (100 percent).

Purposes: pursuant to the Consolidated and Further Continuing Appropriations Act of 2015, to strengthen communities' ability to prevent and end homelessness and reduce avoidable incarceration by increasing the provision of Permanent Supportive Housing (PSH), a proven evidenced-based practice. Funds may be used to carry out a Pay for Success (PFS) model for the provision of PSH for the target population.

Eligible applicants/beneficiaries: federal, state, local, tribal, and territorial nonprofits.

Range/Average: N.A.

Activity: N.A.

HQ: Office of Special Needs Assistance Programs, HUD, Rm. 7262, Washington, DC 20410. Phone: (202) 708-1226.

Internet: HUDExchange.info. (Note: no field offices for this program.)

14.275 HOUSING TRUST FUND

Assistance: formula grants. (100 percent).

Purposes: pursuant to the Housing and Economic Recovery Act of 2008, Section 1131, Public Law 110-289, to expand and preserve the supply of affordable housing, particularly rental housing, for extremely low-income and very low income households. Funds may be used by states for new construction or rehabilitation of public housing. Eighty percent of the funds must be used for rental housing, and up to 10 percent may be used for homebuyers, and 10 percent may be used for administrative costs.

Eligible applicants/beneficiaries: states.

Range: $12,321 to $10,128,143. **Average:** $3,099,842.

Activity: N.A.

HQ: HUD, 541 7th St., SW, Rm. 7164, Washington, DC 20410. Phone: 202-402-3941; FAX: 202-708-1744.

Internet: www.hudexchange.info/program/htf.

14.276 YOUTH HOMELESSNESS DEMONSTRATION PROGRAM

Assistance: direct payments/specified use. (75 percent/to 2 years).

Purposes: pursuant to the McKinney-Vento Homeless Assistance Act, to promote a community-wide commitment to the goal of ending youth homelessness. The program provides funding to quickly re-house homeless unaccompanied youth. Funds may be used to pay for the eligible costs used to establish and operate projects for permanent housing, transitional housing, supportive services only, Homeless Management Information Systems (HMIS), and homelessness prevention.

Eligible applicants: federal state, and local institutions/organizations, public and private nonprofits, hospitals, IHEs.

Eligible beneficiaries: applicants and homeless youth.

Range/Average: N.A.

Activity: N.A.

HQ: Office of Special Needs Assistance Programs, Community Planning and Development, HUD, 451 7th St., SW, Rm. 7262, Washington, DC 20410. Phone: (202) 708-4300; FAX: (202) 401-0053.

Internet: www.hudexchange.info/programs/coc.

14.278   VETERANS HOME REHABILITATION PROGRAM

Assistance: project grants. (50 percent/to 3 years).

Purposes: pursuant to the Consolidated Appropriations Act, 2016, to award grants to nonprofit veterans service organizations to rehabilitate and modify the primary residence of disabled and low-income veterans. Funds may be used to modify and rehabilitate the primary residence of disabled and low-income veterans; rehabilitate such residence that is in a state of interior or exterior disrepair; and install energy-efficient features or equipment.

Eligible applicants: nonprofit organizations serving veterans and low-income individuals.

Eligible beneficiaries: disabled and low-income veterans.

Range: to $1,000,000. **Average:** N.A.

Activity: N.A.

HQ: Office of Community Planning and Development, HUD, 451 7th St., SW, Rm. 7240, Washington, DC 20410. Phone: (877) 787-2526.

Internet: www.hud.gov/ruralgateway.

14.311   SINGLE FAMILY PROPERTY DISPOSITION

Assistance: sale, exchange, donation of property and goods.

Purposes: pursuant to NHA as amended, to reduce the inventory of HUD-acquired properties, expand homeownership opportunities, and strengthen neighborhoods and communities, especially in revitalization areas established in consultation with local governments and nonprofit organizations, in urban or rural areas. Discounts of 30 percent off the list price are granted to sponsors in designated areas—and ten percent outside such areas. Ultimate eligible purchasers acquire and occupy one- to four-unit properties with low down payments, under the FHA Section 203(b) or 203(k) programs, and agree to rehabilitate the properties according to specified standards with funds included in the mortgage amount; generally, such loans include up to $5,000 placed in escrow, to improve the property to minimum standards. In addition, FHA may sell such homes to HUD contractors that, in turn, offer them to the general public. The collective "Good Neighbor Initiative" includes **14.198** and the "Discount Sales to Nonprofits" and Local Governments" and "$ HOME to Local Governments Sales" (**14.313**) programs. Funding for this program includes **14.313**.

Eligible applicants: local governments and nonprofit organizations; others on a competitive basis.

Eligible beneficiaries: purchasers meeting FHA requirements.

Range/Average: N.A.

Activity: N.A.

HQ: Asset Management and Disposition Division, Housing-HUD, 451 7th St., SW, Washington, DC 20410. Phone: (800) 225-5342.

Internet: www.hud.gov/offices/hsg/sfh/reo/reo_home.cfm.

14.313   DOLLAR HOME SALES

Assistance: sale, exchange, or donation of property and goods.

Purposes: to expand HUD's partnership with local governments to foster housing opportunities for low- to moderate-income families. Under the program, FHA-foreclosed single-family homes, remaining unsold for at least six months, may be sold to local governments for $1.00 plus closing costs—and then sold or rented to low- to moderate-income families, first-time homebuyers, or groups that will use the homes to provide such services as child care, shelters, or job training centers. Funding for this program is included in **14.311**.

Eligible applicants: local governments.

Eligible beneficiaries: low- to moderate- income families and communities.

Range/Average: N.A.

Activity: N.A.

HQ: Asset Management and Disposition Division, Housing-HUD, 451 7th St., SW, Washington, DC 20410. Phone: (800) 225-5342.

Internet: www.hud.gov/offices/hsg/sfh/reo/goodn/dhmabout.cfm.

14.314 ASSISTED LIVING CONVERSION FOR ELIGIBLE MULTIFAMILY HOUSING PROJECTS ("ALCP")

Assistance: project grants.

Purposes: pursuant to the HUD Reform Act of 1989 and Housing Act of 1959 as amended, to enable owners of eligible elderly housing developments to convert some or all units in such facilities into Assisted Living Facilities (ALFs) serving frail elderly and disabled persons, designed to accommodate persons able to live independently but needing assistance with activities of daily living. ALFs must provide support services such as personal care, transportation, meals, housekeeping, and laundry. Funds may be used: for physical reconfiguration of individual units; to develop common, services, and administrative spaces, including central kitchens and dining areas, lounges, and recreation spaces; for necessary remodeling. Funding for the supportive services must be provided by the owners or borrowers, either directly or through a third party. Funding for this program is included in **14.157**.

Eligible applicants/beneficiaries: private nonprofit owners of certain unused or under-utilized commercial structures.

Range: $2,000,000 to $6,000,000. **Average:** $4,000,000.

Activity: N.A.

HQ: Office of Grant Policy and Management, Housing-HUD, 451 7th St., SW, Rm. 6152, Washington, DC 20410. Phone: (202) 708-3000.

Internet: www.hud.gov/offices/hsg/mfh/progdesc/alcp.cfm.

14.316 HOUSING COUNSELING TRAINING PROGRAM

Assistance: project grants (100 percent).

Purposes: pursuant to Housing and Urban Development Act of 1968, as amended, to support the training of counselors of HUD-approved housing counseling agencies.

Eligible applicants: public or private nonprofit organizations with at least 2 years nationwide housing-counseling training. Although the program has no matching requirements, applicants are required to demonstrate funding from other sources.

Eligible beneficiaries: housing counselors from HUD-approved counseling agencies.

Range: N.A. **Average:** $666,666.

Activity: N.A.

HQ: Asset Management and Disposition Division, Housing-HUD, 451 7th St., SW, Washington, DC 20410. Phone: (800) 225-5342.

Internet:
portal.hud.gov/hudportal/HUD?src=/program_offices/housing/sfh/hcc/hcc _home. (Note: no field offices for this program.)

14.317 SECTION 8 HOUSING ASSISTANCE PAYMENTS PROGRAM SPECIAL ALLOCATIONS

Assistance: direct payments/specified use (100 percent/1 year).

Purposes: pursuant to United States Housing Act of 1937, to make payments to existing owners of project-based Section 8 housing for 12 month periods; to reduce claims on the Department's insurance fund by aiding projects with FHA-insured or Secretary-held mortgages that have immediate or potentially serious financial difficulties; and to provide decent, safe and sanitary housing for low-income families through the provision of housing assistance payments. No new projects are being approved, but assistance is currently available on a renewal basis, i.e., projects currently assisted may receive a 1-year renewal, or multiple years, up to twenty years, upon expiration of the Section 8 contract. The assistance is paid by HUD to the owner of an assisted unit on behalf of an income-eligible family who pay no more than 30 percent of their monthly adjusted income for rent.

Eligible applicants/beneficiaries: anyone/general public.

Range/Average: N.A.

Activity: N.A.

HQ: Office of Housing Assistance and Grant Administration-HUD, 451 7th St., SW, Washington 20410. Phone: (202) 708-2495.

Internet: www.hud.gov/offices/hsg/mfh/mfhsec8.cfm.

14.318 ASSISTED HOUSING STABILITY AND ENERGY AND GREEN RETROFIT INVESTMENTS PROGRAM

Assistance: project grants (50 - 100 percent/ to 2 years).

Purposes: pursuant to ARRA 2009 Title XII, to provide grants or loans for specific energy retrofit and green investments to certain, eligible assisted, affordable multifamily properties, including incentives for participating property owners, a set-aside for administrative functions, and a set-aside for due diligence and underwriting support.

Eligible applicants/beneficiaries: eligible homeowners.

Range: to $15,000 per housing unit. **Average:** $12,000 per housing unit.

Activity: N.A.

HQ: Office of Affordable Housing Preservation-HUD, 451 7th St., SW, Ste. 6230, Washington, DC 20410.Phone: (202) 708-0001.

Internet: www.hud.gov/recovery.

14.319 MULTIFAMILY ENERGY INNOVATION FUND

Assistance: cooperative agreements (33 to 50 percent/to 2 years).

Purposes: pursuant to the Consolidated Appropriations Act of 2010, to stimulate innovative approaches for increasing the energy efficiency of existing multifamily residential properties that can be replicated by others with resulting savings for families, property owners, possibly the federal government, and lower greenhouse gas emissions.

Eligible applicants/beneficiaries: 35 IHEs selected by the CDC as Prevention Research Centers (PRCs).

Range: $2,500,000 to $7,000,000. **Average:** N.A.

Activity: N.A.

HQ: Program Director, Office of Housing-Federal Housing Commissioner, HUD, 451 7th St., SW, Washington, DC 20410. Phone: (202) 402-8395.

Internet: www.hud.gov. (Note: no field offices for this program.)

14.321 FHA TECHNICAL ASSISTANCE TRAINING—TRANSFORMATION INITIATIVE

Assistance: training (100 percent/to 3 years).

Purposes: pursuant to the Consolidated Appropriations Act, to provide training for direct technical assistance to Federal Housing Administration's (FHA) industry and housing partners in the areas of Originations, Compliance and Servicing to give a comprehensive and consistent understanding of policies, procedures, and goals with respect to FHA's single family (SF) mortgage insurance programs, housing counseling requirements, special real estate owned (REO) programs, and Real Estate Settlement Procedures Act (RESPA) requirements; and to mitigate counterparty risk to the FHA insurance fund.

Eligible applicants/beneficiaries: FHA industry partners.

Range/Average: N.A.

Activity: N.A.

HQ: Asset Management and Disposition Division, Housing-HUD, 451 7th St., SW, Washington, DC 20410. Phone: (800) 225-5342.

Internet: www.hud.gov. (Note: no field offices for this program.)

14.326 PROJECT RENTAL ASSISTANCE DEMONSTRATION (PRA Demo) PROGRAM OF SECTION 811 SUPPORTIVE HOUSING FOR PERSONS WITH DISABILITIES

Assistance: projects grants (100 percent/20 to 30 years).

Purposes: pursuant to Section 811 of the Cranston-Gonzalez National Affordable Housing Act as amended by the Frank Melville Supportive Housing

Investment Act, to implement requirements for the new project rental assistance authority provided by the Melville Act. PRA Demo funds are to aid development of supportive housing units for low-income persons with disabilities in multifamily properties by covering the difference between the units' approved rents and the tenants' contributions toward rent (30 percent of income). Eligible applicants will provide these PRA Demo project-based rental assistance funds to not more than 25% of the units in multifamily developments housing eligible beneficiaries.

Eligible applicants: eligible states must partner with state health care and human service agencies and the state Medicaid agency; eligible housing agencies allocating Low Income Housing Tax Credits (LIHTC) under IRS Section 42 or housing/community development agencies allocating and overseeing HOME Funds, Section 8 or similar programs. One housing agency per state is eligible.

Eligible beneficiaries: low-income (18-62 years of age) disabled persons eligible for community-based, long-term care provided through Medicaid waivers, Medicaid state plan options or other appropriate services.

Range/Average: N.A.

Activity: N.A.

HQ: Director, Office of Housing-Federal Housing Commissioner, HUD, 451 7th St., SW, Washington, DC 20410. Phone: (202) 708-3000.

Internet: N.A.

14.327 PERFORMANCE BASED CONTRACT ADMINISTRATOR PROGRAM (PBCA)

Assistance: direct payments/specified use (100 percent/1 year).

Purposes: pursuant to the United States Housing Act of 1937,to assist States and their political subdivisions (e.g., PHAs) for aiding lower income families in obtaining a decent place to live and of promoting economically mixed housing, assistance payments may be made with respect to existing housing in accordance with the provisions of the above reference section.

Eligible applicants: the fifty United States, the District of Columbia, the United States Virgin Islands, or the Commonwealth of Puerto Rico.

Eligible beneficiaries: families currently receiving assistance as long as their income does not exceed 80 percent of area median income adjusted for family size.

Range/Average: N.A.

Activity: N.A.

HQ: Director, 451 7th St. SW, Washington, DC 20410. Phone: (202) 402-2768.

Internet: portal.hud.gov/hudportal/hud?src=/program_offices/housing/mfh/rfp/sec8rfp.

14.400 EQUAL OPPORTUNITY IN HOUSING ("Fair Housing")

Assistance: investigation of complaints.

Purposes: pursuant to the Fair Housing Act, to enforce the protection of the right to choose housing suited to one's needs and financial ability, in areas where one chooses to live, without discrimination because of race, color, religion, sex, family status, handicap, or national origin, in the sale, lease, advertising, financing, or appraisal—including multifamily housing occupied after 13 March 1991, which must comply with accessibility guidelines. Complaints are investigated and conciliated; if discrimination is established and conciliation is unsuccessful, complainants receive legal representation in taking further legal action. Suits may be filed in a federal court, seeking injunctive relief and actual or punitive damages together with court costs and reasonable attorney fees. Litigation may be initiated by the individual, by HUD on behalf of the individual, or, under certain conditions, by the Attorney General. Technical assistance is available to attorneys, developers, real estate brokers, and the general public.

Eligible applicants/beneficiaries: aggrieved persons may file a complaint with HUD or with a HUD-approved state or local fair housing agency.

Range/Average: N.A.

Activity: N.A.

HQ: OFHEO-HUD, 451 7th St., SW, Rm. 5208, Washington, DC 20410. Phone: (202) 402-5995; *complaint lines*, (800) 669-9777, TTY (800) 927-9275.

Internet: www.hud.gov/complaints/housediscrim.cfm.

14.401 FAIR HOUSING ASSISTANCE PROGRAM—STATE AND LOCAL (FHAP)

Assistance: project grants (100 percent).

Purposes: pursuant to the Fair Housing Act, for state and local complaint processing, technical assistance, training, education, outreach, data and information systems, special enforcement efforts, and for the National Fair Housing Training Academy—to handle complaints regarding violations of fair housing laws.

Eligible applicants/beneficiaries: state and local enforcement agencies administering state and local fair housing laws and ordinances certified by HUD as providing substantially equivalent rights and remedies as those provided by the Fair Housing Act.

Range/Average: N.A.

Activity: 6,843 complaints investigated in FY 2014.

HQ: Director, FHAP Support Division, OFHEO-HUD, 451 7th St. SW, Rm. 5221, Washington, DC 20410. Phone: (202) 708-2288, ext.7044.

Internet: www.hud.gov/offices/fheo/partners/FHAP/index.cfm.

14.408 FAIR HOUSING INITIATIVES PROGRAM (FHIP)

Assistance: project grants. (100 percent/to 5 years).

Purposes: pursuant to the Housing and Community Development Acts of 1987 and 1992 as amended, to develop, execute, or coordinate specialized programs or activities designed to obtain enforcement of the Fair Housing Act or state or local laws certified by HUD as providing substantially equivalent rights and remedies for discriminatory housing practices.

Eligible applicants/beneficiaries: experienced state and local fair housing agencies.

Range: $125,000 to $2,000,000. **Average:** N.A.

Activity: N.A.

HQ: FHIP Support Division, OFHEO-HUD, 451 7th St., SW, Rm. 5222, Washington, DC 20410. Phone: (202) 402-7054.

Internet: www.hud.gov/offices/fheo/partners/FHIP/fhip.cfm.

14.416   EDUCATION AND OUTREACH INITIATIVES ("FHIP EOI")

Assistance: project grants/cooperative agreements (100 percent/12-18 months).

Purposes: pursuant to Housing and Community Development Act of 1987 and 1992, as amended, to fund public education projects in order to prevent or eliminate discriminatory housing practices in accordance with the Fair Housing Act, 42 U.S.C. 3601-3619, or state or local laws that provide substantially equivalent rights and remedies for alleged discriminatory housing practices.

Eligible applicants/beneficiaries: state and local governments, IHEs, and private institutions/organizations.

Range: $125,000 to 1,500,000. **Average:** N.A.

Activity: N.A.

HQ: FHIP Support Division, OFHEO-HUD, 451 7th St., SW, Rm. 5222, Washington, DC 20410. Phone: (202) 402-7054.

Internet: www.hud.gov/offices/fheo/partners.FHIP/fhip.cfm.

14.417   FAIR HOUSING ORGANIZATION INITIATIVES ("FHIP FHOI")

Assistance: project grants/cooperative agreements (100 percent/12-36 months).

Purposes: pursuant to Housing and Community Development Act of 1987 and 1992, as amended to assist in organizing fair housing enforcement in accordance with fair housing rights under the Fair Housing Act; 42 U.S.C. 3601-3619 or state or local laws that provide substantially equivalent rights and remedies for alleged discriminatory housing practices. Objectives include provisions for strengthening existing fair housing enforcement organizations as well as establishing new ones.

Eligible applicants: state and local government agencies, other qualified fair housing enforcement institutions/organizations.

Eligible beneficiaries: private nonprofit institutions/organizations.

Range/Average: N.A.

Activity: N.A.

HQ: FHIP Support Division, OFHEO-HUD, 451 7th St., SW, Rm. 5222, Washington, DC 20410. Phone: (202) 402-7054.

Internet: www.hud.gov/office/fheo/partners.FHIP/fhip.cfm.

14.418 PRIVATE ENFORCEMENT INITIATIVES ("FHIP PEI")

Assistance: project grants/cooperative agreements (100 percent/12-36 months).

Purposes: pursuant to Housing and Community Development Act of 1987 and 1992, as amended, to assist private and tax exempt fair housing enforcement in the investigation and enforcement of all alleged violations under the Fair Housing Act; 42 U.S.C. 3601-3619 or state or local laws that provide substantially equivalent rights and remedies for alleged discriminatory housing practices. Objectives include carrying out testing and other investigative activities.

Eligible applicants: private, tax-exempt, fair housing enforcement organizations.

Eligible beneficiaries: anyone/general public, especially minority and/or disabled individuals.

Range: $325,000 to $975,000. **Average:** N.A.

Activity: N.A.

HQ: FHIP Support Division, OFHEO-HUD, 451 7th St., SW, Rm. 5222, Washington, DC 20410. Phone: (202) 402-7054.

Internet: www.hud.gov/offices/fheo/partners/FHIP/fhip.cfm.

14.506 GENERAL RESEARCH AND TECHNOLOGY ACTIVITY

Assistance: project grants.

Purposes: pursuant to the Housing Act of 1970 as amended, for research, demonstration, and program evaluation and monitoring, in such HUD program-related areas as national housing needs, advancing technology, government-sponsored enterprises, international activities, and urban economic development.

Eligible applicants/beneficiaries: researchers, research organizations, state and local governments, academic institutions, public and private profit and nonprofit organizations.

Range: $15,000 to $20,000,000. **Average:** N.A.

Activity: N.A.

HQ: Budget, Contracts, and Program Control Division, OPDR-HUD, 451 7th St. SW, Washington, DC 20410. Phone: (202) 402-5840.

Internet: www.huduser.org. (Note: no field offices for this program.)

14.516 DOCTORAL DISSERTATION RESEARCH GRANTS

Assistance: project grants (2 years).

Purposes: pursuant to the Housing and Community Development Act of 1970, to assist Ph.D. candidates in completing their research and dissertations on housing and urban development issues. Funds may be used for stipends, software, data purchases, travel, compensation for interviews— but not for tuition, computer hardware, or meals.

Eligible applicants/beneficiaries: graduate students with approved dissertation proposals, whose institutions provide support.

Range: to $25,000 per grant. **Average:** N.A.

Activity: N.A.

HQ: Director, Office of Policy Development and Research, HUD, 451 7th St., SW, Rm. 8226, Washington, DC 20410. Phone: (202) 402-3852.

Internet: www.oup.org and www.hud.gov. (Note: no field offices for this program.)

14.523 TRANSFORMATION INITIATIVE RESEARCH GRANTS: SUSTAINABLE COMMUNITY RESEARCH GRANT PROGRAM

Assistance: cooperative agreements (100 percent/to 2 years).

Purposes: pursuant to the Consolidated Appropriations Act of 2010, to fill key data and information gaps and begin to develop and evaluate policy alternatives that communities can adopt to facilitate decision making about various community investments. HUD seeks to sponsor cutting edge research in the areas of: affordable housing development and preservation; transportation-related issues; economic development and job creation; land use planning and urban design; green and sustainable energy practices; and a range of issues related to sustainability.

Eligible applicants/beneficiaries: 35 IHEs selected by the CDC as Prevention Research Centers (PRCs).

Range: $200,000 to $575,000. **Average:** N.A.

Activity: N.A.

HQ: Director, Office of Policy Development and Research, HUD, 451 7th St., SW, Rm. 8226, Washington, DC 20410. Phone: (202) 402-3852.

Internet: N.A.

14.524 TRANSFORMATION INITIATIVE RESEARCH GRANTS: NATURAL EXPERIMENTS

Assistance: projects grants (100 percent/to 24 years).

Purposes: pursuant to the Consolidated Appropriations Act of 2010, to support scientific research that makes use of natural experiments to evaluate impact on local, state, and federal policies. Funded projects may focus on policy relevant to HUD's mission of increasing homeownership, supporting community development, increasing access to affordable, discrimination-free housing and the development of evaluations that can help determine the best utilization of taxpayer dollars. Funds may not be used specifically for dissertation support, internationally-oriented research, or demonstration projects.

Eligible applicants: nonprofit/for-profit organizations located in the U.S, foundations, think tanks, consortia, DEA-accredited IHEs, and other entities sponsoring a researcher, expert or analyst. HUD will not directly fund individual researchers.

Eligible beneficiaries: eligible researchers, general public.

Range: $100,000 to $250,000 per award. **Average:** N.A.

Activity: N.A.

HQ: Director, Office of Policy Development and Research, HUD, 451 7th St., SW, Rm. 8226, Washington, DC 20410. Phone: (202) 402-3852.

Internet: N.A. (Note: no field offices for this program.)

14.525 TRANSFORMATION INITIATIVE RESEARCH GRANTS: DEMONSTRATION AND RELATED SMALL GRANTS

Assistance: projects grants (100 percent/to 3 years).

Purposes: pursuant to the Consolidated Appropriations Act of 2010, to conduct several major demonstrations through contract studies in the following areas: Family Self-Sufficiency, Pre-Purchase Counseling, Sustainable Building Practices, and Homeless Families Intervention. To enhance demonstrations, funding is provided for a number of small research projects aimed at collecting additional/supplemental information and analyses. Eligible costs include: salaries, project assistants, computer software, purchase of data, travel expenses to collect data or to make presentations at meetings, transcription services, compensation for interviews, and protected/release time for eligible researchers who can demonstrate the need for a period of intensive research.

Eligible applicants: nonprofit/for-profit organizations located in the U.S, foundations, think tanks, consortia, DEA-accredited IHEs, and other entities sponsoring a researcher, expert or analyst.

Eligible beneficiaries: eligible researchers, general public.

Range: $25,000 to $500,000 per grant. **Average:** N.A.

Activity: N.A.

HQ: Director, Office of Policy Development and Research, HUD, 451 7th St., SW, Rm. 8226, Washington, DC 20410. Phone: (202) 402-3852.

Internet: N.A.

14.534 STRONG CITIES STRONG COMMUNITIES (SC2) NATIONAL RESOURCE NETWORK

Assistance: cooperative agreements (100 percent/to 3 years).

Purposes: pursuant to the Consolidated and Further Continuing Appropriations Act of 2012, to provide economically distressed communities with short-term technical assistance in basic operational areas as well as programmatic issues, dictated by local need. In addition, the SC2 Network will aggregate public and private resources to serve a wide range of governments and connect them through a peer-to-peer learning network.

Eligible applicants/beneficiaries: 35 IHEs selected by the CDC as Prevention Research Centers (PRCs).

Range/Average: N.A.

Activity: N.A.

HQ: Program Director, Office of Policy Development and Research, HUD, 451 7th St., SW, Rm. 8116, Washington, DC 20410. Phone: (202) 402-4986; FAX: (202) 708-0573.

Internet: N.A. (Note: no field offices for this program.)

14.535 TRANSFORMATION INITIATIVE: RENTAL ASSISTANCE DEMONSTRATION SMALL RESEARCH GRANT PROGRAM

Assistance: project grants/cooperative agreements (100 percent/3 years).

Purposes: pursuant to the Transformation Initiative (TI) account, Public Law 112-55, and the Consolidated and Further Continuing Appropriations Act of 2012, funds to support direct and indirect costs incurred in the timely completion of research projects that will produce policy-relevant new knowledge about the implementation and consequences of HUDs Rental Assistance Demonstration (RAD), which allows proven financing tools to be applied to at-risk public and assisted housing. HUD will not directly fund individual researchers.

Eligible applicants: Organizations located in the U.S., foundations, think tanks, consortia, U.S. Department of Education-recognized IHEs and other entities that will sponsor a researcher, expert or analyst.

Eligible beneficiaries: principal investigator and other research associates and assistants.

Range: to $200,000. **Average:** N.A.

Activity: N.A.

HQ: Director, Office of Policy Development and Research, HUD, 451 7th St., SW, Rm. 8226, Washington, DC 20410. Phone: (202) 402-3852.

Internet: N.A. (Note: no field offices for this program.)

14.850 PUBLIC AND INDIAN HOUSING

Assistance: direct payments/specified use.

Purposes: pursuant to the Housing Act of 1937 as amended, to support lower-income housing projects operated by local public housing agencies. For projects approved prior to 1 October 1986, HUD may award payments for up to 30 years (to 20 years for modernization) to meet debt service requirements that cannot be paid with rental revenue; for contracts executed after 1 October 1986, for up to 40 years. Operating subsidies may be used to achieve and maintain adequate operating and maintenance services and reserves. Localities make contributions through forgiveness of property taxes or payments in lieu of taxes (PILOTs). Note: development and reconstruction projects now are financed through **14.866**.

Eligible applicants: public housing agencies. (Note: per the Native American Housing Assistance and Self-Determination Act of 1996 (NAHASDA), Indian housing authorities now are ineligible.)

Eligible beneficiaries: lower-income families including families with or without children, the elderly and near-elderly, remaining members of a tenant family, certain single persons, the handicapped, and the displaced.

Range: $2,510 to $900,775,513. **Average:** $1,423,394.

Activity: anticipate operating subsidies for 1.1 million public housing units in FY 2016.

HQ: Assistant Secretary/Public and Indian Housing-HUD, 451 7th St., SW, Washington, DC 20410. Phone: (202) 402-2769.

Internet: www.hud.gov/offices/pih/programs/ph/am.

14.856   LOWER INCOME HOUSING ASSISTANCE PROGRAM—SECTION 8 MODERATE REHABILITATION
("Section 8 Housing Assistance")

Assistance: direct payments/specified use.

Purposes: pursuant to the Housing Act of 1937, Housing and Urban- Rural Recovery Act of 1983, Department of Housing and Urban Development Reform Act of 1989, Housing Opportunity Program Extension Act of 1996, Multifamily Assisted Housing Reform and Affordability Act of 1997, and other housing acts and amendments, to pay rent subsidies to property owners, covering the difference between very-low-income renters' adjusted family income and the market rent for moderately rehabilitated housing. Payments to owners may be made for up to 180 days, and extended for 12 months at a time. Families must pay toward the rent the highest of: 30 percent of their adjusted monthly family income; ten percent of gross monthly family income; or, the portion of welfare assistance designated for their monthly housing cost. The program is inactive; no new projects are being approved.

Eligible applicants/beneficiaries: state, county, municipal, or other authorized public housing agencies. Housing owners coordinate with HUD and/or local agencies to obtain the subsidies for their tenants.

Range: $4,426 to $19,549,245. **Average:** $1,135,021.

Activity: projected to serve 21,215 families in FY 2016.

HQ: Housing Voucher Management and Operations Division, Housing and Voucher Programs, HUD, 451 7th St., SW, Rm. 4210, Washington, DC 20410. Phone: (202) 708-0477.

Internet: www.hud.gov/progdesc/pihindx.html.

14.862   INDIAN COMMUNITY DEVELOPMENT BLOCK GRANT PROGRAM

Assistance: project grants. (100 percent/to 2 years).

Purposes: pursuant to the Housing and Community Development Act of 1974 as amended, to provide assistance to Indian tribes and Alaska Native villages in the development of viable Indian communities using a broad range of activities designed to result in decent housing and suitable living environments, neighborhood revitalization, economic development, and improved community facilities and services. Program policy requires that the "principal benefit" of projects be to low- and moderate-income persons—i.e., at least 70 percent of the grant allocation. Projects may be operated by the locality or through subgrantees, including public or nonprofit agencies, neighborhood-based organizations, local development corporations, small business investment companies, and other groups. Permitted uses of funds include: virtually any aspect of residential or nonresidential rehabilitation, including historic preservation and energy conservation; energy development; grants or loans to businesses; revolving loan funds for rehabilitation or for economic development purposes; real property acquisition; relocation of households or businesses; demolition; redevelopment site clearance and preparation for re-use; improvement or installation of public works; certain public service programs; housing code enforcement; meeting urgent community needs that present an immediate threat to health or welfare; city planning and related studies. Ineligible uses include: facilities for the general conduct of government; community-wide facilities; new housing construction; housing subsidies paid directly to occupants; income maintenance payments. Cities must: include citizen participation in program planning; have an approved comprehensive housing assistance plan. For "entitlement" communities, CDBG grant amounts are based on a statutory formula.

Eligible applicants/beneficiaries: any tribe, band, group, or nation, including Alaska Indians, Aleuts, and Eskimos, and any Alaskan native village eligabible for assistance under the Indian Self Determination and Education Assistance Act or, previously, under the Local Fiscal Assistance Act of 1972.

Range: $25,000 to $5,500,000. **Average:** $605,000.

Activity: N.A.

HQ: Office of Native American Programs, Public and Indian Housing-HUD, Public and Indian Housing-HUD, 451 7th St., SW, Rm. 4126, Washington, DC 20410. Phone: (202) 401-7914.

Internet: www.hud.gov/offices/pih/ih/grants/icdbg.cfm.

14.865 PUBLIC AND INDIAN HOUSING—INDIAN LOAN GUARANTEE PROGRAM ("Loan Guarantees for Indian Housing")

Assistance: guaranteed/insured loans (to 30 years).

Purposes: pursuant to the Housing and Community Development Act of 1992 as amended, for Native Americans and tribal organizations to acquire new, existing, or rehabilitated homes in Indian areas—using guaranteed mortgage loans available through private financial institutions. Such homes may be sold or rented to families. Individual applicant's total debts should not exceed 41 percent of income, including amount of loan.

Eligible applicants/beneficiaries: native Americans including Alaska natives, or tribes, TDHEs, and Indian housing authorities.

Range: N.A. **Average:** $172,000.

Activity: anticipate guaranteeing 5,776 loans in FY 2016.

HQ: Director, Office of Loan Guaranty, Office of Native American Programs, Public and Indian Housing-HUD, 451 7th St., SW, Rm. 5156, Washington, DC 20410. Phone: (202) 402-4978.

Internet: www.hud.gov/offices/pih/ih/homeownership/184. (Note: no field offices for this program.)

14.867 INDIAN HOUSING BLOCK GRANTS

Assistance: formula grants. (100 percent/2 years).

Purposes: pursuant to NAHASDA as amended, for affordable housing activities such as: Indian housing assistance; development; housing management services; crime prevention and safety; model activities.

Eligible applicants/beneficiaries: tribes or TDHEs.

Range: $50,000 to $84,000,000. **Average:** $278,703.

Activity: anticipate assisting 5,795 families by building, acquiring, or rehabilitating their homes in FY 2016.

HQ: Office of Native American Programs, Public and Indian Housing-HUD, Public and Indian Housing-HUD, 451 7th St., SW, Rm. 4126, Washington, DC 20410. Phone: (202) 401-7914.

Internet: www.hud.gov/offices/pih/ih/grants/ihbg.cfm.

14.869 TITLE VI FEDERAL GUARANTEES FOR FINANCING TRIBAL HOUSING ACTIVITIES

Assistance: guaranteed/insured loans (from 20 years).

Purposes: pursuant to NAHASDA, to assist tribes or TDHEs to obtain financing for affordable housing where an obligation cannot be completed without such guaranty. Assistance is limited to eligible affordable housing activities listed in Section 202 of the Act, including housing assistance, development, services, crime prevention and safety activities, model activities.

Eligible applicants/beneficiaries: federally recognized Indian tribe or TDHE—approved recipients of Indian Housing Block Grants (IHBG) funds.

Range/Average: N.A.

Activity: anticipate guaranteeing 5 loans in FY 2016.

HQ: Director, Office of Loan Guaranty, Office of Native American Programs, Public and Indian Housing-HUD, 451 7th St., SW, Rm. 5156, Washington, DC 20410. Phone: (202) 402-4978.

Internet: www.hud.gov/offices/pih/ih/homeownership/titlevi. (Note: no field offices for this program.)

14.870 RESIDENT OPPORTUNITY AND SUPPORTIVE SERVICES—SERVICE COORDINATORS
("ROSS Service Coordinators")

Assistance: project grants. (some matching/3 years).

Purposes: pursuant to the U.S. Housing Act of 1937, to assist public housing residents through employment development and supportive services activities, including the employment of service coordinators or case managers. The primary focus is on a spectrum of services for families leading to homeownership and to promote independent living for the elderly and disabled.

Eligible applicants/beneficiaries: public and Indian housing agencies, TDHEs, resident management corporations; resident councils or organizations in partnerships to leverage resources.

Range: N.A. **Average:** $360,000.

Activity: anticipate 100 awards in FY 2016

HQ: Director, HOPE VI Community and Supportive Services, Public and Indian Housing-HUD, 451 7th St., SW, Rm. 4238, Washington, DC 20410. Phone: (202) 402-2341.

Internet: www.hud.gov/offices/pih/programs/ph/ross.

14.871 SECTION 8 HOUSING CHOICE VOUCHERS

Assistance: direct payments/specified use.

Purposes: pursuant to the Housing Act of 1937 as amended, Quality Housing and Work Responsibility Act of 1998, and other acts, to consolidate previous Section 8 rental assistance programs into a market-driven program, making tenant-based rental assistance available to low-income families and increasing their housing choices. Payments are made to participating owners, representing the difference between the local standard rent and 30 percent of the family's adjusted income.

Eligible applicants: entities qualifying as public housing agencies including certain public and nonprofit entities that administer Section 8 voucher programs.

Eligible beneficiaries: very low income families—i.e., with income not exceeding 50 percent of the area median); lower income families—i.e., with income not exceeding 80 percent of the area median. Criteria are adjusted for smaller or larger families. For Welfare-to Work vouchers, families must also meet special Welfare-to-Work criteria.

Range: $5,728 to $1,074,563,247. **Average:** $7,142,148.

Activity: anticipate serving 2.3 million families in FY 2016.

HQ: Housing Voucher Management and Operations Division, Housing and Voucher Programs, HUD, 451 7th St., SW, Rm. 4210, Washington, DC 20410. Phone: (202) 708-0477.

Internet: www.hud.gov/offices/pih/programs/hcv/index.cfm.

14.872 PUBLIC HOUSING CAPITAL FUND ("CFP")

Assistance: formula grants. (100 percent/to 4 years).

Purposes: pursuant to the U.S. Housing Act of 1937 as amended and Quality Housing and Work Responsibility Act of 1998, for public housing agencies to pay for their capital and management activities including public housing modernization and development.

Eligible applicants/beneficiaries: public housing agencies.

Range: $5,527 to $300,862,746. **Average:** $583,427.

Activity: anticipate making funds available for 3,100 grantees in FY 2016.

HQ: Assistant Secretary/Public and Indian Housing-HUD, 451 7th St., SW, Rm. 4130, Washington, DC 20410. Phone: (202) 708-1640.

Internet: www.hud.gov/offices/pih/programs/ph/capfund/index.cfm.

14.873 NATIVE HAWAIIAN HOUSING BLOCK GRANTS

Assistance: project grants.

Purposes: pursuant to the Hawaiian Homelands Homeownership Act of 2000, to provide housing assistance to native Hawaiian families. Grants may support development, housing services, crime prevention and safety activities, and model activities.

Eligible applicants: Hawaii Department of Native Hawaiian Home Lands.

Eligible beneficiaries: native Hawaiian families eligible to reside on the Hawaiian Home Lands.

Range/Average: N.A.

Activity: anticipate assisting 65 homeowners in FY 2016.

HQ: Office of Native American Programs, Public and Indian Housing-HUD, 500 Ala Moana Blvd. - Ste. 3A, Honolulu, HI 96813. Phone: (808) 522-8175, ext.223.

Internet: www.hud.gov/offices/pih/ih/codetalk/onap/nhhbgprogram.cfm. (Note: no field offices for this program.)

14.874   LOAN GUARANTEES FOR NATIVE HAWAIIAN HOUSING ("Section 184A")

Assistance: guaranteed/insured loans (to 30 years).

Purposes: pursuant to the Hawaiian Homelands Homeownership Act of 2000 and Housing and Community Act of 1992, for Hawaii natives to construct, purchase, or rehabilitate one- to four-family housing located on Hawaiian Home Lands. Small down payments are required.

Eligible applicants/beneficiaries: native Hawaiian families; Department of Hawaiian Homes Lands; Office of Hawaiian Affairs; experienced private nonprofit organizations.

Range/Average: N.A.

Activity: anticipate guaranteeing 100 loans in FY 2016.

HQ: Director, Office of Loan Guaranty, Office of Native American Programs, Public and Indian Housing-HUD, 451 7th St., SW, Rm. 5156, Washington, DC 20410. Phone: (202) 402-4978.

Internet: www.hud.gov/offices/pih/ih/codetalk/onap/program184a.cfm. (Note: no field offices for this program.)

14.877   PUBLIC HOUSING FAMILY SELF-SUFFICIENCY UNDER RESIDENT OPPORTUNITY AND SUPPORTIVE SERVICES (PH FSS)

Assistance: project grants (100 percent).

Purposes: to develop local strategies to coordinate assistance available under the public housing program with public and private resources, to enable participating families to achieve economic independence and housing self-sufficiency. Funds may support the hiring of a program coordinator.

Eligible applicants/beneficiaries: public housing authorities; tribes and TDHEs.

Range: N.A. **Average:** $60,036.

Activity: N.A.

HQ: Director, HOPE VI Community and Supportive Services, Public and Indian Housing-HUD, 451 7th St., SW, Rm. 4238, Washington, DC 20410. Phone: (202) 402-2341.

Internet: www.hud.gov/offices/pih/programs/ph/ross.

14.878   AFFORDABLE HOUSING DEVELOPMENT IN MAIN STREET REJUVENATION PROJECTS ("Main Street")

Assistance: project grants. (95 percent/30 months).

Purposes: pursuant to the Consolidated Appropriations Act of 2006, HUD Appropriations Act of 2006, and others, to assist small communities in the rejuvenation of historic or traditional central business districts or "Main Street Areas" by replacing unused commercial space with affordable housing units.

Eligible applicants/beneficiaries: units of local government, whose jurisdiction contains a population of no more than 50,000 and have either no Public Housing Agency (PHA) or a PHA that administers less than 101 public housing units.

Range: N.A. **Average:** $500,000.

Activity: N.A.

HQ: Office of Public Housing Investments, Office of Urban Revitalization, HUD, 451 7th St., SW, Rm. 4130, Washington, DC 20410. Phone: (202) 401-8812.

Internet: www.hud.gov/mainstreet. (Note: no field offices for this program.)

14.879 MAINSTREAM VOUCHERS

Assistance: direct payments/specified use. (100 percent/5 years).

Purposes: pursuant to the Cranston Gonzalez National Affordable Housing Act, to provide housing assistance payments to participating owners on behalf of eligible tenants with the goal of providing safe, decent, affordable, and sanitary housing for persons with disabilities and Welfare-to-Work families meeting special criteria. Housing assistance payments are the difference between the local payment standard and 30 percent of the family's adjusted income.

Eligible applicants: authorized Public Housing Agencies (PHAs).

Eligible beneficiaries: disabled families who meet income eligibility requirements and are on the Housing Choice Voucher waiting list.

Range: $26,758 to $2,499,026. **Average:** $530,237.

Activity: anticipate serving 14,811 families in FY 2016.

HQ: Housing Voucher Management and Operations Division, Housing and Voucher Programs, HUD, 451 7th St., SW, Rm. 4210, Washington, DC 20410. Phone: (202) 708-0477.

Internet: www.hud.gov/offices/pih/programs/hcv/about/fact_sheet.cfm.

14.881 MOVING TO WORK DEMONSTRATION PROGRAM

Assistance: formula grants.

Purposes: pursuant to the Omnibus Consolidated Rescissions and Appropriations Act of 1996, to give PHAs and the Secretary of HUD flexibility to design and test various approaches for providing and administering housing assistance that will: reduce federal costs and/or achieve greater cost effectiveness; offer greater incentives to families seeking to gain employment and become economically self-sufficient; and increase housing choices for lower-income families.

Eligible applicants: eligible public housing agencies selected by the Secretary for program participation.

Eligible beneficiaries: low-income public housing residents.

Range/Average: N.A.

Activity: N.A.

HQ: Assistant Secretary for Public and Indian Housing, 451 7th St., SW, Rm. 4130, Washington DC, 20410. Phone:(202) 402-2488.

Internet: www.hud.gov/offices/pih/programs/ph/mtw.

14.889   CHOICE NEIGHBORHOODS IMPLEMENTATION GRANTS

Assistance: project grants (95 percent).

Purposes: pursuant to the Consolidated Appropriations Act of 2010, to fund competitive grants to transform neighborhoods of extreme poverty into sustainable mixed-income neighborhoods with well-functioning services, schools, public assets, transportation and access to jobs.

Eligible applicants: local governments, non-profits, Public Housing Agencies (PHAs), for-profit developers applying jointly with a public entity.

Eligible beneficiaries: residents of severely distressed public/assisted housing projects and surrounding communities.

Range: N.A. **Average:** $30,000,000.

Activity: anticipate making 5 to 8 grant awards in FY 2016.

HQ: Director, Choice Neighborhood Planning Grants, Office of Public and Indian Housing-HUD, 451 7th St., SW, Rm. 4130, Washington, DC 20410. Phone: (202) 402-5461.

Internet: www.hud.gov/cn. (Note: no field offices for this program.)

14.892   CHOICE NEIGHBORHOODS PLANNING GRANTS

Assistance: project grants (95 percent/2 years).

Purposes: Choice Neighborhoods Planning Grants will fund the creation of comprehensive neighborhood Transformation Plans that are intended to become the guiding document for the revitalization of the public and/or assisted housing units while simultaneously directing the transformation of the surrounding neighborhood and outlining the steps necessary to create positive outcomes for families within the targeted neighborhood.

Eligible applicants: public housing authorities (PHAs), local governments, tribal entities, nonprofits, and for-profit developers that apply jointly with a public entity.

Eligible beneficiaries: residents of distressed public and/or assisted housing units and surrounding communities.

Range/Average: N.A.

Activity: HUD plans to award 10 grants in FY15.

HQ: Director, Choice Neighborhood Planning Grants, Office of Public and Indian Housing-HUD, 451 7th St., SW, Rm. 4130, Washington, DC 20410. Phone: (202) 402-5461.

Internet: www.hud.gov/cn. (Note: no field offices for this program.)

14.893   OFFICE OF NATIVE AMERICAN PROGRAMS TRAINING AND TECHNICAL ASSISTANCE FOR INDIAN HOUSING BLOCK GRANT PROGRAM

Assistance: training (100 percent/2 years).

Purposes: pursuant to the Omnibus Appropriations Act, to provide technical assistance for Indian tribes, Alaska Native villages, and tribally designated housing entities (TDHEs) for the development of viable communities.

Eligible applicants: for-profit entities/organizations representing Native American housing interests with the capacity to provide training and technical assistance (T&TA) services to Indian tribes and subrecipients.

Eligible beneficiaries: eligible Indian tribes, Alaska Native villages, tribally designated housing entities (TDHEs).

Range/Average: N.A.

Activity: N.A.

HQ: Director, 451 7th St., SW, Washington, DC 20410. Phone: (202) 402-4507.

Internet: portal.hud.gov/hudportal/hud?src=/program_offices/administration /grants/fundsavail.

14.894 OFFICE OF NATIVE AMERICAN PROGRAMS TRAINING AND TECHNICAL ASSISTANCE FOR NATIVE HAWAIIAN HOUSING BLOCK GRANT PROGRAMS

Assistance: training (100 percent).

Purposes: pursuant to The Department of Defense and Full-Year Continuing Appropriations Act, to provide technical assistance for Native Hawaiians in the development of viable communities.

Eligible applicants/beneficiaries: any national or regional T&TA provider or any organization with the capacity to provide services.

Range: to $350,000. **Average:** N.A.

Activity: N.A.

HQ: Director, 451 7th St., SW, Washington, DC 20410. Phone: (202) 402-4507.

Internet: N.A.

14.895 JOBS-PLUS PILOT INITIATIVE

Assistance: project grants. (75 percent/1 year).

Purposes: pursuant to the Consolidated Appropriations Act of 2014, to create collaboration among local housing authorities, residents of public housing developments, local welfare agencies, local workforce development agencies, and other relevant partners. It is aimed at significantly increasing employment and income of public housing residents by providing intensive, employment-focused programs targeting every able-bodied, working-age welfare recipient at a public housing development.

Eligible applicants: public housing authorities.

Eligible beneficiaries: residents of public housing authorities.

Range: $2,000,000 to $4,000,000. **Average:** N.A.

Activity: N.A.

HQ: Office of Public and Indian Housing, HUD, 451 7th St., SW, Rm. 4116, Washington, DC 20410. Phone: (202) 402-6230.

Internet: N.A. (Note: no field offices for this program.)

14.896　FAMILY SELF-SUFFICIENCY PROGRAM (FSS)

Assistance: project grants (100 percent/1 year).

Purposes: project grants to promote the development of local strategies to coordinate the use of assistance under the Housing Choice Voucher and Public Housing programs with public and private resources to enable participating families to increase earned income and financial literacy, reduce or eliminate the need for welfare assistance, and make progress toward economic independence and self-sufficiency. Funds awarded to public housing agencies (PHAs) or tribes/Tribally Designated Housing Entities (TDHEs) may only be used to pay the annual salary and fringe benefits of FSS program coordinators.

Eligible applicants: public housing agencies (PHAs) and tribes/Tribally Designated Housing Entities (TDHEs).

Eligible beneficiaries: individuals and families who are participants in the Housing Choice Voucher program or Public Housing program.

Range: $7,000 to $1,300,000. **Average:** $105,000.

Activity: anticipate assisting 80,000 families in FY 2016.

HQ: Director, Family Self-Sufficiency Program, Office of Public and Indian Housing-HUD, 451 7th St., SW, Washington, DC 20410. Phone: (202) 402-2341.

Internet: portal.hud.gov/hudportal/HUD?src=/program_offices/public_indian _housing/programs/hcv/fss. (Note: no field offices for this program.)

14.897　JUVENILE REENTRY ASSISTANCE PROGRAM (JRAP)

Assistance: project grants. (75 percent/18 months).

Purposes: pursuant to Section 211 of the Second Chance Act, to fund initiatives to provide legal services to youth with former contact with the juvenile justice system to successfully transition into the community through the expungement and sealing of juvenile records.

Eligible applicants: public housing authorities that have established a partnership with a legal aid organizations, university legal centers, and legal service organizations that have experience providing legal services to juveniles.

Eligible beneficiaries: individuals 24 years old and under who have had contact with the juvenile justice system.

Range/Average: N.A.

Activity: N.A.

HQ: HUD, 451 7th St., SW, Washington, DC 20410. Phone: (202) 402-7154.

Internet: N.A. (Note: no field offices for this program.)

14.898　ROSS SUPPORTIVE SERVICES PROGRAMS

Assistance: project grants. (100 percent/3 years).

Purposes: pursuant to the Consolidated and Further Continuing Appropriations Act of 2015, to address the needs of public housing residents by providing supportive services, resident empowerment activities, and/or by assisting residents of all ages in becoming economically self-sufficient through a variety of innovative programs/initiatives. Funds may be used for academic enrichment, economic development, supportive services activities, organizational development, and mediation, including the employment of service coordinators, case managers, and/or service navigators.

Eligible applicants: public and tribal housing authorities and entities, resident councils, and nonprofits.

Eligible beneficiaries: individuals.

Range/Average: N.A.

Activity: N.A.

HQ: Office of Public and Indian Housing, HUD, 451 7th St., SW, Washington, DC 20410. Phone: (202) 402-2430.

Internet: N.A.

14.900 LEAD-BASED PAINT HAZARD CONTROL IN PRIVATELY-OWNED HOUSING

Assistance: project grants. (90 percent/3 years).

Purposes: pursuant to the Housing and Community Development Act of 1992, for programs to identify and control lead-based paint hazards in housing owned by or rented to by low- or very-low- income families, and to prevent childhood lead poisoning caused by lead-based paint. Program objectives include: capacity building; integrating comprehensive community approaches; establishing public registries of lead-safe housing; promoting related job training and employment for low-income area residents. Projects must be conducted by certified contractors and inspectors.

Eligible applicants/beneficiaries: states, cities, or local general government units and tribes with a current, approved "Consolidated Plan."

Range/Average: N.A.

Activity: N.A.

HQ: Director, 451 7th St., SW, Rm. 8236, Washington, DC 20410. Phone: (202) 402-7180.

Internet: www.hud.gov/healthyhomes. (Note: no field offices for this program.)

14.902 LEAD TECHNICAL STUDIES GRANTS

Assistance: cooperative agreements (100 percent/to 3 years).

Purposes: pursuant to the Housing and Community Development Act of 1992, to improve public knowledge of lead-based paint related health hazards, and improve or develop new hazard assessment and control methods.

Eligible applicants: IHEs, state, local, and federally-recognized tribal governments, U.S. nonprofit and eligible for-profit institutions.

Eligible beneficiaries: homeowners, rental property owners, and rental/public housing residents.

Range: $250,000 to $500,000. **Average:** N.A.

Activity: N.A.

HQ: Office of Healthy Homes and Lead Hazard Control-HUD, 451 7th St. SW, Rm. 8236, Washington, DC 20410. Phone: (202) 755-1785, ext.7595; TTY (800) 877-8339.

Internet: www.hud.gov/offices/lead/techstudies/index.cfm. (Note: no field offices for this program.)

14.905 LEAD HAZARD REDUCTION DEMONSTRATION GRANT PROGRAM

Assistance: project grants. (75 percent/3-4 years).

Purposes: pursuant to the Housing and Community Development Act of 1992, for areas with the highest lead paint abatement needs to undertake programs for abatement, inspections, risk assessments, temporary relocations, and interim control of lead-based hazards in eligible private-owned units and multifamily buildings that are occupied by low-income families. Projects must be conducted using certified contractors and inspectors, as well as workers trained through EPA authorized programs.

Eligible applicants/beneficiaries: states, local government units, tribes with approved Consolidated Plan; consortia.

Range/Average: N.A.

Activity: N.A.

HQ: Director, 451 7th St., SW, Rm. 8236, Washington, DC 20410. Phone: (202) 402-7180.

Internet: www.hud.gov/healthyhomes. (Note: no field offices for this program.)

14.906 HEALTHY HOMES TECHNICAL STUDIES GRANTS

Assistance: project grants. (100 percent/3-4 years).

Purposes: pursuant to the Housing and Urban Development Act of 1970, for technical studies to improve methods for detecting and controlling housing-related health and safety hazards. Funding for FY 07 reported under program **14.902**.

Eligible applicants/beneficiaries: U.S. academic, nonprofit and profit (operating without profit) institutions; state, local governments; tribes.

Range: $300,000 to $1,000,000. **Average:** N.A.

Activity: N.A.

HQ: Office of Healthy Homes and Lead Hazard Control-HUD, 451 7th St. SW, Rm. 8236, Washington, DC 20410. Phone: (202) 755-1785, ext.7595; TTY (800) 877-8339.

Internet: www.hud.gov/offices/lead. (Note: no field offices for this program.)

14.913 HEALTHY HOMES PRODUCTION PROGRAM

Assistance: project grants (100 percent).

Purposes: pursuant to the Omnibus Appropriations Act, to comprehensively address multiple residential health and safety hazards, including mold, carbon monoxide, home safety hazards, pesticides and allergens (from pets and pests).

Eligible applicants/beneficiaries: not-for-profit institutions and for-profit firms, state and local governments, federally-recognized Indian Tribes, and colleges and universities located in the United States.

Range/Average: N.A.

Activity: N.A.

HQ: Director, 451 7th St., SW, Rm. 8236, Washington, DC 20410. Phone: (202) 402-7180.

Internet: N.A. (Note: no field offices for this program.)

14.914 ASTHMA INTERVENTIONS IN PUBLIC AND ASSISTED MULTIFAMILY HOUSING

Assistance: cooperative agreements (100 percent/to 3 years).

Purposes: pursuant to the Omnibus Appropriations Act, 2011, to develop and implement cost effective, replicable interventions and protocols for controlling asthma among residents (particularly children) of federally assisted, multifamily housing; to create sustainable programs/policies that reduce exposure to asthma triggers in the indoor environment; and to evaluate the effectiveness (including cost-effectiveness) of asthma control programs/interventions.

Eligible applicants: IHEs, state, local, and federally-recognized tribal governments, U.S. nonprofit and eligible for-profit institutions.

Eligible beneficiaries: residents of federally-assisted multi-family housing.

Range/Average: N.A.

Activity: N.A.

HQ: Program Director, Office of Healthy Homes and Lead Hazard Control, HUD, 451 7th St., SW, Rm. 8236, Washington, DC 20410. Phone: (202) 402-7696.

Internet: www.hud.gov/Grants. (Note: no field offices for this program.)

DEPARTMENT OF THE INTERIOR

15.020 AID TO TRIBAL GOVERNMENTS

Assistance: direct payments/specified use.

Purposes: pursuant to the Indian Self-Determination and Education Assistance Act (ISDEAA) as amended, for general tribal government operations, to maintain up-to-date tribal enrollment records, to conduct tribal elections, and to develop tribal policies, legislation, and regulations.

Eligible applicants/beneficiaries: recognized tribal governments.

Range: $10,000 to $700,000. **Average:** $80,000.

Activity: N.A.

HQ: Deputy Director, Office of Tribal Services (MS-320 SIB), BIA-DOI, 1849 C St., NW, Washington, DC 20240. Phone: (202) 513-7640.

Internet: www.bia.gov.

15.021 CONSOLIDATED TRIBAL GOVERNMENT PROGRAM

Assistance: direct payments/specified use.

Purposes: pursuant to ISDEAA as amended, to combine funding for certain ongoing programs into a single agreement, thus allowing greater flexibility in planning programs and lowering costs of administration—such as scholarships, adult education, job placement, and training.

Eligible applicants/beneficiaries: recognized tribal governments.

Range: $1,300 to $2,400,000. **Average:** $500,000.

Activity: N.A.

HQ: Deputy Director, Office of Tribal Services (MS-320 SIB), BIA-DOI, 1849 C St., NW, Washington, DC 20240. Phone: (202) 513-7640.

Internet: www.bia.gov.

15.022 TRIBAL SELF-GOVERNANCE

Assistance: direct payments/specified use.

Purposes: pursuant to ISDEAA as amended, for tribal law enforcement, social services, scholarships, welfare payments, housing improvement, road maintenance, and other programs previously administered by DOI—but not for the operation of educational institutions.

Eligible applicants/beneficiaries: recognized tribal governments and consortia.

Range: $9,705 to $27,537,488. **Average:** $434,655.

Activity: N.A.

HQ: Office of Self-Governance (MS-4618 MIB), BIA-OS-DOI, 1951 Constitution Ave., NW, MS 355-G, Washington, DC 20240. Phone: (202) 219-0240.

Internet: www.doi.gov/bureau-indian-affairs.html.

15.024 INDIAN SELF-DETERMINATION CONTRACT SUPPORT

Assistance: direct payments/specified use.

Purposes: pursuant to ISDEAA as amended, to cover indirect costs incurred in administering federal programs.

Eligible applicants/beneficiaries: recognized tribal governments and authorized organization.

Range: $10,000 to $8,000,000. **Average:** $190,000.

Activity: N.A.

HQ: Deputy Director, Office of Tribal Services (MS-320 SIB), BIA-DOI, 1849 C St., NW, Washington, DC 20240. Phone: (202) 513-7640.

Internet: www.bia.gov.

15.025 SERVICES TO INDIAN CHILDREN, ELDERLY AND FAMILIES ("Social Services")

Assistance: direct payments/specified use.

Purposes: pursuant to the Snyder Act of 1921 and ISDEAA as amended, to administer welfare assistance programs for adults and children including foster care placement; to reduce substance abuse. Funds may support case-workers and counselors, staffing and operation of emergency shelters, and similar costs.

Eligible applicants/beneficiaries: recognized tribal governments.

Range: $10,000 to $4,800,000. **Average:** $100,000.

Activity: N.A.

HQ: Chief, Division of Human Services (MS-320 SIB), BIA-DOI, 1849 C St., NW, Washington, DC 20240. Phone: (202) 513-7642.

Internet: www.bia.gov.

15.026 INDIAN ADULT EDUCATION

Assistance: direct payments/specified use.

Purposes: pursuant to the Snyder Act of 1921 and ISDEAA as amended, to provide Indian adult education courses, programs, and related activities promoting opportunities for productive employment.

Eligible applicants/beneficiaries: recognized tribal governments.

Range: $100 to $297,000. **Average:** $35,900.

Activity: N.A.

HQ: Office of Indian Education Programs (MS-3609 MIB), BIA-DOI, 1849 C St., NW, Washington, DC 20240. Phone: (202) 208-5810.

Internet: www.bie.gov.

15.027 ASSISTANCE TO TRIBALLY CONTROLLED COMMUNITY COLLEGES AND UNIVERSITIES

Assistance: project grants (100 percent).

Purposes: pursuant to the Tribally Controlled Community College Assistance Act, to operate and improve tribally controlled community colleges, including expansion of their physical resources.

Eligible applicants/beneficiaries: nonprofit, nonsectarian colleges sponsored by recognized tribal governments and organizations, offering certificates or associate, baccalaureate, or graduate degrees.

Range: $273,790 to $13,598,820. **Average:** $2,467,250.

Activity: N.A.

HQ: Bureau of Indian Education, MS 4657-MIB, BIA-DOI, 1849 C St., NW, Washington, DC 20240. Phone: (202) 208-3559.

Internet: www.bie.edu.

15.028 TRIBALLY CONTROLLED COMMUNITY COLLEGE ENDOWMENTS

Assistance: project grants (50 percent).

Purposes: pursuant to the Tribally Controlled College Assistance Act, to establish endowments for tribally controlled community colleges. Interest earned may be used to defray college operating costs, but not to benefit private persons.

Eligible applicants/beneficiaries: colleges chartered by recognized tribes, offering certificates or associate, baccalaureate, or graduate degrees.

Range: N.A. **Average:** $5,700.

Activity: N.A.

HQ: Bureau of Indian Education, MS 4657-MIB, BIA-DOI, 1849 C St., NW, Washington, DC 20240. Phone: (202) 208-3559.

Internet: www.bie.edu.

15.029   TRIBAL COURTS

Assistance: direct payments/specified use.

Purposes: pursuant to ISDEAA as amended, to operate judicial systems. Funds may support salaries and related expenses of judges, prosecutors, defenders, clerks, probation and juvenile officers, and other court personnel.

Eligible applicants/beneficiaries: recognized tribal governments.

Range: $15,000 to $800,000. **Average:** $50,000.

Activity: N.A.

HQ: Deputy Director, Office of Tribal Services (MS-320 SIB), BIA-DOI, 1849 C St., NW, Washington, DC 20240. Phone: (202) 513-7641.

Internet: www.bia.gov.

15.030   INDIAN LAW ENFORCEMENT
("Law Enforcement")

Assistance: direct payments/specified use.

Purposes: pursuant to ISDEAA as amended and Indian Law Enforcement Reform Act, to operate tribal police departments and detention facilities. Funds may be used for salaries and related expenses of criminal investigators, uniformed officers, detention personnel, radio dispatchers, administrative costs.

Eligible applicants/beneficiaries: recognized tribal governments.

Range: $20,000 to $20,000,000. **Average:** $200,000.

Activity: N.A.

HQ: Deputy Director, Law Enforcement Services, (MS-2429 MIB), BIA-DOI, 1849 C St., NW, Washington, DC 20240. Phone: (202) 208-5787.

Internet: www.bia.gov.

15.031   INDIAN COMMUNITY FIRE PROTECTION
("Community Fire Protection")

Assistance: direct payments/specified use.

Purposes: pursuant to ISDEAA as amended, for fire protection services when tribal governments do not receive support for such services from state or local governments. Funds may cover costs of staff, volunteer firefighters training, equipment purchases and repairs, and to purchase smoke detectors, fire extinguishers, fire escapes, and emergency lighting for public buildings.

Eligible applicants/beneficiaries: recognized tribal governments.

Range: $200 to $138,000. **Average:** $10,000.

Activity: N.A.

HQ: Deputy Director, Office of Tribal Services (MS-320 SIB), BIA-DOI, 1849 C St., NW, Stop 320 SIB, Washington, DC 20240. Phone: (202) 513-7640.

Internet: www.bia.gov.

15.032 INDIAN ECONOMIC DEVELOPMENT

Assistance: direct payments/specified use.

Purposes: pursuant to the Snyder Act of 1921, ISDEAA as amended, and other acts, to administer revolving loan and loan guaranty programs, including assistance to Indian-owned businesses in obtaining private financing—toward improvement of tribal economies. Administered programs may include BIA's Loan Guaranty and Insurance Fund, Indian Business Development Program, and Community and Economic Development Program.

Eligible applicants/beneficiaries: recognized tribal governments.

Range: $5,000 to $300,000. **Average:** $215,000.

Activity: N.A.

HQ: Deputy Assistant Secretary/Policy and Economic Development (MS-4071 MIB), BIA-DOI, 1849 C St., NW, Washington, DC 20240. Phone: (202) 219-0005.

Internet: www.doi.gov/bia/ecodev/index.htm; www.doi.gov/bureau-indian-affairs.html.

15.033 ROAD MAINTENANCE—INDIAN ROADS

Assistance: direct payments/specified use.

Purposes: pursuant to the Federal Highway Act of 1921 and ISDEAA as amended, for limited routine maintenance of roads, bridges, and airstrips serving Indian reservations, emphasizing school bus routes and arterial highways.

Eligible applicants/beneficiaries: recognized tribal governments and authorized organizations.

Range/Average: N.A.

Activity: N.A.

HQ: Division of Transportation, Office of Trust Responsibilities, BIA-DOI, 1849 C St., NW, MS-4532 MIB, Washington, DC 20240. Phone: (202) 513-7714.

Internet: www.doi.gov/bia/otrhome.htm.

15.034 AGRICULTURE ON INDIAN LANDS

Assistance: direct payments/specified use; advisory services/counseling; specialized services.

Purposes: pursuant to ISDEAA as amended and American Indian Agriculture Resource Management Act, to protect and restore agronomic and rangeland resources on trust lands; to facilitate the development of renewable agricultural resources. Noxious weed eradication requires 50 percent local matching funds.

Eligible applicants/beneficiaries: recognized tribal governments and authorized organizations.

Range: agriculture: $200 to $575,000; noxious weed eradication: $500 to $300,000. **Average:** agriculture: $50,000; noxious weed eradication: $6,200.

Activity: N.A.

HQ: Office of Trust Responsibilities (MS-3061 MIB), BIA-DOI, 1849 C St., NW, Washington, DC 20240. Phone: (202) 513-0886.

Internet: www.doi.gov/bia/otrhome.htm.

15.035 FORESTRY ON INDIAN LANDS

Assistance: direct payments/specified use; advisory services/counseling; specialized services.

Purposes: pursuant to the Snyder Act of 1921, ISDEAA as amended, and other acts, to maintain, protect, enhance, and develop Indian forest resources. Funds may be used for reforestation, commercial stand improvement, timber sales management, forest planning, and protection activities.

Eligible applicants/beneficiaries: recognized tribal governments and authorized organizations.

Range: $10,000 to $1,000,000. **Average:** $100,000.

Activity: N.A.

HQ: Division of Forestry, Office of Trust Responsibilities (MS-4513 MIB), BIA-DOI, 1849 C St., NW, Washington, DC 20240. Phone: (202) 208-4837.

Internet: www.doi.gov/bia/otrhome.htm#Forests.

15.036 INDIAN RIGHTS PROTECTION

Assistance: direct payments/specified use.

Purposes: pursuant to ISDEAA as amended and other acts, to protect Indian rights guaranteed through treaty or statute, by obtaining the services or information needed by the federal government to litigate challenges to these rights. Project examples include research and data collection concerning water and land title disputes, hunting and fishing rights, environmental problems.

Eligible applicants/beneficiaries: recognized tribal governments and authorized organizations.

Range: $1,000 to $100,000. **Average:** $25,000.

Activity: N.A.

HQ: Division of Real Estate Services, Office of Trust Responsibilities (MS-4510 MIB), BIA-DOI, 1849 C St., NW, Washington, DC 20240. Phone: (202) 208-7737.

Internet: www.doi.gov/bia/Rightsprot.htm.

15.037   WATER RESOURCES ON INDIAN LANDS

Assistance: direct payments/specified use; advisory services/counseling; specialized services.

Purposes: pursuant to the Snyder Act of 1921 and ISDEAA as amended, to assist tribes in the management, planning, and development of their water and related land resources. Water Management, Planning, and Development funds are awarded competitively. Project examples: geographic, hydrologic quantitative and qualitative analysis of water, ground, surface water monitoring; aquifer classification and stream gauging.

Eligible applicants/beneficiaries: recognized tribal governments and authorized organizations.

Range: $10,000 to $200,000. **Average:** N.A.

Activity: N.A.

HQ: Division Chief, Division of Natural Resources, Office of Trust Services, BIA-DOI, 1849 C St., NW, Washington, DC 20240. Phone: (202) 208-3956.

Internet: www.doi.gov/bia/otrhome.htm.

15.038   MINERALS AND MINING ON INDIAN LANDS

Assistance: direct payments/specified use; specialized services; technical information.

Purposes: pursuant to the Snyder Act of 1921, ISDEAA as amended, and other acts, to assist and support the inventory and development of energy and minerals on Indian lands. Funds may be used to inventory, develop, and produce nonrenewable resources. Mineral Assessment funds, awarded competitively, may be used for inventory programs and to develop baseline data. Project examples: feasibility studies; lease compliance; environmental reviews; training; seismic explorations; mapping systems.

Eligible applicants/beneficiaries: recognized tribal governments and authorized organizations.

Range: $10,000 to $250,000. **Average:** $75,000.

Activity: N.A.

HQ: Division of Energy and Minerals, Office of Trust Responsibilities, BIA-DOI, 12136 W. Bayaud Ave., Ste. 300, Lakewood, CO 80228. Phone: (720) 407-0602.

Internet: www.doi.gov/whoweare/as-ia/ieed.

15.040   REAL ESTATE PROGRAMS—INDIAN LANDS

Assistance: direct payments/specified use.

Purposes: pursuant to ISDEAA as amended, Indian Land Consolidation Act, and other acts, to provide real property management, counseling, and land use planning services to individual Indian allottees and tribal and Alaska native entities owning an interest in the almost 56,000,000 acres of trust land; to provide appraisal services required in processing land transactions; to protect and enhance the Indian leasehold estate by providing individual landowners and tribes with lease compliance activities.

Eligible applicants/beneficiaries: recognized tribal governments and authorized organizations; individual American Indians.

Range/Average: N.A.

Activity: N.A.

HQ: Division of Real Estate Services, Office of Trust Responsibilities (MS-4510 MIB), BIA-DOI, 1849 C St., NW, Washington, DC 20240. Phone: (202) 208-7737.

Internet: www.doi.gov/bia/otrhome.htm#Land.

15.041 ENVIRONMENTAL MANAGEMENT—INDIAN PROGRAMS

Assistance: direct payments/specified use.

Purposes: pursuant to ISDEAA as amended, CERCLA, SWDA, RCRA, and other acts, to determine environmental impacts of federal projects on Indian lands and to identify hazardous waste sites—to determine compliance with the National Environmental Policy Act; to prepare Environmental Assessments; to obtain information for compliance with the National Historic Preservation Act and the Archeological Resources Protection Act.

Eligible applicants/beneficiaries: recognized tribal governments and authorized organizations.

Range: $5,000 to $250,000. **Average:** $25,000.

Activity: N.A.

HQ: Division of Environmental and Cultural Resources Management, Office of Trust Responsibilities (MS-4513 MIB), BIA-DOI, 2051 Mercator Dr., Reston, VA 20191. Phone: (703) 390-6524; FAX: (703) 390-6325.

Internet: www.doi.gov/bureau-indian-affairs.html.

15.042 INDIAN SCHOOL EQUALIZATION PROGRAM (ISEP)

Assistance: direct payments/specified use.

Purposes: pursuant to ISDEAA as amended, Indian Education Amendments of 1978, and Tribally Controlled Schools Act, for primary and secondary education including residential programs for Indian students not served by public or sectarian schools.

Eligible applicants/beneficiaries: recognized tribes or tribal organizations currently served by a BIA-funded school.

Range: $161,000 to $8,930,300. **Average:** $2,007,600.

Activity: N.A.

HQ: Office of Indian Education Programs (MS-3609 MIB), BIA-DOI, 1849 C St., NW, Washington, DC 20240. Phone: (202) 208-7658.

Internet: www.bie.edu.

15.043 INDIAN CHILD AND FAMILY EDUCATION (FACE)

Assistance: project grants; training (100 percent).

Purposes: pursuant to the Indian Education Amendments of 1978, to conduct early childhood education, adult education, and parenting skills programs. Funds may not be used for administration costs.

Eligible applicants/beneficiaries: recognized tribes or tribal organizations currently served by a BIA-funded school.

Range: N.A. **Average:** $289,910 per site.

Activity: N.A.

HQ: Center for School Improvement, Office of Indian Education Programs, BIA-DOI, 1011 Indian School Rd, NW, 3rd Floor, Ste. 332, Albuquerque, NM 87104. Phone: (505) 563-5260.

Internet: www.bie.edu.

15.044 INDIAN SCHOOLS—STUDENT TRANSPORTATION

Assistance: direct payments/specified use.

Purposes: pursuant to ISDEAA as amended, Indian Education Amendments of 1978, and Tribally Controlled Schools Act, to provide round-trip transportation of students between home and schools.

Eligible applicants: recognized tribes or tribal organizations currently served by a BIA-funded school.

Eligible beneficiaries: Indian children age 5 to 21, enrolled in schools eligible for assistance under **15.042**.

Range: $2,800 to $1,630,820. **Average:** $328,061.

Activity: N.A.

HQ: Office of Indian Education Programs (MS-3609 MIB), BIA-DOI, 1849 C St., NW, Washington, DC 20240. Phone: (202) 208-7658.

Internet: www.bie.edu.

15.046 ADMINISTRATIVE COST GRANTS FOR INDIAN SCHOOLS

Assistance: project grants (100 percent).

Purposes: pursuant to ISDEAA as amended, Indian Education Amendments of 1978, and Tribally Controlled Schools Act, to pay school operating costs including administration, property and procurement management, insurance, safety, and related expenses.

Eligible applicants/beneficiaries: recognized tribes or tribal organizations operating BIA-funded schools.

Range: $127,600 to $1,166,200. **Average:** $405,967.

Activity: N.A.

HQ: Office of Indian Education Programs (MS-3609 MIB), BIA-DOI, 1849 C St., NW, Washington, DC 20240. Phone: (202) 208-7658.

Internet: www.bie.edu.

15.047 INDIAN EDUCATION FACILITIES, OPERATIONS, AND MAINTENANCE

Assistance: direct payments/specified use.

Purposes: pursuant to ISDEAA as amended, Indian Education Amendments of 1978, and Tribally Controlled Schools Act, to pay facilities operations and maintenance costs including personnel, utilities, minor repairs, equipment, and similar costs.

Eligible applicants/beneficiaries: recognized tribal governments or organizations currently served by BIA-funded elementary or secondary schools or peripheral dormitories.

Range: $58,374 to $2,385,121. **Average:** $533,888.

Activity: N.A.

HQ: Office of Indian Education Programs (MS-3609 MIB), BIA-DOI, 1849 C St., NW, Washington, DC 20240. Phone: (202) 208-7658.

Internet: www.bie.edu.

15.048 BUREAU OF INDIAN AFFAIRS FACILITIES—OPERATIONS AND MAINTENANCE

Assistance: direct payments/specified use.

Purposes: pursuant to ISDEAA as amended, for basic operating and maintenance services provided to BIA-owned or -operated noneducation facilities, including expenses incurred for personnel, supplies, planning, utility costs, telecommunications equipment, and similar costs.

Eligible applicants/beneficiaries: recognized tribal governments with BIA-owned or -operated facilities on their reservations.

Range/Average: N.A.

Activity: N.A.

HQ: Director, Office of Facilities Management and Construction, BIA-DOI, 201 Third St., NW - Ste. 500, PO Box 1248, Albuquerque, NM 87103. Phone: (505) 346-6522.

Internet: www.doi.gov/bia/ofmc/om.htm.

15.051 ENDANGERED SPECIES ON INDIAN LANDS

Assistance: direct payments/specified use; technical information; advisory services/counseling.

Purposes: pursuant to the Snyder Act of 1921, ISDEAA as amended, and the Endangered Species Act, to enable compliance with the Endangered Species Act, the Northern Spotted Owl Recovery Plan, and to implement the Cheyenne River Prairie Management Plan on Indian lands. Project examples: water impoundments, cross fencing and vegetative management; owl and habitat surveys.

Eligible applicants/beneficiaries: recognized tribal governments and authorized organizations whose reservations are inhabited by specific endangered species.

Range: $20,000 to $140,000. **Average:** $50,000.

Activity: N.A.

HQ: Office of Trust Services, Division of Natural Resources, Branch of Fish and Wildlife Recreation, BIA-DOI, MS 4656 MIB 1849 C St., NW, Washington, DC 20240. Phone: (202) 208-4088.

Internet: www.doi.gov/bia/otrhome.htm.

15.052 LITIGATION SUPPORT FOR INDIAN RIGHTS

Assistance: direct payments/specified use.

Purposes: pursuant to ISDEAA as amended, Indian Claims Limitation Act of 1982, and other acts, to establish or defend Indian property or treaty rights through judicial, administrative, or settlement actions. Funds may be used to pay for expert witnesses, research, data collection, technical support, and other evidence-gathering activities required to defend such rights issues as: hunting, fishing, and gathering; trespass; titles; allotment claims; mineral entry; Equal Access to Justice Act settlements.

Eligible applicants/beneficiaries: recognized tribal governments and authorized organizations.

Range/Average: N.A.

Activity: N.A.

HQ: Division of Real Estate Services, Office of Trust Responsibilities (MS-4510 MIB), BIA-DOI, 1849 C St., NW, Washington, DC 20240. Phone: (202) 208-7737.

Internet: www.doi.gov/bia/otrhome.htm.

15.053   ATTORNEY FEES—INDIAN RIGHTS

Assistance: direct payments/specified use.

Purposes: pursuant to the Indian Claims Limitation Act of 1982 and other acts, to support tribes in protecting their treaty rights and other rights established through executive order or court action, by providing assistance in obtaining legal representation. Project examples: environmental damage claims; water rights negotiation or litigation; boundary disputes.

Eligible applicants/beneficiaries: recognized tribal governments.

Range/Average: N.A.

Activity: N.A.

HQ: Division of Real Estate Services, Office of Trust Responsibilities (MS-4510 MIB), BIA-DOI, 1849 C St., NW, Washington, DC 20240. Phone: (202) 208-7737.

Internet: www.doi.gov/bia/otrhome.htm.

15.057   NAVAJO-HOPI INDIAN SETTLEMENT PROGRAM

Assistance: direct payments/specified use.

Purposes: pursuant to the Navajo-Hopi Settlement Act and ISDEAA as amended, to restore the grazing potential of rangeland within the former Navajo/Hopi Joint Use Area, including: livestock monitoring; issuance of grazing permits; implementation of range management plans and grazing control methods; establishment of range units and grazing capacity; removal of trespass livestock on the Hopi Partitioned Lands; initiation of grazing control on the Navajo Partitioned Lands; natural resources restoration.

Eligible applicants/beneficiaries: recognized tribal governments of the Navajo and Hopi tribes and organizations authorized by either tribe.

Range/Average: N.A.

Activity: N.A.

HQ: Office of Trust Responsibilities (MS-3061 MIB), BIA-DOI, 1849 C St., NW, Washington, DC 20240. Phone: (202) 513-0886.

Internet: www.doi.gov/bureau-indian-affairs.html.

15.058 INDIAN POST SECONDARY SCHOOLS ("Haskell Indian Nations University and Southwestern Indian Polytechnic Institute")

Assistance: training.

Purposes: pursuant to the Snyder Act of 1921, to enable American Indian students to attend either of the BIA-operated postsecondary schools with minimal charge for tuition or room and board: Haskell Indian Nations University and Southwestern Indian Polytechnic Institute (SIPI).

Eligible applicants/beneficiaries: members of recognized tribes.

Range/Average: N.A.

Activity: N.A.

HQ: Bureau of Indian Education, MS 4657-MIB, BIA-DOI, 1849 C St., NW, Washington, DC 20240. Phone: (202) 208-3559.

Internet: www.bie.edu.

15.059 INDIAN GRADUATE STUDENT SCHOLARSHIPS ("Special Higher Education Scholarships")

Assistance: project grants.

Purposes: pursuant to the Snyder Act of 1921, to provide financial aid to Indian students, enabling them to obtain advanced degrees.

Eligible applicants/beneficiaries: Indian students that are members of recognized tribal governments, admitted to a graduate program.

Range: $250 to $4,000. **Average:** $3,947.

Activity: N.A.

HQ: American Indian Graduate Center, BIA-DOI, 4520 Montgomery Blvd. - Ste. 1-B, Albuquerque, NM 87109. Phone: (505) 881-4584.

Internet: www.bie.edu/contact.htm.

15.060 INDIAN VOCATIONAL TRAINING—UNITED TRIBES TECHNICAL COLLEGE

Assistance: training; direct payments/unrestricted use.

Purposes: pursuant to the Snyder Act of 1921, ISDEAA as amended, and Indian Adult Vocational Training Act of 1956, to provide vocational training to American Indians through the United Tribes Technical College in Bismarck, North Dakota.

Eligible applicants: the United Tribes Technical College.

Eligible beneficiaries: members of recognized tribes, residing on or near reservations under BIA jurisdiction and needing financial assistance.

Range: $500 to $3,000. **Average:** $2,500.

Activity: N.A.

HQ: Division of Job Placement and Training, Office of Self-Governance and Self-Determination (MS-2542 MIB), BIA-DOI, 1849 C St., NW, Washington, DC 20240. Phone: (202) 219-5270.

Internet: www.united-tribes.tec.nd.us.

15.061   INDIAN JOB PLACEMENT—UNITED SIOUX TRIBES DEVELOPMENT CORPORATION ("United Sioux Tribes")

Assistance: direct payments/specified use; advisory services/counseling.

Purposes: pursuant to the Snyder Act of 1921, ISDEAA as amended, and Indian Adult Vocational Training Act of 1956, to assist Indians in finding permanent employment through job development programs, counseling, and referrals to job training programs—through the United Sioux Tribes Development Corporation in Pierre, South Dakota. Participants receive stipends.

Eligible applicants: Eligible applicants: United Sioux Tribes Development Corporation.

Eligible beneficiaries: members of federally recognized tribes, residing on or near reservations under BIA jurisdiction.

Range/Average: N.A.

Activity: N.A.

HQ: Division of Job Placement and Training, Office of Economic Development (MS-2412 MIB), BIA-DOI, 1849 C St., NW, Washington, DC 20240. Phone: (202) 219-5270.

Internet: www.doi.gov.

15.062   REPLACEMENT AND REPAIR OF INDIAN SCHOOLS

Assistance: direct payments/specified use.

Purposes: pursuant to ISDEAA and Tribally Controlled Schools Act of 1988 as amended, and Tribal Self-Governance Act of 1994, for advanced planning, design, and construction of major expansion or replacement projects or improvement and repair projects—involving BIA-owned or -funded education facilities for the direct support of primary and secondary schools and dormitories.

Eligible applicants/beneficiaries: recognized tribal governments and organizations, including school boards.

Range/Average: N.A.

Activity: N.A.

HQ: Deputy Director, Office of Facilities Management and Construction, BIA-DOI, 1011 Indian School Rd., Suite 335, Albuquerque, NM 87104. Phone: (505) 563-5142.

Internet: www.bia.gov.

15.063   IMPROVEMENT AND REPAIR OF INDIAN DETENTION FACILITIES

Assistance: direct payments/specified use.

Purposes: pursuant to ISDEAA as amended and Tribal Self- Governance Act of 1994, for advanced planning, design, and construction, and improvements, repair, additions to, BIA adult or juvenile detention facilities.

Eligible applicants/beneficiaries: recognized tribal governments.

Range/Average: N.A.

Activity: N.A.

HQ: Deputy Director, Office of Facilities Management and Construction, BIA-DOI, 1011 Indian School Rd., Suite 335, Albuquerque, NM 87104. Phone: (505) 563-5142.

Internet: www.doi.gov/bia/ofmc/cm.htm#3.

15.065 SAFETY OF DAMS ON INDIAN LANDS

Assistance: direct payments/specified use. (100 percent/1-5 years).

Purposes: pursuant to the Snyder Act of 1921, ISDEAA as amended, and Indian Dams Safety Act of 1994, to improve the structural integrity of the 116 dams on Indian lands, for which BIA has responsibility, including inspection, hazard classification, and modification construction.

Eligible applicants/beneficiaries: recognized tribal governments and authorized organizations.

Range/Average: N.A.

Activity: N.A.

HQ: Branch of Irrigation, Power, and Safety of Dams, Division of Water and Land Resources, Office of Trust Responsibilities (MS-4513 MIB), BIA-DOI, 13922 Denver West Pkwy., Lakewood, Colorado 80401. Phone: (303) 231-5222.

Internet: www.doi.gov/bia/otrhome.htm.

15.066 TRIBAL GREAT LAKES RESTORATION INITIATIVE

Assistance: project grants/discretionary. (100 percent/1 year).

Purposes: pursuant to the Indian Self-determination and Education Assistance Act, as amended, to provide financial assistance to Great Lakes tribes to protect, enhance, and restore the Great Lakes. Funds will be used to address tribal priorities in the following focus areas: toxic substances and areas of concern; invasive species; nonpoint source pollution impacts on nearshore health; habitat and fish and wildlife species protection; and foundations for future restoration actions.

Eligible applicants/beneficiaries: federally-recognized tribal governments and organizations.

Range: $1,000 to $500,000. **Average:** $162,000.

Activity: 36 awards in FY 2015.

HQ: BIA-DOI, 5600 W. American Blvd., Ste. 500, Bloomington, MN 55437. Phone: (612) 725-4529.

Internet: N.A.

15.108 INDIAN EMPLOYMENT ASSISTANCE

Assistance: direct payments/specified use.

Purposes: pursuant to the Snyder Act of 1921, ISDEAA, Indian Adult Vocational Training Act, amendments, and other acts, for American Indians to obtain vocational training and employment opportunities. Funds may be used for subsistence, tuition, and related training costs. Payments may extend for up to two years—three years for registered nurses training.

Eligible applicants: federally recognized tribal governments and authorized organizations.

Eligible beneficiaries: unemployed or under-employed members of recognized tribes, residing on or near an Indian reservation under BIA jurisdiction.

Range/Average: N.A.

Activity: N.A.

HQ: Division of Job Placement and Training, Office of Indian Energy and Economic Development, 1951 Constitution Ave., NW, Stop 20-SIB, Washington, DC 20245. Phone: (202) 208-3100.

Internet: www.doi.gov/bia/ecodev/index.htm.

15.113   INDIAN SOCIAL SERVICES—WELFARE ASSISTANCE

Assistance: direct payments/specified use.

Purposes: pursuant to the Snyder Act of 1921, for cash payments to needy Indians to pay for: food, clothing, shelter, etc.; adult nonmedical institutional or custodial care; foster home care; burial expenses; emergency assistance—when such assistance is unavailable from state or local public agencies. Extra benefits are provided when recipients are receiving general assistance and work under the Tribal Work Experience Program.

Eligible applicants/beneficiaries: needy members of recognized tribes, living on or near reservations.

Range/Average: N.A.

Activity: N.A.

HQ: Deputy Director, Office of Tribal Services (MS-320 SIB), BIA-DOI, 1849 C St., NW, Washington, DC 20245. Phone: (202) 513-7642.

Internet: www.doi.gov/bia/childw~2.htm.

15.114   INDIAN EDUCATION—HIGHER EDUCATION GRANT PROGRAM

Assistance: project grants. (100 percent/to 5 years).

Purposes: pursuant to the Snyder Act of 1921, to provide financial assistance to Indian undergraduate college students, supplementing aid packages awarded by colleges.

Eligible applicants/beneficiaries: recognized tribal governments and authorized organizations; members of tribes in financial need, enrolled in or accepted by an accredited college.

Range: $300 to $5,000. **Average:** $2,700.

Activity: N.A.

HQ: Office of Indian Education Programs (MS-3609 MIB), BIA-DOI, 1849 C St., NW, Washington, DC 20240. Phone: (202) 208-4397.

Internet: www.bie.edu.

15.124   INDIAN LOANS—ECONOMIC DEVELOPMENT
("Loan Guaranty Program")

Assistance: guaranteed/insured loans. (to 90 percent/to 30 years).

Purposes: pursuant to the Snyder Act of 1921, ISDEAA as amended, and other acts, for economic development on or near federal Indian reservations, through projects on or near reservations, involving business, industry, or agriculture. Borrowers must have 20 percent equity in businesses being financed.

Eligible applicants/beneficiaries: recognized tribal governments and authorized organizations; individual American Indians.

Range: individuals and tribal enterprises: $150,000 to $10,500,000; federally-recognized tribal governments and organizations: $10,000,000 to $25,000,000. **Average:** N.A.

Activity: N.A.

HQ: Assistant Secretary Indian Affairs, Office of Indian Energy and Economic Development, (MS 20 SIB), BIA-DOI, 1951 Constitution Ave., NW, Washington, DC 20240. Phone: (202) 513-7683.

Internet: www.doi.gov/bia/ecodev/loanpgm.html.

15.130 INDIAN EDUCATION—ASSISTANCE TO SCHOOLS ("Johnson-O'Malley")

Assistance: direct payments/specified use.

Purposes: pursuant to the Johnson-O'Malley Act of 1934 as amended and ISDEAA, for supplemental education programs for Indians in public schools. Project examples: home-school coordinators; remedial tutoring; educational field trips; cultural programs.

Eligible applicants: tribal organizations, Indian corporations, school districts, or states with eligible Indian Education Committees.

Eligible beneficiaries: children age 3 through grade 12, of one- fourth or more degree of Indian blood and descendants of members of recognized tribes—with priority to those residing on or near reservations.

Range: $100 to $3,360,980. **Average:** $77,300.

Activity: N.A.

HQ: Office of Indian Education Programs (MS-3609 MIB), BIA-DOI, 1849 C St., NW, Washington, DC 20240. Phone: (202) 208-4397.

Internet: www.bie.edu.

15.133 NATIVE AMERICAN BUSINESS DEVELOPMENT INSTITUTE (NABDI)

Assistance: formula grants (100 percent/annual agreements).

Purposes: pursuant to the Indian Self-Determination and Education Assistance Act, as amended, to develop partnerships with U.S. business schools in order to assist tribes in analyzing economic potential and business opportunities; to prepare economic feasibility studies.

Eligible applicants: federally-recognized Indian tribal governments.

Eligible beneficiaries: federally-recognized Indian tribal governments and their members.

Range/Average: N.A.

Activity: N.A.

HQ: Division of Indian Energy Policy Development, Office of Indian Energy and Economic Development, Rm. 20, 1951 Constitution Ave., NW, Washington, DC 20245. Phone: (202) 219-0740; FAX: (202) 208-4564.

Internet: N.A.

15.141   INDIAN HOUSING ASSISTANCE

Assistance: project grants; technical information (grants, 100 percent).

Purposes: pursuant to ISDEAA as amended, for home improvements, for housing construction in certain situations, and for technical assistance in establishing housing plans. The HHS Indian Health Service may supplement this program by funding water and sanitary systems. Program is restricted to use within reservations and approved tribal service areas.

Eligible applicants/beneficiaries: recognized tribal governments and organizations; Indians needing Housing Improvement Program assistance.

Range: repairs and renovations: to $35,000; interim improvements: to $2,500. **Average:** repairs: $17,500; new housing construction: $100,000.

Activity: N.A.

HQ: Deputy Director, Office of Tribal Services (MS-320 SIB), BIA-DOI, 1849 C St., NW, Washington, DC 20240. Phone: (202) 513-7640.

Internet: www.doi.gov/bia/tservices/hip/housing.htm.

15.144   INDIAN CHILD WELFARE ACT—TITLE II GRANTS

Assistance: project grants (100 percent).

Purposes: pursuant to the Indian Child Welfare Act, for the operation and maintenance of counseling programs and facilities related to child and family services, including: family assistance; protective day and after-school care; recreational activities; respite care; foster care subsidies; preparation and administration of child welfare codes, including legal representation; education and training; related services and programs.

Eligible applicants/beneficiaries: recognized tribal governments.

Range: $26,449 to $750,000. **Average:** $60,000.

Activity: N.A.

HQ: Deputy Director, Office of Tribal Services (MS-320 SIB), BIA-DOI, 1849 C St., NW, Washington, DC 20240. Phone: (202) 513-7640.

Internet: www.doi.gov/bia/ots/otshome.htm.

15.146   IRONWORKER TRAINING PROGRAM

Assistance: project grants. (100 percent/to 12 weeks).

Purposes: pursuant to the Snyder Act of 1921 and the Indian Adult Vocational Training Act of 1956 as amended, to pay stipends to native Americans to permit them to obtain vocational training and apprenticeships as ironworkers at the National Ironworker Training Program in Broadview, Illinois, and to provide job placement assistance.

Eligible applicants/beneficiaries: American Indian members of recognized tribes, at least age 20, with a high school diploma or equivalent certificate, residing on or near an Indian reservation under BIA jurisdiction, and in good physical health.

Range: N.A. **Average:** $185/week plus work clothes and tools.

Activity: N.A.

HQ: Division of Job Placement and Training, Office of Economic Development (MS-2412 MIB), BIA-DOI, 1849 C St., NW, Washington, DC 20240. Phone: (202) 219-5270.

Internet: www.doi.gov/bia/ecodev/index.htm.

15.147   TRIBAL COURTS—TRUST REFORM INITIATIVE

Assistance: project grants (formula-based).

Purposes: pursuant to ISDEAA as amended and the American Indian Trust Fund Management Reform Act of 1994, to supplement funds available to tribal governments assuming specific increased responsibilities such as: appointing guardians; determining competency; awarding child support from Indian Individual Money (IIM) accounts; determining paternity; sanctioning adoptions, marriages, and divorces; making presumptions of death; adjudicating claims involving trust assets. Funds may not be used for general operating costs.

Eligible applicants/beneficiaries: federally-recognized tribal governments.

Range: $3,000 to $216,000. **Average:** $50,000.

Activity: N.A.

HQ: Office of Tribal Government Services (MS-320 SIB), BIA-DOI, 1849 C St., NW, Washington, DC 20240. Phone: (202) 513-7641.

Internet: www.doi.gov/bia/ots/otshome.htm.

15.148   TRIBAL ENERGY DEVELOPMENT CAPACITY GRANTS (TEDC)

Assistance: direct payments/specified use (100 percent).

Purposes: pursuant to Title XXVI (Indian Energy) of the Energy Policy Act of 1992, as amended, to provide grants to Indian tribes for use in developing and sustaining the managerial and technical capacity needed to develop their energy resources, and to properly account for resulting energy production and revenues.

Eligible applicants: federally recognized Indian tribal governments.

Eligible beneficiaries: federally recognized Indian tribal governments and their members.

Range/Average: N.A.

Activity: N.A.

HQ: Division of Indian Energy Policy Development, Office of Indian Energy and Economic Development, Rm. 20, 1951 Constitution Ave., NW, Washington, DC 20245. Phone: (202) 219-0740; FAX: (202) 208-4564.

Internet: www.eere.energy.gov/tribalenergy/government_grants.cfm.

15.149   FOCUS ON STUDENT ACHIEVEMENT PROJECT ("FOCUS")

Assistance: project grants.

Purposes: The FOCUS program is intended to target schools where student achievement is close to meeting annual measurable objectives as set by their states achievement test and where additional resources could facilitate achievement of Adequate Yearly Progress (AYP) as required by the No

Child Left Behind Act of 2001. Focus grant funds may be used for staff development and to implement proven instructional strategies designed to achieve annual growth for all students and "catch-up" growth for students performing below grade level expectations in reading and math.

Eligible applicants: federally recognized Indian tribal governments, tribal organizations authorized by Indian tribal governments on reservations with Bureau of Indian Education-funded schools.

Eligible beneficiaries: children between the ages of 5 and 21 who are members of or are at least a one-fourth degree Indian blood descendant of a member of an Indian tribe which is eligible for the special programs and services provided by the United States through the Bureau of Indian Affairs.

Range: $100,000 to $225,000. **Average:** $153,333.

Activity: N.A.

HQ: Director, FOCUS, Bureau of Indian Education, Division of Performance and Accountability, BIA Bldg 2, 1011 Indian School Rd., NW, 3rd Fl., Ste. 332, Albuquerque, NM 87104. Phone: (505) 563-5250.

Internet: www.bie.edu.

15.151   EDUCATION PROGRAM ENHANCEMENTS ("BIE Reads and Math Counts")

Assistance: cooperative agreements (100 percent).

Purposes: pursuant to the Indian Self-Determination and Education Assistance Act, to allow BIE to provide specialized assistance to schools struggling to make Adequate Yearly Progress (AYP) that is targeted to address the schools' unique needs and specific gaps in achievement. Funds must be used for staff development, and approved math and reading enhancement programs, are based on satisfactory performance and remain available until expended by the contractor or grantee.

Eligible applicants: federally-recognized tribal governments/organizations on reservations with Bureau-funded schools.

Eligible beneficiaries: children 5 to 21 years who are members of or are at least a one-fourth degree Indian blood descendant of a member of an Indian tribe.

Range: to $176,038 for Read grants; to $232,507 for Math Counts grants. **Average:** $23,052 for Read grants; $17,353 for Math Counts grants.

Activity: N.A.

HQ: Director, Division of Performance and Accountability, Bureau of Indian Education, DOI, BIA Bldg. 2, 1011 Indian School Rd., NW, 3rd Fl., Suite 332, Albuquerque, New Mexico 87104. Phone: (505) 563-5250.

Internet: www.BIE.EDU, www.doi.gov/bureau-indian-affairs.html.

15.152   LAND BUY-BACK PROGRAM FOR TRIBAL NATIONS ("Buy-Back Program")

Assistance: project grants/cooperative agreements (100 percent).

Purposes: pursuant to the Indian Land Consolidation Act and Claims Resolution Act of 2010, cooperative agreements with eligible tribes to reduce the number of fractional interests in trust or restricted lands by purchasing fractional interests from willing sellers and transferring them to tribe.

Eligible applicants/beneficiaries: federally-recognized Indian tribal governments with jurisdiction over fractionated lands.

Range/Average: N.A.

Activity: N.A.

HQ: Director, Land Buy-Back Program for Tribal Nations, Department of the Interior, 1849 C St., NW, Rm. 7222, Washington, DC 20240. Phone: (202) 219-1335.

Internet: www.doi.gov/buybackprogram. (Note: no field offices for this program.)

15.153 HURRICANE SANDY DISASTER RELIEF—COASTAL RESILIENCY GRANTS

Assistance: project grants (100 percent).

Purposes: pursuant to the Disaster Relief Appropriations Act of 2013, funds for disaster assistance related to Hurricane Sandy. Funds are to be used by recipients to assist Interior and its bureaus/offices to restore and rebuild national parks, national wildlife refuges, and increase the resiliency and capacity of coastal habitat and infrastructure to withstand storms and reduce the amount of damage caused by such storms.

Eligible applicants/beneficiaries: anyone/general public.

Range/Average: N.A.

Activity: N.A.

HQ: Director, Office of the Secretary, DOI, 1849 C St NW, Washington, DC 20240. Phone: (202) 208-5183.

Internet: N.A. (Note: no field offices for this program.)

15.214 NON-SALE DISPOSALS OF MINERAL MATERIAL

Assistance: sale, exchange, or donation of property and goods.

Purposes: pursuant to the Materials Act of 1947 as amended, to grant free use permits to extract mineral material from BLM lands for use in public projects. Such material may not be bartered or sold.

Eligible applicants/beneficiaries: federal or state agencies, municipalities; nonprofit entities.

Range/Average: N.A.

Activity: N.A.

HQ: Director, Solid Minerals Division (WO-320), 1849 C St., NW, Rm. 2134LM, Washington, DC 20240. Phone: (202) 912-7112.

Internet: www.blm.gov/nhp/index.htm.

15.222 COOPERATIVE INSPECTION AGREEMENTS WITH STATES AND TRIBES
("Section 202 Agreements")

Assistance: project grants (to 100 percent).

Purposes: pursuant to the Federal Oil and Gas Royalty Act of 1982, for inspections of oil and gas leases on Indian lands, by tribal inspectors.

Eligible applicants/beneficiaries: tribes with producing oil and gas leases on Indian lands for which the federal government has trust responsibility; states with tribal permission.

Range: $346,000 to $402,600. **Average:** $244,650.

Activity: N.A.

HQ: Assistant Director, Resource Use and Protection, BLM-DOI, 1849 C St., NW, LS 300, Washington, DC 20240. Phone: (202) 208-4201.

Internet: www.blm.gov/nhp/index.htm.

15.224 CULTURAL RESOURCE MANAGEMENT

Assistance: project grants; sale, exchange, donation, of property or goods; use of property, facilities, and equipment; specialized services; advisory services/counseling; technical information; training; investigation of complaints.

Purposes: pursuant to the Federal Land Policy and Management Act, Archaeological Resources Protection Act, and National Historic Preservation Act of 1966 as amended, to manage and protect cultural resources on BLM lands, and to increase public awareness of the resources, mainly in western states and Alaska. Project example: universities conducting management-focused archaeological field schools and scholarly research.

Eligible applicants/beneficiaries: anyone.

Range: $3,000 to $2,000,000. **Average:** $35,000.

Activity: N.A.

HQ: Group Administrator, Cultural and Recreation Group (WO 240), BLM-DOI, 1849 C St., NW, Washington, DC 20240. Phone: (202) 912-7241.

Internet: www.blm.gov.

15.225 RECREATION RESOURCE MANAGEMENT

Assistance: project grants; use of property, facilities, and equipment; specialized services; advisory services/counseling; technical information; training (grants, cost sharing).

Purposes: pursuant to ARRA 2009 and Federal Land Policy and Management Act, to manage and upgrade recreational resources and related facilities on BLM lands, mainly in western states and Alaska; for related public education. Project examples: promotion of effective cave management; Back Country Byways program; "watchable" wildlife and recreational fishing programs.

Eligible applicants/beneficiaries: anyone.

Range: $2,000 to $552,400. **Average:** $60,000.

Activity: N.A.

HQ: Manager, Recreation Group (WO 250), BLM-DOI, 1849 C St., NW, Rm. 2134LM, Washington, DC 20240-9998. Phone: (202) 912-7250.

Internet: www.blm.gov/nhp/index.htm.

15.226 PAYMENTS IN LIEU OF TAXES (PILT)

Assistance: direct payments/unrestricted use; direct payments/restricted use.

Purposes: to compensate local governmental taxing units for the loss of taxes from federal lands. Funds may be used for any governmental purpose.

Eligible applicants/beneficiaries: local government units with eligible lands.

Range/Average: N.A.

Activity: N.A.

HQ: PILT Specialist, Office of Budget, BLM-DOI, 1849 C St., NW, Rm. 4116, Washington, DC 20240. Phone: (202) 513-7785.

Internet: www.doi.gov/pilt. (Note: no field offices for this program.)

15.227 DISTRIBUTION OF RECEIPTS TO STATE AND LOCAL GOVERNMENTS

Assistance: direct payments/specified use; direct payments/unrestricted use.

Purposes: pursuant to the Mineral Lands Leasing Act, Outer Continental Shelf Lands Act, Federal Land Policy and Management Act of 1976, Mineral Revenue Payments Clarification Act of 2000, amendments, and other acts, to share federal revenues from fees charged for sale or use of public lands, minerals, and vegetation. Payments are formula-based.

Eligible applicants/beneficiaries: local government units with eligible lands.

Range/Average: N.A.

Activity: N.A.

HQ: Distribution of Receipts Specialist (OC-621), BLM-DOI, Bldg. 50, Denver Federal Center, Denver, CO 80225. Phone: (303) 236-0144.

Internet: www.blm.gov. (Note: no field offices for this program.)

15.228 NATIONAL FIRE PLAN—WILDLAND URBAN INTERFACE COMMUNITY FIRE ASSISTANCE

Assistance: project grants (matching); use of property, facilities, and equipment; specialized services; advisory services/counseling; technical information; training (grants, matching).

Purposes: to implement the National Fire Plan and assist communities at risk from catastrophic wildland fires affecting BLM-managed lands, through community capability building including: assessment, planning, and mitigation activities; community and homeowner education and action; planning and implementation of hazardous fuels reduction including training, monitoring or maintenance; increasing the effectiveness of rural fire district protection; purchase of protective clothing and equipment.

Eligible applicants/beneficiaries: state and local governments, tribes, public and private education institutions, nonprofit organizations, rural fire departments serving communities under 10,000 population in the wildland/urban interface.

Range: $5,000 to $686,000. **Average:** $47,400.

Activity: anticipate 15 to 20 awards in FY 2016.

HQ: Chief, Division of Fire Planning and Fuels Management, National Interagency Fire Center (FA-600), BLM-DOI, 3833 S. Development Ave., Boise, ID 83705. Phone: (208) 387-5186.

Internet: www.blm.gov/nhp/index.htm.

15.229   WILD HORSE AND BURRO RESOURCE MANAGEMENT

Assistance: project grants; use of property facilities, and equipment; advisory services/counseling; technical information; training (grants, to 100 percent).

Purposes: pursuant to Wild Free-Roaming Horse and Burros Act of 1971 and Federal Land Policy and Management Act, to manage and protect wild free-roaming horses and burros, toward achievement and maintenance of natural ecological balance on public lands. Funds may be used in research activities for improved census techniques and fertility control methods, and for adopting excess animals removed from the range. Project example: development of the National Wild Horse and Burro Foundation and its pertinent activities.

Eligible applicants/beneficiaries: anyone.

Range: $85,000 to $3,180,000. **Average:** $532,300.

Activity: N.A.

HQ: Group Manager, Wild Horses and Burros Group (WO260), BLM, 1849 C St., NW, Rm. 2134LM, Washington, DC 20240-9998. Phone: (202) 912-7296.

Internet: www.wildhorseandburro.blm.gov.

15.230   INVASIVE AND NOXIOUS PLANT MANAGEMENT

Assistance: project grants (matching funds encouraged/1 to 5 years); advisory services and counseling; training.

Purposes: pursuant to Federal Noxious Week Act of 1974, Watershed Restoration and Enhancement Agreements and other acts, to encourage cooperation and consultation among state, federal, local governments and agencies in order to inventory, manage, reduce, and prevent the invasion and establishment of noxious weeds, and to implement integrated pest management plans for invasive species within a specific geographic area. Projects with matching funds are more likely to be awarded grants.

Eligible applicants: state and local governments.

Eligible beneficiaries: anyone/general public.

Range: $1,000 to $567,000. **Average:** $31,600.

Activity: N.A.

HQ: Senior Weeds Specialist, Division of Rangeland Resources, BLM-DOI, 1849 C St., NW, MS: 2134LM, Washington, DC 20240. Phone: (202) 912-7226.

Internet: www.blm.gov/wo/st/en/prog/more/weeds/html.

15.231   FISH, WILDLIFE AND PLANT CONSERVATION RESOURCE MANAGEMENT

Assistance: project grants; use of property facilities, and equipment; advisory services/counseling; technical information; training (grants, to 100 percent).

Purposes: pursuant to ARRA 2009, Federal Land Policy and Management Act of 1976, Endangered Species Act of 1973, Sikes Act, Fish and Wildlife Conservation and Water Resources Development Coordination Act, Oceans Act of 1992, Wyden Amendment, and other amendments, to manage fish, wildlife, and plant conservation resources on the public lands administered by BLM, and on certain other public or private lands. Funds may be used for activities involving protection, restoration, enhancement, and conservation, and to provide related public contact and education opportunities. Most projects are conducted by BLM staff; however, management partnerships are supported through challenge grants. No regular discretionary funding is available.

Eligible applicants/beneficiaries: anyone.

Range: $1,000 to $1,000,000. **Average:** $68,300.

Activity: N.A.

HQ: Division Chief, Fish, Wildlife and Plant Conservation, BLM-DOI, (WO 230), 1849 C St., NW, MS-5115, Washington, DC 20240-9998. Phone: (202) 912-7230.

Internet: www.blm.gov/nhp/index.htm.

15.232 WILDLAND FIRE RESEARCH AND STUDIES PROGRAM

Assistance: project grants (100 percent/1-3 years).

Purposes: pursuant to Federal Land Policy and Management Act and The Joint Fire Science Program Authorization in the Department of the Interior and Related Agencies Appropriation Act of 1998 as amended, to address wildland fire management needs of federal and local government land managers through research, studies, and product and tool development that meet objectives of the National Fire Plan. Joint Fire Science Program applicants must clearly identify a federal cooperator to be considered for funding. Projects with matching funds are more likely to be awarded grants.

Eligible applicants/beneficiaries: general public.

Range: $60,000 to $500,000. **Average:** $350,000.

Activity: N.A.

HQ: Group Manager, Planning and Resources Group, BLM-Office of Fire and Aviation, 3833 S. Development Ave., Boise, ID 83705. Phone: (208) 387-5153. Program Manager, Joint Fire Science Program, Phone: (208) 387-5349.

Internet: www.forestsandrangelands.gov.

15.233 FORESTS AND WOODLANDS RESOURCE MANAGEMENT

Assistance: project grants (100 percent/1-5 years); advisory services and counseling; training.

Purposes: pursuant to Federal Land Policy and Management Act of 1976 as amended, to improve forests on public lands through maintenance of forest health, including: forest regeneration, restoration, rehabilitation, insect and disease control, forest development, implementation of stewardship projects, and biomass utilization of public lands. Applicants are encouraged to contribute matching funds, as these projects are more likely to be funded.

Eligible applicants/beneficiaries: general public.

Range: $1,000 to $450,900. **Average:** $50,000.

Activity: N.A.

HQ: Division Chief, Forest and Woodland Management, (WO270), BLM, 1849 C St., NW, Rm. 204LS, Washington, DC 20240-9998. Phone: (202) 452-0316.

Internet: www.blm.gov/wo/st/en/prog/more/forests_and_woodland.html.

15.234 SECURE RURAL SCHOOLS AND COMMUNITY SELF-DETERMINATION

Assistance: project grants (matching funds encouraged).

Purposes: pursuant to Secure Rural Schools and Community Self-Determination Act of 2000, to restore stability and predictability to annual payments made to states and counties containing Natural Forest System and public domain lands managed by BLM for use by counties. Projects may be used for implementing cooperative agreements with federal agencies, state and local governments, private and public entities, landowners and the general public for the protection, restoration, and enhancement of fish and wildlife habitat, to enhance forest ecosystems, and to restore and improve land health and water quality.

Eligible applicants: state and local governments, private, public, nonprofit and for- profit organizations/institutions, and landowners.

Eligible beneficiaries: anyone/general public.

Range: $1,100 to $596,700. **Average:** $83,600.

Activity: N.A.

HQ: Division Chief, Forest and Woodland Management, (WO270), BLM, 1849 C St., NW, Rm. 2134LM, Washington, DC 20240. Phone: (202) 912-7246.

Internet: www.blm.gov/or/rac/ctypayhistory.php.

15.235 SOUTHERN NEVADA PUBLIC LAND MANAGEMENT

Assistance: project grants (100 percent/to five years).

Purposes: pursuant to Southern Nevada Public Land Management Act of 1998, Clark County Conservation of Public Land and Natural Resources Act of 2002, Department of the Interior and Related Agencies Appropriation Act of 2004, to provide for orderly disposal of certain federal lands in Clark County and other areas in Nevada and for the acquisition of environmentally sensitive lands in the State of Nevada. Cooperative projects may include: the development of parks and trails; development and implementation of hazardous fuels reduction and wildlife fire prevention plans; and sustainable biomass and biofuel energy and production activities. Projects are subject to approval by Secretary of the Interior and may not be more than 10 years in duration. Applicants are encouraged to contribute matching funds, as these projects are more likely to be funded.

Eligible applicants: eligible local and regional government entities within the state of Nevada.

Eligible beneficiaries: anyone/general public.

Range: $30,000 to $12,593,700. **Average:** $240,300.

Activity: N.A.

HQ: Division Chief Division of Lands and Realty, BLM, (WO 350), 20 M St., SE, Rm. 2134, Washington, DC 20003. Phone: (202) 912-7350.

Internet: www.nv.blm.gov/snplma.

15.236 ENVIRONMENTAL QUALITY AND PROTECTION RESOURCE MANAGEMENT

Assistance: project grants (100 percent/1-5 years); advisory services and counseling; dissemination of technical information; training.

Purposes: pursuant to Federal Land Policy and Management Act of 1976 and the Consolidated Appropriations Act of 2008 as amended, to reduce or eliminate environmental pollutants hazardous to human health, water, and air resources; restore damaged or degraded watersheds; and to respond to changing climate. Projects address conditions on public lands located mostly in the western U.S. and Alaska. Applicants are encouraged to contribute matching funds or in-kind services, as these projects are more likely to be funded.

Eligible applicants/beneficiaries: general public.

Range: $1,000 to $1,762,000. **Average:** $62,700.

Activity: N.A.

HQ: Division Chief, Environmental Quality and Protection, (WO280), BLM, 1849 C St., NW - 204 LS, Washington, DC 20240. Phone: (202) 912-7136.

Internet: www.blm.gov.

15.237 RANGELAND RESOURCE MANAGEMENT

Assistance: project grants; advisory services and counseling; training (grants, 100 percent/1-5 years).

Purposes: pursuant to Federal Land Policy and Management Act of 1976, Public Rangelands Improvement Act of 1978, and the Taylor Grazing Act of 1934 as amended, to manage, develop and protect public lands through improvement of rangeland ecosystem health, the understanding of watershed resources, and compliance with rangeland and water quality standards. Applicants are encouraged to contribute matching funds or in-kind services, as these projects are more likely to be funded.

Eligible applicants/beneficiaries: general public.

Range: $5,000 to $180,000. **Average:** $49,300.

Activity: N.A.

HQ: Division Chief, Rangeland Resources, (WO220), BLM, 1849 C St., NW, Rm. 20M, Washington, DC 20240. Phone: (202) 912-7222.

Internet: www.blm.gov/wo/st/en.html.

15.238 CHALLENGE COST SHARE

Assistance: project grants (50 percent/1-5 years); use of property, facilities, and equipment; advisory services and counseling; training.

Purposes: pursuant to Department of the Interior and Related Agencies Appropriation Act for Fiscal year 1991, to work with cooperative partners to support habitat improvement and protection; implement endangered and threatened species recovery plans; survey, monitor, and inventory resources; provide visitor services or facilities; manage heritage resources; conduct public outreach and education projects; and support emerging partnership opportunities.

Eligible applicants/beneficiaries: general public.

Range: $1,500 to $182,000. **Average:** $25,100.

Activity: N.A.

HQ: Assistant Director for Renewable Resources and Planning, (WO200), BLM, 1849 C St., NW, Rm. 2134LM, Washington, DC 20240. Phone: (202) 912-7203.

Internet: www.blm.gov.

15.239   MANAGEMENT INITIATIVES

Assistance: project grants; use of property, facilities, and equipment; advisory services and counseling; training (grants, 100 percent/1-5 years).

Purposes: pursuant to Federal Land Policy and Management Act of 1976 as amended, to provide support for the management, protection and development of public lands administered by BLM, mostly in Western U.S. or Alaska. Assistance may also support outreach and education efforts associated with partnership programs. Awards are not covered by any other program entry and are typically supported by funding one-time specific legislation and internal projects and programs. Applicants are encouraged to contribute matching funds, as these projects are more likely to be funded.

Eligible applicants/beneficiaries: general public.

Range: $2,900 to $800,000. **Average:** $117,400.

Activity: N.A.

HQ: Procurement Analyst, Property, Acquisition, and Headquarters Services Group, (WO850), BLM, 1849 C St., NW, Rm. 1075LS, Washington, DC 20240. Phone: (202) 912-7040.

Internet: www.blm.gov.

15.240   HELIUM RESOURCE MANAGEMENT

Assistance: project grants (100 percent/1-5 years).

Purposes: pursuant to the Helium Privatization Act of 1996, to assist the U.S. government in the upgrade and efficient delivery of crude helium to private helium plants which supply private industry, government agencies and research projects. The purchased helium is used to repay the helium debt.

Eligible applicants: public institutions and organizations and for-profit organizations directly involved with the implementation of the Helium Privatization Act and projects related to the elimination of the helium debt.

Eligible beneficiaries: anyone/general public.

Range: $720,000 and $6,000,000. **Average:** $336,000.

Activity: N.A.

HQ: Group Manger, Fluid Minerals, (WO300), BLM, 1848 C Street, NW, MIB 5625, Washington, DC 20240. Phone: (202) 208-420.

Internet: www.blm.gov/nm/st/en/fo/Amarillo_Field_Office.html.

15.241 INDIAN SELF-DETERMINATION ACT CONTRACTS, GRANTS AND COOPERATIVE AGREEMENTS

Assistance: project grants/cooperative agreements; training; use of property, facilities, and equipment (100 percent).

Purposes: pursuant to ISDEAA, to: provide maximum Indian participation in the government and education of Indian people; encourage development of human resources of the Indian people; and to upgrade Indian education. Funds are authorized for non-construction projects in 17 western states and Alaska for BLM programs and services conducted for the benefit of Indian tribes.

Eligible applicants/beneficiaries: federally-recognized Indian tribal governments.

Range: $12,600 to $1,302,100. **Average:** $244,300.

Activity: N.A.

HQ: Native American Coordinator, BLM-DOI, 1849 C St., NW - 2134LM, Washington, DC 20240. Phone: (202) 912-7245.

Internet: www.blm.gov.

15.242 NATIONAL FIRE PLAN—RURAL FIRE ASSISTANCE

Assistance: project grants; use of property, facilities, and equipment; specialized services; advisory services/counseling; technical information; training (grants, matching).

Purposes: to implement the National Fire Plan by increasing firefighter safety and enhancing the knowledge and fire protection capability of rural fire departments near BLM-managed lands, through: education and training, protective clothing and equipment purchases, public education.

Eligible applicants/beneficiaries: state and local governments, tribes, public and private education institutions, nonprofit organizations, rural fire departments serving communities under 10,000 population in the wildland/urban interface.

Range: $1,600 to $125,000. **Average:** $28,600.

Activity: N.A.

HQ: Director Division of Fire Planning and Fuels Management (FA-600), National Interagency Fire Center, 3833 S. Development Ave., Boise, ID 83705. Phone: (208) 387-5186.

Internet: www.nifc.gov/rfa/index.html.

15.250 REGULATION OF SURFACE COAL MINING AND SURFACE EFFECTS OF UNDERGROUND COAL MINING

Assistance: project grants; direct payments/specified use. (50-100 percent/to 3 years).

Purposes: pursuant to the Surface Mining Control and Reclamation Act of 1977, for regulatory activities to control surface impacts of coal mining.

Grants may be used to develop state legislation, programs, and regulations, as well as for enforcement activities; also, to provide hydrologic and geologic data for small coal operators.

Eligible applicants/beneficiaries: state governors. Small coal mine operators (annual production under 300,000 tons) may apply for assistance in meeting technical permit application requirements.

Range: $39,331 to $12,500,570. **Average:** $2,172,639.

Activity: 24 states received grants in FY 2014.

HQ: Chief, Division of Regulatory Support, Office of Surface Mining Reclamation and Enforcement, DOI, 1951 Constitution Ave., NW, Washington, DC 20240. Phone: (202) 208-2868.

Internet: www.osmre.gov.

15.252 ABANDONED MINE LAND RECLAMATION (AMLR) PROGRAM

Assistance: formula grants; project grants. (100 percent/to 3 years).

Purposes: pursuant to the Surface Mining Control and Reclamation Act of 1977, for reclamation projects to correct environmental damage caused or affected by coal and other mining and related processes on eligible lands and waters—occurring prior to 3 August 1977, and certain post-1977 lands and waters beginning 1 October 1991. Subsidence insurance grants, limited to $3,000,000, are also available to states to insure private property against damages caused by underground coal mining.

Eligible applicants/beneficiaries: states and tribes with eligible lands and coal mining operations, and paying reclamation fees.

Range: $70,806 to $53,847,000. **Average:** $8,728,038.

Activity: N.A.

HQ: Chief, Division of Reclamation Support, Office of Surface Mining Reclamation and Enforcement, DOI, 1951 Constitution Ave., NW, Washington, DC 20240. Phone: (202) 208-2868.

Internet: www.osmre.gov.

15.253 NOT-FOR-PROFIT AMD RECLAMATION

Assistance: project grants (100 percent/2 years).

Purposes: pursuant to the Surface Mining Control and Reclamation Act of 1977, for local acid mine drainage reclamation projects, especially in watershed areas, where lands and water were impacted by coal mining activities. Eligibility is limited to areas where mining and related damage occurred prior to 3 August 1977, and where there is no continuing state or federal legal responsibility.

Eligible applicants/beneficiaries: existing nonprofit organizations.

Range: $22,000 to $200,000. **Average:** $86,905.

Activity: 19 new projects funded in FY 2015.

HQ: Chief, Division of Regulatory Support, Office of Surface Mining Reclamation and Enforcement, DOI, 1951 Constitution Ave., NW, Washington, DC 20240. Phone: (202) 208-2868.

Internet: www.osmre.gov.

15.254 OSM/VISTA AMERICORPS PROGRAM

Assistance: direct payments/specified use (12-24 weeks).

Purposes: pursuant to the Surface Mining Control and Reclamation Act of 1977, work with community and volunteer watershed groups in the Appalachian coal country and in western mining towns impoverished by environmental degradation to build local capacity, strengthen environmental stewardship, enhance outreach and education initiatives, engage economic redevelopment, provide professional development for OSMRE/VISTAs, and build stronger partnerships with agencies and industry.@info - purposes:

Eligible applicants: private and public nonprofit organizations and established watershed organizations in Alabama, Illinois, Indiana, Iowa, Kentucky, Maryland, Missouri, Ohio, Oklahoma, Pennsylvania, Tennessee, Virginia, West Virginia.

Eligible beneficiaries: undergraduate and graduate students.

Range/Average: N.A.

Activity: N.A.

HQ: Office of Surface Mining Reclamation and Enforcement, DOI, 1951 Constitution Ave. NW, Washington, DC 20240. Phone: (202) 208-2585.

Internet: www.osmre.gov.acsi/internindex.htm.

15.255 SCIENCE AND TECHNOLOGY PROJECTS RELATED TO COAL MINING AND RECLAMATION

Assistance: project grants (75-100 percent).

Purposes: pursuant to Surface Mining Control and Reclamation Act of 1977 (SMCRA), to support projects which focus on issues related to mining in the USA and its territories, including: development and demonstration of improved technologies to address public safety and environmental issues; encouragement of efforts to collect, preserve and convert into digital format, maps of underground mines that provide valuable information regarding protection of public and miner safety, mine pool evaluation, and mine subsidence investigation for previously mined areas. Funding will be limited to projects that can be completed without additional funding from the Office of Surface Mining (OSM) beyond those funds awarded in the current fiscal year. Cost sharing by applicants is not required but strongly encouraged.

Eligible applicants/beneficiaries: public, private, nonprofit, state, local or Tribal governments, colleges, and universities located in the USA. Mine Mapping: any US state or Indian Tribal agency or US Territory.

Range/Average: N.A.

Activity: N.A.

HQ: Chief, Division of Regulatory Support, Office of Surface Mining Reclamation and Enforcement, DOI, 1951 Constitution Ave., NW, Washington, DC 20240. Phone: (202) 208-2868.

Internet: www.grants.gov.

15.406 NATIONAL PARK SERVICE CENTENNIAL CHALLENGE

Assistance: formula grants (50 percent/to 2 years).

Purposes: pursuant to the Challenge Cost Share and Centennial Challenge Provisions, to support the ten year effort to prepare national parks for another century of conservation, preservation, and public enjoyment. Applicant must have a partner willing to contribute 50% of the total cost of the project, which must be derived from non-federal funds and can include in-kind services. Projects should address one or more of the areas of emphasis: stewardship, environmental, leadership, recreational experience, educational and professional excellence, and should require little or no additional recurring NPS operating funds in order to be sustainable.

Eligible applicants/beneficiaries: state and local governments, tribes, individuals and private, public, nonprofit and for-profit institutions and organizations.

Range: $5,000 to $15,000. **Average:** $10,000.

Activity: N.A.

HQ: Program Manager, Centennial Initiative, DOI-NPS, 1849 C St., NW, Washington, DC 20240. Phone: (202) 208-6843; FAX: (202) 208-0000.

Internet: www.nps.gov/2016. (Note: no field offices for this program.)

15.407 KEWEENAW NATIONAL HISTORICAL PARK (NHP) AND KEWEENAW NHP ADVISORY COMMISSION PARTNER ENHANCEMENT GRANTS ("Keweenaw Heritage Grants")

Assistance: project grants.

Purposes: pursuant to the National Historic Preservation Act of 1966 and the Historic Sites Act of 1935, to enhance partner projects that will mark, interpret, or restore non-federal properties inside the Keweenaw National Park (NPS Grants) or on the Keweenaw Peninsula (Keweenaw NHP Advisory Commission Grants). The availability of discretionary funding is determined by the Keweenaw NHP Advisory Commission each fiscal year. Matched funds are required for both programs.

Eligible applicants/beneficiaries: NPS grants: owners of properties inside the boundaries of the Keweenaw NHP containing nationally significant historic or cultural resources. Keweenaw NHP Advisory Commission Grants: owners or operators of properties on the Keweenaw Peninsula containing local, state, or nationally significant historic or cultural resources.

Range: to $50,000. **Average:** $6,500.

Activity: N.A.

HQ: Management Assistant, Keweenaw NHP, PO Box 471, 25970 Red Jacket Rd., Calumet, MI 49913. Phone: (906) 483-3040.

Internet: www.nps.gov/kewe/grants. (Note: no field offices for this program.)

15.408 BUREAU OF OCEAN ENERGY MANAGEMENT RENEWABLE ENERGY PROGRAM

Assistance: project grants/cooperative agreements (50 percent cost sharing encouraged/1 to 5 years).

Purposes: pursuant to the Outer Continental Shelf Lands Act (OCSLA) Section 1345, cooperative agreements to acquire information to satisfy the requirements of OCSLA associated with leasing and plan review for renewable energy development on the outer continental shelf including: sharing information, joint utilization of available expertise, formation of joint monitoring arrangements to carry out applicable federal and state laws, regulations, and stipulations relevant to outer continental shelf operations both onshore and offshore.

Eligible applicants: state agencies, public non-profit institutions and organizations, including public IHEs and hospitals.

Eligible beneficiaries: research scientists, federal, state and local decision makers, Native American organizations, and the general public.

Range: $100,000 to $1,000,000. **Average:** $500,000.

Activity: N.A.

HQ: Director, Bureau of Ocean Energy Management-DOI, 381 Elden St., HM 3115, Herndon, VA 20170. Phone: (703) 787-1662; FAX: (703) 787-1708.

Internet: www.boem.gov. (Note: no field offices for this program.)

15.421 ALASKA COASTAL MARINE INSTITUTE ("Alaska CMI")

Assistance: project grants (50 percent/1-4 years).

Purposes: to use highly qualified scientific expertise at local levels to collect and disseminate environmental information needed for Outer Continental Shelf oil, gas and marine minerals decisions; address local and regional environmental and resource issues of mutual interest; strengthen Mineral Management Service-State partnership in addressing OCS information needs. Funds may also be used for alternate energy development projects, national conference attendance, and dissemination of project results, but not for capitalization.

Eligible applicants/beneficiaries: University of Alaska named principal investigator; non-UA scientists may collaborate with a UA principal investigator.

Range: $12,000 to $360,000. **Average:** $170,000.

Activity: N.A.

HQ: Bureau of Ocean Energy Management, 381 Elden St., HM-3115, Herndon, VA 20170. Phone: (703) 787-1087; FAX: (703) 787-1053.

Internet: www.boem.gov.

15.422 LOUISIANA STATE UNIVERSITY (LSU) COASTAL MARINE INSTITUTE (CMI)

Assistance: project grants (50 percent/1-4 years).

Purposes: to use highly qualified scientific expertise at local levels to collect and disseminate environmental information needed for Outer Continental Shelf oil, gas and marine minerals decisions; address local and regional environmental and resource issues of mutual interest; strengthen Mineral Management Service-State partnership in addressing OCS information needs. Funds may also be used for national conference attendance, alternate energy development projects, and dissemination of project results, but not for capitalization.

Eligible applicants/beneficiaries: Louisiana State University named principal investigator; non-LSU scientists may collaborate with a LSU principal investigator.

Range: $200,000 to $360,000. **Average:** $210,000.

Activity: N.A.

HQ: Bureau of Ocean Energy Management, 381 Elden St., HM-3115, Herndon, VA 20170. Phone: (703) 787-1087; FAX: (703) 787-1053.

Internet: www.boem.gov.

15.423 BUREAU OF OCEAN ENERGY MANAGEMENT (BOEM) ENVIRONMENTAL STUDIES PROGRAM (ESP)

Assistance: project grants (from 50 percent/1-8 years).

Purposes: to obtain information needed for assessment and management of environmental impacts; to predict impacts on marine biota; to monitor human, marine, and coastal environments in order to provide time series and data trend information. Funds may also be used for alternate energy development projects, national conference attendance, and dissemination of project results, but not for capitalization. Matched funding is strongly encouraged.

Eligible applicants/beneficiaries: state agencies and public IHEs; institutions may apply collaboratively.

Range: $100,000 to $750,000. **Average:** $380,000.

Activity: N.A.

HQ: Bureau of Ocean Energy Management, 381 Elden St., HM-3115, Herndon, VA 20170. Phone: (703) 787-1087; FAX: (703) 787-1053.

Internet: www.boem.gov. (Note: no field offices for this program.)

15.424 MARINE MINERALS ACTIVITIES—HURRICANE SANDY ("Marine Minerals Activities")

Assistance: project grants (50 percent).

Purposes: pursuant to the Outer Continental Shelf Lands Act, to evaluate OCS sand deposits for beach nourishment projects and to foster good working relationships with coastal states regarding OCS mineral issues.

Eligible applicants/beneficiaries: coastal states in need of coastal restoration.

Range: $30,000 to $760,000. **Average:** N.A.

Activity: N.A.

HQ: Chief BOEM, Leasing Division, 45600 Woodland Rd., Stop 3120, Sterling, VA 20166. Phone: (703) 787-1215.

Internet: www.boem.gov/MarineMineralsProgram.

15.427 FEDERAL OIL AND GAS ROYALTY MANAGEMENT—STATE AND TRIBAL COORDINATION ("FOGRMA")

Assistance: project grants (100 percent).

Purposes: pursuant to Federal Oil and Gas Royalty Management Act of 1982, to ensure that all oil, gas, and solid minerals originated on public lands and the Outer Continental Shelf are properly accounted for.

Eligible applicants/beneficiaries: state and tribal governments only.

Range: $200,000 to $3,000,000. **Average:** $500,000.

Activity: N.A.

HQ: Associate Director, Minerals Revenue Management, MMS, 1849 C St., NW, Stop 4211, Washington, DC 20240. Phone: (202) 513-0600.

Internet: www.onrr.gov.

15.428 MARINE GAS HYDRATE RESEARCH ACTIVITIES

Assistance: project grants (1 year).

Purposes: pursuant to the Outer Continental Shelf (OCS) Lands Act, Gas Hydrates Research Act, and Marine Minerals Research Act, to characterize and monitor gas hydrate deposits on the Outer Continental Shelf in the Gulf of Mexico. Matching grants are for research and scientific sensory equipment for the monitoring station.

Eligible applicants: only applications from Center for Marine Resources and Environmental Technology (CMRET) or from qualified subcontractors through CMRET will be accepted. Applicants must have experience in marine gas hydrates.

Eligible beneficiaries: participating organizations and general public.

Range/Average: N.A.

Activity: N.A.

HQ: BOEM Resource Evaluation Division, 381 Elden St., MS-4070, Herndon, VA 20170-4817. Phone: (703) 787-1514.

Internet: www.boem.gov.

15.429 STATE SELECT

Assistance: direct payments/specified use (100 percent).

Purposes: pursuant to Public Lands, 43 U.S.C 852 (a)(4), to share 90 percent of oil and gas royalties with the State to be paid monthly subject to late disbursement interest.

Eligible applicants: revenue from public land leasing will trigger automatic payment distribution computed in accordance with the law.

Eligible beneficiaries: lease lands must be located within State selected area.

Range/Average: N.A.

Activity: N.A.

HQ: Director U.S. Department of Interior, Office of Natural Resources Revenue, 1849 C St., NW, Stop 4211, Washington, DC 20240. Phone: (202) 513-0600.

Internet: www.onrr.gov.

15.430 8(G) STATE COASTAL ZONE

Assistance: direct payments/specified use (100 percent).

Purposes: pursuant to Minerals, Lands and Mining, Title 43, Part 256.47(g), 30 U.S.C 191a; to share 27 percent of mineral leasing revenue derived from any lease issued after September 18, 1978, of any Federal tract which lies wholly or partially within 3 nautical miles of the Seaward boundary of any coastal state. Shared revenue is paid monthly.

Eligible applicants: revenue from qualified leasing will trigger automatic payment distribution computed in accordance with the law.

Eligible beneficiaries: leased Outer Continental Shelf Lands must be located within the 8(g) zone of a coastal state.

Range/Average: N.A.

Activity: N.A.

HQ: Director U.S. Department of Interior, Office of Natural Resources Revenue, 1849 C St., NW, Stop 4211, Washington, DC 20240. Phone: (202) 513-0600.

Internet: www.onrr.gov.

15.431 ALASKA SETTLEMENT AGREEMENT

Assistance: direct payments/unrestricted use (100 percent).

Purposes: pursuant to Public Lands; January 12, 1990 Settlement, 43 U.S.C 1635(l), to share 100 percent with the State of Alaska to be paid monthly subject to late disbursement interest for contracts, leases, permits, rights-of-way, or easements under Section 6 of the Alaska Statehood Act.

Eligible applicants: revenue from effected leases will trigger automatic payment distribution computed in accordance with the law.

Eligible beneficiaries: limited to Leases A-028056, A-028063, A-028135, A-028143, A-028103, A-028140, A-19230, A028055, and A-028047.

Range/Average: N.A.

Activity: N.A.

HQ: Director U.S. Department of Interior, Office of Natural Resources Revenue, 1849 C St., NW, Stop 4211, Washington, DC 20240. Phone: (202) 513-0600.

Internet: www.onrr.gov.

15.432 CALIFORNIA REFUGE ACCOUNT

Assistance: direct payments/unrestricted use (100 percent).

Purposes: pursuant to Public Lands; Settlement agreement dated March 25, 1997, 43 U.S.C 1337(g)(2), (3), to share 40.87 percent with the State of California.

Eligible applicants/beneficiaries: states.

Range/Average: N.A.

Activity: N.A.

HQ: Director U.S. Department of Interior, Office of Natural Resources Revenue, 1849 C St., NW, Stop 4211, Washington, DC 20240. Phone: (202) 513-0600.

Internet: www.onrr.gov.

15.433   FLOOD CONTROL ACT LANDS

Assistance: direct payments/specified use (100 percent).

Purposes: pursuant to Minerals, Lands and Mining, to share 75 percent of mineral leasing revenue with the State, paid monthly and is subject to late disbursement interest. To be used as the State legislature may prescribe for the benefit of public schools and public roads of the county or counties in which such property is situated, or for defraying any of the expenses of county government in such county or counties, including public obligations of levee and drainage districts for flood control and drainage improvements.

Eligible applicants: revenue from acquired Flood Control land leasing will trigger automatic payment distribution computed in accordance with the law.

Eligible beneficiaries: leased acquired lands must be located within the State.

Range/Average: N.A.

Activity: N.A.

HQ: Director U.S. Department of Interior, Office of Natural Resources Revenue, 1849 C St., NW, Stop 4211, Washington, DC 20240. Phone: (202) 513-0600.

Internet: www.onrr.gov.

15.434   GEOTHERMAL RESOURCES

Assistance: direct payments/specified use (100 percent).

Purposes: pursuant to Minerals, Lands, and Mining, 30 U.S.C 191a, 1019, to share 50 percent of mineral leasing revenue with the State, and 25 percent with the county. To be used as the legislature directs giving priority to those subdivisions of the State that are socially or economically impacted by the development of minerals leased, for (1) planning, (2) construction and maintenance of public facilities, (3) provision of public service.

Eligible applicants: revenue from government owned land leasing will trigger automatic payment distribution computed in accordance with the law.

Eligible beneficiaries: leased lands must be located within State/County.

Range/Average: N.A.

Activity: N.A.

HQ: Director U.S. Department of Interior, Office of Natural Resources Revenue, 1849 C St., NW, Stop 4211, Washington, DC 20240. Phone: (202) 513-0600.

Internet: www.onrr.gov.

15.435   GOMESA

Assistance: direct payments/specified use (100 percent).

Purposes: pursuant to Public Law 109-432, 120 STAT 3000, to share 37.5 percent of selected revenue with Gulf producing states and political subdivisions; payable annually during the year after receipt in accordance with 30 CFR Part 219.414. To be used in accordance with all applicable Federal and State laws, only for 1 or more of the following purposes: A) Projects and activities for the purposes of coastal protection, including conservation, coastal restoration, hurricane protection, and infrastructure directly affected by coastal wetland losses; B) mitigation of damage to fish, wildlife or natural resources; C) implementation of a federally-approved marine, coastal or comprehensive conservation management plan; D) Mitigation of the impact of Outer Continental Shelf activities through the funding of onshore infrastructure projects; E) Planning assistance and the administrative costs of complying with this section. Limitation: Not more than 3 percent of amount received may be spent on planning assistance and compliance administrative costs.

Eligible applicants/beneficiaries: eligible states and political subdivisions with Louisiana, Texas, Alabama, and Mississippi.

Range/Average: N.A.

Activity: N.A.

HQ: Director U.S. Department of Interior, Office of Natural Resources Revenue, 1849 C St., NW, Stop 4211, Washington, DC 20240. Phone: (202) 513-0600.

Internet: www.onrr.gov.

15.436 LATE DISBURSEMENT INTEREST

Assistance: direct payments/unrestricted use (100 percent).

Purposes: pursuant to Minerals, Lands and Mining, Public Law 108-447, 30 U.S.C 1721 (b), to pay late disbursement interest on subject payments made to States after the due date.

Eligible applicants: Late disbursements will trigger automatic payment distribution computed in accordance with the Law.

Eligible beneficiaries: ONRR pays late disbursement interest on subject payments made to States after the due date.

Range/Average: N.A.

Activity: N.A.

HQ: Director U.S. Department of Interior, Office of Natural Resources Revenue, 1849 C St., NW, Stop 4211, Washington, DC 20240. Phone: (202) 513-0600.

Internet: www.onrr.gov.

15.437 MINERALS LEASING ACT

Assistance: direct payments/specified use (100 percent).

Purposes: pursuant to the Minerals Leasing Act, the Office of Natural Resources Revenue (ONRR) shares 50 percent (90 percent for Alaska) of mineral leasing revenue with States. Priority is given to those subdivisions of the State that are socially or economically impacted by the development of minerals leased for: planning, construction and maintenance of public facilities, and provision of public service.

Eligible applicants/beneficiaries: state governments in which leased Federal lands and minerals are located.

Range/Average: N.A.

Activity: N.A.

HQ: Director U.S. Department of Interior, Office of Natural Resources Revenue, 1849 C St., NW, Stop 4211, Washington, DC 20240. Phone: (202) 513-0600.

Internet: www.onrr.gov.

15.438 NATIONAL FOREST ACQUIRED LAND

Assistance: direct payments/specified use (100 percent/monthly).

Purposes: pursuant to Minerals, Lands and Mining, 30 U.S.C 191(a). 355(b), ONRR shares 25 percent of minerals leasing revenue with the State in which such National Forest is situated. Revenue is paid monthly and is subject to late disbursement interest. To be used as the state legislature prescribed for the benefit of the public schools and public roads of the country or counties in which such National Forest is situated.

Eligible applicants: revenue from acquired National Forest land leasing will trigger automatic payment distribution computed in accordance with the Law.

Eligible beneficiaries: leased acquired lands must be located within the State.

Range/Average: N.A.

Activity: N.A.

HQ: Director U.S. Department of Interior, Office of Natural Resources Revenue, 1849 C St., NW, Stop 4211, Washington, DC 20240. Phone: (202) 513-0600.

Internet: www.onrr.gov.

15.439 NATIONAL PETROLEUM RESERVE—ALASKA

Assistance: direct payments/specified use (100 percent).

Purposes: pursuant to Public Lands, 43 Stat. 3231.5(f); Public Health and Welfare, 42 U.S.C 6508, ONRR shares 50 percent of mineral leasing revenue with the State of Alaska, to be paid monthly (oil and gas royalties) subject to late disbursement interest. Other than oil and gas royalties are paid semi-annually. To be used for (1) planning; (2) construction, maintenance, and operation of essential public facilities; and (3) other necessary provisions of public service, giving priority to use by subdivisions of the State most directly or severely impacted by development of oil and gas leasing.

Eligible applicants: revenue from public land leasing will trigger automatic payment distribution computed in accordance with the Law.

Eligible beneficiaries: lease lands must be located in the National Petroleum Reserve-Alaska.

Range/Average: N.A.

Activity: N.A.

HQ: Director U.S. Department of Interior, Office of Natural Resources Revenue, 1849 C St., NW, Stop 4211, Washington, DC 20240. Phone: (202) 513-0600.

Internet: www.onrr.gov.

15.440 SOUTH HALF OF THE RED RIVER

Assistance: direct payments/specified use (100 percent).

Purposes: pursuant to Minerals, Lands and Mining, 65 Stat. 252, 30 U.S.C 191(a), 355(b), ONRR shares 37.5 percent of mineral leasing revenue with the State of Oklahoma paid monthly and is subject to late disbursement interest. To be used by the State as the legislature directs giving priority to those subdivisions of the State that are socially or economically impacted by the development of minerals leased, for (1) planning, (2) construction and maintenance of public facilities, and (3) provision of public service.

Eligible applicants: revenue from public land leasing will trigger automatic payment distribution computed in the accordance with the Law.

Eligible beneficiaries: leased lands must be located within the south half of the Red River.

Range/Average: N.A.

Activity: N.A.

HQ: Director U.S. Department of Interior, Office of Natural Resources Revenue, 1849 C St., NW, Stop 4211, Washington, DC 20240. Phone: (202) 513-0600.

Internet: www.onrr.gov.

15.441 SAFETY AND ENVIRONMENTAL ENFORCEMENT RESEARCH AND DATA COLLECTION FOR OFFSHORE ENERGY AND MINERAL ACTIVITIES

Assistance: cooperative agreements (50 percent/1 to 5 years).

Purposes: to conduct technical research (projects must be within the BSEE area of responsibility) associated with oil and gas, alternate energy and marine animal development on the outer continental shelf. Funds support research for exploration and production techniques to enhance safe operations and oil-spill prevention and cleanup from oil and gas, marine minerals, alternate energy development projects and for attendance at national conferences for the dissemination of project results.

Eligible applicants: state agencies and public IHEs. More than one institution may collaborate in the preparation of an application for assistance.

Eligible beneficiaries: federal, state and local governments, research scientists, general public.

Range: $100,000 to $5,000,000. **Average:** $300,000.

Activity: N.A.

HQ: Program Director, OORP, Bureau of Safety and Environmental Enforcement, DOI, 45600 Woodland Rd., MS-E3313, Sterling, VA 20166. Phone: (703) 787-1611; FAX: : (703) 787-1555.

Internet: www.bsee.gov. (Note: no field offices for this program.)

15.504 TITLE XVI WATER RECLAMATION AND REUSE PROGRAM

Assistance: formula grants (25 to 50 percent).

Purposes: pursuant to the Reclamation Wastewater and Groundwater Study and Facilities Act as amended other acts, for appraisals and feasibility studies (50 percent federal funding) on water reclamation and re-use projects, mainly in the western states; for research and demonstration programs and for construction of re-use projects (25 percent federal funding).

Eligible applicants/beneficiaries: projects—legally organized nonfederal entities such as irrigation districts, municipalities. Research—IHEs; architectural and engineering firms.

Range: $50,000 to $4,000,000. **Average:** N.A.

Activity: N.A.

HQ: Office of the Commissioner (D-5000), Bureau of Reclamation-DOI, Denver Federal Center, PO Box 25007, Denver, CO 80225. Phone: (303) 445-3577.

Internet: www.usbr.gov/WaterSMART/title/index.html.

15.506   WATER DESALINATION RESEARCH AND DEVELOPMENT PROGRAM

Assistance: project grants (to 50 percent).

Purposes: pursuant to the Water Desalination Act of 1966, for water desalination studies, research, demonstrations, development projects, and related activities—to develop more cost- effective, technologically efficient, and implementable methods of producing usable water from saline or otherwise contaminated water.

Eligible applicants/beneficiaries: individuals, academic institutions, commercial and industrial organizations; other profit, nonprofit and public entities including state, local, and tribal governments.

Range: $150,000 to $200,000. **Average:** N.A.

Activity: 9 projects funded in FY 2014.

HQ: Water Treatment Engineering and Research Group, Bureau of Reclamation-DOI, Federal Center (81-10000), PO Box 25007, Denver, CO 80225. Phone: (303) 445-2265; FAX: (720) 544-5682.

Internet: www.usbr.gov/pmts/water/desalination/index.html. (Note: no field offices for this program.)

15.507   WATER SMART—SUSTAINING AND MANAGE AMERICA'S RESOURCES FOR TOMORROW ("Water SMART Grants")

Assistance: project grants (50-100 percent/from 2 years).

Purposes: to prevent crisis and conflict over water in western United States through projects (50 percent funding) that will conserve water, increase water use efficiency, or enhance water management—using advanced technology, improvements to existing facilities, and water banks and markets. Up to 100 percent funding may be available for water use efficiency research.

Eligible applicants/beneficiaries: projects—irrigation or water districts in the western U.S. Research grants—IHEs and nonprofit institutions.

Range: $50,000 to $1,000,000. **Average:** N.A.

Activity: 36 projects funded in FY 2014

HQ: Bureau of Reclamation, Office of Policy and Administration, Mail Code: 84-51000, P.O. Box 25007, Denver Federal Center, Denver, CO 80225. Phone: (303) 445-2906; FAX: (720) 544-4207.

Internet: www.usbr.gov/WaterSMART/grants.html.

15.508   PROVIDING WATER TO AT-RISK NATURAL DESERT TERMINAL LAKES
("Desert Terminal Lakes")

Assistance: project grants (100 percent).

Purposes: pursuant to FSRIA and appropriations acts, for activities to provide water only to Walker Lake, Pyramid Lake, and Summit Lake in Nevada.

Eligible applicants/beneficiaries: state and local public agencies, tribes, nonprofit organizations, individuals.

Range: $35,720 to $311,200,000. **Average:** $46,986,688.

Activity: N.A.

HQ: *technical program information,* Lahontan Basin Area Office, Bureau of Reclamation-DOI, 705 N. Plaza St., Rm. 320, Carson City, NV 89701-4015. Phone: (775) 882-3436; FAX: (775) 882-7592.

Internet: www.usbr.gov/mp/lbao/desert_terminal/index.html.

15.509   COLORADO RIVER BASIN SALINITY CONTROL PROGRAM
("Basinwide Program")

Assistance: project grants (100 percent/1-5 years).

Purposes: pursuant to Colorado River Basin Salinity Control Act, as amended, and other laws, to provide financial and technical assistance which help decrease salinity levels in the Colorado River and enhance water quality in the U.S. and Mexico.

Eligible applicants/beneficiaries: eligible owners or operators in approved project area.

Range: $100,000 to $500,000. **Average:** N.A.

Activity: N.A.

HQ: Technical Contact, Bureau of Reclamation, 2764 Compass Dr., Grand Junction, CO 20240. Phone: (970) 248-0637; FAX: (970) 248-0601.

Internet: www.usbr.gov/dataweb/html/crwq.html.

15.510   COLORADO UTE INDIAN WATER RIGHTS SETTLEMENT ACT
("Colorado Ute Settlement Act/Animas La Plata")

Assistance: cooperative agreements; direct payments/specified use; project grants (100 percent/to 5 years).

Purposes: pursuant to ARRA, to supply municipal and industrial water supply to the Ute Mountain Ute, Southern Ute Indian Tribe, the Navajo Nation and non-tribal participants from the Animas-La Plata Project in settlement of water rights claims for the tribes. Funds may be used to complete the construction of a reconfigured Animas-La Plata Project, consisting of facilities to divert and store water from the Animas River to provide for an average annual depletion of 57,100 acre-feet of water and to supply

4,680 acre-feet per year to the Navajo Nation through a pipeline from Farmington to Shiprock, NM.

Eligible applicants: state, local, federally-recognized Indian tribal governments, small businesses, individuals, for-profit organizations.

Eligible beneficiaries: federally-recognized tribal government members and the general public in southwestern Colorado and northwestern New Mexico.

Range: N.A. **Average:** $182,704.

Activity: N.A.

HQ: Contracting Officer, FCCO 100, Four Corners Construction Office, 103 Everett St., Durango, CO 81303. Phone: (505) 325-1794; FAX: (505) 326-4388.

Internet: www.usbr.gov/library/annual_reports/FY2008/MDAPart1.pdf.

15.512 CENTRAL VALLEY PROJECT IMPROVEMENT ACT, TITLE XXXIV

Assistance: project grants (50 percent).

Purposes: pursuant to Lower Rio Grande Valley Water Resources Conservation and Improvement Act of 2000 and Lower Rio Grande Valley Water Resources Conservation and Improvement Act of 2002, as amended, to improve the supply of water in the program area known as Region M (Texas counties in the Rio Grande Regional Water Planning Area). Cost ceiling for conservation and improvements (section 3(g) is $8,000,000; $47,000,000 for construction (section 4(c). A substantial portion of this program is directed toward funding 19 construction projects specifically identified in the Lower Rio Grande Valley Water Resources Act, as amended.

Eligible applicants/beneficiaries: State of Texas, water users in the program area, specified irrigation districts, and other nonfederal entities.

Range: $10,000 to $15,000,000. **Average:** N.A.

Activity: N.A.

HQ: none provided, see listing of field offices.

Internet: www.usbr.gov/mp/cvpia.

15.514 RECLAMATION STATES EMERGENCY DROUGHT RELIEF
("Emergency Drought Relief and Drought Contingency Planning")

Assistance: project grants; specialized services; advisory services/counseling (generally, 6 months).

Purposes: pursuant to Reclamation States Emergency Drought Relief Act of 1991, as amended and the Hawaii Water Resources Act of 2000, for planning assistance that would minimize and mitigate losses and damages resulting from drought conditions.

Eligible applicants/beneficiaries: state and local entities and Federally Recognized Indian Tribal Governments within the following 17 Western U.S. States: Arizona, California, Colorado, Idaho, Kansas, Montana, Nebraska, Nevada, New Mexico, North Dakota, Oklahoma, Oregon, South Dakota, Texas, Wyoming, Utah, and Washington) and Hawaii. All 50 U.S. States and most U.S. territories are eligible for technical assistance.

Range: $10,000 to $1,000,000. **Average:** $666,666.

Activity: N.A.

HQ: Bureau of Reclamation, Office of Program & Policy Services, Bureau of Reclamation, DOI, Mail Code 84-51000, PO Box 25007, Denver Federal Center, Denver, CO 80225. Phone: (303) 445-2906.

Internet: www.usbr.gov/drought.

15.516   FORT PECK RESERVATION RURAL WATER SYSTEM ("Fort Peck Water Supply Project")

Assistance: project grants (76-100 percent/10 years).

Purposes: pursuant to Fort Peck Reservation Rural Water System Act of 2000, to ensure a safe and adequate municipal, rural, and industrial water supply for residents of Fort Peck Indian Reservation in the State of Montana and portions of Roosevelt, Sheridan, Daniels, and Valley Counties that are outside Fort Peck Indian Reservation. Presently, no new project awards are being made under this authority. Funds only available for continuation of existing agreements.

Eligible applicants/beneficiaries: The Fort Peck Tribal Executive Board, Dry Prairie Rural Water Association Incorporated (or any successor non-Federal entity).

Range: $2,029,000 to $6,921,000. **Average:** N.A.

Activity: N.A.

HQ: Tribal and Financial Assistance Officer, Bureau of Reclamation, DOI, PO Box 36900, Billings, MT 59107. Phone: (406) 247-7710; FAX: (406) 247-7695.

Internet: N.A.

15.517   FISH AND WILDLIFE COORDINATION ACT

Assistance: project grants (100 percent/1 to 5 years).

Purposes: pursuant to Fish and Wildlife Coordination Act of 1934, Public Law 85-624, as amended and limited by the Secretary of the Interior delegation of authority at 255 DM 14, to provide financial assistance to public or private organizations for the improvement of fish and wildlife habitats associated with water systems or water supplies affected by Bureau of Reclamation projects.

Eligible applicants/beneficiaries: state and local governments, public, private, nonprofit and for-profit organizations and institutions, Federally recognized Indian Tribal governments, individuals, small businesses, and Native American organizations.

Range: $15,000 to $8,374,000. **Average:** N.A.

Activity: N.A.

HQ: Director Bureau of Reclamation, 1849 C St., NW, Washington, DC 20240. Phone: (202) 208-3100.

Internet: www.usbr.gov.

15.518   GARRISON DIVERSION UNIT ("Garrison Diversion Unit Project")

Assistance: project grants.

Purposes: pursuant to Garrison Diversion Unit, Missouri River Basin Project, Public Law 89-108, Energy and Water Development Appropriation Act of 1985, and The Dakota Water Resources Act of 2000, as amended, to plan and construct a multi-purpose water resource development project within the State of North Dakota for; irrigation; municipal, rural, and industrial water; fish, wildlife, and other natural resource conservation and development; recreation; flood control; augmented stream flows; ground water recharge; and other project purposes.

Eligible applicants/beneficiaries: the State of North Dakota, the Garrison Conservancy District, the Standing Rock Sioux, the Three Affiliated Tribes, the Spirit Lake Nation, and the Turtle Mountain Band of Chippewa.

Range: $123,000 to $4,116,217. **Average:** N.A.

Activity: N.A.

HQ: Tribal and Financial Assistance Officer, Bureau of Reclamation, DOI, PO Box 36900, 316 North 26th St., Billings, MT 59101-6900. Phone: (406) 247-7606.

Internet: www.usbr.gov/gp.

15.519 INDIAN TRIBAL WATER RESOURCES DEVELOPMENT, MANAGEMENT, AND PROTECTION
("Indian Tribal Water Resources")

Assistance: project grants (100 percent/1 to 2 years).

Purposes: pursuant to Consolidated Appropriations Resolution, 2003, Division D - Energy and Water Development Appropriations, Title II, Section 201, Public Law 108-7, to increase opportunities for Indian tribes to develop, manage, and protect their water resources. Examples of funded projects include: well closures, drought relief, aquifer studies, water quality monitoring.

Eligible applicants/beneficiaries: Federally recognized Indian tribes, institutions of higher education, national Indian organizations, and tribal organizations located in the 17 western States identified in the Act of June 17, 1902, as amended; specifically, Arizona, California, Colorado, Idaho, Kansas, Montana, Nebraska, Nevada, New Mexico, North Dakota, Oklahoma, Oregon, South Dakota, Texas, Utah, Washington, and Wyoming.

Range: $2,000 to $300,000. **Average:** N.A.

Activity: N.A.

HQ: Director Native American and International Affairs Office, 1849 C St., NW, Washington, DC 20240. Phone: (202) 513-0550.

Internet: www.usbr.gov/native.

15.520 LEWIS AND CLARK RURAL WATER SYSTEM
("Lewis and Clark Project")

Assistance: project grants. (50-80 percent/until funds are expended).

Purposes: pursuant to Lewis and Clark Rural Water System, Public Law 106-246, and others, to plan and construct a bulk water supply system which will provide safe and adequate municipal, rural, and industrial water supplies, mitigation of wetland areas and water conservation for the Lewis and Clark Rural Water System member entities located in southeastern South Dakota, southwestern Minnesota, and northwestern Iowa. Presently, no new awards are being made. Funds are only available for continuation of existing agreements.

Eligible applicants/beneficiaries: Lewis and Clark Rural Water Supply System, Inc., and member entities (rural water systems in the following counties: Lake, McCook, Minnehaha, Turner, Lincoln, Clay, and Union, in southeastern South Dakota; Rock and Nobles, in Southwestern Minnesota; and Lyon, Sioux, Osceola, O'Brien Dickinson, and Clay, in northwestern Iowa).

Range/Average: N.A.

Activity: N.A.

HQ: Program Director, Bureau of Reclamation, DOI, Great Plains Regional Office, PO Box 36900, 316 North 26th St., Billings, MT 59101. Phone: (406) 247-7684.

Internet: www.lcrws.org.

15.521 LOWER RIO GRANDE VALLEY WATER RESOURCES CONSERVATION AND IMPROVEMENT
("Lower Rio Grande Valley Irrigation Projects")

Assistance: project grants (50 percent).

Purposes: pursuant to Lower Rio Grande Valley Water Resources Conservation and Improvement Act of 2000, and Lower Rio Grande Valley Water Resources Conservation and Improvement Act of 2002, as amended, to improve the supply of water in the program area identified as Region M (Texas counties in Rio Grande Regional Water Planning Area). Cost ceiling for conservation is $8,000,000; for improvements, $47,000,000.

Eligible applicants/beneficiaries: The State of Texas, water users in the program area, specified irrigation districts, and other non-Federal entities.

Range/Average: N.A.

Activity: N.A.

HQ: Tribal and Financial Assistance Officer, Bureau of Reclamation, DOI, PO Box 36900, 316 North 26th St., Billings MT 59101. Phone: (406) 247-7710; FAX: (406) 247-7695.

Internet: www.usbr.gov/gp.

15.522 MNI WICONI RURAL WATER SUPPLY PROJECT
("Mni Wiconi Project")

Assistance: project grants (80-100 percent).

Purposes: pursuant to Mni Wiconi Rural Project Act of 1988, as amended; Yavapai-Prescott Indian Tribe Water Rights Settlement Act of 1994, Title VIII, and Mni Wiconi Act Amendments of 1994, to ensure a safe and adequate municipal, rural, and industrial water supply for the residents of the Pine Ridge Indian, Rosebud Indian, and Lower Brule Indian Reservations and certain other counties located in South Dakota. Cooperative agreements are limited to planning, designing, constructing, operating, maintaining, and replacing the Oglala Sioux, the Rosebud, and the Lower Brule Sioux Rural Water Supply Systems; for planning and construction of the West River/Lyman-Jones Rural Water System. Presently, funds are only available for continuation of existing agreements; no new project awards are being made.

Eligible applicants: West River/Lyman-Jones Water Systems and the Oglala, Rosebud, and Lower Brule Sioux tribes.

Eligible beneficiaries: citizens of the southwest quarter of the State of South Dakota, including the Oglala, Rosebud, and Lower Brule Indian Reservations.

Range: $32,700 to $1,233,000. **Average:** N.A.

Activity: N.A.

HQ: Tribal and Financial Assistance Officer, Bureau of Reclamation, DOI, PO Box 36900, Billings, MT 59107. Phone: (406) 247-7710; FAX: (406) 247-7695.

Internet: www.usbr.gov.

15.524 RECREATION RESOURCES MANAGEMENT ("Title XXVIII")

Assistance: project grants (50-75 percent/to 5 years).

Purposes: pursuant to Federal Water Projects Recreation Act of 1965, and Reclamation Recreation Act of 1992, as amended, to provide opportunities for public recreation at Bureau of Reclamation or other publicly-owned water projects. Cost sharing agreements may be used by state, county, and local government for planning, construction and other facets of improving recreation access and assets at these project areas.

Eligible applicants/beneficiaries: state and local government entities willing to manage/maintain publicly-owned recreation facilities and assets.

Range: $1,432 to $720,000. **Average:** N.A.

Activity: N.A.

HQ: Bureau of Reclamation, DOI, PO Box 25007 (84-53000), Denver, Colorado 80225-0007. Phone: (303) 445-2711; FAX: (303) 445-6690.

Internet: www.usbr.gov/recreation.

15.525 ROCKY BOY'S/NORTH CENTRAL MONTANA REGIONAL WATER SYSTEM

Assistance: project grants (80-100 percent/until funds are expended).

Purposes: pursuant to ARRA 2009, Indian Financing Amendments Act of 2002, Title IX and Rocky Boy's/North Central Montana Regional Water System Act of 2002, to develop safe and adequate rural, municipal, and industrial water supplies via construction of a rural water supply system that will serve the Chippewa-Cree of the Rocky Boy's Indian reservation and the surrounding, off-reservation communities in north central Montana. Presently, no new awards are being made; funds are only available for continuation of existing agreements.

Eligible applicants/beneficiaries: Chippewa-Cree of the Rocky Boy's Indian Reservation and the North Central Montana Regional Water Authority.

Range: $850,000 to $3,179,000. **Average:** N.A.

Activity: N.A.

HQ: Tribal and Financial Assistance Officer, Bureau of Reclamation, DOI, PO Box 36900, Billings, MT 59107. Phone: (406) 247-7710; FAX: (406) 247-7695.

Internet: N.A.

15.527   SAN LUIS UNIT, CENTRAL VALLEY PROJECT

Assistance: project grants (cost sharing encouraged).

Purposes: pursuant to San Luis Unit, Central Valley Project Act of June 3, 1960, to be used for projects that will result in construction and operation of drainage facilities in the San Luis Unit and adjacent areas.

Eligible applicants/beneficiaries: any responsible source, including irrigation and/or water districts, State and local entities, public, private, and quasi-public nonprofit and for-profit institutions/organizations, Federally recognized Indian Tribal Governments, and small businesses.

Range: $86,980 to $210,200. **Average:** N.A.

Activity: 4 agreements in FY 2014.

HQ: none provided, see listing of field offices.

Internet: www.mp.usbr.gov.

15.529   UPPER COLORADO AND SAN JUAN RIVER BASINS ENDANGERED FISH RECOVERY PROGRAMS

Assistance: project grants (cost sharing/1-5 years).

Purposes: pursuant to Upper Colorado and San Juan River Basins Endangered Fish Recovery Programs and Upper Colorado and San Juan River Basins Endangered Fish Recovery Programs Extension, as amended, to assist in the implementation of programs for endangered fish recovery in the Upper Colorado and San Juan River Basins. Periodically, the Bureau of Reclamation will have discretionary funding available to make awards for certain types of projects. As they become available, funding opportunity announcements will be posted to www.grants.gov.

Eligible applicants/beneficiaries: Federal, Interstate, Intrastate, State, and Local governments; Public Institution/Organizations, and Federally Recognized Indian Tribal Governments.

Range: $8,000 to $835,000. **Average:** N.A.

Activity: N.A.

HQ: none provided, see listing of field offices.

Internet: www.usbr.gov/uc/wcao/rm/sjrip.

15.530   WATER CONSERVATION FIELD SERVICES PROGRAM (WCFSP)

Assistance: project grants (to 50 percent/2-5 years).

Purposes: pursuant to Soil and Moisture Conservation Act of 1935, Fish and Wildlife Coordination Act, Reclamation Projects Authorization And Adjustment Act of 1992, and Energy and Water Development Appropriations Act, 2006, and other public laws, to actively encourage water conservation and efficient use of water supplies on Federal Reclamation projects, assist water districts with their responsibility to develop and implement water conservation plans, and complement and support State and other conservation programs.

Eligible applicants/beneficiaries: Depending on the authorizing legislation, agricultural and/or municipal/industrial water districts, irrigation districts, water districts or entities, communities, state or local water agencies, water-related non-profit organizations, small entities (public or private) that have contracts for water with Reclamation under the Warren Act, Native American Tribes, universities or educational institutions proposing to conduct water conservation activities within Reclamation boundaries.

Range: $6,938 to $100,000. **Average:** N.A.

Activity: N.A.

HQ: none provided, see listing of field offices.

Internet: www.usbr.gov/waterconservation.

15.531   YAKIMA RIVER BASIN WATER ENHANCEMENT PROJECT (YRBWEP)

Assistance: project grants (grants/cooperative agreements/1 to 5 years).

Purposes: pursuant to Yavapai-Prescott Indian Tribe Water Rights Settlement Act of 1994, within the Yakima River Basin: to protect, mitigate, and enhance fish and wildlife through improved water management; to improve instream flows, and water quality; and to protect, create and enhance wetlands; to improve the reliability of water supply for irrigation; to authorize a Yakima River basin water conservation program; to realize sufficient water savings from the program so that not less than 40,000 acre-feet of water savings per year are achieved by the end of the fourth year of the Basin Conservation Program; to encourage voluntary transactions among public and private entities which result in the implementation of water conservation measures, practices and facilities; and to provide for the implementation by the Yakima Indian Nation at its sole discretion of (A) an irrigation demonstration project on the Yakima Indian Reservation using water savings from system improvements to the Wapato Irrigation Project, and (B) a Toppenish Creek corridor enhancement project integrating agricultural, fish, wildlife, and cultural resources.

Eligible applicants: State of Washington, and Federally Recognized Indian Tribal Governments, water and irrigation districts, and water rights owners located within the project area.

Eligible beneficiaries: anyone/general public, Intrastate, Local, Individual/Family, and Federally Recognized Indian Tribal Governments within the project area.

Range: $5,000 to $44,700,000. **Average:** $5,960,606.

Activity: N.A.

HQ: YRBWEP Manager, Bureau of Reclamation, DOI, 1849 C St., NW, Washington, DC 20240. Phone: (202) 208-3100.

Internet: www.usbr.gov/pn.

15.532 CENTRAL VALLEY PROJECT, TRINITY RIVER DIVISION, TRINITY RIVER FISH AND WILDLIFE MANAGEMENT ("Trinity River Restoration Program")

Assistance: project grants (cost sharing encouraged).

Purposes: pursuant to the Central Valley Project Improvement Act (CVPIA) of 1992, to identify and address impacts of the Central Valley Project on fish and wildlife, and protect, restore and enhance associated habitats in California's Trinity River basin.

Eligible applicants: any responsible source, including irrigation and/or water districts, State and local entities, public, private, and quasi-public nonprofit and for-profit institutions/organizations, Federally recognized Indian Tribal Governments, and small businesses.

Eligible beneficiaries: general public.

Range: $5,000 to $4,000,000. **Average:** N.A.

Activity: N.A.

HQ: none provided, see listing of field offices.

Internet: www.usbr.gov/mp/ncao.

15.533 CALIFORNIA WATER SECURITY AND ENVIRONMENTAL ENHANCEMENT ("CALFED")

Assistance: project grants (50 percent or more/to 2 years).

Purposes: pursuant to Title I of the Water Supply, Reliability, and Environmental Enhancement Act, to expand and protect water supplies; to improve water quality and the health of the Bay-Delta system through restoration and protection of native species and habitats; and to improve levees for flood protection and ecosystem benefits.

Eligible applicants: agencies of the state of California.

Eligible beneficiaries: general public in and around the California Bay-Delta area.

Range: $80,000 to $4,000,000. **Average:** N.A.

Activity: N.A.

HQ: none provided, see listing of field offices.

Internet: www.mp.usbr.gov.

15.534 MISCELLANEOUS PUBLIC LAS 93-638 CONTRACTS, GRANTS, AND COOPERATIVE AGREEMENTS

Assistance: direct payments for specified use; project grants.

Purposes: pursuant to Indian Self-Determination and Education Assistance Act as amended, to provide non-reimbursable funds for activities which will benefit Indians.

Eligible applicants/beneficiaries: federally recognized Indian tribes and tribal organizations in the 17 western states.

Range: $5,000 to $74,000,000. **Average:** $208,801.

Activity: N.A.

HQ: Office of the Commissioner, Bureau of Reclamation, 1849 C St., NW, Washington, DC 20240-0001. Phone: (202) 513-0501.

Internet: www.usbr.gov/native. (Note: no field offices for this program.)

15.535 UPPER COLORADO RIVERBASIN FISH AND WILDLIFE MITIGATION PROGRAM
("Section 314c Projects")

Assistance: project grants (100 percent/1 to 5 years).

Purposes: pursuant to Fish, Wildlife, and Recreation Mitigation and Conservation, ARRA 2009, and Reclamation Projects Authorization and Adjustment Act of 1992, to protect, restore and enhance wetland and upland ecosystems for the conservation of fish and wildlife resources in the upper Colorado River basin adversely affected by the construction and water resource developments authorized by the Colorado River Storage Project Act of 1956.

Eligible applicants: states (includes DC, public IHEs and hospitals); public nonprofit institutions/organizations; federally-recognized Indian tribal governments; and sponsored organizations.

Eligible beneficiaries: general public.

Range: $42,000 to $276,000. **Average:** N.A.

Activity: N.A.

HQ: Assistant Secretary of the Interior for Water and Science-DOI, 1849 C St., NW, Washington, DC 20240. Phone: (801) 379-1254.

Internet: www.cupcao.gov.

15.537 MIDDLE RIO GRANDE ENDANGERED SPECIES COLLABORATIVE PROGRAM

Assistance: project grants (100 percent/to 2 years).

Purposes: pursuant to Energy and Water Development Appropriations Act 2006, ARRA 2009, Consolidated Appropriations Act of 2008, and Energy and Water Development Appropriations Act 2005, to protect and improve the status of endangered listed species (with special emphasis on the Rio Grande silvery minnow and the southwestern willow flycatcher) along the Middle Rio Grande (MRG), simultaneously protecting existing and future regional water uses while complying with state and federal laws, including Rio Grande compact delivery obligations. All appropriated funds are discretionary.

Eligible applicants: federal agencies, private/public/quasi-public nonprofit institutions/organizations (including IHEs and hospitals), and federally-recognized Indian tribal governments.

Eligible beneficiaries: anyone/general public.

Range: $140,000 to $159,000. **Average:** N.A.

Activity: N.A.

HQ: Program Manager, Albuquerque Area Office, Bureau of Reclamation-DOI, 555 Broadway Blvd., Albuquerque, NM 87102. Phone: (505) 462-3540; FAX, (505) 462-3794.

Internet: www.mrgesa.com.

15.538 LOWER COLORADO RIVER MULTI-SPECIES CONSERVATION PROGRAM (MSCP)

Assistance: project grants (100 percent/1 to 3 years).

Purposes: pursuant to ARRA 2009 and Omnibus Public Land Management Act Title IX, to: protect the lower Colorado River environment while ensuring the certainty of existing river water and power operations; address the needs of threatened and endangered wildlife under the Endangered Species Act; and reduce the likelihood of listing additional species along the lower Colorado River.

Eligible applicants/beneficiaries: anyone/general public.

Range: $100,000 to $500,000. Average: N.A.

Activity: 20 agreements awarded or modified in FY 2014.

HQ: Program Manager, Multi-Species Conservation Program, Bureau of Reclamation-DOI, PO Box 61470, Boulder City, NV 89006. Phone: (702) 293-8555.

Internet: www.lcrmscp.gov.

15.539 EQUUS BEDS DIVISION AQUIFER STORAGE RECHARGE PROJECT

Assistance: cooperative agreements (10 years).

Purposes: pursuant to the Wichita Project Equus Beds Division Authorization Act of 2005, to design and construct the City of Wichita's Aquifer Storage and Recovery project to divert excess flow from the Little Arkansas River into the Equus Beds Aquifer in order to recover depleted storage and protect the Aquifer.

Eligible applicants: City of Wichita.

Eligible beneficiaries: municipal, industrial, and agricultural waters users of south-central Kansas.

Range: N.A. Average: $48,952.

Activity: N.A.

HQ: Program Director, Bureau of Reclamation, DOI, Great Plains Regional Office, PO Box 36900, 316 North 26th St., Billings, MT 59101. Phone: (406) 247-7684.

Internet: www.usbr.gov/gp.

15.540 LAKE MEAD/LAS VEGAS WASH PROGRAM ("Las Vegas Wash LVW Program")

Assistance: cooperative agreements/discretionary grants (35 to 65 percent/1 to 3 years).

Purposes: pursuant to the Water Resources Development Act of 2000, to develop and implement management strategies for the Las Vegas Wash to improve water quality, habitat integrity, and reduce the salinity and sediment transport while providing environmental enhancement and recreational opportunities. Cost share is required: The Southern Nevada Water Authority's (SNWA) share is 35 percent, Bureau of Reclamation's is 65 percent.

Eligible applicants: The Southern Nevada Water Authority and Bureau of Reclamation.

Eligible beneficiaries: general public.

Range: $57,680 to $97,888. **Average:** N.A.

Activity: N.A.

HQ: Director, Bureau of Reclamation, Resources Management Office, PO Box 61470, Boulder City, NV 89006. Phone: (702) 293-8109.

Internet: www.usbr.gov.

15.542 ARIZONA WATER SETTLEMENT ACT OF 2004
("Arizona Water Settlement Act")

Assistance: direct payments/specified use; project grants/cooperative agreements (100 percent).

Purposes: pursuant to the Arizona Water Settlement Act of 2004, to provide for adjustments to the Central Arizona Project in Arizona, authorize the Gila River Indian Community water rights settlement, reauthorize and amend the Southern Arizona Water Rights settlement Act of 1982, for the settlement of water rights to the San Carlos Apache Tribe and for other purposes.

Eligible applicants: must have a water allocation and water delivery contract from a Reclamation water resource project.

Eligible beneficiaries: The general public, Arizona, New Mexico, irrigation and water districts, local entities and tribal government.

Range: to $39,926,000. **Average:** N.A.

Activity: N.A.

HQ: Director, Bureau of Reclamation, Phoenix Area Office, 6150 W. Thunderbird Rd., Glendale, Arizona 85306-4001. Phone: (623) 773-6200.

Internet: www.usbr.gov/lc/phoenix.

15.543 LAKE TAHOE REGIONAL WETLANDS DEVELOPMENT PROGRAM

Assistance: cooperative agreements/discretionary grants (100 percent/1 to 3 years).

Purposes: to assist in addressing past degradation of Lake Tahoe and its watershed by undertaking environmental improvement projects to improve water quality and conditions for species and habitats in the Lake Tahoe Basin. Funded activities may include project planning and implementation, program coordination and management, and public outreach.

Eligible applicants: state and local agencies, federally-recognized Indian tribal governments, private/public institutions/organizations, including profit and nonprofit, educational and scientific.

Eligible beneficiaries: anyone, general public.

Range/Average: N.A.

Activity: N.A.

HQ: Director, Bureau of Reclamation, 2800 Cottage Way, Sacramento, CA 95825. Phone: (916) 978-5037.

Internet: www.usbr.gov/mp. (Note: no field offices for this program.)

15.544 PLATTE RIVER RECOVERY IMPLEMENTATION PROGRAM (PRRIP)

Assistance: cooperative agreements/discretionary grants (50 percent).

Purposes: to implement certain aspects of the FWS's recovery plans for four target species (interior least tern, whooping crane, piping plover and pallid sturgeon) listed as threatened or endangered pursuant to the Endangered Species Act. Per authorizing legislation, the states of Colorado, Nebraska, and Wyoming shall contribute not less than 50% of the total contributions necessary to carry out the PRRIP.

Eligible applicants: cooperative agreement entered into by the governors of Wyoming, Nebraska, and Colorado and the Secretary of the Interior.

Eligible beneficiaries: general public, irrigation and/or water districts, state/local entities, farmers, ranchers, agricultural producers, property owners, municipal water and power users.

Range: $8,000,000 to $17,000,000. **Average:** N.A.

Activity: N.A.

HQ: Director, Bureau of Reclamation, Great Plains Region, PO Box 36900, Billings, MT 59107. Phone: (307) 261-5671; FAX: (307) 261-5683.

Internet: www.platteriverprogram.org.

15.546 YOUTH CONSERVATION PROGRAM

Assistance: cooperative agreements/discretionary grants (75 percent/5 years).

Purposes: pursuant to American Recovery and Reinvestment Act of 2009 (ARRA), to promote and stimulate public purposes such as education, job training, development of responsible citizenship, productive community involvement, and further the understanding and appreciation of natural and cultural resources through the involvement of local youth and young adults (ages 15 to 25) in the care and enhancement of public resources on Reclamation-owned lands and facilities.

Eligible applicants: qualified youth, veteran, or conservation corps (any program established by a state, local, or tribal government or nonprofit organization) and are able to involve youth ages 15-25 in the 17 Western United States and the Intern Program in Reclamation projects on a nation-wide basis.

Eligible beneficiaries: youth (aged 15 to 25 in the 17 Western United States), local communities.

Range: $5,000 to $250,000. **Average:** N.A.

Activity: N.A.

HQ: Director, Bureau of Reclamation, MC-D, PO Box 25007, Denver, CO 80255. Phone: (303) 445-2849.

Internet: www.usbr.gov. (Note: no field offices for this program.)

15.548 RECLAMATION RURAL WATER SUPPLY PROGRAM ("Rural Water Program")

Assistance: cooperative agreements/discretionary grants (50 to 100 percent/2 to 5 years).

Purposes: to provide the basic requirements and framework for conducting water and related resource feasibility studies in order to formulate, evaluate, and select project plans for implementation. Applicants must be located in the 17 Western States as identified in the Reclamation Act of June 17, 1902, as amended.

Eligible applicants: eligible states and their political subdivisions (agencies, departments, municipalities, counties), and other regional or local authorities, Indian tribes and tribal organizations, and entities created under state law that have water management or water delivery authority (irrigation or water districts, canal companies, water users associations, rural water associations/districts, joint powers authorities), and any combination of the entities listed above.

Eligible beneficiaries: small communities (population of no more than 50,000) or group of small communities, including Indian tribes and tribal organizations.

Range/Average: N.A.

Activity: N.A.

HQ: Director, Water and Environmental Resources Division, Bureau of Reclamation, DOI, Bldg. 67 PO Box 25007 (84-55000), Denver, CO 80225-0007. Phone: (303) 445-2711.

Internet: www.usbr.gov/ruralwater.

15.550 INCREASING PUBLIC AWARENESS OF RECREATIONAL OPPORTUNITIES AT RECLAMATION RESERVOIRS FOR PHYSICALLY CHALLENGED AND DISADVANTAGED CHILDREN

Assistance: cooperative agreements/discretionary grants (100 percent/5 years).

Purposes: pursuant to the Take Pride in America (TPIA) program, to: provide opportunities for disabled and disadvantaged children to use and enjoy public waters and related lands; assist Reclamation in meeting its goal to provide accessible programs, facilities and activities to create a positive outdoor experience for all citizens; increase awareness of all participants (parents/caregivers, sportsmen, partners, volunteers) to the capabilities of disabled and disadvantaged children.

Eligible applicants: state, county, city, township and special district governments, independent school districts, IHEs, tribal governments, public and Indian housing authorities, non-profits with 501(c)(3) IRA status, individuals, small businesses.

Eligible beneficiaries: disabled and disadvantaged children.

Range: $100,000 to $125,000. **Average:** $106,709.

Activity: N.A.

HQ: Director, Acquisition and Assistance Management Division, Bureau of Reclamation, Group 84-27810, PO Box 25007, Denver Federal Center, Denver, CO 80225. Phone: (303) 445-2444.

Internet: N.A.

15.551 MADERA WATER SUPPLY ENHANCEMENT PROJECT ("Madera Irrigation District WSEP or Madera Ranch")

Assistance: cooperative agreements (25 percent).

Purposes: pursuant to the Omnibus Public Land Management Act of 2009, to assist the Madera Irrigation District in the engineering, design and construction of the project and the administration of related contracts in order to increase water storage capacity and supply reliability for the district.

Eligible applicants: Madera Irrigation District.

Eligible beneficiaries: Madera Irrigation District, general public.

Range: to $22,500,000. **Average:** $613,701.

Activity: N.A.

HQ: Program Director, Bureau of Reclamation, DOI, 2800 Cottage Way, Sacramento, CA 95825. Phone: (916) 978-5148.

Internet: N.A.

15.552 NAVAJO-GALLUP WATER SUPPLY PROJECT

Assistance: project grants (100 percent).

Purposes: pursuant to the Omnibus Public Land Management Act, to provide financial assistance to design and construct portions of the Navajo-Gallup Water Supply Project, a component of a water right settlement with the Navajo Nation. Financial assistance may be specifically directed to the Navajo Nation (Nation) and the City of Gallup, New Mexico (City) because they are uniquely qualified to perform the design and construction work; will ultimately own and operate Project facilities; and, legislative authority exists to provide this financial assistance to the Nation and City.

Eligible applicants/beneficiaries: Native American organization (Navajo Nation) and local government (City of Gallup New Mexico).

Range: $871,931 to $16,459,249. **Average:** $14,135,690.

Activity: N.A.

HQ: Contracting Officer, FCCO 100, Four Corners Construction Office, 103 Everett St., Durango, CO 81303. Phone: (505) 325-1794; FAX: (505) 326-4388.

Internet: N.A.

15.554 COOPERATIVE WATERSHED MANAGEMENT PROGRAM (CWMP)

Assistance: project grants/cooperative agreements (50 to 100 percent/2 years).

Purposes: pursuant to the Omnibus Public Land Management Act, to enhance water conservation including alternative uses, to improve water quality and ecological resiliency of rivers or streams, and to reduce conflicts over water by supporting the formation of watershed groups to develop local solutions addressing water management issues. A non-federal cost-share is not required for Phase I activities to establish or expand an existing watershed group (to develop a mission statement, project concepts and a restoration plan). Phase II and Phase III require a 50% non-federal cost-share for watershed management projects.

Eligible applicants/beneficiaries: states, Indian tribes, local and special districts; (irrigation and water districts, county soil conservation districts, etc.), local governmental entities, and non-profit organizations. Eligible applicants must be located within the 17 western United States or Territories as identified in the Reclamation Act of June 17, 1902.

Range: $25,000 to $100,000. **Average:** N.A.

Activity: N.A.

HQ: Bureau of Reclamation, Office of Program & Policy Services, Bureau of Reclamation, DOI, Mail Code 84-51000, PO Box 25007, Denver Federal Center, Denver, CO 80225. Phone: (303) 445-2906.

Internet: www.usbr.gov/watersmart/cwmp/index.html.

15.555   SAN JOAQUIN RIVER RESTORATION PROGRAM

Assistance: project grants/cooperative agreements (50 to 100 percent).

Purposes: pursuant to the Omnibus Public Land Management Act, to implement the Settlement consistent with and as supplemented by, the San Joaquin River Restoration Settlement Act which indentifies two goals. The Restoration Goal is to restore and maintain fish populations in "good condition" in the main stem of the San Joaquin River below Friant Dam to the confluence of the Merced River, including naturally-reproducing and self-sustaining populations of salmon and other fish. The Water Management Goal is to reduce or avoid adverse water supply impacts to all of the Friant Division long-term contractors that may result from the Interim Flows and Restoration Flows provided for in this Settlement.

Eligible applicants/beneficiaries: state, tribal, and local governmental agencies, private parties, general public.

Range/Average: N.A.

Activity: N.A.

HQ: Director, Bureau of Reclamation, DOI, Mid-Pacific Regional Office, 2800 Cottage Way, MP-170, Sacramento, CA 95825. Phone: (916) 978-5464.

Internet: www.usbr.gov.

15.556   CROW TRIBE WATER RIGHTS SETTLEMENT

Assistance: direct payments/specified use (100 percent).

Purposes: pursuant to the Claims Resolution Act of 2010, to rehabilitate and improve the water diversion and delivery features of the Crow Irrigation Project (CIP). To plan, design and construct a new municipal, rural & industrial (MR&I) water system for the benefit of the Crow Tribe and its members. The project is for the rehabilitation and improvement of the existing Crow Irrigation Project and for the construction of a new MR&I system on the Crow Reservation.

Eligible applicants: the Crow Tribe of Montana.

Eligible beneficiaries: irrigable lands within the Crow Reservation.

Range: $1,108,413 to $4,000,000. **Average:** N.A.

Activity: N.A.

HQ: Director, Great Plains Regional Office, Bureau of Reclamation, 2021 4th Ave. N, Billings, Montana 59101. Phone: (406) 247-7710; FAX: (406) 247-7892.

Internet: N.A.

15.557 DESERT AND SOUTHERN ROCKIES LANDSCAPE CONSERVATION COOPERATIVES
("Landscape Conservation Cooperatives")

Assistance: project Grants/cooperative agreements (50 perent/2 years).

Purposes: The objective of the Desert and Southern Rockies Landscape Conservation Cooperatives (LCCs) is to enhance the management of natural and cultural resources that have a nexus to water resource management. This includes developing tools to assess and adapt to the impacts of climate change and other landscape scale stressors within the geographic boundaries of the Desert and Southern Rockies LCC and adapt to those stressors. The Desert and Southern Rockies LCCs provide cost-shared financial assistance on a competitive basis for the following types of projects: projecting future water availability and quality, projecting the resiliency and vulnerability of natural or cultural resources, and assessing and evaluating natural or cultural resource management practices and opportunities to adapt. Eligible projects are restricted to within the geographic boundaries of the Desert or Southern Rockies LCCs. The federal share of the cost of a project or activity carried out under this program shall not exceed 50% of the total cost of the project or activity.

Eligible applicants: states, tribes, irrigation districts, water districts, or organizations with water or power delivery in Arizona, California, Colorado, Idaho, Kansas, Montana, Nebraska, Nevada, New Mexico, North Dakota, Oklahoma, Oregon, South Dakota, Texas, Utah, Washington, Wyoming, American Samoa, Guam, the Northern Mariana Islands, or the Virgin Islands; universities located in the United States; non-profit research institutions located in the United States; or non-profit organizations whose proposal addresses fish or wildlife habitat in wetland, riparian, or aquatic areas and has a nexus to a Reclamation project.

Eligible beneficiaries: anyone/general public.

Range: $3,000 to $150,000. **Average:** N.A.

Activity: N.A.

HQ: Bureau of Reclamation, Office of Program & Policy Services, Bureau of Reclamation, DOI, Mail Code 84-51000, PO Box 25007, Denver Federal Center, Denver, CO 80225. Phone: (303) 445-2906.

Internet: www.usbr.gov/WaterSMART/lcc/index.html.

15.558 WHITE MOUNTAIN APACHE TRIBE RURAL WATER SYSTEM ("Miner Flat Project")

Assistance: direct payments/specified use (cooperative agreements) (100 percent).

Purposes: pursuant to The White Mountain Apache Tribe Rural Water System Loan Authorization Act, to plan, engineer, design and construct the Miner Flat Project.

Eligible applicants/beneficiaries: white Mountain Apache Tribe.

Range: to $1,049,426. **Average:** $349,808.

Activity: N.A.

HQ: Director, Bureau of Reclamation 6150 W. Thunderbird Rd., Glendale, Arizona 85306-4001. Phone: (623) 773-6200.

Internet: www.usbr.gov/lc/phoenix.

15.559 NEW MEXICO RIO GRANDE BASIN PUEBLOS IRRIGATION INFRASTRUCTURE PROJECT ("New Mexico Pueblos Irrigation Project")

Assistance: direct payments/specified use; project grants (cooperative agreements) (25 percent cost share).

Purposes: pursuant to the Omnibus Public Lands Management Act of 2009, to rehabilitate and repair irrigation infrastructure of the Rio Grande Pueblos to conserve water and help address potential conflicts over water in the Rio Grande Basin.

Eligible applicants/beneficiaries: funds are to prepare a study for Congress on existing conditions and potential irrigation rehabilitation projects, and to construct irrigation rehabilitation projects after the study is approved by Congress.

Range: $40,000 to $360,000. **Average:** N.A.

Activity: N.A.

HQ: Director, Bureau of Reclamation, 1849 C St. NW, Washington, DC 20240-0001. Phone: (202) 513-0550.

Internet: www.usbr.gov/uc/albuq/progact/nmpueblos/index.html.

15.560 SECURE WATER ACT—RESEARCH AGREEMENTS

Assistance: project grants/cooperative agreements (100 percent).

Purposes: pursuant to the Omnibus Public Lands Management Act of 2009, to fund research activities that are designed to conserve water resources, increase the efficiency of the use of water resources, and/or enhance the management of water resources, including increasing the use of renewable energy in the management and delivery of water.

Eligible applicants: eligible applicants include any: university, nonprofit research institution, or other organization with water or power delivery authority.

Eligible beneficiaries: general public; agricultural, municipal and industrial water users; irrigation or water districts; and state governmental entities with water or power delivery authority.

Range: $10,000 to $420,000. Average: N.A.

Activity: N.A.

HQ: Director, Acquisition and Assistance Management Division, Bureau of Reclamation, Group 84-27810, PO Box 25007, Denver Federal Center, Denver, CO 80225. Phone: (303) 445-2444.

Internet: N.A.

15.562 DIXIE VALLEY WATER EXPORT STUDY

Assistance: project grants/cooperative agreements (100 percent/to 5 years).

Purposes: pursuant to the Farm Security and Rural Investment Act of 2002 and Consolidated Appropriations Act, 2008, to provide financial assistance to Churchill County for its participation in the Dixie Ground Water Export Study. The study will determine how much water is available for export from Dixie Valley, and evaluate the feasibility of conveying the water to various points of use within Churchill County, Nevada.

Eligible applicants: Churchill County, NV.

Eligible beneficiaries: water users in the Dixie Valley, Churchill County, NV area.

Range/Average: N.A.

Activity: N.A.

HQ: Director, Financial Assistance Services 84-27850, Bureau of Reclamation, PO Box 25007, Denver Federal Center, Denver, CO 80225.

Internet: N.A. (Note: no field offices for this program.)

15.563 SUISUN MARSH PRESERVATION AGREEMENT (SMPA)

Assistance: project grants/cooperative agreements (construction: lesser of 40 percent or $50,000,000; maintenance, to 40 percent).

Purposes: pursuant to the Small Reclamation Project Act Amendments and the Suisan Marsh Preservation Agreement, cooperative agreements between Department of Interior, state of California, and the Suisun Resource Conservation District to ensure a dependable water supply of adequate quantity and quality for the protection and preservation of Suisan Marsh fish and wildlife habitat. Establishes cost sharing for construction, annual operation and maintenance, and monitoring as required by the SMPA.

Eligible applicants: state of California.

Eligible beneficiaries: state of California and landowners within Suisun Marsh.

Range: to $1,430,000. Average: $908,333

Activity: N.A.

HQ: Director, Bay-Delta Area Office, Bureau of Reclamation, 801 I St., Ste. 140, Sacramento, CA 95814. Phone: (916) 414-2429.

Internet: www.usbr.gov/mp.

15.564 CENTRAL VALLEY PROJECT CONSERVATION PROGRAM (CVPCP)

Assistance: project grants (100 percent).

Purposes: pursuant to the Fish and Wildlife Coordination Act of 1956, funds to support activities to benefit federally listed endangered and threatened species to compensate for impacts to species resulting from the operation and maintenance of the Central Valley Project. Funds may be used for land acquisition, habitat restoration, research, and captive propagation of listed species. Funds must be applied to projects located within a specified geographic area centered on the Central Valley of California. Cannot fund activities required as regulatory mitigation. Projects must directly benefit at least one federally listed species.

Eligible applicants/beneficiaries: anyone/general public.

Range: $25,000 to $1,000,000. **Average:** N.A.

Activity: anticipate 4 awards in FY 2016.

HQ: Assistant Secretary of the Interior for Water and Science, 1849 C S., NW, Stop MIB6640, Washington, DC 20240. Phone: (202) 208-3100.

Internet: www.usbr.gov/mp/cvpcp.

15.565   IMPLEMENTATION OF THE TAOS PUEBLO INDIAN WATER RIGHTS SETTLEMENT

Assistance: project grants/cooperative agreements. (100 percent).

Purposes: pursuant to the Taos Pueblo Indian Water Rights Settlement Act, Title V of Pub. L. 111-291, to provide financial assistance to eligible non-Pueblo entities to plan, permit, design, engineer, and construct the mutual-benefit projects (as defined in section 503(3) of the Settlement Act). These projects are intended to minimize adverse impacts on the Pueblo's water resources by moving future non-Indian ground water pumping away from the Pueblo's Buffalo Pasture and to implement the resolution of a dispute over the allocation of certain surface water flows between the Pueblo and non-Indian irrigation water right owners in the community of Arroyo Seco Arriba.

Eligible applicants/beneficiaries: specific non-Pueblo tribal entities identified in section 503(1) of the Settlement Act.

Range/Average: N.A.

Activity: N.A.

HQ: Denver Federal Center, Bldg. 56 Rm. 1000 25007, Denver, CO 80225. Phone: (303) 445.2490.

Internet: N.A.

15.605   SPORT FISH RESTORATION PROGRAM
("Dingell-Johnson Program")

Assistance: formula grants. (to 75 percent/2 years).

Purposes: pursuant to the Federal Aid in Sport Fish Restoration Act of 1950 as amended, to restore, conserve, manage, or enhance sport fish populations for the preservation and improvement of sport fishing and related uses of fisheries resources. Funds may be used for acquisition of boating access to public waters, fresh water fish habitat improvement, lake and stream rehabilitation, research, operations and maintenance, similar uses.

Eligible applicants/beneficiaries: fish and wildlife agencies in states with laws prohibiting diversion of revenues from fishing licenses to uses other than administration of the agency; territories.

Range: $900,000 to $14,700,000. **Average:** $5,200,000.

Activity: anticipate 600 awards in FY 2016.

HQ: Director, Policy and Program, U.S. Fish and Wildlife Service Headquarters, Wildlife and Sport Fish Restoration Program, Policy and Programs Division, 5275 Leesburg Pike, Falls Church, VA 22041-3803. Phone: (703) 358-2156.

Internet: wsfrprograms.fws.gov.

15.608   FISH AND WILDLIFE MANAGEMENT ASSISTANCE

Assistance: specialized services.

Purposes: pursuant to the Fish and Wildlife Act of 1956 and Sikes Act of 1974 as amended, Fish and Wildlife Coordination Act of 1958, and other acts, for: conservation and management of fish and wildlife resources, based on biological, chemical, and physical examinations of land and waters; stocking of fishes from national fish hatcheries; co-management by Alaska natives of marine mammals for subsistence use. Services are provided on a cost recoverable basis.

Eligible applicants/beneficiaries: state agencies, local governments, native American organizations, public nonprofit and other organizations, federal agencies.

Range: $1,000 to $750,000. **Average:** $75,000.

Activity: supported 43 ANDS plans and over 150 fish passage and fish habitat projects in FY 2014.

HQ: Chief, Division of Fish and Wildlife Management and Habitat Restoration, FWS-DOI, 5275 Leesburg Pike, MS: FAC, Falls Church, VA 22041-3803. Phone: (703) 358-1792.

Internet: www.fws.gov/fisheries.

15.611   WILDLIFE RESTORATION AND BASIC HUNTER EDUCATION ("Pittman-Robertson Program")

Assistance: formula grants. (to 75 percent/2 years).

Purposes: pursuant to the Federal Aid in Wildlife Restoration Act of 1937 as amended, to restore or manage wildlife populations and to provide facilities and services for hunter safety programs. Funds may be used for land acquisition, development, research, and coordination.

Eligible applicants/beneficiaries: fish and wildlife agencies in states with laws prohibiting diversion of hunting license revenues to uses other than administration of the agency; territories.

Range: $268,000 to $7,187,000. **Average:** $2,750,000.

Activity: anticipate 375 awards in FY 2016.

HQ: Chief, Policy and Programs Division, FWS-DOI, 5275 Leesburg Pike, MS: WSFR, Falls Church, VA 22041-3803. Phone: (703) 358-2156.

Internet: wsfrprograms.fws.gov.

15.614   COASTAL WETLANDS PLANNING, PROTECTION AND RESTORATION PROGRAM
("National Coastal Wetlands Conservation Grants")

Assistance: project grants (50-75 percent).

Purposes: pursuant to the act, for coastal wetlands conservation projects. Funds may be used to acquire interests in lands or waters, and for restoration, enhancement, or management of coastal wetlands ecosystems, including conservation of fish and wildlife.

Eligible applicants/beneficiaries: states bordering the Atlantic, Pacific, Great Lakes, or Gulf coasts (except Louisiana); territories and possessions.

Range: $125,000 to $1,000,000. **Average:** $575,000.

Activity: anticipate 20 awards in FY 2016.

HQ: Program Coordinator, Wildlife and Sport Fish Restoration Program, Policy and Programs Division, 5275 Leesburg Pike, MS: WSFR, Falls Church, VA 22041-3803. Phone: (703) 358-2156.

Internet: wsfrprograms.fws.gov.

15.615   COOPERATIVE ENDANGERED SPECIES CONSERVATION FUND

Assistance: project grants (75-90 percent).

Purposes: pursuant to the Endangered Species Act of 1973 as amended, for programs for the conservation of endangered and threatened species of animals and plants. Funds may cover the costs of habitat surveys, research, planning, monitoring, management, land acquisition, habitat protection, and public education.

Eligible applicants/beneficiaries: states and territories with cooperative agreements with DOI.

Range/Average: N.A.

Activity: anticipate 13 awards in FY 2016.

HQ: Chief, Ecological Services Division of Restoration and Recovery, FWS-DOI, 5275 Leesburg Pike, MS: ES, Falls Church, VA 22041-3803. Phone: (703) 358-2171.

Internet: www.fws.gov/endangered/grants/index.html.

15.616   CLEAN VESSEL ACT PROGRAM

Assistance: project grants (75 percent).

Purposes: pursuant to the 1992 act, for surveys and plans for installing pumpout/dump stations to protect sensitive areas in the coastal zone from recreational boat sewage; for station construction; for related public education programs.

Eligible applicants/beneficiaries: states bordering the Atlantic, Pacific, or Gulf coasts, or the Great Lakes; territories and possessions.

Range: to $1,500,000. **Average:** $350,000.

Activity: anticipate 35 to 45 awards in FY 2016.

HQ: Chief, Wildlife and Sport Fish Restoration Program, Policy and Programs Division, FWS-DOI, 5275 Leesburg Pike, MS: WSFR, Falls Church, VA 22041-3803. Phone: (703) 358-2156.7.

Internet: wsfrprograms.fws.gov.

15.619 RHINOCEROS AND TIGER CONSERVATION FUND

Assistance: project grants (some matching).

Purposes: pursuant to the Rhinoceros and Tiger Conservation Act of 1994 as amended by the Rhino and Tiger Product Labeling Act of 1998, for rhinoceros and tiger conservation projects including: surveys and monitoring; conservation training and education; wildlife inspection, law enforcement, and forensic skills; research; protected area management; sustainable development in buffer zones surrounding rhinoceros and tiger habitat; management of human behavior and livestock to decrease conflicts; use of substitutes for tiger and rhinoceros products in oriental medicine.

Eligible applicants/beneficiaries: appropriate government agencies; experienced organizations and individuals.

Range: to $50,000. Average: N.A.

Activity: anticipate 50 awards in FY 2015.

HQ: Chief, Division of International Conservation, FWS-DOI, 5275 Leesburg Pike, MS: IA, Falls Church, VA 22041-3803. Phone: (703) 358-1754; FAX: (703) 358-2115.

Internet: www.fws.gov/international/wildlife-without-borders/rhino-and-tiger-conservation-fund.html.

15.620 AFRICAN ELEPHANT CONSERVATION FUND

Assistance: project grants (some matching).

Purposes: pursuant to the African Elephant Conservation Act, for African elephant conservation projects including research, management, and protection activities. Project examples: meritorious service awards program for game wardens in Africa; training in elephant biology and ecology; providing anti-poaching equipment.

Eligible applicants/beneficiaries: African government agencies; experienced organizations and individuals.

Range: to $50,000. Average: N.A.

Activity: anticipate 20 awards in FY 2015.

HQ: Chief, Division of International Conservation, FWS-DOI, 5275 Leesburg Pike, MS: IA, Falls Church, VA 22041-3803. Phone: (703) 358-1754; FAX: (703) 358-2115.

Internet: www.fws.gov/international/wildlife-without-borders/african-elephant-conservation-fund.html. (Note: no field offices for this program.)

15.621 ASIAN ELEPHANT CONSERVATION FUND

Assistance: project grants (some matching).

Purposes: pursuant to the Asian African Elephant Conservation Act, for Asian elephant conservation projects including research, management, and protection activities.

Eligible applicants/beneficiaries: Asian government agencies; experienced organizations and individuals.

Range: to $50,000. **Average:** N.A.

Activity: anticipate 40 awards in FY 2015.

HQ: Chief, Division of International Conservation, FWS-DOI, 5275 Leesburg Pike, MS: IA, Falls Church, VA 22041-3803. Phone: (703) 358-1754; FAX: (703) 358-2115.

Internet: www.fws.gov/international/wildlife-without-borders/asian-elephant-conservation-fund.html. (Note: no field offices for this program.)

15.622   SPORTFISHING AND BOATING SAFETY ACT

Assistance: project grants (75 percent).

Purposes: pursuant to the act, to construct, renovate, or maintain tie-up facilities for transient, nontrailerable recreational vessels.

Eligible applicants/beneficiaries: states, possessions and territories.

Range: $100,000 to $1,500,000. **Average:** 100,000 for Tier 1; $500,000 for Tier 2.

Activity: anticipate 30 awards in FY 2015.

HQ: Boating Infrastructure Grant Program Coordinator, Division of Federal Aid (MS MBSP-4020), FWS-DOI, 4401 N. Fairfax Dr., Arlington, VA 22203. Phone: (703) 358-2156; FAX: (703) 358-2156.

Internet: wsfrprograms.fws.gov.

15.623   NORTH AMERICAN WETLANDS CONSERVATION FUND (NAWCF)

Assistance: project grants. (50 percent/2 years).

Purposes: pursuant to the North American Wetlands Conservation Act, for wetlands conservation projects in the U.S., Canada, and Mexico, including: acquisition of interests in lands or waters for fish and wildlife protection; restoration, management, or enhancement of wetland ecosystems and habitats—only in coastal wetlands ecosystems in coastal states.

Eligible applicants/beneficiaries: entities and individuals recommended by the North American Wetlands Conservation Council and approved by the Migratory Bird Conservation Commission.

Range: to $75,000 for small grants; $75,000 to $1,000,000 for standard grants. **Average:** $42,000 for small grants; $710,000 for standard grants.

Activity: anticipate funding 130 projects in FY 2016.

HQ: Chief, Division of Bird Habitat Conservation, MS: MB, 5275 Leesburg Pike, Falls Church, VA 22041-3803. Phone: (703) 358-1784; FAX: (703) 358-2282.

Internet: www.fws.gov/birdhabitat/Grants/NAWCA.

15.625 WILDLIFE CONSERVATION AND RESTORATION

Assistance: formula grants (to 75 percent).

Purposes: pursuant to the Department of Transportation and Related Agencies (i.e. Commerce, Justice, State) Appropriations Act of 2001, to plan and implement projects encouraging a diverse array of wildlife and associated habitats, including species that are not hunted or fished and to provide wildlife education and recreation activities. State, Commonwealth or Territory must have an approved Comprehensive Wildlife Conservation Plan on file to receive grant funds.

Eligible applicants: state, commonwealth, or territorial fish and wildlife agencies with lead management responsibility for fish and wildlife resources.

Eligible beneficiaries: general public.

Range: $121,000 to $2,425,000. **Average:** $904,000.

Activity: N.A.

HQ: Wildlife and Sport Fish Restoration Programs-Policy and Programs, FWS-DOI, MS: WSFR, 5275 Leesburg Pike, Falls Church, VA 22041-3803. Phone: (703) 358-2231.

Internet: wsfrprograms.fws.gov.

15.626 ENHANCED HUNTER EDUCATION AND SAFETY PROGRAM

Assistance: formula grants (75 percent).

Purposes: pursuant to the Federal Aid in Wildlife Restoration Act of 1937 as amended, to enhance hunter, bow, and archery education programs, and to construct firearm shooting and archery ranges.

Eligible applicants/beneficiaries: fish and wildlife agencies in states with laws prohibiting diversion of hunting license revenues to uses other than administration of the agency; territories.

Range: $13,300 to $240,000. **Average:** $145,000.

Activity: anticipate issuing 35 awards in FY 2016.

HQ: Director, Policy and Programs, FWS-DOI, 5275 Leesburg Pike, MS: WSFR, Falls Church, VA 22041-3803. Phone: (703) 358-2156.

Internet: wsfrprograms.fws.gov.

15.628 MULTI-STATE CONSERVATION GRANT PROGRAM

Assistance: project grants. (100 percent/to 3 years).

Purposes: pursuant to the Wildlife and Sport Fish Restoration Act of 2000 as amended and other acts, for sport fish and wildlife restoration projects identified by the International Association of Fish and Wildlife Agencies. Funds may be used for research, boating access development, hunter safety, aquatic education, habitat improvements, and similar purposes.

Eligible applicants/beneficiaries: states or groups of states; nongovernmental organizations.

Range: $25,000 to $500,000. **Average:** $140,000.

Activity: 17 awards in FY 2015.

HQ: Director, Policy and Programs, FWS-DOI, 5275 Leesburg Pike, MS: WSFR, Falls Church, VA 22041-3803. Phone: (703) 358-2156.

Internet: wsfrprograms.fws.gov.

15.629 GREAT APES CONSERVATION FUND

Assistance: project grants (matching) (matching).

Purposes: pursuant to the Great Ape Conservation Act of 2000, for great apes research, conservation, management, and protection programs and projects in countries within their range.

Eligible applicants/beneficiaries: appropriate government agencies; experienced organizations and individuals.

Range: to $50,000. **Average:** N.A.

Activity: anticipate 30 awards in FY 2015.

HQ: Chief, Division of International Conservation, FWS-DOI, 5275 Leesburg Pike, MS: IA, Falls Church, VA 22041-3803. Phone: (703) 358-1754; FAX: (703) 358-2115.

Internet: www.fws.gov/international/wildlife-without-borders/great-ape-conservation-fund.html. (Note: no field offices for this program.)

15.630 COASTAL PROGRAM

Assistance: project grants.

Purposes: pursuant to the Fish and Wildlife Act of 1956 and Fish and Wildlife Coordination Act of 1958, to provide financial and technical assistance via partnerships to identify, protect, and restore habitats in priority coastal areas. Funds may be used for assessments and acquisition of private or public lands.

Eligible applicants/beneficiaries: federal, state, interstate, and intrastate agencies; local and tribal governments; sponsored organizations; public nonprofit institutes and organizations such as watershed councils, land trusts, schools and IHEs; territories and possessions; private landowners including individuals and businesses.

Range: $5,000 to $50,000. **Average:** N.A.

Activity: anticipate initiating 40 projects in FY 2016.

HQ: Chief, Branch of Habitat Restoration, FWS-DOI, 5275 Leesburg Pike, MS: NWRS, Falls Church, VA 22041-3803. Phone: (703) 358-2583.

Internet: www.fws.gov/coastal.

15.631 PARTNERS FOR FISH AND WILDLIFE

Assistance: direct payments/specified use (50 percent).

Purposes: pursuant to the Fish and Wildlife Act of 1956 as amended and Fish and Wildlife Coordination Act of 1958, to provide financial and technical assistance to private landowners and tribes to voluntarily restore or improve native fish and wildlife habitats. Landowners must enter into 10-year cooperative agreements.

Eligible applicants/beneficiaries: private landowners, local governments, tribal organizations, educational institutions.

Range: $200 to $25,000. **Average:** $5,400.

Activity: anticipate funding 90 new projects in FY 2016.

HQ: Chief, Branch of Habitat Restoration, FWS-DOI, 5275 Leesburg Pike, MS: NWRS, Falls Church, VA 22041-3803. Phone: (703) 358-2583 FAX: (703)358-2232.

Internet: www.fws.gov/partners.

15.633   LANDOWNER INCENTIVE PROGRAM (LIP)

Assistance: project grants (75 percent).

Purposes: pursuant to the Land and Water Conservation Fund Act of 1965, to establish new or supplement existing landowner incentive programs providing technical or financial assistance for habitat protection, restoration, and management—to benefit federally listed, proposed, or at-risk species on private lands; to encourage states to enhance private landowner conservation efforts.

Eligible applicants/beneficiaries: fish and wildlife agencies of the states, tribes, territories, and possessions.

Range/Average: N.A.

Activity: N.A.

HQ: Chief, Policy and Programs Division, Wildlife and Sport Fish Restoration Programs, FWS-DOI, (MS MBSP-4020), MS: WSFR, 5275 Leesburg Pike, Falls Church, VA 22041-3803. Phone: (703) 358-2231.

Internet: wsfrprograms.fws.gov.

15.634   STATE WILDLIFE GRANTS (SWG)

Assistance: formula grants. (planning, 75 percent; implementation, 50 percent/2 years).

Purposes: to develop and implement programs for the benefit of wildlife and their habitat, including species that are not hunted or fished.

Eligible applicants/beneficiaries: fish and wildlife agencies of the states, tribes, territories, and possessions.

Range: $155,000 to $3,104,000. **Average:** $1,109,000.

Activity: anticipate making 15 awards in FY 2016.

HQ: Director, Policy and Programs, FWS-DOI, 5275 Leesburg Pike, MS: WSFR, Falls Church, VA 22041-3803. Phone: (703) 358-2156.

Internet: wsfrprograms.fws.gov.

15.635   NEOTROPICAL MIGRATORY BIRD CONSERVATION

Assistance: project grants. (25 percent/to 2 years).

Purposes: pursuant to the Neotropical Migratory Bird Conservation Act of 2000, for projects that: enhance the conservation of neotropical bird species in the U.S., Latin America, or the Caribbean; ensure adequate local public participation in project development and implementation; are conducted in consultation with relevant wildlife management authorities and other appropriate government officials; are sensitive to local historic and cultural resources and comply with applicable laws; and, promote sustainable effective, long-term programs. 75 percent of available funds must be expended outside the U.S.

Eligible applicants/beneficiaries: individuals, corporations, partnerships, trusts, or other private entities; officers, employees, agents, departments, or instrumentalities of any state, municipality, or political subdivision of state, or of any foreign government; entities subject to the jurisdiction of the U.S. or any foreign government; international organizations with an interest in neotropical migratory bird conservation.

Range: $2,000 to $200,000. **Average:** $100,000.

Activity: anticipate funding 30 projects in FY 2016.

HQ: Chief, Division of Bird Habitat Conservation, MS: MB, 5275 Leesburg Pike, Falls Church, VA 22041-3803. Phone: (703) 358-1784; FAX: (703) 358-2282.

Internet: www.fws.gov/birdhabitat/Grants/NMBCA. (Note: no field offices for this program.)

15.636 ALASKA SUBSISTENCE MANAGEMENT

Assistance: project grants (100 percent).

Purposes: pursuant to the Alaska National Interest Lands Conservation Act of 1980, for approved fish and wildlife subsistence management, fisheries monitoring, and traditional ecological knowledge projects—involving partnerships within the ranges of designated fish and wildlife species. Project examples include tagging, studies, harvest surveys.

Eligible applicants/beneficiaries: individuals, families, profit and nonprofit organizations, federal and Alaska state employees and agents or instrumentalities, tribal governments.

Range: $10,000 to $600,000. **Average:** N.A.

Activity: anticipate 35 awards in FY 2016.

HQ: Administrative Specialist, Office of Subsistence Management, Fisheries Information Service Division, FWS-DOI, 1011 E. Tudor Rd., MS 121, Anchorage, AK 99503. Phone: (907) 786-3387.

Internet: alaska.fws.gov/asm/index.cfml.

15.637 MIGRATORY BIRD JOINT VENTURES

Assistance: direct payments/specified use; project grants (100 percent/1-5 years).

Purposes: pursuant to the Fish and Wildlife Act of 1956, Fish and Wildlife Coordination Act of 1958, Fish and Wildlife Conservation Act, Migratory Bird Treaty Act, and amendments, to protect, restore, and enhance wetland and upland ecosystems for the conservation of migratory birds. Project funds must be matched by joint ventures and may be used for costs of administration, coordination, bird habitat landscape planning, monitoring, evaluation, applied research, training, communications and outreach, and project implementation.

Eligible applicants/beneficiaries: federal, state, local, and tribal governments; public, private, profit, and nonprofit organizations; inter- and intrastate entities; individuals or families owning lands.

Range: $2,400 to $900,000. **Average:** $225,000.

Activity: N.A.

HQ: Joint Venture Liaison Officer, Division of Bird Habitat Conservation (MS 4075), FWS-DOI, MS: MBSP, 5275 Leesburg Pike, Falls Church, VA 22041-3803. Phone: (703) 358-1784; FAX: (703) 358-2282.

Internet: www.fws.gov/birdhabitat/JointVentures/index.shtm.

15.639 TRIBAL WILDLIFE GRANTS PROGRAM (TWG)

Assistance: project grants (to 100 percent).

Purposes: pursuant to the Land and Water Conservation Fund Act of 1965, to develop and implement programs for the benefit of wildlife and their habitat, including species that are not hunted or fished—whether on tribal trust or private lands.

Eligible applicants/beneficiaries: tribal governments.

Range: to $200,000. **Average:** $167,000.

Activity: anticipate 20 to 25 awards in FY 2016.

HQ: National Native American Programs Coordinator, FWS-DOI, 1211 SE Cardinal Ct., Suite 100, Vancouver, WA 98683. Phone: (360)604-2531; FAX: (360)604-2505.

Internet: www.fws.gov/nativeamerican.

15.640 WILDLIFE WITHOUT BORDERS—LATIN AMERICA AND THE CARIBBEAN

Assistance: project grants (cost sharing).

Purposes: pursuant to the Endangered Species Act of 1973 as amended, for the management of fish, plant, and wildlife resources in the Western Hemisphere. Priority is accorded to projects to strengthen capacity to conserve and use sustainable biological resources, and result in specific measurable on-the- ground management actions in agreement with the Convention on Nature Protection and Wildlife Preservation in the Western Hemisphere (Western Hemisphere Convention, 1940). Activities should be conducted on-site, and may include work such as: academic and technical training; applied research; community- level education; technology transfer and information exchange; promotion of networks, partnerships, and coalitions.

Eligible applicants/beneficiaries: federal, state, and local governments; non-profit, nongovernmental organizations; public and private IHEs.

Range: to $50,000. **Average:** N.A.

Activity: 26 awards in FY 2015.

HQ: Chief, Division of International Conservation, FWS-DOI, 5275 Leesburg Pike, MS: IA, Falls Church, VA 22041-3803. Phone: (703) 358-1754; FAX: (703) 358-2115.

Internet: www.fws.gov/international/wildlife-without-borders/latin-america -and-the-caribbean/index.html. (Note: no field offices for this program.)

15.641   WILDLIFE WITHOUT BORDERS—MEXICO

Assistance: project grants (cost sharing).

Purposes: pursuant to the Endangered Species Act of 1973 as amended, for the conservation and sustainable use of Mexico's wildlife and plant resources through projects that strengthen Mexico's capacity. Activities should be conducted in Mexico, and may include work such as: academic and technical training; applied research; community-level education; technology transfer and information exchange; promotion of networks, partnerships, and coalitions.

Eligible applicants/beneficiaries: federal, state, and local governments; nonprofit, nongovernmental organizations; public and private IHEs.

Range: N.A. **Average:** $35,000.

Activity: 18 awards in FY 2014.

HQ: Chief, Division of International Conservation, FWS-DOI, 5275 Leesburg Pike, MS: IA, Falls Church, VA 22041-3803. Phone: (703) 358-1754; FAX: (703) 358-2115.

Internet: www.fws.gov/international/DIC/regionalprograms/mexico/mexico .html.

15.642   CHALLENGE COST SHARE (CCS)

Assistance: project grants (50 percent).

Purposes: to encourage partnerships to support the mission of the U.S. Fish and Wildlife Service through projects involving conservation, protection, and enhancement of fish, wildlife, and plants, including recreational and educational activities—whether on or off FWS lands.

Eligible applicants/beneficiaries: individuals, families, and virtually any organization, whether public or private, profit or nonprofit—including territories and possessions.

Range/Average: N.A.

Activity: N.A.

HQ: Assistant Director, National Wildlife Refuge System, FWS-DOI, 5275 Leesburg Pike, MS: NWRS, Falls Church, VA 22041-3803. Phone: (703) 358-1744; FAX: (703) 358-2248.

Internet: www.fws.gov.

15.643   ALASKA MIGRATORY BIRD CO-MANAGEMENT COUNCIL (AMBCC)

Assistance: project grants (100 percent).

Purposes: pursuant to the Fish and Wildlife Coordination Act of 1958 and Migratory Bird Treaty Act, to facilitate and administer programs to involve subsistence hunters of migratory birds in the management and regulation of migratory birds.

Eligible applicants/beneficiaries: native American and public nonprofit organizations, other public institutions, tribal and local governments.

Range: $14,800 to $175,000. **Average:** $39,127.

Activity: anticipate issuing 12 continuation awards in FY 2016.

HQ: Office of the Alaska Migratory Bird Co-Management Council (201), FWS-DOI, 1011 E. Tudor Rd., Anchorage, AK 99503. Phone: (907) 786-3499; FAX: (907) 786-3641.

Internet: Alaska.fws.gov/ambcc/index.htm.

15.644 FEDERAL JUNIOR DUCK STAMP CONSERVATION AND DESIGN ("Junior Duck Stamp Contest")

Assistance: direct payments/specified use; sale, exchange, or donation of property and goods.

Purposes: pursuant to the reauthorized Junior Duck Stamp Conservation and Design Program Act of 1994, for a nationwide design contest to teach K-12 students environmental science, wildlife management, wetlands ecology, and the importance of habitat conservation. Assistance may be used to: provide awards and scholarships to student-winners in state-territory contest rounds; provide awards to schools and other participants; pay costs of outreach and marketing. Cash awards are provided for scholarships to national round winners.

Eligible applicants/beneficiaries: U.S. and territorial K-12 students attending public, private, or home schools.

Range: $500 to $2,500. Average: N.A.

Activity: anticipate issuing 53 awards in FY 2016.

HQ: National Program Coordinator, Federal Duck Stamp Office (MBSP-4070), FWS-DOI, 5275 Leesburg Pike, MS: MBSP, Falls Church, VA 22041-3803. Phone: (703) 358-1784; FAX: (703) 358-2009.

Internet: www.fws.gov/juniorduck.

15.645 MARINE TURTLE CONSERVATION FUND

Assistance: project grants (to 100 percent).

Purposes: pursuant to the Marine Turtle Conservation Act of 2004, for foreign countries to conduct projects to conserve marine turtles and their nesting habitats; to address other threats to marine turtle survival. Applied research projects should address specific management needs and activities.

Eligible applicants/beneficiaries: appropriate responsible government agencies; other qualified organizations and individuals.

Range: to $50,000. Average: N.A.

Activity: 48 awards in FY 2014.

HQ: Chief, Division of International Conservation, FWS-DOI, 5275 Leesburg Pike, MS: IA, Falls Church, VA 22041-3803. Phone: (703) 358-1754; FAX: (703) 358-2115.

Internet: www.fws.gov/international/wildlife-without-borders/marine-turtle-conservation-fund.html. (Note: no field offices for this program.)

15.647 MIGRATORY BIRD CONSERVATION

Assistance: project grants; direct payments/specified use (grants, 1-5 years).

Purposes: pursuant to the Fish and Wildlife Act of 1956, Fish and Wildlife Coordination Act of 1958, Fish and Wildlife Conservation Act, Migratory Bird Treaty Act, and amendments, to maintain and enhance populations and habitats of migratory bird species found in the Upper Midwest, including Illinois, Indiana, Iowa, Michigan, Minnesota, Missouri, Ohio, and Wisconsin. Funds may be used for population surveys and monitoring, applied research, compilation of technical information.

Eligible applicants/beneficiaries: federal, state, local, and tribal governments; public, private, profit, and nonprofit organizations.

Range: $5,000 to $99,974. **Average:** $43,108.

Activity: anticipate funding 3 proposals in FY 2016.

HQ: Division of Migratory Birds, FWS-DOI, 5600 American Blvd. West, Suite 990, Bloomington, MN 55437-1458. Phone: (512) 713-5473.

Internet: www.fws.gov/midwest/midwestbird.

15.648 CENTRAL VALLEY PROJECT IMPROVEMENT (CVPI) ANADROMOUS FISH RESTORATION PROGRAM (AFRP) ("CVPI, AFRP")

Assistance: project grants (1-5 years).

Purposes: pursuant to the Central Valley Improvement Act-Title 34 and the Federal Grant and Cooperative Agreement Act, to protect, restore, and enhance fish, wildlife, and associated habitats in the California Central Valley and Trinity River basins; to address environmental impact, improve operational flexibility, increase water-related benefits, and achieve a reasonable balance among competing demands for water use of the Central Valley Project. Funds may be used for research to improve management and increase Anadromous fish resources; spawning area improvement; installation of fish passages; construction of fish protection devices, and data collection.

Eligible applicants/beneficiaries: state, local governments; native American, public or private nonprofit organizations.

Range/Average: N.A.

Activity: N.A.

HQ: CNO-California Nevada Office, 2800 Cottage Way, Rm. W-2606, Sacramento, CA 95825. Phone: (916) 414-6464; FAX: (916) 414-646.4

Internet: www.fws.gov/stockton/afrp.

15.649 SERVICE TRAINING AND TECHNICAL ASSISTANCE (GENERIC TRAINING)

Assistance: project grants; direct payments/specified use (cost sharing encouraged).

Purposes: pursuant to Fish and Wildlife Act of 1956, Fish and Wildlife Coordination Act, Fish and Wildlife Improvement Act of 1978, as amended, to assist in conservation of the Nation's natural resources by providing financial support for training, meetings, workshops and conferences for the promotion of public conservation awareness.

Eligible applicants/beneficiaries: Federal, state and local government agencies; Federally-recognized Tribal governments; private and public nonprofit institutions/organizations.

Range/Average: N.A.

Activity: 36 awards in FY 2014.

HQ: Branch of Financial Assistance Policy & Oversight Division of Wildlife and Sport Fish Restoration, 5275 Leesburg Pike, MS-WSFR, Falls Church, VA 22041-3803. Phone: (703) 358-2701.

Internet: www.fws.gov.

15.650   RESEARCH GRANTS (GENERIC TRAINING)

Assistance: project grants; direct payments/specified use (cost sharing encouraged).

Purposes: pursuant to Fish and Wildlife Improvement Act of 1978, Land and Water Conservation Fund Act of 1965, Endangered Species Act of 1973, as amended, to assist in the conservation of the Nation's natural resources through land management, research, and data collection/analysis in order to further the preservation and management of natural resources.

Eligible applicants/beneficiaries: Federal, State and local government agencies; Federally-recognized Tribal governments; private nonprofit institutions/organizations; public nonprofit institutions/organizations.

Range/Average: N.A.

Activity: 74 awards in FY 2014.

HQ: Branch of Financial Assistance Policy & Oversight Division of Wildlife and Sport Fish Restoration, 5275 Leesburg Pike, MS-WSFR, Falls Church, VA 22041-3803. Phone: (703) 358-2701.

Internet: www.fws.gov.

15.651   WILDLIFE WITHOUT BORDERS-AFRICA PROGRAM

Assistance: project grants (cost sharing encouraged).

Purposes: pursuant to the Endangered Species Act of 1973 as amended, to strengthen the ability of African institutions to manage and conserve species, habitats, and ecological process for the benefit of African people and the world. Some projects of particular interest are ones that would provide training to increase human and institutional capacity to: mitigate the impact of industry, human/wildlife conflict, climate change, illegal trade in bushmeat; provide community outreach and education, human resource and financial management, conflict resolution, and coalition building. Projects should take place in Africa or facilitate protected area conservation and management within Africa.

Eligible applicants: federal, state, and local government agencies; public and private institutions of higher education, nonprofit, nongovernmental organizations, or any of these entities acting on behalf of an eligible individual.

Eligible beneficiaries: federal, state, and local government agencies; public and private institutions of higher education, nonprofit, nongovernmental organizations. All recipients, both individual and institutional, must have a bank account and the ability to receive funds directly.

Range: to $50,000. **Average:** N.A.

Activity: anticipate 28 awards in FY 2015.

HQ: Chief, Division of International Conservation, FWS-DOI, 5275 Leesburg Pike, MS: IA, Falls Church, VA 22041-3803. Phone: (703) 358-1754; FAX: (703) 358-2115.

Internet: www.fws.gov/international/wildlife-without-borders/africa/index .html.

15.652 UNDESIRABLE/NOXIOUS PLANT SPECIES ("Weeds Program")

Assistance: project grants (100 percent/1-5 years).

Purposes: pursuant to the Fish and Wildlife Act of 1956, Fish and Wildlife Coordination Act of 1958, and National Wildlife Refuge System Administration Act, to identify, manage, and eradicate undesirable plant species on FWS lands. Projects will encourage coordinated, integrated efforts between the FWS and interested parties to conserve, protect and enhance fish, wildlife, and plants for the continuing benefit of the American public.

Eligible applicants/beneficiaries: state and local governments, organizations and institutions, and the general public.

Range: $3,000 to $80,500. **Average:** N.A.

Activity: N.A.

HQ: Assistant Director, National Wildlife Refuge System, FWS-DOI, 5275 Leesburg Pike, MS: NWRS, Falls Church, VA 22041-3803. Phone: (703) 358-1744; FAX: (703) 358-2248.

Internet: www.fws.gov.

15.653 NATIONAL OUTREACH AND COMMUNICATION PROGRAM (NOC)

Assistance: project grants (matching encouraged).

Purposes: pursuant to the Transportation Equity Act for the 21st Century of 1998 and the Sportfishing and Boating Safety Act of 1998, to improve communications with the general public regarding angling and boating opportunities, sound practices, and water safety; to educate and encourage conservation and responsible use of the nations' aquatic resources.

Eligible applicants: anyone with the expertise to conduct work within the scope of the Strategic Plan for the Outreach and Communication Program as required by the Sportfishing and Boating Safety Act of 1998.

Eligible beneficiaries: general public.

Range/Average: N.A.

Activity: N.A.

HQ: NOC Program, External Affairs, FWS-DOI, 5275 Leesburg Pike, MS: EA, Falls Church, VA 22041-3803. Phone: (703) 358-2435.

Internet: www.fws.gov/conservationpartnerships. (Note: no field offices for this program.)

15.654   VISITOR FACILITY ENHANCEMENTS—REFUGES AND WILDLIFE

Assistance: project grants (cost sharing encouraged/1-5 years).

Purposes: pursuant to the Fish and Wildlife Coordination Act of 1958, National Wildlife Refuge System Administration Act, and Fish and Wildlife Act of 1956 as amended, to encourage partnerships with interested parties to enhance wildlife viewing opportunities for the public. Projects must conserve, protect and enhance fish, wildlife, and plants and may include trails, scenic overlooks, interpretive pullouts, signs, and kiosks.

Eligible applicants/beneficiaries: any U.S. government, organization or individual supporting the mission of the FWS project.

Range: $1,000 to $1,000,000. **Average:** N.A.

Activity: anticipate 28 awards in FY 2016.

HQ: Assistant Director, National Wildlife Refuge System, FWS-DOI, 5275 Leesburg Pike, MS: NWRS, Arlington, VA 22041-3803. Phone: (703) 358-1744; FAX: (703) 358-2248.

Internet: www.fws.gov.

15.655   MIGRATORY BIRD MONITORING, ASSESSMENT AND CONSERVATION
("Migratory Bird")

Assistance: project grants; direct payments/specified use (100 percent).

Purposes: pursuant to the Fish and Wildlife Coordination Act of 1958, Fish and Wildlife Conservation Act, Migratory Bird Treaty Act, and Fish and Wildlife Act of 1956 as amended, to maintain, enhance, and deepen understanding of the ecology and habitats of migratory bird species. Special emphasis will be placed on bird species listed in USFWS conservation and management priorities documents (e.g. USFWS Birds of Conservation Concern 2002, Focal Species list). Projects related to the priorities identified in the following plans will receive the greatest funding consideration: Implementing national, regional, flyway Bird Conservation Region, and state-level bird conservation plans (e.g., Partners in Flight North American Landbird Conservation (http://www.partnersinflight.org); U.S. Shorebird Conservation Plan (http://shorebirdplan.fws.gov); and North American Waterbird Conservation Plan (http://birdhabitat.fws.gov/NAWMP/nawm php.htm).

Eligible applicants/beneficiaries: any individual or group in the U.S. or territories.

Range/Average: N.A.

Activity: N.A.

HQ: Chief, Division of Migratory Bird Management, FWS-DOI, 5275 Leesburg Pike, MS: MB, Falls Church, VA 22041-3803. Phone: (703) 358-1757.

Internet: www.fws.gov/migratorybirds.

15.657   ENDANGERED SPECIES CONSERVATION

Assistance: project grants (100 percent/to 1 year).

Purposes: pursuant to Endangered Species Act of 1973, to provide federal financial assistance to secure endangered or threatened species information, undertake restoration actions that will lead to delisting of a species; help prevent extinction of a species, or aid in the recovery of species. Subgrant projects are not funded under formula and project grants.

Eligible applicants/beneficiaries: states (includes DC, public IHEs and hospitals); public nonprofit and for profit institutions/organizations; state and federally recognized Indian tribal governments/organizations.

Range/Average: N.A.

Activity: N.A.

HQ: Chief, Ecological Services Division of Restoration and Recovery, FWS-DOI, 5275 Leesburg Pike, MS: ES, Falls Church, VA 22041-3803. Phone: (703) 358-2171.

Internet: www.fws.gov/endangered/recovery/index.html.

15.658 NATURAL RESOURCE DAMAGE ASSESSMENT, RESTORATION AND IMPLEMENTATION (NRDAR)

Assistance: project grants/cooperative agreements (100 percent/1 to 5 years).

Purposes: pursuant to Oil Pollution Act of 1990, CERCLA, Federal Water Pollution Control Act, and Fish and Wildlife Act of 1956, to provide assistance to individuals and groups to fund assessments, implementation, recovery of damages or any related restoration activity necessary to meet the intent of the NRDAR. Cost-sharing by grant recipient is encouraged.

Eligible applicants/beneficiaries: anyone/general public.

Range: $1,000 to $1,000,000. **Average:** N.A.

Activity: N.A.

HQ: Chief, Division of Environmental Restoration and Recovery U.S. Fish and Wildlife Service, 5275 Leesburg Pike, MS: ES, Falls Church, VA 22041-3803. Phone: (703) 358-2171.

Internet: www.fws.gov/contaminants/Issues/Restoration.cfm.

15.659 NATIONAL WILDLIFE REFUGE FUND ("Refuge Revenue Sharing")

Assistance: direct payments/unrestricted use.

Purposes: pursuant to Refuge Revenue Sharing Act and Refuge Revenue Sharing Act of 1978, to provide revenue sharing payments to local governments to offset tax losses for fee and withdrawn domain lands within approved acquisition boundaries, using revenues derived from the sale of products from National Wildlife Refuges and other fee acquisition lands administered solely or primarily by the Service including public domain lands. Congress may appropriate funds to cover any shortfall for payment to counties.

Eligible applicants: federal.

Eligible beneficiaries: interstate, intrastate, state and local units of government.

Range/Average: N.A.

Activity: N.A.

HQ: National Wildlife Refuge System, FWS-DOI, 5275 Leesburg Pike, Falls Church, VA 22041-3803. Phone: (703) 358-2223.

Internet: www.fws.gov/refuges/realty/rrs.html.

15.660 ENDANGERED SPECIES—CANDIDATE CONSERVATION ACTION FUNDS

Assistance: project grants/cooperative agreements (100 percent/to 1 year).

Purposes: pursuant to Endangered Species Act of 1973, as amended in 1978 and 1982, to secure endangered, threatened, candidate and other at-risk species information or undertake restoration actions that will help avert federal listing of species, lead to the recovery of species, or prevent extinction.

Eligible applicants/beneficiaries: anyone/general public.

Range/Average: N.A.

Activity: anticipate 6 awards in FY 2016.

HQ: Chief, Ecological Services Division of Restoration and Recovery, FWS-DOI, 5275 Leesburg Pike, MS: ES, Falls Church, VA 22041-3803. Phone: (703) 358-2171.

Internet: N.A.

15.661 LOWER SNAKE RIVER COMPENSATION PLAN (LSRCP)

Assistance: project grants/cooperative agreements (100 percent).

Purposes: pursuant to Water Resources Development Act of 1976, and Fish and Wildlife Coordination Act, to mitigate losses of fish and wildlife caused by construction of four hydroelectric dams on the lower Snake River by the U.S. Army Corps of Engineers through operation and maintenance of LSRCP authorized fish hatcheries owned by the U.S. Fish and Wildlife Service.

Eligible applicants: federal, state (includes DC, public IHEs and hospitals) and inter-state governments and federally-recognized Indian tribal governments.

Eligible beneficiaries: anyone/general public.

Range: $272,252 to $5,258,402. **Average:** N.A.

Activity: anticipate 11 awards in FY 2016.

HQ: Regional Office, FWS-DOI, 911 NE 11th Ave., Portland, OR 97232-4181. Phone: (503)231-2763.

Internet: www.fws.gov/lsnakecomplan.

15.662 GREAT LAKES RESTORATION
("Great Lakes Restoration Initiative; Great Lakes Restoration Program")

Assistance: project grants/discretionary.

Purposes: pursuant to the Anadromous Fish Conservation Act, to implement the highest priority actions in order to protect and restore the Great Lakes including, identification, protection, conservation, management, enhancement, or restoration of habitat or species on public and private lands within the Great Lakes Basin.

Eligible applicants/beneficiaries: 35 IHEs selected by the CDC as Prevention Research Centers (PRCs).

Range: $1,000 to $1,000,000. **Average:** N.A.

Activity: 65 awards in FY 2014.

HQ: Program Director, Great Lakes Restoration, U.S. Fish and Wildlife Service, DOI, 1849 C St., NW, Washington, DC 20240. Phone: (202) 208-6394; FAX: (202) 208-4674.

Internet: www.fws.gov/glri.

15.663 NATIONAL FISH AND WILDLIFE FOUNDATION (NFWF)

Assistance: project grants (100 percent).

Purposes: pursuant to the National Fish and Wildlife Foundation Establishment Act, to provide Congressionally mandated funding to the NFWF to direct public conservation dollars to the most pressing environmental needs and match (on a one-to-one basis) those investments with private funds. Cost-share conservation projects will further the conservation and management of the fish, wildlife, and plant resources of the U.S., including territories and possessions, for present and future generations of Americans.

Eligible applicants: eligible partners/sub-recipients include: individuals, foundations, government agencies, non-profits, corporations.

Eligible beneficiaries: the general public, international partners, wildlife and natural resources.

Range/Average: N.A.

Activity: N.A.

HQ: Director, Fish and Wildlife Service, Division of Program and Partnership Support, DOI, 5275 Leesburg Pike, MS: AEA, Falls Church, VA 22041-3803. Phone: (703) 358-2541.

Internet: www.nfwf.org.

15.664 FISH AND WILDLIFE COORDINATION AND ASSISTANCE PROGRAMS (FWCA)

Assistance: project grants/discretionary.

Purposes: pursuant to the U. S. Fish and Wildlife Coordination Act of 1958, as amended, to implement legislation mandating specific conservation and/or environmental project activity, including, but not limited to, financial assistance funding for special appropriations projects to designated recipients and/or unfunded Congressional mandates with funding limited to actual program/project implementation costs, not administrative costs. Cost match not required, but encouraged.

Eligible applicants/beneficiaries: 35 IHEs selected by the CDC as Prevention Research Centers (PRCs).

Range/Average: N.A.

Activity: 5 new awards in FY 2014.

HQ: Chief, Branch of Financial Assistance Policy & Oversight Division of Wildlife Sport Fish Restoration, 5275 Leesburg Pike, MS-WSFR, Falls Church, VA 22041-3803. Phone: (703)358-2701.

Internet: N.A.

15.665 NATIONAL WETLANDS INVENTORY (NWI)

Assistance: project grants/discretionary (100 percent).

Purposes: pursuant to Emergency Wetlands Resources Act (EWRA) of 1986, to map wetlands of the nation, digitize the maps, archive and distribute the data, and produce a 10-year national wetlands status and trends report to Congress.

Eligible applicants/beneficiaries: qualified Americans, profit or nonprofit corporations or institutions, domestic organizations, and Federal, State, Tribal, Territorial, and local agencies.

Range/Average: N.A.

Activity: N.A.

HQ: Chief, Division of Budget and Technical Assistance U.S. Fish and Wildlife Service, 5275 Leesburg Pike, MS: AES, Falls Church, VA 22041-3803. Phone: (703) 358-2171.

Internet: www.fws.gov/wetlands.

15.666 ENDANGERED SPECIES CONSERVATION—WOLF LIVESTOCK LOSS COMPENSATION AND PREVENTION

Assistance: project grants/discretionary (50 percent).

Purposes: pursuant to the Fish and Wildlife Coordination Act of 1934, to provide federal financial assistance to livestock producers undertaking proactive, non-lethal activities to reduce the risk of livestock loss due to predation by wolves and to compensate livestock producers for their losses due to such predation.

Eligible applicants: eligible state and tribal governments/agencies.

Eligible beneficiaries: individual/families, small businesses, organizations, farmers, ranchers, agricultural producers, land owners.

Range: $9,000 to $100,000. **Average:** $50,000.

Activity: anticipate 20 awards in FY 2016.

HQ: Chief, Ecological Services Division of Restoration and Recovery, FWS-DOI, 5275 Leesburg Pike, MS: ES, Falls Church, VA 22041-3803. Phone: (703) 358-2171.

Internet: www.fws.gov/endangered/grants/index.html.

15.667 HIGHLANDS CONSERVATION PROGRAM

Assistance: project grants/discretionary (50 percent).

Purposes: to conserve and protect high-priority conservation lands and natural resources, recognizing the importance of the water, forest, agricultural, wildlife, recreational, cultural resources, and national significance of the Highlands region of the United States.

Eligible applicants/beneficiaries: 35 IHEs selected by the CDC as Prevention Research Centers (PRCs).

Range: $646,600 to $1,940,000. **Average:** $970,000.

Activity: 4 awards.

HQ: Program Director, Wildlife and Sport Fish Restoration, U.S. Fish and Wildlife Service, 300 Westgate Center Dr., Hadley, MA 01035. Phone: (413) 253-8200; FAX: (413) 253-8300.

Internet: www.fws.gov/r5fedaid/index.html. (Note: no field offices for this program.)

15.669 COOPERATIVE LANDSCAPE CONSERVATION ("Landscape Conservation Cooperatives LCCs")

Assistance: project grants/discretionary (100 percent/to 5 years).

Purposes: pursuant to the Fish and Wildlife Conservation Act, to inform conservation decisions and actions, to create Landscape Conservation Cooperatives (LCCs), a network of partners working in unison to ensure the sustainability of America's land, water, wildlife and cultural resources. Facilitated by the Department of the Interior (DOI) as part of its collaborative, science-based response to climate change, each of the 22 LCCs operates within a specific landscape, covering the entire United States and portions of Canada, Mexico, the Caribbean and Pacific Islands.

Eligible applicants: state, county, city, township, tribal governments, IHEs, nonprofit organizations.

Eligible beneficiaries: anyone, general public.

Range: to $1,000,000. **Average:** N.A.

Activity: anticipates issuing 50 awards in FY 2015.

HQ: Director, U.S. Fish and Wildlife Service, Department of the Interior, 5275 Leesburg Pike MS: SA, Falls Church, VA 22041-3803. Phone: (703) 358-1881.

Internet: lccnetwork.org.

15.670 ADAPTIVE SCIENCE

Assistance: project grants/discretionary (100 percent/to 5 years).

Purposes: pursuant to the Fish and Wildlife Act of 1956, to support science projects that include species risk and vulnerability assessments, inventory and monitoring, population and habitat assessments, biological planning and conservation design, management evaluation and research, and conservation genetics.

Eligible applicants: state, county, city, township, tribal governments, IHEs, nonprofit organizations.

Eligible beneficiaries: anyone, general public.

Range: to $1,000,000. **Average:** N.A.

Activity: 25 awards.

HQ: Director, U.S. Fish and Wildlife Service, Department of the Interior, 5275 Leesburg Pike MS: SA, Falls Church, VA 22041-3803. Phone: (703) 358-1881.

Internet: www.fws.gov/science.

15.671 YUKON RIVER SALMON RESEARCH AND MANAGEMENT ASSISTANCE ("R&M Fund")

Assistance: project grants/discretionary (100 percent).

Purposes: pursuant to The Yukon River Salmon Act of 2000, to support projects that are focused on improving the understanding of the biology and management of Yukon River Chinook salmon and summer and fall chum salmon, and to improve the understanding of the biology and management of Yukon River salmon species.

Eligible applicants/beneficiaries: projects that benefit the rural and urban American and Canadian public that subsist off of the salmon resources of the Yukon River.

Range: $3,000 to $220,456. **Average:** $40,756.

Activity: N.A.

HQ: Alaska Region Fish and Wildlife Office, 1011 East Tudor Rd., Anchorage, Alaska 99503. Phone: (907) 786-3523.

Internet: alaska.fws.gov/fisheries/fieldoffice/fairbanks/index.htm.

15.672 WILDLIFE WITHOUT BORDERS—AMPHIBIANS IN DECLINE

Assistance: project grants/discretionary (100 percent).

Purposes: pursuant to the Endangered Species Act of 1973 as amended, to conserve the world's rapidly declining amphibian species. Frogs, toads, salamanders, newts, and caecilians that face a very high risk of extinction in the immediate future and meet the criteria to be listed as "Critically Endangered" or "Endangered" on the International Union for the Conservation of Nature (IUCN) Red List are eligible for funding. Species not eligible for funding are those with natural habitat range located primarily within the U.S. and its territories, Canada, and the high income economies of Europe, and non-amphibian species.

Eligible applicants/beneficiaries: 35 IHEs selected by the CDC as Prevention Research Centers (PRCs).

Range: $10,000 to $40,000. **Average:** $25,000.

Activity: anticipate 5 awards in FY 2015.

HQ: Program Director, Division of International Conservation, U.S. Fish and Wildlife Service, 5275 Leesburg Pike, MS: IA, Falls Church, VA 22041-3803. Phone: (703) 358-2115.

Internet: www.fws.gov/international/wildlife-without-borders/amphibians-in-decline.html. (Note: no field offices for this program.)

15.673   WILDLIFE WITHOUT BORDERS—CRITICALLY ENDANGERED ANIMAL CONSERVATION FUND

Assistance: project grants/discretionary (100 percent).

Purposes: pursuant to Endangered Species Act of 1973 as amended, to reduce threats to highly endangered wildlife in their natural habitat by identifying specific conservation actions that have a high likelihood of creating durable benefits, such as: protection of at-risk populations, veterinary/wildlife health interventions, activities related to execution of species survival plans, strengthening local capacity to conserve the target species, actions addressing unsustainable exploitation, efforts to mitigate or stop wildlife-human conflict, and rehabilitation and rescue. Species eligible for funding are those that meet the criteria to be listed as "Critically Endangered" or "Endangered" on the International Union for the Conservation of Nature (IUCN) Red List.

Eligible applicants/beneficiaries: 35 IHEs selected by the CDC as Prevention Research Centers (PRCs).

Range: $10,000 to $40,000. **Average:** $25,000.

Activity: 10 awards in FY 2015.

HQ: Program Director, Division of International Conservation, U.S. Fish and Wildlife Service, 5275 Leesburg Pike, MS: IA, Falls Church, VA 22041-3803. Phone: (703) 358-2115.

Internet: www.fws.gov/international/wildlife-without-borders/critically-endangered-animals-conservation-fund.html. (Note: no field offices for this program.)

15.676   YOUTH ENGAGEMENT, EDUCATION, AND EMPLOYMENT PROGRAMS (YEEEP)

Assistance: project grants.

Purposes: funds to provide experiential, education, and employment program opportunities for youth of all ages (pre-K through early adult life, including students, associates, fellows, interns, members, and volunteers) to participate in conservation activities. Recipients will use the assistance in rural and urban settings to fulfill the need for exposure of youth of all ages to nature and conservation; stewardship of our lands, waters and wildlife; as well as to enhance and sustain cultural heritage. The intent of these education, career and leadership development programs is to engage, educate, and employ youth participants in the various fields of natural resources conservation.

Eligible applicants/beneficiaries: state agencies, local governments, tribal organizations, interstate, intrastate, public nonprofit institution/organizations, other public institution/organization, private nonprofit/organization, or any other organization subject to the jurisdiction of the United States with interests that support the mission of the Service.

Range: $750.00 to $200,000. **Average:** N.A.

Activity: anticipate issuing 225 awards in FY 2016.

HQ: Chief, Division of Education Outreach, National Conservation Training Center, 5275 Leesburg Pike, MC: EA, Falls Church, VA 22041-3803. Phone: (703) 358-2606.

Internet: www.youthgo.gov.

15.677 HURRICANE SANDY DISASTER RELIEF ACTIVITIES—FWS

Assistance: project grants (to 100 percent/cost sharing encouraged).

Purposes: pursuant to the Disaster Relief Appropriations Act of 2013, funds to provide technical and financial assistance to identify, protect, conserve, manage, enhance or restore habitat and structures on both public and private lands that have been negatively impacted by Hurricane Sandy. Assistance is provided to fund projects that relate to relief and rebuilding activities that improve or restore habitat and structures affected by the disaster. These projects may include, but are not limited to assessments, protection, restoration and monitoring activities. No matching is required, however, matching funds are encouraged to allow for additional restoration and may be used as an evaluation factor for the selection of projects to award.

Eligible applicants: state/local governments, Indian tribal governments, non-profits organizations, IHEs, hospitals, for-profit companies.

Eligible beneficiaries: general public.

Range/Average: N.A.

Activity: N.A.

HQ: Director, Hurricane Sandy Disaster Relief Activities, FWS-DOI, 300 Westgate Center Dr., Hadley, MA 01035. Phone: (413) 253-8243.

Internet: N.A.

15.805 ASSISTANCE TO STATE WATER RESOURCES RESEARCH INSTITUTES
("Water Research Institute Program")

Assistance: formula grants; project grants (formula, 33 percent; project, 50 percent).

Purposes: pursuant to the Water Resources Research Act of 1984 as amended, for basic or applied research, conferences, studies, student training, and related activities concerning regional, state, or local water problems. Project funds may not support formal instructional activities, general education, or costs of permanent buildings.

Eligible applicants/beneficiaries: university water research institutes in states and territories. Other IHEs may participate in cooperation with the designated state institute.

Range: $92,335 to $277,005 for formula grants; $140,162 to $249,949 for competitive grants. **Average:** $95,755 for formula grants; 212,950 for competitive grants.

Activity: N.A.

HQ: Chief, Office of External Research, USGS-DOI, 5522 Research Park Dr., Baltimore, MD 21228. Phone: (443) 498-5505.

Internet: water.usgs.gov/wrri. (Note: no field offices for this program.)

15.807 EARTHQUAKE HAZARDS RESEARCH AND MONITORING ASSISTANCE

Assistance: project grants (cost sharing/to 2 years).

Purposes: for mitigation of earthquake losses. Projects may include providing earth science data and assessments, land use planning, engineering design, emergency preparedness systems.

Eligible applicants/beneficiaries: IHEs, profit and nonprofit organizations, state and local governments.

Range: $1,175 to $1,690,000. **Average:** $58,000.

Activity: N.A.

HQ: External Research Program Manager, Earthquakes Hazards Program Office, Geologic Division, USGS-DOI, MS 905 National Center, 12201 Sunrise Valley Dr., Reston, VA 20192. Phone: (703) 648-6701; FAX: (703) 648-6642.

Internet: earthquake.usgs.gov/research/external.

15.808 U.S. GEOLOGICAL SURVEY—RESEARCH AND DATA ACQUISITION

Assistance: project grants (from 50 percent).

Purposes: pursuant to the Organic Act of 1879, for scientific research complementing USGS programs in classification of the public lands and examination of the geological structure, water, mineral, and biological resources and products of the national domain. Most funded research involves enhancing existing, long- term collaborative projects, including coastal and marine geology studies, volcano monitoring, and earth science research facilities.

Eligible applicants/beneficiaries: profit and nonprofit organizations; state and local governments. Note: funding for external projects is limited; applicants are urged to consult USGS prior to submitting proposals.

Range: $1,000 to $1,866,000. **Average:** $70,000.

Activity: 600 awards in FY 2014.

HQ: none provided, see listing of field offices.

Internet: www.usgs.gov/contracts.

15.809 NATIONAL SPATIAL DATA INFRASTRUCTURE COOPERATIVE AGREEMENTS PROGRAM ("NSDI CAP")

Assistance: project grants (from 50 percent).

Purposes: pursuant to the Organic Act of 1879, for collaborative projects to improve the discovery, access, transfer, and use of geospatial data, through the National Geospatial Data Clearinghouse to further development and implementation of the National Spatial Data Infrastructure (NSDI). Project funds may be used: to develop and promulgate the use of standards in data collection, documentation, transfer, and search and query; for educational outreach programs.

Eligible applicants/beneficiaries: collaborations of federal, state, and local government agencies; educational institutions; private firms and foundations; nonprofit organizations; recognized tribes or native American groups.

Range: $25,00 to $70,000. **Average:** $35,000.

Activity: N.A.

HQ: Federal Geographic Data Committee Secretariat (MS 590), USGS-DOI, 12201 Sunrise Valley Dr., Reston, VA 20192. Phone: (703) 648-5514; FAX: (703) 648-5755.

Internet: www.fgdc.gov/grants.

15.810 NATIONAL COOPERATIVE GEOLOGIC MAPPING PROGRAM ("STATEMAP - EDMAP")

Assistance: project grants. (50 percent/1-2 years).

Purposes: pursuant to the National Geologic Mapping Reauthorization Act of 1997, to produce geologic maps of areas important to the economic, social, or scientific welfare of individual states. "STATEMAP" supports projects: (1) producing new geologic maps with attendant explanatory information; (2) compiling existing geologic data in a digital form at a scale of 1 to 100,000 for inclusion in the National Digital Geologic Map Database. "EDMAP" provides funding: (1) for graduate students in academic research programs involving geologic mapping and scientific data analysis as major components; (2) to expand research and educational capacity of graduate programs; (3) for publication and distribution of geologic maps generated in field-based graduate academic research programs.

Eligible applicants/beneficiaries: state geological surveys. State IHEs may apply on behalf of the state survey.

Range: $8,000 to $364,442 for StateMap; $5,572 to $10,948 for EdMap. **Average:** $115,064 for StateMap; $7,971 for EdMap.

Activity: funded 32 students in FY 2015.

HQ: Coordinator, National Cooperative Geologic Mapping Program, USGS-DOI, MS 908 National Center, 12201 Sunrise Valley Dr., Reston, VA 20192. Phone: (703) 648-6937.

Internet: www.ncgmp.usgs.gov.

15.811 GAP ANALYSIS PROGRAM (GAP)

Assistance: project grants.

Purposes: pursuant to the Endangered Species Act of 1973, Fish and Wildlife Act of 1956, and Fish and Wildlife Conservation Act, for studies where native animal species and natural plant communities occur—to identify gaps in their representation in support of the conservation of biodiversity. Studies are used by federal, state, and other governmental organizations to develop land use or acquisition plans that incorporate information about the presence and distribution of biodiversity.

Eligible applicants/beneficiaries: profit organizations, public and private nonprofit organizations, state and local governments.

Range: $25,000 to $400,000. **Average:** $84,000.

Activity: N.A.

HQ: Coordinator, 970 Lusk Ave., Forest and Rangeland Ecosystem Science Center, Snake River Field Station, Boise, ID 83706. Phone: (208) 426-5219.

Internet: gapanalysis.usgs.gov. (Note: no field offices for this program.)

15.812 COOPERATIVE RESEARCH UNITS PROGRAM (CRUP)

Assistance: project grants (to 5 years).

Purposes: pursuant to the Cooperative Research Units Act as amended by the Fish and Wildlife Improvement Act of 1978, for research, technical assistance, and education projects addressing the information needs of local, state, and federal fish, wildlife, and natural resource agencies. Project examples: gopher tortoise relocation; Caspian terns in San Francisco Bay; black bear genetics; fish community response to pump-storage; Great Lakes colonial waterbirds.

Eligible applicants/beneficiaries: universities hosting CRUPs.

Range: $5,000 to $724,623. **Average:** $52,509.

Activity: N.A.

HQ: Cooperative Research Units, USGS-DOI, 12201 Sunrise Valley Dr., Stop 303, Reston, VA 20192. Phone: (703) 648-4261, -4262; FAX: (703) 648-4269.

Internet: www.coopunits.org.

15.814 NATIONAL GEOLOGICAL AND GEOPHYSICAL DATA PRESERVATION PROGRAM

Assistance: project grants (50 percent).

Purposes: pursuant to the Federal Energy Policy Act of 2005, to preserve and provide access to geological, geophysical, and engineering samples (and related data) extracted from the earth.

Eligible applicants: state geological surveys or state universities affiliated with a geological survey.

Eligible beneficiaries: research scientists, engineers, and general public.

Range: $2,972 to $50,006. **Average:** $27,260.

Activity: 30 awards in FY 2014.

HQ: Program Coordinator, Office of the Chief, USGS-DOI, Box 25046, MS 975 Denver Federal Center, Core Science Systems, Denver, CO 80225. Phone: (303) 202-4828.

Internet: datapreservation.usgs.gov/index.shtml. (Note: no field offices for this program.)

15.815 NATIONAL LAND REMOTE SENSING—EDUCATION OUTREACH AND RESEARCH
("National Cooperative Geographic Information System")

Assistance: project grants (100 percent/1-5 years).

Purposes: to provide all users equal and affordable access to space-based land remote sensing data and the means to conduct research using the data through university based and collaborative research projects. Some technologies of interest include: thermal, radar, multi-spectral and hyper-spectral electro-optical.

Eligible applicants/beneficiaries: nonprofit organizations, public and private colleges and universities and state and local governments may make an application for support by a named principal investigator.

Range: N.A. **Average:** $1,217,400.

Activity: N.A.

HQ: Land Remote Sensing Office, Geography Division, USGS-DOI, 516 National Center, Reston, VA 20192. Phone: (703) 648-5551; FAX: (703) 648-5939.

Internet: www.usgs.gov. (Note: no field offices for this program.)

15.816 MINERALS RESOURCES EXTERNAL RESEARCH PROGRAM (MRERP)

Assistance: project grants (100 percent/1-2 years).

Purposes: to conduct research in topics related to non-fuel mineral resources to ensure availability of: up-to-date quantitative assessments of the potential for undiscovered mineral deposits; geoenvironmental assessments of priority federal lands; reliable geological, geochemical, geophysical, and mineral locality data for the United States; and long-term data sets describing mineral production and consumption. Recipients are encouraged to share in the cost of the project.

Eligible applicants: states; IHEs; public and private agencies and organizations.

Eligible beneficiaries: anyone/general public.

Range: $15,000 to $151,000. **Average:** $58,643.

Activity: 4 awards in FY 2014.

HQ: Associate Coordinator, Mineral Resources Program, USGS-DOI, 913 National Center, Reston, VA 20192. Phone: (703) 648-6103; FAX: (703) 648-6057.

Internet: minerals.usgs.gov/mrerp. (Note: no field offices for this program.)

15.817 NATIONAL GEOSPATIAL PROGRAM: BUILDING THE NATIONAL MAP ("National Map")

Assistance: project grants (50 - 100 percent/12 to 18 months).

Purposes: pursuant to Outer Continental Shelf Resource Management, to utilize stimulus funds from the ARRA 2009, to expand employment and business opportunities within a key sector of the geospatial industry while enabling America to revitalize its physical infrastructure, improve public safety, and adapt to climate change through the collection of high resolution lidar and orthoimagery data. The majority of funds are used to support new data collections and existing, long-term collaborative projects that will enhance the datasets and research using those data.

Eligible applicants: state (includes DC, public IHEs, and hospitals), local, and tribal governments.

Eligible beneficiaries: anyone/general public.

Range: $61,000 to $770,500. **Average:** $294,500.

Activity: anticipate funding 18 cooperative agreements in FY 2015.

HQ: National Geospatial Program, Geological Survey-DOI, 12201 Sunrise Valley Dr., MS 510, Reston, VA 20192. Phone: (703) 648-5519.

Internet: www.nationalmap.gov.

15.818 VOLCANO HAZARDS PROGRAM RESEARCH AND MONITORING

Assistance: project grants (100 percent/1 to 5 years).

Purposes: pursuant to Outer Continental Shelf Resource Management and ARRA 2009, to advance the scientific understanding of volcanic processes and lessen the harmful impacts of volcanic activity on the general population. During FY09 and FY10, this program will provide funding under ARRA for equipment replacement and upgrades of seismic and other monitoring systems. Cost sharing by grant recipients is strongly encouraged.

Eligible applicants: state and local governments, private/public profit and nonprofit organizations/institutions; IHEs (includes research) and hospitals.

Eligible beneficiaries: anyone/general public.

Range: $20,000 to $2,000,000. **Average:** $250,000.

Activity: N.A.

HQ: Volcano Hazards Program Office, Geologic Discipline, USGS-DOI, 3A204 National Center, Reston, VA 20192. Phone: (703) 648-4773.

Internet: volcanoes.usgs.gov. (Note: no field offices for this program.)

15.819 ENERGY COOPERATIVES TO SUPPORT THE NATIONAL COAL RESOURCES DATA SYSTEM (NCRDS)

Assistance: project grants (50 - 100 percent/5 years).

Purposes: pursuant to Public Health and Welfare, Public Lands, and Minerals, Lands and Mines, to collect, interpret, correlate, and evaluate coal and other solid fuel energy-related stratigraphic, chemical, and GIS data; to build and maintain national databases of coal-related stratigraphic and chemical data; to conduct research relative to coal and other solid fuel energy and apply knowledge gained to conduct resource assessments within the United States in order to further the understanding of energy resources within a global, geologic, economic and environmental context. Matching funds by states strongly encouraged. Another 5 year cycle of funding due to begin in 2010.

Eligible applicants: states, IHEs, hospitals, public and private organizations/institutions.

Eligible beneficiaries: anyone/general public.

Range: $15,000 to $26,000. **Average:** $15,190.

Activity: 22 grants funded in FY 2015.

HQ: Energy Resources Program, US Geological Survey-DOI, MS 956 National Center, Reston, VA 20192. Phone: (703) 648-6419.

Internet: energy.er.usgs.gov/coal_quality/state_coops. (Note: no field offices for this program.)

15.820   NATIONAL CLIMATE CHANGE AND WILDLIFE SCIENCE CENTER ("NCCWSC and DOI Climate Science Centers DOI CSC")

Assistance: cooperative agreements/discretionary grants (cost share encouraged).

Purposes: pursuant to the Consolidated Appropriations Act of 2008, to be responsive to the research and management needs of federal and state agencies by working with partners to provide science and technical support regarding the impacts of climate change in fish, wildlife, plants and ecological processes and the mechanisms for adaptation to, mitigation of, or prevention of those impacts. In order to develop standardized approaches and to better facilitate this research, the National Climate Change and Wildlife Science Center (NCCWSC) will develop cooperative agreements and/or grants with the eight Department of the Interior Climate Science Centers (DOI CSC) at the primary hosting Universities to conduct specific research, data gathering, data management and similar scientific activities: Alaska CSC: University of Alaska, Fairbanks; Southeast CSC: North Carolina State University, Raleigh; Northwest CSC: Oregon State University, Corvallis; Southwest CSC: University of Arizona, Tucson; North Central CSC: Colorado State University, Ft. Collins; South Central CSC: Oklahoma University, Norman; Northeast CSC: University of Massachusetts, Amherst; Pacific Islands CSC: University of Hawaii, Manoa.

Eligible applicants: eight DOI CSCs and their primary hosting universities.

Eligible beneficiaries: research scientists, policy makers, natural resource managers, educators, general public.

Range: to $1,000,000. **Average:** N.A.

Activity: 80 grants or agreements in FY 2014.

HQ: Director, U.S. Geological Survey, NCCWSC, DOI, MS-300 National Center, 12201 Sunrise Valley Dr., Reston, VA 20192. Phone: (703) 648-4607.

Internet: nccwsc.usgs.gov.

15.850   INDIAN ARTS AND CRAFTS DEVELOPMENT

Assistance: use of property, facilities, and equipment; advisory services/counseling; investigation of complaints.

Purposes: pursuant to the Act to Promote the Development of Indian Arts and Crafts as amended, Indian Arts and Crafts Act of 1990, and Indian Arts and Crafts Enforcement Act of 2000, to provide program planning assistance in promoting the development of American Indian and native Alaskan arts and crafts. Assistance is nonfinancial including: development of innovative educational, promotional, production, and economic concepts related to native culture; investigations of misrepresentation of handicrafts. No financial assistance is provided through this program.

Eligible applicants/beneficiaries: American Indian and Alaska native individuals and organizations; recognized tribal governments; state and local governments; nonprofit organizations.

Range/Average: N.A.

Activity: N.A.

HQ: Director, Indian Arts and Crafts Board, DOI, Main Interior Bldg., Rm. 4004, Washington, DC 20240. Phone: (202) 208-3773.

Internet: www.iacb.doi.gov. (Note: no field offices for this program.)

15.875 ECONOMIC, SOCIAL, AND POLITICAL DEVELOPMENT OF THE TERRITORIES

Assistance: project grants (100 percent).

Purposes: pursuant to the Act of February 20, 1929 and other acts, to promote the economic, social, and political development of the U.S. territories and freely associated states, toward their self-government and self-sufficiency. Operational costs and capital improvements may be funded, such as the construction of water systems, roads, schools, hospitals, and power and sewer facilities. A small percentage of funding may be available for discretionary grants.

Eligible applicants/beneficiaries: Guam, VI, American Samoa, Northern Mariana Islands.

Range/Average: N.A.

Activity: N.A.

HQ: Director, Financial Management Division, Office of Insular Affairs-DOI, 1849 C St., NW, Mail Stop 2429, Washington, DC 20240. Phone: (202) 219-1335; FAX: (202) 208-7585.

Internet: www.doi.gov/oia. (Note: no field offices for this program.)

15.904 HISTORIC PRESERVATION FUND GRANTS-IN-AID (HPF)

Assistance: formula grants; project grants. (project, 60 percent; territories, 100 percent/project grants, to 2 years).

Purposes: pursuant to the National Historic Preservation Act of 1966 as amended, to provide matching grants for the identification, evaluation, and protection of historic properties listed or eligible for listing in the National Register of Historic Places (see **15.914**). Historic properties may include districts, sites, buildings, structures, and objects significant in American history, architecture, archaeology, engineering, and culture at national, state, and local levels. Grants may finance studies and reports, preservation plans, state staff salaries, equipment, materials, necessary travel, acquisition, or repair. Development projects must involve preservation, restoration, rehabilitation, or nonmajor reconstruction. Certain tax incentives are available to owners of listed properties.

Eligible applicants/beneficiaries: states and territories operating programs administered by a state historic preservation officer, which may subgrant to public and private parties including local governments, profit and nonprofit organizations, or individuals to accomplish program objectives. Tribal Grant Program—tribal governments, Alaska or Hawaii native corporations.

Range: $50,000 to $1,400,000. **Average:** $290,000.

Activity: N.A.

HQ: Associate Director, Cultural Resource Stewardship and Partnerships, NPS-DOI, Washington, DC 20240. Phone: (202) 354-2020.

Internet: www.nps.gov/history/hps/hpg.

15.912   NATIONAL HISTORIC LANDMARK

Assistance: advisory services/counseling.

Purposes: pursuant to the Historic Sites Act of 1935, National Historic Preservation Act of 1966, and amendments, to study, identify, and encourage preservation of nationally-significant historic properties. Designation of historic landmarks and registration on the National Register of Historic Places (see **15.914**) renders them eligible for federal protection, some grants-in-aid programs, and certain tax benefits. Properties of only state or local significance do not qualify.

Eligible applicants/beneficiaries: anyone may suggest properties for inclusion. Property owners may be individuals, governments, or corporate bodies.

Range: $22,000 to $220,000. **Average:** $94,000.

Activity: N.A.

HQ: National Historic Landmarks Survey (MS 2280), NRHE-NPS-DOI, 1849 C St., NW, Washington, DC 20240. Phone: (202) 354-2210.

Internet: www.cr.nps.gov/nhl.

15.914   NATIONAL REGISTER OF HISTORIC PLACES ("National Register")

Assistance: advisory services/counseling.

Purposes: pursuant to the Historic Preservation Act of 1966 and Amendments of 1980 and 1992, Economic Recovery Tax Act of 1981, Tax Reform Act of 1986, and other acts, to expand and maintain the National Register of Historic Places which serves as a planning tool and source of information on sites, buildings, districts, structures, and objects of historical, architectural, engineering, archaeological, and/or cultural significance. Designation of historic landmarks and registration on the National Register renders them eligible for federal protection, some grants-in-aid and loan programs, and certain tax benefits. Federal agencies are required to consider and nominate historic properties within their jurisdiction.

Eligible applicants/beneficiaries: states and territories operating programs administered by state historic preservation officers; tribal preservation officers; federal agencies. Applicants eligible for federal tax benefits include owners of individually listed properties and properties certified by NPS as historic and in a district certified as historic.

Range: $20,000 to $111,000. **Average:** $71,000.

Activity: N.A.

HQ: Keeper of the National Register of Historic Places, NRHE-NPS-DOI, 1849 C St., NW (MS 2280), Washington, DC 20240. Phone: (202) 345-2213.

Internet: www.cr.nps.gov/nr.

15.915   TECHNICAL PRESERVATION SERVICES

Assistance: advisory services/counseling; specialized services; technical information.

Purposes: pursuant to the Federal Property and Administrative Services Act of 1949 and National Historic Preservation Act of 1966, amendments, Mining in National Parks Act of 1976, Tax Reform Act of 1986, and other acts, to offer technical information pertaining to the treatment and maintenance of historic properties. The program provides for the development of policies and standards and for distribution of publications on the technical and design aspects of preservation and rehabilitation, as well as for monitoring acquisition and development grant awards under **15.904**; the service also includes general technical assistance concerning preservation efforts, including certification for eligibility for tax credits.

Eligible applicants/beneficiaries: federal agencies, state and local governments, and individual owners.

Range/Average: N.A.

Activity: N.A.

HQ: Chief, Heritage Preservation Services Program (ORG 2255), NPS-DOI, 1849 C St., NW, Washington, DC 20240. Phone: (202) 513-7270.

Internet: www.nps.gov/tps.

15.916 OUTDOOR RECREATION—ACQUISITION, DEVELOPMENT AND PLANNING
("Land and Water Conservation Fund Grants")

Assistance: project grants. (50 percent/to 3 years).

Purposes: pursuant to the Land and Water Conservation Fund Act of 1965 as amended and other acts, to plan, acquire, and develop public outdoor recreation areas and facilities, including picnic areas, inner city parks, campgrounds, tennis courts, boat launching ramps, bike trails, outdoor swimming pools, roads, water supply, etc.; for studies, surveys, and data collection and analysis related to refinement and improvement of Statewide Comprehensive Outdoor Recreation Plans (SCORPs). Grant funds are not available to cover operating and maintenance costs.

Eligible applicants/beneficiaries: planning grants—only state agencies and territories. Acquisition and development grants—state agencies may apply for direct assistance, or on behalf of other state agencies or political subdivisions, such as cities, counties, and park districts; tribes functioning as general purpose units of government.

Range: $50,000 to $2,000,000. **Average:** $105,000.

Activity: N.A.

HQ: Chief, Recreation Programs (2225), NPS-DOI, 1849 C St., NW, Washington, DC 20240. Phone: (202) 354-6900; FAX: (202) 371-5179.

Internet: www.nps.gov/lwcf.

15.918 DISPOSAL OF FEDERAL SURPLUS REAL PROPERTY FOR PARKS, RECREATION, AND HISTORIC MONUMENTS
("Federal Lands to Parks Program, Historic Surplus Property Program")

Assistance: use of property, facilities, and equipment.

Purposes: pursuant to the Federal Property and Administrative Services Act of 1949 as amended and Federal Lands for Parks and Recreation Act, to transfer surplus federal real property for public park and recreation use, or for use as historic real property. Recipients must agree to manage the property in the public interest and for public use. Only properties listed on the National Register or so eligible may be transferred through the Historic Surplus Property Program. Examples of new uses include nature study areas, wildlife conservation areas, youth and senior citizen areas; arts and crafts centers.

Eligible applicants/beneficiaries: only states or local government units.

Range/Average: N.A.

Activity: N.A.

HQ: State and Local Assistance Division, Federal Lands to Parks Program, NPS-DOI, 1201 I St., NW, Org Code 2225, Washington, DC 20005. Phone: (202) 354-6915.

Internet: www.nps.gov/flp.

15.921   RIVERS, TRAILS AND CONSERVATION ASSISTANCE (RTCA)

Assistance: advisory services/counseling.

Purposes: pursuant to the Wild and Scenic Rivers Act of 1968 and National Trails System Act as amended, Outdoor Recreation Act of 1963, and the Federal Power Act, to support activities between government and citizens to conserve rivers, preserve open space, and develop trails and greenways.

Eligible applicants/beneficiaries: private nonprofit organizations; federal, state, and local government agencies.

Range: $3000 to $237,000. **Average:** $45,000.

Activity: 20 awards in FY 2014.

HQ: Chief, Rivers, Trails and Conservation Assistance (ORG 2240), NPS-DOI, 1849 C St., NW, Washington, DC 20240. Phone: (202) 354-6922.

Internet: www.nps.gov/rtca.

15.922   NATIVE AMERICAN GRAVES PROTECTION AND REPATRIATION ACT (NAGPRA)

Assistance: project grants. (100 percent/to 18 months).

Purposes: pursuant to the act of 1990, for the documentation, inventory, and repatriation of native American human remains and cultural items including sacred objects, objects of cultural patrimony, funerary objects. Funds may be used: to involve specialists including lineal descendants, traditional religious leaders, and other officials; for staff training; for travel costs; to construct appropriate containers to transport finds. Ineligible uses of funds include documentation or repatriation of items from the Smithsonian Institution, care and curation of repatriated items, facilities construction or renovation, or real estate purchases.

Eligible applicants/beneficiaries: museum documentation—any institution or state or local government agency including IHEs with possession of, or control over, native American human remains or cultural items. Tribal documentation and repatriation—recognized tribes, Alaska native villages or corporations, native Hawaiian organizations.

Range: $5,000 to $90,000. **Average:** $25,000.

Activity: more than 30 awards in FY 2014.

HQ: National Center for Cultural Resources, NPS-DOI, 1201 Eye St., NW (2253), Washington, DC 20005. Phone: 202-354-2203.

Internet: www.cr.nps.gov/nagpra/grants. (Note: no field offices for this program.)

15.923 NATIONAL CENTER FOR PRESERVATION TECHNOLOGY AND TRAINING

Assistance: project grants (100 percent).

Purposes: pursuant to the National Historic Preservation Act Amendments of 1992, to develop and distribute preservation and conservation skills and technologies for the identification, evaluation, conservation, and interpretation of prehistoric and historic resources; to develop and facilitate training of federal, state, and local professional, managerial, maintenance, and other personnel; and for international cooperation efforts. Funds may support projects involving: information management; training and education in such disciplines as archeology, historic architecture, historic landscapes, object and materials conservation and interpretation; applied and fundamental research; pollutant research and treatment; analytical facilities; conferences; publications. Ineligible projects include: those focused on specific sites, structures, objects, or collections; internships and fellowships when integrated into funded projects; current projects.

Eligible applicants/beneficiaries: IHEs; nonprofit and quasi- public organizations; federal, state, local, and tribal preservation offices; profit organizations.

Range: $19,000 to $465,000. **Average:** $38,000.

Activity: 8 awards in FY 2014.

HQ: Grants Administrator, Heritage Preservation Services Program, National Center for Cultural Resource Stewardship and Partnership, 645 University Parkway, Natchitoches, LA 71457. Phone: (318) 356-7444.

Internet: www.ncptt.nps.gov.

15.925 NATIONAL MARITIME HERITAGE GRANTS PROGRAM

Assistance: project grants. (50 percent).

Purposes: pursuant to the National Maritime Heritage Act of 1994, to provide matching grants for preservation or education projects that foster a greater awareness and appreciation of the role of maritime endeavors in America's history and culture. The grants will help State and local governments and private nonprofit organizations preserve and interpret their maritime heritage.

Eligible applicants/beneficiaries: state, local, and tribal governments, and private nonprofits.

Range: $25,000 to $250,000. **Average:** $55,000.

Activity: more than 20 awards in FY 2015.

HQ: National Maritime Heritage Program, NPS, 1849 C St., NW, Washington, DC 20240. Phone: (202) 354-2266; FAX: 202-371-2229.

Internet: www.nps.gov/history/history/maritime_new.htm.

15.926 AMERICAN BATTLEFIELD PROTECTION ("ABPP Planning Grants")

Assistance: project grants (100 percent).

Purposes: pursuant to the Omnibus Parks and Public Lands Management Act of 1996 and American Battlefield Protection Act of 1996, for the protection and preservation of battlefield lands on American soil by supporting nonacquisition preservation methods such as planning, education, and survey and inventory. Project examples: preparation of Vision and Protection Plan; preparation of National Register nomination; archeological survey. Funds may not be used for such activities as battlefield reenactments, any construction, permanent staff positions, curation, or other ongoing activities.

Eligible applicants/beneficiaries: federal, intrastate, interstate, state, and local agencies; public and private nonprofit organizations; recognized tribal governments and organizations; territories and possessions; public and private IHEs. Multi-organizational applications are encouraged.

Range: $5,000 to $87,000. **Average:** $60,000.

Activity: 14 awards in FY 2014.

HQ: American Battlefield Protection Program (2255), NPS-DOI, 1201 Eye St., NW, (2255) 6th Floor, Washington, DC 20005. Phone: (202) 354-2037.

Internet: www.nps.gov/history/hps/abpp. (Note: no field offices for this program.)

15.927 HYDROPOWER RECREATION ASSISTANCE ("Rivers and Trails, Hydropower Licensing")

Assistance: advisory services/counseling.

Purposes: pursuant to the Federal Power Act, Wild and Scenic Rivers Act of 1968 as amended, and Outdoor Recreation Act of 1963, to serve as a national technical resource to support government, industry, and nonprofit partnerships, concerning applications for hydropower licensing; to meet present and future outdoor recreation needs; to maintain and enhance a project's riparian areas.

Eligible applicants/beneficiaries: private nonprofit organizations; federal, state, and local government agencies; hydropower licensing applicants.

Range/Average: N.A.

Activity: N.A.

HQ: Rivers and Hydro Leader, Rivers, Trails, and Conservation Assistance (2220), NPS-DOI, 1849 C St., NW, Washington, DC 20240. Phone: (202) 354-6900.

Internet: www.nps.gov/hydro.

15.928   CIVIL WAR BATTLEFIELD LAND ACQUISITION GRANTS
("LWCF Battlefield Acquisition Grants")

Assistance: project grants (50 percent).

Purposes: pursuant to the American Battlefield Protection Act of 1996, to help states and communities acquire and preserve threatened Civil War battlefields. Grants may cover costs of fee simple acquisition of land and protective interests in land at Civil War Battlefields listed in the Civil War Sites Advisory Commission's 1993 report on the Nation's Civil War Battlefields. Administrative costs are ineligible.

Eligible applicants/beneficiaries: state and local governments, which may subgrant funds to private nonprofit organizations that convey perpetual protective easements to the state historic preservation officer or other agency acceptable to NPS.

Range: $1,000 to $1,300,000. **Average:** $150,000.

Activity: 15 awards in FY 2014.

HQ: American Battlefield Protection Program (2255), NPS-DOI, 1201 Eye St., NW, (2255) 6th Floor, Washington, DC 20005. Phone: (202) 354-2037.

Internet: www.nps.gov/history/hps/abpp. (Note: no field offices for this program.)

15.929   SAVE AMERICA'S TREASURES

Assistance: project grants. (50 percent/2 years).

Purposes: pursuant to the Omnibus Parks and Lands Management Act of 1996 and National Historic Preservation Act of 1966 as amended, for preservation and conservation work on nationally significant intellectual and cultural artifacts, as well as historic structures and sites listed on the National Register. Funds may not be used for costs of acquisition or rent.

Eligible applicants/beneficiaries: federal, intrastate, interstate, state, and local agencies; public or private nonprofit organizations and IHEs; tribes.

Range: $5,000 to $150,000. **Average:** $25,000.

Activity: N.A.

HQ: Save America's Treasures Program, NPS-DOI, 1849 C St., NW, Washington, DC 20240. Phone: (202) 354-2020; FAX: (202) 371-1794.

Internet: www.nps.gov/history/hpg. (Note: no field offices for this program.)

15.930   CHESAPEAKE BAY GATEWAYS NETWORK
("Chesapeake Bay Gateways")

Assistance: project grants (to 50 percent/to 18 months).

Purposes: pursuant to the Chesapeake Bay Initiative Act of 1993, to aid state and local governments, communities, nonprofit organizations and the private sector in conserving, restoring and interpreting historical, cultural, recreational and natural resources within the Chesapeake Bay Gateways and watershed network.

Eligible applicants: currently designated Gateways, their managing organizations or partners, including state and local governments and nonprofit organizations.

Eligible beneficiaries: general public.

Range: $30,000 to $125,000. **Average:** $70,000.

Activity: N.A.

HQ: Acting Regional Director, N10 Severn Ave., Suite 314, Annapolis, MD 21403. Phone: (410) 260-2478.

Internet: www.baygateways.net.

15.931   CONSERVATION ACTIVITIES BY YOUTH SERVICE ORGANIZATIONS

Assistance: project grants (2 to 3 months).

Purposes: pursuant to ARRA 2009, the Omnibus Consolidated Appropriations Act of 1997, Omnibus Parks and Public Lands Management Act of 1996, Youth Conservation Corps Act of 1970 and other laws as amended, to utilize qualified youth or conservation groups to carry out appropriate conservation projects.

Eligible applicants: organizations that support youth training and development in resource management, conservation, and cultural resources, including: private and quasi-public nonprofit institutions and organizations, state and local government agencies.

Eligible beneficiaries: young people and general public.

Range: $1,000 to $1,000,000. **Average:** $25,000.

Activity: N.A.

HQ: WASO Youth Program Coordinator, NPS-DOI, 1201 I St., NW, Washington, DC 20005. Phone: (202) 513-7146; FAX: (202) 371-2263.

Internet: www.nps.gov/youthprograms/index.html.

15.933   PRESERVATION OF JAPANESE AMERICAN CONFINEMENT SITES ("Japanese American Confinement Sites Grant Program")

Assistance: project grants (66 percent/to 2 years).

Purposes: pursuant to the Preservation of Japanese American Confinement Sites Act, to provide for the preservation and interpretation of historic confinement sites where Japanese Americans were detained during World War II by encouraging projects that identify, research, evaluate, interpret, protect, restore, repair, and acquire historic confinement sites in order that present and future generations may learn and gain inspiration from these sites.

Eligible applicants/beneficiaries: state/local agencies, public/private nonprofit institutions/organizations, federally-recognized Indian tribal governments, state and public/private colleges and universities.

Range: $16,000 to $500,000. **Average:** $150,000.

Activity: 25 awards in FY 2014.

HQ: Intermountain Regional Office, NPS, DOI, 12795 W. Alameda Parkway, Lakewood, CO 80228. Phone: (303) 969-2885.

Internet: www.nps.gov/history/hps/hpg/jacs/index.html.

15.935 NATIONAL TRAILS SYSTEM PROJECTS

Assistance: cooperative agreements (50 to 100 percent/to 5 years).

Purposes: pursuant to ARRA and the National Trails System Act, to preserve, protect, and develop the components of the National Trails System, with a strong emphasis on volunteer involvement. The availability of discretionary funding is determined by individual trail offices each fiscal year.

Eligible applicants/beneficiaries: 35 IHEs selected by the CDC as Prevention Research Centers (PRCs).

Range: $3,000 to $370,000. **Average:** $63,000.

Activity: more than 50 awards in FY 2014.

HQ: Program Director, National Trails, NPS-DOI, 1849 C St., Washington, DC 20240. Phone: (202) 354-6938.

Internet: www.nps.gov.nts.

15.939 NATIONAL HERITAGE AREA FEDERAL FINANCIAL ASSISTANCE ("National Heritage Area Preservation and Conservation Assistance")

Assistance: direct payments/specified use (cooperative agreements) (50 percent).

Purposes: to preserve and interpret for the educational and inspirational benefit of present and future generations the unique and significant contributions to our national heritage of certain historic and cultural lands, waterways, and structures, to encourage a broad range of economic opportunities enhancing the quality of life within the designated area, and provide a management framework to assist in developing policies and programs that will preserve, enhance, and interpret the cultural, historical, natural, recreation, and scenic resources of the heritage area.

Eligible applicants/beneficiaries: states, their political subdivisions, non profits, private entities, the heritage area management/coordinating entity, and other federal agencies.

Range: $4,000 to $650,000. **Average:** $215,000.

Activity: more than 50 awards in FY 2014.

HQ: Director, 1201 Eye St., NW 6th Floor, Washington, DC 20005. Phone: (202) 354-2222.

Internet: www.nps.gov/history/heritageareas.

15.940 NEW BEDFORD WHALING NATIONAL HISTORIC PARK COOPERATIVE MANAGEMENT

Assistance: direct payments/specified use (cooperative agreements) (25 percent).

Purposes: pursuant to the New Bedford Whaling National Historic Park, To work collaboratively with interested entities and individuals to provide for visitor understanding, appreciation and enjoyment.

Eligible applicants: state, local and tribal governments, other public entities, education institutions, and private nonprofit organizations.

Eligible beneficiaries: anyone/general public.

Range: $5,000 to $10,000. **Average:** $7,500.

Activity: 2 awards in FY 2014.

HQ: Park Superintendent, New Bedford Whaling National Historic Park 33 William St., New Bedford, Massachusetts 02740.

Internet: www.nps.gov/nebe.

15.941 MISSISSIPPI NATIONAL RIVER AND RECREATION AREA STATE AND LOCAL ASSISTANCE

Assistance: cooperative agreements (50 percent).

Purposes: pursuant to ARRA, for acquisition and development within the area of lands or waters and to enhance partner planning for and interpretation of non-federal publicly-owned lands within the area. The availability of funding is determined by the Mississippi NRRA each fiscal year.

Eligible applicants/beneficiaries: 35 IHEs selected by the CDC as Prevention Research Centers (PRCs).

Range: $80,000 to $120,000. **Average:** $104,000.

Activity: N.A.

HQ: Program Director, National Park Service, DOI, 111 E. Kellogg Blvd., Suite 105, St. Paul, MN 55101. Phone: (651) 290-3030.

Internet: www.nps.gov/miss. (Note: no field offices for this program.)

15.942 ENVIRONMENTAL EDUCATION AND CONSERVATION—NORTH CASCADES BIOREGION

Assistance: direct payments/specified use (100 percent).

Purposes: pursuant to The Outdoor Recreation Act, to help people learn, enjoy and understand more about Skagit River and the North Cascades. Objectives include field-based environmental education, providing programs of public education, involvement in conservation, natural science, history and related fields of study, and conducting interpretive activities.

Eligible applicants: the North Cascades Institute has a legal relationship with Seattle City Light to provide the facilities and programs that meet the requirements of the FERC to provide the learning center within North Cascades National Park Complex.

Eligible beneficiaries: general Public Education Professional Student/Trainee Graduate Student Scientists/Researcher Education(0-8) Education(9-12) Education(13+) Credentials/Documentation Sponsored Organization Public Nonprofit Institution/Organization Other Public Institution/Organization.

Range: $20,000 to $60,000. **Average:** $21,000.

Activity: N.A.

HQ: Director, National Park Service, Pacific West Regional Office, 1111 Jackson St., Suite 700, Oakland, California 94607. Phone: (360) 854-7302.

Internet: N.A.

15.943 CHALLENGE COST SHARE
("National Park Service Challenge Cost Share")

Assistance: direct payments/specified use (50 percent).

Purposes: pursuant to the Cost Share Arrangements with Partners Public Law, to increase participation by qualified partners in the preservation and improvement of NPS natural, cultural, and recreational resources in all authorized Service programs and activities. All projects and activities receiving these funds must meet a minimum 50:50 match of cash, goods, or services from a non-Federal source. Applications must be approved by appropriate NPS park, program, center, or trails staff.

Eligible applicants: submitted by NPS park, center, or program staff for competitive selection by the Regional Directors. Must also contain a non-Federal partner.

Eligible beneficiaries: general public, trail system users, conservation organizations.

Range: $1,000 to $25,000. **Average:** $20,000.

Activity: N.A.

HQ: Director, National Park Service, National Challenge Cost Share Coordinator, 1201 Eye St., NW, 9th Fl., Org Code 2240, Washington, DC 20005. Phone: (202) 354-6907; FAX: (202) 371-5179.

Internet: www.nps.gov/ccsp. (Note: no field offices for this program.)

15.944 NATURAL RESOURCE STEWARDSHIP

Assistance: cooperative agreements/discretionary grants; direct payments/specified use (cost share expected).

Purposes: pursuant to the Consolidated Natural Resources Act of 2008, to assist the National Park Service (NPS) as it inventories, evaluates, documents, preserves, protects, monitors, maintains, and interprets natural resources at 392 park units, 21 trails and 58 wild and scenic rivers. Funds may be used for all aspects of natural resource (air, water, geological, biological) stewardship and activities are conducted largely at the park level, utilizing park personnel and contractor or cooperative support.

Eligible applicants/beneficiaries: 35 IHEs selected by the CDC as Prevention Research Centers (PRCs).

Range: $4,000 to $213,000. **Average:** $55,000.

Activity: more than 80 awards in FY 2014.

HQ: Director, Natural Resources Science and Stewardship, NPS, 1201 Eye St., Washington, DC 20006. Phone: (202) 513-7204.

Internet: www.nature.nps.gov.

15.945 COOPERATIVE RESEARCH AND TRAINING PROGRAMS— RESOURCES OF THE NATIONAL PARK SYSTEM
("Cooperative Ecosystem Studies Units CESU Network")

Assistance: cooperative agreements/discretionary grants; direct payments/specified use; dissemination of technical information; training; use of property, facilities, and equipment (cost share expected/3 months to 5 years).

Purposes: to develop adequate, coordinated research, offer training programs and/or develop information products and create cooperative ecosystem study units (CESUs) to conduct multidisciplinary research in order to provide a solid science basis for the management of the National Park System.

Eligible applicants: IHEs (including Land Grant schools), nongovernmental conservation organizations, state/local governments, and federally-recognized tribal governments, in partnership with federal natural resource and scientific agencies.

Eligible beneficiaries: IHEs, faculty, students, researchers, experts, instructors, federal employees and the general public.

Range: $5,000 to $970,000. **Average:** $48,500.

Activity: more than 100 awards in FY 2014.

HQ: National Coordinator, Cooperative Ecosystem Studies Units (CESU) Network, 1849 C St., NW, Rm. #2737, Washington, DC 20240. Phone: (202) 208-5972.

Internet: www.cesu.org.

15.946 CULTURAL RESOURCES MANAGEMENT

Assistance: cooperative agreements/discretionary grants; direct payments/specified use (cost share expected).

Purposes: The NPS is authorized by Congress as the principal federal agency to lead the nation's efforts in historic preservation of the nation's historic and cultural resources with the solicitation, award and administration of cooperative agreements done on a project-by-project basis, generally at the park level. Funds may be used for all aspects of cultural resource stewardship activities, including inventory, monitoring, research, rehabilitation, reconstruction, restoration, preservation, documentation, data recovery, education, and climate change mitigation and adaptation.

Eligible applicants/beneficiaries: 35 IHEs selected by the CDC as Prevention Research Centers (PRCs).

Range: $1,000 to $5,500,000. **Average:** $192,000.

Activity: more than 50 awards in FY 2014.

HQ: Director, Cultural Resources Management Program, NPS, DOI, Main Bldg., 1849 C St., NW, Rm. 2737, Washington, DC 20240. Phone: (202) 208-7625.

Internet: www.nps.gov/history.

15.947 BOSTON HARBOR ISLANDS PARTNERSHIP

Assistance: cooperative agreements/discretionary grants (100 percent).

Purposes: pursuant to the Omnibus Parks and Public Lands Management Act of 1996 as amended and the NPS Organic Act, to improve access through use of public water transportation and provide education and visitor information programs regarding natural and cultural resources are specific objectives related to the management of the recreation area.

Eligible applicants: members of the Boston Harbor Islands Partnership, other public entities, education institutions, private nonprofit organizations.

Eligible beneficiaries: anyone, general public.

Range/Average: N.A.

Activity: N.A.

HQ: Superintendent, Boston Harbor Islands National Park Area, 15 Stark St., Suite 1100, Boston, MA 02109.

Internet: www.nps.gov/boha.

15.954 NATIONAL PARK SERVICE CONSERVATION, PROTECTION, OUTREACH, AND EDUCATION

Assistance: cooperative agreements.

Purposes: to support projects complementary to NPS efforts in resource conservation and protection, historical preservation and environmental sustainability. Projects may include research, education, outdoor recreation, and community outreach and safety. Recipients may be required to share some project or program costs.

Eligible applicants: state, tribal, and local governments, nonprofit organizations, IHEs.

Eligible beneficiaries: anyone, general public.

Range: $2,000 to $925,000. **Average:** $67,000.

Activity: over 100 projects funded in FY 2014.

HQ: Program Director, National Park Service, DOI, 12795 W. Alameda Pkwy., Lakewood, Colorado 80228. Phone: 303-969-2065.

Internet: www.nps.gov.

15.955 MARTIN LUTHER KING JUNIOR NATIONAL HISTORIC SITE AND PRESERVATION DISTRICT

Assistance: project grants, advisory services and counseling (to 100 percent).

Purposes: Cooperative agreements with the owners of properties of historical or cultural significance and properties within the Martin Luther King Junior Preservation District, pursuant to which the Secretary of the Interior may mark, interpret, improve, restore, and provide technical assistance with respect to the preservation and interpretation of such properties. The agreements shall contain, but need not be limited to, provisions that the Secretary shall have the right of access at reasonable times to public portions of the property for interpretive and other purposes, and that no changes or alterations shall be made in the property except by mutual agreement. Recipients may share some project or program costs.

Eligible applicants: owners of properties of historical or cultural significance and properties within the Martin Luther King Junior Preservation District.

Eligible beneficiaries: anyone/general public.

Range: $500,000 to $900,000. **Average:** $700,000.

Activity: N.A.

HQ: Director, Martin Luther King Junior National Historic Site and Preservation District, NPS-DOI, 12795 W. Alameda Parkway, Lakewood, CO 80228. Phone: (303) 987-6739.

Internet: www.nps.gov.

15.958   ROUTE 66 CORRIDOR PRESERVATION PROGRAM

Assistance: cooperative agreements. (50 percent).

Purposes: pursuant to Public Law 106-45, section 2, and Public Law 111-11, section 7304, to provide financial assistance for the preservation of the most significant and representative buildings, structures, road segments, and cultural landscapes along the length of the Route 66 corridor, covering Illinois, Missouri, Kansas, Oklahoma, Texas, New Mexico, Arizona, and California.

Eligible applicants/beneficiaries: public and private preservation entities, individuals, and private landowners.

Range: $5,000 to $30,000. **Average:** $15,000.

Activity: N.A.

HQ: Program Director, 1100 Old Santa Fe Trail, PO Box 728, Santa Fe, NM 87505. Phone: (505) 988-6122.

Internet: ncptt.nps.gov/rt66/. (Note: no field offices for this program.)

15.960   TRIBAL TECHNICAL COLLEGES

Assistance: project grants. (100 percent/1 year).

Purposes: pursuant to the Tribally Controlled Postsecondary Career and Technical Institutions Program, to pay the costs, including institutional support costs, of operating postsecondary career and technical education programs for Indian students at tribally controlled postsecondary career and technical institutions. Funds may be used for the general operating costs of the Tribal Technical College to defray expenditures for academic, educational and administrative purposes and for the operation and maintenance of the College. Funds may not be used in connection with religious worship or sectarian instruction.

Eligible applicants/beneficiaries: federally-recognized tribal governments and organizations.

Range/Average: N.A.

Activity: N.A.

HQ: Bureau of Indian Education, DOI, Stop 4657-MIB, 1849 C St., NW, Washington, DC 20240. Phone: (202) 208-3559.

Internet: www.bie.edu.

15.962   NATIONAL WILD AND SCENIC RIVERS SYSTEM

Assistance: cooperative agreements. (50 percent to 5 years).

Purposes: pursuant to the National Wild and Scenic Rivers Act, 16 U.S.C 1281(e) and Section 1282(b)(1), to encourage participation in the acquisition, protection, and management of river resources and to support the National Wild and Scenic Rivers System and general river conservation.

Eligible applicants/beneficiaries: states, landowners, private non-profit organizations, federal agencies or wild and scenic river management councils or committees, duly authorized by a river's enabling legislation.

Range: $20,000 to $350,000. **Average:** $85,000.

Activity: N.A.

HQ: National Wild and Scenic River Steering Committee, NPS, 1849 C St., Washington, DC 20240. Phone: (202) 354-6929.

Internet: www.nps.gov/orgs/1912/Partnership-Wild-and-ScenicRivers.htm.

15.978 UPPER MISSISSIPPI RIVER SYSTEM LONG TERM RESOURCE MONITORING PROGRAM (LTRMP)

Assistance: project grants (100 percent).

Purposes: pursuant to the Upper Mississippi River Management Act of 1986, to maintain the Upper Mississippi River System as a sustainable large river ecosystem—through monitoring of trends and effects related to resources, and through research as specified in the LTRMP Operations Plan.

Eligible applicants/beneficiaries: states, local governments, intra- and interstate agencies, sponsored organizations, private nonprofit organizations.

Range: $389,475 to $785,628. **Average:** $455,294.

Activity: 6 awards in FY 2015.

HQ: none provided, see listing of field offices.

Internet: www.usgs.gov/ltrmp.html.

15.979 HURRICANE SANDY PROGRAM

Assistance: project grants/cooperative agreements (100 percent/to 2 years).

Purposes: pursuant to the Disaster Relief Act, project grants to support research and data collection projects complementary to continued U.S. Geological Survey Hurricane Sandy recovery and restoration efforts. Awards support research and information needs related to coastal topography and bathymetry, impacts to coastal beaches and barriers, impacts of storm surge and estuarine and bay hydrology, impacts on environmental quality and persisting contaminant exposures, and impacts to coastal ecosystems, habitats, and fish and wildlife. Data, tools, and information produced through these research and data collection efforts will further characterize impacts and changes, guide mitigation and restoration of impacted communities and ecosystems, inform a redevelopment strategy aimed at developing resilient coastal communities and ecosystems, improve preparedness and responsiveness to the next hurricane or similar coastal disaster, and enable improved hazard assessment, response, and recovery for future storms along the hurricane prone shoreline of the United States.

Eligible applicants/beneficiaries: state, local, interstate, federally or state-recognized Indian Tribal Governments, U.S. territories and possessions, IHEs, private foundations, and nonprofit organizations.

Range: $9,000 to $220,000. **Average:** $85,600.

Activity: N.A.

HQ: Director, Hurricane Sandy Program, USGS-DOI, 12201 Sunrise Valley Dr., Reston, VA 20192. Phone: (703) 715-7020.

Internet: www.usgs.gov/contracts.

15.980   NATIONAL GROUND-WATER MONITORING NETWORK

Assistance: cooperative agreements/discretionary grants. (100 percent/to 2 years).

Purposes: pursuant to Public Law 111-11, Subtitle F, to support multi-state, state, tribal, or local water-resource agencies which collect groundwater data to serve as data providers for the National Ground-Water Monitoring Network (NGWMN). Funding for new data providers will be to select and categorize their data in accordance with the Framework document guidelines, and to make data for selected sites available to the NGWMN, and support existing data providers. Funding for existing data providers will support work to keep their networks up to date and ensure that data continue to flow to the NGWMN.

Eligible applicants/beneficiaries: federal, state, local, and tribal water-resource agencies, public and private nonprofit and for-profit institutions/ organizations, research scientists and engineers.

Range: $10,000 to $90,000. **Average:** $35,000.

Activity: N.A.

HQ: Geological Survey, Department of the Interior, 411 National Center, 12201 Sunrise Valley Dr., Reston, VA 20192. Phone: (703)648-5005; FAX: (703)648-6693.

Internet: www.usgs.gov/contracts. (Note: no field offices for this program.)

15.981   WATER USE AND DATA RESEARCH

Assistance: cooperative agreements/discretionary grants. (100 percent/to 2 years).

Purposes: pursuant to Public Law 111-11, Subtitle F, Section 9508, to support State Water Resource agencies in improving data collection techniques and methods, data delivery and management, and data integration with each appropriate dataset developed or maintained by the USGS.

Eligible applicants: states.

Eligible beneficiaries: everyone.

Range: $50,000 to $100,000. **Average:** ; $75,000.

Activity: N.A.

HQ: Department of the Interior, Geological Survey, 1770 Corporate Dr., Ste. 500, Norcross, GA 30093. Phone: (678) 524-1544.

Internet: www.usgs.gov/contracts. (Note: no field offices for this program.)

DEPARTMENT OF JUSTICE

16.001   LAW ENFORCEMENT ASSISTANCE—NARCOTICS AND DANGEROUS DRUGS—LABORATORY ANALYSIS

Assistance: specialized services; advisory services/counseling; technical information.

Purposes: pursuant to the Comprehensive Drug Abuse Prevention and Control Act of 1970 (CDAPCA), to provide drug evidence analysis, expert court testimony, and technical assistance to law enforcement agencies concerning narcotics and other abused drugs.

Eligible applicants/beneficiaries: state and local governments, law enforcement officials, forensic laboratories.

Range/Average: N.A.

Activity: N.A.

HQ: Deputy Assistant Administrator, Office of Forensic Sciences, DEA-DOJ, Washington, DC 20537. Phone: (202) 307-8866.

Internet: www.dea.gov.

16.003 LAW ENFORCEMENT ASSISTANCE—NARCOTICS AND DANGEROUS DRUGS TECHNICAL LABORATORY PUBLICATIONS ("Microgram")

Assistance: technical information.

Purposes: pursuant to CDAPCA, to disseminate scientific information on the detection and analysis of narcotics and dangerous drugs, published monthly in "Microgram."

Eligible applicants/beneficiaries: forensic laboratories; scientists working for law enforcement agencies.

Range/Average: N.A.

Activity: N.A.

HQ: Deputy Assistant Administrator, Office of Forensic Sciences, DEA-DOJ, Washington, DC 20537. Phone: (202) 307-8866.

Internet: www.dea.gov.

16.004 LAW ENFORCEMENT ASSISTANCE—NARCOTICS AND DANGEROUS DRUGS TRAINING

Assistance: training.

Purposes: pursuant to CDAPCA, for DEA training of accredited professional and enforcement personnel in: drug investigations techniques; physical security aspects of legitimate drug distribution; evidence analysis; pharmacology, socio-psychology of drug abuse, and drug education; management and supervisory training of drug unit commanders.

Eligible applicants/beneficiaries: state, local, military, and other federal law enforcement and regulatory officials; crime laboratory technicians and forensic chemists.

Range/Average: N.A.

Activity: N.A.

HQ: Office of Training, DEA-DOJ, Quantico, VA 22134-1475. Phone: (703) 632-5167.

Internet: www.usdoj.gov.

16.012 ALCOHOL, TOBACCO, AND FIREARMS—TRAINING ASSISTANCE

Assistance: training.

Purposes: pursuant to OCCSSA as amended, Gun Control Act of 1968, and Organized Crime Control Act of 1970, to provide training in the enforcement of laws relating to alcohol, tobacco, firearms, arson, explosives, and organized crime. Programs include identification of firearms problems, laboratory capability, undercover, interviewing, investigation techniques, case management.

Eligible applicants/beneficiaries: state, county, and local law enforcement agencies. Participation is limited to nonuniformed police personnel.

Range/Average: N.A.

Activity: N.A.

HQ: Chief, National Center for Explosives Training and Research, 99 New York Ave., NE, Washington, DC 20226. Telephone: (202) 648-8401.

Internet: www.atf.gov. (Note: no field offices for this program.)

16.013   VIOLENCE AGAINST WOMEN ACT COURT TRAINING AND IMPROVEMENT GRANTS

Assistance: project grants (to 100 percent).

Purposes: pursuant to Title I, Violence Against Women and Department of Justice Reauthorization Act of 2005, to improve court responses to adult and youth domestic violence, dating violence, sexual assault, and stalking.

Eligible applicants: federal, state, tribal, territorial, local courts or court-based programs; national, state, tribal, territorial, or local private, nonprofit organizations with demonstrated expertise in developing and providing judicial education about domestic violence, dating violence, sexual assault, or stalking.

Eligible beneficiaries: courts and nonprofit organizations.

Range: $50,000 to $ 341,054. **Average:** $227,362.

Activity: N.A.

HQ: Director, 145 N St., NE, Washington DC, 20530. Phone: (202) 307-0344.

Internet: www.ovw.usdoj.gov. (Note: no field offices for this program.)

16.015   MISSING ALZHEIMER'S DISEASE PATIENT ASSISTANCE PROGRAM ("Alzheimer's Initiatives")

Assistance: project grants (100 percent/to 18 months).

Purposes: pursuant to Consolidated Appropriations Act, 2009, to fund projects that aid in the protection and location of missing elderly individuals, including persons living with Alzheimer's disease and related dementias. This national outreach program should include partnerships between national level law enforcement and Alzheimer's disease associations. The successful applicant must address sustainability for any website and/or national registry developed or enhanced beyond federal funding awarded, as there is no guarantee of future funding for this initiative.

Eligible applicants: local and state-recognized tribal governments, IHEs, hospitals, public and private organizations/institutions.

Eligible beneficiaries: public institutions and organizations.

Range/Average: N.A.

Activity: 2 awards in FY 2015.

HQ: Office of Justice Programs, BJA-DOJ, 810 7th St. NW, Washington, DC 20531. Phone: (202) 616-6500.

Internet: www.bja.gov. (Note: no field offices for this program.)

16.016   CULTURALLY AND LINGUISTICALLY SPECIFIC SERVICES PROGRAM

Assistance: project grants (to 100 percent/2 years).

Purposes: pursuant to Title I, Violence Against Women and Department of Justice Reauthorization Act of 2005, to enhance culturally and linguistically specific services for victims of domestic and dating violence, sexual assault, and stalking.

Eligible applicants/beneficiaries: community-based programs whose primary purpose is providing culturally and linguistically specific services to victims of domestic violence, dating violence, sexual assault, and stalking who can partner with a program having demonstrated expertise in serving such victims.

Range: $18,840 to 450,000. **Average:** $294,629.

Activity: N.A.

HQ: Director, Underserved Program, VAW-DOJ, 145 N St., Ste. 10W121, Washington DC, 20530. Phone: (202) 305-1177.

Internet: www.ovw.usdoj.gov. (Note: no field offices for this program.)

16.017   SEXUAL ASSAULT SERVICES FORMULA PROGRAM

Assistance: project grants (one year or more).

Purposes: pursuant to Violence Against Women and Department of Justice Reauthorization Act of 2005, to increase intervention, advocacy, accompaniment, support services, and related assistance for adult, youth, and child victims of sexual assault and their families and household members.

Eligible applicants: states and territories.

Eligible beneficiaries: rape crisis centers and other nonprofit, nongovernmental organizations, including community and faith-based organizations.

Range: $12,678 to $437,011. **Average:** $178,690.

Activity: N.A.

HQ: Director, Underserved Program, VAW-DOJ, 145 N St., Ste. 10W121, Washington DC, 20530. Phone: (202) 305-1177.

Internet: www.ovw.usdoj.gov. (Note: no field offices for this program.)

16.019   TRIBAL REGISTRY

Assistance: project grants (100 percent).

Purposes: pursuant to the Violence Against Women and Department of Justice Reauthorization Act of 2005, to develop and maintain a national tribal sex offender registry and a tribal protection order registry containing civil and criminal orders of protection issued by Indian tribes and participating jurisdictions. Applicants are encouraged to contribute to the cost of the project with cash, in-kind services or a combination of both.

Eligible applicants: tribes, tribal organizations.

Eligible beneficiaries: tribes, tribal law enforcement agencies, and the general public.

Range/Average: N.A.

Activity: N.A.

HQ: Director, Underserved Program, VAW-DOJ, 145 N St., Ste. 10W121, Washington DC, 20530. Phone: (202) 305-1177.

Internet: www.ovw.usdoj.gov. (Note: no field offices for this program.)

16.025   SPECIAL DOMESTIC VIOLENCE CRIMINAL JURISDICTION IMPLEMENTATION

Assistance: project grants/discretionary. (100 percent/at least 1 year).

Purposes: pursuant to the Violence Against Women Reauthorization Act of 2013, to assist tribal governments in implementing the Special Domestic Violence Criminal Jurisdiction. Funds shall be used to strengthen tribal criminal justice systems to assist tribes in exercising special domestic violence criminal jurisdiction; to provide indigent criminal defendants with the effective assistance of licensed defense counsel; to ensure that jurors are summoned, selected, and instructed in a manner consistent with all applicable requirements; and to accord victims of domestic violence, dating violence, and violations of protection orders rights that are consistent with tribal law and custom.

Eligible applicants/beneficiaries: federally recognized tribal governments and organizations.

Range: $350,000 to $450,000. **Average:** N.A.

Activity: N.A.

HQ: Violence Against Women Office, DOJ, 145 N. St., Ste. 10W121, Washington, DC 20530. Phone: 202-305-1177.

Internet: www.justice/gov/tribal/grants.html. (Note: no field offices for this program.)

16.100   DESEGREGATION OF PUBLIC EDUCATION

Assistance: specialized services.

Purposes: pursuant to Title IV of the Civil Rights Act of 1964 (CRA), Equal Educational Opportunities Act of 1974, and amendments, to secure equal educational opportunities in public schools and colleges, for all persons regardless of their race, color, religion, sex, or national origin. DOJ may: seek court orders to desegregate pubic schools or colleges; intervene in cases in which plaintiffs allege discriminatory practices; litigate referrals from DOED involving such discrimination, as well as on the basis of disability pursuant to the Rehabilitation Act of 1973; seek court orders to ensure that local school districts take steps to overcome language barriers in their instructional programs.

Eligible applicants/beneficiaries: public school parents or groups of parents; public college students or their parents.

Range/Average: N.A.

Activity: N.A.

HQ: Educational Opportunities Litigation Section, Civil Rights Division-DOJ, Washington, DC 20530. Phone: (202) 514-4092.

Internet: www.usdoj.gov/crt/edo/index.html. (Note: no field offices for this program.)

16.101   EQUAL EMPLOYMENT OPPORTUNITY

Assistance: specialized services.

Purposes: pursuant to Title VII of CRA as amended, to initiate legal processes enforcing the Act's provisions and regulations concerning equal employment opportunities, including authorized affirmative action programs—for all persons, regardless of their race, religion, national origin, or sex. Discrimination is forbidden by employers, labor organizations, employment agencies, state and local governments, public agencies, and government contractors and subcontractors.

Eligible applicants/beneficiaries: all persons.

Range/Average: N.A.

Activity: N.A.

HQ: Employment Litigation Section, Civil Rights Division-DOJ, Washington, DC 20530. Phone: (202) 514-3831.

Internet: www.usdoj.gov/crt/emp/index.html. (Note: no field offices for this program.)

16.103   FAIR HOUSING AND EQUAL CREDIT OPPORTUNITY

Assistance: specialized services.

Purposes: pursuant to the Acts cited below, to initiate legal processes assuring enforcement of the provisions of: Title VIII of the Civil Rights Act of 1968 as amended by the Fair Housing Amendments Act of 1988—assuring equal housing opportunities for all in the sale, rental, financing, and related housing activities—regardless of race, color, religion, sex, national origin, family status, or handicap (HUD investigates and attempts conciliation of fair housing cases; if unsuccessful, HUD may file administrative charges; DOJ brings suit in federal court); the Equal Credit Opportunity Act (ECOA) which prohibits discrimination in credit transactions on the basis of race, color, religion, sex, national origin, marital status, or age—because any part of the applicant's income is derived from public assistance, or because the applicant has in good faith exercised a right under the Consumer Credit Protection Act; Title II of CRA, prohibiting discrimination in places of public accommodation including hotels, motels, restaurants, gas stations, and places of entertainment; and, Section 2 of the Religious Land Use and Institutionalized Persons Act of 2000 prohibiting local governments from significantly burdening the exercise of religion or discriminating against religious institutions in their land use and zoning decisions.

Eligible applicants/beneficiaries: all persons.

Range/Average: N.A.

Activity: N.A.

HQ: Housing and Civil Enforcement Section, Civil Rights Division-DOJ, Washington, DC 20530. Phone: (202) 514-4713

Internet: www.justice.gov/crt/housing/hcehome.php. (Note: no field offices for this program.)

16.104 PROTECTION OF VOTING RIGHTS ("Voting Section")

Assistance: specialized services.

Purposes: pursuant to the Voting Rights Act of 1965, amendments, and related laws, to enforce the provisions of the Act regarding voter registration and voting in local, state, and federal elections. The laws protect the rights of all persons to register and vote, without discrimination based on race, color, membership in a language minority group, age, handicap, literacy, or residence overseas.

Eligible applicants/beneficiaries: all U.S. citizens of voting age.

Range/Average: N.A.

Activity: N.A.

HQ: Voting Section, Civil Rights Division-DOJ, Washington, DC 20530. Phone: (800) 253-3931.

Internet: www.justice.gov/crt/about/vot. (Note: no field offices for this program.)

16.105 CIVIL RIGHTS OF INSTITUTIONALIZED PERSONS

Assistance: specialized services.

Purposes: pursuant to the Civil Rights of Institutionalized Persons Act (CRIPA), RLUIPA, Freedom of Access to Clinic Entrances Act (FACE), VCCLEA, OCCSSA, and related laws, to enforce the provisions of the Acts. CRIPA assures the right of equal utilization of any public facility owned or operated by any state or subdivision thereof, without regard to race, religion, or national origin—including facilities for the mentally ill or for the retarded or chronically ill, prisons, jails, pretrial detention facilities, juvenile facilities, and homes for the elderly. FACE authorizes the Attorney General to investigate and, where appropriate, to initiate actions for relief from certain violent, threatening, obstructive, and destructive actions intended to injure, intimidate, or interfere with persons seeking reproductive health services, or deny religious freedom or destruction of property at places of religious worship. RLUIPA prohibits government entities from imposing a substantial burden on the religious exercise of a person residing in or confined to a publicly operated institution.

Eligible applicants/beneficiaries: anyone.

Range/Average: N.A.

Activity: N.A.

HQ: Special Litigation Section, Civil Rights Division-DOJ, Washington, DC 20530. Phone: (202) 514-6255.

Internet: www.usdoj.gov/crt/split/index.html. (Note: no field offices for this program.)

16.109 CIVIL RIGHTS PROSECUTION

Assistance: investigation of complaints.

Purposes: to prosecute cases of national significance involving the deprivation of personal liberties that cannot be or are not sufficiently addressed by state or local authorities. The Criminal Section's jurisdiction includes: acts of racial violence; misconduct by local, state, or federal law enforcement officers; violations of the peonage and involuntary servitude statutes protecting migrant workers and others held in bondage; violations of the FACE Act.

Eligible applicants/beneficiaries: all persons.

Range/Average: N.A.

Activity: N.A.

HQ: Criminal Section, Civil Rights Division-DOJ, Washington, DC 20530. Phone: (202) 514-3204.

Internet: www.usdoj.gov/crt/crim/index.html.

16.123 COMMUNITY-BASED VIOLENCE PREVENTION PROGRAM

Assistance: project grants (100 percent/3 to 4 years).

Purposes: the program will work with community-based organizations to develop and implement strategies to reduce and prevent violence by utilizing five core components that address both the community and those individuals who are most at risk of involvement in a shooting or killing: community mobilization, outreach, faith leader involvement, police participation and public education.

Eligible applicants: eligible states, territories, units of local government, federally-recognized tribal governments who demonstrate a significant violent crime problem affecting youth over an extended period of time.

Eligible beneficiaries: individuals, families and communities affected by violence and crime.

Range/Average: N.A.

Activity: N.A.

HQ: Director, Child Protection Division, Office of Juvenile Justice and Delinquency Prevention, DOJ, 810 7th St., NW, Washington, DC 20531. Phone: (202) 307-9963.

Internet: ojjdp.ncjrs.org. (Note: no field offices for this program.)

16.200 COMMUNITY RELATIONS SERVICE (CRS)

Assistance: specialized services.

Purposes: pursuant to CRA as amended, Title X, to provide conciliation, mediation, training, and technical services to communities in resolving community tensions, conflicts, and civil disorders perceived to be based on race, ethnicity, or national origin. Technical assistance, resource materials, and publications are available. No funds are provided.

Eligible applicants/beneficiaries: representatives of groups, communities; federal, state, or local governmental units.

Range/Average: N.A.

Activity: N.A.

HQ: Community Relations Service-DOJ, 600 E St., NW, Ste. 6000, Washington, DC 20520. Phone: (202) 305-2935.

Internet: www.usdoj.gov/crs.

16.203   PROMOTING EVIDENCE INTEGRATION IN SEX OFFENDER MANAGEMENT DISCRETIONARY GRANT PROGRAM

Assistance: project grants (75 percent/to 2 years).

Purposes: pursuant VCCLEA, to implement comprehensive approaches to the effective management of juvenile and adult sex offenders, or to enhance existing programs. Projects must focus on the continuum of activities and services targeted to community reintegration and management of offenders released from incarceration, rather than on institutional services.

Eligible applicants/beneficiaries: state, local, or tribal units of government, including possessions and territories.

Range: N.A. **Average:** $600,000 for implementation sites; $1,500,000 for TTA; $250,000 per fellowship opportunity.

Activity: N.A.

HQ: SMART Office, Office of Justice Programs, DOJ, 810 7th St., NW, Washington, DC 20531. Phone: (202) 514-4689.

Internet: www.ojp.usdoj.gov/smart. (Note: no field offices for this program.)

16.300   LAW ENFORCEMENT ASSISTANCE—FBI ADVANCED POLICE TRAINING
("FBI Academy, Advanced Specialized Courses")

Assistance: training (1-11 weeks).

Purposes: pursuant to the OCCSSA as amended, Crime Control Act of 1973, Comprehensive Crime Control Act of 1984, and VCCLEA, to provide advanced training at the FBI Academy in such topics as criminal law and investigations, behavioral science, forensic science, education, management, and fitness and health—emphasizing development of managers and administrators. Specialized advanced courses and seminars include firearms administration, white-collar and computer related crimes, latent fingerprint examination, police legal issues, hostage negotiations, executive development, technology, laboratory matters, budgeting, scientific technical analysis, death investigations, bombing and arson investigations, violent crimes against the elderly, sexual exploitation of children. Participants may be reimbursed for round-trip travel costs to Washington, DC; housing, food, laundry and dry cleaning are furnished to students at FBI Academy, Quantico, VA.

Eligible applicants/beneficiaries: regular full-time personnel of municipal, county, or state criminal justice agencies; qualified representatives of federal agencies—meeting age, experience, education, physical, and character requirements.

Range/Average: N.A.

Activity: N.A.

HQ: Assistant Director, 935 Pennsylvania Ave., Finance Division, Rm. 6712, Washington, DC 20535. Phone: (202) 324-0495.

Internet: www.fbi.gov.

16.301   LAW ENFORCEMENT ASSISTANCE—FBI CRIME LABORATORY SUPPORT
("FBI Laboratory")

Assistance: specialized services; training.

Purposes: pursuant to OCCSSA as amended, to provide FBI Laboratory facilities and forensic assistance in examining evidence in criminal matters, technology transfer and access to information and forensic data bases, surveillance capabilities, related expert testimony, and specialized training in forensic disciplines.

Eligible applicants/beneficiaries: state and local law enforcement agencies in the U.S. or possessions.

Range/Average: N.A.

Activity: N.A.

HQ: Assistant Director, 935 Pennsylvania Ave., Finance Division, Rm. 6712, Washington, DC 20535. Phone: (202) 324-0495.

Internet: www.fbi.gov.

16.302   LAW ENFORCEMENT ASSISTANCE—FBI FIELD POLICE TRAINING
("FBI Field Police Training")

Assistance: training.

Purposes: pursuant to the OCCSSA as amended, Crime Control Act of 1973, Comprehensive Crime Control Act of 1984, and VCCLEA, to provide training courses by FBI instructors for criminal justice personnel, covering such areas as fingerprinting, legal topics, police-community relations, hostage negotiation, white collar crime, organized crime, computer fraud, management techniques, investigative support.

Eligible applicants/beneficiaries: municipal, county, local, and state criminal justice personnel.

Range/Average: N.A.

Activity: N.A.

HQ: Assistant Director, 935 Pennsylvania Ave., Finance Division, Rm. 6712, Washington, DC 20535. Phone: (202) 324-0495.

Internet: www.fbi.gov.

16.303   LAW ENFORCEMENT ASSISTANCE—FBI FINGERPRINT IDENTIFICATION
("FBI Criminal Justice Information Services Division")

Assistance: specialized services.

Purposes: to provide FBI fingerprint and arrest-record services. Besides criminal identification, services include locating missing persons and identifying unknown living or deceased persons and victims of major disasters.

Eligible applicants/beneficiaries: criminal justice agencies, federal government, and other authorized governmental and nongovernmental entities.

Range/Average: N.A.

Activity: N.A.

HQ: Assistant Director, 935 Pennsylvania Ave., Finance Division, Rm. 6712, Washington, DC 20535. Phone: (202) 324-0495.

Internet: www.fbi.gov.

16.304   LAW ENFORCEMENT ASSISTANCE—NATIONAL CRIME INFORMATION CENTER (NCIC)

Assistance: specialized services.

Purposes: to operate the FBI NCIC, complementing the development of similar metropolitan and statewide criminal justice information systems. Located in Washington, D.C., NCIC is a computerized index of crimes and criminals of nationwide interest, serving as a nucleus of a high-speed communications network that includes criminal justice agencies throughout the U.S., Canada, and some territories and possessions. The service can also be used to locate wanted or missing persons and stolen property. Technical assistance, consultant services, and training are provided to state agencies.

Eligible applicants/beneficiaries: local, state, and federal criminal justice agencies may participate through their individual control terminal agency.

Range/Average: N.A.

Activity: N.A.

HQ: Assistant Director, 935 Pennsylvania Ave., Finance Division, Rm. 6712, Washington, DC 20535. Phone: (202) 324-0495.

Internet: www.fbi.gov. (Note: no field offices for this program.)

16.305   LAW ENFORCEMENT ASSISTANCE—UNIFORM CRIME REPORTS

Assistance: technical information.

Purposes: to collect, analyze, and publish nationwide crime statistics providing such information as crime trends, offenses known to police, demographic characteristics of arrested persons, police disposition of juveniles arrested, police employee information.

Eligible applicants/beneficiaries: all participating law enforcement agencies including state and local governments receive the annual publication and semiannual releases. Limited copies of semiannual releases are available to any interested individual; the annual publication may be purchased from GPO.

Range/Average: N.A.

Activity: N.A.

HQ: Assistant Director, 935 Pennsylvania Ave., Finance Division, Rm. 6712, Washington, DC 20535. Phone: (202) 324-0495.

Internet: www.fbi.gov. (Note: no field offices for this program.)

16.307 COMBINED DNA INDEX SYSTEM ("CODIS")

Assistance: project grants.

Purposes: pursuant to the DNA Identification Act of 1994, to develop and maintain a national data base containing DNA records from convicted offenders, unsolved crime scenes, and missing persons. CODIS software allows storage and matching of DNA records; installation, training, and user support are provided. The FBI administers the Forensic Laboratory Improvement grant program jointly with the DOJ National Institute of Justice, providing funds for required equipment, supplies, and contractual services.

Eligible applicants/beneficiaries: software and technical assistance—publicly funded state or local forensic science laboratories performing DNA analysis, or private laboratories under contract. DNA grants—publicly funded state or local forensic laboratories.

Range/Average: N.A.

Activity: N.A.

HQ: Assistant Director, 935 Pennsylvania Ave., Finance Division, Rm. 6712, Washington, DC 20535. Phone: (202) 324-0495.

Internet: www.fbi.gov. (Note: no field offices for this program.)

16.308 INDIAN COUNTRY INVESTIGATIONS

Assistance: training.

Purposes: pursuant to VCCLEA, to train BIA and tribal law enforcement officers in conducting investigations in Indian country, in coordination with the Federal Law Enforcement Training Center (FLETC) and the BIA—including in death investigations, child sexual/physical abuse, gaming, evidence recovery, supervision and management, street officer safety.

Eligible applicants/beneficiaries: BIA investigators, tribal and other law enforcement officers.

Range/Average: N.A.

Activity: N.A.

HQ: Assistant Director, 935 Pennsylvania Ave., Finance Division, Rm. 6712, Washington, DC 20535. Phone: (202) 324-0495.

Internet: www.fbi.gov. (Note: no field offices for this program.)

16.309 LAW ENFORCEMENT ASSISTANCE—NATIONAL INSTANT CRIMINAL BACKGROUND CHECK SYSTEM ("NICS")

Assistance: specialized services.

Purposes: pursuant to the Gun Control Act and National Firearms Act, to provide a system through which federal firearm licensees may obtain information on whether prospective buyers would violate federal or state laws, by telephone or other electronic means. Background checks are conducted by the NICS Operations Center; also provided are technical and operational support to users and State Points of Contacts.

Eligible applicants/beneficiaries: firearms licensees and purchasers.

Range/Average: N.A.

Activity: N.A.

HQ: Assistant Director, 935 Pennsylvania Ave., Finance Division, Rm. 6712, Washington, DC 20535. Phone: (202) 324-0495.

Internet: www.fbi.gov.

16.320 SERVICES FOR TRAFFICKING VICTIMS

Assistance: project grants; direct payments/specified use. (75 percent/1-3 years).

Purposes: pursuant to the Victims of Trafficking and Violence Prevention Act of 2000 (VTVPA), to provide assistance to victims of severe forms of trafficking, primarily to meet victims' pre- certifications needs as victims, through: comprehensive services awards to support the creation or enhancement of collaborative networks within given regions or communities, providing or coordinating services including shelter and sustenance, general health and mental health care, legal assistance, job skills training, cultural support, and educational services; and, supplemental and specialized services awards to support discrete, rapid response whenever and wherever trafficking victims are identified. Limited funding also is available for training, technical assistance, and research and evaluation projects.

Eligible applicants: state and local governments; tribes; nonprofit, nongovernmental victims services organizations.

Eligible beneficiaries: victims of severe forms of trafficking without regard to the victim's immigration status. Trafficking is defined by DOJ as: sex trafficking in which a commercial sex act is induced by force, fraud, or coercion, or in which the person induced to perform such act is under age 18; or, the recruitment, harboring, transportation, provision, or obtaining of a person for labor or services through the use of force, fraud, or coercion for the purpose of subjection to involuntary servitude, peonage, debt bondage, or slavery.)

Range: $200,000 to $400,000. **Average:** N.A.

Activity: N.A.

HQ: Office for Victims of Crime, OJP-DOJ, 810 7th St., NW, Washington, DC 20531. Phone: (202) 305-2601.

Internet: www.ovc.gov. (Note: no field offices for this program.)

16.321 ANTITERRORISM EMERGENCY RESERVE

Assistance: project grants; direct payments/specified use. (100 percent/to 3 years).

Purposes: pursuant to VOCA, ATEDPA, VTVPA, and USA Patriot Act of 2001, to provide assistance for victims of mass violence and terrorism occurring within and outside the United States, and a compensation program for victims of international terrorism—through: (1) Antiterrorism and Emergency Assistance Program (AEAP), providing assistance and compensation benefits for victims of domestic and international terrorism, mass violence, including emergency relief, crisis response efforts, training and technical assistance; (2) International Terrorism Victim Expense Reimbursement Program (ITVERP), to compensate victims for expenses associated with acts occurring outside the U.S. Victims all may receive appropriate support services and compensation specifically for medical, mental health, funeral and burial, lost wages, and loss of support.

Eligible applicants: AEAP—victim services organizations; federal, state, and local governments; nongovernmental organizations and similar organizations.

Eligible beneficiaries: ITVERP—generally, victims, family members, and dependents that are U.S. nationals or U.S. government officers or employees as of the date on which the international terrorism act occurred—on or after 21 December 1988, with respect to which an investigation or prosecution was ongoing after 24 April 1996. (Final regulations are still being developed.)

Range/Average: N.A.

Activity: N.A.

HQ: Office for Victims of Crime, OJP-DOJ, 810 7th St., NW, Washington, DC 2053. Phone: (202) 307-5983.

Internet: www.ovc.gov. (Note: no field offices for this program.)

16.523 JUVENILE ACCOUNTABILITY BLOCK GRANTS (JABG)

Assistance: formula grants; project grants (formula, 90 percent; project, 100 percent/formula, 3 years; project, 1-3 years).

Purposes: to develop programs promoting greater accountability in the juvenile justice system. Formula grant funds may be used for such purposes as: building, expanding, renovating, or operating temporary or permanent juvenile correction or detention facilities, including personnel training; to develop and administer accountability-based sanctions for juvenile offenders; to hire additional judges, probation officers, court-appointed defenders, and prosecutors; to enable prosecutors to address drug, gang, and youth violence problems more effectively; to acquire related technology, equipment, and training; to establish juvenile "gun courts" and "drug courts;" to establish and maintain interagency information-sharing programs involving the juvenile and criminal justice systems, schools, and social services agencies; for programs to protect students and school personnel from drug, gang, and youth violence; to implement a policy of controlled substance testing for appropriate categories of juveniles. Discretionary project grants may be awarded for pertinent research, demonstrations, evaluations, and training and technical assistance.

Eligible applicants/beneficiaries: formula grants—states, territories and possessions (except Palau), and local government units. Discretionary grants—public or private agencies, organizations, individuals.

Range/Average: N.A.

Activity: N.A.

HQ: OJJDP, OJP-DOJ, 810 7th St., NW, Washington, DC 20531. Phone: (202) 616-9135.

Internet: www.ojjdp.ncjrs.gov. (Note: no field offices for this program.)

16.524 LEGAL ASSISTANCE FOR VICTIMS

Assistance: project grants (100 percent/to 2 years).

Purposes: pursuant to the Violence Against Women Act of 2000 (VAWA), to increase direct legal services available to victims of domestic violence, sexual assault, and stalking—through innovative collaborative programs and services within the civil legal system, promoting victim safety and increased victim economic autonomy, including representation in such matters as protection orders, family law, or housing matters. Funded activities also may include training, technical assistance, and data collection.

Eligible applicants/beneficiaries: private nonprofit entities, tribal governments, publicly funded organizations not acting in their governmental capacity.

Range: $226,000 to $606,812. **Average:** $476,570.

Activity: N.A.

HQ: Director, Underserved Program, VAW-DOJ, 145 N St., Ste. 10W121, Washington DC, 20530. Phone: (202) 305-1177.

Internet: www.ovw.usdoj.gov. (Note: no field offices for this program.)

16.525 GRANTS TO COMBAT DOMESTIC VIOLENCE, DATING VIOLENCE, SEXUAL ASSAULT, AND STALKING ON CAMPUS

Assistance: project grants. (100 percent/to 3 years).

Purposes: pursuant to VAWA and Department of Justice Reauthorization Act of 2005, to develop and strengthen security and investigation strategies to combat violent crimes against women on campuses, including domestic and dating violence, sexual assault, and stalking; for victim services programs. Funds may support such costs as: apprehension, investigation, and adjudication; personnel training; public education for prevention; lighting and communications systems; coordination with local law enforcement. Grant recipients must meet strict crime reporting requirements.

Eligible applicants/beneficiaries: IHEs or IHE consortia Range; $143,000 to $550,000.

Range: $47,540 to $498,138. **Average:** $278,151.

Activity: N.A.

HQ: Director, Underserved Program, VAW-DOJ, 145 N St., Ste. 10W121, Washington DC, 20530. Phone: (202) 305-1177.

Internet: www.ovw.usdoj.gov. (Note: no field offices for this program.)

16.526 OVW TECHNICAL ASSISTANCE INITIATIVE

Assistance: project grants (100 percent/to 2 years).

Purposes: pursuant to VAWA, to provide expertise and support to communities in: responding to violent crimes against women, including domestic violence, sexual assault, or stalking; increasing victim safety; and, bolstering offender accountability. Grantees participate in educational initiatives, conferences, peer-to-peer consultations, and targeted assistance from experts. Program aim also is to build the capacity of national criminal justice and victim advocacy organizations.

Eligible applicants/beneficiaries: public or private nonprofit victim advocacy and national criminal justice constituency organizations, judicial organizations and related agencies.

Range: $116,500 to $1,359,327. **Average:** $465,551.

Activity: N.A.

HQ: Director, Underserved Program, VAW-DOJ, 145 N St., Ste. 10W121, Washington DC, 20530. Phone: (202) 305-1177.

Internet: www.ovw.usdoj.gov. (Note: no field offices for this program.)

16.527 SUPERVISED VISITATION, SAFE HAVENS FOR CHILDREN

Assistance: project grants. (100 percent/to 2 years).

Purposes: pursuant to VTVPA, for projects enabling supervised visitation and safe exchange of children by and between parents, in situations involving domestic violence, child abuse, sexual assault, or stalking. Projects should involve collaborative relationships among courts, local victim coalitions and shelters, and related entities.

Eligible applicants/beneficiaries: states, tribal governments, local government units.

Range: $340,216 to $492,500. **Average:** $386,745.

Activity: N.A.

HQ: Director, 145 N St., NE, Washington DC, 20530. Phone: (202) 307-0344.

Internet: www.ovw.usdoj.gov. (Note: no field offices for this program.)

16.528 ENHANCED TRAINING AND SERVICES TO END VIOLENCE AND ABUSE OF WOMEN LATER IN LIFE
("Abuse in Later Life")

Assistance: project grants (100 percent/to 2 years).

Purposes: pursuant to VTVPA, to train law enforcement officers, prosecutors, and court personnel to recognize, address, investigate, and prosecute cases of elder abuse, neglect, financial exploitation, and violence against individuals with disabilities—including domestic violence and sexual assault. Projects must include coordination among appropriate services agencies and organizations.

Eligible applicants/beneficiaries: states, tribes, local government units; state or local government agencies; private nonprofit victim advocacy organizations; public or private nonprofit service organizations for older persons or the disabled; national criminal justice constituency or judicial organizations.

Range: $275,000 to $400,00. **Average:** $371,542.

Activity: N.A.

HQ: Director, Underserved Program, VAW-DOJ, 145 N St., Ste. 10W121, Washington DC, 20530. Phone: (202) 305-1177.

Internet: www.ovw.usdoj.gov. (Note: no field offices for this program.)

16.529 EDUCATION, TRAINING, AND ENHANCED SERVICES TO END VIOLENCE AGAINST AND ABUSE OF WOMEN WITH DISABILITIES
("Disability Grant Program")

Assistance: project grants. (100 percent/to 3 years).

Purposes: pursuant to VTVPA, to provide education, training, consultation, and information to organizations and programs that provide services to individuals with disabilities that are victims of domestic violence, stalking, or sexual assault—including independent living centers and disability- related service organizations. Funds may support outreach activities and cost-effective ways that shelters and victim services may accommodate the needs of the disabled. Projects must include coordination among appropriate services agencies and organizations.

Eligible applicants/beneficiaries: states, local government units, tribal governments, private nongovernmental entities serving disabled individuals.

Range: $500,000 to $700,000. **Average:** $587,500.

Activity: N.A.

HQ: Director, Underserved Program, VAW-DOJ, 145 N St., Ste. 10W121, Washington DC, 20530. Phone: (202) 305-1177.

Internet: www.ovw.usdoj.gov. (Note: no field offices for this program.)

16.540 JUVENILE JUSTICE AND DELINQUENCY PREVENTION— ALLOCATION TO STATES ("Title II, Part B Formula Grants")

Assistance: formula grants; project grants. (50-100 percent/to 3 years).

Purposes: pursuant to JJDPA as amended, for state and local programs to prevent juvenile delinquency and improve the juvenile justice system, including: deinstitutionalization of status offenders; separation of adults and juveniles in secure custody; removal of juveniles from adult jails and lockups; community- based services such as group homes and halfway houses; personnel education and training; monitoring and evaluation; elimination of disproportionate contact of minority juveniles. Applicants must have three-year comprehensive plans for meeting program purposes. States must distribute two-thirds of formula funds to local governments, private nonprofit agencies, and tribes performing law enforcement functions.

Eligible applicants/beneficiaries: formula grants—designated state and territorial agencies. Technical assistance contracts—experienced organizations, agencies, and individuals.

Range/Average: N.A.

Activity: N.A.

HQ: OJJDP, OJP-DOJ, 810 7th St., NW, Washington, DC 20531. Phone: (202) 616-9135.

Internet: www.ojjdp.ncjrs.gov. (Note: no field offices for this program.)

16.541 PART E—DEVELOPING, TESTING AND DEMONSTRATING PROMISING NEW PROGRAMS

Assistance: project grants; specialized services. (100 percent/to 3 years).

Purposes: pursuant to JJDPA as amended, for programs to design, test, and demonstrate approaches, techniques, and methods of preventing and controlling juvenile delinquency, such as: community-based alternatives to institutional confinement; diverting juveniles from the traditional justice and correctional system; advocacy activities; programs to strengthen the family unit; prevention and treatment programs for juveniles that commit serious crimes; hate crimes, gun and gang violence prevention programs; after-care and reintegration programs.

Eligible applicants/beneficiaries: public and private nonprofit agencies and organizations; individuals; state, local, and tribal government units or combinations thereof.

Range/Average: N.A.

Activity: N.A.

HQ: Child Protection Division, OJJDP-DOJ, Washington, DC 20531. Phone: (202) 514-4817.

Internet: www.ojjdp.ncjrs.org. (Note: no field offices for this program.)

16.543 MISSING CHILDREN'S ASSISTANCE ("MEC Program")

Assistance: project grants (100 percent/1-3 years).

Purposes: pursuant to JJDPA as amended, to coordinate federal programs related to missing and exploited children and to establish and operate a national resource center and clearinghouse to: provide technical assistance and training in locating and recovering missing children; provide a toll-free hotline; disseminate information about innovative and model programs, services, and legislation; conduct national incidence studies. Research, demonstration, or service program contracts may be awarded for public education programs, services to missing children and their families, location and return of adults with Alzheimer's or related diseases, statewide clearinghouses, and related purposes.

Eligible applicants/beneficiaries: state and local governments, public and private nonprofit organizations; individuals.

Range/Average: N.A.

Activity: N.A.

HQ: Child Protection Division, OJJDP-DOJ, 810 7th St., NW, Washington, DC 20531. Phone: (202) 514-5335.

Internet: www.ojjdp.ncjrs.org. (Note: no field offices for this program.)

16.544 YOUTH GANG PREVENTION

Assistance: project grants (100 percent/12 to 18 months).

Purposes: pursuant to Juvenile Justice and Delinquency Prevention Act of 1974, as amended, to facilitate coordination and cooperation among local education, juvenile justice, employment, social service agencies, and community-based programs with a proven record of effectively providing intervention services to juvenile gang members for the purpose of preventing and/or reducing the participation of juveniles in illegal gang activities.

Eligible applicants/beneficiaries: public or private nonprofit agencies, organizations or individuals.

Range/Average: N.A.

Activity: N.A.

HQ: Child Protection Division, OJJDP-DOJ, Washington, DC 20531. Phone: (202) 514-4817.

Internet: www.ojjdp.gov. (Note: no field offices for this program.)

16.548   TITLE V—DELINQUENCY PREVENTION PROGRAM

Assistance: formula grants. (50 percent/3 years).

Purposes: pursuant to Incentive Grants for Local Delinquency Prevention Program Act of 2002, to increase the capacity of state and local governments to support more effective programs in the prevention of juvenile delinquency through risk and protective factor programming approaches—including such activities as mentoring, tutoring, after-school programs, gang prevention outreach, community team training.

Eligible applicants/beneficiaries: designated state and territorial agencies—for transmittal to local government units.

Range/Average: N.A.

Activity: N.A.

HQ: OJJDP, OJP-DOJ, 810 7th St., NW, Washington, DC 20531. Phone: (202) 616-9135.

Internet: www.ojjdp.ncjrs.org/titleV. (Note: no field offices for this program.)

16.550   STATE JUSTICE STATISTICS PROGRAM FOR STATISTICAL ANALYSIS CENTERS (SACs)

Assistance: project grants (100 percent).

Purposes: pursuant to OCCSSA as amended, to establish and operate Statistical Analysis Centers for the collection, analysis, and dissemination of statistics pertaining to crime and criminal justice.

Eligible applicants/beneficiaries: state agencies.

Range/Average: N.A.

Activity: N.A.

HQ: Bureau of Justice Statistics, BJA-DOJ, 810 7th St., NW, Washington, DC 20531. Phone: (202) 307-0765.

Internet: www.bjs.gov/index.cfm?ty=tp&tipd=48. (Note: no field offices for this program.)

16.554   NATIONAL CRIMINAL HISTORY IMPROVEMENT PROGRAM (NCHIP)

Assistance: project grants (80 percent).

Purposes: pursuant to OCCSSA, for states to: establish or improve computerized criminal history record systems; to collect data on stalking and domestic violence; to improve data accessibility and transmission to the National Instant Criminal Background Check System (NICS). Projects are to permit immediate identification of persons prohibited from purchasing firearms, or subject to domestic violence protective orders, or ineligible to hold positions of responsibility involving children, the elderly, or the disabled. Funds may support participation in the Interstate Automated Identification System and the FBI's Sex Offender Registry.

Eligible applicants/beneficiaries: designated state agencies, which may allocate funds to other state or local agencies or courts. Private organizations may receive contracts.

Range/Average: N.A.

Activity: N.A.

HQ: Bureau of Justice Statistics, DOJ, 810 7th St., NW, Washington, DC 20531. Phone: (202) 307-0765.

Internet: bjs.gov/index.cfm?ty=tp&tid=47. (Note: no field offices for this program.)

16.556 STATE DOMESTIC VIOLENCE AND SEXUAL ASSAULT COALITIONS

Assistance: formula grants. (75-100 percent/to 1 year).

Purposes: pursuant to OCCSSA and VAWA, to coordinate state victim services activities and collaborate and coordinate with federal, state, and local entities engaged in violence against women activities. Required matching funds may be provided through in- kind services.

Eligible applicants/beneficiaries: state domestic violence coalitions as determined by HHS under the Family Violence Prevention and Services Act; state sexual assault coalitions as determined by the CDCP's Center for Injury Prevention and Control under PHSA.

Range: N.A. **Average:** $80,390 for DV coalitions; $117,344 for SA coalitions.

Activity: N.A.

HQ: Director, Underserved Program, VAW-DOJ, 145 N St., Ste. 10W121, Washington DC, 20530. Phone: (202) 305-1177.

Internet: www.ovw.usdoj.gov. (Note: no field offices for this program.)

16.557 TRIBAL DOMESTIC VIOLENCE AND SEXUAL ASSAULT COALITIONS GRANT PROGRAM

Assistance: project grants (75-100 percent/to 2 years).

Purposes: pursuant to OCCSSA and VAWA, to increase awareness of domestic violence and sexual assault against American Indian and Alaska native women; to enhance responses to such violence at the tribal, federal, and state levels; to identify and provide technical assistance to coalition membership and tribal communities to enhance victim access to essential services. Required matching funds may be provided through in-kind services.

Eligible applicants/beneficiaries: established nonprofit, nongovernmental tribal coalitions; individuals or organizations proposing to incorporate as nonprofit, nongovernmental coalitions.

Range/Average: N.A.

Activity: N.A.

HQ: Director, Underserved Program, VAW-DOJ, 145 N St., Ste. 10W121, Washington DC, 20530. Phone: (202) 305-1177.

Internet: www.ovw.usdoj.gov. (Note: no field offices for this program.)

16.560   NATIONAL INSTITUTE OF JUSTICE RESEARCH, EVALUATION, AND DEVELOPMENT PROJECT GRANTS

Assistance: project grants; technical information. (100 percent/to 2 years).

Purposes: pursuant to OCCSSA as amended and Anti-Drug Abuse Act of 1988 (ADAA), for research, development, and evaluation projects relating to the causes and correlates of crime and violence and the improvement of the criminal justice system. Priorities include violent crime, alcohol- and drug-related crime, community crime prevention, criminal justice system improvement, forensic science research, and technology development.

Eligible applicants/beneficiaries: state, local, and tribal governments; profit and nonprofit organizations; IHEs; qualified individuals—including in the territories.

Range/Average: N.A.

Activity: N.A.

HQ: National Institute of Justice, OJP-DOJ, 810 7th St., NW, Washington, DC 20531. Phone: (202) 307-2942.

Internet: www.ojp.usdoj.gov/nij. (Note: no field offices for this program.)

16.562   CRIMINAL JUSTICE RESEARCH AND DEVELOPMENT—GRADUATE RESEARCH FELLOWSHIPS
("Graduate Research Fellowship Program")

Assistance: project grants. (100 percent/6-18 months).

Purposes: pursuant to the OCCSSA as amended and ADAA, for fellowships to doctoral candidates to conduct research related to law enforcement, crime, or criminal justice—covering stipends, project costs, and certain university fees.

Eligible applicants/beneficiaries: IHEs.

Range/Average: N.A.

Activity: N.A.

HQ: National Institute of Justice, OJP-DOJ, 810 7th St., NW, Washington, DC 20531. Phone: (202) 307-2942.

Internet: www.usdoj.gov/nij. (Note: no field offices for this program.)

16.566   NATIONAL INSTITUTE OF JUSTICE W.E.B. DUBOIS FELLOWSHIP PROGRAM

Assistance: project grants. (100 percent/6-12 months).

Purposes: pursuant to OCCSSA as amended and ADAA, for research fellowships concerning justice system administration, delinquency prevention, violence reduction, and related topics. Studies are conducted at the National Institute of Justice.

Eligible applicants/beneficiaries: individuals or their parent agencies or organizations on their behalf. Candidates must have a doctoral-level or legal degree of J.D. or higher.

Range/Average: N.A.

Activity: N.A.

HQ: National Institute of Justice, OJP-DOJ, 810 7th St., NW, Washington, DC 20531. Phone: (202) 307-2942.

Internet: www.nij.gov/nij/funding/fellowships/dubois-fellowship/welcome .htm. (Note: no field offices for this program.)

16.571 PUBLIC SAFETY OFFICER'S BENEFITS PROGRAM (PSOB)

Assistance: direct payments/unrestricted use.

Purposes: pursuant to OCCSSA as amended, to pay disability benefits to officers disabled in the line of duty, or death benefits to survivors of federal, state, or local public safety officers whose death results from a personal injury sustained in the line of duty.

Eligible applicants/beneficiaries: totally and permanently disabled officers or their surviving spouses and children (or their parents if there is no spouse or children). Public safety officers, including law enforcement officers, firefighters and public rescue squad or ambulance crew members, both paid and volunteer; law enforcement officers, including police, corrections, probation, parole, and judicial officers; FEMA personnel; state, local, and tribal emergency management and civil defense personnel. Available also in territories and possessions. (Note: eligibility by category of recipient varies by date of incident; a proportional distribution formula applies in instances of multiple beneficiaries. Details are available from the program headquarters.)

Range/Average: N.A.

Activity: N.A.

HQ: Office of Justice Programs, Bureau of Justice Assistance, Public Safety Officers' Benefits Office, 810 7th St., NW, Washington, DC 20531. Phone: (888) 744-6513.

Internet: www.psob.gov. (Note: no field offices for this program.)

16.575 CRIME VICTIM ASSISTANCE

Assistance: formula grants (to 4 years).

Purposes: pursuant to VOCA and Children's Justice and Assistance Act of 1986 (CJAA) as amended, VCCLEA, ADAA, ATEDPA, VTVPA, USA Patriot Act of 2001 (USAPA), and other acts, for crime victim assistance programs. Primary program purposes include: to stimulate state participation and support for victim direct services programs; to promote victim cooperation with law enforcement; to provide direct compensation and services to victims of violent crimes, sexual assault, spousal abuse, or child abuse, or other crimes. Project examples: domestic violence shelter services; rape crisis programs; support groups for survivors of homicide victims and DUI/DWI crash victims.

Eligible applicants: states, all territories and possessions. Funds are subgranted to public agencies and nonprofit organizations.

Eligible beneficiaries: crime victims or their survivors.

Range: $200,000 to $500,000. **Average:** N.A.

Activity: N.A.

HQ: Office for Victims of Crime, OJP-DOJ, 810 7th St., NW Washington, DC 20531. Phone: (202) 307-5983.

Internet: www.ojp.usdoj.gov/ovc. (Note: no field offices for this program.)

16.576   CRIME VICTIM COMPENSATION

Assistance: formula grants (to 4 years).

Purposes: pursuant to VOCA and CJAA as amended, VCCLEA, ADAA, ATEDPA, VTVPA, USAPA, and other acts, for awards by states to crime victims (other than for property damage excluding damage to prosthetic devices, eyeglasses or corrective lenses, or dental devices); to support victim compensation programs, including for survivors of terrorism, drunk driving, and domestic violence. Compensation may be made for such expenses as medical costs including mental health counseling and care, loss of wages, funeral expenses, costs incurred by nonresidents of the jurisdictions with operating programs.

Eligible applicants: states, territories, and possessions with established crime victim compensation programs.

Eligible beneficiaries: victims of crime resulting in death or physical or personal injury.

Range/Average: N.A.

Activity: N.A.

HQ: Director, State Compensation and Assistance Division, Office for Victims of Crime, OJP-DOJ, 810 7th St., NW, Washington, DC 20531. Phone: (202) 307-5983.

Internet: www.ovc.gov. (Note: no field offices for this program.)

16.578   FEDERAL SURPLUS PROPERTY TRANSFER PROGRAM

Assistance: sale, exchange, or donation of property and goods.

Purposes: pursuant to the Comprehensive Crime Control Act of 1984, Surplus Federal Property Amendments of 1984, and other acts, to transfer or convey surplus federal real or other property for use in correctional or law enforcement programs and projects involving the care or rehabilitation of criminal offenders.

Eligible applicants/beneficiaries: state, local, and territorial governments; political subdivisions.

Range/Average: N.A.

Activity: N.A.

HQ: Manager, Special Projects, BJA-OJP-DOJ, 810 7th St., NW - 4th floor, Washington, DC 20531. Phone: (202) 353-2392; (866) 859-2687.

Internet: www.bja.gov/ProgramDetails.aspx?Program_ID=61.

16.582   CRIME VICTIM ASSISTANCE—DISCRETIONARY GRANTS

Assistance: project grants; direct payments/specified use. (grants, 75-90 percent/grants, 6 months to 2 years).

Purposes: pursuant to VOCA and CJAA as amended, VCCLEA, ADAA, ATEDPA, VTVPA, USAPA, and other acts, for programs to improve the overall quality of services delivered to crime victims including victims of terrorism domestically and abroad, through: demonstration projects and technical assistance to and training of services providers; support of victims services programs including direct compensation benefits. Project focus examples: religious organizations response to crime victims; victims of crimes in urban and rural areas and in Indian country (requiring 10 percent local matching share); working with grass roots organizations' to identify and replicate promising practices; practitioners training; special populations programs.

Eligible applicants/beneficiaries: states, U.S. Attorneys offices, university sites and colleges, victim service agencies, private nonprofit agencies; tribes and tribal organizations.

Range: $35,000 to $2,400,000. **Average:** $250,000.

Activity: N.A.

HQ: Office for Victims of Crime, OJP-DOJ, 810 7th St., NW, Washington, DC 20531. Phone: (202) 307-5983.

Internet: www.ovc.gov. (Note: no field offices for this program.)

16.583 CHILDREN'S JUSTICE ACT PARTNERSHIPS FOR INDIAN COMMUNITIES (CJA)

Assistance: project grants; direct payments/specified use. (90 percent/1-3 years).

Purposes: pursuant to VOCA and CJAA as amended, VCCLEA, ADAA, ATEDPA, VTVPA, and other acts, for Indian tribes to develop, establish, and operate programs to improve the handling of child abuse cases, particularly cases of sexual abuse, and to improve the investigation and prosecution of such cases.

Eligible applicants/beneficiaries: tribal governments, nonprofit Indian organizations.

Range/Average: N.A.

Activity: N.A.

HQ: Director, Federal Assistance Division, Office for Victims of Crime, OJP-DOJ, 810 7th St., NW, Washington, DC 20531. Phone: (202) 598-1156.

Internet: www.justice.gov. (Note: no field offices for this program.)

16.585 DRUG COURT DISCRETIONARY GRANT PROGRAM ("Drug Court Program")

Assistance: project grants. (75 percent/2-3 years).

Purposes: pursuant to OCCSSA, to establish and develop drug courts to handle cases involving nonviolent adult and juvenile offenders. Program funds may support projects providing early and continuous judicial supervision and integrated administration of sanctions and services, including: mandatory periodic testing for controlled or addictive substance use during any period of supervised release or probation; treatment; diversion, probation, or other supervised release; offender management and after-care services.

Eligible applicants/beneficiaries: states, local government units, state and local courts, tribal governments; joint applicants.

Range/Average: N.A.

Activity: N.A.

HQ: Associate Deputy Director, BJA-OJP-DOJ, Washington, DC 20531. Phone: (202) 616-6500; (866) 859-2687.

Internet: www.bja.gov. (Note: no field offices for this program.)

16.587 VIOLENCE AGAINST WOMEN DISCRETIONARY GRANTS FOR INDIAN TRIBAL GOVERNMENTS

Assistance: project grants (90 percent).

Purposes: pursuant to VCCLEA and OCCSSA as amended and VAWA, to develop and strengthen law enforcement and prosecution strategies to combat violent crimes against women, and to augment victim services. Funding may be used to pay costs of personnel, training, technical assistance, data collection, equipment, and victim services. (Note: Beginning in 2007, 10 percent of STOP, Arrest, LAV, Transitional Housing, Rural, and Safe Haven is set aside for the Tribal Program.)

Eligible applicants/beneficiaries: tribal governments.

Range: $150,000 to $900,000. **Average:** $556,802.

Activity: N.A.

HQ: Director, Underserved Program, VAW-DOJ, 145 N St., Ste. 10W121, Washington DC, 20530. Phone: (202) 305-1177.

Internet: www.justice/gov/tribal/grants.html. (Note: no field offices for this program.)

16.588 VIOLENCE AGAINST WOMEN FORMULA GRANTS

Assistance: formula grants (75 percent).

Purposes: pursuant to VCCLEA and OCCSSA as amended and VAWA, to develop and strengthen law enforcement and prosecution strategies to combat violent crimes against women, and to augment victim services. Grants may support costs of personnel, training, technical assistance, data collection and other equipment for apprehension, prosecution, and adjudication, and victim services.

Eligible applicants/beneficiaries: states, territories, and possessions. Subgrants will be awarded to local government units, nonprofit nongovernmental victim services programs, and tribal governments.

Range: $616,994 to $12,654,241. **Average:** $2,417,197.

Activity: N.A.

HQ: Director, Underserved Program, VAW-DOJ, 145 N St., Ste. 10W121, Washington DC, 20530. Phone: (202) 305-1177.

Internet: www.ovw.usdoj.gov. (Note: no field offices for this program.)

16.589 RURAL DOMESTIC VIOLENCE, DATING VIOLENCE, SEXUAL ASSAULT, AND STALKING ASSISTANCE PROGRAM

Assistance: project grants. (100 percent/to 2 years).

Purposes: pursuant to VCCLEA as amended and VAWA, for rural states to implement, expand, and establish cooperative efforts and projects among law enforcement officers, prosecutors, victim advocacy groups, and others—to: investigate and prosecute incidents of domestic violence, dating violence, and child victimization, including in immigration matters; provide treatment and counseling to victims; develop community education and prevention strategies.

Eligible applicants/beneficiaries: state agencies; local governments, tribal governments, and public and private entities in rural states—i.e., those with a population density of 52 or fewer persons per square mile, or in which the largest county's population is less than 150,000, including Alaska, Arkansas, Arizona, Colorado, Idaho, Iowa, Kansas, Maine, Montana, Nebraska, Nevada, New Mexico, North Dakota, Oklahoma, Oregon, South Dakota, Utah, Vermont, and Wyoming.

Range: $142,257 to $1,300,000. **Average:** $780,232.

Activity: N.A.

HQ: Director, Underserved Program, VAW-DOJ, 145 N St., Ste. 10W121, Washington DC, 20530. Phone: (202) 305-1177.

Internet: www.ovw.usdoj.gov. (Note: no field offices for this program.)

16.590   GRANTS TO ENCOURAGE ARREST POLICIES AND ENFORCEMENT OF PROTECTION ORDERS PROGRAM

Assistance: project grants. (100 percent/to 2 years).

Purposes: pursuant to VCCLEA as amended and VAWA, to implement mandatory arrest or pro-arrest programs and policies in police departments in cases of domestic violence including for protection order violations, dating violence, and assaults against older persons and the disabled; to develop related educational and training programs; to improve tracking of cases; to centralize and coordinate police enforcement in groups or units of police, probation, and parole officers, prosecutors, or judges; to coordinate computer tracking systems; to strengthen legal advocacy service programs for victims; to improve judicial handling or such cases.

Eligible applicants/beneficiaries: states, local government units, state or local courts, and tribal governments.

Range: $176,735 to $1,167,713. **Average:** $571,816.

Activity: N.A.

HQ: Director, Underserved Program, VAW-DOJ, 145 N St., Ste. 10W121, Washington DC, 20530. Phone: (202) 305-1177.

Internet: www.ovw.usdoj.gov. (Note: no field offices for this program.)

16.593   RESIDENTIAL SUBSTANCE ABUSE TREATMENT FOR STATE PRISONERS (RSAT)

Assistance: formula grants. (75 percent/to 3 years).

Purposes: pursuant to OCCSSA as amended, to develop and implement residential substance abuse treatment programs within state and local correctional facilities, including individual and group programs to develop cognitive, behavioral, social, vocational, and other skills—and lasting six to twelve months.

Eligible applicants/beneficiaries: states, possessions, territories. Subgrants may be awarded to state and local government units.

Range: $34,412 to $908,404. **Average:** N.A.

Activity: N.A.

HQ: Associate Deputy Director, BJA-OJP-DOJ, 810 7th St., NW, Washington, DC 20531. Phone: (202) 616-6500.

Internet: www.bja.gov. (Note: no field offices for this program.)

16.595 COMMUNITY CAPACITY DEVELOPMENT OFFICE ("Weed and Seed Program")

Assistance: project grants; specialized services. (75 percent/to 5 years).

Purposes: in cooperation with several other federal departments and agencies, to implement "Operation Weed and Seed"—a comprehensive, multidisciplinary approach to combat violent crime, drug use, and gang activity in high-crime neighborhoods. The goal is to identify drug activity and then to "seed" the sites with an array of crime and drug prevention programs, along with human service resources to prevent crime from reoccurring. The strategy is to bring together federal, state, and local government, the community, and the private sector in a partnership.

Eligible applicants/beneficiaries: coalitions of community residents and local, county, state, and federal agencies, and the private sector.

Range: $100,000 to $175,000. **Average:** N.A.

Activity: N.A.

HQ: Community Capacity Development Office, OJP-DOJ, 810 7th St., NW, Washington, DC 20531. Phone: (202) 616-1152; FAX: (202) 616-1152.

Internet: www.ojp.usdoj.gov/ccdo. (Note: no field offices for this program.)

16.596 TRIBAL JUSTICE FACILITIES GRANT PROGRAM FOR INDIAN TRIBES

Assistance: project grants. (90 percent/2 years).

Purposes: pursuant to VCCLEA as amended, to construct or expand jails on tribal lands for the incarceration of adult or juvenile offenders subject to tribal jurisdiction.

Eligible applicants/beneficiaries: tribes—defined as any Indian or Alaska native tribe, band, nation, pueblo, village, or community recognized by DOI.

Range/Average: N.A.

Activity: N.A.

HQ: Tribal Justice Policy Advisor, BJA-OJP-DOJ, 810 7th St., NW, Washington, DC 20531. Phone: (202) 616-6500.

Internet: www.bja.gov. (Note: no field offices for this program.)

16.601 CORRECTIONS—TRAINING AND STAFF DEVELOPMENT

Assistance: project grants; specialized services; technical information; training (100 percent).

Purposes: pursuant to JJDPA as amended, to upgrade operation of state and local correctional programs through training seminars, workshops, or other programs for law enforcement officers, judges and judicial personnel, probation and parole personnel, corrections personnel, welfare workers, lay ex-offenders, and paraprofessionals—involved in the treatment and rehabilitation of criminal and juvenile offenders; to develop technical training teams.

Eligible applicants/beneficiaries: states, local government units, public and private agencies, educational institutions, organizations, and individuals.

Range/Average: N.A.

Activity: N.A.

HQ: National Institute of Corrections, DOJ, 500 1st St., NW, Washington, DC 20534. Phone: (202) 307-6687.

Internet: www.usdoj.gov. (Note: no field offices for this program.)

16.602 CORRECTIONS—RESEARCH AND EVALUATION AND POLICY FORMULATION

Assistance: project grants; specialized services; technical information (100 percent).

Purposes: pursuant to JJDPA as amended, for research and evaluation projects on the corrections system, including the causes, prevention, diagnosis, and treatment of criminal offenders. Project examples: classification systems and methods; community corrections options; communications audits.

Eligible applicants/beneficiaries: states, local government units, public and private agencies, educational institutions, organizations, and individuals.

Range/Average: N.A.

Activity: N.A.

HQ: National Institute of Corrections, DOJ, 500 1st St., NW, Washington, DC 20534. Phone: (202) 307-6687.

Internet: www.usdoj.gov. (Note: no field offices for this program.)

16.603 CORRECTIONS—TECHNICAL ASSISTANCE/CLEARINGHOUSE

Assistance: project grants; specialized services; technical information (100 percent).

Purposes: pursuant to JJDPA as amended, to upgrade the operation of state and local correctional facilities, programs, and services for criminal and juvenile offenders; to provide consultation to federal, state, and local courts, departments, and agencies. Examples of funded projects: improved programs for female offenders; evaluation of offender classification systems; development of community sanctions.

Eligible applicants/beneficiaries: states, local government units, public and private agencies, educational institutions, organizations, and individuals.

Range/Average: N.A.

Activity: N.A.

HQ: National Institute of Corrections, DOJ, 500 1st St., NW, Washington, DC 20534. Phone: (202) 307-6687.

Internet: www.usdoj.gov. (Note: no field offices for this program.)

16.606 STATE CRIMINAL ALIEN ASSISTANCE PROGRAM (SCAAP)

Assistance: direct payments/unrestricted use (100 percent).

Purposes: pursuant to the Immigration and Nationality Act as amended and VCCLEA, to reimburse states and localities for costs incurred to imprison undocumented aliens convicted of felonies or of two or more misdemeanors; to expedite the transfer of illegal aliens to federal custody for deportation.

Eligible applicants/beneficiaries: states, DC, PR, Guam, VI; authorized localities and local jurisdictions.

Range/Average: N.A.

Activity: N.A.

HQ: BJA-OJP-DOJ, 810 7th St., Washington, DC 20531. Phone: (877) 758-3787.

Internet: www.bja.gov. (Note: no field offices for this program.)

16.607 BULLETPROOF VEST PARTNERSHIP PROGRAM (BVP)

Assistance: direct payments/specified use. (50 percent/to 4 years).

Purposes: pursuant to the Bulletproof Vest Partnership Grant Act of 1998 and Bulletproof Vest Program Act of 2000, to purchase armored vests for law enforcement officers, including costs of vest carriers, attachments, inserts, essential covers, and fitting, shipping, handling, and tax charges.

Eligible applicants/beneficiaries: chief executives of states, local governments units, recognized tribes, territories, possessions.

Range/Average: N.A.

Activity: 47,511 vests purchased and distributed in FY 2014.

HQ: BJA-OJP-DOJ, 810 7th St., Washington, DC 20531. Phone: (877) 758-3787.

Internet: ojp.gov/bvpbasi/home.html. (Note: no field offices for this program.)

16.608 TRIBAL COURT ASSISTANCE PROGRAM (TCAP)

Assistance: project grants. (100 percent/to 18 months).

Purposes: to develop, enhance, and operate tribal courts, including intertribal systems.

Eligible applicants/beneficiaries: tribal governments.

Range/Average: N.A.

Activity: N.A.

HQ: Senior Policy Advisor, BJA-OJP-DOJ, 810 7th St., NW, Washington, DC 20531. Phone: (202) 307-0581.

Internet: www.bja.gov. (Note: no field offices for this program.)

16.609   PROJECT SAFE NEIGHBORHOODS

Assistance: project grants. (100 percent/to 18 months).

Purposes: pursuant to OCCSSA as amended and the Crime Control Act of 1990, to enable community leaders and residents to work with prosecutors and other justice officials in the identification of local priorities, problem solving, and strategic planning for public safety—through "Community Gun Violence" Prosecution projects. "Project Safe Neighborhoods" is designed to remove gun-wielding criminals from local neighborhoods. Funds may be used: to hire additional prosecutors to work on cases of firearm-related violent crime; for investigations; for training; for outreach efforts.

Eligible applicants/beneficiaries: state, county, city, and tribal public prosecutor offices.

Range: $150,000 to $500,000. **Average:** N.A.

Activity: N.A.

HQ: Associate Deputy Director, BJA-OJP-DOJ, 810 7th St., NW, Washington, DC 20531. Phone: (202) 616-6500.

Internet: www.bja.gov. (Note: no field offices for this program.)

16.610   REGIONAL INFORMATION SHARING SYSTEMS (RISS)

Assistance: project grants (100 percent).

Purposes: pursuant to OCCSSA, to enhance the ability of state and local criminal justice agencies to identify, target, and remove criminal conspiracies and activities that span interjurisdictional boundaries—by exchanging and sharing information among federal, state, and local law enforcement agencies, pertaining to known or suspected criminals or criminal activity; to provide technical resources, specialized equipment, and training.

Eligible applicants/beneficiaries: Middle Atlantic-Great Lakes Organized Crime Law Enforcement Center, Mid-States Organized Crime Information Center, New England State Police Information Network, Regional Organized Crime Information Center, Rocky Mountain Information Network, and the Western States Information Network.

Range/Average: N.A.

Activity: N.A.

HQ: Associate Deputy Director, BJA-OJP-DOJ, 810 7th St., NW, Washington, DC 20531. Phone: (202) 616-6500.

Internet: www.riss.net. (Note: no field offices for this program.)

16.614   STATE AND LOCAL ANTI-TERRORISM TRAINING (SLATT)

Assistance: training; technical information; advisory services/counseling.

Purposes: pursuant to ATEDPA, to provide specialized multi-agency anti-terrorism preparedness training, covering both domestic and international threats and incidents. Training focus includes crisis and consequence management, anti-terrorist research, operational issues development, and technical assistance and support.

Eligible applicants/beneficiaries: state and local law enforcement and prosecution authorities.

Range/Average: N.A.

Activity: N.A.

HQ: Senior Policy Advisor, BJA-OJP-DOJ, 810 7th St., NW, Washington, DC 20531. Phone: (202) 616-6500; Toll Free: (866) 859-2647.

Internet: www.ojp.usdoj.gov/training/training.htm. (Note: no field offices for this program.)

16.615 PUBLIC SAFETY OFFICERS' EDUCATIONAL ASSISTANCE (PSOEA)

Assistance: direct payments/unrestricted use. (100 percent/45 months).

Purposes: to provide financial assistance for higher education to dependents of public safety officers killed or totally disabled in the line of duty.

Eligible applicants/beneficiaries: spouses and surviving children (under age 27) of federal, state, or local public safety officers including those who served public agencies with or without compensation in law enforcement, firefighting, or as members of public rescue squads or ambulance crews; effective November 1, 2000, FEMA personnel and state, local, and tribal emergency management and civil defense employees also became eligible. Categorical eligibility dates vary with service of victim; contact BJA for details.

Range: $255 to $1,018 per month. **Average:** N.A.

Activity: N.A.

HQ: Office of Justice Programs, Bureau of Justice Assistance, Public Safety Officers' Benefits Office, 810 7th St., NW, Washington, DC 20531. Phone: (888) 744-6513.

Internet: www.psob.gov/index.html. (Note: no field offices for this program.)

16.616 INDIAN COUNTRY ALCOHOL AND DRUG PREVENTION

Assistance: project grants. (100 percent/18 months).

Purposes: to assist tribal governments in the development and implementation of programs to reduce alcohol abuse and crime.

Eligible applicants/beneficiaries: tribal governments.

Range/Average: N.A.

Activity: N.A.

HQ: Senior Policy Advisor, BJA-OJP-DOJ, 810 7th St., NW, Washington, DC 20531. Phone: (202) 616-6500.

Internet: www.bja.gov/ProgramDetails.aspx?Program_ID=63. (Note: no field offices for this program.)

16.710 PUBLIC SAFETY PARTNERSHIP AND COMMUNITY POLICING GRANTS
("COPS Grants")

Assistance: project grants. (75-100 percent/3 years).

Purposes: pursuant to OCCSSA as amended and VCCLEA, to increase police presence in communities, to expand and improve cooperation between law enforcement agencies and communities in addressing problems of crime and disorder, and to enhance public safety. Funds may be used to hire or rehire career law enforcement officers and to procure equipment, technology, or support systems. Grants may also cover costs of programs or projects to: increase the number of officers interacting with community members on proactive crime control and prevention; train officers to increase their skills in conflict resolution, mediation, problem solving; increase participation in multidisciplinary early intervention teams; develop new technologies; support similar activities including innovative approaches to fulfilling the duties of police officers.

Eligible applicants/beneficiaries: states, local government units, tribal governments, other public and private entities, multijurisdictional or regional consortia. Available also in territories and possessions.

Range: $1,914 to $19,747,117. **Average:** $647,823.

Activity: N.A.

HQ: Office of Community Oriented Policing Services, DOJ, 145 N St., NE, Washington, DC 20530. Phone: (202) 616-1314.

Internet: www.cops.usdoj.gov. (Note: no field offices for this program.)

16.726 JUVENILE MENTORING PROGRAM

Assistance: project grants. (100 percent/3 years).

Purposes: pursuant to JJDPA as amended, to develop, implement, and pilot-test mentoring strategies and programs for youth in the juvenile justice system, re-entry youth, and those in foster care.

Eligible applicants/beneficiaries: states, territories, and possessions in partnership with mentoring and other public or private nonprofit organizations.

Range/Average: N.A.

Activity: N.A.

HQ: Program Manager, State and Tribal Assistance Division, Office of Juvenile Justice and Delinquency Prevention, DOJ, 810 7th St., NW, Washington, DC 20531. Phone: (202) 514-2189.

Internet: www.ojjdp.ncjrs.gov. (Note: no field offices for this program.)

16.727 ENFORCING UNDERAGE DRINKING LAWS PROGRAM (EUDL)

Assistance: project grants (1-3 years).

Purposes: to enforce state laws prohibiting alcohol purchase, possession, and use by minors—through projects conducted by partnerships among state and local governments, organizations, and agencies, including for training and technical assistance.

Eligible applicants/beneficiaries: states, DC.

Range/Average: N.A.

Activity: N.A.

HQ: OJJDP, OJP-DOJ, 810 7th St., NW, Washington, DC 20531. Phone: (202) 616-9135.

Internet: www.ojjdp.ncjrs.org. (Note: no field offices for this program.)

16.730 REDUCTION AND PREVENTION OF CHILDREN'S EXPOSURE TO VIOLENCE ("Safe Start")

Assistance: project grants (100 percent/1-5 years).

Purposes: for a demonstration initiative to prevent and reduce the impact of family and community violence on young children, primarily from birth to age 6, by expanding existing community partnerships between service providers such as law enforcement, mental health, early childhood education agencies and others. Funds may be used to: establish or enhance a broad range of local intervention and treatment services; develop multi-agency protocols; develop community-wide systems.

Eligible applicants/beneficiaries: public agencies applying on behalf of collaboratives including private agencies and organizations.

Range/Average: N.A.

Activity: N.A.

HQ: Director, Child Protection Division, Office of Juvenile Justice and Delinquency Prevention, DOJ, 810 7th St., NW, Washington, DC 20531. Phone: (202) 307-9963.

Internet: www.ojjdp.ncjrs.gov. (Note: no field offices for this program.)

16.731 TRIBAL YOUTH PROGRAM (TYP)

Assistance: project grants (100 percent/3 years).

Purposes: to reduce, control, and prevent crime by or against native American youth; to provide interventions for court- involved tribal youth; to improve tribal juvenile justice systems; to provide prevention programs focusing on alcohol and drugs.

Eligible applicants/beneficiaries: tribes and Alaska native villages, including partnerships.

Range/Average: N.A.

Activity: N.A.

HQ: Program Manager, State and Tribal Assistance Division, Office of Juvenile Justice and Delinquency Prevention, DOJ, 810 7th St., NW, Washington, DC 20531. Phone: (202) 514-2189.

Internet: www.ojjdp.gov. (Note: no field offices for this program.)

16.734 SPECIAL DATA COLLECTIONS AND STATISTICAL STUDIES ("Statistics")

Assistance: project grants.

Purposes: pursuant to OCCSSA, to produce official national statistics on crime and the administration of justice to guide federal, state, and local policy-making; to improve the quality of and access to the information. Projects may involve: data collection and processing activities; statistical and methodological research; technical assistance to state, local, and tribal governments; dissemination and clearinghouse services.

Eligible applicants/beneficiaries: state, local, and tribal governments; private and public nonprofit and profit organizations, IHEs, and qualified individuals—including in territories.

Range: $50,000 to $600,000. **Average:** N.A.

Activity: N.A.

HQ: Bureau of Justice Statistics, BJA-DOJ, 810 7th St., NW, Washington, DC 20531. Phone: (202)307-0765.

Internet: www.bjs.ojp.usdoj.gov. (Note: no field offices for this program.)

16.735 PREA PROGRAM: DEMONSTRATION PROJECTS TO ESTABLISH ZERO-TOLERANCE CULTURES FOR SEXUAL ASSAULT IN CORRECTIONAL FACILITIES ("Prison Rape Elimination")

Assistance: project grants (100 percent/2 years).

Purposes: pursuant to the Prison Rape Elimination Act of 2003, to protect male and female inmates in adult and juvenile facilities from prison rape; to safeguard communities to which inmates return. Funds may be used for such costs as: under the Protecting Inmates component—personnel, training, technical assistance, data collection, victim service and treatment, and equipment necessary for the proper prevention, investigation, and prosecution; Safeguarding Communities component—training and technical assistance to states on moderating the growth of prison populations, education of state and local governments on the risks of inmate reentry, developing state and local government collaborative efforts, programs reducing rates of parole and probation revocation.

Eligible applicants/beneficiaries: states—in coordination with stakeholders.

Range/Average: N.A.

Activity: N.A.

HQ: Deputy Director, BJA-OJP-DOJ, 810 Seventh St. NW, Washington, DC 20531 Phone: (202) 616-6500.

Internet: www.ojp.usdoj.gov. (Note: no field offices for this program.)

16.736 TRANSITIONAL HOUSING ASSISTANCE FOR VICTIMS OF DOMESTIC VIOLENCE, DATING VIOLENCE, STALKING, OR SEXUAL ASSAULT ("Transitional Housing")

Assistance: project grants. (100 percent/to 3 years).

Purposes: pursuant to the Prosecutorial Remedies and Other Tools to End the Exploitation of Children Today Act of 2003 (PROTECT Act), for transitional housing assistance and related support services to minors, adults, and the dependents that are homeless or in need of such assistance as a result of fleeing from domestic violence, or for whom emergency shelter or other crisis intervention services are unavailable or insufficient. Funds may be used to pay for short-term rental or utilities and related expenses, and for transportation, counseling, child care, case management, employment counseling, and other assistance.

Eligible applicants/beneficiaries: states, local and tribal governments, other organizations.

Range: $232,177 to $300,000. **Average:** $254,466.

Activity: N.A.

HQ: Director, Underserved Program, VAW-DOJ, 145 N St., Ste. 10W121, Washington DC, 20530. Phone: (202) 305-1177.

Internet: www.ovw.usdoj.gov. (Note: no field offices for this program.)

16.737   GANG RESISTANCE EDUCATION AND TRAINING ("GREAT")

Assistance: project grants. (100 percent/to 18 months).

Purposes: to help prevent youth crime, violence, and gang association, while developing positive relationships among law enforcement, families, and young persons. Funds may support personnel training and purchase of program materials and supplies.

Eligible applicants/beneficiaries: state, county, tribal, and municipal law enforcement agencies—including in territories; other special purpose law enforcement agencies (i.e., independent school districts).

Range/Average: N.A.

Activity: N.A.

HQ: Office of Justice Programs, Office of Juvenile Justice and Delinquency Prevention, BJA-OJP-DOJ, 810 7th St., NW, Washington, DC 20531. Phone: (202) 514-3913.

Internet: www.ojjdp.gov.

16.738   EDWARD BYRNE MEMORIAL JUSTICE ASSISTANCE GRANT PROGRAM ("Byrne JAG Program")

Assistance: formula grants; project grants (4 years).

Purposes: to acquire additional personnel, equipment, supplies, contractual support, training, technical assistance, and information systems—related to programs of law enforcement, prosecution and courts, prevention and education, corrections, drug treatment, planning, evaluation.

Eligible applicants/beneficiaries: state, territorial, and local government units.

Range: $10,000 to $37,000,000. **Average:** N.A.

Activity: N.A.

HQ: Programs Office, BJA-OJP-DOJ, 810 7th St., NW, Washington, DC 20531. Phone: (202) 616-6500.

Internet: www.bja.gov/ProgramDetails.aspx?Program_ID=59.

16.739   NATIONAL PRISON RAPE STATISTICS PROGRAM ("PREA")

Assistance: project grants (100 percent/12-18 months).

Purposes: pursuant to OCCSA as amended and Prison Rape Elimination Act, to collect and analyze data on the incidence of sexual assault among individuals held in federal and state prisons, local jails, and juvenile facilities, as well as on former inmates.

Eligible applicants/beneficiaries: state and local governments, private and public nonprofit and profit organizations, IHEs, individuals.

Range: $1,000,000 to $10,000,000. **Average:** N.A.

Activity: N.A.

HQ: Bureau of Justice Statistics (BJA), DOJ, 810 7th Street, NW, Washington, DC 20531. Phone: (202) 307-0765.

Internet: www.ojp.usdoj.gov/bjs. (Note: no field offices for this program.)

16.740   STATEWIDE AUTOMATED VICTIM INFORMATION NOTIFICATION (SAVIN) PROGRAM

Assistance: project grants; technical information. (50 percent/2 years).

Purposes: for states to build, implement, or improve their statewide automated victim notification systems, enabling them to provide critical information to victims in near-real time and to build a nationwide information sharing capability. Funding may support program staffing, facilities, communication infrastructure, and equipment.

Eligible applicants/beneficiaries: designated state agencies, including tribal governments and territories.

Range/Average: N.A.

Activity: N.A.

HQ: Senior Policy Advisor, BJA-OJP-DOJ, 810 7th St., NW-4th floor, Washington, DC 20531. Phone: (202) 616-6500; Toll Free: (866) 859-2687.

Internet: www.bja.gov/ProgramDetails.aspx?Program_ID=87. (Note: no field offices for this program.)

16.741   DNA BACKLOG REDUCTION PROGRAM

Assistance: formula grants (75 percent/12-18 months).

Purposes: to improve the infrastructure and analysis capacity of existing crime laboratories. Eligible project costs include: upgrading, replacing, and purchasing equipment, instrumentation, and computer hardware and software; supplies such as offender- related evidence collection kits; certain contracted services; facilities renovation; accreditation; personnel training and continuing education.

Eligible applicants/beneficiaries: state and local government units with existing crime labs complying with DOJ requirements.

Range/Average: N.A.

Activity: N.A.

HQ: National Institute of Justice, OJP-DOJ, 810 7th St., NW, Washington, DC 20531. Phone: (202) 616-9264.

Internet: www.usdoj.gov/nij. (Note: no field offices for this program.)

16.742 PAUL COVERDELL FORENSIC SCIENCES IMPROVEMENT GRANT PROGRAM

Assistance: formula grants.

Purposes: pursuant to the Paul Coverdell National Forensic Sciences Improvement Act of 2000, to improve the capacity of state and local forensic science and medical examiner services, including elimination of analysis backlogs by training and employing additional personnel. Funds may be used for personnel, computerization, laboratory equipment, supplies, accreditation, education, training, and certification.

Eligible applicants/beneficiaries: state administering agencies and local government units with approved plans.

Range/Average: N.A.

Activity: N.A.

HQ: National Institute of Justice, OJP-DOJ, 810 7th St., NW, Washington, DC 20531. Phone: (202) 307-2942.

Internet: www.usdoj.gov/nij. (Note: no field offices for this program.)

16.745 CRIMINAL AND JUVENILE JUSTICE AND MENTAL HEALTH COLLABORATION PROGRAM (JMHCP)

Assistance: project grants (80 percent).

Purposes: pursuant to Mentally Ill Offender Treatment and Crime Reduction Act, to facilitate collaboration among the criminal justice, juvenile justice, mental health treatment, and substance abuse systems to increase access to treatment of mentally ill offenders. Project funds may be used: to develop comprehensive plans targeting preliminarily qualified offenders; to implement such activities as establishing or expanding mental health courts and diversion/alternative prosecution and sentencing programs including crisis intervention teams and treatment accountability services; for special related training; to provide such services as special housing, in-jail, and transitional services.

Eligible applicants/beneficiaries: joint applicants including mental health agencies and states, local government units, tribes and tribal organizations— responsible for criminal justice activities.

Range/Average: N.A.

Activity: N.A.

HQ: BJA-OJP-DOJ, 810 7th St., NW, Washington, DC 20531. Phone: (202) 616-6500; Toll Free: (866) 859-2647.

Internet: www.bja.gov/ProgramDetails.aspx?Program_ID=66. (Note: no field offices for this program.)

16.746 CAPITAL CASE LITIGATION INITIATIVE

Assistance: project grants (to 18 months).

Purposes: to provide attorneys and judges who litigate death penalty cases with specialized legal training and technical assistance regarding death penalty issues, in an effort to improve the quality of representation, produce reliable jury verdicts, and minimize post conviction litigation.

Eligible applicants/beneficiaries: state-based agencies/organizations and units of local government serving defense counsel, prosecutors and judges located in states that currently enforce death penalty statutes.

Range/Average: N.A.

Activity: N.A.

HQ: Senior Policy Advisor, BJA-OJP-DOJ, 810 7th St., NW, Washington, DC 20531. Phone: (202) 616-6500.

Internet: www.bja.gov/ProgramDetails.aspx?Program_ID=52. (Note: no field offices for this program.)

16.750 SUPPORT FOR ADAM WALSH ACT IMPLEMENTATION GRANT PROGRAM
("Adam Walsh Act")

Assistance: project grants (to 75 percent/12 to 18 months).

Purposes: pursuant to the Adam Walsh Child Protection and Safety Act of 2006, to assist state, local, and tribal jurisdictions with developing and/or enhancing sex offender registration and tracking programs designed to implement requirements of the Sex Offender Registration and Notification Act (SORNA) under AWA.

Eligible applicants: state, local and tribal government agencies who have the intention of substantially implementing the requirements of SORNA are eligible to apply.

Eligible beneficiaries: state, local and tribal government agencies that have sex offender registry and tracking responsibilities and public as well as private organizations participating in collaborative endeavors with such agencies.

Range: $400,000 to $1,000,000. **Average:** N.A.

Activity: N.A.

HQ: SMART Office, Office of Justice Programs, DOJ, 810 7th St., NW, Washington, DC 20531. Phone: (202) 514-4689.

Internet: www.ojp.usdoj.gov/smart. (Note: no field offices for this program.)

16.751 EDWARD BYRNE MEMORIAL COMPETITIVE GRANT PROGRAM
("Byrne Competitive Program")

Assistance: project grants (to 100 percent/12 to 18 months).

Purposes: pursuant to the Consolidated Appropriations Act of 2008, to improve the capacity and function of the criminal justice system and provide for national support efforts such as training and technical assistance projects to strategically address needs, including crime prevention, control, and reduction.

Eligible applicants: state, regional, and local and tribal governments, public and private organizations, including for-profit (commercial) and nonprofit organizations, faith-based and community organizations, and institutions of higher education.

Eligible beneficiaries: state and local governments, public and private organizations, tribal governments and individuals.

Range/Average: N.A.

Activity: N.A.

HQ: Office of Justice Programs, Bureau of Justice Assistance, DOJ, 810 7th St., NW, Washington, DC 20531. Phone: (202) 616-6500; Toll Free: (866) 859-2647.

Internet: www.bja.gov. (Note: no field offices for this program.)

16.752   ECONOMIC HIGH-TECH AND CYBER CRIME PREVENTION

Assistance: project grants (to 100 percent/12 to 18 months).

Purposes: pursuant to the Consolidated Appropriations Act of 2008, to provide a nationwide support system for agencies involved in the prevention, investigation, and prosecution of economic electronic and cyber crimes and to support and partner with other appropriate entities in addressing related homeland security initiatives. Grants provide training, technical assistance, and/or resources to state, local and tribal law enforcement, prosecutor, and other agencies on how to prevent, combat, investigate and prosecute electronic and cyber crimes.

Eligible applicants: state, local, and tribal government agencies and public and private nonprofit organizations including faith-based and community organizations.

Eligible beneficiaries: state, local, and tribal governments and public and private organizations.

Range/Average: N.A.

Activity: N.A.

HQ: Office of Justice Programs, Bureau of Justice Assistance, DOJ, 810 7th St., NW, Washington, DC 20531. Phone: (202) 616-6500.

Internet: www.NW3C.org. (Note: no field offices for this program.)

16.753   CONGRESSIONALLY RECOMMENDED AWARDS

Assistance: project grants (to 100 percent/12 to 18 months).

Purposes: pursuant to the Consolidated Appropriations Act of 2008, to provide leadership and direction in improving the functioning of the criminal justice system.

Eligible applicants/beneficiaries: state, local, and federally-recognized Indian Tribal governments and agencies; public, private nonprofit, faith-based and community organizations.

Range/Average: N.A.

Activity: N.A.

HQ: Office of Justice Programs, Bureau of Justice Assistance, DOJ, 810 7th St., NW, Washington, DC 20531. Phone: (202) 616-6500; Toll Free: (866) 859-2647.

Internet: www.bja.gov. (Note: no field offices for this program.)

16.754   HAROLD ROGERS PRESCRIPTION DRUG MONITORING PROGRAM (PDMP)

Assistance: project grants (100 percent/planning, to 15 months; implementation and enhancement, to 2 years).

Purposes: to enhance the capacity of regulatory and law enforcement agencies to collect and analyze controlled substance prescription data through a centralized database administered by an authorized state agency. Up to 25 % of funding for Enhancement Grants may be used for operating costs, the rest must be used to enhance the functioning of an existing program.

Eligible applicants/beneficiaries: states (including the 50 states, DC, Puerto Rico, Northern Marianas, U.S. Virgin Islands, Guam, and American Samoa). To receive enhancement and implementation grants, states must have in place an enabling statute or regulation requiring the submission of controlled substance prescription data to an authorized state agency. State agencies are eligible for planning grants if they do not have enabling statutes or regulations in place.

Range/Average: N.A.

Activity: N.A.

HQ: Senior Policy Advisor, Bureau of Justice Assistance, State Policy Office, DOJ, 810 7th St., NW, Washington, DC 20531. Phone: (202) 616-6500; (866) 859-2647.

Internet: www.bja.gov/ProgramDetails.aspx?Program_ID=72. (Note: no field offices for this program.)

16.755 SOUTHWEST BORDER PROSECUTION INITIATIVE PROGRAM (SWBPI)

Assistance: direct payments/unrestricted use (100 percent).

Purposes: pursuant to Public Law 106-246, as amended by Public Law 106-554, to reimburse county and municipal governments in CA,TX, AZ, and NM state government, for specific categories of expenses associated with the handling and processing of federally initiated controlled substances cases along the Southwest Border.

Eligible applicants: local (includes state-designated Indian tribes) units of government.

Eligible beneficiaries: state and local governments.

Range/Average: N.A.

Activity: N.A.

HQ: Programs Office, BJA-DOJ, 810 7th St., NW, Washington, DC 20531. Phone: (202) 514-7047; Toll Free: (866) 817-9274.

Internet: www.ojp.usdoj.gov/swbpi. (Note: no field offices for this program.)

16.756 COURT APPOINTED SPECIAL ADVOCATES (CASA)

Assistance: project grants (100 percent).

Purposes: pursuant to Victims of Child Abuse Act, to ensure that abused and neglected children receive high quality, timely representation in dependency court hearings. Grants and training and technical assistance are provided to local and state programs to support existing and new CASA programs across the nation and CASA services in communities where representation rates are low, numbers of abused and neglected children are high, and service systems do not meet the needs of families and children.

Eligible applicants: public and private institutions/organizations.

Eligible beneficiaries: state and local governments; private/public institutions and organizations.

Range/Average: N.A.

Activity: N.A.

HQ: Child Protection Division, OJJDP-DOJ, 810 7th St., NW, Washington, DC 20735. Phone: (202) 305-1270.

Internet: www.ojjdp.ncjrs.org. (Note: no field offices for this program.)

16.757   JUDICIAL TRAINING ON CHILD MALTREATMENT FOR COURT PERSONNEL JUVENILE JUSTICE PROGRAMS

Assistance: project grants (100 percent).

Purposes: pursuant to Victims of Child Abuse Act, to provide technical assistance, information and support to local Court Appointed Special Advocates programs, assist communities in developing new programs, and provide support to existing and developing state organizations.

Eligible applicants: local and state-recognized tribal governments, IHEs, hospitals, public and private nonprofit organizations/institutions.

Eligible beneficiaries: public and private institutions/organizations.

Range/Average: N.A.

Activity: N.A.

HQ: Child Protection Division, OJJDP-DOJ, 810 7th St., NW, Washington, DC 20531. Phone: (202) 616-3646.

Internet: ojjdp.ncjrs.org. (Note: no field offices for this program.)

16.758   IMPROVING THE INVESTIGATION AND PROSECUTION OF CHILD ABUSE AND THE REGIONAL AND LOCAL CHILDREN'S ADVOCACY CENTERS

Assistance: project grants (100 percent).

Purposes: pursuant to Victims of Child Abuse Act, to improve the investigation and prosecution of child abuse and Children's Advocacy Centers. Some of the objectives to be achieved are: train criminal justice system professionals on innovative techniques for investigating, and prosecuting child abuse cases; increase the number of communities utilizing a Children's Advocacy Center approach to the investigation, prosecution and treatment of child abuse cases; assist communities in developing child-focused programs designed to improve the resources available to children and families; provide support to non-offending family members.

Eligible applicants: local and state-recognized tribal governments, IHEs, hospitals, public and private nonprofit organizations/institutions.

Eligible beneficiaries: public and private nonprofit institutions/organizations.

Range/Average: N.A.

Activity: N.A.

HQ: Child Protection Division, OJJDP-DOJ, 810 7th St., NW, Washington, DC 20531. Phone: (202) 514-5335.

Internet: www.ojjdp.gov. (Note: no field offices for this program.)

16.800 INTERNET CRIMES AGAINST CHILDREN TASK FORCE PROGRAM (ICAC)

Assistance: project grants (75-100 percent/1 to 3 years).

Purposes: pursuant to ARRA 2009 and Protect Our Children Act of 2008 Title I, to enable the ICAC task force program to support a national network of multiagency, multijurisdictional task forces and other projects to prevent technology facilitated child sexual exploitation with at least one task force in each of the 50 states. The ICAC task forces provide forensic and investigative technical assistance to law enforcement and prosecutorial officials, as well as community education information to parents, educators, prosecutors, law enforcement, and others concerned with child victimization.

Eligible applicants: federal government.

Eligible beneficiaries: state and local governments; specialized groups, including health professionals, students and veterans.

Range/Average: N.A.

Activity: N.A.

HQ: Director, Child Protection Division, Office of Juvenile Justice and Delinquency Prevention, DOJ, 810 7th St., NW, Washington, DC 20531. Phone: (202) 307-9963.

Internet: ojjdp.ncjrs.org. (Note: no field offices for this program.)

16.801 STATE VICTIM ASSISTANCE FORMULA GRANT PROGRAM

Assistance: project grants (100 percent/1 to 3 years).

Purposes: pursuant to ARRA 2009, Victims of Crime Act Title II, the Office for Victims of Crime (OVC) will award each eligible state victim assistance program a Recovery Act - VOCA victim assistance formula grant to support the provision of services to victims of crime throughout the nation.

Eligible applicants: states (including DC, IHEs and hospitals).

Eligible beneficiaries: specialized groups, including health professionals, students and veterans.

Range/Average: N.A.

Activity: N.A.

HQ: Office for Victims of Crime, OJP-DOJ, 810 7th St., NW Washington, DC 20531. Phone: (202) 307-5983.

Internet: www.ojp.usdoj.gov. (Note: no field offices for this program.)

16.802 STATE VICTIM COMPENSATION FORMULA GRANT PROGRAM

Assistance: project grants (100 percent/1 to 3 years).

Purposes: pursuant to ARRA 2009, Victims of Crime Act Title II, the Office for Victims of Crime (OVC) will award each eligible state victim compensation program a Recovery Act - VOCA victim compensation formula grant to support the provision of crucial financial assistance to victims of crime throughout the nation.

Eligible applicants: states, U.S. territories and possessions (including IHEs and hospitals).

Eligible beneficiaries: specialized groups, including health professionals, students and veterans.

Range/Average: N.A.

Activity: N.A.

HQ: Office for Victims of Crime, OJP-DOJ, 810 7th St., NW Washington, DC 20531. Phone: (202) 307-5983.

Internet: www.ojp.usdoj.gov. (Note: no field offices for this program.)

16.803   EDWARD BYRNE MEMORIAL JUSTICE ASSISTANCE GRANT (JAG) PROGRAM—GRANTS TO STATES AND TERRITORIES

Assistance: project grants (100 percent/to 4 years).

Purposes: pursuant to ARRA 2009, and Omnibus Crime Control and Safe Streets Act of 1968, to allow states and local governments to support a broad range of activities to prevent and control crime and to improve the criminal justice system.

Funds may not be used to supplant state and local funds and not more than 10 percent of the program grant may be to administer the grant.

Eligible applicants: states, U.S. territories and possessions (including IHEs and hospitals), local governments, tribes, sponsored organizations.

Eligible beneficiaries: statc and local governments.

Range: $1,600,000 to $225,000,000. **Average:** N.A.

Activity: N.A.

HQ: State Policy Office, BJA-DOJ, 810 7th St., NW, 4th Fl, Washington, DC 20531. Phone: (202) 616-6500; Toll Free: (866) 859-2687.

Internet: www.ojp.usdoj.gov/recovery. (Note: no field offices for this program.)

16.804   EDWARD BYRNE MEMORIAL JUSTICE ASSISTANCE GRANT (JAG) PROGRAM—GRANTS TO UNITS OF LOCAL GOVERNMENT

Assistance: project grants (to 4 years).

Purposes: pursuant to ARRA 2009 and Omnibus Crime Control and Safe Streets Act of 1968, allow states and local governments to support a broad range of activities to prevent and control crime and to improve the criminal justice system. Grant assistance is calculated according to formula. Matching funds are encouraged at the state and local level.

Eligible applicants: states (including DC, IHEs, hospitals) and U.S. territories and possessions.

Eligible beneficiaries: local governments.

Range/Average: N.A.

Activity: N.A.

HQ: Office of Justice Programs, BJA-DOJ, 810 7th St., NW, 4th Fl., Washington, DC 20531. Phone: (202) 616-6500; Toll Free: (866) 859-2687.

Internet: www.ojp.usdoj.gov/recovery. (Note: no field offices for this program.)

16.807 VOCA CRIME VICTIM ASSISTANCE DISCRETIONARY GRANT PROGRAM

Assistance: direct payments/specified use; project grants (100 percent/1 to 4 years).

Purposes: pursuant to ARRA 2009 and Victims of Crime Act Title II, to improve the capacity of victim service providers and allied practitioners in advancing rights and services for crime victims. Funding will be provided for training, technical assistance, and demonstration projects that are national in scope and either address gaps in the areas of training and technical assistance or develop promising practices, models, or programs through demonstration projects.

All initiatives, whether related to training, technical assistance, or development of promising practices, models, and programs, must focus on improving the capacity of victim service providers and allied practitioners in advancing rights and services to victims in the following areas: Elder abuse, sexual assault, victim restitution, child abuse, youth victimization (including cybercrime victimization), victim services in corrections settings, stalking, the implications of forensic technologies for victims, and training and technical assistance on crime victims' rights.

Eligible applicants: local and tribal governments, private nonprofit organizations/institutions (including IHEs and hospitals) and tribal institutions/organizations.

Eligible beneficiaries: state and local governments; private nonprofit and public institutions/organizations.

Range/Average: N.A.

Activity: N.A.

HQ: Office for Victims of Crime, OJP-DOJ, 810 7th St., NW, Washington, DC 20531. Phone: (202) 616-8715.

Internet: www.ojp.usdoj.gov. (Note: no field offices for this program.)

16.808 EDWARD BYRNE MEMORIAL COMPETITIVE GRANT PROGRAM

Assistance: project grants (100 percent/2 years).

Purposes: pursuant to ARRA 2009 and Consolidated Appropriations Act of 2008, to improve the capacity of criminal justice systems, assist victims of crime (other than compensation), provide youth mentoring, and to focus efforts on programs that emphasize more comprehensive community approaches, stimulate the economy (i.e., workforce development), and other factors that impact economic conditions and provide resources to improve the capacity of state and local criminal justice systems.

Eligible applicants: state (including DC, IHEs and hospitals), local, and state-recognized tribal governments.

Eligible beneficiaries: state, local, and federally-recognized tribal governments; private/public institutions and organizations; individuals/families.

Range/Average: N.A.

Activity: N.A.

HQ: BJA-DOJ, 810 7th St., NW, Washington, DC 20531. Phone: (202) 616-6500; Toll Free: (866) 859-2647.

Internet: www.ojp.usdoj.gov/BJA. (Note: no field offices for this program.)

16.809 STATE AND LOCAL LAW ENFORCEMENT ASSISTANCE PROGRAM: COMBATING CRIMINAL NARCOTICS ACTIVITY STEMMING FROM THE SOUTHERN BORDER OF THE UNITED STATES COMPETITIVE GRANT PROGRAM

Assistance: project grants (100 percent/2 years).

Purposes: pursuant to ARRA 2009, to provide resources, assistance, and equipment to local law enforcement along the Southern border and in High-Intensity Drug Trafficking areas in order to combat criminal narcotics activity stemming from the Southern border of the United States.

Eligible applicants: state (including DC, IHEs and hospitals), local, state-recognized tribal governments, and public profit and nonprofit institutions/organizations.

Eligible beneficiaries: state, local, and interstate governments; private/public institutions and organizations.

Range/Average: N.A.

Activity: N.A.

HQ: Policy Office, BJA-DOJ, 810 7th St., NW, Washington, DC 20531. Phone: (202) 616-6500; Toll Free: (866) 859-2647.

Internet: www.ojp.usdoj.gov/BJA/grant. (Note: no field offices for this program.)

16.810 ASSISTANCE TO RURAL LAW ENFORCEMENT TO COMBAT CRIME AND DRUGS COMPETITIVE GRANT PROGRAM

Assistance: project grants (100 percent/90 days).

Purposes: pursuant to ARRA 2009, to improve the capacity of rural local, tribal, and state law enforcement to prevent and combat crime, especially drug related crime. Funding will focus on comprehensive programs in the following areas: combating rural crime and improving law enforcement investigations; enhancing corrections, detention, and jail operations; facilitating justice information sharing; and training and technical assistance. Funds may be used to hire personnel to accomplish program goals for each category.

Eligible applicants: state (including DC, IHEs and hospitals), local, state-recognized tribal governments, and public profit and nonprofit institutions/organizations.

Eligible beneficiaries: state, local, and federally-recognized tribal governments; private/public institutions and organizations.

Range/Average: N.A.

Activity: N.A.

HQ: Policy Office, BJA-DOJ, 810 7th St., NW, Washington, DC 20531. Phone: (202) 616-6500; Toll Free: (866) 859-2647.

Internet: www.ojp.usdoj.gov/BJA/grant. (Note: no field offices for this program.)

16.811   CORRECTIONAL FACILITIES ON TRIBAL LANDS

Assistance: project grants (90 percent/18 to 60 months).

Purposes: pursuant to ARRA 2009 and Violent Crime Control and Law Enforcement Act of 1994, to provide resources to allow eligible American Indian tribes and Alaska Native villages to construct correctional facilities on tribal lands, with consideration given to the detention bed space needs and violent crime statistics of the applicant tribe or village. Required 10% match may be cash or in-kind.

Eligible applicants/beneficiaries: federally-recognized Indian tribal governments and other Native American organizations.

Range/Average: N.A.

Activity: N.A.

HQ: Policy Office, BJA-DOJ, 810 7th St., NW, Washington, DC 20531. Phone: (202) 616-6500; Toll Free: (866) 859-2647.

Internet: www.ojp.usdoj.gov/recovery. (Note: no field offices for this program.)

16.812   SECOND CHANCE ACT REENTRY INITIATIVE ("Second Chance Act")

Assistance: project grants (12 to 18 months).

Purposes: pursuant to Second Chance Act of 2007, to help ensure the safe and successful transition of ninety-five percent of all incarcerated prisoners who will eventually be released and will return to communities. Match is required for state and local grants.

Eligible applicants/beneficiaries: state (including DC, IHEs and hospitals), local and state-recognized tribal governments, and public profit and nonprofit institutions/organizations.

Range/Average: N.A.

Activity: N.A.

HQ: Office of Justice Programs, BJA-DOJ, 810 7th St., NW, Washington, DC 20531. Phone: (202) 616-6500; Toll Free: (866) 859-2647.

Internet: www.bja.gov. (Note: no field offices for this program.)

16.813   NICS ACT RECORD IMPROVEMENT PROGRAM (NARIP)

Assistance: project grants/cooperative agreements (to 100 percent/to 1 year).

Purposes: pursuant to NICS (National Instant Criminal Background Check System) Improvement Amendments Act of 2007, to improve the completeness, automation and transmittal to state and federal systems of records utilized by NICS, such as: records of criminal history, felony convictions, warrants, protective orders, convictions for misdemeanor involving domestic violence and stalking, and mental health adjudications and others, which may disqualify an individual from possessing or receiving a firearm under federal law.

Eligible applicants: states (includes DC, public IHEs and hospitals), Indian tribes, and U.S. territories/possessions.

Eligible beneficiaries: states, local, U.S. territories/possessions, Indian tribes, public institutions/organizations, and anyone/general public.

Range/Average: N.A.

Activity: N.A.

HQ: Bureau of Justice Statistics, DOJ, 810 7th St., NW, Washington, DC 20531. Phone: (202) 307-0765.

Internet: bjs.gov/index.cfm?ty=tp&tid=49. (Note: no field offices for this program.)

16.814   NORTHERN BORDER PROSECUTION INITIATIVE PROGRAM (NBPI)

Assistance: direct payments/unrestricted use (100 percent).

Purposes: pursuant to Public Law No. 111-8, 123 Stat. 524, 580 authorizes the reimbursement of county and municipal governments in AK, ID, ME, MI, MN, MT, NH, NY, ND, OH, PA, VT, WA, and WI for specific categories of expenses associated with the handling and processing of federally initiated cases along the Northern Border.

Eligible applicants: states (includes DC, public IHEs and hospitals).

Eligible beneficiaries: state and local governments.

Range/Average: N.A.

Activity: N.A.

HQ: State Policy Office, Bureau of Justice Assistance-DOJ, 810 7th St., NW, Washington, DC 20531. Phone: (202) 514-7057; Toll Free: (866) 859-2647.

Internet: www.ojp.usdoj.gov/nbpi. (Note: no field offices for this program.)

16.815   TRIBAL CIVIL AND CRIMINAL LEGAL ASSISTANCE GRANTS, TRAINING AND TECHNICAL ASSISTANCE (TCCLA TTA)

Assistance: project grants (100 percent).

Purposes: pursuant to the Indian Tribal Justice Technical and Legal Assistance Act of 2000, to enhance tribal court systems and improve access to civil and criminal court systems through legal services and support the development and enhancement of tribal justice systems.

Eligible applicants/beneficiaries: non-profit organizations with a tax status of 501(c)(3) under the Internal Revenue Service (IRS) Code, including tribal enterprises and educational institutions (public, private, and tribal colleges or universities) that provide legal assistance services for Federally-recognized Indian tribes, members of Federally-recognized Indian tribes, or tribal justice systems pursuant to Federal poverty guidelines.

Range: $150,000 to $625,000. **Average:** N.A.

Activity: N.A.

HQ: Department of Justice, Office of Justice Programs, Bureau of Justice Assistance, 810 7th St., NW, Washington, DC 20531. Phone: (877) 927-5657.

Internet: www.bja.gov. (Note: no field offices for this program.)

16.817   BYRNE CRIMINAL JUSTICE INNOVATION PROGRAM (BCJI)

Assistance: project grants/discretionary (100 percent/to 3 years).

Purposes: to improve community safety by designing and implementing effective, comprehensive approaches to addressing crime within a targeted neighborhood as part of a broader strategy to advance neighborhood revitalization and deter future crime through cross-sector community-based partnerships.

Eligible applicants/beneficiaries: states, unit of local governments, non-profit organizations, federally-recognized Indian tribal governments.

Range: $175,000 to $1,000,000. **Average:** N.A.

Activity: N.A.

HQ: Office of Justice Programs, Bureau of Justice Assistance, DOJ, 810 7th St., NW, Washington, DC 20531. Phone: (202) 616-6500, (866) 859-2647.

Internet: www.bja.gov. (Note: no field offices for this program.)

16.818   CHILDREN EXPOSED TO VIOLENCE
("Defending Childhood")

Assistance: project grants; discretionary (100 percent/3 to 4 years).

Purposes: pursuant to the Department of Justice Appropriations Act of 2012, funds support prevention, intervention, treatment, and community organizing strategies and to implement a comprehensive continuum of care for children and teens (birth through age 17) and their families exposed to violence in the home, school, and community.

Eligible applicants: states, unit of local governments, non-profit organizations, independent school districts, federally-recognized Indian tribal governments, public housing authorities/Indian housing authorities.

Eligible beneficiaries: children exposed to violence, their families, schools, and communities.

Range: to $2,500,000. **Average:** N.A.

Activity: N.A.

HQ: Director, Office of Justice Programs, Office of Juvenile Justice and Delinquency Prevention, DOJ, 810 7th St., NW, Washington, DC 20531. Phone: (202) 616-3637; FAX: (202) 353-9093.

Internet: ojjdp.ncjrs.org. (Note: no field offices for this program.)

16.819   NATIONAL FORUM ON YOUTH VIOLENCE PREVENTION

Assistance: project grants/discretionary (100 percent/2 to 3 years).

Purposes: pursuant to the Department of Justice Appropriations Act of 2012, to provide training and technical assistance to localities participating in the Forum and to assist the Forum Coordination Team (FCT) with the development and support of new Forum sites with the goals of more effectively addressing youth violence through multi-disciplinary partnerships, balanced approaches, data-driven strategies, comprehensive planning and the sharing of common challenges and promising strategies.

Eligible applicants/beneficiaries: 35 IHEs selected by the CDC as Prevention Research Centers (PRCs).

Range/Average: N.A.

Activity: N.A.

HQ: Director, Office of Justice Programs, Office of Juvenile Justice and Delinquency Prevention, 810 7th St., NW, Washington, DC 20531. Phone: (202) 514-3913.

Internet: ojjdp.ncjrs.org. (Note: no field offices for this program.)

16.820   POSTCONVICTION TESTING OF DNA EVIDENCE TO EXONERATE THE INNOCENT
("Kirk Bloodsworth Program")

Assistance: project grants/discretionary (100 percent/to 2 years).

Purposes: pursuant to the Department of Justice Appropriations Act of 2012, to help defray state costs associated with postconviction DNA testing of cases of violent felony offenses where actual innocence might be demonstrated. Funding may be used to review postconviction violent felony cases (as defined by state law), and to locate and analyze biological evidence samples associated with these cases. Where a strong justification is provided, up to 15 percent of federal award may be used for permissible case identification activities.

Eligible applicants/beneficiaries: 35 IHEs selected by the CDC as Prevention Research Centers (PRCs).

Range/Average: N.A.

Activity: N.A.

HQ: Director, Office of Justice Programs, National Institute of Justice, DOJ, 810 7th St., NW, Washington, DC 20531. Phone: (202) 532-0118.

Internet: www.nij.gov. (Note: no field offices for this program.)

16.822   NATIONAL CENTER FOR CAMPUS PUBLIC SAFETY
("National Center")

Assistance: project grants/cooperative agreements (100 percent/2 years).

Purposes: pursuant to the Consolidated and Further Continuing Appropriations Act of 2013, cooperative agreement to create National Center, a resource for campus police chiefs, directors of public safety, emergency managers, and key campus safety stakeholders. The National Center will be a think tank and clearinghouse for the identification and dissemination of information, research, training, and promising best practices and emerging issues in campus public safety; it will also serve to connect resources with the needs of constituents, and facilitate coordination between major campus public safety entities, and with federal agencies.

Eligible applicants/beneficiaries: state and local governments, public and private organizations.

Range: to $1,000,000. **Average:** N.A.

Activity: 1 award.

HQ: Office of Justice Programs, Bureau of Justice Assistance, DOJ, 810 7th St., NW, Washington, DC 20531. Phone: (202) 616-6500; Toll Free: (866) 859-2647.

Internet: www.bja.gov. (Note: no field offices for this program.)

16.824   EMERGENCY LAW ENFORCEMENT ASSISTANCE GRANT (EFLEA)

Assistance: project grants (100 percent).

Purposes: pursuant to the Justice Assistance Act of 1984, assistance to (and through) a state government to provide an adequate response to an uncommon situation that requires law enforcement or threatens to become of serious or epidemic proportions, and in which state and local resources are inadequate to protect the lives and property of citizens or to enforce the criminal law. Assistance can be used for personnel costs, to include overtime or straight time for officers affected by the emergency situation. The funds may not be used for planning or other activities related to crowd control for general public safety projects, or for a situation requiring the enforcement of laws associated with scheduled public events, including political conventions and sporting events.

Eligible applicants: states.

Eligible beneficiaries: state/local governments, Indian tribal governments.

Range/Average: N.A.

Activity: N.A.

HQ: Programs Office, BJA-OJP-DOJ, 810 7th St., NW, Washington, DC 20531. Phone: (202) 616-6500.

Internet: www.bja.gov. (Note: no field offices for this program.)

16.825   SMART PROSECUTION INITIATIVE

Assistance: project grants (100 percent).

Purposes: funds to support research and evaluation of prosecutors use of innovative, best practice or evidenced-based approaches to achieving the goals of promoting the fair, impartial and expeditious pursuit of justice; ensuring safer communities; and promoting integrity in the prosecution profession and effective coordination in the criminal justice system. The Smart Prosecution program seeks to encourage exploration of new solutions to public safety concerns, as well as internal operations and organizational structure, while employing a research partner at the problem-definition stage through assessment of strategies and solutions. Smart Prosecution applicants will identify a problem to be addressed and enlist a local research partner to help assess the effectiveness of their Smart Prosecution Effort.

Eligible applicants: for site-based awards, applicants limited to state, local, and tribal prosecutor agencies or a government agency acting as fiscal agent for the applicant. For training and technical assistance funds, applicants are limited to for-profit (commercial) organizations, nonprofit organizations, and IHEs that support national initiatives to improve the functioning of the criminal justice system. For-profit organizations must agree to waive any profit or fees for services.

Eligible beneficiaries: anyone/general public.

Range/Average: N.A.

Activity: N.A.

HQ: Director, Office of Justice Programs, BJA-DOJ, 810 7th St., NW, Washington, DC 20531. Phone: (202) 616-6500.

Internet: www.bja.gov. (Note: no field offices for this program.)

16.826 VISION 21

Assistance: project grants (100 percent).

Purposes: pursuant to the Department of Justice Appropriations Act of 2014, funds to improve assistance and services for victims of crime by addressing the need for more victim-related data, research and program evaluation, holistic legal assistance for crime victims, resources for tribal victims, and capacity building to provide technology and evidence-based training and technical assistance. The Office for Victims of Crime will undertake several initiatives related to Vision 21 and grantees must address one of these initiatives. These include: tribal assistance for victims of violence, funding and enhancing the provision of direct victim services, funding to states to address victims multiple legal issues through a coordinated community network of "wraparound" pro bono legal services, and to help jurisdictions build their technological infrastructure to improve provision of services to victims of crime.

Eligible applicants: victim assistance and compensation programs in the states, the District of Columbia, Puerto Rico, the U.S. Virgin Islands, American Samoa, Guam, and the Northern Mariana Islands; public and private nonprofit organizations, colleges and universities, and other public institutions or organizations; federally recognized Indian tribal governments, tribal consortia consisting of two or more federally recognized Indian tribes, and tribal designees.

Eligible beneficiaries: state, local government agencies, federally recognized Indian tribal governments, U.S. territories, public and private nonprofit institution/organizations, other public and private institution/organizations, Native American organizations, anyone/general public.

Range: $250,000 to $1,000,000. **Average:** N.A.

Activity: N.A.

HQ: Director, Vision 21, OVC-DOJ, 810 7th St., NW, Washington, DC 20531. Phone: (800) 363-0441.

Internet: ojp.gov/ovc. (Note: no field offices for this program.)

16.827 JUSTICE REINVESTMENT INITIATIVE (JRI)

Assistance: project grants (50 to 100 percent).

Purposes: funds to support the Justice Reinvestment Race to the Top program (JRR2T), which is designed to cement or amplify the goals of states efforts under the Justice Reinvestment Initiative (JRI). The JRI convenes states justice system stakeholders and policy leaders to devise data-driven approaches to criminal justice reform designed to generate cost savings that can be reinvested in high-performing public safety strategies. The objectives of the JRR2T Program are to: increase corrections costs saved or avoided by reducing unnecessary confinement; increase reinvestment in evidence-based practices that reduce recidivism; support justice reinvestment reform efforts by promoting and increasing collaboration among agencies and officials who work in criminal justice; and enhance the translation of evidence into practice by supporting the use of data analysis results to inform policy decisions.

Eligible applicants: state and tribal governments.

Eligible beneficiaries: anyone/general public.

Range/Average: N.A.

Activity: N.A.

HQ: Director, JRI, BJA-DOJ, 810 7th St., NW, Washington, DC 20531. Phone: (202) 616-6500.

Internet: www.bja.gov/jri. (Note: no field offices for this program.)

16.828 SWIFT, CERTAIN, AND FAIR (SCF) SANCTIONS PROGRAM—REPLICATING THE CONCEPTS BEHIND PROJECT HOPE

Assistance: project grants/cooperative agreements (100 percent/12 to 18 months).

Purposes: project grants to support the implementation and enhancement of SAC/HOPE program models of supervision of offenders in the community. SAC models are intended to: improve supervision strategies that reduce recidivism; promote and increase collaboration among agencies and officials who work in community corrections and related fields; enhance the offenders perception that the supervision decisions are fair, consistently applied and consequences are transparent; and improve the outcomes of individuals participating in these initiatives. The goals of this program are to develop and enhance SAC initiatives and implement these SAC models with fidelity, resulting in reduced recidivism and better outcomes for program participants. Funds may be used to help state, local, and tribal agencies develop or improve their SAC programs.

Eligible applicants: states, local units of government, federally recognized Indian tribes.

Eligible beneficiaries: anyone/general public.

Range: to $350,000. **Average:** N.A.

Activity: N.A.

HQ: Director, SAC/HOPE, BJA-DOJ, 810 7th St., NW, Washington, DC 20531. Phone: (202) 616-6500.

Internet: www.bja.gov. (Note: no field offices for this program.)

16.835 BODY WORN CAMERA POLICY AND IMPLEMENTATION

Assistance: cooperative agreements. (50 percent/to 2 years).

Purposes: pursuant to the Consolidated and Further Continuing Appropriations Act of 2016, to improve law enforcement's interactions with the public and to increase both trust and communication between the police and the communities they serve through the use of body-worn cameras by police.

Eligible applicants/beneficiaries: federal, state, local, and tribal criminal justice agengies.

Range/Average: N.A.

Activity: N.A.

HQ: BWC Policy Advisor, Office of Justice Programs, Bureau of Justice Assistance, DOJ, 810 7th St., NW, Washington, DC 20531. Phone: (202) 616-6500.

Internet: www.bja.gov. (Note: no field offices for this program.)

16.836 INDIGENT DEFENSE

Assistance: cooperative agreements/discretionary grants. (100 percent/to 3 years).

Purposes: pursuant to the Consolidated Appropriations Act of 2016, to develop strategic plans to enhance the state's capacity to deliver high-quality, fair, and comprehensive legal services to youth who have come into contact with the juvenile justice system. Funds may be used for a broad range of related activities including engaging key leaders, building staff knowledge, developing new programs, services, policies, practices and procedures, and developing training and outreach materials on the new policies.

Eligible applicants: states and territories, tribal governments, nonprofit and for-profit organizations and IHEs.

Eligible beneficiaries: youth and juvenile delinquents.

Range: $125,000 to$1,280,000. **Average:** N.A.

Activity: N.A.

HQ: Office of Justice Programs, Office of Juvenile Justice and Delinquency Prevention, DOJ, 810 7th St., NW, Washington, DC 20531. Phone: (202) 514-4817.

Internet: www.ojjdp.gov. (Note: no field offices for this program.)

16.888 CONSOLIDATED AND TECHNICAL ASSISTANCE GRANT PROGRAM TO ADDRESS CHILDREN AND YOUTH EXPERIENCING DOMESTIC AND SEXUAL VIOLENCE AND ENGAGE MEN AND BOYS AS ALLIES

Assistance: project grants (100 percent).

Purposes: pursuant to the Consolidated and Further Continuing Appropriations Act, to provide services to advocate for and respond to youth victims of domestic violence, dating violence, sexual assault, and stalking; assistance to children and youth exposed to such violence; programs to encourage men and youth in preventing such violence; and assistance to middle and high school students through educating and other services related to such violence.

Eligible applicants/beneficiaries: nonprofit, nongovernmental entities with the demonstrated primary goal of providing services to children or youth exposed to or victims of domestic violence, dating violence, sexual assault, or stalking; Non-profit, nongovernmental entities with demonstrated histories of providing comprehensive services to children or youth exposed to or victims of domestic violence, dating violence, sexual assault, or stalking; Nonprofit, nongovernmental entities with demonstrated histories of creating effective public education and/or community organizing campaigns to encourage men and boys to work as allies with women and girls to prevent sexual assault, domestic violence, dating violence, and stalking; Indian Tribes or tribal nonprofit organizations that provides services to tribal children and youth exposed to or are of domestic violence, dating violence, sexual assault, or stalking; Territorial, Tribal or unit of local government entities.

Range/Average: N.A.

Activity: N.A.

HQ: Director, 145 N St., NE, Washington DC, 20530. Phone: (202) 307-0344.

Internet: N.A. (Note: no field offices for this program.)

16.889   GRANTS FOR OUTREACH AND SERVICES TO UNDERSERVED POPULATIONS
("Underserved Program")

Assistance: project grants (to 100 percent).

Purposes: Project grants to develop and implement outreach strategies targeted at adult or youth victims of domestic violence, dating violence, sexual assault, or stalking in underserved populations and to provide victim services. Grants can be used for the following program purpose areas: working with Federal, State, tribal, territorial and local governments, agencies, and organizations to develop or enhance population specific services; strengthening the capacity of underserved populations to provide population specific services; strengthening the capacity of traditional victim service providers to provide population specific services; strengthening the effectiveness of criminal and civil justice interventions by providing training for law enforcement, prosecutors, judges and other court personnel on domestic violence, dating violence, sexual assault, or stalking in underserved populations; or working in cooperation with an underserved population to develop and implement outreach, education, prevention, and intervention strategies that highlight available resources and the specific issues faced by victims of domestic violence, dating violence, sexual assault, or stalking from underserved populations.

Eligible applicants: public or private nonprofit organizations/institutions, and Native American organizations with demonstrated experience and expertise in providing population specific services in the relevant underserved communities, or population specific organizations working in partnership with a victim service provider or domestic violence or sexual assault coalition.

Eligible beneficiaries: anyone/general public.

Range: to $300,000. **Average:** N.A.

Activity: N.A.

HQ: Director, Underserved Program, VAW-DOJ, 145 N St., Ste. 10W121, Washington DC, 20530. Phone: (202) 305-1177.

Internet: www.ovw.usdoj.gov. (Note: no field offices for this program.)

16.922 EQUITABLE SHARING PROGRAM

Assistance: direct payments/specified use (cooperative agreements) (100 percent).

Purposes: pursuant to The Controlled Substances Act, to remove the tools of crime from criminal organizations, deprives wrongdoers of the proceeds of their crimes, recovers property that may be used to compensate victims, and deters crime. Authorizes the Attorney General to share federally forfeited property with participating and local law enforcement agencies.

Eligible applicants/beneficiaries: state or local law enforcement agency.

Range/Average: N.A.

Activity: N.A.

HQ: AFMLS ACA, 1400 New York Ave., NW, Washington DC, 20005. Phone: (202) 514-1263.

Internet: www.justice.gov/criminal/afmls/equitable-sharing. (Note: no field offices for this program.)

DEPARTMENT OF LABOR

17.002 LABOR FORCE STATISTICS

Assistance: project grants; technical information (100 percent).

Purposes: to provide statistical data on and analyses of labor force activities—e.g., employment and unemployment, wages, occupations, layoffs, plant closings. Quarterly and monthly reports are produced, providing national, state, and local analyses. The data and analyses appear in BLS publications such as "Monthly Labor Review," "Unemployment in States and Local Areas," and "Handbook of Labor Statistics" published by BLS.

Eligible applicants/beneficiaries: cooperative agreement grants—State Workforce Agencies (SWAs) or alternate agencies. Information—anyone (from SWAs and BLS).

Range: $78,500 to $7,385,000. **Average:** $1,355,000.

Activity: N.A.

HQ: Office of Employment and Unemployment Statistics, BLS-DOL, 2 Massachusetts Ave., NE, Washington, DC 20212. Phone: (202) 691-6400.

Internet: www.bls.gov.

17.003   PRICES AND COST OF LIVING DATA

Assistance: technical information.

Purposes: to provide statistical data for use in evaluating consumer, producer, export, and import prices and price changes, and consumer expenditures. Data are published periodically in the "Consumer Price Index," "Producer Price Index," international price indexes, and "Consumer Expenditure Surveys," as well as in other research and study reports.

Eligible applicants/beneficiaries: general public.

Range/Average: N.A.

Activity: N.A.

HQ: Office of Prices and Living Conditions, BLS-DOL, 2 Massachusetts Ave., NE, Washington, DC 20212. Phone: (202) 606-6960.

Internet: www.bls.gov.

17.004   PRODUCTIVITY AND TECHNOLOGY DATA

Assistance: technical information.

Purposes: to provide and analyze data and trends on productivity and technology in major sectors of the U.S. economy and specific industries, and in selected countries. Pertinent reports are published, found in "Major Programs-Bureau of Labor Statistics." Also produced periodically are: consumer price indexes in foreign countries; international comparisons of productivity, labor costs, and the labor force and unemployment.

Eligible applicants/beneficiaries: general public.

Range/Average: N.A.

Activity: N.A.

HQ: Office of Productivity and Technology, BLS-DOL, 2 Massachusetts Ave., NE, Washington, DC 20212. Phone: (202) 691-6304.

Internet: www.bls.gov.

17.005   COMPENSATION AND WORKING CONDITIONS

Assistance: project grants (cooperative grants); technical information (50 percent).

Purposes: to develop and publish data on levels and trends in wages, employee benefits, compensation, occupational safety and health, and work stoppages.

Eligible applicants/beneficiaries: cooperative agreements—state and local governments to operate statistical programs concerning occupational health and safety. Technical information—general public.

Range: $8,000 to $718,000. **Average:** $128,000.

Activity: N.A.

HQ: Office of Productivity and Technology, BLS-DOL, 2 Massachusetts Ave., NE, Washington, DC 20212. Phone: (202) 691-6300.

Internet: www.bls.gov.

17.150   EMPLOYEE BENEFITS SECURITY ADMINISTRATION (EBSA)

Assistance: technical information.

Purposes: pursuant to the Employee Retirement Income Security Act of 1974 as amended (ERISA), to protect the pension, health care, and other employee benefit plans of workers and their families, by: requiring reporting and disclosure of plan and financial information; developing and enforcing fiduciary standards; providing technical assistance, advisory and informational services, workshops and conferences; deterring and correcting violations of statutes through education, voluntary compliance, and civil and criminal enforcement actions. More than $4.8 trillion in assets are under control of ERISA, covering some 6,700,000 benefit plans with 150,000,000 participants.

Eligible applicants/beneficiaries: plan administrators, trustees, participants, beneficiaries.

Range/Average: N.A.

Activity: N.A.

HQ: EBSA-DOL, 200 Constitution Ave., NW, Rm. N5623, Washington, DC 20210. Phone: (866) 444-3272.

Internet: www.dol.gov/ebsa.

17.201   REGISTERED APPRENTICESHIP
("Fitzgerald Act")

Assistance: advisory services/counseling; project grants.

Purposes: pursuant to the National Apprenticeship Act of 1937 as amended, to assist industry in developing, expanding, and improving apprenticeship and other training programs; to register apprentices and programs; to provide technical assistance to state apprenticeship councils; to ensure equal employment opportunities in registered apprenticeship and other training programs. (Apprentice wage rates are exempt from prevailing wages requirements of the Davis-Bacon Act and the Service Contract Act when federal and state programs are registered.)

Eligible applicants: employers, groups or associations of employers, and individual employers—with or without union participation; for grants: community- and faith- based organizations.

Eligible beneficiaries: individuals at least age 16 with sufficient ability, aptitude, and education to master the rudiments of the trade or occupation and to satisfactorily complete required theoretical instruction.

Range/Average: N.A.

Activity: 500,000 active apprentices in FY 2016.

HQ: Administrator, Office of Apprenticeship Training, Employer and Labor Services (OATELS), ETA-DOL, Frances Perkins Bldg., 200 Constitution Ave., NW, N-5311, Washington, DC 20210. Phone: (202) 693-2796; FAX: (202) 693-3799.

Internet: www.doleta.gov/oa.

17.207   EMPLOYMENT SERVICE—WAGNER-PEYSER FUNDED ACTIVITIES ("Wagner-Peyser Act")

Assistance: formula grants; project grants. (100 percent/formula grants, to 3 years).

Purposes: pursuant to the Wagner-Peyser Act of 1933 as amended, ARRA, 2009 and Workforce Investment Act of 1998 (WIA), for states to provide "One-Stop" job finding, counseling, recruitment, referral, re-employment, and placement services, including a computerized interstate listing of hard-to-fill openings, and testing services for job seekers and employers seeking qualified workers—in cooperation with the DOL's U.S. Employment Service nationwide network of public employment offices. Specialized services may be provided for groups such as veterans, migrant and seasonal farm workers, ex-offenders, and the disabled, disadvantaged, youth, minorities, and older workers.

Eligible applicants: states, DC, VI, PR, Guam.

Eligible beneficiaries: employers seeking workers; persons seeking employment; associated groups. Veterans receive priority, with handicapped veterans receiving preferential treatment.

Range/Average: N.A.

Activity: N.A.

HQ: Administrator, Office of Workforce Security, U.S. Employment Service, ETA-DOL, 200 Constitution Ave., NW, Rm. C-4526, Washington, DC 20210. Phone: 202-693-3052; FAX: 202-693-3981.

Internet: www.doleta.gov. (Note: no field offices for this program.)

17.225   UNEMPLOYMENT INSURANCE

Assistance: formula grants; direct payments/unrestricted use.

Purposes: pursuant to SSA, Trade Act of 1974, Federal Unemployment Tax Act, Federal Employees and Ex-Service Members Act, ARRA 2009, Robert T. Stafford Disaster Relief and Emergency Assistance Act, and amendments, to administer state programs providing unemployment compensation, trade adjustment and disaster unemployment assistance, and unemployment compensation for eligible workers, federal employees, and ex-service members. State unemployment insurance tax collections fund benefit payments; federal unemployment insurance tax collections fund state administrative costs, and reimburse states for one-half the costs of extended benefits paid under SSA and the Federal Unemployment Tax Act; benefits to former federal civilian employees and ex-service members are paid out of the Federal Employees Compensation Account in the Unemployment Trust Fund, and reimbursed by the former employing agency; Trade Adjustment Assistance payments and training costs are paid out of the Federal Unemployment Benefits and Allowance Appropriation account in the Unemployment Trust Fund; Disaster Unemployment Assistance is paid by FEMA.

Eligible applicants: state workforce agencies, including in DC, PR, and VI.

Eligible beneficiaries: workers with wages subject to state unemployment laws, federal civilian employees, ex-servicemembers, workers whose unemployment resulted from trade imports, workers whose unemployment resulted from a Presidentially declared disaster—all are eligible if they are involuntarily unemployed, able to and available for work, and meet state eligibility and qualifying requirements. Individual state eligibility requirements are available from local "One Stop" career centers.

Range: $1,500,000 to $366,000,000. **Average:** $50,000,000.

Activity: anticipate 9.2 million beneficiaries in FY 2016.

HQ: Administrator, Office of Workforce Security, ETA-DOL, 200 Constitution Ave., NW, Rm. S4524, Washington, DC 20210. Phone: (202) 693-3029.

Internet: ows.doleta.gov/unemploy.

17.235 SENIOR COMMUNITY SERVICE EMPLOYMENT PROGRAM ("SCSEP - Older Worker Program")

Assistance: formula grants; project grants (90 percent).

Purposes: pursuant to ARRA and Older Americans Act of 1965 as amended, to provide, foster, and promote useful part-time (usually 20 hours weekly) training and work opportunities for unemployed persons age 55 or over—in community service activities such as schools, hospitals, day care centers, park systems, public housing projects, weatherization and nutrition programs, libraries, etc. Training, counseling, and other supportive services may be provided. The program also assists and promotes the transition of enrollees into unsubsidized employment.

Eligible applicants: states; national public and private nonprofit agencies and organizations other than political parties; tribal organizations.

Eligible beneficiaries: adults age 55 or older, with family income at or below 125 percent of the HHS poverty level.

Range: $324,965 to $84,200,000. **Average:** N.A.

Activity: N.A.

HQ: Division of Adult Services, Office of Workforce Investment, ETA-DOL, 200 Constitution Ave., NW, Rm. C-4510, Washington, DC 20210. Phone: (202) 693-3645; FAX: (202) 693-3015.

Internet: www.doleta.gov/seniors.

17.245 TRADE ADJUSTMENT ASSISTANCE

Assistance: direct payments/unrestricted use; formula grants (to 78 weeks).

Purposes: pursuant to the Trade Act of 1974 as amended, Omnibus Trade and Competitiveness Act of 1988, North American Free Trade Agreement Implementation Act, and other acts, to provide "adjustment assistance" payments to and assistance for workers adversely affected by increased imports—including relocation allowances, job testing, counseling, training, and placement services. Payments may be made only after state unemployment compensation benefits have been exhausted. The maximum number of weeks of state unemployment compensation, extended benefits, and trade readjustment allowances may not exceed 52—except that benefits may be paid for an additional 26 weeks to workers participating in approved training.

Eligible applicants: groups of three of more workers, or their union or authorized representative, working with designated state agencies.

Eligible beneficiaries: unemployed workers certified by DOL as eligible to apply for adjustment assistance, and meeting specific other requirements.

Range/Average: N.A.

Activity: N.A.

HQ: Director, Division of Trade Adjustment Assistance, ETA-DOL, 200 Constitution Ave., NW, Washington, DC 20210. Phone: (202) 693-3628.

Internet: www.doleta.gov/tradeact.

17.258 WIA/WIOA ADULT PROGRAM

Assistance: formula grants. (100 percent/to 3 years).

Purposes: pursuant to ARRA 2009 and WIA, for workforce investment activities that increase the unsubsidized employment, retention and earnings, and occupational skill attainment of participants, through One Stop Career Centers providing three levels of services: (1) "core," including outreach, job search and placement assistance, and labor market information; (2) "intensive," with comprehensive assessments, individual employment plans, counseling, and career planning; (3) "training," including occupation and basic skills, linked to job opportunities. Such supportive services as transportation and child care may also be provided.

Eligible applicants: states, DC, PR, and outlying areas, which allocate funds to Workforce Investment Boards.

Eligible beneficiaries: adults age 18 or older, with priority to public assistance recipients and other low-income individuals.

Range/Average: N.A.

Activity: N.A.

HQ: Director, ETA, DOL, 200 Constitution Ave., NW, Rm. C-4526, Washington, DC 20210. Phone: (202) 693-3937.

Internet: www.doleta.gov.

17.259 WIA/WIOA YOUTH ACTIVITIES

Assistance: formula grants (to 3 years).

Purposes: pursuant to ARRA 2009 and WIA, to help low-income youth acquire the educational and occupational skills, training, and support needed to achieve academic and employment success and make the transition to successful careers and productive adulthood. Funds may be used by local workforce investment boards for: employment and training activities; mentoring; supportive services; and, to develop opportunities for leadership development, citizenship, and community service.

Eligible applicants: state governors.

Eligible beneficiaries: individuals age 14-21 whose total family income does not exceed the higher of the poverty line or 70 percent of the lower living standard income, and are deficient in basic literacy skills, or school dropouts, homeless, runaways, foster children, pregnant or parents, offenders or require additional assistance to complete their education or secure and hold employment.

Range/Average: N.A.

Activity: N.A.

HQ: Division of Youth Services, Office of Workforce Investment, ETA-DOL, 200 Constitution Ave., NW, Washington, DC 20210. Phone: (202) 693-3377; FAX: (202) 693-3861.

Internet: www.doleta.gov/youth_services.

17.260   WIA DISLOCATED WORKERS

Assistance: formula grants; project grants. (100 percent/formula, 3 years).

Purposes: pursuant to WIA, to assist dislocated workers in obtaining the services that increase the unsubsidized employment, retention and earnings, and occupational skill attainment of participants, through One Stop Career Centers providing three levels of services: (1) "core," including outreach, job search and placement assistance, and labor market information; (2) "intensive," with comprehensive assessments, individual employment plans, counseling, and career planning; (3) "training," including occupation and basic skills, linked to job opportunities. Such supportive services as transportation and child care may also be provided. National Emergency Grant funds also are available under this program (see eligibility factors below).

Eligible applicants: states, DC, PR, and outlying areas, including for National Emergency Grant funds.

Eligible beneficiaries: workers that have lost their jobs, including those dislocated because of plant closings or mass layoffs, and unlikely to return to their previous industry or occupations; formerly self-employed individuals; displaced, dependent homemakers no longer supported by the other's income. National Emergency Grant Funds—same eligibility; also includes certain military defense employees and individuals affected by mass layoffs, natural disasters, federal government actions, and other specified circumstances.

Range/Average: N.A.

Activity: N.A.

HQ: Office of Workforce Investments, ETA-DOL, 200 Constitution Ave., NW, Rm. S-4209, Washington, DC 20210. Phone: (202) 693-3587.

Internet: www.doleta.gov.

17.261   WIA/WIOA PILOTS, DEMONSTRATIONS, AND RESEARCH PROJECTS

Assistance: project grants. (to 100 percent/1-2 years).

Purposes: pursuant to WIA, for pilot and demonstration projects with interstate validity, addressing national employment and training problems. Projects must include direct services to individuals to enhance employment opportunities, and an evaluation component. Eligible activities include: establishing advanced manufacturing technology skill centers involving local partnerships; training to upgrade the skills of employed workers or to increase employment of out-of-school youth residing in enterprise communities or empowerment zones; joint programs with DOD to develop training programs using innovative learning technology; distance learning projects; partnerships with national organizations experienced in employment and training programs; assistance to public housing authorities providing resident job training; local project evaluation.

Eligible applicants/beneficiaries: state and local governments, federal agencies, private nonprofit and profit organizations including religious and community-based, and educational institutions.

Range: $200,000 to $1,000,000. **Average:** $500,000.

Activity: N.A.

HQ: Division of Pilots, Demonstrations and Research, Office of Policy and Research, ETA-DOL, 200 Constitution Ave., NW, Rm. N-5641, Washington, DC 20210. Phone: (202) 693-3179.

Internet: www.doleta.gov.

17.264 NATIONAL FARMWORKER JOBS PROGRAM (NFJP)

Assistance: formula grants; project grants. (100 percent/1-4 years).

Purposes: pursuant to WIA, for individual employability development assistance and related services to migrant and seasonal farm workers and their dependents suffering chronic unemployment and under-employment. Services may include initial assessment, "One-Stop Center" services, job placement, eligibility determination, intensive case management, basic education, drop-out prevention assistance, allowance payments, training including classroom and on-the-job, and emergency and other supportive services.

Eligible applicants: public agencies and state and local government units; private nonprofit organizations.

Eligible beneficiaries: individuals who, during any consecutive 12 months in the prior 24-month period, were seasonal or migrant farm workers, and are legally available for work in compliance with Selective Service Act requirements.

Range/Average: N.A.

Activity: N.A.

HQ: Division of Adult Services, Office of Workforce Investment, ETA-DOL, 200 Constitution Ave., NW, Rm. C-4510, Washington, DC 20210. Phone: (202) 693-3639.

Internet: www.doleta.gov/Farmworker/html/NFJP.cfm.

17.265 NATIVE AMERICAN EMPLOYMENT AND TRAINING ("Section 166 Program")

Assistance: project grants. (100 percent/1-3 years).

Purposes: pursuant to ARRA 2009 and WIA, for employment and training activities for native Americans, including classroom and on-the-job training, work experience, youth employment programs. Grant funds may be used to pay for such services as day care, health care, job search, relocation and transportation allowances.

Eligible applicants/beneficiaries: tribes, bands, or groups; Alaska native villages or groups; Hawaiian native communities; consortia of the foregoing groups.

Range: $1,000 to $5,000,000. **Average:** N.A.

Activity: N.A.

HQ: Indian and Native American Programs, Division of Adult Services, Office of Workforce Investment, ETA-DOL, 200 Constitution Ave., NW, Rm. S-4209, Washington, DC 20210. Phone: (972) 850-4637; FAX: (972) 850-4605.

Internet: www.doleta.gov/dinap. (Note: no field offices for this program.)

17.267 INCENTIVE GRANTS—WIA SECTION 503 ("WIA Incentive Grants ")

Assistance: formula grants; project grants. (100 percent/to 3 years).

Purposes: pursuant to WIA and the Carl D. Perkins Vocational and Applied Technology Education Amendments of 1998, for innovative programs furthering the purposes of the authorizing acts—including services and activities beyond those provided with regular WIA funding. Applicants should plan activities promoting cooperation and collaboration among administering agencies.

Eligible applicants/beneficiaries: states, DC, VI, PR, Guam—provided their performance under WIA exceeds expected outcome levels.

Range: N.A. **Average:** $3,000,000.

Activity: N.A.

HQ: Chief, Division of System Accomplishments and Accountability, Office of Performance and Technology, ETA-DOL, 200 Constitution Ave., NW, Rm. N-5641, Washington, DC 20210. Phone: (202) 693-3733.

Internet: www.doleta.gov/performance.

17.268 H-1B JOB TRAINING GRANTS

Assistance: project grants. (from 50 percent/1-3 years).

Purposes: pursuant to the American Competitiveness and Workforce Improvement Act of 1998, to engage business, educational and the workforce investment system to work together to develop solutions to the workforce challenges facing high growth industries. The ETA has identified 14 sectors that are projected to add substantial numbers of jobs to the economy or are existing or emerging businesses being transformed by technology or innovation and require new skills for workers: Advanced Manufacturing, Aerospace, Automotive, Biotechnology, Construction, Energy, Financial Services, Geospatial Technology, Health Care, Homeland Security, Hospitality, Information Technology, Retail, and Transportation.

Eligible applicants/beneficiaries: generally, public and private for-profit and non-profit organizations, including businesses, trade associations, Workforce Investment Boards, One-Stop Career Centers, units of state and local government, economic development agencies, education and training providers including community colleges and other faith-based organizations.

Range: $1,000,000 to $5,000,000. **Average:** N.A.

Activity: N.A.

HQ: Business Relations Group, Office of Workforce Investment, ETA-DOL, 200 Constitution Ave., NW - Rm. N-4526, Washington, DC 20210. Phone: (202) 693-2822.

Internet: www.doleta.gov.

17.270   REINTEGRATION OF EX-OFFENDERS

Assistance: project grants. (100 percent/1-3 years).

Purposes: pursuant to WIA, to reduce prisoner recidivism by helping inmates find work when they return to their communities through employment-centered programs that incorporate mentoring, job training and placement, and other comprehensive transitional services.

Eligible applicants: religious and other community organizations located or with a staff presence in the urban community being served, and with the capacity to serve as the lead project agencies.

Eligible beneficiaries: individuals age 18 or older that have been convicted as an adult and imprisoned pursuant to an Act of Congress or state law, and that have never been convicted of a violent or sex-related offense—including those residing in a halfway house.

Range/Average: N.A.

Activity: N.A.

HQ: Division of Youth Services, Office of Workforce Investment, ETA-DOL, 200 Constitution Ave., NW, Rm. N-4511, Washington, DC 20210. Phone: (202) 693-3603.

Internet: www.doleta.gov. (Note: no field offices for this program.)

17.271   WORK OPPORTUNITY TAX CREDIT PROGRAM (WOTC)

Assistance: formula grants (100 percent).

Purposes: pursuant to Small Business Job Protection Act of 1996, Taxpayer relief Act of 1997 and Working Families Tax Relief Act of 2004, as amended, to assist individuals from 10 target groups who face significant barriers to employment move from economic dependency to self-sufficiency by encouraging employment by private-sector businesses in the form of a tax credit against the wages paid to new hires during the first year of employment.

Eligible applicants: states, DC, VI, PR; individuals may not apply.

Eligible beneficiaries: employers seeking WOTC and/or WTWTC target group workers and target group workers seeking employment. Workers must be verified by state workforce agencies before certification will be issued to employer.

Range: $66,000 to $2,420,358. **Average:** N.A.

Activity: N.A.

HQ: Division of Adult Services, Office of Workforce Investment, ETA-DOL, 200 Constitution Ave., NW, Rm. C-4510, Washington, DC 20210. Phone: (202) 693-3639.

Internet: www.doleta.gov/wotc.

17.272 PERMANENT LABOR CERTIFICATION FOR FOREIGN WORKERS

Assistance: specialized services.

Purposes: pursuant to Immigration and Nationality Act of 1952, as amended, to assist employers by supplementing the U.S. workforce with needed skills and assure that the jobs, wages, and working conditions of American workers will not be adversely affected by the admission of foreign workers.

Eligible applicants/beneficiaries: any employer who is unable to find qualified U.S. workers and who seeks to employ foreign workers in employment categories listed in DOL Schedule A (Part 656.10, Title 20, Code of Regulations).

Range/Average: N.A.

Activity: N.A.

HQ: Administrator, Office of Foreign Labor Certification, DOL, 200 Constitution Ave., NW, Washington, DC 20210. Phone: (202) 693-2865.

Internet: www.foreignlaborcert.doleta.gov. (Note: no field offices for this program.)

17.273 TEMPORARY LABOR CERTIFICATION FOR FOREIGN WORKERS

Assistance: formula grants; specialized services.

Purposes: pursuant to Immigration and Nationality Act of 1952, Immigration Act of 1990, and Immigration Reform and Control Act of 1986, as amended, to provide greater protection for U.S. and foreign workers without interfering with an employer's right to obtain temporary foreign workers to work in specialty occupations; to enable agricultural employers to obtain temporary seasonal employees when domestic workers are not available; to protect domestic workers against unfair competition from foreign workers; and to assure adequate working and living conditions for all workers.

Eligible applicants/beneficiaries: individual employers, partnership, corporation, association of agricultural producers, and other authorized agents may file on behalf of their employers or members. Grants related to H-2A and H-2B programs: State Workforce Agencies.

Range/Average: N.A.

Activity: N.A.

HQ: Administrator, Office of Foreign Labor Certification, DOL, 200 Constitution Ave., NW, Washington, DC 20210. Phone: (202) 693-2865.

Internet: www.foreignlaborcert.doleta.gov.

17.274 YOUTHBUILD

Assistance: project grants. (100 percent/2-3 years).

Purposes: pursuant to ARRA 2009, Workforce Investment Act (WIA) of 1998, Title I, Subtitle D, Section 173A, and other laws, to provide disadvantaged youth with: the education and employment skills necessary to achieve economic self sufficiency in occupations in high demand and postsecondary education and training opportunities; opportunities for meaningful work and service to their communities; and opportunities to develop employment and leadership skills and a commitment to community development among youth in low-income communities.

Eligible applicants: public or private nonprofit agency/organization (including a consortium of such agencies or organizations), including: community-based or faith-based organizations; an entity carrying out activities under this WIA, such as a local workforce investment board or One-Stop Career Center; a community action agency; a State or local housing development agency; an Indian tribe or other agency primarily serving Indians; a community development corporation; a State or local youth service conservation corps; or any other public or private non-profit entity that provides education or employment training and can meet the required elements of the grant.

Eligible beneficiaries: individuals who are between the ages of 16 and 24 on the date of enrollment, a member of a disadvantaged youth population (such as a member of a low-income family, or in foster care), a youth offender, an individual with a disability, a child of an incarcerated parent, a migrant youth and a school dropout. Up to 25 percent of the participants in the program may be youth who do not meet the education and disadvantaged criteria above but who are: basic skills deficient, despite attainment of a secondary school diploma, General Education Development (GED) credential, or other State-recognized equivalent; or have been referred by a local secondary school for participation in a YouthBuild program leading to the attainment of a secondary school diploma.

Range: $700,000 to $1,100,000. **Average:** N.A.

Activity: N.A.

HQ: Division of Youth Services, Office of Workforce Investment, Employment and Training Administration, DOL, 200 Constitution Ave., NW, Rm. N-4508 Washington, D.C. 20210. Phone: (202) 693-3110.

Internet: www.doleta.gov.

17.275 PROGRAM OF COMPETITIVE GRANTS FOR WORKER TRAINING AND PLACEMENT IN HIGH GROWTH AND EMERGING INDUSTRY SECTORS

Assistance: project grants (100 percent/1 to 3 years).

Purposes: pursuant to ARRA 2009, to provide competitive grants to used for worker training and placement in high-growth and emerging industry sectors: $500 million for research, labor exchange, and job training projects that prepare workers for careers in energy efficiency and renewable energy; $250 million for worker training and placement projects with a priority to projects that prepare workers for careers in the health sector.

Eligible applicants/beneficiaries: private/public institutions and organizations; small businesses.

Range/Average: N.A.

Activity: N.A.

HQ: Business Relations Group, Office of Workforce Investment, ETA-DOL, 200 Constitution Ave., NW, Washington, DC 20210. Phone: (202) 693-3177.

Internet: www.doleta.gov.

17.276   HEALTH CARE TAX CREDIT—NATIONAL EMERGENCY GRANTS

Assistance: project grants (100 percent).

Purposes: pursuant to ARRA 2009 and Trade Act of 1974 , as amended, Trade Adjustment Assistance (TAA) Reform Act of 2002, and Trade and Globalization Assistance Act of 2009, to provide health insurance coverage assistance and support-related services to eligible TAA-impacted workers and other eligible individuals. HCTC is administered by the IRS, equal to 80 percent of the amount paid by an eligible individual for qualified health coverage as specified in section 35 of the Internal Revenue Code. Monthly payments are made directly to a health plan administrator on behalf of participants, allowing them to receive the benefit on the tax credit at the time of need.

Eligible applicants: states (includes DC, public IHEs and hospitals).

Eligible beneficiaries: specialized group (ex. health professionals, students, veterans).

Range: $1,058,000 to $2,000,000. **Average:** $1,414,564.

Activity: N.A.

HQ: Administrator, Office of National Response, ETA-DOL, 200 Constitution Ave., NW, Rm. N-4702, Washington, DC 20210. Phone: (202) 693-2757.

Internet: www.doleta.gov/neg.

17.277   WIOA NATIONAL DISLOCATED WORKER AND WIA NATIONAL EMERGENCY GRANTS
("National Emergency Grants")

Assistance: project grants (100 percent/to 2 years).

Purposes: pursuant to ARRA of 2009, Title VIII and WIA of 1998 Title I, to temporarily expand service capacity at state and local levels by providing time-limited funding assistance in response to: plant closures; mass layoffs affecting 50 or more workers; special assistance, including health insurance coverage assistance to trade impacted workers and other individuals eligible under the Trade and Globalization Adjustment Assistance Act of 2009; or other significant dislocation events that cannot be accommodated within on-going operations of the formula-funded Dislocated Worker program.

Eligible applicants: states (includes DC, public IHEs and hospitals) and non-profit institutions/organizations.

Eligible beneficiaries: displaced workers and their families.

Range: $200,000 to $13,154,140. **Average:** $3,091,991.

Activity: N.A.

HQ: Director, ETA, DOL, 200 Constitution Ave., NW, Rm. C-4526, Washington, DC 20210. Phone: (202) 693-3937.

Internet: www.doleta.gov/neg.

17.278 WIA/WIOA DISLOCATED WORKER FORMULA GRANTS

Assistance: formula grants (100 percent).

Purposes: pursuant to ARRA of 2009, Title VIII and WIA of 1998 Title I, to reemploy dislocated workers through authorization of three levels of service, available to all job seekers from a qualified training provider: "core" services include outreach, job search and placement assistance, and labor market information; "intensive" services include more comprehensive assessments, development of individual employment plans and counseling, and career planning, available to those who could not find employment through core services; "training" services linked to community job opportunities, including both occupational training and training in basic skills, available to those who cannot find employment through intensive services. The Act also authorizes the provision of supportive services (e.g., transportation and child care assistance) to enable an individual to participate in the program.

Eligible applicants: states (includes DC, public IHEs and hospitals) and U.S. territories/possessions.

Eligible beneficiaries: unemployed.

Range/Average: N.A.

Activity: N.A.

HQ: Director, ETA, DOL, 200 Constitution Ave., NW, Rm. C-4526, Washington, DC 20210. Phone: (202) 693-3937.

Internet: www.doleta.gov.

17.280 WORKFORCE INVESTMENT ACT (WIA) DISLOCATED WORKER NATIONAL RESERVE DEMONSTRATION GRANTS

Assistance: project grants (100 percent/to 2 years).

Purposes: pursuant to the Workforce Investment Act, to carry out demonstration and pilot projects for the purpose of developing and implementing techniques and approaches, and demonstrating the effectiveness of specialized methods, in addressing the employment and training needs of Dislocated Workers.

Eligible applicants: state and local governments, federal agencies, private non-profit/for-profit organizations, including faith-based and community-based organizations, and educational institutions.

Eligible beneficiaries: dislocated and incumbent workers.

Range: $1,700,000 to $5,000,000. **Average:** N.A.

Activity: N.A.

HQ: Director, ETA, DOL, 200 Constitution Ave., NW, Rm. C-4526, Washington, DC 20210. Phone: (202) 693-3937.

Internet: www.doleta.gov.

17.281 WORKFORCE INVESTMENT ACT (WIA) DISLOCATED WORKER NATIONAL RESERVE TECHNICAL ASSISTANCE AND TRAINING

Assistance: formula grants; cooperative agreements (to 3 years).

Purposes: pursuant to the Workforce Investment Act of 1998, to help dislocated workers become reemployed through job search assistance and/or training that builds their occupational skills to meet labor market needs. The Act authorizes three levels of service for dislocated workers. Core services include outreach, job search, placement assistance, and labor market information. Intensive services include more comprehensive assessments, development of individual employment plans and counseling, and career planning. Training services are linked to job opportunities in workers' communities, including occupational and basic skills training. Funds are allotted based on a statutory formula and states, in turn, allocate funds to local workforce investment boards (approximately 600), by a formula prescribed by their governors.

Eligible applicants: states, DC, PR, VI, Guam.

Eligible beneficiaries: unemployed workers, including dislocated, formerly self-employed and displaced homemakers. Priority of service is given to veterans and other covered persons.

Range: $3,150 to $10,800,000. **Average:** N.A.

Activity: N.A.

HQ: Director, ETA, DOL, 200 Constitution Ave., NW, Rm. C-4526, Washington, DC 20210. Phone: (202) 693-3937.

Internet: www.doleta.gov.

17.282 TRADE ADJUSTMENT ASSISTANCE COMMUNITY COLLEGE AND CAREER TRAINING (TAACCCT) GRANTS

Assistance: project grants/discretionary (100 percent/3 to 4 years).

Purposes: pursuant to the Trade Act of 1974 as amended by ARRA, to expand and improve the ability of community colleges and other eligible IHEs to deliver education and career training programs that can be completed in two years or less, are suited for workers eligible for training under the Trade Adjustment Assistance for Workers program, and prepare participants for employment in high-wage, high-skill occupations. This program targets workers who have lost their jobs or are threatened with job loss as a result of foreign trade.

Eligible applicants: accredited community colleges and other eligible IHEs who offer worker training programs able to be completed in two years of less.

Eligible beneficiaries: workers in the 50 States, DC and PR who are eligible for training under the TAA for Workers program.

Range: to $2,400,000. **Average:** N.A.

Activity: N.A.

HQ: Director, ETA, DOL, 200 Constitution Ave., NW, Rm. C-4526, Washington, DC 20210. Phone: (202) 693-3937.

Internet: www.doleta.gov/taaccct.

17.283 WORKPLACE INNOVATION FUND

Assistance: project grants (100 percent/3 years).

Purposes: the Workforce Innovation Fund will fund projects that demonstrate innovative strategies or replicate effective evidence-based strategies for the design and delivery of employment and training services that generate long-term improvements in the performance of the public workforce system, both in terms of outcomes for job-seeker and employer customers and cost-effectiveness.

Eligible applicants: individual or consortia of state workforce agencies, individual or consortia of local workforce investment boards, individual or consortia of entities eligible to apply for WIA Section 166 grants.

Eligible beneficiaries: anyone/general public.

Range/Average: N.A.

Activity: N.A.

HQ: Director, Workplace Innovation Fund, ETA-DOL, 200 Constitution Ave., NW, S4209, Washington, DC 20210. Phone: (202) 693-3763.

Internet: www.doleta.gov/workforce_innovation.

17.284 HURRICANE SANDY DISASTER RELIEF APPROPRIATIONS ACT SUPPLEMENTAL—NATIONAL EMERGENCY GRANTS (NEGs)

Assistance: project grants (100 percent).

Purposes: pursuant to the Disaster Relief Appropriations Act of 2013, time-limited funding assistance to states for the creation of disaster relief employment for workers in Federal Emergency Management Agency (FEMA) declared disaster areas affected by Hurricane Sandy. Funds can be used to create temporary disaster employment to assist with clean up and humanitarian activities as well as to provide employment services (including some supportive services) to eligible participants.

Eligible applicants: designated state Workforce Investment Act (WIA) program grantee agencies in states that have been affected by Hurricane Sandy and have received a public assistance declaration from the Federal Emergency Management Agency (FEMA) for Hurricane Sandy.

Eligible beneficiaries: individuals who been temporarily or permanently laid off as a consequence of Hurricane Sandy, other dislocated workers, or those who are long-term unemployed, as defined by the state.

Range/Average: N.A.

Activity: N.A.

HQ: Director, ETA, DOL, 200 Constitution Ave., NW, Rm. C-4526, Washington, DC 20210. Phone: (202) 693-3937.

Internet: www.doleta.gov.

17.285 APPRENTICESHIP USA GRANTS

Assistance: project grants/discretionary. (100 percent).

Purposes: pursuant to the National Apprenticeship Act of 1937 (Fitzgerald Act) and the 2016 Omnibus Budget, to help states develop and implement strategies to drive apprenticeship expansion; engage industry and other partners to expand apprenticeship to new sectors and new populations; enhance state capacity to conduct outreach and work with employers to start new programs; and to expand participation in apprenticeship through state innovations, incentives and system reforms.

Eligible applicants/beneficiaries: states and territories.

Range: $700,000 to $3,000,000. **Average:** $1,550,000.

Activity: N.A.

HQ: Employment Training Administration, DOL, NW, 200 Constitution Ave., Rm. C5321, Washington, DC 20210. Phone: (202) 693 2796.

Internet: www.dol.gov/apprenticeship.

17.301 NON-DISCRIMINATION AND AFFIRMATIVE ACTION BY FEDERAL CONTRACTORS AND FEDERALLY ASSISTED CONSTRUCTION CONTRACTORS ("OFCCP")

Assistance: investigation of complaints.

Purposes: pursuant to ARRA 2009, Rehabilitation Act of 1973, Vietnam Era Readjustment Assistance Act of 1974, Veterans Codification Act of 1991, ADA, Immigration Reform and Control Act of 1986, and amendments, to enforce nondiscrimination and affirmative action regulations covering employment by federal contractors including subcontractors and those involved in federally-assisted construction. Complaints alleging employment discrimination on the basis of race, sex, religion, color, national origin, disability, or covered veteran status may be filed with OFCCP. Technical advice and assistance are available to employers.

Eligible applicants/beneficiaries: employment applicants, employees, and former employees of federal contractors or federally involved contractors performing work in the U.S., Panama Canal Zone, and possessions and territories—including those recruited in the U.S. to perform work abroad.

Range/Average: N.A.

Activity: N.A.

HQ: Deputy Assistant Secretary, OFCCP, Employment Standards Administration, DOL, Washington, DC 20210. Phone: (202) 693-0101.

Internet: www.dol.gov/ofccp.

17.302 LONGSHORE AND HARBOR WORKERS' COMPENSATION

Assistance: direct payments/unrestricted use.

Purposes: pursuant to the Longshore and Harbor Workers Compensation Act as extended, to replace and supplement income to compensate for permanent disability or death resulting from injury, including occupational disease; to provide benefits for certain medical expenses including hospital care, and funeral expenses up to $3,000. Benefits are paid by private insurers or self-insured employers; federal funds are available in certain cases of permanent total disability and death.

Eligible applicants/beneficiaries: longshore and harbor workers; certain maritime employees working on U.S. navigable waters and in pier and dock areas; employees working on the Outer Continental Shelf, of nonappropriated fund instrumentalities, of private employers working in DC within specified periods or abroad under U.S. government contracts; survivors. PR is not covered.

Range/Average: N.A.

Activity: N.A.

HQ: Division of Longshore and Harbor Workers' Compensation, 200 Constitution Ave., NW, Washington, DC 20210. Phone: (202) 693-0038.

Internet: www.dol.gov/esa/owcp/dlhwc.

17.303   WAGE AND HOUR STANDARDS ("Federal Wage-Hour Laws")

Assistance: advisory services/counseling; investigation of complaints.

Purposes: pursuant to the Fair Labor Standards Act, Walsh-Healy Public Contracts Act, Davis-Bacon Act, Immigration and Nationality Acts, Family and Medical Leave Act of 1993, amendments, and other acts, to provide and enforce standards protecting wages and working conditions of working persons with respect to minimum rate of pay, overtime pay, prevailing hourly wage rates, fringe benefits, child labor, and family and medical leave including for adoptive parents; to enforce wage payment standards for professional performers and related professional employees, as well as for students, nonimmigrant agricultural and certain nonagricultural workers and employees, seasonal workers, handicapped workers, apprentices, and other employment categories; to curtail employer use of lie detector tests. Generally, federal wage and hour standards apply to employees engaged in interstate or foreign commerce, or in the production of goods for such commerce, and to government employees at all levels. Funding for this program includes **17.306** and **17.308**.

Eligible applicants/beneficiaries: any covered employee in the U.S., territories, possessions, and Outer Continental Shelf lands. Family and medical leave provisions apply to all public employers and private employers with 50 or more employees within 75-mile radius of work site.

Range/Average: N.A.

Activity: N.A.

HQ: Administrator, Wage and Hour Division, Employment Standards Administration-DOL, 200 Constitution Ave., NW, Washington, DC 20210. Phone: (202) 693-0539.

Internet: www.dol.gov.

17.306   CONSUMER CREDIT PROTECTION ("Federal Wage Garnishment Law")

Assistance: advisory services/counseling; investigation of complaints.

Purposes: pursuant to the Consumer Credit Protection Act as amended, to enforce federal restrictions on the amount of a person's earnings that may be garnisheed, and prohibiting employers from discharging employees by reason of garnishment for any one indebtedness. Earnings are defined as compensation paid or payable for personal services, whether as wages, salary, commission, bonuses, including periodic payments under a pension or retirement program. Funding for this program is included in **17.303**.

Eligible applicants/beneficiaries: persons with earnings subjected to garnishment—in the U.S., territories, and possessions.

Range/Average: N.A.

Activity: N.A.

HQ: Administrator, Wage and Hour Division, Employment Standards Administration-DOL, 200 Constitution Ave., NW, Washington, DC 20210. Phone: (202) 693-0539.

Internet: www.dol.gov./WHD/garnishment/index.htm.

17.307 COAL MINE WORKERS' COMPENSATION ("Black Lung")

Assistance: direct payments/unrestricted use.

Purposes: pursuant to the Federal Mine Safety and Health Amendments Act of 1977 as amended, to pay monthly cash benefits to coal miners totally disabled with black lung disease, and to their surviving dependents.

Eligible applicants/beneficiaries: disabled coal miners; widows, and other surviving dependents. Included are some workers involved in coal transportation in and around mines, and in coal mine construction. Beneficiaries must have become "totally disabled" from coal workers' pneumoconiosis, as defined in the Act. Applicants may work in areas other than coal mines and remain eligabible for benefits. Benefits may be reduced in cases of excess earnings.

Range/Average: N.A.

Activity: N.A.

HQ: Director, Office of Workers' Compensation Programs, Division of Coal Mine Workers' Compensation, DOL, 200 Constitution Ave., NW, Washington, DC 20210. Phone: (202) 693-0046.

Internet: www.dol.gov/esa/owcp/dcmwc/index.htm.

17.308 FARM LABOR CONTRACTOR REGISTRATION ("Crew Leader")

Assistance: advisory services/counseling; investigation of complaints.

Purposes: pursuant to the Migrant and Seasonal Agricultural Worker Protection Act as amended, to enforce regulations covering farm labor contractors, agricultural employers, and agricultural associations regarding such factors as wages, records, transportation, health, safety, liability insurance, and housing provided for migrant and seasonal agricultural workers. Funding for this program is included in **17.303**.

Eligible applicants/beneficiaries: contractors and their full-time or regular employees that recruit, solicit, hire, furnish, or transport migrant or seasonal agricultural workers for employment for a fee in any form must register with DOL.

Range/Average: N.A.

Activity: N.A.

HQ: Administrator, Wage and Hour Division, Employment Standards Administration-DOL, 200 Constitution Ave., NW, Washington, DC 20210. Phone: (202) 693-0539.

Internet: www.dol.gov.whd/mspa/index.htm.

17.309 LABOR ORGANIZATION REPORTS ("Landrum-Griffin Act")

Assistance: advisory services/counseling; technical information; investigation of complaints.

Purposes: pursuant to the Labor-Management Reporting and Disclosure Act of 1959 as amended, to provide for reporting and disclosure of financial transactions and administrative practices of labor organizations, employers, labor consultants, and others required to report under the Landrum-Griffin Act; to provide standards for the election of union officers, administration of trusteeships, fiduciary responsibilities of union officers, and rights of union members; for court enforcement of safeguards pertaining to union organizations.

Eligible applicants/beneficiaries: union officers, members, organizations. All required reports are available for disclosure to the general public.

Range/Average: N.A.

Activity: N.A.

HQ: Office of Labor-Management Standards, DOL, 200 Constitution Ave., NW, Rm. N-5119, Washington, DC 20011. Phone: (202) 693-1182.

Internet: www.dol.gov/olms.

17.310 ENERGY EMPLOYEES OCCUPATIONAL ILLNESS COMPENSATION

Assistance: direct payments/unrestricted use.

Purposes: pursuant to Energy Employees Occupational Illness Compensation Program Act of 2000 as amended, to provide lump-sum payments and medical benefits to: covered DOE employees and their survivors; certain DOE vendors, contractors, and subcontractors; individuals and survivors found eligible by DOJ under the Radiation Exposure Compensation Act, as well as eligible uranium miners, millers, and ore transporters. Benefits are variable, reflecting degree of impairment and years of qualifying wage- loss.

Eligible applicants/beneficiaries: employees and survivors, as applicable, of DOE others (as cited under "Purposes").

Range: N.A. **Average:** lump-sum payments: Part B, $150,000 per covered employee; Part E, $250,000 per covered employee.

Activity: N.A.

HQ: Office of Workers' Compensation Programs, Division of Energy Employees Occupational Illness Compensation, 200 Constitution Ave., NW, Washington, DC 20210. Phone: (202) 693-0081.

Internet: www.dol.gov.

17.401 INTERNATIONAL LABOR PROGRAMS

Assistance: project grants (100 percent/3 to 4 years).

Purposes: project grants to support programs that combat exploitative child labor internationally and address worker rights issues through technical assistance in countries with which the United States has free trade agreements or trade preference programs. The mission of the program is to use all available international channels to ensure that workers around the world are treated fairly and to improve working conditions, raise living standards, protect workers ability to exercise their rights, and address the workplace exploitation of children and other vulnerable populations.

Eligible applicants: commercial, international, educational, or non-profit organizations, including any faith-based, community-based, or public international organizations.

Eligible beneficiaries: anyone/general public.

Range/Average: N.A.

Activity: N.A.

HQ: Director, International Labor Programs, BILA-DOL, 200 Constitution Ave., NW, Washington, DC 20210. Phone: (202) 693-4876.

Internet: N.A. (Note: no field offices for this program.)

17.502 OCCUPATIONAL SAFETY AND HEALTH—SUSAN HARWOOD TRAINING GRANTS

Assistance: project grants.

Purposes: pursuant to the Occupational Safety and Health Act, to provide occupational safety and health training and education to employees and employers, particularly in the recognition, avoidance, and abatement of workplace hazards.

Eligible applicants/beneficiaries: nonprofit organizations.

Range: $48,000 to $650,000. Average: N.A.

Activity: anticipate 71 awards in FY 2016.

HQ: Assistant Secretary, OSHA-DOL, 200 Constitution Ave., NW, Washington, DC 20210. Phone: (847) 759-7769; FAX: (202) 693-1696.

Internet: www.osha.gov.

17.503 OCCUPATIONAL SAFETY AND HEALTH—STATE PROGRAM ("State Plan Grant Awards")

Assistance: project grants (50 percent).

Purposes: pursuant to the Occupational Safety and Health Act, for state administration and enforcement of approved occupational safety and health programs.

Eligible applicants/beneficiaries: designated state agencies.

Range: $195,000 to $26,425,000. **Average:** N.A.

Activity: anticipate 47,567 state inspections in FY 2016.

HQ: Assistant Secretary, OSHA-DOL, 200 Constitution Ave., NW, Washington, DC 20210. Phone: 202-693-2422; FAX: 202-693-1696.

Internet: www.osha.gov.

17.504 CONSULTATION AGREEMENTS ("Consultation Grant Program")

Assistance: project grants (90 percent).

Purposes: pursuant to the Occupational Safety and Health Act, for consultative workplace safety and health services by states to smaller employers, primarily those with hazardous operations.

Eligible applicants: designated state agencies.

Eligible beneficiaries: any private employer.

Range: $196,000 to $5,543,000. **Average:** N.A.

Activity: anticipate 26,745 consultation visits in FY 2016.

HQ: Assistant Secretary, OSHA-DOL, 200 Constitution Ave., NW, Washington, DC 20210. Phone: 202-693-2422; FAX: 202-693-1696.

Internet: www.osha.gov.

17.505 OSHA DATA INITIATIVE ("OSHA Data Collection Award")

Assistance: project grants (100 percent).

Purposes: pursuant to the Occupational Safety and Health Act, for cooperative agreements for the collection of injury and illness data from employers in specified industries—for OSHA use in targeting interventions.

Eligible applicants/beneficiaries: designated state agencies.

Range/Average: N.A.

Activity: N.A.

HQ: Assistant Secretary, OSHA-DOL, 200 Constitution Ave., NW, Washington, DC 20210. Phone: 202-693-2422; FAX: 202-693-1696.

Internet: www.osha.gov.

17.506 DISASTER RELIEF APPROPRIATIONS ACT, SUSAN HARWOOD TRAINING GRANTS

Assistance: project grants (100 percent/18 months).

Purposes: pursuant to the Disaster Relief Appropriations Act of 2013, funds to provide occupational safety and health training and education to employees and employers, particularly in the recognition, avoidance, and abatement of workplace hazards related to Hurricane Sandy disaster relief.

Eligible applicants: nonprofit organizations in priority areas designated by OSHA that are limited to the state of New Jersey and New York City.

Eligible beneficiaries: individuals employed in workplaces affected by Hurricane Sandy.

Range/Average: N.A.

Activity: N.A.

HQ: Director, Disaster Relief Appropriations Act-Susan Harwood Training Grants, OSHA-DOL, 200 Constitution Ave., NW, N-3419, Washington, DC 20210. Phone: (847) 297-4810.

Internet: www.osha.gov.

17.600 MINE HEALTH AND SAFETY GRANTS

Assistance: project grants (80 percent).

Purposes: pursuant to the Federal Mine Safety and Health Amendments Act of 1977 as amended, to develop and enforce state laws and regulations related to the health and safety of miners; to improve workmen's compensation and occupational disease laws and programs; for miner training.

Eligible applicants/beneficiaries: any mining state.

Range: $27,141 to $634,622. Average: $179,595.

Activity: N.A.

HQ: Director, Educational Policy and Development, Mine Safety and Health, Mine Safety and Health Administration, DOL, 201 12th St. S, Arlington, VA 22202. Phone: (202) 693-9570.

Internet: www.msha.gov. (Note: no field offices for this program.)

17.601 MINE HEALTH AND SAFETY COUNSELING AND TECHNICAL ASSISTANCE

Assistance: advisory services/counseling; technical information.

Purposes: pursuant to the Federal Mine Safety and Health Amendments Act of 1977 as amended, to establish or improve health and safety conditions in and around coal, metal, and nonmetallic mines and mineral facilities— through special studies, technical assistance, investigations, equipment testing.

Eligible applicants/beneficiaries: states, organizations, or individuals.

Range/Average: N.A.

Activity: N.A.

HQ: Office of the Director, Technical Support, 201 12th St. S, Arlington, VA 22202. Phone: (202) 693-9470.

Internet: www.msha.gov.

17.602 MINE HEALTH AND SAFETY EDUCATION AND TRAINING

Assistance: training.

Purposes: pursuant to the Federal Mine Safety and Health Amendments Act of 1977 as amended, to provide initial and advanced technical mine safety and health training of federal mine inspectors, miners, and others. Curriculum materials and audiovisual programs are available.

Eligible applicants/beneficiaries: mine operators, miners, or their agents.

Range/Average: N.A.

Activity: N.A.

HQ: Director, Educational Policy and Development, Mine Safety and Health, Mine Safety and Health Administration, DOL, 201 12th St. S, Arlington, VA 22202. Phone: (202) 693-9570.

Internet: www.msha.gov.

17.603 BROOKWOOD-SAGO GRANT

Assistance: project grants (100 percent).

Purposes: pursuant to the Mine Improvement and New Emergency Response Act of 2006 (Miner Act), to provide training and other educational programs or develop training materials for employers and miners concerning safety and health topics in priority areas designated by MSHA.

Eligible applicants: any mining state of the United States and nonprofit public and private organizations.

Eligible beneficiaries: miner-training program recipients, miners, any organization employing these individuals, and mine operators.

Range: to $50,000. **Average:** N.A.

Activity: N.A.

HQ: Director, Educational Policy and Development, Mine Safety and Health, Mine Safety and Health Administration, DOL, 1201 12th St. S, Arlington, VA 22202. Phone: (202) 693-9570.

Internet: www.msha.gov. (Note: no field offices for this program.)

17.604 SAFETY AND HEALTH GRANTS

Assistance: project grants (100 percent/1 year).

Purposes: pursuant to Federal Mine Safety and Health Amendments Act of 1977 (Mine Act), Mine Improvement and New Emergency Response Act of 2006 (MINER Act), to provide mine safety, health training, and education to miners, mine operators and other individuals who work at a mine; to develop training and other programs to improve health and safety conditions at mines. Grants are restricted to use, services, mine type or other priorities designated or legislated by the Mine Safety and Health Administration.

Eligible applicants: any U.S. mining state, nonprofit public and private organizations, commercial or legislatively mandated entity.

Eligible beneficiaries: individuals, owners, and employers associated with workplaces covered by the Mine and/or MINER Acts.

Range/Average: N.A.

Activity: N.A.

HQ: Director, Educational Policy and Development, Mine Safety and Health, Mine Safety and Health Administration, DOL, 201 12th St. S, Arlington, VA 22202. Phone: (202) 693-9570.

Internet: www.msha.gov. (Note: no field offices for this program.)

17.700 WOMEN'S BUREAU

Assistance: advisory services/counseling.

Purposes: to develop training and employment policies and programs affecting the employment of women and their retirement security; to expand employment opportunities for women and promote their entry into better paying jobs, especially in new technology and nontraditional occupations. Project examples: online newsletter; apprenticeship programs; Work and Family projects; planning for employer-sponsored child care; Girls E-Mentoring in Science, Engineering & Technology, and in nursing.

Eligible applicants/beneficiaries: any individual or group, including in territories.

Range/Average: N.A.

Activity: N.A.

HQ: Director, Women's Bureau, OS-DOL, 200 Constitution Ave., NW Rm. S3002, Washington, DC 20210. Phone: (202) 693-6710.

Internet: www.dol.gov/wb.

17.720 DISABILITY EMPLOYMENT POLICY DEVELOPMENT ("ODEP")

Assistance: project grants.

Purposes: to promote employment opportunities for persons with disabilities by providing disability employment policy leadership to DOL and other federal agencies, through: research and dissemination activities; outreach initiatives; coordination with such other initiatives as Workforce Investment Act projects and programs; technical information about the provisions of the ADA to business leaders, organized labor, and others; and, a range of related activities.

Eligible applicants/beneficiaries: varies according to grant.

Range: $100,000 to $2,500,000. **Average:** N.A.

Activity: N.A.

HQ: Office of Disability Employment Policy, DOL, 200 Constitution Ave., NW, Rm. S1303, Washington, DC 20210. Phone: (202) 693-7880; FAX: (202) 693-7888.

Internet: www.dol.gov/odep. (Note: no field offices for this program.)

17.801 DISABLED VETERANS' OUTREACH PROGRAM (DVOP)

Assistance: formula grants (100 percent).

Purposes: pursuant to the Veterans' Rehabilitation and Education Amendments of 1980, to pay the salaries and expenses of DVOP specialists assigned to meet the employment needs of eligible veterans, with emphasis on those that are economically or educationally disadvantaged including the homeless and those with barriers to employment.

Eligible applicants/beneficiaries: state employment security agencies.

Range: $114,000 to $13,748,000. **Average:** $2,171,611.

Activity: N.A.

HQ: Assistant Secretary, DOL, 200 Constitution Ave., NW, Washington, DC 20210. Phone: 202-693-4733; FAX: 202-693-4755.

Internet: www.dol.gov/vets.

17.802   VETERANS' EMPLOYMENT PROGRAM
("Veterans' Workforce Investment Program - VWIP")

Assistance: project grants (to 100 percent).

Purposes: pursuant to WIA, to enhance services to veterans in employment and training programs and related services; to provide innovative employment and training services and projects; for outreach and public information programs.

Eligible applicants: governors, state and local Workforce Investment Boards, public agencies, private nonprofit and community-based organizations.

Eligible beneficiaries: service-connected disabled veterans, veterans with significant employment barriers, and those recently separated from military service (48 months).

Range/Average: N.A.

Activity: N.A.

HQ: Assistant Secretary, DOL, 200 Constitution Ave., NW, Washington, DC 20210. Phone: 202-693-4733; FAX: 202-693-4755.

Internet: www.dol.gov/vets. (Note: no field offices for this program.)

17.803   UNIFORMED SERVICES EMPLOYMENT AND REEMPLOYMENT RIGHTS
("USERRA")

Assistance: advisory services/counseling; technical information; investigation of complaints.

Purposes: to assist in the employment and reemployment of non- career veterans or candidates for the uniformed services. (Discrimination in employment and acts of reprisal by employers are prohibited—against persons because of their obligation in the uniformed services, filing a claim, seeking assistance concerning an alleged violation, testifying in a proceeding, or otherwise participating in an investigation.) Unresolved complaints are referred to DOJ or to the DOL Office of Special Counsel for representation in federal district courts.

Eligible applicants/beneficiaries: persons that have served voluntarily or involuntarily on active duty, active duty for training, or training duty with the uniformed services, including reservists and National Guard members. Entitlement ceases upon termination of service with a bad conduct or dishonorable discharge, or upon separation under other then honorable conditions.

Range/Average: N.A.

Activity: N.A.

HQ: Assistant Secretary/Veteran's Employment and Training, DOL, 200 Constitution Ave., NW, Washington, DC 20210. Phone: (202) 693-4729.

Internet: www.dol.gov/dol/vets.

17.804   LOCAL VETERANS' EMPLOYMENT REPRESENTATIVE PROGRAM
("LVER Program")

Assistance: formula grants (100 percent).

Purposes: pursuant to the Servicemen's Readjustment Act of 1944, to fund salaries and expenses of Local Veterans Employment Representatives assigned to conduct outreach to employers concerning employment, training, and job placement services and opportunities for veterans.

Eligible applicants/beneficiaries: state employment agencies.

Range: to $6,057,000. **Average:** $1,107,225.

Activity: N.A.

HQ: Assistant Secretary, DOL, 200 Constitution Ave., NW, Washington, DC 20210. Phone: 202-693-4733; FAX: 202-693-4755.

Internet: www.dol.gov/vets.

17.805 HOMELESS VETERANS REINTEGRATION PROJECT (HVRP)

Assistance: project grants (100 percent).

Purposes: pursuant to the SBMHAA as amended, for projects to reintegrate homeless veterans into the labor force—through activities including employment and training services, support services, linkages with other service providers, and outreach performed by formerly homeless veterans.

Eligible applicants/beneficiaries: state and local Workforce Investment Boards and public agencies, private nonprofit and profit organizations and entities.

Range: $92,000 to $300,000. **Average:** $230,000.

Activity: N.A.

HQ: Assistant Secretary, DOL, 200 Constitution Ave., NW, Washington, DC 20210. Phone: 202-693-4733; FAX: 202-693-4755.

Internet: www.dol.gov/dol/vets.

17.806 VETERAN'S PREFERENCE IN FEDERAL EMPLOYMENT

Assistance: federal employment.

Purposes: pursuant to the Veterans Preference Act of 1944, to assist persons who perform services in the uniformed services to secure federal employment and to ensure a higher retention standing in the event of reduction-in-force; to assist veterans, employers, labor organizations, and others concerned with such preference; to investigate related complaints. A point system accords levels of preference to eligible veterans, based on such factors as when they served, receipt of the Purple Heart medal, disability if any, conditions of discharge. Details are available from federal agencies.

Eligible applicants/beneficiaries: veterans and certain of their dependents and survivors. Applicants should indicate their level of preference on job application forms.

Range/Average: N.A.

Activity: N.A.

HQ: Assistant Secretary/Veterans' Employment and Training, DOL, 200 Constitution Ave., NW, Washington, DC 20210. Phone: (202) 693-4729.

Internet: www.dol.gov/dol/vets/public/programs/programs/preference/main .htm.

17.807   TRANSITION ASSISTANCE PROGRAM (TAP)

Assistance: training.

Purposes: pursuant to the Defense Reauthorization Act of 1991, to provide employment instruction, information, and assistance to separating military personnel ad their spouses by offering job search and related services such as resume preparation and service benefits—through TAP workshops at military installations worldwide. Funding is not appropriated separately, and is derived from other funded accounts.

Eligible applicants: state employment agencies; contractors.

Eligible beneficiaries: service members within two years of retirement or one year of separation.

Range/Average: N.A.

Activity: N.A.

HQ: Assistant Secretary, DOL, 200 Constitution Ave., NW, Washington, DC 20210. Phone: 202-693-4733; FAX: 202-693-4755.

Internet: www.dol.gov/vets. (Note: no field offices for this program.)

DEPARTMENT OF STATE

19.009   ACADEMIC EXCHANGE PROGRAMS—UNDERGRADUATE PROGRAMS

Assistance: project grants (100 percent).

Purposes: pursuant to Fulbright-Hays Act of 1961, as amended, to increase mutual understanding between people of the U.S. and people of other countries by means of educational and cultural exchange programs, including exchange of scholars, researchers, professionals, students, and educators. Undergraduate programs include: the Global Undergraduate Exchange Program UGRAD; Study of the US Institutes for foreign student leaders; Critical Language Scholarships for Intensive Summer Institutes; and the Community College Initiatives.

Eligible applicants: nonprofit organizations and IHEs.

Eligible beneficiaries: students and general public.

Range: $153,454 to $6,500,000. **Average:** N.A.

Activity: N.A.

HQ: Bureau of Educational and Cultural Affairs, Office of Academic Exchange Programs, 2200 C St., NW, SA-5, 4th Floor, Rm. 4B07, Washington, DC 20037. Phone: (202) 632-9265.

Internet: exchanges.state.gov. (Note: no field offices for this program.)

19.010   ACADEMIC EXCHANGE PROGRAMS—HUBERT H. HUMPHREY FELLOWSHIP PROGRAM

Assistance: project grants (100 percent).

Purposes: pursuant to Fulbright-Hays Act of 1961, to increase mutual understanding between people of the U.S. and people of other countries by means of educational and cultural exchange programs, including exchange of scholars, researchers, professionals, students, and educators. The Hubert H. Humphrey Fellowship Program is a Fulbright exchange activity that provides mid-career professionals from developing or transitional countries ten months of non-degree academic study and related professional experiences in the United States. Humphrey Fellows are selected based on their potential for leadership and their commitment to public service in either the public or private sector. Fifteen major U.S. host universities are chosen for their excellence in relevant fields of study and for the resources and support they offer Humphrey Fellows.

Eligible applicants: nonprofit organizations/institutions (includes IHEs and hospitals), international organizations/institutions.

Eligible beneficiaries: private/public institutions and organizations, IHEs, federally-recognized tribal governments, specialized groups, education and other professionals.

Range/Average: N.A.

Activity: N.A.

HQ: Office of Global Educational Programs, Humphrey and Institutional Linkages Branch, BECA-Department of State, 2200 C St., NW, SA-5, Rm. 4CC13, Washington, DC 20037. Phone: (202) 632-6328.

Internet: www.exchanges.state.gov/non-us/program/hubert-h-humphrey-fellowship-program. (Note: no field offices for this program.)

19.011   ACADEMIC EXCHANGE PROGRAMS—SPECIAL ACADEMIC EXCHANGE PROGRAMS

Assistance: project grants (100 percent).

Purposes: pursuant to Fulbright-Hays Act of 1961, to increase mutual understanding between the people of the U.S. and people of other countries by means of educational and cultural exchange programs, including the exchange of scholars, researchers, professionals, students, and educators. Special Academic Exchange Programs support participants in undergraduate, graduate, and non-degree professional development programs, targeting underserved populations from developing or strategically important areas.

The programs include: Benjamin A Gilman Scholarship Program; Edmund's Muskie Fellowship Program; Junior Faculty Development Program; South Pacific Exchanges; and Timor Leste Scholarship Program.

Eligible applicants: public and private organizations/institutions (includes IHEs and hospitals), international organizations/institutions.

Eligible beneficiaries: public and private organizations/institutions, anyone/general public.

Range: $422,400 to $12,100,000. **Average:** N.A.

Activity: N.A.

HQ: Council for International Exchange of Scholars, 2200 C St., NW, SA-5, 4th Floor, Rm. 4B07, Washington, DC 20037. Phone: (202) 632-3238.

Internet: exchanges.state.gov. (Note: no field offices for this program.)

19.012 PROFESSIONAL AND CULTURAL EXCHANGE PROGRAMS—SPECIAL PROFESSIONAL AND CULTURAL PROGRAMS

Assistance: project grants (100 percent).

Purposes: pursuant to Fulbright-Hays Act of 1961 as amended, to increase mutual understanding between the people of the U.S. and the people of other countries by means of educational and cultural exchange programs, including the exchange of scholars, researchers, professionals, students, and educators.

Eligible applicants: eligible non-profit organizations and IHEs.

Eligible beneficiaries: anyone/general public.

Range: N.A. **Average:** $287,500.

Activity: N.A.

HQ: BECA-Department of State, 2200 C St., NW, SA-05, Rm. 3B14, Washington, DC 2003. Phone: (202) 632-6070.

Internet: N.A. (Note: no field offices for this program.)

19.013 THOMAS R. PICKERING FOREIGN AFFAIRS FELLOWSHIP PROGRAM
("Pickering Fellowship Program")

Assistance: project grants/cooperative agreements (100 percent).

Purposes: pursuant to 1990-1991 Department of State Authorization Bill and State Dept. Basic Authorities Act of 1956, to attract outstanding students who represent all ethnic and social backgrounds, who have an interest in pursuing a Foreign Service career in the U.S. Department of State. The Pickering Program has an undergraduate and graduate component and funding supports activities and financial obligations such as: tuition costs; room and board; student travel; books, fees and costs associated with student summer internship programs including stipends, travel, passport fees, inoculation and visa fees. Funding supports program administration as well as coordinating program logistics.

Eligible applicants/beneficiaries: college students who are U.S. citizens, especially women and minorities.

Range/Average: N.A.

Activity: N.A.

HQ: Student Programs, Department of State SA-1, 2401 E St., NW, Rm. 518, Washington, DC 20522. Phone: (202) 261-8958.

Internet: www.careers.state.gov/students/programs.html#TRP. (Note: no field offices for this program.)

19.015 CULTURAL, TECHNICAL AND EDUCATIONAL CENTERS

Assistance: project grants/cooperative agreements (100 percent).

Purposes: pursuant to Fulbright-Hays Act of 1961, as amended, Department of State, Foreign Operations, and Related Programs Appropriations Act and others, to assist various organizations identified by Congress to achieve objectives specified by Congress. Funding is provided to the Center for Cultural and Technical Interchange Between East and West (East-West Center) to promote better relations and understanding between the United States and the nations of Asia and the Pacific through cooperative study, training, and research.

Eligible applicants: eligible organizations identified by Congress.

Eligible beneficiaries: public nonprofit and private institutions/organizations.

Range: $985,180 to $16,700,000. **Average:** N.A.

Activity: N.A.

HQ: Council for International Exchange of Scholars, 2200 C St., NW, SA-5, 4th Floor, Rm. 4B07, Washington, DC 20037. Phone: (202) 632-3238.

Internet: exchanges.state.gov. (Note: no field offices for this program.)

19.016 IRAQ ASSISTANCE PROGRAMS

Assistance: project grants/cooperative agreements (50 percent/to 7 years).

Purposes: pursuant to Foreign Assistance Act of 1961 as amended, to promote democracy, political development and reconciliation, economic development and rule of law in Iraq. Funds are discretionary and may not be used for police, military or para-military activities or to influence Iraqi national policy.

Eligible applicants: nongovernment entities, IHEs, private nonprofit institutions/organizations.

Eligible beneficiaries: anyone/general public.

Range: $500,000 to $4,000,000. **Average:** N.A.

Activity: N.A.

HQ: Bureau of Near Eastern Affairs-Department of State, 22430 E St., NW, Washington, DC 20037. Phone: (202) 776-8691; FAX: (202) 776-8500.

Internet: www.state.gov. (Note: no field offices for this program.)

19.018 OVERSEAS PROCESSING ENTITIES (OPEs) FOR U.S. REFUGEE RESETTLEMENT
("PRM")

Assistance: cooperative agreements (100 percent/to 3 years).

Purposes: pursuant to the Immigration and Nationality Act, as amended by the Refugee Act of 1980, to assist the Bureau in preparing the necessary casework for persons eligible for interview by U.S. Citizenship and Immigration Services (USCIS) of the Department of Homeland Security (DHS) under the U.S. Refugee Admissions Program and, for those approved, to provide assistance in completing the additional requirements for refugee admission under Section 207 of the Immigration and Nationality Act.

Eligible applicants: international (IOs) and non-governmental organizations (NGOs).

Eligible beneficiaries: eligible refugees.

Range/Average: N.A.

Activity: N.A.

HQ: Program Director, Bureau of Population, Refugees and Migration (PRM), Department of State, 2401 E St., NW, L505, Washington, DC 20522. Phone: (202) 663-1055; FAX: (202) 663-1364.

Internet: www.state.gov/g/prm/index.htm. (Note: no field offices for this program.)

19.020 CHARLES B. RANGEL INTERNATIONAL AFFAIRS PROGRAM ("Rangel Program")

Assistance: cooperative agreements/discretionary grants; project grants/fellowships (100 percent).

Purposes: pursuant to the State Department Basic Authorities Act of 1956, to increase the number of minorities interested in and being prepared for international service, particularly a Foreign Service career in the Department of State. In addition to a designated amount used for program administrative costs, funding supports tuition costs, room and board, student travel, books, fees, and costs associated with student summer internship programs including stipends, travel, passport fees, inoculation and visa fees.

Eligible applicants: private IHEs.

Eligible beneficiaries: minority students.

Range/Average: N.A.

Activity: N.A.

HQ: Department of State, HR/REE, Rm. H-518, SA-1, 2401 E St., NW, Washington, DC 20522. Phone: (202) 261-8950; FAX: (202) 261-8842.

Internet: careers.state.gov. (Note: no field offices for this program.)

19.021 INVESTING IN PEOPLE IN THE MIDDLE EAST AND NORTH AFRICA

Assistance: cooperative agreements (100 percent).

Purposes: pursuant to the Fulbright Hays Act - The Mutual Educational and Cultural Exchange Act of 1961, to support programs, projects and activities to include (but not limited to) cultural, educational, alumni, information and media efforts in the Middle East and North Africa. NEA Public Diplomacy objectives are focused on active promotion of projects which promote mutual understanding and invest in people.

Eligible applicants: non-profit organizations subject to 501(c)(3) of the U.S. tax code or registered as a non-profit organization in the entity's home country with demonstrated experience in working with vendors, suppliers, contractors, etc. and appropriately staffed offices in country.

Eligible beneficiaries: local organizations, citizens of countries in the Middle East and North Africa, and the U.S.

Range: $10,000 to $5,000,000. **Average:** $500,000.

Activity: N.A.

HQ: Program Director, Bureau of Near Eastern Affairs, Department of State, 2201 C St., NW, HST Bldg., Washington, DC 20520. Phone: (202) 776-8682; FAX: (202) 776-8869.

Internet: N.A. (Note: no field offices for this program.)

19.025 U.S. AMBASSADORS FUND FOR CULTURAL PRESERVATION ("AFCP, USAFCP")

Assistance: cooperative agreements; project grants/discretionary (100 percent/to 5 years).

Purposes: pursuant to the Mutual Educational and Cultural Exchange Act of 1961 (Fulbright-Hays Act), to protect the values of other countries' cultural sites, objects or collections, or forms of traditional cultural expression (intangible heritage) as they are understood by stakeholders, who may include: national, regional, or local cultural authorities, the local community, and others with vested interests in the site and the outcome of a project.

Eligible applicants: 130 eligible countries around the world who may apply through U.S. embassies.

Eligible beneficiaries: anyone, general public.

Range: $10,000 to $700,000. **Average:** $109,000.

Activity: N.A.

HQ: Program Director, ECA/P/C, SA-5, C2, Department of State, Washington, DC 20522-0582. Phone: (202) 632-6308; FAX: (202) 632-6300.

Internet: go.usa.gov/jeUC.

19.026 GLOBAL PEACE OPERATIONS INITIATIVE (GPOI)

Assistance: project grants: capacity building and complaint processing; training; cooperative agreements/contracts; discretionary; collaborative curriculum design; special (100 percent).

Purposes: pursuant to the Foreign Assistance Act of 1961, during Phase I (FY 2005-2009) GPOI helped address major gaps in international capacity to conduct peace support operations (PSOs), with a focus on Africa by increasing the number of peacekeepers available for deployment. During Phase II (FY 2010-2014), program emphasis shifted from the direct training of peacekeepers by U.S. personnel to building sustainable, indigenous PSO training capabilities in partner countries/organizations, with most training handled indigenously by GPOI-trained instructors. Funded activities include: peacekeeping capacity building as it relates to training, courses, course materials, staffing, program management, deployment support, construction and refurbishment of peacekeeping centers, equipment requirements, studies, workshops, conferences, and regional exercises.

Eligible applicants/beneficiaries: governments, NGOs, public/private non-profits.

Range/Average: N.A.

Activity: N.A.

HQ: Director, GPOI, Department of State, 2201 C St., NW, Suite 2811, Washington, DC 20520. Phone: (202) 647-0904.

Internet: N.A. (Note: no field offices for this program.)

19.029 THE U.S. PRESIDENTS EMERGENCY PLAN FOR AIDS RELIEF PROGRAMS (PEPFAR)

Assistance: project grants/cooperative agreements (100 percent/1 to 5 years).

Purposes: the objective of this program is to provide support in achieving the HIV/AIDS care, treatment, and prevention goals of PEPFAR as detailed in the PEPFAR Blueprint.

Eligible applicants: non-governmental, health/medical.

Eligible beneficiaries: anyone/general public.

Range/Average: N.A.

Activity: N.A.

HQ: Director, PEPFAR, GAC-Department of State, 2100 Pennsylvania Ave., NW, Rm. 200, Washington, DC 20037. Phone: (202) 663-2109.

Internet: www.pepfar.gov. (Note: no field offices for this program.)

19.030 ANTITERRORISM ASSISTANCE—DOMESTIC TRAINING PROGRAMS

Assistance: cooperative agreements; cooperative agreements/discretionary grants (100 percent).

Purposes: pursuant to the Foreign Assistance Act of 1961, the Office of Antiterrorism Assistance (ATA) assesses training needs, develops curriculum, and provides the resources to train civilian security and law enforcement personnel from partner nations to enhance their capacity to detect, deter, counter, and investigate terrorist activities with the ultimate goal of helping nations effectively establish the conditions and capacity for achieving peace, security, and stability.

Eligible applicants/beneficiaries: 35 IHEs selected by the CDC as Prevention Research Centers (PRCs).

Range/Average: N.A.

Activity: N.A.

HQ: Director, Antiterrorism Assistance-Domestic Training Programs, Diplomatic Security, Department of State, 1800 N Kent St., Arlington, VA 22209. Phone: (703) 875-6998.

Internet: N.A. (Note: no field offices for this program.)

19.031 RESEARCH AND DEVELOPMENT—PHYSICAL SECURITY PROGRAMS

Assistance: cooperative agreements (100 percent/5 years).

Purposes: pursuant to the Omnibus Diplomatic Security and Antiterrorism Act of 1986 as amended, to design and evaluate physical security countermeasures against terrorism threat for blast mitigation, anti-ram barriers, and forced-entry ballistic-resistant systems.

Eligible applicants: state and local government institutions certified by OSHA and ASTM standards, federally-recognized tribal governments.

Eligible beneficiaries: USG personnel and facilities.

Range/Average: N.A.

Activity: N.A.

HQ: Program Director, Diplomatic Security, Department of State, 1400 Wilson Blvd., Arlington, VA 22209. Phone: (703) 312-3125.

Internet: N.A. (Note: no field offices for this program.)

19.033   GLOBAL THREAT REDUCTION (GTR)

Assistance: cooperative agreements; project grants/including travel grants; (100 percent).

Purposes: pursuant to the Foreign Assistance Act of 1961, as amended, to support programs aimed at reducing the threat posed by terrorist organizations or states of concern seeking to acquire weapons of mass destruction (WMD) expertise, material, and equipment. Funded projects will aim to enhance biological, chemical, and nuclear security practices and productively engage scientists with WMD-applicable expertise.

Eligible applicants/beneficiaries: 35 IHEs selected by the CDC as Prevention Research Centers (PRCs).

Range: N.A. **Average:** $500,000.

Activity: N.A.

HQ: Program Director, HST 3327 - ISN/CTR, 2201 C St., NW, Washington, DC 20520. Phone: (202) 736-4961; FAX: (202) 736-7698.

Internet: www.state.gov/t/isn/58381.htm. (Note: no field offices for this program.)

19.123   EUR/ACE HUMANITARIAN ASSISTANCE PROGRAM

Assistance: project grants.

Purposes: pursuant to the Freedom Support Act, funds to U.S. based nonprofit organizations to provide humanitarian assistance, including food, clothing, medicine, and structural repairs to buildings, for vulnerable populations in countries of the former Soviet Union.

Eligible applicants/beneficiaries: public non-profit organizations based in the United States.

Range: $100,000 to $,600,000. **Average:** N.A.

Activity: N.A.

HQ: Director, EUR/ACE Humanitarian Assistance Program, Dept. of State, 2201 C St., NW, Washington, DC 20003. Phone: (202) 647-7272.

Internet: N.A. (Note: no field offices for this program.)

19.124   EAST ASIA AND PACIFIC GRANTS PROGRAM

Assistance: cooperative agreements/discretionary grants; project grants/fellowships (100 percent/to 2 years).

Purposes: pursuant to the Foreign Assistance Act of 1961, Bureau of East Asian Affairs, to support the foreign assistance goals and objectives of the Department of State, Bureau of Near Eastern Affairs (EAP), as delineated in the FY Bureau Strategic and Resource Plan.

Eligible applicants/beneficiaries: 35 IHEs selected by the CDC as Prevention Research Centers (PRCs).

Range/Average: N.A.

Activity: N.A.

HQ: Director, East Asia and Pacific Grants Program, Bureau of East Asian and Pacific Affairs, Department of State, 2201 C St., NW, Rm. 5313, Washington, DC 20520. Phone: (202) 647-9446.

Internet: N.A. (Note: no field offices for this program.)

19.204 FISHERMEN'S GUARANTY FUND ("Section 7")

Assistance: insurance.

Purposes: pursuant to the Fishermen's Protective Act of 1967 as amended and other acts, to reimburse U.S. commercial fishing vessel owners for losses resulting from the seizure of the vessel by a foreign country on the basis of rights or claims in territorial waters or on the high seas, not recognized by the U.S. (Effective 28 November 1990, the U.S. acknowledges the authority of coastal states to manage highly migratory species, reducing the basis for claims.)

Eligible applicants/beneficiaries: U.S. citizen-owners or -charterers of a documented or certified fishing vessel. Claimants must have paid a premium for the year in which the seizure occurs, if required.

Range/Average: N.A.

Activity: N.A.

HQ: Office of Marine Conservation, Bureau of Oceans and International Environmental and Scientific Affairs, Department of State, Rm. 5806, Washington, DC 20520-7818. Phone: (202) 647-3941; FAX: (202) 736-7350.

Internet: www.state.gov. (Note: no field offices for this program.)

19.221 IRAN ASSISTANCE PROGRAM

Assistance: project grants (100 percent).

Purposes: pursuant to the Foreign Assistance Act of 1961, to support democracy and human rights in the Near East region. Funds can only be used to promote democracy and human rights.

Eligible applicants/beneficiaries: non-profit, for-profit organizations or state and local governments interested in partnering with the Middle East Partnership Initiative to promote democratic change in the Near East.

Range: $500,000 to $2,500,000. **Average:** $1,500,000.

Activity: N.A.

HQ: Director, 2430 E Street NW, Washington, DC 20037. Phone: (202) 776-8627; FAX: (202) 776-8500.

Internet: N.A. (Note: no field offices for this program.)

19.300 PROGRAM FOR STUDY OF EASTERN EUROPE AND THE INDEPENDENT STATES OF THE FORMER SOVIET UNION ("Title VIII")

Assistance: project grants. (100 percent/to 3 years).

Purposes: pursuant to the Research and Training for Eastern Europe and the Independent States of the Former Soviet Union Act of 1983 as amended, for advanced research, graduate training, language training, and related activities—toward the development of American expertise on the countries of the former Soviet Union and Southeast Europe. Funds may support short-term research projects, fellowships, conferences, travel, and publication costs.

Eligible applicants: nonprofit organizations, IHEs.

Eligible beneficiaries: graduate students, scholars.

Range: N.A. **Average:** $500,000.

Activity: N.A.

HQ: Executive Director *or* Program Officer, Program for Study of Eastern Europe and the Independent States of the Former Soviet Union (INR/RES), Department of State, 2201 C St., Washington, DC 20520. Phone: (202) 736-4661.

Internet: www.state.gov/s/inr/grants. (Note: no field offices for this program.)

19.301 THE SECRETARY'S OFFICE OF THE GLOBAL PARTNERSHIP INITIATIVE (S/GPI) GRANT PROGRAMS ("Global Partnership Initiative")

Assistance: project grants/specified projects (100 percent/1-3 years).

Purposes: pursuant to The Foreign Assistance Act of 1961, to support the foreign assistance goals and objectives of the Department of State, Secretary's Office of the Global Partnership Initiative (S/GPI), as delineated in the FY Bureau Strategic and Resource Plan and other strategic planning document.

Eligible applicants: domestic and international entities that implement programs abroad.

Eligible beneficiaries: residents of any community abroad where program activities are taking place.

Range: to $1,000,000. **Average:** N.A.

Activity: N.A.

HQ: Director, 2201 C St. NW, Ste 6817, Washington, DC 20520. Phone: (202) 647-9097.

Internet: www.state.gov/partnerships. (Note: no field offices for this program.)

19.322 ECONOMIC STATECRAFT

Assistance: project grants.

Purposes: funds for projects that place economics and market forces at the center of U.S. foreign policy by both harnessing global economic forces to advance Americas foreign policy and employing the tools of foreign policy to shore up our economic strength. Projects can range in topic and method and may include central themes such as addressing consumer concerns; U.S. business practices and values; renewable energy; good governance and anti-corruption; travel and tourism; regional economic integration; elevating women as economic multipliers; and entrepreneurship.

Eligible applicants/beneficiaries: public and private non-profit organizations, non-governmental organizations, anyone/general public.

Range/Average: N.A.

Activity: N.A.

HQ: Director, Economic Statecraft, BEBA-Dept. of State, 2201 C St., Rm. 3741, Washington, DC 20520. Phone: (202) 647-4032.

Internet: www.state.gov/e/eb/econstatecraft/index.htm. (Note: no field offices for this program.)

19.400 ACADEMIC EXCHANGE PROGRAMS—GRADUATE STUDENTS ("Fulbright Program")

Assistance: project grants. (100 percent/from 1 year).

Purposes: pursuant to the Mutual Educational and Cultural Exchange Act of 1961 (MECEA) as amended, for one-year scholarships to graduate students for one year of academic studies abroad, in the humanities and social sciences—covering costs of tuition, maintenance, transportation, books, insurance. Travel grants may supplement awards obtained from others.

Eligible applicants/beneficiaries: U.S. citizens with: B.A. degree or equivalent, with certain exceptions; no doctoral degree; the majority of their high school and undergraduate college education received at U.S. institutions; language proficiency; good health.

Range: $1,900,000 to $91,404,461. **Average:** N.A.

Activity: N.A.

HQ: Council for International Exchange of Scholars, 2200 C St., NW, SA-5, 4th Floor, Rm. 4B07, Washington, DC 20037. Phone: (202) 632-3238.

Internet: exchanges.state.gov. (Note: no field offices for this program.)

19.401 ACADEMIC EXCHANGE PROGRAMS—SCHOLARS

Assistance: project grants. (100 percent/3 months to 1 year).

Purposes: pursuant to MECEA as amended, for lectureships for university lecturers to serve as visiting professors abroad, and for research grants for scholars for postdoctoral work abroad—covering costs of travel for the grantee (and, in some cases, dependents), maintenance, books, and services.

Eligible applicants/beneficiaries: U.S. citizens with foreign language proficiency and, for lecturing, college or university teaching experience. Research grants—doctoral degree or, in some fields, recognized professional standing as demonstrated by faculty rank, publications, compositions, exhibition record, concerts, etc.

Range: $239,183 to $33,399,192. **Average:** N.A.

Activity: N.A.

HQ: Council for International Exchange of Scholars, 2200 C St., NW, SA-5, 4th Floor, Rm. 4B07, Washington, DC 20037. Phone: (202) 632-3238.

Internet: exchanges.state.gov. (Note: no field offices for this program.)

19.402   INTERNATIONAL VISITORS PROGRAM

Assistance: project grants (cost sharing).

Purposes: pursuant to MECEA as amended, to plan and conduct programs of travel, observation, consultation, study, and practical experience for foreign visitors selected and assigned by the Department of State upon recommendations from U.S. embassies—to bring visitors into contact with influential Americans and representative organizations and institutions, and increase communication and mutual understanding between the foreign and domestic parties.

Eligible applicants/beneficiaries: incorporated U.S. nonprofit organizations with at least four years experience.

Range: $349,996 to $6,459,358. **Average:** N.A.

Activity: N.A.

HQ: Community Relations Branch, Office of International Visitors, BECA-Department of State, 2200 C St., NW, SA-05, Rm. 03BB06, Washington, DC 20037. Phone: (202) 632-6162.

Internet: eca.state.gov/ivlp. (Note: no field offices for this program.)

19.408   ACADEMIC EXCHANGE PROGRAMS—TEACHERS

Assistance: project grants. (100 percent/2 weeks to 1 year).

Purposes: pursuant to MECEA as amended, to enable U.S. and foreign educators to live and teach in a foreign country. Participants from primary, secondary, or junior/community colleges exchange classroom assignments for six weeks, one semester, or one academic year. Generally, participants receive leave with pay and benefits from their respective employers; grants support transportation, maintenance, accident and health insurance.

Eligible applicants/beneficiaries: teachers and administrators with at least a B.A., 3 years full-time experience, English and foreign language proficiency, and U.S. citizenship (for U.S. participants).

Range: $433,557 to $6,949,813. **Average:** N.A.

Activity: N.A.

HQ: Bureau of Educational and Cultural Affairs, Office of Global Educational Programs, Teacher Exchange Branch, Department of State, 2200 C St., NW, SA-05, Rm. 4S17, Washington, DC 20037. Phone: (202) 632-6346.

Internet: exchanges.state.gov. (Note: no field offices for this program.)

19.415   PROFESSIONAL AND CULTURAL EXCHANGE PROGRAMS—CITIZEN EXCHANGES

Assistance: project grants (cost sharing).

Purposes: pursuant to MECEA as amended, to foster, improve, and strengthen U.S. international relations by promoting mutual understanding among the peoples of the world through educational and professional exchanges. Grant funds should support: development of lasting institutional links; establishment of consortia, associations, and information networks; information transfer; development of internships.

Eligible applicants: public and private nonprofit organizations meeting the provisions of IRS regulation 26CFR1.501(c).

Eligible beneficiaries: U.S. citizens and foreign nationals.

Range: $110,664 to $16,200,000. **Average:** N.A.

Activity: N.A.

HQ: Bureau of Educational and Cultural Affairs, Office of Citizen Exchange Programs, 2200 C St., NW, SA-05, Rm. 3B14, Washington, DC 20037. Phone: (202) 632-6070.

Internet: eca.state.gov/about-bureau-0/organizational-structure/office-citizen-exchanges. (Note: no field offices for this program.)

19.421 ACADEMIC EXCHANGE PROGRAMS ("English Language Programs")

Assistance: project grants. (100 percent/to 1 year).

Purposes: pursuant to MECEA as amended, to provide highly qualified ESL/EFL teachers abroad to offer professional expertise in current English language methods and theory to host institutions; to provide specially designed courses for targeted high level groups, such as members and staffs of parliaments, and judicial, finance, and business officials; to develop communication skills among teachers and students that they need to participate in the global economy, to improve their access to diverse perspectives on a broad variety of issues, and to better understand America and its values and institutions. Grants support costs of participant travel, medical insurance, related living and project expenses, and a basic stipend.

Eligible applicants/beneficiaries: U.S. citizens with an M.A. or Ph.D. in TESL/TEFL, applied linguistics, or closely related field, and with specific teacher training experience.

Range: $1,800,000 to $25,000,000. **Average:** N.A.

Activity: N.A.

HQ: Department of State, Bureau of Educational and Cultural Affairs, Office of English Language Programs, English Language Fellow Program, 2200 C St., NW, SA-05, Rm. 4B14, Washington, DC 20037. Phone: (202) 632-9412.

Internet: americanenglish.state.gov. (Note: no field offices for this program.)

19.432 ACADEMIC EXCHANGE PROGRAMS—EDUCATIONAL ADVISING AND STUDENT SERVICES

Assistance: project grants.

Purposes: pursuant to MECEA as amended, to establish an overseas network of "Education USA" educational advising and information centers, to ensure that prospective students in specific locations abroad receive unbiased, ethical, and current information on U.S. higher education. Project funds support program implementation including adviser orientation and training.

Eligible applicants/beneficiaries: experienced incorporated U.S. nonprofit organizations.

Range: $500,000 to $6,018,229. **Average:** N.A.

Activity: N.A.

HQ: Bureau of Educational and Cultural Affairs, Educational Information and Resources (ECA/A/S/A), Department of State, 2200 C St., NW, SA-05, Rm. 04W12, Washington, DC 20037. Phone: (202) 632-6353.

Internet: educationusa.state.gov. (Note: no field offices for this program.)

19.450   ECA INDIVIDUAL GRANTS

Assistance: project grants (including individual awards); (100 percent).

Purposes: pursuant to the Fulbright-Hays Act, to increase mutual under-standing between the people of the United States and the people of other countries by means of educational and cultural exchange; to strengthen the ties which unite us with other nations by demonstrating the education-al and cultural interests, developments, and achievements of the people of the United States and other nations, and the contributions being made toward a peaceful and more fruitful life for people throughout the world; to promote international cooperation for educational and cultural advancement; and thus to assist in the development of friendly, sympa-thetic, and peaceful relations between the United States the other coun-tries of the world.

Eligible applicants: individuals in fields of specialized knowledge or skill, and other influential or distinguished persons.

Eligible beneficiaries: selected participants and the people of participating countries.

Range: $2,800 to $4,800. **Average:** N.A.

Activity: N.A.

HQ: Director, Bureau of Educational and Cultural Affairs, Department of State, SA-5, Rm. C2CC17, Washington, DC 20037. Phone: (202) 632-6382.

Internet: hppt://exchanges.statc.gov. (Note: no field offices for this program.)

19.500   MIDDLE EAST PARTNERSHIP INITIATIVE (MEPI)

Assistance: project grants.

Purposes: pursuant to the Foreign Assistance Act of 1961 as amended, to support economic, political, and educational reform efforts in the Middle East and North Africa, promoting opportunity especially for women and youth. Projects usually involve partnerships to provide training programs and projects involving local nongovernmental organizations (NGOs) and government officials. Some cost sharing is expected.

Eligible applicants: experienced nonprofit and profit organizations, state and local governments.

Eligible beneficiaries: countries covered by State Department's Bureau of Near Eastern Affairs, not currently subject to foreign assistance restrictions, such as: Morocco, Algeria, Tunisia, Egypt, West Bank/Gaza, Jordan, Lebanon, Kuwait, Iraq, Saudi Arabia, Qatar, Bahrain, UAE, Oman, and Yemen.

Range: $10,000 to $23,000,000. **Average:** N.A.

Activity: N.A.

HQ: Bureau of Near Eastern Affairs-Department of State, 22430 E St., NW, Washington, DC 20037. Phone: (202) 776-8691; FAX: (202) 776-8500.

Internet: mepi.state.gov. (Note: no field offices for this program.)

19.501 PUBLIC DIPLOMACY PROGRAMS FOR AFGHANISTAN AND PAKISTAN

Assistance: cooperative agreements (100 percent/to 3 years).

Purposes: pursuant to the Fulbright Hays Act - The Mutual Educational and Cultural Exchange Act of 1961, to promote diplomatic solutions, through language training, critical skills development and other public diplomacy programs. These resources support the people, platforms, and programs necessary to meet the international challenges to American security and welfare.

Eligible applicants: non-profit organizations subject to 501(c)(3) of the U.S. tax code or registered as a non-profit organization in the entity's home country with demonstrated experience in working with vendors, suppliers, contractors, etc. and appropriately staffed offices in country.

Eligible beneficiaries: citizens of Afghanistan, Pakistan, and the U.S.

Range: $300,000 to $2,000,000. **Average:** N.A.

Activity: N.A.

HQ: Director, Public Diplomacy Programs for Afghanistan and Pakistan, Department of State, 2201 C St., NW, Washington, DC 20520. Phone: (202) 647-8667.

Internet: N.A. (Note: no field offices for this program.)

19.510 U.S. REFUGEE ADMISSIONS PROGRAM

Assistance: project grants.

Purposes: pursuant to the Immigration and Nationality Act and Migration and Refugee Assistance Act of 1962 as amended (MRA), to provide initial reception and placement services for refugees approved for admission in the U.S., including: resettlement activities; providing basic necessities and core services for a 90-day period; employment services coordinated with publicly sponsored assistance programs. The program provides a fixed $800 reimbursement per resettled refugee; sponsors are expected to contribute private funds toward actual costs.

Eligible applicants/beneficiaries: state governments, private nonprofit organizations.

Range: N.A. **Average:** $1,021,203.

Activity: N.A.

HQ: Office of Refugee Admissions, Bureau of Population, Refugees, and Migration, Department of State, 2401 E St., NW, L505, Washington, DC 20522-0105. Phone: (202) 663-1052; FAX: (202) 663-1364.

Internet: www.state.gov/g/prm. (Note: no field offices for this program.)

19.511 OVERSEAS REFUGEE ASSISTANCE PROGRAMS FOR EAST ASIA

Assistance: project grants.

Purposes: pursuant to MRA, for humanitarian activities and services for refugees in East Asia—particularly in Thailand along the Burmese border. Projects must be complementary to and coordinated with United Nations programs, as well as other organizations.

Eligible applicants/beneficiaries: United Nations; international and non-governmental organizations.

Range/Average: N.A.

Activity: N.A.

HQ: Bureau of Population, Refugees, and Migration, Office of Assistance for Asia and the Near East, Department of State, 2401 E St., NW, L505, Washington, DC 20522-0105. Phone: (202) 663-3104; FAX: (202) 663-1061.

Internet: www.state.gov/g/prm. (Note: no field offices for this program.)

19.515 CONTRIBUTIONS TO INTERNATIONAL ORGANIZATIONS FOR OVERSEAS ASSISTANCE

Assistance: direct payments/specified use; project grants (100 percent).

Purposes: pursuant to the Migration and Refugee Assistance Act of 1962, to provide contributions to contributions to Public International Organizations to carry out humanitarian assistance activities overseas benefitting refugees, victims of conflict, and other persons of concern.

Eligible applicants/beneficiaries: public International Organizations that provide assistance to refugees and victims of conflict overseas.

Range/Average: N.A.

Activity: N.A.

HQ: Director, 2025 E. St., NW, 8th Floor, SA-9, Washington, DC 20522-0908. Phone: (202) 453-9232.

Internet: www.state.gov/g/prm. (Note: no field offices for this program.)

19.517 OVERSEAS REFUGEE ASSISTANCE PROGRAMS FOR AFRICA

Assistance: project grants.

Purposes: pursuant to MRA, for humanitarian activities and services for refugees across the African continent. Project must be complementary to and coordinated with United Nations programs.

Eligible applicants/beneficiaries: United Nations; international and non-governmental organizations.

Range/Average: N.A.

Activity: N.A.

HQ: Bureau of Population, Refugees, and Migration, Department of State, 2401 C St., NW, Ste. L505, Washington, DC 20522-0105. Phone: (202) 663-1041.

Internet: www.state.gov/g/prm. (Note: no field offices for this program.)

19.518 OVERSEAS REFUGEE ASSISTANCE PROGRAMS FOR WESTERN HEMISPHERE

Assistance: project grants.

Purposes: pursuant to MRA, for humanitarian activities and services for refugees in the Western Hemisphere—particularly in Columbia. Projects must be complementary to and coordinated with United Nations programs, as well as other organizations.

Eligible applicants/beneficiaries: United Nations; international and nongovernmental organizations.

Range/Average: N.A.

Activity: N.A.

HQ: Bureau of Population, Refugees, and Migration, Department of State, 2401 E St., NW, L505 , Washington, DC 20522-0105. Phone: (202) 663-1040. FAX: (202) 663-1530.

Internet: www.state.gov/g/prm. (Note: no field offices for this program.)

19.519 OVERSEAS REFUGEE ASSISTANCE PROGRAM FOR NEAR EAST AND SOUTH ASIA

Assistance: project grants.

Purposes: pursuant to MRA, for humanitarian activities and services for refugees in the Near East and South Asia—including those in and from Afghanistan, India, Iran, Iraq, Palestine, and Tibet. Projects must be complementary to and coordinated with United Nations programs.

Eligible applicants/beneficiaries: United Nations; international and nongovernmental organizations.

Range/Average: N.A.

Activity: N.A.

HQ: Bureau of Population, Refugees, and Migration, Office of Assistance for Asia and Near East, Department of State, 2401 E St., NW, L505, Washington, DC 20522-0105. Phone: (202) 663-3834; FAX: (202) 663-1061.

Internet: www.state.gov/g/prm. (Note: no field offices for this program.)

19.520 OVERSEAS REFUGEE ASSISTANCE PROGRAMS FOR EUROPE

Assistance: project grants.

Purposes: pursuant to MRA, for humanitarian activities and services for refugees in Europe and Central Asia, including Armenia, Azerbaijan, the Balkans, the North and South Caucasus, Chechnya, Georgia, Kosovo, Macedonia, Serbia-Montenegro. Projects must be complementary to and coordinated with United Nations programs, as well as other organizations.

Eligible applicants/beneficiaries: United Nations; international and nongovernmental organizations.

Range/Average: N.A.

Activity: N.A.

HQ: Office of Assistance to Europe, Central Asia and the Americas, Bureau of Population, Refugees, and Migration, Department of State, 2401 E St., NW,

L505, Washington, DC 20522-0105. Phone: (202) 663-1064. FAX: (202) 663-1530.

Internet: www.state.gov/g/prm. (Note: no field offices for this program.)

19.522 OVERSEAS REFUGEE ASSISTANCE PROGRAMS FOR STRATEGIC GLOBAL PRIORITIES

Assistance: project grants.

Purposes: pursuant to MRA, for humanitarian activities and services promoting PRM's initiatives in areas that are cross- cutting, core priorities— including refugee women and children, prevention and response to gender-based violence, enhancing refugee protection and health including HIV/AIDS protection. Projects must be complementary to and coordinated with United Nations programs, as well as other organizations. (Most funding under this program is allocated to the United Nations High Commissioner for Refugees and the International Committee of the Red Cross.)

Eligible applicants/beneficiaries: United Nations; international and nongovernmental organizations.

Range/Average: N.A.

Activity: N.A.

HQ: Bureau of Population, Refugees, and Migration, Department of State, 2401 E St., NW, L505, Washington, DC 20522-0105. Phone: (202) 663-1482; Fax: (202) 663-1002.

Internet: www.state.gov/g/prm. (Note: no field offices for this program.)

19.600 BUREAU OF NEAR EASTERN AFFAIRS

Assistance: cooperative agreements/discretionary grants; project grants/specified projects (100 percent/to 2 years).

Purposes: pursuant to the Foreign Assistance Act of 1961, as amended, to support the foreign assistance goals and objectives of the Department of State, Bureau of Near Eastern Affairs (NEA), as delineated in the FY Bureau Strategic and Resource Plan.

Eligible applicants/beneficiaries: 35 IHEs selected by the CDC as Prevention Research Centers (PRCs).

Range/Average: N.A.

Activity: N.A.

HQ: Director, Bureau of Near Eastern Affairs, 2430 E Street NW, Washington, DC 20037. Phone: (202) 776-8627; FAX: (202) 776-8500.

Internet: www.state.gov/p/nea. (Note: no field offices for this program.)

19.666 EUR/ACE NATIONAL ENDOWMENT FOR DEMOCRACY SMALL GRANTS
("National Endowment for Democracy NED Small Grants Program in Europe, Eurasia and Central Asia")

Assistance: project grants/discretionary (100 percent/2 to 5 years).

Purposes: pursuant to the Department of State, Foreign Operations, and Related Programs Appropriations Act of 2010, to advance democracy in Europe, Eurasia and Central Asia by providing support to indigenous civil society organizations. This program is awarded on a non-competitive basis.

Eligible applicants: National Endowment for Democracy (NED).

Eligible beneficiaries: sub-grants issued to indigenous civil society organizations in Europe, Eurasia and Central Asia.

Range/Average: N.A.

Activity: N.A.

HQ: Program Director, EUR/ACE NED Small Grants, Department of State, 2201 C St., NW, Washington, DC 20520. Phone: (202) 647-7703.

Internet: N.A. (Note: no field offices for this program.)

19.700 GENERAL DEPARTMENT OF STATE ASSISTANCE ("General Assistance Programs")

Assistance: cooperative agreements/discretionary grants; project grants/capacity building and complaint processing, training, discretionary, fellowships, specified projects (100 percent).

Purposes: pursuant to the Immigration and Nationality Act, as amended by the Refugee Act of 1980, to fulfill the mission of the U.S. Department of State. Programs provide information about Department of State programs that are not elsewhere classified.

Eligible applicants/beneficiaries: 35 IHEs selected by the CDC as Prevention Research Centers (PRCs).

Range/Average: N.A.

Activity: N.A.

HQ: Director, General Assistance Programs, Department of State, 2201 C St., Washington, DC 20522. Phone: (703) 516-1989.

Internet: N.A. (Note: no field offices for this program.)

19.750 BUREAU OF WESTERN HEMISPHERE AFFAIRS (WHA) GRANT PROGRAMS

Assistance: project grants/specified projects (100 percent/1-3 years).

Purposes: pursuant to the Foreign Assistance Act of 1961, to support the foreign assistance goals and objectives of the Department of State, Bureau of Western Hemisphere Affairs (WHA), as delineated in the FY Bureau Strategic and Resource Plan and other strategic planning documents.

Eligible applicants: entities that implement programs in WHA countries.

Eligible beneficiaries: residents of any community abroad where program activities are taking place.

Range: to $3,000,000. **Average:** N.A.

Activity: N.A.

HQ: Director, Harry S. Truman Bldg., Rm. 6913, 2201 C St., NW, Washington, DC 20520. Phone: (202) 647-5506.

Internet: N.A. (Note: no field offices for this program.)

19.901 EXPORT CONTROL AND RELATED BORDER SECURITY ("EXBS Program")

Assistance: cooperative agreements; project grants/including travel grants; (100 percent).

Purposes: pursuant to the Foreign Assistance Act of 1961, as amended, to assist existing and potential proliferation source, transit, and transshipment countries with strengthening their strategic trade controls and border security. With over 50 active partner countries on five continents, EXBS focuses on capacity-building through legislation development outreach, licensing and regulatory workshops, enforcement training, provision of inspection and detection equipment, and assistance with government-industry outreach and interagency coordination.

Eligible applicants: IHEs, nonprofits, others.

Eligible beneficiaries: brokers and freight forwarders.

Range: N.A. **Average:** $85,000.

Activity: N.A.

HQ: Program Director, Office of Export Control Cooperation (ISN/ECC), U.S. Department of State, 2201 C St., NW, Rm. 3317, Washington, DC 20520. Phone: (202) 647-1778; FAX: (202) 647-1810.

Internet: www.state.gov/t/isn/ecc/index.htm. (Note: no field offices for this program.)

DEPARTMENT OF TRANSPORTATION

20.106 AIRPORT IMPROVEMENT PROGRAM (AIP)

Assistance: project grants; advisory services/counseling (75-95 percent).

Purposes: pursuant to ARRA 2009, for planning, construction, or rehabilitation of public-use airports and related facilities and equipment, including for commercial passenger and cargo service, heliports, and seaplane landing bases. Eligible expenditures include airport master planning, land acquisition, site preparation, runway and related construction and improvement, noise reduction programs, weather reporting equipment, security and snow-removal equipment, firefighting and rescue equipment, lighting, and projects to comply with the ADA, Clean Air Act, and Federal Water Pollution Control. Ineligible uses of funds include hangar and most automobile parking facilities, buildings unrelated to safety, landscaping or artwork, routine maintenance and repair.

Eligible applicants/beneficiaries: development grants for airports listed in the National Plan of Integrated Airport Systems (NPIAS)—states, counties, municipalities, territories and possessions, and other public agencies including tribes or pueblos; private owners of public-use reliever airports or airports enplaning over 2,500 passengers annually. Noise compatibility grants—certain government units.

Range: $22,500 to $52,814,122. **Average:** $1,773,450

Activity: N.A.

HQ: Financial Assistance Division (APP-500), Office of Airport Planning and Programming, FAA-DOT, 800 Independence Ave., SW, Washington, DC 20591. Phone: (202) 267-7436.

Internet: www.faa.gov/airports_airtraffic/AIP.

20.108 AVIATION RESEARCH GRANTS

Assistance: project grants; use of property, facilities, and equipment. (to 100 percent/6 month minimum).

Purposes: pursuant to the Federal Aviation Administration Research, Engineering and Development Authorization and the Aviation Security Improvement Act of 1990, for advanced applied research and development projects in: Capacity and Air Traffic Management Technology; Communications, Navigation, and Surveillance; Aviation Weather; Airport Technology; Aircraft Safety Technology; System Security Technology; Human Factors and Aviation Medicine; Environment and Energy; Systems Science and Operations Research; Commercial Space Transportation.

Eligible applicants/beneficiaries: IHEs, nonprofit institutions.

Range: $15,000 to $5,000,000. **Average:** N.A.

Activity: N.A.

HQ: Aviation Research Grants Program (ACT-50), FAA-DOT, Hughes Technical Center, Atlantic City International Airport, NJ 08405. Phone: (609) 485-4962; FAX: (609) 485-4088.

Internet: N.A. (Note: no field offices for this program.)

20.109 AIR TRANSPORTATION CENTERS OF EXCELLENCE ("FAA Centers of Excellence")

Assistance: project grants; use of property, facilities, and equipment; specialized services. (50 percent/to 10 years).

Purposes: pursuant to the Federal Aviation Administration Research, Engineering and Development Authorization Act of 1990, for centers conducting long-term continuing research in such areas as catastrophic failure of aircraft, airspace and airport planning and design, airport capacity enhancement techniques, human performance, aviation safety and security, air transportation personnel training.

Eligible applicants/beneficiaries: IHEs, which may partner with industry affiliates and other government laboratories.

Range: from $500,000. **Average:** N.A.

Activity: 16 new cooperative agreements in FY 2014.

HQ: Director, Centers of Excellence Program Office, FAA William J. Hughes Technical Center, Bldg. 300, L28, Atlantic City International Airport, NJ 08405. Phone: (609) 485-5043; FAX: (609) 485-4753.

Internet: www.faa.gov/go/coe. (Note: no field offices for this program.)

20.200   HIGHWAY RESEARCH AND DEVELOPMENT PROGRAM

Assistance: project grants.

Purposes: pursuant to Safe, Accountable, Flexible, Efficient, Transportation Equity Act-a Legacy for Users (SAFETEA-LU), to conduct research needed to maintain and expand our vital transportation infrastructure and address challenges facing the transportation system such as, improving safety and efficiency in freight movement, reducing traffic congestion, increasing intermodal connectivity, and protecting the environment. Funding for this program is included in **20.205**.

Eligible applicants/beneficiaries: teams of state transportation, local government, and/or Canadian provinces who represent a Region (e.g. at least two states or a state and Canadian province).

Range/Average: N.A.

Activity: anticipate 30 to 40 awards in FY 2016.

HQ: Office of Acquisition Management (HAAM), FHWA-DOT, 1200 New Jersey Ave., SE, Washington, DC 20590. Phone: 202-366-4211.

Internet: www.fhwa.dot.gov.

20.205   HIGHWAY PLANNING AND CONSTRUCTION ("Federal-Aid Highway Program")

Assistance: formula grants; project grants. (80-100 percent/to 4 years).

Purposes: for highway and related projects in the interstate and national highway systems, and for bridge and safety improvements on nonfederal-aid roads and within federal lands. Eligible fund uses include costs of planning, design, right-of-way acquisition, relocation assistance, construction, reconstruction, repair (but not maintenance), improvement of interstate and primary and secondary highways, bridge repairs, roads, and streets in urban systems, congestion mitigation and air quality improvement, and research. Related projects may involve railroad grade crossings, roadside beautification, bridges, bicycle paths, pedestrian walkways, carpool projects, fringe and corridor parking, wetland mitigation, forest highways, rest areas, scenic and historic highway improvements. In some cases, funds may be used for public mass transit improvements. Funding is derived from the Highway Trust Fund. Funding for this program includes **20.215** and **20.219**.

Eligible applicants/beneficiaries: state transportation agencies; territories, possessions. Projects related to Indian reservations, parkways and park roads, and public lands highways, certain projects in urban areas or off the state highway systems—tribal governments, counties, other political subdivisions or agencies and federal agencies applying through state agencies.

Range/Average: N.A.

Activity: N.A.

HQ: Director, Office of Program Administration, FHWA-DOT, 1200 New Jersey Ave., SE, Washington, DC 20590. Phone: (202) 366-5330.

Internet: www.fhwa.dot.gov.

20.215 HIGHWAY TRAINING AND EDUCATION

Assistance: project grants; training. (80-100 percent/3 months to 5 years).

Purposes: pursuant to the Transportation Equity Act for the 21st Century, to develop and administer training, educational, and technical assistance programs related to federal-aid highway work. Faculty, graduate, research, and minority fellowships may be awarded under the Dwight David Eisenhower Transportation Fellowship Program. Courses and study programs may be obtained from IHEs, government agencies, private entities, or the National Highway Institute. Funding for this program is included in **20.205**.

Eligible applicants/beneficiaries: training—state and local transportation agency employees. Fellowships—persons matriculating at U.S. IHEs in transportation-related disciplines.

Range/Average: N.A.

Activity: anticipate 200 to 40 awards in FY 2015.

HQ: Director, National Highway Institute, FHWA-DOT, 1310 N Courthouse Rd., Suite 300, Arlington, VA 22201. Phone: (703) 235-0500.

Internet: www.nhi.fhwa.dot.gov.

20.218 NATIONAL MOTOR CARRIER SAFETY ("MCSAP")

Assistance: formula grants (to 80-100 percent).

Purposes: pursuant to the Surface Transportation Assistance Act of 1982, Motor Carrier Safety Act of 1991, and Transportation Equity Act for the 21st Century, for programs involving the development and enforcement of uniform rules, regulations, and standards concerning inter- and intrastate commercial motor vehicle safety, and of state hazardous materials regulations compatible with federal standards.

Eligible applicants/beneficiaries: states; territories and possessions (100 percent funding).

Range/Average: N.A.

Activity: N.A.

HQ: State Programs Division (MC-ESS), FMCSA-DOT, 1200 New Jersey Ave., SE, Washington, DC 20590. Phone: (202) 366-0710.

Internet: www.fmcsa.dot.gov.

20.219 RECREATIONAL TRAILS PROGRAM

Assistance: formula grants; project grants. (80-95 percent/to 4 years).

Purposes: to provide new and maintain existing recreational trails and related facilities for motorized and nonmotorized uses. Project funds may be used to: maintain and restore existing trails; construct new trails; develop trail-side and trail-head facilities and trail linkages; acquire easements identified in state trail plans; acquire fee simple title from willing sellers; pay limited administrative and public education costs. Funds may not be used for property condemnation, nor to provide access by motorized users to trails used mainly by nonmotorized users. Funding for this program is included in **20.205**.

Eligible applicants/beneficiaries: state agencies, which may accept applications from private organizations, or city, county, or other governmental organizations including federal agencies. States must have an advisory committee representing both motorized and nonmotorized users.

Range: $816,847 to $5,698,627. **Average:** $1,614,838.

Activity: N.A.

HQ: Office of Planning and Environment (HEPN-50), FHWA-DOT, 1200 New Jersey Ave., SE, Washington, DC 20590. Phone: (202) 366-5013; FAX: (202) 366-3409.

Internet: www.fhwa.dot.gov/environment/recreational_trails.

20.223   TRANSPORTATION INFRASTRUCTURE FINANCE AND INNOVATION ACT (TIFIA) PROGRAM
("TIFIA Credit Program")

Assistance: direct loans; guaranteed loans; lines of credit (to 35 years).

Purposes: pursuant to legislation codified within sections 601 through 609 of title 23 of the United States Code (23 U.S.C. 601-609), and others, to finance projects of national or regional significance by filling market gaps and leveraging substantial non-Federal and private co-investment. TIFIA credit assistance is intended to facilitate financing of projects that would otherwise be significantly delayed because of funding limitations or difficulties accessing capital markets. Through TIFIA, the DOT provides Federal credit assistance to eligible highway, transit, rail, and intermodal freight projects, including access to seaports. All projects receiving TIFIA assistance must comply with generally applicable Federal laws and regulations, including title VI of the Civil Rights Act of 1964, the National Environmental Policy Act of 1969, and the Uniform Relocation Assistance and Real Property Acquisition Policies Act of 1970. Principal amount of requested credit assistance must not exceed 33 percent of eligible project costs.

Eligible applicants/beneficiaries: Public or private entities seeking to finance, design, construct, own, or operate an eligible surface transportation project may apply for TIFIA assistance, such as state departments of transportation; local governments; transit agencies; special authorities; special districts; railroad companies; and private firms or consortia that may include companies specializing in engineering, construction, materials, and/or the operation of transportation facilities.

Range/Average: N.A.

Activity: closed 6 loans in FY 2015.

HQ: TIFIA Joint Program Office (HCFT-1), Federal Highway Administration, DOT, 1200 New Jersey Ave. Rm. E-64-302, Washington, DC 20590. Phone:(202) 366-9644.

Internet: www.fhwa.dot.gov/ipd/tifia. (Note: no field offices for this program.)

20.224   FEDERAL LANDS ACCESS PROGRAM (FLAP)

Assistance: formula grants; projects grants. (80 percent to 4 years).

Purposes: pursuant to the Fixing America's Surface Transportation Act, Public Law 114-94, 23 U.S.C 204 and Section 1119 of the Moving Ahead for Progress in the 21st Century Act, Public Law 112-141, 23 U.S.C 204, to improve transportation facilities that provide access to, are adjacent to, or are located within Federal lands. Funds shall be used to pay the cost of transportation planning, research, engineering, operation, preventive maintenance, rehabilitation, restoration, construction, and reconstruction of federal lands access transportation facilities located on or adjacent to, or that provide access to, federal lands.

Eligible applicants: the owner of the affected transportation asset(s).

Eligible beneficiaries: state transportation departments and other federal, state, and local agencies.

Range/Average: N.A.

Activity: N.A.

HQ: Director, FHWA-DOT, 1200 New Jersey Ave., Washington, DC 20590. Phone: (202) 493-0271.

Internet: flh.fhwa.dot.gov/programs/flap/reports/.

20.231   PERFORMANCE AND REGISTRATION INFORMATION SYSTEMS MANAGEMENT (PRISM)

Assistance: project grants (100 percent/to 2 years).

Purposes: pursuant to Motor Carrier Safety Act of 1991, Transportation Equity Act for the 21st Century, and Flexible, Efficient Transportation Act of 2006, to identify motor carriers responsible for the safety of commercial motor vehicles, and to monitor their safety fitness—by linking the vehicle registration process to safety performance monitoring and enforcement, which records the DOT vehicle number to the motor carrier. Funds may cover training, outreach, and development of system requirements.

Eligible applicants/beneficiaries: states, DC.

Range: $100,000 to $750,000. **Average:** N.A.

Activity: N.A.

HQ: Office of Enforcement and Compliance (MC-ECE), FMCSA-DOT, 1200 New Jersey Ave., SE, Washington, DC 20590. Phone: (202) 366-0710.

Internet: www.fmcsa.dot.gov/safety-security/prism/prism.htm.

20.232   COMMERCIAL DRIVER'S LICENSE PROGRAM IMPROVEMENT GRANT

Assistance: project grants (100 percent).

Purposes: to prevent truck and bus accidents, fatalities, and injuries through programs requiring drivers to have a single commercial motor vehicle license, and by disqualifying drivers that operate commercial motor vehicles in an unsafe manner. Project examples: Social Security online verification; covert operations for third-party tester.

Eligible applicants/beneficiaries: states, DC.

Range: $20,000 to $1,500,000. **Average:** N.A.

Activity: N.A.

HQ: State Programs Division (CDL Team-MC-ESL), FMCSA-DOT, 1200 New Jersey Ave., SE, Washington, DC 20590. Phone: (202) 366-0710.

Internet: www.fmcsa.dot.gov/safety-security/grants/CDLPI/index.aspx. (Note: no field offices for this program.)

20.233 BORDER ENFORCEMENT GRANTS

Assistance: project grants (100 percent/2 years).

Purposes: pursuant to the Safe, Accessible, Feasible, and Efficient Equity Act, to ensure that commercial motor carriers entering the U.S. from foreign country comply with U.S. commercial vehicle safety and financial standards, regulations, and requirements, and that their drivers are qualified and properly licensed; for enforcement activities and projects.

Eligible applicants/beneficiaries: entities and states sharing a land border with a foreign country.

Range: $22,000 to $18,000,000. **Average:** N.A.

Activity: N.A.

HQ: Borders Division, (MC-ESB), FMCSA-DOT, 1200 New Jersey Ave., SE, Washington, DC 20590. Phone: (202) 366-0710.

Internet: www.fmcsa.dot.gov.

20.234 SAFETY DATA IMPROVEMENT PROGRAM ("SaDIP")

Assistance: project grants (80 percent).

Purposes: pursuant to Safe, Accountable, Flexible, Efficient, Transportation Equity Act: A Legacy for Users (SAFETEA-LU), to improve the overall data quality in the collection and analysis of truck and bus crash and inspection data. Funds may be used to: meet staffing requirements; train law enforcement officers; develop and acquire appropriate software.

Eligible applicants/beneficiaries: states, DC.

Range: $5,000 to $500,000. **Average:** $250,000.

Activity: N.A.

HQ: Analysis Division, Office of Research and Analysis (MC-RRA), FMCSA-DOT, 1200 New Jersey Ave., SE, Washington, DC 20590. Phone: (202) 366-0710.

Internet: www.fmcsa.dot.gov/safety-security/grants/grants.aspx.

20.235 COMMERCIAL MOTOR VEHICLE OPERATOR TRAINING GRANTS (CMV-OST)

Assistance: project grants (80 percent/to 2 years).

Purposes: pursuant to SAFETEA-LU, to train present and future operators of commercial motor vehicles.

Eligible applicants/beneficiaries: state and local governments, public or private IHEs, vocational-technical schools, truck driver training schools.

Range: N.A. **Average:** $100,000.

Activity: N.A.

HQ: State Programs Division (MC-ESS), FMCSA-DOT, 1200 New Jersey Ave., SE, Washington, DC 20590. Phone: (202) 366-0710.

Internet: www.fmcsa.dot.gov. (Note: no field offices for this program.)

20.237 COMMERCIAL VEHICLE INFORMATION SYSTEMS AND NETWORKS (CVISN)

Assistance: project grants (to 80 percent).

Purposes: pursuant to SAFETEA-LU, to focus state commercial vehicle safety enforcement on high-risk operators, to enable more effective HAZ-MAT safety compliance and enforcement, and to incorporate homeland security safeguards, through programs that: integrate data systems that improve the accuracy, integrity, and verifiability of credentials; improve electronic screening of commercial vehicles; and, enable on-line application for and issuance of credentials.

Eligible applicants/beneficiaries: states, DC meeting strict DOT requirements and criteria.

Range: $50,000 to $1,000,000. **Average:** N.A.

Activity: N.A.

HQ: Office of Research and Analysis (MC-RRT), FMCSA-DOT, 1200 New Jersey Ave., SE, Washington, DC 20590. Phone: (202) 366-0710.

Internet: www.fmcsa.dot.gov.

20.239 MOTOR CARRIER RESEARCH AND TECHNOLOGY PROGRAMS

Assistance: cooperative agreements; project grants/contracts (100 percent/1 to 3 years).

Purposes: pursuant to the Surface Transportation Assistance Act of 1982, to implement the Specialized Heavy Vehicle Inspection (SHVI) Study Cooperative Agreement which will provide funding to collect safety data from roadside inspections on commercial motor vehicles (CMV) exceeding certain weight levels to determine if there are any correlations between violations of legal weight limits and violations of motor carrier safety regulations, particularly regulations that are referenced in the out-of-service criteria.

Eligible applicants/beneficiaries: 35 IHEs selected by the CDC as Prevention Research Centers (PRCs).

Range: $100,000 to $3,000,000. **Average:** $400,000.

Activity: N.A.

HQ: Director, Motor Carrier Research and Technology Programs, FMSCA-DOT, 1200 New Jersey Ave., SE, Washington, DC 20590. Phone: (202) 366-2364.

Internet: www.fmcsa.dot.gov. (Note: no field offices for this program.)

20.240   FUEL TAX EVASION-INTERGOVERNMENTAL ENFORCEMENT EFFORT

Assistance: project grants (to 2 years).

Purposes: pursuant to Safe, Accountable, Flexible, Efficient, Transportation Equity Act: A Legacy for Users (SAFETEA-LU), to increase intergovernmental activities and enforcement efforts among public agencies to reduce Federal fuel tax evasion. Funds my be used only to expand or enhance efforts to increase motor fuel tax enforcement and payments, examinations and criminal investigations, and increase research and training in the area of Federal fuel tax evasion.

Eligible applicants/beneficiaries: states, DC, U.S. territories and possessions, other public agencies, including tribal or pueblo, republics of Marshall Islands and Palau, and the Federated States of Micronesia.

Range: $10,000 to $250,000. **Average:** N.A.

Activity: N.A.

HQ: Program Manager, Office of Transportation Policy Studies (HTPS), FHWA-DOT, 1200 New Jersey Ave., SE, Washington, DC 20590. Phone: (202) 366-9234.

Internet: www.fhwa.dot.gov/policy/otps/fueltax.htm. (Note: no field offices for this program.)

20.301   RAILROAD SAFETY

Assistance: investigation of complaints.

Purposes: pursuant to Department of Transportation Act of 1966 and Federal Railroad Safety Act of 1970, as amended, to reduce railroad-related casualties and accidents through investigation of safety-related complaints and evaluations of petitions requesting waivers from standards, rules, and regulations.

Eligible applicants/beneficiaries: anyone concerned with railroad safety.

Range: $4,329 to $9,490,500. **Average:** $2,035,157.

Activity: N.A.

HQ: Associate Administrator for Safety, Federal Railroad Administration-DOT, 1200 New Jersey Ave., SE, Washington, DC 20590. Phone: (202) 493-6139.

Internet: www.fra.dot.gov.

20.313   RAILROAD RESEARCH AND DEVELOPMENT

Assistance: project grants.

Purposes: for research advancing rail safety, by university organizations.

Eligible applicants/beneficiaries: academic research institutions with at least five years relevant experience.

Range: N.A. **Average:** $350,000.

Activity: N.A.

HQ: Office of Research and Development (RDV-31), Federal Railroad Administration-DOT, 1200 New Jersey Ave., S.E., Washington, DC 20590. Phone: (202) 493-6359.

Internet: www.fra.dot.gov. (Note: no field offices for this program.)

20.314 RAILROAD DEVELOPMENT

Assistance: project grants.

Purposes: pursuant to SAFETEA-LU, to provide financial assistance for planning and developing railroad corridors (including environmental studies); rail line relocation and improvement; construction projects that improve rail lines, enhance service, and add capacity to the national rail system; capital construction, rehabilitation, and improvements benefiting train operations.

Eligible applicants/beneficiaries: state, regional, and local governments; for-profit organizations, such as railroads.

Range: $10,000 to $10,000,000. **Average:** N.A.

Activity: N.A.

HQ: Passenger Rail Programs, Office of Railroad Development (RDV-13), Federal Railroad Administration-DOT, 1200 New Jersey Ave., SE, Washington, DC 20590. Phone: (202) 493-6393.

Internet: www.fra.dot.gov. (Note: no field offices for this program.)

20.315 NATIONAL RAILROAD PASSENGER CORPORATION GRANTS ("Amtrak Grants")

Assistance: project grants.

Purposes: to support the operation of and capital investment in U.S. intercity passenger rail service. Funds may be used for operating expenses, capital investment activities, and/or payment of debt service obligations.

Eligible applicants/beneficiaries: National Railroad Passenger Corporation, as authorized by appropriating statute.

Range: $789,000 to $1,129,300,000. **Average:** N.A.

Activity: N.A.

HQ: Passenger Programs Division (RDV-13), Office of Railroad Development, Federal Railroad Administration-DOT, 1200 New Jersey Ave., S.E., Washington, DC 20590. Phone: (202) 493-6454.

Internet: www.fra.dot.gov. (Note: no field offices for this program.)

20.316 RAILROAD REHABILITATION AND IMPROVEMENT FINANCING PROGRAM ("RRIF Loan Program")

Assistance: direct loans (25 years).

Purposes: pursuant to the Railroad Revitalization and Regulatory Reform Act of 1976, to provide direct loans and loan guarantees in order to: acquire, improve, or rehabilitate intermodal, rail freight or passenger equipment or facilities, including track, components of track, bridges, yards, buildings and shops; to develop or establish new intermodal or railroad facilities; and to refinance outstanding debt incurred for described purposes. The maximum loan amount will be based on the remaining available funds under the Program's authorization. The interest rate on direct loans will be equal to the rate on Treasury securities of a similar term.

Eligible applicants/beneficiaries: state and local governments, government-sponsored authorities and corporations, railroads, and joint ventures that include at least one railroad.

Range/Average: N.A.

Activity: anticipate closing 2 loans in FY 2016.

HQ: Chief, Credit & Financial Analysis Division-DOT, 1200 New Jersey Ave., SE, Washington , DC 20590 Phone: (202) 493-6051.

Internet: www.fra.dot.gov/Page/P0128.

20.317 CAPITAL ASSISTANCE TO STATES—INTERCITY PASSENGER RAIL SERVICE
("IPR Program")

Assistance: project grants/matching (50 percent).

Purposes: pursuant to the Transportation, Housing and Urban Development, and Related Agencies Appropriations Act of 2008, to provide financial assistance to fund capital improvements and related planning activities necessary to support improved or new intercity passenger rail service. Only proposed planning projects which lead to a programmatic Environmental Impact Statement for the purpose of route selection and/or a corridor transportation plan prepared in accordance with the methodologies set forth in FRA's publication, entitled Railroad Corridor Transportation Plans: A Guidance Manual," will be considered for possible funding.

Eligible applicants: state departments of transportation (including DC) that include intercity passenger rail service as an integral part of statewide transportation planning as required under section 135 of Title 23, United States Code.

Eligible beneficiaries: general public, both users and non-users of intercity passenger rail service; state departments of transportation and other public agencies; private transportation companies that participate through contractual arrangements with a state DOT.

Range/Average: N.A.

Activity: N.A.

HQ: Office of Railroad Development, 1200 New Jersey Ave., SE, Washington, DC 20590. Phone: (202) 493-6139.

Internet: www.fra.dot.gov.

20.318 MAGLEV PROJECT SELECTION PROGRAM—SAFETEA—LU

Assistance: project grants (80 percent/to 5 years).

Purposes: pursuant to the Safe, Accountable, Flexible, Efficient Transportation Equity Act: A Legacy for Users (SAFETEA-LU) and SAFETEA-LU Technical Corrections Act, to provide financial assistance for a demonstration magnetic levitation transportation project. Eligible project costs include: preconstruction planning, capital cost of fixed guideway infrastructure; propulsion equipment and other components attached to guideways; power distribution, control, communication, storage repair, and maintenance facilities. Costs incurred for a new station are not eligible.

Eligible applicants/beneficiaries: state governments with existing maglev projects located east of the Mississippi River.

Range: $13,000,000 to $28,000,000. **Average:** N.A.

Activity: N.A.

HQ: Office of Railroad Development, 1200 New Jersey Ave., SE, Washington, DC 20590. Phone: (202) 493-6393.

Internet: www.fra.dot.gov. (Note: no field offices for this program.)

20.319 HIGH-SPEED RAIL CORRIDORS AND INTERCITY PASSENGER RAIL SERVICE—CAPITAL ASSISTANCE GRANTS ("HSR/IPR Program")

Assistance: project grants (100 percent/to 5 years).

Purposes: pursuant to ARRA 2009, as amended by Passenger Rail Investment and Improvement Act of 2008, to assist in financing the capital costs of facilities, infrastructure, and equipment necessary to provide or improve high-speed rail and intercity passenger rail service.

Eligible applicants: private (including profit) organizations/institutions.

Eligible beneficiaries: states and profit organizations.

Range/Average: N.A.

Activity: N.A.

HQ: Federal Railroad Administration-DOT, 1200 New Jersey Ave., SE, Washington, DC 20590. Phone: (202) 493-6139.

Internet: www.fra.dot.gov. (Note: no field offices for this program.)

20.320 RAIL LINE RELOCATION AND IMPROVEMENT ("Rail Line Relocation")

Assistance: project grants/cooperative agreements (90 percent).

Purposes: pursuant to Safe, Accountable, Flexible, Efficient Transportation Equity Act: A Legacy for Users (SAFETEA-LU), to provide financial assistance for rail line relocation and improvement projects, including: rehabilitation, relocation or construction of railroads, planning activities.

Eligible applicants: government.

Eligible beneficiaries: states.

Range: $152,664 to $4,000,000. **Average:** $2,050,000.

Activity: 23 awards in FY 2014.

HQ: FRA-DOT, 1200 New Jersey Ave., SE, Washington, DC 20590. Phone: (202) 493-6067.

Internet: www.fra.dot.gov/us/content/2008.

20.321   RAILROAD SAFETY TECHNOLOGY GRANTS

Assistance: project grants (80 percent).

Purposes: pursuant to the Rail Safety Improvement Act of 2008, to facilitate the deployment of train control technologies, train control component technologies, processor-based technologies, electronically controlled pneumatic brakes, rail integrity inspection systems, rail integrity warning systems, switch position indicators and monitors, remote control power switch technologies, track integrity circuit technologies, and other new or novel railroad safety technology.

Eligible applicants/beneficiaries: passenger and freight railroad carriers, railroad suppliers, State and local governments, and IHEs.

Range/Average: N.A.

Activity: N.A.

HQ: Director, Office of Railroad Safety, Federal Railroad Administration, Stop 25, 1200 New Jersey Ave SE., Washington, DC 20590. Phone: (202) 493-1332.

Internet: www.fra.dot.gov.

20.323   FISCAL YEAR 2013 HURRICANE SANDY DISASTER RELIEF GRANTS TO THE NATIONAL RAILROAD PASSENGER CORPORATION

Assistance: project grants (100 percent).

Purposes: pursuant to the Disaster Relief Appropriations Act of 2013, project grants to provide supplemental assistance to the National Passenger Railroad Corporation for disaster assistance related to Hurricane Sandy. Funds may be used for repair expenses or resiliency projects.

Eligible applicants/beneficiaries: the National Railroad Passenger Corporation.

Range: $30,248,000 to $185,000,000. **Average:** N.A.

Activity: N.A.

HQ: Director, Hurricane Sandy Disaster Relief Grants to the National Railroad Passenger Corporation. FRA-DOT, 1200 New Jersey Ave., S.E., Washington, DC 20590. Phone: (202) 493-6454.

Internet: www.fra.dot.gov. (Note: no field offices for this program.)

20.500   FEDERAL TRANSIT—CAPITAL INVESTMENT GRANTS ("New Starts, Small Starts, and Core Capacity")

Assistance: formula grants; project grants (80-90 percent).

Purposes: pursuant to ARRA 2009, for public transportation project costs in the following categories: fixed guideway modernization formula grants; bus and bus facilities discretionary grants and "New Starts" discretionary grants covering new systems and extensions, if specifically designated by Congress. Eligible costs include: acquisition, construction, reconstruction, and improvement of facilities and equipment; purchases of land, buses or other rolling stock; planning and engineering; new technological methods and techniques; park-and-ride lots; projects to meet the needs of the elderly and the disabled; certain projects enhancing urban economic development.

Eligible applicants/beneficiaries: public agencies including states, municipalities, and other state subdivisions; public agencies and instrumentalities of one or more states; public corporations, boards, and commissions established under state law. Private transportation companies may participate through contracts.

Range/Average: N.A.

Activity: N.A.

HQ: Office of Transit Programs, FTA-DOT, 1200 New Jersey Ave., SE, Washington, DC 20590. Phone: (202) 366-0870.

Internet: www.fta.dot.gov.

20.505 METROPOLITAN TRANSPORTATION PLANNING AND STATE AND NON-METROPOLITAN PLANNING AND RESEARCH

Assistance: formula grants. (80 percent/3 years).

Purposes: pursuant to the Moving Ahead for Progress in the 21st Century Act, to develop transportation improvement projects, long- range transportation plans, and other technical studies related to management systems, capital requirements, and economic feasibility.

Eligible applicants/beneficiaries: states (for distribution to metropolitan planning organizations).

Range: $20,000 to $5,000,000. **Average:** N.A.

Activity: anticipate 47 awards in FY 2015.

HQ: Office of Planning and Environment 1200 New Jersey Ave., SE, Washington, DC 20590. Phone: (202) 366-2996.

Internet: www.fta.dot.gov.

20.507 FEDERAL TRANSIT—FORMULA GRANTS ("Urbanized Area Formula Program")

Assistance: formula grants. (50-90 percent/3 years).

Purposes: pursuant to ARRA 2009, to plan, acquire, construct or reconstruct, improve, and maintain transit facilities and equipment. Transit projects may involve bringing equipment into compliance with the ADA and the Clean Air Act; also, they may involve bicycles (90 percent funding). Grants subsidizing operating costs may not exceed 50 percent.

Eligible applicants/beneficiaries: urbanized areas of 200,000 or more population—public entities jointly designated by the governor, responsible local officials, and publicly-owned operators of mass transportation services. Urbanized areas of 50,000 to 200,000 population—governors or their designees.

Range/Average: N.A.

Activity: anticipate 1,500 awards in FY 2015.

HQ: Director, Office of Resource Management and State Programs, Office of Program Management, FTA-DOT, 1200 New Jersey Ave., SE, Washington, DC 20590. Phone: (202) 366-2623.

Internet: www.fta.dot.gov.

20.509 FORMULA GRANTS FOR RURAL AREAS ("Rural Area Program")

Assistance: formula grants. (50-90 percent/2 years).

Purposes: pursuant to ARRA 2009, for public transportation systems in nonurbanized areas—i.e., rural and small areas under 50,000 population, for uses similar to **20.507**.

Eligible applicants/beneficiaries: designated state agencies. Sub-grants may be awarded to state agencies, local public bodies and agencies, nonprofit organizations, tribes, and operators of public transportation services, including intercity bus service—in rural and small urban areas. Private operators may receive subcontracts.

Range/Average: N.A.

Activity: N.A.

HQ: Office of Capital and Formula Assistance, Office of Program Management, FTA-DOT, 1200 New Jersey Ave., SE, Washington, DC 20590. Phone: (202) 366-2677.

Internet: www.fta.dot.gov.

20.513 ENHANCED MOBILITY OF SENIORS AND INDIVIDUALS WITH DISABILITIES

Assistance: formula grants. (80 percent/3 years).

Purposes: to cover capital costs of providing specialized transportation services for elderly and handicapped persons. Specially designed vehicles may be purchased with grant funds. Awards favor projects involving private profit operators.

Eligible applicants/beneficiaries: designated states. Subgrants may be awarded to private nonprofit organizations or public bodies.

Range/Average: N.A.

Activity: N.A.

HQ: Program Coordinator, Office of Resource Management and State Programs, Office of Program Management, FTA-DOT, 1200 New Jersey Ave., SE, Washington, DC 20590. Phone: (202) 366-2150.

Internet: www.fta.dot.gov.

20.514 PUBLIC TRANSPORTATION RESEARCH, TECHNICAL ASSISTANCE, AND TRAINING

Assistance: project grants; technical information; training (to 100 percent).

Purposes: for research on mobility management, transit operational efficiency, safety and emergency preparedness, transit capacity building, energy independence and environmental protection, infrastructure and equipment protection and innovation, and strategic program planning. Projects may involve research, development, demonstrations, training, planning studies, and human resource programs.

Eligible applicants/beneficiaries: public bodies, state and local agencies, nonprofit institutions, universities, profit organizations, and operators of public transportation services.

Range/Average: N.A.

Activity: N.A.

HQ: Associate Administrator/Research, Demonstration and Innovation (TRI-1), FTA-DOT, 1200 New Jersey Ave., SE, Washington, DC 20590. Phone: (202) 366-4052.

Internet: www.fta.dot.gov/research. (Note: no field offices for this program.)

20.516   JOB ACCESS—REVERSE COMMUTE

Assistance: project grants (50-80 percent/to 4 years).

Purposes: pursuant to the Transportation Equity Act for the 21st Century, to develop transportation services to connect welfare recipients and low-income persons to employment and support services. Funds may be used: for capital projects; to finance equipment, facilities, and associated support costs related to providing access to jobs—associated with adding reverse commute bus, train, carpool or service from urban areas, urbanized areas, and other areas to suburban work places.

Eligible applicants/beneficiaries: state and local government agencies, nonprofit agencies, transit providers.

Range: $10,890 to $1,293,611. **Average:** $180,588.

Activity: N.A.

HQ: Office of Program Management, FTA-DOT, 41200 New Jersey Ave., SE, Washington, DC 20590. Phone: (202) 366-2677.

Internet: www.fta.dot.gov/funding/grants/grants_financing_3550.html.

20.518   CAPITAL AND TRAINING ASSISTANCE PROGRAM FOR OVER-THE-ROAD BUS ACCESSIBILITY

Assistance: project grants. (to 90 percent/3 years).

Purposes: pursuant to the Transportation Equity Act for the 21st Century, for private operators of over-the-road buses to finance the incremental capital and training costs of complying with DOT's "Transportation for Individuals with Disabilities" rule. Project costs may cover: adding wheelchair lifts and other accessibility components to new vehicle purchases; retrofitting existing vehicles; training in equipment operation and maintenance, boarding assistance, handling, and storage.

Eligible applicants/beneficiaries: certain private operators of over-the-road buses.

Range: $25,000 to $180,000. **Average:** $25,000.

Activity: N.A.

HQ: Program Manager, Office of Program Management, FTA-DOT, 1200 New Jersey Ave., SE, Washington, DC 20590. Phone: (202) 366-3800.

Internet: www.fta.dot.gov.

20.519 CLEAN FUELS

Assistance: project grants (80-90 percent).

Purposes: for the acquisition of approved "clean fuel buses" and related facilities by agencies providing public transportation in urbanized areas designated as non-attainment or maintenance area for ozone or carbon monoxide.

Eligible applicants/beneficiaries: public agencies including states and municipalities; public corporations, boards, and commissions established under state laws. States are applicants in urbanized areas of under 200,000 population.

Range: $69,720 to $5,000,000. Average: $2,165,596.

Activity: N.A.

HQ: Office of Program Management, FTA-DOT, 1200 New Jersey Ave., SE, Washington, DC 20590. Phone: (202) 366-4818.

Internet: www.fta.dot.gov.

20.521 NEW FREEDOM PROGRAM

Assistance: formula grants (50-100 percent).

Purposes: pursuant to SAFETEA-LU, for new public transportation services or alternatives available to persons with disabilities, beyond ADA requirements. Funds may cover capital and operating expenses within certain limits.

Eligible applicants/beneficiaries: governor-designated recipients. Eligible subrecipients include public and nonprofit agencies, public transportation providers, human services transportation providers.

Range: $111,000 to $2,200,000 for urbanized areas; $644,000 to $1,500,000 for states; $459,000 to $701,000 for rural areas. Average: $150,000 for urbanized areas; $115,000 for states; $160,000 for rural areas.

Activity: N.A.

HQ: Office of Program Management, FTA-DOT, 1200 New Jersey Ave., SE, Washington, DC 20590. Phone: (202) 366-2160.

Internet: www.fta.dot.gov/funding/grants/grants_financing_3549.html. (Note: no field offices for this program.)

20.522 ALTERNATIVES ANALYSIS

Assistance: project grants (80 percent).

Purposes: to conduct analyses of modal and multimodal alternatives and general alignment options for identified transportation needs in particular, broadly defined travel corridors, as part of the early planning for capital projects for new or extensions of existing fixed guideway systems.

Eligible applicants/beneficiaries: public agencies including states and municipalities; public corporations, boards, and commissions established under state laws.

Range/Average: N.A.

Activity: N.A.

HQ: Office of Program Management, FTA-DOT, 1200 New Jersey Ave., SE, Washington, DC 20590. Phone: (202) 366-1636.

Internet: www.fta.dot.gov.

20.523 CAPITAL ASSISTANCE PROGRAM FOR REDUCING ENERGY CONSUMPTION AND GREENHOUSE GAS EMISSIONS ("TIGGER Grants")

Assistance: project grants/discretionary (100 percent).

Purposes: pursuant to the Consolidated Appropriations Act of 2010, to assist public agencies that provide transit service in financing the acquisition of capital assets to reduce energy consumption or greenhouse gas emissions. Applicants must have the legal, financial, and technical capacity to carry out the proposed project and maintain, in a state of good repair, any facilities/equipment purchased with federal assistance.

Eligible applicants/beneficiaries: 35 IHEs selected by the CDC as Prevention Research Centers (PRCs).

Range: $250,000 to $10,800,000. **Average:** $2,300,000.

Activity: N.A.

HQ: Program Director, "TIGGER" Grants, FTA-DOT, 1200 New Jersey Ave., SE, Washington, DC 20590. Phone: (202) 366-3052.

Internet: www.fta.dot.gov/research.

20.527 PUBLIC TRANSPORTATION EMERGENCY RELIEF PROGRAM ("Transit ER Program")

Assistance: project grants/discretionary; special grants (80 percent).

Purposes: pursuant to the Moving Ahead for Progress in the 21st Century Act, to provide operating assistance and capital funding to aid recipients and subrecipients in restoring public transportation service, and in repairing and reconstructing public transportation assets as expeditiously as possible following an emergency or major disaster.

Eligible applicants: public transportation service entity that receives federal transit funds directly from FTA, operating in an area declared an emergency or major disaster by a gubernatorial or presidential declaration.

Eligible beneficiaries: public transportation operators, general public.

Range: $25,000 to $800,000,000. **Average:** N.A.

Activity: 40 awards in FY 2014.

HQ: Program Director, ER Programs, FTA-DOT, 1200 New Jersey Ave., SE, Washington, DC 20590. Phone: (202) 366-0778.

Internet: www.fta.gov. (Note: no field offices for this program.)

20.530 PUBLIC TRANSPORTATION INNOVATION

Assistance: direct payments/specified use. (50 to 100 percent to 2 years).

Purposes: pursuant to the Fixing America's Surface Transportation (FAST) Act of 2015, to advance innovative public transportation research and development of national significance. The program supports research not undertaken by the private sector. Cost sharing will vary based on type of project and direct financial benefit to the participating entity.

Eligible applicants: federal, state, and local government entities, providers of transportation, public and private nonprofit organizations, for-profit organizations, and IHEs.

Eligible beneficiaries: state, local, public and private nonprofit institutions/ organizations.

Range: $200,000 to $1,000,000. **Average:** $400,000.

Activity: N.A.

HQ: FTA-DOT, 1200 New Jersey Ave. SE, Washington, DC 20590. Phone: (202) 366-2204.

Internet: www.fta.dot.gov/research. (Note: no field offices for this program.)

20.531   TECHNICAL ASSISTANCE AND WORKFORCE DEVELOPMENT

Assistance: direct payments/specified use; project grants. (100 percent).

Purposes: pursuant to the Fixing America's Surface Transportation (FAST) Act of 2015, to more effectively and efficiently provide public transportation service, administer funds received in compliance with Federal law, and improve public transportation. Funds will support technical assistance, training, workforce projects, and standards development not undertaken by the private sector, and assistance to comply with federal law. Funds will also support innovative workforce development activities targeting areas with high unemployment, provide training related to the maintenance of alternative-energy-efficient or zero-emission vehicles, and to address current or projected workforce shortages in areas that require technical expertise.

Eligible applicants: federal, state, and local government entities, providers of transportation, public and private nonprofit organizations, for-profit organizations, and IHEs.

Eligible beneficiaries: state, local, public and private nonprofit institutions/organizations.

Range/Average: N.A.

Activity: N.A.

HQ: FTA-DOT, 1200 New Jersey Ave. SE, Washington, DC 20590. Phone: (202) 366-2204.

Internet: www.fta.dot.gov/research. (Note: no field offices for this program.)

20.600   STATE AND COMMUNITY HIGHWAY SAFETY

Assistance: formula grants (80 percent).

Purposes: pursuant to the Highway Safety Act of 1966 as amended, for highway traffic safety enforcement program costs, such as police equipment purchases, training, and overtime pay; emergency medical services training and equipment purchases; public education projects. Program priority areas include alcohol and other drug countermeasures, police traffic services, occupant protection, traffic records, emergency medical services, motorcycle safety, pedestrian/bicycle safety, speed control, roadway safety, pupil transportation safety.

Eligible applicants/beneficiaries: states, tribes, territories, possessions.

Range/Average: N.A.

Activity: N.A.

HQ: Associate Administrator/Injury Control Operations and Resources, National Highway Traffic Safety Administration-DOT, 1200 New Jersey Ave., S.E., NTI-200, Washington, DC 20590. Phone: (202) 366-2121.

Internet: www.nhtsa.whatsup/fedassist/index.html.

20.602 OCCUPANT PROTECTION INCENTIVE GRANTS

Assistance: project grants. (25-100 percent/to 6 years).

Purposes: pursuant to the Highway Safety Act of 1998 as amended, for states to implement and enforce automobile occupant protection programs.

Eligible applicants/beneficiaries: states, DC, PR, VI, Samoa, Northern Marianas, Guam, BIA.

Range: $74,843 to $3,109,419. **Average:** N.A.

Activity: N.A.

HQ: Associate Administrator/Injury Control Operations and Resources, National Highway Traffic Safety Administration-DOT, 1200 New Jersey Ave., S.E., NTI-200, Washington, DC 20590. Phone: (202) 366-2121.

Internet: www.nhtsa.gov.

20.607 ALCOHOL OPEN CONTAINER REQUIREMENTS

Assistance: project grants (to 6 years).

Purposes: pursuant to the Highway Safety Act of 1998 as amended, to encourage states to enact and enforce alcohol open container laws. Funding is based on the calculated annual savings in medical costs to the federal government, including in the Medicare and Medicaid programs.

Eligible applicants/beneficiaries: states, DC, and PR—provided they have no Repeat Intoxicated Driver Laws in effect.

Range/Average: N.A.

Activity: N.A.

HQ: Associate Administrator/Injury Control Operations and Resources, National Highway Traffic Safety Administration-DOT, 1200 New Jersey Ave., S.E., NTI-200, Washington, DC 20590. Phone: (202) 366-2121.

Internet: www.nhtsa/whatsup/fedassist/index.html.

20.608 MINIMUM PENALTIES FOR REPEAT OFFENDERS FOR DRIVING WHILE INTOXICATED

Assistance: project grants (to 6 years).

Purposes: pursuant to the Highway Safety Act of 1998 as amended, to encourage states to enact Repeat Intoxicated Driver Laws. Program funding is based on the calculated annual savings in medical costs to the federal government, including in the Medicare and Medicaid programs.

Eligible applicants/beneficiaries: states, DC, and PR—provided they have no Repeat Intoxicated Driver Laws in effect.

Range: $2,489,000 to $54,546,000. **Average:** N.A.

Activity: N.A.

HQ: Associate Administrator/Injury Control Operations and Resources, National Highway Traffic Safety Administration-DOT, 1200 New Jersey Ave., S.E., NTI-200, Washington, DC 20590. Phone: (202) 366-2121.

Internet: www.nhtsa/whatsup/fedassist/index.html.

20.609 SAFETY BELT PERFORMANCE GRANTS

Assistance: project grants (100 percent).

Purposes: pursuant to SAFETEA-LU, Section 406, for states to adopt and implement programs improving the efficiency, completeness, uniformity, in-state, interstate, and national compatibility, integration, and accessibility of state data on trends—enabling observation and analysis of national trends in crash occurrences, rates, outcomes, and circumstances; for evaluations. Project examples include such activities as: highly visible enforcement of impaired driving and safety belt violations; paid and earned media campaigns supporting mobilizations and crackdowns; motorcycle rider education; pedestrian safety; speed management; DWI courts; technical training of law enforcement officers, prosecutors, and state highway safety officials.

Eligible applicants/beneficiaries: states, DC, PR, VI, Samoa, Northern Marianas, Guam.

Range: N.A. **Average:** $1,000,000.

Activity: N.A.

HQ: Associate Administrator/Injury Control Operations and Resources, National Highway Traffic Safety Administration-DOT, 1200 New Jersey Ave., S.E., NTI-200, Washington, DC 20590. Phone: (202) 366-2121.

Internet: www.nhtsa.gov.

20.610 STATE TRAFFIC SAFETY INFORMATION SYSTEM IMPROVEMENT GRANTS

Assistance: project grants (to 4 years).

Purposes: pursuant to SAFETEA-LU, to encourage sates to adopt and implement effective programs to improve the timelines, accuracy, completeness, uniformity, integration, and accessibility of state data; to link state data systems with other systems within the state, and with other state and national data systems and improve compatibility between systems; to enhance the ability to observe and analyze trends in crash occurrences, rates, outcomes, and circumstances. Funds may be used only to implement data improvement programs.

Eligible applicants/beneficiaries: states, DC, PR, VI, Guam, American Samoa, Northern Mariana Islands, tribes. Applicants must meet certain NHTSA criteria.

Range: $500.00 to $2,344,000. **Average:** N.A.

Activity: N.A.

HQ: Associate Administrator/Injury Control Operations and Resources, National Highway Traffic Safety Administration-DOT, 1200 New Jersey Ave., S.E., NTI-200, Washington, DC 20590. Phone: (202) 366-2121.

Internet: www.nhtsa.gov.

20.611 INCENTIVE GRANT PROGRAM TO PROHIBIT RACIAL PROFILING ("Section 1906")

Assistance: project grants. (80 percent/to 2 years).

Purposes: pursuant to SAFETEA-LU, Section 1906, for states to enact and enforce laws prohibiting racial profiling in the enforcement of laws on federal-aid highways, and to maintain and allow public inspection of statistics on motor vehicle stops by officers in the enforcement of state laws. "Law states" may use funds to; collect, maintain, and evaluate pertinent data; develop and implement programs to reduce racial profiling, including training of law enforcement officers. "Assurances states" may use funds for: activities to prohibit racial profiling in the enforcement of state laws regulating the use of federal-aid highways; activities permitted to law states; providing public access to traffic stop data and evaluating the results of such data.

Eligible applicants/beneficiaries: states, DC, PR, VI, Samoa, Northern Marianas, Guam.

Range: $454,170 to $885,460. **Average:** $668,544.

Activity: N.A.

HQ: Associate Administrator/Injury Control Operations and Resources, National Highway Traffic Safety Administration-DOT, 1200 New Jersey Ave., S.E., NTI-200, Washington, DC 20590. Phone: (202) 366-2121.

Internet: www.nhtsa.gov.

20.612 INCENTIVE GRANT PROGRAM TO INCREASE MOTORCYCLIST SAFETY ("Section 2010")

Assistance: project grants (100 percent).

Purposes: pursuant to SAFETEA-LU, Section 2010, for states to adopt and implement programs to reduce the number of single and multi-vehicle crashes involving motorcyclists. Funds may be used for safety training and motorcyclist awareness programs including: improving training curricula and program delivery in urban and rural areas; acquiring practice motorcycles and suitable training facilities; instruction materials; mobile training units; recruitment and retention of instructors; public service announcements and other outreach methods. States may sub- allocate funds to nonprofit organizations.

Eligible applicants/beneficiaries: states, DC, PR.

Range: $100,000 to $482,959. **Average:** N.A.

Activity: N.A.

HQ: Associate Administrator/Injury Control Operations and Resources, National Highway Traffic Safety Administration-DOT, 1200 New Jersey Ave., S.E., NTI-200, Washington, DC 20590. Phone: (202) 366-2121.

Internet: www.nhtsa.gov.

20.613   CHILD SAFETY AND CHILD BOOSTER SEATS INCENTIVE GRANTS ("Section 2011")

Assistance: project grants (50-75 percent).

Purposes: pursuant to SAFETEA-LU, Section 2010, for states to enact and enforce child restraint laws requiring children under age 8 and weighing up to 65 pounds to be properly restrained, unless they are 4'9" tall. No more than 50 percent of grant amounts may be used to purchase and distribute child safety seats and restraints to low-income families; remaining amounts may be used for program costs including: enforcement; training passenger safety personnel, educators, and parents; public education.

Eligible applicants/beneficiaries: states, DC, PR.

Range: $100,000 to $700,000. **Average:** N.A.

Activity: N.A.

HQ: Associate Administrator/Injury Control Operations and Resources, National Highway Traffic Safety Administration-DOT, 1200 New Jersey Ave., S.E., NTI-200, Washington, DC 20590. Phone: (202) 366-2121.

Internet: nhtsa.dot.gov.

20.614   NATIONAL HIGHWAY TRAFFIC SAFETY ADMINISTRATION (NHTSA) DISCRETIONARY SAFETY GRANTS

Assistance: project grants.

Purposes: pursuant to Highway Safety Act of 1966, as amended, to provide funds to conduct research and development on transportation safety and related issues, specifically projects identified in DOT's Annual Appropriation Legislation.

Eligible applicants/beneficiaries: grantee application eligibility will be developed on an individual grant or cooperative agreement basis by NHTSA Purchase Team.

Range: $100,000 to $482,959. **Average:** N.A.

Activity: N.A.

HQ: Office of Acquisition Management, NHTSA-DOT, 1200 New Jersey Ave., SE, Washington, DC 20590. Phone: (202) 366-9561.

Internet: N.A. (Note: no field offices for this program.)

20.700   PIPELINE SAFETY PROGRAM STATE BASE GRANT

Assistance: formula grants (to 50 percent).

Purposes: pursuant to the Natural Gas Pipeline Safety Act of 1968 as amended and related acts, to pay personnel, inspection, equipment, training, and research costs related to natural gas, liquefied natural gas, and hazardous liquids pipeline safety programs.

Eligible applicants/beneficiaries: state agencies.

Range: $22,027 to $4,949,150. **Average:** $767,764.

Activity: N.A.

HQ: State Program Director, Pipelines and Hazardous Materials Safety Administration-DOT, 1200 New Jersey Ave., SE, Washington, DC 20590. Phone: (405) 834-8344.

Internet: www.phmsa.dot.gov. (Note: no field offices for this program.)

20.701 UNIVERSITY TRANSPORTATION CENTERS PROGRAM

Assistance: project grants. (50 percent/3 to 5 years).

Purposes: to provide assistance to nonprofit IHEs for the purpose of establishing and operating university transportation centers that conduct research, education, and technology transfer programs addressing regional and national transportation issues.

Eligible applicants/beneficiaries: public and private nonprofit IHEs; to apply for competitive grant, IHEs must have established transportation research programs.

Range: $1,000,000 to $3,000,000. **Average:** N.A.

Activity: N.A.

HQ: Office of Innovation, Research, and Education (RDT-30), Research and Innovative Technology Administration (RITA) DOT, 1200 New Jersey Ave., SE, Washington, DC 20590. Phone: (202) 493-2993.

Internet: www.rita.dot.gov/utc. (Note: no field offices for this program.)

20.703 INTERAGENCY HAZARDOUS MATERIALS PUBLIC SECTOR TRAINING AND PLANNING GRANTS ("HMEP")

Assistance: project grants. (80 percent/to 6 years).

Purposes: pursuant to the Federal Hazardous Materials Transportation Act, for the development, improvement, and implementation of emergency response plans to handle hazardous materials accidents and incidents; to enhance implementation of the Emergency Planning and Community Right-to-Know Act of 1986 (EPCRA); for related training of public sector employees.

Eligible applicants/beneficiaries: states, tribes, territories.

Range: $4,795 to $3,500,000. **Average:** N.A.

Activity: funded 50 states, 5 territories, 6 tribes, and 5 nonprofit organizations in FY 2014.

HQ: HMEP Grants Manager, 1200 New Jersey Ave., SE, Washington, DC 2059. Phone: (202) 366-0579; FAX: (202) 366-3753.

Internet: www.phmsa.dot.gov. (Note: no field offices for this program.)

20.710 TECHNICAL ASSISTANCE GRANTS ("TAG Program")

Assistance: project grants/discretionary; technical assistance (100 percent/to 1 year).

Purposes: pursuant to Pipeline Inspection, Protection, Enforcement, and Safety Act of 2006, to offer funding for communities and groups of individuals (excluding for-profit entities) for technical assistance in the form of engineering or other scientific analysis of pipeline safety issues and to help promote public participation in official proceedings. Grant funds may not be used for lobbying or in direct support of litigation.

Eligible applicants: communities/groups of individuals working on pipeline safety.

Eligible beneficiaries: local, public nonprofit institution/organization, anyone/general public.

Range: to $100,000. **Average:** N.A.

Activity: 31 awards in FY 2014.

HQ: FRA-DOT, 1200 New Jersey Ave., SE, Washington, DC 20590. Phone: (202) 366-6855.

Internet: primis.phmsa.dot.gov/tag. (Note: no field offices for this program.)

20.720 STATE DAMAGE PREVENTION PROGRAM GRANTS ("SDPP Grants")

Assistance: project grants.

Purposes: to improve State Damage prevention programs, which are intended to protect underground facilities from excavation damage. Grant funds may not be used for lobbying or in direct support of litigation.

Eligible applicants: any state, territory, or possession authority designated by the Governor with appropriate US DOT Pipeline and Hazardous Materials Safety Administration (PHMSA) certification or agreement.

Eligible beneficiaries: states, territories and possessions.

Range: $20,265 to $100,000. **Average:** $86,395.

Activity: 19 awards in FY 2014.

HQ: Pipelines and Hazardous Materials Safety Administration-DOT, Rm. E-22-103, 1200 New Jersey Ave., SE, Washington, DC 20590. Phone: (202) 366-0568.

Internet: www.phmsa.dot.gov. (Note: no field offices for this program.)

20.721 PHMSA PIPELINE SAFETY PROGRAM ONE CALL GRANT

Assistance: project grants (100 percent).

Purposes: pursuant to the Pipeline Safety Act of 1979, Pipeline Safety Reauthorization Act of 1988, Pipeline Safety Act of 1992, Accountable Pipeline Safety and Partnership Act of 1996, and Natural Gas Pipeline Safety Act of 1968 as amended, to provide funding to state agencies in promoting damage prevention, including changes with theirs state underground damage prevention laws, related compliance activities, and training and public education. State agencies who participate in the pipeline safety program are eligible to apply for One Call grant funding on an annual basis. This optional grant program has a maximum amount request of $50,000 per state and supports initiatives to further promote efforts specifically for damage prevention, including one-call legislation, related compliance activities, training and public education.

Eligible applicants: states that have a certification or agreement with US DOT Pipeline and Hazardous Materials Safety Administration (PHMSA) to do pipeline safety inspections.

Eligible beneficiaries: state agencies.

Range: $10,000 to $45,000. **Average:** N.A.

Activity: N.A.

HQ: State Program Director, Pipelines and Hazardous Materials Safety Administration-DOT, 1200 New Jersey Ave., SE, Washington, DC 20590. Phone: (405) 834-8344.

Internet: www.phmsa.dot.gov.

20.723 PHMSA PIPELINE SAFETY RESEARCH AND DEVELOPMENT OTHER TRANSACTION AGREEMENTS ("PHMSA Pipeline Safety Research and Development")

Assistance: project grants (30 percent).

Purposes: pursuant to the Accountable Pipeline Safety and Partnership Act, to sponsor research and development projects focused on providing near-term solutions that will improve the safety, reduce environmental impact, and enhance the reliability of the nation's pipeline transportation system.

Eligible applicants: universities and other academic institutions, individual, profit organization, nonprofit organization, State (includes D.C.), U.S. Territories and possessions, Indian tribes, local governments.

Eligible beneficiaries: general public can receive benefits from the eligible applicant.

Range: $40,000 to $856,000. **Average:** $189,000.

Activity: N.A.

HQ: Director, U.S. DOT, Pipeline and Hazardous Materials Safety Administration, Office of Pipeline Safety, 793 Countrybriar Ln., Highlands Ranch, CO 80129. Phone: (303) 683-3117; FAX: 303-346-9192.

Internet: www.phmsa.dot.gov. (Note: no field offices for this program.)

20.724 PIPELINE SAFETY RESEARCH COMPETITIVE ACADEMIC AGREEMENT PROGRAM (CAAP) ("CAAP Program")

Assistance: project grants (100 percent/18-24 months).

Purposes: pursuant to Authority for Cooperative Agreements, to spur innovation by enabling an academic research focus on high-risk and high pay-off solutions for pipeline safety challenges, deliver solutions that can be "hand-offs" to further investigations in the CAAP program or in PHMSA's core research program, and to validate proof of concept of a thesis or theory all the way to commercial penetration into the market.

Eligible applicants/beneficiaries: nonprofit IHEs located in the United States.

Range: N.A. **Average:** $300,000.

Activity: N.A.

HQ: Director, Pipeline & Hazardous Materials Safety Administration, Office of Acquisition Services, PHA-30, 1200 New Jersey Ave., SE, Washington, DC 20590. Phone: (202) 366-4429 or (303) 693-3117.

Internet: www.phmsa.dot.gov/pipeline. (Note: no field offices for this program.)

20.761 BIOBASED TRANSPORTATION RESEARCH ("Biobased R & D")

Assistance: project grants (50 percent/4 years).

Purposes: pursuant to SAFTEA- LU, to carry out biobased research of national importance at the National Biodiesel Board and at research centers identified in section 9011 of the Farm Security and Rural Investment Act of 2002. No new grants will be awarded during the program's remaining authorization (through 2009).

Eligible applicants: applicants as designated in SAFTEA- LU.

Eligible beneficiaries: public and private nonprofit institutions of higher learning and industry trade groups.

Range: $9,000,000 to $13,000,000. **Average:** N.A.

Activity: N.A.

HQ: Research and Research and Innovative Technology Administration, Research Development and Technology (RDT) DOT, 1200 New Jersey Ave., SE, E33-470, Washington, DC 20590. Phone: (202) 366-1762.

Internet: www.rita.dot.gov. (Note: no field offices for this program.)

20.762 RESEARCH GRANTS

Assistance: project grants. (80 percent/1-4 years).

Purposes: grants awarded to three institutions/organizations: to develop a research facility in Lewiston, Montana for basic and applies research and testing on surface transportation issues facing rural and cold regions; to carry out the Rural Transportation Research Initiative in at North Dakota State University; and to conduct a feasibility study for the creation of a system of inland ports and distributions centers in Appalachia.

Eligible applicants/beneficiaries: legislated grants in SAFETEA-LU, Section 5513(d)(g) (i), to the following institutions: Western Montana Transportation Institute, Upper Great Plains Transportation Institute, and Appalachian Regional Commission.

Range: $500,000 to $5,000,000. **Average:** $2,250,000.

Activity: N.A.

HQ: Office of Intermodalism, Research and Innovative Technology Administration (RITA) DOT, 1200 New Jersey Ave., E33-464, Washington, DC 20590. Phone: (202) 366-1300.

Internet: www.rita.dot.gov. (Note: no field offices for this program.)

20.802 FEDERAL SHIP FINANCING GUARANTEES ("Title XI")

Assistance: guaranteed/insured loans. (87.5 percent/to 25 years).

Purposes: pursuant to the Merchant Marine Act of 1936 as amended, to finance or refinance: construction, reconstruction, reconditioning, or refinancing of ships built in U.S. shipyards, used in foreign or domestic commerce, in research, or as ocean thermal energy conversion facilities—in coast-wide or intercostal trade, on the Great Lakes or on bays, sounds, rivers, harbors, inland lakes, or as floating dry-docks; for advanced shipbuilding technology of general shipyard facilities. Vessels must be larger than five net tons—other than towboats, barges, scows, lighters, car floats, canal boats, or tank vessels of less than 25 gross tons.

Eligible applicants/beneficiaries: qualified individuals, U.S. shipyards, U.S. and foreign ship owners.

Range/Average: N.A.

Activity: 2 projects approved in FY 2014.

HQ: Associate Administrator/Shipbuilding, Office of Ship Financing, Maritime Administration-DOT, 1200 New Jersey Ave., SE, Washington, DC 20590. Phone: (202) 366-2118.

Internet: www.marad.dot.gov.

20.803 MARITIME WAR RISK INSURANCE ("Title XII, MMA, 1936")

Assistance: insurance.

Purposes: pursuant to the Merchant Marine Act of 1936 as amended, to provide war risk insurance binders or policies on vessels in operation or under construction. Insurance is available at nominal cost in peacetime.

Eligible applicants/beneficiaries: owners of U.S. flag vessels and certain foreign flag vessels.

Range/Average: N.A.

Activity: N.A.

HQ: Director, Office of Insurance and Shipping Analysis, Maritime Administration-DOT, 1200 New Jersey Ave., SE, Washington, DC 20590. Phone: (202) 366-1915.

Internet: www.dot.gov.

20.806 STATE MARITIME SCHOOLS

Assistance: direct payments/specified use; use of property, facilities, and equipment (50 percent).

Purposes: for the operation and maintenance of state maritime schools; for loans to the schools of training vessels by the federal government, as well as their maintenance and repair; for incentive payments to selected cadets. States must admit out-of- state students.

Eligible applicants/beneficiaries: states (limited to one academy per state).

Range: N.A. Average: $600,000 annually per school; $8,000 per academic year for up to four years for selected students.

Activity: anticipate 660 graduates in FY 2015.

HQ: Director, Office of Policy and Plans, Maritime Administration-DOT, 1200 New Jersey Ave., SE, Washington, DC 20590 Phone: (202) 366-5469.

Internet: www.dot.gov.

20.807 U.S. MERCHANT MARINE ACADEMY ("Kings Point")

Assistance: training.

Purposes: for the operation and maintenance of the federal maritime academy, including subsistence payments to students training to become merchant marine officers—as well as their quarters, medical care, program travel, and other expenses.

Eligible applicants/beneficiaries: U.S. citizens that are high school graduates; eligible international students.

Range/Average: N.A.

Activity: anticipate graduating 210 new licensed merchant marine officers in FY 2015.

HQ: Director, Office of Policy and Plans, Maritime Administration-DOT, 1200 New Jersey Ave., SE, Washington, DC 20590. Phone: (202) 366-5111.

Internet: www.dot.gov. (Note: no field offices for this program.)

20.808 CAPITAL CONSTRUCTION FUND (CCF)

Assistance: direct payments/specified use.

Purposes: pursuant to the Merchant Marine Act of 1936 as amended, to provide tax deferment incentives to shipbuilders to acquire, construct, or reconstruct vessels built in the U.S. for use in the U.S. foreign, Great Lakes, or noncontiguous domestic trades.

Eligible applicants/beneficiaries: U.S. citizens that own or lease one or more eligible vessels, with appropriate plans and financial capabilities.

Range/Average: N.A.

Activity: N.A.

HQ: Associate Administrator/Shipbuilding, Office of Ship Financing, Maritime Administration-DOT, 1200 New Jersey Ave., SE, Washington, DC 20590. Phone: (202) 366-1859.

Internet: www.dot.gov.

20.812 CONSTRUCTION RESERVE FUND (CRF)

Assistance: direct payments/specified use.

Purposes: pursuant to the Merchant Marine Act of 1936 as amended, to provide tax deferment incentives to shipbuilders to construct, reconstruct, recondition, or acquire vessels necessary for national defense or U.S. commerce.

Eligible applicants/beneficiaries: U.S. citizens that own in whole or in part one or more vessels operating in the foreign or domestic commerce of the

U.S. or in the fisheries; citizens operating such vessel or vessels owned by another individual.

Range/Average: N.A.

Activity: N.A.

HQ: Associate Administrator/Shipbuilding, Office of Ship Financing, Maritime Administration-DOT, 1200 New Jersey Ave., SE, Washington, DC 20590. Phone: (202) 366-1859.

Internet: www.marad.dot.gov.

20.813   SHIP OPERATIONS COOPERATIVE PROGRAM ("Maritime Security Program")

Assistance: direct payments/specified use.

Purposes: pursuant to the Merchant Marine Act of 1936 as amended and Maritime Security Act of 2003, to maintain a U.S. flag merchant fleet crewed by U.S. citizens to serve both commercial and national security needs, including container ships, lighter- aboard ships, and roll-on/roll-off vessels.

Eligible applicants/beneficiaries: U.S. citizens and operators of U.S. flag vessels.

Range/Average: N.A.

Activity: N.A.

HQ: Director, Office of Sealift Support, Maritime Administration-DOT, 1200 New Jersey Ave., SE, Washington, DC 20590. Phone: (202) 366-2625.

Internet: www.dot.gov. (Note: no field offices for this program.)

20.814   ASSISTANCE TO SMALL SHIPYARDS ("Small Shipyard Grants")

Assistance: direct payments/specified use (75 percent).

Purposes: to award grants for capital and related infrastructure improvements at qualified shipyards that will facilitate the efficiency, cost effectiveness, and quality of domestic ship construction for commercial and Federal Government use. Federal funds can only exceed 75 percent of project cost if the cost is less than $26,075, or if a determination is made that project merits support and requires additional assistance.

Eligible applicants: shipyard; state or local government on behalf of a shipyard. The shipyard must be located in or near a maritime community, in a single geographical location and must be: a small business concern (section 3 of the Small Business Act) that has 600 or less production employees.

Eligible beneficiaries: shipyards.

Range: to $9,980,000. **Average:** N.A.

Activity: N.A.

HQ: Associate Administrator/Business and Workforce Development, Maritime Administration-DOT, 1200 New Jersey Ave., SE-Rm. W21-318, Washington, DC 20590. Phone: (202) 366-5737; FAX: (202) 366-6988.

Internet: www.marad.dot.gov. (Note: no field offices for this program.)

20.817   AIR EMISSIONS AND ENERGY INITIATIVE

Assistance: cooperative agreements (100 percent).

Purposes: pursuant to National Defense Authorization Act of 2010, to fund studies in the development of air emissions reduction and alternative fuels/ technologies that will be used to evaluate public benefits of providing incentives to adopt new technologies and alternative energy in the maritime sector. Shore-side equipment upgrade or shore power projects are not eligible for funding.

Eligible applicants: vessel owners, operators, or public sponsors.

Eligible beneficiaries: federal government, general public.

Range/Average: N.A.

Activity: N.A.

HQ: Program Director, Maritime Administration (MARAD), DOT, 1200 New Jersey Ave., SE, W26/410, Washington, DC Columbia 20590. Phone: (202) 366-1913; FAX: (202) 366-3029.

Internet: N.A. (Note: no field offices for this program.)

20.818   GREAT SHIPS INITIATIVE

Assistance: cooperative agreements (100 percent).

Purposes: pursuant to the Defense Authorizations Act of 2011, to further the current efforts that address the curtailment of aquatic invasive species associated with ballast water operations and commercial shipping within the Great Lakes.

Eligible applicants: eligible applicants will possess: a current EPA-approved Quality Management Plan (QMP); qualified facilities and equipment; personnel available for engineering support and conducting biological analyses according to standard protocols; and the ability to write and follow a rigorous quality assurance plan that maximizes the production of credible results.

Eligible beneficiaries: anyone, general public.

Range/Average: N.A.

Activity: N.A.

HQ: Program Director, Maritime Administration (MARAD), DOT, 1200 New Jersey Ave., SE, W26/410, Washington, DC Columbia 20590. Phone: (202) 366-1913; FAX: (202) 366-3029.

Internet: N.A. (Note: no field offices for this program.)

20.819   BALLAST WATER TREATMENT TECHNOLOGIES

Assistance: cooperative agreements (100 percent/4 years).

Purposes: pursuant to the National Defense Authorization Act of 2012, to further current efforts that address the curtailment of aquatic invasive species associated with the ballast water operations of commercial shipping within the Chesapeake Bay and U.S. coastal waters. Applicants must be able to provide technical services and equipment and to support the testing, evaluation, and demonstration of treatment methods, practices, systems and equipment.

Eligible applicants/beneficiaries: 35 IHEs selected by the CDC as Prevention Research Centers (PRCs).

Range/Average: N.A.

Activity: N.A.

HQ: Program Director, Maritime Administration (MARAD), DOT, 1200 New Jersey Ave., SE, W26/410, Washington, DC Columbia 20590. Phone: (202) 366-1913; FAX: (202) 366-3029.

Internet: N.A. (Note: no field offices for this program.)

20.901 PAYMENTS FOR ESSENTIAL AIR SERVICES (EAS)

Assistance: direct payments/specified use.

Purposes: to subsidize air carriers providing commuter services to unserved communities, covering operating losses and a profit element.

Eligible applicants/beneficiaries: carriers selected by DOT.

Range: $491,205 to $4,710,683. **Average:** $2,189,355.

Activity: N.A.

HQ: Director, Office of Aviation Analysis (X-50), DOT, 1200 New Jersey Ave., SE, Washington, DC 20590. Phone: (202) 366-3176.

Internet: www.dot.gov/policy/aviation-policy/small-community-rural-air-se rvice/essential-air-service. (Note: no field offices for this program.)

20.904 BONDING ASSISTANCE PROGRAM

Assistance: insurance.

Purposes: to enhance opportunities for Small Disadvantaged Business Enterprises (SDBEs) to obtain bid, performance and payment bonds for transportation-related contracts emanating from DOT, its grantees, recipients, their contractors and subcontractors.

Eligible applicants/beneficiaries: certified minority, women-owned and disadvantaged business enterprises.

Range/Average: N.A.

Activity: program offered in 28 cities in FY 2015.

HQ: Bonding Manager, Office of Small and Disadvantaged Business Utilization (S-40), Office of the Secretary-DOT, 1200 New Jersey Ave., SE, Washington, DC 20590. Phone: (202) 366-3403.

Internet: osdbu.dot.gov. (Note: no field offices for this program.)

20.905 DISADVANTAGED BUSINESS ENTERPRISES—SHORT TERM LENDING PROGRAM

Assistance: direct loans (1 year).

Purposes: to provide lines of credit to disadvantaged business enterprises to obtain accounts receivable financing for the performance of transportation-related contracts from DOT, its grantees, and recipients, and their contractors and subcontractors—including for maintenance, rehabilitation, restructuring, improvement, or revitalization of any mode of transportation with any public or commercial provider of transportation or any federal, state, or local transportation agency.

Eligible applicants/beneficiaries: certified disadvantaged business enterprises, minority-and women-owned enterprises; all SBA "Section 8(a)" firms; HUBZONE Empowerment-eligabible and disabled veterans. Applicant must be in business for 2-3 years; not for start-up business.

Range: to $750,000. **Average:** N.A.

Activity: approved 9 loans in FY 2014.

HQ: Office of Small and Disadvantaged Business Utilization (S-40), Office of the Secretary-DOT, 1200 New Jersey Ave., SE, Washington, DC 20590. Phone: (800) 532-1169.

Internet: www.osdbuweb.dot.gov. (Note: no field offices for this program.)

20.910 ASSISTANCE TO SMALL AND DISADVANTAGED BUSINESSES

Assistance: project grants (100 percent).

Purposes: DOT's Office of Small and Disadvantaged Business Utilization (OSDBU) was established in accordance with Public Law 95-507, an amendment to the Small Business Act and the Small Business Investment Act of 1958. OSDBU ensures that small and disadvantaged business policies and goals of the Secretary of Transportation are developed and implemented in a fair, efficient and effective manner to serve small and disadvantaged businesses throughout DOT and the country. The DOT Short Term Lending Program provides assistance to enable small businesses to participate in transportation-related contracts and subcontracts funded by DOT, its grantees and recipients. Financial assistance provides lines of credit to finance accounts receivable arising from transportation-related contracts.

Eligible applicants: established 501 C(6) tax-exempt Chambers of Commerce, Trade Associations and 501 C(3) non-profit organizations, community colleges, minority educational institutions, tribal colleges and universities that have documented experience and capacity necessary to successfully operate and administer a coordinated, Small Business Transportation Resource Center (SBTRC) within their regions.

Eligible beneficiaries: small businesses, businesses owned and operated by socially/economically disadvantaged persons, and businesses owned and operated by women.

Range: N.A. **Average:** $150,000.

Activity: N.A.

HQ: Office of Small and Disadvantaged Business Utilization, S-40, Office of the Secretary, DOT, 1200 New Jersey Ave., SE, Washington, DC 20590. Phone:(202) 366-1930; FAX: (202) 366-7228.

Internet: www.dot.gov/osdbu. (Note: no field offices for this program.)

20.930 PAYMENTS FOR SMALL COMMUNITY AIR SERVICE DEVELOPMENT

Assistance: project grants. (to 100 percent/to 3 years).

Purposes: pursuant to the Wendell H. Ford Aviation Investment and Reform Act for the 21st Century and Vision 100-Century in Aviation Reauthorization Act, for smaller communities to enhance their air service and increase access to the national transportation system—through such activities as: marketing, advertising, and promotion; air service deficiency studies, measuring traffic loss or diversion to other communities; providing financial incentives including subsidies or revenue guarantees to cover air carrier's prospective operating losses or to ground service access providers.

Eligible applicants/beneficiaries: communities or consortia with airports not larger than a small hub airport, including in territories and possessions.

Range: $50,000 to $1,000,000. **Average:** $450,000.

Activity: N.A.

HQ: Associate Director/Small Community Air Service Development Program, Office of Aviation Analysis (X-50), OS-DOT, 1200 New Jersey Ave., SE, W86-307, Washington, DC 20590. Phone: (202) 366-0577; FAX: (202) 366-7638.

Internet: www.dot.gov/policy/aviation-policy/small-community-rural-air-service/SCASDP. (Note: no field offices for this program.)

20.931 TRANSPORTATION PLANNING, RESEARCH AND EDUCATION ("Innovative and Advanced Transportation Research")

Assistance: project grants.

Purposes: pursuant to DOT's FY 06 Appropriation Bill, to provide funds to conduct research and development on transportation, inter-modal systems and related issues. Examples of funded projects include: Evaluation of Shipper Requirement and Rail Services; Infrastructure and Transportations Support; Agriculture Transportation Pilot Project; and Eastern Seaboard Intermodal Transportation Study.

Eligible applicants/beneficiaries: mandated by Congress; only organizations identified in legislation may apply.

Range: $500,000 to $1.500,000. **Average:** N.A.

Activity: N.A.

HQ: Acquisition Services, OST-DOT, 1200 New Jersey Ave., SE, Washington, DC 20950. Phone: (202) 366-3252.

Internet: N.A. (Note: no field offices for this program.)

20.934 NATIONALLY SIGNIFICANT FREIGHT AND HIGHWAY PROJECTS ("FASTLANE Grants")

Assistance: project grants. (80 percent/to 3 years).

Purposes: pursuant to the Fixing America's Surface Transportation (FAST) Act of 2015, to support freight and highway projects of national significance. Funds may be used to for the construction, reconstruction, rehabilitation, and acquisition of property; environmental mitigation, construction contingencies, equipment acquisition, and operational improvements directly related to system performance; and for phase activities, including planning, feasibility analysis, revenue forecasting, environmental review, preliminary engineering, design, and other preconstruction activities.

Eligible applicants/beneficiaries: state, local, and tribal transportation agencies.

Range/Average: N.A.

Activity: N.A.

HQ: Office of the Secretary of Transportation, DOT, 1200 New Jersey Ave., SE, Washington, DC 20590. Phone: (202) 366-7687.

Internet: www.transportation.gov/NSFHP. (Note: no field offices for this program.)

DEPARTMENT OF THE TREASURY

21.004   EXCHANGE OF FEDERAL TAX INFORMATION WITH STATE TAX AGENCIES

Assistance: specialized services.

Purposes: to increase taxpayer compliance and to reduce duplication of resources—through the confidential exchange of tax data, models, and extracts with states and municipalities for tax administration purposes.

Eligible applicants/beneficiaries: states, territories, and municipalities with over 250,000 population that impose taxes on income or wages.

Range/Average: N.A.

Activity: N.A.

HQ: Director, Governmental Liaison and Disclosure, IRS, 15 New Sudbury St., JFK Room 825, Boston, MA 02138. Phone: (617) 316-2254.

Internet: www.irs.gov.

21.006   TAX COUNSELING FOR THE ELDERLY

Assistance: project grants.

Purposes: pursuant to the Revenue Act of 1978, to reimburse volunteers for their out-of-pocket expenses in receiving training and in providing tax counseling to elderly taxpayers.

Eligible applicants/beneficiaries: experienced private or public nonprofit organizations. Governmental agencies are ineligible.

Range/Average: N.A.

Activity: 1,366,162 federal returns prepared in FY 2015.

HQ: Grant Program Office - TCE, Internal Revenue Service, 5000 Ellin Rd., NCFB C4-110, Lanham, MD 20706. Phone: (404) 338-7894.

Internet: www.irs.gov/Individuals/Tax-Counseling-for-the-Elderly. (Note: no field offices for this program.)

21.008   LOW-INCOME TAXPAYER CLINICS

Assistance: project grants. (50 percent/to 3 years).

Purposes: to enable organizations to represent low-income taxpayers in controversies with the IRS, or to inform individuals with limited English language abilities of their tax rights and responsibilities.

Eligible applicants/beneficiaries: private nonprofit organizations; educational institutions with accredited law, business, or accounting schools.

Range: $10,000 to $100,000. **Average:** $77,651.

Activity: N.A.

HQ: Taxpayer Advocate Service, IRS, 1111 Constitution Ave., NW, Rm. 1034, Washington, DC 20224. Phone: (949) 389-4118.

Internet: www.irs.gov/advocate. (Note: no field offices for this program.)

21.009   VOLUNTEER INCOME TAX ASSISTANCE (VITA) MATCHING GRANT PROGRAM

Assistance: project grants (100 percent/1 year).

Purposes: pursuant to Treasury Appropriations Act and Omnibus Appropriations Act, to extend services to underserved populations and hardest-to-reach areas, both urban and non-urban; increase the capacity to file returns electronically; and heighten quality control, enhance volunteer training, and improve the accuracy rate of returns prepared by VITA sites.

Eligible applicants: local (includes state-designated Indian tribes), public and private nonprofit institutions/organizations, and federally-recognized Indian tribal governments.

Eligible beneficiaries: Native American organizations, senior citizens, and low-income individuals.

Range/Average: N.A.

Activity: 1,702,375 returns prepared in FY 2015.

HQ: Grant Program Office, IRS, 401 W. Peachtree St., NW - Stop 420-D, Atlanta, GA 30308. Phone: (404) 338-7894.

Internet: www.irs.gov/Individuals/IRS-VITA-Grant-Program. (Note: no field offices for this program.)

21.012   NATIVE INITIATIVES

Assistance: project grants (100 percent/3 years).

Purposes: pursuant to the Riegle Community Development and Regulatory Improvement Act of 1994, project grants to promote economic revitalization and community development through financial and technical assistance to Native Community Development Financial Institutions (CDFIs) and a complementary series of training programs called Expanding Native Opportunities. Under the Native American CDFI Assistance (NACA) Program, Financial Assistance (FA) and Technical Assistance (TA) awards are provided to build the capacity of new or existing Native CDFIs serving Native Communities. Under the Expanding Native Opportunities, the complementary capacity-building initiatives foster the development of Native CDFIs through training and technical assistance.

Eligible applicants/beneficiaries: Only certified Native CDFIs are eligible to apply for Financial Assistance awards. Organizations that are Certified

Native CDFIs, Emerging Native CDFIs, or Sponsoring Entities may apply for Technical Assistance awards. However, non-certified organizations must be able to become certified within two years after receiving a TA award. Awards may not be issued to Federal agencies, departments, or instrumentalities, state governments, local governments, or any agency or instrumentalities thereof.

Range/Average: N.A.

Activity: N.A.

HQ: Director, Native Initiatives, Community Development Financial Institutions Fund-Dept of Treasury, 1801 L St., NW, 6th Fl., Washington, DC 20036. Phone: (202) 653-0329; FAX: (202) 508-0002.

Internet: www.cdfifund.gov. (Note: no field offices for this program.)

21.014 COMMUNITY DEVELOPMENT FINANCIAL INSTITUTIONS BOND GUARANTEE PROGRAM
("CDFI Bond Guarantee Program")

Assistance: guaranteed/insured loans.

Purposes: pursuant to the Small Business Jobs Act of 2010, funds to provide a new source of long-term capital to certified Community Development Financial Institutions (CDFIs) for economic and community development in low-income communities and underserved rural areas. Through the CDFI Bond Guarantee Program, the U.S. Department of the Treasury will provide a 100 percent guarantee on the principal and interest of bonds issued by qualified issuers. No guarantee amount may be less than $100,000,000, provided the total of all such guarantees in any one fiscal year may not exceed $1 billion (subject to appropriations). Qualified issuers will lend the bond proceeds to eligible CDFIs, which must use the proceeds for lending activities in low-income communities and underserved rural areas such as: multi-family housing projects, charter schools, and municipal and community entity lending, among others. The maximum maturity of the bonds is 30 years and the bonds are taxable. Bond and bond loan rates and terms will vary.

Eligible applicants: qualified issuers as determined by the Community Development Financial Institutions Fund.

Eligible beneficiaries: eligible Community Development Financial Institutions as defined by the Small Business Jobs Act of 2010.

Range/Average: N.A.

Activity: N.A.

HQ: Director, CDFI Bond Guarantee Program, Community Development Financial Institutions Fund-Dept of Treasury, 1801 L St., NW, 6th Fl., Washington, DC 20036. Phone: (202) 653-0323; FAX: 202-508-0034.

Internet: www.cdfifund.gov. (Note: no field offices for this program.)

21.015 RESOURCES AND ECOSYSTEMS SUSTAINABILITY, TOURIST OPPORTUNITIES, AND REVIVED ECONOMIES OF THE GULF COAST STATES ("Gulf RESTORE")

Assistance: formula grants (100 percent).

Purposes: pursuant to the Resources and Ecosystems Sustainability, Tourist Opportunities, and Revived Economies of the Gulf Coast States Act of 2012, grants to fund projects to restore and protect the natural resources, ecosystems, fisheries, marine and wildlife habitats, beaches, coastal wetlands, and economy of the Gulf Coast Region.

Eligible applicants: states of Alabama, Florida, Louisiana, Mississippi, and Texas.

Eligible beneficiaries: people and wildlife of the Gulf Coast Region.

Range/Average: N.A.

Activity: N.A.

HQ: Director, Gulf RESTORE, Dept. of the Treasury,1500 Pennsylvania Ave., NW, Washington, DC 20016. Phone: (202) 622-8951.

Internet: N.A. (Note: no field offices for this program.)

21.020 COMMUNITY DEVELOPMENT FINANCIAL INSTITUTIONS PROGRAM (CDFI)

Assistance: project grants. (50 percent/to 3 years).

Purposes: pursuant to ARRA 2009, to provide financial and technical assistance through CDFIs, promoting economic revitalization and community development, including for: CDFI staff training; acquiring products and services including technology; consulting services.

Eligible applicants/beneficiaries: private nonprofit institutions and organizations, and profit organizations that are or seek to become CDFIs. Governmental entities are ineligible.

Range/Average: N.A.

Activity: N.A.

HQ: Program Manager, CDFI Fund, Department of the Treasury, 1801 L St., NW, 6th Floor, Washington, DC 20036. Phone: 202-653-0329; FAX: 202-508-0002.

Internet: www.cdfifund.gov. (Note: no field offices for this program.)

21.021 BANK ENTERPRISE AWARD PROGRAM (BEA)

Assistance: project grants (100 percent).

Purposes: to encourage insured depository institutions to increase their level of community development activities in the form of loans, investments, services, and technical assistance within distressed communities; to provide assistance to community development financial institutions through grants, stock purchases, loans, deposits, and other forms of financial and technical assistance. Award amounts are based on a percentage of increases by the institutions in qualifying activities. Project example: multifamily housing financing.

Eligible applicants/beneficiaries: Federal Deposit Insurance Corporation-insured depository institutions.

Range/Average: N.A.

Activity: N.A.

HQ: Program Manager, CDFI Fund, Department of the Treasury, 1801 L St., NW, 6th Fl., Washington, DC 20036. Phone: (202) 653-0356; FAX: (202) 508-0077.

Internet: www.cdfifund.gov. (Note: no field offices for this program.)

APPALACHIAN REGIONAL COMMISSION

23.001 APPALACHIAN REGIONAL DEVELOPMENT (SEE INDIVIDUAL APPALACHIAN PROGRAMS) ("Appalachian Program")

Assistance: project grants.

Purposes: pursuant to the Appalachian Regional Development Act of 1965 (ARDA) and amendments, for programs and projects to stimulate public investments in public services, facilities, and institutions in the Appalachian region, through federal-state- local efforts. Priorities are established by the Appalachian Regional Commission, comprising the 13 state governors within the region or their alternates. All proposed projects must meet the requirements of the state Appalachian plan and the annual state investment program, both of which must be approved annually by the commission. (See individual Appalachian program descriptions). Funding is through the commission's various programs (**23.002 - 23.011**).

Eligible applicants/beneficiaries: only in the Appalachian region—states and, through the states, public bodies and private nonprofit organizations.

Range/Average: N.A.

Activity: N.A.

HQ: Executive Director, Appalachian Regional Commission, 1666 Connecticut Ave., NW, Washington, DC 20009. Phone: (202) 884-7668.

Internet: www.arc.gov.

23.002 APPALACHIAN AREA DEVELOPMENT

Assistance: project grants (10-80 percent).

Purposes: pursuant to ARDA and amendments, to supplement other federal project funding supporting self-sustaining development in the region's most distressed counties. Projects must hold high priority in the state's Appalachian development plan. Examples include water and sewer systems, industrial parks, entrepreneurship, export promotion, training, vocational education, health care, child development, revolving loan funds, and business incubator projects—in conjunction with private sector commitments.

Eligible applicants/beneficiaries: (Appalachia only) states, state subdivisions and instrumentalities, private nonprofit agencies.

Range: to $178,112. **Average:** $6,804.

Activity: N.A.

HQ: Executive Director, Appalachian Regional Commission, 1666 Connecticut Ave., NW, Washington, DC 20009. Phone: (202) 884-7668.

Internet: www.arc.gov.

23.003 APPALACHIAN DEVELOPMENT HIGHWAY SYSTEM ("Appalachian Corridors")

Assistance: project grants (80 percent).

Purposes: pursuant to ARDA as amended, to develop a highway system within the Appalachian region where commerce and communication have been inhibited by inadequate access. Grants may cover preliminary engineering, right-of-way acquisition, and construction costs. Additional funding for this program may be provided from the DOT Highway Trust Fund.

Eligible applicants/beneficiaries: (Appalachia only) state governments.

Range/Average: N.A.

Activity: to open 25 miles of the ADHS to traffic in FY 2016.

HQ: Executive Director, Appalachian Regional Commission, 1666 Connecticut Ave., NW, Washington, DC 20009. Phone: (202) 884-7668.

Internet: www.arc.gov.

23.009 APPALACHIAN LOCAL DEVELOPMENT DISTRICT ASSISTANCE (LDD)

Assistance: project grants (50-75 percent).

Purposes: pursuant to ARDA and amendments, for development planning and activities relating to local economic development. Funds may be used for: administrative expenses including technical services of local development districts; with ARC approval, real estate and vehicle purchases, construction and space improvement.

Eligible applicants/beneficiaries: (Appalachia only) multicounty organizations certified by the state.

Range: to $318,000. **Average:** $7,229.

Activity: N.A.

HQ: Executive Director, Appalachian Regional Commission, 1666 Connecticut Ave., NW, Washington, DC 20009. Phone: (202) 884-7668.

Internet: www.arc.gov.

23.011 APPALACHIAN RESEARCH, TECHNICAL ASSISTANCE, AND DEMONSTRATION PROJECTS ("State Research")

Assistance: project grants.

Purposes: pursuant to ARDA and amendments, for research, planning, demonstration, and technical assistance projects relating to concerted economic and community development. Priority is on technical assistance projects leading to job creation.

Eligible applicants/beneficiaries: Appalachian states, state consortia; local public bodies; state instrumentalities.

Range: to $298,817. **Average:** $2,709.

Activity: N.A.

HQ: Executive Director, Appalachian Regional Commission, 1666 Connecticut Ave., NW, Washington, DC 20009. Phone: (202) 884-7668.

Internet: www.arc.gov.

OFFICE OF PERSONNEL MANAGEMENT

27.001 FEDERAL CIVIL SERVICE EMPLOYMENT

Assistance: federal employment.

Purposes: pursuant to the Civil Service Reform Act of 1978, to fill federal job vacancies, usually through competitive exams and without discrimination on any nonmerit basis. Veterans receive preference. Special programs help place the physically handicapped, the mentally retarded or mentally restored, and the disadvantaged.

Eligible applicants/beneficiaries: U.S. citizens age 18 or older (age 16 in certain cases).

Range/Average: N.A.

Activity: N.A.

HQ: Office of Personnel Management, 1900 E St., NW, Rm. 2445, Washington, DC 20415. Phone: (202) 606-2700; *nation-wide,* (912) 757-3000; TDD Service, (912) 744-2299.

Internet: www.opm.gov. (Note: no field offices for this program.)

27.002 FEDERAL EMPLOYMENT ASSISTANCE FOR VETERANS

Assistance: federal employment.

Purposes: pursuant to the Veterans Preference Act of 1944, to assist veterans in obtaining federal employment, with preferences according to their discharge status.

Eligible applicants/beneficiaries: nondisabled and disabled veterans, and certain spouses, widows, widowers, and mothers of veterans.

Range/Average: N.A.

Activity: N.A.

HQ: Disabled Veterans Affirmative Action Programs, Office of Diversity, Employment Service, OPM, 1900 E St., NW, Rm. 2445, Washington, DC

20415. Phone: (202) 606-1059; *veterans preference and special hiring programs,* Office of Staffing Reinvention, Employment Service. Phone: (202) 606-0830.

Internet: www.opm.gov. (Note: no field offices for this program.)

27.003   FEDERAL STUDENT TEMPORARY EMPLOYMENT PROGRAM

Assistance: federal employment (to 1 year).

Purposes: to provide temporary federal employment for youth during school terms (full-time during extended vacation periods). OPM coordinates this program, but it is carried out by other participating federal agencies.

Eligible applicants/beneficiaries: students accepted for or enrolled at least half-time in a secondary, vocational, or technical school or IHE through the graduate level.

Range/Average: N.A.

Activity: N.A.

HQ: *information available from personnel offices of the agencies of interest. For inquiries on policy issues,* Staffing Reinvention Office, Employment Service, OPM, 1900 E St., NW, Washington, DC 20415. Phone: (202) 606-0830.

Internet: www.opm.gov. (Note: no field offices for this program.)

27.005   FEDERAL EMPLOYMENT FOR INDIVIDUALS WITH DISABILITIES ("Selective Placement Program")

Assistance: federal employment.

Purposes: pursuant to the Rehabilitation Act of 1973 as amended, to provide special OPM assistance to federal agencies to assist persons with disabilities, including veterans, in obtaining or retaining federal employment. Federal agencies have coordinators responsible for expanding employment opportunities under this program, to work with state vocational rehabilitation agencies, DVA facilities, and other public and private agencies. Funding is by the accounts of individual agencies.

Eligible applicants/beneficiaries: persons with physical, cognitive, or mental disabilities.

Range/Average: N.A.

Activity: N.A.

HQ: Director, Diversity Office, Employment Service, Office of Personnel Management, 1900 E St., NW, Rm. 2445, Washington, DC 20415. Telephone: (202) 606-1059.

Internet: www.opm.gov. (Note: no field offices for this program.)

27.006   FEDERAL SUMMER EMPLOYMENT ("Summer Jobs in Federal Agencies")

Assistance: federal employment.

Purposes: pursuant to the Civil Service Reform Act of 1978, to provide summer employment primarily for college and high school students, in clerical, craft or trade, administrative, and subprofessional jobs. Summer jobs are filled through agency staffing plans, with funding by the participating agencies.

Eligible applicants/beneficiaries: any U.S. citizen at least age 16 at time of appointment.

Range/Average: N.A.

Activity: N.A.

HQ: Office of Personnel Management, 1900 E St., NW, Rm. 2445, Washington, DC 20415. Phone: (202) 606-2700; *nation-wide,* (912) 757-3000; TDD Service, (912) 744-2299.

Internet: www.opm.gov. (Note: no field offices for this program.)

27.011 INTERGOVERNMENTAL PERSONNEL ACT (IPA) MOBILITY PROGRAM

Assistance: specialized services; advisory services/counseling (to 4 years).

Purposes: pursuant to the Act of 1970 as amended and ISDEAA, to enable temporary assignments of professional, administrative, or technical personnel back and forth between federal, state, local, and tribal governments, IHEs, and other organizations. Assignments may be for up to two years, with one two-year extension. Upon completion of assignments, assigned federal employees must serve in the Civil Service for a period equal to that of the assignment. Cost sharing is negotiable.

Eligible applicants/beneficiaries: federal agencies; state, local, and tribal governments; IHEs. Other organizations include: national, regional, statewide, areawide, or metropolitan organizations of state or local governments; associations of state or local public officials; nonprofit organizations offering professional advisory, research, educational, or developmental services, or related services to governments or universities concerned with public management.

Range/Average: N.A.

Activity: N.A.

HQ: Office of Merit Systems Oversight and Effectiveness, OPM, 1900 E St., NW, Rm. 7463, Washington, DC 20415-0001. Phone: (202) 606-1181.

Internet: www.opm.gov.

27.013 PRESIDENTIAL MANAGEMENT INTERN PROGRAM

Assistance: federal employment; training; specialized services.

Purposes: to attract graduate students of exceptional potential to the federal service. Two-year internships may be awarded for work in federal agencies (exceptionally, for three years). Awardees may be assigned to work temporarily for state or local governments. Nominations for awards are submitted by deans of graduate level programs. Participating entities reimburse OPM for certain program costs through a revolving loan fund.

Eligible applicants/beneficiaries: federal agencies; state, local, and tribal governments; IHEs. Other organizations include: national, regional, statewide, areawide, or metropolitan organizations of state or local governments; associations of state or local public officials; nonprofit organizations offering professional advisory, research, educational, or developmental services, or related services to governments or universities concerned with public management.

Range/Average: N.A.

Activity: N.A.

HQ: Presidential Management Intern Program, Philadelphia Service Center, OPM, 600 Arch St., Philadelphia, PA 19106. Phone: (215) 597-7136, (215) 597-1920.

Internet: www.opm.gov. (Note: no field offices for this program.)

COMMISSION ON CIVIL RIGHTS

29.001 CLEARINGHOUSE SERVICES, CIVIL RIGHTS DISCRIMINATION COMPLAINTS

Assistance: technical information.

Purposes: pursuant to the Civil Rights Commission Reauthorization Act of 1991, to serve as a national clearinghouse concerning the civil rights of individuals, entitling them to equal protection of the laws regardless of their race, color, religion, sex, age, handicap, or national origin; to provide related research, liaison, publications, and public information services to private and public groups and the media; and to process complaints for referral to appropriate federal agencies.

Eligible applicants/beneficiaries: anyone may seek information.

Range/Average: N.A.

Activity: N.A.

HQ: Commission on Civil Rights, 624 Ninth St., NW, Washington, DC 20425. Phone: (202) 376-8177, TDD (202) 376-8116; *complaints,* (202) 376-8582, (800) 552-6843.

Internet: www.opm.gov.

EQUAL EMPLOYMENT OPPORTUNITY COMMISSION

30.001 EMPLOYMENT DISCRIMINATION—TITLE VII OF THE CIVIL RIGHTS ACT OF 1964

Assistance: advisory services/counseling; investigation of complaints.

Purposes: pursuant to the Acts of 1964 and 1991 and amendments, to provide for education, technical assistance, and enforcement of federal prohibitions against employment discrimination in the public and private sectors, based on race, sex, color national origin, or religion. Complaints are investigated and, if reasonable cause is found, mediation is offered; if mediation is not used or successful, charges are conciliated; if unsuccessful, civil action may be brought against named respondents. If conciliation fails on a charge against a state or local government, EEOC may refer the case to DOJ for further action. Funding for this program includes **30.008**, **30.010**, and **30.011**.

Eligible applicants/beneficiaries: any individual or any labor union, association, legal representative, or organization filing on behalf of an individual with reason to believe that an unlawful employment practice has been committed by an employer with 15 or more employees, an employment agency, a labor organization, or a joint labor-management committee controlling apprenticeship or other training activities.

Range/Average: N.A.

Activity: N.A.

HQ: Communications Staff, Office of Communications and Legislative Affairs, EEOC, 131 M St., NE Washington, DC 20507. Phone: (202) 663-4191, TTY (202) 663-4494.

Internet: www.eeoc.gov.

30.005 EMPLOYMENT DISCRIMINATION—PRIVATE BAR PROGRAM

Assistance: specialized services.

Purposes: pursuant to the Civil Rights Acts of 1964 and 1991 and amendments, to assist aggrieved individuals in locating lawyers to represent them in suits involving employment discrimination under provisions of Title VII of the Civil Rights Act of 1964, the Equal Pay Act, the Age Discrimination in Employment Act, or the ADA; to provide technical assistance to aggrieved parties and their attorneys.

Eligible applicants/beneficiaries: individuals filing charges.

Range/Average: N.A.

Activity: N.A.

HQ: Office of General Counsel, EEOC, 131 M St., NE, Washington, DC 20507. Phone: (202) 663-4719.

Internet: www.eeoc.gov.

30.008 EMPLOYMENT DISCRIMINATION—AGE DISCRIMINATION IN EMPLOYMENT

Assistance: advisory services/counseling; investigation of complaints.

Purposes: pursuant to the Age Discrimination in Employment Act of 1967, amendments, and Civil Rights Act of 1991, to enforce regulations concerning arbitrary employment discrimination on the basis of age; to promote the employment of older workers. Individuals age 40 or older are protected from discrimination by: private commercial employers with 20 or more employees; federal, state, local governments; employment agencies; labor organizations. Funding for this program is included in **30.001**.

Eligible applicants/beneficiaries: persons age 40 or over.

Range/Average: N.A.

Activity: N.A.

HQ: Communications Staff, Office of Communications and Legislative Affairs, EEOC, 131 M St., NE Washington, DC 20507. Phone: (202) 663-4191, TTY (202) 663-4494.

Internet: www.eeoc.gov.

30.010 EMPLOYMENT DISCRIMINATION EQUAL PAY ACT

Assistance: advisory services/counseling; investigation of complaints.

Purposes: pursuant to the Equal Pay Act of 1963 as amended and Fair Labor Standards Act Amendment of 1974, to enforce laws prohibiting discrimination on the basis of sex in the payment of wages to men and women performing equal work in the same establishment, which is illegal for: employers engaged in commerce or in the production of goods; federal, state, and local governments. Also, labor organizations are prohibited from causing or attempting to cause employers to violate the law. Exceptions are permitted only where payments are based on systems recognizing seniority, merit, quantity or quality of production, or differentials based on factors other than sex. Funding for this program is included in **30.001**.

Eligible applicants/beneficiaries: employees believing that they or others have been or are being paid in violation of the Act, in any state, territory, or possession.

Range/Average: N.A.

Activity: N.A.

HQ: Communications Staff, Office of Communications and Legislative Affairs, EEOC, 131 M St., NE Washington, DC 20507. Phone: (202) 663-4191, TTY (202) 663-4494.

Internet: www.eeoc.gov.

30.011 EMPLOYMENT DISCRIMINATION—TITLE I OF THE AMERICANS WITH DISABILITIES ACT

Assistance: advisory services/counseling; investigation of complaints.

Purposes: to enforce the ADA as amended, prohibiting employment discrimination by private employers and state and local governments against qualified individuals with disabilities. The commission investigates complaints and, if reasonable cause is found, mediation is offered; if mediation is not used or successful, charges are conciliated; if unsuccessful, legal action may be taken by DOJ against private respondents. If conciliation fails on a charge against a state or local government, EEOC refers the case to DOJ for further action. Funding for this program is included in **30.001**.

Eligible applicants/beneficiaries: any individual or any labor union, association, legal representative, or organization filing on behalf of an individual with reason to believe that an unlawful employment practice has been committed by an employer with 15 or more employees, an employment agency, a labor organization, or a joint labor-management committee controlling apprenticeship or other training activities.

Range/Average: N.A.

Activity: N.A.

HQ: Communications Staff, Office of Communications and Legislative Affairs, EEOC, 131 M St., NE Washington, DC 20507. Phone: (202) 663-4191, TTY (202) 663-4494.

Internet: www.eeoc.gov.

EXPORT-IMPORT BANK

31.007 EXPORT—LOAN GUARANTEE—INSURED LOANS

Assistance: direct loans; guaranteed/insured loans (1-7+ years).

Purposes: pursuant to The Export-Import Bank Act of 1945, as amended, the Export-Import Bank of the U.S. (Ex-Im Bank or the Bank) is an independent executive agency and a wholly-owned U.S. government corporation. Ex-Im Bank's objective is to finance the export of goods and services made in the United States for the purpose of maintaining and creating U.S. jobs. Goods must comply with applicable U.S. content restrictions. There is no minimum transaction size.

Eligible applicants/beneficiaries: anyone/general public, especially small businesses.

Range: $25,000 to $500,000,000. **Average:** N.A.

Activity: N.A.

HQ: Trade Advisor-Export-Import Bank of the United States, 811 Vermont Ave., NW, Washington, DC 20571. Phone: (202) 565-3946; Toll Free: (800) 565-3946.

Internet: www.exim.gov.

FEDERAL COMMUNICATIONS COMMISSION

32.001 COMMUNICATIONS INFORMATION AND ASSISTANCE AND INVESTIGATION OF COMPLAINTS

Assistance: technical information; investigation of complaints.

Purposes: pursuant to the Communications Act of 1934 as amended, for public information, education, and investigation of complaints concerning public communications systems. FCC services relate to rates, broadcast signal interference, equal time for political candidates, and the presentation of issues.

Eligible applicants/beneficiaries: anyone.

Range/Average: N.A.

Activity: N.A.

HQ: Public Service Division, Federal Communications Commission, 1919 M St., NW, Rm. 244, Washington, DC 20554. Phone: (*fees,* Phone: (202) 418-0220; *cable,* (202) 418-0190.

Internet: www.fcc.gov.

FEDERAL MARITIME COMMISSION

33.001 SHIPPING—DISPUTE RESOLUTION AND INVESTIGATION OF COMPLAINTS

Assistance: investigation of complaints.

Purposes: pursuant to the Shipping Act of 1984 as amended, to provide a forum for settling disputes between carriers, shippers concerning maritime shipping and ocean transportation, including: cruise passengers seeking reimbursement of deposits when a cruise is canceled; complaints about unlawful rates or practices. Reparations may be awarded for violations.

Eligible applicants/beneficiaries: anyone.

Range/Average: N.A.

Activity: N.A.

HQ: Director, Office of Consumer Complaints, Federal Maritime Commission, 800 N. Capitol St., NW, Washington, DC 20573. Phone: (202) 523-5807; FAX: (202) 275-0059.

Internet: www.fmc.gov.

FEDERAL MEDIATION AND CONCILIATION SERVICE

34.001 LABOR MEDIATION AND CONCILIATION

Assistance: specialized services; advisory services/counseling.

Purposes: pursuant to the Labor-Management Relations Act of 1947 as amended and other acts, to prevent or minimize work stoppages caused by disputes between labor and management in industries affecting commerce, including federal labor disputes—through mediation of collective bargaining disputes, arbitration assistance, public education, conciliation.

Eligible applicants/beneficiaries: employers involved in interstate commerce, related labor organizations, federal agencies.

Range/Average: N.A.

Activity: N.A.

HQ: FMCS, 2100 K St., NW, Washington, DC 20427. Phone: (202) 606-8100.

Internet: www.fmcs.gov.

34.002 LABOR-MANAGEMENT COOPERATION

Assistance: project grants (12-18 months).

Purposes: pursuant to the Labor-Management Cooperation Act of 1978, to establish, expand, and operate joint labor-management committees in the public or private sectors at the work-site, area, and industry-wide levels—to improve labor-management relations and productivity.

Eligible applicants/beneficiaries: private nonprofit labor- management committees; labor organizations and private companies or public agencies applying jointly; private nonprofit entities.

Range: to $400,000. **Average:** N.A.

Activity: N.A.

HQ: Grants Program Office, Labor Management Cooperation Program, FMCS, 2100 K St., NW, Washington, DC 20427. Phone: (202) 606-8181.

Internet: www.fmcs.gov. (Note: no field offices for this program.)

FEDERAL TRADE COMMISSION

36.001 FAIR COMPETITION COUNSELING AND INVESTIGATION OF COMPLAINTS

Assistance: advisory services/counseling; investigation of complaints.

Purposes: pursuant to the Federal Trade Commission Act of 1914, amendments, and related acts, to prevent and eliminate anticompetitive, deceptive, and other practices adversely affecting consumers. The FTC's concerns include price-fixing, boycotts, price discrimination, illegal mergers and acquisitions, false and misleading advertising, consumer credit transactions and reporting, debt collection practices, food and drug advertising, and other practices affecting the consuming public.

Eligible applicants/beneficiaries: anyone.

Range/Average: N.A.

Activity: N.A.

HQ: Federal Trade Commission, 600 Pennsylvania Ave., NW, Washington, DC 20580. Phone: Director, Bureau of Consumer Protection, (202) 326-3240; Director, Bureau of Competition, (202) 326-3175.

Internet: www.ftc.gov.

GENERAL SERVICES ADMINISTRATION

39.002 DISPOSAL OF FEDERAL SURPLUS REAL PROPERTY

Assistance: sale, exchange, or donation of property and goods.

Purposes: pursuant to the Federal Property and Administrative Services Act of 1949, Surplus Property Act of 1944, SBMHAA, and amendments, to dispose of surplus federal real and related personal property for public purposes, at discounts of up to 100 percent, through leases, permits, sale, exchange, or donation. Applicants for property coordinate with appropriate other federal agencies. Surplus property not deeded to public bodies is generally offered for sale to the public on a competitive bid basis.

Eligible applicants/beneficiaries: surplus real property for park, recreation, correctional facility, historic monument, public airport uses, for health, educational, or homeless programs, and for replacement housing and general public purposes—state and local government agencies. Property for wildlife conservation use—states. Property for health education and homeless program uses—tax-supported and nonprofit medical and educational institutions exempt from taxation under IRS Section 501(c)(3).

Range/Average: N.A.

Activity: N.A.

HQ: Assistant Commissioner, Office of Property Disposal, Public Building Service, GSA, 1800 F St., NW, Washington, DC 20405. Phone: (202) 208-0324.

Internet: Rc.gsa.gov.

39.003   DONATION OF FEDERAL SURPLUS PERSONAL PROPERTY ("Donation Program")

Assistance: sale, exchange, or donation of property and goods.

Purposes: pursuant to the Federal Property and Administrative Services Act of 1949, Surplus Property Act of 1944, Older Americans Act of 1965, and amendments, to donate surplus federal personal property to state and local public agencies for public purposes, to qualifying nonprofit entities for tax-exempt activities, or for educational and research activities. Examples of surplus property include office machines and supplies, furniture, hardware, textiles, special purpose motor vehicles, boats, airplanes, construction equipment. Participation requires prior GSA approval of state plans for distribution to eligible recipients. Items not donated are made available for sale to the general public (see **39.007**).

Eligible applicants/beneficiaries: state and local agencies, departments, instrumentalities, economic development districts, instrumentalities; multi-jurisdictional substate districts; tribes, bands, groups, pueblos; nonprofit, tax-exempt organizations such as schools, colleges, universities, public libraries, schools for the handicapped, educational radio or TV stations, child care centers, museums, hospitals, health centers, clinics, programs for the elderly or homeless; public airports; private service and educational organizations.

Range/Average: N.A.

Activity: N.A.

HQ: Director, Property Management Division, Office of Transportation and Property Management, Federal Supply Service, GSA, 1800 F St., N.W., Washington, DC 20405. Phone: (202) 501-1700.

Internet: www.gsa.gov/property.

39.007 SALE OF FEDERAL SURPLUS PERSONAL PROPERTY ("Sales Program")

Assistance: sale, exchange, or donation of property and goods.

Purposes: pursuant to the Federal Property and Administrative Services Act of 1949 as amended, to sell surplus federal personal property on behalf of most federal civil agencies—including vehicles, aircraft, hardware, electronic and electrical equipment, office supplies and equipment, scrap goods. Disposal is by competitive bid.

Eligible applicants/beneficiaries: general public.

Range/Average: N.A.

Activity: N.A.

HQ: Director, Property Management Division, Office of Transportation and Property Management, Federal Supply Service, GSA, 1800 F St., N.W., Washington, DC 20405. Phone: (202) 501-1700.

Internet: www.govsales.gov.

39.012 PUBLIC BUILDINGS SERVICE

Assistance: provision of specialized services.

Purposes: pursuant to the Consolidated Appropriations Act of 2008 and the Division D-Financial Services and General Government Appropriations Act of 2008, to cultivate innovative regional coordination, design, research, and planning practices for accommodating federal offices in the Washington DC area over the next half-century. Inherent in the development of this intelligent urban planning vision, the federal government encourages guidance by mutual regional concerns including: sustainability, transportation infrastructure, security, new technologies and the changing regional economics of land, housing, and workforce issues.

Eligible applicants/beneficiaries: IHEs, nonprofit and commercial organizations, state and local governments, or individuals with experience in analysis or coordination of the planning issues described in the purpose. Joint ventures between eligible applicants are welcome.

Range/Average: N.A.

Activity: N.A.

HQ: Director of Urban Development/Good Neighbor Program, GSA, 1800 F St., Washington, DC 20405. Phone: (202) 501-1856.

Internet: www.gsa.gov. (Note: no field offices for this program.)

GOVERNMENT PRINTING OFFICE

40.001 DEPOSITORY LIBRARIES FOR GOVERNMENT PUBLICATIONS

Assistance: technical information.

Purposes: to provide government publications and other information products, including electronic products, for public reference in 1,270 depository libraries in the U.S. and its possessions.

Eligible applicants: libraries designated by members of Congress (two Representative designations in each congressional district, four Senatorial designations in each state). By law, all state, highest state appellate court, land-grant college, and law school libraries are also eligible for designation.

Eligible beneficiaries: general public.

Range/Average: N.A.

Activity: N.A.

HQ: Information Dissemination Department, Superintendent of Documents, GPO, 732 N. Capitol St., Washington, DC 20402. Phone: (202) 512-1114; GPO Contact Center; Phone: (202) 512-1800; FAX: (202) 512-2104; Toll-Free (866) 512-1800.

Internet: www.access.gpo.gov/su_docs/fdlp/libpro.html. (Note: no field offices for this program.)

40.002 GOVERNMENT PUBLICATIONS SALES AND DISTRIBUTION ("The Government Bookstore")

Assistance: sale, exchange, or donation of property and goods; technical information.

Purposes: to make available government publications, including 233 subscription services, for sale to the general public. Discounts are available to dealers and other purchasers of large quantities. A revolving fund supports this program.

Eligible applicants/beneficiaries: general public.

Range/Average: N.A.

Activity: N.A.

HQ: Superintendent of Documents, GPO, 732 N. Capitol St., Washington, DC 20402. Phone: (Order Desk, (866) 512-1800; FAX: (202) 512-2104.

Internet: bookstore.gpo.gov. (Note: no field offices for this program.)

LIBRARY OF CONGRESS

42.001 BOOKS FOR THE BLIND AND PHYSICALLY HANDICAPPED

Assistance: use of property, facilities, and equipment.

Purposes: to provide library services to blind and physically handicapped persons—consisting of books on cassette, music scores, discs, and instructional materials in braille, large type, and on recorded formats, in 57 regional and 77 subregional libraries.

Eligible applicants/beneficiaries: U.S. residents and citizens living abroad, providing a certificate of inability to read or manipulate conventional printed material, from a competent authority.

Range/Average: N.A.

Activity: N.A.

HQ: Director, National Library Service for the Blind and Physically Handicapped, LC, 1291 Taylor St., NW, Washington, DC 20542. Phone: (202) 707-5100.

Internet: www.loc.gov/nls.

42.002 COPYRIGHT SERVICE

Assistance: technical information.

Purposes: to administer the U.S. Copyright Law, including: processing of applications, renewals, transfers, searches, and distribution of regulations; processing of compulsory licenses for satellite carriers and cable systems, and digital audio recording products, and collection and distribution of royalties; to administer the Copyright Arbitration Royalty Panels. Fees are charged for certain services. Funding for this program also supports **42.008**.

Eligible applicants/beneficiaries: anyone. Registration may be made by authors, their assignees, or their exclusive licensees, and others designated by law, or by their agents.

Range/Average: N.A.

Activity: N.A.

HQ: Register of Copyrights, Copyright Office, James Madison Memorial Bldg., Library of Congress, 101 Independence Ave., SE, Washington, DC 20559-6000. Phone: (202) 707-1497.

Internet: www.copyright.gov. (Note: no field offices for this program.)

42.008 SEMICONDUCTOR CHIP PROTECTION SERVICE

Assistance: technical information.

Purposes: to administer the provisions of the Semiconductor Chip Protection Act of 1984. The Copyright Office staff: examines and decides on the acceptability of applications and identifying materials for registration of claims of protection; records and publishes legal facts or data pertaining to registered works; furnishes pertinent information to the public; and, records transfer documents. Fees are charged for some services. Program operating costs are absorbed in the budget of the Copyright Office; fees collected are returned to the U.S. Treasury to offset program costs.

Eligible applicants: general public.

Eligible beneficiaries: owners of qualified mask works.

Range/Average: N.A.

Activity: N.A.

HQ: Register of Copyrights, Copyright Office, James Madison Memorial Bldg., Library of Congress, 101 Independence Ave., SE, Washington, DC 20559-6000. Phone: (202) 707-1497.

Internet: www.copyright.gov. (Note: no field offices for this program.)

42.009 VESSEL HULL DESIGN PROTECTION SERVICE

Assistance: technical information.

Purposes: to administer the Vessel Hull Design Protection Act of 1998. The LC Copyright Office: examines and decides the acceptability of applications and identifying material for registration of claims; records and publishes legal facts or data pertaining to registered works. Fees are charged for services. Program operating costs are absorbed in the budget of the Copyright Office; fees collected are returned to the U.S. Treasury to offset program costs.

Eligible applicants/beneficiaries: registration may be made by owners of qualified vessel hull designs, or their agents. Information is available to anyone.

Range/Average: N.A.

Activity: N.A.

HQ: Register of Copyrights, Copyright Office, James Madison Memorial Bldg., Library of Congress, 101 Independence Ave., SE, Washington, DC 20559-6000. Phone: (202) 707-1497.

Internet: www.copyright.gov. (Note: no field offices for this program.)

NATIONAL AERONAUTICS AND SPACE ADMINISTRATION

43.001 NASA—SCIENCE

Assistance: technical information.

Purposes: pursuant to the National Aeronautics and Space Act of 1958 as amended, to support instruction and to initiate systemic change in mathematics, science, and technology education, using NASA specialists to provide inservice and preservice workshops for K-12 teachers, lectures, classroom demonstrations, and media broadcasts.

Eligible applicants/beneficiaries: schools, teacher training institutions, IHEs, civic groups, museums, planetaria.

Range/Average: N.A.

Activity: N.A.

HQ: Office of Education, NASA, 300 E St., SW, Stop LH010, Washington, DC 20546. Phone: (202) 358-3911; FAX: (202) 358-3082.

Internet: www.nasa.gov.

43.002 NASA—AERONAUTICS

Assistance: technical information.

Purposes: pursuant to the National Aeronautics and Space Act of 1958 as amended, to disseminate information about government- sponsored civilian aerospace research and development, including inventions, discoveries, innovations, and other improvements—through: NASA's "TechTracs" data system, via the Internet; publications including "Tech Briefs;" Regional Technology Transfer Centers; commercial technology field center offices.

Eligible applicants/beneficiaries: Tech Briefs subscriptions (no charge)—engineers, domestic enterprise managers, professionals, and others involved in technology transfer. Technical information search and retrieval services and computer programs/documentation—domestic organizations (fees charged for services beyond those available on the Internet); Technology Transfer Projects—those demonstrating a national public need.

Range/Average: N.A.

Activity: N.A.

HQ: Innovative Partnerships Program, Office of Exploration Systems, NASA, 300 E St., SW, Stop LH010, Washington, DC 20546. Phone: (202) 358-3911; FAX: (202) 358-3082.

Internet: www.nasa.gov.

43.003 EXPLORATION

Assistance: cooperative agreements/discretionary grants; project grants; direct payments/specified use; dissemination of technical information (100 percent/to 3 years).

Purposes: pursuant to the Aeronautics and Space Act of 1958, for basic research, educational outreach, or training opportunities in the area of exploration.

Eligible applicants/beneficiaries: 35 IHEs selected by the CDC as Prevention Research Centers (PRCs).

Range/Average: N.A.

Activity: N.A.

HQ: Director, Exploration Program, NASA, 3300 E St., SW, Stop LH010, Washington, DC 20546. Phone: (202) 358-3911; FAX: (202) 358-3082.

Internet: www.nasa.gov.

43.007 SPACE OPERATIONS

Assistance: cooperative agreements/discretionary grants; project grants/contracts, fellowships (100 percent/to 3 years).

Purposes: pursuant to the Aeronautics and Space Act of 1958, for basic research, educational outreach, or training opportunities in the area of Space Operations.

Eligible applicants/beneficiaries: 35 IHEs selected by the CDC as Prevention Research Centers (PRCs).

Range/Average: N.A.

Activity: N.A.

HQ: Director, Space Operations Program, NASA, 300 E St., SW, Stop LH010, Washington, DC 20546. Phone: (202) 358-3911; FAX: (202) 358-3082.

Internet: www.nasa.gov.

43.008 NASA—EDUCATION

Assistance: cooperative agreements/discretionary grants; project grants/discretionary grants; contracts (100 percent/to 3 years).

Purposes: pursuant to the Aeronautics and Space Act of 1958, for basic research, educational outreach, or training opportunities in the area of education.

Eligible applicants/beneficiaries: 35 IHEs selected by the CDC as Prevention Research Centers (PRCs).

Range/Average: N.A.

Activity: N.A.

HQ: Director, Education Program, NASA, 300 E St., SW, Stop LH010, Washington, DC 20546. Phone: (202) 358-3911; FAX: (202) 358-3082.

Internet: www.nasa.gov.

43.009 CROSS AGENCY SUPPORT

Assistance: cooperative agreements/discretionary grants; direct payments/specified use; project grants/collaborative design and production of curriculum, specified projects, travel grants, dissemination of technical information (100 percent/to 3 years).

Purposes: pursuant to the Aeronautics and Space Act of 1958, for basic research, educational outreach, or training opportunities in the area of cross agency support.

Eligible applicants/beneficiaries: 35 IHEs selected by the CDC as Prevention Research Centers (PRCs).

Range/Average: N.A.

Activity: N.A.

HQ: Director, Cross Agency Support Program, NASA, 300 E St., SW, Stop LH010, Washington, DC 20546. Phone: (202) 358-3911; FAX: (202) 358-3082.

Internet: www.nasa.gov.

43.010 CONSTRUCTION & ENVIRONMENTAL COMPLIANCE & REMEDIATION

Assistance: cooperative agreements/discretionary grants; direct payments/specified use; project grants/contracts, fellowships, collaborative design and production of curriculum, specified projects, travel grants, dissemination of technical information (100 percent/to 3 years).

Purposes: pursuant to the Aeronautics and Space Act of 1958, for basic research, educational outreach, or training opportunities in the area of Construction & Environmental Compliance & Remediation.

Eligible applicants/beneficiaries: 35 IHEs selected by the CDC as Prevention Research Centers (PRCs).

Range/Average: N.A.

Activity: N.A.

HQ: Director, Construction & Environmental Compliance & Remediation Program, NASA, 300 E St., SW, Stop LH010, Washington, DC 20546. Phone: (202) 358-3911; FAX: (202) 358-3082.

Internet: www.nasa.gov.

NATIONAL CREDIT UNION ADMINISTRATION

44.002 COMMUNITY DEVELOPMENT REVOLVING LOAN FUND PROGRAM FOR CREDIT UNIONS ("CDRLF, CDCU")

Assistance: direct loans. (50-67 percent/1 to 3 percent interest/to 5 years).

Purposes: to stimulate economic development activities by: increasing income, business ownership, and employment opportunities among the low-income; providing basic financial and related services to community residents, such as financial counseling, membership and participation drives. Loans can also involve housing, including cooperatives and self-help. Funding is derived from a revolving loan fund.

Eligible applicants/beneficiaries: established state- and federally-chartered credit unions serving low-income communities. Available also in territories and possessions.

Range: $500 to $25,000 for grants. $10,000 to $500,000 for loans. **Average:** N.A.

Activity: 381 awards in FY 2015.

HQ: Community Development Revolving Loan Program for Credit Unions, NCUA, 1775 Duke St., Alexandria, VA 22314. Phone: (703) 518-6645.

Internet: www.ncua.gov. (Note: no field offices for this program.)

NATIONAL ENDOWMENT FOR THE ARTS

45.024 PROMOTION OF THE ARTS—GRANTS TO ORGANIZATIONS AND INDIVIDUALS

Assistance: project grants. (organizations,50 percent; individuals, 100 percent/both, to 2 years).

Purposes: pursuant to ARRA 2009 and NFAHA of 1965 as amended, to foster and preserve excellence in the arts, provide public access to the arts, and advance arts education for children and youth. Funds support national, regional, and field-wide organizations in the visual, literary, media, design, and performing arts—in projects involving one of more aspects of: creativity; organizational capacity including technology; heritage and preservation; access; arts learning; international exchanges; and, for national arts programs for television or radio. Also, to support published writers through fellowships for creative writing (fiction and nonfiction), poetry, and literary translations.

Eligible applicants/beneficiaries: organizations—nonprofit tax-exempt entities such as arts institutions and arts service organizations, local arts agencies, state and local governments, tribal organizations; consortia. Individuals—U.S. citizens or permanent residents with exceptional talent; currently, only published creative writers are eligible.

Range: $10,000 to $100,000. **Average:** N.A.

Activity: anticipate 2,200 awards in FY 2016.

HQ: NEA, 400 7th St., SW, Washington, DC 20506. Phone: 202-682-5635.

Internet: www.arts.gov. (Note: no field offices for this program.)

45.025 PROMOTION OF THE ARTS—PARTNERSHIP AGREEMENTS

Assistance: formula grants, project grants; advisory services/counseling (project grants, 50 percent).

Purposes: pursuant to NFAHA, as amended and ARRA 2009, for development of basic state arts plans; for elements of state plans addressing arts learning and fostering arts in underserved areas; to provide basic support through Partnership Agreements for regional arts planning and for presenting and touring. Limited partnership funds are available for national services provided by membership organizations of state and regional arts organizations.

Eligible applicants/beneficiaries: state arts agencies in the states and in six special U.S. jurisdictions; regional and national arts organizations.

Range: $289,500 to $1,089,900 for SAAs; $1,027,700 to $1,649,000 for RAO awards. **Average:** $725,000 for SAAs; $1,330,000 for RAO awards.

Activity: anticipate making 63 partnership awards n FY 2016.

HQ: State and Regional Director, NEA, 400 7th St., SW, Washington, DC 20506. Phone: (202) 682-5583.

Internet: www.arts.gov. (Note: no field offices for this program.)

NATIONAL ENDOWMENT FOR THE HUMANITIES

45.129 PROMOTION OF THE HUMANITIES—FEDERAL/STATE PARTNERSHIP

Assistance: project grants (50 percent/3 years).

Purposes: pursuant to NFAHA as amended, for humanities councils for regranting to local groups and individuals to conduct local, statewide, and regional projects. Project examples: youth partnership programs with Boy and Girl Scouts of America, Boys and Girls Clubs, YMCA-YWCA; traveling exhibits; scholar-led seminars; elder reading initiative.

Eligible applicants: state and territorial nonprofit citizen councils. If the state matches a certain percentage of the federal grant, the governor may designate the existing council as a state agency.

Eligible beneficiaries: state and local governments, sponsored organizations, public and private nonprofit organizations, tribal governments, native American organizations, territories, minority organizations and other specialized groups, quasi-public nonprofit institutions.

Range: $330,880 to $2,202,840. **Average:** $763,756.

Activity: N.A.

HQ: Federal/State Partnership, NEH, 1100 Pennsylvania Ave., Rm. 603, Washington, DC 20506. Phone: (202) 606-8254.

Internet: www.neh.gov/divisions/fedstate. (Note: no field offices for this program.)

45.130 PROMOTION OF THE HUMANITIES—CHALLENGE GRANTS

Assistance: project grants. (20-25 percent/1-4 years).

Purposes: pursuant to NFAHA as amended, for educational and cultural institutions and organizations to increase their financial stability and to sustain or improve humanities programs, services, or resources. Principally, project funds are used to establish endowments; also, for library acquisitions, technological enhancement, construction and renovation, or debt retirement. Grants may not fund general operating costs, projects eligible for other NEH support, or undergraduate scholarships or prizes.

Eligible applicants/beneficiaries: public or private nonprofit organizations including: two-and four-year IHEs; museums; historical or professional societies; research or public libraries; advanced study centers; university presses; media organizations; other similar and related organizations. States, local governments, and territories may apply on their own behalf or on behalf of organizations within their jurisdictions. Individuals and public and private elementary and secondary schools are ineligible.

Range: $250,000 to $750,000 over 4 years. **Average:** $470,000

Activity: N.A.

HQ: Office of Challenge Grants, NEH (Rm. 420), Washington, DC 20506. Phone: (202) 606-8309.

Internet: www.neh.gov. (Note: no field offices for this program.)

45.149 PROMOTION OF THE HUMANITIES—DIVISION OF PRESERVATION AND ACCESS

Assistance: project grants. (cost sharing/to 5 years).

Purposes: pursuant to NFAHA as amended, for the preservation of and activities to provide intellectual access to library, museum, archival, and other humanities collections, including still and moving images and recorded sound collections; for preservation practices and activities including microfilming, archival surveys, cataloguing; for a national program to catalog and preserve U.S. newspapers; for training; for research; for related uses.

Eligible applicants/beneficiaries: state and local governments, sponsored organizations, public and private nonprofit organizations, tribal governments, native American organizations, territories, minority organizations and other specialized groups, quasi-public nonprofit institutions.

Range: $6,000 to $500,000. Average: $74,000.

Activity: N.A.

HQ: Division of Preservation and Access, NEH (Rm. 411), Washington, DC 20506. Phone: (202) 606-8570.

Internet: www.neh.gov/divisions/preservation. (Note: no field offices for this program.)

45.160 PROMOTION OF THE HUMANITIES—FELLOWSHIPS AND STIPENDS

Assistance: project grants. (100 percent/2 months to 2 years).

Purposes: pursuant to NFAHA as amended, for six- to twelve-month fellowships and two-month summer stipends to scholars to undertake full-time independent research and writing in the humanities. Two-year faculty research awards are available to historically black, Hispanic-serving, and tribal IHEs.

Eligible applicants/beneficiaries: college, university, and other institutional faculty and staff, and independent scholars and writers that have completed their professional training. Degree candidates are ineligabible. All applicants must be U.S. citizens or nationals, or foreign nationals with at least three years of U.S. legal residence.

Range: N.A. Average: fellowships/faculty: $4,200 per month for 3 to 12 months; summer stipend: $6,000 for 8 weeks.

Activity: anticipate 185 awards in FY 2015.

HQ: Division of Research Programs, NEH, 1100 Pennsylvania Ave., Washington, DC 20506. Phone: (202) 606-8200.

Internet: www.neh.gov. (Note: no field offices for this program.)

45.161 PROMOTION OF THE HUMANITIES—RESEARCH

Assistance: project grants. (cost sharing/to 3 years).

Purposes: pursuant to NFAHA as amended, to support collaboration by scholars, and postdoctoral fellowship programs at independent humanities research centers. Grants may cover the costs of salaries, travel, supplies, and appropriate research assistance and consultation.

Eligible applicants: collaborative research, scholarly editions—U.S. IHEs, nonprofit professional associations, scholarly societies, other nonprofit organizations. Fellowships—U.S. independent research centers, scholarly societies, and international research organizations with existing fellowship programs.

Eligible beneficiaries: U.S. citizens and residents, state and local governments, sponsored organizations, public and private nonprofit organizations, tribal governments, native American organizations, territories, minority organizations and other specialized groups, quasi-public nonprofit institutions.

Range: $70,000 to $415,000. **Average:** $210,000.

Activity: 47 awards in FY 2014.

HQ: Division of Research Programs, NEH, 1100 Pennsylvania Ave., Washington, DC 20506. Phone: (202) 606-8200.

Internet: www.neh.gov/divisions/research. (Note: no field offices for this program.)

45.162 PROMOTION OF THE HUMANITIES—TEACHING AND LEARNING RESOURCES AND CURRICULUM DEVELOPMENT

Assistance: project grants (to 3 years).

Purposes: pursuant to NFAHA as amended, to fund curriculum and materials development projects to create durable tools for teachers at all educational levels, to engage their students in substantive study in the humanities. Institutional grants are available to historically black, Hispanic-serving, and tribal IHEs, for faculty study programs, institutional planning, construction, acquisition of library and advanced technology resources.

Eligible applicants/beneficiaries: state and local governments, sponsored organizations, public and private nonprofit organizations, tribal governments, native American organizations, territories, minority organizations and other specialized groups, quasi-public nonprofit institutions. Institutional grants—historically black, Hispanic-serving, and tribal IHEs designated by the White House.

Range: to $100,000 for historically black, Hispanic-serving, and tribal colleges and universities; to $38,000 for Enduring Questions Course grants. **Average:** N.A.

Activity: 31 awards in FY 2014.

HQ: Division of Education Programs, NEH, 400 7th St., SW, DC 20505. Phone: (202) 606-8463.

Internet: hi@neh.gov. (Note: no field offices for this program.)

45.163 PROMOTION OF THE HUMANITIES—PROFESSIONAL DEVELOPMENT

Assistance: project grants (to 18 months).

Purposes: pursuant to NFAHA as amended, to promote better teaching and research in the humanities through summer seminars and national institutes, as well Landmarks of American History workshops. Grants may support salaries, participant stipends, travel, and related direct costs. Projects dealing with pedagogical theory or intended to improve writing and speaking normally are not supported.

Eligible applicants: distinguished humanities scholars and teachers applying through sponsoring institutions to direct a program for teachers. Landmarks of American History and Faculty Humanities workshops—state and local governments, sponsored organizations, public and private nonprofit organizations, tribal governments, Native American organizations, territories, minority organizations and other specialized groups, quasi-public nonprofit institutions.

Eligible beneficiaries: teachers in grades K-12 or colleges.

Range/Average: N.A.

Activity: 69 awards in FY 2014.

HQ: Division of Education Programs, NEH, 400 7th St., SW, DC 20505. Phone: (202) 606-8463.

Internet: www.neh.gov. (Note: no field offices for this program.)

45.164 PROMOTION OF THE HUMANITIES—PUBLIC PROGRAMS

Assistance: project grants (6-24 months).

Purposes: pursuant to NFAHA as amended, for planning and implementation costs of humanities programs in museums, historical organizations, libraries, community centers, as well as on public television and radio.

Eligible applicants/beneficiaries: state and local governments, sponsored organizations, public and private nonprofit organizations, tribal governments, native American organizations, territories, minority organizations and other specialized groups, quasi-public nonprofit institutions.

Range: $40,000 to $600,000. **Average:** $213,636.

Activity: N.A.

HQ: Division of Public Programs, NEH, 400 7th St., SW, DC 20505. Phone: (202) 606-8269.

Internet: www.neh.gov/divisions/public. (Note: no field offices for this program.)

45.169 PROMOTION OF THE HUMANITIES—OFFICE OF DIGITAL HUMANITIES

Assistance: project grants. (to 100 percent/to 18 months).

Purposes: pursuant to National Foundations for the Arts and Humanities Act of 1965, as amended, to support projects that utilize or study the impact of digital technology, including those that deploy digital technologies and methods to enhance our understanding of a topic or issue, or the humanities; those that explore the ways in which digital technology changes how we read, write, think, and learn; those that support increasing the public's ability to search and access humanities information.

Eligible applicants/beneficiaries: U.S. nonprofit organizations/institutions; state, local and tribal governments; U.S. citizens or foreign nationals with at least three years residency.

Range/Average: N.A.

Activity: N.A.

HQ: Office of Digital Humanities, NEH, 1100 Pennsylvania Ave., NW, Rm. 402, Washington, DC 20506. Phone: (202) 606-8400.

Internet: www.neh.gov. (Note: no field offices for this program.)

45.201   ARTS AND ARTIFACTS INDEMNITY

Assistance: insurance.

Purposes: pursuant to NFAHA as amended, to provide indemnification against loss or damage to eligible art works, artifacts, and objects exhibited abroad or borrowed from abroad for display in the U.S. Deductibles and maximum amounts apply.

Eligible applicants/beneficiaries: federal, state, and local government entities; nonprofit agencies, institutions; individuals.

Range/Average: N.A.

Activity: anticipate issuing 38 certificates of indemnity in FY 2016.

HQ: Indemnity Administrator, Museum Program, NEA, 400 7th St., SW, Washington, DC 20506. Phone: (202) 682-5541.

Internet: www.arts.gov. (Note: no field offices for this program.)

45.301   MUSEUMS FOR AMERICA

Assistance: project grants; direct payments/unrestricted use. (50 percent/to 3 years).

Purposes: pursuant to the Museum and Library Services Act of 1996 (MSLA), for museums to conserve the nation's historic, scientific, and cultural heritage; to maintain and expand the educational roles of museums and libraries in their educational role. Funds may be used for projects to: sustain cultural heritage; support lifelong learning; or serve as centers of community.

Eligible applicants/beneficiaries: generally, museums in the states, territories, and possessions that have provided museum services for at least two years. Public or private nonprofit agencies, such as a municipality, college, or university responsible for operating a museum, may apply on behalf of museums. Under the IMS definition, a museum is a public or private nonprofit institution organized on a permanent basis for educational or aesthetic purposes, and which: owns or uses and cares for tangible objects, whether animate or inanimate; exhibits them to the general public on a regular basis. "Museums" includes aquariums and zoological parks, botanical gardens and arboreta, and nature centers; art, history (including historic buildings and sites), natural history, children's general, and specialized museums; science and technology centers; and planetariums. Federal museums are ineligible.

Range: $5,000 to $150,000. **Average:** N.A.

Activity: N.A.

HQ: IMLS, 955 L'Enfant Plaza North, SW, Suite 4000, Washington, DC 20024. Phone: (202) 653-4636.

Internet: www.imls.gov. (Note: no field offices for this program.)

45.308   NATIVE AMERICAN/NATIVE HAWAIIAN MUSEUM SERVICES PROGRAM

Assistance: project grants (to 2 years).

Purposes: pursuant to MSLA as amended, for strengthening of museum programming, professional development, and museum services provided to Native Americans and Hawaii natives.

Eligible applicants/beneficiaries: Indian tribes, bands, nations, or other organized groups or communities including Alaska native villages, regional corporations, or village corporations—eligible for BIA programs; nonprofit organizations serving and representing Hawaii natives. Museums, libraries, schools, and IHEs are ineligible; however, they may participate in project partnerships.

Range: $5,000 and $50,000. **Average:** N.A.

Activity: N.A.

HQ: IMLS, Office of Library Services, State Library Program, 955 L'Enfant Plaza North, SW, Suite 4000, Washington, DC 20024. Phone: (202) 653-4634.

Internet: www.imls.gov. (Note: no field offices for this program.)

45.309   MUSEUM GRANTS FOR AFRICAN AMERICAN HISTORY AND CULTURE

Assistance: project grants. (50 percent/to 2 years).

Purposes: pursuant to Museum and Library Services Act, to develop and/or strengthen knowledge, skills, and other expertise of current staff at African American museums; to attract new staff and retain skilled professionals. Grant funds may not be used for: construction, endowment fund contributions, social activities, ceremonies, entertainment, collection acquisition, or pre-grant costs.

Eligible applicants/beneficiaries: a unit of state or local government or a private not-for-profit organization with IRS tax-exempt status, located in 50 states, territories or possessions and a museum whose primary purpose is African American life, art, history and/or culture, or a historically black college or university. Museums located within a parent organization may also qualify if they meet certain criteria.

Range: $5,000 to $150,000. **Average:** N.A.

Activity: N.A.

HQ: IMLS, 955 L'Enfant Plaza North, SW, Suite 4000, Washington, DC 20024. Phone: (202) 653-4667.

Internet: www.imls.gov. (Note: no field offices for this program.)

45.310 GRANTS TO STATES

Assistance: formula grants (66 percent).

Purposes: pursuant to MSLA, to support a broad range of library and information services, either directly or through subgrants, including: establishing or enhancing electronic linkages among or between libraries and with educational, school, or information services; promoting targeted services to diverse geographic, cultural, and socio-economic audiences in urban and rural communities; acquiring or sharing computer systems and telecommunications technologies. Recipients must have an approved five-year state plan.

Eligible applicants/beneficiaries: state library administrative agencies, including in territories and possessions.

Range/Average: N.A.

Activity: N.A.

HQ: Office of Library Services, IMLS, 955 L'Enfant Plaza North, SW, Suite 4000, Washington, DC 20024. Phone: (202) 653-4650.

Internet: www.imls.gov. (Note: no field offices for this program.)

45.311 NATIVE AMERICAN AND NATIVE HAWAIIAN LIBRARY SERVICES

Assistance: project grants. (100 percent/to 2 years).

Purposes: pursuant to the Museum and Library Services Act of 2003, to provide library services to Native Americans, including: support of core library operations; technical assistance projects for training tribal library staff; establishing or enhancing electronic linkages among libraries and with educational, school, or information services; acquiring or sharing computer systems and telecommunications technologies; targeted services to those having difficulty using a library and to under-served communities.

Eligible applicants/beneficiaries: recognized tribes, Alaska native villages, organizations primarily serving Hawaii natives.

Range/Average: N.A.

Activity: N.A.

HQ: Office of Library Services, IMLS, 955 L'Enfant Plaza North, SW, Suite 4000, Washington, DC 20024. Phone: (202) 653-4730.

Internet: www.imls.gov. (Note: no field offices for this program.)

45.312 NATIONAL LEADERSHIP GRANTS

Assistance: project grants (67 percent; above $250,000, 50 percent/to 3 years).

Purposes: pursuant to MSLA, to enhance the quality of library and museum services nationwide and to provide coordination between libraries and museums. Funded activities may include: research and demonstration projects; preservation or digitization of library materials and resources; model cooperative library-museum programs; Building Digital Resources projects.

Eligible applicants/beneficiaries: libraries including those that are nonfederal, public, school, academic, archives, and private nonprofit; also, special libraries, research libraries, library agencies; consortia, and IHEs—applying individually or in partnerships, including with other public, nonprofit organizations. "Museums" includes aquariums and zoological parks, botanical gardens and arboreta, and nature centers; art, history (including historic buildings and sites), natural history, children's general, and specialized museums; science and technology centers; and planetariums. Federal museums are ineligible.

Range: $10,000 to $2,000,000. **Average:** N.A.

Activity: N.A.

HQ: IMLS, 955 L'Enfant Plaza North, SW, Suite 4000, Washington, DC 20024. Phone: (202) 653-4779.

Internet: www.imls.gov. (Note: no field offices for this program.)

45.313 LAURA BUSH 21st CENTURY LIBRARIAN PROGRAM

Assistance: project grants (to 4 years).

Purposes: pursuant to Museum and Library Services Act of 2003, to recruit and educate new librarians and faculty prepared to teach masters of library science students; to support pertinent research. Current priorities include master's level programs, doctoral programs, preprofessional programs, research, building institutional capacity, continuing education. Grants require a 50 percent match, minus funds for student support; the matching requirement is waived for projects involving research only.

Eligible applicants/beneficiaries: libraries including those that are nonfederal, public, school, academic, archives, and private nonprofit; also, special libraries, research libraries, library agencies; consortia, and IHEs—applying individually or in partnerships, including with other public, nonprofit organizations.

Range: $50,000 and $1,000,000. **Average:** N.A.

Activity: N.A.

HQ: IMLS, 955 L'Enfant Plaza North, SW, Suite 4000, Washington, DC 20024. Phone: (202) 653-4730.

Internet: www.imls.gov. (Note: no field offices for this program.)

45.400 PEACE CORPS GLOBAL HEALTH AND PEPFAR INITIATIVE PROGRAM

Assistance: project grants/cooperative agreements.

Purposes: funds to support the U.S. Presidents Emergency Plan for AIDS Relief (PEPFAR)s goals and programmatic strategy. The Peace Corps intends to award multiple cooperative agreements and grants with PEPFAR funding for vital global health programming and training enhancements. Assistance can be used by non-federal entities to plan, develop and implement programmatic activities that support PEPFARs goals through overseas volunteer service, to identify and implement appropriate evidence-based practices and programs related to global health and HIV, and to develop staff capacity to implement global health and PEPFAR programs.

Eligible applicants/beneficiaries: Public or private nonprofit institutions/organizations, quasi-public nonprofit institutions/organizations.

Range/Average: N.A.

Activity: N.A.

HQ: Director, Peace Corps Global Health and PEPFAR Initiative Program, 1111 20th St., NW, Rm. 4432, Washington, DC 20526. Phone: (202) 692-1235.

Internet: www.peacecorps.gov. (Note: no field offices for this program.)

NATIONAL SCIENCE FOUNDATION

47.041 ENGINEERING GRANTS ("ENG")

Assistance: project grants (6 months-3 years).

Purposes: pursuant to the National Science Foundation Act of 1950 (NSFA) as amended, for engineering research and education programs in virtually all phases of engineering science and technological innovation and practice. Funding may support such activities as: research in emerging areas; industry-university cooperative research centers; biomedical engineering research; research equipment and instrumentation grants; undergraduate student research; graduate fellowships; faculty enhancement; inter-disciplinary studies; small business innovation research; small business technology transfer programs. Cost sharing is required except for solicited proposals, conferences, publications, travel, and logistical support. Funds may not support inventions, product development, marketing, or research requiring security classifications.

Eligible applicants/beneficiaries: public and private IHEs; nonprofit institutions; profit organizations including small businesses; state, and local government agencies; unaffiliated individuals.

Range: $3,000 to $1,250,000. **Average:** $1,143,774.

Activity: anticipate 2,300 awards in FY 2016.

HQ: Program Director, Grant Opportunities for Academic Liaison with Industry, Directorate for Engineering-NSF, 4201 Wilson Blvd., Stafford I-505, Arlington, VA 22230. Phone: (703) 292-9013.

Internet: nsf.gov/dir/index.jsp?org=eng. (Note: no field offices for this program.)

47.049 MATHEMATICAL AND PHYSICAL SCIENCES (MPS)

Assistance: project grants. (to 100 percent/3-5 years).

Purposes: pursuant to NSFA as amended, for mostly basic research in physics, chemistry, astronomical and mathematical sciences, and materials, including multidisciplinary research. Grants may support: start-of-the-art user facilities; science and technology centers; institutes; undergraduate student research; developing research opportunities for women, minority, and disabled scientists and engineers; instrumentation; laboratory improvement; research workshops, symposia, and conferences; faculty enhancement; curriculum development. Cost sharing is required, except for symposia, conferences, publications, travel, education, training, or facilities.

Eligible applicants/beneficiaries: public and private IHEs; nonprofit, nonacademic research institutions; private profit organizations; foreign institutions; state and local governments; other federal agencies; certain unaffiliated scientists.

Range: $3,000 to $51,287,774. **Average:** $168,416.

Activity: anticipate 2,500 awards in FY 2016.

HQ: Assistant Director, MPS-NSF, 4201 Wilson Blvd., Stafford I-1005, Arlington, VA 22230. Phone: (703) 292-9151.

Internet: nsf.gov/dir/index.jsp?org=mps. (Note: no field offices for this program.)

47.050 GEOSCIENCES ("GEO")

Assistance: project grants (1-5 years).

Purposes: pursuant to NSFA as amended, for basic research and studies in the atmospheric (e.g., meteorology, climate, paleoclimate), earth, and ocean sciences and in related biological, chemical, and physical disciplines. Grants may support science and technology centers, undergraduate student research, facility enhancement, instrumentation, laboratory equipment, and research opportunities for women, minority, and disabled scientists and engineers. Cost sharing is required, except for symposia, conferences, publications, travel, education, training, facilities, ship operations, or equipment.

Eligible applicants/beneficiaries: public and private IHEs, nonprofit nonacademic research institutions, private profit organizations, certain unaffiliated scientists.

Range: $3,010 to $65,712,130. **Average:** $262,316.

Activity: anticipate 1,600 awards in FY 2016.

HQ: NSF, 4201 Wilson Blvd., Stafford I-705, Arlington, VA 22230. Phone: (703) 292-8500; FAX: (703) 292-9042.

Internet: nsf.gov/dir/index.jsp?org=geo. (Note: no field offices for this program.)

47.070 COMPUTER AND INFORMATION SCIENCE AND ENGINEERING (CISE)

Assistance: project grants. (cost sharing/6 months-3 years).

Purposes: pursuant to NSFA as amended, for research improving the fundamental understanding of computer and information science and engineering; to enhance the training and education of scientists and engineers; and, to provide access to very advanced computing and networking capabilities. Ineligible uses of funds include fellowships, scholarships, product development and marketing.

Eligible applicants/beneficiaries: public and private IHEs; nonprofit and profit organizations; small businesses; state and local government agencies; certain unaffiliated scientists.

Range: $2,430 to $15,000,000. Average: $186,053.

Activity: N.A.

HQ: Assistant Director, CISE-NSF, 4201 Wilson Blvd., Rm. 1105, Arlington, VA 22230. Phone: (703) 292-9074.

Internet: nsf.gov/dir/index.jsp?org=cise. (Note: no field offices for this program.)

47.074 BIOLOGICAL SCIENCES

Assistance: project grants. (to 100 percent/to 5 years).

Purposes: pursuant to NSFA as amended, for mostly basic research in the biological sciences, including cellular and molecular biosciences, integrative organismal biology, environmental biology, biological infrastructure, and plant genomes. Grants may be used to purchase multi-user scientific equipment and for instrument development; research workshops, symposia, and conferences; doctoral, postdoctoral fellowships including for minority scientists. Cost sharing is required, except for symposia, conferences, publications, travel, education, or training.

Eligible applicants/beneficiaries: public and private IHEs, nonprofit nonacademic research institutions, private profit organizations, certain unaffiliated scientists.

Range: $4,800 to $110,824,767. Average: $206,124.

Activity: anticipate 1,300 awards in FY 2016.

HQ: Assistant Director, BIO-NSF, 4201 Wilson Blvd., Stafford I-605, Arlington, VA 22230. Phone: (703) 292-7162.

Internet: nsf.gov/dir/index.jsp?org=bio. (Note: no field offices for this program.)

47.075 SOCIAL, BEHAVIORAL, AND ECONOMIC SCIENCES (SBE)

Assistance: project grants. (to 100 percent/to 5 years).

Purposes: pursuant to NSFA as amended, for basic research in the social, behavioral and economic sciences in such disciplines as: anthropological and geographic sciences; cognitive, psychological, and language science; economic, decision, and management sciences; social and political science; infrastructure, methods, and science studies; educational attainment in science, mathematics, and engineering. Grants may support: science and technology centers, including climate change; science of learning centers, workshops, symposia, and conferences; doctoral and postdoctoral fellowships; junior faculty research; graduate traineeships; mid-career development; undergraduate student research; research opportunities for women, minorities, and disabled scientists and engineers.

Eligible applicants/beneficiaries: public and private IHEs, nonprofit nonacademic research institutions, private profit organizations, certain unaffiliated scientists.

Range: $1,175 to $2,958,735. Average: $93,332.

Activity: anticipate 1,100 awards in FY 2016.

HQ: Directorate for Social, Behavioral and Economic Sciences-NSF, 4201 Wilson Blvd., Rm. 905, Arlington, VA 22230. Phone: (703) 292-8700.

Internet: nsf.gov/dir/index.jsp?org=sbe. (Note: no field offices for this program.)

47.076   EDUCATION AND HUMAN RESOURCES (EHR)

Assistance: project grants (to 5 years).

Purposes: pursuant to NSFA as amended, for programs improving the effectiveness of science, mathematics, engineering, and technology education—through programs that support research and the development of models and strategies, including in: elementary, secondary, informal science education, and lifelong learning; undergraduate, graduate, and postdoctoral education; human resource development; research, evaluation, and dissemination; experimental programs. Grants may support fellowships for up to three years, scholarships, equipment purchases, salaries, and other expenses.

Eligible applicants: public and private two- and four-year IHEs; SEAs and LEAs; tribal entities; nonprofit and private organizations; professional societies; science academies and centers; science museums and zoological parks; research laboratories; other informal science education institutions.

Eligible beneficiaries: pre-school, elementary, secondary, and undergraduate science, mathematics, and engineering teachers and faculty; secondary, undergraduate, and graduate students.

Range: $25,741 to $7,000,000. **Average:** $298,072.

Activity: N.A.

HQ: Assistant Director, EHR-NSF, 4201 Wilson Blvd. Rm. 805, Arlington, VA 22230. Phone: (703) 292-7306.

Internet: www.nsf.gov/dir/index.jsp?org=ehr. (Note: no field offices for this program.)

47.078   POLAR PROGRAMS
("OPP")

Assistance: project grants. (to 100 percent/1-3 years).

Purposes: pursuant to NSFA as amended, for basic research in the Arctic and Antarctic regions, focused on the solid earth, glacial and sea ice, terrestrial ecosystems, the oceans, the atmosphere and beyond. Support is available for science and technology centers, undergraduate student research, postdoctoral fellowships, facility enhancement, instrumentation, laboratory equipment, and research opportunities for women, minority, and handicapped scientists and engineers. Cost sharing is required, except for symposia, conferences, publications, travel, education, training, facilities, ship operations, or equipment.

Eligible applicants/beneficiaries: public and private IHEs, nonprofit nonacademic research institutions, private profit organizations, certain unaffiliated scientists.

Range: $1,000 to $41,400,000. **Average:** $313,000.

Activity: N.A.

HQ: National Science Foundation, 4201 Wilson Blvd., Stafford I-740, Arlington, VA 22230. Phone: (703) 292-8033; FAX: (703) 292-9079.

Internet: nsf.gov/dir/index.jsp?org=opp. (Note: no field offices for this program.)

47.079 OFFICE OF INTERNATIONAL SCIENCE AND ENGINEERING

Assistance: project grants. (to 100 percent/to 3 years).

Purposes: pursuant to NSFA as amended, for international partnerships fostering scientific basic research collaborations, discovery, and education abroad for U.S. students and junior faculty. Activities eligible for funding include graduate traineeships, postdoctoral fellowships, undergraduate research experiences, workshops, planning visits, and research opportunities for women, minorities, and scientists and engineers with disabilities— in all disciplinary fields supported by NSF.

Eligible applicants/beneficiaries: public and private IHEs, nonprofit nonacademic research institutions, profit organizations, certain unaffiliated scientists, multilateral science and technology organizations.

Range: $2,305 to $2,610,000. **Average:** $29,931.

Activity: N.A.

HQ: Office of the Director, National Science Foundation, 4201 Wilson Blvd., Stafford I-935, Arlington, VA 22230. Phone: (703) 292-7216.

Internet: nsf.gov/dir/index.jsp?org=oise. (Note: no field offices for this program.)

47.080 OFFICE OF CYBERINFRASTRUCTURE (OCI)

Assistance: project grants (to 3 years).

Purposes: pursuant to NSFA as amended, to acquire, develop, and provide state-of-the-art cyberinfrastructure resources, tools, and services essential to 21st-century science and engineering research and education. Major program focus: the "OptiPuter" project's inventions and applications in such areas as next-generation access grids available to science, engineering, teaching and education, Doppler radar weather forecasting, and other enhancements of the possibilities of cyberinfrastructure.

Eligible applicants/beneficiaries: public and private IHEs; nonprofit and profit organizations including small businesses; federal, state, and local government agencies—with most funding allocated to academic institutions.

Range: $13,000 to $192,781,000. **Average:** $544,000.

Activity: N.A.

HQ: Office of the Director, OCI-NSF, 4201 Wilson Blvd., Rm. 1145, Arlington, VA 22230. Phone: (703) 292-9060.

Internet: nsf.gov/dir/index.jsp?org=oci. (Note: no field offices for this program.)

47.081 OFFICE OF EXPERIMENTAL PROGRAM TO STIMULATE COMPETITIVE RESEARCH ("EPSCoR")

Assistance: project grants (6 months to 3 years).

Purposes: pursuant to the National Science Foundation Act of 1950 as amended, to assist those jurisdictions that have historically received lesser amounts of academic research and development funding and accelerate the movement of more researchers and institutions from EPSCoR jurisdictions into the mainstream of NSF support. Funds may be used for research, product development, resources, tools and services, salaries and wages, equipment and supplies, travel, publication costs, and other direct and indirect costs.

Eligible applicants/beneficiaries: public and private colleges and universities; non-profit, non-academic organizations; for-profit organizations; state and local governments; and unaffiliated scientists under special circumstances.

Range: $100,000 to $20,000,000. **Average:** $1,640,000.

Activity: N.A.

HQ: Office of the Director, National Science Foundation, 4201 Wilson Blvd., Stafford I-935, Arlington, VA 22230. Phone: (703) 292-7216.

Internet: nsf.gov/dir/index.jsp?org=oia. (Note: no field offices for this program.)

47.082 TRANS-NSF RECOVERY ACT RESEARCH SUPPORT

Assistance: project grants.

Purposes: pursuant to ARRA 2009, to advance the national health, prosperity, and welfare by supporting research and education in all fields of science and engineering. Funds may be used for conducting research or studies (including: salaries and wages, permanent equipment, expendable materials and supplies, travel, participant support, publication costs, and other direct and indirect costs. Applicant cost sharing may be required.

Eligible applicants: private/public institutions and organizations; IHEs and hospitals; scientists/researchers.

Eligible beneficiaries: state and local governments; private/public institutions and organizations; scientists/researchers.

Range: $1,000 to $60,000. **Average:** $158,000.

Activity: N.A.

HQ: NSF, 4201 Wilson Blvd., Stafford II, Rm. 655, Arlington, VA 22230. Phone: (703) 292-7028.

Internet: www.nsf.gov. (Note: no field offices for this program.)

47.083 OFFICE OF INTEGRATIVE ACTIVITIES

Assistance: project grants. (100 percent/to 5 years).

Purposes: pursuant to the National Science Foundation Act of 1950, as amended, to advance research excellence and innovation, develop human and infrastructure capacity critical to the U.S. science and engineering enterprise, and promote engagement of scientists and engineers at all career stages. Funds may be used to pay the costs of conducting research, product development, resources, tools and services, salaries and wages, equipment and supplies, travel, publication costs, other direct costs, and indirect costs.

Eligible applicants/beneficiaries: state and local governments, nonprofit and for-profit institutions/organizations, individuals, and IHEs.

Range: $5,000 to $692,081. **Average:** $139,570.

Activity: 8 awards in FY 2014.

HQ: Office of Integrative Activities, NSF, 4201 Wilson Blvd., Stafford I, Ste. 935, Arlington, VA 22230. Phone: (703) 292-7216; FAX: (703) 292-9040.

Internet: N.A. (Note: no field offices for this program.)

RAILROAD RETIREMENT BOARD

57.001 SOCIAL INSURANCE FOR RAILROAD WORKERS

Assistance: direct payments/unrestricted use.

Purposes: pursuant to the Social Security Act, Railroad Unemployment Insurance Act, Railroad Retirement Act of 1974, and amendments, to pay benefits to railroad workers and their beneficiaries, including retirement, death, disability, unemployment, or sickness insurance.

Eligible applicants/beneficiaries: Railroad Retirement Act benefits—for employee, spouse, and survivor benefits, the employee must have had 10 or more years of railroad service. Annuities—beginning January 2002 or later, 5 years of railroad service rendered after 1995. For survivors, the employees must have been insured at death. Railroad Unemployment Insurance Act—employees with certain minimum earnings in railroad wages; new employees must have worked for a railroad at least five months in a calendar (base) year.

Range/Average: N.A.

Activity: anticipate 554,000 to receive benefits in FY 2016.

HQ: Public Affairs, Railroad Retirement Board, 844 N. Rush St., Chicago, IL 60611-2092. Phone: (312) 751-4777.

Internet: www.rrb.gov.

SECURITIES AND EXCHANGE COMMISSION

58.001 SECURITIES—INVESTIGATION OF COMPLAINTS AND SEC INFORMATION
("Complaints and Inquiries")

Assistance: technical information; investigation of complaints.

Purposes: pursuant to the Securities Act of 1933, Securities and Exchange Act of 1934, Securities Investor Protection Act of 1970, amendments, and related acts, to provide assistance to or on behalf of securities investors, including educational materials and public educational activities; to represent individual investors in SEC rule-making proceedings. SEC's public files contain financial and other information about companies, broker- dealers, investment companies, investment advisers, transfer agents, and banks, which may be examined at SEC offices; or, copies may be obtained from SEC's Public Reference Branch. Investors believing they have been defrauded, or that another party has violated the federal securities laws, may present their complaint and/or information to the SEC. A public action taken by SEC does not necessarily result in monetary benefits to investors; however, aggrieved investors may find the information disclosed by the commission in its actions helpful in any private action brought to recover losses.

Eligible applicants/beneficiaries: anyone may seek information or file a complaint.

Range/Average: N.A.

Activity: N.A.

HQ: Office of Investor Education and Assistance, SEC, 100 F St. NE, Washington, DC 20549-0213. Phone: (202) 551-6551; FAX: (202) 772-9295.

Internet: www.sec.gov.

SMALL BUSINESS ADMINISTRATION

59.006 8(A) BUSINESS DEVELOPMENT PROGRAM ("Section 8(a) Program")

Assistance: specialized services (to 9 years).

Purposes: pursuant to the Small Business Act of 1953 as amended, for SBA to enter into procurement contracts with other federal agencies and for subcontracts, in turn, with socially and economically disadvantaged businesses. The program incorporates contract, technical, and managerial assistance to participants, and access to financial resources.

Eligible applicants/beneficiaries: small businesses at least 51 percent owned, controlled, and managed by U.S. citizens, determined by SBA to be socially and economically disadvantaged; disadvantaged tribes, Alaska native corporations, or native Hawaiian organizations.

Range/Average: N.A.

Activity: N.A.

HQ: Associate Administrator/8(a) Business Development, SBA, 409 3rd St., SW, Washington, DC 20416. Phone: (202) 205-5852.

Internet: www.sba.gov.

59.007 7(J) TECHNICAL ASSISTANCE

Assistance: project grants (100 percent).

Purposes: pursuant to the Small Business Act of 1953 as amended, for projects conducted by qualified entities to provide business management, technical assistance, and services in obtaining financing—to businesses that are socially and economically disadvantaged, located in areas of high unemployment or low income, or participants in program **59.006**. Funds also may be used to establish and strengthen business service agencies including trade associations and cooperatives.

Eligible applicants/beneficiaries: state and local governments; educational institutions; public or private organizations and businesses; lending and financial institutions and sureties; tribes; qualified individuals.

Range/Average: N.A.

Activity: N.A.

HQ: Associate Administrator/Management and Technical Assistance, Office of Business Development, SBA, 409 3rd St., SW, Ste. 8000, Washington, DC 20416. Phone: (202) 205-1904.

Internet: www.sba.gov.

59.008   DISASTER ASSISTANCE LOANS ("DL - Section 7(b) Loans")

Assistance: direct loans. (to 4-8 percent/3-30 years).

Purposes: pursuant to the Small Business Act of 1953 as amended and the Disaster Relief Act of 1970, for victims of declared physical disasters to restore or replace uninsured damaged or destroyed real or personal property. Loan terms depend on the applicant's access to credit. Provisions of the Flood Disaster Protection Act of 1973 and National Flood Insurance Reform Act of 1994 apply. Collateral is required on loans of more than $10,000.

Eligible applicants/beneficiaries: homeowners, renters, businesses, and charitable and nonprofit organizations. Agricultural enterprises are ineligible.

Range/Average: N.A.

Activity: N.A.

HQ: Office of Disaster Assistance, SBA, 409 3rd St., SW, 6th Fl., Washington, DC 20416. Phone: (202) 205-6098.

Internet: www.sba.gov/Disaster.

59.011   SMALL BUSINESS INVESTMENT COMPANIES ("SBIC - SSBIC")

Assistance: direct loans; guaranteed/insured loans; advisory services/counseling (guaranteed/insured loans, to 10-15 years).

Purposes: pursuant to the Small Business Investment Act of 1958 as amended, for privately owned and managed SBA-licensed small business investment companies, including specialized SBICs (SSBICs) assisting socially or economically disadvantaged enterprises, to provide equity capital, in turn, to small businesses—through long-term loans or equity purchases. SBA guarantees debentures issued by the investment companies to maximize leveraging of private funds, by up to 300 percent within maximums established by SBA and for terms of 10 years; participating securities may be guaranteed for up to 15 years. The investment companies provide continuing management and other assistance to firms that obtain the loans.

Eligible applicants: chartered SBICs with private capital of at least $3,000,000 for those not receiving SBA leveraging, or $5,000,000 if receiving SBA leveraging.

Eligible beneficiaries: small businesses (single proprietorship, partnership, or corporation); SSBIC beneficiaries must also be socially or economically disadvantaged enterprises.

Range/Average: N.A.

Activity: N.A.

HQ: Associate Administrator/Investment, Investment Division, SBA, 409 3rd St., SW, 6th Fl., Washington, DC 20416. Phone: (202) 205-6694.

Internet: www.sba.gov.

59.012   7(A) LOAN GUARANTEES ("Section 7(a) Loans")

Assistance: guaranteed/insured loans.

Purposes: pursuant to the Small Business Act of 1953 as amended, for small businesses to construct, expand, or convert business facilities; to purchase equipment or materials; for working capital. Eligible loan uses also include design, manufacture, marketing, installation, or servicing of specific energy measures. Program components include SBA's Low Documentation Loan Program (Low Doc); Cap Line Program; SBAExpress Program; International Trade.

Eligible applicants/beneficiaries: small businesses that meet eligibility standards.

Range/Average: N.A.

Activity: N.A.

HQ: Director, Loan Programs Division, SBA,409 3rd St., SW, 8th Fl., Washington, DC 20416. Phone: (202) 205-3647.

Internet: www.sba.gov/7a-loan-program.

59.016   SURETY BOND GUARANTEES

Assistance: insurance (70-90 percent).

Purposes: pursuant to the Small Business Act of 1953 as amended and the Inspector General Act of 1978, to guarantee bonds issued by commercial surety companies for bid, payment, and performance or other bonds provided to small businesses on contracts up to $2,000,000.

Eligible applicants: surety companies holding certificates of authority from the Secretary of the Treasury.

Eligible beneficiaries: small contractors with gross annual receipts of no more than $6,000,000 as averaged for the last three fiscal years; certain manufacturers. (Applications are submitted directly to insurance agents or brokers.)

Range/Average: N.A.

Activity: N.A.

HQ: Associate Administrator, Office of Surety Guarantees, SBA, 409 3rd St., SW, 8th Fl., Washington, DC 20416. Phone: (202) 401-8275.

Internet: www.sba.gov/osg.

59.026   SERVICE CORPS OF RETIRED EXECUTIVES (SCORE)

Assistance: advisory services/counseling; training.

Purposes: pursuant to the Small Business Act of 1953 as amended, to operate the SCORE program through which retired or active business executives volunteer their services to counsel and train new and existing small business persons. Out-of-pocket expenses of volunteers may be reimbursed.

Eligible applicants/beneficiaries: existing and potential small businesses.

Range/Average: N.A.

Activity: N.A.

HQ: Office of Business and Community Initiatives, SBA, 409 3rd St., SW, 6th Fl., Washington, DC 20416. Phone: (202) 205-8052.

Internet: www.sba.gov.

59.037   SMALL BUSINESS DEVELOPMENT CENTERS (SBDC)

Assistance: project grants; specialized services; advisory services/counseling; technical information (formula based, 50 percent).

Purposes: pursuant to the Small Business Act of 1953 as amended, for SBDCs to provide management counseling, training, and technical assistance to existing or potential small businesses.

Eligible applicants/beneficiaries: public or private IHEs including land grant, community, or junior colleges; certain existing SBDCs.

Range/Average: N.A.

Activity: N.A.

HQ: SBDC Office, SBA, 409 3rd St., SW, 6th Fl., Washington, DC 20416. Phone: (202) 205-7159.

Internet: www.sba.gov/sbdc.

59.041   504 CERTIFIED DEVELOPMENT LOANS ("Section 504 Loans")

Assistance: guaranteed/insured loans (10-20 years).

Purposes: pursuant to the Small Business Investment Act of 1958 as amended, to assist small businesses in acquiring fixed assets, through the sale of debentures to private investors. Loans may cover acquisition of land, buildings, equipment, construction, expansion, renovation, or modernization. Ten percent of project costs must be provided by the small business concern, and 50 percent by a private lender.

Eligible applicants/beneficiaries: nonprofit certified development companies.

Range/Average: N.A.

Activity: N.A.

HQ: Office of Financial Assistance, SBA, 409 3rd St., SW, 8th Fl., Washington, DC 20416. Phone: (202) 205-9949.

Internet: www.sba.gov.

59.043 WOMEN'S BUSINESS OWNERSHIP ASSISTANCE

Assistance: project grants (50-67 percent/to 5 years).

Purposes: pursuant to the Small Business Act of 1953 as amended, Women's Business Ownership Act of 1988, and Women's Business Center Sustainability Act of 1999, to establish women's business centers to assist new or existing small businesses owned and controlled by women, through financial, management, procurement, marketing, training, and counseling services. Services are also provided through the Online Women's Business Center.

Eligible applicants/beneficiaries: experienced private nonprofit organizations.

Range/Average: N.A.

Activity: N.A.

HQ: Office of Women's Business Ownership, SBA, 409 3rd St., SW, 6th Fl., Washington, DC 20416. Phone: (202) 205-7532.

Internet: www.sba.gov/onlinewbc.

59.044 VETERANS OUTREACH PROGRAM ("VBOP")

Assistance: project grants (matching/1-5 years).

Purposes: pursuant to the Small Business Act of 1953 as amended, to establish and operate Veterans Business Outreach Centers to provide long-term training, counseling, and mentoring to veterans starting or operating small businesses.

Eligible applicants/beneficiaries: educational institutions; private businesses; veterans nonprofit community-based organizations; federal, state, and local entities.

Range/Average: N.A.

Activity: N.A.

HQ: Associate Administrator, Office of Veterans Business Development, SBA, 409 3rd St., SW, 5th Floor, Washington, DC 20416. Phone: (202) 205-6257.

Internet: www.sba.gov.

59.046 MICROLOAN PROGRAM

Assistance: formula grants; direct loans (loans, to 10 years).

Purposes: to provide loan funds or loan guaranties to eligible intermediary lenders that, in turn, will make short-term, fixed- rate loans to newly established or growing small businesses for working capital or for the acquisition of supplies or equipment; to make grants to intermediaries to provide intensive marketing, management, and technical assistance to borrowers; to make grants to nonprofit entities to assist low-income individuals in obtaining private sector financing for their businesses.

Eligible applicants: intermediary lenders meeting SBA requirements.

Eligible beneficiaries: small businesses, minority entrepreneurs, nonprofit entities, women, low-income and other persons.

Range/Average: N.A.

Activity: N.A.

HQ: Microenterprise Development Branch, Office of Financial Assistance, SBA, 409 3rd St., SW, 8th Fl., Washington, DC 20416. Phone: (202) 205-0628.

Internet: www.sba.gov.

59.050 PRIME TECHNICAL ASSISTANCE ("PRIME")

Assistance: project grants. (50 percent/1-5 years).

Purposes: pursuant to the Riegle Community Development and Regulatory Improvement Act of 1994 as amended and Gramm-Leach- Bliley Act, to increase the number of microenterprises and enhance their management capabilities, by: providing training and technical assistance in starting or expanding their businesses; providing training and capacity building services to enhance existing or new microenterprise development organizations (MDOs) that provide training programs and services; conducting research and development of "best practices" in the field.

Eligible applicants: established nonprofit MDOs or programs, including collaboratives, that are accountable to local communities and working in conjunction with a state or local government or tribe; certain tribes acting on their own.

Eligible beneficiaries: disadvantaged entrepreneurs and microenterprises.

Range/Average: N.A.

Activity: N.A.

HQ: Office of Financial Assistance, SBA, 409 3rd St., SW, 8th Fl., Washington, DC 20416. Phone: (202) 205-3645.

Internet: www.sba.gov.

59.052 NATIVE AMERICAN OUTREACH

Assistance: project grants.

Purposes: pursuant to the Small Business Act as amended, for entrepreneurial development programs and services provided to American Indians and Alaska and Hawaii natives, located in disadvantaged and under-served reservations and tribal areas, and seeking to establish, develop, and expand small businesses. Projects must include a strong outreach component stressing participation in under-served areas. Project examples: small business incubator activities; training; marketing outreach.

Eligible applicants/beneficiaries: organizations with experience in training, counseling, developing, and measuring small business development in Indian country.

Range/Average: N.A.

Activity: N.A.

HQ: Office of Native American Affairs, SBA, 409 3rd St., SW, 8th Fl., Washington, DC 20416. Phone: (202) 619-0621.

Internet: www.sba.gov/naa.

59.053 OMBUDSMAN AND REGULATORY FAIRNESS BOARDS

Assistance: project grants.

Purposes: pursuant to the Small Business Regulatory Fairness Act of 1996, to serve the small business community by receiving comments regarding unfair or excessive actions by federal agencies or agency employees conducting compliance or enforcement activities. Comments may be confidential or not, and be discussed with appropriate federal agency personnel to seek a timely response to an excessive or unfair federal regulatory issue. Hearings may be held throughout the country to receive testimony and commentary. Comments also may be submitted online, by FAX, mail, or personal delivery.

Eligible applicants/beneficiaries: small businesses, nonprofit organizations, or small government entities (representing fewer than 50,000 persons).

Range/Average: N.A.

Activity: N.A.

HQ: Office of the National Ombudsman, SBA, 409 3rd St., SW, 8th Fl., Washington, DC 20416. Phone: (202) 205-6918.

Internet: www.sba.gov/ombudsman.

59.054 7(A) EXPORT LOAN GUARANTEES

Assistance: guaranteed/insured loans.

Purposes: pursuant to the Small Business Act of 1953 as amended, for small businesses to increase their ability to compete in international markets by enhancing their ability to export, through: the Export Working Capital Program, providing 90 percent loan guarantees; the Export Express Loan Program, with 85 percent loan guarantees; the International Trade Loan Program, with 75 percent loan guarantees. Loans may be used: to construct, expand, or convert facilities; to purchase building equipment or materials; for export working capital.

Eligible applicants/beneficiaries: small businesses meeting SBA size standards, that are independently owned and operated, and not dominant in their field.

Range/Average: N.A.

Activity: N.A.

HQ: Associate Administrator, Office of International Trade, SBA, 409 3rd St., SW, 8th Fl., Washington, DC 20416. Phone: (202) 205-3645.

Internet: www.sba.gov.

59.055 HISTORICALLY UNDERUTILIZED BUSINESS ZONES ("HUBZone")

Assistance: project grants.

Purposes: pursuant to the HUBZone Act of1997, SBA Authorization and Manufacturing Assistance Act of 2004, and HUBZones in Native America Act of 2000, to provide federal contracting assistance for qualified SBCs located in historically underutilized business zones in an effort to increase employment opportunities, investment, and economic development in such areas.

Eligible applicants/beneficiaries: firms who are: SBA-defined small business; at least 51 percent owned/controlled by one or more U.S. citizens, a

Community Development Corporation, agricultural cooperative, or Indian tribe; principle office located in a HUBZone; and at least 35 percent of employees are residents of a HUBZone.

Range/Average: N.A.

Activity: N.A.

HQ: Director, HUBZone Program, SBA, 409 3rd St., SW, 8th Fl., Washington, DC 20416. Phone: (202) 205-2985.

Internet: www.sba.gov/hubzone.

59.058 FEDERAL AND STATE TECHNOLOGY PARTNERSHIP PROGRAM

Assistance: cooperative agreements (50 to 100 percent).

Purposes: pursuant to the Small Business Act, to strengthen the technological competitiveness of small business concerns in the U.S. Only one proposal from each state or territory may be submitted to the SBA for consideration and this application must have an original, signed Letter of Endorsement from the state governor (mayor for DC).

Eligible applicants: state and local economic development agencies, IHEs and small business development centers.

Eligible beneficiaries: technology-based small business owners.

Range/Average: N.A.

Activity: N.A.

HQ: Executive Secretariat, SBA, 409 3rd St., SW, 6th Fl., Washington, DC 20416. Phone: (202) 619-0511.

Internet: www.sba.gov. (Note: no field offices for this program.)

59.062 INTERMEDIARY LOAN PROGRAM (ILP)

Assistance: direct loans (100 percent/3 years).

Purposes: pursuant to the Small Business Jobs Act of 2010, to make direct loans of up to $1 million at an interest rate of 1 percent to up to 20 nonprofit lending intermediaries each year, subject to the availability of funds. Term of ILP loans will be for a maximum period of 20 years with deferred payments for the first two years. Intermediaries will then use the ILP loan funds to make loans of up to $200,000 to startup, newly established, or growing small business concerns.

Eligible applicants/beneficiaries: private nonprofit entity with not less than one year of experience of making loans to startups, newly established or growing small businesses.

Range: N.A. **Average:** $1,000,000.

Activity: N.A.

HQ: Director, SBA, 409 3rd St., SW, 8th Fl., Washington, DC 20416. Phone: (202) 205-7516.

Internet: www.sba.gov.

59.063 DISASTER ASSISTANCE LOANS—DISASTER RELIEF APPROPRIATIONS ACT

Assistance: direct loans (100 percent/3 to 30 years).

Purposes: pursuant to the Disaster Relief Appropriations Act, to provide loans to the victims of declared disasters to repair or replace damaged or destroyed real property and/or personal property. In some cases, home-owners and businesses may be eligible for refinancing of existing loan. Applicants must demonstrate an ability and willingness to repay the loan. Collateral is required on loans greater than $10,000. Loan limits may be increased in some circumstances to provide protective measures from damages caused by physical disasters.

Eligible applicants/beneficiaries: individuals, businesses, or charitable and nonprofit organizations that have suffered physical property loss as a result of a disaster which occurred in an area declared by the President or SBA.

Range/Average: N.A.

Activity: N.A.

HQ: Director, Disaster Assistance Loans, SBA Executive Secretariat, 409 3rd St., SW, 6th Fl., Washington, DC 20416. Phone: (202) 205-6098.

Internet: www.sba.gov/disaster.

59.065 GROWTH ACCELERATOR FUND COMPETITION

Assistance: direct payments/specified use. (20 percent).

Purposes: pursuant to the America COMPETES Reauthorization Act of 2010, to enable accelerators and other entrepreneurial ecosystem models to fund operating budgets. For the purpose of this competition, growth accelerators include accelerators, incubators, co-working startup communities, shared tinker-spaces or other models to accomplish similar goals.

Eligible applicants/beneficiaries: private nonprofit and for-profit institutions/ organizations.

Range: $50,000 to $80,000 for individual awards; $2,500,000 to $4,000,000 for group awards. **Average:** N.A.

Activity: N.A.

HQ: SBA, 409 3rd St., SW, 6th Floor, Washington, DC 20416. Phone: (202) 205-6694; FAX: (202) 481-1869.

Internet: www.sba.gov/accelerators. (Note: no field offices for this program.)

DEPARTMENT OF VETERANS AFFAIRS

64.005 GRANTS TO STATES FOR CONSTRUCTION OF STATE HOME FACILITIES ("State Home Construction")

Assistance: project grants. (to 65 percent/to 5 years).

Purposes: to acquire or construct state domiciliary or nursing home facilities for veterans; to expand, remodel, alter, or equip existing buildings to provide domiciliary, nursing home, or hospital care to veterans in state homes.

Eligible applicants/beneficiaries: states.

Range/Average: N.A.

Activity: N.A.

HQ: Chief Consultant, Geriatrics and Extended Care Strategic Healthcare Group, DVA, 810 Vermont Ave., NW, Washington, DC 20420. Phone: (202) 461-6751.

Internet: www.va.gov. (Note: no field offices for this program.)

64.007 BLIND REHABILITATION CENTERS ("Blind Center")

Assistance: specialized services.

Purposes: to provide personal and social adjustment programs and medical or health-related services to blind veterans at DVA medical centers with blind rehabilitation centers.

Eligible applicants/beneficiaries: blind veterans meeting certain general requirements. Active duty armed forces personnel may be transferred to a center.

Range/Average: N.A.

Activity: N.A.

HQ: Blind Rehabilitation Service (117B), Patient Care Services, DVA, Washington, DC 20420. Phone: (202)461-7317.

Internet: www.va.gov/blindrehab.

64.008 VETERANS DOMICILIARY CARE ("DRRTP")

Assistance: specialized services.

Purposes: to provide inpatient medical care and physical, social, and psychological support services to ambulatory veterans disabled by age or illness, and not requiring acute care or skilled nursing services; for rehabilitation services preparing veterans for independent community living, or assisting them in reaching their optimal level of functioning in a protective environment.

Eligible applicants/beneficiaries: veterans meeting specific criteria.

Range/Average: N.A.

Activity: N.A.

HQ: Chief Consultant, Office of Mental Health Services (116), DVA, Washington, DC 20420. Phone: (202) 273-8443, -8446.

Internet: www.va.gov.

64.009 VETERANS MEDICAL CARE BENEFITS ("Hospitalization and Medical Services")

Assistance: specialized services.

Purposes: to provide hospital outpatient medical, dental, medicine, medical supplies, home health, podiatric, optometric, surgical, and mental health services to enrolled veterans and their dependents, including reimbursement for some travel costs. Services are provided at DVA facilities or under fee-basis hometown care programs when properly authorized.

Eligible applicants/beneficiaries: veterans meeting specific criteria veterans dependents and survivors that are ineligible for Medicare, CHAMPUS (Civilian Health and Medical Program of the Uniformed Service), or CHAMPVA (Civilian Health and Medical Program, Veterans Affairs).

Range/Average: N.A.

Activity: N.A.

HQ: Director, Health Administration Services (10C3), DVA, 810 Vermont Ave., NW, Washington, DC 20420. Phone: (202) 273-8302, -8303.

Internet: www.va.gov.

64.010   VETERANS NURSING HOME CARE

Assistance: specialized services.

Purposes: to provide skilled nursing home care to veterans in DVA, state, or contracts facilities. Also provided are related medical services, supportive personal care, and individual adjustment services.

Eligible applicants/beneficiaries: veterans requiring skilled nursing care and related medical services, and meeting specific criteria.

Range/Average: N.A.

Activity: N.A.

HQ: Nursing Home Care Program Chief, Geriatrics and Extended Strategic Health Group (114), DVA, Washington, DC 20420. Phone: (202) 273-8540.

Internet: www.va.gov.

64.011   VETERANS DENTAL CARE

Assistance: specialized services.

Purposes: to provide dental services for veterans.

Eligible applicants/beneficiaries: veterans meeting specific criteria.

Range/Average: N.A.

Activity: N.A.

HQ: Director, Health Administration Services (10C3), DVA, Washington, DC 20420. Phone: (202) 273-8302, -8303.

Internet: www.va.gov.

64.012   VETERANS PRESCRIPTION SERVICE
("Medicine For Veterans")

Assistance: sale, exchange, or donation of property and goods.

Purposes: to provide prescription drugs and expendable medical supplies from DVA pharmacies to veterans and certain dependents and survivors. Small co-payments may be required.

Eligible applicants/beneficiaries: veterans meeting specific criteria; wives and dependent children under CHAMPVA (Civilian Health and Medical Program, Veterans Affairs).

Range/Average: N.A.

Activity: N.A.

HQ: Chief Consultant, Pharmacy Benefits Management, DVA, Washington, DC 20420. Phone: (202) 273-8429.

Internet: www.va.gov.

64.013 VETERANS PROSTHETIC APPLIANCES ("Prosthetics Services")

Assistance: sale, exchange, or donation of property and goods.

Purposes: to provide prosthetic and related appliances, equipment, and services to disabled veterans, including artificial limbs, artificial eyes, wheelchairs, aids for the blind, hearing aids, braces, orthopedic shoes, eyeglasses, crutches and canes, automobile adaptive equipment, and medical equipment, implants, and supplies—as well as training in the use of the foregoing.

Eligible applicants/beneficiaries: disabled veterans meeting specific criteria.

Range: $10 to $25,000. **Average:** $118.

Activity: N.A.

HQ: Chief, Prosthetic and Clinical Logistics Officer (10f), DVA, Washington, DC 20420. Phone: (202) 254-0440; FAX: (202) 254-0470.

Internet: vaww1.va.gov/prosthetics.

64.014 VETERANS STATE DOMICILIARY CARE

Assistance: formula grants (to 50 percent).

Purposes: pursuant to the Act of August 27, 1888 as amended, to provide domiciliary care services in state homes to veterans disabled by age or illness—to assist them in attaining physical, mental, and social well-being through rehabilitative programs.

Eligible applicants: states.

Eligible beneficiaries: veterans meeting specific criteria including state admission requirements.

Range: $5,000 to $3,600,000. **Average:** $427,000.

Activity: N.A.

HQ: Chief, State Home Per Diem Program, Assistant Chief Medical Director/Geriatrics and Extended Care (114B), DVA, Washington, DC 20420. Phone: (202) 461-6771.

Internet: www.va.gov.

64.015 VETERANS STATE NURSING HOME CARE

Assistance: formula grants (to 50 percent).

Purposes: to provide skilled nursing home care and related medical services to veterans in state veterans homes.

Eligible applicants: states.

Eligible beneficiaries: veterans eligible for care in a DVA facility, needing nursing home care, and meeting other specific criteria ,including state admission requirements.

Range: $267,590 to $11,448,271. **Average:** $5,857,931.

Activity: N.A.

HQ: Chief, State Home Per Diem Program, Assistant Chief Medical Director/Geriatrics and Extended Care (114), DVA, Washington, DC 20420. Phone: (202) 461-6771.

Internet: www.va.gov.

64.016 VETERANS STATE HOSPITAL CARE

Assistance: formula grants (to 50 percent).

Purposes: to provide inpatient hospital care to veterans in state veterans homes.

Eligible applicants: states.

Eligible beneficiaries: veterans meeting specific criteria , including state requirements.

Range: $2,022 to $3,217,481. **Average:** $1,609,752.

Activity: N.A.

HQ: Chief, State Home Per Diem Program, Assistant Chief Medical Director/Geriatrics and Extended Care (114), DVA, Washington, DC 20420. Phone: (202) 461-6771.

Internet: www.va.gov.

64.018 SHARING SPECIALIZED MEDICAL RESOURCES

Assistance: specialized services.

Purposes: for exchanges between DVA and communities, or mutual use of, advanced medical techniques and specialized resources which otherwise might not be available to DVA or to the communities.

Eligible applicants/beneficiaries: medical schools; federal, state, local, public or private hospitals; clinics; research centers; blood and organ banks.

Range/Average: N.A.

Activity: N.A.

HQ: Director, Sharing and Purchasing Office (175), Veterans Health Administration, DVA, 810 Vermont Ave., NW, Washington, DC 20420. Phone: (202) 273-8406.

Internet: www.va.gov.

64.019 VETERANS REHABILITATION—ALCOHOL AND DRUG DEPENDENCE ("Substance Abuse Treatment Program")

Assistance: specialized services.

Purposes: to provide medical, social, vocational, and rehabilitation therapies to alcohol- and drug-dependent veterans, in DVA medical centers and clinics. Services include detoxification, substance abuse rehabilitation, individual and group and family therapy, psychotropic medications, psychiatric counseling, social services, vocational rehabilitation.

Eligible applicants/beneficiaries: veterans meeting specific criteria.

Range/Average: N.A.

Activity: N.A.

HQ: Director, Mental Health and Behavioral Sciences Services (11C), DVA, 810 Vermont Ave., NW, Washington, DC 20420. Phone: (202) 461-7352.

Internet: www.va.gov.

64.022 VETERANS HOME BASED PRIMARY CARE

Assistance: specialized services.

Purposes: to provide primary health care services through DVA interdisciplinary teams to homebound veterans whose caregivers are capable and willing to assist in their care.

Eligible applicants/beneficiaries: veterans requiring intermittent skilled nursing care and related medical services, and meeting specific criteria.

Range/Average: N.A.

Activity: N.A.

HQ: Home Based Primary Care Program Coordinator, Geriatrics and Extended Care Strategic Healthcare Group (114), DVA, Washington, DC 20420. Phone: (202) 273-6488, -8540.

Internet: www.va.gov. (Note: no field offices for this program.)

64.024 VA HOMELESS PROVIDERS GRANT AND PER DIEM PROGRAM

Assistance: project grants (to 65 percent).

Purposes: pursuant to the Homeless Veterans Comprehensive Service Programs Act of 1992, to establish new programs and service centers to provide supportive housing and services for homeless veterans. Funds may be used to: acquire, renovate, or alter facilities; provide outreach and transportation services; pay operating costs. Per diem payments may be provided on behalf of VA-referred or -authorized veterans. Operating costs may be partially supported with grant funds.

Eligible applicants/beneficiaries: project grants—public or private nonprofit entities. For per diem payments, programs must have been established after 10 November 1992.

Range: $12,610 to $541,000. **Average:** N.A.

Activity: N.A.

HQ: Program Manager, Homeless Providers Grant and Per Diem Program, Mental Health Strategic Healthcare Group (116E), DVA, 810 Vermont Ave., NW, Washington, DC 20420. Phone: (202) 273-8966; Toll Free: (877) 322-0334.

Internet: www.va.gov. (Note: no field offices for this program.)

64.026 VETERANS STATE ADULT DAY HEALTH CARE

Assistance: project grants (50 percent).

Purposes: for community-based, nonresidential programs providing skilled nursing and rehabilitative therapy services to veterans with medical or disabling conditions, including at least physical or occupational therapy, or speech-language pathology or audiology, and personal and psychological or counseling services as appropriate.

Eligible applicants/beneficiaries: veterans meeting state as well as DVA requirements.

Range: $22,686 to $165,077. **Average:** $93,882.

Activity: N.A.

HQ: Chief, State Home Per Diem Program, Assistant Chief Medical Director/Geriatrics and Extended Care (114), DVA, Washington, DC 20420. Phone: (202) 461-6771.

Internet: www.va.gov.

64.027 POST-9/11 VETERANS EDUCATIONAL ASSISTANCE ("Post 9/11 GI Bill")

Assistance: direct payments/specified use (100 percent).

Purposes: pursuant to the Post-9/11 Veterans Educational Assistance Act of 2008, to help servicepersons adjust to civilian life after separation from military service, assist in the recruitment and retention of highly qualified personnel in the active and reserve components in the Armed Forces by providing education benefits, and to provide educational opportunities to the dependents of certain service members and veterans.

Eligible applicants/beneficiaries: individuals who entered active duty after September 10, 2001.

Range/Average: N.A.

Activity: N.A.

HQ: Director, DVA, 810 Vermont Ave., NW, Washington, DC 20420. Phone: (202) 461-9800.

Internet: www.gibill.va.gov.

64.028 POST-9/11 VETERANS EDUCATIONAL ASSISTANCE ("Post-9/11 GI Bill")

Assistance: direct payments/unrestricted use (100 percent).

Purposes: pursuant to the Supplemental Appropriations Act of 2008, to help servicepersons adjust to civilian life after separation from military service, assist in the recruitment and retention of highly qualified personnel in the active and reserve components in the Armed Forces by providing education benefits, and to provide educational opportunities to the dependents of certain service members and veterans. Participants may pursue approved programs of education offered by an institution of higher learning (IHL).

Eligible applicants/beneficiaries: individuals who entered active duty after September 10, 2001.

Range/Average: N.A.

Activity: N.A.

HQ: Director, DVA, 810 Vermont Ave., NW, Washington, DC 20420. Phone: (202) 461-9800.

Internet: www.gibill.va.gov.

64.029   PURCHASE CARE PROGRAM
("Purchase Care Program")

Assistance: direct payments/specified use (100 percent).

Purposes: pursuant to the Department of Veterans Affairs and Housing and Urban Development and Independent Agencies Appropriations Act, to develop the administrative processes, policies, regulations, and directives associated with the delivery of VA health benefit programs. Generally covers medically necessary health care for eligible recipients.

Eligible applicants/beneficiaries: veterans of the U.S. armed forces.

Range/Average: N.A.

Activity: N.A.

HQ: Director, Department of Veterans Affairs, Chief Business Office (16), 810 Vermont Ave., NW, Washington, DC 20420. Phone: (303) 370-5061.

Internet: vaww1.va.gov/CBO/index.asp.

64.030   LIFE INSURANCE FOR VETERANS—FACE AMOUNT OF NEW LIFE INSURANCE POLICIES ISSUED

Assistance: insurance (100 percent).

Purposes: pursuant to The Servicemen's Indemnity and Insurance Act of 1951, to provide life insurance protection for other than dishonorably discharged Veterans who are service-disabled separated from active duty on or after April 25, 1951, and to provide mortgage protection life insurance for Veterans and Servicemembers who have received a grant for specially adapted housing.

Eligible applicants/beneficiaries: a Veteran discharged under other than dishonorable conditions from active military duty, on or after April 25, 1951, who has been granted a service connection for a new disability, and who, if not for the disability would be otherwise insurable in accordance with the established standards of good health, applies for coverage within 2 years from the date of notice of the VA service-connected rating.

Range/Average: N.A.

Activity: N.A.

HQ: Director, PO Box 42954, Philadelphia, Pennsylvania 19101. Phone: (1-800) 669-8477.

Internet: www.insurance.va.gov.

64.031   LIFE INSURANCE FOR VETERANS—DIRECT PAYMENTS FOR INSURANCE

Assistance: insurance (100 percent).

Purposes: pursuant to the War Risk Insurance Act, to provide direct insurance payments, including advance payments disbursed as loans, to Veterans and their beneficiaries for claims based on death or other qualifying circumstance. Payments may be authorized for Veterans of World War I, World War II, Korean conflict, Vietnam conflict, Gulf era conflicts and service-disabled Veterans separated from active duty on or after April 25, 1951, and for mortgage protection life insurance for those disabled Veterans who are given a VA grant to secure specially adapted housing under Chapter 21, Title 38, U.S.C.

Eligible applicants: veterans who have purchased one of the named life insurance policies and their beneficiaries. Payment cannot be made if it would cause the insurance proceeds to revert back to a State (in the case where there are no heirs to pay).

Eligible beneficiaries: payment may be made on a claim to a principal beneficiary, a contingent beneficiary, a representative of the estate, a minor or incompetent, or another designee filing for benefits. A beneficiary may assign all or a portion of his or her share of the insurance to a restricted class of the insured's relatives. Payments may also be made to the policyholder for loan or dividend amounts.

Range/Average: N.A.

Activity: N.A.

HQ: Director, PO Box 42954, Philadelphia, PA 19101. Phone: (1-800-669-8477.

Internet: www.insurance.va.gov.

64.033   VA SUPPORTIVE SERVICES FOR VETERAN FAMILIES PROGRAM

Assistance: project grants (100 percent).

Purposes: pursuant to the Veterans' Mental Health and Other Care Improvements Act of 2008, to provide supportive services grants to private non-profit organizations and consumer cooperatives who will coordinate or provide supportive services to very low-income Veteran families who are residing in permanent housing, are homeless and scheduled to become residents of permanent housing within a specified time period, or after exiting permanent housing within a specified time period, are seeking other housing that is responsive to such very low-income Veteran family's needs and preferences.

Eligible applicants: private non-profit organizations or a consumer cooperatives.

Eligible beneficiaries: very-low income veteran families.

Range/Average: N.A.

Activity: N.A.

HQ: Director, VA National Center on Homelessness Among Veterans, SSVF, 4100 Chester Ave., Suite 201, Philadelphia, PA 19104. Phone: (877) 737-0111.

Internet: www.va.gov/homeless/ssvp.asp. (Note: no field offices for this program.)

64.036   VETERANS RETRAINING ASSISTANCE PROGRAM (VRAP)

Assistance: direct payments/specified use (100 percent/monthly).

Purposes: pursuant to the Veterans Retraining Assistance Program (VRAP), to provide training in a program that leads to a high demand occupation and employment assistance to unemployed Veterans.

Eligible applicants/beneficiaries: eligible Veterans must: Be at least 35 but not more than 60 years old, Be unemployed, Have last been discharged under other than dishonorable conditions, Not be eligible for any other VA education benefit programs, Not be in receipt of VA compensation due to unemployability, and Not be or have been in the last 180 days, enrolled in a Federal or state job training program.

Range/Average: N.A.

Activity: N.A.

HQ: Director, Department of Veterans Affairs 810 Vermont Ave., NW, Washington, DC 20420. Phone: (202) 461-9800.

Internet: vabenefits.vba.va.gov.

64.037 VA U.S. PARALYMPICS MONTHLY ASSISTANCE ALLOWANCE PROGRAM

Assistance: direct payments/unrestricted use (100 percent).

Purposes: pursuant to Veterans' Benefits Improvement Act of 2008, to promote lifelong health, motivate, encourage and sustain participation and competition in adaptive sports among disabled veterans and members of the armed forces through partnerships with VA clinical personnel, national and community-based adaptive sports programs. A monthly assistance allowance will be provided to a disabled veteran who qualifies, whether categorized as a developing, elite, or national team athlete.

Eligible applicants/beneficiaries: eligible disabled veterans.

Range: $554 to $1,046 per month, per athlete. **Average:** N.A.

Activity: N.A.

HQ: Director, Department of Veterans Affairs, 90 K St. NE, Rm. 707, Washington, DC 20002. Phone: (202) 632-7136.

Internet: www.va.gov/adaptivesports. (Note: no field offices for this program.)

64.038 GRANTS FOR THE RURAL VETERANS COORDINATION PILOT (RVCP)

Assistance: project grants (100 percent/2 years).

Purposes: pursuant to the Caregivers and Veterans Omnibus Health Services Act of 2010, funds for two-year pilot programs to assess the feasibility of using community-based organizations and local, state, and tribal government entities to provide outreach, coordination, increased availability of high quality medical and mental health services, and assistance to veterans and their families as they transition from the military to civilian life. The programs will be carried out in five locations and the grants are for a two-year period. The locations that must be considered shall be rural areas with high proportions of minorities in the population with limited access to health care and not in close proximity to an active duty military installation.

Eligible applicants: private non-profit organizations or state, local, and tribal governments, that provide services to veterans.

Eligible beneficiaries: veterans and their families transitioning from military to rural areas. Eligible veterans are those who are eligible for VA benefits and have transitioned form active duty military service within last two years. Eligible family members are those who reside in veterans home and are part of established household.

Range/Average: $2,000,000 for two years.

Activity: N.A.

HQ: Director, RVCP, Dept of Veterans Affairs, 810 Vermont Ave., Washington, DC 20420. Phone: (202) 461-4178.

Internet: www.grants.gov. (Note: no field offices for this program.)

64.051   SPECIALLY ADAPTED HOUSING ASSISTIVE TECHNOLOGY GRANT PROGRAM

Assistance: project grants. (100 percent).

Purposes: pursuant to the Veterans' Benefit Act of 2010, to encourage the development of new assistive technologies for specially adapted housing. The goal technologies are defined as an advancement the Secretary determines could aid or augment the ability of a veteran or servicemember to live in an adapted home.

Eligible applicants/beneficiaries: everyone.

Range/Average: N.A.

Activity: N.A.

HQ: SAHAT Grant Program, VA, 810 Vermont Ave., NW, Washington, DC 20420. Phone: (202) 632-8801.

Internet: www.benefits.va.gov/homeloans/adaptedhousing.asp. (Note: no field offices for this program.)

64.100   AUTOMOBILES AND ADAPTIVE EQUIPMENT FOR CERTAIN DISABLED VETERANS AND MEMBERS OF THE ARMED FORCES

Assistance: direct payments/specified use.

Purposes: for disabled veterans and service-persons to purchase automobiles or other conveyances with adaptive equipment. Funds also may be used for repairs, replacements, or reinstallation. Adaptive equipment may be provided for no more than two conveyances during any four-year period, unless one of the vehicles becomes unavailable to the veteran.

Eligible applicants/beneficiaries: active duty personnel and veterans with honorable service and service-persons with a service-connected disability caused by loss of use or permanent loss of one or both feet, one or both hands, or a permanent impairment.

Range: to $11,000. **Average:** N.A.

Activity: N.A.

HQ: Department of Veterans Affairs, 810 Vermont Ave., NW, Washington, DC 20420. Telephone: (202) 461-9500.

Internet: www.va.gov.

64.101   BURIAL EXPENSES ALLOWANCE FOR VETERANS

Assistance: direct payments/specified use.

Purposes: for the plot or internment expenses of certain veterans not buried in a national cemetery; for funeral and burial expenses of veterans whose death results from a service-connected disability; for transportation of the remains of service- connected, disabled veterans to a national cemetery. Headstones or markers and an American flag to drape the casket may also be provided.

Eligible applicants/beneficiaries: burial and plot allowances—the person bearing the veteran's burial expense or the funeral director, if unpaid, on behalf of veterans: discharged under other than dishonorable conditions; discharged or released from active duty for a disability incurred or aggravated in line of duty; or, at time of death, entitled to compensation or pension or indigent or properly hospitalized at VA expense. Flags—next of kin, friend, or associate.

Range: to $2,000. **Average:** N.A.

Activity: N.A.

HQ: DVA, 810 Vermont Ave., NW, Washington, DC 20420. Phone: (202) 461-9700.

Internet: www.va.gov.

64.103   LIFE INSURANCE FOR VETERANS ("GI Insurance")

Assistance: direct loans; insurance.

Purposes: pursuant to the War Risk Insurance Act, World War Veterans Act, National Service Life Insurance Act, and Servicemen's Indemnity and Insurance Act, and amendments, to provide: life insurance protection for veterans of WW-I and -II, the Korean, Vietnam, and Gulf era conflicts, and for those with service-connected disabilities, separated from active duty on April 25, 1951 or later, and current members of the uniformed services and their spouses; mortgage protection life insurance for veterans receiving specially adapted housing; policy loans at varying interest rates. The programs are closed for new issues except Service-Disabled Veterans Insurance, Mortgage Protection Life Insurance, Service Members' Group Life Insurance, and Veterans Group Life Insurance.

Eligible applicants/beneficiaries: veterans meeting specific criteria. If the eligible applicant is mentally incompetent, a fiduciary recognized by DVA may apply on behalf of the veteran for Service-Disabled Veterans Insurance—benefits of which may also be granted under certain conditions for mentally incompetent veterans who were otherwise eligible for such insurance but, due to their incompetence, died without filing an application. Spouses and dependent children are automatically covered unless the member declines or reduces the coverage.

Range/Average: N.A.

Activity: N.A.

HQ: Regional Office and Insurance Center, DVA, PO Box 42954, Philadelphia, PA 19101. Phone: (800) 669-8477.

Internet: www.insurance.va.gov.

64.104   PENSION FOR NON-SERVICE-CONNECTED DISABILITY FOR VETERANS

Assistance: direct payments/unrestricted use.

Purposes: for wartime veterans with total and permanent nonservice-connected disabilities. Income and asset restrictions are prescribed.

Eligible applicants/beneficiaries: veterans with 90 days or more of honorable active wartime service in the Armed Forces or, if less than 90 days, released or discharged from service because of a service-connected disability, or permanently and totally disabled for reasons not due to service. Pension is not payable to those whose estates are so large that it is reasonable they use the estate for maintenance.

Range/Average: N.A.

Activity: N.A.

HQ: DVA, 810 Vermont Ave., NW, Washington, DC 20420. Phone: (202) 461-9700.

Internet: www.va.gov.

64.105   PENSION TO VETERANS SURVIVING SPOUSES, AND CHILDREN ("Death Pension")

Assistance: direct payments/unrestricted use.

Purposes: for needy dependents of deceased wartime veterans whose deaths were not due to service.

Eligible applicants/beneficiaries: unmarried surviving spouses and children of deceased veterans with at least 90 days of honorable active wartime service or, if less than 90 days, discharged for a service-connected disability. A child must be unmarried and under age 18, between age 18 and 23 if in school, or disabled before age 18 and continuously incapable of self-support. Pensions are not payable to those whose estates are so large that it is reasonable they use the estate for maintenance.

Range/Average: N.A.

Activity: N.A.

HQ: Department of Veterans Affairs, 810 Vermont Ave., NW, Washington, DC 20420. Telephone: (202) 461-9500.

Internet: www.va.gov.

64.106   SPECIALLY ADAPTED HOUSING FOR DISABLED VETERANS ("Paraplegic Housing")

Assistance: direct payments/specified use.

Purposes: to provide suitable adapted housing with special fixtures and facilities to severely disabled veterans, including construction, remodeling, or mortgage reduction payments.

Eligible applicants/beneficiaries: veterans with permanent, total, and compensable disabilities.

Range: to $50,000 for housing, land, fixtures, and expenses; to $10,000 for adaptation of residence. **Average:** N.A.

Activity: N.A.

HQ: Department of Veterans Affairs, 810 Vermont Ave., NW, Washington, DC 20420. Telephone: (202) 461-9500.

Internet: www.homeloans.va.gov/SAH.

64.109 VETERANS COMPENSATION FOR SERVICE-CONNECTED DISABILITY

Assistance: direct payments/unrestricted use.

Purposes: for disabled veterans, in amounts reflecting the average impairment in the earning capacity the disability would cause in civilian occupations.

Eligible applicants/beneficiaries: persons suffering disabilities during service in the Armed Forces, incurred in or aggravated by service in the line of duty. Separation from service must have been under other than dishonorable conditions.

Range: $117 to $7,232 per month. **Average:** N.A.

Activity: N.A.

HQ: Department of Veterans Affairs, 810 Vermont Ave., NW, Washington, DC 20420. Telephone: (202) 461-9500.

Internet: www.va.gov.

64.110 VETERANS DEPENDENCY AND INDEMNITY COMPENSATION FOR SERVICE-CONNECTED DEATH ("DIC and Death Compensation")

Assistance: direct payments/unrestricted use.

Purposes: for survivors of deceased veterans whose death resulted from a service-connected disability or while on active duty.

Eligible applicants/beneficiaries: surviving spouses, children, and parent(s) of deceased veterans.

Range/Average: N.A.

Activity: N.A.

HQ: Department of Veterans Affairs, 810 Vermont Ave., NW, Washington, DC 20420. Telephone: (202) 461-9500.

Internet: www.va.gov.

64.114 VETERANS HOUSING—GUARANTEED AND INSURED LOANS ("VA Home Loans")

Assistance: guaranteed/insured loans.

Purposes: for housing for veterans, certain service personnel, or their surviving unremarried spouses—covering home construction or purchases, repairs, improvements, or refinancing. Eligible loans include those covering standard single-family units, condominiums, or manufactured homes and lots—for their own use; also, for solar heating or cooling or other energy conservation improvements. Applicants must have sufficient present and prospective income to meet loan repayment terms, and a satisfactory credit record.

Eligible applicants/beneficiaries: veterans meeting specific criteria. Also, unremarried surviving spouses of eligible veterans deceased in service or as a result of service-connected disabilities.

Range/Average: N.A.

Activity: N.A.

HQ: Department of Veterans Affairs, 810 Vermont Ave., NW, Washington, DC 20420. Telephone: (202) 461-9500.

Internet: www.va.gov.

64.115 VETERANS INFORMATION AND ASSISTANCE ("Veterans Services")

Assistance: advisory services/counseling.

Purposes: to provide information and assistance to all veterans—including of the PHS, NOAA, and certain WW-II Merchant Marines—relating to the full range of benefits to which they are entitled.

Eligible applicants/beneficiaries: generally, veterans, their dependents or beneficiaries, their representatives or other interested parties.

Range/Average: N.A.

Activity: over 21 million contacts completed annually.

HQ: Department of Veterans Affairs, 810 Vermont Ave., NW, Washington, DC 20420. Telephone: (202) 461-9500.

Internet: www.va.gov.

64.116 VOCATIONAL REHABILITATION FOR DISABLED VETERANS

Assistance: direct payments/unrestricted use; direct payments/specified use; direct loans; advisory services/counseling.

Purposes: pursuant to the Veterans' Rehabilitation and Education Amendments of 1980, to provide counseling, no-interest loans, and payments for tuition, fees, related costs, and subsistence for up to four years to disabled veterans and hospitalized service- members pending discharge—to obtain vocational training and suitable employment and to achieve maximum independence in daily living.

Eligible applicants/beneficiaries: veterans of WW-II and later service, with a compensable service-connected disability; certain hospitalized service-members pending discharge or release from service, in need of vocational rehabilitation because of an employment handicap.

Range/Average: N.A.

Activity: N.A.

HQ: Vocational Rehabilitation and Employment Service (28), Veterans Benefits Administration, DVA, 810 Vermont Ave., NW, Washington, DC 20420. Phone: (202) 461-9600.

Internet: www.va.gov. www.vetsuccess.gov.

64.117 SURVIVORS AND DEPENDENTS EDUCATIONAL ASSISTANCE

Assistance: direct payments/specified use.

Purposes: to provide educational opportunities for dependents of certain deceased or disabled veterans—covering pursuit of associate, bachelor, or graduate degree, licensing and certification tests, diplomas, apprenticeships and on-the-job training, preparatory courses, restorative or vocational training. Education must be completed within ten years of the date that the disability was incurred, or from the date of death of the veteran.

Eligible applicants/beneficiaries: spouses, surviving spouses, and children between age 18 and 26—of veterans deceased because of service-connected disabilities; of living veterans with service-connected disabilities considered permanently and totally disabling; of those deceased because of any cause while such disabilities were in existence; of service-members listed for more than 90 days as missing in action; or, of prisoners of war.

Range/Average: N.A.

Activity: N.A.

HQ: Director, Department of Veterans Affairs 810 Vermont Ave., NW, Washington, DC 20420. Phone: (202) 461-9800.

Internet: www.gibill.va.gov.

64.118 VETERANS HOUSING—DIRECT LOANS FOR CERTAIN DISABLED VETERANS

Assistance: direct loans (below-market interest).

Purposes: for disabled veterans to purchase, construct, or improve homes, including farm residences, with specially adapted features and facilities. Loans are coordinated with grants obtained under **64.106** (Specially Adapted Housing for Disabled Veterans).

Eligible applicants/beneficiaries: disabled veterans serving on active duty on or after September 16, 1940, and eligabible under **64.106** (Specially Adapted Housing for Disabled Veterans).

Range: to $33,000. **Average:** N.A.

Activity: N.A.

HQ: Department of Veterans Affairs, 810 Vermont Ave., NW, Washington, DC 20420. Telephone: (202) 461-9500.

Internet: www.va.gov.

64.119 VETERANS HOUSING—MANUFACTURED HOME LOANS

Assistance: guaranteed/insured loans. (to 95 percent/15-25 years).

Purposes: for manufactured homes (new or used), or homes and lots, or lots only—purchased or refinanced for their own use by veterans, servicemembers, and certain unremarried surviving spouses of veterans.

Eligible applicants/beneficiaries: veterans meeting specific criteria. Also, unremarried surviving spouses of eligible veterans deceased in service or as a result of service-connected disabilities.

Range: N.A. **Average:** $20,000 or 40 percent of loan amount, whichever is less.

Activity: N.A.

HQ: Department of Veterans Affairs, 810 Vermont Ave., NW, Washington, DC 20420. Telephone: (202) 461-9500.

Internet: www.va.gov.

64.120 POST-VIETNAM ERA VETERANS' EDUCATIONAL ASSISTANCE ("Voluntary-Contributory Matching Program")

Assistance: direct payments/specified use.

Purposes: for educational, vocational, or professional training to persons entering the Armed Services after 31 December 1976 and before 1 July 1985, as well as those who served during certain other periods. Payments are provided on the basis of a $2 to $1 match of federal to participant contribution. Enrollments in avocational or recreational courses may not be covered. Participants must have satisfactorily contributed to the program, consisting of a monthly deduction of $25 to $100 from military pay, up to a maximum of $2,700, for deposit in a special training fund. Participants may make lump-sum contributions. Applicants must complete their education within ten years after release from service, with certain exceptions.

Eligible applicants/beneficiaries: basically, veterans serving honorably on active duty for more than 180 days beginning on or after 1 January 1977, or discharged after such date because of a service-connected disability; veterans serving for more than 180 days and continuing on active duty and completing their first period of obligated service (or six years of active duty, whichever comes first). No persons on active duty may initiate contributions to this program after March 31, 1987. Certain more recent veterans may elect Montgomery GI Bill benefits (see 64.124), provided their basic pay was reduced by $1,200, based on dates of duty periods.

Range/Average: N.A.

Activity: N.A.

HQ: DVA, 810 Vermont Ave., NW, Washington, DC 20420. Phone: (202) 461-9700.

Internet: www.GIBILL.va.gov.

64.124 ALL-VOLUNTEER FORCE EDUCATIONAL ASSISTANCE ("Montgomery GI Bill Active Duty - MGIB - Chapter 30")

Assistance: direct payments/specified use.

Purposes: for the educational expenses of veterans enrolling in approved educational, professional, or vocational programs, including flight training if already licensed. Participants must have agreed to reductions in their military pay while in service, as nonrefundable contributions toward their participation. $100 monthly is deducted from the basic pay for the first twelve months, unless the veteran specifically elects not to participate in the program; such deductions are nonrefundable except in the case of the death of the veteran within a certain time frame. DOD may provide supplementary contributions to participants' funds as inducements to reenlist, paid while they are enrolled in educational programs. Applicants must complete their education within ten years after release from service, with certain exceptions.

Eligible applicants/beneficiaries: basically, veterans with an honorable discharge and military personnel on active duty on or after 1 July 1985, and with a minimum of two years service. Participants without the required obligated service must have been discharged for a service-related disability, for hardship, for a pre-existing medical or physical or mental condition, for involuntary separation due to reduction in force. Certain others may also meet eligability requirements as described in 64.120; full criteria may be obtained from DVA.

Range/Average: N.A.

Activity: N.A.

HQ: Director, Department of Veterans Affairs 810 Vermont Ave., NW, Washington, DC 20420. Phone: (202) 461-9800.

Internet: www.gibill.va.gov. (Note: no field offices for this program.)

64.125 VOCATIONAL AND EDUCATIONAL COUNSELING FOR SERVICEMEMBERS AND VETERANS ("Chapter 36 Counseling")

Assistance: advisory services/counseling.

Purposes: pursuant to Veterans Education and Employment Programs Amendments, to provide vocational and educational counseling to service-members or veterans, in the identification of personal objectives including the development of employment plans.

Eligible applicants/beneficiaries: service-members applying within 180 days of projected discharge or release from active duty; veterans within one year of discharge or release.

Range/Average: N.A.

Activity: N.A.

HQ: Vocational Rehabilitation and Employment Service (28), Veterans Benefits Administration, DVA, 810 Vermont Ave., NW, Washington, DC 20420. Phone: (202) 273-9600.

Internet: www.va.gov.

64.126 NATIVE AMERICAN VETERAN DIRECT LOAN PROGRAM ("VA Native American Veterans Housing Loan Program")

Assistance: direct loans.

Purposes: for certain native American veterans to purchase, construct, improve, or refinance homes that they will occupy, including manufactured homes, located on trust lands.

Eligible applicants/beneficiaries: qualifying native American veterans certified by a recognized tribal government, and certain surviving unremarried spouses of native American veterans.

Range: to $625,500. **Average:** N.A.

Activity: N.A.

HQ: Department of Veterans Affairs, 810 Vermont Ave., NW, Washington, DC 20420. Telephone: (202) 461-9500.

Internet: www.va.gov.

64.127 MONTHLY ALLOWANCE FOR CHILDREN OF VIETNAM VETERANS BORN WITH SPINA BIFIDA

Assistance: direct payments/unrestricted use.

Purposes: to provide financial assistance to children of Vietnam veterans, born with spina bifida.

Eligible applicants/beneficiaries: natural children of Vietnam veterans, born with spina bifida, except spina bifida occulta, regardless of age or marital status, conceived after the date on which the veteran first served in Vietnam (between 9 January 1962 and 7 May 1975).

Range: $270 to $1,586 per month. **Average:** N.A.

Activity: N.A.

HQ: Department of Veterans Affairs, 810 Vermont Ave., NW, Washington, DC 20420. Telephone: (202) 461-9500.

Internet: www.va.gov.

64.128 VOCATIONAL TRAINING AND REHABILITATION FOR VIETNAM VETERANS' CHILDREN WITH SPINA BIFIDA AND OTHER COVERED BIRTH DEFECTS

Assistance: direct payments/specified use.

Purposes: to provide vocational training and rehabilitation to certain children of Vietnam and Korea veterans, born with spina bifida or other covered birth defects.

Eligible applicants/beneficiaries: natural children of Vietnam veterans, born with spina bifida, except spina bifida occulta, regardless of age or marital status, conceived after the date on which the veteran first served in Vietnam (between 9 January 1962 and 7 May 1975); and some Korea veterans. DVA must determine that it is feasible for the child to achieve a vocational goal within 2 to 4 years.

Range/Average: N.A.

Activity: N.A.

HQ: DVA, 810 Vermont Ave., NW, Washington, DC 20420. Phone: (202) 461-9700.

Internet: www.va.gov.

64.201 NATIONAL CEMETERIES

Assistance: specialized services.

Purposes: pursuant to the National Cemeteries Act of 1973, to provide burial space, headstones and markers, and perpetual care for deceased veterans, members of the Armed Forces, Reservists, and National Guard members whose service was terminated other than dishonorably, and certain dependents—in national cemeteries.

Eligible applicants/beneficiaries: next of kin or, if there is no living kin, a friend of the decedent or public assistance officer on their behalf, of deceased: veterans, members of the Armed Forces (Army, Navy, Air Force, Marine Corps, Coast Guard) dying while on active duty; members of the Reserve or Army or National Guard dying while on active duty for training; 20-year reservists and National Guard and certain other of their dependents; enlisted personnel entering military duty after September 7, 1980, and/or becoming commissioned officers after October 16, 1981, and serving for a minimum of two years; spouses of eligible veterans or members of the Armed Forces lost or buried at sea or determined to be permanently missing or missing in action; minor children and certain unmarried adult children of eligible veterans; U.S. citizens serving in the Armed Forces of any government allied with the U.S. during any wars, and holding U.S. citizenship at time of death; certain commissioned officers of the PHS, NOAA, and others.

Range/Average: N.A.

Activity: N.A.

HQ: Director, Memorial Programs Service (41A), National Cemetery Administration-DVA, 810 Vermont Ave., NW, Washington, DC 20420. Phone: (202) 461-6248.

Internet: www.va.gov.

64.202 PROCUREMENT OF HEADSTONES AND MARKERS AND/OR PRESIDENTIAL MEMORIAL CERTIFICATES

Assistance: direct payments/specified use; specialized services.

Purposes: pursuant to the National Cemeteries Act of 1973 and Veterans' Disability Compensation and Survivors' Benefits Act of 1978, for headstones and markers for the graves or memorial plots in national, post, and state veterans cemeteries, or for the unmarked graves or memorial plots in private cemeteries—of deceased eligible veterans; also, costs of transportation and installation and maintenance, replacement of illegible markers. Presidential Memorial Certificates may also be provided.

Eligible applicants: private cemetery burials—next of kin or nonmembers of the deceased's family, after ascertaining that the grave is unmarked and that a government monument is preferred over a privately purchased one. Monuments must be of a type permitted on the grave of the deceased. If burial or memorial plot is in a national cemetery or state veterans cemetery, the director of the cemetery orders the headstone or marker, after completion of the interment in the cemetery, or upon need for replacement.

Eligible beneficiaries: deceased veterans of wartime or peacetime service, discharged under conditions other than dishonorable; members of the Reserve and the Army and Air National Guard dying while performing or as a result of performing active duty for training; commissioned officers of the PHS and the NOAA, Merchant Marine Seamen, and certain others participating in wartime activities. Spouses and certain dependents also may be eligible.

Range/Average: N.A.

Activity: N.A.

HQ: Memorial Programs Service, National Cemetery Administration 5109 Russell Rd., Quantico, VA 22134 Phone: 202-501-3112.

Internet: www.va.gov.

64.203 STATE CEMETERY GRANTS

Assistance: project grants. (to 100 percent/to 3 years).

Purposes: pursuant to the Veterans Housing Benefits Act of 1978, to establish, expand, or improve state-owned veterans cemeteries for the interment of eligible veterans and their dependents.

Eligible applicants/beneficiaries: states.

Range/Average: N.A.

Activity: N.A.

HQ: Director, State Cemetery Grants Service (41E), National Cemetery Administration-DVA, 810 Vermont Ave., NW, Washington, DC 20420. Phone: (202) 565-48947; FAX: (202) 565-6141.

Internet: www.va.gov. (Note: no field offices for this program.)

ENVIRONMENTAL PROTECTION AGENCY

66.001 AIR POLLUTION CONTROL PROGRAM SUPPORT

Assistance: formula grants (60 percent; tribes, 90-95 percent).

Purposes: pursuant to the Clean Air Act of 1990 (CAA) as amended, to plan, establish, improve, and maintain air pollution prevention and control programs. Funding priorities: attain and maintain national ambient standards for criteria pollutants (ozone, particulate matter, visibility, carbon monoxide, lead, sulfur dioxide, and nitrogen dioxide) that endanger human health and the environment; eliminate unacceptable risks of cancer and other health problems from air toxics emissions; reduce the destructive effects of acid rain deposition on land and water systems. Projects involve such strategies as: regulation of stationary sources, mobile source emissions testing and trip reduction measures, participation in interstate emissions trading program, and other innovative early reduction and voluntary measures taken locally. Funding supports cost of monitoring, personnel, training, and operations; construction costs are ineligible.

Eligible applicants/beneficiaries: municipal, intermunicipal, state, tribal, interstate, intertribal agencies, including possessions and territories.

Range: $70,000 to $7,000,000. **Average:** $1,545,000.

Activity: N.A.

HQ: National Air Grant Coordinator (MC 6102A), OAR-EPA, 09 T.W. Alexander Dr., MC C404-02, Research Triangle Park, North Carolina 27709. Phone: (919) 541-5523.

Internet: www.epa.gov/air.

66.032   STATE INDOOR RADON GRANTS (SIRG)

Assistance: project grants. (to 50 percent; tribes, 100 percent/to 5 years).

Purposes: pursuant to the Indoor Radon Abatement Act and Toxic Substances Control Act (TSCA), to develop and implement programs and projects to reduce radon risks in homes, schools, and other buildings. Eligible activities include radon surveys, public information and educational materials, radon control programs, purchase and maintenance of analytic equipment, training, administrative costs, data storage and management, mitigation demonstrations, toll-free hotlines, and promotion of environmental justice through outreach to low-income and culturally-diverse populations. Financial assistance may be provided to individuals only if such costs relate to demonstration projects or to the purchase and analysis of radon measurement devices.

Eligible applicants: states, territories and possessions, tribes.

Eligible beneficiaries: local, municipal, district, or areawide organizations; IHEs; nonprofit organizations; low-income persons, homeowners.

Range: $15,000 to $805,100. **Average:** $170,000.

Activity: 52 awards in FY 2014.

HQ: Office of Radiation and Indoor Air (6604J), OAR-EPA, 1310 L St., NW, Stop 6609J, Washington, DC 20005. Phone: (202) 343-9117; FAX: (202) 343-9431.

Internet: www.cpa.gov/radon/sirgprogram.html.

66.033   OZONE TRANSPORT COMMISSION (OTC)

Assistance: project grants. (60-100 percent/to 2 years).

Purposes: pursuant to Section 106 (interstate pollution) and Section 111 (interstate ozone pollution) of CAA of 1990 as amended, to develop or recommend regional air quality control implementation plans for reducing ozone pollution. Funds may be used to support interstate pollution projects, including public education and outreach.

Eligible applicants/beneficiaries: state agencies or commissions designated by the governors of the New England and Mid-Atlantic states, and DC, representing affected states and political subdivisions.

Range: $600,000 to $650,000. **Average:** $639,000.

Activity: N.A.

HQ: OAR-EPA (6102A), 1200 Pennsylvania Ave., NW, Stop 6102A, Washington, DC 20460. Phone: (202) 564-1668.

Internet: www.otcair.org.

66.034 SURVEYS, STUDIES, RESEARCH, INVESTIGATIONS, DEMONSTRATIONS, AND SPECIAL PURPOSE ACTIVITIES RELATING TO THE CLEAN AIR ACT

Assistance: project grants. (100 percent/to 5 years).

Purposes: pursuant to CAA of 1963 as amended, for surveys, studies, investigations, demonstrations, and special purpose assistance relating to the causes, effects (including upon health and welfare), extent, prevention, and control of air pollution—including air quality, acid deposition, climate change, global programs, indoor environments, mobile source technology, and community-driven approaches to transportation. Funding priorities include: indoor environments, especially those affecting children; air toxics, including the National Air Toxics Assessment program, National Toxics Inventory, and Air Toxics Monitoring Network; mobile source technologies; truck engine idle reduction technologies; National Clean Diesel Campaign; climate protections, including outreach and public education efforts; other issues.

Eligible applicants/beneficiaries: states, territories and possessions, tribes; international organizations; IHEs; other public and private nonprofit institutions.

Range: $5,000 to $750,000. **Average:** $150,000.

Activity: N.A.

HQ: *Program information,* OAR-EPA (6102A), 1200 Pennsylvania Ave., NW, Stop 6102A, Washington, DC 20460. Phone: (202) 564-1306.

Internet: www.epa.gov/air.

66.037 INTERNSHIPS, TRAINING AND WORKSHOPS FOR THE OFFICE OF AIR AND RADIATION

Assistance: project grants. (100 percent/to 3 years).

Purposes: pursuant to CAA as amended, for internships, training, workshops, fellowships, and technical monitoring supporting the Clean Air Act, including: developing career-oriented personnel; technical training of state, local, territorial, and tribal environmental control agencies; pertinent academic training; student support, traineeships, internships; personnel recruitment.

Eligible applicants/beneficiaries: states, territories and possessions, tribes, tribal governments; international organizations; IHEs; other public and private nonprofit institutions including hospitals, laboratories.

Range: $50,000 to $250,000. **Average:** $200,000.

Activity: N.A.

HQ: *Program information,* OAR-EPA (6102A), 1200 Pennsylvania Ave., NW, Stop 6102A, Washington, DC 20460. Phone: (202) 564-1306.

Internet: www.epa.gov/air.

66.038   TRAINING, INVESTIGATIONS, AND SPECIAL PURPOSE ACTIVITIES OF FEDERALLY-RECOGNIZED INDIAN TRIBES CONSISTENT WITH THE CLEAN AIR ACT (CAA), TRIBAL SOVEREIGNTY AND THE PROTECTION AND MANAGEMENT OF AIR QUALITY ("Tribal CAA 103 Project Grants")

Assistance: project grants (to 5 years).

Purposes: Clean Air Act of 1963, Section 103, as amended to support federally-recognized Indian Tribes' efforts to understand, assess and characterize air quality, and design methods and plans to protect and improve air quality on tribal lands through surveys, studies, research, training, investigations, and special purpose activities. Funding is available to support recipient's allowable direct costs for approved Tribal air resource activities that will protect public health and the environment or that are in accordance with established EPA policies and regulations. Assistance agreement awards under this program may involve or relate to geospatial information (see, http://geodata.epa.gov).

Eligible applicants/beneficiaries: federally-recognized Indian Tribes and Intertribal Consortia.

Range: $25,000 to $500,000. **Average:** $75,000.

Activity: funding provided to 115 tribal governments in FY 2014.

HQ: Grants and Interagency Agreement Management Division, EPA, 1200 Pennsylvania Ave., NW, MC 6103A, Washington, DC 20460 Phone: (202) 564-1082.

Internet: www.epa.gov/air/tribal.

66.039   NATIONAL CLEAN DIESEL FUNDING ASSISTANCE PROGRAM ("DERA National Funding Assistance Program")

Assistance: project grants (to 5 years).

Purposes: pursuant to the Interior, Environment and Related Agencies Appropriations Act of 2008, ARRA 2009, and the Energy Policy Act of 2005, to award grants and low-cost revolving loans to eligible entities in order to fund the costs of a retrofit technology that significantly reduces emissions through development and implementation of a certified engine configuration, verified technology, or emerging technology for buses (including school buses), medium-duty or heavy-duty trucks, marine engines, locomotives, or nonroad engines or vehicles used in construction, handling of cargo (including at port or airport), agriculture, mining, or energy production. Funds may also be used for programs or projects to reduce long-duration idling using verified technology involving a vehicle or equipment described above, or the creation of low-cost revolving loan programs to finance diesel emissions reduction projects. (Note: funding priorities the same as **66.040**.)

Eligible applicants: qualified regional, state, local, tribal agency, port authority, city, county, municipal agency, school district, or metropolitan planning organization (MPO) with jurisdiction over transportation or air quality; nonprofit organizations or institutions that represent or provide pollution reduction or educational services to persons or organizations that own or operate diesel fleets or have as its principal purpose, the promotion of transportation or air quality.

Eligible beneficiaries: state, local, public nonprofit institution/organization, general public.

Range: $100,000 to $2,000,000. **Average:** N.A.

Activity: 28 awards in FY 2014.

HQ: Environmental Protection Agency, 1200 Pennsylvania Ave., NW - MS 6405J, Washington, DC 20460. Phone: (202) 343-9541.

Internet: www.epa.gov/cleandiesel.

66.040   STATE CLEAN DIESEL GRANT PROGRAM ("DERA State Program")

Assistance: project grants (to 7 years).

Purposes: pursuant to ARRA 2009 and Interior, Environment and Related Agencies Appropriations Act of 2008 and the Energy Policy Act of 2005, to award assistance agreements to States to develop and implement such grant and low-cost revolving loan programs in the state as are appropriate to meet state needs and goals relating to the reduction of diesel emissions. Priority shall be given to projects which: maximize public health benefits; are most cost-effective; serve areas with the highest population density, that are poor air quality areas; serve areas that receive a disproportionate quantity of air pollution from diesel fleets or that use a community-based multi-stakeholder collaborative process to reduce toxic emissions; include a certified engine configuration, verified technology, or emerging technology that has a long expected useful life; will maximize the useful life of any certified engine configuration, verified technology, or emerging technology used or funded by the eligible entity; conserve diesel fuel; and utilize ultra low sulfur diesel fuel.

Eligible applicants: 50 states.

Eligible beneficiaries: state, local, public nonprofit institution/organization, general public.

Range: $28,000 to $168,000. **Average:** $120,000.

Activity: 42 awards in FY 2015.

HQ: Environmental Protection Agency, 1200 Pennsylvania Ave., NW - MS 6405J, Washington, DC 20460. Phone: (202) 343-9541.

Internet: www.epa.gov/cleandiesel.

66.042   TEMPORALLY INTEGRATED MONITORING OF ECOSYSTEMS (TIME) AND LONG-TERM MONITORING (LTM) PROGRAM ("TIME/LTM")

Assistance: project grants (100 percent/1 year).

Purposes: pursuant to the National Environmental Policy Act, to conduct and promote the coordination and acceleration of research, investigations, experiments, demonstrations, surveys, studies relating to the causes, effects, extent, prevention and control of air pollution.

Eligible applicants/beneficiaries: state and local governments in acid-sensitive regions of the U.S., IHEs, scientific research community, general public.

Range: $175,000 to $200,000. **Average:** $190,000.

Activity: N.A.

HQ: Director, US Environmental Protection Agency, 1200 Pennsylvania Ave., NW, Mail Code: 6204J, Washington, DC 20460. Phone: (202) 343-9622.

Internet: www.epa.gov/airmarkets/assessments/surfacewater.html. (Note: no field offices for this program.)

66.043 REGIONAL HEALTHY INDOOR AIR PROJECTS FOR COMMUNITY OUTREACH AND EDUCATION, SURVEYS, STUDIES, RESEARCH, INVESTIGATIONS, DEMONSTRATIONS, AND SPECIAL PURPOSE ACTIVITIES RELATING TO THE CLEAN AIR ACT

Assistance: project grants (100 percent/to 5 years).

Purposes: funds to support surveys, studies, research, training, outreach, education, investigations or demonstrations performed by organizations that lead to effective outreach strategies to educate key audiences about indoor air pollutants, their associated health risks and encourage effective mitigation and control strategies. Program focus areas include, but are not limited to reducing the exposure of children and others with asthma to indoor triggers that worsen their health condition; promoting the adoption of operation and maintenance practices in schools, homes, and other buildings throughout the nation to reduce the harmful effects of poor indoor air quality on the health of the occupants; promoting voluntary radon testing by homeowners and building operators to identify elevated levels and fix them when they are found as well as working with homebuilders to incorporate radon resistant and improved indoor air quality construction features into new and remodeled homes; and encouraging adult smokers to protect their children from the adverse health effects of environmental exposure to secondhand smoke by making a conscious decision to keep their homes and cars smoke-free. Projects should also focus on addressing environmental justice and/or disproportionately impacted community concerns.

Eligible applicants/beneficiaries: state and local governments, U.S. territories and possessions, Indian tribes, universities and colleges, hospitals, laboratories, and other public and private nonprofit institutions.

Range: $5,000 to $750,000. **Average:** $50,000.

Activity: N.A.

HQ: Director, Regional Healthy Indoor Air Projects for Community Outreach and Education, OAR-EPA,1200 Pennsylvania Ave., NW, Mail Code 6609J, Washington, DC 20460. Phone: (202) 343-9489.

Internet: www.epa.gov/iaq.

66.110 HEALTHY COMMUNITIES GRANT PROGRAM

Assistance: project grants. (95 percent/1-2 years).

Purposes: pursuant to CAA, CWA, Resource Conservation and Recovery Act (RCRA), TSCA, SDWA, FIFRA, National Environmental Education Act, Pollution Prevention Act (PPA), MPRSA, CERCLA, Indian Environmental General Assistance Program Act, and amendments, for projects only in the New England states that: are located in and directly benefit one or more EPA-designated "Target Investment Areas," "Environmental Justice Areas of Potential Concern," "Places with High Risks from Toxic Air Pollution," "Sensitive Populations," or "Urban Areas;" and, that will achieve measurable environmental and public health results as defined by EPA. Current program priorities include projects involving asthma, capacity building, healthy indoor/outdoor environments, healthy schools, preserving and restoring urban natural resources and open/green space, smart growth, and water quality monitoring or analyses. Projects may provide or support educational opportunities for students, interns, or citizens to learn more about science, biology, and water quality monitoring.

Eligible applicants/beneficiaries: for activities only within the New England states—local public, private, quasi-public nonprofit institutions and organizations; tribal governments; K-12 schools or school districts; grass-roots and community-based organizations; IHEs with substantial community involvement.

Range: $17,000 to $25,000. **Average:** $24,331.

Activity: N.A.

HQ: Region 1-EPA, 1 Congress St., Ste. 1100, Boston, MA 02114. Phone: (617) 918-1797.

Internet: www.epa.gov/region01/index.html.

66.121   PUGET SOUND PROTECTION AND RESTORATION: TRIBAL IMPLEMENTATION ASSISTANCE PROGRAM

Assistance: cooperative agreements (50 to100 percent).

Purposes: pursuant to the Omnibus Appropriations Act of 2009, to restore and maintain the Puget Sound estuarine environment by 2020 so that it will support balanced indigenous populations of shellfish, fish (especially salmon) and wildlife and support the extensive list of recognized uses of Puget Sound. Continued funding is provided to support each tribe and consortium to participate in the Puget Sound Management Conference.

Eligible applicants: federally-recognized tribes or consortia of tribes and eligible intertribal consortia within the greater Puget Sound Basin.

Eligible beneficiaries: federally-recognized tribes or consortia of tribes and general public within the greater Puget Sound Basin.

Range: $150,000 to $160,563. **Average:** N.A.

Activity: 11 awards in FY 2014.

HQ: Director, Puget Sound Team, Office of Ecosystems, Tribal and Public Affairs, EPA Region 10, 1200 Sixth Ave., Suite 900, ETPA-086, Seattle, WA 98101. Phone: (206) 553-0332.

Internet: www.epa.gov/pugetsound/funding/index.html.

66.122 PUGET SOUND ACTION AGENDA OUTREACH, EDUCATION AND STEWARDSHIP SUPPORT PROGRAM

Assistance: cooperative agreements (to 5 years).

Purposes: pursuant to the Omnibus Appropriations Act of 2009 and the Clean Water Act, the Puget Sound National Estuary Program's approved Comprehensive Conservation and Management Plan (CCMP) has a goal to restore and maintain the Puget Sound estuary's environment by 2020, thus assuring protection of public water supplies, protection and propagation of a balanced, indigenous population of shellfish, fish and wildlife, and recreational activities in and on the water.

Eligible applicants/beneficiaries: 35 IHEs selected by the CDC as Prevention Research Centers (PRCs).

Range/Average: N.A.

Activity: N.A.

HQ: Director, Puget Sound Team, Office of Ecosystems, Tribal and Public Affairs, EPA Region 10, 1200 Sixth Ave., Suite 900, ETPA-086, Seattle, WA 98101. Phone: (206) 553-0332.

Internet: www.epa.gov/pugetsound/funding/index.html.

66.123 PUGET SOUND ACTION AGENDA: TECHNICAL INVESTIGATIONS AND IMPLEMENTATION ASSISTANCE PROGRAM

Assistance: cooperative agreements (50 to 100 percent).

Purposes: pursuant to the Clean Water Act, to implement the 2020 Action Agenda for Puget Sound, including development and implementation of programs that will improve water and air quality and minimize the adverse impacts of rapid development in the Puget Sound Basin, including activities linked to nonpoint sources or habitat restoration projects.

Eligible applicants/beneficiaries: 35 IHEs selected by the CDC as Prevention Research Centers (PRCs).

Range/Average: N.A.

Activity: 4 awards.

HQ: Director, Puget Sound Team, Office of Ecosystems, Tribal and Public Affairs, EPA Region 10, 1200 Sixth Ave., Suite 900, ETPA-086, Seattle, WA 98101. Phone: (206) 553-0332.

Internet: www.epa.gov/pugetsound/funding/index.html.

66.124 COASTAL WETLANDS PLANNING PROTECTION AND RESTORATION ACT
("CWPPRA -The Breaux Act")

Assistance: cooperative agreements (85 to 90 percent).

Purposes: pursuant to the Clean Water Act, to assist the state and local governments and IHEs in planning and implementing projects that create, protect, restore and enhance wetlands in coastal Louisiana through strategic "natural" reintroduction of river water, barrier island/shoreline restoration and application of innovative technologies such as pipeline delivery of new sediment.

Eligible applicants/beneficiaries: 35 IHEs selected by the CDC as Prevention Research Centers (PRCs).

Range: $100,000 to $300,000. **Average:** N.A.

Activity: 1 award in FY 2014.

HQ: Project Director, 6WQ-AT, EPA Region 6, 1445 Ross Ave., Dallas, TX 75202. Phone: (214) 665-7187.

Internet: www.epa.gov/region6/water/at/sttribal.htm.

66.126   THE SAN FRANCISCO BAY WATER QUALITY IMPROVEMENT FUND ("SF Bay Grant Program")

Assistance: project grants (50 percent/3-4 years).

Purposes: pursuant to the Clean Water Act, to protect and restore the water quality and aquatic habitat of the San Francisco Bay and its watersheds through comprehensive watershed management.

Eligible applicants/beneficiaries: state, local government agencies, districts, and councils; regional water pollution control agencies and entities; State coastal zone management agencies; and public and private universities and colleges, public or private non-governmental, and non-profit institutions.

Range: $200,000 to $5,000,000. **Average:** $2,000,000.

Activity: N.A.

HQ: Director, USEPA Region 9, 75 Hawthorne St., San Francisco, CA 94105. Phone: (415) 972-3400.

Internet: www2.epa.gov/sfbay-delta/sf-bay-water-quality-improvement-fund.

66.128   SOUTHEASTERN MULTI-MEDIA AND GEOGRAPHIC PRIORITY PROJECTS

Assistance: project grants (100 percent).

Purposes: pursuant to the Pollution Prevention Act, to fund projects (including surveys, studies, investigations, demonstrations, training, outreach, human health and the environment) to prevent, reduce and eliminate pollution through the promotion of environmental sustainability; build capacity on environmental sustainability and public health issues; support the development and implementation of sustainability strategies and enhance environmental literacy; promote coordination and collaboration between and among federal, state, and local governmental and non-governmental organizations as well as build environmental education capacity at institutions of higher education.

Eligible applicants/beneficiaries: interstate, state, tribal, intrastate, and local government agencies, districts, and councils; public and private universities and colleges, laboratories, and research facilities; and public or private non-governmental, non-profit institutions.

Range: N.A. **Average:** $15,000.

Activity: N.A.

HQ: Director, Office of the Regional Administrator, Region 4, U.S. Environmental Protection Agency, 61 Forsyth St., SW, Atlanta, GA 30303. Phone: (404) 562-8976.

Internet: www2.epa.gov/aboutepa/about-epa-region-4-southeast.

66.129 SOUTHEAST NEW ENGLAND COASTAL WATERSHED RESTORATION

Assistance: cooperative agreements. (100 percent).

Purposes: pursuant to the Consolidation and Further Continuing Appropriations Act of 2016, to develop and support the Southeast New England Program (SNEP) for coastal watershed restoration. Funding priority will be projects that protect, improve, or restore water quality through innovative projects and partnerships that address nutrients in coastal ecosystems; integrate habitat and ecological restoration with water quality improvement; develop and invest in innovative, cost-effective restoration and protection practices; identify and sustain ecosystem services and functions; and/or contribute directly or indirectly to increased regional ecosystem resiliency.

Eligible applicants/beneficiaries: state, local, tribal, and territorial governments, nonprofit institutions/organizations, and IHEs.

Range: $250,000 to $1,000,000. **Average:** $500,000.

Activity: N.A.

HQ: EPA, 1200 Penn Ave., NW, Washington, DC 20460. Phone: (202) 564-6004.

Internet: www.epa.gov/region1.

66.202 CONGRESSIONALLY MANDATED PROJECTS ("Congressional Earmarks")

Assistance: project grants.

Purposes: for investigations, experiments, training, demonstrations, and surveys directed by Congress in the EPA annual appropriation or in the annual Appropriations Conference Report—pertaining to activities within EPA's broad purview.

Eligible applicants/beneficiaries: as designated by Congress.

Range/Average: N.A.

Activity: N.A.

HQ: USEPA, 1200 Pennsylvania Ave., NW, Mail Code: 2732A , Washington, DC 20460. Phone: (202) 564-1230.

Internet: www.epa.gov/ocfo/budget/index.htm.

66.203 ENVIRONMENTAL FINANCE CENTER GRANTS ("EFC Grant Program")

Assistance: project grants (100 percent/1-7 years).

Purposes: pursuant to Clean Water Act, SDWA, SWDA, Clean Air Act and others as amended, to provide education, technical assistance, and analytical support to state and local officials and businesses to address the growing costs of environmental protection. Certain activities may not be funded under this program, including: fundraising costs, research within the purview of the EPA's Office of Research and Development, activities associated with brownfield sites. Cost sharing may be required when specified in the announcement for competitive funding opportunity. Starting in FY 2010, the EPA plans to open this program up to competition.

Eligible applicants: public and private nonprofit universities and colleges, nonprofit organizations.

Eligible beneficiaries: anyone/general public.

Range: N.A. **Average:** $125,000.

Activity: N.A.

HQ: Grants and Interagency Agreements Management Division, Environmental Protection Agency, 1200 Pennsylvania Ave., NW - 3903R, Washington, DC 20460. Phone: (202) 564-4996; FAX: (202) 564-2587.

Internet: www2.epa.gov.

66.305 COMPLIANCE ASSISTANCE SUPPORT FOR SERVICES TO THE REGULATED COMMUNITY AND OTHER ASSISTANCE PROVIDERS ("Compliance Assistance Centers")

Assistance: project grants. (to 100 percent/to 5 years).

Purposes: pursuant to SWDA as amended and RCRA, to develop projects to improve environmental compliance within identified commercial or industrial sectors. Funds may be used to create compliance assistance tools utilizing industry and commercial communication channels to deliver the assistance tools, including internet communications, toll-free telephone assistance lines, satellite training, other interactive technologies.

Eligible applicants/beneficiaries: nonprofit organizations, IHEs, and state, local, and tribal governments.

Range: $5,000 to $110,000. **Average:** $27,000.

Activity: N.A.

HQ: USEPA Headquarters, Ariel Rios Bldg., 1200 Pennsylvania Ave., NW, Mail Code: 2224 , Washington, DC 20460. Phone: (202) 564-7076.

Internet: epa.gov/compliance/assistance/centers/index.html.

66.309 SURVEYS, STUDIES, INVESTIGATIONS, TRAINING AND SPECIAL PURPOSE ACTIVITIES RELATING TO ENVIRONMENTAL JUSTICE ("EJSS")

Assistance: project grants (100 percent/1-5 years).

Purposes: pursuant to the CWA, SDWA, SWDA, CAA, TSCA, FIFRA, MPRSA, and CERCLA, for surveys, studies, investigations, and special activities addressing broad environmental and public health issues, emphasizing environmental justice.

Eligible applicants/beneficiaries: states, territories, possessions, tribes and public and private IHEs, hospitals, libraries, and other institutions.

Range: $15,000 to $450,000. **Average:** $25,000

Activity: 2 awards in FY 2015.

HQ: Office of Environmental Justice, 1200 Pennsylvania Ave., NW, Mail Code 2201A, Washington, DC 20460. Phone: (202) 564-0152.

Internet: www.epa.gov/environmentaljustice.

66.310 CAPACITY BUILDING GRANTS AND COOPERATIVE AGREEMENTS FOR COMPLIANCE ASSURANCE AND ENFORCEMENT ACTIVITIES IN INDIAN COUNTRY AND OTHER TRIBAL AREAS

Assistance: project grants. (100 percent/multi-year).

Purposes: pursuant to CWA, FIFRA, CAA, SWDA, SDWA, TSCA, MPRSA, National Environmental Policy Act, and Indian Environmental General Assistance Program Act, to build and improve the capacity to foster environmental enforcement and compliance assurance activities in Indian country and other tribal areas including in Alaska. Eligible project activities include: inspections; assessment; surveys; performance measurement; data quality improvement; enforcement; training including through fellowships, scholarships, traineeships, conferences, and technical assistance; experiments and demonstrations; construction; dissemination and information exchange. Funds should support activities directly related to the National Tribal Compliance Assurance Priority and other specified priorities in Indian country.

Eligible applicants/beneficiaries: responsible tribal, federal, and state organizations; consortia.

Range: $3,000 to $40,000. Average: N.A.

Activity: N.A.

HQ: Office of Compliance, OECA-EPA, 1200 Pennsylvania Ave., NW, Washington, DC 20460. Phone: (202) 564-2516.

Internet: www.epa.gov/compliance/state/grants/index.html.

66.418 CONSTRUCTION GRANTS FOR WASTEWATER TREATMENT WORKS

Assistance: project grants (55-85 percent; insular areas, 100 percent).

Purposes: pursuant to ARRA 2009 and CWA as amended, for construction of municipal wastewater treatment works, including privately owned individual systems, required to meet state or federal water quality standards. Projects may include industrial wastes, provided pretreatment or entry prevention into funded projects is included. Users must be charged.

Eligible applicants/beneficiaries: any municipal, intermunicipal, state, or interstate agency; Indian tribal governments. Also available to each U.S. territory and possession. (Currently, only DC, VI, and Outer Pacific Islands being newly funded; others apply to state revolving funds—see 66.458.

Range: $100,000 to $10,000,000. Average: $5,000,000.

Activity: anticipate 10 awards in FY 2015.

HQ: Municipal Assistance Branch (4204M), Municipal Support Division, Office of Wastewater Management, OW-EPA, 1200 Pennsylvania Ave., NW, Washington, DC 20460. Phone: (202) 564-6186.

Internet: water.epa.gov/grants_funding.

66.419   WATER POLLUTION CONTROL STATE, INTERSTATE, AND TRIBAL PROGRAM SUPPORT ("106 Grants")

Assistance: formula (matching).

Purposes: pursuant to CWA as amended, for activities to prevent and abate surface- and groundwater pollution from point and nonpoint sources, including: planning, monitoring, assessments, permitting, studies, surveillance and enforcement, training, technical assistance, and public information; restoration of impaired watersheds. Funds may not be used for waste treatment plant construction, operation, or maintenance.

Eligible applicants/beneficiaries: state, interstate, tribal, and territorial agencies.

Range: $30,000 to $11,854,000. **Average:** $5,000,000.

Activity: N.A.

HQ: State, Interstate and Tribal Coordinator, Office of Wastewater Management (4201M), OW-EPA, 1200 Pennsylvania Ave., NW, Washington, DC 20460. Phone: (202) 564-3880; FAX: (202) 501-2399.

Internet: www2.epa.gov/water-pollution-control-section.

66.424   SURVEYS, STUDIES, INVESTIGATIONS, DEMONSTRATIONS, AND TRAINING GRANTS—SECTION 1442 OF THE SAFE DRINKING WATER ACT

Assistance: project grants.

Purposes: pursuant to SDWA Section 1442 as amended, to support research, studies, and demonstrations associated with source water and drinking water; to develop and expand capabilities of pertinent programs. Priorities include: contaminants in drinking water; source water protection and treatment methods; measures to protect water quality in the distribution system and at the tap; tribal source water program support; tribal operator certification program; tribal capacity development; tribal administration of the Drinking Water Infrastructure Grants to identify health effects associated with drinking water contaminants.

Eligible applicants/beneficiaries: states, territories and possessions, tribes, IHEs, hospitals, laboratories, other public and private nonprofit institutions, and individuals.

Range: $300,000 to $6,900,000. **Average:** $1,150,000.

Activity: N.A.

HQ: *Program information,* Office of Groundwater and Drinking Water (4604M), OW-EPA, 1200 Pennsylvania Ave., NW, Washington, DC 20460. Phone: (202) 564-3817.

Internet: water.epa.gov/drink/index.cfm.

66.432   STATE PUBLIC WATER SYSTEM SUPERVISION

Assistance: formula grants (75 percent).

Purposes: pursuant to the Public Health Service Act (PHSA), SDWA, and amendments, to develop and implement programs implementing public water system supervision adequate to enforce SDWA provisions, including program plan development, adoption of applicable regulations, data management, system inventories, public participation, technical assistance, laboratory certification, and enforcement.

Eligible applicants/beneficiaries: state agencies, territories and possessions, tribes treated as states.

Range: $120,000 to $6,591,000. **Average:** $1,534,758.

Activity: 55 awards in FY 2014.

HQ: Office of Ground Water and Drinking Water (4606M), OW-EPA, Washington, DC 20460. Phone: (202) 564-4588.

Internet: www.epa.gov/safewater/pws/pwsgrant.html.

66.433 STATE UNDERGROUND WATER SOURCE PROTECTION

Assistance: formula grants (75 percent; tribes, 90 percent).

Purposes: pursuant to SDWA and amendments, to develop and implement underground injection control programs. Funds may be used for such purposes as state regulation review, plan development, data management, inventory of injection facilities, identification of aquifers, technical assistance, public participation, enforcement activities.

Eligible applicants/beneficiaries: states, tribes.

Range: $13,000 to $973,000. **Average:** $176,000.

Activity: N.A.

HQ: Prevention Branch, Drinking Water Protection Division (4606M), Office of Ground Water and Drinking Water, OW-EPA, 1200 Pennsylvania Ave., NW, Washington, DC 20460. Phone: (202) 564-3879.

Internet: water.epa.gov/type/groundwater/uic/grants.cfm.

66.436 SURVEYS, STUDIES, INVESTIGATIONS, DEMONSTRATIONS, AND TRAINING GRANTS AND COOPERATIVE AGREEMENTS—SECTION 104(B)(3) OF THE CLEAN WATER ACT

Assistance: project grants.

Purposes: pursuant to CWA Section 104(b)(3) as amended, for coordination and acceleration of research, investigations, experiments, training, demonstrations, surveys, and studies relating to the causes, effects including health and welfare effects, extent, prevention, reduction, and elimination of water pollution. Priorities include: water quality improvement, watersheds management, aquatic ecosystem restoration, pollutant trading, fish contamination and consumption, nonpoint source management, wetlands protection, coastal and estuarine management, treatment technologies, and environmental management systems. Project examples: watershed education program for broadcast meteorologists; atmospheric mercury deposition study; watershed protection and restoration guides.

Eligible applicants/beneficiaries: states, territories and possessions, tribes, IHEs, hospitals, laboratories, other public and private nonprofit institutions, and individuals.

Range: $10,000 to $580,000. **Average:** $295,000.

Activity: 10 awards in FY 2014.

HQ: Office of Groundwater and Drinking Water (3903R), OW-EPA,1200 Pennsylvania Ave., NW, Washington, DC 20460. Phone: (202) 564-0783.

Internet: water.epa.gov/grants_funding.

66.437   LONG ISLAND SOUND PROGRAM ("LISS")

Assistance: project grants (50-95 percent).

Purposes: pursuant to CWA as amended by the Long Island Sound Restoration Act of 2000, to implement elements of the Long Island Sound Study (LISS) Comprehensive Conservation and Management Plan (CCMP), with special emphasis on implementation projects, research and planning, enforcement, and citizen involvement and education projects.

Eligible applicants/beneficiaries: state, interstate, and regional water control agencies and organizations.

Range: $20,000 to $1,432,877. **Average:** $438,611.

Activity: N.A.

HQ: Ocean and Coastal Protection Division, Office of Wetlands, Oceans and Watersheds, OW-EPA, (MC 5404T); 1200 Pennsylvania Ave., NW, Washington, DC 20460. Phone: (202) 566-1200; FAX: (202) 566-1334.

Internet: longislandsoundstudy.net.

66.439   TARGETED WATERSHEDS GRANTS

Assistance: project grants (75 percent; tribes, to 100 percent).

Purposes: pursuant to CWA as amended, for watershed partnerships to develop innovative, community-based approaches aimed at preventing, reducing, or eliminating water pollution—involving local, state, tribal, and interstate agencies and other public or nonprofit organizations. Funds may be used for research, investigations, experiments, training, demonstrations, surveys, and studies.

Eligible applicants/beneficiaries: state, local, interstate, public agencies; private nonprofit institutions and organizations; tribal governments; territories, possessions; IHEs, individuals.

Range: $400,000 to $900,000 for national targeted watersheds; $90,000 to $280,000 for western estuaries. **Average:** $650,000 for national targeted watersheds; $185,000 for western estuaries; $600,000 for urban waters.

Activity: N.A.

HQ: Office of Wetlands, Oceans, and Watersheds, OW-EPA, MC 4501T, 1200 Pennsylvania Ave. NW, Washington DC, 20460. Phone: (202) 566-5382; FAX: (202) 566-1326.

Internet: water.epa.gov/grants_funding/twg/initiative_index.cfm.

66.440   URBAN WATERS SMALL GRANTS

Assistance: project grants (100 percent).

Purposes: pursuant to the National Environmental Policy Act, to fund projects that will foster a comprehensive understanding of local urban water issues, identify and address these issues at the local level, and educate and empower the community. Seeks to help restore and protect urban water quality and revitalize adjacent neighborhoods by engaging communities in activities that increase their connection to, understanding of, and stewardship of local urban waterways.

Eligible applicants/beneficiaries: residents of urban areas adversely impacted by water pollution, State and local governments, U.S. territories and possessions, Indian Tribes, other public and private nonprofit institutions, intertribal consortia, and interstate agencies.

Range: $40,000 to $60,000. **Average:** $50,000.

Activity: N.A.

HQ: Director, Office of the Assistant Administrator (Mail Code 4101M), Office of Water, U.S. Environmental Protection Agency, Washington, DC 20460. Phone: (202) 566-0730.

Internet: www.epa.gov/urbanwaters. (Note: no field offices for this program.)

66.454 WATER QUALITY MANAGEMENT PLANNING ("Section 205(j)(2)")

Assistance: formula grants (100 percent).

Purposes: pursuant to ARRA 2009 and CWA as amended and Water Quality Act of 1987, for water quality management planning, with priority encouraged for watershed restoration. States must allocate 40 percent of funds to regional and interstate agencies. Program examples: performing waste load allocations; point and nonpoint source planning.

Eligible applicants/beneficiaries: state water quality management agencies.

Range: $100,000 to $1,563,000. **Average:** $273,000.

Activity: 56 awards in FY 2015.

HQ: Assessment and Watershed Protection Division (4503T), OW-EPA, 1200 Pennsylvania Ave., NW, Washington, DC 20004. Phone: (202) 566-1202.

Internet: water.epa.gov/aboutow/owow/funding.cfm.

66.456 NATIONAL ESTUARY PROGRAM (NEP)

Assistance: project grants (50-75 percent/to 3 years).

Purposes: pursuant to CWA as amended, to develop and implement comprehensive conservation and management plans to protect and restore the coastal resources of 28 estuaries holding priority for funding. Funds must be used to develop master environmental plans based on relationships between pollutant loading and ecological impacts.

Eligible applicants/beneficiaries: within the priority geographic areas— regional, interstate, state water pollution control agencies; state coastal zone management agencies; public or private nonprofit organizations; individuals.

Range: N.A. **Average:** $600,000.

Activity: N.A.

HQ: Chief, Coastal Management Branch, Oceans and Coastal Protection Division, Office of Wetlands, Oceans, and Watersheds (4504T), OW-EPA, Washington, DC 20460. Phone: (202) 566-1244; FAX: (202) 566-1336.

Internet: water.epa.gov/type/oceb/nep/index.cfm.

66.458 CAPITALIZATION GRANTS FOR CLEAN WATER STATE REVOLVING FUNDS
("CW State Revolving Fund")

Assistance: formula grants (80 percent).

Purposes: pursuant to ARRA 2009, CWA as amended and Water Quality Act of 1987, to establish state revolving loan funds to finance wastewater treatment facilities and other water quality management activities. Capitalization grants deposited in the revolving funds may be used to provide loans to finance construction of publicly owned wastewater treatment works, to execute a nonpoint source management program, and to develop and execute estuary conservation and management plans.

Eligible applicants: states, PR; (DC, possessions, tribes and territorial agencies use **66.418**.)

Eligible beneficiaries: loans from revolving funds—community, intermunicipal, interstate, and tribal agencies.

Range: $6,500,000 to $147,000,000. Average: $26,000,000.

Activity: 51 awards in FY 2014.

HQ: State Revolving Fund Branch, Municipal Support Division (4204M), Office of Wastewater Management, OW-EPA, 1200 Pennsylvania Ave., NW, Washington, DC 20460. Phone: (202) 564-0686; FAX: (202) 501-2403.

Internet: water.epa.gov/grants_funding/cwsrf/cwsrf_index.cfm.

66.460 NONPOINT SOURCE IMPLEMENTATION GRANTS
("319 Program")

Assistance: formula grants (60-90 percent).

Purposes: pursuant to Clean Water Act, Title III, to assist in implementing EPA-approved Section 319 nonpoint source management programs that promote the development and implementation of watershed-based plans, focusing on watersheds with water quality impairments caused by nonpoint sources, which result in improved water quality in impaired waters.

Eligible applicants/beneficiaries: states (including DC, VI, PR, American Samoa, Northern Marianas, Pacific Trust Territories), tribes and intertribal consortia.

Range: $30,000 to $8,361,000. Average: N.A.

Activity: 56 awards in FY 2014.

HQ: Assessment and Watershed Protection Division, Nonpoint Source Control Branch, Office of Wetlands, Oceans and Watersheds (4503T), EPA, Ariel Rios Bldg, 1200 Pennsylvania Ave., NW, Washington, DC 20460. Phone: (202) 566-0340; FAX: (202) 566-1333.

Internet: water.epa.gov/polwaste/nps/index.cfm.

66.461 REGIONAL WETLAND PROGRAM DEVELOPMENT GRANTS

Assistance: project grants (75 percent).

Purposes: pursuant to CWA as amended, to develop new or enhance existing regional wetlands protection management and restoration programs, with priority to: strengthening comprehensiveness of programs; monitoring and assessment; compensatory mitigation; protection of vulnerable wetlands and aquatic resources. Funds may support research, investigations, experiments, training, demonstrations, surveys, and studies—relating to the causes, effects, extent, prevention, reduction and elimination of water pollution.

Eligible applicants/beneficiaries: appropriate state, interstate, and local agencies—including those involved with wetlands or water quality regulation, planning offices, wild and scenic rivers, fish and wildlife, agriculture and transportation departments, coastal zone management, similar functions; inter-tribal consortia; IHEs that are agencies of the state.

Range: $20,000 to $600,000. **Average:** $220,000.

Activity: N.A.

HQ: Wetlands Division, Office of Wetlands, Oceans and Watersheds (4502T), OW-EPA, 1200 Pennsylvania Ave., NW, Washington, DC 20460. Phone: (202) 566-1225.

Internet: water.epa.gov/type/wetlands/initiative_index.cfm.

66.462 NATIONAL WETLAND PROGRAM DEVELOPMENT GRANTS AND FIVE-STAR RESTORATION TRAINING GRANT

Assistance: project grants (to 75 percent).

Purposes: pursuant to CWA as amended, for comprehensive national wetlands program development by promoting the coordination and acceleration of research, investigations, experiments, training, and studies—relating to the causes, effects, extent, prevention, reduction and elimination of water pollution. Projects also may involve such activities as training and information dissemination.

Eligible applicants/beneficiaries: nonprofit, nongovernmental capable of advancing programs on a national basis; interstate and intertribal agencies.

Range: $75,000 to $300,000 for wetlands development every 2 years. **Average:** $160,500 for wetlands development every 2 years; $1,000,000 for restoration training every 4 years.

Activity: 7 awards in FY 2014.

HQ: Wetlands Division, Office of Wetlands, Oceans and Watersheds (4502T), OW-EPA, 1200 Pennsylvania Ave. NW, Washington, DC 20460 Phone: (202) 566-1225.

Internet: water.epa.gov/type/wetlands/index.cfm. (Note: no field offices for this program.)

66.466 CHESAPEAKE BAY PROGRAM

Assistance: project grants (50-95 percent).

Purposes: pursuant to CWA, for research, experiments, investigations, training, demonstrations, surveys, or studies related to reducing pollution and improving the quality of living resources in the Chesapeake Bay; for the implementation of Chesapeake Bay interstate management programs; for small watershed grants to local organizations to build citizen-based stewardship. Project examples: nonpoint source implementation programs; biological nutrient removal; living resources restoration studies and surveys; mainstem monitoring.

Eligible applicants/beneficiaries: within the Chesapeake Bay basin—state and local governments, interstate agencies, IHEs, other nonprofit organizations, individuals.

Range: $73,333 to $10,000,000. **Average:** $1,100,000.

Activity: 9 new awards and 45 existing projects funded in FY 2014.

HQ: EPA Chesapeake Bay Program Office, 410 Severn Ave., Suite 112, Annapolis, Maryland 21403. Phone: 410-267-5743; FAX: 410-267-5777.

Internet: www.epa.gov/region03/chesapeake.

66.467 WASTEWATER OPERATOR TRAINING GRANT PROGRAM—TECHNICAL ASSISTANCE

Assistance: project grants. (75 percent/to 3 years).

Purposes: pursuant to the Federal Water Pollution Control Act as amended, to provide on-site technical assistance to operations and maintenance (O&M) personnel at publicly owned wastewater treatment works, as well as classroom training.

Eligible applicants/beneficiaries: state agencies; possessions, territories, and tribes; state-designated nonprofit agencies.

Range: $12,000 to $40,000. **Average:** $25,000.

Activity: N.A.

HQ: Office of Wastewater Management (4204M), OW-EPA, 1200 Pennsylvania Ave NW, Washington, DC 20460. Phone: (202) 564-0634.

Internet: water.epa.gov/type/watersheds/wastewater/training.cfm.

66.468 CAPITALIZATION GRANTS FOR DRINKING WATER STATE REVOLVING FUND (DWSRF)

Assistance: formula grants (80 percent).

Purposes: pursuant to ARRA 2009 and SDWA Amendments of 1966, to capitalize DWSRFs to finance infrastructure needed to achieve and maintain compliance with SDWA requirements, through loans or other assistance; to establish new programs to prevent contamination through source water protection and enhanced water systems management.

Eligible applicants: capitalization grants—states, PR. Direct grants—DC, territories, tribes.

Eligible beneficiaries: loans—public, private, or nonprofit community drinking water systems.

Range/Average: N.A.

Activity: N.A.

HQ: Infrastructure Branch (4606M), Drinking Water Protection Division, Office of Groundwater and Drinking Water, OW-EPA, 1200 Pennsylvania Ave., NW, Washington, DC 20460. Phone: (202) 564-3848; FAX: (202) 564-1836.

Internet: water.epa.gov/drink/index.cfm.

66.469 GREAT LAKES PROGRAM ("GLNPO")

Assistance: project grants; use of property, facilities, and equipment; technical information. (grants, 65-100 percent/grants, 1-2 years).

Purposes: pursuant to CWA, to restore and maintain the chemical, physical, and biological integrity of the Great Lakes Basin Ecosystem. Funds may be used for such activities as surveys, research, experiments, training, studies, and demonstrations relating to: contaminated sediment remediation; pollution prevention, reduction, or elimination; habitat protection and restoration; invasive aquatic and terrestrial species, emphasizing prevention; and, similar efforts. Great Lakes Legacy Act projects, requiring a 35 percent match, entail cooperative agreements for contaminant remediation.

Eligible applicants/beneficiaries: state water pollution control agencies; interstate and other public and private nonprofit agencies; institutions; organizations; tribes; individuals.

Range: $8,000 to $5,900,000. **Average:** $600,000.

Activity: N.A.

HQ: Great Lakes National Program Office (G-17J), OW-EPA, 77 W. Jackson Blvd., Chicago, IL 60604-3590. Phone: (312) 886-4013.

Internet: www.epa.gov/glnpo/fund.

66.472 BEACH MONITORING AND NOTIFICATION PROGRAM IMPLEMENTATION GRANTS ("BEACH Act Program")

Assistance: project grants.

Purposes: pursuant to CWA as amended and Beaches Environmental Assessment and Coastal Health Act of 2000, to develop and implement water quality monitoring and public notification programs for coastal recreation waters adjacent to beaches or similar points of public access— including developing protocols, public outreach and education to users.

Eligible applicants/beneficiaries: coastal and Great Lakes states, territories, tribes. Local governments may receive grants after the first year of program operation.

Range: $150,000 to $516,000. **Average:** $280,000.

Activity: N.A.

HQ: OW-EPA (4305T), 1200 Pennsylvania Ave., NW, Washington, DC 20460. Phone: (202) 566-0387; FAX: (202) 566-0409.

Internet: www.epa.gov/waterscience/beaches.

66.473 DIRECT IMPLEMENTATION TRIBAL COOPERATIVE AGREEMENTS (DITCA)

Assistance: project grants. (100 percent/1-3 years).

Purposes: to build tribal capacity to carry out EPA-approved environmental programs for tribes, including such activities as developing protocols for interfacing inspections, permit and enforcement actions, training tribal employees to receive federal credentials.

Eligible applicants/beneficiaries: tribes and inter-tribal consortia.

Range: $10,000 and $100,000. **Average:** $55,000.

Activity: 13 awards in FY 2014.

HQ: American Indian Environmental Office (2690M), OW-EPA, 1200 Pennsylvania Ave., NW, Washington, DC 20460. Phone: (202) 564-0292.

Internet: www.epa.gov/indian/index.htm.

66.474 WATER PROTECTION GRANTS TO THE STATES

Assistance: formula grants (from 1 year).

Purposes: pursuant to SDWA and Department of Defense and Emergency Supplemental Appropriations for Recovery from and Response to Terrorist Acts on the Unites States Act of 2002, for coordination of protection activities pertaining to critical water infrastructure, including work with water utilities and local, state, and federal agencies. Funded activities may include vulnerability assessments and related security enhancements, communications improvement, duty officer programs, toll-free numbers, emergency response and recovery planning, technical assistance, training, and education.

Eligible applicants/beneficiaries: states, tribes, territories, possessions.

Range/Average: N.A.

Activity: N.A.

HQ: Water Security Division (Mail Code 140), U.S. EPA, (4608T), 1200 Pennsylvania Ave., NW, Washington, DC 20460. Phone: (202) 564-4189; FAX: (202) 566-0055.

Internet: water.epa.gov/infrastructure/watersecurity/funding/index.cfm.

66.475 GULF OF MEXICO PROGRAM

Assistance: project grants.

Purposes: pursuant to CWA, to expand and strengthen cooperative efforts to restore and protect the health and productivity of the Gulf of Mexico and its region—including activities in the Mississippi River Basin designed to reduce Gulf hypoxia. Funded activities may include surveys, studies, investigations, research, and demonstrations that are approved by the Gulf of Mexico Program Office. Project examples include: implementation of restoration actions for impaired coastal segments; shellfish habitat restoration; water quality monitoring; characterization of mercury data.

Eligible applicants/beneficiaries: state and local governments, interstate agencies, tribes, IHEs, individuals, and other public or nonprofit organizations.

Range: $30,000 to $300,000. **Average:** $165,000.

Activity: anticipate 15 awards in FY 2015.

HQ: EPA/Gulf of Mexico Program Office, Mail Code EPA/GMPO, Stennis Space Cntr., MS 39529. Phone: (228) 688-1281; FAX: (228) 688-2709.

Internet: www.epa.gov/gmpo.

66.481   LAKE CHAMPLAIN BASIN PROGRAM

Assistance: project grants (75 percent).

Purposes: pursuant to CWA as amended, to assist the states of New York and Vermont in protecting and preserving the "Lake Champlain ecosystem, through implementation of elements of the Lake Champlain Basin Management Plan, Opportunities for Action." Funds may be used to assist research, surveys, studies, modeling, technical, field, restoration, and other supporting work.

Eligible applicants/beneficiaries: state, interstate, and regional water pollution control agencies; public or nonprofit agencies and organizations. (Awards are made in consultation with the Lake Champlain Program Steering Committee.)

Range: $20,000 to $2,712,841. **Average:** $1,356,421.

Activity: N.A.

HQ: US EPA Region 1, 5 Post Office Square, Ste. 100, Mail Code OEP 6-1, Boston, MA 02109. Phone: (617) 918-1686; FAX: (617) 918-0686.

Internet: www.epa.gov/NE/eco/lakechamplain/index.html.

66.508   SENIOR ENVIRONMENTAL EMPLOYMENT PROGRAM (SEE)

Assistance: project grants (100 percent/1-3 years).

Purposes: pursuant to the Environmental Programs Assistance Act of 1984, to employ older Americans in temporary full- or part- time jobs to provide technical assistance in pollution prevention, abatement, and control projects. Funded project examples: nonagricultural pesticide surveys; monitoring asbestos compliance in schools; research, general administrative, and clerical tasks; review and monitoring of the import car program.

Eligible applicants: nonprofit organizations designated by DOL under the Older Americans Act of 1965.

Eligible beneficiaries: federal, state, and local environmental agencies; individuals age 55 or older.

Range: $1,543 to $1,994,761. **Average:** $998,152.

Activity: 126 awards in FY 2015.

HQ: Director, SEE Program (3600A), Office of Administration and Resources Management, EPA, 1200 Pennsylvania Ave., NW, Washington, DC 20460. Phone: (202) 564-4390.

Internet: epa.gov/epahrist/see/brochure.

66.509   SCIENCE TO ACHIEVE RESULTS (STAR) RESEARCH PROGRAM

Assistance: project grants (2-5 years).

Purposes: pursuant to CAA, CWA, SWDA, SDWA, FIFRA, and TSCA, for research: to determine the environmental and human health effects of air and water quality, hazardous waste, toxic substances, and pesticides; to identify, develop, and demonstrate effective pollution control techniques; to explore and develop strategies and mechanisms for use by those in economic, social, governmental, and environmental systems in decision-making. Support may be provided for environmental research centers. Awards are made only in response to requests for competitive proposals; unsolicited proposals are not accepted.

Eligible applicants/beneficiaries: U.S. IHEs, hospitals, and nonprofit organizations; state, local, tribal governments, territories, and possessions.

Range: $183,000 to $6,000,000. **Average:** $900,000.

Activity: anticipate 24 awards in FY 2015.

HQ: Grants Administration Division2777 Crystal Dr., Arlington, VA 22202. Phone: (703) 308-0442; FAX: (202) 233-0680.

Internet: www.epa.gov/ncer.

66.510 SURVEYS, STUDIES, INVESTIGATIONS AND SPECIAL PURPOSE GRANTS WITHIN THE OFFICE OF RESEARCH AND DEVELOPMENT

Assistance: project grants. (100 percent/to 5 years).

Purposes: pursuant to CAA, CWA, SWDA, RCRA, SDWA, FIFRA, TSCA, amendments, and MPRSA, to determine the environmental effects of air quality, drinking water, water quality, hazardous waste, toxic substances, and pesticides; to identify, develop, and demonstrate effective pollution control techniques. Generally, awards are made only in response to requests for competitive proposals, and unsolicited proposals are not funded.

Eligible applicants/beneficiaries: state, local, tribal governments and agencies; territories, possessions; IHEs, hospitals, laboratories, nonprofit organizations; individuals.

Range/Average: N.A.

Activity: anticipate 6 awards in FY 2015.

HQ: Office of Research and Development-EPA, 1200 Pennsylvania Ave., NW, Washington, DC 20460. *Applications, procedures information,* Phone: (202) 564-4763; FAX: (202) 565-2903.

Internet: www.epa.gov/ord/htm/grantopportunity.htm.

66.511 OFFICE OF RESEARCH AND DEVELOPMENT CONSOLIDATED RESEARCH/TRAINING

Assistance: project grants. (100 percent/to 5 years).

Purposes: pursuant to CAA, CWA, SWDA, RCRA, SDWA, FIFRA, TSCA, CERCLA, amendments, and MPRSA, for research and engineering to determine the environmental effects of air quality, drinking water, water quality, hazardous waste, toxic substances, and pesticides; to identify, develop, and demonstrate effective pollution control techniques; to perform risk assessments to characterize the potential adverse health effects of human exposures to environmental hazards—in broad areas such as environmental chemistry and physics, environmental engineering, health and ecological effects of pollution, environmental economics and decision sciences. Generally, unsolicited proposals are not funded.

Eligible applicants/beneficiaries: state, local, tribal governments and agencies; territories, possessions; IHEs, hospitals, laboratories, nonprofit organizations; individuals.

Range/Average: N.A.

Activity: anticipate 6 awards in FY 2015.

HQ: Office of Research and Development-EPA, 1201 Pennsylvania Ave., NW, MC: 8201R, Washington, DC 20460. Phone: (202) 564-4756.

Internet: www.epa.gov/ord/htm/grantopportunity.htm.

66.513 GREATER RESEARCH OPPORTUNITIES (GRO) FELLOWSHIPS FOR UNDERGRADUATE ENVIRONMENTAL STUDY

Assistance: project grants (100 percent).

Purposes: pursuant to CAA, CWA, SWDA, SDWA, TSCA, and FIFRA, to provide graduate and undergraduate fellowships in fields of study related to the environment, including environmental engineering, atmospheric sciences, geology, economics, geography, urban/regional planning, biochemistry, biological sciences, genetics, public health, ecological sciences, and related fields—to strengthen the research capacity especially of IHEs that receive limited funding in the field, including particularly institutions with substantial minority enrollment. Two years of study in specific disciplines may be supported for undergraduates and master's students; doctoral candidates, for three years. Awards are competitive.

Eligible applicants/beneficiaries: U.S. citizens and lawfully admitted permanent residents demonstrating high scientific ability.

Range: to $50,000 for life of fellowship. **Average:** N.A.

Activity: anticipate 13 awards in FY 2015.

HQ: *Grants management information*, USEPA, Potomac Yards South, 2777 Crystal Dr., Rm. S6336, Arlington, VA 22202. Phone: (703) 347-8083.

Internet: www.epa.gov/ncer.

66.514 SCIENCE TO ACHIEVE RESULTS (STAR) FELLOWSHIP PROGRAM ("STAR Program")

Assistance: project grants (100 percent).

Purposes: pursuant to CAA, CWA, SWDA, SDWA, TSCA, and FIFRA, to provide graduate fellowships in the fields of study cited under **66.514**. Two years of study may be supported for master's students; doctoral candidates, for three years. Awards are competitive.

Eligible applicants/beneficiaries: U.S. citizens and lawfully admitted permanent residents demonstrating high scientific ability.

Range: $55,000 to $126,000. **Average:** $80,000.

Activity: 100 awards in FY 2014.

HQ: USEPA, Potomac Yards South, 2777 Crystal Dr., Rm. S11772, Arlington, VA 22202. Phone: (703) 347-8053.

Internet: www.epa.gov/ncer.

66.516 P3 AWARD: NATIONAL STUDENT DESIGN COMPETITION FOR SUSTAINABILITY ("P3 Award")

Assistance: project grants.

Purposes: pursuant to CAA, CWA, SWDA, SDWA, TSCA, and FIFRA, for design projects in wide-ranging categories, conducted by interdisciplinary student teams to: define a technical challenge to environmental sustainability; discuss the relationship of the challenge to people, prosperity, and the planet; and, develop a design approach to address the challenge. Categories may include such topics as water quality and quantity, protection of ecosystem health, green chemistry and engineering, biotechnology, energy production and distribution, conservation of materials and energy, product design, mobility, information technology, and delivery of resources.

Eligible applicants/beneficiaries: teams of graduate and undergraduate students attending U.S. IHEs (*For additional details, see request for applications at web site*: http://www.epa.gov.ncer).

Range: $5,000 to $15,000 for Phase I; $87,000 to $90,000 for Phase II. Average: $14,750 for Phase I; $89,000 for Phase II.

Activity: N.A.

HQ: Grants Administration Division, USEPA Potomac Yards S, 2777 Crystal Dr., Rm. S11781, Arlington, VA 22202. Phone: (703) 347-8102.

Internet: www.epa.gov/ncer/p3.

66.517 REGIONAL APPLIED RESEARCH EFFORTS (RARE)

Assistance: project grants (to 5 years).

Purposes: pursuant to National Environmental Policy Act of 1969, Clean Air Act, Clean Water Act, Solid Waste Disposal Act, Resource Conservation and Recovery Act of 1976, Safe Drinking Water Act, and others, as amended, to determine the environmental effects of air quality, drinking water, water quality, hazardous waste, toxic substances, and pesticides and identify, develop, and demonstrate effective pollution control techniques. Some funding priorities for Fiscal Year 2007 include: conducting high priority air pollutants research, ecological risk assessment, water quality, watersheds and drinking water research, research to improve human health (including children's) risk assessment, pollution prevention and new technologies. Assistance agreement awards under this program may involve or relate to geospatial information (refer to http://geodata.epa.gov).

Eligible applicants/beneficiaries: states, territories and possessions, and U.S. Tribal nations, including DC, public and private state universities and colleges, hospitals, laboratories, state and local government departments, other public or private nonprofit institutions, and in some cases, individuals who have demonstrated unusually high scientific ability.

Range: to $60,000. **Average:** N.A.

Activity: N.A.

HQ: EPA, 1201 Pennsylvania Ave., Washington, DC 20460. Phone: (202) 564-5264.

Internet: www.epa.gov/osp/regions/rare.htm.

66.518 STATE SENIOR ENVIRONMENTAL EMPLOYMENT PROGRAM (SSEE)

Assistance: project grants (100 percent/1-3 years).

Purposes: pursuant to the Environmental Programs Assistance Act of 1984, for states to employ Americans, age 55 or older, in temporary full- or part-time positions to provide technical assistance to federal, state, and local environmental agencies for projects involving pollution prevention, abatement, and control—ranging from inspections of large capacity cesspools to clerical work for environmental staff offices.

Eligible applicants: private, nonprofit organizations designated by the DOL secretary under OAA.

Eligible beneficiaries: state environmental agencies; individuals age 55 or older.

Range: $61,000 to $280,000. **Average:** $170,500.

Activity: 4 awards in FY 2015.

HQ: Office of Human Resources, Program Management and Communications Staff, Office of Administration and Resources Management, EPA, 1200 Pennsylvania Ave, N.W., Washington, DC 20460. Phone: (202) 564-0410, (202) 564-4390.

Internet: epa.gov/see.

66.600 ENVIRONMENTAL PROTECTION CONSOLIDATED GRANTS FOR THE INSULAR AREAS—PROGRAM SUPPORT
("Consolidated Program Support Grants")

Assistance: project grants.

Purposes: pursuant to CAA, CWA, SWDA, RCRA, SDWA, FIFRA, SWDA, MPRSA, CERCLA, amendments, and other acts, to provide an alternative funding mechanism to territories and possessions within the purview of EPA Regions 2 and 9 to develop an integrated approach to pollution control programs, by consolidating activities funded under such programs as **66.001, 66.418, 66.419, 66.432, 66.433, 66.454, 66.468, 66.473, 66.700, 66.801.** Applicants eligible for two or more of the programs may consolidate applications into one, and receive a single total award. Funding for this program is the aggregate total of the programs that may be consolidated; it is not appropriated separately.

Eligible applicants/beneficiaries: agencies in territories and possessions within the purview of EPA Regions 2 and 9.

Range: $2,000,000 to $3,300,000. **Average:** N.A.

Activity: N.A.

HQ: Grants Management Office, USEPA Region 9, 75 Hawthorne St., San Francisco, CA 94105. Phone: (415) 972-3667.

Internet: www2.epa.gov/aboutepa/epa-region-9-pacific-southwest.

66.604 ENVIRONMENTAL JUSTICE SMALL GRANT PROGRAM (EJCGP)

Assistance: project grants. (100 percent/2 years).

Purposes: pursuant to pursuant to CWA, SDWA, SWDA, CAA, TSCA, FIFRA, MPRSA, AND CERCLA, to design, demonstrate, or disseminate practices, methods, or techniques related to environmental justice, including multi-media projects. Funding is available for activities that examine issues related to a community's exposure to multiple environmental harms and risks, extending to socio- economic, institutional, and public policy issues and the natural sciences. Research training may be supported. Ineligible uses of funds include: research related only to contamination from petroleum products unless other issues also are involved; organizational support; capacity building; program development; any construction activities; lobbying; underwriting legal actions.

Eligible applicants/beneficiaries: only affected nonprofit, incorporated community-based organizations unaffiliated with larger national, state, or regional organizations.

Range: $20,000 to $50,000. **Average:** $30,000.

Activity: anticipate 40 awards in FY 2015.

HQ: Office of Environmental Justice, 1200 Pennsylvania Ave., NW, Mail Code 2201A, Washington, DC 20460. Phone: (202) 564-0152.

Internet: www.epa.gov/compliance/environmentaljustice/grants/ej-smgrants .html.

66.605 PERFORMANCE PARTNERSHIP GRANTS (PPGs)

Assistance: formula grants; project grants.

Purposes: to provide an alternative assistance delivery mechanism giving grant recipients greater flexibility in addressing environmental priorities; to improve environmental performance; to achieve savings in administrative costs; and, to strengthen partnerships between EPA and grant recipients. For application and administrative purposes, recipients may combine two or more grant programs specifically identified by EPA. Funding for this program is included in the grant programs that may be involved; it is not appropriated separately.

Eligible applicants/beneficiaries: states, interstate agencies; territories; tribes—eligible to combine two or more of 20 specific EPA categorical grant programs.

Range/Average: N.A.

Activity: N.A.

HQ: Office of Congressional and Intergovernmental Relations (1306A), Office of the Administrator-EPA, 1200 Pennsylvania Ave., NW, Washington DC 20460. Phone: (202) 564-3792; FAX: (202) 501-1545; *tribes,* Office of Water, American Indian Environmental Office, Phone: (202) 564-3792.

Internet: www.epa.gov/ocir/nepps.

66.608 ENVIRONMENTAL INFORMATION EXCHANGE NETWORK GRANT PROGRAM AND RELATED ASSISTANCE

Assistance: project grants. (100 percent/2 years).

Purposes: to develop a nationwide Environmental Information Exchange Network, an internet- and standards-based information network—facilitating electronic reporting, exchange, and integration of environmental data from many sources, concerning the natural environment and related human health issues. Funds support development of: related information technology infrastructure and management capabilities; exchanging data with EPA and other users, through the development of data standards and formats; collaborative innovative projects address the business needs of government agencies at all levels.

Eligible applicants/beneficiaries: states, territories and possessions, tribes and tribal consortia; authorized regional air pollution control agencies.

Range/Average: N.A.

Activity: N.A.

HQ: Office of Environmental Information, Environmental Protection Agency, 1200 Pennsylvania Ave., NW, Mail Code (2823-T), Washington, DC 20460. Phone: (202) 566-1984.

Internet: N.A. (Note: no field offices for this program.)

66.609 PROTECTION OF CHILDREN FROM ENVIRONMENTAL HEALTH RISKS
("Children's Environmental Health")

Assistance: project grants (cost sharing/to 5 years).

Purposes: pursuant to CAA, CWA, SDWA, TSCA, SWDA, FIFRA, MPRSA, CERCLA, and National Environmental Policy Act, to reduce environmental health threats to children or the elderly, through such activities as: supporting efforts to create health school environments; building capacity to address childhood asthma and other children's environmental health issues, as well as to reduce environmental health hazards affecting older persons; implementing a National Agenda for the Environment and the Aging to help protect the health of older persons; civic engagement in pertinent activities and projects; related international efforts; public outreach and communications.

Eligible applicants/beneficiaries: states and state agencies, territories and possessions, tribes, IHEs, hospitals, laboratories, public and private nonprofit organizations.

Range: $10,000 to $150,000 for 2 years. **Average:** $100,000 for 2 years.

Activity: N.A.

HQ: Office of Children's Health Protection, USEPA; Stop 1107T, 1200 Pennsylvania Ave., NW, Washington, DC 20460. Phone: (202) 564-2711.

Internet: yosemite.epa.gov/ochp/ochpweb.nsf/content/homepage.htm.

66.610   SURVEYS, STUDIES, INVESTIGATIONS AND SPECIAL PURPOSE GRANTS WITHIN THE OFFICE OF THE ADMINISTRATOR

Assistance: project grants. (cost sharing/to 5 years).

Purposes: pursuant to CAA, CWA, SDWA, TSCA, SWDA, FIFRA, MPRSA, CERCLA, and National Environmental Policy Act, for surveys, studies, investigations, and special purpose assistance associated with air quality, acid deposition, drinking water quality, hazardous waste, toxic substances, and pesticides; to identify, develop and demonstrate necessary pollution control techniques; to evaluate the economic and social consequences of alternative strategies and mechanisms. Current funding priorities include: providing environmental health information and analysis to state legislatures; building state capacity to reduce environmental hazards affecting health and the environment; supporting environmental education training.

Eligible applicants/beneficiaries: states and state agencies, territories and possessions, tribes, IHEs, hospitals, laboratories, public and private nonprofit organizations.

Range: $500 to $500,000. **Average:** $100,000.

Activity: N.A.

HQ: Grants Administration Division (3903R), USEPA, 1200 Pennsylvania Ave., NW, Washington, DC 20460. Phone: (202) 564-1397.

Internet: www2.epa.gov/aboutepa.

66.611   ENVIRONMENTAL POLICY AND INNOVATION GRANTS

Assistance: project grants (cost sharing/to 5 years). (cost sharing/to 5 years).

Purposes: pursuant to CAA, CWA, SDWA, TSCA, SWDA, FIFRA, and CERCLA, for analyses, studies, evaluations, and conferences leading to reduced pollutants generated and to conservation of natural resources; to improve economic information and analytic methods to support studies, surveys, analyses, evaluations, conferences, workshops, and demonstration projects relating to the benefits, costs, and impacts of environmental programs, as well as of incentive-based and voluntary environmental management strategies and mechanisms. Current funding priorities include innovative projects relating to smart growth, performance result demonstrations, economic analysis, economic analytical and statistical methods development.

Eligible applicants/beneficiaries: states, tribes, territories, possessions; IHEs, hospitals, laboratories, other public or private nonprofit institutions; individuals.

Range: $25,000 to $200,000. **Average:** $100,000.

Activity: N.A.

HQ: Director, USEPA Headquarters, Ariel Rios Bldg., 1200 Pennsylvania Ave., NW, Mail Code: 1809T, Washington, DC 20460. Phone: (202) 566-2261.

Internet: www2.epa.gov/aboutepa/about-office-policy-op.

66.612 SURVEYS, STUDIES, INVESTIGATIONS, TRAINING DEMONSTRATIONS AND EDUCATIONAL OUTREACH RELATED TO ENVIRONMENTAL INFORMATION AND THE RELEASE OF TOXIC CHEMICALS

Assistance: project grants.

Purposes: pursuant to the Clean Water Act, Federal Insecticide, Fungicide, and Rodenticide Act, Clean Air Act, Solid Waste Disposal Act, Safe Drinking Water Act, Toxic Substances Control Act, to provide funding in support of surveys, studies, investigations, training/demonstrations, educational outreach and special purpose assistance as they relate to environmental information and the release of toxic chemicals.

Eligible applicants: states, District of Columbia, U.S. territories, federally recognized Indian tribes and intertribal consortia, public and private colleges and universities, and other public or private nonprofit organizations. Nonprofit organizations exempt from taxation under Section 501(c)(4) of the Internal Revenue Code that lobby are not eligible for financial assistance.

Eligible beneficiaries: general public; state, territory, city, town, county, regional governments, federally recognized Indian tribes and intertribal consortia, and public institutions and industries subject to EPA regulatory reporting requirements.

Range: $175,000 to $225,000. **Average:** $200,000.

Activity: N.A.

HQ: Grants and Interagency Agreements Management Division, EPA, 1200 Pennsylvania Ave., NW, Mail Code: 2842T, Washington, DC 20460. Phone: 202-566-0671.

Internet: www.epa.gov/oei.

66.700 CONSOLIDATED PESTICIDE ENFORCEMENT COOPERATIVE AGREEMENTS

Assistance: project grants (100 percent).

Purposes: pursuant to FIFRA as amended, to develop and maintain comprehensive pesticide programs addressing all aspects of enforcement, and special initiatives; to sponsor cooperative surveillance, monitoring, and analytical procedures; to encourage state regulatory activities. Funding priorities include: worker protection; pesticides used to protect public health; inspection of production facilities, retailing, and application practices; civil and criminal prosecution of violations. Grant funds may be used to pay for inspection and laboratory equipment and supplies, personnel salaries, other administrative costs.

Eligible applicants/beneficiaries: state agencies, territories and possessions, tribes.

Range: $32,000 to $710,000. **Average:** $250,000.

Activity: 72 awards in FY 2014.

HQ: OECA-EPA, 1200 Pennsylvania Ave., NW, Washington, DC 20460. Phone: (202) 564-5940; FAX: (202) 564-0050.

Internet: www.epa.gov/compliance/state/grants/fifra.html.

66.701 TOXIC SUBSTANCES COMPLIANCE MONITORING COOPERATIVE AGREEMENTS

Assistance: project grants (75-100 percent).

Purposes: pursuant to TSCA as amended, to: establish and operate compliance toxic substance monitoring and enforcement programs, including PCBs, asbestos in schools, lead-based paint, and sector-based activities; encourage state regulatory activities; establish worker training and accreditation standards. Grant funds may cover costs of inspection supplies and equipment, personnel, and administration.

Eligible applicants/beneficiaries: state agencies, territories and possessions, tribes.

Range: $32,000 to $710,000. **Average:** $113,000 for PCB and asbestos; $43,000 for lead.

Activity: 320 inspections conducted in FY 2014.

HQ: OECA-EPA, 1200 Pennsylvania Ave., NW, Washington, DC 20460. Phone: (202) 564-5940; FAX: (202) 564-0050.

Internet: epa.gov/compliance/monitoring/programs/tsca/index.html.

66.707 TSCA TITLE IV STATE LEAD GRANTS CERTIFICATION OF LEAD-BASED PAINT PROFESSIONALS
("State Lead Certification Grants")

Assistance: project grants.

Purposes: pursuant to TSCA as amended, to develop and conduct accredited training and certification programs for persons and contractors engaged in lead-based paint activities, and accredit training programs; for pre-renovation education programs, requiring distribution of lead-hazard information prior to building renovations.

Eligible applicants/beneficiaries: state agencies, territories and possessions, tribes.

Range: $16,000 to $350,000. **Average:** $200,000.

Activity: N.A.

HQ: Director, National Program Chemicals Division (7404T), Office of Pollution Prevention and Toxics, OPPTS-EPA, 1200 Pennsylvania Ave., NW, Washington, DC 20460. Phone: (202) 566-0744.

Internet: www2.epa.gov/lead.

66.708 POLLUTION PREVENTION GRANTS PROGRAM
("P2 Grant Program")

Assistance: project grants. (50 percent/to 3 years).

Purposes: pursuant to the Pollution Prevention Act of 1990, to support two programs. Pollution Prevention Grants cover innovative activities promoting preventative approaches to environmental performance and addressing various sectors of concern, including industrial toxics, agriculture, energy, transportation; projects focus on institutionalizing multimedia pollution prevention, establishing prevention goals, providing direct technical assistance and outreach to businesses, and collecting and analyzing data. Pollution Prevention Information Network (PPIN) Grants seek to coordinate work among technical assistance providers, to minimize duplication of effort in information collection, synthesis, dissemination, and training.

Eligible applicants/beneficiaries: state agencies and universities, territories and possessions, tribes. Participation is encouraged through partnerships with business and other environmental assistance providers.

Range: $12,500 to $180,000 for P2 grants; $96,000 to $130,000 for PPIN grants. **Average:** $85,000 for P2 grants; $106,000 for PPIN grants.

Activity: 43 awards in FY 2014.

HQ: Pollution Prevention Division, Office of Pollution Prevention, Pesticides and Toxics (7409-M), OPPTS-EPA, 1200 Pennsylvania Ave., NW, Washington, DC 20460. Phone: (202) 564-8857; FAX: (202) 564-8901.

Internet: epa.gov/p2/pubs/grants/index.htm.

66.714 REGIONAL AGRICULTURAL INTEGRATED PEST MANAGEMENT GRANTS
("Regional AG Grants")

Assistance: project grants. (100 percent/to 2 years).

Purposes: pursuant to FIFRA as amended, to reduce risk from the use of pesticides in agricultural and nonagricultural settings, through research, monitoring, demonstration, and related activities.

Eligible applicants/beneficiaries: states, state universities, territories, possessions, tribes.

Range/Average: N.A.

Activity: N.A.

HQ: Pesticide Environmental Stewardship Program, Biopesticides and Pollution Prevention Division (7511-C), OPPTS-EPA, 1200 Pennsylvania Ave., NW, Washington, DC 20460. Phone: (703) 305-5659.

Internet: www.epa.gov/pestwise/grants.

66.716 RESEARCH, DEVELOPMENT, MONITORING, PUBLIC EDUCATION, OUTREACH, TRAINING, DEMONSTRATIONS, AND STUDIES

Assistance: project grants.

Purposes: pursuant to FIFRA and TSCA, to protect the public health, the environment, ecosystems, and most threatened species from potential risk from future toxic chemicals; to explore such emerging issues as risks to the environment and ecosystems from biotechnology, endocrine disrupters, and lead poisoning.

Eligible applicants/beneficiaries: states, territories, possessions, tribal governments, native American organizations; public and private IHEs, hospitals, laboratories, and other nonprofit institutions; individuals.

Range: $25,000 to $147,000. **Average:** $60,860.

Activity: 15 awards in FY 2014.

HQ: USEPA Headquarters, Ariel Rios Bldg., 1200 Pennsylvania Ave., NW, Mail Code: 2224 , Washington, DC 20460. Phone: (202) 564-3810.

Internet: www.epa.gov/oppts.html.

66.717   SOURCE REDUCTION ASSISTANCE

Assistance: project grants. (95 percent/to 2 years).

Purposes: pursuant to CAA, CWA, FIFRA, SDWA, SWDA, TSCA, amendments, and Executive Orders, for source reduction, pollution prevention, and resource conservation activities that: promote integration of pollution prevention into environmental media regulatory programs; disseminate pollution prevention news, innovative technologies, and technical assistance; encourage and promote activities to assist in the purchasing of environmentally preferable products and services; support the pollution prevention information network through work in measurement of "P2" information activities and services (re: 66.708).

Eligible applicants/beneficiaries: state, local, tribal, and special districts governments, territories and possessions, independent school districts, state IHEs, nonprofits including community-based grassroots organizations.

Range: $25,000 to $147,000. Average: $60,860.

Activity: 15 awards in FY 2014.

HQ: Pollution Prevention Division, Office of Pollution Prevention, Pesticides and Toxics (7409-M), OPPTS-EPA, 1200 Pennsylvania Ave., NW, Washington, DC 20460. Phone: (202) 564-8857.

Internet: www.epa.gov/p2/pubs/grants/index.htm.

66.801   HAZARDOUS WASTE MANAGEMENT STATE PROGRAM SUPPORT

Assistance: formula grants (75 percent).

Purposes: pursuant to SWDA and RCRA as amended, to develop and implement authorized hazardous waste management programs to control the generation, transportation, treatment, storage, and disposal of hazardous wastes, including: permitting; oversight of corrective actions; facilities inspection; inspection of wastes generators; waste minimization.

Eligible applicants/beneficiaries: state agencies, territories, possessions.

Range: $350,000 to $8,500,000. Average: $2,000,000.

Activity: N.A.

HQ: Office of Solid Waste (5303P), OSWER-EPA, 1200 Pennsylvania Ave., NW, Washington, DC 20460. Phone: (703) 308-8630.

Internet: www.epa.gov/epawaste.

66.802   SUPERFUND STATE, POLITICAL SUBDIVISION, AND INDIAN TRIBE SITE-SPECIFIC COOPERATIVE AGREEMENTS
("Superfund")

Assistance: project grants (50-100 percent; tribes, 100 percent).

Purposes: pursuant to ARRA 2009 and CERCLA as amended, to conduct site characterization activities at potential or confirmed hazardous waste sites; to undertake remedial planning and implementation at sites on the

National Priorities List (NPL) of the National Oil and Hazardous Substances Contingency Plan. Project funds may be used to: conduct nontime-critical removal actions; inspect, assess, investigate, study, and prepare remedial designs; conduct remedial actions at uncontrolled sites listed on the NPL; identify responsible parties, conduct settlement negotiations, and take enforcement actions. Matching fund requirements: none if site was privately owned and operated at time of waste disposal prior to development of the NPL, and 10 percent for subsequent activities; 50 percent for sites state or locally operated; 10 percent for infrastructure development.

Eligible applicants/beneficiaries: states, political subdivisions, tribal governments, territories and possessions.

Range: $35,000 to $10,500,000. **Average:** $263,500.

Activity: 55 awards in FY 2014.

HQ: Assessment and Remediation Division, Office of Superfund Remediation and Technology Innovation, Mail Code 5204P, EPA, Washington, DC 20460. Phone: (703) 603-8835.

Internet: www.epa.gov/superfund.

66.804   UNDERGROUND STORAGE TANK PREVENTION, DETECTION AND COMPLIANCE PROGRAM ("UST Program")

Assistance: formula grants (75 percent; tribes, 100 percent).

Purposes: pursuant to SWDA, RCRA, Demonstration Cities and Metropolitan Development Act, and amendments, to develop and implement underground hazardous substances storage tank programs to operate in lieu of the federal program. Funds may be used to: promote effective compliance; ensure routine and correct monitoring by owners and operators; establish state statutory and regulatory authority.

Eligible applicants/beneficiaries: state and territorial agencies, tribes, inter-tribal consortia.

Range/Average: N.A.

Activity: anticipate 100 awards in FY 2015.

HQ: Immediate Office, Office of Underground Storage Tanks (5401P), OSWER-EPA, 1200 Pennsylvania Ave., NW, Washington, DC 20460. Phone: (703) 603-7148.

Internet: www.epa.gov/swerust1/index.htm.

66.805   LEAKING UNDERGROUND STORAGE TANK TRUST FUND CORRECTIVE ACTION PROGRAM

Assistance: formula grants (90 percent; tribes, 100 percent).

Purposes: pursuant to ARRA 2009, SWDA, RCRA, Demonstration Cities and Metropolitan Development Act, and amendments, to correct releases of petroleum from underground storage tanks; to conduct related enforcement and cost recovery activities; to oversee clean-ups by responsible parties. Trust funds may be used for responses where tank owners and operators are unknown, unwilling, or unable to undertake corrective actions;

owners and operators are liable to states for costs incurred when the trust fund is used, and are subject to cost recovery actions.

Eligible applicants/beneficiaries: state and territorial agencies, tribes, inter-tribal consortia.

Range: $41,000 to $3,200,000. **Average:** territory: $46,250.

Activity: anticipate 60 awards in FY 2015.

HQ: Immediate Office, Office of Underground Storage Tanks (5401P), OSWER-EPA, 1200 Pennsylvania Ave., NW, Washington, DC 20460. Phone: (703) 603-7148.

Internet: www.epa.gov/swerust1/index.htm.

66.806 SUPERFUND TECHNICAL ASSISTANCE GRANTS (TAG) FOR COMMUNITY GROUPS AT NATIONAL PRIORITY LIST (NPL) SITES

Assistance: project grants. (from 80 percent/3 years).

Purposes: pursuant to CERCLA and SARA as amended, for community groups to hire technical advisors to assist in: interpreting technical information concerning the assessment of potential hazards at waste sites; selecting and designing appropriate remedies at sites eligible for clean-up under the Superfund program; providing community information. Grant funds may not pay the costs of developing new information, underwriting legal actions or political activity, or travel by recipients.

Eligible applicants/beneficiaries: qualified, incorporated groups affected by an actual or threatened release at any Superfund facility.

Range: to $50,000. **Average:** N.A.

Activity: N.A.

HQ: Community Involvement and Outreach Center, Office of Superfund Remediation and Technology Innovation (5204G), OSWER-EPA, 1200 Pennsylvania Ave., NW, Washington, DC 20460. Phone: (703) 603-8889.

Internet: www.epa.gov/superfund.

66.808 SOLID WASTE MANAGEMENT ASSISTANCE GRANTS

Assistance: project grants (95-100 percent/3 years).

Purposes: pursuant to SWDA and RCRA as amended, to promote use of integrated solid waste management systems to solve municipal generation and management problems at the local, regional, and national levels. Funds may be used for training, surveys, public education materials and programs, studies, and demonstrations. Funding priorities include developing partnerships and education and outreach activities.

Eligible applicants/beneficiaries: federal, state, interstate, intrastate, and local public authorities; private nonprofit organizations and agencies, institutions (including non-profit hospitals and educational institutions); tribes.

Range: $10,000 to $25,000. **Average:** $17,325.

Activity: anticipate 2 awards in FY 2015.

HQ: USEPA Headquarters, Ariel Rios Bldg., 1200 Pennsylvania Ave., NW, Mail Code: 2224 , Washington, DC 20460. Phone: (202) 308-8460.

Internet: www.epa.gov/epawaste/index.htm.

66.809 SUPERFUND STATE AND INDIAN TRIBE CORE PROGRAM COOPERATIVE AGREEMENTS

Assistance: project grants (90 percent).

Purposes: pursuant to CERCLA as amended, for CERCLA response actions that are not site-specific. Funding supports personnel hiring and training, emergency response procedural planning, enforcement, legislative development.

Eligible applicants/beneficiaries: states, territories and possessions, tribal governments, tribal consortia.

Range: $8,000 to $400,000. **Average:** $122,574.

Activity: 12 awards in FY 2014.

HQ: Assessment and Remediation Division, Office of Superfund Remediation and Technology Innovation, Mail Code 5204P, EPA, Washington, DC 20460. Phone: (703) 603-8835.

Internet: www.epa.gov/superfund.

66.812 HAZARDOUS WASTE MANAGEMENT GRANT PROGRAM FOR TRIBES

Assistance: project grants (100 percent).

Purposes: to develop and implement hazardous waste management programs, including: building capacity to improve and maintain regulatory compliance; developing solutions to address waste mismanagement affecting tribal lands.

Eligible applicants/beneficiaries: tribal governments, including those involving Alaska natives; consortia.

Range: $18,000 to $100,000. **Average:** $56,000.

Activity: 7 awards in FY 2014.

HQ: Office of Solid Waste (5303W), OSWER-EPA, Washington, DC 20460. Phone: (703) 308-8458; FAX: (703) 308-8638.

Internet: www.epa.gov/epawaste/wyl/tribal/index.htm.

66.813 ALTERNATIVE OR INNOVATIVE TREATMENT TECHNOLOGY RESEARCH, DEMONSTRATION, TRAINING, AND HAZARDOUS SUBSTANCE RESEARCH GRANTS

Assistance: project grants. (cost sharing/to 5 years).

Purposes: pursuant to CERCLA as amended, for programs involving: research, evaluation, testing, development, and demonstration of alternative or innovative treatment technologies that may be used in response actions to achieve more permanent protection of human health and welfare and the environment; technology transfer including the development, collection, evaluation, coordination, and dissemination of information for response action; training and evaluation of training needs in handling and removal of hazardous substances; research on the detection, assessment, and evaluation of human health and environmental risks of hazardous substances.

Eligible applicants/beneficiaries: states, territories, possessions, tribes; public and private IHEs, hospitals, laboratories, and other nonprofits; individuals; certain projects by profit organizations.

Range: $50,000 to $1,000,000. **Average:** $500,000.

Activity: N.A.

HQ: Contracts Management Branch, Resources Management Division, Office of Superfund Remediation & Technology Innovation, USEPA (5202-P), 1200 Pennsylvania Ave., NW, Washington, DC 20460. Phone: (703) 603-9042.

Internet: www.epa.gov/superfund/index.htm.

66.814 BROWNFIELDS TRAINING, RESEARCH, AND TECHNICAL ASSISTANCE GRANTS AND COOPERATIVE AGREEMENTS ("Brownfields 104k6 Grants")

Assistance: project grants (to 100 percent/1-5 years).

Purposes: pursuant to CERCLA as amended, for training, research, and technical assistance to individuals and organizations to facilitate the inventory of brownfield properties, assessments, clean-up, community involvement, or site preparation. Grant matching requirements have not been established.

Eligible applicants/beneficiaries: general purpose local government units; land clearance authorities or other quasi-governmental entities operating under the supervision of, or as agent of a local government; regional councils or groups of local governments; redevelopment agencies established by state legislatures; tribes, Alaska native corporations, and the Metlakatla Indian Community; nonprofit organizations including IHEs.

Range: to $200,000 per year. **Average:** N.A.

Activity: anticipate 20 awards in FY 2015.

HQ: Office of Brownfields Cleanup and Redevelopment, OSWER-EPA, 1200 Pennsylvania Ave., NW, Washington, DC 20460. Phone: (202) 566-2777.

Internet: www.epa.gov/brownfields.

66.815 ENVIRONMENTAL WORKFORCE DEVELOPMENT AND JOB TRAINING COOPERATIVE AGREEMENTS

Assistance: project grants. (to 100 percent/2 years).

Purposes: pursuant to CERCLA as amended, for training, research, and technical assistance to individuals and organizations to facilitate the inventory of brownfield properties, assessments, clean-up, community involvement, or site preparation. Proposed projects showing evidence of leveraged funding receive priority consideration for approval.

Eligible applicants/beneficiaries: general purpose local government units; land clearance authorities or other quasi-governmental entities operating under the supervision of, or as agent of a local government; regional councils or groups of local governments; redevelopment agencies established by state legislatures; tribes, Alaska native corporations, and the Metlakatla Indian Community; nonprofit organizations including IHEs.

Range: N.A. Average: $200,000 for 3-year project.

Activity: 19 awards in FY 2015.

HQ: Office of Brownfields Cleanup and Redevelopment, OSWER-EPA, Washington, DC 20460 Phone: (202) 566-2777; FAX: (202) 566-2757.

Internet: www.epa.gov/brownfields.

66.816 HEADQUARTERS AND REGIONAL UNDERGROUND STORAGE TANKS PROGRAM

Assistance: project grants (100 percent/to 5 years).

Purposes: pursuant to SWDA, Hazardous and Solid Waste Amendments of 1984, SARA, RCRA, Demonstration Cities and Metropolitan Development Act, and amendments, for activities promoting the prevention, identification, corrective action, enforcement, and management of releases from underground storage tank systems, including: training on a regional and national scale; an electronic newsletter to provide technical information to state and tribal regulators, the general public, and the regulated community; state-federal partnerships providing technical assistance and forums for information exchange.

Eligible applicants/beneficiaries: public authorities including state, inter- and intrastate, tribal, intertribal, and local consortia; public and private nonprofit agencies and institutions.

Range: $199,800 to $370,000. Average: $277,000.

Activity: 4 awards in FY 2015.

HQ: Immediate Office, Office of Underground Storage Tanks (5401P), OSWER-EPA, 1200 Pennsylvania Ave., NW, Washington, DC 20460. Phone: (703) 603-7148.

Internet: www.epa.gov/swerust1/index.htm.

66.817 STATE AND TRIBAL RESPONSE PROGRAM GRANTS

Assistance: formula grants (80-100 percent).

Purposes: pursuant to CERCLA as amended and Small Business Liability Relief and Brownfields Revitalization Act, to establish or enhance state and tribal capacity for brownfields response programs; to capitalize revolving loan funds for clean-up activities; and, to support insurance mechanisms. Programs must ensure maintenance of a public record of completed projects and of planned sites. Applicants must provide a 20 percent share of the cost projects that capitalize a revolving loan fund; otherwise, the federal share is 100 percent.

Eligible applicants/beneficiaries: states and tribes.

Range: $50,000 to $1,000,000. Average: $450,000.

Activity: 160 awards in FY 2015.

HQ: Office of Brownfields Cleanup and Redevelopment, OSWER-EPA, 1200 Pennsylvania Ave., NW, Washington, DC 20460. Phone: (202) 566-2777.

Internet: www.epa.gov/brownfields.

66.818   BROWNFIELDS ASSESSMENT AND CLEANUP COOPERATIVE AGREEMENTS

Assistance: project grants. (80-100 percent/3-5 years).

Purposes: pursuant to ARRA 2009 and CERCLA as amended by the Small Business Liability Relief and Brownfields Revitalization Act, to conduct inventories, characterizations, assessments, planning, and community involvement activities related to brownfield sites; to capitalize revolving loan funds and provide subgrants (maximum, 40 percent of grants funds) for clean-up activities; to carry out clean-up activities at brownfield sites owned by the grant recipient. Assessment grants do not require matching funds; grants to establish revolving loan funds or provide subgrants require a 20 percent match, which may be waived by EPA in cases of financial hardship.

Eligible applicants/beneficiaries: general purpose local government units; land clearance authorities or other quasi-governmental entities operating under the supervision of, or as agent of a local government; regional councils or groups of local governments; redevelopment agencies established by state legislatures; tribes, Alaska native corporations, and the Metlakatla Indian Community; nonprofit organizations including IHEs.

Range/Average: N.A.

Activity: 129 properties cleaned up in FY 2015.

HQ: Office of Brownfields Cleanup and Redevelopment, OSWER-EPA, 1200 Pennsylvania Ave., NW, Washington, DC 20460. Phone: (202) 566-2777.

Internet: www.epa.gov/brownfields.

66.926   INDIAN ENVIRONMENTAL GENERAL ASSISTANCE PROGRAM (GAP) ("GAP for Tribes")

Assistance: project grants. (100 percent/to 4 years).

Purposes: pursuant to the Indian Environmental General Assistance Program Act of 1992 as amended, to administer environmental regulatory programs on Indian lands; to provide EPA technical assistance in the development of multimedia programs to address environmental issues. Funds may be used: to plan, develop, and establish capability to implement environmental protection programs including development and implementation of solid and hazardous waste programs; to conduct assessments and monitoring; to foster compliance with federal environmental statutes. Project examples: water quality assessment program; environmental assessment inventory; establishment of environmental codes; radon and underground storage tank projects.

Eligible applicants/beneficiaries: tribal governments, including those involving Alaska natives; consortia.

Range: $75,000 to $400,000. **Average:** $110,000.

Activity: N.A.

HQ: American Indian Environmental Office (2690M), EPA, 1200 Pennsylvania Ave., NW, Washington, DC 20460. Phone: (202) 564-4013.

Internet: www.epa.gov/indian/grantsandfunding/index.htm.

66.931   INTERNATIONAL FINANCIAL ASSISTANCE PROJECTS SPONSORED BY THE OFFICE OF INTERNATIONAL AND TRIBAL AFFAIRS

Assistance: project grants. (to 100 percent/to 5 years).

Purposes: pursuant to CWA, SWDA, RCRA, CAA, TSCA, FIFRA, SDWA, amendments, National Environmental Policy Act, and MPRSA, for multilateral international efforts to reduce significant risks to human health and ecosystems, caused by pollution that crosses national boundaries—including: issues concerning air quality, water, and toxins relating to the borders between the U.S. and Mexico, Canada (particularly the Great Lakes region), and the Arctic region; reviews and analytical studies of environmental aspects of international trade issues; and, providing technical assistance, capacity building, and on-the-ground projects in priority countries—including those conducted in cooperation with such organizations as the World Health Organization and the United Nations Environment Program, concerning such issues as global climate and clean fuels.

Eligible applicants/beneficiaries: states, territories, possessions, tribes; public and private IHEs, hospitals, laboratories, and other nonprofit organizations.

Range: $15,000 to $300,000. **Average:** $200,000.

Activity: N.A.

HQ: *grants information,* Grants Administration Division, USEPA, 1200 Pennsylvania Ave., NW, Washington, DC 20460. Phone: (202) 566-1680.

Internet: www.epa.gov/oia.

66.950   NATIONAL ENVIRONMENTAL EDUCATION TRAINING PROGRAM ("Teacher Training Program")

Assistance: project grants (75 percent/5 years).

Purposes: pursuant to the National Environmental Education Act, to train professionals in the development and delivery of environmental education programs. Funds may be used to develop programs involving such activities as: classroom training; demonstration projects; program and curriculum development; international exchanges involving the U.S., Mexico, and Canada; library acquisitions; conferences; networking.

Eligible applicants/beneficiaries: IHEs, nonprofit organizations or consortia of institutions to deliver environmental training and support for education professionals.

Range: N.A. **Average:** $10,947,000 for 5 year project.

Activity: N.A.

HQ: Environmental Education Specialist, Office of Environmental Education (1704A), EPA, 1200 Pennsylvania Ave., NW, Washington, DC 20460. Phone: (202) 564-2642.

Internet: www2.epa.gov/education/national-environmental-education-training-program.

66.951   ENVIRONMENTAL EDUCATION GRANTS

Assistance: project grants. (75 percent/1-2 years).

Purposes: pursuant to the National Environmental Education Act, to design, demonstrate, or disseminate practices, methods, or techniques related to environmental education and training, including: development of curricula and educational tools and materials; teacher and faculty training programs; international exchanges involving the U.S., Mexico, and Canada; projects to understand and assess specific environmental and ecological issues or problems. Funding priorities include: capacity building across a state or multiple states; education reform; community issues focus; health and threats to health from environmental pollution, especially as children are affected; teaching skills; career development; environmental justice.

Eligible applicants/beneficiaries: IHEs, local and state education agencies, environmental agencies, nonprofit organizations or consortia, licensed noncommercial educational broadcasting entities.

Range: N.A. **Average:** $192,000 for Model grant; $88,000 for Local grant.

Activity: 38 awards in FY 2014.

HQ: Environmental Education Grant Program (1704A), Office of Environmental Education, EPA, 1200 Pennsylvania Ave., NW, Washington, DC 20460. Phone: (202) 564-2194.

Internet: www.epa.gov/enviroed.

66.952 NATIONAL NETWORK FOR ENVIRONMENTAL MANAGEMENT STUDIES FELLOWSHIP PROGRAM ("NNEMS Fellowship Program")

Assistance: project grants. (100 percent/to 3 years).

Purposes: pursuant to CAA, CWA, SDWA, SWDA, FIFRA, CERCLA, and amendments, to enable students to participate in research projects directly related to their fields of study. Current priorities include: environmental policy, regulation, and law; environmental management and administration; environmental science; public relations and communications; computer programming and development. Stipends are awarded for three months full-time to three years part-time, throughout the fellowship period—for work performed at EPA headquarters, regional offices, or laboratories.

Eligible applicants/beneficiaries: U.S. citizens and permanent residents enrolled at accredited IHEs as graduate or undergraduate students, with satisfactory educational performance and appropriate related course completion.

Range: $7,400.00 to $12,600.00. **Average:** $12,000.00.

Activity: N.A.

HQ: Environmental Education Grant Program (1703A), Office of Environmental Education, EPA, 1200 Pennsylvania Ave., NW, Washington, DC 20460. Phone: (202) 564-0453.

Internet: www.epa.gov/enviroed.

NATIONAL GALLERY OF ART

68.001 NATIONAL GALLERY OF ART EXTENSION SERVICE

Assistance: use of property, facilities, and equipment.

Purposes: to provide educational materials from the National Gallery of Art for use in art and humanities programs. Available audiovisual materials relate to collections of paintings, sculptures, and special exhibitions in the gallery; included are video cassettes, CD-ROMS, DVDs, slide programs, teaching packets. The service is free of charge, except for return mailing costs.

Eligible applicants/beneficiaries: schools, colleges, libraries, museums, clubs, community organizations, noncommercial educational television stations, and individuals.

Range/Average: N.A.

Activity: N.A.

HQ: Department of Education Resources, National Gallery of Art, Washington, DC 20565. Phone: (202) 842-6273, (202) 737-4215.

Internet: www.nga.gov/education/classroom/loanfinder. (Note: no field offices for this program.)

OVERSEAS PRIVATE INVESTMENT CORPORATION

70.002 FOREIGN INVESTMENT FINANCING

Assistance: guaranteed/insured loans (5-15 years).

Purposes: pursuant to the Foreign Assistance Act of 1969, to finance investments in developing countries and emerging economies. Projects must contribute to the economic and social development of host countries and have a positive impact on the U.S. economy. Borrowers must provide a significant equity investment. Direct loans may be approved only for private sector projects with significant involvement by U.S. small businesses. Examples of funded projects include power generation, cellular telephone networks, retail petroleum.

Eligible applicants/beneficiaries: U.S. citizens, corporations, partnerships, other associations beneficially owning more than 50 percent of the entity, or foreign corporations at least 95 percent owned be such entity, or any other 100 percent U.S.-owned foreign entity.

Range: $200,000 to $400,000,000. **Average:** $27,067,770.

Activity: N.A.

HQ: Information Officer, OPIC, 1100 New York Ave., NW, Washington, DC 20527. Phone: (202) 336-8651.

Internet: www.opic.gov. (Note: no field offices for this program.)

70.003 FOREIGN INVESTMENT INSURANCE ("Political Risk Insurance")

Assistance: insurance. (90 percent/to 20 years).

Purposes: pursuant to the Foreign Assistance Act of 1969, to insure U.S. investments in developing countries and emerging markets against the political risks of inconvertibility, expropriation, and political violence. The investments must contribute to the economic and social development of host countries, and not adversely affect U.S. employment or the economy. Special programs insure: contractors and exporters against arbitrary drawings of letters of credit posted as bid, performance, or advance payment guarantees; petroleum exploration, development, and production; leasing operations; debt financing including securities.

Eligible applicants/beneficiaries: U.S. citizens, corporations, partnerships, other associations beneficially owning more than 50 percent of the entity, or foreign corporations at least 95 percent owned be such entity, or any other 100 percent U.S.-owned foreign entity.

Range: to $250,000,000. **Average:** $12,244,695.

Activity: N.A.

HQ: Information Officer, OPIC, 1100 New York Ave., NW, Washington, DC 20527. Phone: (202) 336-8799.

Internet: www.opic.gov. (Note: no field offices for this program.)

NUCLEAR REGULATORY COMMISSION

77.006 U.S. NUCLEAR REGULATORY COMMISSION NUCLEAR EDUCATION GRANT PROGRAM

Assistance: project grants.

Purposes: pursuant to Energy Policy Act of 2005, to provide assistance to IHEs in support or improvement of courses, studies, training, curricula, and disciplines relevant to fields that the NRC determines critical to its mission, including: nuclear safety, security, and environmental protection. Funds may be used for salaries, materials and supplies, equipment, travel, and publication, research, and training costs.

Eligible applicants/beneficiaries: U.S. public and private IHEs.

Range: $87,000 to $200,000. **Average:** N.A.

Activity: N.A.

HQ: U.S. Nuclear Regulatory Commission, Two White Flint North, 11545 Rockville Pike, Rockville, MD 20852; Stop T-7-1-2 Washington, DC 20555-0001. Phone: (301) 415-6869.

Internet: www.nrc.gov. (Note: no field offices for this program.)

77.007 U.S. NUCLEAR REGULATORY COMMISSION MINORITY SERVING INSTITUTIONS PROGRAM (MSIP)

Assistance: project grants; direct payments/specified use.

Purposes: pursuant to Energy Policy Act of 2005, to provide assistance to minority serving programs, activities, symposiums, and training for the exchange and transfer of knowledge and skills regarding fields that the NRC determines critical to its mission, including: nuclear safety, security, and environmental protection. Funds may be used for instruction, training, developmental learning, research and development, program evaluation, technical assistance, facilities and equipment acquisition, internships, fellowships, scholarships, tuition and housing assistance.

Eligible applicants/beneficiaries: U.S. public and private Minority Serving Institutions, their students and faculty and organizations that provide services to Minority Serving Institutions.

Range: $5,000 to $400,000. **Average:** N.A.

Activity: N.A.

HQ: U.S. Nuclear Regulatory Commission, Two White Flint North, 11545 Rockville Pike, Rockville, MD 20852; Stop T-7-1-2 Washington, DC 20555-0001. Phone: (301) 415-6869.

Internet: www.nrc.gov. (Note: no field offices for this program.)

77.008 U.S. NUCLEAR REGULATORY COMMISSION SCHOLARSHIP AND FELLOWSHIP PROGRAM

Assistance: grants.

Purposes: pursuant to Energy Policy Act of 2005 (Section 243), to provide scholarships and fellowships to qualified students interested in pursuing an education in science, engineering, or another field of study in a critical skill area related to the Commission's regulatory mission. Recipients must be enrolled in a professional degree or graduate program offered by a four year institution of higher education in the United States and must commit to employment by the Commission.

Eligible applicants: four year U.S. public and private institutions of higher education.

Eligible beneficiaries: undergraduate and graduate students.

Range: $150,000 to $450,000. **Average:** N.A.

Activity: N.A.

HQ: U.S. Nuclear Regulatory Commission, Two White Flint North, 11545 Rockville Pike, Rockville, MD 20852; Stop T-7-1-2 Washington, DC 20555-0001. Phone: (301) 415-6869.

Internet: www.nrc.gov. (Note: no field offices for this program.)

77.009 U.S. NUCLEAR REGULATORY COMMISSION OFFICE OF RESEARCH FINANCIAL ASSISTANCE PROGRAM ("NRC Office of Research Grant Program")

Assistance: cooperative agreements/discretionary grants; project grants (100 percent/5 years).

Purposes: pursuant to the Energy Policy Act of 2005, the Office of Nuclear Regulatory Research (RES) furthers the regulatory mission of the NRC by providing technical advice, technical tools and information for identifying and resolving safety issues, making regulatory decisions, and promulgating regulations and guidance.

Eligible applicants/beneficiaries: 35 IHEs selected by the CDC as Prevention Research Centers (PRCs).

Range: $5,000 to $225,000. **Average:** N.A.

Activity: N.A.

HQ: U.S. Nuclear Regulatory Commission, Two White Flint North, 11545 Rockville Pike, Rockville, MD 20852; Stop T-7-1-2 Washington, DC 20555-0001. Phone: (301) 415-6869.

Internet: www.nrc.gov. (Note: no field offices for this program.)

COMMODITY FUTURES TRADING COMMISSION

78.004 COMMODITY FUTURES REPARATIONS CLAIMS

Assistance: investigation of complaints.

Purposes: pursuant to the Commodity Exchange Act as amended, Futures Trading Acts, Commodity Futures Modernization Act of 2000, related acts, and amendments, to respond to customer complaints and inquiries concerning commodity futures trading; to conduct hearings and rulings on reparations complaints regarding monetary damages resulting from violations of the acts or regulations, by persons or firms registered under the Act.

Eligible applicants/beneficiaries: market users and the general public.

Range/Average: N.A.

Activity: N.A.

HQ: Office of the Executive Director, Office of Proceedings, Commodity Futures Trading Commission, 1155 21st St., NW, Washington, DC 20581. Phone: (202) 418-5250.

Internet: www.cftc.gov.

DEPARTMENT OF ENERGY

81.003 GRANTING OF PATENT LICENSES

Assistance: technical information.

Purposes: pursuant to the Atomic Energy Act of 1954 and Department of Energy Organization Act of 1977 (DOEOA) as amended, to license some

1,200 DOE-owned U.S. and 200 foreign patents, encouraging widespread use of the licensed inventions. Licenses usually are nonexclusive and revocable, but may be exclusive or partially so under some circumstances such as for commercialization. Copies of patents may be obtained for a modest fee from the U.S. Patent and Trademark Office (see **11.900**).

Eligible applicants/beneficiaries: individuals, firms, or corporations with satisfactory commercialization plans.

Range/Average: N.A.

Activity: N.A.

HQ: Office of Assistant General Counsel/Technology Transfer and Intellectual Property, DOE, 1000 Independence Ave., SW, Washington, DC 20585. Phone: (202) 586-2802.

Internet: www.doe.gov. (Note: no field offices for this program.)

81.022 LABORATORY EQUIPMENT DONATION PROGRAM ("Used Equipment Grants")

Assistance: sale, exchange, or donation of property and goods.

Purposes: pursuant to the Atomic Energy Act of 1954, DOEOA, and Energy Reorganization Act of 1974 as amended, to grant used energy-related laboratory equipment for use in energy-oriented research or instructional programs in the life, physical, and environmental sciences and engineering.

Eligible applicants/beneficiaries: U.S. nonprofit IHEs, hospitals, technical institutes, museums.

Range/Average: N.A.

Activity: N.A.

HQ: Office of Science, DOE, 1000 Independence Ave., SW, Washington, DC 20585. Phone: (202) 586-9742.

Internet: www.osti.gov/ledp/index.jsp.

81.036 INVENTIONS AND INNOVATIONS (I&I)

Assistance: project grants; technical information; advisory services/counseling. (grants, to 100 percent/grants, 1-2 years).

Purposes: pursuant to the Federal Nonnuclear Energy Research and Development Act of 1974 and DOEOA as amended, to support development and commercialization of energy-saving inventions, by providing limited financial assistance and technical assistance in evaluating and launching promising concepts. Funding may not include equity capital.

Eligible applicants/beneficiaries: U.S. citizens and small businesses.

Range: $500,000 to $1,000,000. **Average:** N.A.

Activity: N.A.

HQ: OEERE-DOE, 15013 Denver West Pkwy., Golden, Colorado 80401. Phone: 240-562-1456.

Internet: www.eere.energy.gov. (Note: no field offices for this program.)

81.041 STATE ENERGY PROGRAM (SEP)

Assistance: formula grants (100 percent).

Purposes: pursuant to ARRA 2009, Energy Policy and Conservation Act, DOEOA as amended, and related acts, to develop, implement, or modify state energy conservation plans. Funds may cover costs of plan development or modification, but not research, demonstrations, subsidies, or tax credits.

Eligible applicants/beneficiaries: states, territories, possessions.

Range: to $5,000,000. **Average:** N.A.

Activity: N.A.

HQ: OEERE-DOE, 15013 Denver West Pkwy., Golden, Colorado 80401. Phone: 240-562-1456.

Internet: www.eere.energy.gov. (Note: no field offices for this program.)

81.042 WEATHERIZATION ASSISTANCE FOR LOW-INCOME PERSONS ("WAP")

Assistance: formula grants (100 percent).

Purposes: pursuant to ARRA 2009, Energy Conservation and Production Act, DOEOA, Energy Security Act of 1980, State Energy Efficiency Programs Improvement Act of 1990, amendments, and other acts, for weatherization measures in the homes of low-income households, especially the elderly and the handicapped. Funds may cover such costs as attic insulation, storm windows, furnace and cooling system modifications, replacement furnaces and boilers.

Eligible applicants/beneficiaries: states and certain tribal organizations. If a state does not apply, general purpose local government units, community action agencies, or other nonprofit agencies may apply.

Range: $2,500 to $6,500 per dwelling unit. **Average:** N.A.

Activity: N.A.

HQ: OEERE-DOE, 15013 Denver West Pkwy., Golden, Colorado 80401. Phone: 240-562-1456.

Internet: www.eere.energy.gov. (Note: no field offices for this program.)

81.049 OFFICE OF SCIENCE FINANCIAL ASSISTANCE PROGRAM

Assistance: project grants. (to 100 percent/to 5 years).

Purposes: pursuant to ARRA 2009, Atomic Energy Act of 1954, Federal Nonnuclear Energy Research and Development Act of 1974, DOEOA, Energy Reorganization Act of 1974, and amendments, for fundamental energy research, training, and related activities in the basic sciences and in advanced technology concepts and assessments in related fields. Funds may be obtained for work in such fields as basic energy sciences, high energy and nuclear physics, fusion energy, biological and environmental research, advanced scientific computing. Graduate student support may be provided.

Eligible applicants/beneficiaries: IHEs, profit and nonprofit organizations, state and local governments, unaffiliated individuals.

Range: $10,000 to $2,500,000. **Average:** $250,000.

Activity: N.A.

HQ: Grants and Contracts Division, Office of Science-DOE, 1000 Independence Ave., SW, Washington, DC 20585. Phone: (301) 903-7433.

Internet: science.energy.gov/grants.

81.057 UNIVERSITY COAL RESEARCH

Assistance: project grants. (75-100 percent/to 3 years).

Purposes: pursuant to the Atomic Energy Act of 1954 as amended, Federal Nonnuclear Energy Research and Development Act of 1974, DOEOA, and Energy Reorganization Act of 1974, for research on the physics and chemistry involved in the conversion and utilization of coal. Projects must involve teaching faculty and funded student participation.

Eligible applicants/beneficiaries: U.S. IHEs.

Range: to $300,000 for 3 year project. **Average:** N.A.

Activity: 6 awards in FY 2015.

HQ: Office of Advanced Research, Assistant Secretary/Fossil Energy-DOE, Washington, DC 20585. Phone: (301) 903-2827.

Internet: www.netl.doe.gov/technologies/coalpower/advresearch.

81.064 OFFICE OF SCIENTIFIC AND TECHNICAL INFORMATION (OSTI)

Assistance: technical information.

Purposes: for OSTI to conduct its centralized technical information management program for the collection, organization, preservation, and distribution of domestic and international nuclear and other energy research findings in electronic and printed form; to provide pertinent technical services and information to DOE and its contractors.

Eligible applicants/beneficiaries: state and local governments, universities that are DOE contractors, and other organizations. Public access is available through NTIS and GPO.

Range/Average: N.A.

Activity: N.A.

HQ: Office of Program Integration, OSTI-DOE, 1 Science.gov Way, Oak Ridge, TN 37831. Phone: (865) 576-1146.

Internet: www.osti.gov. (Note: no field offices for this program.)

81.079 REGIONAL BIOMASS ENERGY PROGRAMS

Assistance: project grants. (to 100 percent/2 months-1 year).

Purposes: pursuant to DOEOA as amended, to develop and transfer biomass energy technologies to the scientific and industrial communities; for outreach, public education, and behavior modification activities. Regional programs are tailored to specific regions for feedstock production, conversion technologies, and feasibility studies.

Eligible applicants/beneficiaries: profit and nonprofit organizations; intrastate, interstate, state, local government agencies; universities.

Range/Average: N.A.

Activity: N.A.

HQ: OEERE-DOE, 15013 Denver West Pkwy., Golden, Colorado 80401. Phone: 240-562-1456.

Internet: www.eere.energy.gov. (Note: no field offices for this program.)

81.086 CONSERVATION RESEARCH AND DEVELOPMENT ("Energy Efficiency")

Assistance: project grants. (to 100 percent/2 months to 2 years).

Purposes: pursuant to DOEOA as amended and Federal Nonnuclear Energy Research and Development Act of 1974, for long-term research in energy conservation technology in buildings, industry, FreedomCAR and vehicle technologies and hydrogen, fuel cells, and infrastructure. Project examples include research on high-performance heat pumps, thermally efficient commercial buildings, vehicle engines, high temperature materials, industrial separation processes.

Eligible applicants/beneficiaries: profit and nonprofit organizations, state and local governments.

Range/Average: N.A.

Activity: N.A.

HQ: OEERE-DOE, 15013 Denver West Pkwy., Golden, Colorado 80401. Phone: 240-562-1456.

Internet: www.eere.energy.gov. (Note: no field offices for this program.)

81.087 RENEWABLE ENERGY RESEARCH AND DEVELOPMENT ("Renewable Energy")

Assistance: project grants. (to 100 percent/2 months-1 year).

Purposes: pursuant to DOEOA, for research and development projects in energy technologies, including solar, distributed energy and electric reliability, biomass, wind and hydropower, hydrogen, and geothermal.

Eligible applicants/beneficiaries: profit and nonprofit organizations; intrastate, interstate, and local agencies; universities.

Range/Average: N.A.

Activity: N.A.

HQ: OEERE-DOE, 15013 Denver West Pkwy., Golden, Colorado 80401. Phone: 240-562-1456.

Internet: www.eere.doe.gov. (Note: no field offices for this program.)

81.089 FOSSIL ENERGY RESEARCH AND DEVELOPMENT

Assistance: project grants.

Purposes: pursuant to the Federal Nonnuclear Energy Research and Development Act of 1974, Energy Policy and Conservation Act, DOEOA, and other acts, for fundamental research and technology development to promote the use of environmentally and economically superior technologies for supply, conversion, delivery, and utilization of fossil fuels.

Eligible applicants/beneficiaries: states, local governments, universities, governmental entities, consortia, nonprofit institutions, commercial corporations, joint federal-industry corporations, territories, individuals.

Range: $200,000 to $10,000,000. **Average:** N.A.

Activity: anticipate 73 awards in FY 2016.

HQ: Fossil Energy Program, DOE, 1000 Independence Ave., SW, Washington, DC 20585. Phone: (202) 9586-7661.

Internet: N.A. (Note: no field offices for this program.)

81.104 ENVIRONMENTAL REMEDIATION AND WASTE PROCESSING AND DISPOSAL

Assistance: project grants. (to 100 percent/to 5 years).

Purposes: pursuant to the Atomic Energy Act, DOEOA, Hazardous Materials Transportation Uniform Safety Act of 1990, amendments, and other acts, to develop new or improved technology systems to: eliminate or reduce known or recognized potential risks to the public and to the environment; reduce overall clean-up costs; develop new clean-up methods. Major remediation and waste management areas include: transuranic waste; high-level waste; groundwater and soils; deactivation and decommissioning; nuclear materials.

Eligible applicants/beneficiaries: public and quasi-public agencies, private industry, individuals, groups, educational institutions, nonprofit organizations, state and local governments, tribal governments, territories and possessions.

Range/Average: N.A.

Activity: N.A.

HQ: Office of Soil and Groundwater Remediation, EM-12, 1000 Independence Ave., SW, Washington, DC 20585. Phone: (301) 903-7654.

Internet: www.em.doe.gov. (Note: no field offices for this program.)

81.105 NATIONAL INDUSTRIAL COMPETITIVENESS THROUGH ENERGY, ENVIRONMENT, AND ECONOMICS ("NICE3")

Assistance: project grants. (50 percent/to 3 years).

Purposes: pursuant to DOEOA and Energy Policy Act of 1992 as amended, to develop new processes and/or equipment to reduce the generation of high-volume wastes and greenhouse gases in industry, including agriculture and mining, and to conserve energy and energy-intensive feed stocks. Emphasis is on states with industries with the highest energy consumption and the greatest levels of generation of pollutants. State funding must include industrial partner monies.

Eligible applicants/beneficiaries: commercial firms with proposals endorsed by state agencies; state agencies, territories, possessions, tribes.

Range/Average: N.A.

Activity: N.A.

HQ: OEERE-DOE, 15013 Denver West Pkwy., Golden, Colorado 80401. Phone: 240-562-1456.

Internet: www.eere.energy.gov. (Note: no field offices for this program.)

81.106 TRANSPORT OF TRANSURANIC WASTES TO THE WASTE ISOLATION PILOT PLANT: STATES AND TRIBAL CONCERNS, PROPOSED SOLUTIONS

Assistance: project grants (100 percent).

Purposes: pursuant to the National Security and Military Application of Nuclear Energy Authorization Act and Waste Isolation Pilot Land Withdrawal Act as amended, to support cooperative efforts among the tribes, states, and DOE on the Waste Isolation Pilot Plant shipping corridors in developing plans and procedures for the safe transportation of transuranic waste from temporary storage facilities to the plant. Project elements include accident prevention, emergency preparedness training, and public information activities.

Eligible applicants/beneficiaries: Western Governors' Association, Southern Governors' Association, State of New Mexico, and affected tribal governments.

Range: $50,000 to $7,000,000. **Average:** N.A.

Activity: N.A.

HQ: Federal Disposition Options, Office of Environmental Management-DOE, Washington, DC 20585. Phone: (301) 903-8466.

Internet: www.wipp.energy.gov. (Note: no field offices for this program.)

81.108 EPIDEMIOLOGY AND OTHER HEALTH STUDIES FINANCIAL ASSISTANCE PROGRAM

Assistance: project grants (100 percent).

Purposes: pursuant to the Atomic Energy Act of 1954, Federal Nonnuclear Energy Research and Development Act of 1977, Energy Reorganization Act of 1974, and amendments, for research, education, conferences, communication, and other activities relating to the health of DOE workers and others potentially exposed to health hazards associated with energy production, transmission, and use. Grant funds may support costs relating to project administration, training, publications, and epidemiological studies and research.

Eligible applicants/beneficiaries: IHEs, businesses, nonprofit institutions.

Range: $10,000 to $6,000,000. **Average:** $1,500,000.

Activity: N.A.

HQ: Office of Health Programs-DOE, 1000 Independence Ave., SW, Washington, DC 20623. Phone: (301) 903-1244.

Internet: energy.gov/ehss/environment-health-safety-security. (Note: no field offices for this program.)

81.112   STEWARDSHIP SCIENCE GRANT PROGRAM ("Defense Science")

Assistance: project grants (100 percent).

Purposes: pursuant to the Atomic Energy Act of 1954, Federal Nonnuclear Energy Research and Development Act of 1974, DOEOA, amendments, and other laws, for basic and applied research in science and technology relevant to stockpile stewardship; to promote inter-action among researchers and scientists at DOE laboratories; to train scientists in specific areas related to long-term research; to complement the DOE Advanced Simulation and Computing Academic Strategic Alliances Program by emphasizing primarily experimental research in forefront areas.

Eligible applicants/beneficiaries: U.S. public and private IHEs.

Range: $50,000 to $750,000 for grants; $1,000,000 to $63,000,000 for cooperative agreements. **Average:** N.A.

Activity: N.A.

HQ: Office of Defense Science-DOE, 19901 Germantown Rd., Germantown, Maryland 20874. Phone: (301) 903-7423.

Internet: www.nnsa.energy.gov. (Note: no field offices for this program.)

81.113   DEFENSE NUCLEAR NONPROLIFERATION RESEARCH

Assistance: project grants. (100 percent/to 3 years).

Purposes: pursuant to the Atomic Energy Act of 1954, Federal Nonnuclear Energy Research and Development Act of 1974, DOEOA, National Defense Authorization Act of 2000, amendments, and other acts, for basic and applied research and development on verification technologies that enhance U.S. national security and reduce global danger from the proliferation of special nuclear materials and weapons of mass destruction.

Eligible applicants/beneficiaries: public and private nonprofit IHEs and non-governmental organizations; federal agencies.

Range: N.A. **Average:** $5,000,000 per year for 5 years.

Activity: 1 award in FY 2016.

HQ: Office of Nonproliferation Research and Engineering (NA-22), Office of Defense Nuclear Nonproliferation, National Nuclear Security Administration-DOE, Washington, DC 20585. Phone: (202) 586-2485.

Internet: www.nnsa.doe.gov/na-20. (Note: no field offices for this program.)

81.117   ENERGY EFFICIENCY AND RENEWABLE ENERGY INFORMATION DISSEMINATION, OUTREACH, TRAINING AND TECHNICAL ANALYSIS/ASSISTANCE

Assistance: project grants. (to 100 percent/6 months-5 years).

Purposes: pursuant to DOEOA, Energy Policy Act of 1992, Energy Reorganization Act of 1974, and amendments, to stimulate increased energy efficiency and use of renewable and alternative energy in transportation, buildings, industry, and the federal sector through information dissemination, outreach, training, and related technical assistance.

Eligible applicants/beneficiaries: public and private profit and nonprofit organizations, state and local governments, tribal organizations, Alaska native American organizations, universities.

Range/Average: N.A.

Activity: N.A.

HQ: OEERE-DOE, 15013 Denver West Pkwy., Golden, Colorado 80401. Phone: 240-562-1456.

Internet: www.eere.energy.gov. (Note: no field offices for this program.)

81.119   STATE ENERGY PROGRAM SPECIAL PROJECTS ("SEP Competitive Grants")

Assistance: project grants (to 100 percent).

Purposes: pursuant to DOEOA and National Energy Conservation Policy Act of 1978, amendments, and other acts, to assist states in implementing specific DOE deployment activities and initiatives in such programmatic areas as building codes and standards, alternative fuels, industrial efficiency, and solar and renewable energy technologies.

Eligible applicants/beneficiaries: states, territories, and possessions.

Range: $500,000 to $1,000,000. **Average:** N.A.

Activity: N.A.

HQ: OEERE-DOE, 15013 Denver West Pkwy., Golden, Colorado 80401. Phone: 240-562-1456.

Internet: www.eere.energy.gov. (Note: no field offices for this program.)

81.121   NUCLEAR ENERGY RESEARCH, DEVELOPMENT AND DEMONSTRATION (NE RD&D)

Assistance: project grants (to 100 percent).

Purposes: pursuant to the Atomic Energy Act of 1954, DOEOA, amendments, and Energy Reorganization Act of 1974, for research, development, demonstrations, and deployment in science and technology fields related to nuclear energy to address key issues affecting the future world-wide use of nuclear energy including such areas as advanced reactors, proliferation-resistant fuel and reactor concepts, modeling and analysis, reactor physics. Projects may include development, demonstrations, studies, economic analyses, new regulatory or licensing requirements, and similar activities.

Eligible applicants/beneficiaries: federal, state, and local governments; public or private nonprofit or profit organizations, IHEs; consortia; individuals.

Range: $400,000 to $1,000,000. **Average:** $800,000.

Activity: N.A.

HQ: Office of Nuclear Energy, Office of Advanced Nuclear Research, 1000 Independence Ave., SW, Washington, DC 20585. Phone: (301) 903-3723.

Internet: www.ne.doe.gov. (Note: no field offices for this program.)

81.122   ELECTRICITY DELIVERY AND ENERGY RELIABILITY, RESEARCH, DEVELOPMENT AND ANALYSIS

Assistance: project grants. (100 percent/to 3 years).

Purposes: pursuant to DOEOA as amended, Energy Tax Act of 1978, Energy Security Act of 1980, Superconductivity and Competitiveness Act of 1988, Energy Policy Act of 1992, and ARRA 2009, for research, development, demonstration, technology transfer, and education and outreach activities intended to: modernize and expand the national electricity delivery system; assure the security of the energy infrastructure and reduce its vulnerability; develop an effective emergency response system to protect and restore its capabilities in case of disruption or attack.

Eligible applicants/beneficiaries: private profit and nonprofit organizations, state and local governments.

Range/Average: N.A.

Activity: N.A.

HQ: OEERE-DOE, 15013 Denver West Pkwy., Golden, Colorado 80401. Phone: 240-562-1456.

Internet: www.oe.energy.gov. (Note: no field offices for this program.)

81.123 NATIONAL NUCLEAR SECURITY ADMINISTRATION (NNSA) MINORITY SERVING INSTITUTIONS (MSI) PROGRAM

Assistance: project grants. (100 percent/to 3 years).

Purposes: pursuant to the Atomic Energy Act of 1954, DOEOA, Energy Reorganization Act of 1974, National Nuclear Security Administration Act, and amendments, to establish a research partnership with HBCUs, HSIs, and TCUs to increase their participation in national security-related research, and to train HBCU graduates for NNSA employment.

Eligible applicants/beneficiaries: HBCUs, HSIs, and TCUs.

Range: $750,000 to $5,000,000 per year for 3 to 5 years. **Average:** N.A.

Activity: N.A.

HQ: Office of Diversity and Outreach (NA-61), NNSA-DOE, 1000 Independence Ave., SW, Washington, DC 20585. Phone: (202) 586-8023; FAX: (202) 586-6019.

Internet: www.nnsa.doe.gov. (Note: no field offices for this program.)

81.124 PREDICTIVE SCIENCE ACADEMIC ALLIANCE PROGRAM

Assistance: project grants.

Purposes: pursuant to Atomic Energy Act of 1954, Energy Reorganization Act of 1974, Federal Nonnuclear Energy Research and Development Act of 1974, and others, as amended, to foster the science of building integrated, multi-scale, and multi-physics codes with the primary focus on code validation and verification to help advance the newly emergent predictive science in academia; to promote and sustain scientific interactions between the academic community and scientists at the NNSA laboratories; and to train scientists in specific areas of long-term research relevant to DOE stockpile stewardship. Funds are used to explore research ideas that do not unnecessarily duplicate work already in progress or contemplated by DOE.

Eligible applicants/beneficiaries: U.S. public/private education institutions with Ph.D. granting programs.

Range/Average: N.A.

Activity: N.A.

HQ: Office of Advanced Simulation and Computing, Pennsylvania & H Ave., KAFB-E , Albuquerque, New Mexico 87116. Phone: (505) 845-6462.

Internet: www.sandia.gov/NNSA/ASC/univ/psaap.html. (Note: no field offices for this program.)

81.126 FEDERAL LOAN GUARANTEES FOR INNOVATIVE ENERGY TECHNOLOGIES

Assistance: guaranteed/insured loans (to 30 years).

Purposes: pursuant to Energy Policy Act of 2005 and Title XVII, to encourage early commercial use in the U.S. of new or significantly improved technologies in energy projects that avoid, reduce, or sequester air pollutants or anthropogenic emissions of greenhouse gases through the use of Federal loan guarantees. This is a "self-pay" program and applicants will pay the subsidy costs as determined by the credit subsidy calculation.

Eligible applicants/beneficiaries: corporations, companies, partnerships, associations, societies, trusts, joint ventures or stock companies, or governmental nonfederal entities that have the authority to enter into a loan guarantee for a loan or other debt obligation of an eligabible Project. Examples of funded projects include: renewable energy systems, such as wind photovoltaics, biomass and hydropower projects, advanced fossil energy technology including gasification, efficient end use technologies and hydrogen fuel cell technology.

Range/Average: N.A.

Activity: completed 17 loans in FY 2016.

HQ: Loan Guarantee Program Office, DOE, 1000 Independence Ave., SW, Washington, DC 20585. Phone: (202) 287-1750.

Internet: www.energy.gov/lpo/loan-programs-office. (Note: no field offices for this program.)

81.127 ENERGY EFFICIENT APPLIANCE REBATE PROGRAM (EEARP)

Assistance: formula grants (100 percent/24 months).

Purposes: Energy Policy Act (EPAct) of 2005, to reduce fossil fuel emissions and improve energy efficiency in the residential sector by providing financial and technical assistance for the establishment or continuation of energy star rated appliance rebate programs.

Eligible applicants: states (includes DC, public IHEs and hospitals); US territories and possessions.

Eligible beneficiaries: individuals/families.

Range: $500,000 to $6,000,000. **Average:** N.A.

Activity: N.A.

HQ: OEERE-DOE, 15013 Denver West Pkwy., Golden, Colorado 80401. Phone: 240-562-1456.

Internet: energy.gov/eere/office-energy-efficiency-renewable-energy.

81.128 ENERGY EFFICIENCY AND CONSERVATION BLOCK GRANT PROGRAM (EECBG)

Assistance: formula grants/special project grants (100 percent/18 months).

Purposes: pursuant to Energy Independence and Security Act (EISA) of 2007 Title V, to provide financial and technical assistance to assist state and local governments in creating and implementing a variety of energy efficiency and conservation projects. There is no local match requirements for the EECBG, however, leveraging of funds on the part of the recipient is encouraged.

Eligible applicants: states (includes DC, public IHEs and hospitals); US territories and possessions.

Eligible beneficiaries: individuals/families.

Range/Average: N.A.

Activity: N.A.

HQ: OEERE-DOE, 15013 Denver West Pkwy., Golden, Colorado 80401. Phone: 240-562-1456.

Internet: www.eere.energy.gov.

81.129 ENERGY EFFICIENCY AND RENEWABLE ENERGY TECHNOLOGY DEPLOYMENT, DEMONSTRATION AND COMMERCIALIZATION

Assistance: project grants (50 percent).

Purposes: pursuant to Energy Policy Act of 1992, Energy Policy Act of 2005, Energy Independence and Security Act (EISA) of 2007, ARRA 2009. to provide financial assistance for the technology deployment, demonstration, and commercialization of Energy Efficiency and Renewable Energy technologies, including: biomass; federal energy management; projects involving hydrogen; building, geothermal, fuel cell, infrastructure, industrial, solar energy, vehicle, weatherization and intergovernmental, and wind and hydropower technologies.

Eligible applicants/beneficiaries: anyone/general public.

Range/Average: N.A.

Activity: N.A.

HQ: OEERE-DOE, 15013 Denver West Pkwy., Golden, Colorado 80401. Phone: 240-562-1456.

Internet: www.eere.energy.gov. (Note: no field offices for this program.)

81.135 ADVANCED RESEARCH PROJECTS AGENCY—ENERGY

Assistance: project grants (80 percent).

Purposes: pursuant to America COMPETES Act of 2007, to support the President's National Objectives for DOE, especially transformational energy related technologies. Federally-funded R&D development centers may submit proposals as part of a collaboration, consortium, or other team arrangement.

Eligible applicants: technology R&D entities, (including, but not limited to, companies, IHEs, research foundations, nonprofit entities, and consortia).

Eligible beneficiaries: anyone/general public.

Range: $250,000 to $10,000,000. **Average:** $2,000,000.

Activity: N.A.

HQ: DOE, 1000 Independence Ave., SW, Washington, DC 20585. Phone: (202) 287-6583.

Internet: www.arpa-e.energy.gov. (Note: no field offices for this program.)

81.136 LONG-TERM SURVEILLANCE AND MAINTENANCE

Assistance: project grants/cooperative agreements.

Purposes: pursuant to SARA of 1986, Uranium Mill Tailings Radiation Control Act of 1978, RCRA, and Atomic Energy Act of 1954, CERCLA, and Department of Energy Organization Act of 1977, as amended, to manage DOE's post-closure responsibilities and ensure future protection of human health and the environment according to Office of Legacy Management's objectives. Cost-sharing may be required.

Eligible applicants/beneficiaries: state and local governments, U.S. territories/possessions, state and federally recognized Indian tribes, public and private institutions/organizations.

Range: $4,000 to $450,000. **Average:** $89,736.

Activity: 26 grants and 10 cooperative agreements in FY 2013.

HQ: Office of Legacy Management-DOE, 1000 Independence Ave., SW, Washington, DC 20623. Phone: (202) 586-8018.

Internet: www.lm.doe.gov. (Note: no field offices for this program.)

81.139 ENVIRONMENTAL MANAGEMENT R&D AND VALIDATION TESTING ON HIGH EFFICIENCY PARTICULATE AIR (HEPA) FILTERS ("Environmental Management R&D")

Assistance: cooperative agreements (100 percent).

Purposes: pursuant to the Department of Energy Act, to research and develop improved, safer advanced HEPA filters. Funds will also be used to support technical methods and new technologies needed for high level tank waste mixing, assessment/sampling, waste treatment processes, systems, aerosol/particulate/gas filtering, individual components, and modeling algorithms.

Eligible applicants: publicly owned agency/organization established to perform specialized functions or services for the benefit of all or part of the general public either without charge or at cost, making no profits and having no shareholders to receive dividends, including IHEs and hospitals.

Eligible beneficiaries: anyone working in a radioactive environment or in proximity to radioactive facilities.

Range/Average: N.A.

Activity: N.A.

HQ: Program Director, Environmental Management R&D, US. Dept. of Energy, EM-23, Cloverleaf 1000 Independence Ave. SW, Washington, DC 20585. Phone: (202) 287-5502.

Internet: www.energy.gov. (Note: no field offices for this program.)

81.214   ENVIRONMENTAL MONITORING/CLEANUP, CULTURAL AND RESOURCE MANAGEMENT, EMERGENCY RESPONSE RESEARCH, OUTREACH, TECHNICAL ANALYSIS

Assistance: cooperative agreements/discretionary grants (100 percent, but cost share encouraged).

Purposes: pursuant to the National Historic Preservation Act of 1966, to manage cultural resources and commitments in order to insure that implemented DOE programs: protect human health, the environment, educational training; uphold EM's goals to reduce legacy footprint, lifecycle cost, and accelerate cleanup; and offer research opportunities in science technology, engineering and mathematical (STEM) fields.

Eligible applicants: state/local government entities for the conduct of projects/activities to support DOE missions.

Eligible beneficiaries: state/local governments, U.S. territories/possessions, researchers in science technology, engineering and mathematical (STEM) fields.

Range/Average: N.A.

Activity: N.A.

HQ: Director, Savannah River Operations Office, Department of Energy, P. O. Box A, Aiken, SC 29802. Phone: (803) 952-9175.

Internet: www.srs.gov.

DEPARTMENT OF EDUCATION

84.002   ADULT EDUCATION—STATE GRANT PROGRAM

Assistance: formula grants. (75 percent; territories, 88 percent/to 27 months).

Purposes: pursuant to the Adult Education and Family Literacy Act, Chapter 2, and WIA, for education and workplace, family, and English literacy services, and civics education programs for adults and out-of-school youth at least age 16 lacking mastery of basic educational skills or without a high school diploma or English language proficiency. Portions of grant amounts may be spent for: state leadership activities; professional development; teacher training; correctional education and services to other institutionalized individuals.

Eligible applicants: designated State agencies, LEAs, other public or private nonprofit organizations, including libraries, public housing authorities, IHEs, literacy organizations.

Eligible beneficiaries: out-of-school adults age 16 and older lacking basic educational skills, a high school diploma, or proficiency of English.

Range: $16,678 to $89,375,087. **Average:** $9,981,666.

Activity: N.A.

HQ: Division of Adult Education and Literacy, OVAE-DOED, 400 Maryland Ave., SW, Washington, DC 20202. Phone: (202) 245-6836.

Internet: www2.ed.gov/about/offices/list/ovae/pi/AdultEd/index.html. (Note: no field offices for this program.)

84.004 CIVIL RIGHTS TRAINING AND ADVISORY SERVICES

Assistance: project grants. (100 percent/3 years).

Purposes: pursuant to the Civil Rights Act of 1964 as amended, Title IV, for educational equity assistance centers to provide technical assistance and training services to school districts, relating to compliance with civil rights laws pertaining to race, gender, and national origin. Project funds may be used for information dissemination, staff and community training, and developing curriculum materials specifically for the instruction of students with limited English proficiency relevant to program purposes.

Eligible applicants: private nonprofit organizations, public agencies.

Eligible beneficiaries: educational personnel and elementary and secondary students.

Range: N.A. **Average:** $657,500.

Activity: N.A.

HQ: School Support and Technology Programs, OESE-DOED, 400 Maryland Ave., SW, Rm. 3E201, Washington, DC 20202. Phone: (202) 205-4513.

Internet: www.ed.gov/programs/equitycenters/index.html. (Note: no field offices for this program.)

84.007 FEDERAL SUPPLEMENTAL EDUCATIONAL OPPORTUNITY GRANTS (FSEOG)

Assistance: direct payments/specified use (75 percent).

Purposes: pursuant to the Higher Education Act of 1965 (HEA) as amended, Title IV, for undergraduate postsecondary study by students in financial need. Institutions may receive an administrative cost allowance.

Eligible applicants: public, private nonprofit, postsecondary vocational, and proprietary IHEs.

Eligible beneficiaries: needy undergraduate students meeting citizenship or residency requirements, enrolled or enrolling as regular students, maintaining satisfactory academic progress, in compliance with Selective Service requirements, and neither owing a refund on a Title IV grant or in default on a Title IV loan.

Range: N.A. **Average:** $599.

Activity: anticipate 1,629,000 recipients in FY 2016.

HQ: OFSA-DOED, PO Box 84, Washington, DC 20044-0084 Phone: (800) 433-3243.

Internet: ifap.ed.gov.

84.010   TITLE I GRANTS TO LOCAL EDUCATIONAL AGENCIES

Assistance: formula grants (100 percent).

Purposes: pursuant to the Elementary and Secondary Education Act of 1965 (ESEA), Title I, Part A, to supplement state and local funding for extra instructional activities for children failing to meet academic standards or at-risk. Programs in schools with at least a 40 percent poverty rate may be operated on a schoolwide basis; other schools must operate targeted assistance programs for children failing or at-risk of failing to meet challenging state academic standards.

Eligible applicants: SEAs including in outlying areas; BIA. LEAs and tribal schools are subgrantees.

Eligible beneficiaries: children at risk of failing to meet State academic standards.

Range: $6,595,094 to $1,684,976,704. **Average:** $255,546,643.

Activity: N.A.

HQ: Compensatory Education Programs, OESE-DOED, 400 Maryland Ave., SW, Washington, DC 20202. Phone: (202) 260-1824.

Internet: www.ed.gov/programs/titleiparta/index.html. (Note: no field offices for this program.)

84.011   MIGRANT EDUCATION—STATE GRANT PROGRAM

Assistance: formula grants (100 percent).

Purposes: pursuant to ESEA as amended, Title I, Part C, for comprehensive educational programs for migratory children, including: academic, remedial, bilingual, compensatory, multicultural, and vocational instruction; preschool services; health services; career education services.

Eligible applicants: SEAs; consortia.

Eligible beneficiaries: children age 0-21, of migratory agricultural workers or fishers that have moved across school districts during the last 36 months.

Range: to $128,657,713. **Average:** N.A.

Activity: N.A.

HQ: Office of Migrant Education, OESE-DOED, 400 Maryland Ave., SW, Washington, DC 20202-6135. Phone: (202) 260-1386.

Internet: www.ed.gov/programs/mep/index.html. (Note: no field offices for this program.)

84.013   TITLE I STATE AGENCY PROGRAM FOR NEGLECTED AND DELINQUENT CHILDREN AND YOUTH

Assistance: formula grants (100 percent).

Purposes: pursuant to ESEA as amended, Title I, Part D, for education programs and related services for institutionalized neglected or delinquent children, including children under age 21 in state institutions, adult correctional institutions, or state- operated community day schools. Funds may cover supplemental instruction in core academic subjects, tutoring, counseling, services facilitating transition to schools. Juvenile institutions must provide at least 20 hours of instruction per week; adult institutions, at least 15 hours from nonfederal funds.

Eligible applicants: SEAs. Related state agencies may receive subgrants.

Eligible beneficiaries: children under age 21 in an adult correctional institution, a community day school, or a State institution for neglected or delinquent children.

Range: $122,712 to $2,763,707. **Average:** $892,763.

Activity: N.A.

HQ: Student Achievement and School Accountability Programs, OESE-DOED, Rm. 3E241, 400 Maryland Ave., SW, Washington, DC 20202. Phone: (202) 453-6348.

Internet: www.ed.gov/programs/titleipartd/index.html. (Note: no field offices for this program.)

84.015 NATIONAL RESOURCE CENTERS AND FELLOWSHIPS PROGRAM FOR LANGUAGE AND AREA

Assistance: project grants. (100 percent/to 3 years).

Purposes: pursuant to HEA as amended, Title VI, for instruction in modern foreign languages and in area and international studies. Center grants may be awarded for undergraduate training only, or they may be comprehensive involving undergraduate, graduate, and professional training—supporting costs of instruction programs, administration, library resources and staff, lectures and conferences. Fellowships may be awarded for graduate language study combined with area studies and world affairs, covering tuition, fees, and basic subsistence.

Eligible applicants: accredited US IHEs with resources and commitment to language and international studies.

Eligible beneficiaries: graduate students that are U.S. citizens, nationals, or permanent residents.

Range/Average: N.A.

Activity: N.A.

HQ: International and Foreign Language Education, Office of Postsecondary Education, DOE, 1990 K St., NW, Washington, DC 20006. Phone: (202) 502-7634.

Internet: www.ed.gov/programs/iegpsflasf. (Note: no field offices for this program.)

84.016 UNDERGRADUATE INTERNATIONAL STUDIES AND FOREIGN LANGUAGE PROGRAMS

Assistance: project grants. (50 percent/1-3 years).

Purposes: pursuant to HEA as amended, Title VI, for undergraduate international studies and foreign language program strengthening and improvement. Funds may cover costs of administration, curriculum and faculty development, lectures and conferences, library enhancement, travel.

Eligible applicants/beneficiaries: accredited IHEs, public and private nonprofit agencies and organizations.

Range/Average: N.A.

Activity: N.A.

HQ: International Studies Branch, International Education and Graduate Programs Service, Office of International Education and Foreign Language Studies, OPE-DOED, 1990 K St., NW, Washington, DC 20006. Phone: (202) 502-7631.

Internet: www.ed.gov/programs/iegpsugisf. (Note: no field offices for this program.)

84.018 OVERSEAS PROGRAMS—SPECIAL BILATERAL PROJECTS

Assistance: project grants. (100 percent/4-6 weeks).

Purposes: pursuant to MECEA as amended, to pay the travel and tuition costs of educators participating in short-term training seminars abroad, on topics in the social sciences and humanities.

Eligible applicants/beneficiaries: U.S. citizens or permanent residents with appropriate language proficiency and a bachelor's degree, that are: undergraduate faculty members or full-time elementary or junior high school teachers, administrators, supervisors, curriculum development specialists, or administrators.

Range/Average: N.A.

Activity: N.A.

HQ: International Studies Branch, International Education and Graduate Programs Service, Office of International Education and Foreign Language Studies, OPE-DOED, 1990 K St., NW, 6th Fl., Washington, DC 20006. Phone: (202) 219-7001.

Internet: www.ed.gov/programs/iegpssap. (Note: no field offices for this program.)

84.021 OVERSEAS PROGRAMS—GROUP PROJECTS ABROAD

Assistance: project grants. (100 percent/5 weeks to 36 months).

Purposes: pursuant to MECEA, for groups of teachers, faculty, and graduate or upper-classmen to conduct studies abroad in modern foreign languages and area studies. Funds may cover costs incurred abroad including round-trip travel, rent for instructional facilities, maintenance stipends, books, teaching materials, clerical, and related costs.

Eligible applicants: IHEs; state departments of education; private nonprofit educational organizations; consortia.

Eligible beneficiaries: U.S. citizens, nationals, or permanent residents that are faculty members or teachers at all levels, or graduate students or upper-classmen planning teaching careers in foreign language or area studies.

Range/Average: N.A.

Activity: N.A.

HQ: International Education and Graduate Programs Service, OPE-DOED, 1990 K St., 6th Fl., NW, Washington, DC 20006. Phone: (202) 502-7626.

Internet: www.ed.gov/programs/iegpsgpa. (Note: no field offices for this program.)

84.022   OVERSEAS PROGRAMS—DOCTORAL DISSERTATION RESEARCH ABROAD

Assistance: project grants. (100 percent/6-12 months).

Purposes: pursuant to MECEA as amended, for fellowships to graduate students to complete dissertation research abroad in modern foreign languages and area studies, to develop research knowledge and capability in areas not widely included in American curricula. Generally, no grants are available for projects focusing primarily on Western Europe, nor in countries where the U.S. has no formal diplomatic relations. Grants may cover stipends, travel costs, tuition to host institutions, dependents allowances, insurance, project expenses.

Eligible applicants: IHEs.

Eligible beneficiaries: U.S. citizens, nationals, or permanent residents that are graduate students already admitted to a doctoral degree candidacy program, plan teaching careers in the U.S. upon graduation, and have appropriate language skills. (DOED recommends applicants to the Fulbright scholarship board for approval.)

Range/Average: N.A.

Activity: N.A.

HQ: International Education Programs Service, OPE-DOED, 1990 K St. NW, room 6100, Washington, DC 20006. Phone: (202) 502-7704.

Internet: www.ed.gov/programs/iegpsddrap. (Note: no field offices for this program.)

84.027   SPECIAL EDUCATION—GRANTS TO STATES

Assistance: formula grants (100 percent).

Purposes: pursuant to the Individuals with Disabilities Act (IDEA) as amended, to provide special education and related services to children and youth, age 3-21, with disabilities, including those in private schools.

Eligible applicants: SEAs; territories and possessions; BIA. LEAs apply to SEAs for funds.

Eligible beneficiaries: children with disabilities.

Range: $4,000,000 to $1,200,000,000. **Average:** $218,000,000.

Activity: N.A.

HQ: Office of Special Education Programs, OSERS-DOED, 400 Maryland Ave., SW, Washington, DC 20202. Phone: (202) 245-7309.

Internet: www.ed.gov/about/offices/list/osers/osep/index.html. (Note: no field offices for this program.)

84.031   HIGHER EDUCATION—INSTITUTIONAL AID

Assistance: project grants. (50-100 percent/to 5 years).

Purposes: pursuant to HEA as amended, Title III, to help colleges and universities address their fiscal and management problems. The Strengthening Institutions Program includes tribally controlled and Alaska native- and Hawaii native-serving institutions; funds may be used to plan, develop, and implement programs for faculty development, and for administrative expenses, improvement of academic programs, library and equipment purchases, and student services. The Historically Black Colleges and Universities (HBCU) Program provides funds for undergraduate and graduate programs, which may be used: to acquire scientific equipment; to construct, maintain, and improve classroom, library, and other instructional facilities; for faculty exchanges and fellowships; to purchase library materials; to provide tutoring, counseling, and other student services; for administrative management and equipment. Graduate HBCU program funds may be used to establish or maintain endowments. HBCU projects over $1,000,000 require a 50 percent match.

Eligible applicants/beneficiaries: IHEs with a low average educational and general expenditure, substantial percentage of students receiving Pell Grants or other federal need-based financial aid; HBCUs established prior to 1964.

Range/Average: N.A.

Activity: N.A.

HQ: Office of Higher Education Programs, OPE-DOED, 1990 K St., NW, Washington, DC 20006. Phone: (202) 502-7549.

Internet: www.ed.gov/about/offices/list/ope/idues. (Note: no field offices for this program.)

84.033 FEDERAL WORK-STUDY PROGRAM

Assistance: direct payments/specified use (50-75 percent).

Purposes: pursuant to ARRA 2009 and HEA as amended, Title IV, to provide part- time employment to postsecondary students. The program contributes up to 75 percent of student earnings in jobs in public or nonprofit organizations, or 50 percent when a profit organization hires the student-plus administrative cost allowances to the educational institution. At least 5 percent of allocated funds must support students employed in community service.

Eligible applicants: public, private nonprofit, postsecondary vocational, and proprietary IHEs.

Eligible beneficiaries: undergraduate, graduate, or professional students meeting citizenship and residency requirements, demonstrating financial need, maintaining satisfactory academic progress, in compliance with Selective Service requirements, and neither owing a refund or in default on a Title IV loan.

Range: N.A. **Average:** $1,673.

Activity: anticipate 703,000 recipients in FY 2016.

HQ: OFSA-DOED, PO Box 84, Washington, DC 20044-0084 Phone: (800) 433-3243.

Internet: www.ifap.ed.gov.

84.040 IMPACT AID—FACILITIES MAINTENANCE

Assistance: project grants (100 percent).

Purposes: pursuant to ESEA as amended, Title VIII, to construct, enlarge, maintain, restore, or improve school facilities owned by DOED and operated by LEAs, and to transfer such facilities to LEAs.

Eligible applicants: LEAs.

Eligible beneficiaries: public elementary and secondary school children.

Range/Average: N.A.

Activity: N.A.

HQ: Impact Aid Programs, OESE-DOED, 400 Maryland Ave., SW, Rm. 3E105 (FB-6), Washington, DC 20202. Phone: (202) 260-3858.

Internet: www.ed.gov/about/offices/list/oese/impactaid/index.html. (Note: no field offices for this program.)

84.041   IMPACT AID

Assistance: formula grants (100 percent).

Purposes: pursuant to ESEA as amended, Title VIII, for operating costs of LEAs where enrollments or the tax base are adversely affected by federal activities including: federal acquisition of real property; employment of parents on federal property or in the uniformed services; significant numbers of children residing on federal land including Indian lands; sudden increases in school enrollment. Special additional funds are provided based on related enrollments of handicapped children, which must be used for special programs. Payments for construction may be used for construction and renovation, debt service, or other capital fund activities.

Eligible applicants: LEAs.

Eligible beneficiaries: public elementary and secondary school children.

Range: to $52,700,000 for basic support payments; to $1,220,000 for payments for children with disabilities. **Average:** $1,010,000 for basic support payments; $54,000 for children with disabilities; $100,000 for impact aid construction.

Activity: N.A.

HQ: Impact Aid Programs, OESE-DOED, 400 Maryland Ave., SW, Rm. 3E105 (FB-6), Washington, DC 20202. Phone: (202) 260-3858.

Internet: www.ed.gov/about/offices/list/oese/impactaid/index.html. (Note: no field offices for this program.)

84.042   TRIO—STUDENT SUPPORT SERVICES

Assistance: project grants. (100 percent/4-5 years).

Purposes: pursuant to HEA as amended, Title IV, to provide supportive services to disadvantaged college students to enhance their potential to complete their programs, to facilitate their transition from two-year to four-year programs of study, or to graduate or professional programs. Projects may include personal and academic counseling, career guidance, instruction, mentoring, tutoring, and special services to students with limited language proficiency. Grants may be awarded to students under certain conditions. At least two-thirds of project participants must be physically handicapped or low-income, first-generation college students.

Eligible applicants: IHEs and consortia.

Eligible beneficiaries: low-income, first generation college students or disabled students.

Range: $58,140 to $1,387,251. **Average:** $281,044.

Activity: N.A.

HQ: Federal TRIO Programs, OPE-DOED, 1990 K St., NW, 7th Fl., Washington, DC 20006. Phone: (202) 502-7674.

Internet: www.ed.gov/programs/triostudsupp. (Note: no field offices for this program.)

84.044 TRIO—TALENT SEARCH

Assistance: project grants. (100 percent/to 5 years).

Purposes: pursuant to HEA as amended, Title IV, to identify disadvantaged youth with potential for postsecondary education; to encourage them to return to or continue in and graduate from secondary schools and enroll in postsecondary education; to publicize the availability of financial aid; to provide special tutoring. Two-thirds of project participants must be low-income, potential first-generation college students.

Eligible applicants: IHEs; public and private agencies and organizations; combinations of IHEs and others; some secondary schools.

Eligible beneficiaries: individuals residing in target areas or attending a target school. Participants must be age 11-27 (exceptions allowed).

Range: $102,984 to $681,210. **Average:** $299,142.

Activity: N.A.

HQ: Federal TRIO Programs, OPE-DOED, 1990 K St., NW, 7th Fl., Washington, DC 20006-8510. Phone: (202) 502-7640.

Internet: www.ed.gov/programs/triotalent.

84.047 TRIO—UPWARD BOUND

Assistance: project grants. (100 percent/to 5 years).

Purposes: pursuant to HEA as amended, Title IV, for programs providing academic instruction, personal and academic counseling, tutoring, career guidance, and special instruction to prepare participants for postsecondary education and for careers in which persons from disadvantaged backgrounds are under-represented. Stipends may be paid to students ($40 monthly during the academic year, $60 monthly during special summer residential programs). Two-thirds of the participants must be low-income, potential first-generation college students.

Eligible applicants: IHEs; public and private agencies and organizations; combinations of IHEs and others; some secondary schools.

Eligible beneficiaries: low-income individuals and potential first-generation college students. Except for veterans, eligible regardless of age, participants must be age 13-19 and have completed the eighth grade but not have entered the twelfth grade (exceptions allowed).

Range: $169,913 to $852,958. **Average:** $313,843.

Activity: N.A.

HQ: Federal TRIO Programs, OPE-DOED, 1990 K St., NW, 7th Fl., Washington, DC 20006. Phone: (202) 502-7586.

Internet: www.ed.gov/programs/trioupbound.

84.048   CAREER AND TECHNICAL EDUCATION—BASIC GRANTS TO STATES

Assistance: formula grants. (states, 50 percent; outlying areas, 100 percent/states, 27 months).

Purposes: pursuant to the Carl D. Perkins Vocational and Technical Education Act of 1998 (CDPVTEA), Title I, to expand and improve vocational education programs, including special programs for single parents, single pregnant women, displaced homemakers, criminal offenders in correctional institutions, and for individuals participating in programs to eliminate sex bias and stereotyping.

Eligible applicants: states, outlying areas. Subgrants may be awarded to LEAs and postsecondary institutions.

Eligible beneficiaries: wide range of individuals pursuing vocational education and training.

Range: $567,534 to $120,256,718. **Average:** N.A.

Activity: N.A.

HQ: Division of High School, Postsecondary and Career Education, OVAE-DOED, 400 Maryland Ave., SW, Washington, DC 20202. Phone: (202) 245-7846.

Internet: www.ed.gov/about/offices/list/ovae/pi/cte/index.html. (Note: no field offices for this program.)

84.051   CAREER AND TECHNICAL EDUCATION—NATIONAL PROGRAMS

Assistance: project grants. (100 percent/to 5 years).

Purposes: pursuant to CDPVTEA as amended, for research, development, demonstration, dissemination, evaluation, and assessment activities to improve vocational and technical education.

Eligible applicants/beneficiaries: universities; university consortia and a public or private nonprofit organization.

Range/Average: N.A.

Activity: N.A.

HQ: Policy, Research and Evaluation Staff, OVAE-DOED, 400 Maryland Ave., SW, Washington, DC 20202. Phone: (202) 245-7818.

Internet: www2.ed.gov/about/offices/list/ovae/programs.html. (Note: no field offices for this program.)

84.060   INDIAN EDUCATION—GRANTS TO LOCAL EDUCATIONAL AGENCIES

Assistance: formula grants; project grants. (100 percent/to 5 years).

Purposes: pursuant to ESEA as amended, Title VII, for education programs serving Indian students to assure that they are based on state content and student performance standards. Among the types of activities that may be funded are culturally related programs including native languages, early childhood and family programs emphasizing school readiness, enrichment programs, school-to-work transition, drop-out prevention.

Eligible applicants: LEAs that enroll at least 10 Indian children or in which Indians constitute at least 25 percent of the total enrollment, except those serving Indian children in Alaska, California, and Oklahoma or located on or near an Indian reservation.

Eligible beneficiaries: Indian children, BIA funded schools.

Range: $4,000 to $2,823,022. **Average:** $78,024.

Activity: N.A.

HQ: Office of Indian Education, OESE-DOED, 400 Maryland Ave., SW, Washington, DC 20202. Phone: (202) 260-1454.

Internet: www.ed.gov/about/offices/list/oese/oie/programs.html. (Note: no field offices for this program.)

84.063   FEDERAL PELL GRANT PROGRAM

Assistance: direct payments/specified use.

Purposes: pursuant to ARRA 2009 and HEA as amended, Title IV, for grants to undergraduate postsecondary students demonstrating financial need, to attend public or private nonprofit colleges, vocational-technical schools, universities, hospital schools of nursing, or for-profit proprietary institutions. Award amount reflects family income and assets.

Eligible applicants/beneficiaries: U.S. citizens or eligible noncitizens with a high school diploma, enrolled as undergraduate students and making satisfactory academic progress. Eligible males, age 18 or over and born after December 31, 1959, must have registered with the Selective Service.

Range: $591 to $5,915. **Average:** $3,844.

Activity: anticipate 8,411,000 recipients in FY 2016.

HQ: OFSA-DOED, PO Box 84, Washington, DC 20044-0084 Phone: (800) 433-3243.

Internet: www.ifap.ed.gov.

84.066   TRIO—EDUCATIONAL OPPORTUNITY CENTERS

Assistance: project grants. (100 percent/to 5 years).

Purposes: pursuant to HEA as amended, Title IV, to establish and operate educational opportunity centers to provide academic and financial information to qualified adults interested in pursuing postsecondary education, and to assist them in applying for admission. Tutoring and counseling may be provided for participants not enrolled in an Upward Bound or a Student Support Services project. Two-thirds of the participants must be low-income potential first-generation college students.

Eligible applicants: IHEs; public and private agencies and organizations; combinations of IHEs and others; some secondary schools.

Eligible beneficiaries: residents of target areas, at least age 19 (exceptions allowed).

Range: $214,127 to $1,172,518. **Average:** $372,036.

Activity: N.A.

HQ: Federal TRIO Programs, OPE-DOED, 1990 K St., NW, 7th Fl., Washington, DC 20006. Phone: (202) 502-7655.

Internet: www.ed.gov/programs/trioeoc. (Note: no field offices for this program.)

84.101   CAREER AND TECHNICAL EDUCATION—GRANTS TO NATIVE AMERICANS AND ALASKA NATIVES

Assistance: project grants. (100 percent/to 2 years).

Purposes: pursuant to CDPVTEA, Title I, to plan, conduct, and administer Indian vocational and technical education programs or portions of programs.

Eligible applicants/beneficiaries: tribes, tribal organizations, Alaska native entities.

Range: $300,000 to $600,000. **Average:** $400,000.

Activity: N.A.

HQ: Division of High School, Postsecondary and Career Education, OVAE-DOED, 400 Maryland Ave., SW, Washington, DC 20202. Phone: (202) 245-7792.

Internet: www2.ed.gov/about/offices/list/ovae/programs.html. (Note: no field offices for this program.)

84.103   TRIO STAFF TRAINING PROGRAM

Assistance: project grants. (100 percent/1-2 years).

Purposes: pursuant to HEA as amended, Title IV, to train present or new staff and leadership personnel for federal TRIO programs (special programs for students from disadvantaged backgrounds - **84.042**, **84.044**, **84.047**, **84.066**, **84.217**). Grants support seminars, workshops, internships, and publications.

Eligible applicants: IHEs, public and nonprofit private agencies and organizations.

Eligible beneficiaries: leadership personnel, staff of projects under the federal TRIO programs, individuals preparing for TRIO leadership.

Range: $125,000 to $325,000. **Average:** $190,625.

Activity: N.A.

HQ: Federal TRIO Programs, OPE-DOED, 1990 K St., 7th Fl., NW, Washington, DC 20006. Phone: (202) 502-7789.

Internet: www.ed.gov/programs/triotrain. (Note: no field offices for this program.)

84.116   FUND FOR THE IMPROVEMENT OF POSTSECONDARY EDUCATION (FIPSE)

Assistance: project grants. (to 100 percent/1-3 years).

Purposes: pursuant to HEA as amended, Title VII, to develop innovative programs to improve access to and quality of postsecondary education.

Examples of funded projects include cooperation between colleges and business, uses of technology, improved access for Blacks, Hispanics, and other minorities.

Eligible applicants/beneficiaries: two- and four-year IHEs, community organizations, libraries, museums, consortia, student groups, local government agencies.

Range: $1,627,322 to $3,999,955. **Average:** $3,110,000.

Activity: N.A.

HQ: FIPSE, OPE-DOED, 1990 K St., 6th Fl., NW, Washington, DC 20006. Phone: (202) 502-7621.

Internet: www2.ed.gov/about/offices/list/ope/fipse/index.html. (Note: no field offices for this program.)

84.120 MINORITY SCIENCE AND ENGINEERING IMPROVEMENT ("MSEIP")

Assistance: project grants. (to 100 percent/1-3 years).

Purposes: pursuant to HEA as amended, Title III, to improve undergraduate science and engineering education programs at predominantly minority institutions to better prepare their students, particularly women, for graduate work or careers in which they are under-represented. Eligible uses of funds include salaries, purchase of equipment and instructional materials, faculty development, and inservice training.

Eligible applicants/beneficiaries: private and public nonprofit two-and four-year IHEs whose enrollments are predominantly American Indian, Alaska native, Black, Hispanic, Pacific Islander, or any combination of these or other underrepresented minority; nonprofit science organizations; professional scientific societies; private organizations with science and engineering facilities; quasi-governmental entities with a significant scientific or engineering mission.

Range: $68,000 to $169,000. **Average:** $255,000.

Activity: N.A.

HQ: Institutional Development and Undergraduate Education Service, OPE-DOED, 1990 K St., NW, 6th Fl., Washington, DC 20006. Phone: (202) 502-7616.

Internet: www.ed.gov/programs/iduesmsi. (Note: no field offices for this program.)

84.126 REHABILITATION SERVICES—VOCATIONAL REHABILITATION GRANTS TO STATES

Assistance: formula grants (79 percent).

Purposes: pursuant to the Rehabilitation Act of 1973 as amended, for vocational rehabilitation services to persons with mental and/or physical disabilities resulting in employment handicaps that may reasonably be expected to increase their employability. Services include: assessment; counseling; vocational and other training; reader services for the blind, interpreter services for the deaf; job placement; medical and related services, prosthetic and orthotic devices; rehabilitation technology; transportation to obtain services; construction and establishment of community rehabilitation facilities; services to families of handicapped persons.

Eligible applicants: state agencies, territories, possessions.

Eligible beneficiaries: individuals with physical and/or mental impairments which constitute or result in a substantial impediment to employment.

Range: $900,000 to $301,600,000. **Average:** $41,800,000.

Activity: assisted 200,000 individuals in FY 2014.

HQ: Rehabilitation Services Administration, OSERS-DOED, 400 Maryland Ave., SW, Washington, DC 20202. Phone: (202) 245-7325.

Internet: www.rsa.ed.gov/programs.cfm. (Note: no field offices for this program.)

84.129 REHABILITATION LONG-TERM TRAINING

Assistance: project grants. (90 percent/to 5 years).

Purposes: pursuant to the Rehabilitation Act of 1973 as amended, for academic training programs for personnel involved in vocational rehabilitation for the disabled. Training grants cover such specialties as rehabilitation counseling, independent living, rehabilitation medicine, physical and occupational therapy, prosthetics-orthotics, speech-language, pathology and audiology, rehabilitation of the deaf and the blind, rehabilitation technology. At least 75 percent of grant funds must be used for scholarships.

Eligible applicants: IHEs, state vocational rehabilitation agencies including territories and possessions; other public or nonprofit agencies and organizations.

Eligible beneficiaries: individuals preparing for employment in the field of rehabilitation for the disabled.

Range/Average: N.A.

Activity: N.A.

HQ: Rehabilitation Services Administration, OSERS-DOED, 400 Maryland Ave., SW, Washington, DC 20202. Phone: (202) 245-7343.

Internet: www.ed.gov/offices/OSERS/RSA. (Note: no field offices for this program.)

84.141 MIGRANT EDUCATION—HIGH SCHOOL EQUIVALENCY PROGRAM (HEP)

Assistance: project grants. (100 percent/to 5 years).

Purposes: pursuant to HEA, Title IV, to assist migrant students obtain the equivalent of a secondary school diploma and subsequently to gain employment or to attend college or obtain other postsecondary education or training. Program funds may be used to recruit students and to provide academic and support services and stipends.

Eligible applicants: IHEs or private nonprofit agencies in cooperation with IHEs.

Eligible beneficiaries: students age 16 or older, lacking a high school diploma, in migrant or seasonally employed families, or that participated or were eligible to participate in the Title I Migrant Education Program or JTPA 402.

Range: $180,000 to $475,000. **Average:** $446,438.

Activity: N.A.

HQ: Office of Migrant Education, OESE-DOED, 400 Maryland Ave., SW, Rm. 3E309, Washington, DC 20202. Phone: (202) 260-2063.

Internet: www.ed.gov/program/hep/index.html. (Note: no field offices for this program.)

84.144   MIGRANT EDUCATION—COORDINATION PROGRAM

Assistance: project grants. (100 percent/to 5 years).

Purposes: pursuant to ESEA, Title I, to improve interstate and intrastate coordination of migrant education among SEAs and LEAs. Incentive grants may be provided to SEAs that participate in an approved consortium.

Eligible applicants: SEAs, LEAs, IHEs, other public or nonprofit private entities.

Eligible beneficiaries: migratory children of migratory agricultural workers or fishers.

Range: $60,000 to $120,000. **Average:** N.A.

Activity: N.A.

HQ: Office of Migrant Education, OESE-DOED, 400 Maryland Ave., SW, Rm. 3E257, Washington, DC 20202. Phone: (202) 453-7060.

Internet: www.ed.gov/about/offices/list/oese/ome/index.html. (Note: no field offices for this program.)

84.145   FEDERAL REAL PROPERTY ASSISTANCE PROGRAM

Assistance: sale, exchange, or donation of property and goods (to 30 years).

Purposes: pursuant to the Federal Property and Administrative Services Act of 1949 as amended and Department of Education Organization Act of 1979, to convey surplus federal real property for educational purposes, including all educational levels, vocational education or rehabilitation, libraries, central administration facilities, educational radio and television, rehabilitation and training, research, correctional education centers. Examples include: improved or unimproved land; former Nike sites; total military bases.

Eligible applicants/beneficiaries: states and their political subdivisions and instrumentalities; tax-supported or tax-exempt organizations or private nonprofit institutions.

Range/Average: N.A.

Activity: N.A.

HQ: Federal Real Property Assistance Program, Office of the Administrator/Management Services, DOED, 400 Maryland Ave., SW, Washington, DC 20202. Phone: (202) 260-4558.

Internet: www.ed.gov.

84.149 MIGRANT EDUCATION—COLLEGE ASSISTANCE MIGRANT PROGRAM (CAMP)

Assistance: project grants (100 percent/to 5 years).

Purposes: pursuant to HEA, Title IV, to provide supportive and instructional services and other assistance to migrants enrolling full-time in college for the first academic year. Funds may be used to provide tutoring, counseling, assistance in obtaining financial aid, follow-up services, and inservice training for project staff.

Eligible applicants: IHEs or private nonprofit agencies in cooperation with IHEs.

Eligible beneficiaries: first-year college students engaged, or whose families are engaged, in migrant or other seasonal farm work, or that participated or were eligible to participate in the Title I Migrant Education Program or JTPA 402.

Range: $180,000 to $425,000. **Average:** $410,615.

Activity: N.A.

HQ: Office of Migrant Education, OESE-DOED, 400 Maryland Ave., SW, Rm. 3E309, Washington, DC 20202. Phone: (202) 260-82063.

Internet: www.ed.gov/programs/camp/index.html. (Note: no field offices for this program.)

84.160 TRAINING INTERPRETERS FOR INDIVIDUALS WHO ARE DEAF AND INDIVIDUALS WHO ARE DEAF-BLIND

Assistance: project grants (cost sharing/to 5 years).

Purposes: pursuant to the Rehabilitation Act of 1973 as amended, to train prospective or improve the skills of present manual, oral, and cued speech interpreters providing services to deaf or deaf-blind persons—through classroom instruction, workshops, seminars, and field placement. Curriculum may include such specialty areas as interpreting in medical, legal, or rehabilitation settings.

Eligible applicants/beneficiaries: public or private nonprofit agencies and organizations; IHEs.

Range/Average: N.A.

Activity: N.A.

HQ: Rehabilitation Services Administration, OSERS-DOED, 400 Maryland Ave., SW, Washington, DC 20202. Phone: (202) 245-7343.

Internet: www.ed.gov/students/college/aid/rehab/catinter.html. (Note: no field offices for this program.)

84.161 REHABILITATION SERVICES—CLIENT ASSISTANCE PROGRAM (CAP)

Assistance: formula grants (100 percent).

Purposes: pursuant to the Rehabilitation Act of 1973 as amended, to help persons with disabilities obtain information about and benefits of Rehabilitation Act and ADA projects, programs, facilities, and services, whether as clients or applicants for services—and to help them overcome problems with service delivery systems including assistance and advocacy in pursuing legal, administrative, and other appropriate remedies. Grants may not support class action suits.

Eligible applicants/beneficiaries: states and territories, through public or private agencies designated by the governor.

Range/Average: N.A.

Activity: N.A.

HQ: Rehabilitation Services Administration, OSERS-DOED, 400 Maryland Ave., SW, Washington, DC 20202. Phone: (202) 245-6630.

Internet: www.rsa.ed.gov/programs.cfm. (Note: no field offices for this program.)

84.165 MAGNET SCHOOLS ASSISTANCE

Assistance: project grants. (100 percent/to 3 years).

Purposes: pursuant to ESEA as amended, Title V, for magnet school projects that are part of approved desegregation plans designed to bring together students from different social, economic, racial, and ethnic backgrounds. Funds may be used for planning and promotional activities to develop, expand, continue, or enhance academic instruction; to pay or subsidize teacher and staff salaries; to purchase books, materials, equipment. Funds may not be used for transportation or activities that do not augment academic improvement. Project examples: science and math magnet projects; performing arts magnet programs; Montessori programs.

Eligible applicants/beneficiaries: LEAs.

Range: $350,000 to $4,000,000. **Average:** N.A.

Activity: N.A.

HQ: OESE-DOED, 400 Maryland Ave., SW, Washington, DC 20202. Phone: (202) 260-1816.

Internet: www.ed.gov/programs/magnet/index.html. (Note: no field offices for this program.)

84.173 SPECIAL EDUCATION—PRESCHOOL GRANTS

Assistance: formula grants. (100 percent/15 months).

Purposes: pursuant to IDEA as amended, for free appropriate public educational programs for preschool children with disabilities, requiring special education and related services. States may also use funds to develop and implement elements of comprehensive statewide service delivery systems.

Eligible applicants: SEAs, DC, PR.

Eligible beneficiaries: children age 3-5 (optionally, age 2 and to reach age 3 during the school year), determined to be mentally retarded, hearing impaired, speech or language impaired, visually handicapped, seriously emotionally disturbed, autistic, orthopedically impaired, or other health-impaired.

Range: $217,082 to 35,217,658. **Average:** $6,793,038.

Activity: N.A.

HQ: Office of Special Education Programs, OSERS-DOED, 400 Maryland Ave., SW, Washington, DC 20202. Phone: (202) 245-7309.

Internet: www.ed.gov/about/offices/list/osers/osep/programs.html. (Note: no field offices for this program.)

84.177 REHABILITATION SERVICES—INDEPENDENT LIVING SERVICES FOR OLDER INDIVIDUALS WHO ARE BLIND

Assistance: project grants. (90 percent/to 5 years).

Purposes: pursuant to the Rehabilitation Act of 1973 as amended, to provide independent living services for blind persons age 55 or older, whose vision impairments make competitive employment extremely difficult, but for whom independent living in their own homes or communities is feasible. Program funds may be used to pay such costs as: vision correction or modification; eyeglasses or other visual aids; services and equipment to enhance mobility and self-care; training in braille; teaching services in household management; public education activities.

Eligible applicants/beneficiaries: state agencies, territories, possessions.

Range: $40,000 to $3,350,574. **Average:** $584,509.

Activity: N.A.

HQ: Rehabilitation Services Administration, OSERS-DOED, 400 Maryland Ave., Washington, DC 20202. Phone: (202) 245-7303.

Internet: www.rsa.ed.gov/programs.cfm. (Note: no field offices for this program.)

84.181 SPECIAL EDUCATION—GRANTS FOR INFANTS AND FAMILIES

Assistance: formula grants. (100 percent/to 27 months).

Purposes: pursuant to IDEA as amended, to develop and implement statewide, comprehensive, coordinated, multidisciplinary, inter- agency systems to provide early intervention services for handicapped infants and toddlers and their families. Grants may support expanded or improved services.

Eligible applicants/beneficiaries: states, territories, possessions.

Range: $2,148,926 to $53,043,814. **Average:** $8,211,297.

Activity: N.A.

HQ: Office of Special Education Programs, OSERS-DOED, 400 Maryland Ave., SW, Washington, DC 20202. Phone: (202) 245-7309.

Internet: www.ed.gov/about/offices/list/osers/osep/programs.html. (Note: no field offices for this program.)

84.184 SAFE AND DRUG-FREE SCHOOLS AND COMMUNITIES—NATIONAL PROGRAMS

Assistance: project grants. (to 100 percent/1-4 years).

Purposes: pursuant to ESEA as amended, Title IV, for prevention and education activities concerning the illegal use of drugs and violence at all educational levels.

Eligible applicants/beneficiaries: public and private and nonprofit organizations, individuals.

Range/Average: N.A.

Activity: 105 continuation awards in FY 2015.

HQ: Office of Safe and Drug-Free Schools, DOED, 400 Maryland Ave., SW, Rm. 3E328, Washington, DC 20202. Phone: (202) 453-6722.

Internet: www2.ed.gov/about/offices/list/oese/oshs/index.html. (Note: no field offices for this program.)

84.187   SUPPORTED EMPLOYMENT SERVICES FOR INDIVIDUALS WITH THE MOST SIGNIFICANT DISABILITIES ("Supported Employment State Grants")

Assistance: formula grants (100 percent).

Purposes: pursuant to the Rehabilitation Act of 1973 as amended, for time-limited services leading to supported employment for severely handicapped persons whose potential to engage in a training program has been properly evaluated. Funds may be used for most program operating costs including systematic client training, skilled job trainers to accompany workers for intensive on-the-job training, job development, follow-up services.

Eligible applicants/beneficiaries: state vocational rehabilitation agencies, territories and possessions.

Range: $34,435 to $2,760,353. **Average:** $308,254.

Activity: assisted 17,000 individuals in FY 2014.

HQ: Rehabilitation Services Administration, OSERS-DOED, 400 Maryland Ave., SW, Washington, DC 20202. Phone: (202) 245-7325.

Internet: www.rsa.ed.gov/programs.cfm. (Note: no field offices for this program.)

84.191   ADULT EDUCATION—NATIONAL LEADERSHIP ACTIVITIES

Assistance: project grants. (100 percent/12-18 months).

Purposes: pursuant to the Adult Education and Family Literacy Act as amended, for the improvement and expansion nationally of adult basic education through applied research, development, demonstration, dissemination, evaluation, and related activities. Project examples: evaluations of "what works" for adult basic education and ESL, the funding set-aside for corrections education, and distance learning initiative.

Eligible applicants/beneficiaries: public or private agencies, institutions, organizations; business concerns; individuals.

Range/Average: N.A.

Activity: N.A.

HQ: Division of Adult Education and Literacy, OVAE-DOED, 400 Maryland Ave., SW, Washington, DC 20202-7240. Phone: (202) 245-7717.

Internet: www.ed.gov/about/offices/list/ovae/pi/AdultEd/index.html. (Note: no field offices for this program.)

84.196 EDUCATION FOR HOMELESS CHILDREN AND YOUTH

Assistance: formula grants (100 percent).

Purposes: pursuant to MVHAA, to develop and implement plans to coordinate and improve education programs for homeless children and youth; to identify homeless children and ensure that they enroll in, attend, and achieve success in school. States may provide subgrants to LEAs for direct services to homeless children and youth including tutoring, summer enrichment programs, purchases of supplies, school personnel training.

Eligible applicants/beneficiaries: state departments of education and outlying areas; schools funded by DOI, serving Indian students.

Range: N.A. **Average:** states: $1,216,980.

Activity: N.A.

HQ: OESE-DOED, 400 Maryland Ave., SW, Washington, DC 20202. Phone: (202) 401-0962.

Internet: www.ed.gov/programs/homeless/index.html. (Note: no field offices for this program.)

84.200 GRADUATE ASSISTANCE IN AREAS OF NATIONAL NEED

Assistance: project grants. (75 percent/3-5 years).

Purposes: pursuant to HEA as amended, Title VII, for graduate fellowships for up to five years that will help sustain and enhance the capacity for teaching and research in academic areas of national need, designated by the Secretary of Education.

Eligible applicants: IHEs.

Eligible beneficiaries: needy graduate students with excellent academic records and planning teaching or research careers. They must be U.S. citizens, nationals, permanent residents, or permanent residents of the Trust Territory of the Pacific Islands or citizens of Freely Associated States.

Range/Average: N.A.

Activity: N.A.

HQ: International Education and Graduate Programs Service, OPE-DOED, 1990 K St., NW, 7th Fl., Washington, DC 20006. Phone: (202) 502-7779.

Internet: www.ed.gov/programs/gaann. (Note: no field offices for this program.)

84.215 FUND FOR THE IMPROVEMENT OF EDUCATION (FIE)

Assistance: project grants (100 percent).

Purposes: pursuant to ESEA as amended, Title V, for projects of national significance to improve the quality of education, to assist all students to meet challenging state content standards, and contribute to the achievement of elementary and secondary students. Projects may support a wide range of activities.

Eligible applicants/beneficiaries: SEAs, LEAs, IHEs, public and private organizations.

Range/Average: N.A.

Activity: N.A.

HQ: OERI-DOED, 400 Maryland Ave., SW, Washington, DC 20202. Phone: (202) 401-4942.

Internet: www2.ed.gov/programs/fie/index.html. (Note: no field offices for this program.)

84.217 TRIO—MCNAIR POST-BACCALAUREATE ACHIEVEMENT

Assistance: project grants. (100 percent/4-5 years).

Purposes: pursuant to HEA as amended, Title IV, to prepare low- income, first-generation college students and students from under-represented groups for graduate study. Services may include: opportunities for research and other scholarly activities; summer internships; seminars; tutoring; academic counseling; securing graduate admission and financial assistance; mentoring; exposure to cultural events.

Eligible applicants/beneficiaries: IHEs or combinations of IHEs.

Range: $160,000 to $367,750. **Average:** $235,764.

Activity: N.A.

HQ: Federal TRIO Programs, OPE-DOED, 1990 K St., NW, 7th Fl., Washington, DC 20006. Phone: (202) 219-7138.

Internet: www.ed.gov/programs/triomcnair. (Note: no field offices for this program.)

84.220 CENTERS FOR INTERNATIONAL BUSINESS EDUCATION

Assistance: project grants. (50-90 percent/3 years).

Purposes: pursuant to HEA as amended, Title VI, for inter- disciplinary faculty research to promote international competitiveness of U.S. business. Activities must include: center advisory councils to plan and design activities and programs; collaboration in the center's establishment and operation among the business, management, foreign language, international studies, and other professional schools or departments; assurance that the center's programs are open to students concentrating in these areas.

Eligible applicants/beneficiaries: public and nonprofit private IHEs, or combinations thereof.

Range/Average: N.A.

Activity: N.A.

HQ: International Studies Branch, Center for International Education, 1990 K St., NW, Washington, DC 20006. Phone: (202) 502-7628.

Internet: www.ed.gov/programs/iegpscibe. (Note: no field offices for this program.)

84.229 LANGUAGE RESOURCE CENTERS

Assistance: project grants. (100 percent/to 3 years).

Purposes: pursuant to HEA as amended, Title VI, to establish, strengthen, and operate foreign language resource centers to improve teaching and learning at IHEs, through: research on the use of advanced educational technology; development of new teaching materials based on the research;

development and application of performance testing; teacher training; publication of instructional materials in the less commonly taught languages; dissemination of project results.

Eligible applicants/beneficiaries: IHEs or combinations of IHEs.

Range/Average: N.A.

Activity: N.A.

HQ: International Education and Graduate Programs Service, OPE-DOED, 1990 K St., 6th Fl., NW, Washington, DC 20006. Phone: (202) 502-7626.

Internet: www.ed.gov/programs/iegpslrc. (Note: no field offices for this program.)

84.235 REHABILITATION SERVICES DEMONSTRATION AND TRAINING PROGRAMS

Assistance: project grants (100 percent/to 5 years).

Purposes: pursuant to the Rehabilitation Act of 1973 as amended, to expand and improve vocational rehabilitation and related services for the disabled and severely disabled. Projects may include demonstrations involving such activities as: increasing client choice; service delivery; technical assistance; systems change; special studies and evaluations; transition services; supportive employment; services to unserved, underserved, or populations, and to low-incidence disabilities; transportation; parent information and training; Braille training.

Eligible applicants/beneficiaries: states, public or nonprofit organizations.

Range/Average: N.A.

Activity: N.A.

HQ: Rehabilitation Services Administration, OSERS-DOED, 400 Maryland Ave., SW, Washington, DC 20202. Phone: (202) 245-7343.

Internet: www.ed.gov/offices/OSERS/RSA/Programs/Discretionary/demo train.html. (Note: no field offices for this program.)

84.240 PROGRAM OF PROTECTION AND ADVOCACY OF INDIVIDUAL RIGHTS

Assistance: project grants (100 percent).

Purposes: pursuant to the Rehabilitation Act of 1973 as amended, for systems for protection and advocacy of the rights of persons with disabilities—including services upholding their individual legal and human rights beyond the scope of the Client Assistance Program, and for persons ineligible for programs under the Developmental Disabilities Assistance (DDA) and Bill of Rights Act and the Protection and Advocacy for Individuals with Mental Illness Act (PAIMI).

Eligible applicants/beneficiaries: state-designated protection and advocacy agencies, including territories.

Range/Average: N.A.

Activity: N.A.

HQ: Rehabilitation Services Administration, OSERS-DOED, 400 Maryland Ave., SW, Washington, DC 20202. Phone: (202) 245-6493.

Internet: www.rsa.ed.gov/programs.cfm. (Note: no field offices for this program.)

84.245 TRIBALLY CONTROLLED POSTSECONDARY CAREER AND TECHNICAL INSTITUTIONS

Assistance: project grants. (100 percent/to 5 years).

Purposes: pursuant to CDPVTEA, for the maintenance and operation of tribally controlled postsecondary vocational and technical institutions.

Eligible applicants/beneficiaries: chartered and accredited tribally controlled postsecondary vocational institutions that: have operated for at least three years; enroll at least 100 full-time students (a majority of which are Indians); and, meet other requirements.

Range: $2,343,546 to $5,361,454. **Average:** $3,852,500.

Activity: N.A.

HQ: OVAE Division of Adult and Technical Education, OVAE-DOED, 400 Maryland Ave., SW, Washington, DC 20202. Phone: (202) 245-7790.

Internet: www2.ed.gov/about/offices/list/ovae/programs.html. (Note: no field offices for this program.)

84.246 REHABILITATION SHORT-TERM TRAINING

Assistance: project grants. (cost sharing/1-3 years).

Purposes: pursuant to the Rehabilitation Act of 1973 as amended, for special training seminars, institutes, workshops, and other short-term courses in technical matters relating to the delivery of vocational, medical, social, and psychological services—in fields directly related to the vocational and independent living rehabilitation of persons with disabilities.

Eligible applicants/beneficiaries: IHEs, state vocational rehabilitation agencies including territories and possessions; other public or nonprofit agencies and organizations.

Range/Average: N.A.

Activity: N.A.

HQ: Rehabilitation Services Administration, OSERS-DOED, 400 Maryland Ave., SW, Washington, DC 20202. Phone: (202) 245-7343.

Internet: www.ed.gov/offices/OSERS/RSA. (Note: no field offices for this program.)

84.250 REHABILITATION SERVICES—AMERICAN INDIANS WITH DISABILITIES

Assistance: project grants. (90 percent/to 5 years).

Purposes: pursuant to the Rehabilitation Act of 1973 as amended, to establish and operate tribal vocational rehabilitation service projects serving American Indians with disabilities, residing on reservations.

Eligible applicants/beneficiaries: tribal governments or consortia on federal or state reservations.

Range: $300,000 to $600,000. **Average:** $450,000.

Activity: assisted 2,100 individuals in FY 2014.

HQ: Rehabilitation Services Administration, OSERS-DOED, 400 Maryland Ave., SW, Washington, DC 20202. Phone: (202) 245-7410.

Internet: www.ed.gov/about/offices/list/osers/rsa/index.html. (Note: no field offices for this program.)

84.256 TERRITORIES AND FREELY ASSOCIATED STATES EDUCATION GRANT PROGRAM

Assistance: project grants. (100 percent/3 years).

Purposes: pursuant to ESEA as amended, Title I, for educational activities including teacher training, curriculum development, instructional materials, general school improvement, and schoolwide reform.

Eligible applicants/beneficiaries: LEAs in Micronesia, Marshall Islands, Palau.

Range/Average: N.A.

Activity: N.A.

HQ: School Support and Technology Programs, OESE-DOED, 400 Maryland Ave., SW, Rm. 3E201, Washington, DC 20202. Phone: (202) 205-4513.

Internet: www.ed.gov/programs/tfasegp/index.html. (Note: no field offices for this program.)

84.259 NATIVE HAWAIIAN CAREER AND TECHNICAL EDUCATION

Assistance: project grants (100 percent/to 5 years).

Purposes: pursuant to CDPVTEA, for vocational education projects conducted by organizations primarily serving and representing Hawaii natives.

Eligible applicants/beneficiaries: organizations recognized by the governor, primarily serving and representing Hawaii natives.

Range: $258,219 to $513,638. **Average:** $362,220.

Activity: N.A.

HQ: Division of High School, Postsecondary and Career Education, OVAE-DOED, 400 Maryland Ave., SW, Washington, DC 20202. Phone: (202) 245-7792.

Internet: www2.ed.gov/about/offices/list/ovae/programs.html. (Note: no field offices for this program.)

84.264 REHABILITATION TRAINING—CONTINUING EDUCATION

Assistance: project grants (cost sharing/to 5 years).

Purposes: pursuant to the Rehabilitation Act of 1973 as amended, for regional or area training centers providing continuing education for rehabilitation counselors, administrators, independent living specialists, audiologists, rehabilitation teachers for the blind, and rehabilitation technology specialists—providing vocational, independent living, and client assistance services to the disabled.

Eligible applicants/beneficiaries: IHEs, state vocational rehabilitation agencies including territories and possessions; other public or nonprofit agencies and organizations.

Range/Average: N.A.

Activity: N.A.

HQ: Rehabilitation Services Administration, OSERS-DOED, 400 Maryland Ave., SW, Washington, DC 20202. Phone: (202) 245-7343.

Internet: www.ed.gov/offices/OSERS/RSA. (Note: no field offices for this program.)

84.268 FEDERAL DIRECT STUDENT LOANS

Assistance: direct loans (10-30 years).

Purposes: pursuant to HEA as amended, Title IV, to provide education loans for any school year to vocational, undergraduate, professional, and graduate postsecondary students and their parents—directly from DOED rather than through private lenders. Subsidized loans are based on financial need; unsubsidized loans are not. Standard, extended, consolidated, and graduated repayment plans are available. Generally, repayment begins six months after termination of at least half-time enrollment.

Eligible applicants/beneficiaries: U.S. citizens, nationals, or permanent residents enrolled or accepted for at least half-time enrollment at a participating postsecondary school. Parents may borrow for dependent students under the Direct PLUS program. School enrollment is not required for Direct Consolidation Loans which are available to students, married couples, or parents if they are unable to obtain consolidated loans under 84.032 (Federal Family Education Loans). Students must maintain satisfactory academic progress, be in compliance with Selective Service requirements, and neither owe a refund nor be in default on a Title IV grant or loan.

Range/Average: N.A.

Activity: N.A.

HQ: OFSA-DOED, PO Box 84, Washington, DC 20044-0084 Phone: (800) 433-3243.

Internet: www.ifap.cd.gov.

84.274 AMERICAN OVERSEAS RESEARCH CENTERS

Assistance: project grants. (100 percent/3 years).

Purposes: pursuant to HEA as amended, Title VI, to establish or operate overseas research centers that are consortia of IHEs to promote postgraduate research, exchanges, and area studies. Funds may cover the costs of: faculty and staff stipends, salaries, travel, and research; student travel; maintenance and operations; teaching and research materials; conferences; publications.

Eligible applicants/beneficiaries: tax-exempt permanent overseas centers receiving over 50 percent of their funding from public or private U.S. sources.

Range/Average: N.A.

Activity: N.A.

HQ: International Education and Graduate Programs Service, OPE-DOED, 1990 K St., NW, Washington, DC 20006. Phone: (202) 502-7634.

Internet: www.ed.gov/programs/iegpsaorc. (Note: no field offices for this program.)

84.282 CHARTER SCHOOLS

Assistance: project grants. (100 percent/to 3 years).

Purposes: pursuant to ESEA as amended, Title V, for the planning, development, and initial implementation of charter schools which provide enhanced parental choice while exempt from many statutory and regulatory requirements, in return for which the schools establish plans to improve student academic achievement and stimulate the creativity and commitment of teachers, parents, and the public.

Eligible applicants/beneficiaries: SEAs. If SEAs do not participate, authorized public chartering agencies or other public entities may apply.

Range: $100,000 to $45,000,000. **Average:** N.A.

Activity: N.A.

HQ: Parental Options and Information, OII-DOED, 400 Maryland Ave., SW, Washington, DC 20202. Phone: (202) 453-6384.

Internet: www.ed.gov/programs/charter/index.html. (Note: no field offices for this program.)

84.283 COMPREHENSIVE CENTERS

Assistance: project grants; technical information. (grants, 100 percent/grants, to 5 years).

Purposes: pursuant to the Education Sciences Reform Act of 2002, to support not less than 20 comprehensive centers provide training, technical assistance, and professional development in reading, mathematics, and technology—particularly to school districts and schools that fail to meet their state's definition of adequate yearly progress. Sixteen centers focus on such areas as: implementation and administration of programs authorized under ESEA; using scientifically valid teaching methods and assessment tools in mathematics, science, reading and language arts, English language acquisition, education technology; facilitating communication between education experts, school officials, teachers, parents, and librarians; related information dissemination. Five content centers focus on accountability, instruction, teacher quality, innovation and improvement, and high schools.

Eligible applicants/beneficiaries: public or private nonprofit entities or consortia.

Range: $759,708 to $4,511,622. **Average:** $2,201,741.

Activity: N.A.

HQ: School Support and Technology Programs, OESE-DOED, 400 Maryland Ave., SW, Rm. 3E201, Washington, DC 20202. Phone: (202) 205-4513.

Internet: www.ed.gov/programs/newccp/index.html. (Note: no field offices for this program.)

84.287 TWENTY-FIRST CENTURY COMMUNITY LEARNING CENTERS

Assistance: formula grants (100 percent).

Purposes: pursuant to ESEA as amended, Title IV, for community learning centers to provide academic enrichment opportunities in core subjects for children and literacy programs for families, in rural and inner-city areas.

Eligible applicants: state departments of education.

Eligible beneficiaries: residents within communities served by learning centers.

Range: $5,643,198 to $131,075,439. **Average:** $21,704,607.

Activity: N.A.

HQ: 21st Century Community Learning Centers, OESE-DOED, 400 Maryland Ave., SW, Washington, DC 20202. Phone: (202) 205-1909.

Internet: www.ed.gov/programs/21stcclc/index.html. (Note: no field offices for this program.)

84.295   READY-TO-LEARN TELEVISION

Assistance: project grants. (100 percent/to 5 years).

Purposes: pursuant to ESEA as amended, Title II, to develop: educational programming for preschool and early elementary school children and their families; educational television, programming, and ancillary materials to increase school readiness for young children with limited English proficiency; family literacy programs; support materials and services promoting effective use of educational programming.

Eligible applicants: qualified public telecommunications entities.

Eligible beneficiaries: young children, their parents, child care workers, Head Start providers.

Range/Average: N.A.

Activity: N.A.

HQ: Technology in Education Programs, OII-DOED, 500 Maryland Ave., SW, Washington, DC 20202. Phone: (202) 205-5633.

Internet: www.ed.gov/programs/rtltv/index.html. (Note: no field offices for this program.)

84.299   INDIAN EDUCATION—SPECIAL PROGRAMS FOR INDIAN CHILDREN

Assistance: project grants (100 percent/to 4 years).

Purposes: pursuant to ESEA of 1965, as amended, Title VII, to support early childhood and kindergarten projects, high school projects that aim to aid students in the transition from secondary to postsecondary education, and professional development projects that increase the number and skills of qualified Indian teachers and principals who serve Indian people.

Eligible applicants: SEAs, LEAs, IHEs, Indian tribes and organizations/institutions (including Indian IHEs and federally supported elementary and secondary schools for Indian students) or a consortium.

Eligible beneficiaries: Indian students and education professionals.

Range/Average: N.A.

Activity: N.A.

HQ: Director, Office of Indian Education, OESE-Dept. of Education, 400 Maryland Ave., SW, Washington, DC 20202. Phone: (202) 401-0767.

Internet: www.ed.gov/programs/indiandemo/index.html. (Note: no field offices for this program.)

84.305 EDUCATION RESEARCH, DEVELOPMENT AND DISSEMINATION

Assistance: project grants. (100 percent/1-5 years).

Purposes: pursuant to the Education Sciences Reform Act of 2002, to develop and distribute research-based information supporting learning and improved academic achievement. Grants may fund basic and applied research, development, dissemination, evaluations, and demonstrations.

Eligible applicants/beneficiaries: SEAs, LEAs, IHEs, public and private agencies and organizations, institutions, individuals, or consortia.

Range: $50,000 to $2,000,000. **Average:** N.A.

Activity: 108 awards in FY 2014.

HQ: Institute of Education Sciences, DOED, 400 Maryland Ave., SW, Washington, DC 20202. Phone: (202) 219-1201.

Internet: ies.ed.gov/ncer. (Note: no field offices for this program.)

84.315 CAPACITY BUILDING FOR TRADITIONALLY UNDERSERVED POPULATIONS

Assistance: project grants. (100 percent/1-5 years).

Purposes: pursuant to the Rehabilitation Act of 1973 as amended, to enhance the capacity and increase the participation of HBCUs, Hispanic serving IHEs, other IHEs where minority enrollment is at least 50 percent, and tribes in competitions for Rehabilitation Act funds. Projects should focus on recruiting minorities into vocational rehabilitation and related service careers.

Eligible applicants/beneficiaries: states; public and nonprofit agencies; profit organizations.

Range/Average: N.A.

Activity: N.A.

HQ: Rehabilitation Services Administration, OSERS-DOED, 400 Maryland Ave., SW, Washington, DC 20202-2649. Phone: (202) 245-7300.

Internet: www.ed.gov/about/offices/list/osers/rsa/index.html. (Note: no field offices for this program.)

84.323 SPECIAL EDUCATION—STATE PERSONNEL DEVELOPMENT

Assistance: project grants. (100 percent/1-5 years).

Purposes: pursuant to IDEA as amended, to reform and improve systems for providing educational, early intervention, and transitional services to infants, toddlers, and children with disabilities and their families—including professional development, technical assistance, and information dissemination about best practices.

Eligible applicants: SEAs.

Eligible beneficiaries: infants, toddlers, and children with disabilities and their families.

Range: $500,000 to $1,750,000. **Average:** $1,000,000.

Activity: N.A.

HQ: Office of Special Education Programs, OSERS-DOED, 400 Maryland Ave., SW, Washington, DC 20202. Phone: (202) 245-6673.

Internet: www.ed.gov/about/offices/list/osers/osep/index.html. (Note: no field offices for this program.)

84.324 RESEARCH IN SPECIAL EDUCATION

Assistance: project grants. (to 100 percent/1-5 years).

Purposes: pursuant to the Education Sciences Reform Act of 2002, for applied research to improve services provided and results achieved under IDEA, for infants, toddlers, and children with disabilities—including educational and early intervention services and professional practices.

Eligible applicants: SEAs, LEAs, IHEs, public agencies, private nonprofit organizations, tribes and tribal organizations, profit organizations, outlying areas.

Eligible beneficiaries: infants, toddlers, children, and others with disabilities and their families.

Range: $300,000 to $4,000,000. **Average:** N.A.

Activity: anticipate 50 awards in FY 2016.

HQ: Office of Special Education Programs, OSERS-DOED, 400 Maryland Ave., SW, Washington, DC 20202. Phone: (202) 219-2234.

Internet: ies.ed.gov/ncser. (Note: no field offices for this program.)

84.325 SPECIAL EDUCATION—PERSONNEL DEVELOPMENT TO IMPROVE SERVICES AND RESULTS FOR CHILDREN WITH DISABILITIES

Assistance: project grants. (to 100 percent/1-5 years).

Purposes: pursuant to IDEA as amended, to prepare personnel to serve infants, toddlers, and children with disabilities—in special and regular education, related services, and early intervention. Projects must emphasize use of skills and knowledge derived from research and experience.

Eligible applicants: SEAs, LEAs, IHEs, public agencies, private nonprofit organizations, tribes and tribal organizations, profit organizations, outlying areas.

Eligible beneficiaries: infants, toddler, and children with disabilities and their families.

Range/Average: N.A.

Activity: N.A.

HQ: Office of Special Education Programs, OSERS-DOED, 550 12th St., SW, Washington, DC 20202. Phone: (202) 245-7395.

Internet: www.ed.gov/about/offices/list/osers/osep/index.html. (Note: no field offices for this program.)

84.326 SPECIAL EDUCATION—TECHNICAL ASSISTANCE AND DISSEMINATION TO IMPROVE SERVICES AND RESULTS FOR CHILDREN WITH DISABILITIES

Assistance: project grants. (to 100 percent/1-5 years).

Purposes: pursuant to IDEA as amended, to provide technical assistance and disseminate information to improve early intervention, education, and transitional services and results for children with disabilities and their families—through institutes, regional resource centers, clearinghouses, and similar methods.

Eligible applicants: SEAs, LEAs, IHEs, public agencies, private nonprofit organizations, tribes and tribal organizations, profit organizations, outlying areas.

Eligible beneficiaries: infants, toddler, and children with disabilities and their families.

Range/Average: N.A.

Activity: N.A.

HQ: Office of Special Education Programs, OSERS-DOED, 400 Maryland Ave., SW, Washington, DC 20202. Phone: (202) 245-6209.

Internet: www.ed.gov/about/offices/list/osers/osep/index.html. (Note: no field offices for this program.)

84.327 SPECIAL EDUCATION—TECHNOLOGY AND MEDIA SERVICES FOR INDIVIDUALS WITH DISABILITIES

Assistance: project grants. (to 100 percent/1-5 years).

Purposes: pursuant to IDEA as amended, for the development, demonstration, and utilization of technology; for educational media activities designed to be of educational value; and, for captioning, video description, and cultural activities—for children with disabilities and their families.

Eligible applicants: SEAs, LEAs, IHEs, public agencies, private nonprofit organizations, tribes and tribal organizations, profit organizations, outlying areas.

Eligible beneficiaries: infants, toddler, and children with disabilities and their families.

Range/Average: N.A.

Activity: N.A.

HQ: Office of Special Education Programs, OSERS-DOED, 400 Maryland Ave., SW, Washington, DC 20202. Phone: (202) 245-7527.

Internet: www2.ed.gov/programs/oseptms/index.html. (Note: no field offices for this program.)

84.328 SPECIAL EDUCATION—PARENT INFORMATION CENTERS

Assistance: project grants. (to 100 percent/1-5 years).

Purposes: pursuant to IDEA as amended, to ensure that children with disabilities and their parents: receive training and information on their rights under the Act; can participate effectively in planning and decision-making related to early intervention, special education, and transitional services, including the development of Individual Education Programs (IEPs).

Eligible applicants: parent organizations as defined in IDEA, SEAs, LEAs, public charter schools that are LEAs under state law, IHEs, public agencies, private nonprofit organizations, outlying areas, freely associated states, Indian tribes or tribal organizations, for-profit organizations.

Eligible beneficiaries: infants, toddlers, and other individuals with disabilities and their families.

Range/Average: N.A.

Activity: N.A.

HQ: Office of Special Education Programs, OSERS-DOED, 400 Maryland Ave., SW, Rm. 4057, Washington, DC 20202. Phone: (202) 245-6595.

Internet: www2.ed.gov/programs/oseppic/index.html. (Note: no field offices for this program.)

84.329 SPECIAL EDUCATION—STUDIES AND EVALUATIONS

Assistance: project grants. (to 100 percent/1-5 years).

Purposes: pursuant to IDEA as amended, to evaluate progress in implementing IDEA. Projects cover state and local efforts to provide a free appropriate public education to children with disabilities and early intervention services to infants and toddlers that would be at risk of having substantial development delays without such services.

Eligible applicants: SEAs, LEAs, IHEs, public agencies, private nonprofit organizations, tribes and tribal organizations, profit organizations, outlying areas.

Eligible beneficiaries: infants, toddlers, children, and others with disabilities and their families.

Range: N.A. **Average:** $7,500,000.

Activity: N.A.

HQ: Office of Special Education Programs, OSERS-DOED, 555 New Jersey Ave., NW, Ste. 500J, Washington, DC 20208. Phone: (202) 208-3876.

Internet: ies.ed.gov/ncee. (Note: no field offices for this program.)

84.330 ADVANCED PLACEMENT PROGRAM

Assistance: project grants.

Purposes: pursuant to ESEA as amended, Title I, to cover part or all of the cost of Advanced Placement Test Fees for low-income persons enrolled in an advanced placement class and planning to take a test.

Eligible applicants: SEAs, LEAs, nonprofit organizations.

Eligible beneficiaries: low-income individuals who are enrolled in an advanced placement class and plan to take an advanced placement test.

Range: N.A. **Average:** $678,167.

Activity: N.A.

HQ: Improvement Programs, OII-DOED, 400 Maryland Ave., SW, Washington, DC 20202. Phone: (202) 260-2502.

Internet: www.ed.gov/programs/apfee/index.html. (Note: no field offices for this program.)

84.334   GAINING EARLY AWARENESS AND READINESS FOR UNDERGRADUATE PROGRAMS ("GEAR-UP")

Assistance: project grants. (50 percent/to 5 years).

Purposes: pursuant to HEA, Title IV, to assist low-income students with a secondary diploma, or equivalent, in obtaining the financial assistance necessary to attend an IHE; to provide supportive services to elementary, middle, and secondary students at risk of becoming school drop-outs, including counseling, mentoring, academic support; to provide outreach and relevant information to students and their parents. Services are provided under the Early Intervention Component. Federal grants may be provided under the Scholarship Component, to students participating in the Early Intervention component or in a TRIO program.

Eligible applicants: states; partnerships of LEAs, IHEs, and at least two community organizations including businesses, professional associations, philanthropic organizations, state agencies, parent groups.

Eligible beneficiaries: low-income students and students in high-poverty schools.

Range: N.A. **Average:** $3,682,378 for state grants; $1,827,674 for partnership grants.

Activity: N.A.

HQ: GEAR-UP, OPE-DOED, 1990 K St., NW, Washington, DC 20006. Phone: (202) 502-7802.

Internet: www.ed.gov/programs/gearup/index.html. (Note: no field offices for this program.)

84.335   CHILD CARE ACCESS MEANS PARENTS IN SCHOOL

Assistance: project grants (4 years).

Purposes: pursuant to HEA as amended, Title IV, to support participation of low-income parents in postsecondary education by providing campus-based child care services. Grants may be used to support or establish child care programs, including before or after-school services—but not for construction other than minor renovations. Grant amounts may not exceed one percent of the total amount of Pell grants awarded by the IHE for the preceding year.

Eligible applicants: IHEs that awarded $350,000 or more in Pell grants for the preceding year.

Eligible beneficiaries: low-income students enrolled in postsecondary programs.

Range: $10,000 to $300,000. **Average:** N.A.

Activity: N.A.

HQ: Higher Education Programs, OPE-DOED, 1990 K St., NW, Washington, DC 20006. Phone: (202) 502-7583.

Internet: www.ed.gov/programs/campisp. (Note: no field offices for this program.)

84.336 TEACHER QUALITY ENHANCEMENT GRANTS

Assistance: project grants. (50-75 percent/3-5 years).

Purposes: pursuant to HEA, Title II, for projects to reform teacher preparation programs and certification and licensure requirements, providing alternatives to traditional preparation for teaching, and to develop and implement effective mechanisms for teacher recruitment, pay, removal, and social promotion.

Eligible applicants/beneficiaries: states and partnerships with LEAs with high percentages of households below the poverty line and of secondary teachers not teaching within their specialty, and high rate of teacher turnover. IHEs must demonstrate specific teacher training performance standards.

Range: N.A. **Average:** $1,500,000.

Activity: N.A.

HQ: Teacher Quality Programs, OPE-DOED, 400 Maryland Ave., SW, Washington, DC 20202. Phone: (202) 260-2614.

Internet: www2.ed.gov/programs/tqpartnership/index.html. (Note: no field offices for this program.)

84.350 TRANSITION TO TEACHING

Assistance: project grants. (100 percent/3 years).

Purposes: pursuant to ESEA, Title II, to recruit, train, and place talented individuals from other fields, as well as recent college graduates, into licensed teaching positions in K-12 classrooms in high-need areas, and to support them during their first years in the classroom.

Eligible applicants/beneficiaries: LEA, SEAs, educational service centers, nonprofit agencies and other organizations; partnerships of the foregoing.

Range: $200,000-$2,500,000. **Average:** $454,000.

Activity: N.A.

HQ: Teacher Quality Programs, OII-DOED, 400 Maryland Ave., SW, Washington, DC 20202. Phone: (202) 205-5009.

Internet: www.ed.gov/programs/transitionteach/index.html. (Note: no field offices for this program.)

84.351 ARTS IN EDUCATION

Assistance: project grants. (100 percent/3-5 years).

Purposes: pursuant to ESEA as amended, Title V, to improve systemic education reform by strengthening arts education as an integral part of elementary and secondary school curricula; to assist students in learning to challenge state content standards in the arts; to enable students to demonstrate competence in the arts in accordance with the National Education Goals; to improve the educational performance and future potential of at-risk students; to provide comprehensive and coordinated educational and cultural services. Project selection is coordinated with NEA, NEH, and other arts organizations.

Eligible applicants/beneficiaries: SEAs, LEAs, IHEs; museums and other cultural institutions; other public and private agencies; private profit organizations for certain activities.

Range: $100,000 to $6,700,000. **Average:** N.A.

Activity: N.A.

HQ: OESE-DOED, 400 Maryland Ave., SW, Washington, DC 20202. Phone: (202) 260-1816.

Internet: www2.ed.gov/programs/artsnational/index.html. (Note: no field offices for this program.)

84.354 CREDIT ENHANCEMENT FOR CHARTER SCHOOL FACILITIES

Assistance: project grants. (100 percent/to 5 years).

Purposes: pursuant to ESEA as amended, Title V, for charter schools to leverage funds to finance the cost of acquiring, constructing, and renovating facilities. Grant funds must be deposited in approved reserve accounts, to be used to access private sector capital through bond or other financing instruments.

Eligible applicants/beneficiaries: public governmental or private nonprofit entities, or consortia.

Range: $5,000,000 to $8,000,000. **Average:** $7,500,000.

Activity: N.A.

HQ: Parental Options and Information, OII-DOED, 400 Maryland Ave., SW, Washington, DC 20202. Phone: (202) 453-6384.

Internet: www.ed.gov/programs/charterfacilities/index.html. (Note: no field offices for this program.)

84.356 ALASKA NATIVE EDUCATIONAL PROGRAMS

Assistance: project grants (100 percent).

Purposes: pursuant to ESEA as amended, Title VII, for projects that recognize and address the unique education needs of Alaska native students, parents, and teachers. Activities eligible for funding include: curriculum and education development programs; student enrichment programs in science and mathematics; professional development; Even Start and Headstart activities; family literacy services; dropout prevention programs.

Eligible applicants/beneficiaries: Alaska native educational organizations or entities with experience in developing programs, or partnerships including Alaska native organizations.

Range: $200,000 to $1,000,000. **Average:** $550,000.

Activity: N.A.

HQ: School Improvement Programs, OESE-DOED, 400 Maryland Ave., SW, Washington, DC 20202. Phone: (202) 260-1979.

Internet: www.ed.gov/programs/alaskanative/index.html. (Note: no field offices for this program.)

84.358 RURAL EDUCATION

Assistance: formula grants.

Purposes: pursuant to ESEA as amended, Title VI, to help improve the quality of teaching and learning in rural school districts. Components include: "Small, Rural School Achievement Program," for activities including Improving Teacher Quality, Educational Technology, Language Instruction for Limited English Proficient and Immigrant Students, Safe and Drug-Free Schools and Communities, 21st Century Community Learning Centers, and Innovative Programs; "Rural and Low-Income School Program," for teacher recruitment and retention, professional development, educational technology, and parental involvement.

Eligible applicants/beneficiaries: Small, Rural Achievement—essentially, LEAs where average daily attendance at all schools is less than 600, or in counties with population density less than 10 persons per square mile. Rural and Low-Income Schools—SEAs, for redistribution to LEAs ineligible for Small, Rural Achievement funds and meeting other criteria. If an SEA does not apply, funds may be awarded to eligible LEAs.

Range: to $60,000 for SRSA; $1,000 to $485,000 for RLIS. **Average:** $20,000 for SRSA; $42,000 for RLIS.

Activity: N.A.

HQ: School Support and Technology Programs, OESE-DOED, 400 Maryland Ave., SW, Washington, DC 20202. Phone: (202) 260-7349.

Internet: www.ed.gov/programs/reapsrsa/index.html. (Note: no field offices for this program.)

84.360 HIGH SCHOOL GRADUATION INITIATIVE

Assistance: project grants. (100 percent/to 3 years).

Purposes: pursuant to ESEA as amended, Title I, to help schools implement effective dropout prevention and re-entry programs, including: identifying at-risk students including in middle schools; providing special services to at-risk students; identifying drop-outs and encouraging them to re-enter school; implementing other comprehensive approaches such as breaking large schools into smaller learning communities. Authorized activities include: professional development; reduction in pupil- teacher ratios; counseling and mentoring for at-risk students; implementing comprehensive school reform models.

Eligible applicants/beneficiaries: SEAs and LEAs serving communities with dropout rates above the state average.

Range: N.A. **Average:** $1,652,392.

Activity: N.A.

HQ: Improvement Programs, OII-DOED, 400 Maryland Ave., SW, Washington, DC 20202. Phone: (202) 260-2502.

Internet: www.ed.gov/programs/dropout/index.html. (Note: no field offices for this program.)

84.362 NATIVE HAWAIIAN EDUCATION

Assistance: project grants. (100 percent/to 5 years).

Purposes: pursuant to ESEA as amended, Title VII, to develop innovative educational programs to assist native Hawaiians and to supplement and expand education programs and authorities. Funds may support: early education and care programs; operation of family-based education centers; beginning reading and literacy activities; programs addressing the needs of gifted and talented students; professional development; assistance enabling students to enter and complete postsecondary education.

Eligible applicants/beneficiaries: native Hawaiian educational organizations or community-based organizations; experienced public and private nonprofit organizations, agencies, and institutions; consortia.

Range: $250,000 to $950,000. **Average:** $425,000.

Activity: N.A.

HQ: Academic Improvement and Teacher Quality Programs, OESE-DOED, 400 Maryland Ave., SW, Rm. 3W215, Washington, DC 20202. Phone: (202) 260-1265.

Internet: www.ed.gov/programs/nathawaiian/index.html. (Note: no field offices for this program.)

84.363 SCHOOL LEADERSHIP

Assistance: project grants.

Purposes: pursuant to ESEA as amended, Title II, to develop innovative programs that recruit, train, and mentor principals and assistant principals. Funds may be used for: financial incentives to aspiring new principals; stipends to principals to mentor new principals; professional development programs in instructional leadership and management; incentives for teachers or individuals from other fields wanting to become principals and that are effective in training new principals.

Eligible applicants/beneficiaries: high-need LEAs applying singly or in consortia or partnerships that include nonprofit organizations and IHEs.

Range: $252,000 to $2,472,000. **Average:** $814,000.

Activity: N.A.

HQ: Teacher Quality Programs, OII-DOED, 400 Maryland Ave., SW, Washington, DC 20202. Phone: (202) 205-5009.

Internet: www.ed.gov/programs/leadership/index.html. (Note: no field offices for this program.)

84.365 ENGLISH LANGUAGE ACQUISITION STATE GRANTS

Assistance: formula grants; project grants.

Purposes: pursuant to ESEA as amended, Title III, to ensure that limited English proficient (LEP) children and youth, including immigrants, attain proficiency and meet the same state academic content and achievement standards as all children. Outlying areas and native American applicants may use project funds for appropriate special activities for up to five years, including: hiring tutors and for special professional development and training; developing students' native language skills. Training must be based upon scientifically based research and improve teacher instruction and enhance their ability to understand and use curricula, assessment measures, and instruction strategies for LEP students.

Eligible applicants/beneficiaries: formula funds (95 percent of which must be allocated as subgrants to SEAs)—states and outlying areas with approved state plans. Project grants—tribal educational authorities, BIA-operated or-funded elementary or secondary schools, nonprofit native Hawaiian or native American Pacific Islander language organizations.

Range: $93,373 to $146,895,715. **Average:** $11,972,661.

Activity: N.A.

HQ: Office of English Language Acquisition, OESE-DOED, 400 Maryland Ave., SW, Washington, DC 20202. Phone: (202) 401-9795.

Internet: www2.ed.gov/programs/sfgp/index.html. (Note: no field offices for this program.)

84.366 MATHEMATICS AND SCIENCE PARTNERSHIPS

Assistance: project grants. (100 percent/to 3 years).

Purposes: pursuant to ESEA as amended, Title II, to improve student academic achievement in mathematics and science through projects supporting partnerships of organizations representing preschool through higher education. Funds may be used for such activities as: developing more rigorous curricula aligned with state and local content standards; distance learning projects for teachers; teacher recruitment among mathematics, science, and engineering majors through the use of signing and performance incentives, stipends, and scholarships.

Eligible applicants/beneficiaries: partnerships of SEAs with IHE mathematics, science, or engineering departments, and a high-need LEA. Other organizations may participate.

Range/Average: N.A.

Activity: N.A.

HQ: Academic Improvement and Teacher Quality Programs, OESE-DOED, 400 Maryland Ave., SW, Washington, DC 20202. Phone: (202) 260-7813.

Internet: www.ed.gov/programs/mathsci/index.html. (Note: no field offices for this program.)

84.367 IMPROVING TEACHER QUALITY STATE GRANTS

Assistance: formula grants (to 2 years).

Purposes: pursuant to ESEA as amended, Title II, to increase student achievement by improving teacher and principal quality and increasing their numbers, through such efforts as: recruiting and retaining highly qualified teachers, principals, and assistant principals; professional development addressing subject matter knowledge and related activities.

Eligible applicants/beneficiaries: states with approved consolidated state plans.

Range: $10,516,243 to $246,544,093. **Average:** $42,254,010.

Activity: N.A.

HQ: OESE-DOED, 400 Maryland Ave., SW, Washington, DC 20202. Phone: (202) 453-7019.

Internet: www.ed.gov/programs/teacherqual/index.html. (Note: no field offices for this program.)

84.368   GRANTS FOR ENHANCED ASSESSMENT INSTRUMENTS

Assistance: project grants (100 percent/to 4 years).

Purposes: funds to enhance the quality of assessment instruments and systems used by states for measuring the achievement of all students. Funded projects must meet one or more of the following priorities: improve the quality, validity, and reliability of state academic assessments; measure student academic achievement using multiple measures of student academic achievement from multiple sources; chart student progress over time; and/or evaluate student academic achievement through the development of comprehensive academic assessment instruments, such as performance and technology-based academic assessments.

Eligible applicants: state educational agencies (SEAs) and/or consortia of SEAs.

Eligible beneficiaries: state educational agencies (SEAs) and/or consortia of SEAs, local educational agencies, and local schools.

Range: N.A. **Average:** $7,500,000.

Activity: N.A.

HQ: Director, Student Achievement and School Accountability Programs, OESE-Dept. of Education, 400 Maryland Ave., SW, Washington, DC 20202. Phone: (202) 401-5245.

Internet: www.2.ed.gov/programs/eag/index.html. (Note: no field offices for this program.)

84.369   GRANTS FOR STATE ASSESSMENTS AND RELATED ACTIVITIES

Assistance: formula grants (to 27 months).

Purposes: pursuant to ESEA as amended, Title VI, for the development of the additional state assessments and standards required currently by ESEA—or, if a state has developed those assessments, to support their administration or to carry out other activities related to ensuring that the state's schools and LEAs are held accountable for results.

Eligible applicants/beneficiaries: states.

Range: $3,279,231 to $28,595,203. **Average:** $7,026,172.

Activity: N.A.

HQ: Compensatory Education Programs, OESE-DOED, 400 Maryland Ave., SW, Washington, DC 20202. Phone: (202) 260-1824.

Internet: www2.ed.gov/admins/lead/account/saa.html. (Note: no field offices for this program.)

84.370   DC SCHOOL CHOICE INCENTIVE PROGRAM

Assistance: project grants. (100 percent/to 5 years).

Purposes: pursuant to the DC School Choice Incentive Act of 2003, to establish scholarship programs to provide students with expanded elementary and secondary school choice options. Scholarship funds may be used to pay tuition and fees and transportation expenses to participating DC nonpublic schools of their choice.

Eligible applicants: an educational entity of the District of Columbia government; a nonprofit organizations or a consortium of same.

Eligible beneficiaries: elementary and secondary students residing in DC, from households with income not exceeding 185 percent of the poverty line.

Range/Average: N.A.

Activity: N.A.

HQ: OII-DOED, 400 Maryland Ave., SW, Washington, DC 20202. Phone: (202) 205-5482.

Internet: www.ed.gov/programs/dcchoice/index.html. (Note: no field offices for this program.)

84.371 STRIVING READERS

Assistance: project grants. (100 percent/to 5 years).

Purposes: pursuant to ESEA as amended, Title I, to raise student achievement by improving the reading skills of middle and high school students reading below grade level, in Title I-eligible schools that are at risk of not meeting or not meeting ESEA annual progress requirements—including implementation and evaluation of research-based reading interventions. Project grants support costs such as: supplemental literacy intervention strategies; cross-disciplinary strategies including professional development for subject matter teachers; additional staff time for extra periods of instruction; age-appropriate reading materials; assessment instruments.

Eligible applicants: one or more LEAs receiving Title I funds with one or more high schools or middle schools with significant numbers of students reading below grade level; or, intermediate service agencies on behalf of eligible LEAs; or, partnerships that may include public or private institutions of higher education, eligible nonprofit or for-profit organizations, and LEAs that have one or more high schools or middle schools with significant numbers of students reading below grade level.

Eligible beneficiaries: students in grades 6-12.

Range/Average: N.A.

Activity: N.A.

HQ: OESE-DOED, 400 Maryland Ave., SW, Washington, DC 20202. Phone: (202) 260-2551.

Internet: www.ed.gov/programs/strivingreaders/index.html. (Note: no field offices for this program.)

84.372 STATEWIDE LONGITUDINAL DATA SYSTEMS

Assistance: project grants. (100 percent/1-3 years).

Purposes: pursuant to Educational Technical Assistance Act of 2002, for SEAs to design, develop, and implement statewide, longitudinal data systems to manage, analyze, disaggregate, and use individual student data—consistent with ESEA.

Eligible applicants/beneficiaries: SEAs.

Range: $2,500,000 to $7,000,000 for 4 years. **Average:** N.A.

Activity: N.A.

HQ: Institute of Education Sciences, National Center for Education Statistics, DOED, 1990 K St., NW, Rm. 9112, Washington, DC 20006. Phone: (202) 502-7494.

Internet: nces.ed.gov/programs/slds. (Note: no field offices for this program.)

84.373 SPECIAL EDUCATION—TECHNICAL ASSISTANCE ON STATE DATA COLLECTION

Assistance: project grants. (100 percent/1-5 years).

Purposes: pursuant to IDEA, to provide technical assistance to improve state capacity to meet IDEA data collection requirements.

Eligible applicants: SEAs, LEAs, public charter schools that are LEAs under state law, IHEs, other public agencies, private nonprofit and profit organizations, tribes and tribal organizations, outlying areas, freely associated states.

Eligible beneficiaries: infants, toddler, and children with disabilities, and other individuals with disabilities, and their families.

Range/Average: N.A.

Activity: N.A.

HQ: Division of Research to Practice, OSERS-DOED, 400 Maryland Ave., SW, Washington, DC 20202. Phone: (202) 245-7334.

Internet: www.ed.gov/about/offices/list/osers/osep/index.html. (Note: no field offices for this program.)

84.374 TEACHER INCENTIVE FUND (TIF)

Assistance: project grants. (100 percent/to 5 years).

Purposes: pursuant to ESEA as amended, Title V, for programs that develop and implement performance-based teacher and principal compensation systems in high-need schools, including incentives to assume individual responsibilities and leadership roles. Programs must include gains in student achievement as well as classroom evaluations conducted multiple times during each school year.

Eligible applicants/beneficiaries: LEAs, public charter schools that are LEAs under state law, SEAs; or, partnerships of an LEA, an SEA, or both, and at least one profit organization.

Range: N.A. **Average:** $7,388,000.

Activity: N.A.

HQ: OESE-DOED, 400 Maryland Ave., SW, Washington, DC 20202. Phone: (202) 205-5471.

Internet: www2.ed.gov/programs/teacherincentive/index.html. (Note: no field offices for this program.)

84.377   SCHOOL IMPROVEMENT GRANTS

Assistance: project grants (100 percent/to 27 months).

Purposes: pursuant to the Elementary and Secondary Education Act (ESEA), as amended to strengthen the capacity of states to carry out their program improvement responsibilities required under Sections 1116 and 1117 of Title I of the ESEA by implementing effective school improvement strategies and providing resources to LEAs to carry out those strategies. An SEA must allocate at least 95 percent of the amount of the funds it receives directly to LEAs for schools that have been identified for improvement, corrective action, or restructuring to carry out activities under Section 1116(b), while retaining up to 5 percent of the grant amount received for administration, evaluation, and technical assistance expenses. At the LEA level, these funds may be used for any reasonable costs associated with carrying out school improvement, corrective action, or restructuring activities described in Section 1116(b).

Eligible applicants: SEAs with approved state plan amendments.

Eligible beneficiaries: LEAs must have one or more schools identified for school improvement, corrective action, or restructuring under Section 1116(b) of Title I.

Range: $1,092,596 to $59,959,653. **Average:** $9,153,038.

Activity: N.A.

HQ: Office of Elementary and Postsecondary Education-DOED, 400 Maryland Ave., SW, Washington, DC 20202. Phone: (202) 401-9737.

Internet: www.ed.gov/oese. (Note: no field offices for this program.)

84.378   COLLEGE ACCESS CHALLENGE GRANT PROGRAM

Assistance: formula grants (to 66 percent/to 2 years).

Purposes: pursuant to the Higher Education Act of 1965, as amended to foster partnerships among federal, state and local government entities and philanthropic organizations through matching challenge grants aimed at increasing the number of underrepresented students who enter and remain in postsecondary education. No more than 6 percent of the total amount of the sum of the federal share provided and nonfederal share required may be used for administrative purposes. The minimum allotment for each State for a fiscal year cannot be an amount that is less than 0.5 percent of the total amount appropriated for the program.

Eligible applicants: state agencies with jurisdiction over higher education, or other agencies designated by the Governor of each state. In cases where the State fails to meet program requirements, the Secretary may award funds to philanthropic organizations.

Eligible beneficiaries: underrepresented students and families.

Range/Average: N.A.

Activity: N.A.

HQ: College Access Challenge Grant Program, Office of Postsecondary Education-DOED, 1990 K St., NW, Washington, DC 20006. Phone: (202) 502-7807.

Internet: www.ed.gov/programs/cacg. (Note: no field offices for this program.)

84.379   TEACHER EDUCATION ASSISTANCE FOR COLLEGE AND HIGHER EDUCATION GRANTS ("TEACH Grants")

Assistance: direct payments/specified use (100 percent).

Purposes: pursuant to the College Cost Reduction and Access Act of 2007 and Higher Education Act of 1965, as amended to provide annual grants of up to $4,000 to eligible undergraduate and graduate students who agree to teach specified high-need subjects at schools serving primarily disadvantaged populations for four years within eight years of graduation.

Eligible applicants/beneficiaries: undergraduate and graduate students with a 3.25 GPA completing coursework or requirements necessary to begin a career in teaching. Graduate students must be teachers or retirees from another occupation with expertise in a field in which there is a shortage of teachers or pursuing high-quality alternative certification. Students must attend an IHE that provides high-quality teacher preparation and professional development services; is financially sound; and provides, or assists in the provision, of pedagogical coursework, supervision and support services to teachers.

Range/Average: N.A.

Activity: anticipate 334,000 awards in FY 2016.

HQ: OFSA-DOED, PO Box 84, Washington, DC 20044-0084 Phone: (800) 433-3243.

Internet: www.ifap.ed.gov. (Note: no field offices for this program.)

84.380   SPECIAL EDUCATION—OLYMPIC EDUCATION PROGRAMS

Assistance: project grants (to 5 years).

Purposes: pursuant to the Special Olympic Sports and Empowerment Act, to promote the expansion of Special Olympics and the design and implementation of Special Olympics education programs.

Eligible applicants: Special Olympics.

Eligible beneficiaries: individuals with intellectual disabilities.

Range/Average: N.A.

Activity: N.A.

HQ: Office of Special Education Programs, OSERS-DEOD, 400 Maryland Ave., SW, Rm. 4103-PCP, Washington, DC 20202. Phone: (202) 245-6039.

Internet: www2.ed.gov/programs/osepoly/index.html. (Note: no field offices for this program.)

84.382   STRENGTHENING MINORITY-SERVING INSTITUTIONS

Assistance: project grants (100 percent/to 2 years).

Purposes: pursuant to the Higher Education Act of 1965 as amended by section 802 of the College Cost Reduction and Access Act (CCRAA) of 2007, to strengthen Predominantly Black Institutions (PBI); Asian American and Native American Pacific Islander-Serving Institutions (AANAPISI); and Native American-Serving Non-tribal Institutions (NASNTI) that propose to carry out activities to improve and expand the capacity to serve minority students.

Eligible applicants: PBIs: undergraduate enrollment of at least 40 percent Black American students; AANAPISI and NASNTI: undergraduate enrollment not less than 10 percent Asian American and Native American Pacific Islander and Native American students, respectively.

Eligible beneficiaries: undergraduates who are low-income, first-generation, and/or minority students.

Range/Average: N.A.

Activity: N.A.

HQ: Teacher and Student Development Services Program, Office of Postsecondary Education-DOED, 1900 K St. NW, 6th Fl., Washington, DC 20006. Phone: (202) 502-7549.

Internet: www2.ed.gov/about/offices/list/ope/idues/index.html. (Note: no field offices for this program.)

84.403 CONSOLIDATED GRANT TO THE OUTLYING AREAS

Assistance: formula grants (100 percent/1 year).

Purposes: pursuant to ESEA of 1965, as amended, Title V, to allow insular areas to direct funds to their greatest educational needs and priorities through utilization of one or more eligible programs described in Section 76.125 (c) of the Education Department General Administrative Regulations (EDGAR) during the entitled fiscal year.

Eligible applicants: U.S. territories and possessions (includes IHEs and hospitals).

Eligible beneficiaries: U.S. territories and possessions, schools.

Range: $12,000,000 to $26,000,000. **Average:** N.A.

Activity: N.A.

HQ: School Support and Technology Programs, OESE-DOED, 400 Maryland Ave., SW, Rm. 3E201, Washington, DC 20202. Phone: (202) 205-4513.

Internet: www.ed.gov/about/offices/list/oese/sst/index.html. (Note: no field offices for this program.)

84.407 TRANSITION PROGRAMS FOR STUDENTS WITH INTELLECTUAL DISABILITIES INTO HIGHER EDUCATION

Assistance: cooperative agreements; project grants/discretionary (75 percent/ to 5 years).

Purposes: pursuant to the Higher Education Act of 1965, as amended, to support model demonstration programs that promote the successful transition of students with intellectual disabilities into higher education. Coordinating centers established at the IHEs will: offer inclusive comprehensive transition and postsecondary programs for these students, provide recommendations related to the development of standards, technical assistance and evaluations for model demonstration programs and assist in the development, evaluation, funding, outreach, and continuous improvement of model transition programs.

Eligible applicants: eligible IHEs or a consortia of IHEs.

Eligible beneficiaries: post-secondary students with intellectual disabilities.

Range/Average: N.A.

Activity: N.A.

HQ: Director, Transition Programs for Students with Intellectual Disabilities Into Higher Education, Office of Postsecondary Education, Department of Education, 1990 K St., NW, Washington, DC 20006. Phone: (202) 502-7676.

Internet: N.A. (Note: no field offices for this program.)

84.408 POSTSECONDARY EDUCATION SCHOLARSHIPS FOR VETERAN'S DEPENDENTS ("IASG")

Assistance: direct payments/specified use (100 percent/to 18 semesters).

Purposes: pursuant to the Higher Education Act of 1965, to provide eligible veteran's dependent undergraduate and postsecondary students with non-need based grant assistance to help meet educational expenses. The student must be an eligible veteran's dependent and whose parent or guardian was a member of the Armed Forces of the U.S. and died as a result of performing military service in Iraq or Afghanistan after September 11, 2001. At the time of the parent or guardian's death, the student was less than 24 years of age or had been accepted for enrollment in and is making satisfactory academic progress at an eligible IHE (colleges, universities, vocational-technical schools, hospital schools of nursing). Graduate students and students who have already earned a bachelor's degree are not eligible for assistance, except those enrolled in a program leading to a professional certification in teaching. Applicants must apply annually using the Free Application for Federal Student Aid (FAFSA), meet all IAS Grant eligibility requirements, and must not have a Federal Pell Grant eligible Expected Family Contribution (EFC).

Eligible applicants/beneficiaries: eligible students who are dependents of eligible veterans.

Range: $591 to $5,915. **Average:** $5,535.

Activity: fewer than 1,000 recipients expected in FY 2016.

HQ: OFSA-DOED, PO Box 84, Washington, DC 20044-0084 Phone: (800) 433-3243.

Internet: www.ifap.ed.gov.

84.411 INVESTING IN INNOVATION (i3) FUND

Assistance: project grants (50 percent).

Purposes: pursuant to the American Recovery and Reinvestment Act of 2009, to expand the implementation of, and investment in, innovative practices that are demonstrated to have an impact on improving student achievement or student growth, closing achievement gaps, decreasing dropout rates, increasing high school graduation rates, or increasing college enrollment and completion rates.

Eligible applicants: LEAs and nonprofit organizations in partnership with (a) one or more LEAs or (b) a consortium of schools.

Eligible beneficiaries: high-need students in LEAs.

Range: $3,000,000 to $25,000,000. **Average:** $7,727,000.

Activity: N.A.

HQ: Director, 400 Maryland Ave. S.W., Washington, DC 20202. Phone: (202) 205-3010.

Internet: www.ed.gov/programs/innovation/index.html. (Note: no field offices for this program.)

84.414 GRADUATE RESEARCH OPPORTUNITIES FOR MINORITY STUDENTS

Assistance: project grants (100 percent/1 year).

Purposes: pursuant to the Social Security Act, to support competitive post-graduate grants to apprentice scholars at selected minority serving graduate institutions in the area of retirement security (financial literacy, personal savings, labor force planning, spending patterns, personal debt, etc.) for low- to moderate-income individuals.

Eligible applicants: IHE grantees receiving grants from Historically Black Graduate Institutions, Historically Black Colleges and Universities Masters, Promoting Postbaccalaureat Opportunities for Hispanic Americans, and the Predominantly Black Institutions programs.

Eligible beneficiaries: researchers and graduate students researching retirement security.

Range: N.A. **Average:** $120,000.

Activity: N.A.

HQ: Director, Institutional Service, Higher Education Programs, Office of Postsecondary Education, 1990 K St., NW, Rm. 6062, Washington, DC 20006. Phone: (202) 502-7562.

Internet: N.A. (Note: no field offices for this program.)

84.415 STATE TRIBAL EDUCATION PARTNERSHIP (STEP)

Assistance: project grants (100 percent/to 3 years).

Purposes: pursuant to the Elementary and Secondary Education Act (ESEA), funds for the implementation of collaborative agreements, entered into by Tribal Educational Agencies (TEAs) and State Educational Agencies (SEAs) under which the TEAs perform certain state-level functions under state-administered ESEA formula grant programs for schools located on reservations. The purpose of the program is to promote increased collaboration between TEAs and SEAs in the administration of the ESEAs state-administered formula grant programs, and build the capacity of TEAs to perform certain state-level functions under those programs for schools located on reservations, and thereby increase TEAs role in the education of American Indian/Alaska Native (AI/AN) students, including education to meet their unique educational and cultural needs, and improve the achievement of AI/AN children.

Eligible applicants: eligible entities include a Tribal Educational Agency (TEA) in partnership with a State Educational Agency (SEA) or a consortium of TEAs in partnership with an SEA.

Eligible beneficiaries: Tribal Educational Agencies, State Educational Agencies, Indian students, and teachers.

Range: N.A. **Average:** $240,000 for single TEA; $400,000 for consortium of TEAs.

Activity: N.A.

HQ: Director, Office of Indian Education, OESE-Dept. of Education, 400 Maryland Ave., SW, Washington, DC 20202. Phone: (202) 401-0767.

Internet: www2.ed.gov/about/offices/list/oese/oie/index.html. (Note: no field offices for this program.)

84.417 DIRECTED GRANTS AND AWARDS

Assistance: direct payments/specified use (100 percent).

Purposes: pursuant to Act to Promote the Education of the Blind, Education for the Deaf Act, and Higher Education Act, to award specified institutions for purposes specified in the appropriations or authorization bills.

Eligible applicants/beneficiaries: National Technical Institute for the Deaf (NTID), American Printing House for the Blind (APHB), Gallaudet University, Howard University, other institutions and organizations.

Range/Average: N.A.

Activity: N.A.

HQ: Director, Department of Education, 400 Maryland Ave., SW, Rm. 5W327, Washington, DC 20202. Phone: (202) 401-0292.

Internet: N.A. (Note: no field offices for this program.)

84.419 PRESCHOOL DEVELOPMENT GRANTS

Assistance: project grants. (100 percent).

Purposes: pursuant to the American Recovery and Reinvestment Act of 2009, to support efforts to build, develop, and expand voluntary, high-quality preschool programs. Awards may be limited to activities that develop or enhance state infrastructure, including quality improvement activities. States may subgrant a portion of the funds to local educational agencies and other early learning providers including but not limited to Head Start programs and licensed child care providers.

Eligible applicants: state educational agencies.

Eligible beneficiaries: children age 4 from families at or below 200 percent of the federal poverty line.

Range: $5,000,000 to $35,000,000. **Average:** $20,000,000.

Activity: N.A.

HQ: Office of Early Learning, Office of Elementary and Secondary Education, 400 Maryland Ave., SW, Washington, DC 20202. Phone: (202) 260-7803.

Internet: www.ed.gov/earlylearing. (Note: no field offices for this program.)

84.421 DISABILITY INNOVATION FUND (DIF)

Assistance: project grants. (100 percent/to 5 years).

Purposes: pursuant to the Department of Education Appropriations Acts of 2014 and 2015, to support innovative activities aimed at improving the outcomes of individuals with disabilities.

Eligible applicants: states, tribes, public and nonprofit agencies/organizations, and IHEs.

Eligible beneficiaries: individuals with disabilities.

Range/Average: N.A.

Activity: N.A.

HQ: Office of Special Education and Rehabilitative Services, Department of Education, 400 Maryland Ave., SW, Washington, DC 20202. Phone: (202) 245-7343.

Internet: N.A. (Note: no field offices for this program.)

SCHOLARSHIP AND FELLOWSHIP FOUNDATIONS

85.001 HARRY S TRUMAN SCHOLARSHIP PROGRAM

Assistance: direct payments/specified use.

Purposes: pursuant to the Harry S Truman Memorial Scholarship Act, for scholarships for full-time students pursuing careers in public service, financed by a permanent trust fund endowment.

Eligible applicants/beneficiaries: U.S. citizens or nationals in their college junior year, nominated by their IHEs. Applicants must rank in the upper quarter of their class, and their studies should permit admission to a graduate or professional program for a career in public service.

Range: $2,000 to $15,000. **Average:** $12,000.

Activity: 2,405 students have received scholarship assistance since inception.

HQ: Executive Secretary, Harry S Truman Scholarship Foundation, 712 Jackson Pl. NW, Washington, DC 20006. Phone: (202) 395-4831.

Internet: www.truman.gov. (Note: no field offices for this program.)

85.002 MCC FOREIGN ASSISTANCE FOR OVERSEAS PROGRAMS

Assistance: direct payments/specified use; project grants (to 5 years).

Purposes: pursuant to the Millennium Challenge Act of 2003, to provide U.S. assistance for global development through the Millennium Challenge Corporation. Funds are authorized through grants and cooperative agreements to carry out activities in the world's poorest countries demonstrating commitment to good governance, economic freedom, and investments in their citizens. MCC provides eligible countries with large-scale grants (compacts) to fund country-led solutions for reducing poverty through sustainable economic growth. Threshold programs are smaller grants awarded to countries that come close to passing MCC's eligibility criteria and are firmly committed to improving their policy performance.

Eligible applicants/beneficiaries: eligible foreign governments, educational institutions, public/private institutions, or organizations or individuals.

Range/Average: N.A.

Activity: N.A.

HQ: Director, Millennium Challenge Corporation, Contracts and Grants Management Division, 875 15th St., NW, Washington, DC 20005. Phone: (202) 521-3600.

Internet: www.mcc.gov. (Note: no field offices for this program.)

85.003 MCC DOMESTIC ASSISTANCE FOR OVERSEAS PROGRAMS

Assistance: direct payments/specified use; project grants (to 5 years).

Purposes: pursuant to the Millennium Challenge Act of 2003, to provide U.S. assistance for global development through the Millennium Challenge Corporation. Funds authorized through grants and cooperative agreements are to carry out activities in the world's poorest countries demonstrating commitment to good governance, economic freedom, and investments in their citizens. MCC provides eligible countries with large-scale grants (compacts) to fund country-led solutions for reducing poverty through sustainable economic growth. Threshold programs are smaller grants awarded to countries that come close to passing MCC's eligibility criteria and are firmly committed to improving their policy performance.

Eligible applicants/beneficiaries: eligible foreign governments, educational institutions, public/private institutions, or organizations or individuals.

Range/Average: N.A.

Activity: N.A.

HQ: Director, Millennium Challenge Corporation, Contracts and Grants Management Division, 875 15th St., NW, Washington, DC 20005. Phone: (202) 521-3600.

Internet: www.mcc.gov. (Note: no field offices for this program.)

85.102 CHRISTOPHER COLUMBUS AWARDS

Assistance: project grants/Special (100 percent/12-18 months).

Purposes: pursuant to the Christopher Columbus Quincentenary Coins and Fellowship Foundation, to challenge students to work in teams of three to four with an adult coach, to identify an issue in their community and apply the scientific method to create an innovative solution to the problem.

Eligible applicants: teams of three to four students in sixth through eighth grade with a coach, who identify a problem in their community and solve it using the scientific method.

Eligible beneficiaries: U.S. citizens, middle school students.

Range: N.A. **Average:** $2,000 for monetary awards; $25,000 for grants.

Activity: N.A.

HQ: Director, 110 Genesee St., Ste. 390, Auburn, New York 13021. Phone: (315) 258-0090; FAX: (315) 258-0093.

Internet: www.christophercolumbusawards.com or www.columbusfdn.org. (Note: no field offices for this program.)

85.104 LIFE SCIENCES AWARDS

Assistance: direct payments/unrestricted use (100 percent).

Purposes: Christopher Columbus Quincentenary Coins and Fellowship Foundation in public/private partnership with the U.S. Chamber of Commerce presents four Life Sciences Awards to encourage and promote "cutting edge" innovation in the field of life sciences. Monetary awards will be presented to the following nominees: a scientist, a high school educator, and two high school students n Biology, Chemistry or other life sciences courses.

Eligible applicants/beneficiaries: eligible scientists, high school educators, current high school students.

Range: $1,000 to $10,000. Average: N.A.

Activity: N.A.

HQ: Director, 110 Genesee St., Ste. 390, Auburn, New York 13021. Phone: (315) 258-0090; FAX: (315) 258-0093.

Internet: www.ccolumbusfoundationawards.org. (Note: no field offices for this program.)

85.105 AGRISCIENCE AWARDS

Assistance: direct payments/unrestricted use (100 percent).

Purposes: Christopher Columbus Quincentenary Coins and Fellowship Foundation In public/private partnership with the American Farm Bureau Federation will present eight Agriscience Awards to encourage and promote "cutting edge" innovation in the field of Agriscience. Monetary awards will be presented to the following nominees: a scientist, a high school educator with at least 5 years of teaching experience, and two high school students making or have recently made significant and positive contributions related to the study of agriscience.

Eligible applicants/beneficiaries: eligible scientists, high school educators, current high school students.

Range: $1,000 to $10,000. Average: N.A.

Activity: N.A.

HQ: Director, 110 Genesee St., Ste. 390, Auburn, New York 13021. Phone: (315) 258-0090; FAX: (315) 258-0093.

Internet: www.agriscienceawards.com or http;://columbusfdn.org. (Note: no field offices for this program.)

85.200 BARRY M. GOLDWATER SCHOLARSHIP PROGRAM

Assistance: direct payments/specified use.

Purposes: for scholarships to outstanding students to pursue careers in mathematics, the natural sciences, and engineering—financed by a permanent trust fund endowment.

Eligible applicants/beneficiaries: U.S. citizens, nationals, or lawful resident aliens that are full-time college sophomores and juniors at two- and four-year IHEs, ranking in the upper fourth of their class.

Range: to $7,500. **Average:** $6,650.

Activity: N.A.

HQ: President, Barry M. Goldwater Scholarship Foundation, 6225 Brandon Ave., Ste. 315, Springfield, VA 22150-2519. Phone: (703) 756-6012; FAX: (703) 756-6015.

Internet: www.act.org/goldwater. (Note: no field offices for this program.)

85.300 WOODROW WILSON CENTER FELLOWSHIPS IN THE HUMANITIES AND SOCIAL SCIENCES

Assistance: project grants (4-9 months).

Purposes: pursuant to the Woodrow Wilson Memorial Act of 1968, to foster scholarship and promote exchange of views between scholars and decision makers. The Center sponsors research, meetings, and publications in such areas as history, economics, politics, international relations, the environment, the humanities, and other areas. Fellows are in residence at the Center's main offices in Washington, D.C., where they receive office space, use of special libraries and personal computers, part-time research assistance, and publications services.

Eligible applicants/beneficiaries: citizens of any country, with backgrounds in government, business, the professions, or academia—with English language proficiency. For academic participants, eligability is limited to the postdoctoral level.

Range/Average: N.A.

Activity: N.A.

HQ: Woodrow Wilson International Center for Scholars, 1300 Pennsylvania Ave., NW, Washington, DC 20004. Phone: (202) 691-4000.

Internet: www.wilsoncenter.org. (Note: no field offices for this program.)

85.400 MORRIS K. UDALL SCHOLARSHIP PROGRAM ("Udall Undergraduate Scholarship")

Assistance: direct payments/specified use.

Purposes: pursuant to the Morris K. Udall Scholarship and Excellence in National Environmental and Native American Public Policy Act of 1992, for internships, scholarships, and fellowships to develop increased opportunities for young Americans to prepare for careers related to the environment; for native Americans and Alaska natives intending to pursue careers in health care and tribal public policy. The program is financed by a permanent trust fund endowment.

Eligible applicants/beneficiaries: U.S. citizens, nationals, or permanent resident aliens that are college sophomores or juniors, nominated by accredited IHEs.

Range: $2,000 to $5,000. **Average:** $4,800.

Activity: N.A.

HQ: Executive Director, Morris K. Udall Foundation, 130 S. Scott Ave., Tucson, AZ 85701. Phone: (520) 901-8654; FAX: (520) 901-8570.

Internet: www.udall.gov. (Note: no field offices for this program.)

85.402 MORRIS K. UDALL NATIVE AMERICAN CONGRESSIONAL INTERNSHIP PROGRAM ("Udall Internship Program")

Assistance: direct payments/specified use.

Purposes: pursuant to the Morris K. Udall Scholarship and Excellence in National Environmental and Native American Public Policy Act of 1992, for internships, scholarships, and fellowships to develop increased opportunities for young Americans to prepare for careers related to the environment; for native Americans and Alaska natives intending to pursue careers in health care and tribal public policy. The program is financed by a permanent trust fund endowment. Interns receive round- trip air fare to Washington, D.C., lodging, a per diem for meals and incidentals, and a $1,200 stipend at the conclusion of the internship.

Eligible applicants/beneficiaries: members of recognized tribes or Alaska natives that are matriculated college seniors or graduate or law students with a minimum 3.2 GPA, and interested in tribal government and policy.

Range: N.A. **Average:** $9,500.

Activity: N.A.

HQ: Executive Director, Morris K. Udall Foundation, 130 S. Scott Ave., Tucson, AZ 85701. Phone: (520) 901-8500; FAX: (520) 901-8570.

Internet: www.udall.gov. (Note: no field offices for this program.)

85.500 JAMES MADISON MEMORIAL FELLOWSHIP PROGRAM

Assistance: direct payments/specified use.

Purposes: pursuant to the James Madison Memorial Fellowship Act, for fellowships to future and current secondary school (grades 7- 12) American history, government, or social studies teachers—toward a deeper understanding of American government, as well the spirit of civic participation that inspired the nation's founders. Recipients are obligated to perform one year of teaching for each year of study supported by a fellowship. Payments cover actual costs of tuition, room and board, fees, and books.

Eligible applicants/beneficiaries: Junior Fellows (2-year maximum)—college seniors or college graduates. Senior Fellows (5-year maximum)—experienced, full-time teachers of grades 7-12, pursuing a Master's level degree. All candidates must be U.S. citizens or nationals.

Range: $12,000 to $24,000. **Average:** N.A.

Activity: N.A.

HQ: Director of Administration and Finance, James Madison Memorial Fellowship Foundation, 2000 K St., NW, Ste. 303, Washington, DC 20006. Phone: (202) 653-6109; FAX: (202) 653-6045.

Internet: www.jamesmadison.com. (Note: no field offices for this program.)

85.601 SMITHSONIAN INSTITUTION FELLOWSHIP PROGRAM

Assistance: project grants (10 weeks to 1 year).

Purposes: for graduate and predoctoral students and postdoctoral and senior investigators to conduct research in association with Smithsonian professional staff. Fellowships and internships presently cover: animal behavior; ecology; environmental science emphasizing the tropics; anthropology and archaeology; astrophysics and astronomy; earth sciences and paleobiology; evolutionary and systemic biology; history of science and technology, history of art, especially American, contemporary African, and Asian art, American crafts, decorative arts; social and cultural history of the U.S.; folklife.

Eligible applicants/beneficiaries: postdoctoral fellowships—scholars holding the degree or equivalent for less than 7 years. Senior fellowships—scholars holding the degree or equivalent for 7 years of more. Predoctoral fellowships—candidates who have completed preliminary coursework and exams. Graduate Student fellowships—candidates enrolled in a graduate program of study with at least one semester completed.

Range: $4,500 to $40,000. **Average:** N.A.

Activity: N.A.

HQ: Office of Fellowships, Smithsonian Institution, Victor Bldg. - Ste. 9300, Washington, DC 20013-7012. Phone: (202) 275-0655.

Internet: www.si.edu/research+study. (Note: no field offices for this program.)

85.802 VIETNAM EDUCATION FOUNDATION FELLOWSHIP PROGRAM ("VEF Fellowship Program")

Assistance: project grants/fellowships (to 100 percent).

Purposes: pursuant to the Vietnam Education Foundation Act of 2000, funding for fellowships to Vietnamese nationals to pursue Masters and doctoral degrees in the STEMM fields at U.S. universities. Funds may be used for tuition, fees, living expenses, and professional development costs for the fellow. A grant of $27,000 is provided to the U.S. educational institution during each of the first two years of study toward a Masters or doctoral degree. The U.S. graduate institution is responsible for providing any additional funds needed to cover all required tuition, fees, books, insurance, and a monthly living stipend to the student. Fellows also receive a $1,000 professional development grant that may be used for attendance at professional conferences, books, editing of papers for publishing, and other expenses that directly relate to the program of study.

Eligible applicants/beneficiaries: Vietnamese nationals who enroll in Masters and doctoral degree programs in STEMM fields at an accredited U.S. university.

Range/Average: $28,000.

Activity: N.A.

HQ: Director, VEF Fellowship Program, 2111 Wilson Blvd, Ste. 700, Arlington, VA 22201. Phone: (703) 351-5053; FAX: 703-351-1423.

Internet: www.vef.gov. (Note: no field offices for this program.)

PENSION BENEFIT GUARANTY CORPORATION

86.001   PENSION PLAN TERMINATION INSURANCE ("ERISA")

Assistance: insurance.

Purposes: pursuant to the Employee Retirement Income Security Act of 1974 as amended (ERISA), Pension Protection Act of 1987, Retirement Protection Act of 1994, Job Creation and Worker Assistance Act of 2002, Pension Funding Act Equity Act of 2004, and other acts, to insure voluntary private pension plans; to provide for uninterrupted payment of pension benefits to participants and beneficiaries in PBGC-covered plans; to maintain premiums charged by PBGC at the lowest level consistent with fulfilling its obligations. Insurance coverage is mandatory for any pension plan established or maintained by an employer or an employee organization engaged in or affecting commerce, except such plans as those covering: individual accounts; federal, state, local employees; church employees; nonresident aliens; select groups of management or highly compensated employees; professional service employers with fewer than 25 participants; other specific groups. Single-employer plans may terminate in a standard termination only if sufficient assets exist to provide all benefits—and in a voluntary distress termination only if the sponsoring employer can satisfy specified distress criteria. Benefits are paid within limits specified by law.

Eligible applicants/beneficiaries: private businesses and organizations that maintain defined benefit plans; participants in such plans.

Range/Average: N.A.

Activity: N.A.

HQ: Pension Benefit Guaranty Corporation, 1200 K St., NW, Washington, DC 20005-4026. Phone: (202) 326-4000.

Internet: www.pbgc.gov.

ARCHITECTURAL AND TRANSPORTA- TION BARRIERS COMPLIANCE BOARD

88.001   ARCHITECTURAL AND TRANSPORTATION BARRIERS COMPLIANCE BOARD ("Access Board")

Assistance: technical information.

Purposes: pursuant to the ADA, Rehabilitation Act of 1973, and Architectural Barriers Act of 1968 as amended, and other laws, to enforce federal laws requiring accessibility for physically handicapped persons in federally funded buildings and facilities; to establish related guidelines and requirements; to provide technical assistance and training on design guidelines and standards; to conduct pertinent research.

Eligible applicants/beneficiaries: general public; federal, state, and local agencies.

Range/Average: N.A.

Activity: N.A.

HQ: Director, Office of Technical and Information Services, ATBCB, 1331 F St., NW, Ste. 1000, Washington, DC 20004-1111. Phone: (202) 272-0080, TTY (202) 272-0082; FAX: (202) 272-0081; *technical assistance,* (800) 872-2253, TTY (800) 993-2822.

Internet: www.access-board.gov. (Note: no field offices for this program.)

NATIONAL ARCHIVES AND RECORDS ADMINISTRATION

89.001 NATIONAL ARCHIVES REFERENCE SERVICES—HISTORICAL RESEARCH

Assistance: use of property, facilities, and equipment; advisory services/counseling; technical information.

Purposes: pursuant to the National Archives and Records Administration Act of 1984 and other acts, to provide reference services to the public and researchers in obtaining access to records and historical materials of the federal government in the National Archives, Presidential Libraries, and Regional Records Services. Conferences, workshops, and other outreach activities may be conducted. Restrictions apply to records subject to the Freedom of Information Act, such as national security.

Eligible applicants/beneficiaries: general public.

Range/Average: N.A.

Activity: anticipate providing 1,087,837 reference responses in FY 2016.

HQ: Office of Records Services, National Archives and Records Administration, 8601 Adelphi Rd., College Park, MD 20740. Phone: (301) 837-1910.

Internet: www.archives.gov.

89.003 NATIONAL HISTORICAL PUBLICATIONS AND RECORDS GRANTS

Assistance: project grants.

Purposes: pursuant to the National Archives and Records Administration Act of 1984 and other acts, for preservation, publication, and use of documentary sources relating to U.S. history. Projects may involve: collaborative efforts with the states, including training; publication in book, microform, or electronic editions of papers and documents of national historical significance.

Eligible applicants/beneficiaries: state and local governments, territorial agencies, tribes; educational and other nonprofit institutions including IHEs, libraries, historical societies, museums, university presses, archives; individuals.

Range: $4,320 to $243,950. **Average:** $68,442.

Activity: anticipate 72 awards in FY 2016.

HQ: Office of Records Services, National Archives and Records Administration, 8601 Adelphi Rd., College Park, MD 20740. Phone: (301) 837-1910.

Internet: www.archives.gov/nhprc. (Note: no field offices for this program.)

INDEPENDENT BOARDS
AND COMMISSIONS

90.100   DENALI COMMISSION PROGRAM

Assistance: project grants.

Purposes: pursuant to the Denali Commission Act of 1998, to support the Denali Commission as a federal-state partnership to provide critical utilities and infrastructure throughout Alaska, particularly in distressed communities. Project examples: bulk fuel tank storage at isolated site; remote hydroelectric generation; health care infrastructure planning and construction.

Eligible applicants/beneficiaries: Alaska state and local government agencies, public and private profit and nonprofit organizations, individuals.

Range/Average: N.A.

Activity: N.A.

HQ: Denali Commission, 510 L St., Ste. 410, Anchorage, AK 99501. Phone: (907) 271-3099.

Internet: www.denali.gov. (Note: no field offices for this program.)

90.200   DELTA REGIONAL DEVELOPMENT
("Delta Program")

Assistance: project grants.

Purposes: pursuant to FSRIA, for 240 specific counties in the eight states in the Delta Region (Mississippi River), in partnership with the federal government, to remedy severe and chronic economic distress by stimulating economic development in distressed communities—by leveraging other federal and state programs focused on: basic infrastructure development transportation improvements; business development; and job training services. States each prepare annual development plans related to a strategic program for which funding is requested in that year; the plans are submitted for approval to the Delta Regional Authority (DRA) which is led by a federal co-chairman and the eight state governors; once approved, individual projects are administered by the federal agency involved, a local development district, or the DRA. Funding is reflected in programs **90.201** and **90.202**.

Eligible applicants/beneficiaries: eight states, public and nonprofit entities in the Delta region. Inquiries and proposals should be submitted to appropriate Local Development Districts (listed on the DRA web site, below).

Range/Average: N.A.

Activity: N.A.

HQ: Executive Director, Delta Regional Authority, 236 Sharkey Ave., Ste. 400, Clarksdale, MS 38614. Phone: (662) 624-8600.

Internet: www.dra.gov. (Note: no field offices for this program.)

90.201 DELTA AREA ECONOMIC DEVELOPMENT

Assistance: project grants. (50-90 percent/to 18 months).

Purposes: pursuant to FSRIA, to provide supplemental funds under federal grant-in-aid programs for high-priority projects in state development plans as described in **90.200**. Projects must involve: basic public infrastructure in distressed counties and isolated areas of distress; transportation infrastructure to facilitate economic development; business development emphasizing entrepreneurship; job training or employment-related education, using existing public educational institutions in the region. Recent project examples: water and sewer systems for industrial parks, with tenants committed; IHE workforce training with committed company participation; business incubators.

Eligible applicants/beneficiaries: eight states, public and nonprofit entities in the Delta region. Inquiries and proposals should be submitted to appropriate Local Development Districts (listed on the DRA web site, below).

Range/Average: N.A.

Activity: N.A.

HQ: Executive Director, Delta Regional Authority, 236 Sharkey Ave., Ste. 400, Clarksdale, MS 38614. Phone: (662) 624-8600.

Internet: www.dra.gov. (Note: no field offices for this program.)

90.202 DELTA LOCAL DEVELOPMENT DISTRICT ASSISTANCE (LDD)

Assistance: project grants. (50 percent/1 year).

Purposes: pursuant to FSRIA, for the administrative and technical services costs of certified development districts in multicounty districts, including pertinent professional and technical development—in furtherance of projects and programs outlined in **90.200**.

Eligible applicants/beneficiaries: certified multicounty organizations in the Delta Region.

Range/Average: N.A.

Activity: N.A.

HQ: Executive Director, Delta Regional Authority, 236 Sharkey Ave., Ste. 400, Clarksdale, MS 38614. Phone: (662) 624-8600.

Internet: www.dra.gov. (Note: no field offices for this program.)

90.300 JAPAN-U.S. FRIENDSHIP COMMISSION GRANTS

Assistance: project grants. (cost sharing/6-18 months).

Purposes: to promote educational, artistic, and cultural exchange and research between Japan and the U.S.

Eligible applicants/beneficiaries: public, state, and private IHEs; "501(c)(3)" organizations other than IHEs.

Range/Average: N.A.

Activity: N.A.

HQ: Japan-US. Friendship Commission, 1201 15th St., NW, Ste. 330, Washington, DC 20005. Phone: (202) 653-9800.

Internet: www.jusfc.gov. (Note: no field offices for this program.)

90.400 HELP AMERICA VOTE COLLEGE PROGRAM

Assistance: project grants.

Purposes: pursuant to the Help America Vote Act of 2002, to recruit and train college students to assist state and local governments in the administration of elections by serving as nonpartisan poll workers or assistants.

Eligible applicants/beneficiaries: state and private IHEs; "501(c)(3)" organizations other than IHEs; other nonprofit organizations.

Range/Average: N.A.

Activity: N.A.

HQ: Director, EAC Research Grants, U.S. Election Assistance Commission, 1201 New York Ave., Ste. 300, Washington, DC 20005. Phone: (202) 566-2166.

Internet: www.eac.gov. (Note: no field offices for this program.)

90.401 HELP AMERICA VOTE ACT REQUIREMENTS PAYMENTS

Assistance: direct payments/specified use (95 percent).

Purposes: pursuant to the Help America Vote Act of 2002, to reimburse states for costs incurred in obtaining voting equipment and in meeting standards required by the Act.

Eligible applicants/beneficiaries: states, DC, and outlying areas.

Range/Average: N.A.

Activity: N.A.

HQ: Director, Help America Vote College Program, U.S. Elections Assistance Commission, 1225 New York Ave., NW, Ste. 1100, Washington, DC 20005. Phone: (202) 566-3100.

Internet: www.eac.gov. (Note: no field offices for this program.)

90.402 HELP AMERICA VOTE MOCK ELECTION PROGRAM

Assistance: project grants (100 percent).

Purposes: pursuant to the Omnibus Appropriations Act for Fiscal Year 2008, to promote voter participation and education in American elections through a program of simulated Federal elections (held at least 5 days before the actual general Federal election) that permits participation by students enrolled in a secondary education program. Nonallowable activities and expenditures include: construction, indirect costs, voter registration and Get-Out-The-Vote (GOTV) efforts.

Eligible applicants: state election offices and non-profit organizations, including faith-based, community-based, and tribal organizations who can demonstrate prior experience operating a program of simulated elections aimed at students enrolled in a secondary education program.

Eligible beneficiaries: students in secondary education programs.

Range/Average: N.A.

Activity: N.A.

HQ: Help America Vote Mock Election Program, Election Assistance Commission, 1225 New York Ave., NW, Ste. 1100, Washington, DC 20005. Phone: (202) 566-3100.

Internet: www.eac.gov. (Note: no field offices for this program.)

90.403 U.S. ELECTION ASSISTANCE COMMISSION RESEARCH GRANTS ("EAC Research Grants")

Assistance: cooperative agreements/discretionary grants; project grants (100 percent/to 5 years).

Purposes: pursuant to the Consolidated Appropriations Act of 2010, to carry out research and development to improve the quality, reliability, accuracy, accessibility, affordability and security of voting equipment, election systems and technology. Funds cover: research and development grants, dissemination of research findings, accessibility research, logic and accuracy testing of voting systems, and post election audit research.

Eligible applicants: state/local/tribal governments, IHEs, public nonprofit institutions/organizations.

Eligible beneficiaries: U.S. citizens.

Range/Average: N.A.

Activity: N.A.

HQ: Director, EAC Research Grants, U.S. Election Assistance Commission, 1201 New York Ave., Ste. 300, Washington, DC 20005. Phone: (202) 566-2166.

Internet: www.eac.gov. (Note: no field offices for this program.)

90.500 INTERNATIONAL BROADCASTING INDEPENDENT GRANTEE ORGANIZATIONS

Assistance: project grants (100 percent).

Purposes: to promote freedom and democracy and enhance understanding of accurate, objective, and balanced news, information and other programming about America and the world to overseas audiences.

Eligible applicants: three existing nonprofit organizations: Radio Free Europe/Radio Liberty, Radio Free Asia, and Middle East Broadcasting Networks as identified in the authorizing language.

Eligible beneficiaries: three existing nonprofit entities based and incorporated in the U.S. and overseas listeners who benefit from an alternative news source.

Range/Average: N.A.

Activity: N.A.

HQ: Broadcasting Board of Governors, 330 Independence Ave., SW, Washington, DC 20237. Phone: (202) 321-4194.

Internet: www.bbg.gov. (Note: no field offices for this program.)

INSTITUTE OF PEACE

91.001 UNSOLICITED GRANT PROGRAM

Assistance: project grants.

Purposes: pursuant to the United States Institute of Peace Act and the Department of Defense Authorization Act of 1985, for education, training, research, and public information projects in international peace and conflict resolution. Unsolicited grant awards may support: research by scholars; curricula and materials development for secondary through postgraduate programs; media programming, including materials for television and radio; development of data bases, bibliographies, collections.

Eligible applicants/beneficiaries: domestic or foreign nonprofit organizations; official public institutions; individuals including U.S. citizens and foreign nationals.

Range/Average: N.A.

Activity: N.A.

HQ: Annual Grant Program, U.S. Institute of Peace, 1200 17th St., NW, Ste. 200, Washington, DC 20036. Phone: (202) 429-3842.

Internet: www.usip.org. (Note: no field offices for this program.)

91.002 PRIORITY GRANT COMPETITION

Assistance: project grants (100 percent).

Purposes: pursuant to the United States Institute of Peace Act and the Department of Defense Authorization Act of 1985, for competitive grants to support research, education, library and information technology—on international peace and conflict resolution and on themes and topics identified by the Institute.

Eligible applicants/beneficiaries: domestic or foreign nonprofit organizations; official public institutions; individuals including U.S. citizens and foreign nationals.

Range/Average: N.A.

Activity: N.A.

HQ: Priority Grant Program, U.S. Institute of Peace, 1200 17th St., NW, Ste. 200, Washington, DC 20036. Phone: (202) 429-3842.

Internet: www.usip.org. (Note: no field offices for this program.)

DEPARTMENT OF HEALTH AND HUMAN SERVICES

93.001 CIVIL RIGHTS AND PRIVACY RULE COMPLIANCE ACTIVITIES

Assistance: investigation of complaints.

Purposes: pursuant to the Civil Rights Act, Age Discrimination Act of 1975, ADA, Small Business Job Protection Act of 1996 (SBJPA), Health Insurance Portability and Accountability Act of 1996 (HIPAA), related acts, and amendments, to ensure equal opportunities for, and nondiscrimination on any basis against, applicants for or beneficiaries of HHS assistance through any HHS-assisted program or facility—and that the privacy of their health information will be protected under the HIPAA Privacy Rule; to encourage compliance with nondiscrimination regulations by providing technical assistance to recipients of HHS assistance, through workshops, designing model compliance plans, and training responsible state and local officials. Under SBJPA, the Office of Civil Rights investigates complaints and takes steps to assure that individuals are not discriminated against in adoption or foster care placement decisions.

Eligible applicants/beneficiaries: anyone believing that they have been discriminated against in any HHS program, or wanting information or technical assistance to assure compliance with applicable laws.

Range/Average: N.A.

Activity: N.A.

HQ: Deputy Director, Management Operations Division, Office for Civil Rights, OS-HHS, HHH Bldg., Rm. 509-F6, 200 Independence Ave., SW, Washington, DC 20201. Phone: (202) 619-1333; Director, Office for Civil Rights, (same address), (202) 619-0403.

Internet: www.hhs.gov/ocr.

93.004 COOPERATIVE AGREEMENTS TO IMPROVE THE HEALTH STATUS OF MINORITY POPULATIONS

Assistance: project grants. (100 percent/to 5 years).

Purposes: pursuant to PHSA as amended, for activities to improve the health status and quality of life of racial and ethnic minorities, consistent with the mission of the HHS Office of Minority Health. Funds may not be used to provide health care, for construction, or to supplant ongoing project activities. Project example: provider education and sensitivity training on cultural practices and their influence on patient compliance with medication and therapeutic treatment interventions.

Eligible applicants/beneficiaries: public and private nonprofit entities; faith based organizations.

Range/Average: N.A.

Activity: 21 awards in FY 2014.

HQ: Director, Division of Program Operations, Office of Minority Health, Office of Public Health and Science, OS-HHS, 1101 Wootton Pkwy., Ste. 550, Rockville, MD 20852. Phone: (240) 453-8822.

Internet: minorityhealth.hhs.gov. (Note: no field offices for this program.)

93.006 STATE AND TERRITORIAL AND TECHNICAL ASSISTANCE CAPACITY DEVELOPMENT MINORITY HIV/AIDS DEMONSTRATION PROGRAM ("CTA/CD")

Assistance: project grants. (100 percent/to 3 years).

Purposes: pursuant to PHSA as amended, for demonstrations involving state offices of minority health and community-based organizations in HIV/AIDS health education and prevention strategies—to coordinate statewide responses to the crisis in minority communities; to increase access to services and treatment for minorities; to provide technical assistance and capacity development to minority community-based organizations. Funds may not be used to provide health care, for construction, or to supplant ongoing project activities.

Eligible applicants/beneficiaries: state and territorial offices of minority health, or agencies functioning in that capacity; minority-serving community-based organizations.

Range/Average: N.A.

Activity: N.A.

HQ: Director, Division of Program Operations, Office of Minority Health, Office of Public Health and Science, OS-HHS, 1101 Wootton Pkwy., Ste. 550, Rockville, MD 20852. Phone: (240) 453-8822.

Internet: minorityhealth.gov. (Note: no field offices for this program.)

93.007 PUBLIC AWARENESS CAMPAIGNS ON EMBRYO ADOPTION ("Embryo Donation/Adoption")

Assistance: project grants. (100 percent/to 1 year).

Purposes: for public awareness campaigns on embryo adoption.

Eligible applicants/beneficiaries: "particular" experienced public agencies, nonprofit, and profit organizations; collaboratives. Subgrants may be awarded.

Range: $150,000 to $300,000. **Average:** N.A.

Activity: N.A.

HQ: Office of Population Affairs, Office of Public Health and Science, OS-HHS, 1101 Wootton Pkwy., Ste. 550, Rockville, MD 20852. Phone: (240) 453-8822.

Internet: www.opa.gov.

93.008   MEDICAL RESERVE CORPS SMALL GRANT PROGRAM (MRC)

Assistance: project grants. (100 percent/to 3 years).

Purposes: pursuant to PHSA as amended, for development of community Medical Reserve Corps (MRCs) units to increase capacity at the community level to respond to emergencies that have medical consequences, and to improve public health through volunteerism on an ongoing basis. Funds may be used: to establish community-based, citizen-volunteer MRCs; for organizing, volunteer recruitment, assessment of risks and vulnerability, strategy development, planning, training, drills and practices, supplies, and equipment.

Eligible applicants/beneficiaries: local government entities; local nonprofit, nongovernmental community-based organizations, including nonprofit Citizen Corps Councils of the USA Freedom Corps.

Range: N.A. **Average:** $6,775,000.

Activity: N.A.

HQ: Office of the Surgeon General, USPHS, OS-HHS, 1101 Wootton Pkwy., Ste. 550, Rockville, MD 20852. Phone: (240) 453-8822.

Internet: www.medicalreservecorps.gov/HomePage.

93.009   COMPASSION CAPITAL FUND (CCF)

Assistance: project grants. (80-100 percent/to 3 years).

Purposes: pursuant to SSA as amended, for charitable organizations to emulate model social service programs; for research on the "best practices" of social service organizations. Funds are provided to intermediary organizations, experienced in capacity building, to provide long-term technical assistance to smaller so-called faith-based and community organizations in such areas as strategic planning, financial management, board development, fund development, and outcome measurement. The intermediary organizations provide one-time $50,000 (unmatched) sub-awards to the smaller organizations, with priority to those that: have not received federal funds; will serve the homeless, elders in need, families in transition from welfare to work, at-risk youth, those in need of intensive rehabilitation such as addicts or prisoners, provide marriage education and preparation services. The sub-awards may not fund direct services; rather, they must improve efficiency and capacity.

Eligible applicants/beneficiaries: intermediaries—county, municipal, special district, and tribal governments; IHEs; profit and nonprofit "501(c)(3)" organizations; faith-based organizations. Sub-awards—nonprofit organizations with and without "501(c)(3)" status, other than IHEs; tribal governments; faith-based organizations.

Range/Average: N.A.

Activity: N.A.

HQ: Team Leader, Division of Community Discretionary Programs, Office of Community Services, ACF-HHS, 370 L'Enfant Promenade, SW, 5th Fl. West, Washington, DC 20447. Phone: (202) 401-5115; FAX: (202) 401-4687.

Internet: www.acf.hhs.gov/programs/ccf. (Note: no field offices for this program.)

93.011 NATIONAL ORGANIZATIONS OF STATE AND LOCAL OFFICIALS (NOSLO)

Assistance: cooperative agreements (100 percent).

Purposes: pursuant to the Public Health Service Act, as amended, to support national organizations that represent the following: state, territorial and local government health department officials, state Medicaid directors, and state legislatures to address cross-cutting, publicly-funded health program integration and health access issues identified by the states and local governments and entities.

Eligible applicants: eligible nonprofit national service organizations that can provide training and technical assistance on a national level to state and local governments and health departments.

Eligible beneficiaries: anyone, general public.

Range: $350,000 to $600,000. **Average:** N.A.

Activity: N.A.

HQ: Program Director, 5600 Fishers Ln., Rm. 10C-03, Rockville, MD 20895. Phone: (301) 443-6204; FAX: (301) 443-2286.

Internet: N.A. (Note: no field offices for this program.)

93.015 HIV PREVENTION PROGRAMS FOR WOMEN

Assistance: project grants. (100 percent/to 2 years).

Purposes: to increase awareness of HIV prevention information, of access to related services, and of testing of women in specific categories of women: Living in the Rural South; Attending Minority Institutions; Living in the Rural and Frontier Indian Country; Incarcerated and Newly Released; Living in the U.S. Virgin Islands and Puerto Rico. Funding is through cooperative agreements, and may not be used for direct health care services or equipment.

Eligible applicants/beneficiaries: public IHEs; HBCUs; Hispanic- Serving Institutions; tribal IHEs; private nonprofit community- based organizations; tribal organizations; religious organizations.

Range/Average: N.A.

Activity: N.A.

HQ: Office on Women's Health, HHS, Tower Bldg., 1101 Wootton Parkway, Suite 550, Rockville, MD 20852. Phone: (240) 453-8822.

Internet: www.womenshealth.gov.

93.018 STRENGTHENING PUBLIC HEALTH SERVICES AT THE OUTREACH OFFICES OF THE U.S.-MEXICO BORDER HEALTH COMMISSION

Assistance: project grants (100 percent).

Purposes: pursuant to PHSA, to improve the health of residents along the U.S.-Mexico border, through: targeted outreach and health promotion activities; evaluation and assessments; health data analysis; Health Border/Healthy Gente activities. Funding is through cooperative agreements covering costs of personnel, consultants, educational materials, software, and related travel—but not direct patient care services or equipment, nor real estate-related improvements.

Eligible applicants/beneficiaries: border state departments of health, working with the U.S.-Mexico Border Health Commission.

Range: $400,000 to $475,000. **Average:** N.A.

Activity: N.A.

HQ: Office of Global Affairs-HHS, 1101 Wootton Pkwy., Ste. 550, Rockville, MD 20852. Phone: (240) 453-8822.

Internet: www.globalhealth/world-regions/americas/us-mexico-border-health/index.html.

93.019 TECHNICAL ASSISTANCE AND PROVISION FOR FOREIGN HOSPITALS AND HEALTH ORGANIZATIONS

Assistance: project grants (100 percent/1 year).

Purposes: pursuant to Public Health Service Act, and Division F of the Consolidate Appropriations Act of 2005, to: provide support for a quality of care improvement project based in a partner healthcare institution in Afghanistan; continue education and refresher training to physicians and other staff at Women's and Children's hospitals and other Health Organizations in Afghanistan; and provide support to strengthen management of Women's and Children's hospitals by the Afghan Ministries of Public Health (MOPH) in Afghanistan.

Eligible applicants: U.S. based organizations/institutions with partner health organization in Afghanistan.

Eligible beneficiaries: medically underserved communities/individuals in Afghanistan.

Range: $650,000.00 to $7,900,000. **Average:** N.A.

Activity: N.A.

HQ: Office of Global Affairs-HHS, 200 Independence Ave., SW, Washington, DC 20201. Phone: (202) 205-1435.

Internet: www.phe.gov. (Note: no field offices for this program.)

93.041 SPECIAL PROGRAMS FOR THE AGING—TITLE VII, CHAPTER 3— PROGRAMS FOR PREVENTION OF ELDER ABUSE, NEGLECT, AND EXPLOITATION

Assistance: formula grants. (100 percent/1-4 years).

Purposes: pursuant to the Older Americans Act of 1965 (OAA) as amended, to develop, strengthen, and carry out comprehensive and coordinated programs for the prevention and treatment of abuse, neglect, and exploitation of older persons. Eligible project activities include public education and outreach, counseling, development and analysis of information and data systems, technical assistance and training for professionals and paraprofessionals. States must submit plans covering 2-4 years.

Eligible applicants/beneficiaries: states and territories with state agencies on aging, designated by the governors.

Range: $2,958 to $471,073. **Average:** $84,500.

Activity: N.A.

HQ: Director, Office of Deputy Assistant Secretary/Policy and Programs, AOA-HHS, One Massachusetts Ave., NW, Washington, DC 20001. Phone: (202) 357-3519; FAX: (202) 357-3459.

Internet: www.acl.gov.

93.042 SPECIAL PROGRAMS FOR THE AGING—TITLE VII, CHAPTER 2— LONG-TERM CARE OMBUDSMAN SERVICES FOR OLDER INDIVIDUALS

Assistance: formula grants.

Purposes: pursuant to OAA as amended, to develop or strengthen ombudsman services programs for older persons living or seeking to live in nursing homes or long-term care facilities, to: provide for the investigation and resolution of complaints by or on behalf of residents; promote policies and practices to improve the quality of life and care; consumer and provider education activities. States must submit plans covering 2-4 years.

Eligible applicants/beneficiaries: states and territories with state agencies on aging, designated by the governors.

Range: $9,829 to $1,618,546. **Average:** $283,266.

Activity: completed resolution work on 191,533 complaints and provided 491,373 consultations in FY 2014.

HQ: Director, Administration for Community Living, AOA-HHS, Washington, DC 20201. Phone: (202) 357-3503.

Internet: www.acl.gov.

93.043 SPECIAL PROGRAMS FOR THE AGING—TITLE III, PART D— DISEASE PREVENTION AND HEALTH PROMOTION SERVICES

Assistance: formula grants. (85 percent/1-4 years).

Purposes: pursuant to OAA as amended, to develop or strengthen programs for preventive health services ineligible for reimbursement under Medicare and for health promotion, at senior centers or alternative sites. Eligible project activities include health risk assessments, routine health and nutrition screening, home injury control and safety screening, physical fitness programs, coordination of community mental health services, gerontological counseling, referrals and follow-ups. States must submit plans covering 2-4 years.

Eligible applicants/beneficiaries: states and territories with state agencies on aging, designated by the governors.

Range: $12,281 to $1,992,449. **Average:** $350,884.

Activity: N.A.

HQ: Office for Community-Based Services, AOA-HHS, One Massachusetts Ave., Washington, DC 20001. Phone: 202-357-3508.

Internet: www.aoa.gov.

93.044   SPECIAL PROGRAMS FOR THE AGING—TITLE III, PART B— GRANTS FOR SUPPORTIVE SERVICES AND SENIOR CENTERS

Assistance: formula grants. (85 percent/1-4 years).

Purposes: pursuant to OAA as amended, to provide comprehensive and coordinated supportive services and to operate multipurpose facilities for older persons, including senior centers, developed according to approved 2-4 year state plans; to maximize support provided to older Americans to enable them to remain in their homes and communities. In addition to supportive nutrition services, funds may cover transportation service, in-home services, and caregiver support, as well as acquisition, construction, or renovation costs.

Eligible applicants/beneficiaries: states and territories with state agencies on aging, designated by the governors.

Range: N.A. **Average:** $6,511,854.

Activity: N.A.

HQ: Office for Community-Based Services, AOA-HHS, One Massachusetts Ave., Washington, DC 20001. Phone: (202) 357-3545.

Internet: acl.gov.

93.045   SPECIAL PROGRAMS FOR THE AGING—TITLE III, PART C— NUTRITION SERVICES

Assistance: formula grants. (85 percent/1-4 years).

Purposes: pursuant to OAA as amended, to provide meals, nutrition education, and related services for the elderly—including at least one hot or other appropriate meal per day, five or more days per week (except in rural areas). Meals may be served in a congregate setting or delivered to the home.

Eligible applicants: states and territories with state agencies on aging, designated by the governors.

Eligible beneficiaries: persons age 60 and over and their spouses; certain disabled or handicapped persons under age 60.

Range: $283,444 to $46,294,011 for congregate nutrition services; $146,271 to $29,229,113 for home-delivered nutrition services. **Average:** $8,098,394 for congregate nutrition services; $4,179,161 for home-delivered nutrition services.

Activity: N.A.

HQ: Office for Community-Based Services, AOA-HHS, Washington, DC 20001. Phone: (202) 357-0145.

Internet: www.aoa.gov.

93.047   SPECIAL PROGRAMS FOR THE AGING—TITLE VI, PART A, GRANTS TO INDIAN TRIBES—PART B, GRANTS TO NATIVE HAWAIIANS

Assistance: project grants (100 percent (formula-based).

Purposes: pursuant to OAA as amended, for supportive services to older Indians and Alaska and Hawaii natives, including nutrition services, multipurpose center improvements and staffing, transportation, information and referral assistance, and multifaceted caregiver services.

Eligible applicants: tribal organizations and public or private nonprofit organizations that serve native Hawaiian elders, serving at least 50 clients.

Eligible beneficiaries: Indians age 60 or older and, for nutrition services, their spouses; certain others under age 60.

Range: $63,990 to $156,070. Average: N.A.

Activity: N.A.

HQ: Director, Office of American Indian, Alaskan Native, and Native Hawaiian Programs, AOA-HHS, One Massachusetts Ave, NW , Washington, DC 20201. Phone: 202-357-0148.

Internet: www.acl.gov.

93.048   SPECIAL PROGRAMS FOR THE AGING—TITLE IV—AND TITLE II— DISCRETIONARY PROJECTS

Assistance: project grants. (75 percent/1-3 years).

Purposes: pursuant to OAA as amended, for development and testing of innovative programs in the field of aging—to develop knowledge of the problems and needs of the elderly. Funds may be used to: demonstrate new methods and practices; evaluate existing programs and services; conduct applied research and analysis; train professionals.

Eligible applicants/beneficiaries: public or private nonprofit agencies, organizations, and institutions.

Range/Average: N.A.

Activity: N.A.

HQ: Administration for Community Living, AOA-HHS, One Massachusetts Ave., NW, Washington, DC 20001. Phone: (202) 357-3505.

Internet: www.acl.gov.

93.051   ALZHEIMER'S DISEASE DEMONSTRATION GRANTS TO STATES ("Alzheimer's Demonstration Program")

Assistance: project grants. (55-75 percent/3 years).

Purposes: pursuant to PHSA as amended, Home Health Care and Alzheimer's Disease Amendments Act of 1990, and HPEPA, to plan, establish, and operate model programs for persons with Alzheimer's disease and related disorders, their families, and care-givers, including home health and personal care, companion services, short-term care in health facilities, other respite care services.

Eligible applicants: state agencies.

Eligible beneficiaries: individuals with Alzheimer's disease, families of those individuals, and care providers of those individuals.

Range/Average: N.A.

Activity: N.A.

HQ: Center for Wellness and Community-Based Services, AOA-HHS, One Massachusetts Ave., NW, Washington, DC 20001. Phone: (202) 357-3448.

Internet: www.acl.gov.

93.052 NATIONAL FAMILY CAREGIVER SUPPORT, TITLE III, PART E

Assistance: formula grants; project grants. (formula, 75 percent; project grants, 100 percent/formula grants, 1-4 years).

Purposes: pursuant to OAA as amended, to provide multi-faceted systems of support services for family caregivers and grandparents or older individuals who are relative-caregivers, including: information about, and assistance in gaining access to, available services; individual counseling, organizational support groups, caregiver training in making decisions and solving problems relating to their roles; temporary respite care relief for the caregivers; supplemental complementary services.

Eligible applicants: formula grants—state and territorial governments, with subgrants to area agencies on aging. Project grants—tribal organizations, native Hawaiian organizations.

Eligible beneficiaries: family caregivers.

Range/Average: N.A.

Activity: N.A.

HQ: Office of Home and Community-Based Services, Administration for Community Living, DHHS, One Massachusetts Ave., NW, Washington, DC 20201. Phone: (202) 357-3545.

Internet: www.acl.gov.

93.053 NUTRITION SERVICES INCENTIVE PROGRAM (NSIP)

Assistance: formula grants.

Purposes: pursuant to OAA as amended, to reward effective performance by states and tribes in the efficient delivery or meals to older adults, through the use of cash or USDA commodities in congregate or home-delivered meals. The funding incentives are based on the number of meals served in the prior fiscal year in proportion to all other states and tribes.

Eligible applicants/beneficiaries: state agencies and tribal organizations receiving funds through OAA Titles III and VI.

Range: $779 to $16,113,431. **Average:** $496,766.

Activity: N.A.

HQ: Office for Community-Based Services, AOA-HHS, Washington, DC 20001. Phone: (202) 357-0145.

Internet: www.aoa.gov.

93.054 NATIONAL FAMILY CAREGIVER SUPPORT, TITLE VI, PART C, GRANTS TO INDIAN TRIBES AND NATIVE HAWAIIANS

Assistance: project grants (100 percent).

Purposes: pursuant to the Older Americans Act as amended, to assist Indian Tribal Organizations in providing multifaceted systems of support services for family caregivers, grandparents or older individuals who are relative caregivers. Services may include: information about and assistance and access to services for caregivers, individual counseling and caregiver training, respite care, and supplemental services, on a limited basis, to complement caregiver services.

Eligible applicants: approved Indian Tribal and Native Hawaiian organizations.

Eligible beneficiaries: family caregivers, grandparents, and older individuals who are relative caregivers.

Range: $11,480 to $45,900. **Average:** $28,694

Activity: N.A.

HQ: Director, Office of American Indian, Alaskan Native, and Native Hawaiian Programs, AOA-HHS, One Massachusetts Ave, NW , Washington, DC 20201. Phone: 202-357-0148.

Internet: www.acl.gov.

93.055 APPLIED LEADERSHIP FOR COMMUNITY HEALTH IMPROVEMENT

Assistance: cooperative agreements (100 percent/to 5 years).

Purposes: pursuant to the Public Health Service Act, as amended, to establish a national health applied leadership training program to provide customized public health leadership training to local and state public health officials and their allies. Funds support Assembling, training and providing technical assistance to local teams of 3 to 5 leaders to effectively address local public health problems as part of a Community Health Improvement Project.

Eligible applicants: one currently funded grantee, The Public Health Institute.

Eligible beneficiaries: anyone, general public.

Range/Average: N.A.

Activity: N.A.

HQ: Program Director, CDC, HHS, 1825 Century Blvd., Atlanta, GA 30345. Phone: (404) 498-2762.

Internet: www.cdc.gov. (Note: no field offices for this program.)

93.056 INITIATIVE TO EDUCATE STATE AND TERRITORIAL OFFICIALS ABOUT MAINTAINING AND STRENGTHENING PUBLIC HEALTH IN A CHANGING ENVIRONMENT

Assistance: cooperative agreements (100 percent).

Purposes: pursuant to the Public Health Service Act, as amended, to ensure that legislators and relevant legislative health committee experts from all 50 states and territories have the knowledge, information, and other resources they need to identify, develop, and support policies that maintain essential public health services, while also facilitating the changes needed in the public health system to increase effectiveness and efficiency through better use of resources.

Eligible applicants: Category 1: non-profit organizations with requisite memberships representing governors from all 50 states and territories and must have provided information, education, publications, and networking forums to governors and their staff. Category 2: non-profit organizations that work with state legislators and relevant health committee experts with requisite memberships representing legislatures from all 50 states and territories and must have provided information, education, publications, and networking forums to state legislatures, relevant legislative committees and their staff.

Eligible beneficiaries: anyone, general public.

Range: $150,000 to $300,000. **Average:** N.A.

Activity: N.A.

HQ: Program Director, CDC, HHS, 4770 Buford Hwy., MS E70, Atlanta, GA 30341. Phone: (404) 498-6792.

Internet: www.grants.gov. (Note: no field offices for this program.)

93.059 TRAINING IN GENERAL, PEDIATRIC, AND PUBLIC HEALTH DENTISTRY

Assistance: project grants (100 percent).

Purposes: pursuant to the Public Health Service Act, to support pre-doctoral training, pediatric or public health dentistry, and dental hygiene; post-doctoral training, pediatric and public health dentistry; faculty development training, pediatric and public health dentistry and dental hygiene; and dental faculty loan repayment.

Eligible applicants/beneficiaries: accredited dental or dental hygiene schools, public or private not-for-profit hospitals, or other pubic or not for profit entities.

Range: $93,000 to $735,000. **Average:** $353,000.

Activity: N.A.

HQ: Director, Division of Medicine and Dentistry, Bureau of Health Professions, HRSA, DHHS 5600 Fishers Ln., Rm. 12C-06, Rockville, MD 20857. Phone: (301) 443-1945.

Internet: www.hrsa.gov. (Note: no field offices for this program.)

93.060 COMPETITIVE ABSTINENCE EDUCATION ("SRAE")

Assistance: project grants (100 percent/1 year).

Purposes: pursuant to the Social Security Act, to promote abstinence education, as defined by Section 510(b)(2) in Title V of the Social Security Act, for adolescents. To educate young people and create an environment within communities that supports teen decisions to postpone sexual activity until marriage.

Eligible applicants: public and private entities.

Eligible beneficiaries: adolescents, with a focus on those adolescents that are most likely to bear children out-of-wedlock or who live in areas with high birth rates to adolescents.

Range: $350,000 to $450,000. **Average:** N.A.

Activity: N.A.

HQ: Director, 330 C St., SW, Rm. 3614, Washington, DC 20024. Phone: (202) 205-9605; FAX: (202) 260-9345.

Internet: www.acf.hhs.gov/programs/fysb. (Note: no field offices for this program.)

93.061 INNOVATIONS IN APPLIED PUBLIC HEALTH RESEARCH

Assistance: project grants. (100 percent/to 3 years).

Purposes: pursuant to PHSA as amended, for applied public health research to translate biomedical science results into effective programs that directly affect the quality and length of life. Preference in project selection is given to proposals with participatory research involving affected communities.

Eligible applicants/beneficiaries: public and private profit and nonprofit organizations; governments and their agencies including territories and possessions; IHEs, hospitals, community-based organizations, women-and minority-owned businesses, Indian tribes and tribal organizations, research institutions, faith-based organizations.

Range/Average: N.A.

Activity: N.A.

HQ: Office of Public Health Research, CDCP-HHS, 1600 Clifton Rd., Atlanta, GA 30333. Phone: (404) 693-4639.

Internet: www.cdc.gov. (Note: no field offices for this program.)

93.062 BIOMONITORING PROGRAMS FOR STATE PUBLIC HEALTH LABORATORIES

Assistance: cooperative agreements (100 percent/to 5 years).

Purposes: pursuant to the Public Health Service Act, to develop or expand state-based biomonitoring programs. Funding may be used for personnel salaries, laboratory instruments and supplies, training, travel, and indirect costs.

Eligible applicants/beneficiaries: 35 IHEs selected by the CDC as Prevention Research Centers (PRCs).

Range/Average: N.A.

Activity: N.A.

HQ: Director, Agency for Toxic Substances and Disease Registry, HHS, 4770 Buford Hwy. NE, MS F61, Atlanta, GA 30341-3717. Phone: (770) 488-0572.

Internet: www.cdc.gov. (Note: no field offices for this program.)

93.064 LABORATORY TRAINING, EVALUATION, AND QUALITY ASSURANCE PROGRAMS

Assistance: project grants. (100 percent/to 3 years).

Purposes: pursuant to PHSA as amended, to improve laboratory genetic testing practices relevant to clinical and public health settings; to determine standardized approaches to quality assurance in pathology and laboratory medicine, applicable in diverse settings including community hospitals, academic medical centers, and independent laboratories.

Eligible applicants/beneficiaries: public and private nonprofit organizations, IHEs, research institutions, hospitals, community organizations; state and local governments and their agents, including in territories and possessions.

Range: $100,000 to $500,000. **Average:** $250,000.

Activity: N.A.

HQ: CDCP-HHS, 1600 Clifton Rd., NE; Stop G25, Atlanta, GA 30329-4027. Phone: (404) 498-0233; FAX: (404) 498-2707.

Internet: www.cdc.gov. (Note: no field offices for this program.)

93.065   LABORATORY LEADERSHIP, WORKFORCE TRAINING AND MANAGEMENT DEVELOPMENT, IMPROVING PUBLIC HEALTH LABORATORY INFRASTRUCTURE
("APHL-CDC Partnership for Quality Lab Practice")

Assistance: project grants. (100 percent/to 5 years).

Purposes: pursuant to PHSA as amended, to improve public health laboratory infrastructure; for state-of-the-art training to prepare laboratorians to deal with public health threats with emerging infectious diseases or other biologic and chemical threats; to improve laboratory leadership capabilities; to enhance inter-laboratory communications.

Eligible applicants/beneficiaries: state governments, specifically state public health laboratories; organizations representing state public health laboratories with an established training network.

Range/Average: N.A.

Activity: N.A.

HQ: Project Officer, CDCP-HHS, 1600 Clifton Rd., Stop E21, Atlanta, GA 30333. Phone: (404) 498-6399.

Internet: www.cdc.gov.

93.066   STATE VITAL STATISTICS IMPROVEMENT PROGRAM

Assistance: project grants. (100 percent/1-3 years).

Purposes: pursuant to PHSA as amended, to assist states in improving the timeliness, quality, and sustainability of the decentralized vital statistics system by adopting national consensus standards and guidelines, in all 57 registration areas. These will be systems that can: provide quality and timely data for public health surveillance and medical research; meet citizen needs for legal copies of their birth and death records, as well as meet federal needs for related record verification and authentication; produce comparable vital registration and statistics systems in each state; use national standards and guidelines, including certificates of birth, death, and fetal death; support national security and privacy requirements; integrate with other public health systems; use internet technology.

Eligible applicants/beneficiaries: appropriate public and private nonprofit organizations.

Range: N.A. **Average:** $745,000 per year for 5 years.

Activity: N.A.

HQ: Project Officer, Division of Vital Statistics, National Center for Health Statistics, CDCP-HHS, 3311 Toledo Rd., Rm. 7319, Hyattsville, MD 20782. Phone: (301) 458-4323.

Internet: www.cdc.gov. (Note: no field offices for this program.)

93.067 GLOBAL AIDS

Assistance: project grants. (100 percent/1-5 years).

Purposes: pursuant to PHSA as amended, for activities conducted with other countries, international organizations, U.S. Department of State, USAID, and other partners to achieve the United Nations General Assembly Special Session on HIV/AIDS goal of reducing prevalence among persons age 15-24. Research may not be funded under this program.

Eligible applicants/beneficiaries: limited competition, or single eligibility by authorizing legislation.

Range: $25,000 to $134,000,000. **Average:** $2,200,000.

Activity: N.A.

HQ: Branch Chief, International Branch, CDCP-HHS, 1600 Clifton Rd., NE, Stop E-84, Atlanta, GA 30333. Phone: (404) 498-1613.

Internet: www.cdc.gov.

93.068 CHRONIC DISEASES—RESEARCH, CONTROL, AND PREVENTION

Assistance: project grants. (100 percent/1-5 years).

Purposes: pursuant to PHSA as amended, to prevent and control chronic diseases and disorders through research, development, capacity building, and intervention; to use research data to improve detection, diagnosis, treatment, and care of chronic diseases and their complications; to develop new related knowledge that will improve health and quality of life and eliminate health disparities among segments of the population. CDCP will have substantial involvement in project activities.

Eligible applicants/beneficiaries: state and local governments or their bona fide agents, including in territories and possessions; public, private, profit, and nonprofit organizations including small, minority and women-owned businesses, IHEs, research institutions, faith-based organizations, Indian tribes and tribal organizations; some foreign institutions may be eligible for certain programs.

Range/Average: N.A.

Activity: N.A.

HQ: Office of Extramural Research, National Center for Chronic Disease Prevention and Health Promotion, CDCP-HHS, 1600 Clifton Rd., Atlanta, GA 3033. Phone: (770) 488-8390.

Internet: www.cdc.gov. (Note: no field offices for this program.)

93.069 PUBLIC HEALTH EMERGENCY PREPAREDNESS

Assistance: project grants (100 percent/5 years).

Purposes: pursuant to Public Health Service Act, to develop emergency-ready public health departments intended to support the National Response Plan (NRP) and the National Incident Management System (NIMS) by working with state, local, and tribal governments, the private sector, and non-governmental agencies to upgrade, evaluate and integrate state and local public health jurisdictions and prepare for and respond to terrorism, pandemic influenza, and other public health emergencies.

Eligible applicants/beneficiaries: state health departments of all 50 states, DC, the nation's three largest municipalities (New York, Chicago, Los Angeles county), PR, VI, American Samoa, Guam, Micronesia, Palau, Marshall Islands and Northern Marianas.

Range/Average: N.A.

Activity: N.A.

HQ: Program Director, CDC-HHS, 1600 Clifton Rd. MS D-29, Atlanta, GA 30029. Phone: (404) 639-5276.

Internet: www.cdc.gov. (Note: no field offices for this program.)

93.070 ENVIRONMENTAL PUBLIC HEALTH AND EMERGENCY RESPONSE

Assistance: cooperative agreements (100 percent/to 5 years).

Purposes: pursuant to the Public Health Service Act, to bring public health and epidemiologic principles together to identify, clarify, and reduce the impact of complex environmental threats, including terrorist threats and natural disasters, on populations, domestic and foreign.

Eligible applicants: state, county and tribal governments.

Eligible beneficiaries: state and local health departments, U.S. territories and Native American tribal public health agencies.

Range: $10,000 to $1,500,000. **Average:** N.A.

Activity: N.A.

HQ: Program Director, CDC, HHS, 4770 Buford Hwy, NE, Stop F45, Atlanta, GA 30341-3717. Phone: (770) 488-0711.

Internet: www.cdc.gov. (Note: no field offices for this program.)

93.071 MEDICARE ENROLLMENT ASSISTANCE PROGRAM ("MIPPA")

Assistance: formula grants (100 percent/1 year); project grants (100 percent/1-5 years).

Purposes: pursuant to Medicare Improvements for Patients and Providers Act of 2008, to provide outreach to eligible Medicare beneficiaries regarding benefits available under title XVIII of the Social Security Act and the Medicare Savings Program and to coordinate efforts to inform older Americans about benefits available under federal and state programs.

Eligible applicants: Formula grants: state and U.S. territory governments, with distribution to designated area agencies on aging and tribal organizations through an approved state plan. Project grants: any public or nonprofit private agency, organization, or institution.

Eligible beneficiaries: individuals eligible for Medicare, including Part D drug benefits and older persons eligible for benefits and services under federal and state programs.

Range: N.A. **Average:** $61,464.

Activity: N.A.

HQ: Administration on Aging, HHS, One Massachusetts Ave., Washington, DC 20001. Phone: (202) 357-3589.

Internet: www.acl.gov.

93.072 LIFESPAN RESPITE CARE PROGRAM ("Lifespan Respite")

Assistance: project grants/cooperative agreements (75 percent/to 5 years).

Purposes: pursuant to Lifespan Respite Care Act of 2006, to expand and enhance respite care services to family caregivers, improve statewide dissemination and coordination of respite care, and to provide, supplement, or improve access and quality of respite care services to family caregivers. Funds may also be used to establish a National Resource Center on Lifespan Respite Care designed to maintain a national database on lifespan respite care. Matching funds are required and funds may not be used to supplant other federal, state, or local funds available for respite care services.

Eligible applicants: states (includes DC, public IHEs and hospitals).

Eligible beneficiaries: anyone/general public, especially unpaid family caregivers.

Range: N.A. **Average:** $220,456.

Activity: N.A.

HQ: AOA-HHS, One Massachusetts Ave., NW, Washington, DC 20201. Phone: (202) 357-3414.

Internet: www.acl.gov.

93.073 BIRTH DEFECTS AND DEVELOPMENTAL DISABILITIES— PREVENTION AND SURVEILLANCE

Assistance: cooperative agreements (100 percent/to 5 years).

Purposes: pursuant to the Public Health Service Act, to plan, implement, coordinate, or evaluate programs, research or surveillance activities related to improved birth outcomes, prevention of birth defects and developmental disabilities, and the improvement of infant and child health and developmental outcomes.

Eligible applicants: state health agencies, IHEs, nonprofit organizations.

Eligible beneficiaries: state, local and federally-recognized tribal governments, nonprofit institution/organizations, individual and families.

Range: $5,000 to $1,500,000. **Average:** N.A.

Activity: N.A.

HQ: Program Director, CDC, HHS, 1600 Clifton Rd., NE, Atlanta, GA 30333. Phone: (404) 498-2416.

Internet: www.cdc.gov/ncbddd. (Note: no field offices for this program.)

93.075 SYSTEMS INTEROPERABILITY—HEALTH AND HUMAN SERVICES

Assistance: project grants (100 percent/12 months).

Purposes: pursuant to the Consolidated Appropriations Act, to improve the administration of federal assistance programs by: reducing improper payments; improving administrative efficiency; improving service delivery; and protecting and improving program access for eligible beneficiaries. Grantees can explore systems design and implementation options, determine the costs and benefits of different options, the potential client outcomes and impacts of each option, and develop concrete implementation plans and options for the grantee to consider.

Eligible applicants/beneficiaries: state (including the District of Columbia, Guam, Puerto Rico, and the Virgin Islands) human services agencies.

Range: $977,047 to $1,125,000. **Average:** N.A.

Activity: N.A.

HQ: Director, Office of Child Support Enforcement, Administration for Children and Families, Department of Health and Human Services, 370 L'Enfant Promenade, SW, 4th Fl. East, Washington, DC 20447. Phone: (202) 401-4975; FAX: (202) 205-4582.

Internet: www.acf.hhs.gov/programs/cse. (Note: no field offices for this program.)

93.076 TANF PROGRAM INTEGRITY INNOVATION GRANTS

Assistance: cooperative agreements (100 percent/to 17 months).

Purposes: pursuant to the Consolidated Appropriations Act of 2010, to fund pilot projects for improving the stewardship of federal dollars in assistance programs through the following measures: reducing improper payments; improving administrative efficiency; improving service delivery; and protecting and improving program access for eligible beneficiaries.

Eligible applicants/beneficiaries: 35 IHEs selected by the CDC as Prevention Research Centers (PRCs).

Range: $400,000 to $1,000,000. **Average:** $784,000.

Activity: N.A.

HQ: Director, Office of Family Assistance, Administration for Children and Families, HHS, 370 L'Enfant Promenade SW, Washington, DC 20447. Phone: (202) 401-5488; FAX: (202) 205-5887.

Internet: www.acf.hhs.gov/programs/ofa. (Note: no field offices for this program.)

93.077 FAMILY SMOKING PREVENTION AND TOBACCO CONTROL ACT REGULATORY RESEARCH
("NIH-FDA Tobacco Control Regulatory Research")

Assistance: cooperative agreements; project grants/contracts; training (100 percent/1 to 5 years).

Purposes: pursuant to the Public Health Service Act and the Family Smoking Prevention and Tobacco Control Act, to encourage biomedical, behavioral, and social science research that will inform the development and evaluation of regulations on tobacco product manufacturing, distribution, and marketing.

Eligible applicants/beneficiaries: 35 IHEs selected by the CDC as Prevention Research Centers (PRCs).

Range/Average: N.A.

Activity: N.A.

HQ: Program Director, NIH-FDA Tobacco Control Regulatory Research, NIH, HHS, 6100 Executive Blvd., Rm. 3B01, MSC 7530, Bethesda, MD 20892-7530. Phone: (301) 451-8681 Fax: (301) 480-7660.

Internet: prevention.nih.gov/tobacco-regulatory-science-program. (Note: no field offices for this program.)

93.079 COOPERATIVE AGREEMENTS TO PROMOTE ADOLESCENT HEALTH THROUGH SCHOOL-BASED HIV/STD PREVENTION AND SCHOOL-BASED SURVEILLANCE

Assistance: cooperative agreements (100 percent/to 5 years).

Purposes: pursuant to the Public Health Service Act, to support state, territorial, and local health education agency efforts to reduce new HIV/STD infections among adolescents and to reduce disparities in HIV/STD infections experienced by youth at disproportionate risk, especially targeting large urban school districts with student enrollment greater than 40,000 students, the highest burden of HIV/STD, and the high levels of poverty.

Eligible applicants: states, DC, and territories, large urban school districts, public/private non-profit organizations.

Eligible beneficiaries: state, DC, territorial, and local education agencies, national private sector organizations and their constituents, school-aged youth, and school personnel.

Range: 7,000 to $650,000. **Average:** $375,000.

Activity: N.A.

HQ: Program Director, CDC, HHS, 1600 Clifton Rd. NE, MS E-75, Atlanta, GA 30333. Phone: (404) 718-8333.

Internet: www.cdc.gov. (Note: no field offices for this program.)

93.082 SODIUM REDUCTION IN COMMUNITIES

Assistance: cooperative agreements (100 percent/to 5 years).

Purposes: pursuant to the Public Health Service Act, to implement and evaluate population-based strategies to increase access to lower sodium food in communities, and decrease sodium intake. Funds may be used for planning, organizing, conducting, and supporting sodium reduction strategies at the community and/or state level.

Eligible applicants: state, territorial, official local health department or its bona fide agent or qualified equivalent, tribal governments, tribes, tribal health boards or organizations or inter-tribal councils.

Eligible beneficiaries: states, political subdivisions and U.S. territories, other public entities.

Range: $250,000 to $350,000. **Average:** N.A.

Activity: N.A.

HQ: Program Director, CDC, HHS, 4770 Buford Hwy. NE, MS-F72, Atlanta, GA 30341. Phone: (770) 488-2047.

Internet: www.cdc.gov. (Note: no field offices for this program.)

93.083 PREVENTION OF DISEASE, DISABILITY, AND DEATH THROUGH IMMUNIZATION AND CONTROL OF RESPIRATORY AND RELATED DISEASES

Assistance: project grants (100 percent/1 to 5 years).

Purposes: pursuant to the Public Health Service Act, funds for costs associated with planning, organizing, conducting, and supporting programs directed towards prevention of disease, disability, and death through immunization and control of respiratory and related diseases, and for the implementation of programs whose objectives include, but are not limited to: increase the population of children and adults who are free from respiratory infectious disease complications; strengthen local, state, and national capacity for the early detection, investigation, response and control of respiratory infections in order to accelerate early recognition of respiratory threats and to mitigate the impact of their spread; control the rise in antimicrobial resistant respiratory infections in the community; strengthen prevention and control of respiratory infections in institutional settings, such as health care facilities and workplaces; reduce mortality from pneumonia and other severe respiratory infections; strengthen capacity for early detection, investigation, response, and control of respiratory infectious threats.

Eligible applicants/beneficiaries: IHEs, nonprofit organizations, state/local governments, Indian/Native American tribal organizations, eligible federal agencies, U.S. territory or possession, independent school districts, public housing authorities, Native American tribal organizations, faith-based or community organizations, regional organizations, bona fide agents of state/local governments.

Range/Average: N.A.

Activity: N.A.

HQ: Director, Prevention of Disease, Disability, and Death by Infectious Diseases Program, CDC, 1600 Clifton Rd., Stop E-60, Atlanta, GA 30333. Phone: (404) 718-8833.

Internet: N.A.

93.084 PREVENTION OF DISEASE, DISABILITY, AND DEATH BY INFECTIOUS DISEASES

Assistance: project grants (100 percent/1 to 5 years).

Purposes: pursuant to the Public Health Service Act, funds for costs associated with planning, organizing, conducting, and supporting programs directed towards prevention of disease, disability, and death by control of infectious diseases, and for the implementation of programs whose objectives include, but are not limited to: strengthen public health fundamentals, including infectious disease surveillance, laboratory detection, and epidemiologic investigation; identify and implement high-impact public health interventions to reduce infectious diseases; develop and advance policies to prevent, detect, and control infectious diseases.

Eligible applicants/beneficiaries: IHEs, nonprofit organizations, state/local governments, Indian/Native American tribal organizations, eligible federal agencies, U.S. territory or possession, independent school districts, public housing authorities, Native American tribal organizations, faith-based or community organizations, regional organizations, bona fide agents of state/local governments.

Range/Average: N.A.

Activity: N.A.

HQ: Director, Prevention of Disease, Disability, and Death by Infectious Diseases Program, CDC, 1600 Clifton Rd., Stop E-60, Atlanta, GA 30333. Phone: (404) 718-8833.

Internet: N.A.

93.085   RESEARCH ON RESEARCH INTEGRITY

Assistance: project grants (100 percent/1 year).

Purposes: pursuant to The Public Health and Welfare Act, to foster research on research integrity in areas that have been inadequately explored by evaluating the effectiveness of education and training in the responsible conduct of research, identifying mechanisms other than traditional RCR education institutions might effectively employ to foster the responsible conduct of research and discourage misconduct, evaluating factors affecting the behavior of researchers.

Eligible applicants: public (including city, county, regional, and State government) organizations and private nonprofit entities.

Eligible beneficiaries: anyone/general public.

Range: $50,000 to $150,000. **Average:** N.A.

Activity: N.A.

HQ: Director, Tower Bldg., 2201 Wootton Parkway, Suite 550, Rockville, MD 20852. Phone: (240) 453-8822.

Internet: ori.hhs.gov.

93.086   HEALTHY MARRIAGE PROMOTION AND RESPONSIBLE FATHERHOOD GRANTS (HMRF)

Assistance: project grants; technical information (project grants, to 5 years).

Purposes: pursuant to SSA (as included in the Deficit Reduction Act of 2005), for: (1) healthy marriage promotion activities helping couples that chose marriage for themselves have access to marriage education services; (2) responsible fatherhood promotion activities designed to reverse the rise in father absence; (3) demonstration projects to test the effectiveness of tribal governments and consortia in coordinating services to tribal families at risk of child abuse, or neglect of child welfare services; (4) federal technical assistance to grant recipients. Projects must assure voluntary participation by services recipients; they must also incorporate strong domestic violence prevention components.

Eligible applicants/beneficiaries: "Healthy Marriage Grants"—public and private entities including state, local, and special district government entities, public and private IHEs, tribes and tribal organizations, nonprofit and profit organizations, faith-based and community organizations.

Range/Average: N.A.

Activity: anticipate 135 grants will be awarded in FY 2016.

HQ: Office of Family Assistance, ACF-HHS, 370 L'Enfant Promenade, SW, 5th Fl., East, Washington, DC 20447. Phone: (202) 401-5587.

Internet: www.acf.hhs.gov. (Note: no field offices for this program.)

93.087 ENHANCE SAFETY OF CHILDREN AFFECTED BY SUBSTANCE ABUSE

Assistance: project grants (75-85 percent/3-5 years).

Purposes: pursuant to Child and Family Service Improvement Act of 2006, to provide through interagency collaboration and integration of program activities that are designed to increase the well-being of, improve permanency outcomes for, and enhance the safety of children who are in an out-of-home placement or are at risk of being placed in an out-of-home placement as a result of parent's or caretaker's methamphetamine or other substance abuse. Funding may include: family-based comprehensive long-term substance abuse treatment; early intervention and preventative services; children/family counseling; mental health services; and parenting skills training.

Eligible applicants/beneficiaries: public and private entities including state, local, and special district government entities, public and private IHEs, tribes and tribal organizations, nonprofit and profit organizations/institutions.

Range: $500,000 to $1,000,000. **Average:** $669,231.

Activity: anticipate 21 continuation grants in FY 2016.

HQ: Director, Office on Child Abuse and Neglect, Children's Bureau, ACF-HHS, 1250 Maryland Ave., SW, Washington, DC 20024. Phone: (202) 205-7941.

Internet: www.acf.hhs.gov/programs/cb. (Note: no field offices for this program.)

93.088 ADVANCING SYSTEM IMPROVEMENTS FOR KEY ISSUES IN WOMEN'S HEALTH

Assistance: project grants (100 percent/to 3 years).

Purposes: to provide three years of additional support to existing public health systems/collaborative partnerships to enable them to add a gender focus to Healthy People 2010 (HP 2010) objectives that track the health status of women and/or men. Funds may not be used for construction, building alterations, equipment, printing, food, or medical treatment.

Eligible applicants: applicant must be part of an existing public health system or collaborative partnership and at least one third of the partners should possess demonstrated experience addressing gender differences through appropriate interventions, programs, or research related to the selected objectives of the Office on Women's Health.

Eligible beneficiaries: anyone/general public.

Range: $200,000 to $2,200,000. **Average:** N.A.

Activity: N.A.

HQ: Office on Women's Health, HHS, Tower Bldg., 1101 Wootton Parkway, Suite 550, Rockville, MD 20852. Phone: (240) 453-8822.

Internet: www.womenshealth.gov.

93.089 EMERGENCY SYSTEM FOR ADVANCE REGISTRATION OF HEALTH PROFESSIONAL VOLUNTEERS ("ESAR-VHP")

Assistance: project grants/discretionary (100 percent/to 5 years).

Purposes: pursuant to Public Health Service Act, Title III, Section 319I, as amended, to establish and maintain a national interoperable network of state systems (each system being maintained by a state or group of states) for the purpose of verifying credentials, certifications, licenses, accreditations, relevant training, and hospital privileges of health care professionals who volunteer to provide health services during a public health emergency.

Eligible applicants: local governments (includes state-designated Indian tribes).

Eligible beneficiaries: states, U.S. territories, major urban area (over 250,000).

Range: $58,478 to $200,000. **Average:** N.A.

Activity: N.A.

HQ: ESAR-VHP, National Healthcare Preparedness Programs, Office of Preparedness and Emergency Operations, HHS, 200 C St., SW, Washington, DC 20024. Phone: (202) 245-0722.

Internet: www.phe.gov/esarvhp.

93.090 GUARDIANSHIP ASSISTANCE

Assistance: formula grants.

Purposes: pursuant to Social Security Act, Title IV, Part E, as amended, to provide Federal Financial Participation (FFP) to states and tribes opting to provide assistance payments for care of children by relatives who have assumed legal guardianship of eligible children for whom they previously cared as foster parents.

All relatives assuming guardianship of such children are eligible for the non-recurring expenses associated with obtaining legal guardianship up to $2000. Beginning in FY 2010, funds will be available to Indian tribes, organizations and consortia with approved title IV-E plans to operate a guardianship assistance program.

Eligible applicants: state title IV-E agencies and Indian tribes.

Eligible beneficiaries: children, individuals/families.

Range: $49,338 to $32,577,392. **Average:** $2,990,233.

Activity: anticipate 37 awards in FY 2016.

HQ: Administration For Children And Families-HHS, 1250 Maryland Ave., SW, Washington, DC 20024. Phone: (202) 205-8086.

Internet: www.acf.hhs.gov/programs/cb.

93.091 SOCIAL SERVICES AND INCOME MAINTENANCE BENEFITS ENROLLMENT COORDINATION GRANTS ("SSIMB Grants")

Assistance: project grants/discretionary (100 percent/1 year).

Purposes: pursuant to the Social Security Act, to support ongoing facilitated outreach and enrollment assistance to low-income individuals and families to access already existing Federal, State, and local benefit programs.

Eligible applicants/beneficiaries: private-nonprofit organizations with 501(c)(3) or 501(c)(4) status, and faith-based and community organizations.

Range/Average: N.A.

Activity: N.A.

HQ: Director, Office of Community Services, Administration for Children and Families, Department of Health and Human Services, 370 L'Enfant Promenade, 5th Fl. West, Washington, DC 20447. Phone: (202) 401-5281; FAX: (202) 401-5718.

Internet: www.acf.hhs.gov/programs/ocs/index.html. (Note: no field offices for this program.)

93.093 AFFORDABLE CARE ACT (ACA) HEALTH PROFESSION OPPORTUNITY GRANTS (HPOG)

Assistance: project grants (100 percent/5 years).

Purposes: pursuant to the Social Security Act, to provide education and training to Temporary Assistance for Needy Families (TANF) recipients and other low-income individuals for occupations in the health care field that pay well and are expected to either experience labor shortages or be in high demand.

Eligible applicants: states, Indian tribes or tribal organizations, IHEs, local workforce investment boards established under section 117 of the Workforce Investment Act of 1998, sponsors of an apprenticeship program registered under the National Apprenticeship Act, or community-based organizations.

Eligible beneficiaries: individuals receiving assistance under the State TANF program or other low-income individuals described by the eligible entity in its application for a grant.

Range: $600,000 to $3,000,000. **Average:** $1,800,000.

Activity: anticipate 40 continuation grants only in FY 2016.

HQ: Director, 370 L'Enfant Promenade, SW, Aerospace Bldg., 5th Fl., East, Washington, DC 20447. Phone: (202) 401-5457; FAX: (202) 205-5887.

Internet: www.acf.hhs.gov/programs/ofa/programs/hpog. (Note: no field offices for this program.)

93.095 HHS PROGRAMS FOR DISASTER RELIEF APPROPRIATIONS ACT—NON CONSTRUCTION

Assistance: project grants/cooperative agreements, formula grants (100 percent/to 2 years).

Purposes: pursuant to the Disaster Relief Appropriations Act of 2013, program will fund disaster response and recovery, and other expenses directly related to Hurricane Sandy, which are in the FEMA-declared major disaster states, relevant to the following: the Head Start program; Social Services Block Grant, in addition to the entitlement grants; health services (including mental health services); costs of renovating, repairing, or rebuilding health care facilities, child care facilities, or other social services facilities; supporting the repair or rebuilding of non-federal biomedical or behavioral research facilities.

Eligible applicants: eligible applicants and/or co-applicants must be based or have significant operations in one of the following major FEMA-declared disaster areas: Connecticut, Delaware, Maryland, Massachusetts, New Hampshire, New Jersey, New York, Ohio, Pennsylvania, Rhode Island, Virginia, West Virginia and the District of Columbia. Non-state applicants must partner with 1 or more state, tribal, or local public health agency in one of these disaster area states or DC. Head Start and Social Services Block Grant applicants must be current grantees. Applicants will be required to attest that requested program funds will not be used for costs that are reimbursed by the FEMA under a contract for insurance or by self-insurance.

Eligible beneficiaries: those impacted by Hurricane Sandy in 2012.

Range/Average: N.A.

Activity: N.A.

HQ: Director, HHS Programs for Disaster Relief Appropriations Act—Non Construction, Department of Health and Human Services, 200 Independence Ave., SW, Washington, DC 20201. Phone: (202) 690-6574.

Internet: www.hhs.gov. (Note: no field offices for this program.)

93.096 HHS PROGRAMS FOR DISASTER RELIEF APPROPRIATIONS ACT—CONSTRUCTION

Assistance: project grants (100 percent/to 24 months).

Purposes: pursuant to the Relief Appropriations Act of 2013, funds for disaster response and recovery, and other expenses directly related to Hurricane Sandy, which are in the FEMA-declared major disaster states, relevant to the following: costs of renovating, repairing, or rebuilding health care facilities, child care facilities, or other social services facilities; and supporting the repair or rebuilding of non-Federal biomedical or behavioral research facilities. These funds may be used for research, renovation and repair, constructions, and training. Funds may not be used for costs that are reimbursed by FEMA, or under a contract for insurance, or by self-insurance.

Eligible applicants: governments (including tribal governments), public or private non-profit or for-profit organizations, small businesses, public or private institutions.

Eligible beneficiaries: those impacted by Hurricane Sandy in the FEMA-declared major disaster states, which are: Connecticut, Delaware, Maryland, Massachusetts, New Hampshire, New Jersey, New York, Ohio, Pennsylvania, Rhode Island, Virginia, West Virginia and the District of Columbia.

Range/Average: N.A.

Activity: N.A.

HQ: Director, HHS Programs for Disaster Relief Appropriations Act, HHS, 200 Independence Ave., SW, Washington, DC 20201. Phone: (202) 205-1226.

Internet: www.hhs.gov. (Note: no field offices for this program.)

93.097 STRENGTHENING THE NATIONS PUBLIC HEALTH SYSTEM THROUGH A NATIONAL VOLUNTARY ACCREDITATION PROGRAM FOR STATE, TRIBAL, LOCAL AND TERRITORIAL HEALTH DEPARTMENTS

Assistance: project grants/cooperative agreements (100 percent).

Purposes: pursuant to the Public Health Service Act, funds used for costs associated with planning, organizing, conducting, and supporting the National Voluntary Accreditation Program for State, Tribal, Local and Territorial Health Departments, and for the implementation of the Public Health Accreditation Board (PHAB) program. Specific objectives may/will include but are not limited to: support communications and education regarding the accreditation program; establish a process of continuous improvement of the accreditation standards, tools, and processes to ensure a relevant, current and smoothly functioning program; strengthen strategic partnerships to support accreditation; strengthen the evidence base for accreditation.

Eligible applicants/beneficiaries: the Public Health Accreditation Board (PHAB), a 501(c)3 independent accrediting body that administers the national voluntary public health department accreditation program.

Range/Average: N.A.

Activity: N.A.

HQ: Director, National Voluntary Accreditation Program for State, Tribal, Local and Territorial Health Departments, CDC-DHHS, 1600 Clifton Rd., MS-E70, Atlanta, GA 30333. Phone: (770) 488-1523.

Internet: www.cdc.gov. (Note: no field offices for this program.)

93.098 TRIBAL PUBLIC HEALTH CAPACITY BUILDING AND QUALITY IMPROVEMENT

Assistance: project grants/cooperative agreements (100 percent).

Purposes: pursuant to the Public Health Service Act, funding to improve tribal health systems quality, effectiveness, and efficiency in the delivery of public health services to American Indians/Alaska Natives (AI/AN). Funds may be used for costs associated with planning, organizing, conducting, and supporting the implementation of The Tribal Public Health Capacity Building and Quality Improvement (CBQI) program. All applicants must describe their experience in effectively delivering AI/AN culturally-specific programs and have a proven record of demonstrated success in monitoring and evaluation of the same AI/AN culturally-specific programs.

Eligible applicants: federally recognized tribes and/or tribally designated organizations including non-profit organizations, IHEs, and hospitals.

Eligible beneficiaries: Native American organizations.

Range: N.A. **Average:** $97,500.

Activity: N.A.

HQ: Director, Tribal Public Health Capacity Building and Quality Improvement, CDC-DHHS, 1825 Century Blvd., Atlanta, GA 30345. Phone: (404) 498-0182.

Internet: www.cdc.gov. (Note: no field offices for this program.)

93.103 FOOD AND DRUG ADMINISTRATION—RESEARCH

Assistance: project grants. (100 percent/1-5 years).

Purposes: pursuant to PHSA and Small Business Innovation Research Program Reauthorization Act of 1992 (SBIRPRA) as amended and Radiation Control for Health Safety Act of 1968, for research, demonstration, education, and dissemination activities in a broad range of areas, AIDS, biologics, blood and blood products, therapeutics, vaccine and allergenic projects, drug hazards, human and veterinary drugs, medical devices and diagnostics products, orphan product development, and radiation-emitting devices and materials, food safety and additives. SBIR awards are made.

Eligible applicants/beneficiaries: public or private nonprofit IHEs, institutions, state and local governments, hospitals, laboratories, commercial and nonprofit organizations.

Range/Average: N.A.

Activity: N.A.

HQ: Chief Grants Management Officer, Division of Contracts and Procurement Management, Office of Acquisition and Grant Services, FDA-HHS (HFA-500), 5630 Fishers Ln., Rockville, MD 20852. Phone: (240) 402-7610.

Internet: www.fda.gov. (Note: no field offices for this program.)

93.104 COMPREHENSIVE COMMUNITY MENTAL HEALTH SERVICES FOR CHILDREN WITH SERIOUS EMOTIONAL DISTURBANCES (SED) ("CMHS Child Mental Health Service Initiative")

Assistance: project grants. (33-75 percent/to 6 years).

Purposes: pursuant to PHSA as amended, for community-based care systems for children and adolescents with serious emotional disturbances, and their families—ensuring that: services are provided collaboratively across child-serving systems; each child or adolescent served receives an individualized service plan developed with the participation of the family and, where appropriate, of the child; each plan designates a case manager; funding is provided for the required mental health services. Project funds may be used to pay: administrative costs including staff salaries, travel, supplies, communications, and space and equipment rental; for pertinent training including in providing therapeutic foster or group home care, intensive home-based or intensive day treatment services. Ineligible expenses include real estate-related costs, residential care or services in centers serving more than 10 children, unrelated training, non- mental health services including medical and educational services, and protection and advocacy.

Eligible applicants: states and their political subdivisions, tribal governments.

Eligible beneficiaries: children under age 22 with diagnosed SED or serious behavioral or mental disorders.

Range: $376,096 to $2,000,000. **Average:** $1,329,454.

Activity: anticipate 14 awards will be made in FY 2016.

HQ: Chief, Child Adolescent and Family Branch, Division of Knowledge Development and Systems Change, CMHS-SAMHSA-HHS, 1 Choke Cherry Rd., Rockville, MD 20850. Phone: (240) 276-1418.

Internet: www.samhsa.gov. (Note: no field offices for this program.)

93.107 AREA HEALTH EDUCATION CENTERS POINT OF SERVICE MAINTENANCE AND ENHANCEMENT AWARDS

Assistance: formula grants. (50 percent/to 3 years).

Purposes: pursuant to PHSA as amended and HPEPA, to encourage region-alization of health professions schools by establishing model Area Health Education Centers (see **93.824**), involving collaborative partnerships of university health centers with local planning, educational, and clinical resources; for health careers programs for students in grades 9-12. Emphasis is on recruitment and community-based training of primary care students, residents, and providers.

Eligible applicants/beneficiaries: schools of allopathic medicine or osteopathy and consortia operating AHECs and no longer receiving assistance under **93.824**.

Range: $102,000 to $1,224,000. **Average:** $470,000.

Activity: N.A.

HQ: Chief, AHEC Branch, Division of State, Community and Public Health, Bureau of Health Professions, HRSA-HHS, Parklawn Bldg. - Rm. 9-05, 5600 Fishers Lane, Rockville, MD 20857. Phone: (301) 443-6950. *grants management information*: Director, Division of Grants Management, Health Resources and Services Administration-HHS, 5600 Fishers Ln., Rm. 11A-16, Rockville, MD 20857. Phone: (301) 443-6950.

Internet: bhw.hrsa.gov/grants/areahealtheducationcenters/index.html.

93.110 MATERNAL AND CHILD HEALTH FEDERAL CONSOLIDATED PROGRAMS ("SPRANS, CISS")

Assistance: project grants.

Purposes: pursuant to the Social Security Act of 1935 (SSA) as amended, for special projects of regional or national significance involving training, services, research, and demonstrations in maternal and child health services, including: genetic disease testing, counseling, and information dissemination; operation of comprehensive hemophilia diagnosis and treatment centers. A portion of grant funds, if appropriated, may be used to provide other services including home visitations, increased participation of obstetricians and pediatricians, maternal and child health centers for women and infants, rural health services, community-based services for children with special health care needs.

Eligible applicants/beneficiaries: training grants—public or private nonprofit IHEs. Research grants—public or private nonprofit IHEs, agencies, and organizations. Hemophilia and genetics grants and other special project grants—any public or private entity.

Range: $3,419 to $3,996,711. **Average:** $267,663.

Activity: N.A.

HQ: Associate Administrator, Maternal and Child Health Bureau, HRSA-HHS, 5600 Fishers Ln., Rm. 18-05, Rockville, MD 20857. Phone: (301) 443-2170.

Internet: www.hrsa.gov.

93.113   ENVIRONMENTAL HEALTH

Assistance: project grants. (100 percent/to 5 years).

Purposes: pursuant to PHSA as amended and Small Business Research and Development Enhancement Act of 1992 (SBRDEA), for research and research training on the chemical and physical causes of pathological changes in molecules, cells, tissues, and organs, toward the prevention of neurological, behavioral, and developmental abnormalities, and respiratory diseases, cancer, and other disorders. Grants also support studies of toxicity in metals, natural and synthetic chemicals, pesticides, asbestos and silica, and natural toxins—and their effects on human organ systems, metabolism, endocrine and immune systems, and other biological functions. The Environmental Health Sciences Education Program may fund projects to improve student understanding of environmental health issues and to expand career awareness in health sciences research and services occupations, by developing educational materials for grades K-12. Independent Scientist Awards, Mentored Research Scientist Development Awards, Mentored Clinical Scientist Development Awards, Academic Career Awards, and other programs may also be funded including centers on children's health and disease. SBIR and STTR awards are made.

Eligible applicants/beneficiaries: research grants and cooperative agreements, science education grants, independent scientist awards, mentored clinical and research scientist awards, academic career awards—IHEs, hospitals, state or local governments, nonprofit research institutions, or profit organizations for research by a named principal investigator. Candidates for academic career development awards must have a clinical or research doctorate and peer-reviewed independent research support, and they must devote at least 75 percent effort. Candidates for mentored clinical scientist awards must have clinical training; those holding a Ph.D. degree are ineligible, as are researchers that have served as principal investigators on PHS-supported research projects.

Range: $3,429 to $1,793,611. **Average:** $344,497.

Activity: anticipate 766 awards in FY 2016.

HQ: Director, Superfund Hazardous Substance Basic Research and Training Program, Division of Extramural Research and Training, NIEHS-NIH-HHS, 111 TW Alexander Dr., Research Triangle Park, NC 27709. Phone: (919) 541-5147.

Internet: N.A. (Note: no field offices for this program.)

93.116 PROJECT GRANTS AND COOPERATIVE AGREEMENTS FOR TUBERCULOSIS CONTROL PROGRAMS

Assistance: projects grants. (100 percent/to 5 years).

Purposes: pursuant to PHSA as amended, TB Prevention Amendments Act of 1990 as amended, and other acts, for tuberculosis control and prevention activities. Funds may cover such costs as patient outreach, directly observed therapy to assure its completion, morbidity surveillance, personnel, equipment, supplies, program assessment, and services. Costs of construction and inpatient care are ineligible uses.

Eligible applicants/beneficiaries: official public health agencies of state and local governments, territories and possessions.

Range: $86,938 to $9,317,764. **Average:** $1,454,714.

Activity: anticipate continued support of 62 cooperative agreements in FY 2016.

HQ: National Center for HIV, STD, and TB Prevention, CDCP-HHS, 1600 Clifton Rd., NE, Stop E10, Atlanta, GA 30333. Phone: (404) 639-8958.

Internet: www.cdc.gov/DTBE. (Note: no field offices for this program.)

93.117 PREVENTIVE MEDICINE RESIDENCY WITH INTEGRATIVE HEALTH CARE TRAINING PROGRAM

Assistance: project grants. (100 percent/3 years).

Purposes: pursuant to PHSA as amended and HPEPA, to plan, develop, maintain, or improve postgraduate training programs in preventive medicine. Financial assistance may be provided to residency trainees. Grants may not used for construction or direct patient services.

Eligible applicants: public or private schools of medicine, osteopathy, or public health.

Eligible beneficiaries: U.S. citizens, nationals, and lawful permanent residents.

Range/Average: N.A.

Activity: N.A.

HQ: Division of State, Community, and Public Health, Center for Public Health, Bureau of Health Professions, HRSA-HHS, Parklawn Bldg., Rm. 12-C-05, 5600 Fishers Ln., Rockville, MD 20857. Phone: (301) 443-6950.

Internet: www.hrsa.gov. (Note: no field offices for this program.)

93.118   ACQUIRED IMMUNODEFICIENCY SYNDROME (AIDS) ACTIVITY

Assistance: project grants. (100 percent/to 5 years).

Purposes: pursuant to PHSA as amended, to develop and implement HIV prevention programs of public education and information.

Eligible applicants/beneficiaries: public and private nonprofit and profit organizations including IHEs and research institutions; state and local governments, territories and possessions; small and minority-and women-owned businesses.

Range/Average: N.A.

Activity: N.A.

HQ: Division of HIV/AIDS Prevention (A43), CDCP-HHS, 1600 Clifton Rd., Stop E-07, Atlanta, GA 30333. Phone: (404) 639-8531.

Internet: www.cdc.gov/hiv. (Note: no field offices for this program.)

93.121   ORAL DISEASES AND DISORDERS RESEARCH ("Dental and Craniofacial Research")

Assistance: project grants. (100 percent/to 5 years).

Purposes: pursuant to PHSA as amended and SBRDEA, for research and research training in the oral health sciences, in such areas as craniofacial, oral, and dental health promotion and disease prevention, diagnostics, and therapeutics. Grant programs support basic, clinical, and transitional research, from molecular biology to patient-oriented and community-based clinical investigations—including etiology, pathogenesis, epidemiology, prevention, diagnosis, and treatment—within overlapping programs: Inherited Diseases and Disorders (e.g., cleft lip and palate, other craniofacial birth defects, developmentally related disorders), as well as occlusion defects acquired through trauma; Infectious Diseases such as dental caries, periodontitis, oral manifestations of HIV/AIDS, herpes, hepatitis, and other diseases; Neoplastic Diseases; Chronic Disabling Diseases; Biomaterials, Biomimetics and Tissue Engineering; Behavior, Health Promotion and Environment. Also supported are: Comprehensive Oral Research Centers of Discovery; Research Training and Careers; Diversity in Research; Clinical Trials and Clinical Core Centers; and Technology Transfer. NRSA, SBIR, and STTR awards are available.

Eligible applicants/beneficiaries: research grants—scientists at universities, medical and dental schools, hospitals, laboratories, other public, private, nonprofit, or profit institutions. Career development award candidates must comply with requirements similar to those applying to the NRSA program.

Range/Average: N.A.

Activity: N.A.

HQ: Division of Extramural Research, National Institute of Dental and Craniofacial Research, NIH-HHS, 701 Democracy Blvd., MSC 4878, Bethesda, MD 20892. Phone: (301) 594-4890; FAX: (301) 480-8303.

Internet: www.nidcr.nih.gov. (Note: no field offices for this program.)

93.123 HEALTH PROFESSIONS PREGRADUATE SCHOLARSHIP PROGRAM FOR INDIANS

Assistance: project grants (100 percent).

Purposes: pursuant to the Indian Health Care Improvement Act as amended, for four-year scholarships for American Indians and Alaska natives to complete pregraduate education leading to a baccalaureate degree in pre-medicine or pre-dentistry. Part-time attendance may be supported for a maximum of eight years.

Eligible applicants/beneficiaries: American Indians or Alaska natives accepted or enrolled in a pregraduate program.

Range: $22,035 to $71,672. **Average:** $37,951.

Activity: N.A.

HQ: Grants Policy Office, IHS-HHS, 801 Thompson Ave., Suite TMP 360, Rockville, MD 20852. Phone: (301) 443-5204.

Internet: www.ihs.gov. (Note: no field offices for this program.)

93.124 NURSE ANESTHETIST TRAINEESHIPS (NAT)

Assistance: project grants. (100 percent/1 year).

Purposes: pursuant to PHSA as amended and HPEPA, for nurse anesthetist traineeships for up to 18 months of full-time study by registered nurses in nurse anesthetist master's education programs.

Eligible applicants: accredited schools of nursing, academic health centers, and other public and private nonprofit institutions.

Eligible beneficiaries: U.S. citizens, noncitizen nationals, or permanent residents with 12 months of completed nurse anesthetist master's training.

Range: $6,078 to $125,087. **Average:** $33,536.

Activity: N.A.

HQ: Division of Nursing, Bureau of Health Professions, HRSA-HHS, Parklawn Bldg., Rm. 9-89, 5600 Fishers Ln., Rockville, MD 20857. Phone: (301) 443-5787.

Internet: www.hrsa.gov. (Note: no field offices for this program.)

93.127 EMERGENCY MEDICAL SERVICES FOR CHILDREN ("EMS for Children")

Assistance: project grants. (100 percent/to 3 years).

Purposes: pursuant to PHSA as amended, for demonstration projects to expand and improve emergency medical services for children needing critical care or treatment for trauma.

Eligible applicants/beneficiaries: states, schools of medicine.

Range: $130,000 to $3,000,000. **Average:** $234,345.

Activity: 78 awards in FY 2016.

HQ: EMSC Program Director, Maternal and Child Health Bureau, HRSA-HHS, 5600 Fishers Ln., Rm. 18A-38, Rockville, MD 20857. Phone: (301) 443-8930.

Internet: www.hrsa.gov.

93.129   TECHNICAL AND NON-FINANCIAL ASSISTANCE TO HEALTH CENTERS

Assistance: project grants. (100 percent/to 5 years).

Purposes: pursuant to PHSA as amended, to provide technical and nonfinancial assistance to health centers and NHSC delivery sites, relative to: collaborative activities on state or market area levels; involvement of state agencies in providing primary care to medically underserved populations; developing shared services and joint purchasing arrangements; providing training, assessment of community health needs, expertise in dealing with the homeless, public housing residents, farm workers, and rural and other special populations, as well as in managing and maximizing nonfederal resources; expanding the health center network.

Eligible applicants/beneficiaries: state primary care associations currently working with BHPC-supported providers; other community-based providers.

Range: $300,000 to $6,375,000. **Average:** $1,032,485.

Activity: N.A.

HQ: HRSA-HHS, 5600 Fishers Ln., Rm. 17C-26, Rockville, MD 20857. Phone: (301) 594-4300.

Internet: www.hrsa.gov.

93.130   COOPERATIVE AGREEMENTS TO STATES/TERRITORIES FOR THE COORDINATION AND DEVELOPMENT OF PRIMARY CARE OFFICES ("State Primary Care Offices")

Assistance: project grants.

Purposes: pursuant to PHSA, to coordinate local, state, and federal resources contributing to primary care service delivery and workforce issues to meet the needs of medically under-served populations, through health centers and other community-based providers. Emphasis is on: coordination of Medicaid, Children's Health Insurance program, state offices of rural health, and other health care financing services, maternal and child health; health systems development; National Health Service Corps monitoring; and recruitment and retention of primary care practitioners.

Eligible applicants/beneficiaries: states, state agencies, statewide public or nonprofit entities operating in one state only.

Range: $152,056 to $438,871. **Average:** $201,189.

Activity: 54 awards annually.

HQ: Shortage Designation Branch, Office of Workforce, Evaluation and Quality Assurance, Bureau of Health Professions, HRSA-HHS, 5600 Fishers Ln., Rm. 11SWH03, Rockville, MD 20852. Phone: (301) 594-5168.

Internet: www.hrsa.gov.

93.134   GRANTS TO INCREASE ORGAN DONATIONS

Assistance: project grants. (100 percent/3 years).

Purposes: pursuant to PHSA as amended, for activities to increase the number of organ donors. Funds may not be used for activities reimbursable under Medicare.

Eligible applicants/beneficiaries: public and private nonprofit organ procurement, donation, and transplantation organizations.

Range/Average: N.A.

Activity: N.A.

HQ: Division of Transplantation, Healthcare Systems Bureau, HRSA-HHS, 5600 Fishers Ln., Rockville, MD 20857. Phone: (301) 443-7577.

Internet: www.hrsa.gov.

93.135 CENTERS FOR RESEARCH AND DEMONSTRATION FOR HEALTH PROMOTION AND DISEASE PREVENTION ("Prevention Research Centers")

Assistance: project grants. (100 percent/1-5 years).

Purposes: pursuant to PHSA as amended, to establish, maintain, and operate academic-based centers for research and demonstration programs in health promotion and disease prevention; to establish linkages between ongoing related basic and applied research; for field testing and evaluation of new methods and strategies; to streamline the development and delivery of new techniques; to involve communities in prevention research.

Eligible applicants/beneficiaries: schools of medicine, osteopathy, and public health.

Range/Average: N.A.

Activity: N.A.

HQ: Director, Prevention Research Center Program, Division of Adult and Community Health (K-45), National Center for Chronic Disease Prevention and Health Promotion, CDCP-HHS, 4770 Buford Hwy. NE, Atlanta, GA 30341. Phone: (770) 488-6384.

Internet: www.cdc.gov/prc. (Note: no field offices for this program.)

93.136 INJURY PREVENTION AND CONTROL RESEARCH AND STATE AND COMMUNITY BASED PROGRAMS

Assistance: project grants. (100 percent/1-5 years).

Purposes: pursuant to PHSA as amended and other acts, for injury prevention and control research and demonstrations; to integrate aspects of engineering, public health, behavioral sciences, medicine, and other disciplines; to apply and evaluate current and new interventions, methods, and strategies; for injury control research centers in academic institutions to develop improved approaches to research and training; for public health programs for injury control; to develop and evaluate existing and new methods and techniques of injury surveillance, and to develop, expand, or improve injury control programs to reduce morbidity, mortality, severity, disability, and cost from injuries.

Eligible applicants/beneficiaries: research and centers grants—nonprofit and profit organizations. State and community program grants—official state public health agencies; territories and possessions; jurisdictions of more than 1,000,000 population. Community-based programs—public and private nonprofit and profit organizations.

Range/Average: N.A.

Activity: N.A.

HQ: National Center for Injury Prevention and Control, CDCP-HHS, 4770 Buford Hwy. NE, Atlanta, GA 30341-3724. Phone: (770) 488-1324.

Internet: www.cdc.gov. (Note: no field offices for this program.)

93.137 COMMUNITY PROGRAMS TO IMPROVE MINORITY HEALTH GRANT PROGRAM

Assistance: project grants. (100 percent/3 years).

Purposes: pursuant to PHSA as amended, for demonstration projects conducted by minority community health coalitions to modify behavioral or environmental conditions implicated in the health problems of minority groups—including HIV/AIDS, cancer, cardiovascular disease and stroke, chemical dependency, diabetes, homicide, suicide, unintentional injuries, infant mortality. Projects involve: coordination of integrated community-based screening and outreach services to minority groups and low-income communities; linkages for access and treatment to those at high risk; overcoming socio-cultural and linguistic barriers; working with nontraditional partners in projects to increase educational understanding of health issues. No health care services are provided under this program.

Eligible applicants/beneficiaries: private nonprofit community-based organizations serving Asians, Pacific islanders, African Americans, Latinos, Hispanics, native Americans, Alaska natives, native Hawaiians, or subgroups.

Range: $190,000 to $500,000. **Average:** N.A.

Activity: N.A.

HQ: Director, Division of Program Operations, Office of Minority Health, Office of Public Health and Science, OS-HHS, 1101 Wootton Pkwy., Ste. 550, Rockville, MD 20852. Phone: (240) 453-8822.

Internet: www.minorityhealth.gov. (Note: no field offices for this program.)

93.138 PROTECTION AND ADVOCACY FOR INDIVIDUALS WITH MENTAL ILLNESS (PAIMI)

Assistance: formula grants. (100 percent/2 years).

Purposes: pursuant to PHSA, Protection and Advocacy for Individuals with Mental Illness Act of 1986, and Developmental Disabilities Assistance and Bill of Rights Act, as amended, to plan, develop, administer, and expand programs to protect and advocate the rights of the mentally ill, and to investigate incidents of their abuse and neglect including in public and private care and treatment facilities and nonmedical community- based facilities for children and youth. Limited funds may be used for training and technical assistance provided to staff.

Eligible applicants: state and local government agencies, public or private organizations designated by governors; territories, possessions.

Eligible beneficiaries: mentally ill persons with severe emotional impairments while inpatients or residents in care or treatment facilities, in their own homes, or living in the community; persons in process of being admitted or transported to such facilities, or involuntarily confined in detention facilities, jails, or prisons.

Range: $229,300 to $3,156,787. **Average:** $619,556.

Activity: anticipate 57 awards will be made in FY 2016.

HQ: PATH Program, Homeless Programs Branch, Division of Knowledge Development and Systems Change, CMHS-SAMHSA-HHS, 1 Choke Cherry Rd., 7-1091, Rockville, MD 20857. Phone: (240) 276-1422.

Internet: www.samhsa.gov. (Note: no field offices for this program.)

93.140 INTRAMURAL RESEARCH TRAINING AWARD (IRTA)

Assistance: project grants.

Purposes: pursuant to HPEPA, to provide developmental training and practical research experience at the NIH for pre- or post- doctoral participants, in disciplines related to biomedical research, medical library research, and related fields. IRTA components include: postdoctoral (1-5 years), for physicians and other doctoral researchers; predoctoral (1 month-3 years), for students enrolled in doctoral degree programs in biomedical sciences, or accepted into graduate, doctoral, or medical degree programs; postbaccalaureate (1-2 years), for recent college graduates, particularly minorities, women, and persons with disabilities; technical (2-3 years), for training of professionals; student (1 month-1 year), for promising high school, undergraduate, and graduate students.

Eligible applicants/beneficiaries: postdoctoral awards—candidates with a Ph.D., M.D., D.D.S., D.M.D., D.V.M., or equivalent degree and not more than five years of postdoctoral research experience; predoctoral awards— students applying for, enrolled in, or accepted into graduate, doctoral, or medical degree programs; postbaccalaureate—candidates that graduated no more than one year prior to activation of the traineeship and intending to apply to graduate or medical school in biomedical research within one year; technical—candidates that graduated from a U.S. college or university with a bachelor's or master's degree in any discipline; student—candidates at least age 16 and enrolled at least half-time in high school, or accepted for or enrolled in an accredited U.S. college or university. Recipients must be U.S. citizens or permanent resident aliens.

Range/Average: N.A.

Activity: N.A.

HQ: Executive Director/Intramural Research, NIH-HHS, 2 Center Dr., Bethesda, MD 20892. Phone: (301) 594-2053.

Internet: www.training.nih.gov. (Note: no field offices for this program.)

93.142 NIEHS HAZARDOUS WASTE WORKER HEALTH AND SAFETY TRAINING ("Superfund Worker Training Program")

Assistance: project grants. (100 percent/to 5 years).

Purposes: pursuant to PHSA and SARA as amended, to develop and administer model education and training programs in worker health and safety practices for persons involved in hazardous waste generation, treatment, storage, removal, disposal, containment, transportation, or emergency response. Direct costs of classroom and practical training may be supported. Some SBIR and STTR awards may be made.

Eligible applicants/beneficiaries: public or private nonprofit entities. Small business may apply for SBIR and STTR awards.

Range: $124,719 to $3,401,129. **Average:** $1,000,200.

Activity: N.A.

HQ: Director, Superfund Hazardous Substance Basic Research and Training Program, Division of Extramural Research and Training, NIEHS-NIH-HHS, 111 TW Alexander Dr., Research Triangle Park, NC 27709. Phone: (919) 541-5147.

Internet: www.niehs.nih.gov/careers/hazmat/about_wetp/index.cfm. (Note: no field offices for this program.)

93.143 NIEHS SUPERFUND HAZARDOUS SUBSTANCES—BASIC RESEARCH AND EDUCATION
("NIEHS Superfund Research Program")

Assistance: project grants. (100 percent/to 5 years).

Purposes: pursuant to PHSA, CERCLA, and SARA, as amended, to establish linkages between biomedical research and related engineering, geoscience, and ecological research. Funds may support basic research and advanced or graduate training activities on an inter-disciplinary, multi-project basis, covering: methods and technologies to detect hazardous substances in the environment; advanced techniques for the detection, assessment, and evaluation of the effects of hazardous substances on humans; environmental and occupational health and safety and the engineering aspects of hazardous waste control; related graduate training in the geosciences. SBIR awards are available.

Eligible applicants/beneficiaries: IHEs. Subcontracts are permitted with state and local governments, public or private organizations, or persons or organizations involved with the generation, assessment, treatment of hazardous substances, or operation or ownership or facilities containing hazardous substances.

Range: $5,625 to $2,988,361. **Average:** $795,343.

Activity: N.A.

HQ: Director, Superfund Hazardous Substance Basic Research and Training Program, Division of Extramural Research and Training, NIEHS-NIH-HHS, 111 TW Alexander Dr., Research Triangle Park, NC 27709. Phone: (919) 541-5147.

Internet: www-apps.niehs.nih.gov/sbrp. (Note: no field offices for this program.)

93.145 AIDS EDUCATION AND TRAINING CENTERS

Assistance: project grants. (100 percent/3-5 years).

Purposes: pursuant to PHSA as amended and Ryan White CARE Act Amendments of 2000, for the education and training of primary care providers and others, on the diagnosis, treatment and prevention of HIV disease; for faculty training in related disciplines; to develop and disseminate pertinent curricula and resource materials; to develop protocols for the medical care of women with HIV disease, including prenatal and other gynecological care.

Eligible applicants/beneficiaries: public and private nonprofit entities, schools, academic health science centers.

Range/Average: N.A.

Activity: N.A.

HQ: Division of Training and Technical Assistance/AIDS ETCs, HIV/AIDS Bureau, HRSA-HHS, 5600 Fishers Ln., Rm. 7-90, Rockville, MD 20857. Phone: (301) 443-8109.

Internet: www.hrsa.gov.

93.150 PROJECTS FOR ASSISTANCE IN TRANSITION FROM HOMELESSNESS (PATH)

Assistance: formula grants (75 percent; territories, 100 percent).

Purposes: pursuant to PHSA as amended and SBMHAA, to support services for homeless persons with serious mental illness, with serious mental illness and substance abuse, or at imminent risk of so becoming. Funds may support such services as: outreach; community mental health; screening and diagnosis; habilitation and rehabilitation; substance abuse treatment services; referrals to housing, primary health, job training; staff training; case management; supportive and supervisory services in residential settings. Funds may not be used for emergency shelters or construction, inpatient psychiatric of substance abuse treatment, cash payments to recipients of mental health or substance abuse services.

Eligible applicants/beneficiaries: states, territories, possessions. Subgrants must be provided to political subdivisions and private nonprofit entities including veterans and other community-based organizations.

Range: $50,000 to $8,810,000. **Average:** $1,093,946.

Activity: anticipate 56 awards will be made in FY 2016.

HQ: PATH Program, Homeless Programs Branch, Division of Knowledge Development and Systems Change, CMHS-SAMHSA-HHS, 1 Choke Cherry Rd., 7-1091, Rockville, MD 20857. Phone: (240) 276-1422.

Internet: www.samhsa.gov. (Note: no field offices for this program.)

93.153 COORDINATED SERVICES AND ACCESS TO RESEARCH FOR WOMEN, INFANTS, CHILDREN, AND YOUTH ("Ryan White Program Part D, WICY Program")

Assistance: project grants. (100 percent/to 5 years).

Purposes: pursuant to PHSA as amended and Ryan White CARE Amendments Act of 2000, to improve access to primary medical care, research, and support services within for women, infants, children, and youth with HIV/AIDS or at risk, and to provide support services for their families; to link care systems with proven clinical research; to provide related client education.

Eligible applicants/beneficiaries: public and private nonprofit entities providing primary care.

Range: $100,000 to $2,260,049. **Average:** N.A.

Activity: N.A.

HQ: Division of Community Based Programs, HIV-AIDS Bureau, HRSA-HHS, 5600 Fishers Ln., Rm. 6NWH04, Rockville, MD 20857. Phone: (301) 443-3944.

Internet: www.hrsa.gov.

93.155   RURAL HEALTH RESEARCH CENTERS

Assistance: project grants. (100 percent/to 4 years).

Purposes: to operate rural health research centers and to provide one-year research grants to new investigators to establish an information base and policy analysis capability on the full range of rural health issues, including financing, recruitment and retention of health professionals, access to care, and rural delivery systems.

Eligible applicants/beneficiaries: public and private nonprofit and profit entities including IHEs, research organizations, foundations, and community entities.

Range/Average: N.A.

Activity: N.A.

HQ: Outreach Program Coordinator or Network Development Program Coordinator, Office of Rural Health Policy, Director, Rural Research Centers, Office of Rural Health Policy, HRSA-HHS, Parklawn Bldg., Rm. 17W59-D, 5600 Fishers Ln., Rockville, MD 20857. Phone: (301) 443-0835.

Internet: www.hrsa.gov/ruralhealth.

93.156   GERIATRIC TRAINING FOR PHYSICIANS, DENTISTS AND BEHAVIORAL/MENTAL HEALTH PROFESSIONALS (GTPD)

Assistance: project grants. (100 percent/5 years).

Purposes: pursuant to PHSA as amended and HPEPA, for training programs for current and future faculty in geriatric medicine, dentistry, and behavioral and mental health professionals. Funds may support: one-year retraining programs for physician faculty members in departments of internal or family medicine, gynecology, geriatrics, behavioral or mental health, and dentist faculty members at schools of dentistry or hospital departments of dentistry; two-year fellowships for physicians and dentists with relevant advanced training or experience in medical or dental education.

Eligible applicants/beneficiaries: public or private nonprofit schools of medicine or osteopathy, teaching hospitals, graduate medical education programs.

Range/Average: N.A.

Activity: N.A.

HQ: Division of State, Community, and Public Health, Bureau of Health Professions, HRSA-HHS, Parklawn Bldg., Rm. 12C-05, 5600 Fishers Ln., Rockville, MD 20857. Phone: (301) 443-7762.

Internet: www.hrsa.gov. (Note: no field offices for this program.)

93.157 CENTERS OF EXCELLENCE (COEs)

Assistance: project grants. (100 percent/3 years).

Purposes: pursuant to PHSA as amended and HPEPA, to establish, strengthen, or expand programs to enhance the academic performance of underrepresented minority students in the health professions, though linkages with IHEs, local school districts, and other community-based entities. Funds may be used for such costs as: faculty recruitment, training, and retention, including through the payment of stipends and fellowships; library resource development and enhancement; student recruitment and academic performance enhancement programs; curriculum development; facilitating faculty and student research on issues particularly affecting minority groups; student stipends.

Eligible applicants/beneficiaries: schools of medicine, osteopathy, dentistry, pharmacy; private nonprofit schools with graduate training programs in behavioral and mental health; certain HBCUs.

Range: $2,340,000 to $3,500,000 for HBCUs; $860,000 to $900,000 for non-HBCUs. **Average:** $3,000,000 for HBCUs; $860,000 to $891,000 for non-HBCUs.

Activity: N.A.

HQ: Chief, Diversity Branch, Division of Health Careers Diversity and Development, Bureau of Health Professions, HRSA-HHS, 5600 Fishers Ln., Rm. 9C-105, Rockville, MD 20857. Phone: (301) 443-6950.

Internet: bhw.hrsa.gov/grants/diversity/coe.html. (Note: no field offices for this program.)

93.161 HEALTH PROGRAM FOR TOXIC SUBSTANCES AND DISEASE REGISTRY

Assistance: project grants. (100 percent/1-5 years).

Purposes: pursuant to CERCLA and RCRA as amended, to reduce or eliminate illness, disability, and death resulting from public or worker exposure to toxic substances at spill and waste disposal sites. Services may include: health assessments; health effects studies; exposure and disease registries; technical assistance; consultation; information dissemination; specialized services and assistance including responses to public health emergencies; training; research of chemical toxicity.

Eligible applicants/beneficiaries: states and their political subdivisions, territories, possessions, IHEs, tribal governments.

Range: $130,000 to $300,000. **Average:** N.A.

Activity: N.A.

HQ: Director, Agency for Toxic Substances and Disease Registry, HHS, 4770 Buford Hwy. NE, MS F61, Atlanta, GA 30341-3717. Phone: (770) 488-0572.

Internet: www.cdc.gov. (Note: no field offices for this program.)

93.162   NATIONAL HEALTH SERVICE CORPS LOAN REPAYMENT PROGRAM ("NHSC Loan Repayment Program")

Assistance: project grants.

Purposes: pursuant to PHSA as amended and National Health Service Corps Amendments Act of 1987, for the repayment of NHSC participants' qualifying government and commercial health professions undergraduate and graduate education loans. Up to $25,000 per year may be awarded during the first two years of practice at selected NHSC service sites, and up to $35,000 in the third and subsequent years—plus a 39 percent tax assistance payment. Priority currently is given to primary care physicians, dentists, certified nurse-midwives and nurse practitioners, physician assistants, clinical psychologists, clinical social workers, psychiatric nurse specialists, marriage and family therapists, licensed professional counselors, dental hygienists.

Eligible applicants/beneficiaries: U.S. citizens with a degree in health professions or in professional practice, licensed in a state, and eligible for appointment in the federal civil service or holding a commission in the PHS. Applicants may not: be in default on any federal debt; have a court judgment against them; have an existing service obligation.

Range/Average: N.A.

Activity: N.A.

HQ: Chief, Applications and Award Branch, NHSC Division, Bureau of Health Professions, HRSA-HHS, 5600 Fishers Ln., Rm. 8C-26, Rockville, MD 20857. Phone: (301) 594-4400.

Internet: nhsc.hrsa.gov.

93.164   INDIAN HEALTH SERVICE EDUCATIONAL LOAN REPAYMENT ("IHS Loan Repayment Program")

Assistance: project grants (100 percent).

Purposes: pursuant to the Indian Health Care Amendments of 1988, for payments of up to $20,000 annually toward participants' health professions education loans during each year of service at IHS priority sites or certain other sites—plus 20 percent for tax liability on the grant award. A minimum of two years of service is required.

Eligible applicants/beneficiaries: students enrolled in their final year in a program leading to a degree, or graduate students enrolled in approved programs; or, degreed and licensed professionals, eligible for or holding a PHS or civil service appointment in the HIS; or employees of an Indian health program.

Range: $3,000 to $51,672 for 2 years. Average: $44,120.

Activity: N.A.

HQ: Grants Policy Office, IHS-HHS, 801 Thompson Ave., Suite TMP 360, Rockville, MD 20852. Phone: (301) 443-5204.

Internet: www.ihs.gov.

93.165   GRANTS TO STATES FOR LOAN REPAYMENT PROGRAM ("State Loan Repayment Program")

Assistance: project grants. (50 percent/to 5 years).

Purposes: pursuant to PHSA, for state educational loan repayment programs for health professionals agreeing to serve full-time for a minimum of two years in a health manpower shortage area. State programs must be similar to 93.162.

Eligible applicants/beneficiaries: states.

Range: $80,000 to $1,000,000. Average: $335,129.

Activity: N.A.

HQ: Division of State, Community and Public Health, Bureau of Health Professions, HRSA-HHS, 5600 Fishers Ln., Rm. 8C-26, Rockville, MD 20857. Phone: (301) 594-4400.

Internet: nhsc.hrsa.gov. (Note: no field offices for this program.)

93.172   HUMAN GENOME RESEARCH ("Human Genome Project")

Assistance: project grants. (100 percent/1-5 years).

Purposes: pursuant to PHSA as amended and SBRDEA, to obtain genetic and physical maps and to determine the deoxyribonucleic acid (DNA) sequences of the genomes of humans and model organisms to be used as resources in biomedical research, medicine, and biotechnology—including consideration of the ethical, legal, and social implications. NRSA, SBIR, and STTR awards are available.

Eligible applicants/beneficiaries: public or private, profit or nonprofit IHEs, hospitals, laboratories, other institutions; state and local governments; small businesses.

Range: $70,000 to $4,900,000. Average: $594,689.

Activity: N.A.

HQ: National Human Genome Research Institute, NIH-HHS, 5635 Fishers Ln., Ste. 4076, Bethesda, MD 20892. Phone: (301) 496-7531.

Internet: www.genome.gov. (Note: no field offices for this program.)

93.173   RESEARCH RELATED TO DEAFNESS AND COMMUNICATION DISORDERS

Assistance: project grants. (100 percent/to 5 years).

Purposes: pursuant to PHSA as amended and SBRDEA, to investigate solutions to problems of patients with deafness or disorders of human communication such as hearing, balance, voice, speech, language, and the senses of taste, touch, and smell. Focus may be on etiology, pathology, detection, treatment, and prevention of all forms of hearing disorders and other communication processes, primarily through basic and applied research in anatomy, audiology, biochemistry, bioengineering, epidemiology, genetics, immunology, microbiology, molecular biology, the neurosciences, otolaryngology, psychology, pharmacology, physiology, speech and language pathology, and other scientific disciplines. Funds may support research centers, as well as mentored and unmentored career awards. NRSA, SBIR, and STTR awards are available.

Eligible applicants/beneficiaries: public, private, nonprofit, or profit institutions; SBIR firms; individuals.

Range: $1,728 to $2,350,556. **Average:** $326,904.

Activity: anticipate 1,013 awards in FY 2016.

HQ: National Institute on Deafness and Other Communication Disorders, NIH-HHS, 6001 Executive Blvd., Rm. 8328-MSC 9670, Bethesda, MD 20892-9670. Phone: (301) 496-8693; FAX: (301) 402-6250.

Internet: www.nidcd.nih.gov. (Note: no field offices for this program.)

93.178 NURSING WORKFORCE DIVERSITY (NWD)

Assistance: project grants. (100 percent/3 years).

Purposes: pursuant to PHSA as amended and HPEPA, to increase nursing education opportunities for individuals from disadvantaged backgrounds, by providing student $250 monthly stipends, with a $7,000 annual maximum scholarship, and pre-entry preparation and retention activities. Funds also may be used for project personnel salaries, consultant fees, supplies and equipment, travel, and related costs.

Eligible applicants/beneficiaries: schools of nursing, nursing centers, academic health centers, state and local governments, and other public and nonprofit private entities—with above average rates of admission, retention, and graduation of individuals from disadvantaged backgrounds and ethnic and racial minorities, or with plans for improving such rates.

Range: N.A. **Average:** $316,000.

Activity: N.A.

HQ: Division of Nursing, Bureau of Health Professions, HRSA-HHS, Parklawn Bldg., Rm. 9-89, 5600 Fishers Ln., Rockville, MD 20857. Phone: (301) 443-5688.

Internet: www.hrsa.gov. (Note: no field offices for this program.)

93.184 DISABILITIES PREVENTION
("Disability and Health")

Assistance: project grants. (to 100 percent/3-5 years).

Purposes: pursuant to PHSA as amended, to provide a national focus for the prevention of secondary conditions in persons with selected disability domains, including mobility, personal care, communication, and learning—through cooperative agreements and research projects designed to: build state capacity to coordinate prevention and education activities and to conduct surveillance; provide related technical assistance to communities; employ epidemiological methods to set priorities and target interventions; conduct research on the disabled and their physical, medical, cognitive, emotional, or psychosocial conditions; support a national limb loss information center to serve as an information clearinghouse and to conduct peer education and training sessions with hospitals and limb loss support groups; support the National Center on Physical Activity and Disability to provide information and promote physical activity for the disabled; conduct related activities.

Eligible applicants/beneficiaries: cooperative agreements—state health departments or other state agencies, including in territories or possessions with existing agreements. Research grants—public and private nonprofit entities, universities, nonprofit medical centers, rehabilitation hospitals, disability service organizations, tribal governments.

Range: N.A. **Average:** $300,000.

Activity: N.A.

HQ: Project Officer, Division of Human Development and Disability, National Center on Birth Defects and Developmental Disabilities, CDCP-HHS, 1825 Century Center Blvd., Rm. 4074, Atlanta, GA 30345. Phone: (404) 498-0274.

Internet: www.cdc.gov/ncbddd/disabilityandhealth/index.html. (Note: no field offices for this program.)

93.185 IMMUNIZATION RESEARCH, DEMONSTRATION, PUBLIC INFORMATION AND EDUCATION—TRAINING AND CLINICAL SKILLS IMPROVEMENT PROJECTS

Assistance: project grants. (100 percent/1-5 years).

Purposes: pursuant to PHSA as amended, for research, demonstration, and information dissemination projects on vaccine- preventable diseases and conditions. Funds may be used to conduct project activities including, in certain circumstances, purchasing vaccine.

Eligible applicants/beneficiaries: states and their political subdivisions, other public and private nonprofit entities.

Range/Average: N.A.

Activity: N.A.

HQ: Associate Director/Management and Operations, National Immunization Program (E-05), CDCP-HHS, 1600 Clifton Rd. NE, Atlanta, GA 30333. Phone: (404) 639-9113.

Internet: www.cdc.gov. (Note: no field offices for this program.)

93.186 NATIONAL RESEARCH SERVICE AWARD IN PRIMARY CARE MEDICINE

Assistance: project grants. (100 percent/3-5 years).

Purposes: pursuant to PHSA as amended and the National Institutes of Health Revitalization Act of 1993, for postdoctoral research training programs in primary medical care. Individuals receiving awards incur one month of service obligation for each of the first 12 months of the NRSA support, after which no further service obligation is incurred; the continued training serves to discharge the payback obligation.

Eligible applicants/beneficiaries: domestic public or private nonprofit organizations; state or local governments and territories. Individuals must be U.S. citizens, noncitizen nationals, or lawful permanent residents.

Range: $110,353 to $400,000. **Average:** N.A.

Activity: N.A.

HQ: Dentistry, Psychology and Special Projects Branch, Division of Medicine and Dentistry, Bureau of Health Professions, HRSA-HHS, 5600 Fishers Ln., Rm. 12C-06, Rockville, MD 20857. Phone: (301) 443-7271.

Internet: www.hrsa.gov. (Note: no field offices for this program.)

93.187 UNDERGRADUATE SCHOLARSHIP PROGRAM FOR INDIVIDUALS FROM DISADVANTAGED BACKGROUNDS ("NIH UGSP")

Assistance: project grants. (100 percent/to 4 years).

Purposes: pursuant to PHSA as amended, for scholarships to persons from disadvantaged backgrounds, pursuing undergraduate education preparing them for professions in the biomedical or bio-behavioral sciences at NIH. Recipients must agree: to serve full-time for at least ten consecutive weeks as an NIH employee during each year of the scholarship period; within 60 days of obtaining a degree, to serve one year as a full-time NIH employee for each year of scholarship assistance received, unless deferred.

Eligible applicants/beneficiaries: U.S. citizens, nationals, or permanent residents from disadvantaged backgrounds, enrolled or accepted at IHEs for full-time study, and maintaining good academic standing.

Range: $2,000 to $20,000. **Average:** $9,000.

Activity: N.A.

HQ: Office of Intramural Research, NIH-HHS, 2 Center Dr., Rm. 2E20, Bethesda, MD 20892. Phone: (301) 594-2222.

Internet: www.training.nih.gov/programs/ugsp. (Note: no field offices for this program.)

93.191 GRADUATE PSYCHOLOGY EDUCATION PROGRAM AND PATIENT NAVIGATOR AND CHRONIC DISEASE PREVENTION PROGRAM

Assistance: project grants. (100 percent/3 years).

Purposes: pursuant to PHSA as amended and HPEPA, to establish and expand training programs in the allied health professions that will: expand enrollments in disciplines in short supply or most needed by the elderly; provide rapid transition training programs for participants with baccalaureate degrees in health-related sciences; provide career advancement training for practicing allied health professionals; establish or expand clinical training sites in medically underserved or rural communities; develop curriculum in prevention and health promotion, geriatrics, long-term care, home health and hospice care, and ethics; expand or establish interdisciplinary and training programs; link academic centers to clinical centers; support graduate programs in behavioral and mental health practice. Funds may be used for the costs of personnel, equipment, consultants, guest lecturers, space rental, or renovation—but not for construction, land acquisition, financial support to students.

Eligible applicants/beneficiaries: health professions schools, academic health centers, state or local governments, public or private nonprofit entities.

Range/Average: N.A.

Activity: N.A.

HQ: Division of State, Community and Public Health, Bureau of Health Professions, HRSA-HHS, 5600 Fishers Ln., Parklawn Bldg., Rm. 9-89, Rockville, MD 20857. Phone: 301-443-7661.

Internet: www.hrsa.gov.

93.193   URBAN INDIAN HEALTH SERVICES

Assistance: project grants. (100 percent/to 5 years).

Purposes: pursuant to the Indian Health Care Improvement Act as amended, for health-related services to Indians residing in urban areas, including: alcohol and substance abuse prevention, treatment, rehabilitation, and education; mental health needs assessment and services; health promotion and disease prevention; immunization.

Eligible applicants/beneficiaries: urban Indian organizations.

Range: $149,950 to $1,096,176. **Average:** $280,678.

Activity: N.A.

HQ: Grants Policy Office, IHS-HHS, 801 Thompson Ave., Suite TMP 360, Rockville, MD 20852. Phone: (301) 443-5204.

Internet: www.ihs.gov. (Note: no field offices for this program.)

93.197   CHILDHOOD LEAD POISONING PREVENTION PROJECTS—STATE AND LOCAL CHILDHOOD LEAD POISONING PREVENTION AND SURVEILLANCE OF BLOOD LEAD LEVELS IN CHILDREN (CLPPP)

Assistance: project grants. (100 percent/to 3 years).

Purposes: pursuant to PHSA as amended, Preventive Health Amendments of 1992, and Children's Health Act of 2000, for childhood lead poisoning prevention projects in communities with demonstrated high-risk populations. Funds are to be used: for screening and testing; to identify sources of lead exposure; to monitor medical and environmental management of cases, including follow-up; for public and technical education activities, including staff training; to enhance primary prevention activities in collaboration with other government and community- based organizations; to establish state-based surveillance systems. Ineligible uses of funds include medical care or treatment, remediation of lead sources; however, an acceptable plan must be submitted with assurances that such activities will be carried out.

Eligible applicants/beneficiaries: state health or other departments or agencies; territories and possessions; tribal governments; consortia of the foregoing; five specified local governments.

Range/Average: N.A.

Activity: N.A.

HQ: Program Services Team Leader, Lead Poisoning Prevention Branch, National Center for Environmental Health, CDCP-HHS, 4770 Buford Hwy., NE, MS F45, Atlanta, GA 30341-3717. Phone: 770-488-0711 .

Internet: www.cdc.gov.

93.209 CONTRACEPTION AND INFERTILITY RESEARCH LOAN REPAYMENT PROGRAM (CIR LRP)

Assistance: direct payments/specified use.

Purposes: pursuant to PHSA as amended, to provide incentives to health professionals to work in reproductive research related to contraceptive development or infertility diagnosis and treatment, by providing assistance in repaying their education loans. The program pays up to $35,000 of loan principal and interest for each year of service commitment, not to exceed one-half of remaining loan balance—plus up to 39 percent to offset tax liability. Participants must agree to commit to a period of obligated service of at least two years.

Eligible applicants/beneficiaries: U.S. citizens, nationals, or permanent residents that are health and allied health professionals, including physicians, Ph.D.-level scientists, nurses, physician assistants, or graduate students and postgraduate research fellows.

Range: $9,085 to $70,000. **Average:** $67,708.

Activity: anticipate awarding 16 contracts in FY 2016.

HQ: Director, Office of Extramural Research, National Institute of Child Health and Human Development, NIH-HHS, 6100 Executive Blvd., Rm. 2C01, Bethesda, MD 20892-7510. Phone: (301) 496-6856.

Internet: nichd.nih.gov. (Note: no field offices for this program.)

93.210 TRIBAL SELF-GOVERNANCE PROGRAM: IHS COMPACTS— FUNDING AGREEMENTS ("OTSG Compacts")

Assistance: project grants.

Purposes: pursuant to ISDEAA as amended, to establish and operate programs to provide planning and negotiation resources to tribes interested in participating in the Tribal Self-Governance Program—enabling them to enter into compacts to assume programs, services, and functions of the IHS and HHS that are otherwise available to Indians or tribes.

Eligible applicants/beneficiaries: recognized tribes.

Range: $79,000 to $153,000,000. **Average:** $16,653,000.

Activity: N.A.

HQ: Grants Policy Office, IHS-HHS, 801 Thompson Ave., Suite TMP 360, Rockville, MD 20852. Phone: (301) 443-5204.

Internet: www.ihs.gov. (Note: no field offices for this program.)

93.211 TELEHEALTH PROGRAMS

Assistance: project grants. (100 percent/to 3 years).

Purposes: pursuant to PHSA as amended by the Health Care Safety Net Amendments of 2002, to demonstrate the use of telehealth technologies to support and promote long-distance clinical health care, patient and professional health-related education; to collect information for a systematic evaluation of such projects. Projects are meant for rural areas, frontier communities, and medically-underserved populations. Up to 40 percent of grant funds may be used for equipment (non-transmission).

Eligible applicants/beneficiaries: public nonprofit health care providers or consortia, that are members of an existing or proposed telemedicine network including for-profit entities.

Range/Average: N.A.

Activity: N.A.

HQ: Office for the Advancement of Telehealth, HRSA-HHS, 5600 Fishers Ln., Rm. 17W29-C, Rockville, MD 20857. Phone: (301) 443-0076.

Internet: www.hrsa.gov/ruralhealth/about/telehealth.

93.213   RESEARCH AND TRAINING IN COMPLEMENTARY AND ALTERNATIVE MEDICINE
("National Center for Complementary and Alternative Medicine")

Assistance: project grants. (100 percent/to 5 years).

Purposes: pursuant to PHSA as amended, to foster collaboration between biomedical researchers and practitioners of alternative, complementary, or unconventional medical treatments, by: supporting and coordinating evaluations of alternative medical practices; identifying areas of clinical and preclinical research needing further development; developing clinical databases in conjunction with the National Library of Medicine; developing further international contacts; establishing an intra- and extramural clinical research fellowship program in alternative medicine. Grants may support costs of personnel, consultants, equipment, supplies, patient costs, animals, travel, and related items.

Eligible applicants/beneficiaries: IHEs, hospitals, public agencies, nonprofit research institutions, profit organizations, individuals.

Range: $25,165 to $2,216,251. **Average:** $381,701.

Activity: anticipate 229 grants in FY 2015.

HQ: Division of Extramural Research, National Center for Complementary and Alternative Medicine, NIH-HHS, 6707 Democracy Blvd. - Ste. 401, Bethesda, MD 20817. Phone: (301) 594-2014.

Internet: nccih.nih.gov. (Note: no field offices for this program.)

93.217   FAMILY PLANNING—SERVICES
("Title X")

Assistance: project grants. (from 90 percent/3-5 years).

Purposes: pursuant to PHSA as amended and Family Planning Services and Population Research Acts, for educational, counseling, and comprehensive medical and social services involving family planning, with priority to the low-income. Grants may be used for contraceptive, infertility, and special services to adolescents. Funds may not be used in programs where abortion is a method of family planning, nor for personnel salaries paid from other federal funds, nor for building construction.

Eligible applicants/beneficiaries: city, county, local, regional, or state governmental or private nonprofit entities in states, territories, and possessions; faith-based organizations.

Range: $125,000 to $19,000,000. **Average:** N.A.

Activity: N.A.

HQ: Director, Office of Family Planning, Office of Population Affairs, 1101 Wootton Pkwy., Ste. 550, Rockville, MD 20852. Phone: (240) 453-8822.

Internet: www.hhs.gov/opa. (Note: no field offices for this program.)

93.220   CLINICAL RESEARCH LOAN REPAYMENT PROGRAM FOR INDIVIDUALS FROM DISADVANTAGED BACKGROUNDS (CR-LRP)

Assistance: project grants. (100 percent/2 years minimum).

Purposes: pursuant to PHSA as amended, for repayment of extant educational loans incurred by persons from disadvantaged backgrounds, engaged in clinical research as employees of the NIH. Payments may be made up to $35,000 per year, plus $13,650 annually for tax reimbursements.

Eligible applicants/beneficiaries: U.S. citizens, nationals, or permanent residents from disadvantaged backgrounds, with: an M.D., Ph.D., D.O., D.D.S., D.M.D., D.P.M., B.S.N., A.D.N., or equivalent degree; qualified undergraduate or graduate educational loan debt exceeding 20 percent of their NIH salary; a contract commitment of at least two years of service to NIH; no existing service obligation to federal, state, or other entities.

Range: $4,000 to $70,000 for loan repayments; $1,977 to $34,598 for tax reimbursements. **Average:** loan and tax reimbursements: $68,454.

Activity: anticipate 2 awards in FY 2016.

HQ: Office of Intramural Training and Education, NIH-HHS, Bldg. 2, Rm. 2E18, 2 Center Dr., Bethesda, MD 20892-0230. Phone: (301) 402-1283; FAX: (301) 480-2942.

Internet: www.lrp.nih.gov. (Note: no field offices for this program.)

93.223   DEVELOPMENT AND COORDINATION OF RURAL HEALTH SERVICES

Assistance: project grants. (100 percent/3 years).

Purposes: pursuant to PHSA, to develop and disseminate information to assist rural communities and rural health care organizations in developing and coordinating rural health care services—including information from federal and state agencies, workshops, conferences, research reports, recruitment efforts, and reports from national health care associations.

Eligible applicants/beneficiaries: nonprofit private organizations representing national, state, and local rural health constituencies.

Range: N.A. **Average:** $1,941,349.

Activity: N.A.

HQ: Director, Rural Research Centers, Office of Rural Health Policy, HRSA-HHS, Parklawn Bldg., Rm. 17W-61, 5600 Fishers Ln., Rockville, MD 20857. Phone: (301) 443-0835.

Internet: www.hrsa.gov/ruralhealth.

93.224 CONSOLIDATED HEALTH CENTERS (COMMUNITY HEALTH CENTERS, MIGRANT HEALTH CENTERS, HEALTH CARE FOR THE HOMELESS, AND PUBLIC HOUSING PRIMARY CARE) ("Health Center Program")

Assistance: project grants (to 5 years).

Purposes: pursuant to PHSA and Health Centers Consolidation Act of 1996, to increase access to comprehensive primary and preventive health care and improve the health status of underserved and vulnerable populations, including at centers providing care through or to community, migrant, homeless, public housing, and school-based populations. Projects should improve the availability, accessibility, and organization of health care. Project funds may not be used for inpatient services or to make cash payments to service recipients.

Eligible applicants/beneficiaries: public or private nonprofit entities.

Range: $200,000 to $11,000,000. **Average:** $2,398,666.

Activity: N.A.

HQ: HRSA-HHS, 5600 Fishers Ln., Rm. 17C-26, Rockville, MD 20857. Phone: (301) 594-4300.

Internet: www.hrsa.gov.

93.225 NATIONAL RESEARCH SERVICE AWARDS—HEALTH SERVICES RESEARCH TRAINING

Assistance: project grants. (100 percent/3-5 years).

Purposes: pursuant to PHSA, for fellowships for full-time postdoctoral training in health services research for up to three years, and to predoctoral candidates from under-represented minority groups for up to five years—with grants to institutions providing the training. Training is in health services research and research methods, epidemiology, biostatistics, geriatrics, health administration and public health, medical information sciences, health policy and management, organizational behavior, clinical outcomes and effectiveness, primary care, health care quality, health economics and financing, child health, and vulnerable populations. Postdoctoral fellowship recipients must meet service payback requirements.

Eligible applicants/beneficiaries: domestic public or private nonprofit organizations including state and local governments and territories—with existing training programs. Fellowship recipients must be U.S. citizens, noncitizen nationals, or lawful permanent residents.

Range: $17,558 to $67,622 for individual fellowships; $160,312 to $594,673 for institutions. **Average:** $56,080 for individual fellowships; $394,464 for institutions.

Activity: anticipate 24 to 26 awards in FY 2015.

HQ: Division of Research Education, Agency for Healthcare Research and Quality, HHS, 540 Gaither Rd., Rockville, MD 20850. Phone: (301) 427-1528.

Internet: www.ahrq.gov. (Note: no field offices for this program.)

93.226   RESEARCH ON HEALTHCARE COSTS, QUALITY AND OUTCOMES

Assistance: project grants. (100 percent/to 5 years).

Purposes: pursuant to PHSA as amended, for research and evaluations, demonstration projects, research networks, multidisciplinary centers, and information dissemination on health care and systems for delivery of care. Major issue categories include: quality measurement and improvement; outcomes and cost-effectiveness; clinical practice including primary and practice-oriented research; health care technologies, facilities, and equipment; costs, productivity, organization, and market forces; health promotion and disease prevention, including clinical preventive services; health statistics, surveys, data base development, epidemiology; medical liability.

Eligible applicants/beneficiaries: federal, state, local government agencies; tribal governments; territories and possessions; sponsored organizations; public or private nonprofit organizations; minority and specialized groups; IHEs; individuals; and, profit organizations for cooperative agreements.

Range: $5,000 to $3,999,999. Average: $307,215.

Activity: anticipate funding 352 grants in FY 2016.

HQ: Division of Research Education, Agency for Healthcare Research and Quality, HHS, 540 Gaither Rd., Rockville, Maryland 20850. Phone: (301) 427-1447.

Internet: www.ahrq.gov. (Note: no field offices for this program.)

93.228   INDIAN HEALTH SERVICE—HEALTH MANAGEMENT DEVELOPMENT PROGRAM
("Indian Health")

Assistance: project grants.

Purposes: pursuant to ISDEAA, to increase the capability of American Indians and Alaska natives to operate existing IHS health care programs involving curative, preventive, and rehabilitative health services. Funds may be used for feasibility studies, planning, tribal health management structure development, evaluation.

Eligible applicants/beneficiaries: tribes and tribal organizations.

Range: $50,000 to $100,000. Average: N.A.

Activity: N.A.

HQ: Grants Policy Office, IHS-HHS, 801 Thompson Ave., Suite TMP 360, Rockville, MD 20852. Phone: (301) 443-5204.

Internet: www.ihs.gov. (Note: no field offices for this program.)

93.231   EPIDEMIOLOGY COOPERATIVE AGREEMENTS

Assistance: project grants. (100 percent/to 3 years).

Purposes: pursuant to the Indian Health Care Improvement Act as amended, to develop tribal epidemiology centers and public health infrastructure to coordinate and participate in disease surveillance and prevention projects, as well as investigations and studies of national scope. Project activities include convening of meetings, technical assistance and consultation, training, site visits, coordination on a national basis.

Eligible applicants/beneficiaries: tribes; tribal, urban tribal organizations; consortia.

Range: $380,200 to $523,600. **Average:** $420,250.

Activity: N.A.

HQ: Grants Policy Office, IHS-HHS, 801 Thompson Ave., Suite TMP 360, Rockville, MD 20852. Phone: (301) 443-5204.

Internet: www.ihs.gov. (Note: no field offices for this program.)

93.232 LOAN REPAYMENT PROGRAM FOR GENERAL RESEARCH ("NIH GR-LRP")

Assistance: project grants. (100 percent/3 years).

Purposes: pursuant to PHSA as amended, for repayment of extant educational loans incurred by scientific professionals engaged in laboratory or clinical research as employees of the NIH for a minimum of three years.

Eligible applicants/beneficiaries: U.S. citizens, nationals, or permanent residents from disadvantaged backgrounds, with: an M.D., Ph.D., D.O., D.D.S., D.M.D., D.P.M., B.S.N., A.D.N., or equivalent degree; qualified undergraduate or graduate educational loan debt exceeding 20 percent of their NIH salary; a contract commitment of at least two years of service to NIH; no existing service obligation to federal, state, or other entities.

Range: $6,000 to $105,000 for loan repayments; $3,679 to $48,825 for tax reimbursements. **Average:** $102,000 total for loan and tax.

Activity: anticipate 75 awards in FY 2016.

HQ: Office of Intramural Training and Education, NIH-HHS, Bldg. 2, Rm. 2E18, 2 Center Dr., Bethesda, MD 20892-0230. Phone: (301) 402-1283; FAX: (301) 480-2942.

Internet: www.lrp.nih.gov. (Note: no field offices for this program.)

93.233 NATIONAL CENTER ON SLEEP DISORDERS RESEARCH

Assistance: project grants. (100 percent/1-5 years).

Purposes: pursuant to PHSA, for research, training, information dissemination, and other activities relating to sleep and sleep disorders, including biological and circadian rhythm research, basic understanding of sleep, chronobiological and other sleep related research; to coordinate center activities with other federal agencies and with public and nonprofit organizations. NRSA, SBIR, and STIR funding is available.

Eligible applicants/beneficiaries: nonprofit and profit organizations; individuals.

Range: $5,000 to $2,297,146 for grants; to $1,000,000 for SBIR Phase II. **Average:** grants: $430,737 for grants; $150,000 for SBIR Phase I; $100,000 for STTR Phase I; $750,000 for STTR Phase II.

Activity: anticipate 119 awards in FY 2016.

HQ: Director, Division of Blood Diseases and Resources, National Heart, Lung, and Blood Institute, NIH-HHS, 6701 Rockledge Dr., Rm. 7176, Bethesda, MD 20892. Phone: 301-435-0314.

Internet: www.nhlbi.nih.gov/sleep. (Note: no field offices for this program.)

93.234   TRAUMATIC BRAIN INJURY STATE DEMONSTRATION GRANT PROGRAM (TBI)

Assistance: project grants. (67 percent/1-3 years).

Purposes: pursuant to PHSA as amended, to improve access to health and other TBI-related service for persons of all ages and their families. Planning grants support development of four state-level core capacity components to provide TBI services. Implementation grants are for states with the four core capacity components in place. Post-demonstration grants fund activities begun during the state implementation phase.

Eligible applicants/beneficiaries: state governments.

Range: $100,000 to $250,000. **Average:** $249,911.

Activity: N.A.

HQ: Division of Services for Children with Special Health Care Needs, Maternal and Child Health Bureau, 5600 Fishers Ln., Rm. 13-10, Rockville, MD 20857. Phone: (301) 443-5934.

Internet: www.hrsa.gov.

93.235   ABSTINENCE EDUCATION PROGRAM (ACA)

Assistance: formula grants (57 percent).

Purposes: pursuant to SSA, Section 510, to provide abstinence education and, at state option, mentoring, counseling, and adult supervision to promote abstinence from sexual activity outside of marriage—focusing on groups most likely to bear children out of wedlock. (Note: program provisions approximate **93.010**.)

Eligible applicants/beneficiaries: governor-designated agencies.

Range: $45,559 to $4,861,789. **Average:** $804,237.

Activity: anticipate 59 awards in FY 2016.

HQ: Family and Youth Services Bureau, ACF-HHS, 1250 Maryland Ave., SW, Washington, DC 20024. Phone: (202) 205-9605.

Internet: www.acf.hhs.gov/programs/fysb. (Note: no field offices for this program.)

93.236   GRANTS TO STATES TO SUPPORT ORAL HEALTH WORKFORCE ACTIVITIES

Assistance: project grants. (100 percent/3 years).

Purposes: pursuant to PHSA and HPEPA, to plan and develop new or to maintain and improve existing dental public health residency training programs; to provide financial assistance to trainees. Grants may not be used for construction or for direct patient services.

Eligible applicants/beneficiaries: public or private schools of public health or dentistry; experienced, qualified nonprofit and community-based organizations.

Range: $423,000 to $500,000. **Average:** $451,000.

Activity: N.A.

HQ: Division of Medicine and Dentistry, Bureau of Health Professions, HRSA-HHS, 5600 Fishers Ln., Rm. 12C-06, Rockville, MD 20857. Phone: (301) 443-2564; FAX: (301) 443-1945.

Internet: www.hrsa.gov.

93.237 SPECIAL DIABETES PROGRAM FOR INDIANS—DIABETES PREVENTION AND TREATMENT PROJECTS ("Indian Health")

Assistance: project grants. (100 percent/to 5 years).

Purposes: for primary, secondary, and tertiary diabetes prevention and treatment services and related data collection among American Indians and Alaskan natives.

Eligible applicants/beneficiaries: tribes, tribal and urban Indian organizations operating IHS health programs.

Range/Average: N.A.

Activity: N.A.

HQ: Grants Policy Office, IHS-HHS, 801 Thompson Ave., Suite TMP 360, Rockville, MD 20852. Phone: (301) 443-5204.

Internet: www.ihs.gov. (Note: no field offices for this program.)

93.239 POLICY RESEARCH AND EVALUATION GRANTS

Assistance: project grants (to 100 percent).

Purposes: pursuant to the Social Security Act, for research relevant to policy development and evaluation of current and proposed programs, covering: issues of long-term care, disability, and personal assistance services including informal care giving; health care delivery issues including financing; welfare reform outcomes and policies affecting children and youth; community development; science policy development; reduction of poverty.

Eligible applicants/beneficiaries: nonprofit organizations, state and local government agencies, IHEs, individuals, some profit organizations.

Range: N.A. **Average:** $908,830.

Activity: N.A.

HQ: Grants Officer, Assistant Secretary/Planning and Evaluation, OS-HHS, HHH Bldg., Rm. 405F, 200 Independence Ave., SW, Washington, DC 20201. Phone: (202) 690-8410.

Internet: aspe.hhs.gov. (Note: no field offices for this program.)

93.240 STATE CAPACITY BUILDING

Assistance: project grants. (100 percent/3-5 years).

Purposes: pursuant to CERCLA, SARA, and RCRA as amended, for public health agency capacity building in coordination with the Agency for Toxic Substances and Disease Registry, to conduct: health consultations; public health assessments; exposure investigations; community involvement; health education; public health studies.

Eligible applicants/beneficiaries: state public health agencies including possessions and territories, tribal governments.

Range: $150,000 to $350,000. **Average:** N.A.

Activity: N.A.

HQ: Director, Agency for Toxic Substances and Disease Registry, HHS, 4770 Buford Hwy. NE, MS F61, Atlanta, GA 30341-3717. Phone: (770) 488-0572.

Internet: www.atsdr.cdc.gov. (Note: no field offices for this program.)

93.241 STATE RURAL HOSPITAL FLEXIBILITY PROGRAM

Assistance: project grants.

Purposes: for states to work with rural communities and hospitals to develop and implement rural health plans and integrated care networks, to improve emergency medical services, and to designate critical access hospitals.

Eligible applicants/beneficiaries: states with rural health plans already submitted to the Centers for Medicare and Medicaid Services (CMS). Other states submit applications to CMS regional offices.

Range: $287,000 to $700,000. **Average:** $492,987.

Activity: N.A.

HQ: Outreach Program Coordinator or Network Development Program Coordinator, Office of Rural Health Policy, Director, Rural Research Centers, Office of Rural Health Policy, HRSA-HHS, Parklawn Bldg., Rm. 17W45-C, 5600 Fishers Ln., Rockville, MD 20857. Phone: (301) 443-0835.

Internet: www.hrsa.gov.

93.242 MENTAL HEALTH RESEARCH GRANTS

Assistance: project grants. (100 percent/to 5 years).

Purposes: pursuant to PHSA as amended and SBRDEA, for research on basic brain and behavioral processes underlying mental and behavioral disorders and mental health—employing theoretical, laboratory, clinical, methodological, and field studies involving clinical, subclinical, and normal subjects and populations of all age ranges, as well as animal, computational, and mathematical models. Areas eligible for support include HIV/AIDS behavior, neurosciences including molecular genetics, behavioral sciences, epidemiology, clinical assessment, etiology, treatment, prevention, and services. Grants support clearly defined projects or small groups of related research activities, and research conferences. Program Project and Center grants support large- scale, broad-based interdisciplinary research programs. Small grants (to $50,000 for two years) support small-scale exploratory and pilot studies or exploration of an unusual research opportunity. SBIR and STTR awards are made.

Eligible applicants/beneficiaries: public, private, profit, or nonprofit agencies including state and local governments, federal agencies, IHEs, hospitals, academic or research institutions.

Range: to $8,990,611. **Average:** $350,679.

Activity: anticipate 2,781 in FY 2015.

HQ: Division of Extramural Activities, NIMH, NIH-HHS, 6001 Executive Blvd., Rm. 6160, Bethesda, MD 20892. Phone: (301) 443-5047.

Internet: www.nimh.nih.gov. (Note: no field offices for this program.)

93.243 SUBSTANCE ABUSE AND MENTAL HEALTH SERVICES—PROJECTS OF REGIONAL AND NATIONAL SIGNIFICANCE (PRNS)

Assistance: project grants. (100 percent/1-5 years).

Purposes: pursuant to PHSA as amended and Children's Health Act of 2000, to address priority substance abuse treatment, prevention, and mental health needs of regional and national significance, through grants and cooperative agreements for: knowledge, development, and application projects for treatment and rehabilitation, and their evaluation; training and technical assistance; targeted capacity response programs; systems change, including projects involving statewide family networks and client-oriented and consumer-run self-help activities; programs to foster child health and development.

Eligible applicants/beneficiaries: state and local governments; private non-profit and profit entities such as community-based organizations, IHEs, and hospitals.

Range: $17,692 to $7,099,783. **Average:** $417,410.

Activity: anticipate 506 awards in FY 2016.

HQ: SAMHSA-HHS, 1 Choke Cherry Rd., Rockville, MD 20850. Phone: (240) 276-1418.

Internet: www.samhsa.gov. (Note: no field offices for this program.)

93.247 ADVANCED EDUCATION NURSING GRANT PROGRAM ("ANE")

Assistance: project grants. (100 percent/3 years).

Purposes: pursuant to PHSA as amended and HPEPA, to enhance advanced nursing education and practice including: master's and doctoral programs; combined RN and master's degree programs; post-nursing master's certificate programs; or, for nurse midwives, in certificate programs existing on 12 November 1998, to serve as nurse practitioners, clinical nurse specialist, nurse midwives, nurse administrators, public health nurses, or other specialties.

Eligible applicants/beneficiaries: schools of nursing, academic health centers; other public or private nonprofit or profit entities including community-based organizations.

Range: N.A. Average: $388,458.

Activity: N.A.

HQ: Division of Nursing, Bureau of Health Professions, HRSA-HHS, Parklawn Bldg., Rm. 9-89, 5600 Fishers Ln., Rockville, MD 20857. Phone: (301) 443-5688.

Internet: www.hrsa.gov.

93.250 GERIATRIC ACADEMIC CAREER AWARDS

Assistance: direct payments/specified use. (100 percent/5 years).

Purposes: pursuant to PHSA as amended and HPEPA, to provide financial incentives for junior faculty at schools of allopathic and osteopathic medicine to pursue academic careers in geriatrics.

Eligible applicants/beneficiaries: junior faculty members of accredited schools of allopathic and osteopathic medicine who: are board-certified or-eligible in internal medicine, family practice, or psychiatry; have completed geriatrics fellowship programs; are U.S. citizens, nationals, or lawful permanent residents.

Range/Average: N.A.

Activity: N.A.

HQ: Division of State, Community, and Public Health, Bureau of Health Professions, HRSA-HHS, Parklawn Bldg., Rm. 12-C-05, 5600 Fishers Ln., Rockville, MD 20857. Phone: (301) 443-3353.

Internet: www.hrsa.gov.

93.251 UNIVERSAL NEWBORN HEARING SCREENING

Assistance: project grants. (100 percent/3-5 years).

Purposes: pursuant to PHSA, to implement universal newborn child hearing screening prior to hospital discharge with linkage to a medical home, and diagnostic evaluation and enrollment in a program of early intervention.

Eligible applicants/beneficiaries: states; one technical assistance organization.

Range: $155,000 to $250,000. Average: $235,000.

Activity: N.A.

HQ: Integrated Services Branch, Division of Services for Children with Special Needs, Maternal and Child Health Bureau, HRSA-HHS, 5600 Fishers Ln., Rm. 18A-18, Rockville, MD 20857. Phone: (301) 443-9023.

Internet: www.hrsa.gov.

93.253 POISON CONTROL STABILIZATION AND ENHANCEMENT GRANTS ("Poison Control Centers")

Assistance: project grants.

Purposes: pursuant to the Poison Control Center Enhancement and Awareness Act, Amendments of 2003, to strengthen poisoning prevention and treatment programs and services; to enable non- certified or new centers to obtain certification; to create collaborative approaches among PCCs and with other health entities; to expand access to services. Previous projects also have established a toll-free phone number and nationwide media campaign, developed uniform patient management guidelines.

Eligible applicants/beneficiaries: state-designated poison control centers.

Range: $12,466 to $2,083,401. **Average:** $331,509.

Activity: N.A.

HQ: Poison Control Program, Healthcare Systems Bureau, HRSA-HHS, 5600 Fishers Ln., Rm. 08W-44, Rockville MD 20857. Phone: (301) 443-8177.

Internet: www.hrsa.gov.

93.254   INFANT ADOPTION AWARENESS TRAINING ("IAATP")

Assistance: project grants. (100 percent/1-3 years).

Purposes: pursuant to PHSA and Children's Health Act of 2000, to develop and implement programs to train designated health center staff in providing adoption information and referrals to pregnant women on an equal basis, with all other courses of action included in nondirective counseling.

Eligible applicants/beneficiaries: private nonprofit national, regional, or local organizations whose primary purposes are adoption.

Range/Average: N.A.

Activity: N.A.

HQ: Administration on Children, Youth and Families, Children's Bureau, 1250 Maryland Ave., SW, 8th Fl., Washington, DC 20024. Phone: (202) 205-7270; FAX: (202) 260-9345.

Internet: www.acf.hhs.gov/programs/cb. (Note: no field offices for this program.)

93.255   CHILDREN'S HOSPITALS GRADUATE MEDICAL EDUCATION PAYMENT PROGRAM ("CHGME Payment Program")

Assistance: direct payments/specified use.

Purposes: pursuant to SSA, PHSA as amended, Children's Health Act of 2000, and Healthcare Research and Quality Act of 1999, to operate graduate medical residency programs in pediatrics and other specialties at children's teaching hospitals—to help offset the disparity in funding levels versus other types of federally supported teaching hospitals.

Eligible applicants/beneficiaries: public or private nonprofit and profit children's teaching hospitals with accredited residency training programs, with a Medicare provider agreement in effect and excluded from the Medicare Inpatient Prospective Payment system.

Range: $31,000 to $17,952,000. **Average:** $4,425,000.

Activity: N.A.

HQ: Division of Medicine and Dentistry, Bureau of Health Professions, HRSA-HHS, 5600 Fishers Ln., Rm. 9A-27, Rockville, MD 20857. Phone: (301) 443-6190; FAX (301) 443-8890.

Internet: www.bhpr.hrsa.gov/childrenshospitalgme.

93.257 GRANTS FOR EDUCATION, PREVENTION, AND EARLY DETECTION OF RADIOGENIC CANCERS AND DISEASES

Assistance: project grants.

Purposes: pursuant to PHSA, for new or expanded programs to: screen individuals, as described in the Radiation Exposure Compensation Act, for cancer as a preventative health measure; provide referrals for medical treatment and provide follow-up services; develop and disseminate public information and education for the detection, prevention, and treatment of radiogenic cancers and diseases; facilitate putative applicants in the documentation of claims under the Radiation Exposure Compensation Act. Project funds may not support inpatient services or cash payments to patients.

Eligible applicants/beneficiaries: within states with uranium mines or mills or involved in uranium transport (Arizona, Colorado, Idaho, New Mexico, North Dakota, Oregon, South Dakota, Texas, Utah, Washington, and Wyoming)—cancer centers designated by the National Cancer Institute, DVA health facilities, federally qualified health centers, state or local agencies currently providing health care services, IHS health care facilities, nonprofit organizations.

Range: $118,105 to $223,184. **Average:** $197,046

Activity: N.A.

HQ: Director, Division of Health Center Management, Bureau of Primary Health Care, HRSA-HHS, 5600 Fishers Ln., Rm. 17W29-C, Rockville, MD 20857. Phone: (301) 443-0835.

Internet: www.hrsa.gov/ruralhealth/about/community/resepgrant.html.

93.259 RURAL ACCESS TO EMERGENCY DEVICES GRANT AND PUBLIC ACCESS TO DEFIBRILLATION DEMONSTRATION GRANT (RAED)

Assistance: project grants.

Purposes: pursuant to the Cardiac Arrest Survival Act of 2000, for state community partnerships to purchase Access to Emergency Devices (AEDs) and to obtain training on their use. Funds may also support: medical dispatcher training addressing the use of AEDs for the lay person until arrival of EMS personnel; maintenance costs; data reporting costs.

Eligible applicants/beneficiaries: rural community partnerships including first response entities (e.g., fire, EMS, police), profit and nonprofit entities, statewide or regional offices.

Range/Average: N.A.

Activity: N.A.

HQ: Office of Rural Health Policy, HRSA-HHS, Parklawn Bldg., Rm. 5A-05, 5600 Fishers Ln., Rockville, MD 20857. Phone: (301) 443-08-35.

Internet: www.hrsa.gov.

93.260 FAMILY PLANNING—PERSONNEL TRAINING ("FP Training")

Assistance: project grants. (100 percent/to 3-5 years).

Purposes: pursuant to PHSA and the Family Planning Services and Population Research Act of 1970 as amended, to train paramedical and paraprofessional personnel in family planning services, particularly in rural areas. Programs where abortion as a method of family planning are ineligible for assistance.

Eligible applicants/beneficiaries: city, county, local, regional, or state governments and private nonprofit entities in states, territories, and possessions.

Range: $300,000 to $900,000. **Average:** N.A.

Activity: anticipate 7 awards in FY 2015.

HQ: Director, Office of Family Planning, Office of Population Affairs, HHS, 1101 Wootton Pkwy., Ste. 550, Rockville, MD 20852. Phone: (240) 453-8822.

Internet: https://www.hhs.gov/opa. (Note: no field offices for this program.)

93.261 NATIONAL DIABETES PREVENTION PROGRAM—PREVENTING TYPE 2 DIABETES AMONG PEOPLE AT HIGH RISK ("National Diabetes Prevention Program")

Assistance: project grants (100 percent).

Purposes: pursuant to the Public Health Service Act, funds to scale (expand) and sustain the National Diabetes Prevention Program (DPP). Award recipients will be expected to develop, implement, market, and evaluate a comprehensive plan for scaling the DPP lifestyle change program in select communities. Funds may not be used for research, for the provision of health care services, or for construction. Funds may generally not be used for the purchase of furniture or equipment; any such proposed spending must be identified in the budget. The recipient must perform a substantial role in carrying out project objectives and not merely serve as a conduit for an award to another party or provider who is ineligible.

Eligible applicants: nonprofit and for-profit organizations, Indian/Native American tribal governments, faith-based organizations.

Eligible beneficiaries: anyone/general public.

Range: $750,000 to $2,000,000. **Average:** N.A.

Activity: N.A.

HQ: Director, National Diabetes Prevention Program, CDC, 4770 Buford Hwy, Stop K10, Atlanta, GA 30341. Phone: (770) 488-6241.

Internet: www.cdc.gov/diabetes/prevention.

93.262 OCCUPATIONAL SAFETY AND HEALTH PROGRAM

Assistance: project grants. (100 percent/1-5 years).

Purposes: pursuant to PHSA as amended and Occupational Safety and Health Act of 1970, for research in occupational disease and injury prevention, including projects involving new or improved procedures, methods, techniques, or systems; to train specialized professional and paraprofessional personnel in occupational medicine, nursing, safety, and in industrial hygiene and occupational safety. Grants may be used for: educational resource centers to provide primarily graduate multidisciplinary training; long-term training programs for undergraduate, graduate, technical, or professional trainees. SBIR awards are made.

Eligible applicants/beneficiaries: domestic and foreign public or private profit and nonprofit organizations; federal, state, local, tribal governments agencies; IHEs; research institutions; hospitals; individuals, with special encouragement to apply to women, minorities, and persons with disabilities.

Range: $15,000 to $4,924,000. **Average:** N.A.

Activity: N.A.

HQ: Office of Extramural Programs, NIOSH (E74), CDCP-HHS, 1600 Clifton Rd. NE, Atlanta, GA 30333. Phone: (404) 498-2530.

Internet: www.cdc.gov/niosh/oep. (Note: no field offices for this program.)

93.264 NURSE FACULTY LOAN PROGRAM (NFLP)

Assistance: direct loans. (90 percent/1 year).

Purposes: pursuant to PHSA as amended and Nurse Reinvestment Act of 2002, for schools of nursing to capitalize student loan funds to increase the number of nursing faculty. The program provides up to 90 percent funding for such funds; in turn, schools may award loans of to $30,000 per academic year to students, or the amount of the student's financial need. Loan cancellation ensues for students completing a four-year employment service requirement as nursing faculty, up to 85 percent of the total principal and interest.

Eligible applicants: public and private nonprofit and profit schools of nursing offering full-time advanced degree programs.

Eligible beneficiaries: full-time, graduate nursing students that are U.S. citizens, nationals, or lawful permanent residents.

Range: $11,135 to $2,936,106. **Average:** $289,716.

Activity: N.A.

HQ: Division of Nursing, Bureau of Health Professions, HRSA-HHS, Parklawn Bldg., Rm. 9-89, 5600 Fishers Ln., Rockville, MD 20857. Phone: (301) 443-1399.

Internet: www.hrsa.gov.

93.265 COMPREHENSIVE GERIATRIC EDUCATION PROGRAM (CGEP)

Assistance: project grants. (100 percent/3 years).

Purposes: pursuant to PHSA as amended and Nurse Reinvestment Act of 2002, for programs to train and educate nursing personnel in providing geriatric care. Funds may support student and faculty training programs, curriculum development, continuing education, salaries, travel costs, supplies, and equipment.

Eligible applicants/beneficiaries: schools of nursing, academic health centers, health care facilities, programs leading to certified nurse assistant, partnerships, and other public or private nonprofit and profit entities.

Range: $126,000 to $253,000. **Average:** N.A.

Activity: N.A.

HQ: Division of Nursing, Bureau of Health Professions, HRSA-HHS, Parklawn Bldg., Rm. 12C-05, 5600 Fishers Ln., Rockville, MD 20857. Phone: (301) 443-7762.

Internet: www.hrsa.gov.

93.266 HEALTH SYSTEMS STRENGTHENING AND HIV/AIDS PREVENTION, CARE AND TREATMENT UNDER THE PRESIDENT'S EMERGENCY PLAN FOR AIDS RELIEF
("Global HIV/AIDS Program")

Assistance: project grants. (100 percent/1-5 years).

Purposes: pursuant to PHSA as amended and United States Leadership Against HIV/AIDS, Tuberculosis and Malaria Act of 2003, to rapidly expand antiretroviral therapy (ART) to low-income HIV-infected persons in the 15 countries targeted under the President's Emergency Plan for AIDS Relief (PEDFAR); to develop sustainable indigenous capacity to continue such programs after projects end.

Eligible applicants/beneficiaries: organizations with three years experience in providing ART in three or more of the targeted countries.

Range/Average: N.A.

Activity: N.A.

HQ: Global Program, HIV/AIDS Bureau, HRSA-HHS, 5600 Fishers Ln., Ste. 7-90, Rockville, MD 20857. Phone: (301) 443-3650.

Internet: www.hrsa.gov.

93.267 STATE GRANTS FOR PROTECTION AND ADVOCACY SERVICES

Assistance: formula grants. (100 percent/2 years).

Purposes: pursuant to PHSA as amended, for state protection and advocacy systems to provide outreach and services to individuals with traumatic brain injury, including: information, referrals, and advice; individual and family advocacy; legal representation; specific assistance in self-advocacy.

Eligible applicants/beneficiaries: state protection and advocacy systems including in territories.

Range: $20,000 to $145,583. **Average:** $50,000.

Activity: N.A.

HQ: Program Officer, Protection and Advocacy for Traumatic Brain Injury Program, Division of Services for Children with Special Healthcare Needs, 5600 Fishers Ln., Rm. 13-103, Rockville, MD 20857. Phone: (301) 443-5599.

Internet: www.hrsa.gov.

93.268 IMMUNIZATION COOPERATIVE AGREEMENTS
("Vaccines for Children Program")

Assistance: project grants (to 100 percent).

Purposes: pursuant to PHSA as amended, Health Services and Centers Amendments of 1978, Preventive Health Amendments of 1984, and SSA, to plan, organize, and conduct immunization programs for the control of vaccine-preventable diseases; to purchase, store, supply, and deliver vaccine; for assessment, surveillance, outbreak control, information and education, and volunteer activities; compliance with compulsory school immunization laws. Vaccine purchased with grant funds may be given to private practitioners but may not be sold to patients.

Eligible applicants/beneficiaries: states and, in consultation with state health authorities, political subdivisions and other public entities.

Range: $252,725 to $368,026,903. **Average:** $52,334,322.

Activity: N.A.

HQ: Program Director, CDC-HHS, 1600 Clifton Rd. NE, MS A-19, Atlanta, GA 30033. Phone: (404) 639-8715.

Internet: www.cdc.gov/vaccines. (Note: no field offices for this program.)

93.269 COMPLEX HUMANITARIAN EMERGENCY AND WAR-RELATED INJURY PUBLIC HEALTH ACTIVITIES

Assistance: project grants (100 percent/to 5 years).

Purposes: pursuant to the Public Health Service Act, to bring public health and epidemiologic principles to the aid of populations affected by complex humanitarian emergencies and war-related injuries. Grants and cooperative agreements may be used for personnel, salaries, consultant costs, survey costs, training, equipment, supplies, travel, patient costs, miscellaneous items, and indirect costs.

Eligible applicants: only Landmine Survivors Network may apply for non-research activities supported by the CDC.

Eligible beneficiaries: general public.

Range/Average: N.A.

Activity: N.A.

HQ: International Emergency and Refugee Health Branch, CDCP-HHS, 4770 Buford Hwy., Stop F-57, Atlanta, GA 30341. Phone: (770) 488-0697.

Internet: www.cdc.gov.

93.270 ADULT VIRAL HEPATITIS PREVENTION AND CONTROL

Assistance: project grants (to 5 years).

Purposes: pursuant to the Public Health Service Act, to assist State and local health agencies, health related organizations and other governmental and nongovernmental organizations in their efforts to decrease the incidence of new infections of hepatitis A, hepatitis B and hepatitis C viruses and to decrease risks for chronic liver disease including cirrhosis and liver cancer in persons with chronic hepatitis B and hepatitis C infections.

Eligible applicants: local health agencies and other governmental and non-governmental health-related organizations in the states, DC, and territories.

Eligible beneficiaries: general public.

Range: $30,000 to $500,000. **Average:** $150,000.

Activity: anticipate supporting 65 grantees in FY 2015.

HQ: Division of HIV/AIDS Prevention (A43), CDCP-HHS, 1600 Clifton Rd., Stop E-07, Atlanta, GA 30333. Phone: (404) 639-8531.

Internet: www.cdc.gov. (Note: no field offices for this program.)

93.273 ALCOHOL RESEARCH PROGRAMS

Assistance: project grants. (100 percent/to 5 years).

Purposes: pursuant to PHSA as amended and SBRDEA, for research on alcoholism and alcohol-related problems in such disciplines and subject areas as biomedical and genetic factors, psychological and environmental factors, medical disorders, health services, and prevention and treatment. Research Project Grants support clearly defined projects or small groups of related research activities, and research conferences. Program Project grants support large-scale, broad-based interdisciplinary research programs. Small Grants, limited to $50,000 for up to two years, are for small-scale exploratory and pilot studies or exploration of an unusual research opportunity. Exploratory/Developmental Grants are for a maximum of $275,000 total for up to two years. SBIR and STTR awards are available.

Eligible applicants/beneficiaries: public, private profit and nonprofit agencies including state, local, or regional government agencies, IHEs, hospitals, academic or research institutions.

Range/Average: N.A.

Activity: N.A.

HQ: National Institute on Alcohol Abuse and Alcoholism, NIH-HHS, 5635 Fishers Ln., Rm. 2085, Rockville, MD 20852. Phone: (301) 451-2067; FAX: (301) 443-7043.

Internet: www.nih.gov. (Note: no field offices for this program.)

93.275 SUBSTANCE ABUSE AND MENTAL HEALTH SERVICES—ACCESS TO RECOVERY
("ATR I, ATR II, ATRIII")

Assistance: project grants. (100 percent/1-3 years).

Purposes: pursuant to PHSA as amended, to implement voucher programs for substance abuse clinical treatment and recovery support services, enabling clients to obtain free services from providers of their choice.

Eligible applicants/beneficiaries: chief executives of states, territories, and tribal organizations.

Range: $1,676,000 to $3,352,000. **Average:** $3,159,594.

Activity: N.A.

HQ: CSAT-SAMHSA-HHS, 1 Choke Cherry Rd., Rockville, MD 20850. Phone: (240) 276-1418.

Internet: www.samhsa.gov. (Note: no field offices for this program.)

93.276 DRUG-FREE COMMUNITIES SUPPORT PROGRAM GRANTS
("Drug-Free Community Grants")

Assistance: project grants. (to 50 percent/1 year).

Purposes: pursuant to the Drug-Free Communities Act of 1997, to increase the capacity of community coalitions to reduce substance abuse among adults through collaborative activities; to disseminate state-of-the-art information on practices and initiatives proven to be effective in reducing substance abuse among youth.

Eligible applicants/beneficiaries: nonprofit, charitable, educational community coalitions collaborating with community entities, including government agencies, in a substantial voluntary effort—established for at least six months and with a five-year strategic plan. Note: proposals are submitted to the Office of Justice Programs, and approved by OJJDP and the Office of National Drug Control Policy.

Range: $75,000 to $125,000. **Average:** $116,517.

Activity: anticipate 725 awards in FY 2016.

HQ: PATH Program, Homeless Programs Branch, Division of Knowledge Development and Systems Change, CMHS-SAMHSA-HHS, 1 Choke Cherry Rd., 7-1091, Rockville, MD 20857. Phone: (240) 276-1422.

Internet: www.samhsa.gov. (Note: no field offices for this program.)

93.279 DRUG ABUSE AND ADDICTION RESEARCH PROGRAMS

Assistance: project grants. (100 percent/to 5 years).

Purposes: pursuant to PHSA as amended and SBRDEA, for epidemiologic, basic, clinical, and applied research on the etiology, treatment, prevention, and consequences of drug addiction, including HIV/AIDS. Research project grants support clearly defined projects or small groups of related research activities, and research conferences. Program project and center grants support large-scale, broad-based interdisciplinary research programs. Small grants (up to $50,000 per year for up to two years) support less experienced investigators, testing of new methods and techniques, small-scale exploratory and pilot studies or exploration of an unusual research opportunity. SBIR and STTR awards are available.

Eligible applicants/beneficiaries: public, private, profit and nonprofit organizations; foreign or domestic agencies, including state, local or regional government agencies; IHEs; hospitals; academic or research institutions.

Range: $4,244 to $5,968,000. **Average:** $164,921.

Activity: anticipate 2,129 awards in FY 2016.

HQ: National Institute on Drug Abuse, NIH-HHS, Neurosciences Bldg., 6001 Executive Bldg., Rm. 4241Bethesda, MD 20892. Phone:(301) 435-1384.

Internet: www.drugabuse.gov. (Note: no field offices for this program.)

93.280 NATIONAL INSTITUTES OF HEALTH LOAN REPAYMENT PROGRAM FOR CLINICAL RESEARCHERS (NIH LRP-CR)

Assistance: project grants. (100 percent/from 2 years).

Purposes: pursuant to PHSA, to attract and retain health professionals to clinical research careers by offering extant educational loan repayment for participants agreeing to engage in clinical research at least half-time in a qualifying institution for at least two years. Research must be patient-oriented and conducted with human subjects in an out- or inpatient setting to clarify a problem in human physiology, pathophysiology or disease, or epidemiologic or behavioral studies, outcomes or health services research, or developing new technologies, therapeutic interventions, or clinical trials. Maximum annual benefit is $35,000 in loan repayment and $13,650 in federal tax reimbursement.

Eligible applicants/beneficiaries: U.S. citizens, nationals, or permanent residents with: a Ph.D., M.D., D.D.S., D.M.D., D.O., D.P.M., Pharm.D., D.C., N.D., or equivalent doctoral degree from an accredited institution; qualifying educational debt in excess of 20 percent of annual salary (half of which must be paid by program participant); a contract to conduct research supported by a nonprofit foundation, professional association, or other institution, or a U.S. or other state or local government agency. Full-time federal employees are ineligible.

Range: to $35,000 for loan repayment per year. **Average:** N.A.

Activity: anticipate 800 awards in FY 2016.

HQ: Division of Loan Repayment, NIH, 6011 Executive Blvd., Rm. 206, Bethesda, MD 20892-7650. Phone: (240) 380-3062.

Internet: www.lrp.nih.gov. (Note: no field offices for this program.)

93.281 MENTAL HEALTH RESEARCH CAREER—SCIENTIST DEVELOPMENT AWARDS
("Research Career/Scientist Development")

Assistance: project grants. (100 percent/to 5 years).

Purposes: pursuant to PHSA as amended, for research training in the problems of mental illness, behavioral disorders, and HIV/AIDS—through Mentored Research Scientist, Mentored Clinical Scientist, Mentored Scientist Development for New Minority Faculty, Mentored Patient-Oriented Career Development, Mid-career Investigator in Patient Oriented Research, Independent Scientist, and Senior Scientist Awards. Some research costs may be supported.

Eligible applicants/beneficiaries: research centers, medical schools, departments of psychiatry, nonmedical academic departments, psychiatric hospitals or hospitals with psychiatric services, community mental health centers, biomedical research institutes, and departments of behavioral science. Researchers must have scholastic degree and previous training, and they must be U.S. citizens, nationals, or lawful permanent residents.

Range/Average: N.A.

Activity: N.A.

HQ: Division of Extramural Activities, NIMH, NIH-HHS, 6001 Executive Blvd., Bethesda, MD 20892. Phone: (301) 443-5047.

Internet: www.nimh.nih.gov. (Note: no field offices for this program.)

93.282 MENTAL HEALTH NATIONAL RESEARCH SERVICE AWARDS FOR RESEARCH TRAINING
("NRSA Program")

Assistance: project grants. (100 percent/to 6 years).

Purposes: pursuant to PHSA as amended, for NRSA programs providing research training in mental health problems. Included are: basic biomedical, clinical neuroscience, and behavioral research; epidemiology of mental disorders; etiology, description, diagnosis, and pathogenesis of mental disorders; treatment development, assessment, and evaluation; public health intervention and prevention approaches. Grants for up to six years are directed toward young scientists at the predoctoral or postdoctoral level for full-time work. Career Opportunities in Research (COR) Honors Undergraduate grants are available to minority trainees competing successfully for entry into Ph.D. degree programs. Postdoctoral students receiving support for less than 12 months must meet payback requirements through an equivalent period of research and/or teaching after training is completed.

Eligible applicants/beneficiaries: training grants—domestic public or private nonprofit organizations. Applicants for predoctoral support must have completed at least two years of graduate work and be enrolled in a doctoral degree program. Postdoctoral applicants must have a PhD., Psy.D., M.D., D.D.S., Sc.D., D.N.S., D.O., D.S.W., or equivalent degree. Applicants for individual awards must be U.S. citizens, nationals, or lawful permanent residents. COR Honors Undergraduate program awards—four-year IHEs or health professional schools whose enrollment is drawn substantially from ethnic groups.

Range/Average: N.A.

Activity: N.A.

HQ: Division of Extramural Activities, NIMH, NIH-HHS, 6001 Executive Blvd., Rm. 6160, Bethesda, MD 20892. Phone: (301) 443-5047.

Internet: www.nimh.nih.gov. (Note: no field offices for this program.)

93.283 CENTERS FOR DISEASE CONTROL AND PREVENTION— INVESTIGATIONS AND TECHNICAL ASSISTANCE

Assistance: project grants. (50-100 percent/1-3 years).

Purposes: pursuant to PHSA, Federal Mine Safety and Health Amendments Act of 1977 as amended, and Occupational Safety and Health Act of 1970, to strengthen state and local disease prevention and control programs, including communicable and chronic diseases such as tuberculosis, childhood immunization, tobacco use, diabetes, oral health, and sexually transmitted diseases. Services include investigations, epidemic aid, occupational safety and health programs, epidemiology, consultation, personnel training, responses to public health emergencies.

Eligible applicants/beneficiaries: states and their political subdivisions, local health authorities, and organizations with specialized health interests; IHES and research institutions; certain private, public nonprofit organizations.

Range/Average: N.A.

Activity: N.A.

HQ: Extramural Program Teal Leader, National Center for Chronic Disease Prevention and Health Promotion, CDCP-HHS, 4770 Buford Hwy, Atlanta, Georgia 30341. Phone: (770) 488-5314.

Internet: www.cdc.gov. (Note: no field offices for this program.)

93.284 INJURY PREVENTION PROGRAM FOR AMERICAN INDIANS AND ALASKAN NATIVES—COOPERATIVE AGREEMENTS

Assistance: project grants.

Purposes: pursuant to PHSA as amended, to provide injury prevention health services to American Indians and Alaska natives, through capacity building, implementation of interventions, and training.

Eligible applicants/beneficiaries: tribes, tribal organizations, urban Indian organizations, nonprofit organizations.

Range: to $100,000 for Part I; to $20,000 for Part II. **Average:** N.A.

Activity: N.A.

HQ: Grants Policy Office, IHS-HHS, 801 Thompson Ave., Suite TMP 360, Rockville, MD 20852. Phone: (301) 443-5204.

Internet: www.ihs.gov.

93.285 NATIONAL INSTITUTES OF HEALTH PEDIATRIC RESEARCH LOAN REPAYMENT PROGRAM (PR-LRP)

Assistance: project grants. (100 percent/from 2 years).

Purposes: pursuant to PHSA as amended, to attract and retain health professionals to pediatric research careers by offering repayment of extant education loans for participants agreeing to engage in pediatric research for two years minimum in a qualifying nonprofit institution. Payments may be made up to $35,000 per year, plus $13,650 annually for tax reimbursements.

Eligible applicants/beneficiaries: U.S. citizens, nationals, or permanent residents from disadvantaged backgrounds, with: an M.D., Ph.D., D.O., D.D.S., D.M.D., D.P.M., B.S.N., A.D.N., or equivalent degree; qualified undergraduate or graduate educational loan debt exceeding 20 percent of their salary; a contract commitment of at least two years of service; no existing service obligation to federal, state, or other entities.

Range: to $70,000 plus tax payments. **Average:** N.A.

Activity: anticipate 300 awards in FY 2016.

HQ: Division of Loan Repayment, NIH, 6011 Executive Blvd., Rm. 206, Bethesda, MD 20892-7650. Phone: (240) 380-3062.

Internet: www.lrp.nih.gov. (Note: no field offices for this program.)

93.286 DISCOVERY AND APPLIED RESEARCH FOR TECHNOLOGICAL INNOVATIONS TO IMPROVE HUMAN HEALTH

Assistance: project grants. (100 percent/to 5 years).

Purposes: pursuant to PHSA, for hypothesis-, design-, technology-, or device-driven research relating to the discovery, design, development, validation, and applications of technologies in biomedical imaging and bioengineering. The program includes biomaterials, biosensors and biotransducers, nanotechnology, imaging device development, biomedical imaging technology development, image exploitation, contrast agents, informatics, and computer sciences—related to imaging, molecular and cellular imaging, bio-electrics/biomagnetics, organ and whole body imaging, screening for diseases and disorders, imaging technology assessment, and related disciplines. NRSAs, SBIR, and STTR awards are available.

Eligible applicants/beneficiaries: corporations, public or private institutions, nonprofit or profit entities, individuals.

Range: $3,000 to $2,242,720. **Average:** $376,550.

Activity: anticipate 735 awards in FY 2016.

HQ: National Institute of Biomedical Imaging and Bioengineering, NIH-HHS, 6707 Democracy Blvd., Bethesda, MD 20892. Phone: (301) 451-351.

Internet: www.nibib.nih.gov. (Note: no field offices for this program.)

93.288 NATIONAL HEALTH SERVICE CORPS SCHOLARSHIP PROGRAM ("NHSC Scholarship Program")

Assistance: project grants. (100 percent/1-4 years).

Purposes: pursuant to PHSA, for scholarships to full-time students in the health professions. Disciplines include: allopathic and osteopathic medicine, and dentistry; family nurse practitioners; nurse midwifery; primary care physician assistants; and, other disciplines needed by the NHSC. Scholarship recipients must perform one year of service in a federally-designated health manpower shortage area for each year of support received, or a minimum of two years; however, service deferments may be granted to complete residencies in family practice, internal medicine, pediatrics, and OB/GYN. Service sites also may be located in the territories or possessions.

Eligible applicants/beneficiaries: U.S. citizens or nationals, enrolled or accepted in an accredited U.S. school.

Range/Average: N.A.

Activity: N.A.

HQ: Chief, Applications and Award Branch, NHSC Division, Bureau of Health Professions, HRSA-HHS, 5600 Fishers Ln., Rm. 8C-26, Rockville, MD 20857. Phone: (301) 594-4400.

Internet: nhsc.hrsa.gov.

93.289 PRESIDENT'S COUNCIL ON FITNESS, SPORTS, AND NUTRITION ("PCPFS")

Assistance: advisory services/counseling.

Purposes: to provide professional assistance in the design, development, improvement, and implementation of physical fitness programs, as well as expanded exercise and sports participation opportunities for all age groups. This is accomplished through publications, media campaigns, and a web site, in coordination with school systems, government agencies, employee and industrial organizations, recreation and park departments, communications media, etc.—not with organizations with a commercial interest in physical fitness. No funding is provided.

Eligible applicants/beneficiaries: general public.

Range/Average: N.A.

Activity: N.A.

HQ: Public Affairs Specialist, President's Council on Physical Fitness and Sports, Office of Public Health and Science, OS-HHS, Tower Oaks Bldg.,

Ste. 560, 1101 Wootton Pkwy., Rockville, MD 20852. Phone: (240) 276-9857; FAX: (240) 276-9860.

Internet: www.fitness.gov. (Note: no field offices for this program.)

93.290   NATIONAL COMMUNITY CENTERS OF EXCELLENCE IN WOMEN'S HEALTH
("Coalition for a Healthier Community")

Assistance: project grants. (100 percent/to 5 years).

Purposes: for community-based programs integrating, coordinating, and strengthening linkages in women's health in the following components: comprehensive health service delivery; training for lay and professional health providers; community-based research; public education and outreach; leadership development for women as health care consumers and providers; technical assistance. Funds may be used for staffing, supplies, consultants, equipment, and travel.

Eligible applicants/beneficiaries: public or private nonprofit community-based hospitals or organizations, or community health centers serving underserved women. Note: existing programs and organizations in certain states and PR are ineligible.

Range/Average: N.A.

Activity: N.A.

HQ: Office on Women's Health, HHS, Tower Bldg., 1101 Wootton Parkway, Suite 550, Rockville, MD 20852. Phone: (240) 453-8822.

Internet: www.womenhealth.gov. (Note: no field offices for this program.)

93.291   SURPLUS PROPERTY UTILIZATION
("Federal Property Assistance Program")

Assistance: sale, exchange, or donation of property and goods.

Purposes: pursuant to the Federal Property and Administrative Services Act of 1949 and SBMHAA as amended, to convey or lease surplus federal real properties needed and usable in health programs including research—e.g., land and buildings for use as hospitals, clinics, public health administration, water and sewer systems, rehabilitation programs, and facilities for the homeless. Discounts of up to 100 percent of value may be granted. Deed restrictions apply for 30 years for land, and lesser periods for improvements.

Eligible applicants/beneficiaries: states, political subdivisions and instrumentalities; tax-supported public and nonprofit health institutions.

Range/Average: N.A.

Activity: N.A.

HQ: Director, Division of Property Management, Program Support Center, HHS, Parklawn Bldg., 5600 Fishers Ln., Rockville, MD 20857. Phone: (301) 443-2265.

Internet: www.psc.gov/property_management/federalprop-index.html. (Note: no field offices for this program.)

93.296 STATE PARTNERSHIP GRANT PROGRAM TO IMPROVE MINORITY HEALTH
("State Partnership Program")

Assistance: project grants. (100 percent/to 5 years).

Purposes: pursuant to PHSA, for the development of partnerships with state and territorial offices of minority health—to develop and implement strategies to improve minority health and to eliminate health disparities including in adult and child immunization, asthma, cancer, diabetes, heart disease and stroke, HIV, infant mortality, and mental health. Project activity examples: development of plans of action; strengthened capacity to collect, analyze, and report data and to conduct evaluations; implementation of culturally and linguistically appropriate services; partnering with health professions schools to track progress of minority students to increase the number of minority graduates. Funds may not be used to provide health care treatment, for construction, or to supplant ongoing project activities.

Eligible applicants/beneficiaries: official state and territorial offices of minority health.

Range: $175,000 to $200,000. **Average:** N.A.

Activity: N.A.

HQ: *program information* Director, Division of Program Operations, Office of Minority Health, Office of Public Health and Science, OS-HHS, 11101 Wootton Pkwy., Ste. 550, Rockville, MD 20852. Phone: (240) 453-8822.

Internet: omhrc.gov. (Note: no field offices for this program.)

93.297 TEENAGE PREGNANCY PREVENTION PROGRAM

Assistance: cooperative agreements (100 percent/to 5 years).

Purposes: pursuant to the Consolidated Appropriations Act of 2010, to fund medically accurate and age appropriate programs that reduce teen pregnancy. Most of the available funds (75 percent) must be used for programs that have been proven effective through rigorous evaluation to reduce teenage pregnancy, behavioral risk factors underlying teenage pregnancy, or other associated risk factors. The remaining 25 percent must be used for research and demonstration grants to develop, replicate, refine, and test additional strategies for preventing teenage pregnancy.

Eligible applicants: state, regional, and local units of government, organizations and private nonprofit entities.

Eligible beneficiaries: U.S. teenagers.

Range: $400,000 to $2,000,000. **Average:** N.A.

Activity: anticipate 81 continuation awards in FY 2016.

HQ: Program Director, Office of the Secretary, HHS, 1101 Wootton Pkwy., Ste. 550, Rockville, MD 20852. Phone: (240) 453-8822.

Internet: www.hhs.gov/oah.

93.300 NATIONAL CENTER FOR HEALTH WORKFORCE ANALYSIS (NCHWA)

Assistance: project grants. (to 100 percent/to 5 years).

Purposes: pursuant to PHSA as amended and HPEPA, to develop information describing the health professions workforce and to analyze related issues, enabling decision-making on future directions in the field and in nursing programs in response to societal and professional needs. Funds may be used for targeted information collection and analysis, to develop a nonfederal analytic and research infrastructure, and for program evaluation and assessment.

Eligible applicants/beneficiaries: state and local governments, health professions schools, schools of nursing, academic health centers, community-based health facilities, and other public or private nonprofit entities.

Range: $375,366 to $496,650. **Average:** $439,304.

Activity: N.A.

HQ: NCHWA, Bureau of Health Professions, HRSA-HHS, 5600 Fishers Ln., Rm. 11-103, Rockville, MD 20857. Phone: (301) 443-9846.

Internet: bhw.hrsa.gov/healthworkforce.

93.301 SMALL RURAL HOSPITAL IMPROVEMENT GRANT PROGRAM

Assistance: project grants.

Purposes: pursuant to SSA, to implement "PPS"; to comply with legislative health improvement requirements; to reduce medical errors and support quality improvement.

Eligible applicants/beneficiaries: small rural hospitals, including in territories.

Range: $9,000 to $909,000. **Average:** $303,570.

Activity: N.A.

HQ: Outreach Program Coordinator or Network Development Program Coordinator, Office of Rural Health Policy, Director, Rural Research Centers, Office of Rural Health Policy, HRSA-HHS, Parklawn Bldg., Rm. 17W53-C, 5600 Fishers Ln., Rockville, MD 20857. Phone: (301) 443-0835.

Internet: www.hrsa.gov.

93.303 NURSE CORPS SCHOLARSHIP PROGRAM

Assistance: direct payments/specified use (100 percent/1-4 years).

Purposes: pursuant to the Nurse Reinvestment Act of 2002 and the Public Health Service Act as amended, to increase the supply of registered nurses (RN) in approved health care facilities with a critical shortage of nurses by providing service-obligated scholarships to full and part-time nursing students. Scholarships pay tuition and required fees to the school, a monthly stipend to students and a single annual payment to the student to assist with other reasonable educational expenses, including: books, supplies, equipment, uniforms, travel, for the provision of clinical service, etc. The program requires one year of service with a minimum 2-year service commitment post graduation.

Eligible applicants: U.S. citizen or national, enrolled or accepted for enrollment in a fully accredited US academic institution with a graduate, baccalaureate, or associate degree or diploma nursing program. The applicant must be free of any Federal judgment liens or service obligation, have not defaulted on a federal debt and have no conflicting service obligations. Financial need is also reviewed as part of the eligibility determination.

Eligible beneficiaries: U.S. citizens or nationals enrolled or accepted for enrollment in a fully accredited graduate, baccalaureate, associate degree or diploma nursing program.

Range: $22,352 to $278,052. **Average:** $92,289 for new award; $32,937 for continuation.

Activity: N.A.

HQ: Director, Division of Grants Management, HRSA-HHS, 5600 Fishers Ln., Rm. 8A-55, Rockville, MD 20857. Phone: (301) 594-4400.

Internet: www.hrsa.gov/loanscholarships/scholarships/Nursing/index.html. (Note: no field offices for this program.)

93.305 NATIONAL STATE-BASED TOBACCO CONTROL PROGRAMS ("National Tobacco Control Program")

Assistance: project grants (to 80 percent/1 to 5 years).

Purposes: pursuant to the Public Health Service Act, funds for state departments of health for evidence-based tobacco control interventions and strategies to reduce chronic disease morbidity, mortality, and disability related to tobacco use and secondhand smoke exposure. Awardees may only expend funds for reasonable program purposes, including personnel, travel, supplies, and services, such as contractual. In most cases, awardees may not use funding for the purchase of furniture or equipment; any such proposed spending must be clearly identified in the budget. Reimbursement of pre-award costs is not allowed. The direct and primary recipient in a cooperative agreement program must perform a substantial role in carrying out project outcomes and not merely serve as a conduit for an award to another party or provider who is ineligible.

Eligible applicants: state departments of health.

Eligible beneficiaries: general public.

Range/Average: N.A.

Activity: N.A.

HQ: Director, National Tobacco Control Program, CDC,4770 Buford Hwy., NE, Stop F-79, Atlanta, GA 30341. Phone: 770-488-5218.

Internet: www.cdc.gov. (Note: no field offices for this program.)

93.307 MINORITY HEALTH AND HEALTH DISPARITIES RESEARCH

Assistance: project grants. (100 percent/1-5 years).

Purposes: pursuant to PHSA and SBRDEA, to support basic, clinical, social, and behavioral research; to promote research infrastructure and training; to foster emerging programs; to disseminate information—reaching out to minority and other health disparity communities. The Excellence in Partnerships for Community Outreach, Research on Health Disparities and Training Program (Project EXPORT) provides funds to centers conducting inter-disciplinary minority health and other health disparities research intervention activities. The Research Endowment Program grants provide income for: teaching programs in the biomedical and behavioral sciences and related areas; facilities; student and faculty recruitment and retention; instructional delivery systems and information technology; scholarships, tutoring and counseling programs, and student service programs. The Health Disparities Research-Loan Repayment Program (HDR-LRP) provides for repayment of existing educational loan debt incurred by health professionals engaged in research on minority health or other health disparity issues; recipients must contract for two-year periods minimum, with extensions available. The Research Infrastructure in Minority Institutions (RIMI) Program assists nondoctoral degree institutions in developing their research infrastructure through collaborations with research-intensive universities. SBIR and STIR funding also is available.

Eligible applicants/beneficiaries: grants—individuals, public and private nonprofit and profit institutions. Endowment grants—"Section 736" health professions schools with net endowment assets less than 50 percent of the national average for similar institutions. HDR-LRP—U.S. citizens, nationals, or permanent residents, with qualifying outstanding educational loan debt equal to or less than 20 percent of the applicant's annual salary, with no service obligations to federal, state, or other entities, nor judgment liens arising from federal debt.

Range/Average: N.A.

Activity: N.A.

HQ: Director, Division of Research and Training Activities, National Center on Minority Health and Health Disparities (NCMHD), NIH-HHS, 6707 Democracy Blvd. - Ste. 800, Bethesda, MD 20892-5465. Phone: (301) 402-1366.

Internet: www.nimhd.nih.gov. (Note: no field offices for this program.)

93.308   NATIONAL INSTITUTE ON MINORITY HEALTH AND HEALTH DISPARITIES (NIMHD) EXTRAMURAL LOAN REPAYMENT PROGRAMS

Assistance: project grants. (100 percent/2 to 4 years).

Purposes: pursuant to PHSA as amended, for repayment of existing educational loan debt incurred by health professionals from disadvantaged backgrounds, engaged in patient-oriented clinical research with human subjects, or research on the causes and consequences of disease in inpatient or outpatient settings. Recipients must contact for two-year periods minimum, with one-year extensions available.

Eligible applicants/beneficiaries: U.S. citizens, nationals, or permanent residents with: a Ph.D., M.D., D.D.S., D.M.D., D.O., D.P.M., Pharm.D., D.C., N.D., or equivalent doctoral degree from an accredited institution; qualifying educational debt in excess of 20 percent of annual salary (half of which must be paid by program participant); a contract to conduct research supported by a nonprofit foundation, professional association, or other institution, or a U.S. or other state or local government agency. Full-time federal employees are ineligible.

Range: $7,332 to $97,301 for health disparities research; $31,738 to $97,300 for individuals from disadvantaged backgrounds. **Average:** $49,445 for health disparities research; $68,379 for individuals from disadvantaged backgrounds.

Activity: 208 awards in FY 2014.

HQ: NCMHD, Loan Repayment Program, 6707 Democracy Blvd. - Ste. 800, Bethesda, MD 20892-5465. Phone: (301) 402-1366; FAX: (301) 480-4049.

Internet: www.nimhd.nih.gov. (Note: no field offices for this program.)

93.310 TRANS-NIH RESEARCH SUPPORT ("Common Fund Research Support")

Assistance: project grants; training. (project grants, 100 percent/project grants, to 5 years).

Purposes: pursuant to PHSA, for new initiatives addressing major opportunities and gaps in biomedical research that no NIH Institute could address alone, but the which the agency as a whole can pursue to stimulate biomedical research progress and to catalyze changes that will serve to transform new scientific knowledge into tangible public health benefits.

Eligible applicants/beneficiaries: domestic public or private profit and nonprofit organizations, IHEs, hospitals, laboratories, or other institutions, state and local government units, individuals; foreign organizations for certain initiatives.

Range: $10,000 to $15,462,500. **Average:** $737,000.

Activity: N.A.

HQ: Assistant Director/Roadmap Coordination, Office of the Director, NIH-HHS, Bldg. One, Rm. 201, Bethesda, Maryland 20892. Phone: (301) 402-7617; FAX: (301) 435-7268.

Internet: commonfund.nih.gov. (Note: no field offices for this program.)

93.311 MOBILIZATION FOR HEALTH—NATIONAL PREVENTION PARTNERSHIP AWARDS (NPPA)

Assistance: project grants (100 percent/to 3 years).

Purposes: the purpose of the program is to conduct and support research programs, programs in health promotion, disease preventive health services, education and training, and communications to support such work by private non-profit entities. The funds would be targeted on efforts related to preventive, educational and wellness services projects for children, pregnant women, and diverse and adult populations, which are designed to decrease infectious diseases by stimulating immunization rate improvements.

Eligible applicants: public (including local and sate government) organizations and private nonprofit entities.

Eligible beneficiaries: anyone/general public.

Range: $50,000 to $500,000. **Average:** N.A.

Activity: N.A.

HQ: Office on Women's Health, HHS, Tower Bldg., 1101 Wootton Parkway, Suite 550, Rockville, MD 20852. Phone: (240) 453-8422.

Internet: www.hhs.gov/ash/public_health/indexph.html.

93.313   NIH OFFICE OF RESEARCH ON WOMEN'S HEALTH (NIH ORWH)

Assistance: project grants (100 percent/at least 1 year).

Purposes: pursuant to the NIH Revitalization Act of 1993, to identify projects on women's health that should be conducted or supported by national research institutes; identify multi-disciplinary research related to research on women's health that should be conducted or supported; and promote coordination and collaboration among entities conducting research.

Eligible applicants/beneficiaries: domestic, public or private, non-profit or profit organization, university, hospital, laboratory, or other institution including state and local units of government and individuals.

Range/Average: N.A.

Activity: N.A.

HQ: Director, 6707 Democracy Blvd., Suite 400, Bethesda, MD 20817. Phone: (301) 496-9472.

Internet: N.A. (Note: no field offices for this program.)

93.316   PUBLIC HEALTH PREPAREDNESS AND RESPONSE SCIENCE, RESEARCH, AND PRACTICE
("Public Health Preparedness Science")

Assistance: project grants/cooperative agreements (100 percent/1 to 5 years).

Purposes: the goal of this program is to conduct research and related public health preparedness and response program activities to build the scientific evidence base for public health preparedness, response, and recovery and improve and enhance the nations health security. This program is intended to support research, dissemination of research findings and products, translation of new science-based evidence to practice in the public health preparedness and response system, and the evaluation of effective application of science for improved practice as well as other programs, projects, or activities to advance preparedness science.

Eligible applicants/beneficiaries: public and private nonprofit and for profit organizations/institutions, state, local, territorial governments and agencies, Indian tribes, tribal governments and organizations.

Range/Average: N.A.

Activity: N.A.

HQ: Director, Public Health Preparedness Science, CDC,1600 Clifton Rd., Stop D-29, Atlanta, GA 30029-4018. Phone: (404) 639-5276.

Internet: www.cdc.gov/phpr/science/research.htm. (Note: no field offices for this program.)

93.317   EMERGING INFECTIONS PROGRAMS

Assistance: project grants (100 percent/1 to 5 years).

Purposes: the purpose of the Emerging Infections Programs (EIP) is to assist in local, state, and national efforts to prevent, control, and monitor the public health impact of infectious diseases. The EIP is a population-based network of state health agencies and their collaborators, including (but not limited to) academic institutions, local health departments, public health and clinical laboratories, infection control professionals, and healthcare providers. Funding under this program will support active surveillance, applied public health epidemiologic and laboratory activities, implementation and evaluation of pilot prevention/intervention projects, and flexible response to public health emergencies.

Eligible applicants: health departments of U.S. states, territories, and the District of Columbia.

Eligible beneficiaries: state and local health departments, the District of Columbia, U.S. territories, and the general public.

Range: $2,100,000 to $4,600,000. **Average:** $3,000,000.

Activity: anticipate 10 continuation awards in FY 2016.

HQ: Director, Emerging Infections Program, CDC, 1600 Clifton Rd., NE, Stop C-18, Atlanta, GA 30329. Phone: (404) 639-3743.

Internet: www.cdc.gov. (Note: no field offices for this program.)

93.321   DIETARY SUPPLEMENT RESEARCH PROGRAM

Assistance: project grants/cooperative agreements (100 percent).

Purposes: project grants to support research and other projects that strengthen knowledge and understanding of dietary supplements and translation of that knowledge into effective prevention strategies.

Eligible applicants/beneficiaries: domestic, public or private, non-profit or for-profit organizations, IHEs, hospitals, or other institutions including state and local units of government and tribal entities.

Range: to $100,000. **Average:** N.A.

Activity: N.A.

HQ: Director, Dietary Supplement Research Program, NIH, 6100 Executive Blvd, Ste. 3B01, Rockville, MD 20892. Phone: (301) 496-0168.

Internet: ods.od.nih.gov. (Note: no field offices for this program.)

93.322   CSELS PARTNERSHIP: STRENGTHENING PUBLIC HEALTH LABORATORIES

Assistance: cooperative agreements. (100 percent/1 to 5 years).

Purposes: pursuant to the Public Health Service Act, to improve public health laboratory infrastructure, increase their capacity through workforce development, promote quality laboratory practices, expand and improve health security, promote and support informatics, and enhance communication linkages. Funds may be used for costs associated with planning, organizing, conducting, and supporting public health laboratory infrastructure programs, and for the implementation of other program elements.

Eligible applicants/beneficiaries: federal, state, local, tribal, territorial public and private nonprofit and for-profit institutions/organizations.

Range: $7,000,000 to $27,000,000. **Average:** N.A.

Activity: N.A.

HQ: CDC-HHS, 2400 Century Center Blvd., Atlanta, GA 30345. Phone: (404) 498-6669.

Internet: www.cdc.gov.

93.339 PUBLIC HEALTH CONFERENCE SUPPORT

Assistance: cooperative agreements (100 percent).

Purposes: pursuant to the Public Health Service Act, to provide partial support for public health conferences related to the health promotion, education and prevention of HIV, Viral Hepatitis, STD, and TB Prevention. Funds may be used for costs associated with reasonable program planning, including personnel, travel, and supplies.

Eligible applicants/beneficiaries: 35 IHEs selected by the CDC as Prevention Research Centers (PRCs).

Range: $25,000 to $125,000. **Average:** $30,000.

Activity: anticipate 5 to 6 awards in FY 2016.

HQ: Division of HIV/AIDS Prevention (A43), CDCP-HHS, 1600 Clifton Rd., Stop E-07, Atlanta, GA 30333. Phone: (404) 639-8531.

Internet: www.cdc.gov.

93.342 HEALTH PROFESSIONS STUDENT LOANS, INCLUDING PRIMARY CARE LOANS—LOANS FOR DISADVANTAGED STUDENTS

Assistance: direct loans (90 percent).

Purposes: pursuant to PHSA and HPEPA, to capitalize and administer student loan funds to provide long-term, low-interest loans to full-time students in financial need or from disadvantaged backgrounds, preparing for the health professions. Students may borrow amounts annually to cover reasonable living expenses, tuition, and educational expenses. Third- and fourth- year medical and osteopathic medicine students may borrow additional funds to repay earlier educational loans; they must agree to enter and complete a primary health care residency training program not later than four years after graduating, and to practice primary health care until the loan is paid in full. Payback service provisions apply. The loan interest rate is 5 percent.

Eligible applicants: accredited public or nonprofit private schools located in states, territories, or possessions, providing a course of study leading to a degree of doctor of medicine, dentistry, osteopathy, pharmacy, optometry, podiatry, or veterinary medicine, or B.S. in pharmacy—or an equivalent degree. For LDS, applicant schools must have student recruitment and retention programs, minority health issues curricula, clinic services for minority groups, and mentor programs.

Eligible beneficiaries: full-time students in need of a loan, enrolled or accepted in an eligible course of study—that are U.S. citizens, nationals, or permanent residents of a state or territories or possessions.

Range: $1,000 to $4,715,970. **Average:** $305,575.

Activity: N.A.

HQ: Division of Health Careers Diversity and Development, Bureau of Health Professions, HRSA-HHS, 5600 Fishers Ln., Rm. 9-105, Rockville, MD 20857. Phone: (301) 443-1173.

Internet: bhpr.hrsa.gov/scholarshipsloans/index.html.

93.350 NATIONAL CENTER FOR ADVANCING TRANSLATIONAL SCIENCES (NCATS)

Assistance: project grants (100 percent/1 to 5 years).

Purposes: pursuant to the Public Health Service Act, to catalyze the generation of innovative methods and technologies that will enhance the development, testing, and implementation of diagnostics and therapeutics across a wide range of human diseases and conditions.

Eligible applicants/beneficiaries: IHEs, research hospitals, and other institutions capable of carrying out well-designed studies in any preclinical or clinical science.

Range/Average: N.A.

Activity: N.A.

HQ: Director, 6701 Democracy Blvd, Rm. 988, Bethesda, Maryland 20892-4874. Phone: (301) 435-0860.

Internet: www.ncats.nih.gov. (Note: no field offices for this program.)

93.351 RESEARCH INFRASTRUCTURE PROGRAMS

Assistance: project grants (100 percent/1-5 years).

Purposes: pursuant to the Small Business Research and Development Enhancement Act of 1992, to support research infrastructure and related research programs, and coordinate NIH's science education efforts.

Eligible applicants/beneficiaries: biomedical investigators at any nonprofit or for-profit organization, company, or institution engaged in biomedical research.

Range/Average: N.A.

Activity: N.A.

HQ: Director, 6701 Democracy Boulevard, Rm. 956-MSC4874, Bethesda, MD 20892-4874. Phone: (301) 350-0864.

Internet: dpcpsi.nih.gov/orip/index. (Note: no field offices for this program.)

93.358 ADVANCED EDUCATION NURSING TRAINEESHIPS (AENT)

Assistance: project grants.

Purposes: pursuant to PHSA as amended and HPEPA, to provide financial support through traineeships for 36 months to nurses at the master's or doctoral level, preparing full-time for careers as nurse educators, clinical specialists, practitioners, administrators, midwives, public health nurses, and other approved specialties—and for nurse anesthetists for one year only.

Eligible applicants: schools of nursing, academic health centers, public or private nonprofit entities.

Eligible beneficiaries: U.S. citizens, nationals, or permanent residents licensed as registered nurses, enrolled full-time in graduate courses toward a master's degree or doctoral program.

Range: $100,155 to $350,000. **Average:** $225,078.

Activity: N.A.

HQ: Division of Nursing, Bureau of Health Professions, HRSA-HHS, Parklawn Bldg., Rm. 9-89, 5600 Fishers Ln., Rockville, MD 20857. Phone: (301) 443-6739.

Internet: www.hrsa.gov.

93.359   NURSE EDUCATION, PRACTICE QUALITY AND RETENTION GRANTS

Assistance: project grants. (100 percent/to 5 years).

Purposes: pursuant to PHSA as amended and Nurse Reinvestment Act of 2002, to expand enrollment in baccalaureate nursing programs; to develop and implement internship and residency programs to encourage mentoring and the development of specialties; to provide education in new technologies including distance learning methodologies. Practice methodologies include: establishing or expanding nursing practice arrangements in non-institutional settings to demonstrate methods to improve access to primary health care in medically underserved areas; providing care for underserved populations and other high-risk groups such as the elderly, persons with HIV-AIDS, substance abusers, the homeless, and victims of domestic violence; providing managed care, quality improvement, and other skills needed to practice in existing and emerging organized health care systems; developing cultural competencies; promoting career mobility, cross training, or specialty training.

Eligible applicants/beneficiaries: collegiate schools of nursing, health care facilities, or partnerships involving academic health centers, state and local governments, and other public or private nonprofit or profit entities and community-based organizations.

Range/Average: N.A.

Activity: N.A.

HQ: Division of Nursing, Bureau of Health Professions, HRSA-HHS, Parklawn Bldg., Rm. 9-89, 5600 Fishers Ln., Rockville, MD 20857. Phone: (301) 443-0791.

Internet: www.hrsa.gov.

93.360   BIOMEDICAL ADVANCED RESEARCH AND DEVELOPMENT AUTHORITY (BARDA), BIODEFENSE MEDICAL COUNTERMEASURE DEVELOPMENT

Assistance: cooperative agreements/discretionary grants; project grants/discretionary (100 percent/to 5 years).

Purposes: pursuant to the Consolidated Appropriations Act of 2010, to support international in-country and domestic advanced development and industrialization of human pandemic influenza vaccine, including activities related to the mitigation of the global shortage of influenza vaccines through awards and sub-awards to developing countries with the potential and capacity to manufacture various influenza vaccines. Funds may not be used for basic research (e.g. scientific or medical experiments).

Eligible applicants: eligible entities, including highly-qualified foreign nationals outside the U.S. either alone or in collaboration with American participants.

Eligible beneficiaries: general public, especially at-risk individuals including children, pregnant women, and the elderly.

Range: $250,000 to $15,000,000. **Average:** N.A.

Activity: N.A.

HQ: Director, Biomedical Advanced Research and Development Authority, 330 Independence Ave., SW, Rm. G-640, Washington, DC 20201. Phone: (202) 260-8535.

Internet: www.medicalcountermeasures.gov. (Note: no field offices for this program.)

93.361 NURSING RESEARCH

Assistance: project grants. (100 percent/to 5 years).

Purposes: pursuant to PHSA as amended and SBRDEA, for clinical and basic research to establish a scientific basis for the care of individuals across the life span—from management of patients during illness and recovery to the reduction of risks for disease and disability and the promotion of healthy lifestyles, and extending to: patients, families, and care givers; special needs of at-risk and underserved populations; improving clinical care settings; translating scientific advances into cost-effective health care; bioethical issues. The Centers Program: promotes interdisciplinary research; supports research training and career development activities; concentrates research resources on selected research areas through Core Centers for Nursing Research. NRSA, SBIR, and STTR awards are available.

Eligible applicants/beneficiaries: research—any corporation, public or private institution or agency, SBIR firm, or other legal entity whether profit or nonprofit; individuals. NRSA applicants must be registered professional nurses with a baccalaureate or master's degree in nursing or a related field.

Range/Average: N.A.

Activity: anticipates 264 research grants, 57 NRSA individual awards, 151 NRSA institutional awards in FY 2016.

HQ: National Institute of Nursing Research, NIH-HHS, 31 Center Dr., Bethesda, MD 20892. Phone: (301) 496.8230.

Internet: www.ninr.nih.gov. (Note: no field offices for this program.)

93.364 NURSING STUDENT LOANS (NSL)

Assistance: direct loans (90 percent).

Purposes: pursuant to PHSA as amended and HPEPA, for nursing schools to make 5 percent interest, long-term loans to full- or half-time students with financial needs. The maximum loan in any one year is $2,500, except

$4,000 for each of the final two years of study; the total borrowed may not exceed $13,000.

Eligible applicants/beneficiaries: accredited public and private nonprofit schools of nursing. Students must be U.S. citizens, nationals, or permanent residents.

Range: $3,420 to $345,790. **Average:** $50,619.

Activity: N.A.

HQ: Division of Health Careers Diversity and Development, Bureau of Health Professions, HRSA-HHS, 5600 Fishers Ln., Rm. 9-105, Rockville, MD 20857. Phone: (301) 443-1173.

Internet: bhw.hrsa.gov/scholarshipsloans/index.html.

93.365 SICKLE CELL TREATMENT DEMONSTRATION PROGRAM (SCTDP)

Assistance: project grants (100 percent).

Purposes: pursuant to American Jobs Creation Act of 2004, to develop and establish partnerships to enhance the prevention and treatment of sickle cell disease through coordination of service delivery, genetic counseling and testing, bundling of technical services, training of health professionals, and patient and provider education.

Eligible applicants/beneficiaries: federally-qualified health centers, nonprofit hospitals or clinics, university health centers providing primary care.

Range:Average: $356,618.

Activity: N.A.

HQ: Genetic Services Branch, Division of Services for Children with Special Health Needs, Maternal and Child Health Bureau, HRSA-HHS, 5600 Fishers Ln., Rm. 18A-19, Rockville MD 20857. Phone: (301) 443-9775.

Internet: www.hrsa.gov.

93.389 NATIONAL CENTER FOR RESEARCH RESOURCES

Assistance: project grants. (50-100 percent/1-5 years).

Purposes: pursuant to PHSA as amended and SBRDEA, for primary research to discover and develop critical resources, models, and technologies; to provide biomedical researchers with access to diverse instrumentation, technologies, basic and clinical research facilities, animal models, genetic stocks, biomaterials, and similar resources—enabling advances in biomedicine leading to lifesaving drugs, devices, and therapies. Awards are provided through program mechanisms including: Biomedical Technology Resource (BTR) grants; research project grants; Shared Instrumentation Grants (SIG); High End Instrumentation (HEI); Exploratory Grants. The Division of Clinical Research Resources helps translate scientific knowledge into effective patient care through General Clinical Research Centers (GCRC); such programs as Research Career Development, Mentored Clinical Research Scholar, National Gene Vector Laboratories (NGVL), Science Educational Partnership Award (SEPA); NRSA, SBIR, and STTR awards are available. The Division of Comparative Medicine (DCM) supports National Primate Research Centers (NPRC), Biological

Models and Materials Research (BMMR), and Laboratory Animal Science (LAS) programs. The Division of Research Infrastructure (DRI) supports enhancement of the research environment at minority institutions through grants supporting programs including: Research Centers in Minority Institutions (RCMI); Clinical Research Infrastructure Initiative (RCRII); Institutional Development Awards (IDA); Animal Facilities Improvement; and, Research Facilities Improvement Program (RFIP).

Eligible applicants/beneficiaries: BTR grants—U.S. nonprofit health professional schools, other academic institutions, hospitals, state and local health agencies, research organizations. SIG and HEI awards—institutions only. GCRCs—schools, research hospitals, and other institutions. Research career development—public or private domestic, nonfederal organizations, and IHEs on behalf of candidates. SEPA—IHEs, professional organizations, school systems, scientific societies, science museums, and similar applicants. DCM—IHEs, hospitals, nonprofit and profit organizations. DRI programs—predominantly minority institutions, organizations with historically low success rate in obtaining NIH funding, and nonprofit and some profit organizations, depending on program.

Range/Average: N.A.

Activity: N.A.

HQ: National Center for Research Resources, NIH-HHS, 6701 Democracy Boulevard, Rm. 956-MSC4874, Bethesda, MD 20892-4874. Phone: (301) 350-0864.

Internet: www.nih.gov. (Note: no field offices for this program.)

93.393   CANCER CAUSE AND PREVENTION RESEARCH

Assistance: project grants. (100 percent/to 5 years).

Purposes: pursuant to PHSA as amended and SBRDEA, for research into the causes of cancer and to develop prevention mechanisms. Programs include: epidemiology; chemical, physical, and biological carcinogenesis; nutrition; immunology; field studies and statistics; organ site. Grant funds may be used for personnel and consultants, equipment, patient costs, laboratory animals, alterations, and renovations. SBIR and STTR awards are made.

Eligible applicants/beneficiaries: IHEs, hospitals, public agencies, nonprofit research institutions, or profit organizations.

Range: $5,887 to $5,022,000. **Average:** $433,732.

Activity: anticipate 1,348 awards in FY 2016.

HQ: National Cancer Institute, NIH-HHS, 9609 Medical Center Dr., 7th Fl., West Tower, 7W532, MSC 9750, Rockville, MD 20850. Phone: 240-276-6443; FAX: 240-276-7682.

Internet: www.cancer.gov. (Note: no field offices for this program.)

93.394   CANCER DETECTION AND DIAGNOSIS RESEARCH

Assistance: project grants. (100 percent/to 5 years).

Purposes: pursuant to PHSA as amended and SBRDEA, for research to improve cancer screening, early detection, and diagnostic techniques and methods. Grant funds may be used for patient costs, laboratory animals, equipment, renovations, alterations, personnel and consultant costs. SBIR and STTR awards are made.

Eligible applicants/beneficiaries: IHEs, hospitals, public agencies, nonprofit research institutions, or profit organizations.

Range: $3,941 to $2,528,000. **Average:** $408,935.

Activity: anticipate that 707 awards will be made in FY 2016.

HQ: Associate Director, Cancer Diagnosis Program, Division of Cancer Treatment and Diagnosis, National Cancer Institute, NIH-HHS, 69609 Medical Center Dr., 7th Fl., West Tower, 7W532, MSC 9750, Rockville, MD 20850. Phone: 240-276-6443; FAX: 240-276-7682.

Internet: prevention.cancer.gov. (Note: no field offices for this program.)

93.395 CANCER TREATMENT RESEARCH

Assistance: project grants. (100 percent/to 5 years).

Purposes: pursuant to PHSA as amended and SBRDEA, for fundamental, applied, and clinical cancer treatment research in all modes of therapy including surgery, radiotherapy, chemotherapy, and biological therapy. Supportive approaches include nutrition, stem cell and bone marrow transplantation, blood component replacement, toxicology, pharmacology. Grant funds may be used for patient costs, laboratory animals, alterations, renovations, personnel and consultant costs. SBIR and STTR awards are made.

Eligible applicants/beneficiaries: IHEs, hospitals, public agencies, nonprofit research institutions, or profit organizations.

Range: $3,975 to $6,300,000. **Average:** $427,084.

Activity: anticipate 1,146 awards will be made in FY 2016.

HQ: Division of Cancer Treatment and Diagnosis, National Cancer Institute, NIH-HHS, 9609 Medical Center Dr., 7th Fl., West Tower, 7W532, MSC 9750, Rockville, MD 20850. Phone: 240-276-6443; FAX: 240-276-7682.

Internet: www.cancer.gov/cancertopics/treatment. (Note: no field offices for this program.)

93.396 CANCER BIOLOGY RESEARCH

Assistance: project grants. (100 percent/to 5 years).

Purposes: pursuant to PHSA as amended and SBRDEA, for cancer biology research, including in the areas of nutrition, tumor biology, genetics, and immunology—toward the prevention, detection, diagnosis, and treatment of neoplastic diseases. Grant funds may be used for patient costs, laboratory animals, renovations, alterations, personnel and consultant costs. SBIR and STTR awards are made.

Eligible applicants/beneficiaries: IHEs, hospitals, public agencies, nonprofit research institutions, or profit organizations.

Range: $2,332 to $4,222,000. **Average:** $353,936.

Activity: anticipate 1,433 awards will be made in FY 2016.

HQ: Deputy Director, Division of Cancer Biology, National Cancer Institute (EPN-5050), NIH-HHS, 9609 Medical Center Dr., 7th Fl., West Tower, 7W532, MSC 9750, Rockville, MD 20850. Phone: 240-276-6443; FAX: 240-276-7682.

Internet: dcb.nci.nih.gov. (Note: no field offices for this program.)

93.397 CANCER CENTERS SUPPORT GRANTS

Assistance: project grants. (100 percent/to 5 years).

Purposes: pursuant to PHSA as amended, to provide core funding for comprehensive and specialized cancer centers, supporting the coordination of interdisciplinary programs ranging from basic research to clinical investigation to population science. Funds may be used for professional staff, centralized shared resources and services, and recruitment. Generally, research projects are not supported as such; rather, grants enhance ongoing research.

Eligible applicants/beneficiaries: U.S. nonprofit institutions with a peer-reviewed cancer research base of $4,000,000.

Range: $1,000 to $12,353,000. **Average:** $2,105,271.

Activity: anticipate 258 awards in FY 2016.

HQ: Chief, Cancer Centers Branch, Office of Centers, Training and Resources, NIH-HHS, 9609 Medical Center Dr., 7th Fl., West Tower, 7W532, MSC 9750, Rockville, MD 20850. Phone: 240-276-6443; FAX: 240-276-7682.

Internet: cancercenters.cancer.gov. (Note: no field offices for this program.)

93.398 CANCER RESEARCH MANPOWER

Assistance: project grants. (100 percent/to 5 years).

Purposes: pursuant to PHSA as amended, for biomedical training programs in basic, clinical, and cancer prevention research, and for fellowships to trainees under the NRSA program. Cancer Education Grants are also available to promote cancer education programs. Various career awards provide short-term support for students.

Eligible applicants/beneficiaries: IHEs, hospitals, public agencies, or nonprofit research institutions; U.S. citizens or permanent residents. Cancer Education Grants, career awards—profit organizations.

Range: $6,36 to $1,358,000. **Average:** $151,630.

Activity: anticipate that 1,114 awards will be made in FY 2016.

HQ: Chief, Cancer Training Branch, National Cancer Institute, NIH-HHS, 9609 Medical Center Dr., 7th Fl., West Tower, 7W532, MSC 9750, Rockville, MD 20850. Phone: 240-276-6443; FAX: 240-276-7682.

Internet: www.cancer.gov/researchandfunding/training. (Note: no field offices for this program.)

93.399 CANCER CONTROL
("Cancer Control Grants")

Assistance: project grants. (100 percent/to 5 years).

Purposes: pursuant to PHSA as amended, for basic and applied research in cancer prevention and interventions. Programs include chemo-prevention; cancer communications; diet, nutrition, and physical activity; screening and early detection; biobehavioral mechanisms; tobacco control; special populations research; cancer survivorship; health services and outcomes research; surveillance research. Grant funds may be used for patient costs, renovations, alterations, personnel and consultant costs, and laboratory animals. SBIR and STTR awards are made.

Eligible applicants/beneficiaries: IHEs, hospitals, public agencies, nonprofit research institutions, or profit organizations.

Range/Average: N.A.

Activity: 1 award made in FY 2014.

HQ: Director, Division of Cancer Prevention, National Cancer Institute, NIH-HHS, 9609 Medical Center Dr., 7th Fl., West Tower, 7W532, MSC 9750, Rockville, MD 20850. Phone: 240-276-6443; FAX: 240-276-7682.

Internet: cancercontrol.cancer.gov. (Note: no field offices for this program.)

93.400 NATIONAL HEALTH SERVICE CORPS SCHOLARSHIP PROGRAM

Assistance: direct payments/specified use (100 percent/to 4 years).

Purposes: pursuant to ARRA 2009, to increase supply of primary care physicians, dentists, behavioral and mental health professionals, certified nurse midwives, certified family nurse practitioners, and physician assistants as needed by NHSC in Health Professional Shortage Areas (HPSA) within the U.S. by providing service-obligated scholarships to health professions students. Each year of support incurs 1 year of service with a 2 year minimum service commitment requirement post graduation. A maximum of 4 years of support may be awarded.

Eligible applicants/beneficiaries: students of health professions/U.S. citizens.

Range/Average: N.A.

Activity: N.A.

HQ: Office of Financial Management, HRSA-HHS, 5600 Fishers Ln., Rm. 8C-26, Rockville, MD 20857. Phone: (301) 594-4400.

Internet: nhsc.hrsa.gov.

93.401 NATIONAL HEALTH SERVICE CORPS LOAN REPAYMENT (ARRA)

Assistance: direct payments/specified use (from 2 years).

Purposes: pursuant to ARRA of 2009, to increase supply of health care professionals (especially primary care physicians, dentists, dental hygienist, behavioral and mental health professionals, certified nurse midwives, certified family nurse practitioners, and physician assistants) in Health Professional Shortage Areas (HPSA) within the U.S. and territories by assisting the repayment of qualifying educational loans in return for service at an approved NHSC community site.

Eligible applicants/beneficiaries: specialty-specific, certified and licensed health professionals who are US citizens.

Range/Average: N.A.

Activity: N.A.

HQ: HRSA-HHS, 5600 Fishers Ln., Rm. 8C-26, Rockville, MD 20857. Phone: (301) 594-4400.

Internet: nhsc.hrsa.gov.

93.403 GRANTS FOR TRAINING IN PRIMARY CARE MEDICINE AND DENTISTRY TRAINING AND ENHANCEMENT

Assistance: project grants (100 percent/2 years).

Purposes: pursuant to ARRA of 2009, to plan, develop, and operate or maintain programs for training physician assistants or individuals who teach in programs of such training; to provide grants to dental schools, approved residency and advanced education programs in general or pediatric dentistry for planning, developing or operating programs; to provide financial assistance to residents in such programs; and to develop, implement and disseminate innovative curriculum through means of cooperative agreements or contracts. Grants may not be used for new construction or patient services.

Eligible applicants: public and private nonprofit IHEs, schools, institutions/organizations.

Eligible beneficiaries: health/education professionals.

Range/Average: N.A.

Activity: N.A.

HQ: HRSA-HHS, 5600 Fishers Ln., Rm. 12C-06, Rockville, MD 20857. Phone: (301) 443-6190.

Internet: www.hrsa.gov.

93.409 FACULTY LOAN REPAYMENT PROGRAMS (FLRP)

Assistance: direct payments/specified use (to 2 years).

Purposes: pursuant to ARRA 2009 and PHSA, Title VII, Executive Order, as amended, to provide a financial incentive for degree-trained health professionals from disadvantaged backgrounds to pursue academic careers in allopathic medicine, nursing (RN only), osteopathic medicine, dentistry, pharmacy, podiatric medicine, optometry, veterinary medicine, public or allied health or graduate programs in behavioral and mental health practice for a minimum of 2 years. Eligible educational loans incurred by the applicant will be repaid in return for serving a minimum of 2 years as a full-time or part-time faculty member at one of the qualified accredited health profession colleges or universities. FLRP will pay up to $20,000 a year (maximum amount: $40,000 for 2 years) in return for a two year service commitment obligation, based on the participant's outstanding balance of eligible educational loans.

Eligible applicants/beneficiaries: degree-trained health professionals from disadvantaged backgrounds.

Range/Average: N.A.

Activity: N.A.

HQ: HRSA-HHS, 5600 Fishers Ln., Rm. 9C-14, Rockville, MD 20857. Phone: (301) 594-4130.

Internet: www.hrsa.gov/loanscholarships/repayment/faculty. (Note: no field offices for this program.)

93.433 NATIONAL INSTITUTE ON DISABILITY, INDEPENDENT LIVING, AND REHABILITATION RESEARCH

Assistance: cooperative agreements. (99 percent/to 5 years).

Purposes: pursuant to the Rehabilitation Act of 1973, Title II, as amended, to support and coordinate research and its utilization in order to improve the lives of people of all ages with physical and mental disabilities, especially persons with severe disabilities. Funds are awarded for research, demonstration, dissemination/utilization projects of national significance, and career training projects.

Eligible applicants: state, local, and tribal institutions/organizations, and public and private nonprofits.

Eligible beneficiaries: individuals with disabilities.

Range/Average: N.A.

Activity: N.A.

HQ: Administration for Community Living, HHS, 330 C St., SW, Washington, DC 20201. Phone: (202) 795-7313.

Internet: N.A. (Note: no field offices for this program.)

93.441 INDIAN SELF-DETERMINATION ("638 Contracts")

Assistance: direct payments/specified use.

Purposes: pursuant to Contract Disputes Act of 1978 and ISDEAA, as amended, to enable Indian tribes to assume the management and operation of programs, functions, services, and activities for delivery of health care to Indian people through self-determination contracts.

Eligible applicants/beneficiaries: federally-recognized tribes or tribal organizations.

Range: $31,963 to $25,950,652. **Average:** $1,722,872.

Activity: N.A.

HQ: Grants Policy Office, IHS-HHS, 801 Thompson Ave., Suite TMP 360, Rockville, MD 20852. Phone: (301) 443-5204.

Internet: www.ihs.gov. (Note: no field offices for this program.)

93.442 SPECIAL DIABETES PROGRAM FOR INDIANS (SDPI) DIABETES PREVENTION AND HEALTHY HEART INITIATIVE

Assistance: project grants. (100 percent/5 years).

Purposes: for demonstration projects to implement and evaluate primary prevention of diabetes or prevention of cardiovascular disease in Indians with diabetes.

Eligible applicants/beneficiaries: IHS hospitals or clinics; tribes; Urban Indian Health Programs; consortia.

Range: $137,500 to $397,000. **Average:** $340,915.

Activity: N.A.

HQ: Grants Policy Office, 5600 Fishers Ln., Stop: 09E70, Rockville, MD 20852. Phone: (301) 443-5204.

Internet: www.ihs.gov.

93.444 TRIBAL SELF-GOVERNANCE PROGRAM: PLANNING AND NEGOTIATION COOPERATIVE AGREEMENT ("Tribal Self Governance")

Assistance: project grants (100 percent/1 year).

Purposes: pursuant to Indian Self-Determination and Education Assistance Act as amended, to enable Indian tribes to assume programs, functions, services, and activities that will benefit tribes or Indians as primary or significant beneficiaries. These programs will be administered by HHS through IHS.

Eligible applicants: federally-recognized Indian tribes who have completed specific applicant prerequisites.

Eligible beneficiaries: Indian tribes.

Range: $48,000 to $120,000. **Average:** N.A.

Activity: anticipate 10 awards in FY 2016.

HQ: Grants Policy Office, IHS-HHS, 801 Thompson Ave., Suite TMP 360, Rockville, MD 20852. Phone: (301) 443-5204.

Internet: www.ihs.gov. (Note: no field offices for this program.)

93.448 FOOD SAFETY AND SECURITY MONITORING PROJECT ("FERN Grant Program")

Assistance: project grants. (100 percent/1-3 years).

Purposes: pursuant to the Public Health Security and Bioterrorism Preparedness and Response Act of 2002, to expand participation in networks to enhance federal, state, tribal, and local food safety and security testing programs; to promote a continuing, reliable capability and capacity for laboratory sample analyses of foods and food products for the rapid detection and identification of toxic chemicals or toxins. Funding supports provision of supplies, personnel, facility upgrades, training, and participation in proficiency testing to establish additional reliable laboratory sample analysis capacity and analysis of surveillance samples.

Eligible applicants/beneficiaries: state, local, and tribal government food emergency response laboratories.

Range: $240,000 to $618,000. **Average:** N.A.

Activity: N.A.

HQ: Division of Field Science, Office of Regulatory Affairs, FDA-HHS, 12420 Parklawn Dr., Rm. 3042, Rockville, MD 20857. Phone: 301-796-5830.

Internet: www.fda.gov/ForFederalStateandLocalOfficials/CooperativeAgreementsCRADAsGrants/default.htm.

93.449 RUMINANT FEED BAN SUPPORT PROJECT ("BSE Grant Program")

Assistance: project grants. (100 percent/to 3 years).

Purposes: pursuant to the Public Health Security and Bioterrorism Preparedness and Response Act of 2002, to increase surveillance throughout commercial feed channels to prevent the introduction or amplification of "BSE" in the U.S.A. Funds must supplement annual state program appropriations, and may be used for inspections or salvagers of food and feed and transporters of animal feed and ingredients, supplies, training, laboratory equipment for feed sample testing.

Eligible applicants/beneficiaries: state and tribal feed/BSE regulatory programs.

Range: $250,000 to $350,000 per award, per year.

Activity: N.A.

HQ: Division of Federal-State Relations, Office of Regulatory Affairs, 12420 Parklawn Dr., Rm. 3042, Rockville, MD 20857. Phone: (301) 796-5830.

Internet: www.fda.gov/ForFederalStateandLocalOfficials/CooperativeAgre ementsCRADAsGrants/ucm234348.htm.

93.452 HEALTH IMPROVEMENT FOR RE-ENTERING EX-OFFENDERS INITIATIVE (HIRE) HIV/AIDS ("HIRE Program")

Assistance: cooperative agreements (100 percent/to 3 years).

Purposes: pursuant to the Public Health Service Act, as amended, to support projects or activities consistent with the mission of the Office of Minority Health of the U.S. Public Health Service, that facilitate improvement in the HIV/AIDS health outcomes of ex-offenders re-entering the mainstream population.

Eligible applicants: local and tribal governments, private nonprofit community-based, minority-serving organizations which address health, human, or correctional services or faith-based organizations which provide comprehensive pre-release, transitional or reentry services. Eligible applicants must be located within one of the three targeted states of New York, Florida, or Texas with a minimum of five years experience providing HIV/AIDS related health and support services.

Eligible beneficiaries: reentry populations in the three targeted states, with special emphasis on the following reentry subpopulations: substance abusers, men who have sex with men, and individuals impacted by mental health disorders.

Range: $200,000 to $250,000. **Average:** N.A.

Activity: N.A.

HQ: Office on Women's Health, HHS, Tower Bldg., 1101 Wootton Parkway, Suite 550, Rockville, MD 20852. Phone: (240) 453-8822.

Internet: www.minorityhealth.hhs.gov.

93.464 ACL ASSISTIVE TECHNOLOGY

Assistance: project grants/discretionary. (100 percent/1 year).

Purposes: pursuant to the Assistive Technology Act of 1998, to support State efforts to improve the provision of assistive technology to individuals with disabilities through comprehensive statewide programs of technology-related assistance.

Eligible applicants: states and territories.

Eligible beneficiaries: individuals with disabilities.

Range/Average: N.A.

Activity: N.A.

HQ: Administration for Community Living, DHHS, One Massachusetts Ave., NW, 4th Fl., Washington, DC 20201. Phone: (202) 245-7393.

Internet: www.acl.gov. (Note: no field offices for this program.)

93.501   AFFORDABLE CARE ACT (ACA) GRANTS FOR SCHOOL-BASED HEALTH CENTER CAPITAL EXPENDITURES (SBHCC)

Assistance: project grants (100 percent/2 years).

Purposes: pursuant to the Patient Protection and Affordable Care Act of 2010, to expand capacity to provide primary healthcare services to school-aged children. Competitive funding will be available to new and existing school-based health centers to address significant and pressing capital improvement needs. An eligible school-based health center is a health clinic that is: located in or near a school facility of a school district or board of an Indian tribe/tribal organization, organized through school, community, and health provider relationships, administered by a sponsoring facility and that provides primary health services to children in accordance with state/local law (including licensure and certification).

Eligible applicants: school-based health centers or their sponsoring facilities (including hospitals, public health departments, community health centers, non-profit health care agencies, school or school systems, programs administered by the Indian Health Service, Bureau of Indian Affairs or operated by an Indian tribe/tribal organizations).

Eligible beneficiaries: school-aged children, their communities.

Range: $11,000 to $500,000. **Average:** $350,000.

Activity: N.A.

HQ: HRSA-HHS, 5600 Fishers Ln., Rm. 17C-26, Rockville, MD 20857. Phone: (301) 443-1034.

Internet: www.hrsa.gov. (Note: no field offices for this program.)

93.502   AFFORDABLE CARE ACT (ACA) INFRASTRUCTURE TO EXPAND ACCESS TO CARE (IEAC)

Assistance: project grants (40 percent/5 years).

Purposes: pursuant to the Patient Protection and Affordable Care Act of 2010, to meet the cost of projects for debt service on, or direct construction or renovation of a health care facility that provides research, inpatient tertiary care, or outpatient clinical services and is affiliated with an academic health center at a public research university that contains a state's sole public academic medical and dental school. Eligible states must have an established funding mechanism to provide the required 60 percent funding to complete the project.

Eligible applicants: eligible IHEs.

Eligible beneficiaries: eligible IHEs, general public.

Range/Average: N.A.

Activity: N.A.

HQ: Chief, Facilities Services Branch, Division of Poison Control and Healthcare Facilities, Healthcare Systems Bureau, Health Resources and Services Administration, HHS, Parklawn Bldg., Rm. 08W-50, 5600 Fishers Ln., Rockville, MD 20857. Phone: (301) 443-5656.

Internet: www.hrsa.gov.

93.504   FAMILY TO FAMILY HEALTH INFORMATION CENTERS ("F2F HICs")

Assistance: project grants (100 percent/3 years).

Purposes: pursuant to the Social Security Act, Title V, Section 501(c)(A) as amended by the Patient Protection and Affordable Care Act of 2010, to carry out special maternal and child health (MCH) projects of regional and national significance for the development and support of Family to Family Health Information Centers that: assist families of children and youth with special health care needs (CYSHCN) in making informed choices about health care, including promoting good treatment decisions, cost-effectiveness, and improved health outcomes for their children; develop a model for collaboration between families of CYSHCN and health professionals; and are staffed by health professionals and families with expertise in federal and state public/private health care systems.

Eligible applicants: eligible public/private entities including Indian tribes/tribal organizations, faith-based and community-based organizations focused on families of CYSHCN located in the 50 States and DC.

Eligible beneficiaries: eligible public/private agencies, organizations/ institutions, CYSHCN, their families and communities.

Range: N.A. **Average:** $95,700.

Activity: 51 projects funded in FY 2016.

HQ: Director, Integrated Services Branch, Division of Services for Children with Special Health Needs, Health Resources and Services Administration, HHS, 5600 Fishers Ln., Rm. 13-103, Rockville, MD 20857. Phone: (301) 443-2372.

Internet: www.mchb.hrsa.gov.

93.506   AFFORDABLE CARE ACT (ACA) NATIONWIDE PROGRAM FOR NATIONAL AND STATE BACKGROUND CHECKS FOR DIRECT PATIENT ACCESS EMPLOYEES OF LONG TERM CARE FACILITIES AND PROVIDERS

Assistance: project grants (75 percent/to 3 years).

Purposes: pursuant to the Affordable Care Act (ACA), funding for a nationwide program to identify efficient, effective, and economical procedures for long term care facilities and providers to conduct background checks on a statewide basis on all prospective direct patient access employees. Participating states must require fingerprint checks as part of the criminal background check for all direct patient access employees. Participating states must also have a plan to implement the program statewide and in all long term care entities specified in the ACA, although the State may phase in the program over a multi-year period. In order to participate in this program, a state must guarantee that it will make available non-Federal funds to cover a portion of the program costs.

Eligible applicants: states and U.S. territories.

Eligible beneficiaries: providers of long term care services as designated by participating states.

Range: $1,500,000 to $3,000,000. **Average:** N.A.

Activity: N.A.

HQ: Director, ACA Nationwide Program for National and State Background Checks for Direct Patient Access Employees of Long Term Care Facilities and Providers, CMS-HHS, 7500 Security Blvd., Baltimore, MD 21244. Phone: 410-786-3270.

Internet: N.A. (Note: no field offices for this program.)

93.507 NATIONAL PUBLIC HEALTH IMPROVEMENT INITIATIVE

Assistance: cooperative agreements (100 percent/1 to 5 years).

Purposes: pursuant to the Public Health Act and Prevention and Public Health Fund (PPHF), this program is part of the CDC's larger effort to increase the performance management capacity of public health departments in order to ensure that public health goals are effectively and efficiently met. Continuation funding is available to all current awardees to provide support for accelerating public health accreditation readiness activities, providing additional support for performance management and improvement practices and developing, identifying and disseminating innovative and evidence-based policies and practices. Cross-jurisdictional collaborations are encouraged.

Eligible applicants/beneficiaries: 35 IHEs selected by the CDC as Prevention Research Centers (PRCs).

Range: $100,000 to $400,000 for Component I; $1,000,000 to $2,950,000 for Component II. **Average:** N.A.

Activity: N.A.

HQ: Program Director, CDC, HHS, 2500 Century Pkwy., Atlanta, GA 30329. Phone: (404) 498-6792.

Internet: www.cdc.gov.

93.508 AFFORDABLE CARE ACT (ACA) TRIBAL MATERNAL, INFANT, AND EARLY CHILDHOOD HOME VISITING PROGRAM

Assistance: project grants (100 percent/to 5 years).

Purposes: pursuant to the Affordable Care Act (ACA), funding to strengthen and improve maternal and child health programs, improve service coordination for at-risk communities, and identify and provide comprehensive evidence-based home visiting services to families who reside in at-risk communities. Funds under the Tribal Maternal, Infant, and Early Childhood Home Visiting Program (TMIECHV) will support: conducting a

Tribal needs assessment that considers community characteristics; the quality and capacity of existing home visiting programs, and other supportive services; coordinates with other relevant needs assessments; and involves community stakeholders as appropriate; collaborative planning efforts to address identified needs by developing capacity and infrastructure to fully plan, adopt, implement, and sustain high-quality home visiting programs that have strong fidelity to evidence-based and promising home visiting models; providing high-quality evidence-based home visiting services to pregnant women and families with young children aged birth to kindergarten entry; and conducting rigorous local evaluations that may include examining effectiveness of home visiting models in serving Tribal populations; adaptations of home visiting models for Tribal communities; or questions regarding implementation or infrastructure necessary to support evidence-based home visitation models.

Eligible applicants: federally-recognized Indian tribes (or a consortium of Indian tribes), tribal organizations, or urban Indian organizations, as defined by Indian Health Care Improvement Act.

Eligible beneficiaries: pregnant women and families with young children aged birth to kindergarten residing in at-risk American Indian/Alaskan Native communities who have been determined to be in need of services, in a needs assessment.

Range: $265,000 to $600,000. **Average:** $300,000.

Activity: it is estimated that 21 grants will be awarded in FY 2016.

HQ: Director, Tribal Home Visiting (HV) Program and Tribal Research Center for Early Childhood (TRCEC), Child Care Bureau, Office of Family Assistance, ACF-HHS, 901 D St., SW, 2nd Fl., West 2B002, Washington, DC 20447. Phone: (202) 260-8515.

Internet: www.acf.hhs.gov/programs. (Note: no field offices for this program.)

93.510 AFFORDABLE CARE ACT (ACA) PRIMARY CARE RESIDENCY EXPANSION PROGRAM ("ACA-PCRE")

Assistance: project grants (100 percent/5 years).

Purposes: pursuant to Public Health Service Act as amended by the Patient Protection and Affordable Care Act, to increase the number of physicians trained in family medicine, general internal medicine, and general pediatrics residency programs. Grantees are primary care residency programs that commit to increasing their number of training positions by one to four new post-graduate year positions for five consecutive years and may request support for only one residency program (discipline). Funds are for resident salary including fringe benefits, indirect costs, training expenses, and resident physician travel.

Eligible applicants: eligible applicants include public/nonprofit private hospitals, schools of medicine or osteopathic medicine or public/private nonprofit entities.

Eligible beneficiaries: primary care/family medicine residency training programs, general internal medicine, and general pediatrics.

Range: $960,000 to $3,840,000. **Average:** $1,440,000 for 5 year project.

Activity: N.A.

HQ: Project Officer, Medical Training and Geriatrics Branch, Division of Medicine and Dentistry, Bureau of Health Workforce, HHS, 5600 Fishers Ln., Rm. 9A-27, Rockville, MD 20857. Phone: (301) 443-3870; FAX: (301) 443-8437.

Internet: www.hrsa.gov.

93.513   AFFORDABLE CARE ACT (ACA) ADVANCED NURSING EDUCATION EXPANSION INITIATIVE ("ACA-ANEE")

Assistance: project grants (100 percent/to 5 years).

Purposes: pursuant to the Public Health Service Act as amended by the Affordable Care Act, to increase the number of students enrolled full-time in accredited primary care Nurse Practitioner and Nurse Midwifery programs and accelerate the graduation of part-time students in such programs by encouraging full-time enrollment. Stipend grant funds may be used to support eligible student stipends that cannot exceed $22,000 per year, including full tuition and fees, reasonable living expenses and other educational costs. The grantee is responsible for the disbursement of grant funds to eligible students.

Eligible applicants: DOED-accredited collegiate schools of nursing, academic health centers, and other private/public entities, offering primary care nurse practitioner and/or a nurse-midwifery programs.

Eligible beneficiaries: eligible students must be U.S. citizens, non-citizen nationals, or foreign nationals with permanent residence visas.

Range/Average: N.A.

Activity: N.A.

HQ: Director, Division of Nursing, Bureau of Health Professions, Health Resources and Services Administration, HHS, 5600 Fishers Ln., Rm. 9C-05, Rockville, MD 20857. Phone: (301) 443-5688.

Internet: bhpr.hrsa.gov/nursing/grants/anee.html.

93.514   AFFORDABLE CARE ACT (ACA) EXPANSION OF PHYSICIAN ASSISTANT TRAINING PROGRAM ("ACA-EPAT")

Assistance: project grants (100 percent/to 5 years).

Purposes: pursuant to the Public Health Service Act as amended by the Patient Protection and Affordable Care Act, to increase the number of physician assistants in the primary care workforce. Awards facilitate the expansion of eligible physician assistant education programs (those that commit to sustaining an increased number of students for five consecutive years) through funding for new student stipends, including: educational expenses, reasonable living expenses, and indirect costs.

Eligible applicants: eligible public/nonprofit academically-affiliated physician assistant education programs.

Eligible beneficiaries: eligible physician assistant students in training who are U.S. citizens, non-citizen nationals, or foreign nationals who possess permanent U.S. residence visas.

Range/Average: N.A.

Activity: N.A.

HQ: Division of Medicine and Dentistry, Bureau of Health Professions, HRSA, HHS, 5600 Fishers Ln., Rm. 9A-27, Rockville, MD 20857. Phone: (301) 443-7662; FAX: (301) 443-8890.

Internet: www.hrsa.gov.

93.516 AFFORDABLE CARE ACT (ACA) PUBLIC HEALTH TRAINING CENTERS PROGRAM ("Regional PHTC Program")

Assistance: cooperative agreements (100 percent/3 to 5 years).

Purposes: pursuant to the Public Health Act, to improve the Nation's public health system by strengthening the technical, scientific, managerial and leadership competencies and capabilities of the current and future public health workforce. To help fund the development and implementation of Public Health Training Centers.

Eligible applicants/beneficiaries: 35 IHEs selected by the CDC as Prevention Research Centers (PRCs).

Range: $705,000 to $1,005,000 for regional PHTCs; to $850,000 for national coordinating center. **Average:** N.A.

Activity: N.A.

HQ: Program Director, Division of Public Health and Interdisciplinary Education, Bureau of Health Professions, Health Resources and Services Administration, HHS, Rm. 9-C-05, 5600 Fishers Ln., Rockville, MD 20857. Phone: (301) 443-3875.

Internet: bhpr.hrsa.gov/grants/publichealth/phtc.html.

93.517 AGING AND DISABILITY RESOURCE CENTER ("ACA ADRC")

Assistance: cooperative agreements/discretionary grants (100 percent/to 2 years).

Purposes: pursuant to the Patient Protection and Affordable Care Act, to help states further develop and strengthen their statewide systems of person-centered information, counseling and access. Aging and Disability Resource Centers (ADRCs) are designed to serve as "visible and trusted" sources where people can turn for objective information about and streamlined access to their publicly supported long-term services, support options and their Medicare benefits and for "one-on-one" counseling and consumer advice in order to fully understand how available options relate to their particular needs.

Eligible applicants: states and local aging and disability programs.

Eligible beneficiaries: older adults and other individuals who access ADRCs counseling, advice and outreach services regarding long-term/support options and Medicare benefits.

Range/Average: N.A.

Activity: N.A.

HQ: Director, Administration for Community Living, HHS, One Massachusetts Ave., NW, Washington, DC 20001. Phone: (202) 357-3417; FAX: (202) 357-3469.

Internet: www.acl.gov. (Note: no field offices for this program.)

93.521   BUILDING EPIDEMIOLOGY, LABORATORY, AND HEALTH INFORMATION SYSTEMS CAPACITY IN THE EPIDEMIOLOGY AND LABORATORY CAPACITY FOR INFECTIOUS DISEASE (ELC) AND EMERGING INFECTIONS PROGRAM (EIP) COOPERATIVE AGREEMENTS

Assistance: cooperative agreements (100 percent).

Purposes: pursuant to the Patient Protection and Affordable Care Act, programs strengthen national infectious disease infrastructure by serving as collaborative platforms for state and local health departments, CDC programs, and academic and various other public health partners to improve the ability to detect and respond to emerging infectious disease EIDs and other public health threats. Specifically, the programs build epidemiology, laboratory, and information systems capacity, integrate epidemiology and laboratory practice, implement active surveillance, and conduct targeted research aimed at improving methods and informing national surveillance and response activities.

Eligible applicants: 50 states, DC, largest local health departments (Chicago, Houston, New York City, Philadelphia, San Antonio) and U.S. territories.

Eligible beneficiaries: anyone, general public.

Range/Average: N.A.

Activity: N.A.

HQ: Director, Scientific and Program Services Branch, Division of Preparedness and Emerging Infections, National Center for Emerging and Zoonotic Diseases, CDC-HHS, 1600 Clifton Rd. NE, MS-C18, Atlanta, GA 30333. Phone: (404) 639-4180; FAX: (404) 639-3106.

Internet: www.cdc.gov. (Note: no field offices for this program.)

93.524   BUILDING CAPACITY OF THE PUBLIC HEALTH SYSTEM TO IMPROVE POPULATION HEALTH THROUGH NATIONAL, NON-PROFIT ORGANIZATIONS

("CBA to Strengthen Public Health Infrastructure and Performance")

Assistance: cooperative agreements (100 percent).

Purposes: pursuant to the Public Health Service Act, to provide capacity building assistance (including training, technical consultation and services, and information transfer) with the goal of strengthening state, tribal, local, and territorial public health infrastructure investments.

Eligible applicants: U.S. non-profit, public health professional organizations, including: the Association of State and Territorial Health Officials (ASTHO), the National Association of County and City Health Officials (NACCHO), the American Public Health Association (APHA), the Council of State and Territorial Epidemiologists (CSTE), the Public Health Foundation (PHF), the National Network of Public Health Institutes (NNPHI), the National Association of Local Boards of Health (NALBOH), and the Association of Maternal and Child Health Programs (AMCHP).

Eligible beneficiaries: state, territorial, and local health departments, tribal health organizations, general public.

Range: $100,000 to $9,000,000. **Average:** N.A.

Activity: N.A.

HQ: Program Director, CDC, HHS, 4770 Buford Hwy. NE, MS: K-90, Atlanta, GA 30345. Phone: 770-488-1523; FAX: 770-488-1600.

Internet: www.cdc.gov/stltpublichealth/funding/rfaot13.html. (Note: no field offices for this program.)

93.525 STATE PLANNING AND ESTABLISHMENT GRANTS FOR THE AFFORDABLE CARE ACT (ACA) EXCHANGES

Assistance: cooperative agreements (100 percent/to 2 years).

Purposes: pursuant to the Patient Protection and Affordable Care Act, to provide assistance for activities related to establishing a Health Insurance Exchange that facilitates the purchase of qualified health plans, provides for the establishment of a Small Business Health Options Program (SHOP Exchange), and meets the requirements set forth by the Secretary and the ACA.

Eligible applicants/beneficiaries: 35 IHEs selected by the CDC as Prevention Research Centers (PRCs).

Range/Average: N.A.

Activity: N.A.

HQ: Director, Office of Acquisition and Grants Management, Centers for Medicare and Medicaid Services, HHS, 200 Independence Ave., SW, Washington DC 20201. Phone: (301) 492-4312.

Internet: www.cciio.cms.gov. (Note: no field offices for this program.)

93.526 AFFORDABLE CARE ACT (ACA) GRANTS FOR CAPITAL DEVELOPMENT IN HEALTH CENTERS ("ACA Capital Development Grants")

Assistance: project grants (100 percent/to 3 years).

Purposes: pursuant to the Affordable Care Act (ACA), project grants to existing health centers under the Public Health Service Acts Health Center Program for immediate facility improvements or building capacity. Funds will be used to address immediate and pressing capital needs or to support the costs of alteration/renovation or construction of a facility that is consistent with the Health Center Programs mission—to provide comprehensive, culturally competent, quality primary healthcare services to medically underserved communities and vulnerable populations.

Eligible applicants: existing health centers currently receiving operational funding under the Health Center Program authorized by the Public Health Service Act.

Eligible beneficiaries: populations in medically underserved areas.

Range/Average: N.A.

Activity: N.A.

HQ: HRSA-HHS, 5600 Fishers Ln., Rm. 17C-26, Rockville, MD 20857. Phone: (301) 594-4300.

Internet: www.hrsa.gov.

93.527 AFFORDABLE CARE ACT (ACA) GRANTS FOR NEW AND EXPANDED SERVICES UNDER THE HEALTH CENTER PROGRAM

Assistance: project grants (100 percent).

Purposes: pursuant to the Public Health Service Act, Section 330, to provide for expanded and sustained national investment in community health centers and to improve the availability, accessibility and provision of primary health care services. Funds may not be used for inpatient services, or to make cash payments to intended recipients of services.

Eligible applicants: public/private non-profit entities, including faith-based and community-based organizations that are currently funded Health Centers under section 330 of the Public Health Service Act.

Eligible beneficiaries: medically underserved communities.

Range/Average: N.A.

Activity: N.A.

HQ: HRSA-HHS, 5600 Fishers Ln., Rm. 17C-26, Rockville, MD 20857. Phone: (301) 594-4300.

Internet: www.hrsa.gov.

93.528 NATIONAL FORUM FOR STATE AND TERRITORIAL CHIEF EXECUTIVES ("National Forum")

Assistance: cooperative agreements (100 percent/to 3 years).

Purposes: pursuant to the Public Health Service Act, the National Forum will work with their constituencies to address cross-cutting publicly-funded health program integration and health access issues identified by the governors and their representatives, including overall goals to: seek alignment of HRSA's ACA-funded programs with state/territorial programs; promote integration of primary care and public health; strengthen the health workforce; and reduce health disparities and improve health equity.

Eligible applicants: Nonprofit, bipartisan or nonpartisan organization that represents governors and their staff from a broad cross section of states, DC, and eligible territories.

Eligible beneficiaries: states, DC, and Commonwealths of the Northern Mariana Islands and Puerto Rico, U.S. flag territories of American Samoa, Guam, U.S. Virgin Islands.

Range/Average: N.A.

Activity: N.A.

HQ: Program Director, 5600 Fishers Ln., Rm. 10C-03, Rockville, MD 20895. Phone: (301) 443-6204; FAX: (301) 443-2286.

Internet: www.hrsa.gov. (Note: no field offices for this program.)

93.529 PRE-EXISTING CONDITION INSURANCE PROGRAM (PCIP)

Assistance: direct payment/specified use.

Purposes: pursuant to Patient Protection and Affordability Care Act and the Health Care and Education Reconciliation Act (collectively known as the Affordable Care Act), to require the Secretary of the Department of Health and Human Services (HHS) to establish, either directly or through contracts with states or nonprofit private entities, a temporary high risk health insurance program to provide access to coverage for uninsured Americans with pre-existing conditions.

Eligible applicants: states.

Eligible beneficiaries: U.S. citizens or legal residents who have been uninsured for at least six months and have a pre-existing condition or have been denied health coverage because of a health condition.

Range/Average: N.A.

Activity: N.A.

HQ: Director, Centers for Medicare and Medicaid Services, HHS, 200 Independence Ave., SW, Washington, DC 20201. Phone: (301) 492-4312.

Internet: www.pcip.com. (Note: no field offices for this program.)

93.531 COMMUNITY TRANSFORMATION GRANTS AND NATIONAL DISSEMINATION AND SUPPORT FOR COMMUNITY TRANSFORMATION GRANTS

Assistance: cooperative agreements (100 percent/1 to 5 years).

Purposes: pursuant to the Public Health Service Act, for Community Transformation Grants: to reduce death and disability from the five leading causes of death through the prevention and control of these conditions and their risk factors. National Dissemination and Support for Community Transformation Grants will support the efforts of the CTG program by funding national non-governmental organizations with a network of community based organizations.

Eligible applicants: state, DC, territorial, local, and tribal governments, small, minority and women-owned businesses, IHEs, research institutions, hospitals, profit/non profit, community-based, faith-based, and tribal organizations.

Eligible beneficiaries: anyone, general public.

Range: $50,000 to $500,000 for grants; $350,000 to $3,500,000 for support. **Average:** N.A.

Activity: N.A.

HQ: Program Director, CDC, HHS, 4770 Buford Hwy. NE, MS-K40, NCCD-PHP, Atlanta, GA 30333. Phone: (770) 488-2524; FAX: (770) 488-5964.

Internet: www.cdc.gov. (Note: no field offices for this program.)

93.533 ENHANCED SURVEILLANCE FOR NEW VACCINE PREVENTABLE DISEASE
("NVSN")

Assistance: cooperative agreements (100 percent).

Purposes: pursuant to the Public Health Service Act, to support a network of sites that provide surveillance and data collection on new vaccine use, the impact of new and upcoming vaccines and other immunoprophylaxis, new vaccine policies or policies under consideration, through enhanced inpatient and Emergency Department (ED) surveillance, applied epidemiologic research, and investigator-initiated investigations.

Eligible applicants/beneficiaries: 35 IHEs selected by the CDC as Prevention Research Centers (PRCs).

Range: $450,000 to $550,000. Average: $500,000.

Activity: N.A.

HQ: Program Director, CDC, HHS, 1600 Clifton Rd. NE, MS A-47, Atlanta, GA 30333. Phone: (404) 639-2102.

Internet: N.A.

93.534 AFFORDABLE CARE ACT PROGRAM FOR EARLY DETECTION OF CERTAIN MEDICAL CONDITIONS RELATED TO ENVIRONMENTAL HEALTH HAZARDS

Assistance: project grants/discretionary (100 percent/to 5 years).

Purposes: pursuant to the Affordable Care Act (ACA), this program provides screening, health education, and outreach services for residents of a geographic area subject to declared public health emergencies under the Comprehensive Environmental Response, Compensation, and Liability Act (CERCLA).

Eligible applicants/beneficiaries: hospital, community or federally-qualified health centers, Indian Health Service facilities, National Cancer Institute-designated cancer centers, state/local government agencies, nonprofit organizations.

Range: $2,000,000 to $3,000,000. Average: N.A.

Activity: N.A.

HQ: Director, Agency for Toxic Substances and Disease Registry, HHS, 4770 Buford Hwy. NE, MS F61, Atlanta, GA 30341-3717. Phone: (770) 488-0572.

Internet: N.A. (Note: no field offices for this program.)

93.535 CHILDHOOD OBESITY RESEARCH DEMONSTRATION (ACA)
("Childhood Obesity Research Demonstration")

Assistance: cooperative agreements (100 percent/4 years).

Purposes: pursuant to the Children's Health Insurance Program Reauthorization Act of 2009, to determine whether an integrated model of primary care and public health approaches in the community, such as policy, systems, and environmental supports for nutrition and physical activity, can improve risk factors for obesity for underserved children ages 2-12 years and their families.

Eligible applicants: state, DC, territorial, local, and tribal governments, IHEs, research institutions, hospitals, profit/non profit, community-based, faith-based, and tribal organizations and consortia.

Eligible beneficiaries: general public, specifically low income children eligible for services under titles XIX and XXI of the SSA, children and their families living at or below the federal poverty level or areas where 50% of students are in schools eligible for the National School Lunch Program.

Range: N.A. **Average:** $1,750,000 for Component A; $1,000,000 for Component B.

Activity: N.A.

HQ: Office of Extramural Research, National Center for Chronic Disease Prevention and Health Promotion, CDCP-HHS, 1600 Clifton Rd., Atlanta, GA 3033. Phone: (770) 488-8390.

Internet: N.A. (Note: no field offices for this program.)

93.537 AFFORDABLE CARE ACT MEDICAID EMERGENCY PSYCHIATRIC DEMONSTRATION

Assistance: direct payment/specified use (to 3 years).

Purposes: pursuant to the Affordable Care Act, to establish a demonstration project under which eligible states shall provide payment to eligible, privately-owned institutions for mental diseases (IMDs) with 17 or more beds. Program funds enable these IMDs to provide medical assistance to Medicaid beneficiaries aged 21 to 65 years who require stabilization for an emergency medical psychiatric condition.

Eligible applicants: state Medicaid agencies.

Eligible beneficiaries: eligible Medicaid beneficiaries aged of 21 to 65 years.

Range/Average: N.A.

Activity: N.A.

HQ: Director, Centers for Medicare and Medicaid Services, HHS, 7500 Security Blvd., Baltimore, Maryland 21244. Phone: (410) 786-4631.

Internet: innovation.cms.gov/initiatives/medicaid-emergency-psychiatric-demo. (Note: no field offices for this program.)

93.538 NATIONAL ENVIRONMENTAL PUBLIC HEALTH TRACKING PROGRAM—NETWORK IMPLEMENTATION (ACA)

Assistance: cooperative agreements (100 percent/3 years).

Purposes: pursuant to the Public Health Service Act, to establish and maintain a nationwide tracking network to obtain integrated health and environmental data and to use this information in support of actions that improve the health of communities.

Eligible applicants: states and local government health departments or their bona fide agents.

Eligible beneficiaries: anyone, general public.

Range: $500,000 to $1,100,000. **Average:** $700,000.

Activity: N.A.

HQ: Director, Agency for Toxic Substances and Disease Registry, HHS, 4770 Buford Hwy. NE, MS F61, Atlanta, GA 30341-3717. Phone: (770) 488-0572.

Internet: www.cdc.gov/ephtracking. (Note: no field offices for this program.)

93.539   CAPACITY BUILDING ASSISTANCE TO STRENGTHEN PUBLIC HEALTH IMMUNIZATION INFRASTRUCTURE AND PERFORMANCE

Assistance: cooperative agreements (100 percent/to 2 years).

Purposes: pursuant to the Public Health Service Act (Section 3170), as amended, to manage the public health force that implements and supports immunization practices in the public and private sectors and to monitor the effectiveness and impact of vaccines in order to maintain an immunization program that is scientifically and programmatically sound.

Eligible applicants/beneficiaries: 35 IHEs selected by the CDC as Prevention Research Centers (PRCs).

Range/Average: N.A.

Activity: N.A.

HQ: Program Director, CDC-HHS, 1600 Clifton Rd. NE, MS A-19, Atlanta, GA 30033. Phone: (404) 639-8715.

Internet: www.cdc.gov. (Note: no field offices for this program.)

93.541   RACIAL AND ETHNIC APPROACHES TO COMMUNITY HEALTH (REACH)

Assistance: cooperative agreements (100 percent).

Purposes: pursuant to the Patient Protection and Affordable Care Act of 2010, to reduce death and disability from leading causes of death through the prevention and control of these conditions and their risk factors, especially among underserved populations. Health priority areas include: breast and cervical cancer, cardiovascular disease, diabetes mellitus, adult/older adult immunization, hepatitis B and/or tuberculosis, asthma, and infant mortality.

Eligible applicants: state, DC, territorial, local, and tribal governments, small, minority and women-owned businesses, IHEs, research institutions, hospitals, profit/non profit, community-based, faith-based and tribal organizations.

Eligible beneficiaries: anyone, general public.

Range/Average: N.A.

Activity: N.A.

HQ: Program Director, REACH, CDC-HHS, 4770 Buford Hwy. NE, MS K30, Atlanta, GA 30341. Phone: (770) 488-5332; FAX: (770) 488-5974.

Internet: N.A. (Note: no field offices for this program.)

93.542 HEALTH PROMOTION AND DISEASE PREVENTION RESEARCH CENTERS
("Prevention Research Centers")

Assistance: cooperative agreements (100 percent).

Purposes: pursuant to ARRA, to support selected Prevention Research Centers as they perform, oversee, and coordinate community-based participatory research that promotes the field of prevention research due to their established relationships with community partners.

Eligible applicants: Prevention Research Centers approved by CDC under Program Announcement DP-09-001.

Eligible beneficiaries: anyone, general public.

Range/Average: N.A.

Activity: N.A.

HQ: Program Director, CDC-HHS, Chamble Campus, Bldg. 101, 4770 Buford Hwy., Atlanta, GA 30341. Phone: (770) 488-6384.

Internet: www.cdc.gov. (Note: no field offices for this program.)

93.545 CONSUMER OPERATED AND ORIENTED PLAN PROGRAM (CO-OP)

Assistance: direct loans (start-up loans to 5 years; solvency loans to 15 years).

Purposes: pursuant to the Affordable Care Act, to provide assistance for activities related to establishing a consumer operated and oriented, nonprofit health insurance issuer. Start-up Loans help with start-up costs including: renting/developing administrative technology systems and provider networks; hiring actuaries, management staff, and counsel and consultants to assist with state licensure requirements; developing strategic plans to build enrollment and foster quality improvement; and establishing and participating in a private purchasing council. Solvency Loans assist eligible entities with meeting the solvency and reserve requirements of states in which applicants seek to be licensed to issue CO-OP qualified health plans.

Eligible applicants: private nonprofit institutions/organizations, including IHEs and hospitals; Native American organizations, cooperatives, partnerships, and associations.

Eligible beneficiaries: anyone/general public.

Range: $56,656,900 to $265,133,000. **Average:** $100,000,000.

Activity: N.A.

HQ: Director, Centers for Medicare and Medicaid Services, HHS, 200 Independence Ave., SW, Rm. 739H, Washington, DC, 20201. Phone: (301) 492-4104.

Internet: www.cms.gov. (Note: no field offices for this program.)

93.546 EARLY RETIREE REINSURANCE PROGRAM

Assistance: direct payments/specified use.

Purposes: pursuant to the Patient Protection and Affordability Act, to provide reimbursement to sponsors of participating employment-based plans to cover a portion of the cost of health benefits for early retirees and their spouses, surviving spouses, and dependents resulting in health benefits that are more affordable and accessible. Program ends January 1, 2014, or when there are no more funds available for disbursement.

Eligible applicants: eligible organizations that provide health benefits to early retirees.

Eligible beneficiaries: eligible plan sponsors, early retirees and spouses, surviving spouses, and dependents.

Range: to $387,187,080. **Average:** $1,745,809.

Activity: N.A.

HQ: Director, Centers for Medicare and Medicaid Services, HHS, 200 Independence Ave., SW, Washington, DC 20201. Phone: (301) 492-4312.

Internet: www.cms.gov. (Note: no field offices for this program.)

93.547 AFFORDABLE CARE ACT—NATIONAL HEALTH SERVICE CORPS ("ACA-NHSC")

Assistance: direct payments/specified use; project grants (to 4 years).

Purposes: pursuant to the Public Health Service (PHS) Act as amended by the Affordable Care Act, the National Health Service Corps (NHSC) assists Health Professional Shortage Areas (HPSAs) in every state, territory, and possession of the U.S. to meet their primary care, medical, oral, mental and behavioral health service needs by increasing the supply of clinicians through the following programs: Loan Repayment Program (LRP), Scholarship Program (SP), and State Loan Repayment Program (SLRP). The NHSC-LRP offers fully trained primary care clinicians assistance to pay off qualifying educational loans in exchange for service in a HPSA. The NHSC-SP awards scholarships to health professions students committed to a career in primary care and service in underserved communities of greatest need. The Students to Service (S2S) Loan Repayment Program provides assistance to pay off qualifying educational loans to medical students in their last year of school in exchange for service. The NHSC-SLRP provides matching funds (50 percent) in a form of a grant to states to operate their own repayment programs in HPSAs.

Eligible applicants/beneficiaries: states and U.S. territories, U.S. citizens, health professionals, undergraduate and graduate students.

Range/Average: N.A.

Activity: N.A.

HQ: Director, Bureau of Clinician Recruitment and Service (BCRS), Health Resources and Services Administration, HHS, Rm. 8C-26, 5600 Fishers Ln., Rockville, Maryland 20857. Phone: (301) 594-4400.

Internet: nhsc.hrsa.gov. (Note: no field offices for this program.)

93.548 NUTRITION, PHYSICAL ACTIVITY AND OBESITY PROGRAM

Assistance: cooperative agreements (80 percent/1 to 5 years).

Purposes: pursuant to the Public Health Service Act, to ensure public policy leaders have the tools and knowledge to support improvements in the public health infrastructure so that the public health system is prepared to respond to both acute and chronic threats relating to the Nation's health. Program will improve healthful eating and physical activity in order to prevent and control obesity and other chronic diseases by building and sustaining statewide capacity, and implementing population based strategies and interventions.

Eligible applicants: state and territorial health departments.

Eligible beneficiaries: states and their political subdivisions, local health authorities, individuals and organizations with specialized health interests.

Range/Average: N.A.

Activity: N.A.

HQ: Program Director, CDC-HHS, 4773 Buford Hwy. NE, Atlanta, GA 30341. Phone: (404) 867-9697.

Internet: www.Grants.gov. (Note: no field offices for this program.)

93.549 THE PRIMARY CARE SERVICES RESOURCE COORDINATION AND DEVELOPMENT PROGRAM (ACA) ("State Primary Care Offices")

Assistance: cooperative agreements (100 percent/to 5 years).

Purposes: pursuant to the Public Health Service Act, as amended, to facilitate the coordination of activities within a state relating to the delivery of primary care services and the recruitment and retention of critical health care providers. This includes working with other agencies within and organizations outside of the state government whose policies affect health care services.

Eligible applicants/beneficiaries: 35 IHEs selected by the CDC as Prevention Research Centers (PRCs).

Range: $152,056 to $438,871. **Average:** $201,189.

Activity: 54 awards.

HQ: Bureau of Health Professions/Office of Shortage Designation, HHS, 5600 Fishers Ln., Rm. 11SWH03, Rockville, MD 20852. Phone: (301) 594-5168.

Internet: www.hrsa.gov.

93.550 TRANSITIONAL LIVING FOR HOMELESS YOUTH

Assistance: project grants. (90 percent/5 years).

Purposes: pursuant to the Runaway, Homeless, and Missing Children Protection Act of 2003, to establish and operate transitional living projects for homeless youth age 16-21, including pregnant and parenting youth—providing shelter, skills training, and support services to help them make a successful transition toward productive adulthood and self-sufficiency. Living accommodations may be provided as host family homes, agency-supervised apartments, or scattered-site units rented directly by young persons with agency support.

Eligible applicants/beneficiaries: states, localities, private nonprofit entities, and networks unless they are part of the justice system; tribal governments applying as private nonprofit agencies; community-based organizations.

Range: $100,000 to $200,000. **Average:** $191,930.

Activity: anticipate 202 continuation awards in FY 2016.

HQ: Associate Commissioner, Family and Youth Services Bureau, ACF-HHS, 1250 Maryland Ave., SW, Washington, DC 20024. Phone: (202) 205-9560.

Internet: www.acf.hhs.gov/programs/fysb.

93.551 ABANDONED INFANTS

Assistance: project grants. (90 percent/to 4 years).

Purposes: pursuant to the Abandoned Infants Assistance Act of 1988 as amended, for demonstration projects to prevent the abandonment of infants and young children, especially those exposed to HIV/AIDS or drug-affected, and to provide them and their families with appropriate services; to find homes for them, whether with their natural families or in foster care; to conduct residential programs; to provide respite care for families and care givers; to recruit and train service providers including foster parents, case management, and hospital staff; to provide technical assistance in planning, developing and operating projects.

Eligible applicants/beneficiaries: state, local, tribal governments; territories, possessions; nonprofit organizations; universities.

Range: $475,000 to $1,060,000. **Average:** $499,682.

Activity: anticipate 21 awards in FY 2016.

HQ: Children's Bureau, ACF-HHS, 1250 Maryland Ave., SW, Washington, DC 20447. Phone: (202) 401-5073.

Internet: www.acf.hhs.gov/programs/cb. (Note: no field offices for this program.)

93.556 PROMOTING SAFE AND STABLE FAMILIES

Assistance: formula grants (75 percent).

Purposes: pursuant to SSA as amended, Adoption and Safe Families Act of 1997, and Promoting Safe and Stable Families Amendments of 2001, for community-based family support services promoting the safety and well-being of children and families by enhancing family functioning and child development; for family preservation services for those at risk or in crisis, including reunification, adoption promotion and support, preplacement and prevention, follow-up after foster or respite care, and improving parenting skills; for infant safe haven programs.

Eligible applicants/beneficiaries: states, territories, and certain tribes.

Range: $8,429,441 to $33,512,362. **Average:** N.A.

Activity: anticipate 502 formula grants and 12 discretionary grants will be awarded in FY 2016.

HQ: Deputy Associate Commissioner, Children's Bureau, ACF-HHS, 1250 Maryland Ave., SW, Washington, DC 20024. Phone: (202) 205-8438.

Internet: www.acf.hhs.gov/programs/cb.

93.557 EDUCATION AND PREVENTION GRANTS TO REDUCE SEXUAL ABUSE OF RUNAWAY, HOMELESS AND STREET YOUTH ("Street Outreach Program - SOP")

Assistance: project grants. (90 percent/3 years).

Purposes: pursuant to VCCLEA and Runaway, Homeless, and Missing Children Protection Act of 2003, to provide street-based services to runaway, homeless, and "street youth" that have been subjected to or are at risk of sexual abuse, prostitution, or sexual exploitation—including education and outreach, emergency shelter, survival aid, case management, treatment and counseling, information and referral, crisis intervention, and follow-up support.

Eligible applicants/beneficiaries: private nonprofit agencies including non-federally recognized tribes and urban Indian organizations.

Range: $100,000 to $200,000. **Average:** $124,012.

Activity: anticipate awarding 107 grants including 53 new and 54 continuations in FY 2016.

HQ: Associate Commissioner, Family and Youth Services Bureau, ACF-HHS, 1250 Maryland Ave., SW, Washington, DC 20024. Phone: (202) 205-9560.

Internet: www.acf.hhs.gov/programs/fysb.

93.558 TEMPORARY ASSISTANCE FOR NEEDY FAMILIES (TANF)

Assistance: formula grants.

Purposes: pursuant to SSA as amended and PRWORA, to provide cash grants, work opportunities, and other services to needy families so that their children can be cared for in their own homes; to reduce dependency by promoting job preparation, work, and marriage; to reduce and prevent out-of-wedlock pregnancies; and, to encourage the formation and maintenance of two-parent families. Permitted uses of funds are flexible, based on state plans developed in consultation with local governments and private organizations, including: assistance to low-income households in meeting home heating and cooling costs; uses permitted under the predecessor Aid to Families with Dependent Children (AFDC), Job Opportunities and Basic Skills Training (JOBS), and Emergency Assistance (EA) programs; transferring limited amounts to the Child Care and Development Block Grant (CCDBG) and Social Services Block Grant (SSBG) programs; to meet contingencies. "High Performance Bonus" and "Decrease in Illegitimacy Bonus" funds may be awarded to states meeting specific maintenance-of-effort requirements relating to superseded programs. Most families may receive assistance for no more than five years.

Eligible applicants/beneficiaries: states, tribes, specified Alaskan entities, territories.

Range: $77,195 to $3,653,771,968. **Average:** $134,687,331.

Activity: anticipate 126 awards in FY 2016.

HQ: Director, Office of Family Assistance, ACF-HHS, 5th Fl., East, Aerospace Bldg., 370 L'Enfant Promenade, SW, Washington, DC 20447. Phone: (202) 401-4731; FAX: (202) 205-5887.

Internet: www.acf.hhs.gov/programs/ofa.

93.560 FAMILY SUPPORT PAYMENTS TO STATES—ASSISTANCE PAYMENTS ("Adult Programs in the Territories")

Assistance: formula grants (75 percent).

Purposes: to provide the federal share of assistance payments to aged, blind or disabled persons in Guam, PR, and VI—enabling recipients to pay for food, shelter, clothing, and other daily living needs.

Eligible applicants: Guam, PR, and VI.

Eligible beneficiaries: needy aged, blind or disabled persons in Guam, PR, and VI.

Range: $707,436 and $30,560,246. **Average:** $10,829,401.

Activity: 3 awards annually.

HQ: Director, Office of Family Assistance, ACF-HHS, 5th Fl., East, Aerospace Bldg., 370 L'Enfant Promenade, SW, Washington, DC 20447. Phone: (202) 401-4731; FAX: (202) 205-5887.

Internet: www.acf.hhs.gov/programs/ofa.

93.563 CHILD SUPPORT ENFORCEMENT

Assistance: formula grants (66-90 percent).

Purposes: pursuant to SSA, Title IV-D, as amended, to enforce the collection of child support obligations of absent parents, and to locate absent parents, establish paternity, and obtain child, spousal, and medical support.

Eligible applicants: state agencies, DC, PR, VI, and Guam; tribes.

Eligible beneficiaries: all TANF, foster care maintenance, and Medicaid payments applicants or recipients assigning support rights to the states; all ceasing to receive TANF payments; individuals authorizing the continuation of support enforcement services; other individuals authorizing the continuation of support enforcement services; other individuals applying for services.

Range: $4,556,771 to $454,889,578. **Average:** $61,937,487.

Activity: anticipate 54 awards in FY 2016.

HQ: Director, Planning, Research and Evaluation Division, Office of Child Support Enforcement, ACF-HHS, 901 D, St. SW, Washington, DC 20447. Phone: (202) 401-5101.

Internet: www.acf.dhhs.gov/programs/cse.

93.564 CHILD SUPPORT ENFORCEMENT RESEARCH

Assistance: project grants. (to 95 percent/from 17 months).

Purposes: pursuant to SSA as amended, for innovative research and demonstration projects of regional and national significance to improve the administrative and services delivery aspects of child support payment enforcement programs.

Eligible applicants/beneficiaries: state agencies.

Range: $125,000 to $800,000. **Average:** N.A.

Activity: anticipate 8 to 10 awards in FY 2016.

HQ: Director, Planning, Research and Evaluation Division, Office of Child Support Enforcement, ACF-HHS, 370 L'Enfant Promenade, S.W., Washington, DC 20447. Phone: (202) 401-5602.

Internet: www.acf.hhs.gov/programs/cse.

93.566 REFUGEE AND ENTRANT ASSISTANCE—STATE ADMINISTERED PROGRAMS

Assistance: formula grants.

Purposes: pursuant to the Refugee Act of 1980 and Refugee Education Assistance Act of 1980 as amended, for resettlement assistance to eligible refugees from foreign countries including Cuban and Haitian entrants, asylees, victims of a severe form of trafficking, and certain Amerasians from Vietnam—including maintenance payments for up to eight months, medical and social services, English language training, case management, employment services. States may contract with other providers to offer such services.

Eligible applicants/beneficiaries: designated state agencies.

Range: $17,388 to $78,000,000 for cash and medical assistance; $75,000 to $20,644,345 for social services. **Average:** $6,257,133 for cash and medical assistance; $1,598,500 for social services.

Activity: anticipate 96 awards in FY 2016.

HQ: Office of Refugee Resettlement, ACF-HHS, 370 L'Enfant Promenade SW, 8th Fl. West, Washington, DC 20447. Phone: (202) 205-5933; FAX: (202) 205-5888.

Internet: www.acf.hhs.gov/programs/orr. (Note: no field offices for this program.)

93.567 REFUGEE AND ENTRANT ASSISTANCE—VOLUNTARY AGENCY PROGRAMS
("Matching Grant Program")

Assistance: project grants. (67 percent/3 years).

Purposes: pursuant to the Refugee Act of 1980 as amended, to assist refugees in becoming self-supporting. Funds may be used for cash allowances, job training and development, English language training, case management, social services, and medical support. The federal share is up to $2,000 per refugee.

Eligible applicants/beneficiaries: private nonprofit agencies with a Reception and Placement Grant from the Department of State or DHS.

Range: $1,566,400 to $18,977,200. **Average:** $7,256,577.

Activity: anticipate 9 awards in FY 2016.

HQ: Office of Refugee Resettlement, ACF-HHS, 370 L'Enfant Promenade SW, 8th Fl., West, Washington, DC 20447. Phone: (202) 401-4559; FAX: (202) 401-0981.

Internet: www.acf.hhs.gov/programs/orr/programs. (Note: no field offices for this program.)

93.568   LOW-INCOME HOME ENERGY ASSISTANCE

Assistance: formula grants (100 percent).

Purposes: pursuant to the Community Opportunities, Accountability, Training, and Educational Services Act of 1998 (COATES), for Energy Assistance Block Grants to states, enabling them to make payments to or on behalf of eligible low-income households for their home energy costs, either heating or cooling. Recipients may also receive energy crisis and weatherization assistance. Funds may support training and technical assistance to state and other jurisdictions administering the program. Supplemental funds may be allocated to grantees that leverage nonfederal resources with their LIHEAP funds, under the Residential Energy Assistance Challenge Program (REACH).

Eligible applicants/beneficiaries: block grants—states, DC, tribal governments, specified territories. Training and technical assistance grants—states, tribes, tribal organizations, territories, public agencies, private nonprofit organizations, businesses applying jointly with private nonprofit organizations.

Range: N.A. **Average:** $16,363,845.

Activity: anticipate 240 grants will be awarded in FY 2016.

HQ: Director, Division of Energy Assistance, Office of Community Services, ACF-HHS, 370 L'Enfant Promenade, S.W., Washington, DC 20447. Phone: (202) 401-4870; FAX: (202) 401-5661.

Internet: www.acf.hhs.gov/programs/ocs/programs/liheap. (Note: no field offices for this program.)

93.569   COMMUNITY SERVICES BLOCK GRANT (CSBG)

Assistance: formula grants.

Purposes: pursuant to COATES, for anti-poverty programs and projects, conducted by local community action agencies and organizations, to eliminate the causes of poverty—including employment services, elderly services, housing, educational services, health care, emergency health and food assistance, services to migrant and seasonal farm workers, coordination of various governmental and private services.

Eligible applicants: states, territories, tribes, tribal organizations.

Eligible beneficiaries: locally-based nonprofit community anti- poverty agencies and other eligible entities providing services to low-income individuals and families.

Range: $1,019 to $55,942,793. **Average:** $5,242,585.

Activity: anticipate 130 awards will be awarded in FY 2016.

HQ: Division of State Assistance, Office of Community Services, ACF-HHS, 901 D St., SW, 5th Fl., Rm. 5A165, Washington, DC 20447. Phone: (202) 401-4666.

Internet: www.acf.hhs.gov/programs/ocs. (Note: no field offices for this program.)

93.570 COMMUNITY SERVICES BLOCK GRANT—DISCRETIONARY AWARDS ("Community Economic Development")

Assistance: project grants. (100 percent/1-5 years).

Purposes: pursuant to COATES, for program activities to alleviate the causes of poverty in distressed communities. Eligible activities include those that: promote full-time permanent jobs for the poor; provide income or ownership opportunities for community members; address needs for rural water and waste-water treatment; provide character-building activities for youth, including sports and physical fitness; assist migrant and seasonal farm workers; promote electronic communication and access to program information. Special consideration is given to projects designated for Empowerment Zones or Enterprise Communities.

Eligible applicants/beneficiaries: economic development projects—private, locally initiated and governed nonprofit community development corporations.

Range: to $800,000. **Average:** N.A.

Activity: anticipate 43 grants will be awarded in FY 2015.

HQ: Team Leader, Division of Community Discretionary Programs, Office of Community Services, ACF-HHS, 370 L'Enfant Promenade, SW, 5th Fl. West, Washington, DC 20447. Phone: (202) 401-5115; FAX: (202) 401-4687.

Internet: www.acf.hhs.gov/programs/ocs. (Note: no field offices for this program.)

93.575 CHILD CARE AND DEVELOPMENT BLOCK GRANT ("CCDF")

Assistance: formula grants.

Purposes: pursuant to the Child Care and Development Block Grant Act of 1990 and PRWORA, to develop and provide child care policies and fee-based services, mainly for working low-income families. Activities must include: comprehensive consumer education to parents and the public; increasing parental choice; resource and referral services; infant and toddler, and school- age services; implementation of state health, safety, licensing, and registration standards; staff training; research, demonstration, and evaluation projects; to improve resettlement services for refugees. Funds may not support any real estate or major construction costs.

Eligible applicants: states, territories, possessions; tribal governments and organizations, Alaska native and native Hawaiian organizations.

Eligible beneficiaries: children under age 13 (19 if disabled), residing with a family with income not above 85 percent of the state median, in which at least one parent has a job or attends a job training or educational program, or needing or receiving protective services.

Range/Average: N.A.

Activity: anticipate 316 grants will be awarded in FY 2016.

HQ: Child Care Bureau, ACF-HHS, 370 L'Enfant Promenade, SW, 5th Fl. East, Washington, DC 20447. Phone: (202) 690-6782; FAX: (202) 690-5600.

Internet: www.acf.hhs.gov/programs/occ.

93.576 REFUGEE AND ENTRANT ASSISTANCE—DISCRETIONARY GRANTS

Assistance: project grants. (to 100 percent/1-5 years).

Purposes: pursuant to the Refugee Act of 1980 and Refugee Education Assistance Act of 1980 as amended, for projects promoting refugee self-sufficiency or addressing their special needs. Project examples: relocation from high welfare dependency areas to communities with favorable employment prospects; vocational training and employment services; micro-loans for start-up businesses.

Eligible applicants/beneficiaries: state and local governments, private non-profit organizations.

Range: $75,000 to $17,000,000. **Average:** N.A.

Activity: anticipate 228 grants will be awarded in FY 2016.

HQ: Office of Refugee Resettlement, ACF-HHS, 370 L'Enfant Promenade SW, 8th Fl., West, Washington, DC 20447. Phone: (202) 401-4559; FAX: (202) 401-0981.

Internet: www.acf.hhs.gov/programs/orr/programs. (Note: no field offices for this program.)

93.579 U.S. REPATRIATION

Assistance: project grants. (100 percent/5 years).

Purposes: pursuant to SSA, to provide temporary assistance, care, and treatment to citizens returning to the U.S. from foreign travel—required because of physical or mental illness, destitution, or because of war, threat of war, or a similar crisis. Assistance may include money, food, shelter, clothing, and transportation. Costs must be repaid to the federal government.

Eligible applicants/beneficiaries: international social service organizations.

Range: $900,000 to $1,000,000; one award per year. **Average:** N.A.

Activity: 1 award in FY 2016.

HQ: Office of Refugee Resettlement, ACF-HHS, 370 L'Enfant Promenade SW, Aerospace Bldg, 8th Fl. West, Washington, DC 20447. Phone: (202) 401-4845; FAX: (202) 401-0981.

Internet: www.acf.hhs.gov/programs/orr. (Note: no field offices for this program.)

93.581 IMPROVING THE CAPABILITY OF INDIAN TRIBAL GOVERNMENTS TO REGULATE ENVIRONMENTAL QUALITY
("Environmental Regulatory Enhancement")

Assistance: project grants. (80-100 percent/1-3 years).

Purposes: pursuant to the Native American Programs Act of 1974 as amended and Indian Environmental Regulatory Enhancement Act, to plan, develop, and implement tribal environmental regulatory programs pertaining to Indian lands, including: environmental protection regulations, ordinances, and laws; technical and operating capacity relating to both tribal and federal requirements; employee training and education; monitoring and enforcement; tribal court enforcement systems.

Eligible applicants/beneficiaries: tribes, incorporated nonfederally-recognized tribes, Alaska native villages, tribal governments, and consortia.

Range: $100,000 to $300,000. **Average:** $146,872.

Activity: anticipate 8 continuations and 4 new awards in FY 2016.

HQ: Administration for Native Americans, ACF-HHS, 370 L'Enfant Promenade SW, 2nd Fl. West, Washington, DC 204477. Phone: (877) 922-9262.

Internet: www.acf.hhs.gov/programs/ana. (Note: no field offices for this program.)

93.583 REFUGEE AND ENTRANT ASSISTANCE—WILSON-FISH PROGRAM ("Wilson/Fish Program")

Assistance: project grants. (100 percent/to 4 years).

Purposes: pursuant to the Refugee Act of 1980 and Refugee Education Assistance Act of 1980 as amended, for demonstration projects promoting early employment and self-sufficiency of refugees, including certain Amerasian immigrants, asylees, Cuban and Haitian entrants, and certified victims of a severe form of trafficking—developed as innovative approaches to the state- administered program (**93.566**), including the provision of integrated services, cash and medical assistance, social services, case management, and coordination among voluntary resettlement agencies and services providers.

Eligible applicants/beneficiaries: states, voluntary and other nonprofit resettlement organizations.

Range: $372,867 to $7,142,389. **Average:** N.A.

Activity: anticipate 13 awards in FY 2016.

HQ: Office of Refugee Resettlement, ACF-HHS, 370 L'Enfant Promenade SW, 8th Fl. West, Washington, DC 20447. Phone: (202) 205-5933; FAX: (202) 205-5888.

Internet: www.acf.hhs.gov/programs/orr. (Note: no field offices for this program.)

93.584 REFUGEE AND ENTRANT ASSISTANCE—TARGETED ASSISTANCE GRANTS ("Targeted Assistance")

Assistance: formula grants. (100 percent/3 years).

Purposes: pursuant to the Immigration and Nationality Act, Refugee Assistance Extension Act of 1986, VTVPA, amendments, and related acts, for employment-related and other social services for refugees, asylees, Amerasians, victims of a severe form of trafficking, and entrants in areas of high concentrations and high welfare rates, including: job development and placement; on- the-job training; business and employer incentives; job-related and vocational English language training.

Eligible applicants: state agencies providing assistance to counties and similar areas.

Eligible beneficiaries: refugees admitted within last five years, Cuban and Haitian entrants, certain Amerasians from Vietnam and their accompanying family members, certified victims of a severe form of trafficking.

Range: $96,518 to $12,036,939. **Average:** $1,157,862.

Activity: anticipate 38 grants will be awarded in FY 2016.

HQ: Office of Refugee Resettlement, ACF-HHS, 370 L'Enfant Promenade SW, 8th Fl. West, Washington, DC 20447. Phone: (202) 205-5933; FAX: (202) 205-5888.

Internet: www.acf.hhs.gov/programs/orr. (Note: no field offices for this program.)

93.586 STATE COURT IMPROVEMENT PROGRAM

Assistance: formula grants (75 percent).

Purposes: to improve the performance of state courts in their role in the continuum of care provided for families and children at risk. Funds may be used to assess areas in need of correction or added attention and to implement reforms.

Eligible applicants/beneficiaries: the highest state court in each state, DC, and PR.

Range: $92,040 to $572,921 for state grants; $93,055 and $144,890 for tribal grants. **Average:** $160,615 for state grants; $132,569 for tribal grants.

Activity: anticipate 163 grants will be awarded in FY 2016.

HQ: Children's Bureau, ACF-HHS, 1250 Maryland Ave., SW 8th Fl., Washington, DC 20024. Phone: (202) 205-8709.

Internet: www.acf.hhs.gov/programs/cb.

93.587 PROMOTE THE SURVIVAL AND CONTINUING VITALITY OF NATIVE AMERICAN LANGUAGES

Assistance: project grants. (80-100 percent/1-3 years).

Purposes: pursuant to the Native Americans Programs Act of 1974 as amended and Native Americans Languages Act of 1992, to plan and implement programs to assure the survival and continuing vitality of native American languages. Project examples: development of specialized school curricula; language training programs including language immersion camps and master/apprentice programs; compilation and transcription of oral narratives.

Eligible applicants/beneficiaries: tribes; incorporated nonfederally-recognized and state-recognized tribes; Alaska native villages, tribes, or tribal governing bodies; nonprofit Alaska native regional associations or corporations or native organizations or consortia; incorporated nonprofit multipurpose community-based Indian organizations; urban Indian centers; public and private nonprofit agencies, tribally controlled community colleges, post-secondary vocation.

Range: $100,000 to $300,000. **Average:** N.A.

Activity: anticipate awarding 60 grants in FY 2016.

HQ: Administration for Native Americans, ACF-HHS, 370 L'Enfant Promenade SW, 2nd Fl. West, Washington, DC 204477. Phone: (877) 922-9262.

Internet: www.acf.hhs.gov/programs/ana. (Note: no field offices for this program.)

93.590   COMMUNITY-BASED CHILD ABUSE PREVENTION GRANTS

Assistance: formula grants.

Purposes: pursuant to the Child Abuse Prevention and Treatment Act as amended, to establish, operate, or expand statewide networks of community-based family resource programs to prevent child abuse and neglect.

Eligible applicants: states, some territories and possessions.

Eligible beneficiaries: children, families; organizations dealing with family resource programs.

Range: $200,000 to $3,312,634. **Average:** N.A.

Activity: anticipate awarding 56 grants in FY 2015.

HQ: Office on Child Abuse and Neglect, ACF-HHS, 1250 Maryland Ave., SW, 8th Fl., Washington, DC 20024. Phone: (202) 205-7403.

Internet: www.friendsnrc.org. (Note: no field offices for this program.)

93.591   FAMILY VIOLENCE PREVENTION AND SERVICES—STATE DOMESTIC VIOLENCE COALITIONS

Assistance: formula grants (100 percent).

Purposes: pursuant to the Family Violence Prevention and Services Act, Child Abuse Prevention, Adoption and Family Services Act, VCCLEA, VTVPA, Child Abuse Prevention and Treatment Act, Keeping Children and Families Safe Act of 2003, amendments, and other acts, for prevention and intervention activities conducted by state domestic violence coalitions, including: program coordination with and technical assistance to local programs and services providers; encouraging appropriate responses to domestic violence cases; working with judicial and law enforcement officials to develop appropriate responses to child custody and visitation issues involving domestic violence; public education campaigns; training; related activities.

Eligible applicants/beneficiaries: statewide nonprofit coalitions in states, some territories and possessions.

Range: N.A. **Average:** states and territories: $241,071.

Activity: anticipate 56 grants will be awarded in FY 2016.

HQ: Family and Youth Services Bureau, ACF-HHS, 1250 Maryland Ave., Ste. 8212, SW, Washington, DC 20024. Phone: (202) 401-5524.

Internet: www.acf.hhs.gov/programs/fysb/programs/family-violence-prevention-services. (Note: no field offices for this program.)

93.592 FAMILY VIOLENCE PREVENTION AND SERVICES—DISCRETIONARY GRANTS

Assistance: project grants. (varying match/1-5 years).

Purposes: pursuant to the Family Violence Prevention and Services Act, Child Abuse Prevention, Adoption and Family Services Act, Child Abuse Prevention and Treatment Act, VCCLEA, VTVPA, Keeping Children and Families Safe Act of 2003, amendments, and other acts, to prevent family violence through projects and activities intended to improve the design, delivery, and coordination of services addressing the problem. Project activities may involve information gathering, research, demonstrations, evaluation, establishing specialized national resource centers, a national hotline, and public education.

Eligible applicants/beneficiaries: public and private nonprofit agencies, tribes, Alaska native villages or regional corporations.

Range: $114,000 to $4,500,0006. **Average:** N.A.

Activity: anticipate 31 awards in FY 2016.

HQ: Family and Youth Services Bureau, ACF-HHS, 1250 Maryland Ave., SW, Washington, DC 20024. Phone: (202) 205-1476.

Internet: www.acf.hhs.gov/programs/fysb/programs/family-violence-preve ntion-services. (Note: no field offices for this program.)

93.593 JOB OPPORTUNITIES FOR LOW-INCOME INDIVIDUALS ("JOLI Program")

Assistance: project grants. (to 100 percent/to 3 years).

Purposes: pursuant to the Family Support Act as amended and PRWORA, to create new permanent employment and business opportunities for TANF recipients and others through: participant training, supportive, and follow-up activities; expansion of existing businesses through technical and financial assistance; self-employment and micro-enterprises; new business ventures; nontraditional employment initiatives leading to self- sufficiency. Projects must: involve cooperative relationships with local TANF agencies, involving supportive services and client referrals, with encouragement to establish partnerships with child support enforcement agencies; include a strong evaluation component.

Eligible applicants: nonprofit IRS Section 501(c) organizations including community development corporations and charitable and tribal organizations.

Eligible beneficiaries: TANF recipients and other low-income individuals.

Range/Average: N.A.

Activity: N.A.

HQ: Team Leader, Division of Community Discretionary Programs, Office of Community Services, ACF-HHS, 370 L'Enfant Promenade SW, 5th Fl., West, Washington, DC 20447. Phone: (202) 401-9365; FAX: (202) 401-4687.

Internet: www.acf.hhs.gov/programs/ocs/index.html. (Note: no field offices for this program.)

93.594 TRIBAL WORK GRANTS ("Native Employment Works")

Assistance: formula grants.

Purposes: pursuant to SSA as amended, to allow tribes to operate programs to make work available to their members.

Eligible applicants/beneficiaries: tribes or Alaska native organizations that conducted JOBS programs in FY 95.

Range: $5,187 to $1,752,666. **Average:** $96,000.

Activity: anticipate awarding 78 grants in FY 2015.

HQ: Division of Tribal TANF Management, Office of Family Assistance, Administration for Children and Families, HHS, 370 L'Enfant Promenade SW, Washington, DC 20447. Phone: (202) 205-8354.

Internet: www.acf.hhs.gov/programs/ofa/dts.

93.595 WELFARE REFORM RESEARCH, EVALUATIONS AND NATIONAL STUDIES

Assistance: project grants. (75 percent/1-5 years).

Purposes: pursuant to PRWORA, for research on the benefits, effects, and costs of various welfare reform interventions; for studies on the effects of different programs on welfare dependency, illegitimacy, teen pregnancy, employment rates, child well-being, and related areas; for demonstrations; for analyses and evaluations.

Eligible applicants/beneficiaries: governmental entities, IHEs, nonprofit and profit organizations.

Range: $50,000 to $1,000,000. **Average:** $369,991.

Activity: anticipate funding 4 grants in FY 2016.

HQ: Office of Planning, Research and Evaluation, Administration for Children and Families, HHS, 370 L'Enfant Promenade, SW Fl., West, Washington, DC 20447. Phone: (202) 401-4535.

Internet: www.acf.hhs.gov/programs/opre.

93.596 CHILD CARE MANDATORY AND MATCHING FUNDS OF THE CHILD CARE AND DEVELOPMENT FUND (CCDF)

Assistance: formula grants (matching/2 years).

Purposes: pursuant to SSA, PRWORA, Child Care and Development Block Grant Act of 1990, and amendments, to assist low-income families with child care by: developing flexible child care programs and policies; promoting choices by working parents in selecting suitable child care; providing consumer education information to help parents make informed child care choices; implementing state health, safety, licensing, and registration standards. At least 70 percent of grant funds must be used to provide child care assistance to families: receiving assistance under a state TANF program; attempting to work to "transition" off temporary assistance programs through work activities, or at risk of becoming dependent on temporary assistance programs. The matching rate is the same as under the Medicaid program.

Eligible applicants: states, DC, tribal governments and organizations, Alaska native corporations.

Eligible beneficiaries: children under age 13 (19 if disabled), residing with a family with income not above 85 percent of the state median, in which at least one parent has a job or attends a job training or educational program, or needing or receiving protective services.

Range/Average: N.A.

Activity: anticipate 293 grants will be awarded in FY 2016.

HQ: Child Care Bureau, ACF-HHS, 370 L'Enfant Promenade, SW, 5th Fl. East, Washington, DC 20447. Phone: (202) 690-6782; FAX: (202) 690-5600.

Internet: www.acf.hhs.gov/programs/occ.

93.597 GRANTS TO STATES FOR ACCESS AND VISITATION PROGRAMS

Assistance: project grants (90 percent).

Purposes: pursuant to SSA, for programs that support and facilitate access and visitation by noncustodial parents with their children. Eligible project activities include mediation, counseling, education, development of parenting plans, visitation enforcement, and development of guidelines for visitation and alternative custody arrangements.

Eligible applicants/beneficiaries: states, DC, PR, VI, Guam.

Range/Average: N.A.

Activity: anticipate 54 awards in FY 2016.

HQ: Director, Consumer Services, Office of Child Support Enforcement, Aerospace Bldg., 370 L'Enfant Promenade SW - 4th Floor, Washington, DC 20447. Phone: (202) 401-4578.

Internet: www.acf.dhhs.gov/programs/cse.

93.598 SERVICES TO VICTIMS OF A SEVERE FORM OF TRAFFICKING ("Anti-Trafficking in Persons Program")

Assistance: project grants.

Purposes: pursuant to VTVPA, to provide victims of a severe form of trafficking access to benefits and services to the same extent as refugees, including case management, referrals and funded cash, medical assistance, special mental health and other services, and community and local outreach.

Eligible applicants: state and local governments; private nonprofit organizations.

Eligible beneficiaries: adults and children certified by HHS as victims of a severe form of trafficking, in consultation with the Attorney General.

Range: $90,000 to $3,491,385. **Average:** $490,605.

Activity: anticipate awarding 1 new grant and 21 continuation grants in FY 2016.

HQ: Office of Refugee Resettlement, ACF-HHS, 370 L'Enfant Promenade SW - 8th floor, Washington, DC 20447. Phone: (866) 401-5510, (202) 401-4825, -9207.

Internet: www.acf.hhs.gov/trafficking. (Note: no field offices for this program.)

93.599   CHAFEE EDUCATION AND TRAINING VOUCHERS PROGRAM (ETV)

Assistance: formula grants (80 percent).

Purposes: pursuant to SSA, Chafee Foster Care Independence Act of 1999, and Promoting Safe and Stable Families Amendments of 2001, to make vouchers available for education and training, including postsecondary, to youths that have aged out of foster care or that have been adopted from the foster care system after age 16 until they reach age 23—as long as they are participating in the Chafee Foster Care Independence Program (program **93.674**) at age 21. Vouchers in amounts up to $5,000 per year may be used for the cost of attending an IHE.

Eligible applicants: state governments, DC, PR.

Eligible beneficiaries: youth otherwise eligible for services under program **93.674**, including those who have left foster care because they attained age 18 and not yet attained age 21; youth likely to remain in foster care until age 18.

Range: $82,407 to $5,825,141 for states; $4,741 to $12,675 for tribes. **Average:** $818,917 for states; $8,145 for tribes.

Activity: anticipate 55 awards in FY 2016.

HQ: Children's Bureau, Administration for Children and Families, 1250 Maryland Ave., SW, 8th Fl., Washington, DC 20024. Phone: (202) 690-7888.

Internet: www.acf.hhs.gov/programs/cb.

93.600   HEAD START

Assistance: project grants (80 to 100 percent).

Purposes: pursuant to COATES, to promote school readiness through Head Start Programs offering comprehensive health, education, nutrition, social, and other services to economically disadvantaged preschool children, including children of migratory workers and on Indian reservations; to involve parents in the program. Training and technical assistance grants may be awarded to Head Start agencies and to agencies providing services. At least 90 percent of project enrollment must be from families with incomes below OMB poverty guidelines or receiving public assistance; at least 10 percent must be available for children with disabilities.

Eligible applicants: local governments, tribes, public or private nonprofit and profit agencies. Subcontracts with other agencies are permitted.

Eligible beneficiaries: children from birth until their entry into school systems.

Range: $136,000 to $200,351,000. **Average:** $4,300,000.

Activity: anticipate providing early childhood services to 927,275 children and families in FY 2016.

HQ: Head Start Bureau, ACF-HHS, 1250 Maryland Ave., SW, Washington, DC 20024. Phone: (202) 205-7378.

Internet: www.acf.hhs.gov/programs/ohs.

93.601 CHILD SUPPORT ENFORCEMENT DEMONSTRATIONS AND SPECIAL PROJECTS

Assistance: project grants. (100 percent/17 weeks).

Purposes: pursuant to SSA and PRWORA, for regional and national projects and demonstrations to improve the effectiveness of child support enforcement efforts on the regional and national levels, advancing the requirements of PRWORA.

Eligible applicants/beneficiaries: state human services umbrella and other state and local public agencies; nonprofit organizations; tribes and tribal organizations; consortia.

Range: $30,000 to $100,000. **Average:** N.A.

Activity: 5 continuation awards in FY 2014.

HQ: Deputy Director, Division of State, Tribal, and Local Assistance, Office of Child Support Enforcement, ACF-HHS, 370 L'Enfant Promenade SW - 4th Floor, Washington, DC 20447. Phone: (202) 401-4578.

Internet: www.acf.dhhs.gov/programs/cse/grants.

93.602 ASSETS FOR INDEPENDENCE DEMONSTRATION PROGRAM ("AFI Program")

Assistance: project grants. (50 percent/5 years).

Purposes: pursuant to the Assets for Independence Act and COATES as amended, for demonstration projects to establish and evaluate the social, civic, psychological, and economic effects of providing incentives to individuals and families with limited incomes to save a portion of their earned income to: obtain a postsecondary education; purchase first homes; capitalize small businesses; transfer assets to IDAs of family members. 85 percent of federal and matching funds must be used to match deposits in Individual Development Accounts (IDAs) by participants. The maximum federal contribution is $2,000 per individual and $4,000 per household.

Eligible applicants: national, state, regional, and community- based organizations; tax-exempt nonprofit organizations; state or local agencies; tribal governments applying jointly with nonprofit organizations; low-income credit unions; community development financial institutions collaborating with community-based organizations.

Eligible beneficiaries: individuals and members of households eligible for TANF or with adjusted incomes not exceeding the earned income amount specified in Section 32 of the Internal Revenue Code. Maximum net worth provisions apply.

Range: to $1,000,000. **Average:** $350,000.

Activity: anticipate 35 grants will be awarded in FY 2016.

HQ: Office of Community Services, ACF-HHS, 370 L'Enfant Promenade, SW, 5th Fl., West, Washington, DC 20447. Phone: (202) 401-5692.

Internet: www.acf.hhs.gov/programs/ocs/afi. (Note: no field offices for this program.)

93.603   ADOPTION AND LEGAL GUARDIANSHIP INCENTIVE PAYMENTS

Assistance: formula grants.

Purposes: pursuant to SSA and Adoption Promotion Act of 2003, to provide incentives to states to increase the annual number of foster child, special needs, and older child adoptions. Funds may also be used for post-adoption services to children.

Eligible applicants/beneficiaries: states, DC, PR.

Range: to $9,757,199. **Average:** $1,266,375.

Activity: anticipate 40 agencies will receive adoption incentives payments in FY 2016.

HQ: Division of Program Implementation, Children's Bureau, ACF-HHS, 1250 Maryland Ave., SW, 8th Fl., Washington, DC 20024. Phone: (202) 205-8552.

Internet: www.acf.hhs.gov/programs/cb.

93.604   ASSISTANCE FOR TORTURE VICTIMS
("Services for Survivors of Torture")

Assistance: project grants.

Purposes: pursuant to the Torture Victims Relief Act of 1998 and amendments, to provide services and rehabilitation for victims of torture, with special emphasis on applicants for asylum. Eligible uses of funds include treatment, social and legal services, providing research and training for care providers.

Eligible applicants/beneficiaries: public or private organizations and institutions.

Range: $194,000 to $518,000. **Average:** $336,000.

Activity: anticipate 31 awards will be made in FY 2016.

HQ: Office of Refugee Resettlement, Administration for Children and Families, HHS, 370 L'Enfant Promenade, SW, Washington, DC 20447. Phone: (202) 401-5585; FAX: (202) 401-5583.

Internet: www.acf.hhs.gov/programs/orr. (Note: no field offices for this program.)

93.605   FAMILY CONNECTION GRANTS

Assistance: project grants (50-75 percent/1-3 years).

Purposes: pursuant to the Fostering Connections to Success and Increasing Adoptions Act of 2008, to insure the safety and welfare of children and help them reconnect with family members by: making available kinship navigator programs; promoting effective partnerships and utilizing technology among public and private agencies to ensure kinship caregiver families are adequately served; enable parents and children to live in a safe environment for a period of at least six months.

Eligible applicants: state, local or tribal child welfare agencies and private nonprofit organizations that are experienced in working with foster children or children in kinship care arrangements.

Eligible beneficiaries: tribal child welfare agencies and public or private non-profit organizations working with foster children, children in kinship care arrangements, or those at risk of entering foster care that help children reconnect with family members.

Range: $213,937 to $750,000. **Average:** $507,349.

Activity: anticipate 3 awards in FY 2016.

HQ: Children's Bureau, ACF-HHS, 1250 Maryland Ave., SW, Washington, DC 20024. Phone: (202) 205-8172.

Internet: www.acf.hhs.gov/programs/cb. (Note: no field offices for this program.)

93.606 PREPAREDNESS AND EMERGENCY RESPONSE LEARNING CENTERS ("ACA–PERLC")

Assistance: cooperative agreements (100 percent/5 years).

Purposes: pursuant to the Public Health Service Act (PHSA), to improve the nation's public health and medical preparedness and emergency response capabilities. Accredited schools of public health will collaborate, develop, and deliver core competency-based training and education that respond to the public health preparedness and response needs of state, local and tribal public health authorities, and emphasize essential public health security capabilities.

Eligible applicants: eligible Schools of Public Health (as required by section 319F-2(d) of the PHSA) and accredited by the Council on Education for Public Health.

Eligible beneficiaries: general public, federal, state, local, and tribal public health preparedness programs.

Range/Average: N.A.

Activity: N.A.

HQ: Program Director, CDC-HHS, 1600 Clifton Rd. MS D-29, Atlanta, GA 30029. Phone: (404) 639-5276.

Internet: www.cdc.gov. (Note: no field offices for this program.)

93.609 AFFORDABLE CARE ACT (ACA)—MEDICAID ADULT QUALITY GRANTS

Assistance: project grants (100 percent/to 2 years).

Purposes: pursuant to the Affordable Care Act (ACA), grants to support state Medicaid agencies in testing, collecting, and reporting the Initial Core Set of Health Care Quality Measures for Adults Enrolled in Medicaid to Centers for Medicare and Medicaid Services (CMS). The grant funding will also support states efforts to use these data for improving the quality of care for adults covered by Medicaid.

Eligible applicants/beneficiaries: state Medicaid agencies in Medicaid agencies in the U.S. territories.

Range: to $1,000,000 per year for up to 2 years. **Average:** N.A.

Activity: N.A.

HQ: Director, Medicaid Adult Quality Grants, CMS-HHS, 200 Independence Ave., SW, Rm. 733H-02, Washington, DC 20201. Phone: (301) 492-4312.

Internet: www.medicaid.gov/Medicaid-CHIP-Program-Information/By-Topics/Quality-of-Care/Adult-Medicaid-Quality-Grants.html. (Note: no field offices for this program.)

93.610   HEALTH CARE INNOVATION AWARDS (HCIA)

Assistance: cooperative agreements (100 percent/3 years).

Purposes: pursuant to the Social Security Act, to implement and evaluate the service delivery and payment models that support system transformation toward higher quality care at lower costs for Medicare, Medicaid, and Children's Health Insurance Program (CHIP) beneficiaries. Applicants should demonstrate capability to improve care within the first 6 months of the award, while creating a sustainable pathway to net Medicare/ Medicaid/CHIP savings within two to three years.

Eligible applicants: provider groups, health systems, payers, other private sector organizations, faith-based organizations, local governments, public-private partnerships and eligible organizations (such as professional associations) applying as conveners—assembling and coordinating the efforts of a group of participants.

Eligible beneficiaries: Medicare, Medicaid, and CHIP beneficiaries.

Range: $1,000,000 to $30,000,000. **Average:** N.A.

Activity: N.A.

HQ: Director, Center for Medicare & Medicaid Innovation, HHS, 7500 Security Blvd., Baltimore, MD 21207. Phone: (410) 786-7724.

Internet: innovation.cms.gov. (Note: no field offices for this program.)

93.611   STRONG START FOR MOTHERS AND NEWBORNS

Assistance: cooperative agreements (100 percent).

Purposes: pursuant to the Patient Protection and Affordable Care Act, to test new care and payment models that have the potential to improve perinatal outcomes for women enrolled in Medicaid and/or Children's Health Insurance Program (CHIP) who are at high-risk for adverse pregnancy outcomes.

Eligible applicants: clinician groups, hospitals or service providers of obstetrical care services and proposed enhanced prenatal care services. States, managed care organizations (MCOs) and conveners who apply must partner with service providers and supply letters of agreement from their provider partners.

Eligible beneficiaries: women enrolled in Medicaid and/or CHIP.

Range: $190,000 to $1,600,000. **Average:** $436,000.

Activity: N.A.

HQ: Director, Centers for Medicare and Medicaid Services, Office of Acquisition and Grants Management, HHS, 200 Independence Ave., SW, Rm. 733H-02, Washington, DC. Phone: (301) 492-4312.

Internet: innovations.cms.gov/initiatives/Strong-Start/index.html. (Note: no field offices for this program.)

93.612 NATIVE AMERICAN PROGRAMS ("SEDS")

Assistance: project grants. (80-100 percent/1-3 years).

Purposes: pursuant to the Native American Programs Act of 1974, OAA, and amendments, to improve the social and economic conditions of native Americans within their communities. Funds may be used for such activities as: governance projects; economic and social development projects; financial assistance; training and technical assistance; research, demonstration, and evaluation.

Eligible applicants/beneficiaries: public and private nonprofit agencies including governing bodies of tribes on federal and state reservations, Alaska native villages and regional corporations, agencies serving Hawaii natives, organizations in urban or rural non-reservation areas, native American Pacific Islanders.

Range: $50,000 to $400,000. **Average:** $222,539.

Activity: anticipate awarding 30 new grants and 110 continuation grants in FY 2016.

HQ: Administration for Native Americans, ACF-HHS, 370 L'Enfant Promenade SW, 2nd Fl. West, Washington, DC 204477. Phone: (877) 922-9262.

Internet: www.acf.hhs.gov/programs/ana. (Note: no field offices for this program.)

93.613 PRESIDENT'S COMMITTEE FOR PEOPLE WITH INTELLECTUAL DISABILITIES (PCPID)

Assistance: advisory services/counseling.

Purposes: to advise and assist the President on matters pertaining to persons with intellectual disabilities, including mental retardation, through studies and coordination of federal, state, and local efforts; to provide public information; to mobilize support for related activities.

Eligible applicants/beneficiaries: general public.

Range/Average: N.A.

Activity: N.A.

HQ: Executive Director, President's Committee for People with Intellectual Disabilities, ACF-HHS, Washington, DC 20447. Phone: (202) 357-3496.

Internet: www.acl.gov/Programs/AIDD/Programs/PCPID/index.aspx. (Note: no field offices for this program.)

93.616 MENTORING CHILDREN OF PRISONERS (MCP)

Assistance: project grants. (75 percent/3 years).

Purposes: pursuant to the Safe and Stable Families Act of 2001, to establish or expand and operate programs using a network of public and private entities to provide mentoring services for children of prisoners.

Eligible applicants/beneficiaries: state or local government units, tribes and tribal organizations, private nonprofit community groups—in areas with substantial numbers of children or prisoners.

Range/Average: N.A.

Activity: N.A.

HQ: Associate Commissioner, Family and Youth Services Bureau, ACF-HHS, 1250 Maryland Ave., SW, Washington, DC 20024. Phone: (202) 205-8306.

Internet: www.acf.hhs.gov/programs/fysb.

93.617 VOTING ACCESS FOR INDIVIDUALS WITH DISABILITIES—GRANTS TO STATES
("Help America Vote Act")

Assistance: formula grants.

Purposes: pursuant to the Help America Vote Act, to provide greater accessibility to polling places for persons with disabilities. Funds may be used to: make polling places accessible, including the path of travel, entrances, exits, and voting areas of each polling place; provide opportunity for voting access and participation, including privacy and independence; train election officials, poll workers, and election volunteers in elections for federal office; provide appropriate information dissemination.

Eligible applicants/beneficiaries: states, territories and possessions.

Range: from $100,000. **Average:** N.A.

Activity: N.A.

HQ: Administration on Developmental Disabilities, ACF-HHS, One Massachusetts Ave., NW, Washington, DC 20201. Phone: (202) 357-3486.

Internet: www.acf.hhs.gov/programs.add. (Note: no field offices for this program.)

93.618 VOTING ACCESS FOR INDIVIDUALS WITH DISABILITIES—GRANTS FOR PROTECTION AND ADVOCACY SYSTEMS

Assistance: formula grants; project grants.

Purposes: pursuant to the Help America Vote Act, to ensure full participation by persons with disabilities in the electoral process. Funds may be used to improve access and participation, and to provide training and technical assistance to protection and advocacy systems.

Eligible applicants/beneficiaries: states, territories and possessions with an approved Protection and Advocacy System in place.

Range: $35,000 to $323,000. **Average:** $144,000.

Activity: N.A.

HQ: Administration on Developmental Disabilities, ACF-HHS, One Massachusetts Ave., NW, Washington, DC 20201. Phone: (202) 357-3486.

Internet: www.acl.gov/Programs/AIDD/Index.aspxhttp. (Note: no field offices for this program.)

93.621   AFFORDABLE CARE ACT INITIATIVE TO REDUCE AVOIDABLE HOSPITALIZATIONS AMONG NURSING FACILITY RESIDENTS ("Nursing Facility Initiative")

Assistance: project grants/cooperative agreements (100 percent/4 years).

Purposes: pursuant to the Protection and Affordable Care Act, the Centers for Medicare & Medicaid Services (CMS) will select eligible organizations to test a series of evidence-based clinical interventions, with the goal of improving the health and health care among nursing facility residents and ultimately reducing avoidable inpatient hospital admissions. The enhanced care and coordination providers will collaborate with state Medicaid and state survey and certification agencies and participating nursing facilities, with each provider implementing its intervention in at least 15 Medicare-and-Medicaid-certified nursing facilities in the same state. Nursing facilities, entities controlled by nursing facilities are excluded from serving as enhanced care and coordination providers under this cooperative agreement.

Eligible applicants: public/nonprofit organizations (such as Aging and Disability Resource Centers, Area Agencies on Aging, Behavioral Health Organizations, Centers for Independent Living, universities), care coordination/case management organizations, medical care providers (such as physician practices), eligible health plans, integrated delivery networks (must include unaffiliated nursing facilities).

Eligible beneficiaries: fee-for-service Medicare/Medicaid enrollees and other long-stay residents in nursing facilities.

Range: $5,000,000 to $25,000,000. **Average:** N.A.

Activity: N.A.

HQ: 7500 Security Blvd., Centers for Medicare and Medicaid Services, HHS, Baltimore, MD 21214. Phone: (212) 616-2329.

Internet: N.A. (Note: no field offices for this program.)

93.622   COORDINATING CENTER FOR INTERPROFESSIONAL EDUCATION AND COLLABORATIVE PRACTICE ("ACA–CC–IPECP")

Assistance: cooperative agreements (75 percent/5 years).

Purposes: pursuant to the Public Health Service Act, to provide an infrastructure for leadership, expertise, and support to enhance the coordination and capacity building of IPECP among health professions across the U.S. and particularly in medically underserved areas.

Eligible applicants/beneficiaries: 35 IHEs selected by the CDC as Prevention Research Centers (PRCs).

Range/Average: N.A.

Activity: N.A.

HQ: MPH, APRN Office of Health Resources and Services Administration, HHS, 5600 Fishers Ln. Rm. 9-61, Rockville, MD 20857. Phone: (301) 443-1253.

Internet: www.hrsa.gov. (Note: no field offices for this program.)

93.623 BASIC CENTER GRANT (BCP)

Assistance: project grants. (to 90 percent/to 3 years).

Purposes: pursuant to the Runaway, Homeless, and Missing Children Protection Act of 2003, to establish or strengthen the operation of locally controlled, community-based centers for runaway and homeless youth and their families. Grants fund services must be delivered outside the law enforcement, child welfare, mental health, and juvenile justice systems. Centers provide services in residential settings normally accommodating no more than 20 youth, including activities such as individual and family counseling, temporary shelter for youth under age 18 for up to 15 days, food, clothing, transitional and after-care assistance. The program funds a national toll-free communication system, personnel training, research, demonstration, and service projects.

Eligible applicants/beneficiaries: states, localities, private entities, and coordinated networks of such agencies operating outside the law enforcement structure or juvenile justice system; Indian organizations.

Range: $100,000 to $200,000. **Average:** $162,778.

Activity: anticipate 306 grants will be awarded in FY 2016.

HQ: Associate Commissioner, Family and Youth Services Bureau, ACF-HHS, 1250 Maryland Ave., SW, Washington, DC 20024. Phone: (202) 205-9560.

Internet: www.acf.hhs.gov/programs/fysb.

93.624 STATE INNOVATION MODELS: FUNDING FOR MODEL DESIGN AND MODEL TESTING ASSISTANCE (ACA) ("State Innovation Models SIM")

Assistance: cooperative agreements (100 percent/to 4 years).

Purposes: pursuant to Section 1115A of the Social Security Act (added by Section 3021 of the Affordable Care Act), to provide funds for Model Testing awards for states to implement the State Health Care Innovation Plan and to test and evaluate the proposed service delivery and payment models. Model Design awards will support states that need financial and technical support to engage stakeholders and complete a State Health Care Innovation Plan. A comprehensive plan must provide a broad vision of health system transformation and payment reform and describe the state's broad strategy for delivery system evolution into community-integrated health care. States can apply for a Model Design award or a Model Testing award but not both.

Eligible applicants: states, DC and U.S. territories.

Eligible beneficiaries: Medicare, Medicaid, and Children's Health Insurance Program (CHIP) populations.

Range/Average: N.A.

Activity: N.A.

HQ: Program Director, Centers for Medicare and Medicaid Services, HHS, 7205 Windsor Blvd., Baltimore, MD 21244. Phone: (410) 786-9726.

Internet: N.A. (Note: no field offices for this program.)

93.628 IMPLEMENTATION SUPPORT FOR STATE DEMONSTRATIONS TO INTEGRATE CARE FOR MEDICARE/MEDICAID ENROLLEES ("ACA-ISSD")

Assistance: cooperative agreements (75 to 100 percent/2 years).

Purposes: pursuant to the Patient Protection and Affordable Care Act, Centers for Medicare & Medicaid Services (CMS) seeks to fund activities necessary to implement the demonstrations to integrate care for Medicare-Medicaid enrollees, especially those that promote beneficiary engagement and protection of beneficiary rights. Funding will be provided to states that previously had design contracts and also have a signed Memorandum of Understanding (MOU) with CMS to implement a CMS-approved demonstration.

Eligible applicants: only eligible states with a signed Memorandum of Understanding with CMS to implement their demonstration design.

Eligible beneficiaries: Medicare and Medicaid recipients.

Range: $1,000,000 to $15,000,000 for 2 years. **Average:** N.A.

Activity: N.A.

HQ: Program Director, ISSD, Centers for Medicare and Medicaid Service, HHS, 7500 Security Blvd., Baltimore, MD 21244. Phone: (410) 786-2237.

Internet: www.cms.gov. (Note: no field offices for this program.)

93.630 DEVELOPMENTAL DISABILITIES BASIC SUPPORT AND ADVOCACY GRANTS

Assistance: formula grants (75-100 percent).

Purposes: pursuant to the Mental Retardation Facilities and Construction Act of 1963, Developmental Disabilities Assistance and Bill of Rights Act, and amendments, to plan and provide comprehensive and coordinated services to developmentally disabled persons, enabling them to reach their maximum potential in the community and to assure the protection of their legal and human rights. Funds may support state and local costs of planning and administration of services.

Eligible applicants: designated state agencies, territories and possessions.

Eligible beneficiaries: persons with developmental disabilities attributable to a mental and/or physical impairment manifested before age 22, resulting in functional limitations and reflecting lifelong need for services in at least three of seven functional areas—including self-care, receptive and expressive language, learning, mobility, self-direction, capacity for independent living, economic self-sufficiency, infants and children to age 9 showing high probability of a developmental disability.

Range: N.A. **Average:** basic support: $450,000; protection and advocacy: $200,000.

Activity: anticipate 113 grants will be awarded in FY 2015.

HQ: Administration on Developmental Disabilities, ACF-HHS, One Massachusetts Ave., NW, Washington, DC 20201. Phone: (202) 690-5982.

Internet: acl.gov/programs/aidd/Index.aspx.

93.631 DEVELOPMENTAL DISABILITIES PROJECTS OF NATIONAL SIGNIFICANCE

Assistance: project grants (varying match).

Purposes: pursuant to the Mental Retardation Facilities and Construction Act of 1963, Developmental Disabilities Assistance and Bill of Rights Act, and amendments, to increase and support the independence, productivity, and integration into communities of developmentally disabled persons. Grants support such activities as family support activities, education of policy makers, data collection and analysis, federal inter-agency initiatives, technical assistance including for developing information and referral systems, improved supportive services, services to minorities with disabilities, transitional services for youth, nationally significant projects.

Eligible applicants/beneficiaries: state, local, public, or private nonprofit agencies and organizations.

Range: $50,000 to $500,000. **Average:** N.A.

Activity: N.A.

HQ: Administration on Intellectual and Developmental Disabilities, Administration for Community Living, ACF-HHS, One Massachusetts Ave., NW, Washington, DC 20201. Phone: (202) 690-7025.

Internet: www.acl.gov/Programs/AIDD/Index.aspx.

93.632 UNIVERSITY CENTERS FOR EXCELLENCE IN DEVELOPMENTAL DISABILITIES EDUCATION, RESEARCH, AND SERVICE (UCEDD)

Assistance: project grants. (75-90 percent/5 years).

Purposes: pursuant to the Mental Retardation Facilities and Construction Act of 1963, Developmental Disabilities Assistance and Bill of Rights Act, and amendments, to administer and operate university- or college-related programs for the developmentally disabled, including: interdisciplinary training for personnel; basic and applied research; information dissemination; community demonstration projects including direct services to developmentally disabled persons—e.g., family and individual support, educational, vocational, clinical, health and prevention services.

Eligible applicants/beneficiaries: public or nonprofit entities associated with or integral parts of IHEs.

Range: N.A. **Average:** $535,000.

Activity: N.A.

HQ: Administration on Intellectual and Developmental Disabilities, Administration for Community Living, ACF-HHS, One Massachusetts Ave., NW, Washington, DC 20201. Phone: (202) 690-7025.

Internet: www.acf.dhhs.gov/programs/add. (Note: no field offices for this program.)

93.634 AFFORDABLE CARE ACT (ACA) SUPPORT FOR DEMONSTRATION OMBUDSMAN PROGRAMS SERVING BENEFICIARIES OF STATE DEMONSTRATIONS TO INTEGRATE CARE FOR MEDICARE/MEDICAID

Assistance: project grants (100 percent/3 years).

Purposes: pursuant to the Social Security Act and the Patient Protection and Affordable Care Act, funds to states for activities necessary to plan for, develop, and implement ombudsman programs to support the Financial Alignment Demonstration. The program is designed to ensure that beneficiaries of the Financial Alignment Demonstration models, as well as their caregivers and authorized representatives, have access to person-centered assistance in resolving problems related to the plans and providers.

Eligible applicants: states which have signed a Memorandum of Understanding with CMS to implement one of the Financial Alignment Demonstration models.

Eligible beneficiaries: enrollees and caregivers in the Financial Alignment Demonstration.

Range: $275,000 to $3,000,000. **Average:** N.A.

Activity: N.A.

HQ: Director, Support for Demonstration Ombudsman Programs Serving Beneficiaries of State Demonstrations to Integrate Care for Medicare-Medicaid, CMMS-HHS, 7500 Security Blvd., Baltimore, MD 21207. Phone: (410) 786-8200.

Internet: www.cms.gov/Medicare-Medicaid-Coordination/Medicare-and-Medicaid-Coordination/Medicare-Medicaid-Coordination-Office/FinancialModelstoSupportStatesEffortsinCareCoordination.html. (Note: no field offices for this program.)

93.643 CHILDREN'S JUSTICE GRANTS TO STATES

Assistance: formula grants. (100 percent/2 years).

Purposes: pursuant to the Child Abuse Prevention and Treatment Act, VOCA, and amendments, for improved response to, and investigation and prosecution of, child abuse and neglect cases, particularly cases of sexual abuse and exploitation—including experimental, model, and demonstration programs, and legal and procedural reforms. Projects must be designed to achieve reforms in such areas as: investigative, administrative, and judicial handling of cases; inter-jurisdictional matters, with emphasis on reducing trauma to victims and their families; performance of court-appointed attorneys and guardians.

Eligible applicants/beneficiaries: states, territories, possessions.

Range: $53,266 to $1,809,761. **Average:** $314,553.

Activity: anticipate 50 awards in FY 2016.

HQ: Office on Child Abuse and Neglect, ACF-HHS, 1250 Maryland Ave., SW, 8th Fl., Washington, DC 20024. Phone: (202) 205-8879.

Internet: www.acf.dhhs.gov/programs/cb. (Note: no field offices for this program.)

93.645 STEPHANIE TUBBS JONES CHILD WELFARE SERVICES PROGRAM

Assistance: formula grants (75 percent).

Purposes: pursuant to SSA as amended, for state, local, and tribal child welfare services to promote State and Tribal flexibility in the development and expansion of a coordinated child and family services program that utilizes community-based agencies and ensures all children are raised in safe, loving families.

Eligible applicants/beneficiaries: state agencies, tribes, territories and possessions.

Range: $150,265 to $30,793,211 for states; $1,075 to $733,369 for tribes. **Average:** $5,061,089 for states; $33,303 for tribes.

Activity: anticipate 245 grants will be awarded in FY 2016.

HQ: Children's Bureau, ACF-HHS, 1250 Maryland Ave. SW, Washington, DC 20024. Phone: (202) 205-8438.

Internet: www.acf.hhs.gov/programs/cb.

93.647 SOCIAL SERVICES RESEARCH AND DEMONSTRATION (SSRD)

Assistance: project grants. (75 percent/1-3 years).

Purposes: pursuant to SSA as amended, for innovative research projects to test, demonstrate, and evaluate new concepts in social services for children and families.

Eligible applicants/beneficiaries: governmental entities, IHEs, nonprofit or profit organizations.

Range: $25,000 to $120,000. **Average:** $78,643.

Activity: anticipate awarding 3 new and 10 continuation grants in FY 2016.

HQ: Office of Planning, Research and Evaluation, Administration for Children and Families, HHS, 370 L'Enfant Promenade, SW Fl., West, Washington, DC 20447. Phone: (202) 401-4535.

Internet: www.acf.hhs.gov/programs/opre.

93.648 CHILD WELFARE RESEARCH TRAINING OR DEMONSTRATION

Assistance: project grants (to 100 percent).

Purposes: pursuant to SSA as amended, for programs to train current and prospective child welfare program personnel, including traineeship stipends. Previous projects examples include professional education for child welfare practices and cross-program training.

Eligible applicants/beneficiaries: IHEs.

Range: $999,074 to $4,240,690. **Average:** $2,837,807.

Activity: N.A.

HQ: Children's Bureau, ACF-HHS, 1250 Maryland Ave., SW, Washington, DC 20024. Phone: (202) 205-8172.

Internet: www.acf.hhs.gov/programs/cb.

93.649 NUTRITION AND PHYSICAL ACTIVITY PROGRAMS

Assistance: cooperative agreements. (100 percent/1 to 5 years).

Purposes: pursuant to the Public Health Service Act, to improve dietary quality to support healthy child development and reduce chronic disease; increase health-related physical activity for people of all ages; and decrease prevalence of obesity through prevention of weight gain and maintenance of healthy weight. Funds may be used for planning, data collection, organizing, and the implementation of program elements, and for personnel, travel, supplies, and services. Funds may not be used for research, clinical care, or for the purchase of furniture or equipment.

Eligible applicants/beneficiaries: state, local, tribal, and territorial public and private nonprofit and for-profit institutions/organizations.

Range/Average: N.A.

Activity: N.A.

HQ: CDC-HHS, 4770 Buford Hwy., NE, Atlanta, GA 30341. Phone: (404) 867-9697.

Internet: N.A. (Note: no field offices for this program.)

93.650   ACCOUNTABLE HEALTH COMMUNITIES

Assistance: formula grants. (100 percent/5 years).

Purposes: pursuant to the Social Security Act, as amended by section 3021 of the Affordable Care Act, to test innovative payment and service delivery models to reduce Medicare, Medicaid, or CHIP expenditures, while preserving or enhancing the quality of beneficiaries' care.

Eligible applicants/beneficiaries: local, tribal, and territorial government entities, hospitals and health systems, individual and group provider practices, and IHEs.

Range: $200,000 to $450,000. **Average:** N.A.

Activity: N.A.

HQ: Centers for Medicare and Medicaid Services, HHS, 7500 Security Blvd., StopWB-06-05, Baltimore, MD 21244. Phone: (410) 786-8033.

Internet: www.innovation.cms.gov. (Note: no field offices for this program.)

93.651   TRANSFORMING CLINICAL PRACTICE INITIATIVE (TCPI)— SUPPORT AND ALIGNMENT NETWORK (SAN) 2.0

Assistance: formula grants/cooperative agreements. (100 percent).

Purposes: pursuant to Section 1115A of the Social Security Act, and Section 3021 of the Affordable Care Act, to implement and evaluate models that support healthcare design improvements to deliver higher quality care at lower costs in both primary and specialty care. Funds may not be used for specific components, devices, equipment, to build or purchase health information technology or other information technology or to make permanent improvements to property not owned by the federal government.

Eligible applicants: public and private nonprofit and private for-profit health organizations/institutions, and IHEs.

Eligible beneficiaries: anyone.

Range: $500,000 to $2,500,000. **Average:** N.A.

Activity: N.A.

HQ: CMS-HHS, 7500 Security Blvd., Baltimore, MD 21207. Phone: (410) 786-8834.

Internet: www.cms.hhs.gov. (Note: no field offices for this program.)

93.652 ADOPTION OPPORTUNITIES

Assistance: project grants. (to 100 percent/1-5 years).

Purposes: pursuant to the Child Abuse Prevention and Treatment and Adoption Reform Act of 1978 as amended, for projects to improve adoption practices including: adoption education and training; recruitment on the national level; child placement in kinship care arrangements, pre-adoptive, or adoptive homes; operation of national center for special needs adoption; minority recruitment, post-legal adoption services; improving the placement rate in foster care; barrier elimination across jurisdictional boundaries.

Eligible applicants/beneficiaries: state and local government entities, public and private nonprofit licensed agencies, community-based organizations, adoptive family groups, minority groups, sectarian institutions.

Range: $365,744 to $3,669,500. **Average:** $675,715.

Activity: anticipate 33 grants will be awarded in FY 2016.

HQ: Children's Bureau, ACF-HHS, 1250 Maryland Ave., SW, Washington, DC 20024. Phone: (202) 205-8172.

Internet: www.acf.hhs.gov/programs/cb. (Note: no field offices for this program.)

93.658 FOSTER CARE—TITLE IV-E

Assistance: formula grants (50-83 percent).

Purposes: pursuant to SSA as amended, Title IV-E, for the operation of state and local foster child programs, including payments on behalf of the children, and training and administrative costs.

Eligible applicants/beneficiaries: states, DC, PR.

Range: $275,902 to $1,211,401,409 for formula grants. **Average:** $8,922,499 for formula grants; $241,405 for plan development grants.

Activity: anticipate 55 awards in FY 2016.

HQ: Children's Bureau, ACF-HHS, 1250 Maryland Ave., SW, Washington, DC 20024. Phone: (202) 654-2527.

Internet: www.acf.hhs.gov/programs/cb.

93.659 ADOPTION ASSISTANCE

Assistance: formula grants.

Purposes: pursuant to SSA as amended, Title IV-E, for adoption subsidy payments for adopted children with special needs. The subsidies are available from the time of adoption placement to age 18 (or older for certain handicaps).

Eligible applicants: states, DC, PR.

Eligible beneficiaries: children that are recipients of or eligible for AFDC, AFDC-FC, or SSI, and have special needs, e.g., a special factor or condition requiring adoption assistance for placement.

Range: $473,493 to $455,389,089. **Average:** $46,315,056.

Activity: anticipate 54 awards in FY 2016.

HQ: Deputy Associate Commissioner, Children's Bureau, ACF-HHS, 1250 Maryland Ave., SW, Washington, DC 20024. Phone: (202) 205-8438.

Internet: www.acf.hhs.gov/programs/cb.

93.667   SOCIAL SERVICES BLOCK GRANT ("SSBG Program")

Assistance: formula grants (100 percent).

Purposes: pursuant to SSA, Jobs Training Bill, Medicaid and Medicare Patient and Program Act of 1987, Family Support Act of 1988, and amendments, to provide social services to: prevent, reduce, or eliminate dependency; achieve or maintain self- sufficiency; prevent neglect, abuse, or exploitation of persons; prevent or reduce inappropriate institutional care; enable individuals to secure admission or referral for institutional care when other forms of care are inappropriate; supplement comprehensive community revitalization in designated Empowerment Zones and Enterprise Communities (EZ/EC). Funds may be used for activities relating to preventive health, mental health, substance abuse, and maternal and child health, as well as low- income home energy assistance. Ineligible uses include cash payments for subsistence or for room and board, medical care, health or prison facility social services, educational services, and most real estate costs—unless specifically approved by HHS.

Eligible applicants/beneficiaries: states, territories and possessions.

Range: $36,087 to $194,063,454. **Average:** $28,303,508.

Activity: anticipate 57 grants will be awarded in FY 2016.

HQ: Division of State Assistance, Office of Community Services, ACF-HHS, 901 D St., SW, 5th Fl., Rm. 5A165, Washington, DC 20447. Phone: (202) 401-2333.

Internet: www.acf.hhs.gov/programs/ocs/ssbg.

93.669   CHILD ABUSE AND NEGLECT STATE GRANTS

Assistance: formula grants. (100 percent/to 5 years).

Purposes: pursuant to the Child Abuse Prevention, Adoption and Family Services Act of 1988, JJDPA, Child Abuse Prevention and Treatment Act, Keeping Children and Families Safe Act of 2003, amendments, and other acts, to operate, improve, and augment state child protective systems, including such activities as: reporting, investigation, management, legal representation, and prosecution of cases of child abuse and neglect; research; treatment of and services to abused children and their families; personnel training; public education and information; community- based programs.

Eligible applicants/beneficiaries: states, territories and possessions.

Range: $55,182 to $2,842,348. **Average:** $441,680.

Activity: anticipate 56 grants will be awarded in FY 2016.

HQ: Division of Program Implementation, Children's Bureau, ACF-HHS, 1250 Maryland Ave., SW, 8th Fl., Washington, DC 20024. Phone: (202) 205-8552.

Internet: www.acf.dhhs.gov/programs/cb.

93.670   CHILD ABUSE AND NEGLECT DISCRETIONARY ACTIVITIES

Assistance: project grants. (varying match/to 5 years).

Purposes: pursuant to the Child Abuse Prevention and Treatment Act and Child Abuse Prevention, Adoption and Family Services Act of 1988 as amended, and Keeping Children and Families Safe Act of 2003, for research, demonstration service improvement, information dissemination, and technical assistance projects—toward the prevention, identification, assessment, and treatment of child abuse and neglect.

Eligible applicants/beneficiaries: states, local governments, public and private nonprofit agencies and organizations, tribes.

Range: $289,220 to $775,000. **Average:** $421,476.

Activity: anticipate 55 awards in FY 2016.

HQ: Children's Bureau, ACF-HHS, 1250 Maryland Ave., SW, Washington, DC 20024. Phone: (202) 205-8172.

Internet: www.acf.hhs.gov/programs/cb. (Note: no field offices for this program.)

93.671   FAMILY VIOLENCE PREVENTION AND SERVICES—DOMESTIC VIOLENCE SHELTER AND SUPPORTIVE SERVICES

Assistance: formula grants (65-80 percent).

Purposes: pursuant to the Family Violence Prevention and Services Act, Child Abuse Prevention, Adoption and Family Services Act of 1988, VCCLEA, VTVPA, Keeping Children and Families Safe Act of 2003, amendments, and other laws, for the prevention of family violence; to provide immediate shelter and other assistance to victims and their dependents. The program emphasizes community- based projects that provide shelter, counseling, advocacy, and self-help services to victims and their children—without income eligibility standards. Funds may not be used to make payments to victims.

Eligible applicants/beneficiaries: states, tribes, territories and possessions.

Range: $14,897 to $7,994,397. **Average:** N.A.

Activity: anticipate 188 grants will be awarded in FY 2016.

HQ: Family and Youth Services Bureau, ACF-HHS, 1250 Maryland Ave., Ste. 8212, SW, Washington, DC 20024. Phone: (202) 401-5524.

Internet: www.acf.hhs.gov/programs/fysb/programs/family-violence-prevention-services. (Note: no field offices for this program.)

93.674   CHAFEE FOSTER CARE INDEPENDENCE PROGRAM (CFCIP)

Assistance: formula grants (80 percent).

Purposes: pursuant to SSA as amended and Foster Care Independence Act of 1999, and Promoting Safe and Stable Families Amendments of 2001, for state and local programs designed to assist youth receiving foster care maintenance payments to make the transition to independent living. Funds may be used for skill development, mentoring activities, postsecondary education, supportive services, or training related to program purposes, including voucher payments.

Eligible applicants: states, DC, PR.

Eligible beneficiaries: youth age 18 and over, currently or formerly receiving foster care payments, until they reach age 21.

Range: $500,000 to $18,101,906 for states; tribes: $8,871 to $39,389 for tribes. **Average:** $2,650,256 for states; tribes: $21,671 for tribes.

Activity: anticipate 56 grants will be awarded in FY 2016.

HQ: Children's Bureau, Administration for Children and Families, 1250 Maryland Ave., SW, 8th Fl., Washington, DC 20024. Phone: (202) 690-7888.

Internet: www.acf.dhhs.gov/programs/cb.

93.676 UNACCOMPANIED ALIEN CHILDREN PROGRAM

Assistance: project grants.

Purposes: pursuant to the Homeland Security Act of 2002, to develop plans and policies to coordinate and implement care and placement services for unaccompanied alien children in federal custody by reason of their immigration status.

Eligible applicants/beneficiaries: state and local governments, private nonprofit and profit organizations.

Range: $251,775 to $75,629,520. **Average:** $8,603,441.

Activity: placed 25,000 children in FY 2015.

HQ: Director, Division of Unaccompanied Children Services, HHS, 370 L'Enfant Promenade SW, 7th Fl. East, Washington, DC 20447. Phone: (202) 401-4997; FAX: (202) 401-1022.

Internet: www.acf.hhs.gov/programs/orr. (Note: no field offices for this program.)

93.701 TRANS-NIH RECOVERY ACT RESEARCH SUPPORT

Assistance: project grants; capacity building and complaint processing; training (100 percent/ to 2 years).

Purposes: pursuant to PHSA, Title IV, to promote research and other projects that will support fundamental biomedical discovery and translation of that knowledge into effective prevention strategies and new treatments while also providing economic stimulus to the nation.

Eligible applicants: U.S. territories/possessions (includes IHEs and hospitals).

Eligible beneficiaries: anyone/general public.

Range/Average: N.A.

Activity: N.A.

HQ: Division Coordinator, Office of Grants Management, NIH-HHS, 9000 Rockville Pike, Bethesda, MD. Phone: (301) 435-0714.

Internet: www.nih.gov. (Note: no field offices for this program.)

93.702 NATIONAL CENTER FOR RESEARCH RESOURCES, RECOVERY ACT CONSTRUCTION SUPPORT

Assistance: project grants.

Purposes: pursuant to PHSA, to support the facility demands of NIH research programs by renovating existing research facilities and building new research facilities to meet basic and clinical space requirements, laboratory safety, biohazard containment, and animal care standards. The Recovery Act has modified the usual period of federal interest from 20 years to 10 years.

Eligible applicants/beneficiaries: public nonprofit institutions/organizations (includes IHEs and hospitals).

Range/Average: N.A.

Activity: N.A.

HQ: Division Coordinator, Office of Grants Management, NCRR-NIH-HHS, 6701 Democracy Blvd., Rm. 960, Bethesda, MD 20892-4874. Phone: (301) 435-0877.

Internet: www.ncrr.nih.gov. (Note: no field offices for this program.)

93.703   GRANTS TO HEALTH CENTER PROGRAMS (ARRA)

Assistance: project grants.

Purposes: pursuant to ARRA 2009, in order to facilitate medically underserved and uninsured individuals, to increase comprehensive primary and preventive health care services by establishing and supporting new sites and service areas. Funds may not be used to make cash payments to intended recipients of services.

Eligible applicants: public nonprofit institutions/organizations (includes IHEs and hospitals).

Eligible beneficiaries: public and private nonprofit institutions/organizations.

Range/Average: N.A.

Activity: N.A.

HQ: HRSA-HHS, 5600 Fishers Ln., Rm. 17C-26, Rockville, MD 20857. Phone: (301) 594-4300.

Internet: www.grants.gov.

93.704   TRANS-NIH RECOVERY ACT LOAN REPAYMENT SUPPORT

Assistance: direct payments/specified use (to two years).

Purposes: pursuant to PHSA, Title IV and ARRA 2009, to attract and retain health professionals performing research in fields required by NIH to carry out its mission by providing educational loan repayment for participants with substantial educational debt relative to income, who agree by written contract to engage in biomedical, behavioral or clinical research in a qualifying nonprofit institution or as an employee of the NIH for 2 years for new intramural and extramural contracts. Recipients must have qualified educational debt in excess of 20 percent of their annual salary, half of this "debt" threshold must be paid by the program recipients.

Eligible applicants: small business (less than 500 employees).

Eligible beneficiaries: health professionals who are U.S. citizens.

Range: $2,298 to $70,000 for loan repayments; $1,040 to $31,679 for tax reimbursements. **Average:** loan and tax reimbursements$48,718 for loan and tax reimbursements.

Activity: N.A.

HQ: NIH-HHS, 6011 Executive Blvd., Rm. 206, Stop 7650, Bethesda, MD 20892-7650. Phone: (866) 849-4046.

Internet: www.lrp.nih.gov. (Note: no field offices for this program.)

93.706   AGING NUTRITION SERVICES FOR NATIVE AMERICANS

Assistance: project grants (100 percent/to 1 year).

Purposes: pursuant to ARRA 2009 and Older Americans Act of 1965, to provide grants to Native American tribal organizations who are current grantees under Title VI of the OAA, as amended, to support nutrition services including meals, nutrition education and referrals for older Americans in order to maintain health, independence and quality of life. Meals may be served in a congregate setting or delivered to the home, if the older individual is homebound.

Eligible applicants: federally-recognized Indian tribal governments.

Eligible beneficiaries: American Indian senior citizens aged 60 years and over.

Range/Average: N.A.

Activity: N.A.

HQ: Director, Office of American Indian, Alaskan Native, and Native Hawaiian Programs, AOA-HHS, One Massachusetts Ave, NW , Washington, DC 20201. Phone: 202-357-0148.

Internet: www.acl.gov.

93.708   HEAD START (ARRA)
("HS, Recovery Act")

Assistance: project grants (to 80 percent/to 1 year).

Purposes: pursuant to ARRA 2009 and Head Start Act, as amended by Improving Head Start for School Readiness Act of 2007, to promote school readiness of low-income children, by enhancing cognitive, social and emotional development through the provision of comprehensive health, educational, nutritional, social and other services. Head Start emphasizes the significant involvement of parents: in their children's learning; in the administration of their local Head Start programs; and in realizing their own educational, literacy and employment goals.

Eligible applicants: profit and private institutions/organizations, IHEs (includes research).

Eligible beneficiaries: local, public institutions/organizations, and eligible low-income individuals/families.

Range/Average: N.A.

Activity: N.A.

HQ: ACF-HHS, 1250 Maryland Ave., SW, Washington, DC 20024. Phone: (202) 205-7378.

Internet: www.acf.hhs.gov/programs/ohs.

93.709   EARLY HEAD START (EHS)

Assistance: project grants (80 percent/1 year).

Purposes: pursuant to ARRA 2009 and Head Start Act, as amended by Improving Head Start for School Readiness Act of 2007, to promote the development of low-income infant and toddler age children, by enhancing cognitive, social and emotional development through the provision of comprehensive health, educational, nutritional, social and other services. Head Start emphasizes the significant involvement of parents: in their children's learning; in the administration of their local Head Start programs; and in realizing their own educational, literacy and employment goals.

Eligible applicants: profit and private institutions/organizations, IHEs (includes research).

Eligible beneficiaries: local, public institutions/organizations, and eligible low-income individuals/families.

Range/Average: N.A.

Activity: N.A.

HQ: ACF-HHS, 1250 Maryland Ave., SW, Washington, DC 20024. Phone: (202) 205-7378.

Internet: www.acf.hhs.gov/programs/ohs.

93.710   COMMUNITY SERVICES BLOCK GRANT (ARRA) ("CSBG-ARRA")

Assistance: formula grants.

Purposes: pursuant to ARRA 2009 and Community Services Block Grant Act (CSBG Act), as amended by the COATES Act of 1998, to provide assistance to states and local communities, working through a network of community action agencies and other neighborhood-based organizations, for: reduction of poverty; revitalization of low-income communities; and empowerment of low-income families and individuals in rural and urban areas to become fully self-sufficient (particularly families who are attempting to transition off a state program carried out under part A of Title IV of the Social Security Act). States are required to use 99 percent of their ARRA allocations for grants to "eligible entities," as defined in the CSBG Act, with the remaining one percent for benefits enrollment coordination activities to identify and enroll eligible individuals and families.

Eligible applicants: states, (includes public IHEs and hospitals), federally-recognized tribal governments, and U.S. territories/possessions.

Eligible beneficiaries: public nonprofit institutions/organizations and individuals/families.

Range/Average: N.A.

Activity: N.A.

HQ: Division of State Assistance, Office of Community Services, ACF-HHS, 901 D St., SW, 5th Fl., Rm. 5A165, Washington, DC 20447. Phone: (202) 401-2333.

Internet: www.acf.hhs.gov/programs/ocs/csbg. (Note: no field offices for this program.)

93.711   STRENGTHENING COMMUNITIES FUND ("SCF, Recovery Act")

Assistance: project grants/cooperative agreements (80 percent/2 years).

Purposes: pursuant to ARRA 2009, to fund SCF which is composed of two programs: (1) SCF Nonprofit Capacity Building Program which provides training, technical assistance, and financial assistance to local faith-based and community organizations enabling them to more fully participate in economic recovery; and (2) SFC Government Capacity Building Program which builds the capacity of state, local, and tribal governments to provide outreach to faith-based and community-based organizations. Applicants are encouraged to meet their 20 percent match requirements through cash contributions.

Eligible applicants/beneficiaries: state, local, and tribal governments; private/public institutions and organizations.

Range/Average: N.A.

Activity: N.A.

HQ: Office of Community Services, Division of State Assistance, ACF-HHS, 370 L'Enfant Promenade, SW, 5th Fl. West, Washington, DC 20447. Phone: (202) 401-5115; FAX: (202) 401-419.

Internet: www.acf.hhs.gov/programs/ocs/index.html.

93.713   CHILD CARE AND DEVELOPMENT BLOCK GRANT (ARRA) ("CCDBG")

Assistance: formula grants (100 percent/2 years).

Purposes: pursuant to ARRA, 2009 and Child Care and Development Block Grant Act of 1990, to provide child care assistance for low-income families and to: allow each state maximum flexibility in developing child care programs and policies; promote parental choice and empower working parents to make decisions about good child care; encourage states to provide consumer education information for parents about child care choices; assist states in providing child care to parents trying to achieve independence from public assistance; and assist states in implementing their established health, safety, licensing, and registration standards regulations.

Eligible applicants: states (includes DC, public IHEs and hospitals), U.S. territories/possessions, and federally recognized Indian tribal governments.

Eligible beneficiaries: low income individuals/families.

Range/Average: N.A.

Activity: N.A.

HQ: Child Care Bureau, Office of Family Assistance, ACF-HHS, 370 L'Enfant Promenade, S.W., 5th Fl. East, Washington, DC 20447. Phone: (202) 401-4831; FAX: (202) 690-5600.

Internet: www.acf.hhs.gov/programs/ccb.

93.714   EMERGENCY CONTINGENCY FUND FOR TEMPORARY ASSISTANCE FOR NEEDY FAMILIES (TANF) STATE PROGRAMS ("TANF Emergency Fund, Recovery Act")

Assistance: formula grants (100 percent).

Purposes: pursuant to ARRA, 2009 and TANF Emergency Fund, Recovery Act, Title IV, Part A, Section 2101, to promote the economic and social well being of children, youth, families, and communities by providing up to $5 billion for states, territories, and tribes) in FY 2009 and FY 2010 that have increased assistance caseloads and/or certain types of expenditures. This Emergency Fund is in addition to the TANF Contingency Fund in section 403(b) of the Act that currently gives money to qualifying States (but not territories or tribes) during an economic downturn.

Eligible applicants: states (includes DC, public IHEs and hospitals).

Eligible beneficiaries: states, U.S. territories/possessions, federally recognized Indian tribal governments, and Native American organizations.

Range/Average: N.A.

Activity: N.A.

HQ: Director, Office of Family Assistance, ACF-HHS, 5th Fl., East, Aerospace Bldg., 370 L'Enfant Promenade, SW, Washington, DC 20447. Phone: (202) 401-4731; FAX: (202) 205-5887.

Internet: www.acf.hhs.gov/programs/ofa.

93.716   TEMPORARY ASSISTANCE FOR NEEDY FAMILIES (TANF) SUPPLEMENTAL GRANTS

Assistance: formula grants (20 - 25 percent).

Purposes: pursuant to Supplemental Grants for Population Increases in Certain States, Recovery Act, Title IV, Part A, Section 2102, to provide supplemental TANF funds for states with exceptionally high population growth in the early 1990s, historic (1994) welfare grants per poor person lower than 35 percent of the national average, or a combination of those factors. This program carries a maintenance of effort (MOE) requirement wherein funded states spend an applicable percentage of its own money to help eligible families in ways consistent with the purposes of the TANF program.

Eligible applicants: states (includes DC, public IHEs and hospitals).

Eligible beneficiaries: low income individuals/families.

Range/Average: N.A.

Activity: N.A.

HQ: Director, Office of Family Assistance, ACF-HHS, 5th Fl., East, Aerospace Bldg., 370 L'Enfant Promenade, SW, Washington, DC 20447. Phone: (202) 401-4731; FAX: (202) 205-5887.

Internet: www.acf.hhs.gov/programs/ofa/tanf/index.html.

93.718   HEALTH INFORMATION TECHNOLOGY REGIONAL EXTENSION CENTERS PROGRAM

Assistance: project grants/discretionary (50 percent/to 4 years).

Purposes: pursuant to PHSA and ARRA of 2009, to establish Health Information Technology Regional Extension Centers to identify and disseminate best practices and provide technical assistance supporting the adoption and meaningful use of health IT to improve care quality while protecting patient privacy.

Eligible applicants: public nonprofit institutions/organizations (includes IHEs and hospitals).

Eligible beneficiaries: anyone/general public.

Range: N.A. **Average:** $8,500,000.

Activity: N.A.

HQ: Office of the National Coordinator for Health Information Technology, HHS, 330 C St., SW, Ste. 1100, Washington, DC 20201. Phone: (202) 690-7151.

Internet: healthit.gov. (Note: no field offices for this program.)

93.719   ADVANCE INTEROPERABLE HEALTH INFORMATION TECHNOLOGY SERVICES TO SUPPORT HEALTH INFORMATION EXCHANGE

Assistance: project grants/discretionary (to 4 years).

Purposes: pursuant to ARRA of 2009, Division A, Title XIII, HITECH Act, this state-based program will: promote electronic movement and use of health information among organizations using nationally recognized interoperability standards; enable providers to qualify for ARRA-authorized Medicare and Medicaid financial incentives, by providing health information exchange; improve health care quality and efficiency; establish a technical infrastructure to support health care reform.

Eligible applicants: states (includes DC, public IHEs and hospitals).

Eligible beneficiaries: anyone/general public.

Range: N.A. **Average:** $2,470.000, estimated.

Activity: N.A.

HQ: HHS, 330 C St., SW, Ste. 7033A, Washington, DC 20201. Phone: (202) 550-5796.

Internet: www.healthit.gov. (Note: no field offices for this program.)

93.721   HEALTH INFORMATION TECHNOLOGY PROFESSIONALS IN HEALTH CARE (ARRA)
("Health Information Technology Education HITE")

Assistance: cooperative agreements/discretionary grants; project grants/discretionary (100 percent/2 to 4 years).

Purposes: pursuant to ARRA, to provide assistance to IHEs (or consortia thereof) to establish or expand health informatics education programs, including certification, undergraduate, and masters degree programs, for both health care and information technology students to ensure the rapid and effective utilization and development of health information technologies in the U.S. health care infrastructure.

Eligible applicants/beneficiaries: 35 IHEs selected by the CDC as Prevention Research Centers (PRCs).

Range: N.A. **Average:** $966,436.

Activity: N.A.

HQ: Office of the National Coordinator for Health Information Technology, HHS, 330 C St., SW, Ste. 1100, Washington, DC 20201. Phone: (202) 690-7151.

Internet: healthit.gov. (Note: no field offices for this program.)

93.727   BEACON COMMUNITIES—COMMUNITY HEALTH PEER LEARNING PROGRAM

Assistance: cooperative agreements (100 percent/3 years).

Purposes: pursuant to the ARRA of 2009, to support health IT and information exchange infrastructure and implement performance measurement, quality improvement, and care coordination programs to achieve improvements in health care quality, safety, efficiency, and population health with the goal of hospitals, clinicians, communities and patients becoming meaningful users of health IT.

Eligible applicants/beneficiaries: 35 IHEs selected by the CDC as Prevention Research Centers (PRCs).

Range: N.A. **Average:** $2,226,818.

Activity: N.A.

HQ: Office of the National Coordinator for Health Information Technology, HHS, 330 C St., SW, Ste. 1100, Washington, DC 20201. Phone: (202) 690-7151.

Internet: healthit.gov. (Note: no field offices for this program.)

93.728   STRATEGIC HEALTH IT ADVANCED RESEARCH PROJECTS (ARRA) ("SHARP")

Assistance: cooperative agreements (100 percent/4 years).

Purposes: pursuant to ARRA of 2009, to conduct research pinpointing where breakthrough advances are needed to address well-documented problems that have impeded adoption of health IT and to accelerate progress towards achieving meaningful, nationwide use of health IT in support of a high-performing health care system.

Eligible applicants/beneficiaries: 35 IHEs selected by the CDC as Prevention Research Centers (PRCs).

Range/Average: N.A.

Activity: N.A.

HQ: Program Director, SHARP, Office of the Secretary, HHS, 200 Independence Ave., SW, Washington, DC 22209. Phone: (202) 690-7151.

Internet: healthit.gov/policy-researchers-implementers/strategic-health-it-advanced-research-projects-sharp. (Note: no field offices for this program.)

93.732   MENTAL AND BEHAVIORAL HEALTH EDUCATION AND TRAINING GRANTS (MBHET)

Assistance: project grants (100 percent/3 years).

Purposes: pursuant to the Public Health Service Act as amended by the Patient Protection and Affordable Care Act, to support IHEs with accredited programs in social work, psychology (clinical and counseling), marriage and family therapy to recruit students to implement field placement for master's level social workers, psychologists, marriage and family therapists to deliver clinical behavioral health services to high need/high demand populations.

Eligible applicants: with accredited master's level programs social work, psychology (clinical and counseling), and marriage and family therapy.

Eligible beneficiaries: eligible student trainees who are U.S. citizens or nationals or have a permanent resident visa, be enrolled in accredited programs in social work, psychology (clinical and counseling) and/or marriage and family therapy, and commit to field placement with high need/high demand communities.

Range/Average: N.A.

Activity: N.A.

HQ: Director, Division of Public Health and Interdisciplinary Education, HHS, 5600 Fishers Ln., Rm. 9-89, Rockville, MD 20857. Phone: (301) 443-7661.

Internet: www.hrsa.gov.

93.733   CAPACITY BUILDING ASSISTANCE TO STRENGTHEN PUBLIC HEALTH IMMUNIZATION INFRASTRUCTURE AND PERFORMANCE

Assistance: cooperative agreements (100 percent/2 years).

Purposes: pursuant to the Public Health Service Act, as amended, to improve the efficiency, effectiveness, and/or quality of immunization practices by strengthening the immunization information technology infrastructure, building capacity for public health department insurance billing, and expanding immunization delivery partnerships so that more children, adolescents, and adults are protected against vaccine-preventable diseases.

Eligible applicants: current 64 CDC Immunization Program grantees.

Eligible beneficiaries: U.S. states, territories, political subdivisions and other public entities.

Range: $25,000 to $900,000. **Average:** $300,000.

Activity: N.A.

HQ: Program Director, CDC-HHS, 1600 Clifton Rd. NE, MS A-19, Atlanta, GA 30033. Phone: (404) 639-8715.

Internet: N.A. (Note: no field offices for this program.)

93.734   EMPOWERING OLDER ADULTS AND ADULTS WITH DISABILITIES THROUGH CHRONIC DISEASE SELF-MANAGEMENT EDUCATION PROGRAMS

Assistance: cooperative agreements; project grants/discretionary (100 percent/ to 3 years).

Purposes: pursuant to the Affordable Care Act (Prevention and Public Health Fund), to increase the number of older and/or disabled adults with chronic conditions who complete evidence-based chronic disease self-management education (CDSME) programs in order to maintain or improve their health status, and to strengthen and expand integrated, sustainable service systems within states to provide evidence-based CDSME programs.

Eligible applicants: state units on aging and public health departments in U.S. states/territories.

Eligible beneficiaries: older and disabled adults with chronic conditions who are residents of U.S. states/territories.

Range: $300,000 to $9000,000. **Average:** N.A.

Activity: N.A.

HQ: Program Director, Administration for Community Living, HHS, One Massachusetts Ave., Washington, DC 20001. Phone: 202-357-3508.

Internet: www.acl.gov. (Note: no field offices for this program.)

93.735 STATE PUBLIC HEALTH APPROACHES FOR ENSURING QUITLINE CAPACITY

Assistance: cooperative agreements (100 percent).

Purposes: pursuant to the Consolidated Appropriations Act, to ensure and support state quitline capacity, in order to respond to upcoming federal initiatives such as the National Tobacco Education Campaign. This program addresses the "Healthy People 2020" focus area of tobacco use and the goal of reducing illness, disability, and death related to tobacco use and secondhand smoke exposure.

Eligible applicants: state and territorial health departments (includes DC, Guam, and Puerto Rico).

Eligible beneficiaries: state and territorial health departments, and other public entities.

Range: $50,000 to $2,771,803. **Average:** N.A.

Activity: N.A.

HQ: Program Director, CDC-HHS, 4770 Buford Hwy. NE, MS K-50, Atlanta, GA 30341. Phone: (770) 488-1221.

Internet: www.cdc.gov. (Note: no field offices for this program.)

93.736 VIRAL HEPATITIS PREVENTION

Assistance: cooperative agreements (100 percent).

Purposes: pursuant to the Public Health Service Act, as amended, to allow for CDC to partner with multiple organizations to benefit individuals by substantially reducing viral hepatitis (HCV and HBV) transmission, identifying those that are chronically infected and linking infected individuals with treatment if appropriate.

Eligible applicants: state, DC, territorial, local, and tribal governments, small, minority and women-owned businesses, IHEs, research institutions, hospitals, profit/non profit, community-based, faith-based and tribal organizations.

Eligible beneficiaries: anyone, general public.

Range: $1,000,000 to $5,250,000. **Average:** N.A.

Activity: N.A.

HQ: Program Director, CDC-HHS, 1600 Clifton Rd., NE, Stop E-07, Atlanta, GA 30333. Phone: (404) 639-8531.

Internet: www.grants.gov. (Note: no field offices for this program.)

93.738 RACIAL AND ETHNIC APPROACHES TO COMMUNITY HEALTH PROGRAM ("REACH")

Assistance: cooperative agreements (100 percent/5 years).

Purposes: pursuant to the Public Health Service Act, to support the implementation of projects to reduce racial and ethnic health disparities. Program activities will focus on prevention of chronic diseases and conditions across multiple identified health areas, including: cardiovascular disease, diabetes, breast and cervical cancer, infant mortality, asthma, and child and adult immunizations.

Eligible applicants: state, DC, territorial, local, and tribal governments, small, minority and women-owned businesses, IHEs, research institutions, hospitals, profit/non profit, community-based, faith-based and tribal organizations.

Eligible beneficiaries: anyone, general public.

Range/Average: N.A.

Activity: N.A.

HQ: Program Director, CDC-HHS, 4770 Buford Hwy. NE, MS K30, Atlanta, GA 30333. Phone: (404) 498-3058.

Internet: www.cdc.gov. (Note: no field offices for this program.)

93.739 CHRONIC DISEASE INNOVATION GRANTS

Assistance: cooperative agreements (100 percent/4 years).

Purposes: pursuant to the Patient Protection and Affordable Care Act of 2010, to expand the National Diabetes Prevention Program, an evidence-based lifestyle change program in populations at high-risk for developing type 2 diabetes (African American, American Indian/Alaska Native, Hispanic/Latino, women with a history of gestational diabetes, and the economically impoverished).

Eligible applicants: small, minority and women-owned businesses, federally-recognized tribes, profit/non profit, regional, community-based, faith-based and tribal organizations.

Eligible beneficiaries: anyone, general public.

Range/Average: N.A.

Activity: N.A.

HQ: Program Director, CDC-HHS, 4770 Buford Hwy. NE, MS K10, Atlanta, GA 30333. Phone: (770) 488-1097; FAX: : (770) 488-8550.

Internet: www.cdc.gov. (Note: no field offices for this program.)

93.741   BREASTFEEDING PROMOTION AND SUPPORT—IMPROVING MATERNITY CARE PRACTICES

Assistance: cooperative agreements (100 percent/3 years).

Purposes: pursuant to the Consolidated Appropriations Act, to support breastfeeding mothers and support hospitals in promoting breastfeeding as part of national efforts to improve childhood nutrition and address childhood obesity.

Eligible applicants: only grantees previously awarded under Hospital Collaboratives to Improve Maternity Care Practices Related to Breastfeeding in the U.S. are eligible.

Eligible beneficiaries: anyone, general public.

Range/Average: N.A.

Activity: N.A.

HQ: Program Director, Breastfeeding Promotion and Support, CDC-HHS, 4770 Buford Hwy. NE, Atlanta, GA 30341. Phone: (404) 867-9697.

Internet: www.cdc.gov. (Note: no field offices for this program.)

93.742   EARLY CHILDCARE AND EDUCATION OBESITY PREVENTION PROGRAM—OBESITY PREVENTION IN YOUNG CHILDREN

Assistance: cooperative agreements (100 percent/5 years).

Purposes: pursuant to the Consolidated Appropriations Act, to improve the quality of obesity prevention practices through evidence and practice-based policy, environmental, programmatic and infrastructure changes in Early Child Care settings (e.g. child care centers, family care homes, Head Start programs, pre-schools, etc.) and facilities.

Eligible applicants/beneficiaries: 35 IHEs selected by the CDC as Prevention Research Centers (PRCs).

Range/Average: N.A.

Activity: N.A.

HQ: Program Director, Obesity Prevention in Young Children, CDC-HHS, 4770 Buford Hwy. NE, Atlanta, GA 30341. Phone: (770) 488-6042.

Internet: www.cdc.gov. (Note: no field offices for this program.)

93.743   REACH: OBESITY AND HYPERTENSION DEMONSTRATION PROJECTS

Assistance: cooperative agreements (100 percent/5 years).

Purposes: pursuant to the Public Health Service Act, to support the implementation of projects that develop and implement replicable and scalable strategies to assure population-wide policy, systems, and environmental (PSE) changes that will address any racial and ethnic health disparities in obesity and hypertension reduction practices. The program is designed to fund organizations that have a partnership with a local community-based organization, a local public health department (or tribal organization), and a university/academic institution.

Eligible applicants: state, DC, territorial, local, and tribal governments, small, minority and women-owned businesses, IHEs, research institutions, hospitals, local health authorities, profit/non profit, community-based, faith-based and tribal organizations.

Eligible beneficiaries: anyone, general public.

Range/Average: N.A.

Activity: N.A.

HQ: Program Director, CDC, HHS, 4770 Buford Hwy. NE, MS-K40, NCCD-PHP, Atlanta, GA 30333. Phone: (770) 488-2524; FAX: (770) 488-5964.

Internet: N.A.

93.744 BREAST AND CERVICAL CANCER SCREENING OPPORTUNITIES FOR STATES, TRIBES, AND TERRITORIES

Assistance: cooperative agreements (100 percent).

Purposes: pursuant to the Consolidated Appropriations Act, to enhance and leverage existing organized systems for breast and cervical cancer screening in order to provide high quality screening, tracking and follow-up (including patient navigation) to low income, uninsured and under-insured women.

Eligible applicants: states or their bona fide agents, tribes and territories currently funded through Cancer Prevention and Control Programs.

Eligible beneficiaries: anyone, general public.

Range: $15,000 to $700,000. **Average:** N.A.

Activity: N.A.

HQ: Program Director, NCCDPHP, CDC-HHS, 4770 Buford, Hwy. MS F76, Atlanta, GA 30341. Phone: (770) 488-4880; FAX: (770) 488-3230.

Internet: www.cdc.gov. (Note: no field offices for this program.)

93.745 HEALTH CARE SURVEILLANCE/HEALTH STATISTICS—BEHAVIORAL RISK FACTOR SURVEILLANCE SYSTEM

Assistance: cooperative agreements (100 percent/22 months).

Purposes: pursuant to ARRA and the Public Health Service Act, to allocate funds for planning, implementing and data collecting surveillance information through the BRFSS, add six health care access and use questions to the 2013 BRFSS survey, increase the BRFSS landline sample size to restore the number of completed interviews achieved to 2011 levels, and increase the proportion of cell phone interviews.

Eligible applicants/beneficiaries: 35 IHEs selected by the CDC as Prevention Research Centers (PRCs).

Range: $50,000 to $100,000. **Average:** $68,000.

Activity: N.A.

HQ: Program Director, BRFSS, CDC-HHS, 2500 Century Pkwy., Atlanta, GA 30345. Phone: (404) 498-6558.

Internet: www.grants.gov. (Note: no field offices for this program.)

93.747 ELDER ABUSE PREVENTION INTERVENTIONS PROGRAM ("Elder Abuse Prevention Interventions Projects")

Assistance: cooperative agreements/discretionary grants (100 percent/3 years).

Purposes: pursuant to the Patient Protection and Affordable Care Act, to develop, implement, and evaluate successful or promising prevention interventions in elder abuse, neglect, and exploitation.

Eligible applicants: state and tribal governments.

Eligible beneficiaries: older adults.

Range/Average: N.A.

Activity: N.A.

HQ: Director, Administration on Aging, Administration for Community Living, One Massachusetts Ave., NW, Washington, DC 20201. Phone: (202) 357-3519.

Internet: www.acl.gov. (Note: no field offices for this program.)

93.748 COOPERATIVE AGREEMENTS FOR PRESCRIPTION DRUG MONITORING PROGRAM, ELECTRONIC HEALTH RECORD (EHR) INTEGRATION, AND INTEROPERABILITY EXPANSION

Assistance: cooperative agreements (100 percent).

Purposes: pursuant to the Public Health Service Act, as amended, to improve real-time access to PDMP data by integrating Prescription Drug Monitoring Programs (PDMPs) into existing technologies like Electronic Health Records (EHRs), in order to improve the ability of state PDMPs to reduce the nature, scope, and extent of prescription drug abuse, and to strengthen state PDMPs that are currently operational by providing resources to make changes necessary to increase interoperability.

Eligible applicants/beneficiaries: 35 IHEs selected by the CDC as Prevention Research Centers (PRCs).

Range: to $225,000. **Average:** N.A.

Activity: N.A.

HQ: Program Director, SAMHSA-HHS, 1 Choke Cherry Rd., Rockville, MD 20850. Phone: (240) 276-1418.

Internet: www.samhsa.gov. (Note: no field offices for this program.)

93.749 PUBLIC HEALTH LABORATORY INFRASTRUCTURE

Assistance: cooperative agreements (100 percent/to 5 years).

Purposes: pursuant to the Public Health Service Act, funding for the Association of Public Health Laboratories (APHL) to strengthen public health infectious disease laboratory infrastructure by addressing gaps in public health laboratory practice, and to assist with development, implementation and ongoing support of laboratory technologies for use in public health.

Eligible applicants: Association of Public Health Laboratories (APHL), a private nonprofit organization and the current CDC-approved single grantee.

Eligible beneficiaries: states, political subdivisions, U.S. territories, other public entities and students/trainees.

Range: $1,000,000 to $3,000,000. **Average:** $2,000,000.

Activity: N.A.

HQ: Program Director, CDC-HHS, 1600 Clifton Rd., MS-E56, Atlanta, GA 30333. Phone: (404) 498-1307.

Internet: www.cdc.gov. (Note: no field offices for this program.)

93.751 CONSORTIUM FOR TOBACCO USE CESSATION TECHNICAL ASSISTANCE

Assistance: project grants (100 percent/to 5 years).

Purposes: pursuant to the Consolidation Appropriations Act of 2013, the Consolidated and Further Continuing Appropriations Act of 2013, and the Patient Protection and Affordable Care Act, funds to develop a consortium for tobacco use cessation technical assistance. The aim of the cessation consortium is to provide technical assistance to state tobacco control programs and national and state partners by translating the science of tobacco control cessation into public health action in order to increase the rate of cessation among tobacco users in the U.S. The technical assistance will support state tobacco control programs and other partners to promote comprehensive cessation strategies for state tobacco control programs, enhance state "quitline" capacity, promote comprehensive cessation coverage, and promote health systems change. Project funds may be used for costs associated with planning, organizing, conducting, and supporting tobacco cessation technical assistance strategies.

Eligible applicants: state and local governments or their bona fide agents, IHEs, nonprofit and for-profit organizations, Native American tribal governments, Native American organizations.

Eligible beneficiaries: general public.

Range: $75,000 to $450,000. **Average:** $112,500.

Activity: N.A.

HQ: Director, Consortium for Tobacco Use Cessation Technical Assistance, NCCDPH-CDC, 4770 Buford Highway NE, Stop K50, Atlanta, GA 30341. Phone: (770) 488-1172.

Internet: www.cdc.gov.

93.752 CANCER PREVENTION AND CONTROL PROGRAMS FOR STATE, TERRITORIAL AND TRIBAL ORGANIZATIONS FINANCED IN PART BY PREVENTION AND PUBLIC HEALTH FUNDS
("National Breast and Cervical Cancer Early Detection Program")

Assistance: project grants/cooperative agreements (to 75 percent/1 to 5 years).

Purposes: funds to develop comprehensive breast and cervical cancer early detection programs with the goal of increasing screening and follow-up among all groups of women, with special attention to reaching those women who are of low income, uninsured, underinsured and minority, or Native American. Cooperative agreement funds may be used to assure screening of women for breast and cervical cancer as an early detection preventive measure; assure appropriate referrals for follow-up services for women with abnormal screening tests and routine rescreening; develop and disseminate public education and outreach programs for the early detection and control of breast and cervical cancers; improve the education, training and skills of health professionals in the early detection and control of breast and cervical cancers; establish mechanisms through which the States, tribes and territories can monitor the quality of breast and cervical cancer screening procedures, including the interpretation of such procedures; and evaluate program activities through appropriate surveillance and monitoring.

Eligible applicants/beneficiaries: state and territorial health departments, tribal health and organizations.

Range: $242,796 to $8,693,584. **Average:** $2,320,696.

Activity: N.A.

HQ: Director, NBCCEDP, CDC, 4770 Buford Hwy, NE, Atlanta, GA 30341. Phone: (770) 488-1074.

Internet: www.cdc.gov. (Note: no field offices for this program.)

93.753 CHILD LEAD POISONING PREVENTION SURVEILLANCE FINANCED IN PART BY PREVENTION AND PUBLIC HEALTH (PPHF) PROGRAM ("Childhood Lead Poisoning Prevention Surveillance")

Assistance: project grants/cooperative agreements (100 percent/1 to 5 years).

Purposes: funds to support and enhance surveillance capacity at the state and city level to prevent and eliminate childhood lead poisoning. Funds may not be expended for medical care and treatment, or for environmental remediation of lead sources.

Eligible applicants: federal, state, local, territorial, tribal governments, public and private nonprofit and for profit institutions and organizations.

Eligible beneficiaries: anyone/general public.

Range: $250,000 to $500,000.

Activity: N.A.

HQ: Director, Childhood Lead Poisoning Prevention Surveillance, CDC, 4770 Buford Hwy, NE, Stop F45, Atlanta, GA 30341-3717. Phone: (770) 488-0711.

Internet: www.cdc.gov/nceh/lead. (Note: no field offices for this program.)

93.754 PROMOTION AND SUPPORT OF OPTIMAL BREASTFEEDING PRACTICES THROUGHOUT THE UNITED STATES

Assistance: project grants (100 percent/1 to 5 years).

Purposes: project grants to increase capacity to provide new or enhanced services that promote, support, facilitate and implement strategies to improve sub-optimal breastfeeding practices in the U.S. and affect long term changes in the rates of breastfeeding and obesity. Funds may be used for costs associated with planning, data collection, organizing, and the implementation of program elements related to the following objectives: increase breastfeeding rates throughout the United States; promote and support optimal breastfeeding practices; improve the health and well-being of mothers, infants and children; and reduce disparities in breast-feeding.

Eligible applicants: state, territorial, tribal health departments.

Eligible beneficiaries: anyone/general public.

Range: $500,000 to $2,500,000. **Average:** N.A.

Activity: N.A.

HQ: Director, Promotion and Support of Breastfeeding, NCCDPHP-CDC, 4770 Buford Hwy, NE, Atlanta, GA 30341. Phone: (404) 867-9697.

Internet: www.cdc.gov.

93.761   EVIDENCE-BASED FALLS PREVENTION PROGRAMS

Assistance: cooperative agreements/discretionary grants. (100 percent/to 3 years).

Purposes: pursuant to the Consolidated Appropriations Act of 2014, the Public Health Service Act, and the Patient Protection and Affordable Care Act, to significantly increase the number of older adults and adults with disabilities at risk of falls who participate in evidence-based community programs to reduce falls and falls risks.

Eligible applicants: state, local, and tribal governments, public and private nonprofits, community- and faith-based organizations, hospitals and IHEs.

Eligible beneficiaries: older and disabled adults at risk for falls residing in states, tribes, and territories.

Range: $509,000 to $695,000. **Average:** $581,356.

Activity: N.A.

HQ: Administration for Community Living, HHS, 330 C St., Washington, DC 20201. Phone: (202) 795-7438.

Internet: www.acl.gov.

93.767   STATE CHILDREN'S INSURANCE PROGRAM ("CHIP")

Assistance: formula grants (to 85 percent).

Purposes: pursuant to the Medicare, Medicaid and State Children's Health Insurance Program Balanced Budget Refinement Act of 1999, Medicare, Medicaid, and State Children's Health Insurance Program Improvement Act of 2000, for states to initiate and expand child health assistance to uninsured low-income children, including under state Medicaid programs. Coverage may not discriminate on the basis of diagnosis nor pre-existing condition, and must be coordinated with other public and private programs. The cost of abortions may be covered only to save the life of the mother or if the pregnancy resulted from rape or incest.

Eligible applicants: states, possessions and territories with HHS-approved state plans.

Eligible beneficiaries: targeted low-income children whose family income exceeds Medicaid limits by no more than 50 percent, ineligible for Medicaid and not covered by other health insurance—not including families eligible for a state health benefits plan through employment with a state public agency.

Range: $999,756 to $1,57,720,328. **Average:** N.A.

Activity: N.A.

HQ: Center for Medicaid and State Operations, CMS-HHS, 7500 Security Blvd., Baltimore, MD 21244. Phone: (410) 786-3870.

Internet: www.cms.gov. (Note: no field offices for this program.)

93.770 MEDICARE—PRESCRIPTION DRUG COVERAGE ("Medicare Part D")

Assistance: direct payments/specified use.

Purposes: pursuant to SSA and Medicare Prescription Drug, Improvement and Modernization Act of 2003 (Medicare Modernization Act or "MMA"), to provide prescription drugs to Medicare beneficiaries through their voluntary participation in prescription drug plans, with a subsidy provided to low-income beneficiaries.

Eligible applicants: nongovernmental entities organized and licensed under state laws as risk-bearing entities to offer health insurance in state in which they offer plans.

Eligible beneficiaries: individuals entitled to Medicare benefits under Part A or enrolled in Part B, residing in an approved plan's service area, and not enrolled in a Medicare Advantage plan other than a Medicare savings account plan or private fee- for-service plan that does not provide qualified prescription drug coverage.

Range/Average: N.A.

Activity: N.A.

HQ: CMS-HHS, 7500 Security Blvd., Baltimore, MD 21244. Phone: (410) 786-7625.

Internet: www.cms.hhs.gov. (Note: no field offices for this program.)

93.773 MEDICARE—HOSPITAL INSURANCE ("Medicare Part A")

Assistance: direct payments/specified use.

Purposes: pursuant to ARRA 2009, SSA, Medicare, Medicaid, and State Children's Health Insurance Program Improvement Act of 2000, MMA, amendments, and other acts, to provide insurance coverage for treatment in hospitals and other care facilities for covered services to persons age 65 or over, to certain disabled persons, and to those with chronic renal disease. Benefits may be paid to participating and emergency hospitals, skilled nursing facilities, home health agencies, and hospice agencies— for inpatient hospital services and post-hospital extended care services incurred during a benefit period. The beneficiary is responsible for a $1,288 inpatient hospital deductible, and varying coinsurance amounts according to the type and length of care received. Home health services are paid in full.

Eligible applicants/beneficiaries: persons age 65 or over and certain disabled persons. Nearly everyone that reached 65 before 1968 is eligible, including those ineligible for cash Social Security benefits. Those reaching age 65 in 1968 or after and ineligible need some work credit to qualify for hospital insurance benefits, the amount of which depends on their age. Hospital insurance is also available to persons age 65 or over and otherwise ineligible, through payment of a monthly premium. Certain federal, state, and local government employees are also eligible.

Range/Average: N.A.

Activity: N.A.

HQ: Center for Medicare & Medicaid Services, 7500 Security Blvd., Baltimore, MD 212444. Phone: (410) 786-5407.

Internet: www.cms.hhs.gov. (Note: no field offices for this program.)

93.774 MEDICARE—SUPPLEMENTARY MEDICAL INSURANCE ("Medicare Part B")

Assistance: direct payments/specified use (50-100 percent).

Purposes: pursuant to ARRA 2009, SSA as amended, Medicare, Medicaid, and State Children's Health Insurance Program Improvement Act of 2000, MMA, amendments, and other acts, to provide medical insurance protection for covered services furnished by physicians and other suppliers of medical services to elderly or disabled persons and to those with chronic renal disease, including services provided by hospitals, skilled nursing facilities, and home health agencies. The beneficiary is responsible for an annual $166 deductible before benefits may begin, effective in FY 05; thereafter, Medicare pays a percentage of charges for covered services, varying from 50 to 100 percent. The enrollee pays a monthly premium. Some states and other third- parties pay the premium on behalf of qualifying individuals.

Eligible applicants/beneficiaries: all persons age 65 and over, and those under age 65 eligabible for hospital insurance benefits (see 93.773)—voluntarily enrolled for supplementary medical insurance. eligabibility is available to U.S. citizen-residents or lawful permanent residents residing in the U.S. continuously for the previous five years.

Range/Average: N.A.

Activity: anticipate 55,340,000 enrollees in FY 2015.

HQ: Center for Beneficiary Choices, CMS-HHS, 7500 Security Blvd., Baltimore, MD 21207. Phone: (410) 786-5995.

Internet: www.cms.hhs.gov. (Note: no field offices for this program.)

93.775 STATE MEDICAID FRAUD CONTROL UNITS (SMFCU)

Assistance: formula grants (75-90 percent).

Purposes: pursuant to SSA as amended, to investigate and prosecute fraud and patient abuse in state Medicaid programs.

Eligible applicants/beneficiaries: specified state government entities.

Range: $291,136 to $38,191,424. **Average:** $3,964,705.

Activity: N.A.

HQ: Director, Medicaid Fraud Unit Oversight Division, Office of Evaluation and Inspections, Office of Inspector General, OS-HHS, Cohen Bldg., 330 Independence Ave., SW, Washington, DC 20201. Phone: (202) 619-0480.

Internet: www.oig.hhs.gov. (Note: no field offices for this program.)

93.777   STATE SURVEY AND CERTIFICATION OF HEALTH CARE PROVIDERS AND SUPPLIERS

Assistance: formula grants.

Purposes: pursuant to SSA as amended, to monitor health care providers and suppliers to assure their compliance with federal regulatory health and safety standards and conditions of participation in Medicare and Medicaid programs.

Eligible applicants/beneficiaries: designated state agencies.

Range: $598,898 to $45,741,734. **Average:** $6,827,599.

Activity: N.A.

HQ: Director, Survey and Certification Group, CMS-HHS, 7500 Security Blvd., Baltimore, MD 21244. Phone: (410) 786-9493.

Internet: www.cms.hhs.gov/contracts. (Note: no field offices for this program.)

93.778   MEDICAL ASSISTANCE PROGRAM
("Medicaid; Title XIX")

Assistance: formula grants (50-83 percent).

Purposes: pursuant to SSA as amended, for medical assistance payments on behalf of recipients of cash assistance, children, pregnant women, certain elderly, and other eligible groups. States must provide: hospital in- and outpatient care; rural health clinic services; federally qualified health center services; other laboratory and X-ray services; nursing facility services; home health services for persons over age 21; family planning services; early and periodic screening, diagnosis, and treatment for persons under age 21; pediatric or family nurse practitioner services; nurse-midwife services. States may use funds to pay for Medicare premiums, copayments, and deductible payments of eligible beneficiaries.

Eligible applicants: state and local welfare agencies.

Eligible beneficiaries: low-income persons over age 65 or blind or disabled, members of families with dependent children, low-income children and pregnant women; certain Medicare beneficiaries; in some states, medically-needy persons may apply to a state or local welfare agency for medical assistance.

Range: $16,170,000 to $58,353,405,000. **Average:** $6,735,769,321.

Activity: N.A.

HQ: Center for Medicaid and State Operations, CMS-HHS, 7500 Security Blvd., Rm. C4-25-02, Baltimore, MD 21244. Phone: (410) 786-3870.

Internet: www.cms.hhs.gov/contracts. (Note: no field offices for this program.)

93.779 CENTERS FOR MEDICARE AND MEDICAID SERVICES (CMS) RESEARCH, DEMONSTRATIONS AND EVALUATIONS ("CMS Research")

Assistance: project grants. (to 95 percent/to 2 years).

Purposes: pursuant to the SSA and Small Business Innovation Development Act of 1982 as amended, for analyses, experiments, demonstrations, and pilot projects to resolve major health care financing issues or to improve the administration of the Medicare and Medicaid programs. Funds may be provided as SBIR grants , Hispanic health services grants, HBCU grants, IHE grants.

Eligible applicants/beneficiaries: private nonprofit or profit organizations; public agencies including state Medicaid agencies.

Range/Average: N.A.

Activity: N.A.

HQ: Director, Office of Research, Development, and Information, CMS-HHS, Central Bldg., Rm. C3-20-11, 7500 Security Blvd., Baltimore, MD 21244. Phone: (800) 633-4277.

Internet: www.cms.hhs.gov/contracts. (Note: no field offices for this program.)

93.780 GRANTS TO STATES FOR OPERATION OF QUALIFIED HIGH-RISK POOLS

Assistance: formula grants.

Purposes: pursuant to the Trade Act of 2002, for the operation of qualified state high-risk health insurance pools by providing federal funding for up to 50 percent of losses incurred by the pool for a given state fiscal year.

Eligible applicants/beneficiaries: states that: (1) operate a qualified high-risk pool as defined in section 2744(c)(2) of PHSA; restrict premiums charged under the pool to no more than 150 percent of applicable standard risk rates for the state; offer a choice of two or more coverage options through the pool; have in effect a mechanism reasonably designed to ensure continues funding of losses after then end of FY 04; incurred losses in the state's FY 02, 03, or 04.

Range/Average: N.A.

Activity: N.A.

HQ: Centers for Medicare and State Operations, CMS-HHS 200 Independence Ave., SW, Rm. 739H, Washington, DC 20201. Phone: (301) 492-4482.

Internet: www.cms.hhs.gov/HighRiskPools. (Note: no field offices for this program.)

93.784 FEDERAL REIMBURSEMENT OF EMERGENCY HEALTH SERVICES FURNISHED TO UNDOCUMENTED ALIENS

Assistance: direct payments/specified use.

Purposes: pursuant to MMA, to reimburse providers for their otherwise unreimbursed costs associated with furnishing emergency health services required under the Emergency Medical Treatment and Active Labor Act (EMTALA), to undocumented and certain other aliens.

Eligible applicants: states.

Eligible beneficiaries: hospitals, certain physicians, ambulance services that provide emergency health care under EMTALA.

Range/Average: N.A.

Activity: N.A.

HQ: Hospital and Ambulatory Group, Center for Medicare Management, CMS-HHS, 7500 Security Blvd., Baltimore, MD 21244. Phone: (410) 786-0048.

Internet: www.cms.gov/undocaliens.02policy,asp. (Note: no field offices for this program.)

93.791 MONEY FOLLOWS THE PERSON REBALANCING DEMONSTRATION

Assistance: project grants (to 5 years).

Purposes: pursuant to Deficit Reduction Act of 2005, to give states the option to rebalance their long-term support programs to allow Medicaid programs to be more sustainable, while helping individuals to achieve independence by proposing a system of home and community-based care, subject to approval by the CMS. States will be reimbursed for home and community-based services under this program.

Eligible applicants: any single State Medicaid Agency, State Mental Health Agency or instrumentality of the state (meaning states, DC, or U.S. territories or possessions). Only one application per state.

Eligible beneficiaries: individuals who have resided in state for at least 6 months (possibly up to 2 years as specified in some states) previous to start of Money Follows the Person (MFP) Rebalancing Demonstration; who are in an inpatient facility; who receive Medicaid benefits for services furnished by the facility and who would continue to require those services.

Range/Average: N.A.

Activity: N.A.

HQ: CMS-HHS (MS S2-14-26), 7500 Security Blvd., Baltimore, MD 21244. Phone: (410) 786-8287.

Internet: www.cms.gov/CommunityServices/20_MFP.asp. (Note: no field offices for this program.)

93.810 PAUL COVERDELL NATIONAL ACUTE STROKE PROGRAM

Assistance: cooperative agreements. (100 percent/to 5 years).

Purposes: pursuant to the Public Health Services Act, as amended, to improve the quality of acute stroke care and health outcomes for acute stroke patients. Funds may be used to develop and maintain partnerships, implement and support the operation of a hospital based stroke registry, and develop and maintain a quality improvement program. Funds may not be used for research or clinical care.

Eligible applicants/beneficiaries: state health departments.

Range: $700,000 to $800,000. **Average:** N.A.

Activity: N.A.

HQ: CDC-HHS, 4770 Buford Hwy., NE, Stop F72, Atlanta, GA 30341. Phone: (770) 488-6093.

Internet: www.cdc.gov. (Note: no field offices for this program.)

93.813 HEART DISEASE & STROKE PREVENTION PROGRAM AND DIABETES PREVENTION

Assistance: cooperative agreements. (100 percent/to 5 years).

Purposes: pursuant to the Public Health Service Act and the Affordable Care Act, to support the implementation of population-wide and priority population approaches to prevent obesity, diabetes, and heart disease and stroke and reduce health disparities in these areas among adults. Funds may be used for costs associated with planning, implementing, and evaluating chronic disease prevention and control programs.

Eligible applicants: state and local health departments.

Eligible beneficiaries: communities.

Range: $1,300,000 to $3,520,000. **Average:** N.A.

Activity: N.A.

HQ: CDC-HHS, 4770 Buford Hwy., NE, Stop F75, Atlanta, GA 30341. Phone: (770) 488-1431.

Internet: www.cdc.gov. (Note: no field offices for this program.)

93.814 PARTNER SUPPORT FOR HEART DISEASE AND STROKE PREVENTION

Assistance: cooperative agreements. (100 percent).

Purposes: pursuant to the Public Health Service Act, to provide partnership support around cardiovascular disease prevention efforts, including dissemination of evidence-based practices, tools and strategies, creating opportunities for peer learning and sharing of best practices, facilitating community and clinical linkages at the state and local level, and packaging and promoting the use of cardiovascular tools and products.

Eligible applicants/beneficiaries: state, local, tribal, and territorial government organizations and NGOs.

Range: $250,000 to $500,000. **Average:** $400,000.

Activity: N.A.

HQ: CDC-HHS, 4770 Buford Hwy., NE, Stop F-72, Atlanta, GA 30341. Phone: (770) 488-5108.

Internet: www.cdc.gov. (Note: no field offices for this program.)

93.817 HOSPITAL PREPAREDNESS PROGRAM (HPP)—EBOLA PREPAREDNESS AND RESPONSE ACTIVITIES

Assistance: formula grants/cooperative agreements. (100 percent/to 5 years).

Purposes: pursuant to the Consolidated and Continuing Appropriations Act of 2015, and the Public Health Service Act, to improve healthcare system preparedness for Ebola and develop a regional hospital network for Ebola patient care.

Eligible applicants/beneficiaries: states.

Range: $202,989 to $15,229,780. **Average:** $3,250,000.

Activity: N.A.

HQ: Office of the Assistant Secretary for Preparedness and Response, HHS, 200 C St., SW, Rm. C4K12, Washington, DC 20024. Phone: (202) 245-0732.

Internet: www.phe.gov. (Note: no field offices for this program.)

93.822   HEALTH CAREERS OPPORTUNITY PROGRAM (HCOP)

Assistance: project grants. (100 percent/3 years).

Purposes: pursuant to PHSA as amended and HPEPA, to assist students from disadvantaged backgrounds to undertake education preparing them to enter a health or allied health professions schools, including graduate programs. Projects provide preparatory services, including recruitment, counseling, mentoring, preliminary education and health research training, information on financial aid, primary care exposure activities, and stipends.

Eligible applicants/beneficiaries: accredited schools of medicine, osteopathy, public health, dentistry, veterinary medicine, optometry, pharmacy, allied health, chiropractic, podiatry; public and private nonprofit schools with programs to train physician assistants or offering graduate programs in behavioral and mental health.

Range: $400,000 to $650,000. **Average:** $550,000.

Activity: N.A.

HQ: Chief, Diversity Branch, Division of Health Careers Diversity and Development, Bureau of Health Professions, HRSA-HHS, 5600 Fishers Ln., Rm. 9C-105, Rockville, MD 20857. Phone: (301) 443-6950.

Internet: bhw.hrsa.gov/grants/diversity/hcop.html. (Note: no field offices for this program.)

93.823   EBOLA SUPPORT—TRANSMISSION AND PREVENTION CONTROL, PUBLIC HEALTH PREPAREDNESS, VACCINE DEVELOPMENT

Assistance: cooperative agreements. (100 percent/1 to 5 years).

Purposes: pursuant to the Public Health Service Act, to support infection control programs throughout hospitals and other health care facilities to control transmission of Ebola, pathogens similar to Ebola, and those transmitted similarly to Ebola. Funds may be used for costs associated with planning, organizing, conducting, and supporting programs directed towards prevention of disease, disability, and death by control of infectious diseases, and for the implementation of other program elements.

Eligible applicants: state, local, tribal, territorial, public and private nonprofit, and for-profit institutions/organizations.

Eligible beneficiaries: state, local, tribal, and territorial public institutions/organizations, and health professionals.

Range/Average: N.A.

Activity: N.A.

HQ: CDC-HHS, 1600 Clifton Rd., NE , Atlanta, GA 30052. Phone: (404) 718-8839.

Internet: www.cdc.gov.

93.824 AREA HEALTH EDUCATION CENTERS INFRASTRUCTURE DEVELOPMENT AWARDS (AHEC)

Assistance: project grants. (from 50-75 percent/3 years).

Purposes: pursuant to PHSA as amended and HPEPA, to improve the distribution, diversity, supply, and quality of health service delivery system personnel, by encouraging regionalization of health professions schools and involving students in grades 9-12 in health careers programs. Program funds may be used to plan, develop, and operate AHECs, linked with academic resources of university health sciences centers, to initiate education system incentives to attract and retain health care personnel in scarcity areas, emphasizing community-based training of primary care oriented students, residents, and providers—but not for construction, patient services, or stipends.

Eligible applicants/beneficiaries: public or nonprofit schools of medicine or osteopathy, consortia; accredited schools of nursing in states without AHECs.

Range: $232,000 to $1,856,000. **Average:** $891,946.

Activity: N.A.

HQ: Chief, AHEC Branch, Division of State Community and Public Health, Bureau of Health Professions, HRSA-HHS, 5600 Fishers Ln., Rm. 9C-105, Rockville, MD 20857. Phone: (301) 443-6950.

Internet: bhw.hrsa.gov/grants/areahealtheducationcenters/index.html.

93.825 NATIONAL EBOLA TRAINING AND EDUCATION CENTER (NETEC)

Assistance: project grants. (100 percent/to 5 years).

Purposes: pursuant to the Consolidated and Continuing Appropriations Act of 2015, and the Public Health Service Act, to increase the competency of health care and public health workers and the capability of health care facilities to deliver efficient and effective Ebola patient care through the nationwide, regional network for Ebola and other infectious diseases.

Eligible applicants: health care facilities that have safely and successfully evaluated and treated patients with Ebola.

Eligible beneficiaries: public health departments, hospitals and supporting health care systems.

Range/Average: N.A.

Activity: N.A.

HQ: Office of the Assistant Secretary for Preparedness and Response, HHS, 200 C St., SW, Rm. C4K12, Washington, DC 20024. Phone: (202) 692-4673.

Internet: www.phe.gov. (Note: no field offices for this program.)

93.831 STANDARDS DEVELOPMENT ORGANIZATION COLLABORATION TO ENHANCE STANDARDS ALIGNMENT, TESTING, AND MEASUREMENT

Assistance: cooperative agreements. (100 percent).

Purposes: pursuant to the Public Health Service Act, to establish a mechanism for ongoing collaboration among the Office of the National Coordinator of Health and various standards and development organizations (SDOs). Funds for this cooperative agreement can be used to provide a sub-recipient funds through a contract or subgrant. Funds cannot be used for to supplant or replace current public or private funding; supplant ongoing or usual activities of any organization involved in the project; purchase or improve land, or to purchase, construct, or make permanent improvements to any building; or to reimburse pre-award costs.

Eligible applicants: state, local, tribal, territorial public and private nonprofit organizations/institutions.

Eligible beneficiaries: healthcare organizations and patients using electronic records.

Range: N.A. **Average:** $100,000.

Activity: N.A.

HQ: Office of the Secretary, HHS, 330 C St. SW, Washington , DC 20201. Phone: (202) 720-2919.

Internet: www.healthit.gov.

93.832 PROMOTING THE CANCER SURVEILLANCE WORKFORCE, EDUCATION AND DATA USE

Assistance: cooperative agreements. (100 percent).

Purposes: pursuant to the Public Health Service Act, to expand the capacity of the CDC-funded National Program of Cancer Registries (NPCR) through external partners, to pursue activities that impact the national cancer surveillance workforce. Funds may be used for personnel, travel, supplies, and services. Funds may not be used for research.

Eligible applicants/beneficiaries: public and private nonprofit organizations/institutions.

Range/Average: N.A.

Activity: N.A.

HQ: CDC-HHS, 4770 Buford Hwy., NE, Stop F-76, Atlanta, GA 30341. Phone: (770) 488-8430.

Internet: www.cdc.gov. (Note: no field offices for this program.)

93.833 SUPPORTING AND MAINTAINING A SURVEILLANCE SYSTEM FOR CHRONIC KIDNEY DISEASE IN THE UNITED STATES

Assistance: cooperative agreements. (100 percent/to 5 years).

Purposes: pursuant to the Public Health Service Act, to continue developing, supporting and enhancing the chronic kidney disease (CKD) Surveillance System, to monitor the burden and trends of CKD and its risk factors over time, and to monitor and evaluate trends in achieving Healthy People 2020 objectives.

Eligible applicants: state, local, tribal, and territorial government entities, public and private nonprofit and for-profit institutions/organizations, and IHEs.

Eligible beneficiaries: general public.

Range: $200,000 to $400,000. **Average:** N.A.

Activity: anticipate 2 awards in FY 2016.

HQ: CDC-HHS, 4770 Buford Hwy., NE, Stop F-75, Atlanta, GA 30341. Phone: (770) 488-1057.

Internet: www.cdc.gov. (Note: no field offices for this program.)

93.837 CARDIOVASCULAR DISEASES RESEARCH

Assistance: project grants. (100 percent/1-5 years).

Purposes: pursuant to PHSA as amended and SBRDEA, for research and research training in prevention, education, and control activities related to heart and vascular diseases. Project funds may support salaries, equipment, and patient hospitalization costs required to perform the research effort. NRSA, SBIR, and STTR awards are available.

Eligible applicants/beneficiaries: nonprofit and profit organizations engaged in biomedical research.

Range: $2,591 to $13,546,604. **Average:** $511,264.

Activity: anticipate 2,568 research grants and 227 National Research Service awards in FY 2016.

HQ: Director, Division of Blood Diseases and Resources, National Heart, Lung, and Blood Institute, NIH-HHS, 6701 Rockledge Dr., Rm. 7176, Bethesda, MD 20892. Phone: 301-435-0314.

Internet: www.nhlbi.nih.gov/about/dcvs. (Note: no field offices for this program.)

93.838 LUNG DISEASES RESEARCH

Assistance: project grants. (100 percent/to 5 years).

Purposes: pursuant to PHSA as amended and SBRDEA, for research and research training concerning lung diseases, and to improve their prevention and treatment. Project funds may support salaries, equipment, and patient hospitalization costs required to perform the research effort. NRSA, SBIR, and STTR awards are available.

Eligible applicants/beneficiaries: nonprofit and profit organizations engaged in biomedical research.

Range: $3,064 to $14,449,550. **Average:** $473,042.

Activity: anticipate 1,096 research grants and 98 National Research Service awards in FY 2016.

HQ: Director, Division of Blood Diseases and Resources, National Heart, Lung, and Blood Institute, NIH-HHS, 6701 Rockledge Dr., Rm. 7176, Bethesda, MD 20892. Phone: 301-435-0314.

Internet: www.nhlbi.nih.gov/about/dld. (Note: no field offices for this program.)

93.839 BLOOD DISEASES AND RESOURCES RESEARCH

Assistance: project grants. (100 percent/to 5 years).

Purposes: pursuant to PHSA as amended and SBRDEA, for research and research training toward the improved diagnosis, treatment, and prevention of nonmalignant blood diseases; for research on stem cell biology and transplantation; to improve the availability, safety, and use of blood and blood products. Project funds may support salaries, equipment, and patient hospitalization costs required to perform the research effort. NRSA, SBIR, and STTR awards are available.

Eligible applicants/beneficiaries: nonprofit and profit organizations engaged in biomedical research.

Range: $4,972 to $4,704,000. **Average:** $497,972.

Activity: anticipate 664 research grants and 84 National Research Service awards in FY 2016.

HQ: Director, Division of Blood Diseases and Resources, National Heart, Lung, and Blood Institute, NIH-HHS, 6701 Rockledge Dr., Rm. 7176, Bethesda, MD 20892. Phone: 301-435-0314.

Internet: www.nhlbi.nih.gov/about/dbdr. (Note: no field offices for this program.)

93.845 PROMOTING POPULATION HEALTH THROUGH INCREASED CAPACITY IN ALCOHOL EPIDEMIOLOGY

Assistance: cooperative agreements. (100 percent/to 5 years).

Purposes: pursuant to the Public Health Service Act, to support the building of capacity in alcohol epidemiology in state and large city health departments and help provide the tools needed to perform core public health functions, such as public health surveillance. Funds may be used to for staffing, travel, training, supplies, surveys, and/or required analytic software.

Eligible applicants/beneficiaries: state , including the District of Columbia, and large city health departments.

Range/Average: N.A.

Activity: N.A.

HQ: CDC-HHS, 4770 Buford Hwy., NE, Stop F78, Atlanta, GA 30341. Phone: (770) 488-8063.

Internet: www.cdc.gov. (Note: no field offices for this program.)

93.846 ARTHRITIS, MUSCULOSKELETAL AND SKIN DISEASES RESEARCH

Assistance: project grants. (100 percent/to 5 years).

Purposes: pursuant to PHSA as amended and SBRDEA, for basic research, research training, and clinical investigations concerning all aspects and forms of arthritis and musculoskeletal and skin diseases, including a centers program for large-scale research. NRSA, SBIR, and STTR awards are available.

Eligible applicants/beneficiaries: individuals, public and private nonprofit or profit institutions proposing to establish, expand, and improve research activities in health sciences and related fields.

Range: $1,000 to $1,700,000 for research grants; $50,614 to $409,931 for service awards. **Average:** $191,309 for research grants; $239,516 for service awards.

Activity: anticipate 1,342 grants in FY 2016.

HQ: Director, Extramural Program, National Institute of Arthritis and Musculoskeletal and Skin Diseases, NIH-HHS, 6701 Democracy Blvd. - Ste. 800, Bethesda, MD 20892. Phone: (301) 451-6515.

Internet: www.niams.nih.gov. (Note: no field offices for this program.)

93.847 DIABETES, DIGESTIVE, AND KIDNEY DISEASES EXTRAMURAL RESEARCH

Assistance: project grants. (100 percent/to 5 years).

Purposes: pursuant to PHSA as amended and SBRDEA, for basic and clinical biomedical research and research training in: diabetes and related complications, including its etiology, pathogenesis, prevention, diagnosis, and treatment; endocrinology, including the normal and abnormal functions of the pituitary, thyroid, parathyroid, adrenal, pineal, and thymus glands, as well as the action of hormones, hormone biosynthesis, secretion, metabolism, binding to protein carriers and subsequent release, and the kinetics of binding; metabolic processes of diseases such as membrane structure, function, and transport phenomena, as well as inherited disorders including cystic fibrosis, including their causes, prevention, and treatment. NRSA, SBIR, and STTR awards are available.

Eligible applicants/beneficiaries: individuals, public and private nonprofit or profit institutions proposing to establish, expand, and improve research activities in health sciences and related fields.

Range: $597 to $27,443,000 for project grants; $3,955 to $652,000 for NRSAs; $7,000 to $1,655,000 for SBIR. **Average:** $450,000 for grants; $124,000 for NRSAs; 447,000 for SBIR.

Activity: anticipate 3,838 awards in FY 2016.

HQ: Director, Division of Diabetes, Endocrinology, and Metabolic Diseases, National Institute of Diabetes and Digestive and Kidney Diseases, NIH-HHS, 31 Center Dr., Rm. 9A34, Bethesda, MD 20892. Phone: (301) 594-8842.

Internet: www2.niddk.nih.gov. (Note: no field offices for this program.)

93.852 NATIONAL SYNDROMIC SURVEILLANCE PROGRAM COMMUNITY OF PRACTICE (NSSP COP)

Assistance: cooperative agreements. (100 percent/to 5 years).

Purposes: pursuant to the Public Health Service Act, to fund organizations with extensive experience developing and supporting syndromic surveillance practice to develop, implement and maintain a community of practice for CDC's National Syndromic Surveillance Program.

Eligible applicants: organizations with more than a decade of experience in advancing the science and practice of syndromic surveillance and managing a distributed community of practice.

Eligible beneficiaries: state and local health authorities, public and private non-profit, IHEs, research institutions, faith-based organizations, and research centers.

Range/Average: N.A.

Activity: N.A.

HQ: CDC-HHS, 2960 Brandywine Rd., Atlanta, GA 30341. Phone: (404) 498-2441.

Internet: www.cdc.gov.

93.853   EXTRAMURAL RESEARCH PROGRAMS IN THE NEUROSCIENCES AND NEUROLOGICAL DISORDERS

Assistance: project grants. (100 percent/to 5 years).

Purposes: pursuant to PHSA as amended and SBRDEA, for clinical and basic research and research training concerning neurological disorders and stroke, and their diagnosis, prevention, epidemiology, and treatment through development of drugs and neural prostheses. Programs supported include research on stroke, traumatic brain and spinal cord injuries, Parkinson's and Alzheimer's diseases, brain tumors; cellular, molecular, and systems neuroscience, developmental neurobiology and disorders, and neurogenetics, epilepsy, multiple sclerosis, AIDS, immune disorders, and sleep and pain disorders. Special programs include a number of career development awards, including Re-Entry into the Neurological Sciences awards for scientists that have been away from research for a least three years to re-establish their skills. NRSA, SBIR, and STTR awards are available.

Eligible applicants/beneficiaries: research grants—any public or private non-profit or profit institution. Career program awards—U.S. citizens or permanent residents nominated and sponsored by a public or private nonprofit institution.

Range: $50,000 to $10,887,994 for research grants; $15,412 to $459,127 for institutional awards; $2,006 to $59,402 for individual awards. **Average:** $392,000 for research grants; $53,539 for institutional awards; $37,213 for individual awards.

Activity: anticipate 865 awards in FY 2016.

HQ: National Institute of Neurological Disorders and Stroke, NIH-HHS, 6001 Executive Blvd., Ste. 3309, Bethesda, MD 20892. Phone: (301) 402-4370.

Internet: www.ninds.nih.gov. (Note: no field offices for this program.)

93.855   ALLERGY AND INFECTIOUS DISEASES RESEARCH

Assistance: project grants. (100 percent/to 7 years).

Purposes: pursuant to PHSA as amended and SBRDEA, to establish, expand, and improve basic and clinical biomedical research and research training in allergic and immunologic diseases and related areas, including asthma, AIDS, transplantation biology, and related areas including genetics. Research Career Development Awards are available to institutions for up to five years, to train young scientists for independent research careers. NRSA, SBIR, and STTR awards are available.

Eligible applicants/beneficiaries: IHEs, hospitals, laboratories, and other public or private, profit or nonprofit, institutions, state and local governments, small businesses, individuals.

Range: $2,500 to $6,395,901. **Average:** $426,165.

Activity: N.A.

HQ: Director, Division of Extramural Activities, National Institute of Allergy and Infectious Diseases, NIH-HHS, 5601 Fishers Ln., Rm. 5E48, Bethesda, MD 2089. Phone: (240) 669-5429.

Internet: www.niaid.nih.gov. (Note: no field offices for this program.)

93.856   MICROBIOLOGY AND INFECTIOUS DISEASES RESEARCH

Assistance: project grants. (100 percent/to 7 years).

Purposes: pursuant to PHSA as amended and SBRDEA, for basic, applied, and clinical biomedical research and research training related to microbiology and infectious diseases. Program aims include the control of disease caused by infectious or parasitic agents, including AIDS, retroviruses, Reye's Syndrome. Studies are supported on the mechanisms of antibiotics, as well as epidemiological observations in hospitalized patients or community populations. Research Career Development Awards are available to institutions for up to five years, to train young scientists for careers in independent research. NRSA, SBIR, and STTR awards are available.

Eligible applicants/beneficiaries: IHEs, hospitals, laboratories, and other public or private, profit or nonprofit, institutions, state and local governments, small businesses, individuals.

Range/Average: N.A.

Activity: N.A.

HQ: Director, Division of Extramural Activities, National Institute of Allergy and Infectious Diseases, NIH-HHS, 5601 Fishers Ln., Rm. 5E48, Bethesda, MD 2089. Phone: (240) 669-5429.

Internet: www.niaid.nih.gov. (Note: no field offices for this program.)

93.858   NATIONAL COLLABORATION TO SUPPORT HEALTH, WELLNESS AND ACADEMIC SUCCESS OF SCHOOL-AGE CHILDREN

Assistance: cooperative agreements. (100 percent/to 5 years).

Purposes: pursuant to the Public Health Service Act, to improve the health of youth by funding NGOs to assist CDC-funded grantees and the organizations' constituents (e.g., states, school districts and/or schools) to implement environmental and systems changes that support and reinforce healthful behaviors and reduce disparities.

Eligible applicants/beneficiaries: community- and faith-based and American Indian/Alaskan Native organizations/institutions.

Range: $300,000 to $450,000. **Average:** N.A.

Activity: N.A.

HQ: CDC-HHS, 4770 Buford Hwy., Atlanta, GA 30341. Phone: (770) 488-6167.

Internet: www.cdc.gov. (Note: no field offices for this program.)

93.859   BIOMEDICAL RESEARCH AND RESEARCH TRAINING

Assistance: project grants. (100 percent/to 5 years).

Purposes: pursuant to PHSA as amended, for research and research training in basic biomedical sciences not targeted to specific diseases or disorders. Biomedical science fields supported include: cell biology and biophysics; genetics and development biology; pharmacology, physiology, and biological chemistry; bio- informatics and computational biology. Special training programs include: Minority Access to Research Careers which supports research training at the undergraduate, graduate, and faculty levels; Minority Biomedical Research Support.

Eligible applicants/beneficiaries: U.S. citizens, non-citizen nationals, permanent residents.

Range: $20,000 to $10,000,000. **Average:** N.A.

Activity: N.A.

HQ: National Institute of General Medical Sciences, 45 Center Dr., Bethesda, MD 20892-6200. Phone: (301) 496-7301.

Internet: www.nigms.nih.gov. (Note: no field offices for this program.)

93.860   EMERGING INFECTIONS SENTINEL NETWORKS

Assistance: cooperative agreements. (100 percent/to 5 years).

Purposes: pursuant to the Public Health Service Act, to contribute to surveillance for emerging infectious diseases, including drug resistant, foodborne and waterborne, and vaccine-preventable or potentially vaccine-preventable diseases, and to enhance information exchange leading to early identification of and response to trends and outbreaks.

Eligible applicants: organizations currently operating a nationwide provider-based sentinel network that links academically affiliated hospital emergency departments in monitoring a variety of infectious disease problems; and organizations currently operating provider-based sentinel networks that link groups of participating individuals or organizations organized around either infectious disease clinicians or travel medicine in monitoring a variety of infectious disease problems.

Eligible beneficiaries: health professionals and the general public.

Range: $300,000 to $800,000. **Average:** $550,000.

Activity: N.A.

HQ: CDC-HHS, 1600 Clifton Rd., NE, Stop C18, Atlanta, GA 30329. Phone: (404) 639-7087.

Internet: www.cdc.gov. (Note: no field offices for this program.)

93.865   CHILD HEALTH AND HUMAN DEVELOPMENT EXTRAMURAL RESEARCH

Assistance: project grants. (100 percent/to 5 years).

Purposes: pursuant to PHSA as amended and SBRDEA, for fundamental and clinical, biomedical, and behavioral research and research training associated with growth and development biologic and reproductive functions, and population dynamics; also, to conduct research on the impact of disabilities, diseases, and defects, toward the restoration, increase, and maximization of the capabilities of persons so afflicted. NRSA, SBIR, and STTR awards are available.

Eligible applicants/beneficiaries: IHEs; medical, dental, nursing, and public health schools; state and local health departments; hospitals; laboratories; other public or private profit or nonprofit organizations; individuals.

Range: $50,000 to $5,000,000. **Average:** $450,663.

Activity: anticipate 1,576 awards in FY 2016.

HQ: Director, Center for Research for Mothers and Children, National Institute of Child Health and Human Development, NIH-HHS, Bldg. 6100 Executive Blvd., Rm. 2C01, Bethesda, MD 20892-7510. Phone: (301) 496-6856.

Internet: www.nichd.nih.gov/Pages/index.aspx. (Note: no field offices for this program.)

93.866 AGING RESEARCH

Assistance: project grants. (100 percent/to 5 years).

Purposes: pursuant to PHSA as amended and SBRDEA, for biomedical, social, and behavioral research and research training associated with the aging process and the diseases, special problems, and needs people as they age—including geriatric research and research into genetic diseases and Alzheimer's, and social aspects of care and aging. NRSA, SBIR, and STTR awards are available.

Eligible applicants/beneficiaries: IHEs; medical, dental, nursing, and public health schools; state and local health departments; hospitals; laboratories; other public or private profit or nonprofit organizations; individuals.

Range/Average: N.A.

Activity: N.A.

HQ: National Institute on Aging, NIH-HHS, 7201 Wisconsin Ave., Rm. 2C218, Bethesda, MD 20892. Phone: (301) 496-9322 Fax: (301) 402-2945.

Internet: www.nia.nih.gov. (Note: no field offices for this program.)

93.867 VISION RESEARCH

Assistance: project grants. (100 percent/to 5 years).

Purposes: pursuant to PHSA as amended, SBRDEA, and other acts, for basic, clinical, and applied research and research training projects addressing the leading causes of blindness and impaired vision, including retinal and corneal diseases, diabetic retinopathy, macular degeneration, cataract, glaucoma, strabismus, and amblyopia; for related projects including enhancement of the rehabilitation, training, and quality of life of persons who are partially-sighted or blind. Conference grants, core grants, mentored clinical scientist development awards, clinical vision research development awards, clinical study planning grants, and small grants for data analysis may be offered. NRSA, SBIR, and STTR awards are available.

Eligible applicants/beneficiaries: research grants, cooperative agreements, career development awards—IHEs, hospitals, laboratories, federal institutions; other public or private nonprofit and profit organizations including small businesses; state and local governments. Foreign institutions may apply for research grants only.

Range: $26,298 to $5,057,448 for grants and cooperative agreements; $26,298 to $560,041 for NRSA (institutional); $14,476 to $62,002 for NRSA (individual). **Average:** $392,655 for grants and cooperative agreements; $217,314 for NRSA (institutional); $45,355 for NRSA (individual).

Activity: anticipate 1,246 awards in FY 2015.

HQ: Research Resources Officer, National Eye Institute, NIH-HHS, Rm. 1300, 5635 Fishers Ln., Bethesda, MD 20892-9300. Phone: (301) 451-2020.

Internet: www.nei.nih.gov. (Note: no field offices for this program.)

93.875 ASSISTANCE FOR ORAL DISEASE PREVENTION AND CONTROL

Assistance: cooperative agreements. (100 percent/3 to 5 years).

Purposes: pursuant to Sections 317 of the Public Health Service Act as amended, to strengthen state oral health programs and public health core capacity to reduce inequalities in the oral health of targeted populations. Funds may be used for costs associated with planning, implementing, and evaluating oral disease and chronic disease prevention and control programs. Funds may not be used for direct dental and other health care services.

Eligible applicants/beneficiaries: state, territorial and tribal health agencies.

Range/Average: N.A.

Activity: N.A.

HQ: CDC-HHS, 4770 Buford Hwy., NE, Stop F80, Atlanta, GA 30341. Phone: (770) 488-6075.

Internet: www.cdc.gov. (Note: no field offices for this program.)

93.876 ANTIMICROBIAL RESISTANCE SURVEILLANCE IN RETAIL FOOD SPECIMENS
("NARMS Retail Food Surveillance")

Assistance: cooperative agreements. (100 percent/1 to 4 years).

Purposes: pursuant to Section 1702(a) and Section 1703(a) and (c) of the Public Health Service Act, as amended, to improve the detection of and surveillance for antimicrobial resistance among enteric bacteria in raw retail food commodities, particularly fresh retail meat.

Eligible applicants/beneficiaries: federal, state, local, tribal, and territorial institutions/organizations, public and private nonprofit, private for-profit, and indviduals.

Range/Average: N.A.

Activity: anticipate 30 awards in FY 2016.

HQ: FDA-HHS, 8401 Muirkirk Rd., Laurel, MD 20708. Phone: (240) 402-0891.

Internet: www.fda.gov. (Note: no field offices for this program.)

93.879 MEDICAL LIBRARY ASSISTANCE

Assistance: project grants. (100 percent/to 5 years).

Purposes: pursuant to PHSA as amended and SBRDEA, for training programs for professional medical library personnel; for fellowships; to expand or improve existing medical libraries; for biomedical publications; for research in medical informatics and related computer sciences; for similar uses, including computer and telecommunications technology. SBIR and STTR awards are made.

Eligible applicants/beneficiaries: training grants—nonfederal public and nonprofit private institutions. Fellowships—pre-or postdoctoral candidates that are U.S. citizens, nationals, or lawful permanent residents. Other grants—depending on category, domestic public, private, nonprofit, profit health sciences institutions and organizations.

Range: $20,000 to $750,000. Average: $364,360.

Activity: anticipate 320 new and 130 continuing awards in FY 2016.

HQ: Extramural Programs, National Library of Medicine, NIH-HHS, Bethesda, MD 20894. Phone: (301) 496-4621, (301) 594-4882. grants management information: Grants Management Officer, same address. Phone: (301) 496-4221; grant review contact, (301) 496-4253.

Internet: www.nlm.nih.gov/ep. (Note: no field offices for this program.)

93.884 GRANTS FOR PRIMARY CARE TRAINING AND ENHANCEMENT

Assistance: project grants. (100 percent/3 years).

Purposes: pursuant to PHSA as amended and HPEPA, for graduate education and residency programs leading to the practice of family medicine including geriatrics, general internal medicine, general pediatrics, general dentistry, or pediatric dentistry, as well as training of physician assistants in primary care. Grant funds may be used: to plan, develop, and operate or participate in approved programs; provide financial assistance to participants; for faculty development and improving academic administrative units to strengthen clinical instruction. Grants may not be used for construction or patient services.

Eligible applicants/beneficiaries: accredited public or private nonprofit schools of medicine or osteopathy, hospitals, or other entities.

Range: $300,000 to $500,000. Average: N.A.

Activity: N.A.

HQ: Primary Care Medical Education Branch, Division of Medicine and Dentistry, Bureau of Health Professions, HRSA-HHS, Parklawn Bldg., Rm. 12C-06, 5600 Fishers Ln., Rockville, MD 20857. Phone: (301) 443-2354.

Internet: bhpr.hrsa.gov/grants/medicine.index.html.

93.887   HEALTH CARE AND OTHER FACILITIES ("Renovation or Construction Projects")

Assistance: project grants. (100 percent/3-5 years).

Purposes: to construct, renovate, expand, repair, equip, or modernize health care facilities and other related facilities.

Eligible applicants/beneficiaries: state and local governments including their IHEs, quasi-governmental agencies, private IHEs, private profit and non-profit entities. Entities are eligible if specifically earmarked in Congressional appropriation.

Range/Average: N.A.

Activity: N.A.

HQ: Facilities Monitoring Branch, Division of Facilities Compliance and Recovery, Healthcare Systems Bureau, HRSA-HHS, Parklawn Bldg., Rm. 08W-50, 5600 Fishers Ln., Rockville, MD 20857. Phone: (301) 443-7858.

Internet: www.hrsa.gov/hcofconstruction/ . (Note: no field offices for this program.)

93.888   SPECIALLY SELECTED HEALTH PROJECTS

Assistance: project grants. (100 percent/3-5 years).

Purposes: for programs selected by the U.S. Congress as needed for improved health care.

Eligible applicants/beneficiaries: state and local governments including their IHEs, quasi-governmental agencies, private IHEs, private profit and non-profit entities. Entities are eligible if specifically earmarked in Congressional appropriation.

Range/Average: N.A.

Activity: N.A.

HQ: Division of Grants Policy, Office of Federal Assistance Management, HRSA-HHS, Parklawn Bldg., Rm. 17W45C, 5600 Fishers Ln., Rockville, MD 20857. Phone: (301) 443-0835.

Internet: www.rurahealth.hrsa.gov.

93.889   NATIONAL BIOTERRORISM HOSPITAL PREPAREDNESS PROGRAM (HPP)

Assistance: project grants.

Purposes: pursuant to the Public Health Security and Bioterrorism Preparedness and Response Act of 2002, for health care entities to upgrade their ability to deliver coordinated and effective care to victims of terrorism and other public health emergencies requiring mass immunization, treatment, isolation, and quarantine in the aftermath of bioterrorism or other outbreaks of infectious disease; for needs assessment updates; for continuation, refinement, and implementation of approved work plans.

Eligible applicants/beneficiaries: state health departments including territories and possessions; and, New York City, Chicago, and Los Angeles.

Range: $270,000 to $27,000,000. **Average: $5,351,000.**

Activity: N.A.

HQ: Hospital Preparedness Program, Assistant Secretary for Preparedness and Response, HHS, 200 C E St., SW, Concourse C4K17, Washington, DC 20024. Phone: (202) 245-0732.

Internet: www.phe.gov. (Note: no field offices for this program.)

93.908 NURSE CORPS LOAN REPAYMENT PROGRAM

Assistance: project grants (100 percent).

Purposes: pursuant to PHSA as amended and Nurse Reinvestment Act of 2002, to repay education loans on behalf of nurses entering full-time employment at IHS or native Hawaiian health centers, public hospitals, migrant or rural health clinics, or certain other health facilities with critical shortages of nurses. Repayment agreements are made for not less than two consecutive years of service; amounts range from 30 percent of the unpaid initial principal and interest of qualified loans in return for the first year of service, to 85 percent for three years.

Eligible applicants/beneficiaries: licensed or license-eligible registered nurses that: will have received a diploma or academic degree; will begin full-time employment (32 hours or more per week) for two or three years at an eligible health facility; have unpaid educational loans obtained for their nursing education; are U.S. citizens, nationals, or permanent legal residents.

Range: $23,000 to $363,000. **Average:** $50,316.

Activity: 667 awards in FY 2014.

HQ: Chief, Nursing Education Loan Repayment Branch, Division of Nursing, Bureau of Health Professions, HRSA-HHS, Parklawn Bldg., Rm. 9C-14, 5600 Fishers Ln., Rockville, MD 20857. Phone: (301) 594-4130.

Internet: www.hrsa.gov/loanscholarships/repayment/nursing. (Note: no field offices for this program.)

93.910 FAMILY AND COMMUNITY VIOLENCE PREVENTION PROGRAM

Assistance: project grants. (100 percent/4 years).

Purposes: pursuant to PHSA as amended, to establish family life centers on the campuses of 24 minority IHEs, to prevent minority- related violence and to improve health and human services to minorities, through: assessments of, and coordination with, related local community resources; design and implementation of educational interventions addressing interpersonal family violence; outreach services to students from dysfunctional families. Funds may not be used to provide health care, nor for construction or demonstration projects.

Eligible applicants/beneficiaries: an IHE representing four-year, primarily minority undergraduate institutions and a two-year tribal college.

Range: $250,000 to $500,000. **Average:** N.A.

Activity: N.A.

HQ: Director, Division of Program Operations, Office of Minority Health, Office of Public Health and Science, OS-HHS, 1101 Wootton Pkwy., Ste. 550, Rockville, MD 20852. Phone: (240) 453-8822.

Internet: www.minorityhealth.hhs.gov. (Note: no field offices for this program.)

93.912 RURAL HEALTH CARE SERVICES OUTREACH, RURAL HEALTH NETWORK DEVELOPMENT AND SMALL HEALTH CARE PROVIDER QUALITY IMPROVEMENT PROGRAM

Assistance: project grants (100 percent).

Purposes: pursuant to the Health Care Safety Net Amendment, to expand access to, coordinate, restrain the cost of, and improve essential rural health care services by developing integrated systems or networks in rural areas and regions—including mental health services, emergency services, prenatal care, free clinical services, prevention services, professionals training, and transportation services.

Eligible applicants/beneficiaries: rural public or private nonprofit entities that include three or more health care providers; organizations exclusively providing services to migrant and seasonal farm workers; tribal, quasi-tribal entities delivering services on reservations or tribal areas.

Range: $74.954 to $525,000. **Average:** N.A.

Activity: N.A.

HQ: Outreach Program Coordinator or Network Development Program Coordinator, Office of Rural Health Policy, Director, Rural Research Centers, Office of Rural Health Policy, HRSA-HHS, Parklawn Bldg., Rm. 17W29-C, 5600 Fishers Ln., Rockville, MD 20857. Phone: (301) 443-0835.

Internet: www.hrsa.gov/ruralhealth.

93.913 GRANTS TO STATES FOR OPERATION OF OFFICES OF RURAL HEALTH

Assistance: project grants. (to 75 percent/to 5 years).

Purposes: pursuant to PHSA as amended, to improve health care in rural areas by establishing state offices of rural health. Funds must support information clearinghouses, coordination of state and federal programs, technical assistance, health professionals recruitment activities.

Eligible applicants/beneficiaries: states.

Range: $152,267 to $171,598. **Average:** N.A.

Activity: N.A.

HQ: State Office of Rural Health Grant Program, Office of Rural Health Policy, HRSA-HHS, Parklawn Bldg., Rm. 17W45C, 5600 Fishers Ln., Rockville, MD 20857. Phone: (301) 443-0835.

Internet: www.hrsa.gov.

93.914 HIV EMERGENCY RELIEF PROJECT GRANTS

Assistance: project grants.

Purposes: pursuant to PHSA as amended and Ryan White Comprehensive AIDS Resources Emergency (CARE) Act Amendments of 2000, to assist areas most severely affected by the HIV epidemic, in developing, organizing, and operating programs providing a continuum of health and support services—including: HIV- related outpatient and ambulatory services; case management and comprehensive treatment services for patients and their families; substance abuse and mental health treatment; inpatient services to prevent unnecessary hospitalization or to expedite discharge; services to infants, women, and children with or exposed to HIV disease.

Eligible applicants/beneficiaries: metropolitan areas with populations of 500,000 or more, reporting more than 2,000 cases of AIDS during the most recent five years, per CDCP data.

Range: $2,097,353 to $102,094,291. **Average:** $11,786,883.

Activity: N.A.

HQ: Division of Service Systems, HIV/AIDS Bureau, HRSA-HHS, Parklawn Bldg., Rm. 9W-12, 5600 Fishers Ln., Rockville, MD 20857. Phone: (301) 443-7136.

Internet: www.hrsa.gov.

93.917   HIV CARE FORMULA GRANTS

Assistance: formula grants (to 100 percent).

Purposes: pursuant to PHSA as amended and Ryan White Comprehensive AIDS Resources Emergency (CARE) Act Amendments of 2000, to improve the quality, availability, and organization of health care and support services for persons with HIV disease and their families. Funds may be used: to provide outpatient and ambulatory health and support services, including case management and comprehensive treatment services, substance abuse treatment, and mental health treatment; for inpatient case management services to prevent unnecessary hospitalization or to expedite discharge; to establish and operate consortia; to provide home and community-based care services; to assure the continuity of health insurance coverage; to provide therapeutics to treat individuals with HIV disease.

Eligible applicants/beneficiaries: states, territories and possessions.

Range: $41,049 to $146,242,713. **Average:** N.A.

Activity: N.A.

HQ: Division of Service Systems, HIV/AIDS Bureau, HRSA-HHS, Parklawn Bldg., Rm. 09W32, 5600 Fishers Ln., Rockville, MD 20857. Phone: (301) 443-6745.

Internet: www.hrsa.gov.

93.918   GRANTS TO PROVIDE OUTPATIENT EARLY INTERVENTION SERVICES WITH RESPECT TO HIV DISEASE

Assistance: project grants. (100 percent/to 5 years).

Purposes: pursuant to PHSA as amended and the Ryan White Comprehensive AIDS Resources Emergency (CARE) Act Amendments of 2000, to improve the availability, accessibility, and organization of ambulatory services to persons infected with HIV or at high risk, and to offer early intervention services, including: counseling and testing; partner involvement in risk reduction; transmission prevention; primary care diagnosis and treatment; case management. Capacity building funding may be provided to develop new or expanded programs particularly in rural, underserved, and minority areas. Funds may not be used to acquire real property or to provide inpatient or residential care.

Eligible applicants/beneficiaries: public or private nonprofit: community health centers; family planning grantees under PHS Section 1001, other than states; comprehensive programs of primary health care; comprehensive hemophilia diagnostic and treatment centers.

Range: $38,647 to $1,305,534. **Average:** $500,070.

Activity: N.A.

HQ: Division of Community Based Programs, HIV-AIDS Bureau, HRSA-HHS, 5600 Fishers Ln., Rm. 9-74, Rockville, MD 20857. Phone: (770) 488-1172.

Internet: www.hrsa.gov.

93.919   COOPERATIVE AGREEMENTS FOR STATE-BASED COMPREHENSIVE BREAST AND CERVICAL CANCER EARLY DETECTION PROGRAMS ("National Breast and Cervical Cancer Early Detection Program")

Assistance: project grants. (75 percent/1-5 years).

Purposes: pursuant to the Breast and Cervical Cancer Mortality Prevention Act of 1990, to develop comprehensive breast and cervical cancer early detection programs; to increase screening and follow-up among all groups of women, especially those that are low-income, uninsured, under-insured, minority, or native Americans. Funds may be used for public education and outreach, referrals services, staff training, project monitoring and evaluation—but not for treatment services.

Eligible applicants/beneficiaries: state health agencies, territories and possessions, tribes and tribal organizations.

Range: $242,796 to $8,693,584. **Average:** $2,320,696.

Activity: N.A.

HQ: Program Services Branch, Division of Cancer Prevention and Control, National Center for Chronic Disease Prevention and Health Promotion (K57), CDCP-HHS, 4770 Buford Hwy. NE, Atlanta, GA 30341. Phone: (404) 488-4880.

Internet: www.cdc.gov/cancer. (Note: no field offices for this program.)

93.923   DISADVANTAGED HEALTH PROFESSIONS FACULTY LOAN REPAYMENT (FLRP) AND MINORITY FACULTY FELLOWSHIP PROGRAM (MFFP)

Assistance: project grants; direct payments/specified use. (project grants, 50-100 percent/project grants, to 3 years).

Purposes: pursuant to PHSA as amended and HPEPA, to repay educational loans owed by health professionals from disadvantaged backgrounds, or to provide fellowships to minority faculty, serving for at least two years on the full-time or part-time faculty of a school of medicine, nursing, osteopathy, dentistry, pharmacy, podiatry, optometry, veterinary medicine, public health, allied health, or graduate programs in clinical psychology. Unless waived, schools are required to pay 50 percent of the repayment or fellowship amount due for each year of service.

Eligible applicants/beneficiaries: FLRP—health professionals from disadvantaged backgrounds with degrees or enrolled in approved graduate training programs, or enrolled as full-time students in their final course of study. MFFP—health professions schools with programs in the fields designated.

Range/Average: N.A.

Activity: N.A.

HQ: Division of Health Careers Diversity and Development, Bureau of Health Professions, HRSA-HHS, 5600 Fishers Ln., Rm. 9C-14, Rockville, MD 20857. Phone: (301) 594-4130.

Internet: www.hrsa.gov/loanscholarships/repayment/faculty.

93.924 RYAN WHITE HIV/AIDS DENTAL REIMBURSEMENTS AND COMMUNITY BASED DENTAL PARTNERSHIP GRANTS

Assistance: direct payments/specified use; project grants (project grants, to 5 years).

Purposes: pursuant to PHSA as amended and Ryan White CARE Act Amendments of 2000, to reimburse the uncompensated costs incurred for oral health services to patients with HIV/AIDS, by dental schools, and postdoctoral dental education and dental hygiene education programs; to increase access to oral health care services for HIV-positive individuals, while providing education and clinical training for dental and hygiene provided located in community-based settings through "dental partnerships."

Eligible applicants/beneficiaries: public or private nonprofit schools of dentistry and dental hygiene, and accredited postgraduate dental education programs in the states, territories, and possessions.

Range: $907 to $864,222 for dental reimbursement; $219,230 to $364,172 for partnership grants. **Average:** $155,641 for dental reimbursement; $294,876 for partnership grants.

Activity: N.A.

HQ: Division of Community Based Programs, HIV-AIDS Bureau, HRSA-HHS, 5600 Fishers Ln., Rm. 12C-06, Rockville, MD 20857. Phone: (301) 443-6190.

Internet: www.hrsa.gov.

93.925 SCHOLARSHIPS FOR HEALTH PROFESSIONS STUDENTS FROM DISADVANTAGED BACKGROUNDS ("SDS")

Assistance: project grants.

Purposes: pursuant to PHSA as amended and HPEPA, for annual scholarships to full-time students from disadvantaged backgrounds, awarded by health professions schools that maintain special programs for enrollees, including recruiting and retaining students from disadvantaged backgrounds. At least 16 percent of funds must be allocated to schools providing scholarships only to nurses, and giving preference to former EFN and SDS recipients.

Eligible applicants: public or private nonprofit schools of medicine, nursing, osteopathy, dentistry, pharmacy, podiatry, optometry, veterinary medicine, chiropractic, allied health, or offering graduate programs in public health, behavioral and mental health, or physician assistants.

Eligible beneficiaries: U.S. citizens, nationals, or lawful permanent residents of states, territories, or possessions.

Range: $42,840 to $650,000. **Average:** $443,840.

Activity: N.A.

HQ: Division of Health Careers Diversity and Development, Bureau of Health Professions, HRSA-HHS, 5600 Fishers Ln., Rm. 9-105, Rockville, MD 20857. Phone: (301) 443-1173.

Internet: bhw.hrsa.gov/scholarshipsloans/index.html. (Note: no field offices for this program.)

93.926 HEALTHY START INITIATIVE ("Healthy Start")

Assistance: project grants. (100 percent/to 4 years).

Purposes: pursuant to PHSA, to eliminate disparities in perinatal and maternal health by enhancing community service systems and infrastructure, and state infrastructures, directing resources and interventions to improve access to, utilization, and full participation of comprehensive service projects for high-risk women and infants. Funds may be used to implement community- driven, multifaceted approaches integrating various health education, social and support services—including outreach, case management, screening and referral, peer mentoring by trained community members, and home visiting programs to promote access and use of preconceptional, perinatal, and inter- conceptional services. Projects must have a community-base consortium of individuals and organizations, including persons served, to collaborate with their state agency and to implement a local health system action plan.

Eligible applicants/beneficiaries: in urban and rural communities with significant disparities in perinatal health—public or private entities including community-based organizations, tribes, and tribal organizations; states needing to build their infrastructure and capacity to address and support eligible communities.

Range: $750,000 to $2,000,000. **Average:** N.A.

Activity: N.A.

HQ: Division of Healthy Start and Perinatal Services, Maternal and Child Health Bureau, HRSA-HHS, Parklawn Bldg., Rm. 13-91, 5600 Fishers Ln., Rockville, MD 20857. Phone: (301) 368-1019.

Internet: www.hrsa.gov.

93.928 SPECIAL PROJECTS OF NATIONAL SIGNIFICANCE (SPNS)

Assistance: project grants. (100 percent/to 5 years).

Purposes: pursuant to PHSA as amended and Ryan White CARE Act Amendments of 2000, to advance knowledge and skills in the delivery of health and support services to persons with HIV disease. Funds support innovative projects: for which implementation, costs, utilization, and outcomes can be evaluated rigorously; providing models unlikely to exist without SPNS support; that extend the care model to previously underserved or unserved populations.

Eligible applicants/beneficiaries: public and private nonprofit entities including state or local health departments, hospitals, IHEs, community-based service organizations, IHEs; national service provider organizations.

Range: $80,000 to $3,200,000. **Average:** $300,000.

Activity: N.A.

HQ: Chief, Demonstration Project Development and Evaluation Branch, Division of Science and Policy, HIV/AIDS Bureau, HRSA-HHS, 5600 Fishers Ln., Rm. 7-90, Rockville, MD 20857. Phone: (301) 443-8109.

Internet: www.hrsa.gov.

93.932   NATIVE HAWAIIAN HEALTH CARE SYSTEMS

Assistance: project grants. (to 83.3 percent/to 3 years).

Purposes: pursuant to the Native Hawaiian Health Care Improvement Act, for programs raising the health status of native Hawaiians living in Hawaii, by providing comprehensive health promotion and disease prevention and primary health care services. Outreach, case management, and referral components should integrate traditional health concepts with western medicine, employing existing health resources as much as possible.

Eligible applicants/beneficiaries: Papa Ola Lokahi (a consortium of Hawaiian and native Hawaiian organizations); Native American Health Care Systems as specifically defined in Hawaii state laws.

Range: $1,000,000 to $3,000,000. **Average:** $2,000,000.

Activity: N.A.

HQ: HRSA-HHS, 5600 Fishers Ln., Rm. 17C-26, Rockville, MD 20857. Phone: (301) 594-4300.

Internet: www.hrsa.gov.

93.933   DEMONSTRATION PROJECTS FOR INDIAN HEALTH

Assistance: project grants. (100 percent/to 5 years).

Purposes: pursuant to PHSA as amended, to promote improved health care among American Indians and Alaska natives, through research, studies, and demonstration projects addressing such issues as elder care, women's health care, and children and youth initiative.

Eligible applicants/beneficiaries: tribes, tribal organizations, nonprofit intertribal or urban Indian organizations contracting with IHS, public or private nonprofit health and education entities, state and local health agencies.

Range/Average: N.A.

Activity: N.A.

HQ: Grants Policy Office, IHS-HHS, 801 Thompson Ave., Suite TMP 360, Rockville, MD 20852. Phone: (301) 443-5204.

Internet: www.ihs.gov. (Note: no field offices for this program.)

93.936 NATIONAL INSTITUTES OF HEALTH ACQUIRED IMMUNODEFICIENCY SYNDROME RESEARCH LOAN REPAYMENT PROGRAM (AIDS LRP)

Assistance: project grants. (100 percent/from 2 years).

Purposes: pursuant to PHSA as amended, for partial repayment of educational loans owed by physicians, registered nurses, and scientists employed by NIH in AIDS research. Recipients must have qualified educational debt exceeding 20 percent of their annual salary, and they must engage in research for a minimum of two years. Continuation contracts are available.

Eligible applicants/beneficiaries: NIH AIDS researchers with an M.D., Ph.D., D.D.S., D.O., D.M.D., D.V.M., D.P.M., A.D.N., B.S.N., or equivalent degree, that: are U.S. citizens, nationals, or permanent residents; have no existing service obligation to federal, state, or other entities.

Range: loan repayment awards,$4,000 to $70,000; tax reimbursements, $1,977 to $34,598. **Average:** N.A.

Activity: anticipate 5 awards in FY 2016.

HQ: Office of Intramural Training and Education, NIH-HHS, Bldg. 2, Rm. 2E18, 2 Center Dr., Bethesda, MD 20892-0230. Phone: (301) 402-1283; FAX: (301) 480-2942.

Internet: www.lrp.nih.gov. (Note: no field offices for this program.)

93.938 COOPERATIVE AGREEMENTS TO SUPPORT COMPREHENSIVE SCHOOL HEALTH PROGRAMS TO PREVENT THE SPREAD OF HIV AND OTHER IMPORTANT HEALTH PROBLEMS ("SHEPSA")

Assistance: project grants. (100 percent/to 5 years).

Purposes: pursuant to PHSA as amended, to develop and implement health education programs for HIV and other health problems for school-age populations (elementary through college), parents, and school, health, and education personnel. Funds may support personnel salaries, training, data collection, monitoring, preparation and dissemination of information including audiovisuals, technical assistance; special outreach to minority, special needs, and high-risk youth. Funds may not be used for research, surveys, computer or office equipment purchases, office space costs, construction or renovation—unless specifically approved.

Eligible applicants/beneficiaries: states, territories and possessions; large urban school districts with high HIV-AIDS rates; national nongovernmental organizations.

Range: $1,000 to $678,000. **Average:** $283,600.

Activity: N.A.

HQ: Program Development and Services Branch, Division of Adolescent and School Health, National Center for Chronic Disease Prevention and Health Promotion (K31), CDCP-HHS, 1600 Clifton Rd. NE, MS E-75, Atlanta, GA 30333. Phone: (404) 718-8333.

Internet: www.cdc.gov/healthyyouth. (Note: no field offices for this program.)

93.939 HIV PREVENTION ACTIVITIES—NON-GOVERNMENTAL ORGANIZATION BASED

Assistance: project grants. (to 100 percent/to 5 years).

Purposes: pursuant to PHSA as amended, to promote coordination for primary and secondary HIV prevention efforts among community-based organizations, HIV education and prevention service agencies, and national and regional nonprofit organizations. Project examples include street outreach, risk reduction, and community intervention programs.

Eligible applicants/beneficiaries: nongovernmental public and private nonprofit entities.

Range/Average: N.A.

Activity: N.A.

HQ: Division of HIV/AIDS Prevention (A43), CDCP-HHS, 1600 Clifton Rd., Stop E-07, Atlanta, GA 30333. Phone: (404) 639-8531.

Internet: www.cdc.gov/hiv. (Note: no field offices for this program.)

93.940 HIV PREVENTION ACTIVITIES—HEALTH DEPARTMENT BASED ("HIV Prevention Program")

Assistance: project grants. (to 100 percent/1-5 years).

Purposes: pursuant to PHSA as amended, for state and local health departments to develop, implement, and evaluate primary and secondary HIV prevention programs. Project activities may include: health education and risk reduction for drug users; public information; minority initiatives; counseling, testing, referral, and partner notification.

Eligible applicants/beneficiaries: states and, in consultation with state health authorities, political subdivisions, territories and possessions.

Range/Average: N.A.

Activity: N.A.

HQ: Division of HIV/AIDS Prevention (A43), CDCP-HHS, 1600 Clifton Rd., Stop E-07, Atlanta, GA 30333. Phone: (404) 639-8531.

Internet: www.cdc.gov/hiv. (Note: no field offices for this program.)

93.941 HIV DEMONSTRATION, RESEARCH, PUBLIC AND PROFESSIONAL EDUCATION PROJECTS

Assistance: project grants. (to 100 percent/1-5 years).

Purposes: pursuant to PHSA as amended, to develop, test, and disseminate improved HIV prevention strategies at the community level. Applicants are encouraged to involve research groups in the program.

Eligible applicants/beneficiaries: states and political subdivisions, other public and private nonprofit entities.

Range/Average: N.A.

Activity: N.A.

HQ: Division of HIV/AIDS Prevention (A43), CDCP-HHS, 1600 Clifton Rd., Stop E-07, Atlanta, GA 30333. Phone: (404) 639-8531.

Internet: www.cdc.gov/hiv. (Note: no field offices for this program.)

93.942   RESEARCH, PREVENTION, AND EDUCATION PROGRAMS ON LYME DISEASE IN THE UNITED STATES
("Lyme Disease")

Assistance: project grants. (100 percent/to 3 years).

Purposes: pursuant to PHSA as amended, to develop and implement improved measures for the primary and secondary prevention of Lyme disease, including: surveillance activities; ecological and epidemiological studies; diagnostic tests; public education; use of primate models.

Eligible applicants/beneficiaries: public and private nonprofit organizations able to provide services in areas where Lyme disease is found, including IHEs, research institutions, state and local health departments.

Range: $250,000 to $300,000. **Average:** N.A.

Activity: N.A.

HQ: Office of Extramural Research (C-19), National Center for Infectious Diseases, CDCP-HHS, 1600 Clifton Rd. NE, Atlanta, GA 30329-4018. Phone: (404) 718-8845; FAX: (404) 718-8640.

Internet: www.cdc.gov.

93.943   EPIDEMIOLOGIC RESEARCH STUDIES OF ACQUIRED IMMUNODEFICIENCY SYNDROME (AIDS) AND HUMAN IMMUNODEFICIENCY VIRUS (HIV) INFECTION IN SELECTED POPULATION GROUPS

Assistance: project grants. (100 percent/1-3 years).

Purposes: pursuant to PHSA as amended, for research of HIV- related epidemiologic issues concerning risks of transmission, the natural history and transmission of the disease in certain populations, and development and evaluation of behavioral recommendations to reduce AIDS and HIV infection—particularly as they affect minority populations.

Eligible applicants/beneficiaries: states and their political subdivisions, agents, or instrumentalities; public or private nonprofit or profit organizations.

Range/Average: N.A.

Activity: N.A.

HQ: Division of HIV/AIDS Prevention (A43), CDCP-HHS, 1600 Clifton Rd., Stop E-07, Atlanta, GA 30333. Phone: (404) 639-8531.

Internet: www.cdc.gov. (Note: no field offices for this program.)

93.944   HUMAN IMMUNODEFICIENCY VIRUS (HIV)/ACQUIRED IMMUNODEFICIENCY SYNDROME (AIDS) SURVEILLANCE

Assistance: project grants. (100 percent/1-5 years).

Purposes: pursuant to PHSA as amended, to continue and strengthen HIV/AIDS surveillance programs; to effect, maintain, measure, and evaluate the extent of incidence and prevalence throughout the U.S. and its territories; to provide information for targeting and implementing prevention activities. Funds may support staffing costs, purchase of computer hardware and software, laboratory costs.

Eligible applicants/beneficiaries: state and local governments including territories and possessions currently receiving HIV/AIDS surveillance cooperative agreements.

Range/Average: N.A.

Activity: N.A.

HQ: Division of HIV/AIDS Prevention (A43), CDCP-HHS, 1600 Clifton Rd., NE, Stop E-07, Atlanta, GA 30333. Phone: (404) 639-8531.

Internet: www.cdc.gov. (Note: no field offices for this program.)

93.945 ASSISTANCE PROGRAMS FOR CHRONIC DISEASE PREVENTION AND CONTROL

Assistance: project grants (80-100 percent/3-5 years).

Purposes: pursuant to PHSA as amended, to prevent and control chronic diseases, including cardiovascular diseases and arthritis; to establish new chronic disease prevention programs such as Racial and Ethnic Approaches to Community Health (REACH) programs. Funds may support costs associated with planning, implementing, and evaluating programs—but not direct curative or rehabilitative services.

Eligible applicants/beneficiaries: *all programs,* health agencies of the states and U.S. territories and possessions. REACH—public and private community-based organizations.

Range/Average: N.A.

Activity: N.A.

HQ: Deputy Director, Division of Adult and Community Health (K47), National Center for Chronic Disease Prevention and Health Promotion, CDCP-PHS-HHS, 1600 Clifton Rd, Atlanta, Georgia 30333. Phone: (770) 488-5269.

Internet: www.cdc.gov/nccdphp.

93.946 COOPERATIVE AGREEMENTS TO SUPPORT STATE-BASED SAFE MOTHERHOOD AND INFANT HEALTH INITIATIVE PROGRAMS ("Safe Motherhood and Infant Health")

Assistance: project grants. (100 percent/to 5 years).

Purposes: pursuant to PHSA as amended, for: (1) Pregnancy Risk Assessment and Monitoring Systems (PRAMS), to establish and maintain state-specific, population-based surveillance of selected maternal behaviors that occur during pregnancy and early infancy, and to generate state-specific data for planning and assessing perinatal health programs; (2) Maternal and Child Health Epidemiology Programs (MCHEP) to develop state multidisciplinary teams to assist states in using epidemiological and surveillance data to address the health problems of women, infants, and children, related to pregnancy, in vitro fertilization, violence around pregnancy, preterm delivery, and reproductive health complications. Funds also may support related other types of surveillance, research, and demonstration projects.

Eligible applicants/beneficiaries: state and territorial public health agencies designated as vital U.S. registration areas; New York City public health agency; tribal governments. Prevention research—public and private nonprofit agencies including universities.

Range/Average: N.A.

Activity: N.A.

HQ: Division of Reproductive Health, National Center for Chronic Disease Prevention and Health Promotion, CDCP-HHS, Atlanta, GA 30341. Phone: (770) 488-6255.

Internet: www.cdc.gov. (Note: no field offices for this program.)

93.947 TUBERCULOSIS DEMONSTRATION, RESEARCH, PUBLIC AND PROFESSIONAL EDUCATION

Assistance: project grants. (to 100 percent/3-5 years).

Purposes: pursuant to PHSA as amended, for research into the prevention and control of tuberculosis nationally and internationally; for demonstration projects; for public information and education programs; for education, training, and clinical skills improvement for health professionals including allied health personnel. Funds may not be used for inpatient care.

Eligible applicants/beneficiaries: states, political subdivisions; public and private nonprofit entities.

Range: $100,000 to $1,000,000. **Average:** $120,000.

Activity: N.A.

HQ: National Center for HIV, STD, and TB Prevention, CDCP-HHS, 1600 Clifton Rd. NE (Stop E10), Atlanta, GA 30333. Phone: (404) 639-5259.

Internet: www.cdc.gov/DTBE. (Note: no field offices for this program.)

93.958 BLOCK GRANTS FOR COMMUNITY MENTAL HEALTH SERVICES ("MHBG")

Assistance: formula grants.

Purposes: pursuant to PHSA as amended, to provide comprehensive community mental health services to adults with a serious mental illness and to children with serious emotional disturbance; for program monitoring; for technical assistance in related planning and implementation. Services must be provided through qualified community programs including community mental health centers or child mental health, psycho-social rehabilitation, mental health peer-support, or mental health primary consumer-directed programs. Funds may not be used for inpatient services, cash payments to patients, most real estate or major equipment costs.

Eligible applicants/beneficiaries: state and territorial governments; tribal organizations.

Range: $50,000 to $63,093,869. **Average:** $7,750,299.

Activity: anticipate 59 awards will be made in FY 2016.

HQ: PATH Program, Homeless Programs Branch, Division of Knowledge Development and Systems Change, CMHS-SAMHSA-HHS, 1 Choke Cherry Rd., 7-1091, Rockville, MD 20857. Phone: (240) 276-1422.

Internet: www.samhsa.gov. (Note: no field offices for this program.)

93.959   BLOCK GRANTS FOR PREVENTION AND TREATMENT OF SUBSTANCE ABUSE ("SABG")

Assistance: formula grants.

Purposes: pursuant to PHSA as amended, to develop and implement prevention, treatment, and rehabilitation activities directed to the diseases of alcohol and drug abuse. At least 20 percent of funds allocated must support education and counseling programs concerning alcohol and substance abuse and tobacco use, for persons not requiring treatment; at least 5 percent of funds must increase treatment services for pregnant women and women with dependent children. States must require treatment programs for intravenous drug abusers, stipulating prompt admittance of such individuals into treatment. States must provide tuberculosis services such as counseling, testing, treatment, and early intervention for substance abusers at risk for HIV disease—either directly or through public or nonprofit entities.

Eligible applicants/beneficiaries: state and territory governments; the Red Lake Band of Chippewa Indians.

Range: $127,671 to $250,323,608. **Average:** $28,722,431.

Activity: anticipate 60 awards will be made in FY 2016.

HQ: PATH Program, Homeless Programs Branch, Division of Knowledge Development and Systems Change, CMHS-SAMHSA-HHS, 1 Choke Cherry Rd., 7-1097, Rockville, MD 20857. Phone: (240) 276-1422.

Internet: www.samhsa.gov. (Note: no field offices for this program.)

93.964   PUBLIC HEALTH TRAINEESHIPS

Assistance: formula grants. (100 percent/to 3 years).

Purposes: pursuant to PHSA as amended and HPEPA, for traineeships for graduate students of public health. Training must be in: biostatistics; epidemiology; environmental health; toxicology; public health nutrition; maternal and child health.

Eligible applicants/beneficiaries: schools, programs of public health; other accredited public and private nonprofit institutions.

Range: $77,411 to $150,000. **Average:** N.A.

Activity: N.A.

HQ: Director, Division of Nursing, Bureau of Health Professions, Health Resources and Services Administration, HHS, 5600 Fishers Ln., Rm. 9C-05, Rockville, MD 20857. Phone: (301) 443-5688.

Internet: www.hrsa.gov.

93.965   COAL MINERS RESPIRATORY IMPAIRMENT TREATMENT CLINICS AND SERVICES
("Black Lung Clinics")

Assistance: project grants.

Purposes: pursuant to the Federal Mine Safety and Health Act and Black Lung Benefits Act, for broad support of coal miners respiratory impairments treatment clinics and services, including patient and family member education to maximize the patient's ability for self-care.

Eligible applicants/beneficiaries: state, public or private entities.

Range: $100,000 to $626,986. **Average:** $416,842.

Activity: N.A.

HQ: Director, Division of Health Center Management, Bureau of Primary Health Care, HRSA-HHS, 5600 Fishers Ln., Rm. 17W29-C, Rockville, MD 20857. Phone: (301) 443-0835.

Internet: www.hrsa.gov/ruralhealth.

93.969   GERIATRIC EDUCATION CENTERS

Assistance: project grants. (100 percent/5 years).

Purposes: pursuant to PHSA as amended and HPEPA, to develop collaborative arrangements among health professions schools and health care facilities, focusing on multi-disciplinary training of health professionals in geriatric health care, including faculty training and retraining; to provide students with clinical training in nursing homes, chronic and acute care hospitals, ambulatory care centers, and senior centers; to develop and disseminate pertinent curricula; provide continuing education for health professionals. Funds may not be used for trainee costs or for land acquisition or construction activities.

Eligible applicants/beneficiaries: accredited health professions schools; schools of allied health; physician assistant training programs.

Range: $500,000 to $850,000. **Average:** $790,000.

Activity: N.A.

HQ: Division of State, Community, and Public Health, Bureau of Health Professions, HRSA-HHS, Parklawn Bldg., Rm. 12C-06T, 5600 Fishers Ln., Rockville, MD 20857. Phone: (301) 443-5626.

Internet: www.hrsa.gov. (Note: no field offices for this program.)

93.970   HEALTH PROFESSIONS RECRUITMENT PROGRAM FOR INDIANS

Assistance: project grants (100 percent).

Purposes: pursuant to the Indian Health Care Improvement Act as amended, to establish and operate programs to recruit American Indians and Alaska natives into education or training programs at health or allied health professions schools; to increase the number of nurses, nurse midwives, nurse practitioners, and nurse anesthetists delivering health care services to Americans Indians and Alaska natives; to place health professional residents for short-term assignments at IHS facilities.

Eligible applicants/beneficiaries: public or private nonprofit health or educational entities, with preference to tribes and tribal or urban Indian health organizations.

Range/Average: N.A.

Activity: N.A.

HQ: Grants Policy Office, IHS-HHS, 801 Thompson Ave., Suite TMP 360, Rockville, MD 20852. Phone: (301) 443-5204.

Internet: www.ihs.gov. (Note: no field offices for this program.)

93.971 HEALTH PROFESSIONS PREPARATORY SCHOLARSHIP PROGRAM FOR INDIANS

Assistance: project grants.

Purposes: pursuant to the Indian Health Care Improvement Act as amended, for compensatory pre-professional health education scholarships to American Indians and Alaska natives, covering up to two years of full-time study. Eligible disciplines are pre- nursing, -pharmacy, -medical technology, -physical therapy, -engineering, and pre-sanitation.

Eligible applicants/beneficiaries: persons of American Indian or Alaska native descent, with high school completed and accepted into an eligible program.

Range: $16,525 to $55,394. **Average:** $29,409.

Activity: N.A.

HQ: Grants Policy Office, IHS-HHS, 801 Thompson Ave., Suite TMP 360, Rockville, MD 20852. Phone: (301) 443-5204.

Internet: www.ihs.gov.

93.972 HEALTH PROFESSIONS SCHOLARSHIP PROGRAM

Assistance: project grants. (100 percent/to 4 years).

Purposes: pursuant to the Indian Health Care Amendments of 1988, for scholarships to American Indians and Alaska natives enrolling full- or part-time in health professions schools, to prepare them for careers serving Indians in: allopathic or osteopathic medicine; dentistry; baccalaureate or graduate nursing; graduate public health nutrition; graduate medical social work; graduate speech pathology/audiology; optometry; pharmacy; health care administration. Grantees must serve one year in the IHS or an Indian health organization for each year of support received through the program, with a minimum of two years—with deferments for certain types of advanced training.

Eligible applicants/beneficiaries: native American Indians or Alaskans enrolled as members of a tribe, accepted for study at a U.S. educational institution in a medical/health career education program deemed necessary by the IHS, and eligible for or holding an appointment to the PHS or for civil service in IHS.

Range: $17,615 to $125,500. **Average:** $44,877.

Activity: N.A.

HQ: Grants Policy Office, IHS-HHS, 801 Thompson Ave., Suite TMP 360, Rockville, MD 20852. Phone: (301) 443-5204.

Internet: www.ihs.gov.

93.974 FAMILY PLANNING—SERVICE DELIVERY IMPROVEMENT RESEARCH GRANTS (SDI)

Assistance: project grants (100 percent).

Purposes: pursuant to PHSA as amended and Family Planning Services and Population Research Acts, for research studies to improve family planning services delivery. Funds may not be used in programs where abortion is a method of family planning.

Eligible applicants/beneficiaries: public or private nonprofit entities, including in territories and possessions.

Range: $300,000 to $400,000. Average: N.A.

Activity: anticipate 4 awards in FY 2015.

HQ: Office of Population Affairs, HHS, 1101 Wootton Pkwy., Ste. 550, Rockville, MD 20852. Phone: (240) 453-8822.

Internet: www.gov/opa. (Note: no field offices for this program.)

93.977 PREVENTIVE HEALTH SERVICES—SEXUALLY TRANSMITTED DISEASES CONTROL GRANTS
("STD Prevention Grants")

Assistance: project grants. (to 100 percent/1-5 years).

Purposes: pursuant to PHSA and amendments, for surveillance activities to prevent sexually transmitted disease, including reporting, screening, case follow-up including notification of sex partners; interstate epidemiological referral; personnel education and training; studies and demonstrations; development of control strategies and activities.

Eligible applicants/beneficiaries: any state, and in consultation with state authorities, political subdivisions.

Range: $85,762 to $6,406,117. Average: $1,338,726.

Activity: N.A.

HQ: Division of HIV/AIDS Prevention (A43), CDCP-HHS, 1600 Clifton Rd., Stop E-07, Atlanta, GA 30333. Phone: (404) 639-8531.

Internet: www.cdc.gov/std. (Note: no field offices for this program.)

93.982 MENTAL HEALTH DISASTER ASSISTANCE AND EMERGENCY MENTAL HEALTH

Assistance: project grants. (100 percent/9-12 months).

Purposes: pursuant to the Robert T. Stafford Disaster Relief and Emergency Assistance Act, for supplemental emergency mental health counseling services to victims of major disasters; to train workers to provide such counseling.

Eligible applicants/beneficiaries: state or local nonprofit agencies recommended by the state governor.

Range: $694,600 to $2,134,752. **Average:** $1,305,100.

Activity: 8 awards in FY 2014.

HQ: Emergency Services and Disaster Relief Branch, CMHS-SAMHSA-HHS, 1 Choke Cherry Rd., Rockville, MD 20850. Phone: (240) 276-1418.

Internet: www.samhsa.gov. (Note: no field offices for this program.)

93.985 ASSISTANCE FOR ORAL DISEASE PREVENTION AND CONTROL

Assistance: project grants/discretionary. (100 percent/3 to 5 years).

Purposes: pursuant to Public Health Service Act (as amended), and the Patient Protection and Affordable Care Act, to establish oral health leadership and program guidance, oral health data collection and interpretation, a multi-dimensional delivery system for oral and physical health, and to implement science-based programs (including dental sealants and community water fluoridation) to improve oral and physical health.

Eligible applicants: state, local, tribal, and territorial health agencies.

Eligible beneficiaries: local health agencies, and organizations and individuals with specialized health interests.

Range/Average: N.A.

Activity: N.A.

HQ: CDC-HHS, 4770 Buford Hwy., NE, Stop F-80, Atlanta, GA 30341. Phone: 770-488-6075.

Internet: www.cdc.gov. (Note: no field offices for this program.)

93.988 COOPERATIVE AGREEMENTS FOR STATE-BASED DIABETES CONTROL PROGRAMS AND EVALUATION OF SURVEILLANCE SYSTEMS

Assistance: project grants. (80-84 percent/5 years).

Purposes: pursuant to PHSA as amended and Health Services and Centers Amendments Act of 1978, to plan, implement, and evaluate state-based diabetes control programs including: determining the size and nature diabetes-related problems; developing new strategies to prevention; establishing partnerships to prevent diabetes problems; increasing awareness of prevention and control opportunities among the public, health care and business communities, and diabetes patients; improving access to quality care. Direct curative or rehabilitative services to patients may not be provided with grant funds.

Eligible applicants/beneficiaries: official state and territorial health agencies.

Range/Average: N.A.

Activity: N.A.

HQ: Program Development Branch, Division of Diabetes Translation, National Center for Chronic Disease Prevention and Health Promotion, CDCP-HHS, 2877 Brandywine Rd., Williams Bldg., Atlanta, GA 30341. Phone: (770) 488-1094; FAX: (770) 488-5966.

Internet: www.cdc.gov.

93.989 INTERNATIONAL RESEARCH AND RESEARCH TRAINING ("Global Health Research and Research Training")

Assistance: project grants. (100 percent/to 5 years).

Purposes: pursuant to PHSA as amended, for research and research training to reduce disparities in global health and toward the international exchange of ideas and information. Research is supported in the basic biological, behavioral, and social sciences, including economics, demography, and ethics. Grants may support stipends, foreign living allowances, travel, and minimal other costs required to perform research in a foreign country.

Eligible applicants/beneficiaries: IHEs, hospitals, laboratories, federal institutions, state and local governments, and other public or private nonprofit of profit institutions.

Range/Average: N.A.

Activity: N.A.

HQ: Fogarty International Center, NIH-HHS, Bldg. 31, Rm. B2C39, MSC 2220, Bethesda, MD 20892-2022. Phone: (301) 402-5011.

Internet: www.fic.nih.gov. (Note: no field offices for this program.)

93.990 NATIONAL HEALTH PROMOTION

Assistance: project grants. (100 percent/to 3 years).

Purposes: pursuant to PHSA as amended, for national membership organizations from various sectors to participate in the National Health Promotion Program to educate the public about good health habits and programs designed to prevent disease and disability. Funds may be used to develop promotion programs and materials to be used by schools, medical treatment sites, work sites, and community health promotion programs; to identify the needs of special population groups; to fill gaps identified in the "Healthy People 2010: National Health Promotion and Disease Prevention Objectives."

Eligible applicants/beneficiaries: public or private nonprofit organizations.

Range: $500,000 to $900,000. **Average:** N.A.

Activity: N.A.

HQ: Office of Disease Prevention and Health Promotion, OS-HHS, 1101 Wootton Pkwy., Ste. 550, Rockville, MD 20852. Phone: (240) 453-8822.

Internet: www.healthypeople.gov. (Note: no field offices for this program.)

93.991 PREVENTIVE HEALTH AND HEALTH SERVICES BLOCK GRANT ("PHHS Block Grants")

Assistance: formula grants. (100 percent/2 years).

Purposes: pursuant to PHSA, Health Omnibus Programs Extension Act of 1988, and amendments, for state preventive health service programs, including emergency medical services program improvement (but not program operations costs), health incentive activities, hypertension programs, rodent control, fluoridation programs, health education, risk reduction programs, home health services, services for victims of sex offenses including prevention of sex offenses, and other services.

Eligible applicants/beneficiaries: state and Pacific territorial governments, certain tribes.

Range: $21,258 to $7,026,219. **Average:** $1,572,013.

Activity: N.A.

HQ: Project Officer, National Center for Chronic Disease Prevention and Health Promotion (K30), CDCP-HHS, 3005 Chamblee Tucker Rd., Stop K45, Chamblee, GA 30341. Phone: (770) 488-5941; FAX: (770) 488-5974.

Internet: www.cdc.gov/nccdphp/blockgrant. (Note: no field offices for this program.)

93.994 MATERNAL AND CHILD HEALTH SERVICES BLOCK GRANT TO THE STATES
("MCH Block Grants")

Assistance: formula grants (57 percent).

Purposes: pursuant to SSA as amended, for a broad range of health and related services including preventive and primary care services to pregnant women, mothers, infants, and children including children with special health needs. Funds may support such costs as program planning, administration, education, and evaluation. Ineligible uses of funds are most inpatient services, cash payments for health services, major equipment purchases, construction costs, or research or training other than by public or nonprofit entities.

Eligible applicants/beneficiaries: states and insular areas.

Range: $145,808 to $38,964,489. **Average:** $9,153,000.

Activity: 59 awards in FY 2016.

HQ: Division of State and Community Health, Maternal and Child Health Bureau, HRSA-HHS, 5600 Fishers Ln., Rm. 5C-26, Rockville, MD 20857. Phone: (301) 443-2204.

Internet: www.hrsa.gov.

93.995 ADOLESCENT FAMILY LIFE—DEMONSTRATION PROJECTS

Assistance: project grants. (to 70 percent/to 5 years).

Purposes: pursuant to PHSA as amended, to establish innovative, comprehensive, and integrated approaches to the delivery of care services to pregnant and parenting adolescents, especially those under age 17; to promote abstinence from sexual relations through age-appropriate education on sexuality and decision making skills as the most effective method of preventing adolescent pregnancy and avoiding sexually transmitted diseases including HIV/AIDS. Funds may support costs of: care and prevention services; coordination of services among local providers; appropriate supplemental services.

Eligible applicants/beneficiaries: public organizations including city, county, regional, and state governments; private nonprofit organizations.

Range: $400,000 to $600,000. **Average:** N.A.

Activity: N.A.

HQ: Office of Adolescent Pregnancy Programs, Office of Population Affairs, OS-HHS, 1101 Wootton Pkwy. - Ste. 700, Rockville, MD 20852. Phone:

(240) 453-2828. *grants management information*: Director, Office of Grants Management, Office of Public Health and Science, HHS, 1101 Wootton Pkwy., Ste. 550 Rockville, MD 20853. Phone: (240) 453-8822.

Internet: www.opa.gov. (Note: no field offices for this program.)

93.997 ASSISTED OUTPATIENT TREATMENT GRANT PROGRAM FOR INDIVIDUALS WITH SERIOUS MENTAL ILLNESS

Assistance: project grants/discretionary. (100 percent/to 4 years).

Purposes: pursuant to the Protecting Access to Medicare Act of 2014, to improve the health and social outcomes for the individuals served in the program by increasing healthcare utilization, improving behavioral health and other health outcomes, and reducing rates of homelessness and incarceration.

Eligible applicants/beneficiaries: state, county and city mental health systems and mental health courts.

Range: to $1,000,000. **Average:** N.A.

Activity: N.A.

HQ: SAMHSA-HHS, 5600 Fishers Ln., Rockville, MD 20857. Phone: (240) 276-1418.

Internet: www.samhsa.gov. (Note: no field offices for this program.)

93.998 AUTISM AND OTHER DEVELOPMENTAL DISABILITIES, SURVEILLANCE, RESEARCH, AND PREVENTION

Assistance: cooperative agreements. (100 percent/1 to 5 years).

Purposes: pursuant to the Public Health Service Act, Executive Order 317(k)(2), to support public and private nonprofit organizations in the planning, implementing, coordinating, or evaluating programs related to autism and other developmental disabilities and the improvement of infant and child health and developmental outcomes.

Eligible applicants/beneficiaries: state, local, tribal, and territorial public and private nonprofit institutions/organizations.

Range: $5,000 to $1,750,000. **Average:** N.A.

Activity: N.A.

HQ: CDC-HHS, 1600 Clifton Rd., NE, MS-E87, Atlanta, GA 30333. Phone: (404) 498-3860.

Internet: N.A. (Note: no field offices for this program.)

CORPORATION FOR NATIONAL AND COMMUNITY SERVICE

94.002 RETIRED AND SENIOR VOLUNTEER PROGRAM

Assistance: project grants. (70-90 percent/3 years).

Purposes: pursuant to the Domestic Volunteer Service Act of 1973 as amended and National and Community Service Trust Act of 1993 (NCSA), for programs engaging retired persons as volunteers in community service projects—e.g., intergenerational activities, in-home care, consumer education, public safety, and health and human service activities. Grant funds cover program costs including staff salaries and reimbursements to volunteers for their out-of-pocket expenses, primarily for transportation. Technical assistance and materials toward establishing and operating programs are available.

Eligible applicants: public agencies including state and local government agencies, private nonprofit organizations.

Eligible beneficiaries: volunteers at least age 55.

Range: to $768,228. **Average:** $71,695.

Activity: N.A.

HQ: National Senior Service Corps, RSVP, CNCS, 1201 New York Ave., NW, Washington, DC 20525. Phone: (202) 606-5000.

Internet: www.nationalservice.gov/programs/senior-corps.

94.003 STATE COMMISSIONS

Assistance: project grants (cost sharing).

Purposes: pursuant to NCSA as amended, to operate independent, bipartisan state commissions to oversee funded AmeriCorps programs. Commissions generally include 15 to 25 members appointed by governors.

Eligible applicants/beneficiaries: state governments, DC, PR.

Range: $125,000 to $1,000,000. **Average:** N.A.

Activity: N.A.

HQ: CNCS, 1201 New York Ave., NW, Washington, DC 20525. Phone: (202) 606-6930.

Internet: www.nationalservice.org.

94.006 AMERICORPS

Assistance: project grants.

Purposes: pursuant to NCSA as amended, to plan or operate national and community service programs addressing community education, public safety, human, and environmental needs—by encouraging volunteers to serve part- or full-time. AmeriCorps members serve for one year, and receive education awards for postsecondary education or to pay off student loans. Examples include volunteers serving as mentors, tutors, teaching assistants, role models—in after-school, immunization, low- income housing renovation, "crime watch," and environmental projects.

Eligible applicants/beneficiaries: states, tribes, territories, national nonprofit organizations, professional corps, and multi- state organizations.

Range: $200,000 to $3,000,000. **Average:** N.A.

Activity: N.A.

HQ: CNCS, 1201 New York Ave., NW, Washington, DC 20525. Phone: (202) 606-6930.

Internet: www.nationalservice.org.

94.007 PLANNING AND PROGRAM DEVELOPMENT GRANTS

Assistance: project grants.

Purposes: pursuant to NCSA as amended, for innovative demonstration projects that build the ethic of service among Americans of all ages and backgrounds—including through the AmeriCorps Education Award Program, AmeriCorps Promise Fellows Program, and Martin Luther King Day of Service Program, and Disability Outreach grants for programs ensuring participation of the disabled in national and community service.

Eligible applicants/beneficiaries: demonstration grants—state and local government agencies, nonprofit organizations. Disability grants—operating AmeriCorps programs, state commissions, national nonprofit organizations.

Range/Average: N.A.

Activity: N.A.

HQ: CNCS, 1201 New York Ave., NW, 8th Fl., Washington, DC 20525. Phone: (202) 606-6967.

Internet: www.nationalservice.gov. (Note: no field offices for this program.)

94.011 FOSTER GRANDPARENT PROGRAM (FGP)

Assistance: project grants (from 90 percent).

Purposes: pursuant to the Domestic Volunteer Service Act of 1973 as amended and National and Community Service Trust Act of 1993, to engage older volunteers with limited incomes in providing supportive services to infants, children, or youth with special or exceptional needs. Programs may be conducted in the children's homes or in residential or nonresidential facilities including preschools. Grant funds may be used: to pay stipends to low- income foster grandparents serving as volunteers, and to provide their transportation, physical exams, and meals; for staff salaries and travel, equipment, and space costs. Technical assistance and materials toward establishing and operating programs are available.

Eligible applicants: state and local government agencies, private nonprofit organizations.

Eligible beneficiaries: persons at least age 60, low-income, and physically, mentally, and emotionally capable of serving clients on a person-to-person basis; non-low-income individuals may serve as volunteers without stipends.

Range: to $1,917,775. **Average:** $333,362.

Activity: N.A.

HQ: Foster Grandparent Program, National Senior Service Corps, CNCS, 1201 New York Ave., NW, Washington, DC 20525. Phone: (202) 606-5000.

Internet: www.nationalservice.gov/programs/senior-corps.

94.013 VOLUNTEERS IN SERVICE TO AMERICA ("AmeriCorps-VISTA")

Assistance: specialized services.

Purposes: pursuant to the Domestic Volunteer Service Act of 1973 as amended, to provide volunteers from all walks of life and age groups, working in projects addressing the problems of poverty such as health, illiteracy, substance abuse prevention and education, hunger, homelessness, housing, unemployment. Volunteers may be recruited locally or referred by CNCS; they serve full-time for one year, living at subsistence levels of support among the people they serve.

Eligible applicants/beneficiaries: federal, state, or local government agencies or private nonprofit organizations.

Range/Average: N.A.

Activity: anticipate supporting 7,800 VISTA members and summer associates in FY 2015.

HQ: Director, VISTA, CNCS, 1201 New York Ave., NW, Washington, DC 20525. Phone: (202) 606-6849.

Internet: www.americorps.gov/about/programs/vista.asp.

94.016 SENIOR COMPANION PROGRAM (SCP)

Assistance: project grants. (from 90 percent/3 years).

Purposes: pursuant to the Domestic Volunteer Service Act of 1973 as amended and National and Community Service Trust Act of 1993, for the operating costs of the Senior Companion Program, including stipends, transportation, physical exams, insurance, and meals for low-income older volunteers. SCP participants serve as companions to other adults, primarily older persons with special needs. Services to the adults may be provided in their homes or in residential or nonresidential facilities, including such activities as helping hospital patients during their recuperation, arranging for community social services, working with the terminally ill. Respite care services, including to Alzheimer's patients and their families, are also provided.

Eligible applicants: state and local government agencies, private nonprofit organizations.

Eligible beneficiaries: persons at least age 60, low-income, and physically, mentally, and emotionally capable of serving clients on a person-to-person basis; non-low-income individuals may serve as volunteers without stipends.

Range: to $611,758. **Average:** $238,077.

Activity: N.A.

HQ: Senior Companion Program, CNCS, 1201 New York Ave., NW, Washington, DC 20525. Phone: (202) 606-5000.

Internet: www.nationalservice.gov/programs/senior-corps.

94.017 SENIOR DEMONSTRATION PROGRAM

Assistance: project grants/discretionary (100 percent/1 to 3 years).

Purposes: pursuant to the Domestic Volunteer Service Act of 1973, to provide grants to qualified agencies for the purpose of conducting innovative activities involving older Americans as volunteers. Volunteers may not supplant hiring or displace employed workers, or impair existing contracts for service. Volunteers may not be involved in nor may funds be used to support religious activities, labor or anti-labor organization, lobbying, or partisan or non-partisan political activities.

Eligible applicants: non-profit organizations, state and local government agencies/entities.

Eligible beneficiaries: eligible senior volunteers, aged 55 or older.

Range/Average: N.A.

Activity: N.A.

HQ: Director, Corporation for National and Community Service/Senior Demonstration Program, 1201 New York Ave., NW, Washington, DC 20525. Phone: (202) 606-5000.

Internet: www.seniorcorps.gov.

94.019 SOCIAL INNOVATION FUND (SIF)

Assistance: cooperative agreements (to 5 years).

Purposes: pursuant to the Edward M. Kennedy Serve America Act of 2009, to fund and work with existing grant-making institutions to direct resources to innovative community-based nonprofit organizations to identify, validate, and grow promising approaches to overcoming challenges facing local communities. One or more of the following issues should be addressed: prepare America's youth for success in school, active citizenship, productive work, and healthy and safe lives; increase economic opportunities for economically disadvantaged individuals; promote healthy lifestyles, reducing risk factors that can lead to illness. Applicant cost-match required.

Eligible applicants: existing intermediary organizations, grantmaking institutions, or grantmaking partnerships.

Eligible beneficiaries: subgrants issued to promising nonprofit community organizations working to address priority issues in low-income communities across the country.

Range/Average: N.A.

Activity: N.A.

HQ: Program Director, Corporation for National and Community and Service, 1201 New York Ave., Washington, DC 20005. Phone: (202) 606-3223.

Internet: www.nationalservice.gov. (Note: no field offices for this program.)

94.021 VOLUNTEER GENERATION FUND

Assistance: project grants/discretionary (50 to 80 percent/3 years).

Purposes: pursuant to the Edward M. Kennedy Serve America Act, to increase the number of volunteers dedicated to addressing important needs in communities across America. Funds will support the efforts of volunteer connector organizations to recruit, manage, support and retain individuals to serve in high quality assignments, including those aligned with special days of service such as Martin Luther King, Jr. Day and the 9-11 Day of Service and Remembrance.

Eligible applicants: state service commissions (or approved alternative administrative entities) or partnerships/consortia of state service commissions.

Eligible beneficiaries: community-based entities eligible for sub-grants, volunteers and their communities.

Range: from $75,000. **Average:** N.A.

Activity: N.A.

HQ: Director, Corporation for National and Community Service, 10 Causeway St., Suite 473, Boston, MA 02222. Phone: (617) 565-7001.

Internet: N.A. (Note: no field offices for this program.)

94.023 AMERICORPS VISTA TRAINING & LOGISTICS SUPPORT ("VISTA Volunteers in Service to America")

Assistance: dissemination of technical information; training (100 percent/to 2 years).

Purposes: pursuant to the Domestic Volunteer Service Act of 1973, to provide training and technical assistance to the AmeriCorps VISTA program in the professional development of its members and sponsors at community-based, non-profit organization and agency service sites, prior to service. Assistance includes: travel arrangements, fingerprinting for criminal history, background checks, curriculum and instructional design, on-site logistical support, development of training-support materials in multi-media, web and graphic design, server maintenance, marketing/communication strategies, and evaluation.

Eligible applicants/beneficiaries: eligible U.S. citizens or legal residents 18 years or older, eligible organizations willing to sponsor a VISTA member or members.

Range/Average: N.A.

Activity: N.A.

HQ: Director, Corporation for National and Community Service, 1201 New York Ave., NW, Washington, DC 20525. Phone: (202) 606-6816; FAX: (202) 606-3475.

Internet: www.nationalservice.gov. (Note: no field offices for this program.)

94.026 NATIONAL SERVICE AND CIVIC ENGAGEMENT RESEARCH COMPETITION

Assistance: cooperative agreements. (100 percent/3 years or more).

Purposes: pursuant to the National and Community Service Act of 1990, as amended, to increase the nation's understanding and knowledge about the importance and potential of volunteering, national and community service, and civic engagement. Applications are sought to build on existing research in the field, address gaps in knowledge, and provide new ideas and methodological approaches to the study of national service.

Eligible applicants/beneficiaries: public and private nonprofit institutions/organizations.

Range/Average: N.A.

Activity: N.A.

HQ: Corporation for National and Community Service, 1201 New York Ave., NW, Washington, DC 20005. Phone: (202) 606-6772.

Internet: N.A.

EXECUTIVE OFFICE
OF THE PRESIDENT

95.001 HIGH INTENSITY DRUG TRAFFICKING AREAS PROGRAM (HIDTA)

Assistance: project grants (100 percent/2 years).

Purposes: pursuant to the Office of National Drug Control Policy Reauthorization Act of 2006, funding for law enforcement initiatives in areas that have been designated by the Director of The Office of National Drug Control Policy (ONDCP) as High Intensity Drug Trafficking Areas (HIDTAs). The purpose of the program is to reduce drug trafficking and drug production in the United States by: facilitating cooperation among Federal, State, local, and tribal law enforcement agencies to share information and implement coordinated enforcement activities; enhancing law enforcement intelligence sharing among Federal, State, local, and tribal law enforcement agencies; providing reliable law enforcement intelligence to law enforcement agencies needed to design effective enforcement strategies and operations; and supporting coordinated law enforcement strategies which maximize use of available resources to reduce the supply of illegal drugs in designated areas and in the United States as a whole.

Eligible applicants: law enforcement initiatives located and operated in an area designated as a HIDTA by the Director of ONDCP.

Eligible beneficiaries: law enforcement drug task forces, drug related law enforcement Initiatives, drug related intelligence or information centers located in designated HIDTAs.

Range/Average: N.A.

Activity: N.A.

HQ: Director, High Intensity Drug Trafficking Areas Program, Executive Office of the President, 750 17th St., NW, Washington, DC 20503. Phone: (202) 395-6739.

Internet: www.whitehousedrugpolicy.gov. (Note: no field offices for this program.)

95.005 DRUG COURT TRAINING AND TECHNICAL ASSISTANCE

Assistance: project grants (100 percent).

Purposes: pursuant to the Consolidated Appropriations Act of 2012, the Office of National Drug Control Policy (ONDCP) will award one or more grants to establish training, technical assistance, and other resources to promote an improved criminal justice system in order to break the cycle of drug use, crime, incarceration, and recidivism.

Eligible applicants/beneficiaries: eligible organizations with expertise/experience in brokering and developing training and technical assistance for drug court professionals.

Range/Average: N.A.

Activity: N.A.

HQ: Director, Executive Office of the President 750 17th St., NW, Washington, DC 20503. Phone: (202) 395-6739.

Internet: N.A. (Note: no field offices for this program.)

95.006 MODEL STATE DRUG LAWS INITIATIVE

Assistance: project grants (100 percent).

Purposes: pursuant to the Consolidated Appropriations Act of 2012, to assist policymakers and practitioners in developing comprehensive laws, policies and programs on current and emerging drug and alcohol issues facing states and localities.

Eligible applicants/beneficiaries: eligible public nonprofit institutions/organizations with expert knowledge and experience conducting research and analysis, providing technical assistance, and drafting model state drug and alcohol laws, policies, and programs.

Range/Average: N.A.

Activity: N.A.

HQ: Director, Executive Office of the President 750 17th St., NW, Washington, DC 20503. Phone: (202) 395-6739.

Internet: N.A. (Note: no field offices for this program.)

SOCIAL SECURITY ADMINISTRATION

96.001 SOCIAL SECURITY—DISABILITY INSURANCE

Assistance: direct payments/unrestricted or specified use.

Purposes: pursuant to SSA as amended, to replace part of the earnings lost because of a physical or mental impairment preventing a person from working. Disability is defined as a medically determined physical or mental impairment that has lasted or is expected to last at least 12 months, or to result in death. There is a five-month waiting period. Costs of vocational rehabilitation for certain beneficiaries are eligible.

Eligible applicants/beneficiaries: disabled workers under full retirement age (66 for workers age 62 in 2005) if they have worked for a sufficient period of time under Social Security. Certain family members of disabled workers also are eligible for benefits, including: unmarried children under age 18, or 19 for full-time elementary and secondary students; disabled unmarried children under age 22; spouse caring for child under age 16 or disabled, receiving benefits on worker's Social Security record; spouses age 62 or over; divorced spouses age 62 or over, married to the worker for at least 10 years. Benefits are subject to an earnings test, and may be reduced by amounts received under other programs. Certain restrictions apply for impairments: based on drug addiction or alcoholism; based on felony-and confinement-related impairments. Coverage credits under the social security systems of certain foreign governments may be taken into account. Effective after 2003, lawfully admitted aliens may be eligible if they have a work-authorized Social Security Number. Applicants should contact local Social Security offices for additional details.

Range/Average: N.A.

Activity: N.A.

HQ: Office of Public Inquiries, SSA, Annex, Rm. 4100, Baltimore, MD 21235. Phone: (410) 965-2736.

Internet: www.socialsecurity.gov.

96.002 SOCIAL SECURITY—RETIREMENT INSURANCE

Assistance: direct payments/unrestricted use.

Purposes: pursuant to SSA as amended, to pay monthly cash benefits to retired workers and their eligible auxiliaries.

Eligible applicants/beneficiaries: retired workers age 62 and over that have worked the required number of years under Social Security. Certain family members also are eligible for benefits, including: unmarried children under age 18, or 19 for full-time elementary and secondary students; disabled unmarried children under age 22; spouse caring for child under age 16 or disabled, receiving benefits on worker's Social Security record; spouses age 62 or over; divorced spouses age 62 or over, married to the worker for at least 10 years. Benefit payments to eligible workers applying before full-benefit retirement age (66 for workers age 62 in 2005) are reduced permanently. Benefit amounts may be reduced for a spouse receiving a government pension based on his or her work in non-covered employment. Coverage credits under the social security systems of certain foreign governments may be taken into account to meet eligibility requirements. Effective after 2003, lawfully admitted aliens may be eligible if they have a work-authorized Social Security Number. All applicants should contact local Social Security offices for additional details and restrictions.

Range/Average: N.A.

Activity: N.A.

HQ: Office of Public Inquiries, SSA, Annex, Rm. 4100, Baltimore, MD 21235. Phone: (410) 965-2736.

Internet: www.socialsecurity.gov.

96.004 SOCIAL SECURITY—SURVIVORS INSURANCE

Assistance: direct payments/specified or unrestricted uses.

Purposes: pursuant to SSA as amended, to pay monthly cash benefits to a deceased worker's dependents if the deceased was insured for survivors' insurance protection.

Eligible applicants/beneficiaries: widows or widowers age 60 or over; surviving divorced spouses age 60 or over, married to the deceased worker for at least 10 years; survivors with a child in their care under age 16 or disabled; disabled widows, widowers, or divorced spouses age 50-59; unmarried children under age 18, or under 19 if in elementary or secondary school, or age 18 or older if disabled before age 22; dependent parents age 62 or over. Earnings tests and benefit limits apply, except for beneficiaries age 70 or over. Under certain conditions, a lump-sum death payment of $255 is payable to survivors. Benefits are subject to an earnings test, and may be reduced by amounts received under other programs. Benefit amounts are reduced for a spouse receiving a government pension based on his or her work in non-covered employment. Coverage credits under the social security systems of certain foreign governments may be taken into account to meet eligibility requirements. Effective after 2003, lawfully admitted aliens may be eligible if they have a work-authorized Social Security Number. Applicants should contact local Social Security offices for additional details.

Range/Average: N.A.

Activity: N.A.

HQ: Office of Public Inquiries, SSA, Annex, Rm. 4100, Baltimore, MD 21235. Phone: (410) 965-2736.

Internet: www.socialsecurity.gov.

96.006 SUPPLEMENTAL SECURITY INCOME

Assistance: direct payments/unrestricted or specified uses.

Purposes: pursuant SSA as amended, to provide supplemental income to persons aged 65 and over and to blind or disabled persons with incomes and financial resources below specified levels.

Eligible applicants/beneficiaries: persons age 65 or over or blind or disabled, meeting U.S. citizenship or residence requirements, and with income and assets below certain levels.

Range/Average: N.A.

Activity: N.A.

HQ: Office of Public Inquiries, SSA, Annex, Rm. 4100, Baltimore, MD 21235. Phone: (410) 965-2736.

Internet: www.socialsecurity.gov.

96.007 SOCIAL SECURITY—RESEARCH AND DEMONSTRATION ("SSA Research and Demonstration")

Assistance: project grants. (75-95 percent/3 months-5 years).

Purposes: pursuant to SSA as amended, for social, economic, and demographic research and demonstration projects and experiments to improve the management, administration, and effectiveness of facets of SSA programs.

Eligible applicants/beneficiaries: state and local governments, educational institutions, hospitals, public and private nonprofit and profit organizations.

Range/Average: N.A.

Activity: N.A.

HQ: Grants Management Officer, Office of Operations Contracts and Grants, Office of Acquisition and Grants, DCFAM, SSA, 1540 Robert M. Ball Bldg., 6401 Security Blvd., Baltimore, MD 21235. Phone: (410) 965-9534.

Internet: www.ssa.gov. (Note: no field offices for this program.)

96.008 SOCIAL SECURITY—WORK INCENTIVES PLANNING AND ASSISTANCE PROGRAM ("SSA WIPA Program")

Assistance: project grants. (75-95 percent/3 months-5 years).

Purposes: pursuant to SSA, Ticket-to-Work Incentives Improvement Act of 1999, Workforce Improvement Act of 1998, and other acts, for: statewide benefits planning and assistance programs, including information on the availability of protection and advocacy services, to all Social Security Disability Insurance and SSI beneficiaries; ongoing outreach to beneficiaries with disabilities and families eligible to participate in state or federal work incentives programs; to disseminate information to SSA beneficiaries with disabilities, including transition-to-work youth, about work incentives and related issues.

Eligible applicants/beneficiaries: state or local governments; public, private, profit or nonprofit organizations—including such organizations as centers for independent living, protection and advocacy organizations, tribal entities, client assistance programs, state vocational rehabilitation agencies, developmental disabilities councils, Workforce Investment Boards.

Range/Average: N.A.

Activity: N.A.

HQ: Project Officer, Office of Employment Support Programs, ODISP-SSA, 107 Altmeyer Bldg., 1540 Robert M. Ball Bldg., 6401 Security Blvd., Baltimore, MD 21235. Phone: (410) 965-9534.

Internet: www.ssa.gov. (Note: no field offices for this program.)

96.009 SOCIAL SECURITY STATE GRANTS FOR WORK INCENTIVES ASSISTANCE TO DISABLED BENEFICIARIES

Assistance: project grants. (formula based/3 months-5 years).

Purposes: pursuant to SSA, Ticket-to-Work Incentives Improvement Act of 1999, Workforce Improvement Act of 1998, and other acts, to provide information, advice, and advocacy to disabled SSA beneficiaries, about obtaining vocational rehabilitation and other services to help them obtain or regain gainful employment. Some program cost-sharing will be required.

Eligible applicants/beneficiaries: state protection and advocacy systems.

Range/Average: N.A.

Activity: N.A.

HQ: Project Officer, Office of Employment Support Programs, ODISP-SSA, 107 Altmeyer Bldg., 1540 Robert M. Ball Bldg., 6401 Security Blvd., Baltimore, MD 21235. Phone: (410) 965-9534.

Internet: www.ssa.gov. (Note: no field offices for this program.)

96.020 SPECIAL BENEFITS FOR CERTAIN WORLD WAR II VETERANS ("SVB")

Assistance: direct payments/unrestricted use.

Purposes: pursuant to SSA and Foster Care Independence Act of 1999, to pay special benefits to certain World War II veterans that are eligible for SSI benefits and reside outside the U.S.

Eligible applicants/beneficiaries: World War II veterans age 65 or older as of December 14, 1999, residing outside the U.S. (including specific Filipino veterans), meeting length and dates of service requirements, and with other benefit income that is less than 75 percent of the SSI benefit rate.

Range/Average: N.A.

Activity: N.A.

HQ: SSA, Office of Public Inquiries, Windsor Park Bldg., 6401 Security Blvd., Baltimore, MD 21235. Phone: (401) 965-2736.

Internet: www.socialsecurity.gov.

DEPARTMENT OF HOMELAND SECURITY

97.005 STATE AND LOCAL HOMELAND SECURITY NATIONAL TRAINING PROGRAM

Assistance: project grants. (100 percent/to 3 years).

Purposes: pursuant to USAPA, to develop and conduct training programs for state and local first responders to incidents involving WMD domestic terrorist incidents involving nuclear, biological, chemical, incendiary, and explosive devices—for personnel involved in fire-fighting, law enforcement, emergency medical services, emergency management, public works, and public health.

Eligible applicants: the National Domestic Preparedness Consortium. Others that may become eligible will be so notified.

Eligible beneficiaries: state and local government units.

Range/Average: N.A.

Activity: N.A.

HQ: Office of State and Local Government Coordination and Preparedness, Office for Domestic Preparedness-DHS, 800 K St., NW, Ste. 210, Washington, DC 20472. Phone: (800) 368-6498.

Internet: www.fema.gov/government/grant/index.shtm. (Note: no field offices for this program.)

97.007 HOMELAND SECURITY PREPAREDNESS TECHNICAL ASSISTANCE PROGRAM (HSPTAP)

Assistance: project grants. (100 percent/to 3 years).

Purposes: pursuant to USAPA, to enhance the capacity of state and local first responders to respond to WMD terrorist incidents involving nuclear, biological, chemical, incendiary, and explosive devices. Funds may be used to develop, plan, and implement programs and to sustain and maintain specialized equipment.

Eligible applicants: public or private organizations with expertise and experience in providing program assistance.

Eligible beneficiaries: state and local units of government.

Range/Average: N.A.

Activity: N.A.

HQ: Office of State and Local Government Coordination and Preparedness, Office for Domestic Preparedness-DHS, 500 C St., 6th Fl., Washington, DC 20472-3100. Phone: (202) 786-0849.

Internet: www.fema.gov. (Note: no field offices for this program.)

97.008 NON-PROFIT SECURITY PROGRAM ("NSGP")

Assistance: project grants. (100 percent/2.5 years).

Purposes: pursuant to USAPA, to address the unique needs of large urban areas and mass transit authorities to be prepared for and respond to threats of incidents of terrorism. Funds may be used for equipment, training, exercises, and planning.

Eligible applicants/beneficiaries: states containing selected cities.

Range/Average: N.A.

Activity: N.A.

HQ: Office of State and Local Government Coordination and Preparedness, Office for Domestic Preparedness-DHS, 5071 D Techworld Bldg., 500 C St., SW, Washington, DC 20472. Phone: (800) 368-6498.

Internet: www.fema.gov/government/grant/index. (Note: no field offices for this program.)

97.009 CUBAN/HAITIAN ENTRANT PROGRAM

Assistance: project grants. (100 percent/1-4 years).

Purposes: pursuant to the Refugee Education Assistance Act of 1980 as amended, for primary resettlement services to eligible Cubans and Haitians paroled into communities by DHS for humanitarian reasons; for

Cuban and Haitian entrants living in south Florida and requiring secondary resettlement assistance.

Eligible applicants/beneficiaries: public or private nonprofit organizations or agencies; certain profit organizations.

Range/Average: N.A.

Activity: anticipate serving 11,000 Cuban and Haitian entrants in FY 2016.

HQ: Parole and Humanitarian Assistance Branch, Immigration and Customs Enforcement, Office of International Affairs-DHS, 20 Massachusetts Ave. NW, 3rd Fl., Washington, DC 20529. Phone: (800) 375-5283.

Internet: www.dhs.gov.

97.010 CITIZENSHIP EDUCATION AND TRAINING

Assistance: technical information.

Purposes: pursuant to the Immigration and Nationality Act of 1952 as amended, to provide instruction and training materials in citizenship responsibilities for immigrants interested becoming U.S. citizens and in learning English and U.S. history and government. Free federal textbooks on citizenship at various reading levels are provided.

Eligible applicants/beneficiaries: public schools or other educational groups conducting classes under supervision of public schools.

Range/Average: N.A.

Activity: anticipate providing services to 26,000 permanent residents.

HQ: Director, Office of Procurement Operations, Office of Health Affairs, DHS, 245 Murray Ln., SW, Stop 0115, Washington, DC 20523. Phone: (202) 477-5589.

Internet: www.uscis.gov/grants.

97.012 BOATING SAFETY FINANCIAL ASSISTANCE

Assistance: formula grants. (50-100 percent/1 year).

Purposes: for states to develop and operate recreational boating safety programs. Funds may support: education, maintenance, and enforcement activities; costs of facilities acquisition and construction or repair of access sites; personnel training; administration.

Eligible applicants/beneficiaries: states, territories, and possessions with approved boating safety programs; national nonprofit service organizations.

Range/Average: N.A.

Activity: N.A.

HQ: Office of Boating Safety (G-PCB), U.S. Coast Guard-DHS, 2703 Martin Luther King Jr. Ave, SE, Washington, DC 20593-7501. Phone: (202) 372-1055.

Internet: www.uscgboating.org. (Note: no field offices for this program.)

97.018 NATIONAL FIRE ACADEMY TRAINING ASSISTANCE ("Student Stipend Reimbursement Program")

Assistance: direct payments/specified use.

Purposes: pursuant to the Federal Fire Prevention and Control Act of 1974 as amended, for limited stipends, travel expenses, and lodging costs of attending resident or regional programs the National Fire Academy.

Eligible applicants/beneficiaries: members of fire departments and others with significant responsibility for fire prevention and control. Federal and private industry employees and foreign students may attend courses, but are ineligible for payments.

Range/Average: N.A.

Activity: N.A.

HQ: Emergency Preparedness and Response, FEMA-DHS, 500 C St., SW, Washington, DC 20472. Phone: (800) 368-6498.

Internet: www.usfa.fema.gov. (Note: no field offices for this program.)

97.022 FLOOD INSURANCE

Assistance: insurance.

Purposes: pursuant to the National Flood Insurance Act of 1968, to insure property owners against losses from floods, mudflow, and flood-caused erosion—at or below normal actuarial rates; to promote flood plain management practices. Flood insurance must be purchased as a condition of obtaining any form of federal financial assistance, including disaster assistance and mortgage loan insurance from VA, FmHA, and FHA, when projects are located within flood hazard areas where flood insurance is available. Special program provisions apply for properties within the Coastal Barrier Resource System. Maximum amounts of coverage and other requirements apply, according to type and location of structure; details are available from FEMA regional offices or responsible state offices.

Eligible applicants: states and their political subdivisions that submit completed applications to FEMA consistent with program regulations.

Eligible beneficiaries: residential, business, and municipal property owners in states or political subdivisions that have enacted NFIP flood plain management measures.

Range: to $1,900,000. **Average:** $31,802.

Activity: N.A.

HQ: FEMA-DHS, 1800 South Bell St., Arlington, VA 20598-3010. Phone: (800) 621-FEMA (3363).

Internet: www.fema.gov/business/nfip.

97.023 COMMUNITY ASSISTANCE PROGRAM—STATE SUPPORT SERVICES ELEMENT (CAP-SSSE)

Assistance: project grants (75 percent).

Purposes: pursuant to the National Flood Insurance Act of 1968 and Flood Disaster Protection Act of 1973 as amended, to identify, prevent, and resolve flood plain management issues in communities participating in the NFIP, through the adoption of flood loss reduction measures. Project examples: community assistance visits, ordinance assistance, coordination meetings with FEMA regional offices, community rating system application assistance and review workshops.

Eligible applicants/beneficiaries: states and through the states, NFIP communities and local governments.

Range/Average: N.A.

Activity: 52 awards in FY 2016.

HQ: FEMA-DHS, 500 C St., SW, Washington, DC 20472. Phone: (202) 646-4133.

Internet: www.fema.gov.

97.024   EMERGENCY FOOD AND SHELTER NATIONAL BOARD PROGRAM ("EFSP")

Assistance: formula grants.

Purposes: pursuant to SBMHAA as amended, to supplement and expand ongoing programs providing shelter, food, and supportive services for needy families and individuals; for projects to create more effective and innovative local programs; for minimum rehabilitation of existing mass shelter or feeding facilities, bringing them into compliance with local building codes. Eligible expenses include: costs of food and its transport, food preparation and serving equipment; mass shelter and other shelter, such as hotels and motels; rent or mortgage payments assistance for one month only; limited facility repairs; utility payments. Ineligible costs include such expenses as rental security or other deposits, cash payments to the homeless, major property improvements.

Eligible applicants/beneficiaries: jurisdictions approved by the Emergency Food and Shelter Program National Board chaired by FEMA or State Set-Aside Committees, may award grants to: public or private nonprofit organizations, community action agencies, food banks, food pantries; specialized community groups such as domestic violence centers; native American organizations; organizations providing food and shelter to AIDS patients, handicapped persons, the elderly, teenage runaways, and others with emergency needs.

Range/Average: N.A.

Activity: N.A.

HQ: FEMA-DHS, 500 C St., SW, Rm. 614, Washington, DC 20472. Phone: (800) 621-FEMA (3363).

Internet: www.fema.gov.

97.025   NATIONAL URBAN SEARCH AND RESCUE (US&R) RESPONSE SYSTEM

Assistance: project grants (100 percent).

Purposes: pursuant to the Earthquake Hazards Reduction Act of 1977 and Stafford Act as amended, to develop national immediately deployable urban search and rescue task forces to locate, extricate, and provide medical treatment to victims of structural collapse during a disaster. Funds may be used for training, exercises, and to acquire and maintain specialized equipment.

Eligible applicants/beneficiaries: 28 jurisdictions designated by FEMA as members of the National Urban Search and Rescue Response System.

Range: $1,154,582 to $1,312,082. **Average:** N.A.

Activity: N.A.

HQ: FEMA-DHS, 500 C St., SW, Ste. 214, Washington, DC 20472. Phone: (202) 621-646-3796.

Internet: www.fema.gov. (Note: no field offices for this program.)

97.026   EMERGENCY MANAGEMENT INSTITUTE—TRAINING ASSISTANCE ("Student Stipend Reimbursement Program - SEP")

Assistance: direct payments/specified use.

Purposes: pursuant to the Stafford Act, National Security Act of 1947, Defense Production Act of 1950, Earthquake Hazards Reduction Act of 1977, and amendments, for emergency management personnel to obtain training at the Emergency Management Institute and selected other locations. Programs embody the Comprehensive Emergency Management System by unifying the elements of planning, preparedness, mitigation, response, and recovery. Travel and per diem costs are reimbursed for state and local participants.

Eligible applicants/beneficiaries: state, local, and tribal emergency management personnel.

Range/Average: N.A.

Activity: 34,637 students attended EMI courses and 3,711 received a stipend in FY 2014.

HQ: Preparedness Directorate, FEMA-DHS, 16825 South Seton Ave., Emmitsburg, MD 21727. Phone: (301) 447-1200.

Internet: www.training.fema.gov.

97.027   EMERGENCY MANAGEMENT INSTITUTE (EMI)—INDEPENDENT STUDY PROGRAM (ISP)

Assistance: training.

Purposes: pursuant to the Stafford Act, National Security Act of 1947, Defense Production Act of 1950, Earthquake Hazards Reduction Act of 1977, and amendments, to offer home study courses in emergency management practices, of which 32 are available. Examples include: Emergency Program Manager; Radiological Emergency Management; A Citizen's Guide to Disaster Assistance; Building for the Earthquakes of Tomorrow: Engineering Principles and Practices for Retrofitting Flood Prone Residential Buildings; Animals in Disaster; and, refresher and other specialized courses.

Eligible applicants/beneficiaries: general public, emergency management personnel, public officials. Some courses are restricted to certain audiences.

Range/Average: N.A.

Activity: anticipate 2,000,000 course completions in FY 2016.

HQ: Preparedness Directorate, FEMA-DHS, 16825 South Seton Ave., Emmitsburg, MD 21727. Phone: (301) 447-1200.

Internet: www.training.fema.gov.

97.028 EMERGENCY MANAGEMENT INSTITUTE (EMI)—RESIDENT EDUCATIONAL PROGRAM

Assistance: training.

Purposes: pursuant to the Stafford Act, National Security Act of 1947, Defense Production Act of 1950, Earthquake Hazards Reduction Act of 1977, and amendments, to provide training of federal, state, local, and tribal emergency management personnel involved in emergency and disaster response. Training emphasizes planning, mitigation, response, and recovery—embodied in the Comprehensive Emergency Management System.

Eligible applicants/beneficiaries: official emergency management personnel.

Range/Average: N.A.

Activity: anticipate housing 8,000 to 9,000 students in FY 2016.

HQ: Preparedness Directorate, FEMA-DHS, 16825 South Seton Ave., Emmitsburg, MD 21727. Phone: (301) 447-1200.

Internet: www.training.fema.gov.

97.029 FLOOD MITIGATION ASSISTANCE (FMA)

Assistance: project grants. (base amount plus 75 percent/2 years).

Purposes: pursuant to the National Flood Insurance Reform Act of 1994, to implement measures that reduce or eliminate long-term risks of flood damage to buildings, manufactured homes, and other insurable structures under the NFIP. Funds may support planning, engineering and planning services, and such implementation activities as elevation or dry floodproofing of structures, minor structural projects, beach nourishment.

Eligible applicants/beneficiaries: planning and project grants—states and communities participating in the NFIP. Technical assistance grants—state agencies.

Range/Average: N.A.

Activity: N.A.

HQ: FEMA-DHS, 1800 South Bell St., Arlington, VA 20595-3015. Phone: (202) 646-3358.

Internet: www.fema.gov/flood-mitigation-assistance-grant-program.

97.030 COMMUNITY DISASTER LOANS

Assistance: direct loans (generally, 5 years).

Purposes: pursuant to the Stafford Act, for local governments in declared disaster areas, suffering substantial loss of tax and other revenue and demonstrating a need for financial assistance. Funds may be used only to maintain existing municipal operating functions.

Eligible applicants/beneficiaries: local governments in designated disaster areas.

Range/Average: N.A.

Activity: N.A.

HQ: FEMA-DHS, 500 C St., SW, Stop 3163, Washington, DC 20472. Phone: (202) 646-3895.

Internet: www.dhs.gov.

97.031   CORA BROWN FUND

Assistance: direct payments/specified use.

Purposes: pursuant to the Stafford Act as amended, to help victims of natural disasters that will not obtain assistance through other government or private programs. The fund was established by the late Cora C. Brown of Kansas City, Missouri, who left a portion of her estate to the U.S. government to help victims of natural disasters not caused by or attributed to war.

Eligible applicants/beneficiaries: individuals, families, and groups in need of disaster-related home repair and rebuilding and other services.

Range/Average: N.A.

Activity: N.A.

HQ: Emergency Preparedness and Response, FEMA-DHS, 500 C St., SW, 6th Fl., Washington, DC 20472. Phone: (202) 212-1000.

Internet: www.dhs.gov.

97.032   CRISIS COUNSELING ("CCP")

Assistance: project grants. (100 percent/60 days).

Purposes: pursuant to the Stafford Act as amended and the Crisis Counseling Assistance and Training Act, to provide immediate crisis counseling services to victims of major natural disasters to relieve mental health problems, at no cost to the victims. Funding may support: such services as screening, diagnostic and counseling techniques, outreach, and public education; training of providers.

Eligible applicants/beneficiaries: states or public or private agencies designated by the governor.

Range/Average: N.A.

Activity: N.A.

HQ: FEMA-DHS, 500 C St., SW, 6th Fl., Washington, DC 20472-3100. Phone: (202) 212-1117.

Internet: www.samhsa.gov.

97.033   DISASTER LEGAL SERVICES (DLS)

Assistance: direct payments/specified use.

Purposes: pursuant to the Stafford Act as amended, to provide free legal services to persons affected by natural disasters, including legal advice, counseling, and representation in nonfee- generating cases.

Eligible applicants/beneficiaries: low-income individuals, families, groups.

Range/Average: N.A.

Activity: N.A.

HQ: FEMA-DHS, 500 C St., SW, Sixth Fl., Washington, DC 20472-3100. Phone: (202) 212-1117.

Internet: www.fema.gov.

97.034 DISASTER UNEMPLOYMENT ASSISTANCE (DUA)

Assistance: direct payments/specified use; specialized services (to 26 weeks).

Purposes: pursuant to the Stafford Act as amended, to provide weekly unemployment benefits to persons left jobless by natural disasters and ineligible for regular unemployment insurance benefits.

Eligible applicants/beneficiaries: disaster victims.

Range/Average: N.A.

Activity: N.A.

HQ: FEMA-DHS, 500 C St., SW, 6th Fl., Washington, DC 20472-3100. Phone: (202) 212-1117.

Internet: www.fema.gov.

97.036 DISASTER GRANTS—PUBLIC ASSISTANCE ("Presidentially Declared Disasters")

Assistance: project grants (75 percent).

Purposes: pursuant to the Stafford Act, to provide supplemental assistance in alleviating suffering and hardship resulting from declared major disasters or emergencies. Eligible program costs include the removal of wreckage and debris on public and private lands, emergency protective measures, emergency transportation or communications, restoration of eligible facilities.

Eligible applicants/beneficiaries: state and local governments, other state political subdivisions, territories and possessions, tribal governments, Alaska native villages or organizations, certain private nonprofit organizations.

Range/Average: N.A.

Activity: N.A.

HQ: FEMA-DHS, 500 C St., SW, Washington, DC 20472. Phone: (202) 646-4136; Toll Free: (800) 621-3363.

Internet: www.fema.gov.

97.039 HAZARD MITIGATION GRANT ("HMGP")

Assistance: project grants. (75 percent/2 years).

Purposes: pursuant to the Stafford Act, for measures to permanently reduce or eliminate future damages and losses from natural hazards through safer building practices, improving existing structures, and supporting infrastructure. Funds may be used: to acquire, relocate, modify, or demolish structures; for seismic rehabilitation or retrofitting of structures; for initial implementation of vegetation management programs; to provide pertinent training to architects, engineers, building officials, and others; to bring structures into compliance with floodplain management requirements.

Eligible applicants/beneficiaries: state and local governments, other public entities, authorized tribal organizations, Alaska native villages or organizations, private nonprofit organizations.

Range/Average: N.A.

Activity: N.A.

HQ: FEMA-DHS, 1800 South Bell St., Arlington, VA 20595-3015. Phone: (202) 646-3358.

Internet: www.fema.gov/government/mitigation.shtm.

97.040 CHEMICAL STOCKPILE EMERGENCY PREPAREDNESS PROGRAM (CSEPP)

Assistance: projects grants.

Purposes: pursuant to the Department of Defense Authorization Act of 1986, to enhance emergency preparedness capabilities at the eight chemical agent stockpile facilities maintained by DOD. Funding has paid for operational siren systems, demographic surveys, dedicated radio and telephone systems, public training courses and exercises.

Eligible applicants/beneficiaries: the states of Alabama, Arkansas, Colorado, Illinois, Indiana, Kentucky, Maryland, Oregon, Utah, and Washington and the Confederated Tribes Umatilla Indian Reservation. Local governments and tribes may receive subgrants.

Range/Average: N.A.

Activity: N.A.

HQ: FEMA-DHS, 1800 South Bell St., Crystal City, VA 20598-3025. Phone: (703) 605-1379.

Internet: www.dhs.gov.

97.041 NATIONAL DAM SAFETY PROGRAM

Assistance: project grants (100 percent).

Purposes: pursuant to the Water Resources Development Act of 1996, to establish, improve, and maintain safety programs covering nonfederal dams. States meeting specific criteria may use funds for such activities as permitting and approval of project plans, legislative modifications and regulations development, enforcement activities, emergency response, program staffing, public education, and training.

Eligible applicants/beneficiaries: states, PR.

Range/Average: N.A.

Activity: N.A.

HQ: FEMA-DHS, 500 C St. SW, 4th Fl., Rm. 427, Washington, DC 20472. Phone: (1-800) 621-FEMA (3363).

Internet: www.fema.gov.

97.042 EMERGENCY MANAGEMENT PERFORMANCE GRANTS (EMPG)

Assistance: formula grants. (to 50 percent/2 years).

Purposes: pursuant to the Stafford Act as amended, to develop, maintain, and improve comprehensive emergency management capabilities, by combining several funding streams into a consolidated grant. The key functional areas are: Laws and Authorities; Hazard Identification and Risk Assessment; Hazard Management; Resource Management; Planning; Direction, Control, and Coordination; Communications and Warning; Operations and Procedures; Logistics and Facilities; Training; Exercises; Public Education and Information; Finance and Administration.

Eligible applicants/beneficiaries: states, DC, territories, possessions.

Range/Average: N.A.

Activity: N.A.

HQ: Preparedness Directorate, FEMA-DHS, 5071 D Techworld Bldg., 500 C St., SW, Washington, DC 20472. Phone: (800) 368-6498.

Internet: www.fema.gov/government/grant/index.shtm.

97.043 STATE FIRE TRAINING SYSTEMS GRANTS

Assistance: project grants.

Purposes: for state fire training systems to deliver National Fire Academy courses and programs.

Eligible applicants/beneficiaries: 50 state fire training systems.

Range/Average: N.A.

Activity: N.A.

HQ: FEMA-DHS, 16825 South Seton Ave., Emmitsburg, Maryland 21727. Phone: (301) 447-1376.

Internet: www.usfa.fema.gov.

97.044 ASSISTANCE TO FIREFIGHTERS GRANT ("Fire Grants")

Assistance: project grants (70-90 percent).

Purposes: pursuant to the Federal Fire Prevention and Control Act of 1974 as amended by the Defense Authorization Bill of 2001, for direct assistance to fire departments for costs of firefighting operations and firefighter safety. Applicants must compete for grants which may be used for a broad range of eligible expenses including equipment and vehicles, training, public education, personnel, arson prevention, emergency medical services—with funding limits on certain categories.

Eligible applicants/beneficiaries: fire departments in states, territories and possessions, local authorities, tribal nations—including their emergency medical services units.

Range/Average: N.A.

Activity: N.A.

HQ: Preparedness Directorate, FEMA-DHS, 2TechWorld Bldg., South Tower, 5th Fl., 500 C St., SW, Washington, DC 20472. Phone: (866) 274-0960.

Internet: www.fema.gov.

97.045 COOPERATING TECHNICAL PARTNERS (CTP)

Assistance: project grants (100 percent/1-2 years).

Purposes: pursuant to the National Flood Insurance Act of 1968 (Housing and Urban Development Acts of 1968 and 1969), Flood Disaster Protection Act of 1973, amendments, and National Flood Insurance Reform Act of 1994, to increase local involvement in and ownership of the development and maintenance of flood hazard maps produced for the NFIP. Project examples: Refinement of Zone A Boundaries; Digital Flood Insurance Rate Map Preparation.

Eligible applicants/beneficiaries: states, territories, possessions, regional agencies, and communities participating in the NFIP.

Range/Average: N.A.

Activity: N.A.

HQ: FEMA-DHS, 245 Murray Ln. - Bldg. 410, Washington, DC 20523. Phone: (800) 368-6498.

Internet: fema.gov.

97.046   FIRE MANAGEMENT ASSISTANCE GRANT (FMAG)

Assistance: project grants; specialized services (grants, 75 percent).

Purposes: pursuant to the Stafford Act, for the mitigation, management, and control of any fire on public (nonfederal) or privately owned forest or grassland that threatens to become a major disaster.

Eligible applicants/beneficiaries: state and tribal governments.

Range/Average: N.A.

Activity: N.A.

HQ: FEMA-DHS, 500 C St., SW, 4th Fl., Rm. 427, Washington, DC 20472. Phone: (800) 621-FEMA (3363).

Internet: www.fema.gov.

97.047   PRE-DISASTER MITIGATION (PDM)

Assistance: project grants. (75-90 percent/to 2 years).

Purposes: pursuant to the Stafford Act as amended by the Disaster Mitigation Act of 2000, for cost-affective hazard mitigation activities that are part of a comprehensive mitigation program and reduce injuries, fatalities, and property destruction.

Eligible applicants/beneficiaries: states, territories, possessions, tribal governments. Subgrants may be awarded to local and tribal governments participating in the NFIP.

Range/Average: N.A.

Activity: N.A.

HQ: FEMA-DHS, 1800 South Bell St., Arlington, VA 20595-3015. Phone: (202) 646-3358.

Internet: www.fema.gov/pre-disaster-mitigation-grant-program.

97.048   DISASTER HOUSING ASSISTANCE TO INDIVIDUALS AND HOUSEHOLDS IN PRESIDENTIAL DECLARED DISASTER AREAS

Assistance: direct payments/specified use. (75 percent/to 18 months).

Purposes: pursuant to the Stafford Act as amended, for individuals and households affected by disasters to enable them to: obtain temporary housing; make repairs to their primary residences; build replacement new permanent housing; meet such other needs as medical, dental, funeral, personal property, transportation costs.

Eligible applicants/beneficiaries: U.S. citizens, noncitizen nationals, or qualified aliens whose primary residences: have been damaged or destroyed by declared major disasters; are not covered by insurance; are located in an insular area outside continental U.S. or in other remote locations where alternative housing resources are unavailable. (Note: states apply for funds under 94.050.)

Range: to $32,400. **Average:** $4,263.

Activity: N.A.

HQ: Emergency Preparedness and Response, FEMA-DHS, 500 C St., SW, 6th Fl., Washington, DC 20472-3100. Phone: (202) 212-1000.

Internet: www.FEMA.gov.

97.050   PRESIDENTIAL DECLARED DISASTER ASSISTANCE TO INDIVIDUALS AND HOUSEHOLDS—OTHER NEEDS

Assistance: project grants. (75 percent/to 18 months).

Purposes: pursuant to the Stafford Act as amended, for individuals and households affected by disasters to pay necessary expenses and address serious needs that cannot be met through other forms of assistance or through insurance. Assistance may be used to meet medical, dental, funeral, personal property, transportation needs.

Eligible applicants/beneficiaries: states. (NOTE: if states do not apply, assistance to individuals is provided under **97.048**.)

Range: to $32,400. **Average:** $4,263.

Activity: N.A.

HQ: Emergency Preparedness and Response, FEMA-DHS, 500 C St., SW, 6th Fl., Washington, DC 20472-3100. Phone: (202) 212-1000.

Internet: www.dhs.gov.

97.052   EMERGENCY OPERATIONS CENTERS (EOC)

Assistance: project grants (phase I: 100 percent; phase II: 50 percent).

Purposes: pursuant to the Robert T. Stafford Disaster Relief and Emergency Assistance Act (Stafford Act) and the Departments of Veterans Affairs, Housing and Urban Development, and Independent Agencies Appropriations Act of 2000, to supplement and assist state and local capabilities to respond to emergencies or disasters including terrorist attacks. Grants to states are to encourage the development of Emergency Operations Centers (EOCs) that provide flexibility, sustainability, security, survivability, and interoperability. A Phase I grant of $50,000 will be awarded to each state to complete a vulnerability assessment of its existing state EOC. If a state has already completed a vulnerability assessment, it may apply to use the funds to conduct initial assessments of local EOCs. Phase II grants will be used to address the most immediate EOC deficiencies nationwide.

Eligible applicants/beneficiaries: states (including territories) and local governments.

Range/Average: N.A.

Activity: N.A.

HQ: Office of National Preparedness, FEMA-HHS, 500 C St., SW, Washington, DC 20472. Phone: (800) 368-6498.

Internet: www.fema.gov.

97.055 INTEROPERABLE COMMUNICATIONS EQUIPMENT

Assistance: project grants (75 percent).

Purposes: pursuant to the Homeland Security Act of 2002, Federal Fire Prevention and Control Act of 1974, and other acts, for demonstration projects on multidisciplinary and/or inter- jurisdictional uses of equipment and technologies to increase communications inter-operability among fire services, law enforcement, and emergency medical services. Funds may support purchases of equipment or services to participate in public safety, commercial, or other shared networks and portable gateway solutions.

Eligible applicants/beneficiaries: local governments nominated by state or territorial governments.

Range/Average: N.A.

Activity: N.A.

HQ: Office of National Preparedness, FEMA, 500 C St., SW, Washington, DC 20523. Phone: (202) 646-2500; FAX: (202) 646-3061.

Internet: www.fema.gov.

97.056 PORT SECURITY GRANT PROGRAM (PSGP)

Assistance: project grants (75 percent).

Purposes: for regulated seaports and terminals to enhance port security through: security assessments and mitigation strategies; enhanced facility and operational security—e.g., terminal and commuter or ferry vessels access control, and physical, cargo, and passenger security. Funds may support such costs as for planning, training, exercises, equipment, and administration.

Eligible applicants/beneficiaries: federally regulated public and private ports or terminals designated as "critical"; consortia of local stakeholder groups such as river groups, ports, and terminal associations.

Range/Average: N.A.

Activity: N.A.

HQ: Transportation Infrastructure Security Division, Preparedness Directorate, FEMA-DHS, 5071 D Techworld Bldg., 500 C St., SW, Washington, DC 20472. Phone: (800) 368-6498.

Internet: www.fema.gov/government/grant/index.shtm. (Note: no field offices for this program.)

97.057 INTERCITY BUS SECURITY GRANTS

Assistance: project grants.

Purposes: to protect inter-city bus systems and the traveling public from terrorism, especially explosives and nonconventional threats. Funds may support such costs as for planning, training, exercises, equipment, and administration.

Eligible applicants/beneficiaries: private or public operators of over-the-road buses including operators of regular route, charter, tour, and other services; bus associations; other associations related to intercity bus industry—i.e., transportation industry organizations involved directly in training and providing technical assistance with an emphasis on security.)

Range/Average: N.A.

Activity: N.A.

HQ: Transportation Infrastructure Security Division, Preparedness Directorate, FEMA-DHS, 800 K St., NW, Washington, DC 20472-3615. Phone: (800) 368-6498.

Internet: www.fema.gov. (Note: no field offices for this program.)

97.061 CENTERS FOR HOMELAND SECURITY ("COE")

Assistance: project grants. (100 percent/to 3 years).

Purposes: pursuant to the Homeland Security Act of 2002 as amended and Emergency Wartime Supplemental Appropriation Act of 2003, to establish a coordinated, university-based system to enhance homeland security, complementing other DHS and other federal agency activities—to develop and deploy specific homeland security technologies and capabilities. Funds may be used for: targeted research area that leverage the multidisciplinary capabilities of universities; involve U.S. graduate and undergraduate students.

Eligible applicants/beneficiaries: IHEs.

Range/Average: N.A.

Activity: 2 new awards in FY 2016.

HQ: University Programs, DHS, 245 Murray Ln. - Bldg. 410, Washington, DC 20523. Phone: (202) 254-5695.

Internet: www.hsuniversityprograms.org. (Note: no field offices for this program.)

97.062 SCIENTIFIC LEADERSHIP AWARDS

Assistance: direct payments/specified use.

Purposes: pursuant to the Homeland Security Act of 2002 as amended, to develop and increase the number of undergraduate and graduate students attaining advanced degrees and working in areas of importance to homeland security. Tuition and fee payments are paid to universities; students receive monthly stipends.

Eligible applicants/beneficiaries: U.S. citizens enrolled full-time as juniors, graduate students, or postdoctoral fellows in computer science, engineering, life or physical sciences, math, psychology, social sciences, DVM/PhD, and certain humanities.

Range/Average: N.A.

Activity: anticipate 4 to 6 awards in FY 2016.

HQ: University Programs, DHS, 245 Murray Ln. - Bldg. 410, Stop 0217, Washington, DC 20523. Phone: (202) 254-5695.

Internet: www.hsuniversityprograms.org. (Note: no field offices for this program.)

97.067   HOMELAND SECURITY GRANT PROGRAM (HSGP)

Assistance: formula grants (2 years).

Purposes: pursuant to the U.S.A. Patriot Act of 2001, to enhance the capacity of state and local emergency responders to prevent, respond to, and recover from a terrorism incident involving chemical, biological, radiological, nuclear, and explosive (CBRNE) devices and cyber attacks. The program encompasses: (1) State Homeland Security Program (SHSP); (2) Urban Areas Security Initiative (UASI); (3) Law Enforcement Terrorism Prevention Program (LETPP); (4) Citizen Corps Program (CCP); (5) Emergency Management Performance Grants; (6) Metropolitan Medical Response System.

Eligible applicants/beneficiaries: states, territories, possessions. Local government units may receive subgrants.

Range/Average: N.A.

Activity: N.A.

HQ: Office of State and Local Government Coordination and Preparedness, Office for Domestic Preparedness-DHS, 500 C St., SW, Washington, DC 20472. Phone: (800) 368-6498.

Internet: www.FEMA.gov/grants.

97.075   RAIL AND TRANSIT SECURITY GRANT PROGRAM ("TSGP/IPR")

Assistance: project grants. (100 percent/30 months).

Purposes: pursuant to the U.S.A. Patriot Act, for rail and transit systems to develop a sustainable program to enhance their security and overall preparedness to prevent, respond to, and recover from acts of terrorism. Eligible uses of project funds include planning, organization, training, exercises, equipment, and limited management expenses.

Eligible applicants: state administrative agencies.

Eligible beneficiaries: rail and transit operators and industry associations.

Range/Average: N.A.

Activity: N.A.

HQ: Transportation Infrastructure Security Division, Office of Grants and Training, Preparedness Directorate, FEMA-DHS, 5071 D Techworld Bldg., 500 C St., SW, Washington, DC 20472. Phone: (800) 368-6498.

Internet: www.fema.gov/government/grant/index.shtm. (Note: no field offices for this program.)

97.076 CYBERTIPLINE

Assistance: project grants.

Purposes: to prevent the abduction, abuse, and sexual exploitation of children through activities supporting investigative and forensics; to promote awareness of the child pornography tip line and Project Alert; to operate a national resource center and clearinghouse.

Eligible applicants/beneficiaries: a designated nonprofit organization.

Range/Average: N.A.

Activity: N.A.

HQ: NCMEC, U.S. Secret Service-DHS, 11320 Random Hills Rd., Suite 400, Fairfax, VA 22030. Phone: (703) 293-9207.

Internet: www.dhs.gov. (Note: no field offices for this program.)

97.077 HOMELAND SECURITY RESEARCH, DEVELOPMENT, TESTING, EVALUATION, AND DEMONSTRATION OF TECHNOLOGIES RELATED TO NUCLEAR THREAT DETECTION

Assistance: project grants; use of property, facilities, and equipment; sale, exchange, donation of property and goods; technical information.

Purposes: pursuant to the Homeland Security Act of 2002, to provide funding and/or property to conduct testing, evaluation, and demonstration of homeland security technologies intended to identify, counter, or respond to terrorist threats.

Eligible applicants/beneficiaries: state, local, and tribal governments; private, public profit or nonprofit organizations; individuals.

Range/Average: N.A.

Activity: N.A.

HQ: DHS, Domestic Nuclear Detection Office 245 Murray Ln., SW, DNDO Stop 0550, Washington, DC 20528-0550. Phone: (202) 254-7190.

Internet: www.dhs.gov/about-domestic-nuclear-detection-office. (Note: no field offices for this program.)

97.078 BUFFER ZONE PROTECTION PROGRAM (BZPP)

Assistance: project grants.

Purposes: to plan, equip, and manage protective actions toward the protection, securing, and reducing of vulnerabilities of identified critical infrastructure and key resource sites. State Administrative Agencies allocate funds to jurisdictions in which sites are located.

Eligible applicants: State Administrative Agencies, including in territories and possessions.

Eligible beneficiaries: responsible state and local governmental jurisdictions.

Range/Average: N.A.

Activity: N.A.

HQ: Preparedness Directorate, Office of Grants & Training, FEMA-DHS, 245 Murray Ln. - Bldg. 410, Washington, DC 20523. Phone: (800) 368-6498.

Internet: www.fema.gov. (Note: no field offices for this program.)

97.080 INFORMATION ANALYSIS INFRASTRUCTURE PROTECTION (IAIP) AND CRITICAL INFRASTRUCTURE MONITORING AND PROTECTION

Assistance: project grants.

Purposes: pursuant to the Department of Homeland Security Act, to explore the feasibility and viability of commercially available protective measure technology to nonfederal entities, through pilot or demonstration projects, or as directed by Congress, to support monitoring of critical infrastructure, initiatives, programs and projects.

Eligible applicants/beneficiaries: state, local, and tribal governments; private, public profit or nonprofit organizations; individuals.

Range/Average: N.A.

Activity: N.A.

HQ: Office of Procurement Operations, DHS, NPPD 245 Murray Ln., SW, Bldg. 410, Stop 0612, Washington, DC 20525-0612. Phone: (202) 447-5589.

Internet: www.dhs.gov. (Note: no field offices for this program.)

97.082 EARTHQUAKE CONSORTIUM ("ECSS")

Assistance: project grants (100 percent).

Purposes: pursuant to the Earthquake Hazards Reduction Act of 1977 as amended, to develop earthquake preparedness and response plans, prepare inventories, and conduct seismic safety inspection of critical structures and lifelines—including the development of multistate groups for such purposes. Project examples include education and training for community and state officials.

Eligible applicants/beneficiaries: restricted to Central U.S. Earthquake Consortium, Western States Seismic Policy Council, Northeast States Emergency Consortium, and Cascadia Region Earthquake Workgroup.

Range/Average: N.A.

Activity: N.A.

HQ: Mitigation Division, FEMA-DHS, 1800 South Bell St., Arlington, VA 20598. Phone: (202) 646-2810.

Internet: www.fema.gov. (Note: no field offices for this program.)

97.083 STAFFING FOR ADEQUATE FIRE AND EMERGENCY RESPONSE ("SAFER")

Assistance: project grants. (to 90 percent/5 years).

Purposes: to recruit, hire, and retain firefighters in local communities, and help the communities meet industry minimum standards. Grant recipients may not use funds to supplant pre-existing local funding, and they must retain personnel under the program for at least one year beyond the grant period. Matching requirements increase from year to year.

Eligible applicants/beneficiaries: specific jurisdictions in states, possessions, and territories.

Range/Average: N.A.

Activity: N.A.

HQ: Fire Grants Program Office, Office for State and Local Government Coordination and Preparedness-DHS, TechWorld Bldg - South Tower, 5th Fl., 500 C St., SW, Washington, DC 20742. Phone: (866) 274-0960.

Internet: www.fema.gov/firegrants/index.shtm.

97.088 DISASTER ASSISTANCE PROJECTS

Assistance: project grants.

Purposes: pursuant to the Homeland Security Act, Stafford Act, and Public Health Bioterrorism and Public Health Emergencies Act of 2002, for specified projects identified by Congress or a DHS program office.

Eligible applicants/beneficiaries: nonfederal entities invited to apply by DHS or specified in appropriation statute.

Range/Average: N.A.

Activity: N.A.

HQ: FEMA-DHS, 245 Murray Ln. - Bldg. 410, Washington, DC 20523. Phone: (800) 368-6498.

Internet: www.fema.gov.

97.089 DRIVER'S LICENSE SECURITY GRANT PROGRAM

Assistance: project grants.

Purposes: pursuant to the Homeland Security Act and Real ID Act, for projects integrating hardware, software, and information management systems to implement the Real ID Act, establishing national standards for issuing drivers licenses.

Eligible applicants/beneficiaries: state, territorial agencies responsible for issuing drivers licenses.

Range/Average: N.A.

Activity: N.A.

HQ: Office of Grants and Training, Preparedness Directorate, DHS, 500 C St., SW, Washington, DC 20472. Phone: (800) 368-6498.

Internet: www.fema.gov/grants. (Note: no field offices for this program.)

97.091 HOMELAND SECURITY BIOWATCH PROGRAM

Assistance: project grants; use of property, facilities, equipment; sale, exchange, or donation of property and goods; technical information.

Purposes: pursuant to the Homeland Security Act of 2002, to provide funding for testing, evaluation, and demonstration of homeland security technologies intended to identify, counter, or respond to terrorist threats. Financial and non-financial assistance may be used for: salaries, materials and supplies, equipment, travel, publication costs, subcontractor and supporting costs required for technical and other activities.

Eligible applicants/beneficiaries: state and local governments or as specified by U.S. Appropriation Statute.

Range/Average: N.A.

Activity: N.A.

HQ: Director, Office of Procurement Operations, Office of Health Affairs, DHS, 245 Murray Ln., SW, Stop 0115, Washington, DC 20523. Phone: (202) 477-5589.

Internet: www.dhs.gov. (Note: no field offices for this program.)

97.092 REPETITIVE FLOOD CLAIMS (RFC)

Assistance: project grants (1-2 years).

Purposes: pursuant to National Flood Insurance of 1968 and Bunning-Bereuter-Blumenauer Flood Insurance Reform Act of 2004, as amended, to assist states, tribal governments, and communities with the reduction or elimination of long-term risk of flood damage to structures insured under the NFIP that have had one or more claims for flood damages through mitigation activities that are in the best interest of the National Flood Insurance Fund (NFIF).

Eligible applicants/beneficiaries: state emergency management agencies of states, DC, and federally-recognized tribal governments.

Range/Average: N.A.

Activity: N.A.

HQ: FEMA-DHS, 1800 South Bell St., Arlington, VA 20595-3015. Phone: (202) 646-3428.

Internet: www.fema.gov.

97.101 NATIONAL FALLEN FIREFIGHTERS MEMORIAL (NFFM)

Assistance: direct payments/specified use.

Purposes: pursuant to Homeland Security Act of 2002, to provide funding for the planning, directing and managing of the activities of the annual National Fallen Firefighters Memorial Program and identify, investigate, and report on all on-duty firefighter fatalities. With the support of fire and life-safety organizations, the program seeks to reduce line-of-duty firefighter deaths and general vulnerability of communities to natural, technological, and human-caused disasters.

Eligible applicants: National Fallen Firefighter Foundation.

Eligible beneficiaries: firefighters, living and fallen, their families, community members.

Range/Average: N.A.

Activity: N.A.

HQ: Project Officer, National Fallen Firefighters Memorial, Department of Homeland Security, 16825 S. Seton Ave., Emmitsburg, MD 21727. Phone: (301) 447-1422.

Internet: www.fema.gov.

97.103 DEGREES AT A DISTANCE PROGRAM

Assistance: project grants.

Purposes: pursuant to Homeland Security Act of 2002, U.S.A. Patriot Act of 2001, Federal Fire Prevention and Control Act of 1974, and others, to support curriculum development, regional meeting support, program marketing, course material printing, publications and initiation of institutional agreements with local two-year college degree programs and colleges/universities designated by the National Fire Academy, to participate in the Degrees at a Distance Program (DDP).

Eligible applicants: only colleges/universities designated by U.S. Fire Administration are eligible. Unsolicited applications will not be accepted.

Eligible beneficiaries: general public.

Range/Average: N.A.

Activity: N.A.

HQ: U. S. Fire Administration, DHS, 16825 South Seton Ave., Emmitsburg, Maryland 21727. Phone: (301) 447-1376.

Internet: www.usfa.dhs.gov. (Note: no field offices for this program.)

97.104   HOMELAND SECURITY-RELATED SCIENCE, TECHNOLOGY, ENGINEERING AND MATHEMATICS (HS STEM) CAREER DEVELOPMENT PROGRAM
("HS-STEM Career Development Program")

Assistance: project grants (100 percent).

Purposes: to provide funding for the establishment of a scientific career development program at colleges and universities, who, in turn, provide scholarships and fellowships to students.

Eligible applicants: specific information on applicant eligibility is identified in funding opportunity announcement and program guidance.

Eligible beneficiaries: public and private institutions/organizations (colleges and universities).

Range/Average: N.A.

Activity: N.A.

HQ: Chief Procurement Officer, Grants and Financial Assistance Division, Office of Procurement Operations, DHS, 245 Murray Ln. - Bldg. 410, Washington, DC 20523. Phone: (202) 254-5695.

Internet: www.hsuniversityprograms.org. (Note: no field offices for this program.)

97.106   SECURING THE CITIES PROGRAM

Assistance: project grants; use of property, facilities, and equipment; sale, exchange, or donation of property and goods; dissemination of technical information.

Purposes: pursuant to the Homeland Security Act of 2002, as amended to prevent a Radiological/Nuclear (RN) attack on high risk urban areas by enhancing regional capabilities to detect, identify, and interdict illicit radioactive materials in and around urban areas. Financial and non-financial assistance may be provided for the following: salaries, materials and supplies, equipment, travel, publication costs, subcontractor and supporting costs required for technical and other activities necessary to achieve the objective.

Eligible applicants: specific applicant eligibility identified in the funding opportunity announcement and application/program guidance, or as specified by U.S. Appropriation Statute.

Eligible beneficiaries: federal, state, local and Indian tribal governments, interstate or intrastate governmental organizations, private, public or nonprofit organizations.

Range/Average: N.A.

Activity: N.A.

HQ: Assessments, Domestic Nuclear Detection Office, DHS, MS 7100, 245 Murray Drive SW, Stop 0550, Washington, DC 20528-0550. Phone: (202) 254-7443.

Internet: www.dhs.gov. (Note: no field offices for this program.)

97.107   NATIONAL INCIDENT MANAGEMENT SYSTEM (NIMS)

Assistance: project grants (100 percent).

Purposes: pursuant to the Homeland Security Act of 2002 and the Department of Homeland Security Appropriations Act of 2007, to support the development, integration, and deployment of incident management systems. This includes establishing operational, technical and programmatic standards in support of nationwide implementation of the NIMS model, a unified approach to incident management and standard command and management structures.

Eligible applicants: specific applicant eligibility identified in the funding opportunity announcement and application/program guidance.

Eligible beneficiaries: state, local, and Indian Tribal governments, U.S. territories and possessions, public, private and nonprofit institutions and organizations.

Range/Average: N.A.

Activity: N.A.

HQ: FEMA-DHS, 800 K St., NW, Rm. 5154, Washington, DC 20001. Phone: (202) 786-9630.

Internet: www.fema.gov/emergency/nims/index.shtm. (Note: no field offices for this program.)

97.108   HOMELAND SECURITY, RESEARCH, TESTING, EVALUATION, AND DEMONSTRATION OF TECHNOLOGIES

Assistance: project grants; use of property, facilities, and equipment; sale, exchange, or donation of property and goods; dissemination of technical information.

Purposes: pursuant to the Homeland Security Act of 2002, to provide funding and/or property for the purpose of conducting research, testing, evaluation, and demonstration of homeland security technologies intended to identify, counter, or respond to terrorist threats. Financial and nonfinancial assistance may be provided for the following: salaries, materials and supplies, equipment, travel, publication costs, subcontractor and supporting costs required for technical and other activities necessary to achieve the objective.

Eligible applicants: state, local, and Indian Tribal governments, private, public, profit or nonprofit organizations, or individuals specified by U.S. Appropriation Statute, including U. S. and international institutions of higher education and educational laboratories.

Eligible beneficiaries: federal, state, local, and Indian Tribal governments, private, public, profit or nonprofit organizations, and individuals.

Range/Average: N.A.

Activity: N.A.

HQ: Grants and Financial Assistance Division, Office of Procurement Operations, DHS, 245 Murray Ln., S.W., Bldg. 410, Washington, DC 20523. Phone: (202) 447-5522.

Internet: www.dhs.gov. (Note: no field offices for this program.)

97.110 SEVERE LOSS REPETITIVE PROGRAM (SLR)

Assistance: project grants (75-90 percent).

Purposes: pursuant to the National Flood Insurance Act of 1968, as amended by the Bunning-Bereuter-Blumenauer Flood Insurance Reform Act of 2004, to assist states and local governments to reduce or eliminate the long-term risk of flood damage to residential properties insured under the National Flood Insurance Program (NFIP) that meet the definition of severe repetitive loss property, and to reduce losses to the National Flood Insurance Fund (NFIF) by funding projects that result in the greatest savings to the NFIF in the shortest time period. Eligible activities under the SLR program include: acquisition and relocation of at-risk structures and the conversion of property to open space; elevation of existing structures to the Base Flood Elevation (BFE) or an ABFE Advisory Base Flood Elevation (ABFE) or higher (for the SRL program Mitigation Reconstruction is only permitted when traditional elevation cannot be implemented); minor physical localized flood control projects; and dry-flood proofing (historic properties only).

Eligible applicants: state emergency management agencies or a similar state office, DC, U.S. territories, and federally-recognized Indian tribal governments. Specific information on sub-applicant eligibility and application procedures for Indian tribal governments provided in SRL program guidance.

Eligible beneficiaries: states, territories, local, and federally-recognized Indian tribal governments and homeowners.

Range/Average: N.A.

Activity: N.A.

HQ: Chief, Program Implementation Section, Risk Reduction Branch, Mitigation Division, FEMA, 1800 South Bell St., Arlington, VA 20595-3015. Phone: (202) 646-3428.

Internet: www.fema.gov/government/mitigation.shtm.

97.111 REGIONAL CATASTROPHIC PREPAREDNESS GRANT PROGRAM (RCPGP)

Assistance: project grants (75 percent).

Purposes: pursuant to the U.S. Troop Readiness, Veterans' Care, Katrina Recovery, and Iraq Accountability Appropriations Act of 2007, and Consolidated Appropriations Act of 2008, to support an integrated planning system that provides for regional all-hazard planning for catastrophic events and the development of necessary plans, protocols, and procedures to manage a catastrophic event. Objectives include: creating regional planning processes and planning communities through the establishment of a Catastrophic Planning Working Group; identifying and assessing priority areas of concern using both capabilities-based and scenario-based planning models; developing enhanced regional plans and addressing shortcomings in jurisdiction plans to support both the management of a catastrophic incident and to enable enduring government; and linking planning efforts to resource allocations.

Eligible applicants: specific applicant eligibility identified in the funding opportunity announcement and application/program guidance.

Eligible beneficiaries: state and local governments.

Range/Average: N.A.

Activity: N.A.

HQ: Department of Homeland Security, 500 C St., SW, Washington, DC 20472. Phone: (202) 360-1733.

Internet: www.fema.gov. (Note: no field offices for this program.)

97.113 RAIL AND TRANSIT SECURITY GRANT PROGRAM (ARRA) ("Transit Security Grant Program")

Assistance: project grants (100 percent).

Purposes: pursuant to ARRA, 2009 and Implementing Recommendations of the 9/11 Commission Act of 2007, to create sustainable programs for the protection of critical bus and infrastructure from terrorism, with special emphasis on construction projects which address the most significant risks and can be completed in a timely fashion.

Eligible applicants: public nonprofit institutions/organizations.

Eligible beneficiaries: anyone/general public.

Range/Average: N.A.

Activity: N.A.

HQ: DHS-FEMA, Control Desk, 500 C St., SW, Washington, DC 20472. Phone: (800) 368-6498.

Internet: www.fema.gov. (Note: no field offices for this program.)

97.114 EMERGENCY FOOD AND SHELTER NATIONAL BOARD PROGRAM (ARRA)

Assistance: project grants (100 percent).

Purposes: pursuant to ARRA, 2009 and Stewart B. McKinney Homeless Assistance Act of 1987, as amended, Title III, to supplement and expand ongoing efforts to provide shelter, food, and supportive services for needy families and individuals and to conduct minimum rehabilitation of existing mass shelter or mass feeding facilities, making them safe, sanitary and bringing them into compliance with local building codes.

Eligible applicants: quasi-public nonprofit institutions/organizations.

Eligible beneficiaries: public and private/quasi-public nonprofit institutions and organizations.

Range/Average: N.A.

Activity: N.A.

HQ: DHS-FEMA, 500 C St., SW, Rm. 619, Washington, DC 20472. Phone: (800) 621-FEMA (3363).

Internet: www.fema.gov.

97.115 ASSISTANCE TO FIREFIGHTERS GRANT (ARRA) ("Fire Station Construction")

Assistance: project grants (100 percent).

Purposes: pursuant to ARRA 2009, to provide financial assistance in the construction, upgrading or rehabilitation of fire stations. Up to 5 percent of grant may be used for program administration.

Eligible applicants: local fire departments (includes state-designated Indian Tribes).

Eligible beneficiaries: anyone/general public.

Range/Average: N.A.

Activity: N.A.

HQ: Assistance to Firefighters Grant Program, DHS-FEMA, Tech World Bldg. - South Tower 5th Fl., 500 C St SW, Washington, DC 20472. Phone: (866) 274-0960.

Internet: www.fema.gov.

97.116 PORT SECURITY GRANT PROGRAM (ARRA)

Assistance: project grants/cooperative agreements (100 percent).

Purposes: pursuant to ARRA, 2009 and Maritime Transportation Security Act, to create a sustainable program for the protection of regulated ports from terrorism, with priority on construction projects which address the most significant risks and can be completed in a timely fashion.

Eligible applicants: public institutions/organizations.

Eligible beneficiaries: local, anyone/general public.

Range/Average: N.A.

Activity: N.A.

HQ: DHS-FEMA, Control Desk, Techworld Bldg., 500 C St., SW, Washington, DC 20472-3615. Phone: (800) 368-6498.

Internet: www.fema.gov. (Note: no field offices for this program.)

97.123 MULTI-STATE INFORMATION SHARING AND ANALYSIS CENTER (MS-ISAC)

Assistance: cooperative agreements (100 percent).

Purposes: pursuant to the Department of Homeland Security Appropriations Act of 2010, MS-ISAC is a key resource for significantly enhancing state, local, tribal and territorial governments' cyber security posture by providing enhanced expertise and operations. This centralized approach also leverages the economies of scale, thereby maximizing the utilization of scarce state resources to protect the critical systems.

Eligible applicants: The Multi-State Information Sharing and Analysis Center (MS-ISAC).

Eligible beneficiaries: state, local, territorial and tribal governments.

Range/Average: N.A.

Activity: N.A.

HQ: Director, MS-ISAC Program, DHS, 245 Murray Ln. SW, MS 0115, Washington, DC 20528. Phone: (703) 235-5324.

Internet: www.dhs.gov. (Note: no field offices for this program.)

97.128 NATIONAL CYBER SECURITY AWARENESS

Assistance: project grants (100 percent/2 years).

Purposes: pursuant to the Homeland Security Act of 2002, to provide funding for outreach, education, and technical assistance in order to raise public awareness of cybersecurity awareness nationally. Outreach and technical assistance includes: the provision of written information; maintaining a website; development of cybersecurity awareness collateral; establishment and maintenance of metrics to measure effectiveness of awareness efforts; and development of seminars, workshops or training sessions.

Eligible applicants: public/state/private IHEs, eligible nonprofits.

Eligible beneficiaries: anyone/general public.

Range/Average: N.A.

Activity: N.A.

HQ: Director, National Cyber Security Awareness Program, DHS, 245 Murray Ln. SW, Stop 0640, Arlington, VA 20598-0640. Phone: (703) 235-5281.

Internet: www.dhs.gov/cyber. (Note: no field offices for this program.)

97.130 NATIONAL NUCLEAR FORENSICS EXPERTISE DEVELOPMENT PROGRAM (NNFEDP)

Assistance: project grants (100 percent).

Purposes: pursuant to the Nuclear Forensics and Attribution Act, to select an entity to administer the NNFEDP program with the objective of upholding homeland security. By encouraging a diverse and highly talented cadre of new and emerging experts, to increase the workforce to fill specific gaps in the area of nuclear forensics. Grant recipients will issue funds to eligible students or IHEs for the following: materials, supplies, laboratory equipment/facilities upgrades, travel, publications costs, subcontractor and supporting costs required for technical and other activities necessary to achieve the objective.

Eligible applicants: for-profit organizations other than small businesses, non-profits with 501(c)(3) IRS status, other than IHEs.

Eligible beneficiaries: IHEs, eligible students.

Range/Average: N.A.

Activity: N.A.

HQ: Director, DNDO, DHS, 245 Murray Ln. SW, Stop 0550, Washington, DC 20528-0550. Phone: (202) 254-7709.

Internet: www.dhs.gov.

97.131 EMERGENCY MANAGEMENT BASELINE ASSESSMENTS GRANT (EMBAG)

Assistance: direct payments/specified use (100 percent/to 2 years).

Purposes: pursuant to the Homeland Security Act of 2002, to assess the shortfalls in interagency cooperation and continuity of government at the state level in the event of an emergency. Peer-validated assessments using nationally-recognized emergency management program standards and an accreditation system for meeting those standards will be utilized to assess the involvement of relevant state agencies in prevention, protection, mitigation, response, recovery planning, and continuity of government.

Eligible applicants: eligible non-profit organizations with significant experience in providing assessments of state emergency management organizations.

Eligible beneficiaries: state and territory emergency management programs.

Range/Average: N.A.

Activity: 15 EMAP assessments performed in FY 2015.

HQ: Program Officer, Department of Homeland Security, 800 K St., NW, Washington, DC 20472-3630. Phone: (202) 786-9451.

Internet: www.fema.gov. (Note: no field offices for this program.)

97.132 FINANCIAL ASSISTANCE FOR COUNTERING VIOLENT EXTREMISM

Assistance: project grants. (100 percent/2 years).

Purposes: pursuant to the Department of Homeland Security Appropriations Act of 2016, to provide federal assistance to support new and existing community-based efforts to counter violent extremism recruitment and radicalization to violence. Funds may be used for planning, training, exercises and domestic travel, but may not be used for equipment, construction, or international travel.

Eligible applicants/beneficiaries: state, local, and tribal, public nonprofit, and other public institutions/organizations.

Range/Average: N.A.

Activity: N.A.

HQ: DHS, 500 C St., SW, Washington, DC 20472, Phone: (202) 786-0816.

Internet: www.fema.gov. (Note: no field offices for this program.)

AGENCY FOR INTERNATIONAL DEVELOPMENT

98.001   USAID FOREIGN ASSISTANCE FOR PROGRAMS OVERSEAS

Assistance: project grants (to 5 years).

Purposes: pursuant to the Foreign Assistance Act of 1961 as amended, to advance U.S. foreign policy objectives by supporting economic growth, agriculture and trade, global health, democracy, conflict prevention, and humanitarian assistance projects. Funds usually are awarded competitively to U.S. nongovernmental and educational institutions, for projects conducted in developing countries virtually throughout the world.

Eligible applicants: any type of applicant.

Eligible beneficiaries: foreign governments, public or private institutions or organizations, or individuals.

Range/Average: N.A.

Activity: N.A.

HQ: USAID, 1300 Pennsylvania Ave., NW, Washington, DC 20523. Phone: (202) 712-4810.

Internet: www.usaid.gov. (Note: no field offices for this program.)

98.002   COOPERATIVE DEVELOPMENT PROGRAM (CDP)

Assistance: project grants (3-5 years).

Purposes: pursuant to the Foreign Assistance Act of 1961 as amended, to support cooperative development organizations in the establishment and management of cooperatives worldwide. Funds may support feasibility studies and technical assistance or advisory services to cooperatives, private voluntary and other nongovernmental organizations, governments, and groups of individuals interested in developing new or existing cooperatives. Program emphasis is on developing, testing, and implementing solutions to major issues facing international cooperative development, including governance, modern management, cooperatives legislation and regulation, and achieving scale and salience.

Eligible applicants/beneficiaries: U.S. cooperatives and recognized cooperative development organizations.

Range: $1,000,000 to $5,000,000 for 5 years. **Average:** N.A.

Activity: N.A.

HQ: Cooperative Coordinator, Office of Private and Voluntary Cooperation, Bureau for Democracy, Conflict and Humanitarian Assistance, USAID, Washington, DC 20523. Phone: (202) 712-5226.

Internet: www.usaid.gov/hum_response/pvc/coop.html. (Note: no field offices for this program.)

98.003   OCEAN FREIGHT REIMBURSEMENT PROGRAM (OFR)

Assistance: project grants. (100 percent/2 years).

Purposes: pursuant to the Foreign Assistance Act of 1961, to pay transportation charges for overseas shipments of commodities used in privately funded development and humanitarian assistance programs for the relief and rehabilitation of friendly people. Shipments must consist only of approved commodities—e.g., medical and educational supplies, agricultural and building equipment—only to approved countries that receive shipments duty-free.

Eligible applicants/beneficiaries: U.S. private voluntary organizations registered with USAID, receiving at least 20 percent of their funding for international programs from nongovernmental sources.

Range: $2,500 to $150,000. **Average:** N.A.

Activity: N.A.

HQ: Ocean Freight Program Officer, Cooperative Coordinator, Office of Private and Voluntary Cooperation, Bureau for Democracy, Conflict and Humanitarian Assistance, USAID, Washington, DC 20523. Phone: (202) 712-4795.

Internet: www.usaid.gov. USAID keyword: ofr. (Note: no field offices for this program.)

98.004 NON-GOVERNMENTAL ORGANIZATION STRENGTHENING (NGO)

Assistance: project grants (70 percent/to 5 years).

Purposes: pursuant to the Foreign Assistance Act of 1961 as amended, to improve the capacities of local indigenous nongovernmental organizations, networks, and intermediate service organizations in developing countries.

Eligible applicants: U.S. private voluntary organizations registered with USAID, receiving at least 20 percent of their funding for international programs from nongovernment sources, and current matching grant recipients.

Eligible beneficiaries: foreign private institutions or organizations.

Range: $1,300,000 to $3,250,000 for 5 years. **Average:** $2,400,000.

Activity: N.A.

HQ: (no address/phone provided).

Internet: www.usaid.gov/our_work/cross- cutting_programs/private_volun tary_cooperation/ngo.html. (Note: no field offices for this program.)

98.005 INSTITUTIONAL CAPACITY BUILDING (ICB)

Assistance: project grants. (75-90 percent/to 5 years).

Purposes: pursuant to the Foreign Assistance Act of 1961 as amended, to strengthen the capacity of new and experienced "Food for Peace Title II Partners" to plan and implement food security programs, including in emergency situations. Funds may support establishing systems, training, food security assessments and aid logistics, and strengthening mechanisms.

Eligible applicants/beneficiaries: U.S. private voluntary organizations or cooperatives registered with USAID.

Range: to $3,500,000 for 5 years. **Average:** N.A.

Activity: N.A.

HQ: Grants Manager, Program Operations Division, Office of Food for Peace, USAID, 1300 Pennsylvania Ave., NW, Washington, DC 20523. Phone: (no number provided).

Internet: www.usaid.gov. (Note: no field offices for this program.)

98.006 FOREIGN ASSISTANCE TO AMERICAN SCHOOLS AND HOSPITALS ABROAD (ASHA)

Assistance: project grants. (cost sharing/2-5 years).

Purposes: pursuant to the Foreign Assistance Act of 1961 as amended, to strengthen foreign schools and hospitals best demonstrating American ideas and practices. Project examples: upgrading of a training facility; construction and equipping of private health care ward; construction of telecommunication laboratory.

Eligible applicants/beneficiaries: U.S. nonprofit organizations demonstrating a continuing supportive relationship with overseas institutions.

Range: $500,000 to $2,000,000 for up to 5 years. **Average:** N.A.

Activity: N.A.

HQ: Office of American School and Hospitals Abroad, Bureau for Democracy, Conflict and Humanitarian Assistance, USAID, 1300 Pennsylvania Ave., Washington, DC 20523. Phone: (202) 712-0510.

Internet: www.usaid.gov/our_work/cross-cutting_programs/asha. (Note: no field offices for this program.)

98.007 FOOD FOR PEACE DEVELOPMENT ASSISTANCE PROGRAM (DAP)

Assistance: project grants; sale, exchange, or donation of property and goods. (cost sharing/to 5 years).

Purposes: pursuant to the Agriculture, Trade and Development Assistance Act of 1954 as amended, to improve access, availability, and utilization of food in food-insecure environments abroad. Program focus: improving household nutrition and health status, especially in children and mothers; increasing agricultural productivity including field production, post- harvest handling, transformation, and marketing. Applicants may request commodities and cash for program implementation.

Eligible applicants/beneficiaries: U.S. private voluntary organizations or cooperatives registered with USAID; registration with the Office of Food Peace also is required.

Range: $1,000,000 to $25,000,000 for 3-5 years. **Average:** N.A.

Activity: N.A.

HQ: Development Programs Division, Office of Food for Peace, USAID, 1300 Pennsylvania Ave., NW, Washington, DC 20523. Phone: (no number provided).

Internet: www.usaid.gov. (Note: no field offices for this program.)

98.008 FOOD FOR PEACE EMERGENCY PROGRAM

Assistance: project grants; sale, exchange, or donation of property and goods.

Purposes: pursuant to the Agriculture, Trade and Development Assistance Act of 1954 as amended, to improve access, availability, and utilization of food in food-insecure environments abroad—especially in emergency situations in which hunger and malnutrition need to be prevented. Applicants may request commodities and cash for program implementation.

Eligible applicants/beneficiaries: U.S. private voluntary organizations or cooperatives registered with USAID; registration with the Office of Food Peace also is required.

Range/Average: N.A.

Activity: N.A.

HQ: Emergency Programs Division, Office of Food for Peace, USAID, 1300 Pennsylvania Ave., NW, Washington, DC 20523. Phone: (no number provided).

Internet: www.usaid.gov. (Note: no field offices for this program.)

98.009   JOHN OGONOWSKI FARMER-TO-FARMER PROGRAM ("Development Assistance Program")

Assistance: project grants (5-10 years).

Purposes: pursuant to the Farm Security and Rural Investment Act of 2002 and Agriculture, Trade and Development Assistance Act of 1954, to improve global food production and marketing by transferring technical skills of the U.S. agricultural community to farmers in developing and middle-income countries, emerging markets, sub-Saharan African countries, and Caribbean Basin countries.

Eligible applicants/beneficiaries: agricultural producers, agriculturalists, IHEs and their foundations, private agribusinesses willing to waive profits and fees, private organizations—which must be registered with USAID.

Range/Average: N.A.

Activity: N.A.

HQ: Farmer-to-Farmer Program, USAID, Washington, DC 20523. Phone: (202) 712-4086; FAX: (202) 216-3579; Technical Advisor, (202) 712-5837; FAX: (202) 216-3579; Program Analyst, (202) 219-0476; FAX: (202) 219-0508.

Internet: www.usaid.gov/our_work/agriculture/farmer_to_farmer.htm. (Note: no field offices for this program.)

98.010   DENTON PROGRAM

Assistance: specialized services.

Purposes: to use empty space on U.S. military carriers to transport eligible donated goods for humanitarian relief, at little or no cost to nongovernmental organizations. The program is jointly administered by USAID, Department of State, and DOD.

Eligible applicants/beneficiaries: U.S. private voluntary organizations, nongovernmental organizations, or small organizations.

Range: N.A. **Average:** $50,000 per year for inspections.

Activity: N.A.

HQ: Denton Program Officer, Office of Private and Voluntary Cooperation, Bureau for Democracy, Conflict and Humanitarian Assistance, USAID, Washington, DC 20523. Phone: (202) 712-4795.

Internet: www.usaid.gov/hum_response/pvc/ and www.dentonfunded.ida.org. (Note: no field offices for this program.)

98.011   GLOBAL DEVELOPMENT ALLIANCE

Assistance: project grants (50 percent/to 5 years).

Purposes: pursuant to the Foreign Assistance Act of 1961 as amended, for activities by public-private alliances promoting such international objectives as: advancing the growth of democracy and good governance; strengthening world economic growth, development, and stability, while expanding opportunities for U.S. business; improving health, education, environmental conditions for the global population; minimizing the human costs of displacement, conflicts, and natural disasters.

Eligible applicants/beneficiaries: U.S. and non-U.S. nongovernmental organizations, private businesses, foundations, business and trade associations, international organizations, IHEs; U.S. cities and states, other federal agencies, host country parastals, individual and group philanthropies, other similar organizations.

Range: $300,000 to $1,000,000. **Average:** N.A.

Activity: N.A.

HQ: GDA Secretariat, USAID, Washington, DC 20523. Phone: (202) 712-4272.

Internet: www.usaid.gov/our_work/global_partnerships/gda. (Note: no field offices for this program.)

98.012   USAID DEVELOPMENT PARTNERSHIPS FOR UNIVERSITY COOPERATION AND DEVELOPMENT

Assistance: project grants.

Purposes: for U.S. IHEs to collaborate with counterpart institutions in developing countries to conduct projects that address critical development needs in those countries.

Eligible applicants/beneficiaries: U.S. IHEs, including community colleges.

Range/Average: N.A.

Activity: N.A.

HQ: Higher Education Community Liaison, USAID, 1300 Pennsylvania Ave., NW, Washington, DC 20523. Phone: (202) 712-1531; FAX: (202) 216-3229.

Internet: www.usaid.gov; www.HEDProgram.org. (Note: no field offices for this program.)

PART III

Program
Funding Levels

Summary Tables

Two tables are presented:

- *Table 1. Estimated Outlays/Credits for Domestic Assistance Programs, by Federal Department or Agency* (FY 13, 14, 15, 16).

- *Table 2. Summary of Estimated Outlays/Credits, by Federal Department or Agency* (FY 13, 14, 15, 16).

The tables are based on information in the *Catalog of Federal Domestic Assistance 2015,* and prior editions, and updated in July, 2016 based on information found on the *Catalog* website found at https://www.cfda.gov. The tables offer a general perspective of government funding for specific programs and agencies, in relation to one another and to other federal activities. Such a perspective can be useful in several ways to persons or organizations interested in certain programs and in government assistance, including:

- Having identified programs meeting given needs, prospective applicants can use the tables to compare relative funding levels.

- Tables 1 and 2 show funding levels for four federal fiscal years. To our knowledge tables compiled specifically for the domestic assistance programs exist nowhere else—i.e., apart from the costs of other administering agency functions. Perhaps such a compilation adds a new dimension to perspectives of federal domestic assistance.

Important Note on Unavailable Information

In recent years, some departments or agencies have failed to provide updates to funding levels for certain programs and, in some cases, have failed to provide updates to funding levels for all programs administered by that department or agency. For instance, the DEPARTMENT OF VERTERANS AFFAIRS has not updated funding levels for some of its largest programs, and the SOCIAL SECURITY ADMINISTRATION has not updated funding levels for any of its programs.

For this reason, we have eliminated the table of the fifty largest domestic assistance programs and the table of the fifty smallest domestic assistance programs to avoid confusion caused by this lack of information.

Important Notes on the Tables, Footnotes

Certain inconsistencies in the source material cannot be corrected. Therefore, the tables should be used only as a general guide to the availability of funding.

In Table 2, the first two digits in the five-digit number preceding the name of the administering agency correspond to the program number series identifying programs in Part II—e.g., 11.000 preceding DEPARTMENT OF COMMERCE encompasses all department programs including administrative sub-units.

The following footnotes are employed:

* amount shown is a "credit" rather than an actual cash outlay. In the tables, amounts loaned or insured by the government are classified as credits.

(a) funding for the program cannot be separately identified from other agency expenses.

e amount was estimated in the source material, the significance of which is discussed in Part I.

\i includes funding for this and for one or more other programs; program descriptions in Part II explain such cases.

(n) program did not exist during the reported fiscal year.

(nr) the administering agency did not provide funding levels for the reported fiscal year, which differs from the agency *reporting no funding,* in which case a zero is used.

(o) funding is included in an amount reported for another program, as noted in the Part II program descriptions.

\p includes value of property or goods awarded; such amounts are not necessarily appropriated funds.

\r program supports or is supported by a revolving fund.

\t program includes support from or is supported by a federal trust fund.

\u user charges, fees, or other nonfederal funds help support the program, including loan repayments; amounts shown are not necessarily or entirely appropriated funds.

Table 1.   Estimated Outlays/Credits for All Domestic Assistance Programs, by Department or Agency

Program Number	ADMINISTRATIVE ENTITY Program Title (abridged)	FY 2013 in $thousands	FY 2014 in $thousands	FY 2015 in $thousands	FY 2016 in $thousands
	DEPARTMENT OF AGRICULTURE				
10.001	Agricultural Research	32,314	31,392	33,000 e	33,000
10.025	Plant, Animal Disease, Pest Control \ t	185,757	202,222	229,244 e	205,265 e
10.028	Wildlife Services	2,738	6,372	6,436 e	6,501
10.030	Indemnity Program	1,150	3,245	2,395 e	2,395 e
10.051	Commodity Loans, Deficiency Payments \ u	9,524	525	171,639 e	75,833 e
		5,744,195*	3,787,599*	5,995,188*e	7,260,464*e
10.053	Dairy Indemnity	1,648	379	463 e	500 e
10.054	Emergency Conservation	41,507	28,033	40,000 e	56,807 e
10.055	Direct, Counter-Cyclical Payments \ u	1,117	67,446	0 e	0 e
10.056	Farm Storage Facility Loans \ u	240,308*	115,952*	320,000*e	320,000*e
10.069	Conservation Reserve Program	1,769,356	1,841,214	1,772,157 e	1,832,144 e
10.072	Wetlands Reserve	400,192	61,833	226,639 e	290,925 e
10.080	Milk Income Loss Contract	272,175	325	0 e	0 e
10.085	Tobacco Transition Payments \ u	951,718	924,598	0 e	0 e
10.090	Supplemental Revenue Assistance Program	(nr)	32,185	63,036 e	0 e
10.098	Transportation Reimbursement— Geographically Disadvantaged	1,842	1,997	1,996 e	0 e
10.099	Conservation Loans	75*	0*	150,000*e	150,000*e
10.102	Emergency Forest Restoration Program	4,788	3,760	15,000 e	22,249 e
10.105	Emergency Conservation Program— Disaster Relief	0	188	10,000 e	3,193 e
10.106	Emergency Forest Restoration Program	5,152	5,011	15,000 e	5,751 e
10.108	Livestock Indemnity	(n)	71,181	63,300 e	42,100 e
10.109	Livestock Forage	(n)	6,739,854	1,521,000 e	573,000 e
10.110	Livestock—Emergency Assistance	(n)	40,000	38,000 e	19,500 e
10.111	Tree Assistance	(n)	10,400	8,000 e	4,300 e
10.112	Price Loss Coverage	(n)	(n)	(n)	932,000 e
10.113	Agriculture Risk Coverage	(n)	(n)	5,404,000 e	8,445,000 e
10.116	The Margin Protection	(n)	(n)	450 e	500 e
10.117	Biofuel Infrastructure Partnership	(n)	(n)	100,000 e	0 e
10.153	Market News	31,102	32,566	33,975 e	34,325 e
10.155	Marketing Agreements and Orders	20,056	18,994	20,186 e	20,489 e
10.156	Federal-State Marketing Improvement	1,235	1,235	1,235 e	1,235 e
10.162	Inspection Grading, Standardization \ t	150,743	158,344	153,911 e	155,357 e
10.163	Market Protection and Promotion	29,752	13,101	17,268 e	17,323 e
10.164	Wholesale Farmers, Alternative Markets	3,624	4,045	5,386 e	7,187 e
10.165	Perishable Agricultural Commodities	9,775	10,035	10,178 e	10,279 e
10.167	Transportation Services	2,733	2,580	2,731 e	2,756 e
10.168	Farmersí Market Promotion	0	15,000 e	15,000 e	15,000 e
10.170	Farm Bill-Specialty Crop Grants	52,000	73,000 e	74,500 e	75,500 e
10.171	Organic Certification Cost Share Programs	1,326	10,740	11,588 e	11,650 e
10.172	Local Food Promotion	(n)	(n)	15,000 e	15,000 e
10.200	Agricultural Research, Special	22,460	20,417	19,377 e	16,126 e
10.202	Cooperative Forestry Research	28,713	31,979	31,953 e	31,920 e
10.203	Agricultural Experiment Stations	205,663	229,173	228,936 e	0 e
10.205	1890 Land Grant Colleges	44,331	49,394	49,334 e	54,472 e
10.206	Agricultural Research—Competitive	0	0	0 e	e
10.207	Animal Health and Disease Research	3,436	3,713	3,711 e	0 e
10.210	Food, Sciences—Fellowships	2,861	3,106	3,105 e	0 e
10.212	Small Business Innovation Research	16,266	19,253	20,014 e	26,734 e
10.215	Sustainable Agriculture Research	12,501	21,303	21,287 e	21,271 e
10.216	1890 Capacity Building	16,958	18,321	18,257 e	19,348 e
10.217	Higher Education Challenge Grants	4,222	4,563	4,561 e	0 e
10.219	Biotechnology Risk Assessment	2,786	1,901	1,848 e	0 e
10.220	Multicultural Scholars Program	870	947	945 e	0 e
10.221	Tribal Colleges Education Equity	3,084	3,439	3,439 e	3,654 e
10.222	Tribal Colleges Endowment	4,748	4,882	4,876 e	4,421 e
10.223	Hispanic Serving Institutions	8,167	8,841	8,840 e	8,841 e
10.225	Community Food Projects	4,800	4,800	8,640 e	8,640 e

Please see "Important Notes on the Tables, Footnotes," page 888

Table 1. *(continued)*

Program Number	ADMINISTRATIVE ENTITY Program Title (abridged)	FY 2013 in $thousands	FY 2014 in $thousands	FY 2015 in $thousands	FY 2016 in $thousands
10.226	Secondary Agriculture Education	793	858	857 e	0 e
10.227	1994 Institutions Research Program	1,554	1,678	1,677 e	0 e
10.228	Alaska, Hawaii Native Education	2,836	3,066	3,066 e	3,066 e
10.250	Agricultural, Rural Research	1,313	1,438	1,804 e	2,694 e
10.253	Food Assistance, Nutrition Research \ u	1,398	2,733	1,313 e	2,100 e
10.255	Economic Development Grants \ u	500	500	500 e	500 e
10.290	Agricultural Market Research	833	1,418	1,300 e	800 e
10.303	Integrated Programs	13,562	27,122	22,925 e	20,979 e
10.304	Homeland Security-Agricultural	5,296	6,413	6,432 e	6,432 e
10.305	International Science, Education	0	0	0 e	0 e
10.306	Biodiesel	0	960	890 e	960 e
10.307	Organic Agriculture Research	0	18,981	17,561 e	18,968 e
10.308	Instruction/Insular Area Activities	0	0	0 e	0 e
10.309	Specialty Crop Research	0	75,431	69,770 e	75,447 e
10.310	Agriculture and Food Research	254,068	292,741	296,578 e	410,849 e
10.311	Beginning Farmer/Rancher Development	0	19,092	17,599 e	19,092 e
10.312	Biomass Research and Development	0	2,795	2,496 e	2,789 e
10.313	Veterinary Medicine Loan Repayment	3,911	4,239	4,393 e	4,426 e
10.314	New ERA Rural Technology Grants	0	0	0 e	0 e
10.315	TAAF Training Coordination	0	0	0 e	0 e
10.317	Food Aid Nutrition Enhancement Program	0	0	0 e	0 e
10.322	Distance Education Grants—Insular Areas	1,465	1,728	1,728 e	0 e
10.325	Peopleís Garden Program	0	0	0 e	0 e
10.328	National Food Safety Competitive Grants	(n)	(n)	2,336 e	4,800 e
10.331	Food Insecurity Nutrition Incentive Grants	(n)	31,500	0 e	18,000 e
10.350	Assistance/Cooperatives	0	0	0 e	0 e
10.352	Value-Added Producer Grants	(nr)	25,000	40,000 e	40,000 e
10.404	Emergency Loans \ u	33,388*	18,106*	94,556*e	54,683*e
10.405	Farm Labor Housing Loans	18,881*	52,959*	24,000*e	24,000*e
10.406	Farm Operating Loans \ u	1,960,150*	2,201,419*	2,647,997*e	2,654,447*e
10.407	Farm Ownership Loans \ u	1,946,913*	3,102,449*	3,500,000*e	3,500,000*e
10.410	Very Low/Moderate Income Housing \ u	23,190,552*	19,859,354*	19,672,824*e	20,900,000*e
10.415	Rural Rental Housing Loans \ u	35,390*	2,685*	28,000*e	42,000*e
10.417	Housing Repair Loans, Grants \ u	27,168	28,289	28,700 e	25,000 e
		14,335*	13,806*	17,000*e	26,278*e
10.420	Rural Self-Help Housing	25,654	12,363	28,000 e	10,000 e
10.421	Tribal Corporation Loans \ u	(nr)	0*	2,000*e	2,000*e
10.427	Rural Rental Assistance Payments	837,054	1,110,000	1,089,000 e	1,172,000 e
10.433	Rural Housing Preservation Grants	4,086	4,808	0 e	0 e
10.435	State Mediation Grants	4,035	3,470	3,404 e	3,404 e
10.438	Section 538 Rural Rental Housing	52,227*	136,162*	150,000*e	150,000*e
10.443	Outreach/Farmers, Ranchers	0	9,100 e	9,500 e	(nr)
10.446	Rural Community Development \ u	6,800	5,960	10,406 e	10,400 e
10.447	Housing Preservation Restructuring	0	38,000 e	33,000 e	(nr)
10.448	Rural Housing Voucher Demonstration —Multi-Family	13,192	12,734	7,000 e	15,000 e
10.449	Boll Weevil Eradication Loans	0*	0*	60,000*e	60,000*e
10.450	Crop Insurance \ u	20,967,135*	12,732,452*	12,800,503*e	11,193,434*e
10.451	Noninsured Assistance \ u	334,776	177,816	165,000 e	165,000 e
10.456	Non-Insurance Risk Management \ u	0	0	0 e	0 e
10.458	Crop Insurance Education \ u	4,970	4,609	5,000 e	5,000 e
10.475	Intrastate Meat, Poultry Inspection	49,624	50,020	50,020 e	(nr)
10.477	Meat, Poultry and Egg Inspection \ t	975,000	1,015,000	1,001,000 e	(nr)
10.479	Food Safety	3,900	3,900 e	3,900 e	(nr)
10.500	Cooperative Extension Service	120,958	460,752	460,753 e	457,667 e
10.543	Smarter Lunchrooms	(n)	1,500	1,500 e	1,500 e
10.551	Food Stamps	74,007,024	78,363,955	71,508,411 e	(nr)
10.553	School Breakfast Program	3,610,150	3,716,095	3,959,929 e	4,230,498 e
10.555	School Lunch Program \ p	11,052,821	11,289,685	11,996,089 e	11,777,825 e
10.556	Special Milk Program	12,523	10,662	11,216 e	11,314 e
10.557	Nutrition/Women, Infants, Children	13,808,865	13,805,632	14,401,698 e	14,223,445 e
10.558	Child, Adult Care Food Program \ p	3,035,383	3,111,875	3,195,866 e	3,240,646 e
10.559	Summer Food Service \ p	452,457	464,439	511,521 e	602,533 e
10.560	State Expenses/Child Nutrition \ p	292,235	256,646	263,686 e	269,652 e

Please see "Important Notes on the Tables, Footnotes," page 888

Table 1. *(continued)*

Program Number	ADMINISTRATIVE ENTITY Program Title (abridged)	FY 2013 in $thousands	FY 2014 in $thousands	FY 2015 in $thousands	FY 2016 in $thousands
10.561	State Grants/Food Stamp Program	700,946	5,675,834	5,831,448 e	5,973,776 e
10.565	Commodity Supplemental Food \ p	185,879 e	180,929	235,826 e	221,298 e
10.566	Nutrition Assistance/Puerto Rico	2,000,568	2,060,594	1,930,128 e	(nr)
10.567	Food Distribution/Indian \ p	101,127	119,500	145,371 e	145,171 e
10.568	Emergency Food—Administrative	64,322	69,092	49,401 e	49,401 e
10.569	Emergency Food—Commodities \ p	243,848	245,736	270,000 e	270,000 e
10.572	WIC Farmersí Market Nutrition	18,723	19,633	16,548 e	16,548 e
10.574	Team Nutrition Grants	35,619	22,191	5,500 e	5,500 e
10.576	Senior Farmers Market Nutrition	21,987	20,585	20,600 e	20,600 e
10.578	WIC Grants to States	(nr)	103,089	128,636 e	128,636 e
10.579	Child Nutrition Discretionary \ p	44,200	40,706	41,000 e	39,000 e
10.580	Food Stamp Program Outreach	(nr)	5,000	5,000	5,000 e
10.582	Fresh Fruit, Vegetable Program	165,000	172,746	159,000 e	163,000 e
10.585	FNS Food Safety Grants	1,215	1,265	1,280 e	1,265 e
10.586	Nutrition Education Innovations	299	353	296 e	(nr)
10.587	Food Service Management Institute Administration/Staffing	6,300	7,800	8,300 e	7,800 e
10.589	Child Nutrition Direct Certification Awards	4,000	4,000	0 e	0 e
10.594	Nutrition Education Grants—Indian Reservations	916	989	995 e	(nr)
10.595	Farm to School Training and Technical Assistance	0	0	0 e	0 e
10.600	Foreign Market Development \ u	32,741	32,016	32,016 e	(nr)
10.601	Market Access Program \ u	189,800	185,600 e	185,600 e	(nr)
10.602	Dairy Export Incentive Program	(nr)	10,000 e	0 e	(nr)
10.603	Emerging Markets Program \ u	9,490	9,280 e	9,280 e	(nr)
10.604	Assistance/Specialty Crops \ u	8,541	8,352	8,352 e	(nr)
10.605	Quality Samples Program \ u	2,373	2,320	2,320 e	(nr)
10.606	Food for Progress	172,044	132,478	145,488 e	150,000 e
10.608	Food for Education \ u	214,677	183,159	202,200 e	200,000 e
10.609	Trade Adjustment Assistance \ r	90,000	22,500 e	0 e	(nr)
10.610	Export Guarantee Program	6,279*	6,748*	6,748*e	6,748*e
10.612	USDA Local/Regional Food Aid Procurement	0	0	0 e	0 e
10.613	Faculty Exchange Program	190	263	230 e	350 e
10.614	Scientific Cooperation Exchange-China	426	297	297 e	300 e
10.615	Pima Agriculture Cotton Trust Fund	(n)	16,000 e	16,000 e	0 e
10.652	Forestry Research	8,962	8,432	7,331 e	6,248 e
10.664	Cooperative Forestry Assistance	134,299	153,667	127,500 e	(nr)
10.665	Schools and Roads—States	317,464	300,409	285,222 e	270,960 e
10.666	Schools and Roads—Counties	26,664	27,518	4,601 e	4,463 e
10.672	Rural Development, Forestry	0	0	0 e	0 e
10.674	Forest Products Lab: Technology Unit	3,706	7,284	9,000 e	5,000 e
10.675	Urban and Community Forestry	301,701	9,742	10,000 e	(nr)
10.676	Forest Legacy	50,515	44,565	44,417 e	54,600 e
10.678	Forest Stewardship	12,642	12,176	(nr)	(nr)
10.679	Collaborative Forest Restoration	2,868	3,318	3,000	
10.680	Forest Health Protection	37,907	40,225	41,973 e	40,655 e
10.681	Wood Education	0	0	0 e	0 e
10.682	National Forest Foundation	2,850	3,000	3,000 e	3,000 e
10.683	National Fish/Wildlife Foundation Payments	2,850	3,000	3,000 e	3,000 e
10.684	International Forestry Programs	7,500	7,500	7,000 e	7,000 e
10.685	Community Wood Energy	0	0	0 e	0 e
10.689	Forest/Open Space Conservation	1,892	1,683	1,971 e	1,683 e
10.690	Lake Tahoe Erosion Control Grants	10,991	1,500	0 e	0 e
10.691	Good Neighbor Authority	169	0	0 e	0 e
10.692	Emergency Forest Restoration—Disaster Relief	356	0	0 e	0 e
10.694	Southwest Forest Health/Wildfire Prevention	1,500	1,725	1,500 e	(nr)
10.700	National Agricultural Library	21,676	24,000 e	24,000 e	(nr)
10.759	Assistance for Rural Communities and Households	488	3,199	2,304 e	1,500 e
10.760	Water, Waste Disposal Systems \ i, u	0 18,010*	7,249 831,614*	365,408 e 1,518,200*e	365,408 e 1,518,200*e
10.761	Technical Assistance, Training	17,550	19,000	19,214 e	19,000 e
10.762	Solid Waste Management	3,141	4,000	4,000 e	4,000 e
10.763	Community Water Assistance	5,805	14,711	4,798 e	10,000 e

Please see "Important Notes on the Tables, Footnotes," page 888

Table 1. *(continued)*

Program Number	ADMINISTRATIVE ENTITY Program Title (abridged)	FY 2013 in $thousands	FY 2014 in $thousands	FY 2015 in $thousands	FY 2016 in $thousands
10.766	Community Facilities Loans and Grants \ u	12,200	17,000	13,000 e	13,000 e
		1,401,000*	1,574,000*	2,273,000*e	2,273,000*e
10.767	Intermediary Relending Program \ u	17,420*	17,889*	18,890*e	18,890*e
10.768	Business and Industry Loans \ u	939,340*	1,084,020*	590,800*e	758,200*e
10.769	Rural Business Enterprise Grants	25,000 e	23,948	0 e	0 e
10.770	Water, Waste Disposal	32,572	42,298	19,810 e	32,454 e
		0*	0*	0*	0*
10.771	Rural Cooperative Development	10,000	5,800	5,800 e	5,800
10.773	Rural Business Opportunity Grants	3,000	0	0 e	0 e
10.777	Norman E. Borlaug Fellowship	1,089	1,796	1,700 e	2,000 e
10.850	Rural Electrification Loans \ u	4,410,308*	2,239,968*	5,000,000*e	6,000,000*e
10.851	Rural Telephone Loans \ u	196,159*	213,993*	223,824*e	690,000*e
10.854	Rural Economic Development \ r, u	10,000	9,280	9,270 e	9,270 e
		50,287*	85,600*	38,684*e	30,662*e
10.855	Distance Learning, Telemedicine	28,991	20,396	21,000 e	20,000 e
		0*	0*	0*	0*
10.857	State Bulk Fuel Revolving Fund \ r	0	0	1,000 e	0 e
10.858	RUS Denali Commission	2,500	2,310	0 e	0 e
10.859	High Energy Cost Communities	13,833	9,872	10,000 e	0 e
10.862	Household Water Well System	917	765	1,285 e	993 e
10.863	Community Connect Grant Program	20,259	13,686	14,000 e	14,000 e
10.864	Fund/Financing Water, Wastewater \ r	924	1,000	1,000 e	1,000 e
10.866	Repowering Assistance	0	0	0 e	0 e
10.867	Advanced Biofuels	48,000	48,297	15,000 e	15,000 e
10.868	Rural Energy for America Program	72,148*	68,824*	147,278*e	272,273*e
10.870	Rural Microentrepreneur Assistance	10,710*	17,700*	14,190*e	15,000*e
10.874	Delta Health Care Services	2,775	3,000	5,000 e	3,000 e
10.886	Rural Broadband Access Loans	88,935*	0*	0*e	70,000*e
10.902	Soil and Water Conservation	698,655	700,069	787,696 e	733,030 e
10.903	Soil Survey	73,925	81,777	83,910 e	80,094 e
10.904	Watershed Protection	13,923	4,950	20,730 e	200 e
10.905	Plant Materials for Conservation	8,980	8,723	10,291 e	9,170 e
10.907	Snow Survey, Water Forecasting	8,007	9,599	10,136 e	8,937 e
10.912	Environmental Quality Incentives	1,373,859	1,297,068	1,398,685 e	1,413,000 e
10.913	Farm, Ranch Lands Protection	118,129	2,877	93,840 e	69,000 e
10.914	Wildlife Habitat Incentive	63,513	9,612	24,016 e	20,000 e
10.916	Watershed Rehabilitation	15,929	14,109	19,702 e	4,320 e
10.917	Agricultural Management Assistance	2,450	6,570	4,635 e	5,000 e
10.920	Grassland Reserve Program	62,857	1,452	24,976 e	22,000 e
10.921	Conservation Security Program	158,856	120,411	28,299 e	9,000 e
10.922	Healthy Forests Program	6,443	3,047	4,154 e	3,000 e
10.923	Watershed Protection Program	95,062	61,270	67,697 e	0 e
10.924	Conservation Stewardship Program	882,552	1,030,871	1,210,167 e	1,456,221 e
10.925	Agricultural Water Enhancement	55,258	5,384	14,846 e	12,000 e
10.926	Chesapeake Bay Watershed Program	49,399	6,927	6,773 e	5,000 e
10.927	Emergency Watershed Protection— Disaster Relief	5,062	16,060	8,107 e	0 e
10.928	Emergency Watershed Protection— Floodplain Easements	101	1,139	141,474 e	0 e
10.929	Water Bank Program	3	4,330	4,545 e	0 e
10.933	Wetlands Mitigation Banking	(n)	(n)	10,000 e	0 e
10.950	Agricultural Statistics Reports	166,637 e	169,722	172,408 e	180,346 e
10.960	Technical Agricultural Assistance	26,511	18,222	21,347 e	22,250 e
10.961	Scientific Cooperation and Research	240	240	240 e	240 e
10.962	International Training	1,289	4,072	4,100 e	4,100 e
10.999	Storage, Transportation Lease Agreements	(nr)	(nr)	(nr)	(nr)
	DEPARTMENT TOTAL: OUTLAYS	122,719,821	139,140,994	134,460,650	62,332,864
	CREDITS*	61,414,145*	48,163,299*	55,293,682*	57,990,279*

Please see "Important Notes on the Tables, Footnotes," page 888

Table 1. *(continued)*

Program Number	ADMINISTRATIVE ENTITY Program Title (abridged)	FY 2013 in $thousands	FY 2014 in $thousands	FY 2015 in $thousands	FY 2016 in $thousands
	DEPARTMENT OF COMMERCE				
11.001	Census Bureau Data Products	(nr)	(nr)	(nr)	(nr)
11.002	Census Customer Services	(nr)	(nr)	(nr)	(nr)
11.003	Census Geography	(nr)	(nr)	(nr)	(nr)
11.004	Intergovernmental Services	(nr)	(nr)	(nr)	(nr)
11.005	Census Special Tabulations	(nr)	(nr)	(nr)	(nr)
11.006	Personal Census Search	(nr)	(nr)	(nr)	(nr)
11.008	NOAA Mission-Related Education Awards	3,748	3,029	3,875 e	0 e
11.011	Ocean Exploration	9,075	7,312	10,912 e	14,709 e
11.012	Integrated Ocean Observing System	26,305	28,297	29,338 e	29,500 e
11.013	Education Quality Award Ambassadorship	0	35	30 e	0 e
11.014	Band 14 Incumbent Spectrum Relocation	(n)	(n)	(n)	40,000 e
11.016	Statistical, Research, and Methodology	(n)	(n)	(n)	1,000 e
11.025	Measures and Analyses	(nr)	(nr)	(nr)	(nr)
11.026	National Trade Data Bank \ r, u	(nr)	(nr)	(nr)	(nr)
11.106	Antidumping Duty	(nr)	(nr)	(nr)	(nr)
11.108	Commercial Service	(nr)	(nr)	(nr)	(nr)
11.110	Manufacturing and Services	(nr)	(nr)	(nr)	(nr)
11.111	Foreign-Trade Zones/U.S.	(nr)	(nr)	(nr)	(nr)
11.112	Export Market Development	1,910 e	2,000 e	(nr)	(nr)
11.113	ITA Special Projects	6,000	(nr)	(nr)	(nr)
11.150	Licensing Services, Information	(nr)	(nr)	(nr)	(nr)
11.300	Public Works, Economic Development	(nr)	131,798	99,000 e	(nr)
11.302	Support for Planning Organizations	(nr)	29,278	30,000 e	(nr)
11.303	Technical Assistance	(nr)	19,480	11,000 e	(nr)
11.307	Economic Adjustment Assistance	(nr)	59,603	35,000 e	(nr)
11.312	Research and Evaluation	1,469	(nr)	15,000 e	(nr)
11.313	Trade Adjustment Assistance	(nr)	15,000	12,500 e	(nr)
11.400	Geodetic Surveys and Services	7,513	7,168	8,225 e	(nr)
11.407	Interjurisdictional Fisheries	(nr)	(nr)	(nr)	(nr)
11.408	Fishermenís Contingency Fund	350 e	(nr)	(nr)	(nr)
11.413	Fishery Products Inspection	(a)	(a)	(a)	(a)
11.415	Fisheries Finance Program \ u	83,000* e	(nr)	(nr)	(nr)
11.417	Sea Grant Support	57,200 e	67,671	69,505 e	71,290 e
11.419	Coastal Zone Management	61,649	61,949	71,146 e	(nr)
11.420	Estuarine Research Reserves	14,854	16,305	21,300 e	(nr)
11.426	Coastal Ocean Science	189	4 e	10 e	(nr)
11.427	Fisheries Development	(nr)	(nr)	(nr)	(nr)
11.429	Marine Sanctuary Program	4,701	8,676 e	9,500 e	(nr)
11.430	Undersea Research	0	(nr)	(nr)	(nr)
11.431	Climate, Atmospheric Research	(nr)	41,300	48,313 e	(nr)
11.432	Oceanic, Atmospheric Research	1,064 e	180,522	159,845 e	167,838 e
11.433	Marine Fisheries Initiative	2,000 e	(nr)	(nr)	(nr)
11.434	Cooperative Fishery Statistics	(a)	(a)	(a)	(a)
11.435	Southeast Area Monitoring	4,000 e	(nr)	(nr)	(nr)
11.436	Columbia River Fisheries	(a)	(a)	(a)	(a)
11.437	Pacific Fisheries	(a)	(a)	(a)	(a)
11.438	Pacific Coast Salmon Recovery	50,000 e	(nr)	(nr)	(nr)
11.439	Marine Mammal Data Program	(a)	(a)	(a)	(a)
11.440	Environmental Sciences	3,896 e	11,963	(nr)	(nr)
11.441	Fishery Management Councils	(nr)	(nr)	(nr)	(nr)
11.452	Unallied Industry Projects	(a)	(a)	(a)	(a)
11.454	Unallied Management Projects	(a)	(a)	(a)	(a)
11.457	Chesapeake Bay Studies	(a)	(a)	(a)	(a)
11.459	Weather and Air Quality Research	1,064 e	619	4,111 e	2,500 e
11.460	Oceanic and Atmospheric Projects	1,250 e	(nr)	(nr)	(nr)
11.462	Hydrologic Research	800 e	(nr)	(nr)	(nr)
11.463	Habitat Conservation	(a)	(a)	(a)	(a)
11.467	Meteorologic, Hydrologic Projects	300 e	(nr)	(nr)	(nr)
11.468	Applied Meteorological Research	600 e	(nr)	(nr)	(nr)
11.469	Congressionally Identified Projects	(nr)	(nr)	(nr)	(nr)
11.472	Unallied Science Program	(a)	(a)	(a)	(a)

Please see "Important Notes on the Tables, Footnotes," page 888

Table 1. *(continued)*

Program Number	ADMINISTRATIVE ENTITY Program Title (abridged)	FY 2013 in $thousands	FY 2014 in $thousands	FY 2015 in $thousands	FY 2016 in $thousands
11.473	Coastal Services Center	4,130	(nr)	6,500 e	(nr)
11.474	Atlantic Coastal Fisheries	(a)	(a)	(a)	(a)
11.478	Coastal Ocean Program	8,359	8,559	15,000 e	(nr)
11.481	Educational Partnership Program	10,452	12,263	12,500 e	12,500 e
11.483	NOAA Programs for Disaster Relief	16,927	31,283 e	0 e	(nr)
11.549	State and Local Implementation Grants	118,213	4,520 e	2,844 e	(nr)
11.550	Public Telecommunications Facilities	(nr)	(nr)	(nr)	(nr)
11.557	Broadband Technology Opportunities	(nr)	(nr)	(nr)	(nr)
11.558	State Broadband Data/Development Grant	(nr)	(nr)	(nr)	(nr)
11.601	Calibration Program \ r	(nr)	8,077	8,100 e	8,200 e
11.603	Standard Reference Data System \ r	(nr)	7,517	8,121 e	(nr)
11.604	Standard Reference Materials \ r	(nr)	15,870	17,552 e	(nr)
11.606	Weights and Measures Service \ r	(nr)	4,887	4,943 e	4,943 e
11.609	Measurement, Engineering Research \ r	88,951 e	101,000	107,000 e	113,200 e
11.610	Standards and Certification \ r	(nr)	(nr)	(nr)	(nr)
11.611	Manufacturing Extension Partnership	134,960 e	105,986	125,626 e	115,013 e
11.616	Technology Innovation Program	1,414 e	1,074	(nr)	(nr)
11.620	Science, Technology, Business and/or Education Outreach	(nr)	0	0	25,789 e
11.801	Native American Business Development	(nr)	(nr)	(nr)	(nr)
11.900	Patent and Trademark Information	(nr)	(nr)	(nr)	(nr)
11.999	Marine Debris	(n)	(n)	(n)	2,700 e
	DEPARTMENT TOTAL: OUTLAYS	643,343	993,045	946,796	609,182
	CREDITS*	83,000*	0*	0*	0*

DEPARTMENT OF DEFENSE

Program Number	ADMINISTRATIVE ENTITY Program Title (abridged)	FY 2013 in $thousands	FY 2014 in $thousands	FY 2015 in $thousands	FY 2016 in $thousands
12.002	Procurement Technical Assistance	(nr)	(nr)	(nr)	(nr)
12.100	Aquatic Plant Control	(nr)	(nr)	(nr)	(nr)
12.101	Beach Erosion Control Projects	(nr)	(nr)	(nr)	(nr)
12.102	Emergency Flood Control Works	(nr)	(nr)	(nr)	(nr)
12.103	Emergency Flood Response	(nr)	(nr)	(nr)	(nr)
12.104	Flood Plain Management	(nr)	(nr)	(nr)	(nr)
12.105	Essential Highways, Public Works	(nr)	(nr)	(nr)	(nr)
12.106	Flood Control Projects	(nr)	0	16 e	16 e
12.107	Navigation Projects	(nr)	(nr)	(nr)	(nr)
12.108	Snagging and Clearing	(nr)	(nr)	(nr)	(nr)
12.109	Protection, Clearing Channels	(nr)	(nr)	(nr)	(nr)
12.110	Planning Assistance to States	0	6,385	6,000 e	(nr)
12.111	Flood Prevention	(nr)	(nr)	(nr)	(nr)
12.112	Payments to States/Taxes	(nr)	(nr)	(nr)	(nr)
12.113	Reimbursements/Technical Services	(nr)	(nr)	(nr)	(nr)
12.114	Collaborative Research, Development	(nr)	(nr)	(nr)	(nr)
12.116	DOD Appropriation Act of 2003	5,178	6,056	185 e	4,000 e
12.217	Electronic Absentee Systems for Elections	0	0	0 e	0 e
12.218	FVAP Policy Clearinghouse	2,938	752 e	700 e	(nr)
12.219	EASE 2.0	10,532	442	0 e	0 e
12.225	Commercial Technologies for Maintenance Activities Program	0	9,663	5,724 e	8,000 e
12.300	Basic, Applied Scientific Research	589,664	593,806	600,000 e	600,000 e
12.350	DOD HIV/AIDS Prevention	38,050	32,621	32,000 e	32,000 e
12.351	Combating WMD—Basic Research	(nr)	(nr)	(nr)	(nr)
12.352	Combating WMD—Advanced Research	(nr)	(nr)	(nr)	(nr)
12.355	Pest Management and Vector Control	(n)	(n)	1,500 e	2,000 e
12.357	ROTC Language/Culture Training	8,200 e	(nr)	(nr)	(nr)
12.360	Chemical, Biological Defense	2,300 e	(nr)	(nr)	(nr)
12.369	Marine Corps Systems Command Assistance	4,000	4,000	4,000 e	4,000 e
12.400	Military Construction	56,753	60,680	60,000 e	(nr)
12.401	National Guard Operations	1,690,743	1,979,662	1,900,000 e	(nr)
12.404	Civilian Youth Opportunities	(nr)	(nr)	(nr)	(nr)
12.420	Military Medical Research	(nr)	(nr)	(nr)	(nr)
12.431	Basic Scientific Research	455,849	445,745	450,000 e	(nr)

Table 1. *(continued)*

Program Number	ADMINISTRATIVE ENTITY Program Title (abridged)	FY 2013 in $thousands	FY 2014 in $thousands	FY 2015 in $thousands	FY 2016 in $thousands
12.440	Dissertation Year Fellowship	(nr)	20 e	20	20 e
12.550	International Education \ t	25,305	25,305	17,244 e	23,803 e
12.551	National Security—Scholarships \ t	(nr)	2,000	2,000 e	2,000 e
12.552	National Security—Fellowships	(nr)	2,000	2,000 e	2,000 e
12.553	National Flagship Language Fellowships	(nr)	0	0 e	0 e
12.554	Heritage Language Speakers Grants	(nr)	(nr)	(nr)	(nr)
12.555	Heritage Language Speakers Scholarships	(nr)	(nr)	(nr)	(nr)
12.556	Student Achievement at Military-Connected Schools	39,069 e	50,000	(nr)	(nr)
12.557	Invitational Grants/Military-Connected Schools	0	32,151 e	20,000 e	(nr)
12.560	Education Outreach Implementation	4,102	8,866 e	5,000 e	(nr)
12.579	Language Training Center	14,161	14,683	2,800 e	2,000 e
12.598	Centers for Academic Excellence	4,700 e	(nr)	(nr)	(nr)
12.600	Defense-Special Assistance Payments	260,000	94,946	58,000 e	(nr)
12.604	Community Economic Adjustment	0	0	1,500 e	0 e
12.607	Community Economic Planning \ t	15,300	14,907	11,300 e	(nr)
12.610	Joint Land Use Studies \ t	3,200	2,774	6,195 e	(nr)
12.611	Community Planning Assistance	0	5,678	1,000 e	(nr)
12.614	Advance Planning \ t	6,300	3,268	8,230 e	(nr)
12.615	State/Local Research/Technical Assistance	0	1,005	1,400 e	(nr)
12.630	Research/Science, Engineering	(nr)	(nr)	(nr)	(nr)
12.631	Science, Math and Research for Transformation	25,675	10,000 e	10,000 e	(nr)
12.632	Legacy Resource Management	(n)	4,479	2,624 e	4,668 e
12.700	Obsolete DOD Property \ p	(nr)	(nr)	(nr)	(nr)
12.750	USU Medical Research Projects	113,086	224,422	45,000 e	220,000 e
12.800	Defense Research Sciences	436,156	531,340	500,000 e	(nr)
12.900	Language Grant Program	(nr)	(nr)	(nr)	(nr)
12.901	Mathematical Sciences Grants	13,815	0	0 e	0 e
12.902	Information Security	3,885	3,000	3,000 e	(nr)
12.910	Research and Technology	(nr)	(nr)	(nr)	(nr)
	DEPARTMENT TOTAL: OUTLAYS	3,828,961	4,170,656	3,757,438	904,507
	CREDITS*	0*	0*	0*	0*

	DEPARTMENT OF HOUSING AND URBAN DEVELOPMENT				
14.008	Transformation Initiative Research-Choice Neighborhoods	0	(nr)	(nr)	(nr)
14.103	Interest Reduction—Housing \ u	(a)	(a)	(a)	(a)
14.108	Rehabilitation Mortgage Insurance \ u	(o)	(o)	(o)	(o)
14.110	Manufactured Home Loan Insurance \ i, u	39,000*	24,328*	22,000*e	20,000*e
14.117	Mortgage Insurance—Homes \ i, u	240,388,758*	135,087,517*	134,707,000*e	173,600,000*e
14.119	Homes for Disaster Victims \ u	(o)	(o)	(o)	(o)
14.122	Mortgage Insurance—Renewal Areas \ u	(o)	(o)	(o)	(o)
14.123	Mortgage Insurance—Declining Areas \ u	(o)	(o)	(o)	(o)
14.126	Mortgage Insurance—Cooperatives \ u	(o)	(o)	(o)	(o)
14.127	Manufactured Home Parks \ u	9,594* e	(nr)	(nr)	(nr)
14.128	Mortgage Insurance—Hospitals \ u	889,000*	1,050,000*	1,100,000*e	(nr)
14.129	Mortgage Insurance—Nursing Homes \ u	381,000*	521,000*e	521,000*e	(nr)
14.133	Mortgage Insurance—Condominiums \ i, u	(o)	(o)	(o)	(o)
14.134	Mortgage Insurance—Rental Housing \ u	0*	0*	0*	0*
14.135	Mortgage Insurance—Market Rate \ i, u	2,525,080* e	(nr)	(nr)	(nr)
14.138	Mortgage Insurance—Elderly \ u	61,994* e	(nr)	(nr)	(nr)
14.139	Rental Housing/Renewal Areas \ u	390,412* e	(nr)	(nr)	(nr)
14.142	Property Improvement Loans \ u	107,000*	102,000*	101,000*e	101,000*e
14.149	Rent Supplements, Housing	372,000	334,000 e	318,000 e	(nr)
14.151	Supplemental Loan Insurance \ u	0*	(nr)	(nr)	(nr)
14.155	Existing Multifamily Projects \ u	5,457,000* e	(nr)	(nr)	(nr)
14.157	Supportive Housing/Elderly \ i, u	275,618	352,000	393,000 e	(nr)
14.159	Graduated Payment Mortgage \ u	(o)	(o)	(o)	(o)
14.162	Manufactured Home Lot Loans \ u	(o)	(o)	(o)	(o)
14.163	Single Family Cooperative Housing \ u	(o)	(o)	(o)	(o)
14.168	Land Sales	(nr)	(nr)	(nr)	(nr)

Please see "Important Notes on the Tables, Footnotes," page 888

Table 1. *(continued)*

Program Number	ADMINISTRATIVE ENTITY Program Title (abridged)	FY 2013 in $thousands	FY 2014 in $thousands	FY 2015 in $thousands	FY 2016 in $thousands
14.169	Housing Counseling Assistance	45,500 e	(nr)	(nr)	(nr)
14.171	Manufactured Home Standards \ t	(nr)	(nr)	(nr)	(nr)
14.172	Growing Equity Mortgages \ u	(o)	(o)	(o)	(o)
14.175	Adjustable Rate Mortgages \ u	(o)	(o)	(o)	(o)
14.181	Supportive Housing/Disabilities \ u	101,847	132,000 e	128,000 e	(nr)
14.183	Home Equity Conversion Mortgages \ u	14,775,707*	13,493,000*e	15,860,000*e	(nr)
14.184	Mortgages/Single Room Occupancy \ u	(o)	(o)	(o)	(o)
14.188	HFA Risk Sharing Program \ u	233,000* e	(nr)	(nr)	(nr)
14.189	QPE Risk Sharing \ u	100,000* e	(nr)	(nr)	(nr)
14.191	Multifamily Housing Coordinators	86,151	51,000	68,000 e	(nr)
14.195	Section 8—Special Allocations	9,429,000	9,947,000 e	10,365,000 e	(nr)
14.198	Officer Next Door Sales Program \ u	(o)	(o)	(o)	(o)
14.218	CDBG/Entitlement	3,308	2,116	3,066 e	3,066 e
14.225	CDBG/Insular Area	7,000	7,000	7,000 e	7,000 e
14.228	CDBG/State	921,359	906,900	886,531 e	886,531 e
14.231	Emergency Shelter Grants	215,000	250,000	274,000 e	250,000 e
14.239	HOME Investment Partnerships	919,045	1,023,768	848,108	952,347 e
14.241	Housing/Persons with AIDS	302,176	330,000	330,000 e	332,000 e
14.247	Self-Help Homeownership	12,794	10,000 e	10,023	19,978 e
14.248	CDBG—Section 108 Loans	230,895*	110,387*	500,000*e	250,000*e
14.252	Section 4 Capacity Building	33,169	35,000	35,000	35,000 e
14.259	Transformation Initiative Technical Assistance	21,389	51,000	(a)	(a)
14.261	Homeless Management Information Systems	6,634	6,000 e	6,000 e	(nr)
14.267	Continuum of Care Program	1,851,481	1,810,560	1,992,000 e	1,995,000 e
14.268	Rural Housing Stability Assistance	0	0	0 e	0 e
14.269	Hurricane Sandy Disaster Recovery Grants	2,086,236	1,598,360	3,809,604 e	(nr)
14.270	Appalachia Economic Development Initiative	(n)	1,000	550	0 e
14.271	Delta Community Capital Initiative	(n)	1,000	1,478	0 e
14.273	Pay for Success	(n)	5,000	5,000 e	0 e
14.275	Housing Trust Fund	(n)	(n)	(n)	173,591 e
14.276	Youth Homelessness Demonstration	(n)	(n)	(n)	0 e
14.278	Veterans Home Rehabilitation	(n)	(n)	(n)	5,700 e
14.311	Single Family Property Disposition \ i, p	317,379	5,559,195	4,244,454 e	6,268,607 e
14.313	Dollar Home Sales \ p	(o)	(o)	(o)	(o)
14.314	Assisted Living Conversion	26,922	20,000 e	0 e	(nr)
14.316	Housing Counseling Training	6,000 e	(nr)	(nr)	(nr)
14.317	Section 8 Housing Assistance Payments-Special	(nr)	(nr)	(nr)	(nr)
14.318	Assisted Housing Stability/Energy/Green Retrofit Investments	(nr)	(nr)	(nr)	(nr)
14.319	Multifamily Energy Innovation Fund	(nr)	(nr)	(nr)	(nr)
14.321	FHA Technical Assistance Training/ Transformation	1,414	0	0 e	0 e
14.326	Supportive Housing for Persons with Disabilities-Implementation	0	226,000	42,000 e	(nr)
14.327	Performance Based Contract Administrator Program	(nr)	(nr)	(nr)	(nr)
14.400	Equal Opportunity in Housing	66,888	67,356	75,874 e	(nr)
14.401	FHAP—State, Local	16,955	30,727	27,205 e	23,300 e
14.408	Fair Housing Initiatives	38,656	38,867	40,304 e	44,700 e
14.416	Education and Outreach Initiatives	3,816	5,632	4,604 e	7,050 e
14.417	Fair Housing Organization Initiatives	9,790	3,724	6,425 e	2,875 e
14.418	Private Enforcement Initiatives-Fair Housing	25,049	29,510	29,275 e	34,775 e
14.506	General Research and Technology	46,833	48,269 e	50,000 e	(nr)
14.516	Doctoral Dissertation Research	(nr)	(nr)	(nr)	(nr)
14.523	Transformation Initiative Research- Sustainable Community	500	0 e	0 e	0 e
14.524	Transformation Initiative Research Grants-Natural Experiments	(nr)	(nr)	(nr)	(nr)
14.525	Transformation Initiative Research-Small Grants	400	0 e	0 e	0 e
14.534	Strong Cities/Communities Resource Network	9,879	0 e	0 e	0 e
14.535	Rental Assistance Demonstration—Small Research Grants	400	0 e	0 e	0 e

Please see "Important Notes on the Tables, Footnotes," page 888

Table 1. *(continued)*

Program Number	ADMINISTRATIVE ENTITY Program Title (abridged)	FY 2013 in $thousands	FY 2014 in $thousands	FY 2015 in $thousands	FY 2016 in $thousands
14.850	Public and Indian Housing	3,457,380	3,735,442	3,728,626 e	3,829,161 e
14.856	Section 8 Moderate Rehabilitation	184,460	253,080	200,000 e	215,000 e
14.862	Indian CDBG	58,208	70,000	66,000 e	80,000 e
14.865	Indian Housing Loans	642,132*	708,799*	851,000*e	1,150,793*e
14.867	Indian Housing Block Grants	617,571	651,396	642,500 e	658,000 e
14.869	Tribal Housing Activities	16,466*	11,900*	16,500*e	17,500*e
14.870	Residents—Supportive Services	28,785	45,000	44,682	35,000 e
14.871	Section 8 Housing Choice Vouchers	14,701,204	15,653,580	15,889,910 e	17,360,764 e
14.872	Public Housing Capital Fund	1,489,607	1,579,392	1,595,002 e	1,602,904 e
14.873	Hawaii Housing Block Grants	12,036	9,700	8,700 e	0 e
14.874	Native Hawaiian Housing	24,999*	11,300*	11,400*e	20,000*e
14.877	Public Housing, Family Self-Sufficiency	1,764	16,319	0 e	0 e
14.878	Main Street Rejuvenation	500 e	(nr)	(nr)	(nr)
14.879	Mainstream Vouchers	109,889	104,505	114,975 e	107,643 e
14.881	Moving to Work Program	3,942,532	4,347,099	4,446,184 e	4,578,437 e
14.889	Choice Neighborhoods Implementation Grants	112,836	120,200	157,798 e	245,000 e
14.892	Choice Neighborhoods Planning Grants	4,374	5,000 e	5,000 e	(nr)
14.893	Indian Housing Block Grant Training/Assistance	6,033	7,667	5,200 e	0 e
14.894	Native Hawaiian Housing Block Grant Training/Assistance	351	1,066	300 e	0 e
14.895	Jobs-Plus Pilot Initiative	(n)	(n)	30,000 e	100,000 e
14.896	Family Self-Sufficiency Program	0	75,000	75,000 e	85,000 e
14.897	Juvenile Reentry Assistance	(n)	(n)	853 e	900 e
14.898	ROSS Supportive Services	(n)	(n)	2,000 e	900 e
14.900	Lead-Based Paint Hazards	(nr)	(nr)	(nr)	(nr)
14.902	Lead Technical Studies Grants \ i	(nr)	(nr)	(nr)	(nr)
14.905	Lead Hazard Reduction Demonstration	(nr)	(nr)	(nr)	(nr)
14.906	Healthy Homes Technical Studies	(nr)	(nr)	(nr)	(nr)
14.913	Healthy Homes Production Grant Program	0	0	0 e	0 e
14.914	Asthma in Public/Assisted Multifamily Housing	(nr)	(nr)	(nr)	(nr)
	DEPARTMENT TOTAL: OUTLAYS	41,988,118	49,557,430	51,013,231	39,940,229
	CREDITS*	266,272,037*	151,120,231*	153,689,900*	175,159,293*

DEPARTMENT OF THE INTERIOR

Program Number	Program Title	FY 2013	FY 2014	FY 2015	FY 2016
15.020	Aid to Tribal Governments	(nr)	25,839	(nr)	(nr)
15.021	Consolidated Tribal Government	(nr)	74,623	(nr)	(nr)
15.022	Tribal Self-Governance	435,251	535,082	(nr)	(nr)
15.024	Indian Self-Determination	(nr)	242,000	(nr)	(nr)
15.025	Children, Elderly, Families	(nr)	35,763	(nr)	(nr)
15.026	Indian Adult Education	2,336	(nr)	(nr)	(nr)
15.027	Tribally Controlled Colleges	63,254	68,084	68,084 e	68,084 e
15.028	Community College Endowments	103	109	109 e	109 e
15.029	Tribal Courts	(nr)	23,241	(nr)	(nr)
15.030	Indian Law Enforcement	(nr)	6,882 e	(nr)	(nr)
15.031	Indian Community Fire Protection	(nr)	(nr)	(nr)	(nr)
15.032	Indian Economic Development	(nr)	(nr)	(nr)	(nr)
15.033	Road Maintenance	25,155 e	(nr)	(nr)	(nr)
15.034	Agriculture on Indian Lands	27,494 e	(nr)	(nr)	(nr)
15.035	Forestry on Indian Lands	(nr)	(nr)	(nr)	(nr)
15.036	Indian Rights Protection	(nr)	(nr)	(nr)	(nr)
15.037	Water Resources on Indian Lands	13,578 e	11,064	(nr)	(nr)
15.038	Minerals, Mining/Indian Lands	(nr)	(nr)	(nr)	(nr)
15.040	Real Estate Programs-Indian Lands	(nr)	(nr)	(nr)	(nr)
15.041	Environmental Management	(nr)	(nr)	(nr)	(nr)
15.042	Indian School Equalization	229,514 e	240,908	240,908 e	240,908 e
15.043	Indian Child and Family Education	7,280 e	8,178	8,178 e	8,178 e
15.044	Indian Schools—Transportation	33,508 e	52,796	52,945 e	53,145 e
15.046	Administrative Costs/Indian Schools	43,834 e	48,253	62,395 e	75,335 e
15.047	Indian Education Facilities	125,167	118,257	126,619 e	149,982 e

Please see "Important Notes on the Tables, Footnotes," page 888

Table 1. *(continued)*

Program Number	ADMINISTRATIVE ENTITY Program Title (abridged)	FY 2013 in $thousands	FY 2014 in $thousands	FY 2015 in $thousands	FY 2016 in $thousands
15.048	BIA Facilities	(nr)	(nr)	(nr)	(nr)
15.051	Endangered Species/Indian Lands	(nr)	(nr)	(nr)	(nr)
15.052	Litigation Support/Indian Rights	(nr)	(nr)	(nr)	(nr)
15.053	Attorney Fees-Indian Rights	(nr)	(nr)	(nr)	(nr)
15.057	Navajo-Hopi Settlement	(nr)	(nr)	(nr)	(nr)
15.058	Indian Post Secondary Schools	17,477 e	19,611	19,767 e	19,900 e
15.059	Graduate Student Scholarships	2,142 e	2,492	2,742 e	2,992 e
15.060	United Tribes Technical College	(nr)	(nr)	(nr)	(nr)
15.061	United Sioux Tribes	(nr)	(nr)	(nr)	(nr)
15.062	Replacement, Repair—Schools	(nr)	(nr)	(nr)	(nr)
15.063	Improvement—Detention Facilities	(nr)	(nr)	(nr)	(nr)
15.065	Safety of Dams/Indian Lands	(nr)	(nr)	(nr)	(nr)
15.066	Tribal Great Lakes Restoration	(n)	3,813	5,180 e	5,180 e
15.108	Indian Employment Assistance	(nr)	(nr)	(nr)	(nr)
15.113	Indian Social Services—Welfare	(nr)	(nr)	(nr)	(nr)
15.114	Indian—Higher Education	38,133 e	(nr)	(nr)	(nr)
15.124	Indian Loans—Economic \ u	(nr)	(nr)	(nr)	(nr)
15.130	Indian Education—Schools	21,396 e	21,592	21,997 e	24,684 e
15.133	Native American Business Development	(nr)	(nr)	(nr)	(nr)
15.141	Indian Housing Assistance	(nr)	(nr)	(nr)	(nr)
15.144	Indian Child Welfare Act	(nr)	(nr)	(nr)	(nr)
15.146	Ironworker Training Program	(nr)	(nr)	(nr)	(nr)
15.147	Tribal Courts-Trust Reform	(nr)	(nr)	(nr)	(nr)
15.148	Tribal Energy Development Capacity	400 e	(nr)	(nr)	(nr)
15.149	FOCUS on Student Achievement Project	920 e	920	(nr)	(nr)
15.151	Education Program Enhancements	4,768 e	4,768	(nr)	(nr)
15.152	Land Buy-Back Program For Tribal Nations	447	5,000	8,000 e	5,000 e
15.153	Hurricane Sandy Disaster Relief—Coastal Resiliency Grants	(nr)	100,000	(nr)	(nr)
15.214	Disposals of Mineral Material \ p	(nr)	(nr)	6,072	(nr)
15.222	Inspection Agreements	750 e	750	1,497	1,497 e
15.224	Cultural Resource Management	2,601	2,600	924	1,500 e
15.225	Recreation Resource Management	7,780	7,780	1,705	6,392 e
15.226	Payments in Lieu of Taxes	(nr)	(nr)	(nr)	(nr)
15.227	Receipts/State, Local Governments	87,500	87,500	87,500 e	87,500 e
15.228	Wildland Urban Fire Assistance	5,971	5,971	2,300	2,300 e
15.229	Wild Horse, Burro Resource Management	10,000	11,760	11,760 e	12,000 e
15.230	Invasive and Noxious Plant Management	3,500	3,500	2,385	2,400 e
15.231	Fish, Wildlife, Plant Conservation	(a)	(a)	(a)	(a)
15.232	Wildland Fire Research/Studies	2,490	5,118	(nr)	4,500 e
15.233	Forests and Woodlands Resource Management	124	300	1,100	1,210 e
15.234	Secure Rural Schools/Community Self-Determination	3,672	3,317	139	3,000 e
15.235	Southern Nevada Public Land Management	2,904	2,270	(nr)	7,670 e
15.236	Environmental Quality and Protection	0	0	7,392	8,500 e
15.237	Rangeland Resource Management	1,300	1,300	1,612	1,773 e
15.238	Challenge Cost Share/National Parks	2,500	2,500	787	2,423 e
15.239	Land Management Initiatives	2,500	2,500	1,423	500 e
15.240	Helium Resource Management	6,720	9,025	6,696 e	6,696 e
15.241	Indian Self-Determination Act	3,000	3,000	5,470	3,000 e
15.242	National Fire Plan—Rural Assistance	550	550	15,557	1,200 e
15.250	Surface Coal Mining	68,590	71,979	68,590 e	65,500 e
15.252	Abandoned Mine Land Reclamation	321,627	298,318	249,800 e	209,700 e
15.253	Not-for-Profit AMD Reclamation	1,878	1,200	1,651	1,300 e
15.254	Summer Watershed Intern	160	200	200 e	200 e
15.255	Coal Mining, Applied Science Agreements	0	0	0 e	0 e
15.406	National Park Service Centennial Challenge	0	0	10 e	50 e
15.407	Keweenaw National Historical Park Enhancement	3	39	0 e	0 e
15.408	Bureau of Ocean Energy Management Renewable Energy Program	2,000	1,000	(nr)	0 e
15.421	Alaska Coastal Marine Institute	1,000	1,000	981	500 e
15.422	LSU Coastal Marine Institute	1,000	1,000	525	500 e
15.423	Minerals Management Service Studies	6,107	10,000	5,743	6,400 e
15.424	Marine Minerals Activities	500	1,000	(nr)	1,500 e
15.427	Oil and Gas Royalty Management \ t	(nr)	(nr)	11,234	13,283 e

Please see "Important Notes on the Tables, Footnotes," page 888

Table 1. *(continued)*

Program Number	ADMINISTRATIVE ENTITY Program Title (abridged)	FY 2013 in $thousands	FY 2014 in $thousands	FY 2015 in $thousands	FY 2016 in $thousands
15.428	Marine Gas Hydrate Research Activities	0	0	0 e	0 e
15.429	State Select Gas Royalty Payments	(nr)	542	465	343 e
15.430	8(g) State Coastal Zone	(nr)	36,375	22,146	22,154 e
15.431	Alaska State Select	(nr)	603	7	5 e
15.432	California Refuge Account	(nr)	5 e	0	0 e
15.433	Flood Control Act Lands	(nr)	36,380	13,665	25,995 e
15.434	Geothermal Resources	(nr)	7,467	10,809	9,075 e
15.435	GoMESA	(nr)	2,808	2,441	314 e
15.436	Late Disbursement Interest	(nr)	0	328 e	242 e
15.437	Minerals Leasing Act	(nr)	2,090,138	1,780,826	1,313,078 e
15.438	National Forest Acquired Lands	(nr)	8,265	5,359	5,716 e
15.439	National Petroleum Reserve - Alaska	(nr)	3,010	3,085	3,914 e
15.440	South Red River Payments	(nr)	3 e	15	11 e
15.441	Offshore Energy/Mineral Activities Safety/Enforcement	200	(nr)	(nr)	(nr)
15.504	Water Reclamation and Reuse	17,080	26,942	26,000 e	23,365 e
15.506	Desalination Research, Development	1,153	1,500	1,502	1,800 e
15.507	Water 2025	21,400	19,000	23,500 e	20,000 e
15.508	Desert Terminal Lakes	599	1,945	3,428	667 e
15.509	Colorado River Basin Salinity Control	12,398	8,714	10,418	12,046 e
15.510	Water Rights Settlement, Ute	236	200	4,128	400 e
15.512	Central Valley Project Improvement	29,469	25,000	7,544	7,000 e
15.514	Emergency Drought Relief	(nr)	500	5,000	2,500 e
15.516	Fort Peck Water Supply	896	9,200	9,849	3,700 e
15.517	Fish and Wildlife Coordination Act	22,620	25,806	27,938	20,000 e
15.518	Garrison Diversion Unit	25,778	33,463	29,253	23,149 e
15.519	Indian Tribal Water Resources	3,218	2,200	10,691	10,000 e
15.520	Lewis and Clark Rural Water System	4,119	8,350	8,775	2,774 e
15.521	Lower Rio Grande Irrigation Projects	300	30	343	50 e
15.522	Mni Wiconi Water Supply Project	33,149	0	11,215	12,000 e
15.524	Recreation Resources Management	8,519	8,000	12,370	(nr)
15.525	Rocky Boyís Regional Water	3,661	11,400	10,891	4,625 e
15.527	San Luis, Central Valley Project	167	174	210	80 e
15.529	Endangered Fish Recovery	5,657	7,931	4,125	4,208 e
15.530	Water Conservation	1,737	3,437	4,457	4,457 e
15.531	Yakima River Basin Water	5,919	4,620	10,813	5,329 e
15.532	Central Valley Project	6,403	7,361	7,588	9,265 e
15.533	California Water Security	2,243	2,000	3,647	4,102 e
15.534	Miscellaneous Assistance for Native Americans	226	200	10	0 e
15.535	Upper Colorado River Fish/Wildlife Mitigation	33	9 e	(nr)	382 e
15.537	Middle Rio Grande Endangered Species	75	105	(nr)	323 e
15.538	Lower Colorado River Multi-Species Conservation	2,192	2,200	2,500 e	2,500 e
15.539	Equus Beds Aquifer Storage Recharge	2	5 e	(nr)	49 e
15.540	Lake Mead/Las Vegas Wash Program	196	775	(nr)	375 e
15.542	Arizona Water Settlement Act	0	81,327	71,503	75,000 e
15.543	Lake Tahoe Regional Wetlands Development	1,162	835	(nr)	0 e
15.544	Platte River Recovery	17,994	9,749	14,777 e	17,122 e
15.546	Youth Conservation Program	482	400	400	400 e
15.548	Reclamation Rural Water Supply	0	0	0	0
15.550	Recreation-Physically Challenged/Disadvantaged Children	150	70	125 e	125 e
15.551	Madera Water Supply Enhancement Project	0	0	0 e	0 e
15.552	Navajo-Gallup Water Supply Project	32,410	25,763	16,644 e	0 e
15.554	Cooperative Watershed Management	379	250	250 e	250 e
15.555	San Joaquin River Restoration	10,851	7,000	2,800 e	45 e
15.556	Crow Tribe Water Rights Settlement	9,477	7,500	2,000	12,772 e
15.557	Desert and Southern Rockies Landscape Conservation Cooperatives	1,057	700	0	0 e
15.558	White Mountain Apache Tribe Rural Water System	1,200	2,000	0	0 e
15.559	Rio Grande Basin Pueblos Irrigation	247	250	250 e	300 e
15.560	SECURE Water Act-Research	385	350	1,897	2,000 e
15.562	Dixie Valley Water Export Study	0	0	32	19 e
15.563	Suisun Marsh Preservation Agreement	0	1,351 e	1,374 e	(nr)

Please see "Important Notes on the Tables, Footnotes," page 888

Table 1. *(continued)*

Program Number	ADMINISTRATIVE ENTITY Program Title (abridged)	FY 2013 in $thousands	FY 2014 in $thousands	FY 2015 in $thousands	FY 2016 in $thousands
15.564	Central Valley Project Conservation Program	1,419	1,224	1,192	1,492 e
15.565	Taos Pueblo Indian Water Rights	(n)	(n)	(n)	24,250 e
15.605	Sport Fish Restoration \ t	359,800	352,000	350,000 e	345,000 e
15.608	Fish and Wildlife Management	15,704	17,200	17,200	18,700 e
15.611	Wildlife Restoration	620,997	753,255	800,475	804,650 e
15.614	Coastal Wetlands \ t	20,000	16,500	17,000 e	17,000 e
15.615	Endangered Species Fund	43,854	47,388 e	47,388 e	87,673
15.616	Clean Vessel Act \ t	14,757	16,589	16,000 e	14,000 e
15.619	Rhinoceros, Tiger Conservation	2,448	2,632	2,400	3,500
15.620	African Elephant Conservation \ t	1,874	1,805	1,500 e	1,500 e
15.621	Asian Elephant Conservation	1,647	1,450	1,759 e	1,507 e
15.622	Sportfishing, Boating Safety \ t	20,000	10,000	14,300	12,000 e
15.623	Wetlands Conservation	61,580	77,603	78,860	78,000 e
15.625	Wildlife Conservation	60	80	80 e	80 e
15.626	Hunter Education and Safety	7,700	7,700	7,992	7,700 e
15.628	Multi-State Conservation Grants \ t	6,000	6,000	6,000	6,000 e
15.629	Great Apes Conservation	1,812	2,059	1,875	1,875 e
15.630	Coastal Program	6,000	14,000	14,000 e	14,000 e
15.631	Partners for Fish, Wildlife	22,000	22,000	22,000	74,000 e
15.633	Landowner Incentive	5,000	1,200	2,000 e	1,700 e
15.634	State Wildlife Grants	52,200	52,400	52,400 e	52,400 e
15.635	Neotropical Migratory Bird	3,567	3,631	3,600 e	3,600 e
15.636	Alaska Subsistence Management	4,441	4,600	4,728 e	3,851 e
15.637	Migratory Bird Joint Ventures	5,859	4,994	5,000 e	5,000 e
15.639	Tribal Wildlife Grants	4,134	4,666	4,084	4,084 e
15.640	Wildlife—Latin America	262	500	500 e	500 e
15.641	Wildlife—Mexico	612	600	500 e	600 e
15.642	Challenge Cost Share	(nr)	0	0 e	0 e
15.643	Alaska Migratory Bird Co-Management	552	641	681 e	681 e
15.644	Junior Duck Stamp Conservation \ p	60	60	50 e	50 e
15.645	Marine Turtle Conservation	1,777	1,660	1,500 e	1,500 e
15.647	Migratory Bird Conservation	526	345	200 e	200 e
15.648	Anadromous Fish Restoration	4,294	3,046	8,611 e	4,423 e
15.649	National Resource Conservation Training	1,800	902	900 e	900 e
15.650	Research Grants	3,357	1,970	1,500 e	1,000 e
15.651	Wildlife Without Borders—Africa	7,763	17,500	17,000 e	17,000 e
15.652	Undesirable/Noxious Plant Species	201	201	201 e	201 e
15.653	Outreach, Communication Program \ t	12,259	10,920	12,033	12,850 e
15.654	Visitor Facility Enhancements	12,882	1,400	1,500 e	1,700 e
15.655	Migratory Bird Conservation	852	1,064	1,000 e	1,000 e
15.657	Endangered Species Conservation/ Implementation	778	0	0 e	0 e
15.658	Natural Resource Damage Assessment	2,618	3,177	3,500 e	3,500 e
15.659	National Wildlife Refuge Fund	3,000	4,521	4,000 e	3,500 e
15.660	Endangered Species Conservation/Candidates	0	575	575 e	575 e
15.661	Lower Snake River Compensation Plan	29,880	31,000	31,000 e	32,000 e
15.662	Great Lakes Restoration	40,500	49,000	32,000 e	32,000 e
15.663	National Fish/Wildlife Foundation Grants	6,922,000	6,922	7,525 e	7,525 e
15.664	Fish and Wildlife Coordination and Assistance	800	179	175 e	150 e
15.665	National Wetlands Inventory	330	0	0 e	0 e
15.666	Livestock Loss Compensation/Prevention	850	900	900 e	900 e
15.667	Highlands Conservation Program	5,208	3,599	3,000 e	0 e
15.669	Cooperative Landscape Conservation	2,500	1,600	1,600 e	2,000 e
15.670	Adaptive Science	12,000	10,000	10,000 e	24,000 e
15.671	Yukon River Salmon Research/Management	260	259	270 e	270 e
15.672	WWB-Amphibians in Decline	100	111	250 e	250 e
15.673	WWB-Critically Endangered Animal Conservation	302	291	250 e	250 e
15.676	Youth Engagement, Education, and Employment Programs	82	4,311	4,500 e	4,750 e
15.677	Hurricane Sandy Disaster Relief Activities	450	81,565	20,414 e	0 e
15.805	State Water Resources Research	6,165	6,317	6,300 e	6,300 e
15.807	Earthquake Hazards Reduction	38,010	35,000	35,000 e	(nr)
15.808	Geological Survey—Research, Data	38,010	43,562	35,000 e	35,000 e
15.809	National Spatial Data	0	0	0 e	0 e
15.810	National Geologic Mapping Program	6,002	5,982	5,982	6,712 e

Please see "Important Notes on the Tables, Footnotes," page 888

Table 1. *(continued)*

Program Number	ADMINISTRATIVE ENTITY Program Title (abridged)	FY 2013 in $thousands	FY 2014 in $thousands	FY 2015 in $thousands	FY 2016 in $thousands
15.811	GAP Analysis Program	40	760	400 e	400 e
15.812	Cooperative Research Units Program	14,880	13,442	14,000 e	14,000 e
15.814	Geological, Geophysical Data	626	818	835 e	835 e
15.815	National Land Remote Sensing	960	1,217	1,217 e	1,217 e
15.816	Minerals Resources Research	0	208	0	0 e
15.817	National Geospatial Program	1,057	1,548	3,500 e	(nr)
15.818	Volcano Hazards Research/Monitoring	893	376	400 e	400 e
15.819	Energy Cooperatives	292	292	292	300 e
15.820	Climate Change/Wildlife Science Center	8,700	6,500	10,000 e	10,000 e
15.850	Indian Arts, Crafts Development	(nr)	(nr)	(nr)	(nr)
15.875	Economic, Social, Political Development	612,908	678,249	617,451	624,000 e
15.904	Historic Preservation	51,005	42,936	56,410 e	56,410 e
15.912	National Historic Landmarks	387	372	0 e	0 e
15.914	National Register/Historic Places	92	22	0 e	0 e
15.915	Technical Preservation Services	0	0	0 e	0 e
15.916	Outdoor Recreation	20,269	62,877	45,000 e	45,000 e
15.918	Federal Surplus Real Property	701	589	589 e	589 e
15.921	Rivers, Trails Conservation	1,795	3,043	1,900 e	1,900 e
15.922	Native American Graves Protection	1,629	1,557	1,694 e	1,694 e
15.923	Preservation Technology, Training	720	803	750 e	750 e
15.925	National Maritime Heritage Grants	(n)	(n)	(n)	2,000 e
15.926	American Battlefield Protection	1,039	1,333	1,300 e	1,400 e
15.927	Hydropower Recreation Assistance	0	0	0 e	0 e
15.928	Civil War Battlefield Acquisition	9,822	5,211	8,500 e	8,500 e
15.929	Save Americaís Treasures	40	64	42 e	42 e
15.930	Chesapeake Bay Gateways	483	567	500 e	0 e
15.931	Youth Service Conservation Activities	13,693	21,930	20,000 e	20,000 e
15.933	Preservation of Japanese American Confinement Sites	1,776	2,815	3,000 e	3,000 e
15.935	National Trails System Projects	4,248	4,164	4,417 e	4,417 e
15.939	National Heritage Area Financial Assistance	12,447	17,569	17,000 e	17,000 e
15.940	New Bedford Whaling National Historic Park	0	38	10 e	15 e
15.941	Mississippi National River and Recreation Area	208	0	350 e	350 e
15.942	North Cascades Environmental Education/ Conservation	14	34	50 e	50 e
15.943	Challenge Cost Share/Land Management	100	382	104 e	500 e
15.944	Natural Resource Stewardship	8,256	13,912	8,587 e	8,587 e
15.945	Cooperative Research and Training	32,880	43,941	34,196 e	45,000 e
15.946	Cultural Resources Management	11,130	12,167	15,000 e	15,000 e
15.947	Boston Harbor Islands Partnership	162	0	250 e	250 e
15.954	National Park Service Conservation	21,407	20,118	22,263 e	23,000 e
15.955	Martin Luther King Junior National Historic Site and Preservation District	0	728	971 e	971 e
15.958	Route 66 Corridor Preservation	(n)	(n)	(n)	90 e
15.960	Tribal Technical Colleges	(n)	6,465	6,814 e	6,911 e
15.962	National Wild and Scenic Rivers System	(n)	(n)	(n)	1,200 e
15.978	Upper Mississippi Monitoring	2,369	2,788	2,732 e	2,500 e
15.979	Hurricane Sandy Program	(nr)	1,542	4,479 e	(nr)
15.980	National Ground-Water Monitoring Network	(n)	(n)	1,000 e	1,500 e
15.981	Water Use and Data Research	(n)	(n)	(n)	1,500 e
	DEPARTMENT TOTAL: OUTLAYS	11,201,246	7,440,993	5,923,623	5,477,644
	CREDITS*	0*	0*	0*	0*

	DEPARTMENT OF JUSTICE				
16.001	Narcotics, Drugs—Laboratory	4,278 e	605	605 e	605 e
16.003	Narcotics, Drugs/Publications	1	1	1 e	1 e
16.004	Narcotics, Drugs Training	1,437 e	5,753	5,750 e	5,750 e
16.012	ATF-Training Assistance	(nr)	(nr)	(nr)	(nr)
16.013	Court Training Grants	2,607 e	(nr)	(nr)	(nr)
16.015	Missing Alzheimerís Disease Patient Assistance	837	750	0 e	0 e
16.016	Culturally Specific Services	6,402	6,650 e	6,650 e	(nr)

Please see "Important Notes on the Tables, Footnotes," page 888

Table 1. *(continued)*

Program Number	ADMINISTRATIVE ENTITY Program Title (abridged)	FY 2013 in $thousands	FY 2014 in $thousands	FY 2015 in $thousands	FY 2016 in $thousands
16.017	Sexual Assault Services	15,390	15,390	15,000 e	15,000 e
16.019	Tribal Registry	0	0	(nr)	(nr)
16.025	Domestic Violence Criminal Jurisdiction	(n)	(n)	(n)	2,500 e
16.100	Desegregation of Public Education	(nr)	(nr)	(nr)	(nr)
16.101	Equal Employment Opportunity	(nr)	(nr)	(nr)	(nr)
16.103	Fair Housing and Equal Credit	(nr)	(nr)	(nr)	(nr)
16.104	Protection of Voting Rights	(nr)	(nr)	(nr)	(nr)
16.105	Institutionalized Persons	(nr)	(nr)	(nr)	(nr)
16.109	Civil Rights Prosecution	(nr)	(nr)	(nr)	(nr)
16.123	Community-Based Violence Prevention	10,270	5,500	0 e	18,000 e
16.200	Community Relations Service	12,036 e	(nr)	(nr)	(nr)
16.203	Sex Offender Management	(a)	(a)	(a)	(a)
16.300	FBI Advanced Police Training	8,939	8,804	9,405 e	9,318 e
16.301	FBI Crime Laboratory	18,809	23,582	22,022 e	25,627 e
16.302	FBI Field Police Training	21,268	21,291	21,409 e	22,538 e
16.303	FBI Fingerprint Identification	9,785	169,382	97,446 e	79,412 e
16.304	National Crime Information Center	13,327	15,118	25,873 e	17,950 e
16.305	Uniform Crime Reports	10,435	6,240	5,856 e	6,313 e
16.307	DNA Index System	12,901	13,926	11,052 e	11,779 e
16.308	Indian Country Investigations	2,048	2,645	2,195 e	2,935 e
16.309	Law Enforcement Assistance—NICS	29,287	72,323	32,863 e	34,252 e
16.320	Services for Trafficking Victims	(nr)	14,250	10,500 e	(nr)
16.321	Antiterrorism Emergency Reserve	(nr)	50,000	(nr)	(nr)
16.523	Juvenile Accountability Incentives	23,341	30,000 e	30,000 e	(nr)
16.524	Legal Assistance for Victims	29,394	28,000	28,000 e	(nr)
16.525	Crimes Against Women/Campuses	7,355	7,500 e	7,500 e	(nr)
16.526	Technical Assistance, Training	32,970	31,114	30,000 e	(nr)
16.527	Supervised Visitation/Children	6,225 e	(nr)	(nr)	(nr)
16.528	Elder Abuse, Neglect, Exploitation	3,262	3,200	3,200	(nr)
16.529	Violence/Women with Disabilities	4,616	4,600 e	4,600 e	(nr)
16.540	Juvenile Justice—States	41,080 e	56,000	56,000 e	70,000 e
16.541	Developing, Testing—New Programs	1,390	(nr)	(nr)	(nr)
16.543	Missing Childrenís Assistance	62,553	67,000	68,000 e	67,000 e
16.544	Youth Gang Prevention	4,668	2,500	3,000 e	(nr)
16.548	Delinquency Prevention Program	18,673	15,000	15,000 e	42,000 e
16.550	State Justice Statistics Program	(a)	(a)	(a)	(a)
16.554	Criminal History Improvement	4,983	28,121	50,000 e	50,000 e
16.556	State Violence Coalition Grants	10,657	10,000 e	10,000 e	(nr)
16.557	Tribal Violence Coalition Grants	2,493	5,000 e	5,000 e	(nr)
16.560	NIJ Research, Evaluation, Development	30,238	35,645	47,500 e	52,500 e
16.562	Graduate Research Fellowships	(a)	(a)	(a)	(a)
16.566	Dubois Fellowship Program	(a)	(a)	(a)	(a)
16.571	Public Safety Officersí Benefits	61,949	80,928	81,000 e	100,000 e
16.575	Crime Victim Assistance	425,201	745,000	2,361,000 e	1,000,000 e
16.576	Crime Victim Compensation	159,067	(nr)	(nr)	945,000 e
16.578	Federal Surplus Property Transfer	0	(nr)	(nr)	(nr)
16.582	Victim Assistance/Discretionary	15,892	(nr)	(nr)	(nr)
16.583	Childrenís Justice/Indian	(nr)	(nr)	(nr)	(nr)
16.585	Drug Court Program	35,790	40,500	0 e	36,000 e
16.587	Violence Against Women/Indian	28,588	30,000 e	30,000 e	(nr)
16.588	Violence Against Women	128,095	120,000 e	120,000 e	(nr)
16.589	Rural Domestic Violence	22,243	25,000 e	25,000 e	(nr)
16.590	Arrest Policies/Enforcement	30,836	35,000 e	35,000 e	(nr)
16.593	Substance Abuse Treatment/Prisoners	10,962	10,000	14,000 e	14,000 e
16.595	Community Capacity Development Office	(nr)	(nr)	(nr)	(nr)
16.596	Correctional Grant/Tribes	10,286	30,000	0 e	0 e
16.601	Corrections—Training	6,819 e	6,200	500 e	500 e
16.602	Corrections—Research	1,313 e	500	200 e	200 e
16.603	Corrections—Technical Assistance	3,070 e	1,989	300 e	300 e
16.606	Criminal Alien Assistance	237,123 e	180,000	0 e	0 e
16.607	Bulletproof Vest Partnership	16,486	22,500	0 e	40,000 e
16.608	Tribal Court Assistance	3,748	30,000	0 e	0 e
16.609	Community Prosecution	4,649 e	7,565	0 e	0 e
16.610	Regional Information Sharing	29,583	30,000	25,000 e	25,000 e

Please see "Important Notes on the Tables, Footnotes," page 888

Table 1. (continued)

Program Number	ADMINISTRATIVE ENTITY Program Title (abridged)	FY 2013 in $thousands	FY 2014 in $thousands	FY 2015 in $thousands	FY 2016 in $thousands
16.614	Anti-Terrorism Training	1,567	1,000	2,000 e	2,000 e
16.615	Public Safety Educational Assistance	15,962	16,300	16,300 e	16,300 e
16.616	Indian Alcohol and Drug Prevention	15,974	30,000	0 e	0 e
16.710	Public Safety, Community Policing	(nr)	(nr)	(nr)	(nr)
16.726	Juvenile Mentoring Program	84,027	88,500	90,000 e	58,000 e
16.727	Enforcing Underage Drinking Laws	4,668	2,500 e	(nr)	(nr)
16.730	Safe Start	0	0	0 e	0 e
16.731	Tribal Youth Program	3,336	5,000	5,000 e	(nr)
16.734	Special Data Collections	13,474	17,702	55,400 e	59,900 e
16.735	Protecting Inmates, Communities	10,686	12,500	10,500 e	10,500 e
16.736	Transitional Housing/Victims	20,085	20,000 e	20,000 e	(nr)
16.737	Gang Resistance Education, Training	0	(nr)	(nr)	(nr)
16.738	Byrne Memorial Justice Assistance	364,907	376,000	376,000 e	376,000 e
16.739	National Prison Rape Statistics	(a)	(a)	(a)	(a)
16.740	Victim Information Notification	654	0	0 e	0 e
16.741	Forensic DNA Capacity Enhancement	90,451	100,898	100,000 e	100,000 e
16.742	Coverdell Forensic Sciences	9,687	10,505	0 e	0 e
16.745	Criminal and Mental Health Collaboration	7,273	8,250	0 e	14,000 e
16.746	Capital Case Litigation	2,468	2,000	2,000 e	2,000 e
16.750	Adam Walsh Act Grant	17,403	24,079	21,000 e	21,000 e
16.751	Byrne Competitive Grant	12,850	13,500	15,000 e	15,000 e
16.752	High-Tech Crime Prevention	4,944	10,000	15,000 e	15,000 e
16.753	Congressionally Recommended Awards	2,993	75	0 e	0 e
16.754	Harold Rogers Prescription Drug Monitoring	5,528	7,000	7,000 e	11,000 e
16.755	Southwest Border Prosecution Initiative	4,649 e	0	0 e	0 e
16.756	Court Appointed Special Advocates	5,579	6,000	6,000 e	6,000 e
16.757	Judicial Training on Child Maltreatment	1,263	(nr)	(nr)	(nr)
16.758	Improving Investigation/Prosecution of Child Abuse	1,400	19,000	19,000 e	11,000 e
16.800	Internet Crimes against Children Task Force	(nr)	0	0 e	0 e
16.801	State Victim Assistance Grants	(nr)	0	0 e	0 e
16.802	State Victim Compensation Grants	(nr)	0	0 e	0 e
16.803	Edward Byrne Memorial Justice Assistance Grants-State	(nr)	0	0 e	0 e
16.804	Edward Byrne Memorial Justice Assistance Grants-Local	(nr)	0	0 e	0 e
16.807	Crime Victim Assistance-Discretionary	(nr)	0	0 e	0 e
16.808	Edward Byrne Memorial Grants	(nr)	0	0 e	0 e
16.809	State/Local Law Enforcement Assistance- Narcotics	(nr)	0	0 e	0 e
16.810	Rural Law Enforcement Assistance	(nr)	0	0 e	0 e
16.811	Tribal Correctional Facilities	(nr)	0	0 e	0 e
16.812	Second Chance Act Prisoner Reentry Initiative	62,570	67,750	115,000 e	115,000 e
16.813	NICS Act Record Improvement	10,025	10,805	5,000 e	5,000 e
16.814	Northern Border Prosecution Initiative	(a)	(a)	(a)	(a)
16.815	Tribal Civil/Criminal Legal Assistance	1,900	1,596	1,575 e	0 e
16.817	Byrne Criminal Justice Innovation Program	14,881	10,500	29,500 e	29,500 e
16.818	Children Exposed to Violence	12,089	8,000	8,000 e	23,000 e
16.819	Youth Violence Prevention	1,867	0	1,000 e	0 e
16.820	Postconviction DNA Testing	3,316	3,593	0 e	0 e
16.822	National Center for Campus Public Safety	2,302	4,000	2,000 e	0 e
16.824	Emergency Law Enforcement Assistance Grant	(nr)	0	0 e	0 e
16.825	Smart Prosecution Initiative	0	2,500	5,000 e	5,000 e
16.826	Vision 21	(a)	(a)	(a)	(a)
16.827	Justice Reinvestment Initiative	0	27,500	30,000 e	30,000 e
16.828	Swift and Certain Sanctions	0	4,000	10,000 e	10,000 e
16.835	Body Worn Camera Policy	(n)	(n)	(n)	22,500 e
16.836	Indigent Defense	(n)	(n)	5,400	2,500 e
16.888	Consolidated Youth Program	(nr)	7,500 e	7,500 e	(nr)
16.889	Services to Underserved Populations—Outreach Grants	0	4,324	4,324 e	(nr)
16.922	Equitable Sharing Program	657,217	(nr)	(nr)	(nr)
	DEPARTMENT TOTAL: OUTLAYS	3,163,650	3,073,949	4,300,926	3,654,680
	CREDITS*	0*	0*	0*	0*

Please see "Important Notes on the Tables, Footnotes," page 888

Table 1. *(continued)*

Program Number	ADMINISTRATIVE ENTITY Program Title (abridged)	FY 2013 in $thousands	FY 2014 in $thousands	FY 2015 in $thousands	FY 2016 in $thousands
	DEPARTMENT OF LABOR				
17.002	Labor Force Statistics	339,503	338,406	329,070 e	(nr)
17.003	Prices and Cost of Living Data	194,070	200,438	206,012 e	(nr)
17.004	Productivity and Technology Data	11,363	10,151	10,477 e	(nr)
17.005	Compensation, Working Conditions	82,970	87,916	8,699 e	0 e
17.150	Employee Benefits Security	173,573	178,500	181,000 e	207 e
17.201	Registered Apprenticeship, Training	26,000	32,000	32,000 e	37,000 e
17.207	Employment Service \ t	726,000	718,000	720,000 e	720,000 e
17.225	Unemployment Insurance \ t	70,563,000	44,563,000	39,135,000 e	38,795,000 e
17.235	Senior Community Service	426,000	432,000	433,000 e	434,000 e
17.245	Trade Adjustment Assistance	534,000	306,268	235,700 e	450,000 e
17.258	WIA Adult Program	731,000	766,000	775,000 e	813,000 e
17.259	WIA Youth Activities	770,000	806,000	817,000 e	858,000 e
17.260	WIA Dislocated Workers	0	0	0 e	0 e
17.261	Pilots, Demonstration, Research	6,000 e	6,000	10,000 e	0 e
17.264	Migrant, Seasonal Farmworkers	80,000	82,000	82,000 e	82,000 e
17.265	Native American Employment	48,000	50,000	49,000 e	53,000 e
17.267	WIA Incentive Grants—Section 503	10,000 e	10,000	10,000 e	0 e
17.268	H-1B Job Training Grants	22,000	110,000	270,000 e	300,000 e
17.270	Prisoner Reentry	79,000 e	74,000	82,078	88,078 e
17.271	Work Opportunity Tax Credit	18,000	18,000	18,000 e	18,000 e
17.272	Permanent Labor Certification, Foreign	24,000	24,000	24,000 e	31,000 e
17.273	Temporary Labor Certification, Foreign	38,000	38,000	38,000 e	44,000 e
17.274	Youth Build Program	72,000	75,000	77,000 e	81,000 e
17.275	High Growth and Emerging Industry Worker Training	0	0	0 e	0 e
17.276	Health Care Tax Credit National Emergency Grants	4,000	0	0 e	0 e
17.277	WIA-National Emergency Grants	175,000	194,000	169,000 e	178,000 e
17.278	WIA Dislocated Worker Grants	959,000	1,004,000	1,016,000 e	1,021,000 e
17.280	WIA-Dislocated Worker National Reserve Demonstration Grants	0	2,000	20,000 e	20,000
17.281	WIA-Dislocated Worker National Reserve Assistance/Training	6,000	4,000	18,000 e	12,000 e
17.282	Community College/Career Training Grants	489,000	451,000	0 e	0 e
17.283	Workforce Innovation Fund	24,000	51,000	39,000 e	0 e
17.284	Hurricane Sandy—Supplemental National Emergency Grants	20,000	0	0 e	0 e
17.285	Apprenticeship USA Grants	(n)	(n)	(n)	61,500 e
17.301	Federal, Construction Contractors	(nr)	(nr)	(nr)	(nr)
17.302	Longshore and Harbor Workers	129,441	127,084	124,784 e	122,526 e
17.303	Wage, Hour Standards \ i	(nr)	(nr)	(nr)	(nr)
17.306	Consumer Credit Protection	(nr)	(nr)	(nr)	(nr)
17.307	Coal Mine Workersí Compensation \ t	339,615	309,398	258,849 e	237,585 e
17.308	Farm Labor Contractors	(nr)	(nr)	(nr)	(nr)
17.309	Labor Organization Reports	39	39	39	41 e
17.310	Occupational Illness Compensation	1,314,459	1,058,809	1,044,253 e	1,025,978 e
17.401	International Labor Programs	(a)	(a)	(a)	(a)
17.502	Susan Harwood Training	10,149	10,687	10,537	10,537 e
17.503	State Program	98,548	100,000	100,850 e	100,850 e
17.504	Consultation Agreements	54,813	57,775	57,773	57,775 e
17.505	OSHA Data Initiative	281	0	0 e	0 e
17.506	Susan Harwood Training Grants	1,250	0	0 e	0 e
17.600	Mine Health and Safety Grants	2,991	8,441	8,441 e	8,441 e
17.601	Mine Health, Safety Counseling	(nr)	33,791	33,791 e	34,583 e
17.602	Mine Health, Safety Education	13,154	12,943	13,000 e	13,100 e
17.603	Brookwood-Sago Grant	550 e	1,000	1,000 e	1,000 e
17.604	Safety and Health Grants	0	0	125 e	125 e
17.700	Womenís Bureau	10,878	11,536	9,047 e	11,836 e
17.720	Disability Employment Policy	(nr)	(nr)	(nr)	(nr)
17.801	Disabled Veterans Outreach	89,617	108,913	115,916	114,863 e
17.802	Veterans Employment Program	(nr)	(nr)	(nr)	(nr)

Please see "Important Notes on the Tables, Footnotes," page 888

Table 1. *(continued)*

Program Number	ADMINISTRATIVE ENTITY Program Title (abridged)	FY 2013 in $thousands	FY 2014 in $thousands	FY 2015 in $thousands	FY 2016 in $thousands
17.803	Uniformed Services/Rights	(a)	(a)	(a)	(a)
17.804	Local Veterans Employment	67,721	59,362	54,988	57,710 e
17.805	Homeless Veterans Reintegration	36,100	38,100	38,109	38,109 e
17.806	Preference/Federal Employment	(a)	(a)	(a)	(a)
17.807	Transition Assistance Program	12,673	13,418	14,000 e	14,000 e
	DEPARTMENT TOTAL: OUTLAYS	78,833,758	52,582,975	46,690,538	45,945,844
	CREDITS*	0*	0*	0*	0*

DEPARTMENT OF STATE

Program Number	ADMINISTRATIVE ENTITY Program Title (abridged)	FY 2013 in $thousands	FY 2014 in $thousands	FY 2015 in $thousands	FY 2016 in $thousands
19.009	Academic Exchange/Undergraduate	33,238	51,247	51,247 e	51,247 e
19.010	Academic Exchange/Humphrey Fellowship	13,709	10,349	10,349 e	10,349 e
19.011	Academic Exchange/Special	17,629	18,797	18,797 e	18,797 e
19.012	Special Professional/Cultural Exchange Programs	3,876	575	575 e	575 e
19.013	Thomas R. Pickering Foreign Affairs Fellowship	(nr)	(nr)	(nr)	(nr)
19.015	Cultural, Technical and Educational Centers	16,584	17,685	17,685 e	17,685 e
19.016	Iraq Assistance Programs	(nr)	(nr)	(nr)	(nr)
19.018	U.S. Refugee Resettlement	(nr)	(nr)	(nr)	(nr)
19.020	Charles B. Rangel International Affairs Program	(nr)	(nr)	(nr)	(nr)
19.021	Investing in People in The Middle East and North Africa	(nr)	(nr)	(nr)	(nr)
19.025	U.S. Ambassadors Fund-Cultural Preservation	5,750	5,750 e	5,750 e	(nr)
19.026	Global Peace Operations Initiative	(a)	(a)	(a)	(a)
19.029	Emergency Plan for AIDS Relief Programs	0	(nr)	(nr)	(nr)
19.030	Antiterrorism/Domestic Training	1,500 e	1,500	(nr)	(nr)
19.031	Physical Security Programs-Research	2,000 e	(nr)	(nr)	(nr)
19.033	Global Threat Reduction	22,118	41,770	35,000 e	35,000 e
19.123	EUR/ACE Humanitarian Assistance Program	11,000 e	6,000	(nr)	(nr)
19.124	East Asia and Pacific Grants	(nr)	(nr)	(nr)	(nr)
19.204	Fishermenís Guaranty Fund	(nr)	(nr)	(nr)	(nr)
19.221	Near East Regional Democracy	(nr)	(nr)	(nr)	(nr)
19.300	Study/Eastern Europe	(nr)	(nr)	(nr)	(nr)
19.301	Global Partnership Initiative Grants	2,000 e	(nr)	(nr)	(nr)
19.322	Economic Statecraft	(a)	(a)	(a)	(a)
19.400	Educational Exchange—Graduate	131,291	102,328	102,328 e	102,328 e
19.401	Lecturers and Research Scholars	55,909	36,077	36,077 e	36,077 e
19.402	International Visitors Program	61,886	60,335	60,335 e	60,335 e
19.408	Exchange—Secondary, Postsecondary	21,830	21,966	21,966 e	21,966 e
19.415	Professional Exchanges	93,799	98,272	98,272 e	98,272 e
19.421	English Language Fellow Program	36,388	36,800	36,800 e	36,800 e
19.432	Overseas Educational Advising	7,500	7,888	7,888 e	7,888 e
19.450	ECA Individual Grants	917	26	26 e	26 e
19.500	Middle East Partnership Initiative	67,510	70,000	70,000 e	75,000 e
19.501	Diplomacy Programs for Afghanistan/Pakistan	110,000 e	88,900	(nr)	(nr)
19.510	U.S. Refugee Admissions	(nr)	(nr)	(nr)	(nr)
19.511	Refugee Assistance/East Asia	(nr)	(nr)	(nr)	(nr)
19.515	Organizations for Overseas Assistance	(nr)	(nr)	(nr)	(nr)
19.517	Refugee Assistance/Africa	(nr)	(nr)	(nr)	(nr)
19.518	Refugee Assistance/Western Hemisphere	(nr)	(nr)	(nr)	(nr)
19.519	Refugee/Near East, South Asia	(nr)	(nr)	(nr)	(nr)
19.520	Refugee Assistance/Europe	(nr)	(nr)	(nr)	(nr)
19.522	Refugee/Strategic Global Priorities	(nr)	(nr)	(nr)	(nr)
19.600	Bureau of Near Eastern Affairs	(nr)	(nr)	(nr)	(nr)
19.666	National Endowment for Democracy	(nr)	(nr)	(nr)	(nr)
19.700	General Department of State Assistance	(a)	(a)	(a)	(a)
19.750	Bureau of Western Hemisphere Affairs	(nr)	(nr)	(nr)	(nr)
19.901	Export Control and Related Border Security	(nr)	(nr)	(nr)	(nr)
	DEPARTMENT TOTAL: OUTLAYS	716,434	676,265	573,095	572,345
	CREDITS*	0*	0*	0*	0*

Please see "Important Notes on the Tables, Footnotes," page 888

Table 1. *(continued)*

Program Number	ADMINISTRATIVE ENTITY Program Title (abridged)	FY 2013 in $thousands	FY 2014 in $thousands	FY 2015 in $thousands	FY 2016 in $thousands
	DEPARTMENT OF TRANSPORTATION				
20.106	Airport Improvement Program \ t	3,343,300	3,211,717	3,192,650 e	(nr)
20.108	Aviation Research \ t	14,384	16,307	10,000 e	12,000 e
20.109	Air Transportation Centers \ t	13,075	15,508	15,000 e	16,000 e
20.200	Highway Research, Development	110,064	216,713	70,000 e	70,000 e
20.205	Highway Planning, Construction \ i, t	37,785,373	40,474,922	40,600,000 e	49,700,000 e
20.215	Highway Training, Education \ t	18,252	59,347	58,500 e	60,000 e
20.218	National Motor Carrier Safety \ t	211,399	215,000	(nr)	(nr)
20.219	Recreational Trails \ t	71,646	87,825	55,000 e	60,000 e
20.223	Transportation Infrastructure Finance \ u	2,004,663*	7,830,201*	13,396,000*e	12,696,000*e
20.224	Federal Lands Access	(n)	(n)	220,090	225,637 e
20.231	Registration Information Management \ t	5,000	5,000	5,000 e	(nr)
20.232	Commercial Driver License State \ t	29,940	30,000	30,000 e	(nr)
20.233	Border Enforcement Grants \ t	32,000	32,000	32,000 e	(nr)
20.234	Safety Data Improvement Program \ t	2,994	3,000	3,000 e	(nr)
20.235	Commercial Operator Training \ t	973	1,000	1,000 e	(nr)
20.237	Commercial Vehicle Information	25,000	15,000	15,000 e	(nr)
20.239	Motor Carrier Research/Technology	0	0	0	(nr)
20.240	Fuel Tax Evasion Enforcement \ t	2,162	9,193	2,000 e	10,000 e
20.301	Railroad Safety	108,272	11,229	1,303 e	1,303 e
20.313	Railroad Research and Development	40,529	38,310	46,688 e	39,250 e
20.314	Railroad Development	2,208	37,185	39,485 e	(nr)
20.315	Railroad Passenger Corporation Grants	1,399,318	1,387,231	1,410,893 e	(nr)
20.316	Railroad Rehabilitation \ u	600,000*	600,000*e	967,100*e	600,000*e
20.317	Intercity Rail Assistance	3,259	11,020	18,600 e	2,450,000 e
20.318	Maglev Project Selection Program	0	0	63,658 e	(nr)
20.319	High-Speed Rail/Intercity Passenger Rail Service	25,479	31,781	68,459 e	0 e
20.320	Rail Line Relocation and Improvement	20,179	8,577	11,412 e	0 e
20.321	Railroad Safety Technology	0	0	550 e	0 e
20.323	Hurricane Sandy Disaster Relief Grants—National Railroad Passenger Corporation	82,699	151,240	81,701 e	(nr)
20.500	Capital Investment Grants \ t	1,955,000	2,505,015	2,120,000 e	3,250,000 e
20.505	Metropolitan Planning Grants \ t	126,646	170,698	91,007	120,391 e
20.507	Urbanized Area Formula Grants \ t	4,389,154	6,952,847	5,481,481 e	5,062,311 e
20.509	Nonurbanized Areas	598,301	744,926	547,145 e	677,675 e
20.513	Elderly, Persons with Disabilities \ t	133,222	239,804	402,598 e	296,459 e
20.514	Transit Planning, Research \ t	44,000	48,000	37,500 e	60,000 e
20.516	Job Access—Reverse Commute \ t	0	70,291	24,617 e	6,154 e
20.518	Over-the-Road Bus Accessibility \ t	0	3,438	4,532 e	1,133 e
20.519	Clean Fuels	0	24,983	2,617 e	654 e
20.521	New Freedom Program	0	36,461	18,826 e	4,707 e
20.522	Alternatives Analysis	0	7,254	23,576 e	5,894 e
20.523	Reducing Energy Consumption/Greenhouse Gas	0	543	49,605 e	0 e
20.527	Public Transportation Emergency Relief	10,164,300	3,590,000	0 e	0 e
20.530	Public Transportation Innovation	(n)	(n)	33,000	28,000 e
20.531	Workforce Development	(n)	(n)	9,500	9,500 e
20.600	State, Community Highway Safety \ t	234,050	230,653	193,536 e	0 e
20.602	Occupant Protection \ t	0	0	0 e	0 e
20.607	Alcohol Open Container \ t	(nr)	0	18,857 e	0 e
20.608	Penalties/Repeat Offenders \ t	0	0	35,895 e	0 e
20.609	Safety Belt Performance Grants \ t	0	0	0 e	0 e
20.610	Traffic Safety Information System	0	0	0 e	0 e
20.611	Prohibit Racial Profiling Incentive \ t	0	0	0 e	0 e
20.612	Motorcyclist Safety Incentive \ t	0	0	0 e	0 e
20.613	Child Safety/Booster Seats Incentive \ t	0	0	0 e	0 e
20.614	Highway Safety Grants	6,300	5,150	(nr)	(nr)
20.700	Pipeline Safety	38,088	47,601	54,085 e	(nr)
20.701	University Transportation Centers	69,400	68,813	44,645	95,198 e
20.703	Hazardous Materials Training	25,380	24,870	30,197 e	25,000 e
20.710	Pipeline Safety Technical Assistance	948	1,383	1,500 e	(nr)
20.720	State Damage Prevention Grants	1,531	1,538	1,619 e	1,500 e
20.721	Pipeline Safety	1,069	1,066	1,018 e	(nr)

Please see "Important Notes on the Tables, Footnotes," page 888

Table 1. *(continued)*

Program Number	ADMINISTRATIVE ENTITY Program Title (abridged)	FY 2013 in $thousands	FY 2014 in $thousands	FY 2015 in $thousands	FY 2016 in $thousands
20.723	Pipeline Safety Research and Development	8,224	9,824	12,000 e	4,000 e
20.724	Pipeline Safety Research	793	700	2,000 e	(nr)
20.761	Biobased Transportation	0	0	0 e	0 e
20.762	Research Grants	0	0	0 e	0 e
20.802	Federal Ship Financing \ u	0	0	336,630 e	576,700 e
		0*	3,500*	3,200*e	0*e
20.803	Maritime War Risk Insurance \ u	0*	0*	0*	0*
20.806	State Marine Schools	16,206	17,300	18,500 e	(nr)
20.807	U.S. Merchant Marine Academy	81,788	140	146 e	(nr)
20.808	Capital Construction Fund	0	0	0 e	0 e
20.812	Construction Reserve Fund	0	0	0 e	0 e
20.813	Maritime Security Fleet Program	160,289	90,800	0 e	0 e
20.814	Small Shipyard Assistance	9,980	0	0 e	0 e
20.817	Air Emissions and Energy Initiative	1,900	2,127	2,096 e	(nr)
20.818	Great Ships Initiative	2,290	179	200 e	(nr)
20.819	Ballast Water Treatment Technologies	2,944	2,475	1,000 e	0 e
20.901	Essential Air Services \ t	255,000	269,000	266,078 e	(nr)
20.904	Bonding Assistance	7,173	6,245	(nr)	(nr)
20.905	Disadvantaged—Short-Term Lending	8,500*	925*	925*e	925*e
20.910	Small Business Assistance	1,648	1,900	1,900 e	1,900 e
20.930	Small Community Air Service \ t	11,404	6,000	5,500 e	(nr)
20.931	Transportation Planning	1,495	9,743	(nr)	(nr)
20.934	Significant Freight/Highway Projects	(n)	(n)	(n)	800,000 e
	DEPARTMENT TOTAL: OUTLAYS	61,696,028	61,260,872	55,925,395	63,671,366
	CREDITS*	2,613,163*	8,434,626*	14,367,225*	13,296,925*

DEPARTMENT OF THE TREASURY

Program Number	Program Title (abridged)	FY 2013	FY 2014	FY 2015	FY 2016
21.004	Federal Tax Information/States	0	0	(nr)	(nr)
21.006	Tax Counseling/Elderly	5,600	5,300	7,000 e	6,500 e
21.008	Low-Income Taxpayer Clinics	(nr)	10,000	10,000	12,000 e
21.009	Volunteer Income Tax Assistance Grants	12,070	11,600	12,000	15,000 e
21.012	Native Initiatives	(nr)	12,000	(nr)	(nr)
21.014	CDFI Bond Guarantee Program	500* e	500*e	(nr)	(nr)
21.015	Gulf Coast States Resources	(nr)	(nr)	(nr)	(nr)
21.020	Community Development Program	150,000	(nr)	(nr)	(nr)
21.021	Bank Enterprise Award	17,049	18,000 e	(nr)	(nr)
	DEPARTMENT TOTAL: OUTLAYS	184,719	56,900	29,000	33,500
	CREDITS*	500*	500*	0*	0*

APPALACHIAN REGIONAL COMMISSION

Program Number	Program Title (abridged)	FY 2013	FY 2014	FY 2015	FY 2016
23.001	Appalachian Regional Development	73,000 e	(nr)	(nr)	(nr)
23.002	Appalachian Area Development	73,000 e	64,582	79,000 e	84,000 e
23.003	Highway System	470,000 e	(nr)	(nr)	(nr)
23.009	Development District Assistance	7,000 e	7,150	7,000 e	7,000 e
23.011	Research, Technical Assistance	1,000 e	893	1,000 e	1,000 e
	DEPARTMENT TOTAL: OUTLAYS	624,000	72,625	87,000	92,000
	CREDITS*	0*	0*	0*	0*

OFFICE OF PERSONNEL MANAGEMENT

Program Number	Program Title (abridged)	FY 2013	FY 2014	FY 2015	FY 2016
27.001	Federal Civil Service	(a)	(a)	(a)	(a)
27.002	Employment Assistance/Veterans	(a)	(a)	(a)	(a)
27.003	Federal Student Employment	(a)	(a)	(a)	(a)
27.005	Federal Employment/Disabled	(a)	(a)	(a)	(a)
27.006	Federal Summer Employment	(a)	(a)	(a)	(a)
27.011	Intergovernmental Mobility	(a)	(a)	(a)	(a)
27.013	Presidential Management Intern \ r	(a)	(a)	(a)	(a)
	DEPARTMENT TOTAL: OUTLAYS	0	0	0	0
	CREDITS*	0*	0*	0*	0*

Please see "Important Notes on the Tables, Footnotes," page 888

Table 1. *(continued)*

Program Number	ADMINISTRATIVE ENTITY Program Title (abridged)		FY 2013 in $thousands	FY 2014 in $thousands	FY 2015 in $thousands	FY 2016 in $thousands
	COMMISSION ON CIVIL RIGHTS					
29.001	Clearinghouse Services		(nr)	(nr)	(nr)	(nr)
	DEPARTMENT TOTAL:	OUTLAYS	0	0	0	0
		CREDITS*	0*	0*	0*	0*
	EQUAL EMPLOYMENT OPPORTUNITY COMMISSION					
30.001	Title VII/Civil Rights \ i		344,219	364,000	364,500	373,112
30.005	Private Bar Program		(nr)	(nr)	(nr)	(nr)
30.008	Age Discrimination		(nr)	(nr)	(nr)	(nr)
30.010	Discrimination Equal Pay Act		(nr)	(nr)	(nr)	(nr)
30.011	Title I ADA, Investigations		(nr)	(nr)	(nr)	(nr)
	DEPARTMENT TOTAL:	OUTLAYS	344,219	364,000	364,500	373,112
		CREDITS*	0*	0*	0*	0*
	EXPORT-IMPORT BANK					
31.007	Export Loan Guarantee		(nr)	(nr)	(nr)	(nr)
	DEPARTMENT TOTAL:	OUTLAYS	0	0	0	0
		CREDITS*	0*	0*	0*	0*
	FEDERAL COMMUNICATIONS COMMISSION					
32.001	Information, Investigation		(a)	(a)	(a)	(a)
	DEPARTMENT TOTAL:	OUTLAYS	0	0	0	0
		CREDITS*	0*	0*	0*	0*
	FEDERAL MARITIME COMMISSION					
33.001	Shipping—Complaints		1,840	1,761	1,846 e	1,985 e
	DEPARTMENT TOTAL:	OUTLAYS	1,840	1,761	1,846	1,985
		CREDITS*	0*	0*	0*	0*
	FEDERAL MEDIATION AND CONCILIATION SERVICE					
34.001	Labor Mediation, Conciliation		(nr)	(nr)	(nr)	(nr)
34.002	Labor Management Cooperation		0	400	800	400 e
	DEPARTMENT TOTAL:	OUTLAYS	0	400	800	400
		CREDITS*	0*	0*	0*	0*
	FEDERAL TRADE COMMISSION					
36.001	Fair Competition Counseling		(nr)	(nr)	(nr)	(nr)
	DEPARTMENT TOTAL:	OUTLAYS	0	0	0	0
		CREDITS*	0*	0*	0*	0*
	GENERAL SERVICES ADMINISTRATION					
39.002	Real Property Disposal \ p		4,595	8,645 e	8,244 e	(nr)
39.003	Personal Property Donation \ p		8,892	8,164	(nr)	(nr)
39.007	Personal Property Sale \ p, r		8,921	9,108 e	(nr)	(nr)
39.012	Public Buildings Service		(nr)	(nr)	(nr)	(nr)
	DEPARTMENT TOTAL:	OUTLAYS	22,408	25,917	8,244	0
		CREDITS*	0*	0*	0*	0*

Please see "Important Notes on the Tables, Footnotes," page 888

Table 1. *(continued)*

Program Number	ADMINISTRATIVE ENTITY Program Title (abridged)		FY 2013 in $thousands	FY 2014 in $thousands	FY 2015 in $thousands	FY 2016 in $thousands
	GOVERNMENT PRINTING OFFICE					
40.001	Depository Libraries		(nr)	(nr)	(nr)	(nr)
40.002	Government Publications Sales \ p, r		(nr)	(nr)	(nr)	(nr)
	DEPARTMENT TOTAL:	OUTLAYS	0	0	0	0
		CREDITS*	0*	0*	0*	0*
	LIBRARY OF CONGRESS					
42.001	Books for the Blind, Handicapped		(nr)	(nr)	(nr)	(nr)
42.002	Copyright Service \ i, u		(nr)	(nr)	(nr)	(nr)
42.008	Semiconductor Chip Protection \ u		(nr)	(nr)	(nr)	(nr)
42.009	Vessel Hull Design Protection \ u		(nr)	(nr)	(nr)	(nr)
	DEPARTMENT TOTAL:	OUTLAYS	0	0	0	0
		CREDITS*	0*	0*	0*	0*
	NATIONAL AERONAUTICS AND SPACE ADMINISTRATION					
43.001	Aerospace Education Services		(nr)	652,408	654,847 e	653,000 e
43.002	Technology Transfer		(nr)	39,017	41,899 e	40,000 e
43.003	Exploration Research, Outreach, Training		(nr)	27,308	28,680 e	28,000 e
43.007	Space Operations-Education Assistance		(nr)	(nr)	(nr)	(nr)
43.008	NASA Education		(nr)	(nr)	(nr)	(nr)
43.009	Cross Agency Support		(nr)	(nr)	(nr)	(nr)
43.010	Construction and Environmental Compliance		(nr)	(nr)	(nr)	(nr)
	DEPARTMENT TOTAL:	OUTLAYS	0	718,733	725,426	721,000
		CREDITS*	0*	0*	0*	0*
	NATIONAL CREDIT UNION ADMINISTRATION					
44.002	Revolving Loan Program \ u		(nr)	(nr)	2,528 e	2,400 e
			3,000* e	(nr)	1,500* e	1,500* e
	DEPARTMENT TOTAL:	OUTLAYS	0	0	2,528	2,400
		CREDITS*	3,000*	0*	1,500*	1,500*
	NATIONAL FOUNDATION ON THE ARTS AND HUMANITIES					
45.024	Organizations and Individuals		65,655	66,314	68,117 e	69,174 e
45.025	Partnership Agreements		47,172	48,661	49,778 e	49,800 e
45.129	Federal-State Partnership		(nr)	43,432	(nr)	(nr)
45.130	Challenge Grants		7,920 e	8,850 e	(nr)	(nr)
45.149	Preservation and Access		17,442	15,460	15,628	(nr)
45.160	Fellowships and Stipends		4,960	5,045 e	5,056 e	(nr)
45.161	Research		8,422	9,707 e	9,728 e	(nr)
45.162	Teaching, Learning, Curriculum		1,694 e	1,433	(nr)	(nr)
45.163	Professional Development		11,856 e	(nr)	(nr)	(nr)
45.164	Public Programs		14,328	13,684	13,454 e	(nr)
45.169	Digital Humanities Initiative		4,250 e	(nr)	(nr)	(nr)
45.201	Arts and Artifacts Indemnity		(a)	(a)	(a)	(a)
45.301	Museum for America Grants		19,564	20,200	20,200	21,457 e
45.308	Native American/Hawaiian Museum		877	924	924	972 e
45.309	African American History Grants		1,336	1,407	1,407	1,481 e
45.310	State Library Program		150,000	154,848	154,848 e	154,500 e
45.311	Native American, Hawaiian Library		3,667	3,861	3,861	4,063 e
45.312	National Leadership Grants		18,845	19,800	19,800	28,668 e
45.313	Librarians for the 21st Century		10,000	10,000	10,000	10,500 e
45.400	Peace Corps—Global Health and PEPFAR Initiative Program		(nr)	(nr)	(nr)	(nr)
	DEPARTMENT TOTAL:	OUTLAYS	387,988	423,626	372,801	340,615
		CREDITS*	0*	0*	0*	0*

Please see "Important Notes on the Tables, Footnotes," page 888

Table 1. *(continued)*

Program Number	ADMINISTRATIVE ENTITY Program Title (abridged)	FY 2013 in $thousands	FY 2014 in $thousands	FY 2015 in $thousands	FY 2016 in $thousands
	NATIONAL SCIENCE FOUNDATION				
47.041	Engineering Grants	876,330 e	833,122	892,310 e	949,220 e
47.049	Mathematical, Physical Sciences	1,345,180 e	1,267,860	1,336,720 e	1,366,230 e
47.050	Geosciences	2,586,980 e	1,321,320	1,304,390 e	1,365,410 e
47.070	Computer, Information Science	858,530 e	892,726	892,604 e	921,730 e
47.074	Biological Sciences	733,860 e	720,837	731,029 e	747,920 e
47.075	Social, Behavioral, Economic	259,550 e	256,840	272,200 e	291,460 e
47.076	Education and Human Resources	875,610 e	832,023	866,000 e	962,570 e
47.078	Polar Programs	449,740 e	(a)	(a)	(a)
47.079	International Science, Engineering	482,800 e	48,306	48,520 e	51,020 e
47.080	Office of Cyberinfrastructure	218,270 e	(nr)	(nr)	(nr)
47.081	Competitive Research	(a)	(a)	(a)	(a)
47.082	Trans-NSF Recovery Act Research Support	(nr)	(nr)	(nr)	(nr)
47.083	Office of Integrative Activities	(n)	274,933	265,650 e	289,160 e
	DEPARTMENT TOTAL: OUTLAYS	8,686,850	6,447,967	6,609,423	6,944,720
	CREDITS*	0*	0*	0*	0*
	RAILROAD RETIREMENT BOARD				
57.001	Social Insurance/Railroad Workers \ t	11,747,000	12,037,000	12,303,000 e	12,503,000 e
	DEPARTMENT TOTAL: OUTLAYS	11,747,000	12,037,000	12,303,000	12,503,000
	CREDITS*	0*	0*	0*	0*
	SECURITIES AND EXCHANGE COMMISSION				
58.001	Investigation of Complaints	(nr)	(nr)	(nr)	(nr)
	DEPARTMENT TOTAL: OUTLAYS	0	0	0	0
	CREDITS*	0*	0*	0*	0*
	SMALL BUSINESS ADMINISTRATION				
59.006	8(a) Business Development	(nr)	(nr)	(nr)	(nr)
59.007	7(j) Technical Assistance	(nr)	2,723	2,800 e	2,800 e
59.008	Physical Disaster Loans	(nr)	(nr)	(nr)	(nr)
59.011	Small Business Investment Companies	(nr)	2,549,000*	4,000,000*e	4,000,000*e
59.012	Small Business Loans	(nr)	17,875,000*	23,500,000*e	23,500,000*e
59.016	Bond Guarantees \ u	(nr)	1,386,000*	6,000,000*e	6,000,000*e
59.026	Service Corps of Retired Executives	(nr)	7,000	8,000 e	8,000 e
59.037	Small Business Development Center	(nr)	110,514	115,000 e	115,000 e
59.041	Certified Development Company Loans	(nr)	4,184,000*	7,500,000*e	7,500,000*e
59.043	Womenís Business Ownership	(nr)	13,982	15,000 e	16,000 e
59.044	Veterans Entrepreneurial Training	(nr)	3,090	3,000 e	3,000 e
59.046	Microloan Program	(nr)	26,000*	25,000*e	35,000*e
59.050	Microenterprise Development Grants	(nr)	3,500	5,000 e	(nr)
59.052	Native American Economic Development	(nr)	1,589	2,000 e	2,000 e
59.053	Ombudsman, Fairness Boards	(nr)	(nr)	(nr)	(nr)
59.054	7(a) Export Loans	(nr)	1,300,000*	(nr)	(nr)
59.055	Historically Underutilized Business Zones	(nr)	2,248	3,000 e	3,000 e
59.058	Federal and State Technology Partnership	(nr)	2,000	2,000 e	(nr)
59.062	Intermediary Loan Program	(nr)	(nr)	(nr)	(nr)
59.063	Disaster Assistance Loans	0*	302,000*	1,100,000*e	1,100,000*e
59.065	Growth Accelerator Fund Competition	(n)	2,500	4,000 e	5,000 e
	DEPARTMENT TOTAL: OUTLAYS	0	149,146	159,800	154,800
	CREDITS*	0*	27,622,000*	42,125,000*	42,135,000*

Please see "Important Notes on the Tables, Footnotes," page 888

Table 1. *(continued)*

Program Number	ADMINISTRATIVE ENTITY Program Title (abridged)	FY 2013 in $thousands	FY 2014 in $thousands	FY 2015 in $thousands	FY 2016 in $thousands
	DEPARTMENT OF VETERANS AFFAIRS				
64.005	Construction/State Homes	(nr)	(nr)	(nr)	(nr)
64.007	Blind Rehabilitation Centers	(nr)	(nr)	(nr)	(nr)
64.008	Veterans Domiciliary Care	(nr)	(nr)	(nr)	(nr)
64.009	Veterans Medical Care Benefits	(nr)	(nr)	(nr)	(nr)
64.010	Veterans Nursing Home Care	(nr)	(nr)	(nr)	(nr)
64.011	Veterans Dental Care	(nr)	(nr)	(nr)	(nr)
64.012	Veterans Prescription Service \ p	(nr)	(nr)	(nr)	(nr)
64.013	Veterans Prosthetic Appliances \ p	(nr)	(nr)	(nr)	(nr)
64.014	Veterans State Domiciliary Care	(nr)	(nr)	(nr)	(nr)
64.015	Veterans State Nursing Homes	(nr)	(nr)	(nr)	(nr)
64.016	Veterans State Hospital Care	(nr)	(nr)	(nr)	(nr)
64.018	Sharing Specialized Medical Resources	(nr)	(nr)	(nr)	(nr)
64.019	Alcohol and Drug Dependence	(nr)	(nr)	(nr)	(nr)
64.022	Home Based Primary Care	(nr)	(nr)	(nr)	(nr)
64.024	Homeless Providers Grants	(nr)	(nr)	(nr)	(nr)
64.026	State Adult Day Health Care	(nr)	(nr)	(nr)	(nr)
64.027	Post-9/11 Veterans Education Payments	(a)	(a)	(a)	(a)
64.028	Post-9/11 Veterans Education Agreements	(a)	(a)	(a)	(a)
64.029	Purchase Care Program	(nr)	(nr)	(nr)	(nr)
64.030	Life Insurance for Veterans - New Policies	(nr)	(nr)	(nr)	(nr)
64.031	Life Insurance for Veterans - Direct Payments	(nr)	(nr)	(nr)	(nr)
64.033	VA Supportive Services-Veteran Families	(nr)	(nr)	(nr)	(nr)
64.036	Veterans Retraining Assistance	(nr)	(nr)	(nr)	(nr)
64.037	VA Paralympics Monthly Assistance Allowance	2,000 e	(nr)	(nr)	(nr)
64.038	Rural Veterans Coordination Pilot Grants	(a)	(a)	(a)	(a)
64.051	Housing Assistive Technology	(n)	(n)	(n)	1,000 e
64.100	Automobiles, Adaptive Equipment	(nr)	(nr)	(nr)	(nr)
64.101	Burial Expenses Allowance	(nr)	(nr)	(nr)	(nr)
64.103	Life Insurance \ t, u	(nr)	(nr)	(nr)	(nr)
64.104	Pension/Non-Service Connected	(nr)	(nr)	(nr)	(nr)
64.105	Pension/Survivors	(nr)	(nr)	(nr)	(nr)
64.106	Specially Adapted Housing	(nr)	(nr)	(nr)	(nr)
64.109	Service-Connected Disability	(nr)	(nr)	(nr)	(nr)
64.110	Dependency, Indemnity Compensation	(nr)	(nr)	(nr)	(nr)
64.114	Veterans Housing—Loans \ u	(nr)	(nr)	(nr)	(nr)
64.115	Veterans Information, Assistance	(a)	(a)	(a)	(a)
64.116	Vocational Rehabilitation \ u	(nr)	(nr)	(nr)	(nr)
		(nr)	(nr)	(nr)	(nr)
64.117	Dependents Educational Assistance	(nr)	(nr)	(nr)	(nr)
64.118	Housing—Disabled Veterans \ u	(nr)	(nr)	(nr)	(nr)
64.119	Manufactured Home Loans \ u	(nr)	(nr)	(nr)	(nr)
64.120	Post-Vietnam Era Educational \ t	(nr)	(nr)	(nr)	(nr)
64.124	All-Volunteer Force Educational	(nr)	(nr)	(nr)	(nr)
64.125	Vocational, Educational Counseling	(nr)	(nr)	(nr)	(nr)
64.126	Native American Direct Loan \ u	(nr)	(nr)	(nr)	(nr)
64.127	Allowance/Spina Bifida	(nr)	(nr)	(nr)	(nr)
64.128	Training/Spina Bifida	(nr)	(nr)	(nr)	(nr)
64.201	National Cemeteries	(nr)	(nr)	(nr)	(nr)
64.202	Headstones, Markers, Certificates	(nr)	(nr)	(nr)	(nr)
64.203	State Cemetery Grants	(nr)	(nr)	(nr)	(nr)
	DEPARTMENT TOTAL: OUTLAYS	2,000	0	0	1,000
	CREDITS*	0*	0*	0*	0*
	ENVIRONMENTAL PROTECTION AGENCY				
66.001	Air Pollution Control Support	223,437	223,437	228,219 e	243,229 e
66.032	State Indoor Radon Grants	7,626	8,051	8,051 e	8,051 e
66.033	Ozone Transport	639	639	639 e	639 e
66.034	Surveys, Studies/Clean Air Act	5,950	8,202	8,125 e	6,495 e
66.037	Air and Radiation Training	540	450	2,087 e	450 e

Please see "Important Notes on the Tables, Footnotes," page 888

Table 1. *(continued)*

Program Number	ADMINISTRATIVE ENTITY Program Title (abridged)	FY 2013 in $thousands	FY 2014 in $thousands	FY 2015 in $thousands	FY 2016 in $thousands
66.038	Air Quality—Native American	12,560	12,830	12,745 e	11,896 e
66.039	Clean Diesel—National	13,000	15,000	18,000 e	35,000 e
66.040	Clean Diesel—State	4,900	4,400	7,500 e	16,000 e
66.042	Ecosystem Monitoring-TIME/LTM	391	380	380 e	380 e
66.043	Regional Healthy Indoor Air Projects	800	0	0 e	0 e
66.110	Healthy Communities Grant Program	(nr)	341	0 e	0 e
66.121	Puget Sound Protection-Tribal Implementation	7,571	6,440	9,490	(nr)
66.122	Puget Sound Stewardship Support	989	0	0 e	0 e
66.123	Puget Sound Action Agenda Assistance	17,248	15,763	15,672 e	(nr)
66.124	Coastal Wetlands Planning/Protection/ Restoration	2,810	2,560	363 e	(nr)
66.126	San Francisco Bay Water Quality Improvement	5,235	4,819	4,481 e	(nr)
66.128	Southeastern Pollution Prevention	85	15	0 e	15 e
66.129	New England Coastal Watershed Restoration	(n)	2,000	2,500 e	7,000 e
66.202	Congressionally Mandated Projects	0	0	0 e	0 e
66.203	Environmental Finance Center Grants	617	500	1,000 e	2,000 e
66.305	Compliance Assistance-Support	275	360	260 e	260 e
66.309	Surveys, Studies, Investigations \ t	0	0	35 e	0
66.310	Compliance Assurance/Indian Country	185	185	185 e	185 e
66.418	Wastewater Treatment Works	26,848	26,848	27,576 e	27,000 e
66.419	Water Pollution Control	2,259,673	233,509	229,293 e	249,164 e
66.424	Surveys/Safe Drinking Water Act	11,863	11,863	9,800 e	10,000 e
66.432	Public Water System Supervision	94,983	101,963	101,294 e	109,700 e
66.433	Underground Water Source Protection	8,583	89,274	10,291 e	10,291 e
66.436	Surveys, Studies/Clean Water Act	3,861	22,693	4,290 e	3,963 e
66.437	Long Island Sound Program	3,681	3,904	3,904 e	2,488 e
66.439	Targeted Watershed Grants	0	0	0 e	0 e
66.440	Urban Waters Small Grants	794	2,100	0 e	1,600 e
66.454	Water Quality Management Planning	14,131	11,700	14,676 e	11,822 e
66.456	National Estuary Program	14,336	15,065	16,440 e	(nr)
66.458	Clean Water State Revolving Funds \ r	1,396,117	1,992,227	1,394,333 e	1,118,000 e
66.460	Nonpoint Source Implementation	157,767	155,708	159,252 e	169,915 e
66.461	Regional Wetland Program Development	13,053	12,290	14,161 e	19,161 e
66.462	National Wetland Program Development	1,500	1,900	6,600 e	1,000 e
66.466	Chesapeake Bay Program	38,190	42,037	55,066 e	51,111 e
66.467	Wastewater Operator Training	0	0	0 e	0 e
66.468	Drinking Water/Revolving Fund \ r	896,333	972,910	900,950 e	1,182,000 e
66.469	Great Lakes Program	99,984	96,672	89,827 e	90,000 e
66.472	Beach Monitoring and Notification	9,452	9,629	9,549 e	0 e
66.473	Direct Implementation/Tribal	556	612	550 e	550 e
66.474	Water Protection Grants to States	0	0	0 e	0 e
66.475	Gulf of Mexico Program	1,356	3,122	1,547 e	1,228 e
66.481	Lake Champlain Basin Project	2,268	1,399	4,396 e	1,399 e
66.508	Senior Environmental Employment	89,156	48,400	50,000 e	50,000 e
66.509	Science to Achieve Results	37,200	44,200	39,100 e	48,800 e
66.510	Surveys, Studies/Office of Research	1,600	1,700	2,100 e	1,800 e
66.511	Consolidated Research, Training	12,300	21,900	16,800 e	17,000 e
66.513	Greater Opportunities Fellowship	1,700	1,100	1,500 e	0 e
66.514	STAR Fellowship Program	9,300	8,000	7,200 e	0 e
66.516	Design Competition/Sustainability	2,500	1,200	1,000 e	1,000 e
66.517	Regional Applied Research Efforts	500	200	100 e	0 e
66.518	State Senior Environmental Employment	140	280	250 e	250 e
66.600	Consolidated Grants—Program Support	29,300	27,000	28,000 e	28,000 e
66.604	Environmental Justice Small Grant \ t	1,200	0	1,200 e	0 e
66.605	Performance Partnership Grants	421,107	438,000	445,000 e	449,000 e
66.608	Information Exchange Network	9,494	9,860	9,751	9,700
66.609	Health Protection/Children, Elderly	0	0	0 e	0 e
66.610	Surveys/Office of Administrator	155	83	225 e	(nr)
66.611	Environmental Policy, Innovation	635	800	800 e	800 e
66.612	Toxic Chemical Information	275	175	175 e	200 e
66.700	Pesticide Enforcement	17,672	18,050	17,932	18,050 e
66.701	Toxic Substances Compliance	4,816	4,919	4,887 e	4,919 e
66.707	TSCA State Lead Grants	13,755	13,500	14,000	14,049
66.708	Pollution Prevention Grants	4,347	4,790	4,790 e	4,790 e

Please see "Important Notes on the Tables, Footnotes," page 888

Table 1. *(continued)*

Program Number	ADMINISTRATIVE ENTITY Program Title (abridged)	FY 2013 in $thousands	FY 2014 in $thousands	FY 2015 in $thousands	FY 2016 in $thousands
66.714	Pesticide Environmental Stewardship	459	11	0 e	0 e
66.716	Surveys, Studies, Training	7,851	913	1,000 e	1,000 e
66.717	Source Reduction Assistance	744	913	1,000 e	1,000 e
66.801	Hazardous Waste Management	97,777	98,153	99,693 e	99,693 e
66.802	Superfund—Site Specific \ t	48,000	56,000	40,000 e	40,000 e
66.804	Underground Storage Tanks	30,326	54,254	53,714 e	60,714 e
66.805	Leaking Storage Tank Trust Fund\ t	57,290	56,849	56,169 e	54,402 e
66.806	TAG/Community Groups/NPL Sites	370	410	250 e	200 e
66.808	Solid Waste Management Assistance	146	44	50 e	50 e
66.809	Superfund/Core Program	6,300	5,400	7,000 e	7,000 e
66.812	Hazardous Waste Management/Tribes	298	298	295 e	300 e
66.813	Treatment Technology Research	385	490	500 e	500 e
66.814	Brownfields Agreements	6,325	3,663	5,000 e	10,600 e
66.815	Brownfield Job Training	3,200	3,600	3,600 e	(nr)
66.816	Underground Storage Tanks \ t	816	884	1,109 e	(nr)
66.817	State and Tribal Response	46,700	47,745	47,745 e	47,745 e
66.818	Brownfields Assessment, Cleanup	62,500	59,000	(nr)	66,000 e
66.926	Indian Environmental GAP	64,000	65,600	65,000 e	96,400 e
66.931	International Financial Assistance	1,686	1,686	2,500 e	2,500 e
66.950	Environmental Education, Training	2,425	1,828	2,176 e	(nr)
66.951	Environmental Education Grants	2,779	3,307	3,307 e	3,000 e
66.952	Environmental Management Fellowship	250	0	0 e	0 e
	DEPARTMENT TOTAL: OUTLAYS	6,457,966	5,219,002	4,408,445	4,531,454
	CREDITS*	0*	0*	0*	0*

NATIONAL GALLERY OF ART

Program Number	Program Title	FY 2013	FY 2014	FY 2015	FY 2016
68.001	Art Extension Service	(nr)	(nr)	(nr)	(nr)
	DEPARTMENT TOTAL: OUTLAYS	0	0	0	0
	CREDITS*	0*	0*	0*	0*

OVERSEAS PRIVATE INVESTMENT CORPORATION

Program Number	Program Title	FY 2013	FY 2014	FY 2015	FY 2016
70.002	Foreign Investment Financing \ u	(nr)	(nr)	(nr)	(nr)
70.003	Foreign Investment Insurance \ u	(nr)	(nr)	(nr)	(nr)
	DEPARTMENT TOTAL: OUTLAYS	0	0	0	0
	CREDITS*	0*	0*	0*	0*

NUCLEAR REGULATORY COMMISSION

Program Number	Program Title	FY 2013	FY 2014	FY 2015	FY 2016
77.006	Nuclear Education Grants	0	1,800	0 e	(nr)
77.007	Minority Serving Institutions	(nr)	(nr)	1,400 e	(nr)
77.008	Scholarship and Fellowship, Science	14,400	15,000	15,000 e	(nr)
77.009	NRC Office of Research Financial Assistance	1,200	3,200	2,832 e	(nr)
	DEPARTMENT TOTAL: OUTLAYS	15,600	20,000	19,232	0
	CREDITS*	0*	0*	0*	0*

COMMODITY FUTURES TRADING COMMISSION

Program Number	Program Title	FY 2013	FY 2014	FY 2015	FY 2016
78.004	Commodity Futures Reparations	(nr)	(nr)	(nr)	(nr)
	DEPARTMENT TOTAL: OUTLAYS	0	0	0	0
	CREDITS*	0*	0*	0*	0*

DEPARTMENT OF ENERGY

Program Number	Program Title	FY 2013	FY 2014	FY 2015	FY 2016
81.003	Granting of Patent Licenses	(a)	(a)	(a)	(a)
81.022	Energy-Related Equipment \ p	0	0	0 e	0 e

Please see "Important Notes on the Tables, Footnotes," page 888

Table 1. *(continued)*

Program Number	ADMINISTRATIVE ENTITY Program Title (abridged)	FY 2013 in $thousands	FY 2014 in $thousands	FY 2015 in $thousands	FY 2016 in $thousands
81.036	Inventions and Innovations	1,045	0	0 e	0 e
81.041	State Energy Program	36,409	39,000	26,593 e	(nr)
81.042	Weatherization Assistance	118,095	180,420	167,502 e	(nr)
81.049	Office of Science	965,085	1,133,670	1,124,690 e	(nr)
81.057	University Coal Research	2,399	2,396	2,400 e	2,700 e
81.064	Scientific, Technical Information	8,300	8,400 e	8,700 e	(nr)
81.079	Regional Biomass Programs	0	0	0 e	0 e
81.086	Conservation Research, Development	163,991	38,466	0 e	0 e
81.087	Renewable Energy Research	356,633	157,717	0 e	0 e
81.089	Fossil Energy Research, Development	498,715	535,512	547,043 e	495,360 e
81.104	Office of Environmental Cleanup	10,116	17,424	14,000 e	14,510 e
81.105	National Industrial Competitiveness	(nr)	(nr)	(nr)	(nr)
81.106	Transport/Transuranic Waste	(nr)	6,446	11,319 e	11,989 e
81.108	Epidemiology, Health Studies	25,000 e	25,137	25,147 e	25,147 e
81.112	Stewardship Science	97,239	107,750	110,000 e	100,000 e
81.113	Nuclear Nonproliferation Research	(nr)	24,459	5,000 e	15,000 e
81.117	Energy Efficiency—Renewable	36,107	27,078	12,737 e	(nr)
81.119	State Energy Special Projects	1,059	4,815	4,798 e	(nr)
81.121	Nuclear Energy Research, Development	258,945	175,081	172,263 e	180,000 e
81.122	Electricity Delivery, Reliability	27,008	30	0 e	(nr)
81.123	HBCU Program	(nr)	14,531	14,640 e	16,500 e
81.124	Predictive Science	11,600	18,000	18,000 e	18,000 e
81.126	Innovative Energy Loans \ u	(nr)	(nr)	(nr)	(nr)
81.127	Energy Efficient Appliance Rebate	0	0	0 e	0 e
81.128	Energy Efficiency and Conservation	0	0	0 e	0 e
81.129	Renewable Energy Technology Deployment	0	0	0 e	0 e
81.135	Energy Financial Assistance	169	264,222	270,000 e	270,000 e
81.136	Atomic Energy Long-Term Maintenance	3,339 e	(nr)	(nr)	(nr)
81.139	Environmental Management R&D	(nr)	1,000	1,000 e	1,000 e
81.214	Environmental Monitoring/Cleanup	400	7,848	9,216 e	8,792 e
	DEPARTMENT TOTAL: OUTLAYS	2,621,654	2,789,402	2,545,048	1,158,998
	CREDITS*	0*	0*	0*	0*

	DEPARTMENT OF EDUCATION				
84.002	Adult Education—State Grant	594,993	563,955	568,955 e	568,955 e
84.004	Civil Rights Training	6,599	6,598	6,575 e	6,575 e
84.007	Educational Opportunity Grants	926,107	976,513	976,513 e	976,513 e
84.010	Title I Grants	13,760,219	14,384,802	14,384,802 e	14,409,802 e
84.011	Migrant Education	372,751	374,751	374,751 e	374,751 e
84.013	Neglected and Delinquent Children	47,614	47,614	47,614 e	47,614 e
84.015	Language, Area Studies	52,617	53,082	53,082 e	53,082 e
84.016	Undergraduate International Studies	1,570	2,928	2,928 e	2,928 e
84.018	Overseas—Bilateral Projects	639	646	661 e	601 e
84.021	Overseas—Group Projects Abroad	3,288	3,274	3,261 e	3,261 e
84.022	Overseas—Doctoral Dissertation	3,036	3,029	3,012 e	3,012 e
84.027	Special Education—State Grants	10,974,866	11,472,848	11,497,848	11,912,848 e
84.031	Higher Education—Institutional Aid	732,482	745,411	743,299 e	745,394 e
84.033	Work-Study Program	1,100,271	1,158,522	1,176,350 e	1,176,350 e
84.040	Impact Aid—Facilities Maintenance	4,591	4,835	4,835 e	4,835 e
84.041	Impact Aid	1,219,058	1,283,768	1,283,768 e	1,283,768 e
84.042	TRIO—Student Support Services	281,706	281,666	297,494 e	297,494 e
84.044	TRIO—Talent Search	128,117	134,614	135,134 e	134,662 e
84.047	TRIO—Upward Bound	303,082	321,689	322,292 e	322,292 e
84.048	Vocational Education—States	1,047,095	1,099,381	1,099,381 e	1,099,381 e
84.051	Vocational Education—National	7,421	7,421	7,421 e	7,421 e
84.060	Indian Education—LEAs	100,381	100,381	100,381 e	100,381 e
84.063	Pell Grant Program	32,351,695	30,998,135	31,326,815 e	32,333,945 e
84.066	TRIO—Educational Opportunity	44,064	46,880	46,925 e	46,904 e
84.101	Vocational Education—Indians	13,306	13,970	13,970 e	13,970
84.103	TRIO Staff Training Program	1,327	1,525	1,525 e	1,400 e
84.116	Fund/Postsecondary Education	3,311	79,400	67,775 e	200,000 e

Please see "Important Notes on the Tables, Footnotes," page 888

Table 1. *(continued)*

Program Number	ADMINISTRATIVE ENTITY Program Title (abridged)	FY 2013 in $thousands	FY 2014 in $thousands	FY 2015 in $thousands	FY 2016 in $thousands
84.120	Minority Science, Engineering	8,778	8,971	8,971 e	8,971 e
84.126	Rehabilitation Services—State	2,947,422	3,027,104	3,052,454 e	3,121,305 e
84.129	Rehabilitation Training	118	17,075	17,464 e	19,468
84.141	Migrant Education—High School	18,836	18,836	20,387 e	20,387 e
84.144	Migrant Education—Coordination	3,000	3,000	3,000 e	3,000 e
84.145	Federal Real Property Assistance \ p	(a)	(a)	(a)	(a)
84.149	Migrant Education—College	15,614	15,614	16,900 e	16,900 e
84.160	Training Interpreters for Deaf	2,100	2,100	19,800 e	2,100 e
84.161	Rehabilitation—Client Assistance	11,600	12,000	13,000 e	13,000 e
84.165	Magnet Schools	91,647	91,647	91,647 e	91,647 e
84.173	Special Education—Preschool	353,238	353,238	353,238	368,238 e
84.177	Rehabilitation Services—Blind	32,239	33,317	33,317 e	33,317 e
84.181	Infants, Families/Disabilities	419,653	438,498	438,556 e	503,556 e
84.184	Drug Free Schools—National	61,484	90,000	70,000 e	0 e
84.187	Supported Employment	27,548	27,548	27,548 e	30,548 e
84.191	Adult Education—National Leadership	10,712	13,712	13,712 e	19,712 e
84.196	Homeless Children, Youth	61,771	65,042	65,042 e	65,042 e
84.200	Graduate Assistance/National Need	29,293	29,293	29,293 e	29,233 e
84.215	Improvement of Education	38,687	42,376	48,000 e	41,926 e
84.217	TRIO/Post-Baccalaureate	34,060	46,037	30,264 e	30,701 e
84.220	International Business Education	5,468	4,571	4,571 e	4,571 e
84.229	Language Resource Centers	2,431	2,747	2,747 e	2,747 e
84.235	Rehabilitation Services/Training	5,046	5,796	5,796 e	5,796 e
84.240	Protection and Advocacy	17,088	17,650	17,650 e	17,650 e
84.245	Tribal Vocational/Technical	7,705	7,705	7,705 e	7,705 e
84.246	Rehabilitation Short-Term Training	200	200	200 e	200 e
84.250	Rehabilitation—Indians/Disabilities	37,224	37,201	39,160 e	39,825 e
84.256	Freely Associated States—Education	5,000	5,000	5,000 e	5,000 e
84.259	Hawaiian Vocational Education	2,661	2,794	2,794 e	2,794 e
84.264	Rehabilitation Training—Continuing	9,097	9,000	8,300 e	7,500 e
84.268	Federal Direct Student Loans	128,758,682*	135,385,067*	130,490,532*e	136,968,456*e
84.274	Overseas Research Centers	650	650	650 e	650 e
84.282	Charter Schools	241,507	248,172	253,172 e	253,172 e
84.283	Comprehensive Centers	48,445	48,445	48,445 e	48,445 e
84.287	Community Learning Centers	1,091,564	1,149,370	1,151,673 e	1,151,673 e
84.295	Ready-To-Learn TV	25,771	25,741	25,741 e	25,741 e
84.299	Education Programs for Indian Children	17,993	17,993	17,993 e	17,933 e
84.305	Education Research, Development	179,860	179,860	179,860 e	202,273 e
84.315	Capacity Building	1,976	2,027	2,027 e	968 e
84.323	State Personnel Development	41,630	41,630	41,630 e	41,630 e
84.324	Research in Special Education	47,295	54,000	54,000 e	54,000 e
84.325	Personnel/Children with Disabilities	83,700	83,700	83,700 e	83,700 e
84.326	Technical/Children with Disabilities	44,345	44,345	44,345	44,345 e
84.327	Technology/Individuals/Disabilities	28,047	28,047	28,047 e	28,047 e
84.328	Parent Information Centers	27,411	27,411	27,411 e	27,411 e
84.329	Studies, Evaluations	10,818	10,818	10,818 e	13,000 e
84.330	Advanced Placement Program	28,483	28,483	28,483 e	28,483 e
84.334	Awareness, Readiness—Undergraduate	286,435	301,639	301,639 e	301,639 e
84.335	Child Care/Parents in School	15,134	15,134	15,134 e	15,134 e
84.336	Teacher Quality Enhancement Grants	40,592	40,592	40,592 e	0 e
84.350	Transition to Teaching	24,691	13,762	13,700 e	0 e
84.351	Arts in Education	23,648	25,000	25,000 e	25,000 e
84.354	Credit Enhancement/Charter School	13,000	11,930	13,000 e	13,000 e
84.356	Alaska Native Educational Programs	31,449	31,453	31,453 e	23,453 e
84.358	Rural Education	169,840	169,840	169,840 e	169,840 e
84.360	Dropout Prevention Programs	46,267	42,267	0 e	0 e
84.362	Native Hawaiian Education	32,397	32,397	32,397 e	32,397 e
84.363	School Leadership	27,584	25,763	16,368 e	0 e
84.365	English Language Acquisition	643,748	671,379	670,469 e	670,469 e
84.366	Mathematics, Science Partnerships	141,902	149,717	152,717 e	152,717 e
84.367	Improving Teacher Quality	2,337,830	2,348,898	2,349,830 e	2,349,830 e
84.368	Grants for Enhanced Assessment Instruments	8,733	8,949	8,949 e	8,949 e
84.369	State Assessments, Activities	360,167	369,051	369,051 e	369,051 e
84.370	DC School Choice Incentive Program	18,006	15,200	13,199 e	1,200 e

Please see "Important Notes on the Tables, Footnotes," page 888

Table 1. *(continued)*

Program Number	ADMINISTRATIVE ENTITY Program Title (abridged)	FY 2013 in $thousands	FY 2014 in $thousands	FY 2015 in $thousands	FY 2016 in $thousands
84.371	Striving Readers	378	158,000	160,000 e	160,000 e
84.372	Statewide Data Systems	36,085	34,538	34,539 e	70,000 e
84.373	Special Education Data Collection	23,693	15,000	13,000	20,000 e
84.374	Teacher Incentive Funds	283,771	288,771	230,000 e	350,000 e
84.377	School Improvement Grants	505,756	505,756	505,756 e	505,756 e
84.378	College Access Challenge Grant	142,350	139,200	0 e	0 e
84.379	Teacher Education Grants	93,022	91,554	80,423 e	94,318 e
84.380	Special Education—Olympic	7,583	7,583	7,583	10,083 e
84.382	Minority-Serving Institutions	34,639	29,872	23,175 e	23,300 e
84.403	Consolidated Grant to Outlying Areas	65,793	73,391	72,000 e	0 e
84.407	Transition Programs-Students with Intellectual Disabilities	10,384	10,384	11,800 e	11,800 e
84.408	Education Scholarships for Veteranís Dependents	236	331	376 e	476 e
84.411	Investing in Innovation (i3) Fund	141,602	141,602	120,000 e	120,000 e
84.414	Minorities and Retirement Security Program	480	480	480 e	480 e
84.415	State Tribal Education Partnership (STEP)	1,635	2,000	2,000 e	2,000 e
84.417	Directed Grants and Awards	(a)	(a)	(a)	(a)
84.419	Preschool Development Grants	(n)	250,000	250,000 e	750,000 e
84.421	Disability Innovation Fund	(n)	(n)	20,000 e	20,000 e
	DEPARTMENT TOTAL: OUTLAYS	75,830,251	76,607,835	76,746,348	78,933,341
	CREDITS*	128,758,682*	135,385,067*	130,490,532*	136,968,456*

	SCHOLARSHIP AND FELLOWSHIP FOUNDATIONS				
85.001	Truman Scholarship Program \ t	(nr)	(nr)	(nr)	(nr)
85.002	Foreign Assistance for Overseas Programs	(nr)	(nr)	(nr)	(nr)
85.003	Domestic Assistance for Overseas Programs	(nr)	(nr)	(nr)	(nr)
85.102	Christopher Columbus Awards	273 e	273	(nr)	(nr)
85.104	Life Sciences Awards	0	17 e	(nr)	(nr)
85.105	Agriscience Awards	17 e	17 e	(nr)	(nr)
85.200	Goldwater Scholarship Program \ t	(nr)	(nr)	(nr)	(nr)
85.300	Wilson Fellowships	(nr)	(nr)	(nr)	(nr)
85.400	Udall Scholarship Program	254	250 e	250 e	(nr)
85.402	Udall Congressional Internships	129	116 e	120 e	(nr)
85.500	Madison Fellowship Program \ t	(nr)	(nr)	(nr)	(nr)
85.601	Smithsonian Institution Fellowship	(nr)	(nr)	(nr)	(nr)
85.802	Fellowship Program	28 e	28 e	(nr)	(nr)
	DEPARTMENT TOTAL: OUTLAYS	701	701	370	0
	CREDITS*	0*	0*	0*	0*

	PENSION BENEFIT GUARANTY CORPORATION				
86.001	Pension Plan Termination Insurance \ u	(nr)	(nr)	(nr)	(nr)
	DEPARTMENT TOTAL: OUTLAYS	0	0	0	0
	CREDITS*	0*	0*	0*	0*

	ARCHITECTURAL AND TRANSPORTATION BARRIERS COMPLIANCE BOARD				
88.001	Compliance Board	(nr)	(nr)	(nr)	(nr)
	DEPARTMENT TOTAL: OUTLAYS	0	0	0	0
	CREDITS*	0*	0*	0*	0*

	NATIONAL ARCHIVES AND RECORDS ADMINISTRATION				
89.001	Historical Research	40,649	45,447	73,815 e	75,291 e
89.003	National Historical Publications	5,575	5,066	5,309 e	5,000 e
	DEPARTMENT TOTAL: OUTLAYS	46,224	50,513	79,124	80,291
	CREDITS*	0*	0*	0*	0*

Please see "Important Notes on the Tables, Footnotes," page 888

Table 1. *(continued)*

Program Number	ADMINISTRATIVE ENTITY Program Title (abridged)	FY 2013 in $thousands	FY 2014 in $thousands	FY 2015 in $thousands	FY 2016 in $thousands
	INDEPENDENT BOARDS AND COMMISSIONS				
90.100	Denali Commission Program \ t	(nr)	(nr)	(nr)	(nr)
90.200	Delta Regional Development	(o)	(o)	(o)	(o)
90.201	Delta Area Economic Development	(nr)	(nr)	(nr)	(nr)
90.202	Delta Local Development District	(nr)	(nr)	(nr)	(nr)
90.300	Japan-US Friendship Grants	(nr)	(nr)	(nr)	(nr)
90.400	Help America Vote—Pollworker	(nr)	(nr)	(nr)	(nr)
90.401	Help America Vote Act Requirements	(nr)	(nr)	(nr)	(nr)
90.402	Help America Vote—Mock Elections	(nr)	(nr)	(nr)	(nr)
90.403	U.S. Election Assistance Commission Research	(nr)	(nr)	(nr)	(nr)
90.500	International Broadcasting Independent Grantee Organizations	(nr)	(nr)	(nr)	(nr)
	DEPARTMENT TOTAL: OUTLAYS	0	0	0	0
	CREDITS*	0*	0*	0*	0*
	INSTITUTE OF PEACE				
91.001	Unsolicited Grant Program	(nr)	(nr)	(nr)	(nr)
91.002	Solicited Grant Program	(nr)	(nr)	(nr)	(nr)
	DEPARTMENT TOTAL: OUTLAYS	0	0	0	0
	CREDITS*	0*	0*	0*	0*
	DEPARTMENT OF HEALTH AND HUMAN SERVICES				
93.001	Civil Rights, Privacy Rule	38,615	38,798	38,798 e	42,705 e
93.004	Health Status/Minority Populations	4,825	4,475	0 e	(nr)
93.006	Minority HIV/AIDS Demonstration	0	0	0 e	0 e
93.007	Public Awareness/Embryo Adoption	685	735	681 e	(nr)
93.008	Medical Reserve Corps	5,550	4,030	(nr)	(nr)
93.009	Compassion Capital Fund	0	0	0 e	0 e
93.011	National Organizations of State/Local Officials	1,215	2,219	2,400 e	2,400 e
93.015	HIV Prevention, Women	3,705	4,060	0 e	(nr)
93.018	US/Mexico Border Health	1,300	1,300	1,350 e	(nr)
93.019	Foreign Hospitals/Health Organizations	450	312	(nr)	(nr)
93.041	Aging—Prevention of Abuse, Neglect	4,773	4,732	4,732	4,732 e
93.042	Aging—Long-Term Care Ombudsman	15,870	15,863	15,885	15,885 e
93.043	Aging—Disease Prevention	19,743	19,732	19,848 e	19,848 e
93.044	Aging—Senior Centers	345,666	345,694	345,694 e	347,724 e
93.045	Aging—Nutrition Services	617,913	654,588	654,588 e	694,588 e
93.047	Aging—Indian, Native Hawaiian	25,746	25,539	26,158 e	29,100 e
93.048	Aging—Discretionary Projects	36,324	36,324	36,324 e	36,324 e
93.051	Alzheimer's Disease Demonstration	3,099	9,537	3,099 e	(nr)
93.052	National Family Caregiver Support	152,678	152,678	145,586	154,500 e
93.053	Nutrition Services Incentive	157,734	153,311	160,069 e	160,069 e
93.054	Family Caregiver Support	6,023	6,039	6,031 e	6,800 e
93.055	Leadership for Community Health Improvement	1,250	0	0 e	0 e
93.056	Maintaining and Strengthening Public Health	0	0	0 e	0 e
93.059	Training in Dentistry	18,736	17,938	19,480 e	19,399 e
93.060	Competitive Abstinence Education	4,260	4,486	0	9,000 e
93.061	Applied Public Health Research	6,052	0	0 e	0 e
93.062	Biomonitoring/State Public Health Labs	0	699	(o)	(o)
93.064	Laboratory Training, Evaluation	645	579	673 e	1,550 e
93.065	Improving Public Health Laboratory	18,772	1,908	599 e	599 e
93.066	Vital Statistics Re-Engineering	856	695	686 e	0 e
93.067	Global Aids	1,370,667	1,412,727	1,388,124	1,500,000 e
93.068	Research, Control, Prevention	2,978	(nr)	(nr)	(nr)
93.069	Public Health Emergency Preparedness	4,250	4,082	400 e	400 e

Please see "Important Notes on the Tables, Footnotes," page 888

Table 1. *(continued)*

Program Number	ADMINISTRATIVE ENTITY Program Title (abridged)	FY 2013 in $thousands	FY 2014 in $thousands	FY 2015 in $thousands	FY 2016 in $thousands
93.070	Environmental Public Health/Emergency Response	28,719	52,550	50,070 e	50,070 e
93.071	Medicare Enrollment Assistance	16,608	16,608	16,608 e	(nr)
93.072	Lifespan Respite Care Program	2,506	2,273	2,294 e	2,294 e
93.073	Birth Defects/Developmental Disabilities Prevention	12,701	16,895	20,000 e	0 e
93.075	Systems Interoperability and Improvement	0	0	0 e	0 e
93.076	TANF Integrity Innovation Grants	1,581	0	0 e	0 e
93.077	Family Smoking Prevention Regulatory Research	98,415	103,000	108,099 e	109,000 e
93.079	School-Based HIV/STD Prevention	14,812	21,046	17,939 e	17,939 e
93.082	Sodium Reduction in Communities	1,867	2,840	(nr)	0 e
93.083	Prevention through Immunization and Control of Respiratory and Related Diseases	150	1,347	1,332 e	0 e
93.084	Prevention of Disease, Disability, and Death by Infectious Diseases	0	662	3,115 e	0 e
93.085	Responsible Conduct of Research	1,228	1,508	1,500 e	(nr)
93.086	Healthy Marriage and Fatherhood	123,778	147,194	148,102 e	150,000 e
93.087	Childrenís Safety, Parental Drug Use	15,016	14,054	14,115	14,100 e
93.088	Targets for Healthy People	1,915	1,715	3,700 e	(nr)
93.089	Advance Registration/Volunteer Health Professionals	0	0	0 e	0 e
93.090	Guardianship Assistance	77,099	89,707	109,000 e	123,400 e
93.091	Social Services Benefits Enrollment	0	0	0 e	0 e
93.093	Health Profession Opportunity Grants	68,316	65,992	71,420 e	71,420 e
93.095	HHS Programs for Disaster Relief—Non Construction	524,862	104,411	68,754 e	0 e
93.096	HHS Programs for Disaster Relief— Construction	0	66,400	0 e	0 e
93.097	National Voluntary Accreditation Program for Health Departments	900	1,400	900 e	(nr)
93.098	Tribal Public Health Capacity Building and Quality Improvement	587	550	550 e	(nr)
93.103	FDA—Research	93,359	122,487	150,874 e	165,962 e
93.104	CMHS/Serious Emotional Disturbances	46,409	57,585	12,059 e	11,896 e
93.107	Model Area Health Education Centers	21,757	22,409	24,000 e	25,000 e
93.110	Maternal, Child Health Programs	126,137	127,630	127,630 e	(nr)
93.113	Biological Response/Health Hazards	304,675	312,256	311,900 e	320,681 e
93.116	Tuberculosis Control Programs	79,774	81,593	80,991 e	80,911 e
93.117	Preventive Medicine	2,962	5,765	9,837 e	7,136 e
93.118	AIDS Activity	4,162	3,096	3,658 e	(nr)
93.121	Oral Diseases/Disorders Research	287,612	290,101	283,554 e	284,277 e
93.123	Pregraduate Scholarship/Indians	2,654	2,733	2,176	1,837 e
93.124	Nurse Anesthetist Traineeships	2,250	2,250	2,250 e	2,250 e
93.127	Emergency Medical Services/Children	17,639	18,865	18,861 e	18,861 e
93.129	Assistance to Health Centers	65,073	66,579	69,948 e	74,107 e
93.130	State Primary Care Offices	8,407	6,345	6,943 e	7,000 e
93.134	Organ Donations	9,819	8,350	7,065 e	8,720 e
93.135	Centers/Health Promotion	20,901	29,423	19,500 e	19,500 e
93.136	Injury Prevention, Control Research	78,673	79,976	97,668 e	113,812 e
93.137	Community Minority Health	4,515	9,579	15,550 e	(nr)
93.138	Advocacy/Mental Illness	33,571	35,325	35,315 e	35,315 e
93.140	Intramural Research Training	101,964	102,983	105,501	106,556 e
93.142	Hazardous Waste Worker Training	34,349	36,007	36,597 e	36,579 e
93.143	Hazardous Substances Research	45,438	46,925	46,902 e	46,230 e
93.145	AIDS Education, Training Centers	33,736	38,028	38,761 e	36,128 e
93.150	Transition from Homelessness	58,446	61,578	61,573 e	61,573 e
93.153	Research/Women, Infants, Youth	64,565	64,564	66,000 e	67,000 e
93.155	Rural Health Research Centers	8,290	6,384	8,265 e	1,368 e
93.156	Geriatric Fellowships	6,476	7,448	0 e	0 e
93.157	Centers of Excellence	20,482	20,702	20,597 e	20,980 e
93.161	Toxic Substances, Disease Registry	3,513	4,899	4,688 e	4,688 e
93.162	NHSC Loan Repayment	(nr)	(nr)	(nr)	194,500 e
93.164	IHS Loan Repayment	29,878	19,125	29,117	29,440 e

Please see "Important Notes on the Tables, Footnotes," page 888

Table 1. *(continued)*

Program Number	ADMINISTRATIVE ENTITY Program Title (abridged)	FY 2013 in $thousands	FY 2014 in $thousands	FY 2015 in $thousands	FY 2016 in $thousands
93.165	State Loan Repayment	8,990	12,735	13,000 e	13,000 e
93.172	Human Genome Research	378,190	386,926	367,251	377,981 e
93.173	Deafness, Communication Disorders	330,488	329,192	328,672 e	336,741 e
93.178	Nursing Workforce Diversity	13,852	15,008	13,931 e	13,931 e
93.184	Disabilities Prevention	24,740	19,161	12,710 e	(nr)
93.185	Immunization Research, Demonstration	105,810	122,145	111,780 e	111,780 e
93.186	NRSA/Primary Care	6,775	6,923	6,865 e	6,865 e
93.187	Undergraduate Scholarships	3,475	2,862	3,356 e	3,439 e
93.191	Allied Health Special Projects	2,469	6,946	6,946 e	6,946 e
93.193	Urban Indian Health Services	9,577	9,748	9,523	9,423 e
93.197	Childhood Lead Poisoning Prevention	0	375	375 e	375 e
93.209	Contraception, Infertility LRP	1,010	1,016	1,016 e	1,016 e
93.210	Tribal Self-Governance	1,560,942	1,585,900	1,833,200	1,858,200 e
93.211	Telehealth Network Grants	10,107	12,535	13,284 e	13,615 e
93.213	Complementary/Alternative Medicine	88,294	91,227	90,115 e	(nr)
93.217	Family Planning—Services	259,617	253,508	247,800 e	(nr)
93.220	Loan Repayment/Disadvantaged	122	121	0 e	205 e
93.223	Rural Health Services	1,508	1,544	2,100 e	2,100 e
93.224	Consolidated Health Centers	2,382,143	2,523,718	2,478,000 e	2,700,000 e
93.225	Health Services Research Training	7,348	7,493	7,462 e	7,462 e
93.226	Research/Healthcare Cost, Quality	118,783	115,048	112,914 e	112,481 e
93.228	IHS—Health Management	2,442	2,577	2,577	2,577 e
93.231	Epidemiology Agreements	5,043	5,043	4,431	4,679 e
93.232	Loan Repayment/General Research	2,911	4,089	3,340 e	4,089 e
93.233	Sleep Disorders Research	53,387	51,258	51,258 e	51,258 e
93.234	Traumatic Brain Injury	4,985	5,066	5,066 e	9,321 e
93.235	Abstinence Education	36,863	35,842	46,219 e	75,000 e
93.236	Dental Public Health Training	10,538	11,362	11,362 e	11,500 e
93.237	Special Diabetes Program/Indians	112,091	112,091	116,400	138,700 e
93.239	Policy Research	2,895	2,895	2,900 e	2,400 e
93.240	State Capacity Building	10,223	10,092	10,092 e	10,092 e
93.241	State Rural Hospital Flexibility	25,042	23,811	23,811 e	23,811 e
93.242	Mental Health Research	1,089,804	1,110,217	1,108,078	(nr)
93.243	Substance Abuse, Mental Health	668,459	808,414	502,234 e	339,563 e
93.247	Advanced Education Nursing	31,245	25,146	29,134 e	29,134 e
93.250	Geriatric Academic Career Awards	4,354	3,311	0 e	0 e
93.251	Universal Newborn Hearing Screening	16,224	17,818	16,225 e	17,818 e
93.253	Poison Control Centers	16,232	17,239	16,825 e	17,115 e
93.254	Infant Adoption Awareness Training	0	0	0 e	0 e
93.255	Childrenís Hospitals Education	236,338	249,742	248,058 e	100,000 e
93.257	Radiogenic Cancers, Diseases	1,580	1,576	1,590 e	1,590 e
93.259	Rural Access/Emergency Devices	1,813	2,786	3,862 e	2,706 e
93.260	Family Planning—Personnel	6,170	5,829	4,916 e	(nr)
93.261	National Diabetes Prevention Program	2,009	0	2,000 e	2,000 e
93.262	Occupational Safety, Health Program	111,328	118,786	93,000 e	(nr)
93.264	Nurse Faculty Loan Program	22,102	23,242	25,205 e	25,205 e
93.265	Comprehensive Geriatric Education	3,927	3,921	0 e	0 e
93.266	Global AIDS Relief	85,874	106,437	60,000 e	60,000 e
93.267	Protection, Advocacy Services	3,100	3,100	3,100 e	(nr)
93.268	Immunization Grants	306,724	311,097	324,098 e	(nr)
93.269	Humanitarian Public Health	2,480	10,449	8,775 e	8,775 e
93.270	Viral Hepatitis Prevention	16,700	15,544	15,535 e	15,944 e
93.273	Alcohol Research Programs	319,761	327,706	447,453	467,445 e
93.275	Mental Health—Access to Recovery	83,973	0	0 e	0 e
93.276	Drug-Free Communities Support	78,448	83,384	84,475 e	84,475 e
93.279	Drug Abuse, Addiction Research	773,163	793,756	785,813 e	813,881 e
93.280	NIH Loan Repayment/Researchers	38,881	39,025	43,757	43,000 e
93.281	Mental Health/Development Awards	(o)	(o)	(o)	(o)
93.282	Mental Health Research Training	(o)	(o)	(o)	(o)
93.283	Disease Control—Investigations	648,437	445,607	6,566 e	7,000 e
93.284	Injury Prevention—Indians/Alaskans	2,280	2,280	1,800	1,800 e
93.285	NIH Pediatric Research LRP	14,883	17,001	16,892	17,000 e
93.286	Discovery and Applied Research	265,069	271,916	263,165 e	276,764 e
93.288	NHSC Scholarship	(nr)	(nr)	(nr)	(nr)

Please see "Important Notes on the Tables, Footnotes," page 888

Table 1. *(continued)*

Program Number	ADMINISTRATIVE ENTITY Program Title (abridged)	FY 2013 in $thousands	FY 2014 in $thousands	FY 2015 in $thousands	FY 2016 in $thousands
93.289	Physical Fitness and Sports	1,215	1,215	1,215 e	2,100 e
93.290	Centers/Womenís Health	2,991	3,367	3,000 e	(nr)
93.291	Surplus Property Utilization	(a)	(a)	(a)	(a)
93.296	Minority Health Improvement Grants	3,232	3,231	3,000 e	(nr)
93.297	Teenage Pregnancy Prevention	84,794	84,647	87,385 e	(nr)
93.300	Health Workforce Analysis	1,365	1,474	2,905 e	2,668 e
93.301	Small Rural Hospital Improvement	14,870	14,268	14,199 e	14,376 e
93.303	Nursing Scholarship Program	22,688	22,466	23,996 e	23,996 e
93.305	National State Tobacco Control Programs	0	0	58,000 e	58,000 e
93.307	Minority Health, Disparities Research	221,524	228,950	(nr)	(nr)
93.308	Loan Repayment/Clinical Research	11,965	10,606	(nr)	(nr)
93.310	Trans-NIH Research	424,350	452,656	499,586 e	519,586 e
93.311	Mobilization For Health—National Prevention Partnership Awards	(n)	3,385	2,253	(nr)
93.313	Office of Research on Womenís Health	35,000	36,312	34,000 e	34,000 e
93.316	Public Health Preparedness and Response	(n)	(n)	3,685 e	3,685 e
93.317	Emerging Infections Programs	0	2,401	303 e	30,000 e
93.321	Dietary Supplement Research Program	0	0	1,500 e	1,500 e
93.322	Strengthening Public Health Laboratories	(n)	(n)	27,000 e	27,000 e
93.339	Public Health Conference Support	0	0	500 e	500 e
93.342	Health Professions Student Loans	9,444*	18,823*	11,775*e	11,775*e
93.350	National Center for Advancing Translational Sciences	541,973	530,596	528,361 e	546,685 e
93.351	Research Infrastructure Programs	280,694	267,069	265,944 e	263,861 e
93.358	Advanced Nursing Traineeships	22,755	28,854	28,573 e	22,750 e
93.359	Nurse Education, Practice, Retention	34,479	65,015	57,532 e	57,532 e
93.360	Biodefense Medical Countermeasures	23,392	15,455	15,000 e	(nr)
93.361	Nursing Research	111,398	112,394	113,761 e	116,576 e
93.364	Nursing Student Loans \ r	3,781*	3,138*	3,460*e	3,460*e
93.365	Sickle Cell Treatment	3,210	4,455	3,406 e	4,455 e
93.389	National Center/Research Resources	0	0	0 e	0 e
93.393	Cancer Cause, Prevention	637,211	611,442	544,308 e	614,006 e
93.394	Cancer Detection, Diagnosis	328,204	361,700	340,704 e	366,893 e
93.395	Cancer Treatment Research	656,848	797,273	713,416 e	717,341 e
93.396	Cancer Biology Research	502,446	498,475	533,735 e	555,813 e
93.397	Cancer Centers Support	530,339	543,160	549,765 e	552,297 e
93.398	Cancer Research Manpower	167,779	169,674	170,131 e	169,997 e
93.399	Cancer Control	88,138	82	82 e	82 e
93.400	Health Service Corps Scholarships	0	0	0 e	0 e
93.401	National Health Service Corps/Loan Repayment	(nr)	(nr)	(nr)	(nr)
93.403	Primary Care Medicine/Dentistry Training	0	0	0 e	0 e
93.409	Faculty Loan Repayment Programs	0	0	0 e	0 e
93.433	ACL-NIDILRR Research	(n)	(a)	(a)	(a)
93.441	Indian Self-Determination	399,072	458,328	458,328 e	458,328 e
93.442	Special Diabetes Program/Indians	23,182	23,182	27,400	0 e
93.444	Tribal Self-Governance	504	840	840	840 e
93.448	Food Safety, Security Monitoring	9,677	10,103	10,090 e	9,714 e
93.449	Ruminant Feed Ban Support Project	2,316	2,316	0 e	0 e
93.452	Health Improvement for Ex-offenders HIV/AIDS	1,500	1,500	1,500 e	(nr)
93.464	ACL Assistive Technology	(n)	31,000	28,682 e	28,682 e
93.501	School-Based Health Centers	32,257	0	0 e	0 e
93.502	Infrastructure to Expand Access to Care	0	0	0 e	0 e
93.504	Family to Family Health Information Centers	4,893	4,893	5,000 e	5,000 e
93.506	Long Term Care Facilities—Employee Background Checks	11,758	1,306	18,000 e	18,000 e
93.507	National Public Health Improvement Initiative	16,805	0	0 e	0 e
93.508	Tribal Maternal, Infant, and Early Childhood Home Visiting Program	11,533	12,250	12,250 e	12,250 e
93.510	Primary Care Residency Expansion	0	0	0 e	0 e
93.513	Advanced Nursing Education Expansion	0	0	0 e	0 e
93.514	Physician Assistant Training Expansion	0	0	0 e	0 e
93.516	Public Health Training Centers Program	0	9,100	9,100 e	9,100 e

Please see "Important Notes on the Tables, Footnotes," page 888

Table 1. *(continued)*

Program Number	ADMINISTRATIVE ENTITY Program Title (abridged)	FY 2013 in $thousands	FY 2014 in $thousands	FY 2015 in $thousands	FY 2016 in $thousands
93.517	Aging and Disability Resource Center	6,129	0	0 e	0 e
93.521	Emerging Infections Program-Increasing Capacity	41,070	51,389	47,662 e	(nr)
93.524	Building Capacity/Public Health System	19,214	16,243	15,000 e	15,000 e
93.525	State Health Exchange Establishment	2,097,666	654,355	448,619 e	0 e
93.526	Grants for Capital Development in Health Centers	33,494	35,700	150,000 e	0 e
93.527	Health Center Program Expansion	68,033	528,024	523,324 e	75,000 e
93.528	Forum for State/Territorial Chief	460	310	600 e	600 e
93.529	Pre-existing Condition Insurance Executives Program	1,745,603	0	0 e	0 e
93.531	Community Transformation Grants-Support	107,447	0	0 e	0 e
93.533	Surveillance-New Vaccine Preventable Disease	2,741	2,741	2,700 e	(nr)
93.534	Early Detection/Environmental Health Hazards	2,499	2,500	2,500 e	2,500 e
93.535	Childhood Obesity Research	6,238	5,011	0 e	(nr)
93.537	Emergency Psychiatric Demonstration	14,212	29,910	33,104	390 e
93.538	Environmental Public Health Tracking	14,348	250	(nr)	(nr)
93.539	Strengthen Public Health Immunization Infrastructure	8,400	9,415	0 e	(nr)
93.541 Health	Racial/Ethnic Approaches to Community	750	0	0 e	0 e
93.542	Health Promotion/Disease Prevention Research Centers	14,732	2,566	2,300 e	0 e
93.545	CO-OP Program	301,658*	129,670*	87,668*	0*e
93.546	Early Retiree Reinsurance Program	80,580	11,400	817	1,104 e
93.547	National Health Service Corps	216,332	202,075	209,700 e	440,400 e
93.548	Nutrition, Physical Activity and Obesity Program	5,922	48	(nr)	(nr)
93.549	Primary Care Services Coordination/ Development	2,000	4,000	3,921 e	4,000 e
93.550	Transitional Living/Homeless Youth	38,869	41,263	41,278 e	46,219 e
93.551	Abandoned Infants	10,210	10,493	10,510 e	10,434 e
93.556	Promoting Safe and Stable Families	333,842	327,089	330,989 e	330,891 e
93.557	Street Outreach Program	15,151	16,050	15,427 e	15,427 e
93.558	Temporary Assistance/Families	17,176,542	17,144,415	17,174,542 e	17,164,542 e
93.560	Family Support Payments	32,488	32,488	33,000 e	33,000 e
93.563	Child Support Enforcement	3,112,729	3,354,811	3,335,393 e	3,387,743 e
93.564	Child Support Enforcement Research	4,000	3,752	4,000 e	4,000 e
93.566	Refugee and Entrant Assistance	384,398	374,068	365,857 e	378,840 e
93.567	Refugees, Entrants—Agencies	63,448	65,309	65,309 e	87,309 e
93.568	Low-Income Home Energy Assistance	3,252,598	3,398,226	3,387,316 e	3,187,304 e
93.569	Community Services Block Grant	632,697	665,495	671,355 e	668,418 e
93.570	CSBG—Discretionary	30,261	33,017	33,679 e	0 e
93.575	Child Care, Development Block Grant	2,191,255	2,358,000	2,435,000 e	2,805,000 e
93.576	Refugee, Entrant—Discretionary	77,557	78,072	127,715 e	127,715 e
93.579	U.S. Repatriation Program	949	928	927 e	1,000 e
93.581	Indian/Environmental Quality	2,009	1,762	1,750 e	1,750 e
93.583	Refugee, Entrant Assistance-Wilson	31,090	27,000	27,000 e	35,000 e
93.584	Refugee, Entrant Assistance—Targeted	42,841	42,874	42,841 e	42,841 e
93.586	State Court Improvement	31,336	30,740	30,728 e	30,928 e
93.587	Native American Languages	13,183	12,894	12,403 e	13,000 e
93.590	Community-Based Child Abuse Prevention	38,860	41,527	41,527 e	(nr)
93.591	Domestic Violence Coalitions	12,123	13,352	13,500 e	14,500 e
93.592	Family Violence—Discretionary	13,266	14,755	14,325 e	27,513 e
93.593	Job Opportunities/Low-Income	0	0	0 e	0 e
93.594	Tribal Work Grants	7,633	7,633 e	7,633 e	(nr)
93.595	Welfare Reform Research \ i	850	1,850	1,350 e	2,200 e
93.596	Child Care, Development	2,909,708	2,930,000	2,917,000 e	2,917,000 e
93.597	Access and Visitation Programs	10,000	10,000	10,000 e	10,000 e
93.598	Victims of Trafficking	9,123	11,996	13,000 e	13,000 e
93.599	Chafee Vouchers	41,689	42,608	43,257 e	43,257 e

Please see "Important Notes on the Tables, Footnotes," page 888

Table 1. *(continued)*

Program Number	ADMINISTRATIVE ENTITY Program Title (abridged)	FY 2013 in $thousands	FY 2014 in $thousands	FY 2015 in $thousands	FY 2016 in $thousands
93.600	Head Start	7,469,707	8,150,150	8,153,106 e	9,529,407 e
93.601	Child Support Enforcement	498	710	499 e	(nr)
93.602	Assets/Independence Demonstration	13,666	10,890	14,275 e	13,539 e
93.603	Adoption Incentive Payments	37,230	37,943	37,943 e	37,943 e
93.604	Assistance for Torture Victims	10,674	10,724	10,735 e	10,735 e
93.605	Family Connection Grants	13,492	8,625	2,010 e	2,010 e
93.606	Preparedness/Emergency Learning Centers	0	0	0 e	0 e
93.609	Medicaid Adult Quality Grants	25,943	23,296	25,943 e	0 e
93.610	Health Care Innovation Awards	306,600	411,757	0 e	0 e
93.611	Strong Start for Mothers/Newborns	11,744	11,820	11,774	0 e
93.612	Native American Programs	24,239	26,030	28,185 e	28,000 e
93.613	Presidentís Committee/Disabilities	(nr)	166 e	166 e	166 e
93.616	Mentoring Children of Prisoners	0	0	0 e	0 e
93.617	Voting/Individuals with Disabilities	0	4,616	0 e	0 e
93.618	Voting/P & A Systems	4,900	4,616	4,963 e	(nr)
93.621	Reduce Avoidable Hospitalizations/Nursing Facilities	25,763	26,876	26,821 e	4,689 e
93.622	Interprofessional Education/Collaborative Practice	771	788	788 e	788 e
93.623	Basic Center Grant	47,617	50,856	50,915 e	51,495 e
93.624	State Innovation Models/Design, Testing	120,958	90,973	184,172	173,078 e
93.628	Integrate Care for Medicare/Medicaid	(nr)	43,259	15,800 e	8,011 e
93.630	Developmental Disabilities/Basic	108,553	108,553	108,553	110,916 e
93.631	Developmental Disabilities/Projects	6,360	8,317	8,857 e	14,500 e
93.632	Developmental Disabilities/University	37,503	36,674	37,674	38,619 e
93.634	Demonstration Ombudsman Programs	708	1,148	3,874	4,308 e
93.643	Childrenís Justice Grants	17,000	16,986	16,900 e	17,000 e
93.645	Child Welfare Services	262,622	268,735	268,735 e	268,735 e
93.647	Social Services Research	3,404	1,573	1,208 e	813 e
93.648	Child Welfare Services Training	19,912	19,865	6,139 e	6,139 e
93.649	Nutrition and Physical Activity	(n)	(n)	(n)	1,000 e
93.650	Accountable Health Communities	(n)	(n)	(n)	55,700 e
93.651	Transforming Clinical Practice Initiative	(n)	(n)	(n)	3,300 e
93.652	Adoption Opportunities	31,828	32,434	32,434 e	32,000 e
93.658	Foster Care	4,119,576	4,642,376	4,725,996 e	4,527,435 e
93.659	Adoption Assistance	2,278,135	2,449,853	2,510,000 e	2,562,000 e
93.667	Social Services Block Grant	1,613,300	1,577,600	1,575,900 e	2,000,000 e
93.669	Child Abuse, Neglect State Grants	24,734	25,310	25,310 e	25,310 e
93.670	Child Abuse, Neglect Discretionary	17,607	19,809	18,592 e	19,000 e
93.671	Family Violence/States, Indians	96,980	106,817	108,000 e	116,000 e
93.674	Chafee Foster Care Independence	137,933	137,900	137,900 e	137,000 e
93.676	Unaccompanied Alien Children	320,085	910,086	948,000 e	967,000 e
93.701	Trans-NIH Research Support	(nr)	0	0 e	0 e
93.702	Center for Research Resources Construction Support	0	0	0 e	0 e
93.703	Grants to Health Center Programs	0	0	0 e	0 e
93.704	Trans-NIH Repayment Support	0	0	0 e	0 e
93.706	Aging Nutrition/Native Americans	0	0	0 e	0 e
93.708	Head Start	0	0	0 e	0 e
93.709	Early Head Start	0	0	0 e	0 e
93.710	Community Services Block Grant	0	0	0 e	0 e
93.711	Strengthening Communities Fund	0	0	0 e	0 e
93.713	Child Care and Development	0	0	0 e	0 e
93.714	Emergency/Temporary Assistance/Needy Families	0	0	0 e	0 e
93.716	Temporary Assistance/Needy Families/ Supplemental	0	0	0 e	0 e
93.718	Health IT Regional Extension Centers	(nr)	0	0 e	0 e
93.719	State Grants/Health IT	(nr)	0	30,382 e	3,667 e
93.721	IT Professionals/Health Care	0	0	6,765 e	0 e
93.727	Information Technology/Beacon Communities	0	0	2,227 e	537 e
93.728	Strategic Health IT Advanced Research	0	0	0 e	0 e
93.732	Mental/Behavioral Health Education/Training	0	0	0 e	0 e
93.733	Strengthen Immunization Infrastructure	0	43,612	0 e	(nr)

Please see "Important Notes on the Tables, Footnotes," page 888

Table 1. *(continued)*

Program Number	ADMINISTRATIVE ENTITY Program Title (abridged)	FY 2013 in $thousands	FY 2014 in $thousands	FY 2015 in $thousands	FY 2016 in $thousands
93.734	Empowering Older Adults/Disease Management	7,054	7,579	8,000 e	8,000 e
93.735	State Smoking Quitline Capacity	15,630	17,000	0 e	(nr)
93.736	Viral Hepatitis Prevention	0	0	0 e	0 e
93.738	Racial/Ethnic Approaches to Community Health	1,800	27,349	0 e	0 e
93.739	Chronic disease Innovation Grants	2,009	7,000	0 e	0 e
93.741	Breastfeeding Promotion and Support	2,363	0	0 e	0 e
93.742	Obesity Prevention in Young Children	3,778	3,701	3,700 e	(nr)
93.743	Racial/Ethnic Approaches to Obesity/ Hypertension	0	0	0 e	0 e
93.744	Breast and Cervical Cancer Screening	0	0	0 e	0 e
93.745	Behavioral Risk Factor Surveillance	3,855	4,299	(nr)	(nr)
93.747	Elder Abuse Prevention	503	0	0 e	0 e
93.748	Prescription Drug Monitoring Program	0	0	0 e	0 e
93.749	Public Health Laboratory Infrastructure	20	1,305	45,000 e	(nr)
93.751	Consortium for Tobacco Use Cessation— Technical Assistance	450	450	450 e	450 e
93.752	Cancer Prevention and Control Programs	0	97,834	97,834 e	97,834 e
93.753	Child Lead Poisoning Prevention Surveillance	0	11,000	9,452 e	9,452 e
93.754	Optimal Breastfeeding Practices	0	0	0 e	0 e
93.761	Evidence-Based Falls Prevention	(n)	4,849	5,000 e	5,000 e
93.767	State Childrenís Insurance Program	8,939,373	9,513,914	11,291,546	13,499,160 e
93.770	Medicare Prescription Drugs \ t	69,693,000*	64,698,000*	75,321,000*e	97,764,000*e
93.773	Medicare—Hospital Insurance \ t	269,780,000*	266,678,000*	275,569,000*e	295,291,000*e
93.774	Medicare—Supplementary \ t	245,095,000*	262,595,000*	278,226,000*e	303,410,000*e
93.775	Medicaid Fraud Control	222,201	224,479	230,698	243,715 e
93.777	State Survey/Providers, Suppliers	333,492	342,625	358,297	359,356 e
93.778	Medicaid	286,698,295	299,709,844	371,158,762 e	384,450,381 e
93.779	Medicare, Medicaid Research	600	544	650 e	900 e
93.780	Grants to States/High-Risk Pools	41,756	20,420	0	0 e
93.784	Reimbursement/Undocumented Aliens	16,080	5,649	2,252 e	2,000 e
93.791	Money Follows the Person	343,745	367,608	540,592 e	1,538,173 e
93.810	Paul Coverdell Acute Stroke Program	(n)	(n)	4,740 e	4,740 e
93.813	Prevent Obesity, Diabetes, Heart Disease and Stroke	(n)	(n)	69,500 e	69,500 e
93.814	Heart Disease and Stroke Prevention	(n)	(n)	300 e	300 e
93.817	Ebola Preparedness and Response Activities	(n)	(n)	182,375 e	4,739 e
93.822	Health Careers Opportunity Program	11,387	10,098	11,000 e	(nr)
93.823	Ebola Transmission and Prevention Control	(n)	(n)	15,000 e	0 e
93.824	Area Health Education Centers	3,780	6,229	5,104 e	5,104 e
93.825	National Ebola Training and Education Center	(n)	(n)	4,242 e	2,271 e
93.831	Standards Alignment, Testing, and Measurement	(n)	(n)	100 e	0 e
93.832	Promoting the Cancer Surveillance	(n)	(n)	(n)	200 e
93.833	Surveillance for Chronic Kidney Disease	(n)	(n)	1,000 e	1,000 e
93.837	Heart, Vascular Diseases Research	1,357,629	1,315,820	1,315,820 e	1,315,820 e
93.838	Lung Diseases Research	523,483	540,687	540,687 e	540,687 e
93.839	Blood Diseases, Resources Research	335,699	330,654	330,654 e	330,654 e
93.845	Increased Capacity in Alcohol Epidemiology	(n)	(n)	(n)	600 e
93.846	Arthritis/Skin Diseases Research	412,870	423,088	422,480 e	433,354 e
93.847	Diabetes, Endocrinology, Metabolism	1,497,339	1,534,841	1,561,153 e	1,588,222 e
93.852	National Syndromic Surveillance	(n)	(n)	(n)	400 e
93.853	Neuroscience, Neurological Disorders	1,143,817	1,200,453	1,174,263 e	1,264,223 e
93.855	Allergy, Immunology, Transplantation	590,666	2,689,997	2,762,301 e	2,917,357 e
93.856	Microbiology, Infectious Diseases	1,823,479	(o)	(o)	(o)
93.858	Success of School-Age Children	(n)	(n)	(n)	14,000 e
93.859	Biomedical Research, Training	2,188,917	2,262,193	2,206,688 e	2,328,114 e
93.860	Emerging Infections Sentinel Networks	(n)	(n)	(n)	1,500 e
93.865	Child Health, Development Research	874,250	901,630	900,146 e	918,210 e
93.866	Aging Research	823,616	950,607	972,507 e	1,032,273 e
93.867	Vision Research	523,044	542,378	540,137 e	554,259 e
93.875	Oral Disease Prevention and Control-Agreements	(n)	(n)	(n)	2,000 e
93.876	Antimicrobial Resistance—Retail Food	(n)	(n)	(n)	2,500 e

Please see "Important Notes on the Tables, Footnotes," page 888

Table 1. *(continued)*

Program Number	ADMINISTRATIVE ENTITY Program Title (abridged)	FY 2013 in $thousands	FY 2014 in $thousands	FY 2015 in $thousands	FY 2016 in $thousands
93.879	Medical Library Assistance	41,184	42,317	42,318 e	42,318 e
93.884	Primary Care Medicine, Dentistry	36,535	36,924	38,924 e	38,924 e
93.887	Renovation/Health Care Facilities	0	0	0 e	0 e
93.888	Specially Selected Health Projects	0	0	0 e	0 e
93.889	Bioterrorism Hospital Preparedness	(o)	(o)	(o)	(o)
93.908	Nursing Education Loan Repayment	44,818	46,134	47,992 e	47,992 e
93.910	Family Life Centers	2,064	8,797	8,790 e	(nr)
93.912	Rural Health Outreach, Development	42,278	46,057	48,644 e	48,594 e
93.913	Offices of Rural Health	9,080	8,590	8,520 e	8,447 e
93.914	HIV Emergency Relief Project Grants	594,339	618,492	624,705 e	620,080 e
93.917	HIV Care Formula Grants	1,148,790	1,196,564	1,151,817 e	1,151,000 e
93.918	Outpatient Early Intervention/HIV	179,670	191,527	186,000 e	186,500 e
93.919	Breast, Cervical Cancer Detection	1,250	56,174	52,110 e	52,110 e
93.923	Disadvantaged Health Faculty Loan	0	1,090	1,190 e	1,190 e
93.924	HIV/AIDS Dental Reimbursements	11,979	12,255	12,239 e	12,239 e
93.925	Health Professions Scholarships	42,007	42,024	43,940 e	45,970 e
93.926	Healthy Start Initiative	93,382	93,382	93,382 e	102 e
93.928	Projects of National Significance	25,000	25,000	25,000 e	25,000 e
93.932	Hawaiian Health Systems	12,195	12,339	12,339 e	12,339 e
93.933	Demonstration Projects/Indian Health	17,064	13,142	34,400	42,765 e
93.936	AIDS Research Loan Repayment	123	200	80 e	200 e
93.938	School Health Programs/HIV	5,570	1,728	0 e	0 e
93.939	HIV Prevention—Non-Governmental	70,673	74,438	79,557 e	(nr)
93.940	HIV Prevention—Health Department	358,067	358,096	358,096 e	(nr)
93.941	HIV Demonstration, Research	20,182	2,566	1,568 e	(nr)
93.942	Research, Treatment/Lyme Disease	900	675	(nr)	(nr)
93.943	Epidemiologic Research/AIDS, HIV	1,284	2,360	3,560 e	(nr)
93.944	HIV/AIDS Surveillance	68,090	78,911	79,841 e	(nr)
93.945	Chronic Disease Prevention, Control	77,861	58,242	64,261 e	(nr)
93.946	Motherhood, Infant Health Initiative	11,236	11,789	13,401 e	13,401 e
93.947	Tuberculosis Demonstration	2,318	5,835	6,269 e	6,269 e
93.958	Block Grants/Mental Health	408,923	457,386	457,268 e	457,268 e
93.959	Block Grants/Substance Abuse	1,600,200	1,719,701	1,723,346 e	1,723,346 e
93.964	Public Health Traineeships	0	6,392	0 e	0 e
93.965	Coal Miners Respiratory Impairment	6,594	6,612	6,669 e	6,589 e
93.969	Geriatric Education Centers	17,104	19,686	35,716 e	35,716 e
93.970	Health Professions/Indians	3,571	3,507	3,304	3,587 e
93.971	Health Preparatory/Indians	1,069	1,101	855	850 e
93.972	Health Professions Scholarship	15,893	14,037	12,632	12,500 e
93.974	Family Planning—Service Research	1,049	1,852	1,200 e	(nr)
93.977	STD Control	98,998	84,950	98,904 e	0 e
93.982	Mental Health Disaster Assistance	56,995	10,242	0 e	0 e
93.985	Oral Disease Prevention and Control-Grants	(n)	(n)	(n)	2,000 e
93.988	Diabetes Control Programs	0	9,171	(nr)	(nr)
93.989	International Research, Training	51,086	52,625	52,192 e	53,909 e
93.990	National Health Promotion	200	200	125 e	(nr)
93.991	Health Services Block Grant	0	0	0 e	0 e
93.994	Maternal, Child Health Block Grant	512,578	536,556	540,027 e	540,027 e
93.995	Adolescent Family Life	0	0	0 e	0 e
93.997	Assisted Outpatient Treatment	(n)	(n)	(n)	12,000 e
93.998	Autism Surveillance, Research, and Prevention	(n)	6,900	6,325 e	6,325 e
	DEPARTMENT TOTAL: OUTLAYS	387,831,097	402,356,085	474,995,565	490,318,638
	CREDITS*	584,882,883*	594,122,631*	629,218,903*	696,480,235*

CORPORATION FOR NATIONAL AND COMMUNITY SERVICE

Program Number	Program Title	FY 2013	FY 2014	FY 2015	FY 2016
94.002	Retired, Senior Volunteer Program	47,578 e	(nr)	(nr)	(nr)
94.003	State Commissions	(nr)	(nr)	(nr)	(nr)
94.006	AmeriCorps	(nr)	(nr)	(nr)	(nr)
94.007	Planning, Program Development	0	0	0 e	0 e
94.011	Foster Grandparent Program	104,781 e	(nr)	(nr)	(nr)
94.013	Volunteers in Service to America	89,961	92,364	92,364 e	(nr)

Please see "Important Notes on the Tables, Footnotes," page 888

Table 1. *(continued)*

Program Number	ADMINISTRATIVE ENTITY Program Title (abridged)	FY 2013 in $thousands	FY 2014 in $thousands	FY 2015 in $thousands	FY 2016 in $thousands
94.016	Senior Companion Program	44,278 e	(nr)	(nr)	(nr)
94.017	Senior Demonstration Program	0	0	0 e	0 e
94.019	Social Innovation Fund	42,471	48,815	(nr)	(nr)
94.021	Volunteer Generation Fund	(nr)	(nr)	(nr)	(nr)
94.023	AmeriCorps VISTA Training/Logistics Support	(nr)	9,000 e	8,000 e	(nr)
94.026	National Service/Civic Engagement Competition	(n)	(n)	800 e	0 e
	DEPARTMENT TOTAL: OUTLAYS	329,069	150,179	101,164	0
	CREDITS*	0*	0*	0*	0*

EXECUTIVE OFFICE OF THE PRESIDENT

Program Number	Program Title	FY 2013	FY 2014	FY 2015	FY 2016
95.001	High Intensity Drug Trafficking Areas Program	223,487	235,822	242,300	247,300 e
95.005	Drug Court Training/Technical Assistance	1,331	1,400	2,731	2,000 e
95.006	Model State Drug Laws Initiative	1,188	1,250	2,500	1,250 e
	DEPARTMENT TOTAL: OUTLAYS	226,006	238,472	247,531	250,550
	CREDITS*	0*	0*	0*	0*

SOCIAL SECURITY ADMINISTRATION

Program Number	Program Title	FY 2013	FY 2014	FY 2015	FY 2016
96.001	Social Security—Disability \ t	(nr)	(nr)	(nr)	(nr)
96.002	Social Security—Retirement \ t	(nr)	(nr)	(nr)	(nr)
96.004	Survivors Insurance \ t	(nr)	(nr)	(nr)	(nr)
96.006	Supplemental Security Income	(nr)	(nr)	(nr)	(nr)
96.007	Research and Demonstration \ t	(nr)	(nr)	(nr)	(nr)
96.008	Benefits Planning, Outreach \ t	(nr)	(nr)	(nr)	(nr)
96.009	Incentives/Disabled Beneficiaries \ t	(nr)	(nr)	(nr)	(nr)
96.020	Benefits/World War II Veterans	(nr)	(nr)	(nr)	(nr)
	DEPARTMENT TOTAL: OUTLAYS	0	0	0	0
	CREDITS*	0*	0*	0*	0*

DEPARTMENT OF HOMELAND SECURITY

Program Number	Program Title	FY 2013	FY 2014	FY 2015	FY 2016
97.005	State, Local Training Program	75,740	87,000	(nr)	(nr)
97.007	Preparedness Technical Assistance	525	525	525 e	525 e
97.008	Urban Areas Security Initiative	10,000	13,000	13,000 e	13,000 e
97.009	Cuban/Haitian Entrant Program	7,900	7,900	10,776	12,000 e
97.010	Citizenship Education, Training	9,884	9,631	9,985	10,000 e
97.012	Boating Safety Financial \ t	120,895	107,444	112,830	114,326 e
97.018	National Fire Academy Training	1,576	1,522	1,625 e	1,775 e
97.022	Flood Insurance \ r	171,000*	176,300*	179,294*e	181,198*e
97.023	Community Assistance Program \ r	10,400	10,299	10,400 e	10,400 e
97.024	Emergency Food, Shelter	113,805	120,000	120,000 e	100,000 e
97.025	National Urban Search, Rescue	34,012	33,722	33,872 e	27,668 e
97.026	EMI—Training Assistance	1,862	2,024	1,600 e	1,600 e
97.027	EMI—Independent Study	729	853	617 e	642 e
97.028	EMI—Resident Education	2,300	2,025	2,100 e	2,100 e
97.029	Flood Mitigation Assistance	5,178	111,862	45,000 e	60,000 e
97.030	Community Disaster Loans	174,024*	0*	15,452*e	99,000*e
97.031	Cora Brown Fund \ t	7	2,100	(nr)	(nr)
97.032	Crisis Counseling	82,089	5,633	(nr)	(nr)
97.033	Disaster Legal Services	71	25	0	0
97.034	Disaster Unemployment Assistance	30,247	1,091	(nr)	(nr)
97.036	Disaster Grants—Public Assistance	5,730,769	5,910,634	(nr)	(nr)
97.039	Hazard Mitigation Grant	482,000	836,966	700,000 e	(nr)
97.040	Chemical Stockpile Emergency	33,513	14,439	15,359 e	20,380 e
97.041	Dam Safety	7,134	7,575	7,091 e	6,384 e
97.042	Emergency Management Performance	332,456	350,100	350,100 e	350,100 e
97.043	State Fire Training Systems Grants	1,034	1,000	920 e	(nr)
97.044	Assistance to Firefighters Grant	320,920	319,132	305,000 e	(nr)
97.045	Cooperating Technical Partners	24,199	38,447	41,000 e	50,000 e

Please see "Important Notes on the Tables, Footnotes," page 888

Table 1. *(continued)*

Program Number	ADMINISTRATIVE ENTITY Program Title (abridged)	FY 2013 in $thousands	FY 2014 in $thousands	FY 2015 in $thousands	FY 2016 in $thousands
97.046	Fire Management Assistance	109,070	101,607	(nr)	(nr)
97.047	Pre-Disaster Mitigation	31,272	38,238	42,500 e	40,000 e
97.048	Individual, Household Housing	1,740,320	143,408	259,000 e	(nr)
97.050	Individuals, Households/Other	1,478,211	1,766	9,248	25,586 e
97.052	Emergency Operations Centers	0	0	0 e	0 e
97.055	Interoperable Communications	0	0	0 e	0 e
97.056	Port Security Grant Program	93,207	100,000	100,000 e	100,000 e
97.057	Intercity Bus Security	0	0	3,000 e	0 e
97.061	Centers for Homeland Security	30,770	32,700	32,858	30,212 e
97.062	Scholars and Fellows	2,850	2,850	2,827	3,600 e
97.067	Homeland Security Grant Program \ i	968,390	1,043,046	1,044,000 e	1,044,000 e
97.075	Rail and Transit Security	93,209	100,000	97,000 e	97,000 e
97.076	Center/Missing, Exploited Children	305	305	305	305 e
97.077	Testing, Evaluation, Demonstration \ p	10,914	9,834	11,094 e	12,418 e
97.078	Buffer Zone Protection Plan	0	0	0 e	0 e
97.080	IAIP Pilot Projects	2,601	1,187	1,470	0 e
97.082	Earthquake Consortium	2,680	2,916	3,407 e	3,407 e
97.083	Staffing/Fire, Emergency	320,920	340,000	335,000 e	(nr)
97.088	Disaster Assistance Projects	53,568	4,096	(nr)	(nr)
97.089	Real ID Program	0	1,964	0 e	0 e
97.091	Homeland Security Biowatch \ p	27,502	28,830	29,725	17,174 e
97.092	Repetitive Flood Claims	0	0	0 e	0 e
97.101	National Fallen Firefighters Memorial	225	0	0 e	0 e
97.103	Degrees at a Distance	0	0	0 e	0 e
97.104	STEM Career Development	0	0	0 e	0 e
97.106	Securing Cities \ p	21,325	20,100	16,950	19,570 e
97.107	Incident Management System	2,000	2,000	2,000 e	2,000 e
97.108	Homeland Security Technologies \ p	2,008	1,816	650	1,400 e
97.110	Flood Loss Program	0	3,352	0 e	0 e
97.111	Catastrophic Preparedness Grant	0	0	0 e	0 e
97.113	Rail and Transit Security Grant Program	0	0	0 e	0 e
97.114	Emergency Food and Shelter National Board	0	0	0 e	0 e
97.115	Assistance to Firefighters Grant	0	0	0 e	0 e
97.116	Port Security Grant Program	0	0	0 e	0 e
97.123	Multi-State Information Sharing/Analysis Center	8,550	16,091	12,946	9,500 e
97.128	National Cyber Security Awareness	750	550	550	550 e
97.130	Nuclear Forensics Expertise Development	2,450	2,405	1,939	1,495 e
97.131	Emergency Management Baseline Assessments	600	900	300 e	300 e
97.132	Countering Violent Extremism	(n)	(n)	(n)	10,000 e
	DEPARTMENT TOTAL: OUTLAYS	12,442,942	9,994,910	3,788,569	2,199,417
	CREDITS*	345,024*	176,300*	194,746*	280,198*

AGENCY FOR INTERNATIONAL DEVELOPMENT

Program Number	Program Title	FY 2013	FY 2014	FY 2015	FY 2016
98.001	Foreign Assistance Programs	(nr)	(nr)	(nr)	(nr)
98.002	Cooperative Development Program	(nr)	(nr)	(nr)	(nr)
98.003	Ocean Freight Reimbursement	(nr)	(nr)	(nr)	(nr)
98.004	NGO Strengthening	(nr)	(nr)	(nr)	(nr)
98.005	Institutional Capacity Building	(nr)	(nr)	(nr)	(nr)
98.006	American Schools, Hospitals Abroad	(nr)	(nr)	(nr)	(nr)
98.007	Food for Peace DAP \ p	(nr)	(nr)	(nr)	(nr)
98.008	Food for Peace Emergency Program \ p	(nr)	(nr)	(nr)	(nr)
98.009	John Ogonowski Farmer-to-Farmer	(nr)	(nr)	(nr)	(nr)
98.010	Denton Program	(nr)	(nr)	(nr)	(nr)
98.011	Global Development Alliance	(nr)	(nr)	(nr)	(nr)
98.012	USAID/University Partnerships	(nr)	(nr)	(nr)	(nr)
	DEPARTMENT TOTAL: OUTLAYS	0	0	0	0
	CREDITS*	0*	0*	0*	0*
	GRAND TOTAL: OUTLAYS	**832,593,893**	**836,622,353**	**887,187,456**	**821,749,882**
	CREDITS*	1,044,372,434*	965,024,654*	1,025,381,488*	1,122,311,886*
	GRAND TOTAL: OUTLAYS + CREDITS	1,876,966,327	1,801,647,007	1,912,568,944	1,944,061,768

Please see "Important Notes on the Tables, Footnotes," page 888

Table 2.   Summary of Estimated Outlays/Credits, by Federal Department or Agency

Program Number	Department or Agency	FY 2013 in $thousands	FY 2014 in $thousands	FY 2015 in $thousands	FY 2016 in $thousands
10.000	**DEPARTMENT OF AGRICULTURE**				
	Total Outlays	122,719,821	139,140,994	134,460,650	62,332,864
	Total Credits	61,414,145*	48,163,299*	55,293,682*	57,990,279*
	TOTAL OUTLAYS + CREDITS	184,133,966	187,304,293	189,754,332	120,323,143
11.000	**DEPARTMENT OF COMMERCE**				
	Total Outlays	643,343	993,045	946,796	609,182
	Total Credits	83,000*	0*	0*	0*
	TOTAL OUTLAYS + CREDITS	726,343	993,045	946,796	609,182
12.000	**DEPARTMENT OF DEFENSE**				
	Total Outlays	3,828,961	4,170,656	3,757,438	904,507
	Total Credits	0*	0*	0*	0*
	TOTAL OUTLAYS + CREDITS	3,828,961	4,170,656	3,757,438	904,507
14.000	**DEPARTMENT OF HOUSING AND URBAN DEVELOPMENT**				
	Total Outlays	41,988,118	49,557,430	51,013,231	39,940,229
	Total Credits	266,272,037*	151,120,231*	153,689,900*	175,159,293*
	TOTAL OUTLAYS + CREDITS	308,260,155	200,677,661	204,703,131	215,099,522
15.000	**DEPARTMENT OF THE INTERIOR**				
	Total Outlays	11,201,246	7,440,993	5,923,623	5,477,644
	Total Credits	0*	0*	0*	0*
	TOTAL OUTLAYS + CREDITS	11,201,246	7,440,993	5,923,623	5,477,644
16.000	**DEPARTMENT OF JUSTICE**				
	Total Outlays	3,163,650	3,073,949	4,300,926	3,654,680
	Total Credits	0*	0*	0*	0*
	TOTAL OUTLAYS + CREDITS	3,163,650	3,073,949	4,300,926	3,654,680
17.000	**DEPARTMENT OF LABOR**				
	Total Outlays	78,833,758	52,582,975	46,690,538	45,945,844
	Total Credits	0*	0*	0*	0*
	TOTAL OUTLAYS + CREDITS	78,833,758	52,582,975	46,690,538	45,945,844
19.000	**DEPARTMENT OF STATE**				
	Total Outlays	716,434	676,265	573,095	572,345
	Total Credits	0*	0*	0*	0*
	TOTAL OUTLAYS + CREDITS	716,434	676,265	573,095	572,345
20.000	**DEPARTMENT OF TRANSPORTATION**				
	Total Outlays	61,696,028	61,260,872	55,925,395	63,671,366
	Total Credits	2,613,163*	8,434,626*	14,367,225*	13,296,925*
	TOTAL OUTLAYS + CREDITS	64,309,191	69,695,498	70,292,620	76,968,291
21.000	**DEPARTMENT OF THE TREASURY**				
	Total Outlays	184,719	56,900	29,000	33,500
	Total Credits	500*	500*	0*	0*
	TOTAL OUTLAYS + CREDITS	185,219	57,400	29,000	33,500
23.000	**APPALACHIAN REGIONAL COMMISSION**				
	Total Outlays	624,000	72,625	87,000	92,000
	Total Credits	0*	0*	0*	0*
	TOTAL OUTLAYS + CREDITS	624,000	72,625	87,000	92,000
27.000	**OFFICE OF PERSONNEL MANAGEMENT**				
	Total Outlays	0	0	0	0
	Total Credits	0*	0*	0*	0*
	TOTAL OUTLAYS + CREDITS	0	0	0	0

Please see "Important Notes on the Tables, Footnotes," page 888

Table 2. *(continued)*

Program Number	Department or Agency	FY 2013 in $thousands	FY 2014 in $thousands	FY 2015 in $thousands	FY 2016 in $thousands
29.000	**COMMISSION ON CIVIL RIGHTS**				
	Total Outlays	0	0	0	0
	Total Credits	0*	0*	0*	0*
	TOTAL OUTLAYS + CREDITS	0	0	0	0
30.000	**EQUAL EMPLOYMENT OPPORTUNITY COMMISSION**				
	Total Outlays	344,219	364,000	364,500	373,112
	Total Credits	0*	0*	0*	0*
	TOTAL OUTLAYS + CREDITS	344,219	364,000	364,500	373,112
31.000	**EXPORT-IMPORT BANK**				
	Total Outlays	0	0	0	0
	Total Credits	0*	0*	0*	0*
	TOTAL OUTLAYS + CREDITS	0	0	0	0
32.000	**FEDERAL COMMUNICATIONS COMMISSION**				
	Total Outlays	0	0	0	0
	Total Credits	0*	0*	0*	0*
	TOTAL OUTLAYS + CREDITS	0	0	0	0
33.000	**FEDERAL MARITIME COMMISSION**				
	Total Outlays	1,840	1,761	1,846	1,985
	Total Credits	0*	0*	0*	0*
	TOTAL OUTLAYS + CREDITS	1,840	1,761	1,846	1,985
34.000	**FEDERAL MEDIATION AND CONCILIATION SERVICE**				
	Total Outlays	0	400	800	400
	Total Credits	0*	0*	0*	0*
	TOTAL OUTLAYS + CREDITS	0	400	800	400
36.000	**FEDERAL TRADE COMMISSION**				
	Total Outlays	0	0	0	0
	Total Credits	0*	0*	0*	0*
	TOTAL OUTLAYS + CREDITS	0	0	0	0
39.000	**GENERAL SERVICES ADMINISTRATION**				
	Total Outlays	22,408	25,917	8,244	0
	Total Credits	0*	0*	0*	0*
	TOTAL OUTLAYS + CREDITS	22,408	25,917	8,244	0
40.000	**GOVERNMENT PRINTING OFFICE**				
	Total Outlays	0	0	0	0
	Total Credits	0*	0*	0*	0*
	TOTAL OUTLAYS + CREDITS	0	0	0	0
42.000	**LIBRARY OF CONGRESS**				
	Total Outlays	0	0	0	0
	Total Credits	0*	0*	0*	0*
	TOTAL OUTLAYS + CREDITS	0	0	0	0
43.000	**NATIONAL AERONAUTICS AND SPACE ADMINISTRATION**				
	Total Outlays	0	718,733	725,426	721,000
	Total Credits	0*	0*	0*	0*
	TOTAL OUTLAYS + CREDITS	0	718,733	725,426	721,000
44.000	**NATIONAL CREDIT UNION ADMINISTRATION**				
	Total Outlays	0	0	2,528	2,400
	Total Credits	3,000*	0*	1,500*	1,500*
	TOTAL OUTLAYS + CREDITS	3,000	0	4,028	3,900

Please see "Important Notes on the Tables, Footnotes," page 888

Table 2. (continued)

Program Number	Department or Agency	FY 2013 in $thousands	FY 2014 in $thousands	FY 2015 in $thousands	FY 2016 in $thousands
45.000	**NATIONAL FOUNDATION ON THE ARTS AND HUMANITIES**				
	Total Outlays	387,988	423,626	372,801	340,615
	Total Credits	0*	0*	0*	0*
	TOTAL OUTLAYS + CREDITS	387,988	423,626	372,801	340,615
47.000	**NATIONAL SCIENCE FOUNDATION**				
	Total Outlays	8,686,850	6,447,967	6,609,423	6,944,720
	Total Credits	0*	0*	0*	0*
	TOTAL OUTLAYS + CREDITS	8,686,850	6,447,967	6,609,423	6,944,720
57.000	**RAILROAD RETIREMENT BOARD**				
	Total Outlays	11,747,000	12,037,000	12,303,000	12,503,000
	Total Credits	0*	0*	0*	0*
	TOTAL OUTLAYS + CREDITS	11,747,000	12,037,000	12,303,000	12,503,000
58.000	**SECURITIES AND EXCHANGE COMMISSION**				
	Total Outlays	0	0	0	0
	Total Credits	0*	0*	0*	0*
	TOTAL OUTLAYS + CREDITS	0	0	0	0
59.000	**SMALL BUSINESS ADMINISTRATION**				
	Total Outlays	0	149,146	159,800	154,800
	Total Credits	0*	27,622,000*	42,125,000*	42,135,000*
	TOTAL OUTLAYS + CREDITS	0	27,771,146	42,284,800	42,289,800
64.000	**DEPARTMENT OF VETERANS AFFAIRS**				
	Total Outlays	2,000	0	0	1,000
	Total Credits	0*	0*	0*	0*
	TOTAL OUTLAYS + CREDITS	2,000	0	0	1,000
66.000	**ENVIRONMENTAL PROTECTION AGENCY**				
	Total Outlays	6,457,966	5,219,002	4,408,445	4,531,454
	Total Credits	0*	0*	0*	0*
	TOTAL OUTLAYS + CREDITS	6,457,966	5,219,002	4,408,445	4,531,454
68.000	**NATIONAL GALLERY OF ART**				
	Total Outlays	0	0	0	0
	Total Credits	0*	0*	0*	0*
	TOTAL OUTLAYS + CREDITS	0	0	0	0
70.000	**OVERSEAS PRIVATE INVESTMENT CORPORATION**				
	Total Outlays	0	0	0	0
	Total Credits	0*	0*	0*	0*
	TOTAL OUTLAYS + CREDITS	0	0	0	0
77.000	**NUCLEAR REGULATORY COMMISSION**				
	Total Outlays	15,600	20,000	19,232	0
	Total Credits	0*	0*	0*	0*
	TOTAL OUTLAYS + CREDITS	15,600	20,000	19,232	0
78.000	**COMMODITY FUTURES TRADING COMMISSION**				
	Total Outlays	0	0	0	0
	Total Credits	0*	0*	0*	0*
	TOTAL OUTLAYS + CREDITS	0	0	0	0
81.000	**DEPARTMENT OF ENERGY**				
	Total Outlays	2,621,654	2,789,402	2,545,048	1,158,998
	Total Credits	0*	0*	0*	0*
	TOTAL OUTLAYS + CREDITS	2,621,654	2,789,402	2,545,048	1,158,998
84.000	**DEPARTMENT OF EDUCATION**				
	Total Outlays	75,830,251	76,607,835	76,746,348	78,933,341
	Total Credits	128,758,682*	135,385,067*	130,490,532*	136,968,456*
	TOTAL OUTLAYS + CREDITS	204,588,933	211,992,902	207,236,880	215,901,797

Please see "Important Notes on the Tables, Footnotes," page 888

Table 2. *(continued)*

Program Number	Department or Agency	FY 2013 in $thousands	FY 2014 in $thousands	FY 2015 in $thousands	FY 2016 in $thousands
85.000	**SCHOLARSHIP AND FELLOWSHIP FOUNDATIONS**				
	Total Outlays	701	701	370	0
	Total Credits	0*	0*	0*	0*
	TOTAL OUTLAYS + CREDITS	701	701	370	0
86.000	**PENSION BENEFIT GUARANTY CORPORATION**				
	Total Outlays	0	0	0	0
	Total Credits	0*	0*	0*	0*
	TOTAL OUTLAYS + CREDITS	0	0	0	0
88.000	**ARCHITECTURAL AND TRANSPORTATION BARRIERS COMPLIANCE BOARD**				
	Total Outlays	0	0	0	0
	Total Credits	0*	0*	0*	0*
	TOTAL OUTLAYS + CREDITS	0	0	0	0
89.000	**NATIONAL ARCHIVES AND RECORDS ADMINISTRATION**				
	Total Outlays	46,224	50,513	79,124	80,291
	Total Credits	0*	0*	0*	0*
	TOTAL OUTLAYS + CREDITS	46,224	50,513	79,124	80,291
90.000	**INDEPENDENT BOARDS AND COMMISSIONS**				
	Total Outlays	0	0	0	0
	Total Credits	0*	0*	0*	0*
	TOTAL OUTLAYS + CREDITS	0	0	0	0
91.000	**INSTITUTE OF PEACE**				
	Total Outlays	0	0	0	0
	Total Credits	0*	0*	0*	0*
	TOTAL OUTLAYS + CREDITS	0	0	0	0
93.000	**DEPARTMENT OF HEALTH AND HUMAN SERVICES**				
	Total Outlays	387,831,097	402,356,085	474,995,565	490,318,638
	Total Credits	584,882,883*	594,122,631*	629,218,903*	696,480,235*
	TOTAL OUTLAYS + CREDITS	972,713,980	996,478,716	1,104,214,468	1,186,798,873
94.000	**CORPORATION FOR NATIONAL AND COMMUNITY SERVICE**				
	Total Outlays	329,069	150,179	101,164	0
	Total Credits	0*	0*	0*	0*
	TOTAL OUTLAYS + CREDITS	329,069	150,179	101,164	0
95.000	**EXECUTIVE OFFICE OF THE PRESIDENT**				
	Total Outlays	226,006	238,472	247,531	250,550
	Total Credits	0*	0*	0*	0*
	TOTAL OUTLAYS + CREDITS	226,006	238,472	247,531	250,550
96.000	**SOCIAL SECURITY ADMINISTRATION**				
	Total Outlays	0	0	0	0
	Total Credits	0*	0*	0*	0*
	TOTAL OUTLAYS + CREDITS	0	0	0	0
97.000	**DEPARTMENT OF HOMELAND SECURITY**				
	Total Outlays	12,442,942	9,994,910	3,788,569	2,199,417
	Total Credits	345,024*	176,300*	194,746*	280,198*
	TOTAL OUTLAYS + CREDITS	12,787,966	10,171,210	3,983,315	2,479,615
98.000	**AGENCY FOR INTERNATIONAL DEVELOPMENT**				
	Total Outlays	0	0	0	0
	Total Credits	0*	0*	0*	0*
	TOTAL OUTLAYS + CREDITS	0	0	0	0
	GRAND TOTAL: OUTLAYS	832,593,893	836,622,353	887,187,456	821,749,882
	GRAND TOTAL: CREDITS	1,044,372,434*	965,024,654*	1,025,381,488*	1,122,311,886*
	GRAND TOTAL: OUTLAYS + CREDITS	1,876,966,327	1,801,647,007	1,912,568,944	1,944,061,768

Please see "Important Notes on the Tables, Footnotes," page 888

PART IV

Field Office Contacts

NOTE: Field offices manage specific programs, or they may provide information about programs. However, if the program description in Part II states "Note: no field offices for this program," contacts should be with the headquarters office. "PART I - Obtaining Federal Assistance" offers observations concerning field office contacts, especially in the discussion of the entry heading "⑩ *Program headquarters address, phone number, and web sites.*"

DEPARTMENT OF AGRICULTURE

AGRICULTURAL RESEARCH SERVICE

10.001 **REGIONAL OFFICES**

BELTSVILLE—Bldg. 003 - Rm. 03, BARC-West, Beltsville, MD 20705. Phone: (301) 504-7019.

MIDSOUTH—Delta States Research Center, P.O. Box 225, Stoneville, MS 38776. Phone: (601) 686-5345.

MIDWEST—Northern Regional Research Center, 1815 N. University St., Peoria, IL 61604. Phone: (700) 360-4618.

NORTH ATLANTIC—Eastern Regional Research Center, 600 E. Mermaid Lane, Philadelphia, PA 19118. Phone: (215) 233-6551.

NORTHERN PLAINS—Procurement Assistance Officer, 1201 Oakridge Dr. - Ste. 150, Fort Collins, CO 80525-5526. Phone: (303) 229-5513.

PACIFIC WEST—Western Regional Research Center, 800 Buchanan St., Albany, CA 94710. Phone: (510) 559-6016.

SOUTH ATLANTIC—Russell Research Center, College Station Rd., P.O. Box 5677, Athens, GA 30604-5677. Phone: (706) 546-3532.

SOUTHERN PLAINS—7607 Eastmark Dr. - Ste. 30, College Station, TX 77840. Phone: (979) 960-9444.

ANIMAL AND PLANT HEALTH INSPECTION SERVICE

10.025 **REGIONAL OFFICES**
through
10.030 **Plant Protection and Quarantine**

CENTRAL *(Arkansas, Iowa, Kansas, Louisiana, Missouri, Nebraska, North Dakota, Oklahoma, South Dakota, Texas)*—3505 Boca Chica Blvd. - Ste. 60, Brownsville, TX 78521-4065. Phone: (956) 504-4150.

EASTERN *(Connecticut, Delaware, District of Columbia, Illinois, Indiana, Maine, Maryland, Massachusetts, Michigan, Minnesota, New Hampshire, New Jersey, New*

10.025
through
10.030
(cont.)

York, Ohio, Pennsylvania, Rhode Island, Vermont, Virginia, West Virginia, Wisconsin)—Blason II - 2nd fl., 505 S. Lenola Rd., Moorestown, NJ 08057-1549. Phone: (609) 968-4970.

SOUTHEAST *(Alabama, Florida, Georgia, Kentucky, Mississippi, North Carolina, Puerto Rico, South Carolina, Tennessee, Virgin Islands)*—Bldg. 1, 3505 25th Ave., Gulfport, MS 39501. Phone: (601) 863-1813.

WESTERN *(Alaska, Arizona, California, Colorado, Guam, Hawaii, Idaho, Montana, Nevada, New Mexico, Oregon, Utah, Washington, Wyoming)*—9580 Micron Ave. - Ste. I, Sacramento, CA 95827. Phone: (916) 857-6065.

Veterinary Services

CENTRAL *(Arkansas, Iowa, Kansas, Louisiana, Missouri, Nebraska, North Dakota, Oklahoma, South Dakota, Texas)*—100 W. Pioneer Pkwy. - Ste. 00, Arlington, TX 76010. Phone: (817) 276-2201.

NORTHERN *(Illinois, Indiana, Maryland, Massachusetts, Michigan, Minnesota, New Jersey, New York, Ohio, Pennsylvania, Virginia, West Virginia, Wisconsin)*—1 Winner's Circle - Ste. 00, Albany, NY 12205. Phone (518) 453-0103.

SOUTHEAST *(Alabama, Florida, Georgia, Kentucky, Mississippi, North Carolina, Puerto Rico, South Carolina, Tennessee—500 E. Zack St. - Ste. 10, Tampa, FL 33602-3945. Phone: (813) 228-2952.

WESTERN *(Alaska, Arizona, California, Colorado, Hawaii, Idaho, Montana, Nevada, New Mexico, Oregon, Utah, Washington, Wyoming)*—384 Inverness Dr. S. - Ste. 50, Englewood, CO 80112. Phone (303) 784-6202.

Wildlife Service

EASTERN *(Alabama, Arkansas, Connecticut, Delaware, District of Columbia, Florida, Georgia, Illinois, Indiana, Iowa, Louisiana, Kentucky, Maine, Maryland, Massachusetts, Michigan, Minnesota, Mississippi, Missouri, New Hampshire, New Jersey, New York, North Carolina, Ohio, Pennsylvania, Puerto Rico, Rhode Island, South Carolina, Tennessee, Vermont, Virginia, Virgin Islands, West Virginia, Wisconsin)*— 3322 West End Ave. - Ste. 01, Nashville, TN 37203. Phone: (615) 736-2007.

WESTERN *(Alaska, Arizona, California, Colorado, Guam, Hawaii, Idaho, Kansas, Montana, Nebraska, Nevada, New Mexico, North Dakota, Oklahoma, Oregon, South Dakota, Texas, Utah, Washington, Wyoming)*—12345 W. Alameda Pkwy. - Ste. 04, Lakewood, CO 80228. Phone: (303) 969-6560.

■ National Wildlife Research Center, 1201 Oakridge Dr., Ft. Collins, CO 80525. Phone: (970) 223-1588.

FARM SERVICE AGENCY

STATE OFFICES

10.051
through
10.069

Alabama—4121 Carmichael Rd. - Ste. 00, P.O. Box 235013, Montgomery, AL 36106-5013. Phone: (334) 279-3500.

Alaska—800 W. Evergreen - Ste. 16, Palmer, AK 99645-6389. Phone: (907) 745-7982.

Arizona—77 E. Thomas Rd. - Ste. 40, Phoenix, AZ 85012-3318. Phone: (602) 640-5200.

Arkansas—Federal Bldg. - Rm. 416, 700 W. Capitol Ave., Little Rock, AR 72201-3225. Phone: (501) 301-3000.

California—430 G St. - Ste. 161, Davis, CA 95616-4161. Phone: (530) 792-5538.

Caribbean Area—Fernandez Junzos Station, Cobian's Plaza - Ste. 09,P.O. Box 11188, 1607 Ponce DeLeon Ave., Santurce, PR 00909-0001. Phone: (809) 729-6872.

Colorado—655 Parfet St. - Ste. E-305, Lakewood, CO 80215-5517. Phone: (303) 236-2866.

Connecticut—88 Day Hill Rd., Windsor, CT 06095. Phone: (860) 285-8483.

Delaware—1201 College Park Dr. - Ste. 01, Dover, DE 19904-8713. Phone: (302) 678-2547.

Florida—440 NW 25th Place - Ste. , Gainesville, FL 32606. Phone: (352) 379-4500.

Georgia—Federal Bldg. - Rm. 02, 355 E. Hancock Ave., P.O. Box 1907, Athens, GA 30603-1907. Phone: (706) 546-2266.

Hawaii—300 Ala Moana Blvd. - Rm. 106, P.O. Box 50008, Honolulu, HI 96850. Phone: (808) 541-2644.

Idaho—9173 W. Barners - Ste. B, Boise, ID 83705-1511. Phone: (208) 378-5650.

Illinois—3500 W Avenue, P.O. Box 19273, Springfield, IL 62794-9273. Phone: (217) 241-6600.

Indiana—5981 Lakeside Blvd., Indianapolis, IN 46278. Phone: (317) 290-3030, ext.317.

Iowa—10500 Buena Vista Ct., Des Moines, IA 50322. Phone: (515) 254-1540, ext.600.

Kansas—3600 Anderson Ave., Manhattan, KS 66502-2511. Phone: (785) 539-3531.

Kentucky—771 Corporate Dr. - Ste. 00, Lexington, KY 40503-5478. Phone: (606) 224-7601.

Louisiana—3737 Government St., Alexandria, LA 71302-3395. Phone: (318) 473-7721.

Maine—444 Stillwater Ave. - Ste. , Bangor, ME 04402-0406. Phone: (207) 990-9140.

Maryland—River Center - Ste. E, 8335 Guilford Rd., Columbia, MD 21046. Phone: (410) 381-4550.

Massachusetts—445 West St., Amherst, MA 01002-2957. Phone: (413) 256-0232.

Michigan—3001 Coolidge Rd. - Ste. 00, East Lansing, MI 48823-6321. Phone: (517) 337-6659, ext.1201.

Minnesota—400 Farm Credit Service Bldg., 375 Jackson St., St. Paul, MN 55101-1852. Phone: (612) 602-7700.

Mississippi—6310 I-55 North, P.O. Box 14995, Jackson, MS 39211. Phone: (601) 965-4300.

Missouri—Parkade Plaza, 601 Business Loop 70 West - Ste. 25, Columbia, MO 65203. Phone: (573) 876-0925.

Montana—10 E. Babcock - Rm. 57, P.O. Box 670, Bozeman, MT 59715. Phone: (406) 587-6872.

Nebraska—7131 A St., P.O. Box 57975, Lincoln, NE 68510-7975. Phone: (402) 437-5581.

Nevada—1755 E. Plumb Lane - Ste. 02, Reno, NV 89502-3207. Phone: (775) 784-5411.

New Hampshire—22 Bridge St. - 4th fl., P.O. Box 1388, Concord, NH 03302-1338. Phone: (603) 224-7941.

New Jersey—Mastoris Professional Plaza, Bldg. 2 - Ste. E, 163 Rt. 130, Bordentown, NJ 08505-2249. Phone: (609) 298-3446.

New Mexico—6200 Jefferson St. NE, Albuquerque, NM 87109. Phone: (505) 761-4900.

New York—441 S. Salina St. - (5th fl.) Ste. 56, Syracuse, NY 13202-2455. Phone: (315) 477-6303.

North Carolina—4407 Bland Rd. - Ste. 75, Raleigh, NC 27609-6296. Phone: (919) 875-4800.

10.051 through 10.069 (cont.)

North Dakota—1025 28th St. SW, P.O. Box 3046, Fargo, ND 58108. Phone: (701) 239-5205.

Ohio—Federal Bldg. - Rm. 40, 200 N. High St., Columbus, OH 43215. Phone: (614) 469-6735.

Oklahoma—100 USDA - Ste. 02, Farm Rd. and McFarland St., Stillwater, OK 74074-2653. Phone: (405) 742-1130.

Oregon—7620 SW Mohawk, P.O. Box 1300, Tualatin, OR 97062-8121. Phone: (503) 692-6830.

Pennsylvania—One Credit Union Pl. - Ste. 20, Harrisburg, PA 17110-2994. Phone: (717) 237-2113.

Rhode Island—West Bay Office Complex - Rm. 0, 60 Quaker Lane, Warwick, RI 02886-0111. Phone: (401) 828-8232.

South Carolina—1927 Thurmond Mall - Ste. 00, Columbia, SC 29201-2375. Phone: (803) 806-3830.

South Dakota—Federal Bldg. - Rm. 08, 200 4th St. SW, Huron, SD 57350-2478. Phone: (605) 352-1160.

Tennessee—U.S. Courthouse - Rm. 79, 801 Broadway, Nashville, TN 37203-3816. Phone: (615) 736-5555.

Texas—Commerce National Bank Bldg. - 2nd fl., 2405 Texas Ave. S., College Station, TX 77840. Phone: (409) 260-9207. *For mail:* P.O. Box 2900, College Station, TX 77841-0001.

Utah—125 S. State St. - Rm. 239, P.O. Box 11350, Salt Lake City, UT 84147-0350. Phone: (801) 524-5013.

Vermont—Executive Square Office Bldg., 346 Shelburne St., Burlington, VT 05401-4995. Phone: (802) 658-2803.

Virginia—Culpeper Bldg. - Ste. 38, 1606 Santa Rosa Rd., Richmond, VA 23229. Phone: (804) 287-1500.

Washington—Rock Pointe Tower - Ste. 68, 316 W. Boone Ave., Spokane, WA 99201-2350. Phone: (509) 323-3000.

West Virginia—New Federal Bldg. - Rm. 39, 75 High St., P.O. Box 1049, Morgantown, WV 26507-1049. Phone: (304) 291-4351.

Wisconsin—6515 Watts Rd. - Rm. 00, Madison, WI 53719-2797. Phone: (608) 276-8732, ext.100.

Wyoming—951 Werner Ct. - Ste. 30, Casper, WY 82601-1307. Phone: (307) 261-5231.

NATURAL RESOURCES CONSERVATION SERVICE

10.072

REGIONAL OFFICES

EAST—1400 Wilson Blvd. - Ste. 100, Arlington, VA 22209. Phone: (703) 312-7282.

MIDWEST—One Gifford Pinchot Dr. - Rm. 04, Madison, WI 53705-3210. Phone: (608) 264-5281.

NORTHERN PLAINS—100 Centennial Mall North - Rm. 52, Lincoln, NE 68508. Phone: (402) 437-5315.

SOUTH CENTRAL—Bldg. 23, 501 W. Felix St., P.O. Box 6459, Ft. Worth, TX 76115. Phone: (817) 334-5224, ext.3700.

SOUTHEAST—1720 Peachtree Rd. NW - Ste. 16-N, Atlanta, GA 30367. Phone: (404) 347-6105.

WEST—650 Capitol Mall - Rm. 072, Sacramento, CA 95814. Phone: (916) 498-5284.

STATE OFFICES

Alabama—3381 Skyway Dr., Auburn, AL 36830. Phone: (334) 887-4500.

Alaska—949 E. 36 Ave. - Ste. 00, Anchorage, AK 99508-4302. Phone: (907) 271-2424.

Arizona—3003 N. Central Ave. - Ste. 00, Phoenix, AZ 85012-2945. Phone: (602) 280-8808.

Arkansas—Federal Bldg. - Rm. 404, 700 W. Capitol Ave., P.O. Box 2323, Little Rock, AR 72201-3228. Phone: (501) 324-5445.

California—2121-C 2nd St. - Ste. 02, Davis, CA 95616-5475. Phone: (916) 757-8215.

Colorado—655 Parfet St. - Rm.E200C, Lakewood, CO 80215-5517. Phone: (303) 236-2886, ext.202.

Connecticut—16 Professional Park Rd., Storrs, CT 06268-1299. Phone: (203) 487-4014.

Delaware—1203 College Park Dr. - Ste. 01, Dover, DE 19904-8713. Phone: (302) 678-4160.

Florida—2614 NW 43rd St., Box 141510, Gainesville, FL 32606-6611. Phone: (904) 338-9500.

Georgia—Federal Bldg., 355 E. Hancock Ave., P.O. Box 13, Athens, GA 30601-2769. Phone: (706) 546-2272.

Hawaii—300 Ala Moana Blvd. - Rm. 316, P.O. Box 50004, Honolulu, HI 96850-0002. Phone: (808) 541-2601.

Idaho—3244 Elder St. - Rm. 24, Boise, ID 83705-4711. Phone: (208) 378-5700.

Illinois—1902 Fox Dr., Champaign, IL 61820-7335. Phone: (217) 398-5267.

Indiana—6013 Lakeside Blvd., Indianapolis, IN 46278-2933. Phone: (317) 290-3200.

Iowa—Federal Bldg. - Ste. 93, 210 Walnut St., Des Moines, IA 50309-2180. Phone: (515) 284-6655.

Kansas—760 S. Broadway, Salina, KS 67401. Phone: (913) 823-4565.

Kentucky—771 Corporate Dr. - Ste. 10, Lexington, KY 40503-5479. Phone: (606) 224-7350.

Louisiana—3737 Government St., Alexandria, LA 71302-3727. Phone: (318) 473-7751.

Maine—5 Godfrey Dr., Orono, ME 04473. Phone: (207) 866-7241.

Maryland—John Hansen Business Center - Ste. 01, 339 Busch's Frontage Rd., Annapolis, MD 21401-5534. Phone: (410) 757-0861.

Massachusetts—451 West St., Amherst, MA 01002-2995. Phone: (413) 253-4351.

Michigan—1405 S. Harrison Rd. - Rm. 01, East Lansing, MI 48823-5243. Phone: (517) 337-6701, ext.1201.

Minnesota—600 Farm Credit Bldg., 375 Jackson St., St. Paul, MN 55101-1854. Phone: (612) 290-3675.

Mississippi—Federal Bldg. - Ste. 321, 100 W. Capital St., Jackson, MS 39269-1399. Phone: (601) 965-5205.

Missouri—Parkade Center - Ste. 50, 601 Business Loop - 70 West, Columbia, MO 65203-2546. Phone: (573) 876-0901.

Montana—Federal Bldg. - Rm. 43, 10 E. Babcock St., Bozeman, MT 59715-4704. Phone: (406) 587-6813.

Nebraska—Federal Bldg. - Rm. 52, 100 Centennial Mall N., Lincoln, NE 68508-3866. Phone: (402) 437-5327.

Nevada—Bldg. F - Ste. 01, 5301 Longley Lane, Reno, NV 89511-1805. Phone: (702) 784-5863.

10.072
(cont.)

New Hampshire—Federal Bldg., 2 Madbury Rd., Durham, NH 03824-1499. Phone: (603) 433-0505.

New Jersey—1370 Hamilton St., Somerset, NJ 08873-3157. Phone: (908) 246-1205.

New Mexico—6200 Jefferson NE - Rm. 05, Albuquerque, NM 87109-3734. Phone: (505) 761-4400.

New York—441 S. Salina St. - (Ste. 54) Rm. 20, Syracuse, NY 13202-2450. Phone: (315) 477-6504.

North Carolina—4405 Bland Rd. - Ste. 05, Raleigh, NC 27609-6293. Phone: (919) 873-2102.

North Dakota—Federal Bldg. - Rm. 70, 220 E. Rosser Ave. and 3rd St., Bismarck, ND 58502-1458. Phone: (701) 250-4421.

Ohio—Federal Bldg. - Rm. 22, 200 N. High St., Columbus, OH 43215-2478. Phone: (614) 469-6962.

Oklahoma—100 USDA - Ste. 03, Stillwater, OK 74074-2624. Phone: (405) 742-1204.

Oregon—Federal Bldg. - (16th fl.) Ste. 300, 101 SW Main St., Portland, OR 97204-3221. Phone: (503) 414-3201.

Pacific Basin Area—FHB Bldg. - Ste. 01, 400 Route 9, Guam 96927. Phone: (9-011-671)472-7490.

Pennsylvania—One Credit Union Place - Ste. 40, Harrisburg, PA 17110-2993. Phone: (717) 782-2202.

Puerto Rico—IBM Bldg. - Ste. 04, 654 Munoz Rivera Ave., Hato Rey, PR 00918-4123. Phone: (787) 766-5206.

Rhode Island—60 Quaker Lane - Ste. 6, Warwick, RI 02886-0111. Phone: (401) 828-1300.

South Carolina—Thurmond Federal Bldg. - Rm. 50, 1835 Assembly St., Columbia, SC 29201-2489. Phone: (803) 765-5681.

South Dakota—Federal Bldg., 200 4th St. SW, Huron, SD 57350-2475. Phone: (605) 352-1200.

Tennessee—675 U.S. Courthouse, 801 Broadway, Nashville, TN 37203-3878. Phone: (615) 736-5471.

Texas—Poage Federal Bldg., 101 S. Main St., Temple, TX 76501-7682. Phone: (817) 774-1214.

Utah—Bennett Federal Bldg. - Rm. 402, 125 S. State St., Salt Lake City, UT 84147. Phone: (801) 524-5050.

Vermont—69 Union St., Winooski, VT 05404-1999. Phone: (802) 951-6795.

Virginia—Culpeper Bldg. - Ste. 09, 1606 Santa Rosa Rd., Richmond, VA 23229-5014. Phone: (804) 287-1691.

Washington—W. 316 Boone Ave. - Ste. 50, Spokane, WA 99201-2348. Phone: (509) 323-2900.

West Virginia—75 High St. - Rm. 01, Morgantown, WV 26505. Phone: (304) 291-4153.

Wisconsin—6515 Watts Rd. - Ste. 00, Madison, WI 53719-2726. Phone: (608) 264-5577.

Wyoming—Federal Office Bldg. - Rm. 124, 100 E. B St., Casper, WY 82601. Phones: (307) 261-5201, -1911.

10.080
through
10.106

Listed under **10.051.**

AGRICULTURAL MARKETING SERVICE

10.153
through
10.167

COTTON DIVISION

Grading, Marketing Services (including Market News)

3275 Appling Rd., Memphis, TN 38133. Phone: (901) 384-3000.

Standardization and Quality Assurance Branch

3275 Appling Rd., Memphis, TN 38133. Phone: (901) 384-3015.

DAIRY DIVISION

Dairy Inspection, Grading Branch and Laboratory

Bldg. A - Ste. 70, 800 Roosevelt Rd., Glen Ellyn, IL 60137. Phone: (708) 790-6920.

Market News Service

2811 Agricultural Dr., Madison, WI 53704-6777. Phone: (608) 224-5080.

FRUIT AND VEGETABLE DIVISION

Fresh and Processed Products

Alabama—1557 Reeves St., P.O. Box 1368, Dothan, AL 36302. Phone: (334) 792-5185.

Arizona—1688 W. Adams - Rm. 15, Phoenix, AZ 85007. Phone: (602) 542-0880.

California—1320 E. Olympic Ave. - Rm. 12, Los Angeles, CA 90021. Phones: (213) 894-2489, -6553.

■ 1220 N St. - Rm.A-270, P.O. Box 942871, Sacramento, CA 94271-0001. Phones: (916) 654-0810, -0813, -0815.

Colorado—2331 W. 31st Ave., Denver, CO 80211. Phones: (303) 844-4570, 477-0093.

Connecticut—Connecticut Regional Market, 101 Reserve Rd. - Rm. , Hartford, CT 06114. Phone: (860) 240-3446.

Delaware—2320 S. DuPont Hwy., Dover, DE 19901. Phone: (302) 736-4811.

District of Columbia/Maryland—Baltimore-Washington Terminal Market Office, 8610 Baltimore-Washington Blvd. - Ste. 12, Jessup, MD 20794. Phones: (301) 317-4387, -4587.

Florida—Techniport Bldg. - Rm. 56, 5600 NW 36th St., Miami, FL 33122. Phone: (305) 870-9542.

Georgia—Administration Bldg. - Rm. 05, 16 Forest Pkwy., Forest Park, GA 30050. Phone: (404) 366-7522.

Hawaii—1428 S. King St., P.O. Box 22159, Honolulu, HI 96823-2159. Phone: (808) 973-9566.

Idaho—2270 Old Penitentiary Rd., Boise, ID 83712. Phone: (208) 332-8670.

Indiana—P.O. Box 427, Greenfield, IN 46140-0427. Phone: (317) 462-5897.

Kentucky—No. 1 Produce Terminal, Louisville, KY 40218. Phones: (502) 595-4266, -4278.

Louisiana—U.S. Postal Service Bldg. - Rm. 1036, 701 Loyola Ave., New Orleans, LA 70113. Phones: (504) 589-6741, -6742.

Maine—744 Main St. - Ste. , P.O. Box 1058, Presque Isle, ME 04769. Phone: (207) 764-2100.

10.153 through 10.167 (cont.)

Massachusetts—Boston Market Terminal Bldg. - Rm. , 34 Market St., Everett, MA 02149. Phones: (617) 389-2480, -2481.

Michigan—90 Detroit Union Produce Union Terminal, 7201 W. Fort St., Detroit, MI 48209. Phones:(313) 226-6059, -6225.

Minnesota—90 W. Plato Blvd., St. Paul, MN 55107. Phones: (612) 296-8557, -0593.

Missouri—Gumble Bldg. - Rm. 02, 801 Walnut St., Kansas City, MO 64106. Phone: (816) 374-6273.

- Unit 1 Produce Row - (1st fl.) Rm. 00, St. Louis, MO 63102. Phone: (314) 425-4514, -4515.

New Jersey—Federal Bldg. - Rm. 430, 970 Broad St., Newark, NJ 07102. Phone: (201) 645-2636.

New York—Division of Food Safety and Inspection Service, Capital Plaza - Bldg. 2 (2nd fl.), 1 Winners Circle, Albany, NY 12235. Phones: (518) 457-1211, -2090, -1982.

- 465B Hunts Point Market, Bronx, NY 10474. Phones: (718) 991-7665, -7669.

Ohio—3716 Croton Ave., Cleveland, OH 44115. Phone: (216) 522-2135.

- Division of Food, Dairy and Drugs, Bldg. 2, 8995 E. Main St., Reynoldsburg, OH 43068. Phone: (614) 728-6350.

Oklahoma—2800 N. Lincoln Blvd., Oklahoma City, OK 73105. Phone: (405) 521-3864.

Oregon—635 Capitol St. NE, Salem, OR 97310-0110. Phone: (503) 986-4629.

Pennsylvania—2301 N. Cameron St. - Rm. 12, Harrisburg, PA 17110. Phones: (717) 787-5107, -5108.

- 210 Produce Bldg., 3301 S. Galloway St., Philadelphia, PA 19148. Phones: (215) 336-0845, -0846.

- Pittsburgh Produce Terminal Bldg. - Rm. 06, 2100 Smallman St., Pittsburgh, PA 15222. Phones: (412) 261-6435.

Puerto Rico—Federal-State Inspection, GSA Service Center, 651 Federal Dr. - Ste. 03-05, Guaynabo, PR 00965. Phones: (787) 783-2230, -4116.

Tennessee—3211 Alcoa Hwy., Knoxville, TN 37920. Phone: (423) 577-2633.

- Melrose Station, P.O. Box 40627, Nashville, TN 37204. Phone: (615) 360-0169.

Texas—1406 Parker St. - Ste. 03, Dallas, TX 75215. Phones: (214) 767-5337, -5338.

- 8001 E N. Mesa - Ste. 03, El Paso, TX 79932. Phone: (505) 589-3753.

- 3100 Produce Row - Rm. A, Houston, TX 77023. Phones: (713) 923-2557, -2558.

- Administration Bldg. - Rm. 44, 1500 S. Zarzamora St., San Antonio, TX 78207. Phone: (210) 222-2751.

- 1301 W. Expressway, P.O. Box 107, San Juan, TX 78589. Phones: (210) 787-4091, -6881.

Utah—350 N. Redwood Rd. - Rm. 17, Salt Lake City, UT 84116. Phone: (801) 538-7187.

Washington—National Resources Bldg. - 2nd fl., 1111 Washington St., P.O. Box 42560, Olympia, WA 98504-2560. Phone: (360) 902-1831.

Market News Branch

Arizona—522 N. Central Ave. - Rm. 06, Phoenix, AZ 85004. Phone: (602) 379-3066.

California—2202 Monterey St. - Ste. 04-A, Fresno, CA 93721. Phone: (209) 487-5178.

- 1320 E. Olympic Blvd. - Ste. 12, Los Angeles, CA 90021-1907. Phone: (213) 894-3077.

- 630 Sansome St. - Rm. 27, San Francisco, CA 94111. Phone: (415) 705-1300.

Colorado—Greeley Producers Bldg., 711 "O" St., Greeley, CO 80631. Phones: (970) 351-7097, -8256.

Florida—Brickell Plaza Bldg. - Ste. 24, 909 SE 1st Ave., Miami, FL 33131. Phone: (305) 373-2955.

■ (*Seasonal*)775 Warner Ln., Orlando, FL 32803. Phone: (407) 897-5950.

Georgia—203 Administration Bldg., 16 Forest Pkwy., Forest Park, GA 30050. Phones: (404) 763-7297, 361-1376.

■ Georgia State Farmers Market - Stall 39, 502 Smith Ave., U.S. Hwy. 84, P.O. Box 1447, Thomasville, GA 31799. Phone: (912) 228-1208.

Idaho—1820 E. 17th St. - Ste. 30, Idaho Falls, ID 83404. Phone: (208) 526-0166.

Illinois—Kluczynski Bldg. - Rm. 12, 230 S. Dearborn St., Chicago, IL 60604. Phone: (312) 353-0111.

Maryland—Maryland Wholesale Produce Market, Bldg. B - Rm. 01, 7460 Conowingo Ave., Jessup, MD 20794. Phones: (410) 799-4840, -4841; Washington DC only: (301) 621-1261.

Massachusetts—Boston Market Terminal - Rm. 0, 34 Market St., Everett, MA 02149. Phones: (617) 387-4498, -4615, -4681.

Michigan—Federal Bldg. - Rm. 01, 175 Territorial Rd., P.O. Box 1204, Benton Harbor, MI 49023. Phones: (616) 925-3270, -3271.

■ Union Produce Terminal - Rm. 3, 7201 W. Fort St., Detroit, MI 48209. Phone: (313) 841-1111.

Missouri—Unit 1, Produce Row - Rm. 01, St. Louis, MO 63102-1418. Phone: (314) 425-4520.

New York—5A NYC Terminal Market, Halleck St. at Edgewater Rd., Bronx, NY 10474-7355. Phone: (718) 542-2225.

Pennsylvania—3301 S. Galloway St. - Rm. 61, Philadelphia, PA 19148. Phone: (215) 597-4536.

■ 2100 Smallman St. - Rm. 07, Pittsburgh, PA 15222. Phone: (412) 644-5847.

Texas—1406 Parker - Rm. 01, Dallas, TX 75215. Phones: (214) 767-5375, -5376, -5377.

Washington—Interwest Savings Bank - Ste. 02, 15111 8th Ave. SW, P.O. Box 48099, Seattle, WA 98148-0099. Phones: (206) 764-3753, -3804.

■ Agricultural Service Center - Rm. , 2015 S. 1st St., Yakima, WA 98903. Phones: (509) 575-2492, -2493.

Marketing Field Service

California—2202 Monterey St. - Ste. 02-B, Fresno, CA 93721. Phone: (209) 487-5901.

Florida—301 3rd St. NW - Ste. 06, P.O. Box 2276, Winterhaven, FL 33881. Phones: (941) 299-4770, -4886.

Oregon—1220 SW 3rd Ave. - Rm. 69, Portland, OR 97204. Phones: (503) 326-2724, -2725.

Texas—1313 E. Hackberry, McAllen, TX 78501. Phone: (956) 682-2833.

Processed Products Branch

EASTERN—Regional Director, Bldg. A - Ste. 80, 800 Roosevelt Rd., Glen Ellyn, IL 60137-5875. Phone: (630) 790-6957.

Florida—6966 NW 36th Ave., Miami, FL 33147-6506. Phone: (305) 835-7626.

■ 98 3rd St. SW, Winter Haven, FL 33880-2909. Phone: (941) 294-7416.

Georgia—1555 St. Joseph Ave., East Point, GA 30344-2591. Phone: (404) 763-7495.

Indiana—4318 Technology Dr., South Bend, IN 46628-9752. Phone: (219) 287-5407.

10.153 through 10.167 (cont.)

Louisiana (*Inspection Point of East Point, GA*)—Commerce Bldg. - Ste. , 1942 Williams Blvd., Kenner, LA 70062-6285. Phone: (504) 466-0343.

Maine—165 Lancaster St., Portland, ME 04101-2499. Phone: (207) 772-1588.

Maryland (*Inspection Point of Hunt Valley, MD*)—102 Maryland Ave., Easton, MD 21601-3409. Phone: (410) 822-3383.

- Hunt Valley Professional Bldg., 9 Schilling Rd., Hunt Valley, MD 21031-1106. Phone: (410) 962-4946.

Michigan (*Inspection Point of South Bend, IN*)—c/o Vroom Cold Storage, Russell Rd., Hart, MI 49420-0113. Phone: (616) 873-5654.

Minnesota (*Inspection Point of Ripon, WI*)—2126 Hoffman Rd., Mankato, MN 56001-5863. Phone: (507) 387-6101.

New Jersey—Park Plaza, Professional Bldg. - Ste. 04, 622 Georges Rd., North Brunswick, NJ 08902-3313. Phone: (908) 545-0939.

New York (*Inspection Point of North Brunswick, NJ*)—Genesee Valley Regional Market, 900 Jefferson Rd. - Rm. 10, Rochester, NY 14623-3289. Phones: (716) 424-2092, -2096.

Oklahoma (*Inspection Point of Weslaco, TX*)—716 S. 2nd St. - Ste. 06, Stilwell, OK 74960-4806. Phone: (918) 696-6333.

Puerto Rico—Federal State Inspection Service, GSA Center - Ste. 03-05, 651 Federal Dr., Guaynabo, PR 00965-1030. Phones: (809) 783-2230, -4116.

Texas—Federal Bldg. - Rm. 011, 2320 La Branch St., Houston, TX 77004-1036. Phone: (713) 659-3836.

- (*Inspection Point of Weslaco, TX*)—319 Market St., Laredo, TX 78040-8529. Phone: (210) 726-2258.

- 117 S. Westgate, Weslaco, TX 78596-2701. Phones: (210) 968-2772, -2126.

Virginia—No.1 N. 14th St. - Rm. 32, Richmond, VA 23219-3691. Phone: (804) 786-0930.

Wisconsin—742 E. Fond du Lac St., Ripon, WI 54971-9555. Phone: (414) 748-2287.

WESTERN—Regional Director, 2202 Monterey St. - Ste. 02-C, Fresno, CA 93721-3175. Phone: (209) 487-5891.

California—2202 Monterey St. - Ste. 02-A, Fresno, CA 93721-3129. Phone: (209) 487-5210.

- (*Inspection Point of Fresno*)—45-116 Commerce St. - Ste. 5, Indio, CA 92201-3440. Phone: (619) 347-1057.

- 1320 E. Olympic Rd. - Rm. 12, Los Angeles, CA 90021-1948. Phone: (213) 894-3173.

Hawaii—State of Hawaii Department of Agriculture, 1428 S. King St., P.O. Box 22159, Honolulu, HI 96823-2159. Phone: (808) 973-9566.

Oregon (*Inspection Point of Yakima, WA*)—111 S. Main St., Milton-Freewater, OR 97862-1342. Phone: (541) 938-3251.

- 340 High St. NE, Salem, OR 97301-3631. Phone: (503) 399-5761.

Washington—32 N. 3rd St. - Rm. 12, Yakima, WA 98901-2791. Phone: (509) 575-5869.

LIVESTOCK DIVISION

Livestock and Grain Market News Branch

Alabama—1445 Federal Dr. - Rm. 07, P.O. Box 3336, Montgomery, AL 36109-0336. Phone: (334) 223-7488.

Arizona—Stockyards Bldg. - Rm. 02, 5001 E. Washington St., Phoenix, AZ 85034-2010. Phone: (602) 379-4376.

Arkansas—2301 S. University - Rm. 10-B, P.O. Box 391, Little Rock, AR 72203-3910. Phone: (501) 671-2203.

Colorado—711 "O" St., Greeley, CO 80631-9540. Phone: (970) 353-9750.

Florida—775 Warner Lane, Orlando, FL 32803. Phone: (407) 897-2708.

Georgia—Georgia State Farmers Market, 502 Smith Ave. - Stall 38, P.O. Box 86, Thomasville, GA 31792-0086. Phone: (912) 226-2198.

Illinois—Illinois Department of Agriculture, Division of Marketing, State Fairgrounds, P.O. Box 19281, Springfield, IL 62794-9281. Phone: (217) 782-4925.

Iowa—210 Walnut St. - Rm. 67, Des Moines, IA 50309-2106. Phone: (515) 284-4460.

- 800 Cunningham Dr. - Rm. 25, P.O. Box 2437, Sioux City, IA 51107-2437. Phone: (712) 252-3286.

Kansas—100 Military Ave. - Ste. 17, Dodge City, KS 67801-4945. Phone: (316) 227-8881.

Kentucky—1321 Story Ave., Louisville, KY 40206-1884. Phone: (502) 582-5287.

Louisiana—Capitol Station, 5825 Florida Blvd., P.O. Box 3334, Baton Rouge, LA 70821-3334. Phone: (504) 922-1328.

Minnesota—New Livestock Exchange Bldg. - Ste. 08, S. St. Paul, MN 55075-5598. Phone: (612) 451-1565.

Missouri—601 Illinois Ave. - Rm. 10, St. Joseph, MO 64504-1396. Phone: (816) 238-0678.

Montana—Public Auction Yards Bldg. - Rm. 06, 112 S. 18th and Minnesota Ave., P.O. Box 1191, Billings, MT 59103-1191. Phone: (406) 657-6285.

Nebraska—213 Livestock Exchange Bldg., 29th and O St., Omaha, NE 68107-2603. Phone: (402) 731-4520.

New Mexico—2507 N. Telshor Blvd. - Ste. , Las Cruces, NM 88001. Phone: (505) 521-4928.

Oklahoma—Livestock Exchange Bldg. - Rm. 40, 2501 Exchange Ave., Oklahoma City, OK 73108-2477. Phone: (405) 232-5425.

Oregon—1220 SW 3rd Ave. - Rm. 772, Portland, OR 97204-2899. Phone: (503) 326-2237.

Pennsylvania—c/o New Holland Sales Stables, 101 W. Fulton St., P.O. Box 155, New Holland, PA 17557. Phone: (717) 354-2391.

South Carolina—Youngblood Bldg., 1001 Bluff Rd., P.O. Box 13405, Columbia, SC 29201-3405. Phone: (803) 737-4491.

South Dakota—803 E. Rice St. - Rm. 03, Sioux Falls, SD 57103-0193. Phone: (605) 338-4061.

Tennessee—Melrose Station, Ellington Agriculture Center, Hogan Rd., P.O. Box 40627, Nashville, TN 37204-0627. Phone: (615) 781-5406.

Texas—Livestock Exchange Bldg. - 1st fl., 101 S. Manhattan St., P.O. Box 30217, Amarillo, TX 79104-0217. Phone: (806) 372-6361.

- Producers Livestock Auction Bldg., P.O. Box 30160, San Angelo, TX 76903-0160. Phone: (915) 653-1778.

Washington—988 Juniper St., Moses Lake, WA 98837-2250. Phone: (509) 765-3611.

Wyoming—1834 E. A St., Torrington, WY 82240-1813. Phone: (307) 532-4146.

Meat Grading and Certification

Colorado—400 Livestock Exchange Bldg., Denver, CO 80216-2139. Phone: (303) 294-7676.

Illinois—Bldg. A - Ste. 30, 800 Roosevelt Rd., Glen Ellyn, IL 60137-5832. Phone: (708) 790-6905.

10.153
through
10.167
(cont.)

Iowa—210 Walnut St. - Rm. 75-A, Des Moines, IA 50309-2106. Phone: (515) 284-7166.

Nebraska—204 Livestock Exchange Bldg., 29th and O St., Omaha, NE 68107-2603. Phone: (402) 733-4833.

Texas—Livestock Exchange Bldg., 101 S. Manhattan St., P.O. Box 30217, Amarillo, TX 79104. Phone: (806) 373-7111.

POULTRY DIVISION

Poultry Grading Branch

EAST MIDWEST *(Alabama, Arkansas, Louisiana, Mississippi, Oklahoma, Tennessee, Texas)*—1 Natural Resources Dr. - Rm. 10, P.O. Box 8521, Little Rock, AR 72215-8521. Phone: (501) 324-5955.

EASTERN *(Connecticut, Delaware, District of Columbia, Florida, Georgia, Maine, Maryland, Massachusetts, New Hampshire, New Jersey, New York, North Carolina, Pennsylvania, Puerto Rico, Rhode Island, South Carolina, Vermont, Virgin Islands, Virginia, West Virginia)*—635 Cox Rd. - Ste. G, Gastonia, NC 28054-3441. Phone: (704) 867-3871.

WEST MIDWEST *(Illinois, Indiana, Iowa, Kansas, Kentucky, Michigan, Minnesota, Missouri, Nebraska, North Dakota, Ohio, South Dakota, Wisconsin)*—Federal Bldg. - Rm. 77, 210 Walnut St., Des Moines, IA 50309-2100. Phone: (515) 284-4581.

WESTERN *(Alaska, Arizona, California, Colorado, Hawaii, Idaho, Montana, New Mexico, Nevada, Oregon, Utah, Washington, Wyoming)*—2909 Coffee Rd. - Ste. , Modesto, CA 95355-3188. Phone: (209) 522-5251.

Poultry Market News Branch

California—Bldg. 6 - Section E, 5600 Rickenbacker Rd., Bell, CA 90201-6418. Phones: (213) 269-4154; *Recorded messages 24 hrs./day*: (213) 260-4676.

Connecticut—Connecticut Department of Agriculture, Marketing Division, State Office Bldg. - Rm. 63, 165 Capital Ave., Hartford, CT 06106-1688. Phone: (860) 566-3671.

District of Columbia—AMS, PY Division, USDA National Poultry Supervisor/National Egg Supervisor, South Bldg. - Rm. 960, P.O. Box 96456, Washington, DC 20090-6456. Phone: (202) 720-6911.

Georgia—60 Forsyth St. SW - Rm. M80, Atlanta, GA 30303. Phones: FTS (404) 562-5830, -5856.

Iowa—210 Walnut St. - Rm. 51, Des Moines, IA 50309-2103. Phone: (515) 284-4545 *(recorded messages 24 hrs./day)*.

Louisiana—Louisiana Department of Agriculture, Wilson Bldg., P.O. Box 3334, Baton Rouge, LA 70821-3334. Phone: (504) 922-1328.

Mississippi—352 E. Woodrow Wilson, P.O. Box 4629 Jackson, MS 39296-4629. Phone: (601) 965-4662.

North Carolina—North Carolina Department of Agriculture, State Agriculture Bldg. - Rm. 02, 2 W. Edenton St., P.O. Box 27647, Raleigh, NC 27611-7647. Phone: (919) 733-7252.

Texas—Texas Department of Agriculture, Capitol Station, 1700 N. Congress Ave., Austin, TX 78711-2847. Phones: (512) 463-7628; (toll-free within state, 1-800-252-3407).

Virginia—Virginia Department of Agriculture and Consumer Services, 116 Reservoir St., Harrisonburg, VA 22801-4232. Phone: (540) 434-0779.

SCIENCE DIVISION

Alabama—Supervisory Chemist, Aflatoxin Laboratories, 3119 Wesley Way, Dothan, AL 36301-2020. Phone: (334) 794-5070.

- Laboratory Supervisor, 1557 Reeves St., P.O. Box 1368, Dothan, AL 36302. Phone: (334) 792-5185.

Florida—Supervisory Chemist, Eastern Laboratories, 98 3rd St. SW - Ste. 11, Winter Haven, FL 33880-2909. Phone: (941) 299-7958.

Georgia—Laboratory Supervisor, 1211 Schley Ave., Albany, GA 31707. Phone: (912) 430-8490.

- Laboratory Supervisor, P.O. Box 488, Ashburn, GA 31714. Phone: (912) 567-3703.

- Laboratory Supervisor, 610 N. Main St., Blakely, GA 31723. Phone: (912) 723-4570.

- Laboratory Supervisor, P.O. Box 272, Dawson, GA 31742. Phone: (912) 995-7257.

Illinois—Laboratory Director, Midwestern Laboratory, 3570 N. Avondale Ave., Chicago, IL 60618-5391. Phone: (312) 353-6525.

North Carolina—Laboratory Supervisor, 301 W. Pearl St., P.O. Box 279, Aulander, NC 27805. Phone: (919) 345-1661, ext.156.

- Laboratory Director, Eastern Laboratory, 2311-B Aberdeen Blvd., Gastonia, NC 28054-0614. Phone: (704) 867-3873.

- Laboratory Address, 645 Cox Rd., Gastonia, NC 28054-0614. Phone: (704) 867-1882.

Oklahoma—Laboratory Supervisor, 107 S. 4th St., Madill, OK. 73446. Phone: (405) 795-5615.

Virginia—Pesticide Records Branch, 8700 Centreville Rd. - Ste. 00, Manassas, VA 22110-0031, Phones: (703) 330-7826; Residue Branch, (703) 330-2300.

- Laboratory Supervisor, 308 Culloden St., P.O. Box 1130, Suffolk, VA 23434. Phone: (757) 925-2286.

TOBACCO DIVISION

Tobacco Inspection and Market News

LEXINGTON REGION *(Indiana, Kentucky, Maryland, Missouri, North Carolina, Ohio, Tennessee, Virginia, West Virginia (burley), and Connecticut, Massachusetts, Pennsylvania, Wisconsin cigar areas)*—771 Corporate Dr. - Ste. 00, Lexington, KY 40503. Phone: (606) 224-1088.

RALEIGH REGION *(Alabama, Florida, Georgia, North Carolina, South Carolina, Virginia(Flue-cured, Tobacco and Naval Stores Inspection))*—1306 Annapolis Dr. - Rm. 05, Raleigh, NC 27608-0001. Phone: (919) 856-4584.

REGULATORY BRANCH REGIONAL OFFICES (Perishable Agricultural Commodities Act)

Arizona—Federal Bldg. - Rm. , 300 W. Congress St., P.O. Box FB30, Tucson, AZ 85701-1319. Phone: (520) 670-4793.

Illinois—Bldg. A - Ste. 60, 800 Roosevelt Rd., Glen Ellyn, IL 60137-5832. Phone: (630) 790-6929.

New Jersey—622 Georges Rd. - Ste. 03, North Brunswick, NJ 08902-3303. Phone: (908) 846-8222.

Texas—1200 E. Copeland Rd. - Ste. 04, Arlington, TX 76011-4938. Phone: (817) 885-7805.

Virginia—8700 Centerville Rd. - Ste. 06, Manassas, VA 22110. Phone: (703) 330-4455.

RURAL DEVELOPMENT (Rural Housing Service - Rural Business-Cooperative Service)

10.350 through 10.352

STATE OFFICES

Alabama—Sterling Center - Ste. 01, 4121 Carmichael Rd., Montgomery, AL 36106-3683. Phone: (334) 279-3400.

Alaska—800 W. Evergreen - Ste. 01, Palmer, AK 99645-6539. Phone: (907) 745-2176.

Arizona—3003 N. Central Ave. - Ste. 00, Phoenix, AZ 85012-2906. Phone: (602) 280-8700.

Arkansas—700 W. Capitol Ave. - Rm. 416, P.O. Box 2778, Little Rock, AR 72201-3325. Phone: (501) 301-3200.

California—430 G St. - Agency 4169, Davis, CA 95616-4169. Phone: (530) 792-5800.

Colorado—655 Parfet St. - Rm.E-100, Lakewood, CO 80215. Phone: (303) 236-2801.

Connecticut—*See* **Massachusetts**.

Delaware *(Delaware, Maryland)*—5201 S. Dupont Hwy., P.O. Box 400, Camden, DE 19934-9998. Phone: (302) 697-4300.

Florida *(Florida, Virgin Islands)*—Federal Bldg., 4440 NW 25th Place, P.O. Box 147010, Gainesville, FL 32614-7010. Phone: (352) 338-3400.

Georgia—Stephens Federal Bldg., 355 E. Hancock Ave., Athens, GA 30601-2768. Phone: (706) 546-2162.

Hawaii—Federal Bldg. - Rm. 11, 154 Waianuenue Ave., Hilo, HI 96720. Phone: (808) 933-3000.

Idaho—9173 W. Barnes Dr. - Ste. A1, Boise, ID 83709. Phone: (208) 378-5600.

Illinois—Illini Plaza - Ste. 03, 1817 S. Neil St., Champaign, IL 61820. Phone: (217) 398-5235.

Indiana—5975 Lakeside Blvd., Indianapolis, IN 46278. Phone: (317) 290-3100.

Iowa—Federal Bldg. - Rm. 73, 210 Walnut St., Des Moines, IA 50309. Phone: (515) 284-4663.

Kansas—1200 SW Executive Dr., P.O. Box 4653, Topeka, KS 66605. Phone: (785) 271-2700.

Kentucky—771 Corporate Dr. - Ste. 00, Lexington, KY 40503. Phone: (606) 224-7300.

Louisiana—3727 Government St., Alexandria, LA 71302. Phone: (318) 473-7920.

Maine—444 Stillwater Ave. - Ste. , P.O. Box 405, Bangor, ME 04402-0405. Phone: (207) 990-9106.

Maryland— *See* **Delaware**.

Massachusetts *(Connecticut, Massachusetts, Rhode Island)*—451 West St., Amherst, MA 01002. Phone: (413) 253-4300.

Michigan—3001 Coolidge Rd. - Ste. 00, East Lansing, MI 48823. Phone: (517) 337-6635.

Minnesota—410 Agribank Bldg., 375 Jackson St., St. Paul, MN 55101-1853. Phone: (651) 602-7800.

Mississippi—Federal Bldg. - Ste. 31, 100 W. Capitol St., Jackson, MS 39269. Phone: (601) 965-4316.

Missouri—Parkade Center - Ste. 35, 601 Business Loop - 70 West, Columbia, MO 65203. Phone: (573) 876-0976.

Montana—900 Technology Blvd. - (Unit 1) Ste. B, P.O. Box 850, Bozeman, MT 59715. Phone: (406) 585-2580.

Nebraska—Federal Bldg. - Rm. 52, 100 Centennial Mall North, Lincoln, NE 68508. Phone: (402) 437-5551.

Nevada—1390 S. Curry St., Carson City, NV 89703-9910. Phone: (702) 887-1222.

New Hampshire— *See* **Vermont**.

New Jersey—Tarnsfield Plaza - Ste. 2, 790 Woodland Rd., Mt. Holly, NJ 08060. Phone: (609) 265-3600.

New Mexico—6200 Jefferson St. NE - Rm. 55, Albuquerque, NM 87109. Phone: (505) 761-4950.

New York—The Galleries of Syracuse, 441 S. Salina St. - Ste. 57, Syracuse, NY 13202-2541. Phone: (315) 477-6400.

North Carolina—4405 Bland Rd. - Ste. 60, Raleigh, NC 27609. Phone: (919) 873-2000.

North Dakota—Federal Bldg. - Rm. 08, 220 E. Rosser, P.O. Box 1737, Bismarck, ND 58502-1737. Phone: (701) 250-4781.

Ohio—Federal Bldg. - Rm. 07, 200 N. High St., Columbus, OH 43215-2477. Phone: (614) 469-5606.

Oklahoma—100 USDA - Ste. 08, Stillwater, OK 74074-2654. Phone: (405) 742-1000.

Oregon—101 SW Main St. - Ste. 410, Portland, OR 97204-3222. Phone: (503) 414-3300.

Pennsylvania—One Credit Union Pl. - Ste. 30, Harrisburg, PA 17110-2996. Phone: (717) 237-2299.

Puerto Rico—New San Juan Office Bldg. - Rm. 01, 159 Carlos E. Chardon St., Hato Rey, PR 00918-5481. Phone: (787) 766-5095.

Rhode Island— *See* **Massachusetts**.

South Carolina—Thurmond Federal Bldg. - Rm. 007, 1835 Assembly St., Columbia, SC 29201. Phone: (803) 765-5163.

South Dakota Huron Federal Bldg. - Rm. 10, 200 4th St. SW, Huron, SD 57350. Phone: (605) 352-1100.

Tennessee—3322 West End Ave. - Ste. 00, Nashville, TN 37203-1084. Phone: (615) 783-1300.

Texas—Federal Bldg. - Ste. 02, 101 S. Main, Temple, TX 76501. Phone: (254) 742-9700.

Utah—Federal Bldg. - Rm. 311, 125 S. State St., P.O. Box 11350, Salt Lake City, UT 84147-0350. Phone: (801) 524-4063.

Vermont *(New Hampshire, Vermont)*—City Center - 3rd fl., 89 Main St., Montpelier, VT 05602. Phone: (802) 828-6010.

Virgin Islands— *See* **Florida**.

Virginia—Culpeper Bldg. - Ste. 38, 1606 Santa Rosa Rd., Richmond, VA 23229. Phone: (804) 287-1550.

Washington—1835 Black Lake Blvd. SW - Ste. B, Olympia, WA 98512-5715. Phone: (360) 704-7740.

West Virginia—Federal Bldg. - Rm. 20, 75 High St., Morgantown, WV 26505-7500. Phone: (304) 291-4791.

Wisconsin—4949 Kirschling Court, Stevens Point, WI 54481. Phone: (715) 345-7600.

Wyoming—Federal Bldg. - Rm. 005, 100 E. B St., P.O. Box 820, Casper, WY 82602. Phone: (307) 261-6300.

10.404   Listed under **10.051**.

10.405   Listed under **10.350**.

10.406   Listed under **10.051**.
through
10.407

10.410   Listed under **10.350.**
through
10.433

10.435   Listed under **10.051.**

10.438   Listed under **10.350.**
through
10.448

RISK MANAGEMENT AGENCY

10.450   ## REGIONAL SERVICE OFFICES

REGION 1 *(Connecticut, Delaware, Maine, Maryland, Massachusetts, New Hampshire, New Jersey, New York, North Carolina, Pennsylvania, Rhode Island, Vermont, Virginia, West Virginia)*—4407 Bland Rd. - Ste. 60, Raleigh, NC 27609. Phone: (919) 875-4880.

REGION 2 *(Alabama, Florida, Georgia, Puerto Rico, South Carolina, Virgin Islands)*—106 S. Patterson St. - Ste. 50, Valdosta, GA 31601-5609. Phone: (912) 242-3044.

REGION 3 *(Arkansas, Kentucky, Louisiana, Mississippi, Tennessee)*—8 River Bend Place, Jackson, MS 39208. Phone: (601) 965-4771.

REGION 4 *(Illinois, Indiana, Michigan, Ohio)*—3500 W. Wabash - Ste. B, Springfield, IL 62707. Phone: (217) 241-6601.

REGION 5 *(Iowa, Minnesota, Wisconsin)*—Minnesota World Trade Center, 30 E. 7th St. - Ste. 10, St. Paul, MN 55101-4901. Phone: (651) 290-3304.

REGION 6 *(Montana, North Dakota, South Dakota, Wyoming)*—3490 Gabel Rd. - Ste. 00, Billings, MT 59102-6440. Phone: (406) 657-6447.

REGION 7 *(Colorado, Kansas, Missouri, Nebraska)*—3401 SW Van Buren St., Topeka, KS 66611-2227. Phone: (785) 266-0248.

REGION 8 *(New Mexico, Oklahoma, Texas)*—205 NW 63rd St. - Ste. 70, Oklahoma City, OK 73116-8209. Phone: (405) 879-2700.

REGION 9 *(Arizona, California, Hawaii, Nevada, Utah)*—430 G St. - Ste. 168, Davis, CA 95616-4168. Phone: (530) 792-5870.

REGION 10 *(Alaska, Idaho, Oregon, Washington)*—112 N. University Rd. - Ste. 05, Spokane, WA 99206-5295. Phone: (509) 353-2147.

COMPLIANCE FIELD OFFICES

CENTRAL *(Colorado, Kansas, Missouri, Nebraska)*—6501 Beacon Dr., Kansas City, MO 64131. Phone: (816) 926-7963.

EASTERN *(Alabama, Connecticut, Delaware, Florida, Georgia, Maine, Maryland, Massachusetts, New Hampshire, New Jersey, New York, North Carolina, Pennsylvania, Puerto Rico, Rhode Island, South Carolina, Vermont, Virginia, West Virginia)*—4407 Bland Rd. - Ste. 80, Raleigh, NC 27609. Phone: (919) 875-4930.

MIDWEST *(Illinois, Indiana, Ohio, Michigan)*—6045 Lakeside Blvd., Indianapolis, IN 46278. Phone: (317) 290-3050.

NORTHERN *(Iowa, Minnesota, Montana, North Dakota, South Dakota, Wisconsin, Wyoming)*—3440 Federal Dr. - Ste. 00, Eagan, MN 55122-1301. Phone: (612) 725-3730.

SOUTHERN *(Kentucky, Louisiana, Mississippi, New Mexico, Oklahoma, Tennessee, Texas)*—1111 W. Mockingbird Lane - Ste. 280, Dallas, TX 75247-5016. Phone: (214) 767-7700.

WESTERN *(Alaska, Arizona, California, Hawaii, Idaho, Nevada, Oregon, Utah, Washington)*—430 G St. - Ste. 167, Davis, CA 95616-4167. Phone: (530) 792-5850.

10.451   Listed under **10.051**.

FOOD SAFETY AND INSPECTION SERVICE

10.456   Listed under **10.450**.
through
10.458

10.475   **Meat, Poultry, and Egg Products Inspection**
through
10.477   **DISTRICT OFFICES**

Arkansas *(DISTRICT 35: Arkansas, Louisiana, Oklahoma)*—Country Club Center - Ste. 01, 4700 S. Thompson Bldg. B, Springdale, AR 72764. Phone: (501) 751-8412.

California *(DISTRICT 5: California)*—Bldg. 2C, 620 Central Ave., Alameda, CA 94501. Phone: (510) 337-5000.

Colorado *(DISTRICT 15: Alaska, American Samoa, Arizona, Colorado, Guam, Hawaii, Idaho, New Mexico, Nevada, Northern Mariana Islands, Oregon, Utah, Washington)*—Bldg. 45, P.O. Box 25387, Denver, CO 80225-0387. Phone: (303) 236-9800.

Georgia *(DISTRICT 85: Florida, Georgia, Puerto Rico, Virgin Islands)*—Bldg. 1924 - Ste. R90, 100 Alabama St. SW, Atlanta, GA 30303. Phone: (404) 562-5900.

Illinois *(DISTRICT 50: Illinois, Indiana, Ohio)*—1919 S. Highland Ave. - Ste. 15C, Lombard, IL 60148. Phone: (630) 620-7474.

Iowa *(DISTRICT 25: Iowa, Nebraska)*—Federal Bldg. - Rm. 85, 210 Walnut St., Des Moines, IA 50309. Phone: (515) 727-8960.

Kansas *(DISTRICT 30: Kansas, Missouri)*—4920 Bob Billings Pkwy, Lawrence, KS 66049. Phone: (785) 841-5600.

Maryland *(DISTRICT 75: Delaware, Maryland, Virginia, Washington D.C., West Virginia)*—5601 Sunnyside Ave. - Ste. -2288B, Beltsville, MD 20705-5200. Phone: (301) 504-2136.

Minnesota *(DISTRICT 20: Minnesota, Montana, North Dakota, South Dakota, Wyoming)*—Butler Square West - Ste. 89C, 100 N. 6th St., Minneapolis, MN 55403. Phone: (612) 370-2400.

Mississippi *(DISTRICT 90: Alabama, Mississippi, Tennessee)*—715 S. Pear Orchard Rd. - Ste. 01, Ridgeland, MS 39157. Phone: (601) 965-4312.

New York *(DISTRICT 65: Connecticut, Maine, Massachusetts, New Hampshire, New York, Rhode Island, Vermont)*—230 Washington Ave., Albany, NY 12203-6870. Phone: (518) 452-6870.

North Carolina *(DISTRICT 80: Kentucky, North Carolina, South Carolina)*—6020 Six Forks Rd., Raleigh, NC 27609. Phone: (919) 844-8400.

Pennsylvania *(DISTRICT 60: New Jersey, Pennsylvania)*—Mellon Independence Center - Ste. 100-A, 701 Market St., Philadelphia, PA 19106-1576. Phone: (215) 597-4219, ext.106.

Texas *(DISTRICT 40: Texas)*—1100 Commerce - Rm. 16, Dallas, TX 75242-0598. Phone: (214) 767-9116.

Wisconsin *(DISTRICT 45: Michigan, Wisconsin)*—2810 Crossroads Dr. - Ste. 500, Madison, WI 53718-7969. Phone: (608) 240-4080.

FOOD AND NUTRITION SERVICE

10.543   **REGIONAL OFFICES**
through
10.594   **MID-ATLANTIC** *(Delaware, District of Columbia, Maryland, New Jersey, Pennsylvania, Puerto Rico, Virgin Islands, Virginia, West Virginia)*—Mercer Corporate Park, 300 Corporate Blvd., Robinsville, NJ 08691. Phone: (609) 259-5025.

10.543
through
10.594
(cont.)

MIDWEST *(Illinois, Indiana, Michigan, Minnesota, Ohio, Wisconsin)*—77 W. Jackson Blvd - 20th fl., Chicago, IL 60604-3507. Phone: (312) 353-6664.

MOUNTAIN PLAINS *(Colorado, Iowa, Kansas, Missouri, Montana, Nebraska, North Dakota, South Dakota, Utah, Wyoming)*—1244 Speer Blvd. - Ste. 03, Denver, CO 80204. Phone: (303) 844-0300.

NORTHEAST *(Connecticut, Maine, Massachusetts, New Hampshire, New York, Rhode Island, Vermont)*—10 Causeway St. - Rm. 01, Boston MA 02222-1068. Phone: (617) 565-6370.

SOUTHEAST *(Alabama, Florida, Georgia, Kentucky, Mississippi, North Carolina, South Carolina, Tennessee)*—Martin Luther King, Jr. Federal Annex - (1st fl.) Rm. T36, 61 Forsythe St. SW, Atlanta, GA 30303. Phone: (404) 562-1801, -1802

SOUTHWEST *(Arkansas, Louisiana, New Mexico, Oklahoma, Texas)*—1100 Commerce St. - Rm. 55, Dallas, TX 75242. Phone: (214) 290-9800.

WESTERN *(Alaska, American Samoa, Arizona, California, Guam, Hawaii, Idaho, Nevada, Northern Marianas, Oregon, Washington, Freely Associated States of the Pacific)*—550 Kearny St. - Rm. 00, San Francisco, CA 94108. Phone: (415) 705-1310.

10.609
through
10.610

Listed under **10.051.**

FOREST SERVICE

10.652
through
10.692

RESEARCH HEADQUARTERS - Forest and Range Experiment Stations

INTERMOUNTAIN *(Idaho, Montana, Nevada, Utah, Wyoming-western one-third)*—324 25th St., Ogden, UT 84401. Phone: (801) 625-5421.

NORTH CENTRAL *(Illinois, Indiana, Iowa, Michigan, Minnesota, Missouri, Wisconsin)*—1992 Folwell Ave., St. Paul, MN 55108. Phone: (612) 649-5252.

NORTHEASTERN *(Connecticut, Kentucky, Maine, Massachusetts, New Hampshire, New Jersey, New York, Ohio, Pennsylvania, Vermont, West Virginia)*—5 Radnor Corporate Center - Ste. 00, Radnor, PA 19087-4585. Phone: (610) 975-4207.

PACIFIC NORTHWEST *(Alaska, Oregon, Washington)*—P.O. Box 3890, Portland, OR 97208-3890. Phone: (503) 326-5644.

PACIFIC SOUTHWEST *(California, Hawaii)*—P.O. Box 245, Berkeley, CA 94701-0245. Phone: (510) 559-6317.

ROCKY MOUNTAIN *(Arizona, Colorado, Kansas, Nebraska, New Mexico, North Dakota, Oklahoma-Panhandle only, South Dakota, Texas-western, Wyoming-eastern two-thirds)*—240 W. Prospect Rd., Ft. Collins, CO 80526-2098. Phone: (970) 498-1139.

SOUTHERN *((Alabama, Arkansas, Florida, Georgia, Louisiana, Mississippi, North Carolina, Oklahoma-except Panhandle, Puerto Rico, South Carolina, Tennessee, Texas-eastern, Virginia)*—200 Weaver Blvd., P.O. Box 2680, Asheville, NC 28802. Phone: (704) 257-4301.

Forest Products Laboratory: One Gifford Pinchot Dr., Madison, WI 53705-2398. Phone: (608) 231-9315.

REGIONAL OFFICES

Note: to contact local Forest Supervisor or Ranger District Offices, consult the appropriate regional office, following.

REGION 1 *(Idaho-northern, Montana, North Dakota, South Dakota-northwestern corner)*—Federal Bldg., P.O. Box 7669, Missoula, MT 59807. Phone: (406) 329-3347.

REGION 2 *(Colorado, Kansas, Nebraska, South Dakota-except northwestern corner, Wyoming-eastern two-thirds)*—740 Simms St., Golden, CO 80401. Phone: (303) 275-5350.

REGION 3 *(Arizona, New Mexico)*—333 Broadway SE, Albuquerque, NM 87102. Phone: (505) 842-3292.

REGION 4 *(Idaho-southern, Nevada, Utah, Wyoming-western one-third)*—Federal Office Bldg., 324 25th St., Ogden, UT 84401. Phone: (801) 625-5306.

REGION 5 *(California, Hawaii)*—1323 Club Dr., Vallejo, CA 94592. Phone: (707) 562-8737.

REGION 6 *(Oregon, Washington)*—333 SW 1st St., Portland, OR 97204-3440. Phone: (503) 808-2468.

REGION 8 *(Alabama, Arkansas, Florida, Georgia, Kentucky, Louisiana, Mississippi, North Carolina, Oklahoma, Puerto Rico, South Carolina, Tennessee, Texas, Virginia, Virgin Islands)*—1720 Peachtree Rd. NW, Atlanta, GA 30309. Phone: (404) 347-4177.

REGION 9 *(Connecticut, Delaware, Illinois, Indiana, Iowa, Maine, Maryland, Massachusetts, Michigan, Minnesota, Missouri, New Hampshire, New Jersey, New York, Ohio, Pennsylvania, Rhode Island, Vermont, West Virginia, Wisconsin)*—626 East Wisconsin Ave., Milwaukee, WI 53202. Phone: (414) 297-3600.

REGION 10 *(Alaska)*—709 W. 9th St., Juneau, AK 99801-1807. Phone: (907) 586-8807.

State and Private Forestry Areas

NORTHEASTERN AREA *(Covers states Listed under Region 9, foregoing)*—5 Radnor Corporate Center, P.O. Box 6775, Radnor, PA 19087-8775. Phone: (610) 975-4103.

FOREST STEWARDSHIP

ALASKA *(Alaska)*—3301 C St. - Ste. 22, Anchorage, AK 99503. Phones: (907) 271-2550; FAX (907) 271-2897.

INTERMOUNTAIN *(Idaho, Montana, North Dakota, Nevada, Utah)*—Federal Bldg., 324 25th St., Ogden, UT 84401. Phones: (801) 625-5189; FAX (801) 625-5127.

NORTHEASTERN *(Connecticut, Delaware, Illinois, Indiana, Iowa, Massachusetts, Maryland, Maine, Michigan, Minnesota, Missouri, New Jersey, New Hampshire, New York, Ohio, Pennsylvania, Rhode Island, Vermont, Wisconsin, West Virginia)*—11 Campus Blvd. - Ste. 00, Newtown Square, PA 19073. Phones: (610) 557-4029; FAX (610) 557-4136.

PACIFIC NORTHWEST *(Oregon, Washington)*—333 SW 1st Ave., P.O. Box 3623, Portland, OR 97208. Phones: (503) 808-2355; FAX (503) 808-2339.

PACIFIC SOUTHWEST *(California, Hawaii)*—1323 Club Drive, Vallejo, CA 94592. Phones: (707) 562-8918; FAX (707) 562-9054.

ROCKY MOUNTAIN *(Colorado, Kansas, Nebraska, South Dakota, Wyoming)*—P.O. Box 25127, Lakewood, CO 80225. Phones: (303) 275-5239; FAX (303) 275-5754.

SOUTHERN *(Alabama, Arkansas, Florida, Georgia, Kentucky, Louisiana, Mississippi, North Carolina, Oklahoma, South Carolina, Tennessee, Texas, Virginia)*—1720 Peachtree Rd. NW - Ste. 508, Atlanta, GA 30367. Phones: (404) 347-1649; FAX (404) 347-2776.

SOUTHWESTERN *(Arizona, New Mexico)*—517 Gold Ave. SW, Albuquerque, NM 87102. Phone: (505) 842-3229; FAX (505) 842-3800.

10.700 Listed under **10.001.**

10.760   Listed under **10.350.**
through
10.874

10.902   Listed under **10.072.**
through
10.929

NATIONAL AGRICULTURAL STATISTICS SERVICE

10.950   ## FIELD OFFICES

Alabama—Sterling Centre, Suite 200, 4121 Carmichael Rd., Montgomery, AL 36106-2872. Phone: 334-279-3555.

Alaska—1150 S. Colony Way Ste. 11, Palmer, AK 99645. Phone: 907-745-4272.

Arizona—230 N. First Ave. Ste. 303, Phoenix, AZ 85003-1706. Phone: 602-280-8850.

Arkansas—10800 Financial Centre Pkwy. Ste. 110, Little Rock, AR 72211. Phone: 501-228-9926.

California—650 Capitol Mall Ste. 6-100, Sacramento, CA 95814. Phone: 916-498-5161.

Colorado—645 Parfet St. Ste. W-201, Lakewood, CO 80215-5517. Phone: 303-236-2300.

Delaware—Dept of Agriculture Bldg., 2320 South Dupont Hwy., Dover, DE 19901. Phone: 302-698-4537.

Florida—1222 Woodward St., Orlando, FL 32803. Phone: 407-648-6013.

Georgia—Stephens Federal Bldg. Ste. 320, 355 East Hancock Ave., Athens, GA 30601. Phone: 706-546-2236.

Hawaii—State Department of Agriculture Building, 1428 South King St., Honolulu, HI 96814. Phone: 808-973-2907.

Idaho—2224 Old Penitentiary Rd., Boise, ID 83712. Phone: 208-334-1507.

Illinois—Department of Agriculture Bldg. Rm. 4, 801 Sangamon Ave., Springfield, IL 62702. Phone: 217-492-4295.

Indiana—1435 Win Hentschel Blvd. Ste. 110, West Lafayette, IN 47906-4145. Phone: 765-494-8371.

Iowa—833 Federal Building, 210 Walnut St., Des Moines, IA 50309. Phone: 515-284-4340.

Kansas—632 S.W. Van Buren Rm. 00, Topeka, KS 66603. Phone: 785-233-2230.

Kentucky—601 West Broadway Rm. 45, Louisville, KY 40202. Phone: 502-582-5293.

Louisiana—5825 Florida Blvd. Rm. 179, Baton Rouge, LA 70806. Phone: 225-922-1362.

Maryland—50 Harry S Truman Pkwy. - Ste. 202, Annapolis, MD 21401. Phone: 410-841-5740.

Michigan—3001 Coolidge Rd. Ste. 400, East Lansing, MI 48823 Phone: 517-324-5300

Minnesota—55 East 5th St. Ste. 500, St. Paul, MN 55101. Phone: 651-296-2230.

Mississippi—121 North Jefferson St. Ste. 230, Jackson, MS 39201. Phone: 601-965-4575.

Missouri—601 Business Loop 70 West Ste. 240, Columbia, MO 65203. Phone: 573-876-0950.

Montana—10 West 15th St. - Ste. 3100, Helena, MT 59626. Phone: 406-441-1240.

Nebraska—Federal Bldg. Rm. 98, 100 Centennial Mall North, Lincoln, NE 68508. Phone: 402-437-5541.

Nevada—5600 Fox Ave. Rm. 13, Reno, NV 89506-1300. Phone: 775-972-6001.

New Hampshire—53 Pleasant St. Rm. 100, Concord, NH 03301. Phone: 603-224-9639.

New Jersey—Health and Agriculture Bldg. Rm. 05, 369 South Warren St., Trenton, NJ 08625. Phone: 609-292-6385.

New Mexico—2507 North Telshor Blvd. Ste. 4, Las Cruces, NM 88011. Phone: 575-522-6023.

New York—10B Airline Dr., Albany, NY 12235-1004. Phone: 518-457-5570.

North Carolina—2 W. Edenton St., Raleigh, NC 27601-1085. Phone: 919-856-4394.

North Dakota—NDSU - IACC Bld., 1320 Albrecht Blvd., Fargo, ND 58105. Phone: 701-239-5306.

Ohio—Bromfield Admin. Bldg. Rm. 03, 8995 East Main St., Reynoldsburg, OH 43068. Phone: 614-728-2100.

Oklahoma—2800 North Lincoln Boulevard - Third Floor, Oklahoma City, OK 73105-4207. Phone: 405-522-6190.

Oregon—1735 Federal Bld., 1220 SW Third Avenue, Portland, OR 97204. Phone: 503-326-2131.

Pennsylvania—2301 N. Cameron Street Rm.G-19, Harrisburg, PA 17110. Phone: 717-787-3904.

Puerto Rico—Dept. of Ag. of Puerto Rico, 1309 Fernandez Juncos, Santurce, PR 00907-1163. Phone: 787-723-3773.

South Carolina—1835 Assembly Street - Ste. 1008, Columbia, SC 29201. Phone: 803-765-5333.

South Dakota—5020 S Broadband Lane, Sioux Falls, SD 57108. Phone: 605-323-6500.

Tennessee—Holeman Office Bldg., Ellington, Agricultural Ctr., 440 Hogan Rd., Nashville, TN 37220-1626. Phone: 615-781-5300.

Texas—Federal Bldg. Rm. 00, 300 E. 8th St., Austin, TX 78701. Phone: 512-916-5581.

Utah—176 N. 2200 West - Ste. 260, Salt Lake City, UT 84116. Phone: 801-524-5003.

Virginia—102 Governor St. Rm.LL20, Richmond, VA 23219. Phone: 804-771-2493.

Washington—1111 Washington St. SE, Olympia, WA 98501. Phone: 360-902-1940.

West Virginia—1900 Kanawha Blvd. E, Charleston, WV 25305. Phone: 304-345-5958.

Wisconsin—2811 Agriculture Dr., Madison, WI 53718-6777. Phone: 608-224-4848.

Wyoming—308 W. 21st St. - Third Floor, Cheyenne, WY 82001. Phone: 307-432-5600.

10.999 Listed under **10.051**.

DEPARTMENT OF COMMERCE

BUREAU OF THE CENSUS

**11.001
through
11.005**

REGIONAL OFFICES

California—15350 Sherman Way - Ste. 00, Van Nuys, CA 91406-4224. Phones: (818) 267-1700, -1711.

Colorado—6900 W. Jefferson Ave. - Ste. 00, Denver, CO 80235-2032. Phones: (303) 264-0202, 969-6777.

Georgia—101 Marietta St. NW - Ste. 200, Atlanta, GA 30303-2700. Phones: (404) 730-3832, -3835.

11.001
through
11.005
(cont.)

Illinois—1111 W 22nd St. Ste. 400, Oakbrook, IL 60523-1918. Phones: (630) 288-9200, -9288.

Kansas—1211 N. 8th St., Kansas City, KS 66101-2129. Phones: (913) 551-6728, -6789.

Massachusetts—4 Copley Place - Ste. 01, Boston, MA 02117-9108. Phones: (617) 424-4500, -0547.

Michigan—1395 Brewery Park Blvd. - Ste. 00, Detroit, MI 48207-2635. Phones: (313) 259-1158, -5045.

New York—395 Hudson St. - Ste. 00, New York, NY 10014. Phones: (212) 584-3400, 478-4800.

North Carolina—901 Center Park Dr. - Ste. 06, Charlotte, NC 28217-2935. Phones: (704) 424-6400, -6944.

Pennsylvania—833 Chestnut St.- Ste. 04, Philadelphia, PA 19107-4405. Phones: (215) 717-1800, -0755.

Texas—8585 N. Stemmons Fwy. - Ste. 00S, Dallas, TX 75247-3841. Phones: (214) 253-4401, 655-5362.

Washington—601 Union St. - Ste. 800, Seattle, WA 98104-1074. Phones: (206) 381-6200, -6310.

NATIONAL OCEANIC AND ATMOSPHERIC ADMINISTRATION

11.011
through
11.012

REGIONAL OFFICES

ALASKA—P.O. Box 21668, Juneau, AK 99802-1668. Phone: (907) 586-7221.

NORTHEAST—One Blackburn Dr., Gloucester, MA 01930. Phone: (978) 281-9250.

NORTHWEST—7600 Sand Point Way NE, Seattle, WA 98115. Phone: (206) 526-6150.

SOUTHEAST—9721 Executive Center Dr. N. - Ste. 01, St. Petersburg, FL 33702. Phone: (727) 570-5301.

SOUTHWEST—501 W. Ocean Blvd. - Ste. 200, Long Beach, CA 90802-4213. Phone: (562) 980-4001.

- Southwest Fisheries Science Center, P.O. Box 271, La Jolla, CA 92038-0271. Phone: (619) 546-7081.

FIELD AREAS

Virginia—Atlantic Marine Center, 439 W. York St., Norfolk, VA 23510-1114. Phone: (757) 441-6776.

Washington—Pacific Marine Center, 1801 Fairview Ave. E., Seattle, WA 98102. Phone: (206) 553-7656.

11.016   Listed under **11.001.**

INTERNATIONAL TRADE ADMINISTRATION (including Export Assistance Centers)

11.108
through
11.112

Alabama—Medical Forum Bldg. - Rm. 07, 950 22nd St. N., Birmingham, AL 35203. Phones: (205) 731-1331; FAX (205) 731-0076.

Alaska—431 W. 7th Ave. - Ste. 08, Anchorage, AK 99501. Phones: (907) 271-6237; FAX (907) 271-6242.

Arizona—2901 N. Central Ave. - Ste. 70, Phoenix, AZ 85012. Phones: (602) 640-2513; FAX (602) 640-2518.

■ 120 N. Stone Ave. Ste. 200, Tucson, AZ 85701. Phones: (520) 670-5540; FAX (520) 231-1910.

Arkansas—425 W. Capitol Ave. - Ste. 25, Little Rock, AR 72201. Phones: (501) 324-5794; FAX (501) 324-7380.

California—2100 Chester Ave.- Ste. 166, Bakersfield, CA 93301. Phones: (661) 637-0136; FAX (661) 637-0156.

■ 550 E. Shaw Ave. Ste. 155, Fresno, CA 93710. Phones: (559) 227-6582.

■ 84-245 Indio Springs Pkwy., Indio, CA 92203-3499. Phones: (760) 722-3898; FAX (760) 772-0337.

■ 11150 Olympic Blvd. - Ste. 75, Los Angeles, CA 90064. Phones: (310) 235-7104; FAX (310) 235-7220.

■ 444 S. Flower St. 34th Fl., Los Angeles, CA 90071. Phones: (213) 894-4231; FAX (213) 894-8789.

■ c/o Monterey Institute of International Studies, 411 Pacific St. - Ste. 16A, Monterey, CA 93940. Phones: (831) 641-9850; FAX (831) 641-9849.

■ 1301 Clay St. Ste. 630N, Oakland, CA 94612. Phones: (510) 273-7350; FAX (510) 251-7352.

■ Inland Empire Export Assistance Center, 2940 Inland Empire Blvd. - Ste. 21, Ontario, CA 91764. Phones: (909) 466-4134; FAX (909) 466-4140.

■ 333 Ponoma St., Port Hueneme, CA 93041. Phones: (805) 488-4844; FAX (805) 488-7801.

■ 1410 Ethan Way, Sacramento, CA 95825. Phones: (916) 566-7170; FAX (916) 566-7123.

■ 6363 Greenwich Dr. - Ste. 30, San Diego, CA 92122. Phones: (619) 557-5395; FAX (619) 557-6176.

■ 250 Montgomery St. - 14th fl., San Francisco, CA 94104. Phones: (415) 705-2300; FAX (415) 705-2297.

■ 50 Acacia Ave., San Rafael, CA 94901. Phones: (415) 485-6200; FAX (415) 485-6219.

Colorado—World Trade Center, 1625 Broadway - Ste. 80, Denver, CO 80202. Phones: (303) 844-6623; FAX (303) 844-5651.

Connecticut—213 Court St. - Rm. 03, Middletown, CT 06457-3346. Phones: (860) 638-6950; FAX (860) 638-6970.

Delaware—*See* **Pennsylvania**, Philadelphia office.

Florida—1130 Cleveland St., Clearwater, FL 33755. Phones: (727) 893-3738; FAX (727) 449-2889.

■ 200 E. Las Olas Blvd. - Ste. 600, Ft. Lauderdale, FL 33301. Phones: (954) 356-6640; FAX (954) 356-6644.

■ 3 Independent Dr., Jacksonville, FL 32202, Phone: (904) 232-1270; FAX 232-1271.

■ 5835 Blue Lagoon Dr. Ste. 03, Miami, FL 33126-3009. Phones: (305) 526-7425; FAX (305) 526-7434.

■ Entrepreneurial Center, 315 E. Robinson St., Orlando, FL 32801-1912. Phones: (407) 648-6170; FAX (407) 487-1901.

■ 325 John Knox Rd. - Ste. 01 Tallahassee, FL 32303. Phones: (850) 942-9635; FAX (850) 922-9595.

Georgia—Centergy One Bldg. - Ste. 055, 75 5th St., NW, Atlanta, GA 30308. Phones: (404) 897-6090; FAX (404) 652-6085.

■ 111 E. Liberty St. - Ste. 02, Savannah, GA 31405. Phones: (912) 652-4204; FAX (912) 652-5675.

**11.108
through
11.112
(cont.)**

Hawaii—521 Ala Moana Blvd. - Rm. 14, Honolulu, HI 96813. Phones: (808) 522-8040; FAX (808) 522-8045.

Idaho (*Portland, OR district*)—700 W. State St. - 2nd fl., Boise, ID 83720. Phones: (208) 364-7791; FAX (208) 334-2783.

Illinois—200 W. Adams St. - Ste. 450, Chicago, IL 60606. Phones: (312) 353-8040; FAX (312) 353-8120.

  ■ 28055 Ashley Circle - Ste. 12, Libertyville, IL 60048. Phones: (847) 327-9082; FAX (847) 247-0423.

  ■ Jobst Hall Rm. 41, 922 N. Glenwood Ave., Peoria, IL 61606. Phones: (309) 671-7815; FAX (309) 671-7818.

  ■ 605 Fulton Ave. Ste. E103, Rockford, IL 61103. Phones: (815) 316-2380; FAX (815) 628-2571.

Indiana—Indianapolis Export Assistance Center, Pennwood One - Ste. 06, 11405 N. Pennsylvania St., Carmel, IN 46032. Phones: (317) 582-2300; FAX (317) 582-2301.

Iowa—700 Locust St. - Ste. 00, Des Moines, IA 50309-3739. Phones: (515) 288-8614; FAX (515) 288-1437.

Kansas (*Kansas City, MO district*)—150 N. Main St. - Ste. 00, Wichita, KS 67202-4012. Phones: (316) 263-4067; FAX (316) 263-8306.

Kentucky—601 W. Broadway - Rm. 34B, Louisville, KY 40202. Phones: (502) 582-5066; FAX (502) 582-6573.

Louisiana—Delta Export Assistance Center, 2 Canal St. - Ste. 710, New Orleans, LA 70130. Phones: (504) 589-6546; FAX (504) 589-2337.

  ■ Business Education Bldg.- 119H, One University Place, Shreveport, LA 71115-2300. Phones: (318) 676-3064; FAX (318) 676-3063.

Maine (*Boston, MA District*)—511 Congress St., Portland, ME 04101. Phones: (207) 541-7430; FAX (207) 541-7420.

Maryland—300 Pratt St. Ste. 300, Baltimore, MD 21202. Phones: (410) 962-4539; FAX (410) 962-4529.

Massachusetts—World Trade Center - Ste. 07, 164 Northern Ave., Boston, MA 02210-2071. Phones: (617) 424-5990; FAX (617) 424-5992.

Michigan—8109 E. Jefferson Ave. Ste. 101, Detroit, MI 48214. Phones: (313) 226-3650; FAX (313) 226-3657.

  ■ 401 W. Fulton St. - Ste. 49C, Grand Rapids, MI 49504. Phones: (616) 458-3564; FAX (616) 458-3872.

  ■ Oakland Pointe Office Bldg. - Ste. 300 West, 250 Elizabeth Lake Rd., Pontiac, MI 48341. Phones: (248) 975-9600; FAX (248) 975-9606.

  ■ c/o Eastern Michigan University, 300 w. Michigan Ave. Ste. 306G, Ypsilanti, MI 48197 Phones: (734) 487-0259; FAX (734) 485-2432.

Minnesota—100 N. 6th St. - Ste. 10C, Minneapolis, MN 55403. Phones: (612) 348-1638; FAX (612) 965-4132.

Mississippi—175 E. Capitol St. Ste. 255, Jackson, MS 39201. Phones: (601) 965-4130; FAX (601) 857-0026.

Missouri—2509 Commerce Tower, 911 main St., Kansas City, MO 64105. Phones: (816) 421-1876; FAX (816) 471-7839.

  ■ 8235 Forsyth Cntr. Ste. 520, St. Louis, MO 63105. Phones: (314) 425-3302; FAX (314) 425-3381.

Montana—University of Montana, Gallagher Business Bldg. - Ste. 57, Missoula, MT 59812. Phones: (406) 542-6656; FAX (406) 542-6659.

Nebraska—13006 W. Centre Rd., Omaha, NE 68144. Phones: (402) 597-0193; FAX (402) 595-1194.

Nevada—400 S. Fourth St. Ste. 250. Las Vegas, NV 89101 Phones: (702) 388-6694; FAX (702) 388-6469.

■ 1 East 1st St. 16th Fl., Reno, NV 89501. Phones: (775) 784-5203; FAX (775) 784-5343.

New Hampshire *(Boston, MA district)*—17 New Hampshire Ave., Portsmouth, NH 03801-2838. Phones: (603) 334-6074; FAX (603) 334-6110.

New Jersey—744 Broad St. Ste. 1505, Newark, NJ 07102. Phones: (973) 645-4682; FAX (973) 645-4783.

■ 20 West St., P.O. Box 820, Trenton, NJ 08625-0820. Phones: (609) 989-2100; FAX (609) 989-2395.

New Mexico *(Dallas, TX District)*—c/o New Mexico Department of Economic Development, 1100 St. Francis Dr., P.O. Box 20003, Santa Fe, NM 87504. Phones: (505) 231-0075; FAX (505) 827-0211.

New York—130 S. Elmwood Ave. Ste. 530, Buffalo, NY 14202. Phones: (716) 551-4191; FAX (716) 551-5290.

■ Harlem Export Assistance Center, 163 W. 125th St. - Ste. 01, New York, NY 10027. Phones: (212) 860-6200; FAX (212) 860-6203.

■ Long Island Export Assistance Center, 33 Whitehall St. 22nd Fl., New York, NY 10004. Phones: (212) 809-2675; FAX (212) 809-2687.

■ 400 Andrews St. Ste. 10, Rochester, NY 14604. Phones: (585) 263-6480; FAX (585) 325-6505.

■ Westchester Export Assistance Center, 707 W. Chester Ave. - Ste. 09, White Plains, NY 10604. Phones: (914) 682-6712; FAX (914) 682-6698.

North Carolina—521 E. Morehead St. - Ste. 35, Charlotte, NC 28202. Phones: (704) 333-4886; FAX (704) 332-2681.

■ 342 N. Elm St., Greensboro, NC 27401. Phones: (336) 333-5345; FAX (336) 333-5158.

■ 10900 World Trade Blvd. Ste. 110, Raleigh, NC 27617 Phones: (919) 281-2750; FAX (919) 281-2754.

North Dakota—51 Broadway Ste. 505, Fargo, ND 58102. Phones: (701) 0239-5080; FAX (701) 237-9634.

Ohio—36 E. 7th St. - Ste. 650, Cincinnati, OH 45202. Phones: (513) 684-2944; FAX (513) 684-3227.

■ Bank One Center - Ste. 00, 600 Superior Ave. E., Cleveland, OH 44114. Phones: (216) 522-4750; FAX (216) 522-2235.

■ 401 N. Front St. Ste. 200, Columbus, OH 43215. Phones: (614) 365-9510; FAX (614) 365-9598.

■ 300 Madison Ave., Toledo, OH 43604. Phones: (419) 241-0683; FAX (419) 241-0684.

Oklahoma—301 NW 63rd St. - Ste. 30, Oklahoma City, OK 73116. Phones: (405) 608-5302; FAX (405) 608-4211.

■ 700 N. Greenwood Ave. - Ste. 400, Tulsa, OK 74106. Phones: (918) 581-7650; FAX (918) 581-6263.

Oregon—One World Trade Center - Ste. 42, 121 SW Salmon St., Portland, OR 97204. Phones: (503) 326-3001; FAX (503) 326-6351.

Pennsylvania—Millersville University of International Affairs, 2 S. George St., Cumberland House, P.O. Box 40, Millersville, PA 17551-0302. Phones: (717) 872-4386; FAX (717) 871-2132.

■ The Curtis Center - Ste. 80W, Independence Square West, Philadelphia, PA 19106. Phones: (215) 597-6101; FAX (215) 597-6123.

11.108 through 11.112 (cont.)

■ 425 6th Ave. Ste. 2950, Pittsburgh, PA 15222. Phones: (412) 644-2800; FAX (412) 644-2803.

Puerto Rico *(Hato Rey)*—Centro International de Mercadeo, Torre II Ste. 702, San Juan, PR 00968-8058. Phones: (787) 755-1992; FAX (787) 781-7178.

Rhode Island *(Hartford, CT district)*—One West Exchange St., Providence, RI 02903. Phones: (401) 528-5104; FAX (401) 528-5067.

South Carolina—7300 College St., Haribson Hall 2nd Fl., Columbia, SC 29063. Phones: (803) 732-5211; FAX (803) 732-5241.

■ Upstate Export Assistance Center, Park Central Office Park - Bldg. 1 (Ste. 09), 216 S. Pleasantburg Dr. Ste. 243, Greenville, SC 29607. Phones: (864) 250-8429; FAX (864) 250-8513.

■ 5300 International Blvd. - Ste. 01-C, North Charleston, SC 29418. Phones: (843) 760-3794; FAX (843) 760-3798.

■ 1362 McMillan Ave. Ste. 100, North Charleston, SC 29405. Phones: (843) 746-3404; FAX (843) 529-0305.

South Dakota—Siouxland Export Assistance Center, Augustana College - Rm. 22, 2001 S. Summit Ave. Sioux Falls, SD 57197. Phones: (864) 330-4264; FAX (864) 330-4266.

Tennessee—Memphis Export Assistance Center, 22 N. Front St. Ste. 200, Memphis, TN 38103. Phones: (901) 544-0930; FAX (901) 543-4435.

■ 17 Market Square Ste. 201, Knoxville, TN 37902-1405. Phones: (865) 545-4637; FAX (865) 545-4435.

■ 211 Commerce St. - Ste. 00(3rd fl.), Nashville, TN 37201. Phones: (615) 259-6060; FAX (615) 259-6064.

Texas—221 E. 11th St. 4th Fl., P.O. Box 12428, Austin, TX 78711-2428. Phones: (512) 916-5939; FAX (512) 916-5940.

■ 808 Throckmorton St., Ft. Worth, TX 76102. Phones: (817) 392-2673; FAX (817) 392-2668.

■ 1450 Hughes Rd. Ste. 20, Grapevine, TX 78711-2428. Phones: (817) 310-3744; FAX (817) 310-3757.

■ 15600 J.F. Kennedy Blvd. Ste. 530, Houston, TX 77032. Phones: (281) 449-9402.

■ 6401 S. 36th St. Ste. 4, McAllen, TX 78503. Phones: (956) 661-0238; FAX (956) 661-0239.

■ 1400 N. FM 1788 - Rm. 303, Midland, TX 79707-1423. Phones: (432) 552-2490; FAX (432) 552-3490.

■ 203 S. St. Mary St. - Ste. 60, San Antonio, TX 78205. Phones: (210) 228-9878; FAX (210) 228-9874.

Utah—9690 S. 300 West Ste. 331, Sandy, UT 84070. Phones: (801) 225-1871; FAX (801) 255-3147.

Vermont—National Life Bldg. - 6th fl., Drawer 20, Montpelier, VT 05620-0501. Phones: (802) 828-4508; FAX (802) 828-3258.

Virginia—100 N. Glebe Rd.. Ste. 1500, Arlington, VA 22201. Phones: (703) 235-0331; FAX (703) 524-2649.

■ 400 N. 8th St. - Ste. 12, P.O. Box 10026, Richmond, VA 23240. Phones: (804) 771-2246; FAX (804) 524-2649.

Washington—2601 Fourth Ave. Ste. 320, Seattle, WA 98121. Phones: (206) 553-5615; FAX (206) 553-7253.

■ 801 W. Riverside Ave. - Ste. 00, Spokane, WA 99201. Phones: (509) 353-2625; FAX (509) 353-2449.

■ 950 Pacific Ave. - Ste. 10, Tacoma, WA 98402. Phones: (253) 593-6736; FAX (253) 383-4676.

West Virginia—1116 Smith St. - Ste. 14, Charleston, WV 25301. Phones: (304) 347-5123; FAX (304) 347-5408.

- Wheeling Jesuit University/NTTC, 316 Washington Ave., Wheeling, WV 26003. Phones: (304) 243-5493; FAX (304) 243-5494.

Wisconsin—517 E. Wisconsin Ave. - Rm. 96, Milwaukee, WI 53202. Phones: (414) 297-3473; FAX (414) 297-3470.

Wyoming—*See* **Denver, Colorado** Export Assistance Center.

11.150   Bureau of Industry and Security

Western—3300 Irvine Ave. - Ste. 45, Newport Beach, CA 92660. Phone: (949) 660-0144.

- 160 Santa Clara St. - Ste. 25, San Jose, CA 95113. Phone: (408) 998-8806.

ECONOMIC DEVELOPMENT ADMINISTRATION

11.300
through
11.313

REGIONAL OFFICES

Atlanta *(Alabama, Florida, Georgia, Kentucky, Mississippi, North Carolina, South Carolina, Tennessee)*—401 W. Peachtree St. NW - Ste. 820, Atlanta, GA 30308-3510. Phone: (404) 730-3002.

Austin *(Arkansas, Louisiana, New Mexico, Oklahoma, Texas)*—604 Lavaca St. - Ste. 100, Austin, TX 78701-4037. Phone: (512) 381-8144.

Chicago *(Illinois, Indiana, Michigan, Minnesota, Ohio, Wisconsin)*—111 N. Canal St. - Ste. 55, Chicago, IL 60606-7204. Phone: (312) 353-8143.

Denver *(Colorado, Iowa, Kansas, Missouri, Montana, Nebraska, North Dakota, South Dakota, Utah, Wyoming)*—1244 Speer Blvd. - Rm. 70, Denver, CO 80204. Phone: (303) 844-4715.

Philadelphia *(Connecticut, Delaware, District of Columbia, Maine, Maryland, Massachusetts, New Hampshire, New Jersey, New York, Pennsylvania, Puerto Rico, Rhode Island, Vermont, Virgin Islands, Virginia, West Virginia)*—Curtis Center, Independence Square West - Ste. 40 South, Philadelphia, PA 19106. Phone: (215) 597-4603.

Seattle *(Alaska, American Samoa, Arizona, California, Guam, Hawaii, Idaho, Marshall Islands, Micronesia, Nevada, Northern Mariana Islands, Oregon, Washington)*—Jackson Federal Bldg. - Ste. 90, 915 2nd Ave., Seattle, WA 98174. Phone: (206) 220-7660.

11.407
through
11.474

Listed under **11.011.**

MINORITY BUSINESS DEVELOPMENT AGENCY

11.801

REGIONAL AND DISTRICT OFFICES

REGIONS I, II, AND III *(Connecticut, Delaware, District of Columbia, Maine, Maryland, Massachusetts, New Hampshire, New Jersey, New York, Pennsylvania, Puerto Rico, Rhode Island, Vermont, Virgin Islands, West Virginia)*—26 Federal Plaza - Rm. 720, New York, NY 10278. Phone: (212) 264-3262.

Massachusetts—10 Causeway St. - Rm. 18., Boston, MA 02222-1041. Phone: (617) 565-6850.

Pennsylvania—Federal Office Bldg. - Rm. 0128, 600 Arch St., Philadelphia, PA 19106. Phone: (215) 597-9236.

11.801
(cont.)

REGION IV *(Alabama, Florida, Georgia, Kentucky, Mississippi, North Carolina, South Carolina, Tennessee)*—401 W. Peachtree St. NW - Rm. 715, Atlanta, GA 30308-3516. Phone: (404) 730-3300.

Florida—Federal Bldg. - Rm. 314, 51 SW 1st Ave., P.O. Box 25, Miami, FL 33130. Phone: (305) 536-5054.

REGIONS V AND VII *(Illinois, Indiana, Iowa, Kansas, Michigan, Minnesota, Missouri, Nebraska, Ohio, Wisconsin)*—55 E. Monroe St. - Ste. 406, Chicago, IL 60603. Phone: (312) 353-0182.

REGIONS VI AND VIII *(Arkansas, Colorado, Louisiana, Montana, New Mexico, North Dakota, Oklahoma, South Dakota, Texas, Utah, Wyoming)*—1100 Commerce St. - Rm. B23, Dallas, TX 75242. Phone: (214) 767-8001.

REGIONS IX AND X *(Alaska, American Samoa, Arizona, California, Guam, Hawaii, Idaho, Nevada, Oregon, Washington)*—221 Main St. - Rm. 280, San Francisco, CA 94105. Phone: (415) 744-3001.

California—9660 Flair Dr. - Ste. 55, El Monte, CA 91731. Phone: (818) 453-8636.

DEPARTMENT OF DEFENSE

DEPARTMENT OF THE ARMY, CORPS OF ENGINEERS

12.100
through
12.116

Alabama *(Mobile District)*—P.O. Box 2288, Mobile, AL 36628. Phone: (205) 690-2511.

Alaska *(Alaska District)*—P.O. Box 898, Anchorage, AK 99506. Phone: (907) 752-5233.

Arkansas *(Little Rock District)*—P.O. Box 867, Little Rock, AR 72203. Phone: (501) 378-5531.

California *(Los Angeles District)*—P.O. Box 2711, Los Angeles, CA 90053. Phone: (213) 688-5300.

■ *(Sacramento District)*—650 Capitol Mall, Sacramento, CA 95814. Phone: (916) 448-2232.

■ *(San Francisco District)*—211 Main St., San Francisco, CA 94105. Phone: (415) 974-0358.

■ *(South Pacific Division)*—630 Sansome St. - Rm. 20, San Francisco, CA 94111. Phone: (415) 556-0914.

District of Columbia—CDR, USACA/CEMP-RI, 20 Massachusetts Ave. NW, Washington, DC 20314. Phone: (202) 504-4950.

Florida *(Jacksonville District)*—P.O. Box 4970, Jacksonville, FL 32232. Phone: (904) 791-2241.

Georgia *(Savannah District)*—P.O. Box 889, Savannah, GA 31402. Phone: (912) 944-5224, ext.224.

■ *(South Atlantic Division)*—510 Title Bldg., 30 Pryor St. SW, Atlanta, GA 30335. Phone: (404) 221-6711.

Hawaii *(Pacific Ocean Division)*—Ft. Shafter, HI 96858. Phone: (808) 438-1500.

Illinois *(Chicago District)*—219 S. Dearborn St., Chicago, IL 60604. Phone: (312) 353-6400.

■ *(North Central Division)*—536 S. Clark St., Chicago, IL 60605. Phone: (312) 353-6310.

- *(Rock Island District)*—Clock Tower Bldg., P.O. Box 2004, Rock Island, IL 61204. Phone: (309) 788-6361.

- Constitution Engineering Research Laboratory, Champaign, IL 61820-1305. Phone: (217) 373-6789.

Kentucky *(Louisville District)*—P.O. Box 59, Louisville, KY 40201. Phone: (502) 582-5601.

Louisiana *(New Orleans District)*—P.O. Box 60267, New Orleans, LA 70160. Phone: (504) 838-1121.

Maryland *(Baltimore District)*—P.O. Box 1715, Baltimore, MD 21203. Phone: (301) 962-4545.

Massachusetts *(New England Division)*—424 Trapelo Rd., Waltham, MA 02254. Phone: (617) 647-8220.

Michigan *(Detroit District)*—P.O. Box 1027, Detroit, MI 48231. Phone: (313) 226-6762.

Minnesota *(St. Paul District)*—1135 USPO and Custom House, St. Paul, MN 55101. Phone: (612) 725-7501.

Mississippi *(Lower Mississippi Valley Division)*—P.O. Box 80, Vicksburg, MS 39180. Phone: (601) 634-5750.

- *(Vicksburg District)*—P.O. Box 60, Vicksburg, MS 39180. Phone: (601) 634-5010.

- Waterways Experiment Station, Vicksburg, MS 39180-0631. Phone: (601) 634-2424.

Missouri *(Kansas City District)*—700 Federal Bldg., Kansas City, MO 64106. Phone: (816) 374-3201.

- *(St. Louis District)*—210 N. Tucker Blvd., St. Louis, MO 63101. Phone: (314) 263-5660.

Nebraska *(Missouri River Division)*—Downtown Station, P.O. Box 103, Omaha, NE 68101. Phone: (402) 221-7201.

- *(Omaha District)*—USPO and Courthouse - Rm. 014, Omaha, NE 68102. Phone: (402) 221-3900.

New Hampshire—Cold Regions Research and Engineering Laboratory, Hanover, NH 03755-1290. Phone: (603) 646-4390.

New Mexico *(Albuquerque District)*—P.O. Box 1580, Albuquerque, NM 87103. Phone: (505) 766-2732.

New York *(Buffalo District)*—1776 Niagara St., Buffalo, NY 14207. Phone: (716) 876-5454, ext.2200.

- *(New York District)*—26 Federal Plaza, New York, NY 10278. Phone: (212) 264-0100.

- *(North Atlantic Division)*—90 Church St., New York, NY 10007. Phone: (212) 264-7101.

North Carolina *(Wilmington District)*—P.O. Box 1890, Wilmington, NC 28402. Phone: (919) 343-4501.

Ohio *(Ohio River Division)*—P.O. Box 1159, Cincinnati, OH 45201. Phone: (513) 221-6000.

Oklahoma *(Tulsa District)*—P.O. Box 61, Tulsa, OK 74121. Phone: (918) 581-7311.

Oregon *(North Pacific Division)*—P.O. Box 2870, Portland, OR 97208. Phone: (503) 221-3700.

- *(Portland District)*—P.O. Box 2946, Portland, OR 97208. Phone: (503) 221-6000.

Pennsylvania *(Philadelphia District)*—U.S. Custom House, 2nd and Chestnut St., Philadelphia, PA 19106. Phone: (215) 597-4848.

- *(Pittsburgh District)*—Federal Bldg., 1000 Liberty Ave., Pittsburgh, PA 15222. Phone: (412) 644-6800.

12.100
through
12.116
(cont.)

South Carolina *(Charleston District)*—P.O. Box 919, Charleston, SC 29402. Phone: (803) 724-4229.

Tennessee *(Memphis District)*—B-202 Clifford Davis Federal Bldg., Memphis, TN 38103. Phone: (901) 521-3221.

■ *(Nashville District)*—P.O. Box 1070, Nashville, TN 37202. Phone: (615) 251-5626.

Texas *(Ft. Worth District)*—P.O. Box 17300, Ft. Worth, TX 76102. Phone: (817) 334-2300.

■ *(Galveston District)*—P.O. Box 1229, Galveston, TX 77553. Phone: (409) 766-3006.

■ *(Southwestern Division)*—1114 Commerce St., Dallas, TX 75242. Phone: (214) 767-2500.

Virginia *(Norfolk District)*—803 Front St., Norfolk, VA 23510. Phone: (804) 441-3601.

■ Humphreys Engineer Center Support Activity, Ft. Belvoir, VA 22060-5580. Phone: (202) 355-2153.

■ Topographic Engineering Center, Ft. Belvoir, VA 22060-5546. Phone: (202) 355-2659.

Washington *(Seattle District)*—P.O. Box C-3755, Seattle, WA 98124. Phone: (206) 764-3690.

■ *(Walla Walla District)*—City-County Airport - Bldg. 602, Walla Walla, WA 99362. Phone: (509) 522-6506.

West Virginia *(Huntington District)*—502 8th St., Huntington, WV 25721. Phone: (304) 529-5395.

Research and Development Laboratories

USAE Hydrologic Engineering Center, 609 2nd St., Davis, CA 95616-4887. Phone: (916) 756-1104.

USA Construction Engineering Research Laboratory, 2902 Newmark Dr., Champaign, IL 61821-1075. Phones: (800) 872-2375, (800) 252-7122.

USAE Waterways Experiment Station, 3909 Falls Ferry Rd., Vicksburg, MS 39180-6199. Phones: (601) 634-2512, (800) 522-6937.

USA Cold Regions Research and Engineering Laboratory, 72 Lynn Rd., Hanover, NH 03755-1290. Phone: (603) 646-4445.

USA Topographic Engineering Center, Cude Bldg. No. 2592, Ft. Belvoir, VA 22060-5546. Phone: (703) 355-3133.

USAE Institute for Water Resources, Casey Bldg. No. 2594, Ft. Belvoir, VA 22060-5586. Phone: (703) 355-3084.

OFFICE OF THE SECRETARY (ECONOMIC SECURITY)

12.355

WESTERN REGION—Office of Economic Adjustment, OASD(FM&P), 1325 J St. - Ste. 500, Sacramento, CA 95814. Phone: (916) 567-7365.

NATIONAL GUARD BUREAU

12.400
through
12.401

Admin Services, Readiness Center, 111 S. George Mason Dr. Arlington, VA 22204. Phone: (703) 607-7056.

Anti-Terrorism Program, ARNG Readiness Center, 111 S. George Mason Dr., Arlington, VA 22204-1302. Phone: (703) 607-9198.

Aviation Operations, ARNG Readiness Center, 111 S. George Mason Dr., Arlington, VA 22204-1382. Phone: (703) 607-7752.

Distributive Learning Program, ARNG Readiness Center, 111 S. George Mason Dr. Arlington, VA 22204. Phone: (703) 601-9869.

Electronic Security System, ARNG Readiness Center, 111 S. George Mason Dr., Arlington, VA 22204-1382. Phone: (703) 607-7956.

Environmental Resources Management, ARNG Readiness Center, 111 S. George Mason Dr., Arlington, VA 22204-1382. Phone: (703) 607-7340.

Facilities O&M, 3500 Fetcher Ave., Andrews AFB, MD 20331-5157. Phone: (301) 836-8194.

Fire Protection, 3500 Fetchet Ave., Andrews AFB, MD 20331-5157. Phone: (301) 278-8170.

Full Time Dining Facility Operations, ARNG Readiness Center, 111 S. George Mason Dr., Arlington, VA 22204-1382. Phone: (703) 607-7344.

Logistics Facilities, 3500 Fetchet Ave., Andrews AFB, MD 20762-5157. Phone: (301) 836-8338.

Natural & Cultural Resources Mgt, 3500 Fetchel Ave., Andrews AFB, MD 20762-5157. Phone: (301) 836-8427.

Real Property, ARNG Readiness Center, 111 S. George Mason Dr., Arlington, VA 22204-1382. Phone: (703) 607-7916.

Reimbursable Maintenance Operations, ARNG Readiness Center, 111 S. George Mason Dr. Arlington, VA 22204. Phone: (703) 607-7721.

Security Guard Activities, ARNG Readiness Center, 111 S. George Mason Dr., Arlington, VA 22204-1382. Phone: (703) 607-7353.

Security Guard, Andrews AFB, 3500 Fetcher Ave., MD 20331-5157. Phone: (301) 836-7809.

Services Resources Mgt, 3500 Fetchet Ave., Andrews AFB, MD 20762-5157. Phone: (301) 836-8162.

State Family Program Activities, 1411 Jefferson Davis Hwy., Alexandria, VA 22202-3231. Phone: (703) 607-0882.

Sustainable Range Program, ARNG Readiness Center, 111 S. George Mason Dr., Arlington, VA 22204-1382. Phone: (703) 607-7884.

Telecommunications, Readiness Center, 111 S. George Mason Dr., Arlington, VA 22204-1382. Phone: (703) 607-7654.

12.600
through
12.631 Listed under **12.355**

SECRETARIES OF MILITARY DEPARTMENTS

12.700 *Contact nearest military installation. Consult local phone directory.*

DEPARTMENT OF THE AIR FORCE, MATERIAL COMMAND

12.800 Air Force Office of Scientific Research, Bolling AFB - Ste. B115, 110 Duncan Ave., Washington, DC 20332-4990. Phone: (no number provided).

Armstrong Laboratory, 8005 9th St., Brooks AFB, TX 78235-5353. Phone: (no number provided).

Phillips Laboratory, 3651 Lowry Ave. SE, Kirkland AFB, NM 87117-5777. Phone: (505) 846-4979.

Rome Laboratory, 26 Electronics Pkwy., Griffins AFB, NY 13441-4514. Phone: (315) 330-7746.

Wright Laboratory, Bldg. 7, 2530 C St., Wright-Patterson AFB, OH 45433-7607. Phone: (513) 255-4813.

DEPARTMENT OF HOUSING AND URBAN DEVELOPMENT

FEDERAL HOUSING COMMISSIONER

14.103 through 14.525

FIELD OFFICES

Alabama—950 22nd St. N. - Ste. 00, Birmingham, AL 35203-5302. Phones: (205) 731-2617; FAX (205) 731-2593.

Alaska—3000 C St. - Ste. 01, Anchorage, AK 99503. Phones: (907) 677-9800; FAX (907) 677-9803.

Arizona—1 N. Central Ave. - Ste. 00, Phoenix, AZ 85004. Phones: (602) 379-7100; FAX (602) 379-3985.

- 160 N. Stone Ave., Tucson, AZ 85701-1467. Phones: (602) 670-6000; FAX (602) 670-6207.

Arkansas—TCBY Tower, 425 W. Capitol Ave. - Ste. 00, Little Rock, AR 72201-3488. Phones: (501) 324-5931; FAX (501) 324-6142.

California—2135 Fresno St. - Ste. 00, Fresno, CA 93721-1718. Phones: (559) 487-5033; FAX (559) 487-5191.

- AT&T Center - Ste. 00, 611 W. 6th St., Los Angeles, CA 90017-3127. Phones: (213) 894-8000; FAX (213) 894-8110.

- Moss Federal Bldg. Rm. -200, 650 Capitol Mall, Sacramento, CA 95814-2601. Phones: (916) 498-5220, ext.322; FAX (916) 498-5262.

- Symphony Towers - Ste. 600, 750 B St., San Diego, CA 92101-8131. Phones: (619) 557-5310; FAX (619) 557-5312.

- 600 Harrison St. - 3rd fl., San Francisco, CA 94107-1300. Phones: (415) 489-6400; FAX (415) 489-6419.

- Federal Bldg. Rm. 015, 34 Civic Center Plaza, Santa Ana, CA 92701-4003. Phones: (714) 796-5577; FAX (714) 796-1285.

Colorado—1670 Broadway 25th fl.,, Denver, CO 80202. Phones: (303) 672-5440; FAX (303) 672-5004.

Connecticut—One Corporate Center - 19th fl., 20 Church St., Hartford, CT 06103-3220. Phones: (860) 240-9700; FAX (860) 240-4850.

Delaware—One Rodney Square - Ste. 04, 920 King St., Wilmington, DE 19801-3016. Phones: (302) 573-6300; FAX (302) 573-6259.

District of Columbia—820 1st St. NE - Ste. 00, Washington, DC 20002-4205. Phones: (202) 275-9200; FAX (202) 275-9212.

Florida—Bennett Federal Bldg. Ste. 1015, 400 W. Bay St., Jacksonville, FL 32202. Phones: (904) 232-2627; FAX (904) 232-3759.

- Brickell Plaza Bldg., 909 SE 1st Ave., Miami, FL 33131-3028. Phones: (305) 536-4456; FAX (305) 536-5765.

- Langley Bldg. - Ste. 70, 3751 Maguire Blvd., Orlando, FL 32803-3032. Phones: (407) 648-6441; FAX (407) 648-6310.

- Timberlake Federal Bldg. Annex - Ste. 02, 500 E. Zack St., Tampa, FL 33602-3945. Phones: (813) 228-2026; FAX (813) 228-2431.

Georgia—Five Points Plaza, 40 Marietta St., Atlanta, GA 30303-2806. Phones: (404) 331-4111; FAX (404) 730-2392.

Hawaii—3 Waterfront Plaza - Ste. A, 500 Ala Moana Blvd., Honolulu, HI 96813-4918. Phones: (808) 522-8175; FAX (808) 522-8194.

Idaho—Plaza IV - Ste. 20, 800 Park Blvd., Boise, ID 83712-7743. Phones: (208) 334-1990; FAX (208) 334-9648.

Illinois—Metcalfe Federal Bldg., 77 W. Jackson Blvd., Chicago, IL 60604-3507. Phones: (312) 353-5680; FAX (312) 886-2729.

- 500 W. Monroe St. - Ste. SW, Springfield, IL 62704. Phones: (217) 492-4120; FAX (217) 492-4154.

Indiana—151 N. Delaware St. - Ste. 200, Indianapolis, IN 46204-2526. Phones: (317) 226-6303; FAX (317) 226-6317.

Iowa—Federal Bldg.- Rm. 39, 210 Walnut St., Des Moines, IA 50309-2155. Phones: (515) 284-4512; FAX (515) 284-4743.

Kansas—Regional Office, 400 State Ave. - Rm. 07, Kansas City, KS 66101-2406. Phones: (913) 551-5462; FAX (913) 551-5469.

Kentucky—601 W. Broadway, Louisville, KY 40202. Phones: (502) 582-5251; FAX (502) 582-6074.

Louisiana—Boggs Federal Bldg. - 9th fl., 500 Poydras St., New Orleans, LA 70130. Phones: (504) 589-7201; FAX (504) 589-7266.

- 401 Edwards St. - Ste. 510, Shreveport, LA 71101-5513. Phones: (318) 676-3440; FAX (318) 676-3407.

Maine—Smith Federal Bldg. - Rm. 01, 202 Harlow St., Bangor, ME 04401-4919. Phones: (207) 945-0467; FAX (207) 945-0533.

Maryland—City Crescent Bldg. - 5th fl., 10 S. Howard St., Baltimore, MD 21201-2505. Phones: (410) 962-2520; FAX (410) 209-6670.

Massachusetts—O'Neill Jr. Federal Office Bldg. - Rm. 01, 10 Causeway St., Boston, MA 02222-1092. Phones: (617) 994-8200; FAX (617) 565-5257.

Michigan—McNamara Federal Bldg., 477 Michigan Ave., Detroit, MI 48226-2592. Phones: (313) 226-7900; FAX (313) 226-5611.

- Phoenix Bldg., 801 S. Saginaw St., Flint, MI 48502. Phones: (810) 766-5112; FAX (810) 766-5122.

- Trade Center Bldg., 50 Louis St. NW, Grand Rapids, MI 49503-2633. Phones: (616) 456-2100; FAX (616) 456-2114.

Minnesota—Kinnard Financial Center, 920 Second St. S., Minneapolis, MN 55402. Phones: (612) 370-3000, ext.2045; FAX (612) 370-3220.

Mississippi—McCoy Federal Bldg. - Rm. 10, 100 W. Capitol St., Jackson, MS 39269-1096. Phones: (601) 965-4757; FAX (601) 965-4773.

Missouri—Young Federal Bldg. - Ste. 207, 1222 Spruce St., St. Louis, MO 63103-2836. Phones: (314) 539-6583; FAX (314) 539-6384.

Montana—Power Block Bldg., 7 W. 6th Ave., Helena, MT 59601. Phones: (406) 449-5050; FAX (406) 449-4052.

Nebraska—Zorinsky Federal Bldg. - Ste. 329, 1616 Capitol Ave., Omaha, NE 68102-4908. Phones: (402) 492-3101; FAX (402) 492-3150.

Nevada—300 S. Las Vegas Blvd. - Ste. 900, Las Vegas, NV 89101-5833. Phones: (702) 366-2100; FAX (702) 388-6244.

- 745 W. Moana Ln. Ste. 360, Reno, NV 89509-4932. Phones: (775) 824-3703; FAX (775) 784-5005.

New Hampshire—1000 Elm St. - 8th fl., Manchester, NH 03101-1730. Phones: (603) 666-7510; FAX (603) 666-7667.

New Jersey—Bridgeview Bldg. - 2nd fl., 800 Cooper St., Camden, NJ 08102-1156. Phones: (856) 757-5081; FAX (856) 757-5373.

14.103
through
14.525
(cont.)

■ One Newark Center - 13th fl., Newark, NJ 07102-5260. Phones: (973) 622-7900; FAX (973) 645-2323.

New Mexico—625 Silver Ave. SW - Ste. 00, Albuquerque, NM 87102-3185. Phones: (505) 346-6463, ext.7332; FAX (505) 346-6704.

New York—52 Corporate Circle, Albany, NY 12203-5121. Phones: (518) 464-4200; FAX (518) 464-4300.

■ Lafayette Court - 5th fl., 465 Main St., Buffalo, NY 14203-1780. Phones: (716) 551-5755; FAX (716) 551-5752.

■ 26 Federal Plaza - Ste. 541, New York, NY 10278-0068. Phones: (212) 264-8000; FAX (212) 264-3068.

■ 128 Jefferson St., Syracuse, NY 13202. Phones: (315) 477-0616; FAX (315) 477-0196.

North Carolina—Asheville Bldg. - Ste. 01, 1500 Pinecroft Rd., Greensboro, NC 27407-3838. Phones: (336) 547-4001; FAX (336) 547-4138.

North Dakota—Federal Bldg. - Rm. 66, 657 2nd Ave., Fargo, ND 58108-2483. Phones: (701) 239-5136; FAX (701) 239-5249.

Ohio—15 E. 7th St., Cincinnati, OH 45202-2401. Phones: (513) 684-3451; FAX (513) 684-6224.

■ Renaissance Bldg. - Ste. 00, 1350 Euclid Ave., Cleveland, OH 44115-1815. Phones: (216) 522-4058; FAX (216) 522-4067.

■ 200 N. High St., Columbus, OH 43215-2463. Phones: (614) 469-2540; FAX (614) 469-2432.

Oklahoma—301 NW 6th St. - Ste. 00, Oklahoma City, OK 73102. Phones: (405) 609-8509; FAX (405) 609-8588.

■ Williams Center Tower II Ste. 400, 2 W. Second St., Tulsa, OK 74103. Phones: (918) 292-8900; FAX (918) 292-8993.

Oregon—400 SW 6th Ave. - Ste. 00, Portland, OR 97204-1632. Phones: (971) 222-2600; FAX (971) 222-0357.

Pennsylvania—The Wanamaker Bldg., 100 Penn Square East, Philadelphia, PA 19107-3380. Phones: (215) 656-0600; FAX (215) 656-3445.

■ 339 6th Ave. - 6th fl., Pittsburgh, PA 15222-2515. Phones: (412) 644-6428; FAX (412) 644-4240.

Puerto Rico—235 Federico Costa St. Ste. 200, San Juan, PR 00918. Phones: (787) 766-5201; FAX (787) 766-5995.

Rhode Island—121 S. Main St. Ste. 300, Providence, RI 02903-7104. Phones: (401) 277-8300; FAX (401) 528-5312.

South Carolina—Thurmond Federal Bldg. - 13th fl., 1835 Assembly St., Columbia, SC 29201-2480. Phones: (803) 765-5592; FAX (803) 253-3043.

South Dakota—4301 W. 57th St. - Ste. 101, Sioux Falls, SD 57105-6558. Phones: (605) 330-4223; FAX (605) 330-4428.

Tennessee—Duncan Federal Bldg. - 3rd fl., 710 Locust St., Knoxville, TN 37902-2526. Phones: (865) 545-4384; FAX (865) 545-4569.

■ One Memphis Place - Ste. 00, 200 Jefferson Ave., Memphis, TN 38103-2389. Phones: (901) 544-3367; FAX (901) 544-3697.

■ 235 Cumberland Bend Dr. - Ste. 00, Nashville, TN 37228-1803. Phones: (615) 736-5213; FAX (615) 736-7848.

Texas—525 Griffin St. - Rm. 60, Dallas, TX 75202-5032. Phones: (214) 767-8300; FAX (214) 767-8973.

■ 801 Cherry St. Ste. 2500, Ft. Worth, TX 76113-2905. Phones: (817) 978-5965; FAX (817) 978-5567.

- 1301 Fannin - Ste. 200, Houston, TX 77002. Phones: (713) 718-3199; FAX (713) 718-3225.

- Mahon Federal Bldg. and U.S. Courthouse - Rm. 11, 1205 Texas Ave., Lubbock, TX 79401-4093. Phones: (806) 472-7265, ext.3030; FAX (806) 472-7275.

- One Alamo Center Ste. 05, 106 S. St. Mary's St, Antonio, TX 78205. Phones: (210) 475-6806; FAX (210) 472-6804.

Utah—125 S. State St. - Ste. 001, Salt Lake City, UT 84138. Phones: (801) 524-6070; FAX (801) 524-3439.

Vermont—159 Bank St. - 2nd fl., Burlington, VT 05401-4410. Phones: (802) 951-6290; FAX (802) 951-6298.

Virginia—The 3600 Centre, 600 E. Broad St. - 3rd fl., Richmond, VA 23219-4920. Phones: (804) 771-2100; FAX (804) 822-4984.

Washington—Seattle Federal Office Bldg. - Ste. 00, 909 1st Ave., Seattle, WA 98104-1000. Phones: (206) 220-5101; FAX (206) 220-5108.

- US Courthouse Bldg. - Rm. 88, 920 W. Riverside, Spokane, WA 99201-1010. Phones: (509) 353-0674; FAX (509) 353-0682.

West Virginia—Kanawha Valley Bldg. - Ste. 08, 405 Capitol St., Charleston, WV 25301-1795. Phones: (304) 347-7000; FAX (304) 347-7050.

Wisconsin—Reuss Federal Plaza - Ste. 380, 310 W. Wisconsin Ave., Milwaukee, WI 53203-2289. Phones: (414) 297-3214; FAX (414) 297-3947.

Wyoming—Federal Bldg. - Rm. 010, 150 E. B St., Casper, WY 82601-1969. Phones: (307) 261-6250; FAX (307) 261-6245.

OFFICE OF NATIVE AMERICAN PROGRAMS

14.850 through 14.898   FIELD OFFICES

Alaska—3000 C St. - Ste. 01, Anchorage, AK 99503. Phones: (907) 677-9800; FAX (907) 667-9807.

Eastern/Woodlands (*Iowa, all states east of Mississippi River*)—77 W. Jackson Blvd. - Rm. 404, Chicago, IL 60604-3507. Phones: (312) 886-4532, (800) 735-3239; FAX (312) 353-8936.

Northern Plains (*Colorado, Montana, Nebraska, North Dakota, South Dakota, Utah, Wyoming*)—UMB Plaza - 22nd fl., 1670 Broadway, Denver, CO 80202-4801. Phones: (303) 672-5465, (888) 814-2495; FAX (303) 672-5003.

Northwest (*Idaho, Oregon, Washington*)—Seattle Federal Office Bldg. - Ste. 00, 909 1st Ave., Seattle, WA 98104-1000. Phones: (206) 220-5270; FAX (206) 220-5234.

Southern Plains (*Arkansas, Kansas, Louisiana, Missouri, Oklahoma,Texas*)—301 NW 6th St. - Ste. 00., Oklahoma City, OK 73102. Phones: (405) 609-8532; FAX (405) 609-8403.

Southwest (*Arizona, California, Nevada, New Mexico*)—1 N. Central Ave. - Ste. 00, Phoenix, AZ 85004-2361. Phones: (602) 379-7200; FAX (602) 379-3101.

DEPARTMENT OF THE INTERIOR

BUREAU OF INDIAN AFFAIRS

15.020 through 15.025

AREA OFFICES

Alaska—Alaska Regional Office, Juneau, AK 99802-5520. Phone: (907) 586-7177.

Arizona—Western Regional Office, P.O. Box 10 - MS 100, Two Arizona Center - 12th fl., Phoenix, AZ 85001-0010. Phone: (602) 379-6600.

California—Pacific Regional Office, Federal Office Bldg., 2800 Cottage Way, Sacramento, CA 95825-1846. Phone: (916) 979-2600. *See also* **Arizona.**

District of Columbia—Deputy Commissioner of Indian Affairs, (MS 4140 MIB), 1849 C St. NW, Washington, DC 20240. Phone: (202) 208-5116.

Minnesota—Midwest Regional Office, One Federal Dr. - Rm. 50, St. Snelling, MN 55111. Phone: (612) 713-4400, ext.1020.

Montana—Rocky Mountain Regional Office, 316 N. 26th St., Billings, MT 59101-1397. Phone: (406) 247-7943.

New Mexico—Southwest Regional Office, 615 1st St. NW, P.O. Box 26567, Albuquerque, NM 87125-6567. Phone: (505) 346-7590. *See also* **Arizona.**

- Navajo Regional Office, P.O. Box 1060, Gallup, NM 87305. Phone: (505) 863-8314.

New York—*See* **Virginia**—Eastern Regional Office.

North Carolina—*See* **Virginia**—Eastern Regional Office.

North Dakota—*See* **South Dakota.**

Oklahoma—Southern Plains Office, P.O. Box 368, Anadarko, OK 73005-0368. Phone: (405) 247-6673, ext.257.

- Eastern Oklahoma Regional Office, 101 N. 5th St., Muskogee, OK 74401-6206. Phone: (918) 687-2295.

Oregon——Northwest Regional Office, 911 NE 11th Ave., Portland, OR 97232-4169. Phone: (503) 231-6702. *See also* **Arizona.**

South Dakota—Great Plains Regional Office, 115 4th Ave. SE, Aberdeen, SD 57401-4382. Phone: (605) 226-7343.

Utah—*See* **Arizona, New Mexico(Navajo), and Oregon.**

Virginia—**Eastern Regional Office, 3701 N. Fairfax Dr. - Ste. 60, Arlington, VA 22203. Phone: (703) 235-3006.**

Washington—*See* Oregon.

Wisconsin—*See* Minnesota.

Wyoming—*See* Montana.

FIELD AGENCIES

Alaska—Anchorage Field Office, 1675 C St. - Ste. 11, Anchorage, AK 99501-5198. Phone: (907) 271-4088.

- Bethel Field Office, 1675 C St. - Ste. 79, Anchorage, AK 99501-5198. Phone: (907) 271-4086.

- Fairbanks Agency, 101 12th Ave. - Rm. 6, Fairbanks, AK 99701-6270. Phone: (907) 456-0222.

- Metlakatla Field Office, P.O. Box 450, Metlakatla, AK 99926. Phone: (907) 886-3791.

Arizona—Chinle Agency, P.O. Box 7-H, Chinle, AZ 86503. Phone: (520) 674-5100.

■ Colorado River Agency, Rt.1 - Box 9-C, Parker, AZ 85344. Phone: (520) 669-7111.

■ Ft. Apache Agency, P.O. Box 560, Whiteriver, AZ 85941. Phone: (520) 338-5353.

■ Ft. Defiance Agency, P.O. Box 619, Ft. Defiance, AZ 86504. Phone: (520) 729-7217, -7218.

■ Ft. Yuma Field Office, P.O. Box 11000, Yuma, AZ 85366-1000. Phone: (760) 572-0248.

■ Hopi Agency, P.O. Box 158, Keams Canyon, AZ 86034. Phone: (520) 738-2228.

■ Papago Agency, P.O. Box 578, Sells, AZ 85634. Phone: (520) 383-3286.

■ Pima Agency, P.O. Box 8, Sacaton, AZ 85247. Phone: (520) 562-3326.

■ Salt River Field Office, 10000 E. McDowell Rd., Scottsdale, AZ 85256. Phone: (602) 640-2168.

■ San Carlos Agency, P.O. Box 209, San Carlos, AZ 85550. Phone: (520) 475-2321.

■ Truxton Canon Field Office, P.O. Box 37, Valentine, AZ 86437. Phone: (520) 769-2286.

■ Western Navajo Agency, P.O. Box 127, Tuba City, AZ 86045. Phone: (520) 283-2254, -2252.

California—Central California Agency, 1824 Tribute Rd. - Ste. J, Sacramento, CA 95815. Phone: (916) 566-7121.

■ Northern California Field Office, 1900 Churn Creek Rd. - Ste. 00, Redding, CA 96002. Phone: (530) 246-5141.

■ Palm Springs Field Office, 650 E. Tahquitz Canyon Way - Ste. A, P.O. Box 2245, Palm Springs, CA 92262. Phone: (760) 416-2133.

■ Southern California Agency, 2038 Iowa Ave. - Ste. 01, Riverside, CA 92507-0001. Phone: (909) 276-6624.

Colorado—Southern Ute Agency, P.O. Box 315, Ignacio, CO 81137. Phone: (970) 563-4511.

■ Ute Mountain Ute Field Office, P.O. Box KK, Towaoc, CO 81334. Phone: (970) 565-8473.

Florida—Seminole Agency, 6075 Sterling Rd., Hollywood, FL 33024. Phone: (954) 356-7288.

Idaho—Ft. Hall Agency, P.O. Box 220, Ft. Hall, ID 83203. Phone: (208) 238-2301.

■ Northern Idaho Agency, P.O. Drawer 277, Lapwai, ID 83540. Phone: (208) 843-2300.

■ Plummer Subagency, 850 A St., P.O. Box 408, Plummer, ID 83851. Phone: (208) 686-1887.

Kansas—Haskell Indian Nations University, 155 Indian Ave., Lawrence, KS 66046. Phone: (785) 749-8404.

■ Horton Field Office, P.O. Box 31, Horton, KS 66439. Phone: (785) 486-2161.

Michigan—Michigan Field Office, 2901.5 I-75 Business Spur, Sault Ste. Marie, MI 49783. Phone: (906) 632-6809.

Minnesota—Minnesota Agency, Federal Bldg. - Rm. 18, 522 Minnesota Ave. NW, Bemidji, MN 56601-3062. Phone: (218) 751-2011.

■ Red Lake Field Office, Red Lake, MN 56671. Phone: (218) 679-3361.

Mississippi—Choctaw Field Office, 421 Powell St., Philadelphia, MS 39350. Phone: (601) 656-1522.

Montana—Blackfeet Agency, P.O. Box 880, Browning, MT 59417. Phone: (406) 338-7544.

■ Crow Agency, P.O. Box 69, Crow Agency, MT 59022. Phone: (406) 638-2672.

**15.020
through
15.025
(cont.)**

- Flathead Field Office, P.O. Box 40, Pablo, MT 59855-5555. Phone: (406) 675-0242.
- Ft. Belknap Agency, R.R. 1 - P.O. Box 980, Harlem, MT 59526. Phone: (406) 353-2901, ext.23.
- Ft. Peck Agency, P.O. Box 637, Poplar, MT 59255. Phone: (406) 768-5312.
- Northern Cheyenne Agency, P.O. Box 40, Lame Deer, MT 59043. Phone: (406) 477-8242.
- Rocky Boy's Field Office, R.R. 1 - P.O. Box 542, Box Elder, MT 59521. Phone: (406) 395-4476.

Nebraska—Winnebago Agency, P.O. Box 18, Winnebago, NE 68071. Phone: (402) 878-2502.

Nevada—Eastern Nevada Field Office, 1555 Shoshone Circle, Elko, NV 89801. Phone: (775) 738-0569.

- Western Nevada Agency, 1677 Hot Springs Rd., Carson City, NV 89706. Phone: (775) 887-3500.

New Mexico—Eastern Navajo Agency, P.O. Box 328, Crownpoint, NM 87313. Phone: (505) 786-6100.

- Jicarilla Agency, P.O. Box 167, Dulce, NM 87528. Phone: (505) 759-3951.
- Laguna Agency, P.O. Box 1448, Laguna, NM 87026. Phone: (505) 552-6001.
- Mescalero Agency, P.O. Box 189, Mescalero, NM 88340. Phone: (505) 671-4423.
- Northern Pueblos Agency, Fairview Station, P.O. Box 4269, Espanola, NM 87533. Phone: (505) 753-1400.
- Ramah-Navajo Agency, Rt.2 - Box 14, Ramah, NM 87321. Phone: (505) 775-3235.
- Shiprock Agency, P.O. Box 966, Shiprock, NM 87420. Phone: (505) 368-3300.
- Southern Pueblos Agency, P.O. Box 1667, Albuquerque, NM 87103. Phone: (505) 346-2424.
- Zuni Agency, P.O. Box 369, Zuni, NM 87327. Phone: (505) 782-5591.

New York—New York Field Office, P.O. Box 7366, Syracuse, NY 13261-7366. Phone: (315) 448-0620.

North Carolina—Cherokee Agency, Cherokee, NC 28719. Phone: (704) 497-9131.

North Dakota—Ft. Berthold Agency, P.O. Box 370, New Town, ND 58763. Phone: (701) 627-4707.

- Ft. Totten Agency, P.O. Box 270, Ft. Totten, ND 58335. Phone: (701) 766-4545.
- Standing Rock Agency, P.O. Box E, Ft. Yates, ND 58538. Phone: (701) 854-3433.
- Turtle Mountain Agency, P.O. Box 60, Belcourt, ND 58316. Phone: (701) 477-3191.

Oklahoma—Anadarko Agency, P.O. Box 309, Anadarko, OK 73005. Phone: (405) 247-6677.

- Chickasaw Agency, 1500 N. Country Club Rd., P.O. Box 2240, Ada, OK 74821. Phone: (580) 436-0784.
- Concho Field Office, P.O. Box 68, El Reno, OK 73036-0068. Phone: (405) 262-7481.
- Okmulgee Field Office, P.O. Box 370, Okmulgee, OK 74447. Phone: (918) 756-3950.
- Osage Agency, P.O. Box 1539, Pawhuska, OK 74056. Phone: (918) 287-1032.
- Miami Field Office, P.O. Box 391, Miami, OK 74355. Phone: (918) 542-3396.
- Pawnee Agency, Pawnee, P.O. Box 440, OK 74058-0440. Phone: (918) 762-2585.
- Shawnee Field Office, 624 W. Independence - Ste. 14, Shawnee, OK 74801. Phone: (405) 273-0317.
- Talihina Office, Drawer H, Talihina, OK 74571. Phone: (918) 567-2207.

- Wewoka Agency, P.O. Box 1060, Wewoka, OK 74884. Phone: (405) 257-6259.

Oregon—Siletz Field Office, P.O. Box 569, Siletz, OR 97380. Phone: (541) 444-2679.

- Umatilla Agency, P.O. Box 520, Pendleton, OR 97801. Phone: (541) 278-3786.

- Warm Springs Agency, P.O. Box 1239, Warm Springs, OR 97761. Phone: (541) 553-2411.

South Dakota—Cheyenne River Agency, P.O. Box 325, Eagle Butte, SD 57625. Phone: (605) 964-6611.

- Crow Creek Agency, P.O. Box 139, Ft. Thompson, SD 57339. Phone: (605) 245-2311.

- Lower Brule Agency, P.O. Box 190, Lower Brule, SD 57548. Phone: (605) 473-5512.

- Pine Ridge Agency, P.O. Box 1203, Pine Ridge, SD 57770. Phone: (605) 867-5125.

- Rosebud Agency, P.O.Box 550, Rosebud, SD 57570. Phone: (605) 747-2224.

- Sisseton Agency, P.O. Box 688, Agency Village, SD 57262. Phone: (605) 698-3001.

- Yankton Agency, P.O. Box 577, Wagner, SD 57380. Phone: (605) 384-3651.

Utah—Uintah and Ouray Agency, P.O. Box 130, Ft. Duchesne, UT 84026. Phone: (435) 722-4300.

- Southern Paiute Field Office, P.O. Box 720, St. George, UT 84771. Phone: (435) 674-9720.

Washington—Colville Agency, P.O. Box 111, Nespelem, WA 99155-0111. Phone: (509) 634-2316.

- Makah Field Office, P.O. Box 115, Neah Bay, WA 98357. Phone: (360) 645-3232.

- Olympic Peninsula Agency, P.O. Box 48, Aberdeen, WA 98520. Phone: (360) 533-9100.

- Puget Sound Field Office, 2707 Colby Ave. - Ste. 101, Everett, WA 98201. Phone: (425) 258-2651.

- Spokane Agency, P.O. Box 389, Wellpinit, WA 99040. Phone: (509) 258-4561.

- Yakima Agency, P.O. Box 632(BIA) - P.O. Box 151(Tribal), Toppenish, WA 98948. Phone: (509) 865-5121.

Wisconsin—Great Lakes Agency, 615 Main St. W., Ashland, WI 54806-0273. Phone: (715) 682-4527.

Wyoming—Wind River Agency, P.O. Box 158, Ft. Washakie, WY 82514. Phone: (307) 332-7810.

15.026 through 15.028

EDUCATION LINE OFFICES

Alaska—Anchorage Education Field Office, 1675 C St., Anchorage, AK 99501. Phone: (907) 271-4115.

Arizona—Chinle Agency-Education, Navajo Rt. 7, P.O. Box 6003, Chinle, AZ 86503. Phone: (520) 674-5130, ext.201.

- Ft. Apache Agency-Education, Hwy. 73 and Elm St., P.O. Box 920, White River, AZ 85941. Phone: (520) 338-5441.

- Ft. Defiance Agency-Education - Bldg. 38, P.O. Box 110, Blue Canyon Hwy., Ft. Defiance, AZ 86504-0110. Phone: (520) 729-7251.

- Hopi Agency-Education, Hwy. 264, P.O. Box 568, Keams Canyon, AZ 86034. Phone: (520) 738-2262.

- Papago Agency-Education, South Bldg. 49, P.O. Box 38, Sells, AZ 85634. Phone: (520) 383-3292.

- Pima Agency-Education, 400 N. 5th St., P.O. Box 10, Phoenix, AZ 85001. Phone: (602) 379-3944.

15.026
through
15.028
(cont.)

■ Western Navajo Agency-Education, Bldg. 407, Hwy. 160 and Warrior Dr., P.O. Box 746, Tuba City, AZ 86045. Phone: (520) 283-2218.

California—Sacramento Area Education Office, 2800 Cottage Way, Sacramento, CA 95825. Phone: (916) 979-2560, ext.234.

Kansas—Haskell Indian Nations University, 155 Indian Ave. - #1305, Lawrence, KS 66046-4800. Phone: (785) 749-8404.

Minnesota—Minneapolis Area Education Office, 331 S. 2nd Ave., Minneapolis, MN 55401-2241. Phone: (612) 373-1000, ext.1090.

Montana—Billings Area Education Office, 316 N. 26th St., Billings, MT 59101-1397. Phone: (406) 247-7953.

New Mexico—Eastern Navajo Agency Education, Bldg. 222, 1 Main St., P.O. Box 328, Crownpoint, NM 87313. Phone: (505) 786-6150.

■ Northern Pueblos Agency-Education, Fairview Station, 1 Mile N. of Espanola - Hwy. 68, P.O. Box 4269, Espanola, NM 87533. Phone: (505) 753-1465.

■ Shiprock Agency-Education, Hwy. 666N, P.O. Box 3239, Shiprock, NM 87420-3239. Phone: (505) 368-4427, ext.360.

■ Southern Pueblos Agency-Education, 1000 Indian School Rd. NW, P.O. Box 1667, Albuquerque, NM 87103. Phone: (505) 346-2431.

■ Southwestern Indian Polytechnic Institute, 9169 Coors Rd. NW, P.O. Box 10146-9196, Albuquerque, NM 87184. Phone: (505) 346-2343.

North Dakota—Standing Rock Agency-Education, Main St. off Hwy. 106, Agency Ave., P.O. Box E, Ft. Yates, ND 58538. Phone: (701) 854-3497.

■ Turtle Mountain Agency-Education, School St., P.O. Box 30, Belcourt, ND 58316. Phone: (701) 477-6471, ext.211.

Oklahoma—Oklahoma Education Office, 4149 Highline Blvd. - Ste. 80, Oklahoma City, OK 73108. Phone: (605) 945-6051, ext.301, (405) 605-6057.

Oregon—Portland Area Education Office, 911 NE 11th Ave., Portland, OR 97232-4169. Phone: (503) 872-2743.

South Dakota—Cheyenne River Agency-Education, 100 N. Main, P.O. Box 2020, Eagle Butte, SD 51625. Phone: (605) 964-8722.

■ Crow Creek/Lower Brule Agency-Education, 140 Education Ave., P.O. Box 139, Ft. Thompson, SD 57339. Phone: (605) 245-2398.

■ Pine Ridge Agency-Education, 101 Main St., P.O. Box 333, Pine Ridge, SD 57770. Phone: (605) 867-1306.

■ Rosebud Agency-Education, 1001 Ave. D, P.O. Box 669, Mission, SD 57555. Phone: (605) 856-4478, ext.261.

Virginia—South and Eastern States Agency-Education, 3701 N. Fairfax Dr. - Ste. 60, Arlington, VA 22203. Phone: (703) 235-3233.

15.029
through
15.041

Listed under **15.020.**

15.042
through
15.047

Listed under **15.026.**

15.048
through
15.057

Listed under **15.020.**

15.058
through
15.059

Listed under **15.026.**

15.060 through **15.113**	Listed under **15.020**.
15.114	Listed under **15.026**.
15.124	Listed under **15.020**.
15.130	Listed under **15.026**.
15.133 through **15.148**	Listed under **15.020**.
15.149 through **15.151**	Listed under **15.026**.

BUREAU OF LAND MANAGEMENT

15.214 through 15.242

STATE OFFICES

Alaska—6881 Abbott Loop Rd., Anchorage, AK 99507. Phone: (907) 267-1323.

Arizona—222 N. Central Ave., P.O. Box 16563, Phoenix, AZ 95004-2203. Phone: (602) 417-9266.

California—2800 Cottage Way - Ste. W-1834, Sacramento, CA 95825-1886. Phone: (916) 978-4527.

Colorado—2850 Youngfield St., Lakewood, CO 80215-7076. Phone: (303) 239-3677.

District of Columbia - Branch of Procurement Management *(For bureauwide inquiries)*—1849 C St. NW, (MS 1075-LS), Washington, DC 20240. Phone: (202) 452-5170.

Idaho—1387 S. Vinnell Way, Boise, ID 83709-1657. Phone: (208) 373-3909.

Montana—5001 Southgate Dr., P.O. Box 36800, Billings, MT 59107-6800. Phone: (406) 896-5205.

Nevada—1340 Financial Blvd, P.O. Box 12000, Reno, NV 89520-0006. Phone: (702) 861-6417.

New Mexico—435 Montano NE, Albuquerque, NM 87107. Phone: (505) 761-8994.

Oregon—1515 SW 5th Ave., P.O. Box 2965, Portland, OR 97208. Phone: (503) 952-6220.

Utah—324 S. State St. - Ste. 01, Salt Lake City, UT 84111-2303. Phone: (801) 539-4172.

Virginia-Eastern States Office—7450 Boston Blvd., Springfield, VA 22153. Phone: (703) 440-1596.

Wyoming—5353 Yellowstone Rd., P.O. Box 1828, Cheyenne, WY 82005. Phone: (307) 775-6058.

LAW ENFORCEMENT DISTRICTS

DISTRICT I *(All Indian reservations in Michigan, Minnesota, Nebraska, North Dakota, South Dakota, Wisconsin)*—Office of Law Enforcement, Bureau of Indian Affairs, 115 4th Ave. SE, (MC 302), Aberdeen, SD 57401.

DISTRICT II *(All Indian reservations in Kansas and western Oklahoma, all Indian tribes in eastern Oklahoma)*—Office of Law Enforcement, Bureau of Indian Affairs, 101 N. 5th St., Muskogee, OK 74401.

15.214
through
15.242
(cont.)

DISTRICT III *(All Indian reservations in Arizona, northern California, Nevada, Utah (excluding Navajo))*—Office of Law Enforcement, Bureau of Indian Affairs, Bldg. 2 - N. 5th St., Phoenix, AZ 85004. *For mail:* P.O. Box 10, Phoenix, AZ 85001.

DISTRICT IV *(All Indian reservations in southern Colorado, New Mexico, and all Navajo Indian reservations in Arizona, New Mexico, Utah)*—Office of Law Enforcement, Bureau of Indian Affairs, P.O. Box 26567, Albuquerque, NM 87125-6567.

DISTRICT V *(All Indian reservations in Alaska, Idaho, Montana, Oregon, Washington, Wyoming)*—Office of Law Enforcement, Bureau of Indian Affairs, 316 N. 26th St., Billings, MT 59101.

DISTRICT VI *(All Indian reservations in Alabama, Connecticut, Florida, Louisiana, Maine, Mississippi, New York, North Carolina, Rhode Island)*—Office of Law Enforcement, Bureau of Indian Affairs, 1849 C St. NW, (MS 4550 MIB), Washington, DC 20240-0001.

OFFICE OF SURFACE MINING RECLAMATION AND ENFORCEMENT

FIELD OFFICES

15.250
through
15.255

Alabama—135 Gemini Circle - Ste. 15, Homewood, AL 35209. Phone: (205) 290-7282.

District of Columbia—1951 Constitution Ave. NW, Washington, DC 20240. Phone: (202) 208-4006.

Indiana—575 N. Pennsylvania St. - Rm. 01, Indianapolis, IN 46204. Phone: (317) 226-6700.

Kentucky—2675 Regency Rd., Lexington, KY 40503-2922. Phone: (859) 233-2494.

New Mexico—505 Marquette Ave. NW - Ste. 200, Albuquerque, NM 87102. Phone: (505) 248-5070.

Oklahoma—5100 E. Skelly Dr. - Ste. 70, Tulsa, OK 74135. Phone: (918) 581-6431.

Pennsylvania—Harrisburg Transportation Center - Ste. C, 415 Market St., Harrisburg, PA 17101. Phone: (717) 782-4036.

Tennessee—530 Gay St. SW - Ste. 00, Knoxville, TN 37902. Phone: (423) 545-4103.

Virginia—Powell Valley Square Shopping Center, 1941 Neeley Rd. - Ste. 01 (Compartment 116), Big Stone Gap, VA 24219. Phone: (540) 523-4303.

West Virginia—1027 Virginia St. E., Charleston, WV 25301. Phone: (304) 347-7162.

Wyoming—Federal Bldg. - Rm. 128, 100 E. "B" St., Casper, WY 82601-1918. Phone: (307) 261-6555.

REGIONAL COORDINATING CENTERS

APPALACHIAN REGION—Three Parkway Center, Pittsburgh, PA 15220. Phone: (412) 937-2828.

MID-CONTINENT REGION—Alton Federal Bldg., 501 Belle St. - Rm. 16, Alton, IL 62002. Phone: (618) 463-6460.

WESTERN REGION—1999 Broadway - Ste. 320, Denver, CO 80202-5733. Phone: (303) 844-1401.

BUREAU OF OCEAN ENERGY MANAGEMENT

15.421 through 15.428

REGIONAL OFFICES

Alaska OCS Region—3801 Centerpoint Dr., Ste. 500, Anchorage, AK 99503. Phone: (907) 334-5200.

Gulf of Mexico OCS Region & Atlantic OCS Region—1201 Elmwood Park Blvd., New Orleans, LA 70123-2394. Phone: (800) 200-4853.

Pacific OCS Region—760 Paseo Camarillo, Ste. 102 (CM 102), Camarillo, CA 93010. Phone: (805) 384-6305.

BUREAU OF RECLAMATION

15.504 through 15.565

REGIONAL OFFICES

COMMISSIONER'S OFFICE—Denver Federal Center, P.O. Box 25007, Denver, CO 80225-0007. Phone: (303) 445-2692.

GREAT PLAINS—P.O. Box 36900, Billings, MT 59107-6900. Phone: (406) 247-7600.

LOWER COLORADO—P.O. Box 61470, Boulder City, NV 89006-1470. Phone: (702) 293-8411.

MID-PACIFIC—Federal Office Bldg., 2800 Cottage Way, Sacramento, CA 95825-1898. Phone: (916) 978-5000.

PACIFIC NORTHWEST—1150 N. Curtis Rd. - Ste. 00, Boise, ID 83706-1234. Phone: (208) 378-5012.

UPPER COLORADO—125 S. State St. - Rm. 107, Salt Lake City, UT 84138-1102. Phone: (801) 524-3600.

Technical/Program Information:

Bureau of Reclamation, Lahontan Basin Area Office, 705 N. Plaza St. - Rm. 20, Carson City, NV 89701-4015. Phones: (775) 882-3436; FAX (775) 882-7592.

Acquisition Office:

Bureau of Reclamation, Mid-Pacific Regional Office, Acquisition Services, 2800 Cottage Way - Rm.E-1815, Sacramento, CA 95825-1898. Phones: (916) 978-5130; FAX (916) 978-5175, -5182. **Internet:** e-mail, "2WG4@mp.usbr.gov".

U.S. FISH AND WILDLIFE SERVICE

Federal Law Enforcement Training Center, Bldg. 69 - Rm. 00, Glynco, GA 31524. Phone: (912) 267-2370.

15.605 through 15.677

REGIONAL OFFICES

REGION I *(California, Hawaii, Idaho, Nevada, Oregon, Washington)*—911 NE 11th Ave., Portland, OR 97232-4181. Phones: (503) 872-2716; FAX (503) 231-6118.

REGION II *(Arizona, New Mexico, Oklahoma, Texas)*—500 Gold Ave. SW - Rm. 018, P.O. Box 1306, Albuquerque, NM 87103. Phones: (505) 248-6910; FAX (505) 248-6282.

REGION III *(Illinois, Indiana, Iowa, Michigan, Minnesota, Missouri, Ohio, Wisconsin)*—Federal Bldg., 1 Federal Dr., Ft. Snelling, MN 55111. Phones: (612) 713-5284; FAX (612) 713-5301.

REGION IV *(Alabama, Arkansas, Florida, Georgia, Kentucky, Louisiana, Mississippi, North Carolina, Puerto Rico, South Carolina, Tennessee, Virgin Islands)*—1875 Century Blvd., Atlanta, GA 30345. Phones: (404) 679-4006; FAX (404) 679-4000.

15.605
through
15.677
(cont.)

REGION V *(Connecticut, Delaware, District of Columbia, Maine, Maryland, Massachusetts, New Hampshire, New Jersey, New York, Pennsylvania, Rhode Island, Vermont, Virginia, West Virginia)*—300 Westgate Center Dr., Hadley, MA 01035. Phones: (413) 253-8308; FAX (413) 253-8300.

REGION VI *(Colorado, Kansas, Montana, Nebraska, North Dakota, South Dakota, Utah, Wyoming)*—Denver Federal Center, P.O. Box 25486, Denver, CO 80025. Phones: (303) 236-7920; FAX (303) 236-8295.

REGION VII *(Alaska)*—1011 E. Tudor Rd., Anchorage, AK 99503. Phones: (907) 786-3306; FAX (907) 786-3542.

Alabama—Wheeler NWR, 2700 Refuge Hdqtrs. Rd., Decatur, AL 35603. Phone: (256) 350-6639.

Alaska—1011 E. Tudor Rd., MS 201, Anchorage, AK 99503. Phone: (907) 786-3517.

American Samoa— USFWS, P.O. Box 3730, Pago Pago, AS 96799-3730. Phone: 011(684) 633-4456.

Arizona—Imperial National Wildlife Refuge, 12812 North Wildlife Way, P.O. Box 72217, Yuma, AZ 85365. Phone: 928-783-3371.

Arkansas—One 4H Way, Little Rock, AR 72223. Phone: (501) 821-6884.

California—Sacramento NWR Complex, 752 County Rd. 99W, Willows, CA 95988. Phone: (530) 934-2801.

Colorado— Rocky Mountain Arsenal NWR, USFWS Bldg. 121, Commerce City, CO 80022-2108. Phone: (303) 289-0867.

Connecticut—CN Waterfowl Association, 29 Bowers Hill Rd., Oxford, CT 06478. Phone: (203) 888-0352.

Delaware—DE Division/Fish and Wildlife, 4876 Hay Point Landing Rd., Smyrna, DE 19977. Phone: (302) 653-2882, ext.104.

District of Columbia—Patuxent Research Refuge, 10901 Scarlet Tanager Loop, Laurel, MD 20708-4027. Phone: (301) 497-5789.

Florida—J.N. Ding Darling NWR, 1 Wildlife Drive, Sanibel, FL 33957. Phone: (239) 472-1100.

Georgia—USFWS-Migratory Birds, 1875 Century Blvd. Ste. 240, Atlanta, GA 30345. Phone: (404) 679-7051.

Hawaii—USFWS, Pacific Islands Office, Rm. -311, 300 Ala Moana Blvd., Honolulu, HI 96850. Phone: (808) 792-9530.

Idaho—Deer Flat NWR, 13751 Upper Embankment Rd., Nampa, ID 83686. Phone: (208) 467-9278.

Illinois—IL DNR, Division of Education, 1 Natural Resources Way, Springfield, IL 62702. Phone: (217) 782-9741.

Indiana—Muscatatuck NWR, 12985 E. US Hwy. 50, Seymour, IN 47274. Phone: (812) 522-4352.

Iowa—Neal Smith NWR, 9981 Pacific St., P.O. Box 399, Prairie City, IA 50228. Phone: (515) 994-3400.

Kansas—Great Plains Nature Center, 6232 E. 29th N., Wichita, KS 67220. Phone: (316) 683-5499, ext.108.

Kentucky—Clarks River NWR, 91 US HWY 641 North, Benton, KY 42025. Phone: (270) 527-5770.

Louisiana—North Louisiana Refuge Complex, 11372 Hyw. 143, Farmerville, LA 71241. Phone:(318) 387-1114.

Maine—Maine Coastal Islands NWR, P.O. Box 495, 16 Rockport Pk. Ctr., Rockport, ME 04856. Phone: (207) 236-6970, ext.11.

Maryland—Patuxent Research Refuge, 10901 Scarlet Tanager Loop, Laurel, MD 20708-4027. Phone: (301) 497-5789.

Massachusetts—MA Wildlife Federation, One Rabbit Hill Rd., Westboro, MA 01581. Phone: (508) 389-6310.

Michigan—Shiawassee NWR, 6975 Mower Rd., Saginaw, MI 48601. Phone: (989) 759-1669.

Minnesota—MN Valley NWR, 3815 American Blvd. E., Bloomington, MN 55425. Phone: (952) 858-0710.

Mississippi—MS Museum of Natural Science, 2148 Riverside Dr., Jackson, MS 39202. Phone: (601) 354-7303.

Missouri—Big Muddy NWR, 4200 New Haven Dr., Columbia, MO 65201. Phone: (573) 441-2799 or (800) 611-1826.

Montana—Lee Metcalf NWR, Outdoor Recreation Planner, 4567 Wildfowl Ln., Stevensville, MT 59870. Phone: (406) 777-5552.

Nebraska—Crescent Lake NWR Complex, 115 Railway, Scottsbluff, NE 69361. Phone: (308) 635-7851.

Nevada—Stillwater NWR, 1000 Auction Rd., Fallon, NV 89406. Phone: (775) 423-5128.

New Hampshire—NH Fish and Game Department, 11 Hazen Dr., Concord, NH 03301. Phone: (603) 271-3211.

New Jersey—The Wetlands Institute, 1075 Stone Harbor Blvd., Stone Harbor, NJ 08247. Phone: (609) 368-1211.

New Mexico—Bosque del Apache NWR, 1001 NW Hwy. 1, San Antonio, NM 87832. Phone:(575) 835-1828.

New York—Montezuma National Wildlife Refuge, 3395 US Rte. 20, Seneca Falls, NY 13148. Phone: (315) 568-5987.

North Carolina—USFWS Ecological Survey, 551 E. Pylon Dr., Raleigh, NC 27606. Phone: (919) 856-4520, ext.25.

North Dakota—Audubon NWR, 3275 11th Street NW, Coleharbor, North Dakota 58531. Phone: (701) 442-5474, ext.17.

Ohio—Ottawa NWR, 14000 W. State Rte.2, Oak Harbor, OH 43449. Phone: (419) 898-0014.

Oklahoma—Wichita Mountains Wildlife Refuge, 32 Refuge HDQRTS Rd., Indiahoma, OK 73552. Phone: (580) 429-3221.

Oregon—OR Coast NWR Complex, 2127 SE Marine Science Dr., Newport, OR 97365. Phone: (541) 867-4550.

Pennsylvania—John Heinz National Wildlife Refuge, 8601 Lindbergh Blvd., Philadelphia, PA 19153. Phone: (215) 365 3118.

Rhode Island— Rhode Island NWR Complex, 50 Bend Rd., Charlestown, RI 02813. Phone: (401) 364-9124.

South Carolina—SC Dept. of Natural Resources, 1000 Assembly St. #209, Columbia, SC 29202. Phone: (803) 734-3885.

South Dakota— D.C. Booth HNFH, 423 Hatchery Circle, Spearfish, SD 57783. Phone: (605) 642-7730, ext.221.

Tennessee—Tennessee NWR, 3006 Dinkins Lane, Paris, TN 38242. Phone: (731) 642-2091.

Texas—Texas Mid-Coast Refuge Complex, 2547 CR 316, Brazoria, Texas 77422. Phone: (979) 964-4011.

Utah—Bear River Bird Refuge, 2155 W. Forest Rd., Brigham City, UT 84302. Phone: (435) 723-5887.

Vermont—Missisquoi NWR, 29 Tabour Rd., Swanton, VT 05488. Phone: (802) 868-4781.

15.605
through
15.677
(cont.)

Virginia—Chincoteague NWR, P.O. Box 62, Chincoteague, VA 23336. Phone: (757) 336-6122.

Virgin Islands—VI Division of Fish and Wildlife, 45 Mars Hill, Frederiksted, VI 00840. Phone: (340) 713-2422.

Washington—Nisqually NWR, 100 Brown Farm Rd., Olympia, WA 98516. Phone: (360) 753-9467.

West Virginia—Ohio River Islands NWR, 3004 7th St., Parkersburg, WV 26102. Phone: (304) 422-0752.

Wisconsin—Necedah NWR, W7996 20th St. W., Necedah, WI 54646. Phone: (608) 565-2551.

Wyoming—National Museum of Wildlife Art, P.O. Box 6825, 2820 Rungius Rd., Jackson, WY 83002. Phone: (307) 732-5417.

U.S. GEOLOGICAL SURVEY

15.807
through
15.820

REGIONAL OFFICES

Biological Resources Division

CENTRAL *(Arkansas, Colorado, Iowa, Kansas, Louisiana, Minnesota, Missouri, Montana, Nebraska, New Mexico, North Dakota, Oklahoma, South Dakota, Texas, Wyoming)*—Regional Chief Biologist, Denver Federal Center Bldg, 020 - Rm.A1419, (MS 300), Denver, CO 80225. Phone: (303) 236-2739, ext.238.

EASTERN *(Alabama, Connecticut, District of Columbia, Florida, Georgia, Illinois, Indiana, Kentucky, Maine, Maryland, Massachusetts, Michigan, Mississippi, New Hampshire, New Jersey, New York, North Carolina, Ohio, Pennsylvania, Puerto Rico, Rhode Island, South Carolina, Tennessee, Vermont, Virginia, West Virginia, Wisconsin)*—Acting Regional Chief Biologist, National Center - Rm. A100, (MS 300), 12201 Sunrise Valley Dr., Reston, VA 20192. Phone: (703) 648-4060.

WESTERN *(Alaska, Arizona, California, Hawaii, Idaho, Nevada, Oregon, Utah, Washington)*—Regional Chief Biologist, 909 1st Ave. - Ste. 00, Seattle, WA 98104. Phone: (206) 220-4600.

Geologic Division

CENTRAL—Federal Center, (MS 911), Denver, CO 80225. Phone: (303) 236-5435.

EASTERN—953 National Center, Reston, VA 20192. Phone: (703) 648-6662.

WESTERN—345 Middlefield Rd., (MS 919), Menlo Park, CA 94025. Phone: (415) 650-5102.

National Mapping Division

Mapping Application Center—National Center, (MS 567), Reston, VA 20192. Phone: (703) 648-6002.

Midcontinent Mapping Center—1400 Independence Rd., (MS 300), Rolla, MO 65401. Phone: (573) 308-3800.

Rocky Mountain Mapping Center—Denver Federal Center, (MS 508), Bldg. 810, Box 25046, Denver, CO 80225-0046. Phone: (303) 202-4040.

South Dakota - Earth Resources Observation Systems Data Center—Mundt Federal Bldg., Sioux Falls, SD 57198. Phone: (605) 594-6123.

Western Mapping Center—345 Middlefield Rd., (MS 531), Menlo Park, CA 94025-3591. Phone: (415) 329-4254.

Water Resources Division

CENTRAL *(Colorado, Iowa, Kansas, Minnesota, Montana, Nebraska, New Mexico, North Dakota, Oklahoma, South Dakota, Texas, Wyoming)*—Regional Hydrologist, (MS 406), Denver Federal Center, Bldg. 25, Box 25046, Lakewood, CO 80225-0046. Phone: (303) 236-5950, ext.0.

NORTHEAST *(Connecticut, Delaware, Illinois, Indiana, Kentucky, Maine, Maryland, Massachusetts, Michigan, New Hampshire, New Jersey, New York, Ohio, Pennsylvania, Rhode Island, Vermont, Virginia, West Virginia, Wisconsin)*—Regional Hydrologist, (MS 433), 433 National Center, Reston, VA 22092. Phone: (703) 648-5813.

SOUTHEAST *(Alabama, Arkansas, Florida, Georgia, Louisiana, Mississippi, Missouri, North Carolina, Puerto Rico, South Carolina, Tennessee, Virgin Islands)*—Regional Hydrologist, Spalding Woods Office Park - Ste. 60, 3850 Holcomb Bridge Rd., Norcross, GA 30092-2202. Phone: (404) 409-7701.

WESTERN *(Alaska, American Samoa, Arizona, California, Guam, Hawaii, Idaho, Nevada, Oregon, other Pacific Islands, Utah, Washington)*—Regional Hydrologist, (MS 470), 345 Middlefield Rd., Menlo Park, CA 94025-3591. Phone: (415) 329-4414.

NATIONAL PARK SERVICE

For financial assistance information contact the State Historic Preservation Officer in your state, and the appropriate regional office for subgrant eligibility information, following.

15.904 through 15.955

NATIONAL HEADQUARTERS

National Park Service—Professional Services, 1849 C St. NW, Washington, DC 20240. Phone: (202) 208-3264.

REGIONAL OFFICES

ALASKA—2525 Gambell St., Anchorage, AK 99503-2892. Phone: (907) 257-2690.

INTERMOUNTAIN—12795 W. Alameda Pkwy., Denver, CO 80225-0287. Phone: (303) 969-2503.

MIDWEST—Professional Services and Legislation, 1709 Jackson St., Omaha, NE 68102. Phone: (402) 221-3084.

NATIONAL CAPITAL—Finance Management Officer, 1100 Ohio Dr. SW, Washington, DC 20242. Phone: (202) 619-7160.

NORTHEAST—U.S. Custom House, 200 Chestnut St. - 3rd fl., Philadelphia, PA 19106. Phone: (215) 597-7013.

SOUTHEAST—Atlanta Federal Center - 1924 Building, 100 Alabama St. SW, Atlanta, GA 30303. Phone: (404) 562-3100.

PACIFIC WEST—Resources, Stewardship and Partnership, 111 Jackson St. - Ste. 00, Oakland, CA 94607. Phone: (415) 427-1321.

SERVICE CENTERS

Denver Service Center—P.O. Box 25287, Denver, CO 80225. Phone: (303) 969-2100.

Harpers Ferry Center—P.O. Box 50, Harpers Ferry, WV 25425-0050. Phone: (304) 535-6211.

15.960 Listed under **15.026.**

15.962 Listed under **15.904.**

15.978 through 15.979 Listed under **15.807.**

DEPARTMENT OF JUSTICE

DRUG ENFORCEMENT ADMINISTRATION

16.001 through 16.004

FIELD OFFICES

(No phone numbers provided)

Atlanta—75 Spring St. SW - Rm. 40, A53, Atlanta, GA 30303.

Boston—JFK Federal Bldg. - Rm.E-400, 15 Sudbury St., Boston, MA 02203-0402.

Caribbean—Metro Office Park - Bldg.17, Guayanabo, PR 00968.

Chicago—230 S. Dearborn St. - Ste. 200, Chicago, IL 60604.

Dallas—10160 Technology Blvd., East Dallas, TX 75220-4343.

Denver—115 Inverness Dr. E., Englewood, CO 80112-5116.

Detroit—431 Howard St., Detroit, MI 48226.

El Paso—DEA/EPIC, SSG Sims St., El Paso, TX 79908-8098.

■ 600 S. Mesa Hills Dr., El Paso, TX 79912.

Houston—1433 W. Loop South - Ste. 00, Houston, TX 77027-9506.

Los Angeles—Royal Federal Bldg. - 20th fl., 255 E. Temple St., Los Angeles, CA 90012.

Miami—8400 NW 53rd St., Miami, FL 33166.

Newark—80 Mulberry St. - 2nd fl., Newark, NJ 07102-4206.

New Orleans—Three Lakeway Center - Ste. 800, 3838 N. Causeway Blvd., Metairie, LA 70002.

New York—99 10th Ave., New York, NY 10011.

Philadelphia—600 Arch St. - Rm. 0224, Philadelphia, PA 19106.

Phoenix—3010 N. 2nd St. - Ste. 01, Phoenix, AZ 85012.

San Diego—4560 Viewridge Ave., San Diego, CA 92123-1672.

San Francisco—450 Golden Gate Ave., San Francisco, CA 94102.

Seattle—400 2nd Ave. W, Seattle, WA 98119-4140.

St. Louis—7911 Forsythe Blvd. - Ste. 00, St. Louis, MO 63105.

Washington, D.C.—801 K St. NW - Ste. 00, Washington, DC 20001.

Laboratories

MID-ATLANTIC—460 New York Ave. NW, Washington, DC 20532-0001.

NORTH CENTRAL—536 S. Clark St. - Rm. 00, Chicago, IL 60605,

NORTHEAST—99 Tenth Ave. - Rm. 21, New York, NY 10011.

SOUTH CENTRAL—1880 Regal Row, Dallas, TX 75235.

SOUTHEAST—5205 NW 84th Ave., Miami, FL 33166.

SOUTHWEST—410 W.35th St., National City, CA 91950.

SPECIAL TESTING AND RESEARCH—3650 Concorde Pkwy. - Ste. 00, Chantilly, VA 20151.

WESTERN—390 Main St. - Rm. 00, San Francisco, CA 94105.

Office of Training

Drug Enforcement Administration, FBI Academy, P.O. Box 1475, Quantico, VA 22134-1475.

CIVIL RIGHTS DIVISION

16.109   CRIMINAL SECTION

Contact local U.S. Attorney's Office, or FBI (addresses listed under **16.300**).

COMMUNITY RELATIONS SERVICE

16.200   REGIONAL OFFICES

REGION I *(Connecticut, Maine, Massachusetts, New Hampshire, Rhode Island, Vermont)*—408 Atlantic Ave. - Ste. 22, Boston, MA 02110. Phone: (617) 424-5715.

REGION II *(New Jersey, New York, Puerto Rico, Virgin Islands)*—26 Federal Plaza - Rm. 6-118, New York, NY 10278. Phone: (212) 264-0700.

REGION III *(Delaware, District of Columbia, Maryland, Pennsylvania, Virginia, West Virginia)*—2nd and Chestnut St. - Rm. 08, Philadelphia, PA 19106. Phone: (215) 597-2344.

REGION IV *(Alabama, Florida, Georgia, Kentucky, Mississippi, North Carolina, South Carolina, Tennessee)*—75 Piedmont Ave. NE - Rm. 00, Atlanta, GA 30303. Phone: (404) 331-6883.

REGION V *(Illinois, Indiana, Michigan, Minnesota, Ohio, Wisconsin)*—55 W. Monroe St. - Rm. 20, Chicago, IL 60603. Phone: (312) 353-4391.

REGION VI *(Arkansas, Louisiana, New Mexico, Oklahoma, Texas)*—1420 Mockingbird Ln. - Ste. 50, Dallas, TX 75247. Phone: (214) 655-8175.

REGION VII *(Iowa, Kansas, Missouri, Nebraska)*—1100 Main St. - Ste. 320, Kansas City, MO 64105. Phone: (816) 426-7434.

REGION VIII *(Colorado, Montana, North Dakota, South Dakota, Utah, Wyoming)*—1244 Speer Blvd. - Ste. 50, Denver, CO 80204-3584. Phone: (303) 844-2973.

REGION IX *(Arizona, California, Guam, Hawaii, Nevada)*—888 S. Figueroa St. - Ste. 880, Los Angeles, CA 90017. Phone: (213) 894-2941.

REGION X *(Alaska, Idaho, Oregon, Washington)*—915 2nd Ave. - Rm. 808, Seattle, WA 98174. Phone: (206) 220-6700.

FIELD OFFICES

Detroit—211 W. Fort St. - Rm. 404, Detroit, MI 48226. Phone: (313) 226-4010.

Houston—515 Rusk Ave. - Rm. 2605, Houston, TX 77002. Phone: (713) 718-4861.

Miami—51 SW 1st Ave. - Rm. 24, Miami, FL 33130. Phone: (305) 536-5206.

San Francisco—120 Howard St. - Ste. 90, San Francisco, CA 94105. Phone: (415) 744-6565.

FEDERAL BUREAU OF INVESTIGATION

16.300 through 16.309   FIELD OFFICES (Special Agent in Charge)

REGION I *(Connecticut, Maine, Massachusetts, New Hampshire, Rhode Island, Vermont)*:

- Federal Office Bldg., 600 State St., New Haven, CT 06510-2020. Phones: (203) 503-5000, 786-7000.

- 1 Center Plaza - Ste. 00, Boston, MA 02108-1801. Phones: (617) 742-5533, 223-6000.

16.300
through
16.309
(cont.)

REGION II *(New Jersey, New York, Puerto Rico, Virgin Islands)*:

- One Gateway Center - 22nd fl., Newark, NJ 07102-9889. Phone: (973) 792-3000.
- Foley Bldg., 200 McCarty Ave., Albany, NY 12209-2095. Phones: (518) 465-7551, 431-7200.
- One FBI Plaza, Buffalo, NY 14202-2698. Phones: (716) 856-7800, 843-4300.
- Javits Federal Office Bldg., 26 Federal Plaza, New York, NY 10278-0004. Phone: (212) 384-1000.
- U.S. Federal Office Bldg. - Rm. 26, 150 Carlos Chardon, Hato Rey, PR 00918-1716. Phones: (787) 754-6000, -3292.

REGION III *(Delaware, District of Columbia, Maryland, Pennsylvania, Virginia, West Virginia)*:

- Washington Metropolitan Field Office, 601 4th St. NW, Washington, DC 20535-0002. Phone: (202) 278-2000.
- 7142 Ambassador Rd., Baltimore, MD 21244-2754. Phones: (410) 265-8080, 281-0198.
- Federal Office Bldg. - 8th fl., 600 Arch St., Philadelphia, PA 19106-1675. Phones: (215) 418-4500, -4000.
- U.S. Post Office - Ste. 00, 700 Grant St., Pittsburgh, PA 15219-1906. Phones: (412) 471-2000, 456-9100.
- 150 Corporate Blvd., Norfolk, VA 23502-4999. Phones: (757) 455-0100, -0123.
- 111 Greencourt Rd., Richmond, VA 23228-4948. Phones: (804) 261-1044, (700) 923-2000.

REGION IV *(Alabama, Florida, Georgia, Kentucky, Mississippi, North Carolina, South Carolina, Tennessee)*:

- 2121 8th Ave. N. - Rm. 400, Birmingham, AL 35203-2396. Phones: FTS (205) 715-0300; FAX (205) 326-6166.
- St. Louis Centre - 3rd fl., 1 St. Louis St., Mobile, AL 36602-3930. Phones: (334) 438-3674, (334) 219-3555.
- 7820 Arlington Expressway - Ste. 00, Jacksonville, FL 32211-7499. Phones: (904) 721-1211.
- 16320 NW 2nd Ave., North Miami Beach, FL 33169-6508. Phones: (305) 944-9101, 787-6100.
- Federal Office Bldg. - Rm. 10, 500 E. Zack St., Tampa, FL 33602-3917. Phones: (813) 273-4566, 272-8000.
- 2635 Century Pkwy. NE - Ste. 00, Atlanta, GA 30345-3112. Phones: (404) 679-9000, -6100.
- Federal Office Bldg. - Ste. 00, 600 Martin Luther King Place, Louisville, KY 40202-2231. Phones: (502) 583-3941.
- Federal Office Bldg. - Ste. 553, 100 W. Capitol St., Jackson, MS 39269-1601. Phones: (601) 948-5000, 360-7550.
- Wachovia Bldg. - Ste. 00, 400 S. Tyron, Charlotte, NC 28285-0001. Phone: (704) 377-9200, 331-4500.
- 151 W. Park Blvd., Columbia, SC 29210-3857. Phones: (803) 551-4200, 551-4209.
- 710 Locust St. - Ste. 00, Knoxville, TN 37902-2537. Phones: (865) 544-0751, 544-3500.
- Eaglecrest Bldg. - Ste. 000, 225 N. Humphreys Blvd., Memphis, TN 38120-2107. Phones: (901) 747-4300, -9739.

REGION V *(Illinois, Indiana, Michigan, Minnesota, Ohio, Wisconsin)*:

- Dirksen Federal Office Bldg. - Rm. 05, 219 S. Dearborn St., Chicago, IL 60604-1702. Phones: (312) 431-1333, 786-2500.

- 400 W. Monroe St. - Ste. 00, Springfield, IL 62704-1800. Phones: (217) 522-9675, 535-4400.
- Federal Office Bldg. - Rm. 79, 575 N. Pennsylvania St., Indianapolis, IN 46204-1585. Phones: (317) 639-3301, 321-6100.
- McNamara Federal Office Bldg. - 26th fl., 477 Michigan Ave., Detroit, MI 48226-2598. Phones: (313) 965-2323, 237-4355.
- 111 Washington Ave. S. - Ste. 100, Minneapolis, MN 55401-2176. Phones: (612) 376-3200.
- Federal Office Bldg. - Rm. 000, 550 Main St., Cincinnati, OH 45202-8501. Phones: (513) 421-4310, 562-5600.
- Federal Office Bldg. - Rm. 005, 1240 E. 9th St., Cleveland, OH 44199-9912. Phones: (216) 522-1400, 622-6600.
- 330 E. Kilbourn Ave. - Ste. 00, Milwaukee, WI 53202-6627. Phones: (414) 276-4684, 291-4899.

REGION VI *(Arkansas, Louisiana, New Mexico, Oklahoma, Texas)*:
- Two Financial Centre - Ste. 00, 10825 Financial Centre Pkwy., Little Rock, AR 72211-3552. Phones: (501) 221-9100, 228-8400.
- 2901 Leon C. Simon Blvd., New Orleans, LA 70126-1061. Phones: (504) 816-3000.
- 415 Silver Ave. SW - Ste. 00, Albuquerque, NM 87102. Phone: (505) 224-2000.
- 3301 W. Memorial Rd., Oklahoma City, OK 73134. Phones: (405) 290-7770, -3875.
- 1801 N. Lamar - Ste. 00, Dallas, TX 75202-1795. Phones: (214) 720-2200, 922-7475.
- 600 S. Mesa Hills Dr. - Ste. 000, El Paso, TX 79912-5533. Phone: (915) 832-5000.
- 2500 E. T.C. Jester, Houston, TX 77008-1300. Phones: (713) 693-5000, -3800.
- U.S. Post Office and Courthouse Bldg. - Ste. 00, 615 E. Houston St., San Antonio, TX 78205-9998. Phones: (210) 225-6741, 978-5400.

REGION VII *(Iowa, Kansas, Missouri, Nebraska)*:
- U.S. Courthouse - Rm. 00, 1300 Summit, Kansas City, MO 64105-1362. Phones: (816) 221-6100, 512-8200.
- 2222 Market St. - Rm. 704, St. Louis, MO 63103-2516. Phones: (314) 231-4324, 589-2500.
- Federal Office Bldg., 10755 Burt St., Omaha, NE 68114-2000. Phones: (402) 493-8688, 492-3700.

REGION VIII *(Colorado, North Dakota, South Dakota, Utah, Wyoming)*:
- Federal Office Bldg. - Ste. 823 (18th fl.), 1961 Stout St., Denver, CO 80294-1823. Phones: (303) 629-7171, 628-3000.
- 257 Towers Bldg. - Ste. 200, 257 E. 200 S., Salt Lake City, UT 84111-2048. Phones: (801) 579-1400, -4400.

REGION IX *(American Samoa, Arizona, California, Guam, Hawaii, Nevada)*:
- Midtowne Business Centre II - Ste. 00, 201 E. Indianola Ave., Phoenix, AZ 85012-2080. Phones: (602) 279-5511, 650-3300.
- Federal Office Bldg. - Ste. 700, 11000 Wilshire Blvd., Los Angeles, CA 90024-3672. Phones: (858) 565-1255, 514-5500.
- 4500 Orange Grove Ave., Sacramento, CA 95841-4205. Phones: (916) 481-9110, 977-2200.
- Federal Office Bldg., 9797 Aero Dr., San Diego, CA 92123-1800. Phones: (619) 565-1255, 514-5500.
- 450 Golden Gate Ave. - 13th fl., San Francisco, CA 94102-9523. Phones: (415) 553-7400, -2000.

16.300 through 16.309 (cont.)

- Kalanianaole Federal Office Bldg. - Rm. -230, 300 Ala Moana Blvd., Honolulu, HI 96850-0053. Phone: (808) 566-4300.

- John Lawrence Bailey Bldg., 700 E. Charleston Blvd., Las Vegas, NV 89101-1545. Phones: (702) 385-1281, (700) 545-0110.

REGION X *(Alaska, Idaho, Oregon, Washington)*:

- 101 E. 6th Ave., Anchorage, AK 99501-2523. Phones: (907) 258-5322, 276-4441.

- Crown Plaza Bldg. - Ste. 00, 1500 SW 1st Ave., Portland, OR 97201-5828. Phones: (503) 224-4181, 552-5200.

- Federal Office Bldg. - Rm. 10, 915 2nd Ave., Seattle, WA 98101. Phones: (206) 262-2000, (700) 391-8760.

OFFICE OF THE INSPECTOR GENERAL

FIELD INSTALLATIONS

Arizona—*Investigations,* 10 E. Broadway - Ste. 05, Tucson, AZ 85701. Phones: (520) 670-5243; FAX (520) 670-5246. *For mail:* Tucson, AZ 85702-0471.

California—*Investigations,* 321 S. Waterman Ave. - Rm. 08, El Centro, CA 92243. Phones: (760) 335-3549; FAX (760) 335-3534.

- *Investigations,* 330 N. Brand St. - Ste. 55, Glendale, CA 91203. Phones: (818) 543-1172; FAX (818) 637-5082.

- 1200 Bayhill Dr. - Stes.220/201, San Bruno, CA 94066. Phones: *audits,* (650) 876-9220; FAX (650) 876-0902; *investigations,* (650) 876-9058; FAX (650) 876-9083.

- *Investigations,* 701 "B" St. - Ste. 60, San Diego, CA 92101. Phones: (619) 557-5970; FAX(619) 557-6518.

Colorado—*Investigations,* Plaza of the Rockies, 111 S. Tejon St. - Ste. 12, Colorado Springs, CO 80903. Phones: (719) 635-2366; FAX (719) 635-4769.

- *Audits,* The Chancery Bldg. - Ste. 603, 1120 Lincoln St., Denver, CO 80203. Phones: (303) 864-2000; FAX (303) 864-2004.

District of Columbia—1425 New York Ave. NW - Stes.6100/7100, Washington, DC 20530. Phones: *audits,* (202) 616-4688; FAX (202) 616-4581; *investigations and fraud detection unit,* (202) 616-4760; FAX (202) 616-9881. *For mail(investigations):* P.O. Box 27718, Washington, DC 20038-7718.

Florida—*Investigations,* 3800 Inverrary Blvd. - Ste. 12, Ft. Lauderdale, FL 33319. Phones: (954) 535-2859; FAX (954) 535-5436.

Georgia—*Audits,* Russell Federal Bldg. - Ste. 130, 75 Spring St., Atlanta, GA 30303. Phones: (404) 331-5928; FAX (404) 331-5046.

- *Investigations,* 60 Forsyth St. SW - Ste. M45, Atlanta, GA 30303. Phones: (404) 562-1980; FAX (404) 562-1960.

Illinois—Citicorp Center, 500 W. Madison Blvd. - Stes.3510/3510B, P.O. Box 2134, Chicago, IL 60661. Phones: *audits,* (312) 353-1203; FAX (312) 886-0513; *investigations,* (312) 886-7050; FAX (312) 886-7065.

Massachusetts—*Investigations,* 1 Courthouse Way - Rm. 200, Boston, MA 02210. Phones: (617) 748-3218; FAX (617) 748-3965. *For Mail*: Boston, MA 02106-2134.

New York—*Investigations,* JFK Airport, Bldg. 77 - Penthouse no. 2, N. Boundary Rd., Jamaica, NY 11430. Phones: FTS (718) 553-7520; FAX (718) 553-7533. *For mail*: JFK Airport, Jamaica, NY 11430-0999.

Pennsylvania—*Audits,* 701 Market St. - Ste. 01, Philadelphia, PA 19106. Phones: (215) 580-2111; FAX (215) 597-1348.

Texas—207 S. Houston St. - *(audits)* Rm. 75 (Box 4), *(investigations)* Rm. 51 (Box 5), Dallas, TX 75202-4724. Phones: *audits,* (214) 655-5000; FAX (214) 655-5025; *investigations,* (214) 655-5076; FAX (214) 655-5071.

- *Investigations,* 4050 Rio Bravo - Ste. 00, El Paso, TX 79902. Phones: (915) 577-0102; FAX (915) 577-9012.

- *Investigations,* Casey Federal Courthouse - Ste. 307, 515 Rusk Ave., Houston, TX 77002. Phones: (713) 718-4888; FAX (713) 718-4706. *For mail:* P.O. Box 610071, Houston, TX 77208-9998.

- *Investigations,* Texas Commerce Center, Bentsen Tower - Ste. 10, 1701 W. Business Hwy.83, McAllen, TX 78501. Phones: (956) 618-8145; FAX (956) 618-8151.

Washington—*Investigations,* 620 Kirkland Way - Ste. 04, Kirkland, WA 98033-6021. Phones: (425) 828-3998; FAX (425) 827-2183.

BUREAU OF JUSTICE ASSISTANCE

16.578   ## G.R.E.A.T program regional offices

MIDWEST—La Crosse Police Dept., 400 La Crosse St., La Crosse, WI 54601. Phone: (877) 864-7328. **Internet:** e-mail, "contactus@mwgreat.org".

NORTHEAST—Philadelphia Police Department, Community Relations Division, 1328 Race. St. - 2nd fl., Philadelphia, PA 19107. Phone: (215) 686-1477.

NORTHWEST—Portland Police Bureau, 111 SW 2nd Ave., Portland, OR 97204. Phone: (800) 823-7188.

SOUTHEAST—Orange County Sheriff's Office, 2500 W. Colonial Dr. - 2nd fl., Orlando, FL 32804. Phone: (407) 254-7369, (800) 363-5569.

SOUTHWEST—Phoenix Police Dept., 620 W. Washington St., Phoenix, AZ 85003. Phone: (602) 495-0432, (800) 244-7328. **Internet:** e-mail, "GREAT@phoenix.gov".

OFFICE OF JUSTICE PROGAMS

OFFICE OF JUVENILE JUSTICE AND DELINQUENCY PREVENTION

16.737   ### Regional Offices

Southeast Region—Orange County Sheriff's Office, 2500 W. Colonial Dr., 2nd Fl., Orlando, FL 32804. Phone: (407) 254-7369.

Northeast Region—Philadelphia Police Department, Community Relations Division, 1328 Race St., 2nd Floor., Philadelphia, PA 19107. Phone: (215) 686-1477.

Midwest Region—La Crosse Police Department, 400 La Crosse St., La Crosse, WI 54601. Phone: (608) 789-8202.

Southwest Region—Phoenix Police Department, 620 West Washington St., Phoenix, AZ 85003. Phone: (602) 495-0432.

Northwest Region—Portland Police Bureau, 449 NE Emerson, Portland, OR 97211. Phone: (503) 823-2111.

16.738   Listed under **16.578.**

DEPARTMENT OF LABOR

BUREAU OF LABOR STATISTICS

17.002 through 17.005

REGIONAL OFFICES

ATLANTA *(Alabama, Florida, Georgia, Kentucky, Mississippi, North Carolina, South Carolina, Tennessee)*—AFC - Rm. T50, 61 Forsyth St. SW, Atlanta, GA 30303. Phone: (404) 893-4424.

BOSTON/NEW YORK *(Connecticut, Maine, Massachusetts, New Hampshire, New York, Puerto Rico, Virgin Islands, Rhode Island, Vermont)*—JFK Federal Bldg. - E310, Boston, MA 02203. Phone: (617) 565-2324.

- 201 Varick St. - Rm. 08, New York, NY 10014-4811. Phone: (212) 337-2500.

CHICAGO *Illinois, Indiana, Iowa, Michigan, Minnesota, Nebraska, North Dakota, Ohio, South Dakota, Wisconsin)*—Federal Office Bldg. - 9th fl., 230 S. Dearborn St., Chicago, IL 60604-1595. Phone: (312) 353-7200, ext.229.

DALLAS/KANSAS CITY *(Arkansas, Colorado, Kansas, Louisiana, Missouri, Montana, New Mexico, Oklahoma, Texas, Utah, Wyoming)*—A. Maceo Federal Bldg. - Ste. 21, 525 Griffin St., Dallas, TX 75202-5028. Phone: (214) 767-9379.

- 2 Pershing Square Bldg. Ste. 1190, 2300 Main St., Kansas City, MO 64108. Phone: (816) 285-7001.

PHILADELPHIA *(Delaware, District of Columbia, Maryland, Pennsylvania, New Jersey, Virginia, West Virginia)*—The Curtis Center - Ste. 10 E., 170 S. Independence Mall W., Philadelphia, PA 19106-3305. Phone: (215) 861-5603.

SAN FRANCISCO *(Alaska, American Samoa, Arizona, California, Guam, Hawaii, Idaho, Nevada, Oregon, Washington, Trust Territory of the Pacific Islands)*—71 Stevenson St. - 6th fl., P.O. Box 193766, San Francisco, CA 94103. Phone: (415) 625-2285, -2245.

EMPLOYEE BENEFITS SECURITY ADMINISTRATION

17.150

FIELD OFFICES

California—1055 E. Colorado Blvd. - Ste. 00, Pasadena, CA 91106. Phones: (626) 229-1000; FAX (626) 229-1098.

- 90 7th St. Ste. 1-300, San Francisco, CA 94105. Phones: (415) 625-2481; FAX (415) 975-4589.

District of Columbia—1335 East-West Hwy. - Ste. 00, Silver Spring, MD 20910-3225. Phones: (301) 713-2000; FAX (301) 713-2008.

Florida—Bldg. H - Site 104, 8040 Peters Rd., Plantation, FL 33324. Phones: (954) 424-4022; FAX (954) 424-0548.

Georgia—61 Forsyth St. SW - Ste. B54, Atlanta, GA 30303. Phones: (404) 302-3900; FAX (404) 562-2168.

Illinois—200 W. Adams St. - Ste. 600, Chicago, IL 60606. Phones: (312) 353-0900; FAX (312) 353-1023.

Kentucky—1885 Dixie Hwy. - Ste. 10, Ft. Wright, KY 41011-2664. Phones: (859) 578-4680; FAX (859) 578-4688.

Massachusetts—JFK Bldg. - Rm. 75, Boston, MA 02203. Phones: (617) 565-9600; FAX (617) 565-9666.

Michigan—211 W. Fort St. - Ste. 310, Detroit, MI 48226-3211. Phones: (313) 226-7450; FAX (313) 226-4257.

Missouri—1100 Main St. - Ste. 200, Kansas City, MO 64105-5148. Phones: (816) 426-5131; FAX (816) 426-5511.

- Young Federal Bldg. - Rm. 310, 1222 Spruce St., St. Louis, MO 63101-2818. Phones: (314) 539-2693; FAX (314) 539-2697.

New York—33 Whitehall St. - Ste. 200(12th fl.), New York, NY 10004. Phones: (212) 607-8600; FAX (212) 607-8681.

Pennsylvania—170 S. Independence Mall W. - Ste. 70 West, Philadelphia, PA 19106-3317. Phones: (215) 861-5300; FAX (215) 861-5347.

Texas—525 Griffin St. - Rm. 00, Dallas, TX 75202-5025. Phones: (214) 767-6831; FAX (214) 767-1055.

Washington—1111 3rd Ave. - Ste. 60, Seattle, WA 98101-3212. Phones: (206) 553-4244; FAX (206) 553-0913.

EMPLOYMENT AND TRAINING ADMINISTRATION

17.201
through
17.285

BUREAU OF APPRENTICESHIP AND TRAINING (BAT)

Regional Offices

REGION I *(Connecticut, Maine, Massachusetts, New Hampshire, Rhode Island, Vermont)*—JFK Federal Bldg. - Rm.E-370, Boston, MA 02203. Phones: (617) 565-2288; FAX (617) 565-9171.

REGION II *(New Jersey, New York, Puerto Rico, Virgin Islands)*—201 Varick St. - Rm. 02, New York, NY 10014. Phones: (212) 337-2313; FAX (212) 337-2317.

REGION III *(Delaware, Maryland, Pennsylvania, Virginia, West Virginia)*—3535 Market St. - Rm. 3240, Philadelphia, PA 19104. Phones: (215) 596-6417; FAX (215) 596-0192.

REGION IV *(Alabama, Florida, Georgia, Kentucky, Mississippi, North Carolina, South Carolina, Tennessee)*—61 Forsyth St. NW - Rm. M12, Atlanta, GA 30303. Phones: (404) 562-2092; FAX (404) 562-2149.

REGION V *(Illinois, Indiana, Michigan, Minnesota, Ohio, Wisconsin)*—230 S. Dearborn St. - Rm. 08, Chicago, IL 60604. Phones: (312) 353-7205; FAX (312) 353-5506.

REGION VI *(Arkansas, Louisiana, New Mexico, Oklahoma, Texas)*—Federal Bldg. - Rm. 11, 525 Griffin St. Dallas, TX 75202. Phones: (214) 767-4993; FAX (214) 767-4995.

REGION VII *(Iowa, Kansas, Missouri, Nebraska)*—1100 Main St. - Ste. 040, Kansas City, MO 64105-2112. Phones: (816) 426-3856; FAX (816) 426-3664.

REGION VIII *(Colorado, Montana, North Dakota, South Dakota, Utah, Wyoming)*—U.S. Custom House - Rm. 65, 721 19th St., Denver, CO 80202. Phones: (303) 844-4791; FAX (303) 844-4701.

REGION IX *(Arizona, California, Hawaii, Nevada)*—Federal Bldg. - Rm. 30, 71 Stevenson St., P.O. Box 193767, San Francisco, CA 94105. Phones: (415) 975-4007; FAX (415) 975-4010.

REGION X *(Alaska, Idaho, Oregon, Washington)*—1111 3rd Ave. - Rm. 25, Seattle, WA 98101-3212. Phones: (206) 553-5286; FAX (206) 553-1689.

EMPLOYMENT STANDARDS ADMINISTRATION

17.301   OFFICE OF FEDERAL CONTRACT COMPLIANCE PROGRAMS

Regional Offices

REGION I *(Connecticut, Maine, Massachusetts, New Hampshire, Rhode Island, Vermont)*—JFK Federal Bldg. - Rm.E-235, One Congress St., Boston, MA 02203. Phone: (617) 565-2055.

REGION II *(New Jersey, New York, Puerto Rico, Virgin Islands)*—201 Varick St. - Rm. 50, New York, NY 10014. Phone: (212) 337-2007.

REGION III *(Delaware, District of Columbia, Maryland, Pennsylvania, Virginia, West Virginia)*—Curtis Center - Ste. 50W, 170 S. Independence Mall W., Philadelphia, PA 19106-3309 Phone: (215) 861-5763.

REGION IV *(Alabama, Florida, Georgia, Kentucky, Mississippi, North Carolina, South Carolina, Tennessee)*—Atlanta Federal Center - Rm. B75, 61 Forsyth St. SW, Atlanta, GA 30303. Phone: (404) 562-2424.

REGION V *(Illinois, Indiana, Iowa, Kansas, Michigan, Minnesota, Missouri, Nebraska, Ohio, Wisconsin)*—Kluczynski Federal Bldg. - Rm. 70, 230 S. Dearborn St., Chicago, IL 60604. Phone: (312) 596-7010.

REGION VI *(Arkansas, Colorado, Louisiana, Montana, New Mexico, North Dakota, Oklahoma, South Dakota, Texas, Utah, Wyoming)*—Federal Bldg. - Ste. 40, 525 S. Griffin St., Dallas, TX 75202. Phone: (214) 767-2804.

REGION IX *(Arizona, California, Guam, Hawaii, Nevada)*—71 Stevenson St. - Ste. 700, San Francisco, CA 94105. Phone: (415) 975-4720.

REGION X *(Alaska, Idaho, Oregon, Washington)*—1111 3rd Ave. - Ste. 45, Seattle, WA 98101. Phone: (206) 553-7182.

District and Area Offices

Alabama—Medical Forum Bldg. - Ste. 60, 950 22nd St. N., Birmingham, AL 35203. Phone: (205) 731-0820.

Arizona—3221 N. 16th St. - Ste. 03, Phoenix, AZ 85016. Phone: (602) 640-2960.

Arkansas—TCBY Tower - Ste. 35, 425 W. Capitol Ave., Little Rock, AR 72201. Phone: (501) 324-5436.

California—Federal Bldg. - Ste. 103, 11000 Wilshire Blvd., Los Angeles, CA 90024. Phone: (310) 235-6800.

- 1301 Clay St. - Ste. 080N, Oakland, CA 94612. Phone: (510) 637-2938.

- 5675 Ruffin Rd. - Ste. 20, San Diego, CA 92123. Phone: (619) 557-6489.

- 60 S. Market St. - Ste. 10, San Jose, CA 95113. Phone: (408) 291-7384.

- 34 Civic Center Plaza - Ste. 06, P.O. Box 12800, Santa Ana, CA 92712. Phone: (714) 836-2784.

Colorado—1244 Spee Blvd. - Rm. 20, Denver, CO 80204-3584. Phone: (303) 844-4481.

Connecticut—135 High St. - Rm. 11, Hartford, CT 06103. Phone: (860) 240-4277.

District of Columbia—Riddell Bldg. - Ste. 22, 1730 K St. NW, Washington, DC 20006. Phone: (202) 254-2501.

Florida—1851 Executive Center Dr. - Ste. 00, Jacksonville, FL 32207. Phone: (904) 232-3073.

- Brickell Plaza Federal Bldg. - Ste. 22, 909 SE 1st Ave., Miami, FL 33131. Phone: (305) 536-5670.

- Commodore Bldg. - Ste. 60, 3444 McCrory Pl., Orlando, FL 32803. Phone: (407) 648-6181.

Georgia—61 Forsyth St. - Rm. B65, Atlanta, GA 30303. Phone: (404) 562-2444.

Hawaii—300 Ala Moana Blvd. - Rm. 326, P.O. Box 50149, Honolulu, HI 96850. Phone: (808) 541-2933.

Illinois—230 S. Dearborn St. - Rm. 34, Chicago, IL 60604. Phone: (312) 596-7046.

Indiana—429 N. Pennsylvania St. - Rm. 08, Indianapolis, IN 46204. Phones: (317) 226-5860.

Kentucky—Mazzoli Federal Bldg. - Rm. 85, 600 Martin Luther King Place, Louisville, KY 40202. Phone: (502) 582-6275.

Louisiana—701 Loyola Ave. - Rm. 3029, New Orleans, LA 70113. Phone: (504) 589-6575.

Maryland—Appraiser's Store Bldg. - Rm. 02, 103 S. Gay St., Baltimore, MD 21202. Phone: (410) 962-3572.

Massachusetts—JFK Federal Bldg. - Rm.E-235, Boston, MA 02203. Phone: (617) 565-2055.

Michigan—McNamara Federal Bldg. - Rm. 320, 211 W. Fort St., Detroit, MI 48226. Phone: (313) 226-3728.

- 50 Louis St. NW - 2nd fl.(NW-c/o), Ste. 00-HUD, Grand Rapids, MI 49503. Phone: (616) 456-2144.

Minnesota—Bridgeplace Bldg. - Rm. 02, 220 2nd St. S., Minneapolis, MN 55401. Phone: (612) 370-3177.

Mississippi—Millsaps Bldg. - Ste. 00, 201 W. Capitol St., Jackson, MS 39201. Phone: (601) 965-4668.

Missouri—1100 Main St. - Rm. 60, Kansas City, MO 64105. Phone: (816) 426-3860.

- 1222 Spruce St. - Rm. 0207, St. Louis, MO 63103. Phone: (314) 539-6394.

Nebraska—106 S. 15th St. - Rm. 08, Omaha, NE 68116. Phone: (402) 221-3381.

New Jersey—Bldg. 5 - Rm. 03, 3131 Princeton Pike, Lawrenceville, NJ 08648. Phone: (609) 989-2380.

- Diamond Head Bldg. - Rm. 02, 200 Sheffield Dr., Mountainside, NJ 07092. Phone: (201) 645-6104.

New Mexico—505 Marquette Ave. NW - Ste. 10, Albuquerque, NM 87102. Phone: (505) 248-5015.

New York—O'Brien Federal Bldg. - Rm. 40, 19 Aviation Rd., Albany, NY 12205. Phone: (518) 435-0326.

- Six Fountain Plaza - Ste. 00, Buffalo. NY 14202. Phone: (716) 551-5065.

- 26 Federal Plaza - Rm. 6-116, New York, NY 10278. Phone: (212) 264-7742.

North Carolina—Mart Office Bldg. - Rm.BB-401, 800 Briar Creek Rd., Charlotte, NC 28205. Phone: (704) 344-6113.

- 300 Fayetteville Street Mall - Ste. 21, Raleigh, NC 27601. Phone: (919) 856-4058.

Ohio—55 Rennaissance Center - Ste. 50, 1350 Euclid St. - Ste. 50, Cleveland, OH 44114. Phone: (216) 522-7472.

- 200 N. High St. - Rm. 09, Columbus, OH 43215. Phone: (614) 469-5831.

Oklahoma—51 Yale Bldg. - Rm. 04, 5110 S. Yale, Tulsa, OK 74135. Phone: (918) 496-6772.

Oregon—Federal Office Bldg. - Ste. 030, 1515 SW 5th Ave., Portland, OR 97201. Phone: (503) 326-4112.

Pennsylvania—Nix Federal Bldg. - Rm. 11, 9th and Market St., Philadelphia, PA 19107. Phone: (215) 597-4122.

- Federal Bldg. - Rm. 132, 1000 Liberty Ave., Pittsburgh, PA 15222. Phone: (412) 395-6330.

17.301
(cont.)

Puerto Rico—San Patricio Office Center - 4th fl., 7 Tabonuco St., Guaynabo, PR 00968. Phone: (787) 775-1901.

South Carolina—Thurmond Federal Bldg. - Ste. 08, 1835 Assembly St., Columbia, SC 29201. Phone: (803) 765-5244.

Tennessee—167 N. Main St. - Ste. 01, Memphis, TN 38103. Phone: (901) 544-3458.

- 1321 Murfreesboro Rd., Ste. 01, Nashville, TN 37217. Phone: (615) 781-5395.

Texas—Federal Office Bldg. - Rm. 12, 525 S. Griffin St., Dallas, TX 75202. Phone: (214) 767-2911.

- 2320 La Branch St. - Rm. 103, Houston, TX 77004. Phone: (713) 718-3800.

- 800 Dolorosa St. - Rm. 00, San Antonio, TX 78207. Phone: (210) 472-5835.

Utah—Gateway Tower East - Ste. 690, 10 E. South Temple, Salt Lake City, UT 84101. Phone: (801) 524-4470.

Virginia—400 N. 8th St. - Rm. 52, Richmond, VA 23240. Phone: (804) 771-2136.

Washington—Federal Office Bldg. - Ste. 45, 1111 3rd Ave., Seattle, WA 98101. Phone: (206) 553-7182.

Wisconsin—Federal Bldg. - Ste. 115, 310 W. Wisconsin Ave., Milwaukee, WI 53203. Phone: (414) 297-3821.

OFFICE OF WORKERS' COMPENSATION PROGRAMS

17.302

REGIONAL OFFICES

California—71 Stevenson St. - Ste. 705, San Francisco, CA 94105. Phone: (415) 975-4160.

Colorado—1801 California St. - Ste. 20, Denver, CO 80202-2614. Phone: (720) 264-3160.

Florida—214 N. Hogan St. - Ste. 026, Jacksonville, FL 32202. Phone: (904) 357-4725.

Illinois—230 S. Dearborn St. - Rm. 00, Chicago, IL 60604. Phone: (312) 596-7131.

Massachusetts—JFK Federal Bldg. - Rm.E-260, Boston, MA 02203. Phone: (617) 565-2130.

Missouri—City Center Square - Ste. 50, 1100 Main St., Kansas City, MO 64105. Phone: (816) 426-2196.

New York—201 Varick St. - Rm. 50, New York, NY 10014. Phone: (212) 337-2033.

Pennsylvania—Curtis Center - Ste. 80 W., 170 S. Independence Mall W., Philadelphia, PA 19106-3313. Phone: (215) 861-5406.

Texas—525 S. Griffin St. - Rm. 07, Dallas, TX 75202. Phone: (214) 767-4713.

Washington—1111 3rd Ave. - Ste. 15, Seattle, WA 98101-3212. Phone: (206) 553-5508.

LONGSHORE AND HARBOR WORKERS' COMPENSATION

DISTRICT OFFICES

DISTRICT 1 *(Connecticut, Maine, Massachusetts, New Hampshire, Rhode Island, Vermont)*—JFK Federal Bldg. - Rm.E-260, Boston, MA 02203. Phone: (617) 565-2103.

DISTRICT 2 *(New Jersey, New York, Puerto Rico, Virgin Islands)*—201 Varick St. - Rm. 50, P.O. Box 249, New York, NY 10014-0249. Phone: (212) 337-2030.

DISTRICT 3 *(Delaware, Pennsylvania, West Virginia)*—Curtis Center - Ste. 90 W., 170 S. Independence Mall W., Philadelphia, PA 19106-3313. Phone: (215) 861-5459.

DISTRICT 4 *(District of Columbia, Maryland)*—31 Hopkins Plaza - Rm. 10-B, Baltimore, MD 21201. Phone: (410) 962-3677.

DISTRICT 5 *(Virginia)*—200 Granby Mall - Rm. 12, Norfolk, VA 23510. Phone: (757) 441-3071.

DISTRICT 6 *(Alabama, Florida, Georgia, Kentucky, Mississippi, North Carolina, South Carolina, Tennessee)*—214 N. Hogan St. - Ste. 040, Jacksonville, FL 32202. Phone: (904) 357-4757.

DISTRICT 7 *(Arkansas, Louisiana)*—701 Loyola Ave. - Rm. 3032, New Orleans, LA 70113. Phone: (504) 589-2671.

DISTRICT 8 *(Oklahoma, New Mexico, Texas)*—8866 Gulf Freeway - Ste. 40, Houston, TX 77017. Phone: (713) 943-1605.

DISTRICT 10 *(Illinois, Indiana, Iowa, Kansas, Michigan, Minnesota, Missouri, Nebraska, Ohio, Wisconsin)*—230 S. Dearborn St. - Rm. 78, Chicago, IL 60604. Phone: (312) 596-7153.

DISTRICT 13 *(Arizona, California-northern, Nevada)*—71 Stevenson St. - Rm. 705, P.O. Box 3770, San Francisco, CA 94119-3770. Phone: (415) 975-4274.

DISTRICT 14 *(Alaska, Colorado, Idaho, Montana, Oregon, North Dakota, South Dakota, Utah, Washington, Wyoming)*—1111 3rd Ave. - Ste. 20, Seattle, WA 98101-3212. Phone: (206) 553-4471.

DISTRICT 15 *(Hawaii, Pacific Area to 60 east longitude)*—300 Ala Moana Blvd. - Rm. -135, P.O. Box 50209, Honolulu, HI 96850 *(via air mail)*. Phone: (808) 541-1983.

DISTRICT 18 *(Southern California)*—401 E. Ocean Blvd. - Ste. 20, Long Beach, CA 90802. Phone: (562) 980-3578.

DIVISION OF COAL MINE WORKERS' COMPENSATION
DISTRICT OFFICES

Contact nearest Social Security office or appropriate CMWC office, following.

Colorado *(Western United States)*—1801 California St. - Ste. 25, Denver, CO 80202-2614. Phone: (720) 264-3100.

Kentucky *(Kentucky)*—334 Main St. - 5th fl., Pikeville, KY 41501. Phone: (800) 366-4599.

- *(Alabama, Florida, Georgia, Mississippi, North Carolina, South Carolina, Tennessee)*—402 Campbell Way, Spring St., Mt. Sterling, KY 40353. Phone: (800) 366-4628.

Ohio *(Illinois, Indiana, Michigan, Minnesota, Ohio, Wisconsin)*—1160 Dublin Rd. - Ste. 00, Columbus, OH 43215. Phone: (800) 347-3771.

Pennsylvania *(Connecticut, Delaware, District of Columbia, Maine, Massachusetts, New Hampshire, New Jersey, New York, Pennsylvania-eastern, Rhode Island, Vermont)*—S. Main Towers, 105 N. Main St. - Ste. 00, Wilkes-Barre, PA 18701. Phone: (800) 347-3755.

- *(Maryland, Pennsylvania-western)*—Wellington Square - Ste. 05, 1225 S. Main St., Greensburg, PA 15601. Phone: (800) 347-3753.

- *(Pennsylvania-central, Virginia)*—Penn Traffic Bldg. - 2nd fl., 319 Washington St., Johnstown, PA 15901. Phone: (800) 347-3754.

West Virginia *(West Virginia-northern)*—Federal Bldg. - Ste. 116, 425 Juliana St., Parkersburg, WV 26101. Phone: (800) 347-3751.

- *(West Virginia-southern)*—Charleston Federal Center - Ste. 10, 500 Quarrier St., Charleston, WV 25301. Phone: (800) 347-3749.

**17.302
(cont.)**

DIVISION OF ENERGY EMPLOYEES OCCUPATIONAL ILLNESS COMPENSATION

DISTRICT OFFICES

DISTRICT 1 *(Alabama, Florida, Georgia, Kentucky, Mississippi, North Carolina, South Carolina and Tennessee)* 400 W. Bay St. Rm. 22, Jacksonville, FL 32202. Phone: (877) 336-4272.

DISTRICT 2 *(Connecticut, Delaware, District of Columbia, Illinois, Indiana, Iowa, Maine, Maryland, Massachusetts, Michigan, Minnesota, New Hampshire, New Jersey, New York, Ohio, Pennsylvania, Puerto Rico, Rhode Island, Vermont, Virgin Islands, Virginia, West Virginia and Wisconsin)* 1001 Lakeside Ave. Ste. 350, Cleveland, OH 44114. Phone: (888) 859-7211.

DISTRICT 3 *(Arkansas, Colorado, Kansas, Louisiana, Missouri, Montana, Nebraska, North Dakota, Oklahoma, South Dakota, Texas, Utah, Wyoming and all claims from RECA Section 5 awardees)* 1999 Broadway Ste. 1120, Denver, CO 80202-5711. Phone:(888) 805-3389.

DISTRICT 4 *(Alaska, Arizona, California, Idaho, Hawaii, Marshall Islands, Nevada, New Mexico, Oregon and Washington)* 719 2nd Ave. (6th fl.) Ste. 601, Seattle, WA 98104. Phone:(888) 805-3401.

WAGE AND HOUR DIVISION

**17.303
through
17.306**

REGIONAL OFFICES

MIDWEST—230 S. Dearborn St. - Rm. 20, Chicago, IL 60604-1591. Phone: (312) 596-7180.

NORTHEAST—The Curtis Center - Ste. 50 West, 170 Independence Mall W., Philadelphia, PA 19106-3317. Phone: (215) 861-5800.

SOUTHEAST—Atlanta Federal Center - Rm. M40, 61 Forsyth St. SW, Atlanta, GA 30303. Phone: (404) 562-2202.

SOUTHWEST—Federal Bldg. - Rm. 00, 525 S. Griffin St., Dallas, TX 75202-5007. Phone: (214) 767-6895.

WESTERN—71 Stevenson St. - Ste. 30, San Francisco, CA 94105. Phone: (415) 975-4510.

DISTRICT OFFICES

Alabama—Aronov Bldg. - Rm. 08, 474 S. Court St., Montgomery, AL 36104-4158. Phone: (304) 223-7641.

Arizona—3221 N. 16th St. - Ste. 01, Phoenix, AZ 85016-7161. Phone: (602) 640-2990.

Arkansas—TCBY Tower - Ste. 25, 425 W. Capitol Ave., Little Rock, AR 72201. Phones: (501) 324-5377.

California-Los Angelos—300 S. Glendale Ave. - Ste. 00, Glendale, CA 91205-1752. Phones: (213) 894-6375.

■ 2800 Cottage Way - Rm.W-1836, Sacramento, CA 95825. Phone: (916) 978-6120.

■ 5675 Ruffin Rd. - Ste. 20, San Diego, CA 92123-1362. Phone: (619) 557-5606.

■ 455 Market St. - Ste. 00, San Francisco, CA 94105. Phone: (415) 744-5590.

Colorado—1999 Broadway - Ste. 445, P.O. Drawer 3505, Denver, CO 80202. Phone: (720) 264-3250.

Connecticut—135 High St. - Rm. 10, Hartford, CT 06103-1595. Phone: (860) 240-4160.

Florida—Federal Bldg. - Rm. 08, 299 E. Broward Blvd., Ft. Lauderdale, FL 33301-1976. Phone: (954) 356-6896.

■ 3728 Phillips Hwy. - Ste. 19, Jacksonville, FL 32207. Phone: (904) 232-2489.

■ Sunset Center - Rm. 55, 10300 SW Sunset Dr., Miami, FL 33173-3038. Phones: (305) 598-6607; FAX (305) 279-8393.

■ Austin Laurel Bldg. - Ste. 00, 4905 W. Laurel Ave., Tampa, FL 33607-3838. Phone: (813) 288-1242.

Georgia—Atlanta Federal Center - Rm. M10, 61 Forsyth St. SW, Atlanta, GA 30303. Phone: (404) 562-2201.

■ Low Federal Bldg. Complex - Ste. B-210, 124 Barnard St., Savannah, GA 31401-3648. Phones: (912) 652-4221, -4229.

Illinois—230 S. Dearborn - Rm. 12, Chicago, IL 60604-1595. Phone: (312) 596-7182.

■ 509 W. Capitol Ave. - Ste. 05, Springfield, IL 62704-1929. Phone: (217) 492-4060.

Indiana—429 N. Pennsylvania St. - Rm. 03, Indianapolis, IN 46204-1873. Phone: (317) 226-6801.

■ River Glen Plaza - Ste. 60, 501 E. Monroe St., South Bend, IN 46601-1615. Phones:(219) 236-8331, -8332.

Iowa—Federal Bldg. - Rm. 43, 210 Walnut St., Des Moines, IA 50309. Phone: (515) 284-4625.

Kansas—Gateway Tower II - Ste. 010, 400 State Ave., Kansas City, KS 66101. Phone: (913) 551-5721.

Kentucky—Snyder U.S. Courthouse and Custom House - Rm. 1, 601 W. Broadway, Louisville, KY 40202-9570. Phone: (502) 582-5226.

Louisiana—701 Loyola Ave. - Rm. 3028, New Orleans, LA 70113-1931. Phone: (504) 589-6171.

Maryland—207 Appraisers Stores Bldg., 103 S. Gay St., Baltimore, MD 21201-4061. Phone:(410) 962-4984.

Massachusetts—Kennedy Federal Bldg. - Rm. 25, Boston, MA 02203. Phone: (617) 565-2066.

Michigan—211 Fort St. - Rm. 317, Detroit, MI 18226-2799. Phone: (313) 226-7447.

■ 2920 Fuller Ave. NE - Ste. 00, Grand Rapids, MI 49505-3409. Phone: (616) 456-2004.

Minnesota—Midland Square - Ste. 20, 331 2nd Ave S., Minneapolis, MN 55401-2233. Phone: (612) 370-3371.

Mississippi—One Jackson Place - Ste. 020, 188 E. Capitol St., Jackson, MS 39201-2126. Phones: (601) 965-4347, -4348.

Missouri—1222 Spruce St. - Rm. 102-B, St. Louis, MO 63103. Phones: (314) 539-2706, -3014.

Nebraska—Federal Bldg. - Rm. 15, 106 S. 15th St., Omaha, NE 68102. Phone: (402) 221-4682.

New Hampshire—2 Wall St. - 1st fl., Manchester, NH 03101. Phones: (603) 666-7716; FAX (603) 666-7600.

New Jersey—Bldg. 5 - Rm. 16, 3131 Princeton Pike, Lawrenceville, NJ 08648. Phones: (609) 989-2247, -2368.

■ 200 Sheffield St. - Ste. 02, Mountainside, NJ 07092. Phone: (973) 645-2279.

New Mexico—Western Bank Bldg. - Ste. 40, 505 Marquette NW, Albuquerque, NM 87102-2160. Phone: (505) 248-5115.

New York—O'Brien Federal Bldg. - Rm. 22, Albany, NY 12207. Phone: (518) 431-4279.

■ 26 Federal Plaza - Rm. 700, New York, NY 10278. Phone: (212) 264-8185.

■ 1400 Old Country Rd. - Ste. 10, Westbury, NY 11590-5119. Phone: (516) 338-1890.

17.303
through
17.306
(cont.)

North Carolina—800 Briar Creek Rd. - Ste. CC-412, Charlotte, NC 28205-6903. Phone: (704) 344-6298.

■ Somerset Park Bldg. - Ste. 60, 4407 Bland Rd., Raleigh, NC 27609-6296. Phones: (919) 790-2741, -2742.

Ohio—525 Vine St. - Ste. 80, Cincinnati, OH 45202-3268. Phone: (513) 684-2908.

■ Federal Bldg. - Rm. 17, 1240 E. 9th St., Cleveland, OH 44199-2054 Phones: (216) 522-3892, -3893.

■ 646 Federal Bldg., 200 N. High St., Columbus, OH 43215-2475. Phones: (614) 469-5678; FAX (614) 469-5428.

Oregon—1515 SW 5th Ave. - Ste. 040, Portland, OR 97201-5445. Phone: (503) 326-3057.

Pennsylvania—U.S. Customs House - Rm. 00, 2nd and Chestnut St., Philadelphia, PA 19106. Phone: (215) 597-4950.

■ Federal Bldg. - Rm. 13, 1000 Liberty Ave., Pittsburgh, PA 15222. Phone: (412) 395-4996.

■ Stegmaier Bldg. - Ste. 73-M, 7 N. Wilkes-Barre Blvd., Wilkes-Barre, PA 18702-3594. Phone: (570) 826-6316.

Puerto Rico—San Patricio Office Center - 4th fl., 7 Tabonuco St., Guaynabo, PR 00968. Phone: (787) 775-1924.

South Carolina—Federal Bldg. - Rm. 072, 1835 Assembly St., Columbia, SC 29201-9863. Phone: (803) 765-5981.

Tennessee—Executive Plaza - Bldg.511, 1321 Murfreesboro Rd., Nashville, TN 37217-2626. Phones: (615) 781-5343, -5345.

Texas—Smith Federal Bldg. - Rm. 07, 525 S. Griffin St., Dallas, TX 75202-5007. Phone: (214) 767-6294.

■ South Bldg. - Ste. 02, 9990 Richmond Ave., Houston, TX 77042-4546. Phone: (713) 339-5575.

■ Northchase I Office Bldg. - Ste. 40, 10127 Morocco St., San Antonio, TX 78216. Phone: (210) 308-4515.

Utah—10 E. South Temple - Ste. 680, Salt Lake City, UT 84133. Phone: (801) 524-5706.

Virginia—Federal Bldg. - Ste. 16, 400 N. 8th St., Richmond, VA 23240. Phone: (804) 771-2995.

Washington—1111 3rd Ave. - Ste. 55, Seattle, WA 98101-3212. Phone: (206) 553-4482.

West Virginia—500 Quarrier St. - Ste. 20, Charleston, WV 25301. Phone: (304) 347-5206.

Wisconsin—740 Regent St. - Ste. 02, Madison, WI 53715. Phone: (608) 264-5221.

17.307   Listed under **17.302.**

17.308   Listed under **17.303.**

OFFICE OF LABOR-MANAGEMENT STANDARDS

17.309 ## FIELD OFFICES

California—3660 Wilshire Blvd. - Ste. 08, Los Angeles, CA 90010-2713. Phone: (213) 252-7508.

■ 71 Stevenson Pl. - Ste. 25, San Francisco, CA 94105-2997. Phone: (415) 975-4020.

Colorado—1999 Broadway St. - Rm. 435, P.O. Box 46550, Denver, CO 80201-6550. Phone: (720) 264-3231.

District of Columbia—Riddell Bldg. - Ste. 58, 1730 K St. NW, Washington, DC 20006. Phone: (202) 254-6510.

Georgia—61 Forsyth St. SW - Rm. B85, Atlanta, GA 30303-2219. Phone: (404) 562-2083.

Illinois—Federal Office Bldg. - Ste. 74, 230 S. Dearborn St., Chicago, IL 60604-1505. Phone: (312) 596-7160.

Louisiana—701 Loyola Ave. - Ste. 3009, New Orleans, LA 70113-1912. Phone: (504) 589-6174.

Massachusetts—JFK Federal Bldg. - Rm.E-365, Boston, MA 02203-0002. Phone: (617) 565-9880.

Michigan—211 W. Fort St. - Ste. 313, Detroit, MI 48226-3237. Phone: (313) 226-6200.

Missouri—1222 Spruce St. - Ste. .109E, St. Louis, MO 63103-2830. Phone: (314) 539-2667.

New York—Federal Bldg. - Ste. 310, 111 W. Huron St., Buffalo, NY 14202-2379. Phone: (716) 551-4976.

- 201 Varick St. - Ste. 78,, New York, NY 10014-4811. Phone: (212) 337-2580.

Ohio—525 Vine St. - Ste. 50, Cincinnati, OH 45202-3168. Phone: (513) 684-6840.

- Federal Office Bldg. - Ste. 31, 1240 E. 9th St., Cleveland, OH 44199-2053. Phone: (216) 522-3855.

Pennsylvania—The Curtis Center - Rm. 60W, 170 S. Independence Mall West, Philadelphia, PA 19106-3310. Phone: (215) 861-4818.

- Federal Office Bldg. - Ste. 01, 1000 Liberty Ave., Pittsburgh, PA 15222-4004. Phone: (412) 395-6925.

Tennessee—233 Cumberland Bend Dr. - Ste. 10, Nashville, TN 37228-1809. Phone: (615) 736-5906.

Texas—Maceo Smith Federal Bldg. - Ste. 00, 525 Griffin St., Dallas, TX 75202-5007. Phone: (214) 767-6834.

Washington— Federal Office Bldg. - Ste. 05, 1111 3rd Ave., Seattle, WA 98101-3212. Phone: (206) 553-5216.

Wisconsin—517 E. Wisconsin Ave. - Ste. 18, Milwaukee, WI 53202-4504. Phone: (414) 297-1501.

17.310   Listed under **17.302.**

OCCUPATIONAL SAFETY AND HEALTH ADMINISTRATION

17.502 **REGIONAL OFFICES**
through
17.506 **REGION I** *(Connecticut, Maine, Massachusetts, New Hampshire, Rhode Island, Vermont)*—JFK Federal Bldg. - Low Rise Bldg. (Rm.E-340), Boston, MA 02114. Phone: (617) 565-9860.

REGION II *(New Jersey, New York, Puerto Rico)*—201 Varick St. - Ste. 70, New York, NY 10014. Phone: (212) 337-2378.

REGION III *(Delaware, District of Columbia, Maryland, Pennsylvania, Virginia, West Virginia)*—The Curtis Center - Ste. 40 West, 170 Independence Mall W., Philadelphia, PA 19106-3309. Phone: (215) 861-4900.

REGION IV *(Alabama, Florida, Georgia, Kentucky, Mississippi, North Carolina, South Carolina, Tennessee)*—61 Forsyth St. SW - Rm. T50, Atlanta, GA 30303. Phone: (404) 562-2300.

17.502
through
17.506
(cont.)

REGION V *(Illinois, Indiana, Minnesota, Michigan, Ohio, Wisconsin)*—230 S. Dearborn St. - 32nd fl. (Rm. 244), Chicago, IL 60604. Phone: (312) 353-2220.

REGION VI *(Arkansas, Louisiana, New Mexico, Oklahoma, Texas)*—525 Griffin St. - Rm. 02, Dallas, TX 75202. Phone: (972) 850-4145.

REGION VII *(Iowa, Kansas, Missouri, Nebraska)*—City Center Square - Ste. 00, 1100 Main St., Kansas City, MO 64105. Phone: (816) 426-5861.

REGION VIII *(Colorado, Montana, North Dakota, South Dakota, Utah, Wyoming)*— 1999 Broadway St. - Rm. 690, Denver, CO 80202-5716. Phone: (720) 264-6550.

REGION IX *(American Samoa, Arizona, California, Guam, Hawaii, Nevada, Trust Territory of the Pacific Islands)*—Federal Bldg. 90 7th St. Ste. 8100, San Francisco, CA 94103. Phone: (415) 625-2547.

REGION X *(Alaska, Idaho, Oregon, Washington)*—1111 3rd Ave. - Ste. 15, Seattle, WA 98101-3212. Phone: (206) 553-5930.

AREA OFFICES

Alabama—Todd Mall, 2047 Canyon Rd., Birmingham, AL 35216-1981. Phone: (205) 731-1534, ext.133.

- 3737 Government Blvd. - Ste. 00, Mobile, AL 36693-4309. Phone: (251) 441-6131.

Alaska—301 W. Northern Lights Blvd. - Rm. 07, Anchorage, AK 99503-7571. Phone: (907) 271-5152.

Arizona—3221 N. 16th St. - Ste. 00, Phoenix, AZ 85016. Phone: (602) 640-2007.

Arkansas—TCBY Bldg. - Ste. 50., 425 W. Capitol Ave., Little Rock, AR 72201. Phone: (501) 324-6291.

California—Resource Center - Ste. 05, 101 El Camino Blvd., Sacramento, CA 95815. Phone: (916) 566-7470.

- Resource Center, 5675 Ruffin Rd. - Ste. 30, San Diego, CA 92123. Phone: (619) 557-5904.

- Resource Center, 71 Stevenson St. - Ste. 20, San Francisco, CA 94105. Phone: (415) 975-4316.

Colorado—1391 Speer Blvd. - Ste. 10, Denver, CO 80204-2552. Phone: (303) 844-5285.

- 7935 E. Prentice Ave. - Ste. 09, Englewood, CO 80111-2714. Phone: (303) 843-4500.

Connecticut—Clark Bldg. - 4th fl., 1057 Broad St., Bridgeport, CT 06604. Phone: (203) 579-5581.

- Federal Bldg. - Rm. 13, 450 Main St., Hartford, CT 06103. Phone: (860) 240-3152.

Delaware—Caleb Boggs Federal Bldg. - Rm. 209, 844 King St., Wilmington, DE 19801. Phone: (302) 573-6518.

Florida—Bldg. H100, 8040 Peters Rd., Ft. Lauderdale, FL 33324. Phone: (954) 424-0242.

- Ribault Bldg. - Ste. 27, 1851 Executive Center Dr., Jacksonville, FL 32207. Phone: (904) 232-2895.

- 5807 Breckenridge Pkwy. - Ste. A, Tampa, FL 33610. Phone: (813) 626-1177.

Georgia—450 Mall Blvd. - Ste. J, Savannah, GA 31406-1418. Phone: (912) 652-4393.

- 2400 Herodian Way - Ste. 50, Smyrna, GA 30080-2968. Phone: (770) 984-8700.

- La Vista Perimeter Office Park, Bldg. 7 - Ste. 10,, 2183 N. Lake Pkwy., Tucker, GA 30084-4154. Phone: (770) 493-6644.

Hawaii—Resource Center - Ste. -146, 300 Ala Moana Blvd., Honolulu, HI 96850. Phone: (808) 541-2685.

Idaho—1150 N. Curtis Rd. - Ste. 01, Boise, ID 83703. Phone: (208) 321-2960.

Illinois—1600 167th St. - Ste. 2, Calumet City, IL 60409. Phone: (708) 891-3800.

- 701 Lee St. - Ste. 50, Des Plaines, IL 60016. Phone: (847) 803-4800.

- 11 Executive Dr. - Ste. 1, Fairview Heights, IL 62208. Phone: (618) 632-8612.

- 365 Smoke Tree Plaza, North Aurora, IL 60542. Phone: (630) 896-8700.

- 2918 W. Willow Knolls Rd., Peoria, IL 61614. Phone: (309) 671-7033.

Indiana—U.S. Post Office and Courthouse - Rm. 23, 46 E. Ohio St., Indianapolis, IN 46204. Phone: (317) 226-7290.

Iowa—210 Walnut St. - Rm. 15, Des Moines, IA 50309. Phone: (515) 284-4794.

Kansas—8600 Farley - Ste. 05, Overland Park, KS 66212-4677. Phone: (913) 385-7380.

- 271 W. 3rd St. N. - Rm. 00, Wichita, KS 67202. Phone: (316) 269-6644.

Kentucky—Watts Federal Bldg. - Rm. 08, 330 W. Broadway, Frankfort, KY 40601-1922. Phone: (502) 227-7024.

Louisiana—9100 Bluebonnet Centre Blvd. - Ste. 01, Baton Rouge, LA 70809. Phone: (225) 389-0474.

Maine—Muskie Federal Bldg. - Rm.G26, 40 Western Ave., Augusta, ME 04330. Phone: (207) 626-9160.

- 202 Harlow St. - Rm. 11, Bangor, ME 04401-4906. Phone: (207) 941-8177.

Maryland—1099 Winterson Rd. - Ste. 40, Linthicum, MD 21090. Phones: (410) 865-2055, -2056.

Massachusetts—639 Granite St. - 4th fl., Braintree, MA 02184. Phone: (617) 565-6924.

- Valley Office Park - 1st fl., 13 Branch St., Methuen, MA 01844. Phone: (617) 565-8110.

- 1441 Main St. - Rm. 50, Springfield, MA 01103-1493. Phone: (413) 785-0123.

Michigan—801 S. Waverly Rd. - Ste. 06, Lansing, MI 48917-4200. Phone: (517) 327-0904.

Minnesota—330 S. 4th St. - Ste. 205, Minneapolis, MN 55415. Phone: (612) 664-5460.

Mississippi—3780 I-55N. - Ste. 10., Jackson, MS 39211-6323. Phone: (601) 965-4606.

Missouri—6200 Connecticut Ave. - Ste. 00, Kansas City, MO 64120. Phone: (816) 483-9531.

- 911 Washington Ave. - Rm. 20, St. Louis, MO 63101. Phone: (314) 425-4249.

Montana—2900 4th Ave. N. - Ste. 03, Billings, MT 59101. Phone: (406) 247-7494.

Nebraska—Overland-Wolf Bldg. - Rm. 00, 6910 Pacific St., Omaha, NE 68106. Phone: (402) 221-3182.

Nevada—Federal Bldg. - Rm. 04, Resource Center, 705 North Plaza, Carson City, NV 89701. Phone: (702) 885-6963.

New Hampshire—55 Pleasant St. - Rm. 901, Concord, NH 03301. Phone: (603) 225-1629.

New Jersey—Plaza 35 - Ste. 05, 1030 St. Georges Ave., Avenel, NJ 07001 Phone: (732) 750-3270.

- 500 Rt. 17 S. - 2nd fl., Hasbrouck Heights, NJ 07604. Phone: (201) 288-1700.

- Marlton Executive Park, South Bldg. 2 - Ste. 20, 701 Rt. 73, Marlton, NJ 08053. Phone: (856) 757-5181.

- 299 Cherry Hill Rd.- Ste. 04, Parsippany, NJ 07054. Phone: (973) 263-1003.

New Mexico—Western Bank Bldg. - Ste. 20, 505 Marquette Ave. NW, Albuquerque, NM 87102. Phone: (505) 248-5302.

17.502 through 17.506 (cont.)

New York—Tomich Federal Bldg. - Ste. 00, 401 New Karner Rd., Albany, NY 12205-3809. Phone: (518) 464-4338.

- 42-40 Bell Blvd., Bayside, NY 11361. Phone: (718) 279-9060.

- 5360 Genessee St., Bowmansville, NY 14026. Phone: (716) 684-3891.

- 201 Varick St. - Rm. 05, New York, NY 10014. Phone: (212) 620-3200.

- 3300 Vickery Rd., North Syracuse, NY 13212. Phone: (315) 451-0808.

- 660 White Plains Rd. - 4th fl., Tarrytown, NY 10591-5107. Phone: (914) 524-7510.

- 1400 Old Country Rd. - Ste. 08, Westbury, NY 11590. Phone: (516) 334-3344.

North Carolina—Century Station, Federal Bldg. - Rm. 38, 300 Fayetteville Mall, Raleigh, NC 27601-9998. Phone: (919) 856-4770.

North Dakota—Federal Office Bldg., 1640 E. Capitol Ave., Bismarck, ND 58501. Phone: (701) 250-4521.

Ohio—Federal Bldg. - Rm. 028, 36 Triangle Park Dr., Cincinnati, OH 45246. Phone: (513) 841-4132.

- Federal Bldg. - Rm. 99, 1240 E. 9th St., Cleveland, OH 44199. Phone: (216) 522-3818.

- Federal Office Bldg. - Rm. 20, 200 N. High St, Columbus, OH 43215. Phone: (614) 469-5582.

- Ohio Bldg. - Ste. 00, 420 Madison Ave., Toledo, OH 43604. Phone: (419) 259-7542.

Oklahoma—55 N. Robinson - Ste. 15, Oklahoma City, OK 73102. Phone: (405) 278-9560.

Oregon—1220 SW 3rd St. - Rm. 40, Portland, OR 97204. Phone: (503) 326-2251.

Pennsylvania—850 N. 5th St., Allentown, PA 18102. Phone: (610) 776-0592.

- 3939 W. Ridge Rd. - Ste. B-12, Erie, PA 16506. Phone: (814) 833-5758.

- Progress Plaza, 49 N. Progress Ave., Harrisburg, PA 17109. Phone: (717) 782-3902.

- U.S. Customs House - Rm. 42, 2nd and Chestnut St., Philadelphia, PA 19106. Phone: (215) 597-4955.

- Federal Bldg. - Rm. 428, 1000 Liberty Ave., Pittsburgh, PA 15522-4101. Phone: (412) 395-4903.

- 7 N. Wilkes-Barre Blvd. - Ste. 10, Wilkes-Barre, PA 18702. Phone: (570) 826-6538.

Puerto Rico—BBV Plaza Bldg. - Ste. B, 1510 F.D. Roosevelt Ave., Guaynabo, PR 00968. Phone: (787) 277-1560.

Rhode Island—380 Westminster Mall - Rm. 43, Providence, RI 02903. Phone: (401) 528-4669.

South Carolina—1835 Assembly St. - Rm. 468, Columbia, SC 29201. Phone: (803) 765-5904.

Tennessee—2002 Richard Jones Rd. - Ste. C-205, Nashville, TN 37215-2809. Phone: (615) 781-5423.

Texas—903 San Jacinto Blvd. - Ste. 19, Austin, TX 78701. Phone: (512) 916-5783.

- Wilson Plaza West - Ste. 00, 606 N. Carancahua, Corpus Christi, TX 78476. Phone: (361) 888-3420.

- 8344 East R.L. Thornton Fwy. - Ste. 20, Dallas, TX 75228. Phone: (214) 320-2400.

- 700 E. San Antonio - Rm.C-408, El Paso, TX 79901. Phone: (915) 534-6251.

- North Star II - Ste. 02, 8713 Airport Fwy., Ft. Worth, TX 76180-7610. Phone: (817) 428-2470.

- 17625 El Camino Real - Ste. 00, Houston, TX 77058. Phone: (281) 286-0583.

- 507 N. Sam Houston Pkwy. E. - Ste. 00, Houston, TX 77060. Phone: (281) 591-2438.

- Federal Bldg. - Rm. 06, 1205 Texas Ave., Lubbock, TX 79401. Phone: (806) 472-7681.

Utah—1781 South 300 W., P.O. Box 65200, Salt Lake City, UT 84165-0200. Phone: (801) 487-0521.

Virginia—200 Granby Mall - Rm. 14, Norfolk, VA 23510. Phone: (757) 441-3820.

Washington—505 106th Ave. NE - Ste. 02, Bellevue, WA 98004. Phone: (206) 553-7520.

West Virginia—405 Capitol St. - Ste. 07, Charleston, WV 25301. Phone: (304) 347-5937.

Wisconsin—1648 Tri Park Way, Appleton, WI 54914. Phone: (920) 734-4521.

- 1310 W. Clairmont Ave., Eau Claire, WI 54701. Phone: (715) 832-9019.

- 4802 E. Broadway, Madison, WI 53716. Phone: (608) 441-5388.

- Reuss Bldg. - Ste. 180, 310 Wisconsin Ave., Milwaukee, WI 53203. Phone: (414) 297-3315.

MINE SAFETY AND HEALTH ADMINISTRATION

17.601 through 17.602

COAL MINE SAFETY AND HEALTH

District Offices

DISTRICT NO. 1 *(Connecticut, Delaware, Maine, Massachusetts, New Hampshire, New Jersey, New York, Pennsylvania (counties east of and including Susquehanna, Sullivan, Columbia, Montour, Northumberland, Dauphin, York), Rhode Island, Vermont)*—Stegmaier Bldg. - Ste. 34, 7 N. Wilkes-Barre Blvd., Wilkes-Barre, PA 18702. Phone: (570) 826-6321.

DISTRICT NO. 2 *(Pennsylvania counties west of and including Bradford, Lycoming, Union, Snyder, Juniata, Perry, Cumberland, Adams)*—Rural Rt.1 - Box 736, Hunter, PA 15639. Phone: (412) 925-5150, ext.111.

DISTRICT NO. 3 *(Maryland, Ohio, West Virginia counties north of and including Jackson, Roane, Calhoun, Braxton, Randolph, Pendleton)*—5012 Mountaineer Mall, Morgantown, WV 26505. Phone: (304) 291-4277.

DISTRICT NO. 4 *(West Virginia counties south of and including Mason, Putnam, Kanawha, Clay, Nicholas, Webster, Greenbrier, Pocahontas)*—100 Bluestone Rd., Mt. Hope, WV 25880. Phone: (304) 877-3900, ext.125.

DISTRICT NO. 5 *(Virginia)*—P.O. Box 560, Norton, VA 24273. Phone: (540) 679-0230.

DISTRICT NO. 6 *(Kentucky counties east of and including Mason, Robertson, Fleming, Rowan, Menifee, Morgan, Magoffin, Floyd, Pike, Letcher)*—159 N. Mayo Trail, Pikeville, KY 41501-3249. Phone: (606) 432-0943, ext.116.

DISTRICT NO. 7 *(Alabama (counties north and east of, and including, Jackson, Marshall, Etowah, Cherokee), Georgia (counties north of, and including, Polk, Bartow, Cherokee, Forsyth, Hall, Jackson, Madison, Elbert), Kentucky (counties east of and including Boone, Grant, Scott, Woodford, Jessamine, Garrard, Lincoln, Pulaski, Clinton up to District 6 boundary), North Carolina, South Carolina, Tennessee)*—HC 66-Box 1699, Barbourville, KY 40906. Phone: (606) 546-5123.

DISTRICT NO. 8 *(Illinois, Indiana, Iowa, Michigan, Minnesota, Missouri counties north of the Missouri River, Wisconsin)*—2300 Old Decker Rd. - Ste. 00, Vincennes, IN 47591. Phone: (812) 882-7617.

DISTRICT NO. 9 *(All states west of the Mississippi River including Alaska and Hawaii, except Minnesota, Iowa and all counties of Missouri south of the Missouri River)*—Denver Federal Center, P.O. Box 25367, Denver, CO 80225-0367. Phone: (303) 231-5458.

17.601
through
17.602
(cont.)

DISTRICT NO. 10 *(Kentucky counties west of and including Gallatin, Owen, Franklin, Anderson, Mercer, Boyle, Casey, Russell, Cumberland)*—100 YMCA Dr., Madisonville, KY 42431-9019. Phone: (270) 821-4180.

DISTRICT NO. 11 *(Alabama and Georgia (counties south and west of the District 7 boundary) Florida, Mississippi, Puerto Rico, Virgin Islands)*—135 Gemini Circle - Ste. 13, Birmingham, AL 35209. Phone: (205) 290-7300.

METAL AND NONMETAL MINE SAFETY AND HEALTH

District Offices

Alabama *(Southeastern: Alabama, Florida, Georgia, Kentucky, Mississippi, North Carolina, Puerto Rico, South Carolina, Tennessee, Virgin Islands)*—135 Gemini Circle - Ste. 12, Birmingham, AL 35209. Phone: (205) 290-7294.

California *(Western: Alaska, California, Hawaii, Idaho, Nevada, Oregon, Washington)*—2060 Peabody Rd. - Ste. 10, Vacaville, CA 95687-6696. Phone: (707) 447-9844.

Colorado *(Rocky Mountain: Arizona, Colorado, Kansas, Montana, Nebraska, North Dakota, South Dakota, Utah, Wyoming)*—P.O. Box 25367, Denver, CO 80225-0367. Phone: (303) 231-5465.

Minnesota *(North Central: Illinois, Indiana, Iowa, Michigan, Minnesota, Ohio, Wisconsin)*—515 W. 1st St. - #333, Duluth, MN 55802-1302. Phone: (218) 720-5448.

Pennsylvania *(Northeastern: Connecticut, Delaware, District of Columbia, Maine, Maryland, Massachusetts, New Hampshire, New Jersey, New York, Pennsylvania, Rhode Island, Vermont, Virginia, West Virginia)*—230 Executive Dr. - Ste. , Cranberry Township, PA 16066-6415. Phone: (724) 772-2333.

Texas *(South Central: Arkansas, Louisiana, Missouri, New Mexico, Oklahoma, Texas)*—1100 Commerce St. - Rm. C50, Dallas, TX 75242-0499. Phone: (214) 767-8401.

TECHNICAL SUPPORT FIELD CENTERS

Pennsylvania—Safety and Health Technology Center, Cochrans Mill Rd., P.O. Box 18233, Pittsburgh, PA 15236. Phone: (412) 386-6902.

West Virginia—Approval and Certification Center, Industrial Park Rd., Rural Rt. 1 - Box 251, Triadelphia, WV 26059. Phone: (304) 547-2029.

National Mine Health and Safety Academy

1301 Airport Rd., Beaver, WV 25813-9426. Phone: (304) 256-3200.

OFFICE OF THE SECRETARY, WOMEN'S BUREAU

17.700 **REGIONAL OFFICES**

REGION I *(Connecticut, Maine, Massachusetts, New Hampshire, Rhode Island, Vermont)*—JFK Federal Bldg. - Rm.E-270, One Congress St., Boston, MA 02114. Phones: (617) 565-1988, 1-800-518-3585.

REGION II *(New Jersey, New York, Puerto Rico, Virgin Islands)*—201 Varick St. - Rm. 01, New York, NY 10014. Phone: (212) 337-2389.

REGION III *(Delaware, District of Columbia, Maryland, Pennsylvania, Virginia, West Virginia)*—The Curtis Center - Ste. 80 West, 170 S. Independence Mall W., Philadelphia, PA 19104. Phones: (215) 861-4860, 1-800-379-9042.

REGION IV *(Alabama, Florida, Georgia, Kentucky, Mississippi, North Carolina, South Carolina, Tennessee)*—61 Forsyth St. SW - Ste. T95, Atlanta, GA 30367. Phones: (404) 562-2336, 1-800-672-8356.

REGION V *(Illinois, Indiana, Michigan, Minnesota, Ohio, Wisconsin)*—230 S. Dearborn St. - Rm. 022, Chicago, IL 60604. Phones: (312) 353-6985, 1-800-648-8183.

REGION VI *(Arkansas, Louisiana, New Mexico, Oklahoma, Texas)*—Federal Bldg. - Ste. 35, 525 Griffin St., Dallas, TX 75202. Phones: (214) 767-6985, 1-800-887-6794.

REGION VII *(Iowa, Kansas, Missouri, Nebraska)*—City Center City Square - Ste. 45, 1100 Main St., Kansas City, MO 64106. Phones: (816) 426-6108, 1-800-252-4706.

REGION VIII *(Colorado, Montana, North Dakota, South Dakota, Utah, Wyoming)*—Federal Office Bldg. - Ste. 05, 1801 California St., Denver, CO 80202-2614. Phones: (303) 844-1286, 1-800-299-0886.

REGION IX *(Arizona, California, Hawaii, Nevada)*—71 Stevenson St. - Rm. 27, San Francisco, CA 94105. Phone: (415) 975-4750.

REGION X *(Alaska, Idaho, Oregon, Washington)*—1111 3rd Ave. - Rm. 25, Seattle, WA 98101-3211. Phones: (206) 553-1534, 1-888-296-7011.

OFFICE OF THE ASSISTANT SECRETARY FOR VETERANS' EMPLOYMENT AND TRAINING

17.801 through 17.806

REGIONAL AND STATE OFFICES

REGION I *(Connecticut, Maine, Massachusetts, New Hampshire, Rhode Island, Vermont, Virgin Islands)*—Connecticut Department of Labor Bldg., 200 Folly Brook Blvd., Wethersfield, CT 06109. Phone: (860) 263-6490.

- JFK Federal Bldg. - Government Center (Rm.E-315), Boston, MA 02203. Phone: (617) 565-2080.
- Hurley Bldg. - 2nd fl., ES Operations Section, 19 Staniford St., Boston, MA 02114. Phone: (617) 626-6699.
- 5 Mollison Way, P.O. Box 3106, Lewiston, ME 04243. Phone: (207) 753-9090.
- 143 N. Main St. - Rm. 08, Concord, NH 03301. Phone: (603) 225-1424.
- 57 Spruce St., Westerly, RI 02891. Phone: (401) 528-5134.
- Post Office Bldg. - Rm. 03, 87 State St., P.O. Box 603, Montpelier, VT 05602. Phone: (802) 828-4441.

REGION II *(New Jersey, New York, Puerto Rico, Virgin Islands)*—Labor Bldg. - 11th fl. (CN058), Trenton, NJ 08625. Phone: (609) 292-2930.

- Harriman State Campus - Bldg. 12 (Rm. 18), Albany, NY 12240-0099. Phone: (518) 457-7465.
- 201 Varick St. - Rm. 66, New York, NY 10014. Phone: (212) 337-2211.
- 198 Calle Guayama - 20th fl., Hato Rey, PR 00917. Phone: (787) 754-5391.

REGION III *(Delaware, District of Columbia, Maryland, Pennsylvania, Virginia, West Virginia)*—500 C St. NW - Rm. 08, Washington, DC 20001. Phone: (202) 724-7005.

- 4425 N. Market St. - Rm. 20, Wilmington, DE 19809-0828. Phone: (302) 761-8138.
- 1100 N. Eutaw St. - Rm. 10, Baltimore, MD 21201. Phone: (410) 767-2110.
- Labor and Industry Bldg. - Rm. 108,, 7th and Forster Sts., Harrisburg, PA 17121. Phone: (717) 787-5834.
- The Curtis Center - Ste. 70W, 170 S. Independence Mall West, Philadelphia, PA 19106. Phone: (215) 861-5390.
- 703 E. Main St. - Rm. 18, Richmond, VA 23219. Phone: (804) 786-7269.
- Capitol Complex - Rm. 04, 112 California Ave., Charleston, WV 25305-0112. Phone: (304) 558-4001.

**17.801
through
17.806
(cont.)**

REGION IV *(Alabama, Florida, Georgia, Kentucky, Mississippi, North Carolina, South Carolina, Tennessee)*—649 Monroe St. - Rm. 43, Montgomery, AL 36131-6300. Phone: (334) 223-7677.

- P.O. Box 1527, Tallahassee, FL 32302-1527. Phone: (850) 942-8800.

- Nunn Atlanta Federal Center - Rm. -T85, 61 Forsyth St. SW, Atlanta, GA 30303. Phone: (404) 562-2305.

- Sussex Place - Ste. 04, 148 International Blvd. NE, Atlanta, GA 30303-1751. Phone: (404) 656-3127.

- c/o Department for Employment Services, 275 E. Main St., Frankfort, KY 40621-2339. Phone: (502) 564-7062.

- 1520 W. Capitol St., P.O. Box 1699, Jackson, MS 39215-1699. Phone: (601) 965-4204.

- P.O. Box 27625, Raleigh, NC 27611-7625. Phones: (919) 733-7402, -7407.

- P.O. Box 1755, Columbia, SC 29202-1755. Phone: (803) 765-5195.

- 915 8th Ave. N., Nashville, TN 37219-3795. Phone (615) 736-7680.

REGION V *(Illinois, Indiana, Michigan, Minnesota, Ohio, Wisconsin)*—230 S. Dearborn - Rm. 064, Chicago, IL 60604. Phone: (312) 353-0970.

- 401 S. State St. - 744 North, Chicago, IL 60605. Phone: (312) 793-3433.

- 10 N. Senate Ave. - Rm.SE-103, Indianapolis, IN 46204. Phone: (317) 232-6804.

- 7310 Woodward Ave. - Ste. 07, Detroit, MI 48202. Phone: (313) 876-5613.

- 390 Robert St. N. - 1st fl., St. Paul, MN 55101. Phone: (651) 296-3665.

- P.O. Box 1618, Columbus, OH 43216. Phone: (614) 644-3688.

- P.O. Box 8310, Madison, WI 53708-8310. Phone: (608) 266-3110.

REGION VI *(Arkansas, Louisiana, New Mexico, Oklahoma, Texas)*—P.O. Box 128, Little Rock, AR 72203. Phone: (501) 682-3786.

- P.O. Box 94094, Rm. 84, Baton Rouge, LA 70804-9094. Phone: (225) 389-0339.

- P.O. Box 25085, Albuquerque, NM 87125-5085. Phone: (505) 346-7502.

- 201 N. Lincoln Blvd., P.O. Box 52003, Oklahoma City, OK 73152-2003. Phone: (405) 231-5088.

- P.O. Box 1468, Austin, TX 78767. Phone: (512) 463-2814.

- 525 Griffin St. - Rm. 58, Dallas, TX 75202. Phone: (214) 767-4987.

REGION VII *(Iowa, Kansas, Missouri, Nebraska)*—150 Des Moines St., Des Moines, IA 50309-5563. Phone: (515) 281-9061.

- 401 Topeka Blvd., Topeka, KS 66603-3182. Phone: (913) 296-5032.

- 421 E. Dunklin St., Jefferson City, MO 65102-1087. Phone: (573) 751-3921.

- City Center Square - Ste. 50, 1100 Main St., Kansas City, MO 64105-2112. Phone: (816) 426-7151.

- 550 S. 16th St., P.O. Box 94600, Lincoln, NE 68508. Phone: (402) 437-5289.

REGION VIII *(Colorado, Montana, North Dakota, South Dakota, Utah, Wyoming)*— 1999 Broadway - Ste. 730, Denver, CO 80202-2614. Phone: (303) 844-1175.

- 2 Park Central - Ste. 00, 1515 Arapahoe St., Denver, CO 80202-2117. Phone: (303) 844-2151.

- 1215 8th Ave., Helena, MT 59601-4144. Phone: (406) 449-5431.

- 1000 E. Divide Ave., Bismarck, ND 58502-1632. Phone: (701) 328-2865.

- 420 S. Roosevelt St., Aberdeen, SD 57402-4730. Phone: (605) 626-2325.

- 140 E. 300 South, Salt Lake City, UT 84111-2333. Phone: (801) 524-5703.

- 100 W. Midwest Ave., Casper, WY 82602-2760. Phone: (307) 261-5454.

REGION IX *(Arizona, California, Hawaii, Nevada)*—1400 W. Washington St., P.O. Box 6123-SC760E, Phoenix, AZ 85005. Phone: (602) 379-4961.

- 800 Capitol Mall - Rm.W-1142, P.O. Box 826880, Sacramento, CA 94280-0001. Phone: (916) 654-8178.
- 71 Stevenson St. - Ste. 05, San Francisco, CA 94105. Phone: (415) 975-4700.
- P.O. Box 3680, Honolulu, HI 96811. Phone: (808) 522-8216.
- 1923 N. Carson St. - Rm. 05, Carson City, NV 89702. Phone: (702) 687-4632.

REGION X *(Alaska, Idaho, Oregon and Washington)*—1111 W. 8th St., P.O. Box 25509, Juneau, AK 99802-5509. Phone: (907) 465-2723.

- P.O. Box 2697, Boise, ID 83701. Phone: (208) 334-6163.
- 312 Employment Division Bldg. - Rm. 08, 875 Union St. NE, Salem, OR 97311-0100. Phone: (503) 947-1490.
- P.O. Box 165, Olympia, WA 98507-0165. Phone: (360) 438-4600.
- 1111 3rd Ave. - Ste. 00, Seattle, WA 98101-3212. Phone: (206) 553-4831.

DEPARTMENT OF STATE

BUREAU OF EDUCATIONAL AND CULTURAL AFFAIRS

19.025   American Council of Young Political Leaders, 1612 K St. NW - Ste. 00, Washington, DC 20006. Phone: (202) 857-0999.

Young Professionals Component:

CDS International, 330 7th Ave., New York, NY 10001. Phone: (212) 497-3509.

Vocational Component: Nacel/Open Door, 3410 Federal Dr. - Ste. 01, St. Paul, MN 55122. Phone: (651) 686-0080.

Institute of International Education, Southern Regional Office, 515 Post Oak Blvd. Ste. 150, Houston, TX 77027-9407. Phone: (713) 621-6300; FAX (713) 621-9758.

International Education Training:

NAFSA, Association of International Educators, 1307 New York Ave. NW - 8th fl., Washington, DC 20005-4701. Phones:(202) 737-3699; FAX (202) 737-3657.

Research: Institute of International Education, 809 United Nations Plaza, New York, NY 10017. Phone: (212) 984-5331.

DEPARTMENT
OF TRANSPORTATION

FEDERAL AVIATION ADMINISTRATION

20.106   **AVIATION INFORMATION DISTRIBUTION PROGRAM**

Regional Offices

ALASKA—(AHT-200/AAL-17), 222 W. 7th Ave., Box 14, Anchorage, AK 99513-7587. Phones: (202) 267-3436, (907) 271-5377.

CENTRAL—(ACE-4), 601 E. 12th St., Kansas City, M0 64106-2808. Phone: (816) 329-2420.

EASTERN—(ACH-1), Technical Center, Atlantic City International Airport, Atlantic City, NJ 08405. Phone: (605) 485-6515.

■ (AEA-60), JFK International Airport, Federal Bldg. - Rm. 11, Jamaica, NY 11430. Phone: (718) 553-3363.

GREAT LAKES—(AGL-4), O'Hare Lake Office Center, 2300 E. Devon Ave., Des Plaines, IL 60018. Phone: (847) 294-7106.

NEW ENGLAND—(ANE-40), 12 New England Executive Park, Burlington, MA 01803-5299. Phone: (781) 238-7378.

NORTHWEST MOUNTAIN—(ANM-4CL), 1601 Lind Ave. SW, Renton, WA 98055-4056. Phone: (425) 227-1725.

SOUTHERN—(ASO-1), 1701 Columbia Ave., P.O. Box 20636, Atlanta, GA 30320-0631. Phone: (425) 227-1725.

SOUTHWEST—(AMC-3), Aeronautical Center, P.O. Box 25082, Oklahoma City, OK 73135. Phone: (405) 954-5332.

■ (ASW-18B), 2601 Meacham Blvd., Ft. Worth, TX 76137-4298. Phone: (817) 222-5833.

WESTERN PACIFIC—(AWP-4), Worldway Postal Center, P.O. Box 92007, Los Angeles, CA 90009-2007. Phone:(310) 725-3802.

FEDERAL HIGHWAY ADMINISTRATION

20.200
through
20.215   **DIVISION OFFICES**

Alabama—500 Eastern Blvd. - Ste. 00, Montgomery, AL 36117-2018. Phone: (334) 223-7370.

Alaska—709 W. 9th St. - Rm. 51, P.O. Box 21648, Juneau, AK 99802-1648. Phone: (907) 586-7180.

Arizona—234 N. Central Ave. - Ste. 30, Phoenix, AZ 85004-2220. Phone: (602) 379-3646.

Arkansas—700 W. Capitol Ave. - Rm. 130, Little Rock, AR 72201-3298. Phone: (501) 324-5625.

California—980 9th St. - Ste. 00, Sacramento, CA 95814-2724. Phone: (916) 498-5001.

Colorado—555 Zang St. - Rm. 50, Lakewood, CO 80228-1097. Phone: (303) 969-6730, ext.3.

Connecticut—628-2 Hebron Ave. - Ste. 03, Glastonbury, CT 06033-5007. Phone: (860) 659-6703, ext.3009.

Delaware—300 S. New St. - Rm. 101, Dover, DE 19904-0726. Phone: (302) 734-5323.

District of Columbia—Union Center Plaza - Ste. 50, 820 1st St. NE, Washington, DC 20002-4205. Phone: (202) 523-0163.

Florida—227 N. Bronough St. - Rm. 015, Tallahassee, FL 32301-1330. Phone: (850) 942-9650.

Georgia—61 Forsyth St. SW - Ste. 7T100, Atlanta, GA 30303-3104. Phone: (404) 562-3630. **Hawaii**—Kalanianaole Federal Bldg. - Rm. -306, 300 Ala Moana Blvd., P.O. Box 50206, Honolulu, HI 96850-5000. Phone: (808) 541-2700, ext.312.

Idaho—3050 Lakeharbor Lane - Ste. 26, Boise, ID 83703-6243. Phone: (208) 334-9180.

Illinois—3250 Executive Park Dr., Springfield, IL 62703-4514. Phone: (217) 492-4640.

Indiana—575 N. Pennsylvania St. - Rm. 54, Indianapolis, IN 46204-1576. Phone: (317) 226-7475.

Iowa—105 6th St., Ames, IA 50010-6337. Phone: (515) 233-7300.

Kansas—3300 S. Topeka Blvd. - Ste. , Topeka, KS 66611-2237. Phone: (785) 267-7281.

Kentucky—330 W. Broadway, Frankfort, KY 40601-1922. Phone: (502) 223-6720.

Louisiana—5304 Flanders Dr. - Ste. A, Baton Rouge, LA 70808-4348. Phone: (225) 757-7600.

Maine—Muskie Federal Bldg. - Rm. 14, 40 Western Ave., Augusta, ME 04330-6394. Phone: (207) 622-8487, ext.19.

Maryland—711 W. 40th St. - Ste. 20, Baltimore, MD 21211-2108. Phone: (410) 962-4440.

Massachusetts—55 Broadway - 10th fl., Cambridge, MA 02142-1093. Phone: (617) 494-3657.

Michigan—315 W. Allegan St. - Rm. 07, Lansing, MI 48933-1528. Phone: (517) 377-1844.

Minnesota—Galtier Plaza - Ste. 00 (Box 75), 380 Jackson St., St. Paul, MN 55101-2904. Phone: (651) 291-6100.

Mississippi—666 North St. - Ste. 05, Jackson, MS 39202-3199. Phone: (601) 965-4215.

Missouri—209 Adams St., Jefferson City, MO 65101-3203. Phone: (573) 636-7104.

Montana—2880 Skyway Dr., Helena, MT 59602-1230. Phone: (406) 449-5303, ext.235.

Nebraska—Federal Bldg. - Rm. 20, 100 Centennial Mall N., Lincoln, NE 68508-3851. Phone: (402) 437-5765.

Nevada—705 N. Plaza St. - Ste. 20, Carson City, NV 89701-0602. Phone: (775) 687-1204.

New Hampshire—279 Pleasant St. Ste. 04, Concord, NH 03301-7502. Phone: (603) 228-0417.

New Jersey—840 Bear Tavern Rd. - Ste. 10, West Trenton, NJ 08628-1019. Phone: (609) 637-4200.

New Mexico—604 W. San Mateo Rd., Santa Fe, NM 87505-3920. Phone: (505) 820-2021.

New York—O'Brien Federal Bldg. - Rm. 19, Clinton Ave. and N. Pearl St., Albany, NY 12207. Phone: (518) 431-4125.

North Carolina—310 New Bern Ave - Ste. 10, Raleigh, NC 27601-1441. Phone: (919) 856-4346.

**20.200
through
20.215
(cont.)**

North Dakota—1471 Interstate Loop, Bismarck, ND 58503-0567. Phone: (701) 250-4204.

Ohio—200 N. High St. - Rm. 28, Columbus, OH 43215. Phone: (614) 280-6896.

Oklahoma—300 N. Meridan - Ste. 05S, Oklahoma City, OK 73107-6560. Phone: (405) 605-6011.

Oregon—The Equitable Center - Ste. 00, 530 Center St. NE, Salem, OR 97301-3740. Phone: (503) 399-5749.

Pennsylvania—228 Walnut St. - Rm. 58, Harrisburg, PA 17101-1720. Phone: (717) 221-3461.

Puerto Rico—Degetau Federal Bldg. - Rm. 10, 330 Carlos Chardon Ave., San Juan, PR 00916. Phone:(787) 766-5600, ext.223.

Rhode Island—380 Westminster Mall - 5th fl., Providence, RI 02903-3246. Phone: (401) 528-4560.

South Carolina—1835 Assembly St. - Ste. 270, Columbia, SC 29201-2483. Phone: (803) 765-5411.

South Dakota—116 E. Dakota Ave., Pierre, SD 57501-3110. Phone: (605) 224-8033.

Tennessee—640 Grassmere Park Rd. - Ste. 12, Nashville, TN 37211-3658. Phone: (615) 781-5770.

Texas—Federal Office Bldg. - Rm. 26, 300 E. 8th St., Austin, TX 78701-3233. Phone: (512) 536-5900.

Utah—2520 W. 4700 S. - Ste. A, Salt Lake City, UT 84118-1847. Phone: (801) 963-0182.

Vermont—Federal Bldg., 87 State St., P.O. Box 568, Montpelier, VT 05601-0568. Phone: (802) 828-4423.

Virginia—400 N. 8th St. - Rm. 50, P.O. Box 10249, Richmond, VA 23240-0249. Phone: (804) 775-3320.

Washington—Evergreen Plaza, - Ste. 01, 711 S. Capitol Way, Olympia, WA 98501-1284. Phone: (360) 753-9480.

West Virginia—Geary Plaza - Ste. 00, 700 Washington St. E., Charleston, WV 25301-1604. Phone: (304) 347-5928.

Wisconsin—Highpoint Office Park, 567 D'Onofrio Dr., Madison, WI 53719-2814. Phone: (608) 829-7500.

Wyoming—2617 E. Lincolnway - Ste. D, Cheyenne, WY 82001-5662. Phone: (307) 772-2101, ext.40.

Federal Lands Highway Division Offices

CENTRAL—555 Zang St., Lakewood, CO 80228-1010. Phone: (303) 716-2000.

EASTERN—Loudoun Technical Center, 21400 Ridgetop Circle, Sterling, VA 20166-6511. Phone: (703) 404-6201.

WESTERN—610 E. 5th St., Vancouver, WA 98661-3801. Phone: (360) 619-7700.

FEDERAL MOTOR CARRIER SAFETY ADMINISRATION

20.218 ## REGIONAL OFFICES

Eastern Service Center—802 Cromwell Park Dr., Ste. N, Glen Burnie, MD 21061. Phone: (443) 703-2240.

Midwestern Service Center—4749 Lincoln Mall Dr., Suite 300A, Matteson, IL 60443. Phone: (708) 283-3577.

Southern Service Center—1800 Century Blvd., Ste. 1700, Atlanta , GA 30345. Phone: (404) 327-7400.

Western Service Center—Golden Hills Office Centre, 12600 W. Colfax Ave., Ste. B-300, Lakewood, CO 80215. Phone: (303) 407-2350.

20.219 through 20.224   Listed under **20.200.**

20.231 through 20.237   Listed under **20.218.**

FEDERAL RAILROAD ADMINISTRATION

20.301 through 20.321   ## REGIONAL OFFICES

REGION I - **Northeastern** *(Connecticut, Maine, Massachusetts, New Hampshire, New Jersey, New York, Rhode Island, Vermont)*—55 Broadway - Rm. 077, Cambridge, MA 02142. Phone: (617) 494-2302.

REGION II - **Eastern** *(Delaware, District of Columbia, Pennsylvania, Maryland, Virginia, West Virginia, Ohio)*—2 International Plaza - Ste. 50, Philadelphia, PA 19113. Phone: (610) 521-8200.

REGION III - **Southern** *(Alabama, Florida, Georgia, Kentucky, Mississippi, North Carolina, South Carolina, Tennessee)*—Atlanta Federal Center - Ste. 6T20, 61 Forsyth St. SW, Atlanta, GA 30303-3104. Phone: (404) 562-3800.

REGION IV - **Central** *(Illinois, Indiana, Michigan, Minnesota, Wisconsin)*—111 N. Canal St. Ste. 655, Chicago, IL 60606. Phone: (312) 353-6203.

REGION V - **Southwestern** *(Arkansas, Louisiana, New Mexico, Oklahoma, Texas)*— 8701 Bedford Euless Rd. Ste. 425, Hurst, TX 76053. Phone: (817) 284-8142.

REGION VI - **Midwestern** *(Colorado, Iowa, Kansas, Missouri, Nebraska)*—DOT Bldg. - Ste. 64, 901 Locust St., Kansas City, MO 64106-2095. Phone: (817) 329-3840.

REGION VII - **Western** *(Arizona, California, Nevada, Utah)*—801 "I" St. - Ste. 66, Sacramento, CA 95814-2559. Phone: (916) 498-6540.

REGION VIII - **Northwestern** *(Alaska, Idaho, Montana, North Dakota, Oregon, South Dakota, Washington, Wyoming)*—Murdock Executive Plaza - Ste. 50, 703 Broadway, Vancouver, WA 98660. Phone: (360) 696-7536.

FEDERAL TRANSIT ADMINISTRATION

20.500 through 20.523   ## REGIONAL OFFICES

REGION I *(Connecticut, Maine, Massachusetts, New Hampshire, Rhode Island, Vermont)*—c/o Volpe National, Transportation Systems Center, Kendall Square - Ste. 20, 55 Broadway, Cambridge, MA 02142-1093. Phone: (617) 494-2055.

REGION II *(New Jersey, New York, Virgin Islands)*—Metropolitan Office - Ste. 29, One Bowling Green, New York, NY 10004-1415. Phone: (212) 668-2170.

REGION III *(Delaware, District of Columbia, Maryland, Pennsylvania, Virginia, West Virginia)*—1760 Market St. - Ste. 00, Philadelphia, PA 19103-4124. Phone: (215) 656-7100.

REGION IV *(Alabama, Florida, Georgia, Kentucky, Mississippi, North Carolina, Puerto Rico, South Carolina, Tennessee)*—61 Forsyth St. SW - Ste. 7T50, Atlanta, GA 30303-8917. Phone: (404) 562-3500.

REGION V *(Illinois, Indiana, Michigan, Minnesota, Ohio, Wisconsin)*—200 W. Adams St. - Ste. 20, Chicago, IL 60606-5232. Phone: (312) 353-2789.

20.500 through 20.523 (cont.)

REGION VI *(Arkansas, Louisiana, New Mexico, Oklahoma, Texas)*—Lanham Federal Bldg. - Ste. A36, 819 Taylor St., Ft. Worth, TX 76102. Phone: (817) 978-0550.

REGION VII *(Iowa, Kansas, Missouri, Nebraska)*—901 Locust St. - Rm. 04, Kansas City, MO 64106. Phone: (816) 329-3920.

REGION VIII *(Note: grant making activity for Arizona and Nevada falls under Region VIII) (Colorado, Montana, North Dakota, South Dakota, Utah, Wyoming)*—12300 W. Dakota Ave. - Ste. 10, Lakewood, CO 80228-2583. Phone: (720) 963-3300.

REGION IX *(American Samoa, Arizona, California, Guam, Hawaii, Nevada)*—201 Mission St. - Ste. 210, San Francisco, CA 94105-1926. Phone: (415) 744-3133.

REGION X *(Alaska, Idaho, Oregon, Washington)*—Jackson Federal Bldg. - Ste. 142, 915 2nd Ave., Seattle, WA 98174-1002. Phone: (206) 220-7954.

NATIONAL HIGHWAY TRAFFIC SAFETY ADMINISTRATION

20.600 through 20.613

REGIONAL OFFICES

REGION I *(Connecticut, Maine, Massachusetts, New Hampshire, Rhode Island, Vermont)*—Transportation System Center, Kendall Square (Code 903), Cambridge, MA 02142. Phone: (617) 494-3427.

REGION II *(New Jersey, New York, Puerto Rico, Virgin Islands)*—222 Mamaroneck Ave. - Ste. 04, White Plains, NY 10605. Phone: (914) 682-6162.

REGION III *(Delaware, District of Columbia, Maryland, Pennsylvania, Virginia, West Virginia)*—Crescent Bldg. - Ste. 000, 10 S. Howard St., Baltimore, MD 21201. Phone: (410) 962-0077.

REGION IV *(Alabama, Florida, Georgia, Kentucky, Mississippi, North Carolina, South Carolina, Tennessee)*—61 Forsyth St. SW - Ste. 7T30, Atlanta, GA 30303-3104. Phone: (404) 562-3739.

REGION V *(Illinois, Indiana, Michigan, Minnesota, Ohio, Wisconsin)*—19900 Governors Dr. - Ste. 01, Olympia Fields, IL 60461. Phone: (708) 503-8822.

REGION VI *(Arkansas, Indian Nations, Louisiana, New Mexico, Oklahoma, Texas)*—819 Taylor St. - Rm. A38, Ft. Worth, TX 76102-6177. Phone: (817) 978-3653.

REGION VII *(Iowa, Kansas, Missouri, Nebraska)*—P.O. Box 412515, Kansas City, MO 64141. Phone: (816) 822-7233.

REGION VIII *(Colorado, Montana, North Dakota, South Dakota, Utah, Wyoming)*—555 Zang St. - Rm. 30, Denver, CO 80228. Phone: (303) 969-6917.

REGION IX *(American Samoa, Arizona, California, Guam, Hawaii, Mariana Islands, Nevada)*—201 Mission St. - Ste. 230, San Francisco, CA 94105. Phone: (415) 744-3089.

REGION X *(Alaska, Idaho, Oregon, Washington)*—3140 Jackson Federal Bldg., 915 2nd Ave., Seattle, WA 98174. Phone: (206) 220-7640.

PIPELINE AND HAZARDOUS MATERIALS SAFETY ADMINISTRATION

20.721

REGIONAL OFFICES

CENTRAL *(Illinois, Indiana, Iowa, Kansas, Michigan, Minnesota, Missouri, Nebraska, North Dakota, Ohio, South Dakota, Wisconsin)*—Pipeline Safety 901 Locust St. Ste. 62, Kansas City, MO 64106. Phone: (816) 329-3800; FAX (816) 329-3831. *Hazardous Materials Safety* 2300 E. Devon Ave. Ste. 78, Des Plaines, IL 60018-4696. Phone: (847) 294-8580; FAX (847) 294-8590.

EASTERN *(Connecticut, Delaware, District of Columbia, Maine, Maryland, Massachusetts, New Hampshire, New Jersey, New York, Pennsylvania, Rhode Island, Vermont, Virginia, West Virginia)*—820 Bear Tavern Rd. Ste. 06, West Trenton, NJ 08628. Phone: (609) 989-2256; FAX (609) 989-2277.

SOUTHERN *(Alabama, Florida, Georgia, Kentucky, Mississippi, North Carolina, Puerto Rico, South Carolina, Tennessee)*— Pipeline Safety 233 Peachtree St. NE Ste. 600, Atlanta, GA 30303. Phone: (404) 832-1147; FAX (404) 832-1169. *Hazardous Materials Safety* 233 Peachtree St. NE Ste. 602, Atlanta, GA 30303. Phone: (404) 832-1140; FAX (404) 832-1168.

SOUTHWEST *(Arkansas, Louisiana, New Mexico, Oklahoma, Texas)*—8701 S. Gessner Rd. Ste. 1110, Houston, TX 77074. Phones: (713) 272-2820, -2822, -2859; FAX (713) 272-2821, -2831.

WESTERN *(Alaska, American Samoa, Arizona, California, Colorado, Commonwealth of Northern Mariana Islands, Guam, Hawaii, Idaho, Montana, Nevada, Oregon, Utah, Washington, Wyoming)*— Pipeline Safety 12300 W. Dakota Ave. Ste. 110, Lakewood, CO 80228. Phone: (720) 963-3160; FAX (720) 963-3161. *Hazardous Materials Safety* 3401 Centrelake Dr. Ste. 550B, Ontario, CA 91761. Phone: (909) 937-3279; FAX (909) 390-5142.

MARITIME ADMINISTRATION

20.802 through 20.812

REGIONAL OFFICES

CENTRAL *(Alabama, Arkansas, Colorado, Florida (western half), Louisiana, Mississippi, New Mexico, Oklahoma, Tennessee, Texas)*—501 Magazine St. - Rm. 223, New Orleans, LA 70130-3394. Phone: (504) 589-2000.

GREAT LAKES *(Illinois, Indiana, Iowa, Kansas, Kentucky, Michigan, Minnesota, Missouri, Nebraska, New York (lake coastal area), North Dakota, Ohio, Pennsylvania (lake coastal area), South Dakota, West Virginia (western third), Wisconsin)*— 1701 E. Woodfield Rd. Ste. 03, Schaumburg, IL 60173. Phone: (847) 995-0122.

NORTH ATLANTIC *(Connecticut, Delaware, Maine, Maryland, Massachusetts, New Hampshire, New Jersey, New York (except lake coastal area), Pennsylvania (except lake coastal area), Rhode Island, Vermont)*—One Bowling Green Rm. 18, New York, NY 10004-1415. Phone: (212) 668-3330.

SOUTH ATLANTIC *(Florida (eastern half), Georgia, North Carolina, Puerto Rico, South Carolina, Virginia, West Virginia (eastern two-thirds)*—Bldg. 4D - Rm. 11, 7737 Hampton Blvd., Norfolk, VA 23505. Phone: (757) 441-6393.

WESTERN *(Alaska, Arizona, California, Hawaii, Idaho, Montana, Nevada, Oregon, Utah, Washington, Wyoming)*—201 Mission St. - Ste. 200, San Francisco, CA 94105. Phone: (415) 744-3125.

FIELD OFFICE

New York—U.S. Merchant Marine Academy, Kings Point, NY 11024-1699. Phone: (516) 773-5000.

American War Risk Agency, 30 Broad St. - 7th fl., New York, NY 10004. Phone: (212) 405-2814.

■ California Maritime Academy, Vallejo, CA 94591.

■ Great Lakes Maritime Academy, Traverse City, MI 49684.

■ Maine Maritime Academy, Castine, ME 04421.

■ Massachusetts Maritime Academy, Buzzards Bay, MA 02532.

■ State University of New York Maritime College, Ft. Schuyler, NY 10465.

■ Texas State Maritime Program, Galveston, TX 77550.

DEPARTMENT OF THE TREASURY

INTERNAL REVENUE SERVICE

21.004 *Contact:* District Director, Attn: Disclosure Officer, in local IRS offices or via **Internet:** "www.irs.gov/foia/article/0,,id=120681,00.html". *Consult local phone directory under "U.S. Government - Internal Revenue Service."*

APPALACHIAN REGIONAL COMMISSION

23.001 through 23.011

STATE ALTERNATES OFFICES

Alabama—Director, Department of Economic and Community Affairs, P.O. Box 5690, 401 Adams Ave., Montgomery, AL 36104-5690. Phone: (334) 242-8672.

Georgia—Director, Intergovernmental Relations, Office of the Governor, State Capital - Rm. 31, Atlanta, GA 30334. Phone: (404) 463-7775.

Kentucky—Community Holding Company, 220 Main St., P.O. Box 331, Inez, KY 41224. Phone: (606) 298-3510.

Maryland—Director, Maryland Office of Planning, 301 W. Preston St. - Rm. 101, Baltimore, MD 21201. Phone: (410) 767-4510.

Mississippi—Community Assistance, Mississippi Development Authority, P.O. Box 849, Jackson, MS 39205-0849. Phone: (601) 359-6622.

New York—Secretary of State, 41 State St., Albany, NY 12231. Phone: (518) 486-9844.

North Carolina—Director, North Carolina Washington Office, 441 N. Capitol St. - Ste. 32, Washington DC 20001-1512. Phone: (202) 624-5833.

Ohio—Director, Governor's Office of Appalachia, 77 S. High St. - 28th fl., Columbus, OH 43266-1001. Phone: (614) 644-9228.

Pennsylvania—Deputy Secretary/Community Affairs and Development, Department of Community and Economic Development, Commonwealth Keystone Bldg. - 4th fl., 400 North St., Harrisburg, PA 17120. Phone: (717) 787-3003.

South Carolina—Policy Advisor to the Governor, Office of the Governor, P.O. Box 12267, Columbia, SC 29211. Phone: (803) 734-5166.

Tennessee—Commissioner, Department of Economic and Community Development, William R. Snodgrass Tennessee - 11th fl., 312 8th Ave. N., Nashville, TN 37243-0405. Phone: (615) 741-1888.

Virginia—Department of Housing and Community Development, Jackson Center, 501 N. 2nd St., Richmond, VA 23219. Phone: (804) 371-7002

West Virginia—Director/Community Development Division, West Virginia Development Office, State Capitol Complex - Bldg. 6 (Rm. 53), Charleston, WV 25305. Phone: (304) 558-4010.

OFFICE OF
PERSONNEL MANAGEMENT

Contact should be made directly with personnel offices of federal agencies of interest, or through national job information sources listed under the Headquarters office.

27.011 SERVICE CENTERS

REGION I *(Connecticut, Delaware, Maine, Maryland, Massachusetts, New Hampshire, New Jersey, New York, Pennsylvania, Rhode Island, Vermont)—Green Federal Bldg. - Rm. 400, 600 Arch St., Philadelphia, PA 19106-1596. Phone: (215) 597-7670.*

(Puerto Rico)—*Plaza Laz American Tower - Rm. 100, 525 Roosevelt Ave., Hato Rey, PR 00918. Phone: (809) 766-5620.*

REGION II (Alabama, Arkansas, Mississippi, Tennessee)—*520 Wynn Dr. NW, Huntsville, AL 35816-3426. Phone: (205) 837-1271.*

(Florida, Georgia)—*Russell Federal Bldg. - Ste. 56, 75 Spring St. SW, Atlanta, GA 30303-3109. Phone: (404) 331-4588.*

(North Carolina, South Carolina)—*Somerset Park - Ste. 00, 4407 Bland Rd., Raleigh, NC 27609-6296. Phone: (919) 790-2817.*

(Virginia)—*Federal Bldg. - Rm. 00, 200 Granby St., Norfolk, VA 23510-1886. Phone: (804) 441-3373.*

REGION III (Illinois)—*Kluzynski Federal Bldg. - DPN30-3, 230 S. Dearborn St., Chicago, IL 60604-1687. Phone: (312) 353-6234.*

(Indiana, Kentucky, Michigan, northern Ohio)—*477 Michigan Ave. - Rm. 94, Detroit, MI 48226-2574. Phone: (313) 226-2095.*

(Iowa, Kansas, Missouri, Nebraska)—*Federal Bldg. - Rm. 31, 601 E. 12th St., Kansas City, MO 64106-2826. Phone: (816) 426-5706.*

(Minnesota, North Dakota, South Dakota, Wisconsin)—*Whipple Federal Bldg. - Rm. 03, One Federal Dr., Ft. Snelling, MN 55111-4007. Phone: (612) 725-3437.*

(Ohio, Indiana, Kentucky, West Virginia)—*U.S. Courthouse and Federal Bldg. - Rm. 07, 200 W. 2nd St., Dayton, OH 45402-0001. Phone: (513) 225-2576.*

REGION IV (Arizona, Colorado, Montana, New Mexico, Utah, Wyoming)—*12345 W. Alameda Pkwy. - Rm. 16, P.O. Box 25167, Denver, CO 80225-0001. Phone: (303) 969-6931.*

(Arkansas, Louisiana, Nevada, Oklahoma, Texas)—*8610 N. Broadway - Rm. 05, San Antonio, TX 78217-0001. Phone: (210) 805-2423.*

REGION V (California, Nevada)—*20 Howard St. - Rm. 35, San Francisco, CA 94105-0001. Phone: (415) 281-7074.*

(Alaska, Hawaii (Honolulu and Island of Oahu), Pacific Overseas)—*Federal Bldg., 300 Ala Moana Blvd., P.O. Box 50028, Honolulu, HI 96850-0001. Phone: (808) 541-2795.*

(Idaho, Oregon, Washington)—*700 5th Ave. - Ste. 950, Seattle, WA 98104-5012. Phone: (206) 553-0870.*

Students may obtain information from their college career guidance office, or via phone by contacting the Career America Connection at (912) 757-3000. *Internet: "www.opm.gov", under Presidential Management Intern Program. ID NUM = 27.013*

COMMISSION ON CIVIL RIGHTS

29.001   ## REGIONAL OFFICES

CENTRAL—Gateway Tower II - Ste. 08, 400 State Ave., Kansas City, KS 66101. Phones: (913) 551-1400, TDD (913) 551-1414.

EASTERN—624 9th St. NW - Ste. 00, Washington, DC 20425. Phones: (202) 376-7533, TDD (202) 376-8116.

MIDWESTERN—55 W. Monroe St. - Ste. 10, Chicago, IL 60603. Phones: (312) 353-8311, TDD (312) 353-8362.

ROCKY MOUNTAIN—1700 Broadway - Ste. 10, Denver, CO 80290. Phones: (303) 866-1040, TDD (303) 866-1049.

SOUTHERN—61 Alabama St. SW - Ste. 840T, Atlanta, GA 30303. Phones: (404) 562-7000, TDD (404) 562-7004.

WESTERN—3660 Wilshire Blvd. - Ste. 10, Los Angeles, CA 90010. Phones: (213) 894-3437, TDD (213) 894-3435.

EQUAL EMPLOYMENT OPPORTUNITY COMMISSION

30.001 through 30.011   ## DISTRICT OFFICES

Alabama—1130 22nd St. S. - Ste. 000, Birmingham, AL 35205-2397. Phone: (205) 212-2100.

Arizona—Norwest Tower - Ste. 90, 3300 N. Central Ave., Phoenix, AZ 85012-2504. Phone: (602) 640-5000.

California—255 E. Temple Ave. - 4th fl., Los Angeles, CA 90012. Phone: (213) 894-5980.

▪ 350 Embarcadero - Ste. 00, San Francisco, CA 94105-1687. Phone: (415) 625-5600.

Colorado—303 E. 17th Ave. - Ste. 10, Denver, CO 80203-9634. Phone: (303) 866-1300.

District of Columbia—1801 L St. NW - Ste. 00, Washington, DC 20507. Phone: (202) 275-7377.

Florida—One Biscayne Tower, 2 S. Biscayne Blvd. - Ste. 700, Miami, FL 33131. Phone: (305) 536-4491.

Georgia—100 Alabama St. - Ste. R30., Atlanta, GA 30303. Phone: (404) 562-6930.

Illinois—500 W. Madison St. - Ste. 800, Chicago, IL 60661. Phone: (312) 353-2713.

Indiana—Federal Bldg. - Ste. 900, 101 W. Ohio St., Indianapolis, IN 46204-4203. Phone: (317) 226-7212.

Louisiana—701 Loyola Ave. - Ste. 00, New Orleans, LA 70113-9936. Phone: (504) 589-2329.

Maryland—City Crescent Bldg. - 3rd fl., 10 S. Howard St., Baltimore, MD 21201. Phone: (410) 962-3932.

Michigan—McNamara Federal Bldg. - Ste. 65, 477 Michigan Ave., Detroit, MI 48226-9704. Phone: (313) 226-4600.

Missouri—1222 Spruce St. - Rm. 100, St. Louis, MO 63103. Phone: (314) 539-7800.

New York—33 Whitehall St. - 5th fl., New York, NY 10004-2112. Phone: (212) 336-3620.

North Carolina—129 W. Trade St. - Ste. 00, Charlotte, NC 28202. Phone: (704) 344-6682.

Ohio—Tower City, Skylight Office Tower - Ste. 50,, 1660 W. 2nd St., Cleveland, OH 44113-1454. Phone: (216) 522-2001.

Pennsylvania—Bourse Bldg. - Ste. 00, 21 S. 5th St., Philadelphia, PA 19106-2515. Phone: (215) 440-2623.

Tennessee—1407 Union Ave. - Ste. 21, Memphis, TN 38104. Phone: (901) 544-0115.

Texas—207 S. Houston St. - 3rd fl., Dallas, TX 75202-4726. Phone: (214) 253-2700.

- Leland Bldg. - 7th fl., 1919 Smith St., Houston, TX 77002. Phone: (713) 209-3320.

- Mockingbird Plaza II - Ste. 00, 5410 Fredericksburg Rd., San Antonio, TX 78229-3555. Phone: (210) 281-7600.

Washington—Federal Office Bldg. - Ste. 00, 909 1st Ave., Seattle, WA 98104-1061. Phone: (206) 220-6883.

Wisconsin—Reuss Federal Plaza - Ste. 00, 310 W. Wisconsin Ave., Milwaukee, WI 53203-2292. Phone: (414) 297-1111.

AREA OFFICES

Arkansas—820 Louisiana St. - Ste. 00, Little Rock, AR 72201. Phone: (501) 324-5060.

California—410 B St. - Ste. 550, San Diego, CA 92101. Phone: (619) 557-7235.

Florida—501 E. Polk St. - Rm. 000, Tampa, FL 33602. Phone: (813) 228-2310.

Kansas—400 State Ave. - Ste. 05, Kansas City, KS 66101. Phone: (913) 551-5655.

Kentucky—U.S. Post Office and Courthouse - Rm. 68, 600 Martin Luther King Jr. Place, Louisville, KY 40202. Phone: (502) 582-6082.

Massachusetts—Kennedy Federal Bldg. - Rm. 75, One Congress St., Boston, MA 02203-0506. Phone: (617) 565-3200.

Minnesota—330 S. 2nd Ave. - Ste. 30, Minneapolis, MN 55401-2224. Phone: (612) 335-4040.

Mississippi—100 W. Capitol St. - Ste. 07, Jackson, MS 39269. Phone: (601) 965-4537.

New Jersey—One Newark Center - 21st fl., Newark, NJ 07102-5233. Phone: (973) 645-6383.

New Mexico—505 Marquette Ave. NW - Ste. 00, Albuquerque, NM 87102-2189. Phone: (505) 248-5201.

North Carolina—1309 Annapolis Dr., Raleigh, NC 27608-2129. Phone: (919) 856-4064.

Ohio—Peck Federal Office Bldg. - Ste. 0-019, 550 Main St., Cincinnati, OH 45202-3122. Phone: (513) 684-2851.

Oklahoma—Oklahoma Tower - Ste. 350, 210 Park Ave., Oklahoma City, OK 73102-2265. Phone: (405) 231-4911.

Pennsylvania—Federal Bldg. - Ste. 00, 1000 Liberty Ave., Pittsburgh, PA 15222-4187. Phone: (412) 644-3444.

Puerto Rico—Plaza Las Americas - Ste. 20L, 525 F.D Rooseveldt Ave., San Juan PR 00918-8001. Phone: (787) 771-1464.

Tennessee—50 Vantage Way - Ste. 02, Nashville, TN 37228. Phone: (615) 736-5820.

Texas—300 E. Main St. - Ste. 00, El Paso, TX 79901. Phone: (915) 534-6700.

Virginia—Federal Bldg. - Ste. 39, 200 Granby St., Norfolk, VA 23510. Phone: (757) 441-3470.

- 830 E. Main St. - Ste. 00, Richmond, VA 23219. Phone: (804) 771-2200.

30.001
through
30.011
(cont.)

LOCAL OFFICES

California—1265 W. Shaw Ave. - Ste. 03, Fresno, CA 93711. Phone: (559) 487-5793.

- 1301 Clay St. - Ste. 170-N, Oakland, CA 94612-5217. Phone: (510) 637-3230.
- 96 N. 3rd St. - Ste. 00, San Jose, CA 95112. Phone: (408) 291-7353.

Georgia—410 Mall Blvd. - Ste. G, Savannah, GA 31406-4821. Phone: (912) 652-4234.

Hawaii—300 Ala Moana Blvd. - Ste. -127, P.O. Box 50082, Honolulu, HI 96850-0051. Phone: (808) 541-3120.

New York—6 Fountain Plaza - Ste. 50, Buffalo, NY 14202. Phone: (716) 551-4441.

North Carolina—2303 W. Meadowview Dr. - Ste. 01, Greensboro, NC 27407. Phone: (336) 547-4188.

South Carolina—301 N. Main St. - Ste. 402, Greenville, SC 29601. Phone: (803) 241-4400.

EXPORT-IMPORT BANK
OF THE UNITED STATES

31.007

REGIONAL OFFICES

NORTHEAST AND MID-ATLANTIC *(Connecticut, Delaware, Maine, Maryland, Massachusetts, New Hampshire, New Jersey, New York, North Carolina, Pennsylvania, Rhode Island, Vermont, Virginia, Washington DC, West Virginia)*—33 Whitehall St., 22nd Fl. Ste. B, New York, NY 10004. Phone: (212) 809-2650; FAX (212) 809-2687.

SOUTHEAST *(Alabama, Florida, Georgia , Puerto Rico, South Carolina, U.S. Virgin Islands)*— 5835 Blue Lagoon Dr. Ste. 203, Miami, FL 33126. Phone: (305) 526-7436; FAX (305) 526-7435.

MIDWEST *(Chicago-Milwaukee Metro area, Illinois, Indiana, Iowa, Kansas, Kentucky, Michigan, Minnesota, Missouri, Nebraska, North Dakota, Ohio, South Dakota, Wisconsin)*— 200 West Adams St. Ste. 2450, Chicago, IL 60606. Phone: (312) 353-8081; FAX (312) 353-8098.

SOUTHWEST *(Arkansas, Colorado, Houston (east), Houston (west), Katy-Sugarland-Corpus Christi, TX, Mississippi, New Mexico, Oklahoma, San Antonio/Austin, Texas, Tennessee, Texas (south and west)*— 1880 S. Dairy Ashford II Ste. 405 Houston, TX 77077. Phone:(281) 721-0465; FAX (281) 679-0156.

North Texas Branch *(Dallas/Fort Worth, Louisiana, North Texas and Panhandle, Louisiana)*—1650 W. Virginia St. Ste. 110, McKinney, TX 75069. Phone: (214) 551-4959.

WESTERN

Orange County, CA Branch *(Alaska, Hawaii, Los Angeles County, Montana, Nevada (southern), Orange County, San Bernardino County, Utah (southern), Washington State, Wyoming)*—3300 Irvine Ave. Ste. 305, Newport Beach, CA 92660. Phone: (949) 660-1341; FAX (949) 660-9553.

San Diego, CA Branch *(Arizona, Imperial Valley County, Riverside County, San Diego County)*—9449 Balboa Ave. Ste. 111, San Diego, CA 92123. Phone: (858) 467-7035; FAX (858) 467-7043.

San Francisco, CA Branch *(East Bay, Idaho, Monterey, California (northern), Nevada (northern), Utah (northern), Oregon, San Francisco, San Francisco Peninsula, Santa Clara Counties, Santa Cruz, Vancouver WA)*—USEAC, 250 Montgomery St. - 14th Fl., San Francisco, CA 94104. Phone: (415) 705-2285; FAX: (415) 705-1156.

FEDERAL COMMUNICATIONS COMMISSION

32.001 ## REGIONAL OFFICES

California—3777 Depot Rd. - Rm. 20, Hayward, CA 94545-2756. Phone: (510) 732-9046.

Illinois—Park Ridge Office Center - Rm. 06, 1550 Northwest Hwy., Park Ridge, IL 60608-1460. Phone: (708) 298-5405.

Missouri—Brywood Office Tower - Rm. 20, 8800 E. 63rd St., Kansas City, MO 64133-4895. Phone: (816) 353-9035.

DISTRICT OFFICES

Alaska—6721 Raspberry Rd., Anchorage, AK 99502-1896. Phone: (907) 243-2153.

California—18000 Studebaker Rd. - Rm. 60, Cerritos, CA 90701-3684. Phones: (310) 809-2096, (310) 865-0598.

- 3777 Depot Rd. - Rm. 20, Hayward, CA 94545-2725. Phone: (510) 732-9046.
- Interstate Office Park, 4542 Ruffner St. - Rm. 70, San Diego, CA 92111-2216. Phone: (619) 467-0549.

Colorado—165 S. Union Blvd. - Ste. 60, Lakewood, CO 80228-2213. Phones: (303) 969-6497, 776-8026.

Florida—Rochester Bldg. - Rm. 10, 8390 NW 53rd St., Miami, FL 33166-4668. Phone: (305) 526-7420.

- 2203 N. Lois Ave. - Rm. 215, Tampa, FL 33607-2356. Phone: (813) 348-1502.

Georgia—Koger Center-Gwinnett - Rm. 20, 3575 Koger Blvd., Duluth, GA 30136-4958. Phone: (404) 279-4621.

- P.O. Box 85, Powder Springs, GA 30073-0085. Phones: (770) 943-5420, 242-0165.

Hawaii—P.O. Box 1030, Waipahu, HI 96797-1030. Phone: (808) 677-3318.

Illinois—Park Ridge Office Center - Rm. 06, 1550 Northwest Hwy., Park Ridge, IL 60068-1460. Phones: (708) 298-5401, -5402.

Louisiana—800 W. Commerce St. - Rm. 05, New Orleans, LA 70123-3333. Phone: (504) 589-2095.

Maine—P.O. Box 470, Belfast, ME 04915-0470. Phone: (207) 338-4088.

Maryland—P.O. Box 250, Columbia, MD 21045-9998. Phone: (301) 725-3474.

Massachusetts—One Batterymarch Park, Quincy, MA 02169-7495. Phone: (617) 770-4023.

Michigan—P.O. Box 89, Allegan, MI 49010-9437. Phone: (616) 673-2063.

- 24897 Hathaway St., Farmington Hills, MI 48335-1552. Phones: (810) 471-5605; *recorded information,* 471-0052.

Minnesota—2025 Sloan Pl. - Ste. 1, Maplewood, MN 55117-2058. Phone: (612) 774-5175.

Missouri—Brywood Office Tower - Rm. 20, 8800 E. 63rd St., Kansas City, MO 64133-4895. Phone: (816) 353-3773.

Nebraska—Grand Island, NE 68802-1588. Phone: (308) 382-4296 (*recorded information at night*).

New York—1307 Federal Bldg., 111 W. Huron St., Buffalo, NY 14202-2398. Phone: *recorded information,* (716) 551-4511.

- 201 Varick St., New York, NY 10014-4870. Phones: (212) 620-3437, -3438, 660-3437; *recorded information,* (212) 620-3435, 660-3436.

32.001   Oregon—1782 Federal Bldg., 1220 SW 3rd Ave., Portland, OR 97204-2898. Phones:
(cont.)   (503) 326-4114, -4115.

Puerto Rico—San Juan Field Office, Federal Bldg. - Rm. 47, Hato Rey, PR 00918-1731. Phone: (809) 766-5567.

Texas—P.O. Box 632, Kingsville, TX 78363-0632. Phone: (512) 592-2531.

Washington—11410 NE 122nd Way - Ste. 12, Kirkland, WA 98034-6927. Phone: (206) 821-9037.

Equipment Construction and Installation Branch

3600 Hiram-Lithia Spring Rd. SW, P.O. Box 65, Powder Springs, GA 30073. Phone: (404) 943-6425.

FOB Monitoring Assistance

Watch Officer, Signal Analysis Branch, Enforcement Division, 1919 M St. NW - Rm. 49, Washington, DC 20554. Phone: (202) 418-1180.

Field Operations Bureau

Chief, 1919 M St. NW - Rm. 34, Washington, DC 20554-0001. Phone: (202) 418-1100.

FEDERAL MARITIME COMMISSION

33.001   ## DISTRICT OFFICES

Houston—Houston Area Representative, 650 North Sam Houston Pkwy. Ste. 30, Houston, TX 77060. Phone: (281) 591-6088; FAX (281) 591-6099.

Los Angeles—Los Angeles Area Representative, U.S. Customs House Bldg. - Rm. 20, 839 S. Beacon St., San Pedro, CA 90733-0230. Phones: (310) 514-4905; FAX (310) 514-3931.

Miami—South Florida Area Representative, Federal Maritime Commission, Hollywood, FL 33081-3609. Phones: (305) 963-5362; FAX (305) 963-5630.

New Orleans—New Orleans Area Representative, U.S. Customs House - Rm. 09B, 423 Canal St., New Orleans, LA 70130. Phones: (504) 589-6662; FAX (504) 589-6663.

New York—New York Area Representative, JFK International Airport, Bldg. 75 - Rm. 05-B, Jamaica, NY 11430. Phone: (718) 553-2228; FAX (718) 553-2229.

Seattle—Seattle Area Representative, c/o U.S. Customs, 7 S. Nevada St. - Ste. 00, Seattle, WA 98134. Phones: (206) 553-0221; FAX (206) 553-0222.

FEDERAL MEDIATION AND CONCILIATION SERVICE

34.001   ## REGIONAL OFFICES

MIDWESTERN—6161 Oak Tree Blvd. - Ste. 00, Independence, OH 44131. Phones: (216) 522-4805; FAX (216) 522-7541.

NORTHEASTERN—One Newark Center - 16th fl., Newark, NJ 17102. Phones: (973) 645-2200; FAX (973) 297-4860.

SOUTHERN—401 W. Peachtree St. NW - Ste. 72, Atlanta, GA 30308. Phones: (404) 331-3995; FAX (404) 331-4017.

UPPER MIDWESTERN—Broadway Place West - Ste. 950, 1300 Godward St., Minneapolis, MN 55413. Phones: (612) 370-3300; FAX (612) 370-3104.

WESTERN—Westin Bldg. - Ste. 1000, 2001 6th Ave., Seattle, WA 98121. Phones: (206) 553-5800: FAX (206) 553-6653.

FEDERAL TRADE COMMISSION

36.001 ## REGIONAL OFFICES

California—10877 Wilshire Blvd. - Ste. 00, Los Angeles, CA 90024. Phone: (310) 824-4343.

■ 901 Market St. - Ste. 70, San Francisco, CA 94103. Phone: (415) 848-5100.

Georgia—225 Peachtree St. NE - Ste. 500, Atlanta, GA 30303. Phone: (404) 656-1390.

Illinois—55 E. Monroe St. - Ste. 825, Chicago, IL 60603. Phone: (312) 960-5634.

New York—One Bowling Green - Ste. 18, New York, NY 10004. Phone: (212) 607-2829.

Ohio—Eaton Center - Ste. 00, 1111 Superior Ave., Cleveland, OH 44114-2507. Phone: (216) 263-3455.

Texas—1999 Bryan St. - Ste. 150, Dallas, TX 75201-6808. Phone: (214) 979-9350.

Washington—915 2nd Ave. - Ste. 896, Seattle, WA 98174. Phone: (206) 220-6350.

GENERAL
SERVICES ADMINISTRATION

**39.002
through
39.007** ## Offices of Property Sales

NATIONAL CAPITOL REGION *(District of Columbia and the DC, Metropolitan area: In Maryland: Montgomery and Prince Georges counties. In Virginia: Arlington, Fairfax, Loudoun and Prince Williams counties)*—7th and D Sts. SW, Washington, DC 20407. Phone: (202) 260-6438.

REGION I *(Connecticut, Illinois, Indiana, Maine, Massachusetts, Michigan, Minnesota, New Hampshire, New Jersey, New York, Ohio, Puerto Rico, Rhode Island, Vermont, Virgin Islands, Wisconsin)*—10 Causeway St., Boston, MA 02222. Phone:(617) 565-5700.

REGION IV *(Alabama, Delaware, District of Columbia, Florida, Georgia, Kentucky, Maryland, Mississippi, North Carolina, Pennsylvania, South Carolina, Tennessee, Virginia, West Virginia)*—401 W. Peachtree St., Atlanta, GA 30365-2550. Phone: (404) 331-5133.

REGION VII *(Arkansas, Colorado, Iowa, Kansas, Louisiana, Missouri, Montana, Nebraska, New Mexico, North Dakota, Oklahoma, South Dakota, Texas, Utah)*—819 Taylor St., Ft. Worth, TX 76102. Phone: (817) 978-2331.

REGION IX *(American Samoa, Alaska, Arizona, California, Guam, Hawaii, Idaho, Oregon, Nevada, Trust Territory of the Pacific Islands, Washington)*—450 Golden Gate Ave. - 4th fl. E., San Francisco, CA 94102-3429. Phone: (415) 522-3429.

39.002 through 39.007 (cont.)

Federal Supply Service/Property Management Offices

GREAT LAKES REGION *(Illinois, Indiana, Michigan, Minnesota, Ohio, Wisconsin)*—230 S. Dearborn St. - Rm. 430, (MS 34-6), Chicago, IL 60604-1696. Phone: (312) 886-8996.

GREATER SOUTHWEST REGION *(Arkansas, Louisiana, New Mexico, Oklahoma, Texas)*—819 Taylor St. - Rm. A05, Ft. Worth, TX 76102-6105. Phone: (817) 978-3794.

HEARTLAND REGION *(Iowa, Kansas, Missouri, Nebraska)*—1500 E. Bannister Rd. - Rm. 102, Kansas City, MO 64131. Phone: (816) 823-3700.

MID-ATLANTIC REGION *(Delaware, Maryland, Virginia, Pennsylvania, West Virginia (except those areas in the National Capital Region))*—Strawbridge's Bldg. - 10th fl., 20 N. 8th St., Philadelphia, PA 19107-3191. Phone: (215) 446-5065.

NATIONAL CAPITAL REGION *(District of Columbia, the counties of Montgomery and Prince Georges in Maryland, the cities of Alexandria, Fairfax, and Falls Church and the counties of Arlington, Fairfax, Loudoun, and Prince William in Virginia)*—470 L'Enfant Plaza East SW - Ste. 100, Washington, DC 20407. Phone: (202) 619-8975.

- Central Office, GSA-FSS, 1901 S. Bell St. - Rm. 04, Arlington, VA 22202. Phone: (703) 605-5610.

NEW ENGLAND REGION *(Connecticut, Maine, Massachusetts, New Hampshire, Rhode Island, Vermont)*—O'Neill Jr. Federal Bldg. - Rm. 47 (3rd fl.), 10 Causeway St., Boston, MA 02222. Phone: (617) 565-7319.

NORTHEAST AND CARIBBEAN REGION *(New Jersey, New York, Puerto Rico, U.S. Virgin Islands)*—26 Federal Plaza - Rm. 0-112, New York, NY 10278. Phone: (212) 264-3300.

NORTHWEST/ARCTIC REGION *(Alaska, Idaho, Oregon, Washington)*—400 15th St. SW, Auburn, WA 98001-6599. Phone: (253) 931-7934.

PACIFIC RIM REGION *(American Samoa, Arizona, California, Guam, Hawaii, Nevada, Northern Mariana Islands)*—450 Golden Gate Ave., San Francisco, CA 94102-3434. Phone: (415) 522-3029.

ROCKY MOUNTAIN REGION *(Colorado, Montana, North Dakota, South Dakota, Utah, Wyoming)*—Denver Federal Center - Bldg. 41, P.O. Box 25506, Denver, CO 80225-0506. Phone: (303) 236-7700.

SOUTHEAST SUNBELT REGION *(Alabama, Florida, Georgia, Kentucky, Mississippi, North Carolina, South Carolina, Tennessee)*—401 W. Peachtree St. - Rm. 600, Atlanta, GA 30365. Phone: (404) 331-0040.

LIBRARY OF CONGRESS

42.001   *There are 57 regional and 77 subregional libraries in the U.S. Each state has an agency that distributes talking book machines. Local public libraries have information available. Consult local phone directories. Otherwise, contact headquarters office.*

NATIONAL AERONAUTICS AND SPACE ADMINISTRATION

43.001 through 43.010

FIELD CENTERS

Alabama—Marshall Space Flight Center, Huntsville, AL 35812. Phone: (256) 961-0954.

California—Ames Research Center, Moffett Field, CA 94035. Phones: (650) 604-6274, -6497.

- Dryden Flight Research Center, Edwards, CA 93523. Phone: (661) 276-7570.

Florida—John F. Kennedy Space Center, Kennedy Space Center, FL 32899. Phone: (321) 867-2959.

Maryland—Goddard Space Flight Center, Greenbelt, MD 20771. Phone: (301) 286-7205.

Mississippi—Stennis Space Center, Stennis Space Center, MS 39529. Phone: (228) 688-3333.

Ohio—Glenn Research Center, 21000 Brookpark Rd., Cleveland, Ohio 44135. Phone: (216) 433-4000.

Texas—Johnson Space Center, Houston, TX 77058. Phone: (281) 483-7011.

Virginia—Langley Research Center, Langley Station, Hampton, VA 23365. Phone: (757) 864-6300.

TECHNOLOGY UTILIZATION CENTERS

Alabama—Marshall Space Flight Center, (MS CD30), Marshall Space Flight Center, AL 35812. Phone: (205) 544-4266.

California—Ames Research Center, (MS 202A-3), Moffett Field, CA 94035-1000. Phone: (650) 604-1754.

- Dryden Flight Research Center, (MS 4839), Edwards, CA 93253-0273. Phone: (661) 276-3689.

- NASA Management Office-JPL, (MS 301-350), 4800 Oak Grove Dr., Pasadena, CA 91109-8099. Phone: (818) 354-3480.

District of Columbia—NASA Headquarters, Office of Exploration Systems, Washington, DC 20546-0001. Phone: (202) 358-2320.

Florida—Kennedy Space Center, (MS YA-C1), Kennedy Space Center, FL 32899-0001. Phone: (407) 867-6624.

Maryland—Goddard Space Flight Center, (MS 504), Greenbelt, MD 20771-0001. Phone: (301) 286-5810.

Mississippi—Stennis Space Center, (MS JAOO), Stennis Space Center, MS 39529-6000. Phone: (601) 688-1914.

Ohio—Glenn Research Center, (MS 3-7), 21000 Brookpark Rd., Cleveland, OH 44135. Phone: (216) 433-5398.

Texas—Johnson Space Center, (MS HA), 2101 NASA Road 1, Houston, TX 77058-3696. Phone: (281) 483-0474.

Virginia—Langley Research Center, (MS 118), 11 Langley Blvd., Hampton, VA 23681-0001. Phone: (757) 864-6005.

43.001 through 43.010 (cont.)

REGIONAL TECHNOLOGY TRANSFER CENTERS

Persons or organizations desiring comprehensive technical information may contact the Central Network at (800) 642-2872) or regional affiliates, following:

FAR WEST—3716 S. Hope St. - Ste. 00, Los Angeles, CA 90007-4344. Phone: (213) 743-2353.

- Montana State University Techlink Center - Ste. A, 900 Technology Blvd., Bozeman, MT 59718. Phone: (406) 994-7700.

MID-ATLANTIC—Technology Commercialization Center, Inc., 12050 Jefferson Ave. - Ste. 50, Newport News, VA 23606. Phone: (757) 269-0025.

- Research Triangle Institute Center for Technology Applications, P.O. Box 12194, Research Triangle Park, NC 27709. Phone: (919) 541-7205.

MID-CONTINENT—Texas Engineering Extension Service, Texas A and M University System, 301 Tarrow, College Station, TX 77843-8000. Phone: (979) 845-8762.

MIDWEST—Great Lakes Industrial Technology Center, Battelle Memorial Institute, 25000 Great Northern Corporate Center - Ste. 60, Cleveland, OH 44070-5310. Phone: (440) 734-0094.

NATIONAL RTTC—Wheeling Jesuit College, 316 Washington Ave., Wheeling, WV 26003. Phone: (800) 678-6882.

NORTHEAST—Center for Technology Commercialization, Westborough, MA 01581. Phone: (508) 870-0042.

SOUTHEAST—Georgia Tech Research Corp., Georgia Institute of Technology, Office of Sponsored Programs, Atlanta, GA 30332. Phone: (404) 894-6786.

RAILROAD RETIREMENT BOARD

57.001

REGIONAL OFFICES

Colorado—1999 Broadway - Ste. 300 (Box 7), Denver CO 80202-5737. Phone: (303) 844-0800.

Georgia—401 W. Peachtree St. - Ste. 703, Atlanta, GA 30308-3519. Phone: (404) 331-2691.

Pennsylvania—NIX Federal Bldg. - Ste. 04, 900 Market St., Philadelphia, PA 19107-4228. Phone: (215) 597-2647.

SECURITIES AND EXCHANGE COMMISSION

58.001

REGIONAL OFFICES

California—5670 Wilshire Blvd. - 11th fl., Los Angeles, CA 90036-3648. Phone: (213) 965-3998. **Internet:** e-mail, "losangeles@sec.gov".

Colorado—1801 California St. - Ste. 500, Denver, CO 80202-2656. Phone: (303) 844-1000. **Internet:** e-mail, "denver@sec.gov".

Florida—801 Brickell Ave. - Ste. 800, Miami, FL 33131. Phone: (305) 982-6300. **Internet:** e-mail, "miami@sec.gov".

Illinois—175 W. Jackson Blvd. - Ste. 00, Chicago, IL 60604. Phone: (312) 353-7390. **Internet:** e-mail, "chicago@sec.gov".

New York—3 World Financial Cntr. Ste. 400, New York, NY 10281-1022. Phone: (212) 336-1100. **Internet:** e-mail, "newyork@sec.gov".

DISTRICT OFFICES

California—44 Montgomery St. - Ste. 600, San Francisco, CA 94104. Phone: (415) 705-2500. **Internet:** e-mail, "sanfrancisco@sec.gov".

Georgia—3475 Lenox Rd. NE - Ste. 000, Atlanta, GA 30326-1232. Phone: (404) 842-7600. **Internet:** e-mail, "atlanta@sec.gov".

Massachusetts—33 Arch St. 23 fl., Boston, MA 02110-1424. Phone: (617) 573-8900. **Internet:** e-mail, "boston@sec.gov".

Pennsylvania—Mellon Independence Center, 701 Market St., Philadelphia, PA 19106-1532. Phone: (215) 597-3100. **Internet:** e-mail, "philadelphia@sec.gov".

Texas—Burnett Plaza Ste. 900, 801 Cherry St., Unit 18, Ft. Worth, TX 76102. Phone: (817) 978-3821. **Internet:** e-mail, "dfw@sec.gov".

Utah—15 W. South Temple St. - Ste. 800, Salt Lake City, UT. 84101. Phone: (801) 524-5796. **Internet:** e-mail, "saltlake@sec.gov".

SMALL BUSINESS ADMINISTRATION

59.006 through 59.063

REGIONAL AND DISTRICT OFFICES

REGION I *(Connecticut, Maine, Massachusetts, New Hampshire, Rhode Island, Vermont)*—10 Causeway St. - Ste. 12, Boston, MA 02222. Phone: (617) 565-8416; FAX (617) 565-8420.

Connecticut—Federal Bldg., 330 Main St. - 2nd fl., Hartford, CT 06106. Phone: (203) 240-4700.

Maine—Federal Bldg. - Rm. 12, 68 Sewall St., Augusta, ME 04330. Phone: (207) 622-8274, ext.386.

Massachusetts—10 Causeway St. - Rm. 65, Boston, MA 02222-1093. Phone: (617) 565-5561.

- One Federal St. - Bldg.101-R, Springfield, MA 01105. Phone: (413) 785-0484.

New Hampshire—55 Pleasant St. - Ste. 101, Concord, NH 03301-1257. Phone: (603) 225-1400.

Rhode Island—380 Westminster Mall - 5th fl., Providence, RI 02903. Phone: (401) 528-4561.

Vermont—Federal Bldg. - Rm. 05, 87 State St., Montpelier, VT 05602. Phone: (802) 828-4422.

REGION II *(New Jersey, New York, Puerto Rico, Virgin Islands)*—26 Federal Plaza - Ste. 108, New York, NY 10278. Phone: (212) 264-1450.

New Jersey—2 Gateway Center - 15th fl., Newark, NJ 07102. Phone: (973) 645-3680.

New York—Federal Bldg. - Rm. 311, 111 W. Huron St., Buffalo, NY 14202. Phone: (716) 551-4305.

- 333 E. Water St. - 4th fl., Elmira, NY 14901. Phone: (607) 734-1571.

- 35 Pinelawn Rd. - Ste. 07W, Melville, NY 11747. Phone: (516) 454-0750.

**59.006
through
59.063
(cont.)**

■ 26 Federal Plaza - Rm. 1-00, New York, NY 10278. Phone: (212) 264-1318.

■ 100 State St. - Ste. 10, Rochester, NY 14614. Phone: (716) 263-6700.

■ 401 S. Salina St. - 5th fl., Syracuse, NY 13202. Phone: (315) 471-9393.

Puerto Rico and U.S. Virgin Islands—Degatau Federal Bldg. - Ste. 01, 252 Ponce DeLeon Blvd., San Juan, PR 00918. Phone: (787) 766-5002.

REGION III *(Delaware, District of Columbia, Maryland, Pennsylvania, Virginia, West Virginia)*—Parkview Tower, 1150 First Avenue Ste. 1001, King of Prussia, PA 19406. Phone: (610) 383-3092.

Delaware Branch Office—1007 N. Orange St. - Ste. 120, Wilmington, DE 19801. Phone: (302) 573-6294.

District of Columbia—740 15th St. - 3rd fl., Washington, DC 20005. Phone: (202) 272-0340.

Maryland—10 S. Howard St. - Ste. 220, Baltimore, MD 21201-2565. Phone: (410) 962-6195.

Pennsylvania—100 Chestnut St. - Rm. 07, Harrisburg, PA 17101. Phone: (717) 782-3840.

■ 900 Market St. - 5th fl., Philadelphia, PA 19406. Phone: (215) 580-2700.

■ 411 7th Ave. - Ste. 450, Pittsburgh, PA 15219. Phone: (412) 395-6560.

■ 7 N. Wilkes-Barre Blvd., Wilkes-Barre, PA 18702. Phone: (570) 826-6497.

Virginia—400 N. 8th St. - Ste. 150, Richmond, VA 23240-0126. Phone: (804) 771-2400.

West Virginia—320 W. Pike St., Clarksburg, WV 26301. Phone: (304) 623-5631.

REGION IV *(Alabama, Florida, Georgia, Kentucky, Mississippi, North Carolina, South Carolina, Tennessee)*—233 Peachtree Street, NE Suite 1800, Atlanta, GA 30303. Phone: (404) 331-4999; FAX (404) 331-2354.

Alabama—801 Tom Martin Dr. - Ste. 01, Birmingham, AL 35203-2398. Phone: (205) 290-7101.

Florida—7825 Baymeadows Way - Ste. 00-B, Jacksonville, FL 32256-7504. Phone: (904) 443-1900.

■ 100 S. Biscayne Blvd. - 7th fl., Miami FL 33131. Phone: (305) 536-5521.

Georgia—233 Peachtree St., NE, Atlanta, GA 30303. Phone: (404) 331-0100.

Kentucky—Federal Bldg. - Rm. 88, 600 Martin Luther King Jr. Pl., Louisville, KY 40202. Phone: (502) 582-5971.

Mississippi—2510 14th St. - Ste. 01, Gulfport, MS 39501. Phone: (228) 863-4449.

■ 210 E. Capital St. - 210E, Jackson, MS 39201. Phone: (601) 965-4378.

North Carolina—6302 Fairview Rd. - Ste. 00, Charlotte, NC 28210-2227. Phone: (704) 344-6563.

South Carolina—1835 Assembly St. - Rm. 58, Columbia, SC 29201. Phone: (803) 765-5377.

Tennessee—50 Vantage Way - Ste. 01, Nashville, TN 37228-1500. Phone: (615) 736-5850.

REGION V *(Illinois, Indiana, Michigan, Minnesota, Ohio, Wisconsin)*—Citicorp Cntr. - Ste. 240, 500 W. Madison St., Chicago, IL 60661-2511. Phone: (312) 353-0357.

Illinois—500 W. Madison St. - Rm. 250, Chicago, IL 60661-2511. Phone: (312) 353-4508.

■ 511 W. Capitol Ave. - Ste. 02, Springfield, IL 62704. Phone: (217) 492-4416.

Indiana—429 N. Pennsylvania St. - Ste. 00, Indianapolis, IN 46204-1873. Phone: (317) 226-7272.

Minnesota—100 N. 6th St. - Ste. 10C, Minneapolis, MN 55403-1563. Phone: (612) 370-2306.

Michigan—477 Michigan Ave. - Rm. 15, Detroit, MI 48226. Phone: (313) 226-7204.

■ 501 S. Front St., Marquette, MI 49885. Phone: (906) 225-1108.

Ohio—1350 Euclid St. - Ste. 11, Cleveland, OH 44115. Phone: (216) 522-4180.

■ 525 Vine St. - Ste. 70, Cincinnati, OH 45202. Phone: (513) 684-2814.

■ 2 Nationwide Plaza - Ste. 400, Columbus, OH 43215-2592. Phone: (614) 469-6860.

Wisconsin—740 Regent St. - Ste. 00, Madison, WI 53715. Phone: (608) 264-5263.

■ 310 W. Wisconsin Ave. - Ste. 00, Milwaukee, WI 53202. Phone: (414) 297-3941.

REGION VI *(Arkansas, Louisiana, New Mexico, Oklahoma, Texas)*—4300 Amon Carter Blvd. - Ste. 08, Ft. Worth, TX 76155. Phone: (817) 684-5581; FAX (817) 884-5588.

Arkansas—2120 Riverfront Dr. - Ste. 00, Little Rock, AR 72202. Phone: (501) 324-5871.

Louisiana—365 Canal St. - Ste. 250, New Orleans, LA 70130. Phone: (504) 589-6685.

New Mexico—625 Silver Ave. SW, - Ste. 20, Albuquerque, NM 87102. Phone: (505) 346-7909.

Oklahoma—301 N. 6th St. - Ste. 16, Oklahoma City, OK 73102. Phone: (405) 609-8000.

Texas—3649 Leopard St. - Ste. 11, Corpus Christi, TX 78408. Phone: (361) 879-0017.

■ 10737 Gateway West - Ste. 20, El Paso, TX 79935. Phone: (915) 633-7001.

■ 4300 Amon Center Blvd. - Ste. 14, Ft. Worth, TX 76155. Phone: (817) 885-6500.

■ Lower Rio Grande Valley District Office, 222 E. Van Buren St. - Rm. 00, Harlingen, TX 78550. Phone: (956) 427-8533.

■ 8701 S. Gessner Dr. - Ste. 200, Houston, TX 77074. Phone: (713) 773-6500.

■ 1205 Texas Ave. - Rm. 08, Lubbock, TX 79401-2693. Phone: (806) 472-7462.

■ 7319 San Pedro Bldg.2 - Ste. 00, San Antonio, TX 78232. Phone: (210) 403-5904.

REGION VII *(Iowa, Kansas, Missouri, Nebraska)*—1000 Walnut Ste. 530, Kansas City, MO 64106, Phone: (816) 426-4840; FAX (816) 426-4848.

Iowa—215 4th Ave. SE - Ste. 00, Cedar Rapids, IA 52401-1806. Phone: (319) 362-6405.

■ New Federal Bldg. - Rm. 49, 210 Walnut St., Des Moines, IA 50309. Phone: (515) 284-4026.

Kansas—271 W. 3rd St. N. - Ste. 500, Wichita, KS 67202. Phone: (316) 269-6566.

Missouri—323 W. 8th St. - Ste. 01, Kansas City, MO 64105. Phone: (816) 374-6708.

■ 830 E. Primrose - Ste. 01, Springfield, MO 65807. Phone: (417) 890-8501.

■ 200 N. Broadway - Ste. 500, St. Louis, MO 63102. Phone: (314) 539-6600.

Nebraska—11145 Mill Valley Rd., Omaha, NE 68154. Phone: (402) 221-4691.

REGION VIII *(Colorado, Montana, North Dakota, South Dakota, Utah, Wyoming)*—721 19th St. - Ste. 00, Denver, CO 80202-2599. Phone: (303) 844-0500; FAX (303) 844-0506.

Colorado—721 19th St. - Rm. 26, Denver, CO 80202-2599. Phone: (303) 844-2607.

Montana—301 S. Park Ave. - Rm. 34, Helena, MT 59626. Phone: (406) 441-1081.

North Dakota—Federal Bldg. - Rm. 19, 657 2nd Ave. N., Fargo, ND 58108-3086. Phone: (701) 239-5131.

South Dakota—110 S. Phillips Ave. - Ste. 00, Sioux Falls, SD 57104-6727. Phone: (605) 330-4243.

59.006 through 59.063 (cont.)

Utah—Federal Bldg. - Rm. 231, 125 S. State St., Salt Lake City, UT 84138-1195. Phone: (801) 524-5804.

Wyoming—Federal Bldg. - Rm. 001, 100 E. "B" St., Casper, WY 82602-2839. Phone: (307) 261-6500.

REGION IX *(Arizona, California, Hawaii, Nevada, Pacific Islands)*—330 N. Brand Blvd. - Ste. 270, Glendale, CA 91203. Phone: (818) 552-3436; FAX (818) 552-3434.

Arizona—2828 N. Central Ave. - Ste. 00, Phoenix, AZ 85004-1093. Phone: (602) 745-7200.

California—2719 N. Air Fresno Dr. - Ste. 00, Fresno, CA 93727-1547. Phone: (559) 487-5791.

- 330 N. Brand Blvd. - Ste. 200, Glendale, CA 91203-2304. Phone: (818) 552-3210.

- 650 Capital Mall - Ste. -5000, Sacramento, CA 95814. Phone: (916) 930-3700.

- 500 W. C St. - Ste. 50, San Diego, CA 92101-3540. Phone: (619) 557-7250.

- 455 Market St. - 6th fl., San Francisco, CA 94105. Phone: (415) 744-6801.

- 200 W. Santa Ana Blvd. - Ste. 00, Santa Ana, CA 92701. Phone: (714) 550-7420.

Hawaii—300 Ala Moana Blvd. - Rm. -235, Honolulu, HI 96850-4981. Phone: (808) 541-2990.

Guam—400 Route 8 - Ste. 02, Hagatna, GU 96910-2003. Phone: (671) 471-7419.

Nevada—400 S. 4th St. - Ste. 50, Las Vegas, NV 89101. Phone: (702) 388-6611.

REGION X *(Alaska, Idaho, Oregon, Washington)*—2401 4th Ave. Ste. 400, Seattle, WA 98121. Phone: (206) 553-5676. FAX (206) 553-4155.

Alaska—222 W. 8th Ave. - Rm.A36, Anchorage, AK 99513-7559. Phone: (907) 271-4022.

Idaho—1020 Main St. - Ste. 90, Boise, ID 83702-5745. Phone: (208) 334-1696.

Oregon—1515 SW 5th Ave. - Ste. 050, Portland, OR 97201-5494. Phone: (503) 326-2682.

Washington—1200 6th Ave. - Ste. 700, Seattle, WA 98101-1128. Phone: (206) 553-7310.

- 801 W. Riverside Ave. - Ste. 00., Spokane, WA 99201-0901. Phone: (509) 353-2809.

DISASTER AREA OFFICES

Customer Service Center (Nationwide Call Center), 130 South Elmwood Ave. Ste. 516, Buffalo, NY 14202. Phones: Toll Free, 1-800-659-2955, (716) 843-4100, TTY (800) 877-8339; FAX (716) 843-4281. Internet e-mail: disastercustomerservice@sba.gov.

Center East (Regions I V)101 Marietta Street NW Ste. 700, Atlanta, GA 30303-2725. Phones: Toll Free, 1-800-659-2955, (404) 331-0333, TTY (404) 331-7296: FAX 1-800-798-3807, (404) 331-0273.

Center West (Regions VI X)P.O. Box 419004, Sacramento, CA 95841-9004. Phones: Toll Free, 1-800-488-5323, (916) 735-1500, TTY (916) 735-1683.

U.S Export Assistance Centers

California—3300 Irvine Ave. - #305, Newport Beach, CA 92660-3198. Phone: (949) 660-1688, ext.115; FAX (949) 660-1338.

- 6501 Sylvan Rd., Citrus Heights, CA 95610. Phone: (916) 735-1708; Fax (202) 741-6851.

Colorado—1625 Broadway Ave. - Ste. 80, Denver, CO 80202. Phone: (303) 844-6623, ext.218; FAX (303) 844-5651.

Florida—5835 Blue Lagoon Dr. - Ste. 03, Miami, FL 33126. Phone: (305) 526-7425, ext.21; FAX (305) 526-7434.

Georgia—75 5th St. NW - Ste. 055, Atlanta, GA 30308. Phone: (404) 897-6089. FAX(404) 897-6085.

Illinois—200 West Adams St. Ste. 2450, Chicago, IL 60606. Phone: (312) 353-8065; FAX: (202) 481-2281.

Maryland—300 West Pratt St. Ste. 00, Baltimore, MD 21201.

Massachusetts—JFK Federal Bldg. Ste. 1826A, 55 New Sudbury St., Boston, MA 02203. Phone: (617) 565-4305; FAX (617) 565-4313.

Michigan—8109 E. Jefferson Ave. Ste. 110, Detroit, MI 48214. Phone: (313) 226-3670; FAX (313) 226-3657.

Minnesota—100 N. 6th St., 210-C Butler Sq., Minneapolis, MN 55403. Phone: (612) 348-1642; FAX (612) 348-1650.

Missouri—8235 Forsyth Blvd. - Ste. 20, St. Louis, MO 63105. Phone: (314) 425-3304; FAX (314) 425-3381.

New York—33 Whitehall St. - 22nd fl., New York, NY 10004. Phone: (212) 809-2645; FAX (212) 809-2687.

North Carolina—521 E. Morehead St. - Ste. 35, Charlotte, NC 28202. Phone: (704) 333-4886; FAX (704) 332-2681.

Ohio—600 Superior Ave. - Ste. 00, Cleveland, OH 44114. Phone: (216) 522-4731; FAX (216) 522-2235.

Oregon—One World Trade Center - Ste. 42, 121 SW Salmon St., Portland, OR 97204. Phone: (503) 326-5498; FAX (202) 481-2257.

Pennsylvania—The Curtis Center - Ste. 80 W., 601 Walnut St., Philadelphia, PA 19106. Phone: (215) 597-6110; FAX (202) 481-5216.

Texas—1450 Hughes Rd. Ste. 220, Grapevine, TX 76051. Phone: (817) 310-3749; FAX: (817) 310-3757.

Washington—4th and Vine Blvd., 2601 4th Ave. - Ste. 20, Seattle, WA 98121. Phone: (206) 553-0051. FAX (206) 553-7253.

DEPARTMENT OF VETERANS AFFAIRS

VETERANS HEALTH ADMINISTRATION

64.007 through 64.026

VETERANS MEDICAL FACILITIES

Alabama—700 S. 19th St., Birmingham, AL 35233. Phone: (205) 933-8101.

- 215 Perry Hill Rd., Montgomery, AL 36109-3798. Phone: (334) 272-4670.
- Tuscaloosa, AL 35404. Phone: (205) 554-2000.
- Tuskegee, AL 36083. Phone: (304) 727-0550.

Alaska—Medical/Regional Office Center, 235 E. 8th Ave., Anchorage, AK 99508-2989. Phone: (907) 257-4700.

Arizona—7th St. at Indian School Rd., Phoenix, AZ 85012. Phone: (602) 277-5551.

- Prescott, AZ 86313-5000. Phone: (520) 445-4860.
- Tucson, AZ 85723-0001. Phone: (520) 792-1450.

64.007
through
64.026
(cont.)

Arkansas—Fayetteville, AR 72703. Phone: (501) 443-4301.

■ 300 E. Roosevelt Rd., Little Rock, AR 72205. Phone: (501) 660-1202.

California—2615 E. Clinton Ave., Fresno, CA 93703-2223. Phone: (209) 225-6100.

■ Livermore, CA 94550. Phone: (510) 447-2560.

■ 11201 Benton St., Loma Linda, CA 90822-5201. Phone: (909) 825-7084.

■ 5901 E. 7th St., Long Beach, CA 90822-5201. Phone: (310) 494-2611.

■ 3801 Miranda Ave., Palo Alto, CA 94304-1207. Phone: (415) 493-5000.

■ 2800 Contra Costa Blvd., Pleasant Hill, CA 94523-3961. Phone: (510) 372-2000.

■ 3350 La Jolla Village Dr., San Diego, CA 92161-0001. Phone: (619) 552-8585.

■ 4150 Clement St., San Francisco, CA 94121-1598. Phone: (415) 221-4810.

■ Sepulveda, CA 91343-2099. Phone: (818) 891-7711.

■ 11301 Wilshire Blvd., West Los Angeles, CA 90073-1002. Phone: (310) 478-3711.

Colorado—1055 Clermont St., Denver, CO 80220-0166. Phone: (303) 399-8020.

■ Ft. Lyon, CO 81038-5000. Phone: (719) 384-3100.

■ Grand Junction, CO 81501-6499. Phone: (303) 242-0731.

Connecticut—55 Willard Ave., Newington, CT 06111. Phone: (860) 666-6951.

■ West Spring St., West Haven, CT 06516. Phone: (203) 932-5711.

Delaware—1601 Kirkwood Hwy., Wilmington, DE 19805. Phone: (302) 994-2511.

District of Columbia—50 Irving St. NW, Washington, DC 20422. Phone: (202) 745-8000.

Florida—Bay Pines, FL 33744. Phone: (813) 398-6661.

■ Archer Rd., Gainesville, FL 32608-1197. Phone: (325) 376-1611.

■ Lake City, FL 32055-5898. Phone: (904) 755-3016.

■ 1201 NW 16th St., Miami, FL 33125. Phone: (305) 324-4455.

■ Bruce B. Downs Blvd., Tampa, FL 33612. Phone: (813) 972-2000.

■ West Palm Beach, FL 33420-3207. Phone: (561) 882-6700.

Georgia—1670 Clairmont Rd., Atlanta, GA 30033. Phone: (404) 321-6111.

■ 2460 Wrightsboro Rd., Augusta, GA 30904-6285. Phone: (706) 733-0188.

■ 2460 Wrightsboro Rd., Dublin, GA 31021. Phone: (912) 272-1210.

Idaho—5th and Fort St., Boise, ID 83702-4598. Phone: (208) 336-5100.

Illinois—333 E. Huron St., Chicago, IL 60611. Phone: (312) 943-6600.

■ 820 S. Damen Ave., Chicago, IL 60612. Phone: (312) 666-6500.

■ Danville, IL 61832-5198. Phone: (217) 442-8000.

■ Hines, IL 60141-5000. Phone: (708) 343-7200.

■ 2401 W. Main St., Marion, IL 62959. Phone: (618) 997-5311.

■ North Chicago, IL 60064. Phone: (847) 688-1900.

Indiana—1600 Randallia Dr., Ft. Wayne, IN 46805-5100. Phone: (219) 426-5431.

■ 1481 W. 10th St., Indianapolis, IN 46202-2884. Phone: (317) 635-7401.

■ 46952 E. 38th St., Marion, IN 46953-4589. Phone: (317) 674-3321.

Iowa—30th and Euclid Ave., Des Moines, IA 50310-5774. Phone: (515) 699-5999.

■ Highway 6 W., Iowa City, IA 52246-2208. Phone: (319) 338-0581.

■ 1515 W. Pleasant St., Knoxville, IA 50138-3399. Phone: (515) 842-3101.

Kansas—4201 S. 4th St. Traffic Way, Leavenworth, KS 66048. Phone: (913) 682-2000.

■ 2200 Gage Blvd., Topeka, KS 66622. Phone: (913) 272-3111.

■ 5500 E. Kellogg, Wichita, KS 67218. Phone: (316) 685-2221.

Kentucky—Leestown Rd., Lexington, KY 40511-1093. Phone: (606) 233-4511.

■ 800 Zorn Ave., Louisville, KY 40206-1499. Phone: (502) 895-3401.

Louisiana—Shreveport Hwy., Alexandria, LA 71301. Phone: (318) 473-0010.

■ 1601 Perdido St., New Orleans, LA 70146. Phone: (504) 568-0811.

■ 510 E. Stoner Ave., Shreveport, LA 71101-4295. Phone: (318) 221-8411.

Maine—Rt. 17 E., Togus, ME 04330. Phone: (207) 623-8411.

Maryland—Baltimore, Ft. Howard and Perry Point Divisions, 3900 Lock Raven Blvd., Baltimore, MD 21201. Phone: (410) 605-7000.

Massachusetts—200 Spring Rd., Bedford, MA 01730. Phone: (617) 275-7500.

■ 150 S. Huntington Ave., Boston, MA 02130. Phone: (617) 232-9500.

■ 940 Belmont St., Brockton, MA 02401. Phone: (508) 583-4500.

■ N. Main St., Northampton, MA 01060-1288. Phone: (413) 584-4040.

■ 1400 Veterans of Foreign Wars Pkwy., West Roxbury, MA 02401. Phone: (508) 583-4500.

Michigan—2215 Fuller Rd., Ann Arbor, MI 48105-2300. Phone: (313) 769-7100.

■ 5500 Armstrong Rd., Battle Creek, MI 49016-0544. Phone: (616) 966-5600.

■ Detroit, MI 48201-1932. Phone: (313) 576-1000.

■ Iron Mountain, MI 49801. Phone: (906) 779-3150.

■ 1500 Weiss St., Saginaw, MI 48602-5298. Phone: (517) 793-2340.

Minnesota—54th St. and 48th Ave. S., Minneapolis, MN 55417. Phone: (612) 725-2000.

■ 8th St., N. 44th Ave., St. Cloud, MN 56303. Phone: (612) 252-1670.

Mississippi—Pass Rd., Biloxi, MS 39531. Phone: (601) 388-5541.

■ 1500 E. Woodrow Wilson Dr., Jackson, MS 39216. Phone: (601) 362-4471.

Missouri—800 Stadium Rd., Columbia, MO 65201. Phone: (573) 443-2511.

■ 4801 Linwood Blvd., Kansas City, MO 64128. Phone: (816) 861-4700.

■ Hwy. 67 N., Poplar Bluff, MO 63901. Phone: (573) 686-4151.

■ Jefferson Barracks, St. Louis, MO 63125. Phone: (314) 487-0400.

■ 915 N. Grand Blvd., St. Louis, MO 63106. Phone: (314) 652-4100.

Montana—William St. and Hwy. 12 W., Ft. Harrison, MT 59636-1500. Phone: (406) 447-7900

■ 210 S. Winchester, Miles City, MT 59301-4798. Phone: (406) 232-3060.

Nebraska—2201 N. Broad Well, Grand Island, NE 68803-2153. Phone: (308) 382-3660.

■ 600 S. 70th St., Lincoln, NE 68510-2493. Phone: (402) 489-3802.

■ 4101 Woolworth Ave., Omaha, NE 68105-1873. Phone: (402) 346-8800.

Nevada—1703 Charleston Blvd., Las Vegas, NV 89102-2395. Phone: (702) 385-3700.

■ 1000 Locust St., Reno, NV 89520-0111. Phone: (702) 786-7200.

New Hampshire—718 Smyth Rd., Manchester, NH 02104. Phone: (603) 624-4366.

New Jersey—Tremont Ave. and S. Center, East Orange, NJ 07018. Phone: (201) 676-1000.

■ Valley and Knollcroft Rd., Lyons, NJ 07939. Phone: (201) 647-0180.

New Mexico—2100 Ridgecrest Dr. SE, Albuquerque, NM 87108-5138. Phone: (505) 256-2843.

New York—113 Holland Ave., Albany, NY 12208. Phone: (518) 462-3311.

■ Redfield Pkwy., Batavia, NY 14020. Phone: (716) 343-7500.

64.007 through 64.026 (cont.)

- Medical Center, Argonne Ave., Bath, NY 14810. Phone: (607) 776-2111.
- 130 W. Kingsbridge Rd., Bronx, NY 10468. Phone: (718) 584-9000.
- 800 Poly Pl., Brooklyn, NY 11209. Phone: (718) 630-3521.
- 3495 Bailey Ave., Buffalo, NY 14215. Phone: (716) 834-9200.
- Ft. Hill Ave., Canandaigua, NY 14424. Phone: (716) 394-2000.
- Castle Point, NY 12511. Phone: (914) 831-2000.
- Old Albany Post Rd., Montrose, NY 10548. Phone: (914) 737-1216.
- 1st Ave. at E. 24th St., New York, NY 10010. Phone: (212) 951-5959.
- Long Island-Middleville Rd., Northport, NY 11768. Phone: (516) 261-4400.
- Irving Ave. at University Place, Syracuse, NY 13210. Phone: (315) 477-7461.

North Carolina—Asheville, NC 28805. Phone: (704) 299-7431.

- 508 Fulton St., Durham, NC 27705. Phone: (919) 286-0411.
- 2300 Ramsey St., Fayetteville, NC 28301. Phone: (910) 822-7059.
- 1601 Brenner Ave., Salisbury, NC 28144. Phone: (704) 638-9000.

North Dakota—2101 Elm St., Fargo, ND 58102. Phone: (701) 232-3241.

Ohio—17273 State Rt. 104, Chillicothe, OH 45601. Phone: (614) 773-1141.

- 3200 Vine St., Cincinnati, OH 45220. Phone: (513) 475-6300.
- 10701 East Blvd., Cleveland, OH 44106-3800. Phone: (216) 791-3800.
- Medical Center Nursing Home and Domiciliary, 4100 W. 3rd St., Dayton, OH 45428. Phone: (513) 262-2170.

Oklahoma—125 S. Main St., Muskogee, OK 74401. Phone: (918) 683-3261.

- 921 NE 13th St., Oklahoma City, OK 73104. Phone: (405) 270-0501.

Oregon—3710 SW U.S. Veterans Hospital Rd., Portland, OR 97207-1034. Phone: (503) 220-8262.

- New Garden Valley Blvd., Roseburg, OR 97470-6153. Phone: (541) 440-1000.
- Domiciliary, White City, OR 97503-3207. Phone: (541) 826-2111.

Pennsylvania—Pleasant Valley Blvd., Altoona, PA 16602-4377. Phone: (814) 943-8164.

- New Castle Rd., Butler, PA 16001-2480. Phone: (412) 287-4781.
- Coatesville, PA 19320. Phone: (610) 384-7711.
- 135 E. 38th St., Erie, PA 16504. Phone: (814) 868-8661.
- S. Lincoln Ave., Lebanon, PA 17042. Phone: (717) 272-6621.
- University and Woodland Ave., Philadelphia, PA 19104. Phone: (215) 823-5800.
- Highland Dr., Pittsburgh, PA 15206. Phone: (412) 363-4900.
- University Dr., Pittsburgh, PA 15240. Phone: (412) 688-6000.
- 1111 East End Blvd., Wilkes-Barre, PA 18711-0026. Phone: (717) 824-3521.

Puerto Rico—Barrio Monacillos, Rio Piedras, PR 00927-5800. Phone: (787) 758-7575.

Rhode Island—380 Westminster Mall, Providence, RI 02908-4799. Phone: (401) 273-7100.

South Carolina—109 Bee St., Charleston, SC 29401-5799. Phone: (803) 577-5011.

- 1801 Assembly St., Columbia, SC 29201-1639. Phone: (803) 776-4000.

South Dakota—I-90 and Hwy. 34, Ft. Meade, SD 57741. Phone: (605) 745-2000.

- 5th St., Hot Springs, SD 57757. Phone: (605) 745-2000.
- 2501 W. 22nd St., Sioux Falls, SD 57117. Phone: (605) 336-3230.

Tennessee—1030 Jefferson Ave., Memphis, TN 38104-2193. Phone: (901) 523-8990.

- Mountain Home, TN 37684. Phone: (423) 926-1171.

- 3400 Lebanon Rd., Murfreesboro, TN 37129-1236. Phone: (615) 893-1360.
- 1310 24th Ave. S., Nashville, TN 37212-2637. Phone: (615) 327-4751.

Texas—6010 Amarillo Blvd. W., Amarillo, TX 79106. Phone: (806) 355-9703.

- 2400 S. Gregg St., Big Spring, TX 79720. Phone: (915) 263-7361.
- Sam Rayburn Memorial Veterans Center, Bonham, TX 75418. Phone: (903) 583-2111.
- 4500 S. Lancaster Rd., Dallas, TX 75216. Phone: (214) 376-5451.
- 5919 Brook Hollow Dr., El Paso, TX 79925. Phone: (915) 564-6100.
- 2002 Holcombe Blvd., Houston, TX 77030. Phone: (713) 479-1414.
- Memorial Blvd., Kerrville, TX 78028. Phone: (210) 896-2020.
- 1016 Ward St., Marlin, TX 76661. Phone: (817) 883-3511.
- 7400 Merton Minter Blvd., San Antonio, TX 78284. Phone: (210) 617-5300.
- 1901 S. 1st St., Temple, TX 76504. Phone: (817) 778-4811.
- 4800 Memorial Dr., Waco, TX 76711. Phone: (817) 752-6581.

Utah—500 Foothill Blvd., Salt Lake City, UT 84148-0001. Phone: (801) 582-1565.

Vermont—White River Junction, VT 05001-0001. Phone: (802) 295-9363.

Virginia—Emancipation Dr., Hampton, VA 23667. Phone: (804) 722-9961.

- 1201 Broad Rock Rd., Richmond, VA 23249. Phone: (804) 230-0001.
- 1970 Roanoke Blvd., Salem, VA 24153. Phone: (540) 982-2463.

Washington—American Lake, WA 98493. Phone: (206) 762-1010.

- 1660 S. Columbian Way, Seattle, WA 98108. Phone: (206) 762-1010.
- North 4816 Assembly St., Spokane, WA 99205-6197. Phone: (509) 328-4521.
- 77 Wainwright Dr., Walla Walla, WA 99362-3975. Phone: (509) 525-5200.

West Virginia—200 Veterans Ave., Beckley, WV 25801. Phone: (304) 255-2121.

- Milford and Chestnut St., Clarksburg, WV 26301. Phone: (304) 623-3461.
- 1540 Spring Valley Dr., Huntington, WV 25704. Phone: (304) 429-6741.
- Rt. 9, Martinsburg, WV 25401-9809. Phone: (304) 263-0811.

Wisconsin—2500 Overlook Terrace, Madison, WI 53705. Phone: (608) 256-1901.

- 5000 W. National Ave., Milwaukee, WI 53295. Phone: (414) 384-2000.
- Tomah, WI 54660. Phone: (608) 372-3971.

Wyoming—2360 W. Pershing Blvd., Cheyenne, WY 82001-5392. Phone: (307) 778-7300.

- Fort Rd., Sheridan, WY 82801-8320. Phone: (307) 672-1675.

VETERANS BENEFITS ADMINISTRATION

FIELD OFFICES

64.027 through 64.028

Note: DVA provides toll-free phone service throughout the 50 states, Washington DC, and Puerto Rico: (800) 827-1000.

Alabama—345 Perry Hill Rd., Montgomery, AL 36109-3798.

Alaska—2925 DeBarr Rd., Anchorage, AK 99508-2989.

Arizona—3225 N. Central Ave., Phoenix, AZ 85012-2405.

Arkansas—2200 Ft. Roots - Bldg. 65, North Little Rock, AR 72115-1280.

California—Federal Bldg., 11000 Wilshire Blvd., Los Angeles, CA 90024-3602.

- Oakland Federal Bldg., 1301 Clay St., Oakland, CA 94612-5209.
- 8810 Rio San Diego Dr., San Diego, CA 92108-1508.

64.027
through
64.028
(cont.)

Colorado—155 Van Gordon St., Lakewood, CO 80228-1709.

Connecticut—450 Main St., Hartford, CT 06103-3077.

Delaware—1601 Kirkwood Hwy., Wilmington, DE 19805-4988.

District of Columbia—1120 Vermont Ave. NW, Washington, DC 20421-1111.

Florida—9500 Bay Pines Blvd., P.O. Box 1437, St. Petersburg, FL 33731.

Georgia—1700 Clairmont Rd., Decatur, GA 30033-4032.

Hawaii—459 Patterson Rd. - E-Wing, P.O. Box 29020, Honolulu, HI 96820.

Idaho—805 W. Franklin St., Boise, ID 83702-5560.

Illinois—2122 W. Taylor St., Chicago, IL 60612.

Indiana—575 N. Pennsylvania St., Indianapolis, IN 46204-1526.

Iowa—210 Walnut St. - Rm. 063, Des Moines, IA 50309-9825.

Kansas—5500 E. Kellogg, Wichita, KS 67218-1698.

Kentucky—321 W. Main St. Ste. 390, Louisville, KY 40202.

Louisiana—701 Loyola Ave. - Rm. 210, New Orleans, LA 70113-1912.

Maine—1 VA Center, Togus, ME 04330-6795.

Maryland—Federal Bldg. - Rm. 33, 31 Hopkins Plaza, Baltimore, MD 21201-0001.

Massachusetts—JFK Federal Bldg., Government Center - Rm. 265, Boston, MA 02203-0393.

Michigan—McNamara Federal Bldg. - Rm. 400, 477 Michigan Ave., Detroit, MI 48226-2591.

Minnesota—Federal Bldg., Ft. Snelling, St. Paul, MN 55111-4050.

Mississippi—1600 E. Woodrow Wilson Ave., Jackson, MS 39216-5102.

Missouri—400 S. 18th St., St. Louis, MO 63103-2676.

Montana—Williams St., Ft. Harrison, MT 59636-9999.

Nebraska—5631 S. 48th St., Lincoln, NE 68516-4198.

Nevada—1201 Terminal Way, Reno, NV 89520-0118.

New Hampshire—Cotton Federal Bldg., 275 Chestnut St., Manchester, NH 03101-2489.

New Jersey—20 Washington Pl., Newark, NJ 07102-3174.

New Mexico—Chavez Federal Bldg. and U.S. Courthouse, 500 Gold Ave. SW, Albuquerque, NM 87102-3118.

New York—130 South Elmwood Ave., Buffalo, NY 14202.

■ 245 W. Houston St., New York, NY 10014-4805.

North Carolina—Federal Bldg., 251 N. Main St., Winston-Salem, NC 27155-1000.

North Dakota—2101 Elm St., Fargo, ND 58102-2417.

Ohio—1240 E. 9th St., Cleveland, OH 44199-2001.

Oklahoma—Federal Bldg., 125 S. Main St., Muskogee, OK 74401-7025.

Oregon—Federal Bldg. - Rm. 217, 1220 SW 3rd Ave., Portland, OR 97204-2825.

Pennsylvania—5000 Wissahickon Ave., Philadelphia, PA 19101-8079.

■ 1000 Liberty Ave., Pittsburgh, PA 15222-4004.

Philippines—1131 Roxas Blvd., Ermita 0930, Manila, PI 96440.

■ Manila Regional Office and Outpatient Clinic, FPO AP 96515-1100.

Puerto Rico—U.S. Courthouse and Federal Bldg., Carlos E. Chardon St., Hato Rey, San Juan, PR 00936-4867. Phone: (809) 766-5510.

Rhode Island—380 Westminster Mall, Providence, RI 02903-3246.

South Carolina—1801 Assembly St., Columbia, SC 29201-2495.

South Dakota—2501 W. 22nd St., Sioux Falls, SD 57117-5046.

Tennessee—U.S. Courthouse Federal Office Bldg., 110 9th Ave. S., Nashville, TN 37203-3817.

Texas—6900 Almeda Rd., Houston, TX 77030-4200.

- One Veteran Plaza, 701 Clay Ave., Waco, TX 76799-0001.

Utah—Federal Bldg., 125 S. State St., P.O. Box 11500, Salt Lake City, UT 84158.

Vermont—215 Main St., White River Junction, VT 05009-0001.

Virginia—210 Franklin Rd. SW, Roanoke, VA 24011-2204.

Washington—Federal Bldg., 915 2nd Ave., Seattle, WA 98174-1060.

West Virginia—640 4th Ave., Huntington, WV 25701-1340.

Wisconsin—5400 W. National Ave., Milwaukee, WI 53214.

Wyoming—2360 E. Pershing Blvd., Cheyenne, WY 82001.

64.029   Listed under **64.007.**

64.030   Listed under **64.027.**
through
64.128

NATIONAL CEMETERY SYSTEM

64.201   ## AREA OFFICES
through
64.202   **California**—1301 Clay St. - 1230 North, Oakland, CA 94612-5209. Phone: (510) 637-6270.

Colorado—P.O. Box 25126, Denver, CO 80225. Phone: (303) 914-5700.

Georgia—1700 Clairmont Rd. - 4th fl., Decatur, GA 30333-4032. Phone: (404) 929-5899.

Indiana—575 N. Pennsylvania St., Indianapolis, IN 46204. Phone: (317) 226-0205.

Pennsylvania—5000 Wissahickon Ave., Philadelphia, PA 19144. Phone: (215) 381-3787.

MEMORIAL PROGRAMS PROCESSING SITES

Kansas—Ft. Leavenworth National Cemetery, 395 Biddle Blvd., Ft. Leavenworth, KS 66027-2307. Phones: Toll Free, 1-888-460-9709, (913) 758-1805; FAX (913) 758-1839.

Pennsylvania—Lebanon VA Medical Center - Bldg.27, 1700 S. Lincoln Ave., Lebanon, PA 17042. Phones: Toll free, 1-888-574-9107, (717) 270-9424; FAX (717) 270-9428.

Tennessee—Nashville Processing Site, 220 Athens Way - Ste. 102, Nashville, TN 37228-1346. Phones: Toll free, 1-888-367-1330, (615) 736-2841, ext.228; FAX(615) 736-2026.

Virginia—Logistics Management Service, 5105 Russell Rd., Quantico, VA 22134. Phone: (703) 441-4014.

- 5109 Russell Road, Quantico, VA 22134. Phones: *Program Support Unit,* (202) 501-3028; *Applicant Assistance Unit,* (202) 501-3078; *Presidential Certificate Program,* (202) 565-4259.

ENVIRONMENTAL PROTECTION AGENCY

66.001
through
66.472

REGIONAL GRANTS MANAGEMENT CONTACTS

REGION I *(Connecticut, Maine, Massachusetts, New Hampshire, Rhode Island, Vermont)*—One Congress St. - Ste. 100, (MC MGM), Boston, MA 02114-2023. Phones: (617) 918-1972; FAX (617) 918-1929.

REGION II *(New Jersey, New York, Puerto Rico, Virgin Islands)*—Grants Administration Branch, (OPM-GRA), 290 Broadway, New York, NY 10007-1866. Phones: (212) 637-3402; FAX (212) 637-3518.

REGION III *(Delaware, District of Columbia, Maryland, Pennsylvania, Virginia, West Virginia)*—Grants Management Section, Office of the Comptroller, (3PM70), 1650 Arch St., Philadelphia, PA 19103-2029. Phones: (215) 814-5410; FAX (215) 814-5271.

REGION IV *(Alabama, Florida, Georgia, Kentucky, Mississippi, North Carolina, South Carolina, Tennessee)*—Grants and Contracts Administration Section, Management Division, 61 Forsyth St. SW, Atlanta, GA 30303-8960. Phones: (404) 562-8371; FAX (404) 562-8370.

REGION V *(Illinois, Indiana, Michigan, Minnesota, Ohio, Wisconsin)*—Acquisition and Assistance Branch, (MC 10J), 77 W. Jackson Blvd., Chicago, IL 60604-3507. Phones: (312) 886-2400; FAX (312) 353-9096.

REGION VI *(Arkansas, Louisiana, New Mexico, Oklahoma, Texas)*—Grants Audit Section, (6M-PG), Management Division, First International Bldg., 1445 Ross Ave., Dallas, TX 75202-2733. Phones: (214) 665-6510; FAX (214) 665-7284.

REGION VII *(Iowa, Kansas, Missouri, Nebraska)*—Grants Administration Branch, 901 N. 5th St., Kansas City, KS 66101. Phones: (913) 551-7346; FAX (913) 551-7579.

REGION VIII *(Colorado, Montana, North Dakota, South Dakota, Utah, Wyoming)*—Grants Administration Branch, (8PM-GFM), 999 18th St. - Ste. 00, Denver, CO 80202-2466. Phones: (303) 312-6305; FAX (303) 312-6685.

REGION IX *(American Samoa, Arizona, California, Guam, Hawaii, Nevada, Trust Territories of Pacific Islands, Wake Island)*—Grants and Finance Branch, 75 Hawthorne St., San Francisco, CA 94105. Phones: (415) 744-1693; FAX (415) 744-1678.

REGION X *(Alaska, Idaho, Oregon, Washington)*—Grants Administration Unit, 1200 6th Ave., Seattle, WA 98101. Phones: (206) 553-2722; FAX (206) 553-4957.

CHEMICAL EMERGENCY PREPAREDNESS AND PREVENTION OFFICE (CEPP)

Regional Offices

REGION I—One Congress St. - Ste. 100, (MC SEP), Boston, MA 02114-2023. Phone: (617) 918-1804.

REGION II—Bldg. 209, 2890 Woodbridge Ave., Edison, NJ 08837-3679. Phone: (732) 906-6194.

REGION III—1650 Arch St., (MC 3HS33), Philadelphia, PA 19103. Phone: (215) 814-3273.

REGION IV—Air Division - 12th fl., 61 Forsyth St. SW, Atlanta, GA 30303. Phone: (404) 562-9085.

REGION V—77 W. Jackson Blvd., (MC SC-6J), Chicago, IL 60604. Phone: (312) 353-9045.

REGION VI—1445 Ross Ave., (MC 6SF-RO), Dallas, TX 75202-2733. Phone: (214) 665-2270.

REGION VII—901 N. 5th St., (MC ATRDCRIB), Kansas City, KS 66101. Phone: (913) 551-7540.

REGION VIII—One Denver Place, (MC EPR-SA), 999 18th St. - Ste. 00, Denver, CO 80202-2405. Phone: (303) 312-6760.

REGION IX—75 Hawthorne St., (MC SFD 9-3), San Francisco, CA 94105. Phone: (415) 972-3039.

REGION X—1200 6th Ave., (MC ECL-116), Seattle, WA 99101. Phone: (206) 553-8414.

Municipal Solid Waste Primary Contacts

REGION I—One Congress St. - Ste. 100, (MC SPP-SPP), Boston, MA 02114-2023. Phones: (617) 918-1813; FAX (617) 918-1810.

REGION II—290 Broadway, (MC 2DEPP-RPB), New York, NY 10007-1866. Phones: (212) 637-4125; FAX (212) 637 4437.

REGION III—1650 Arch St., (MC 3WC21/3HW60), Philadelphia, PA 19103. Phones: (215) 814-3298; FAX (215) 814-3163.

REGION IV—Atlanta Federal Center, (MC 4WD-RPB/RSS), 61 Forsyth St., Atlanta, GA 30303-3104. Phones: (404) 562-8449; FAX (404) 562-8439.

REGION V—77 W. Jackson Blvd., (MC DRP-8J), Chicago, IL 60604-3590. Phones: (312) 886-0976; FAX (312) 353-4788.

REGION VI—1445 Ross Ave., (MC 6PD-U), Dallas, TX 75202-2733. Phones: (214) 665-6760; FAX (214) 665-7263.

REGION VII—901 N. 5th St., (MC ARTD/SWPP), Kansas City, KS 66101. Phones: (913) 551-7523; FAX (913) 551-7947.

REGION VIII—999 18th St. - Ste. 00, (MC 8P-P3T), Denver, CO 80202-2466. Phones: (303) 312-6099; FAX (303) 312-6044.

REGION IX—75 Hawthorne St., (MC WST-7), San Francisco, CA 94105. Phones: (415) 744-1284; FAX (415) 744-1044.

REGION X—1200 6th Ave., (MC WCM-128), Seattle, WA 98101. Phones: (206) 553-6117; FAX (206) 553-8509.

Pollution Prevention Contacts

REGION I—JFK Federal Bldg. - Rm. 203 (SPN), Boston, MA 02203. Phones: (617) 918-1817; FAX (617) 918-4939.

REGION II—290 Broadway - 25th fl. (2-OPM-PPI), DEPP, New York, NY 10007-1866. Phones: (212) 637-3742; FAX (212) 637-3771.

REGION III—1650 Arch St. (3RA20), Philadelphia, PA 19103-2029. Phones: (215) 814-2761; FAX (215) 566-2782.

REGION IV—Air and Pesticide Center, 61 Forsyth St. SW, Atlanta, GA 30303. Phones: (404) 562-9430; FAX (404) 562-9066.

REGION V—Waste, Pesticide and Toxics Division, 77 W. Jackson Blvd. (DRP-8J), Chicago, IL 60604-3590. Phones: (312) 353-4669; FAX (312) 353-4788.

REGION VI—Compliance Assurance and Enforcement Division, 1445 Ross Ave. - Ste. 200 (6EN-XP), Dallas, TX 75202. Phones: (214) 665-2119; FAX (214) 665-7446.

66.001
through
66.472
(cont.)

REGION VII—Air, RCRA and Toxics Division, 726 Minnesota Ave., (ARTD/TSPP), Kansas City, KS 66101. Phones: (913) 551-7517; FAX (913) 551-7065.

REGION VIII—Office of P2, State and Tribal Assistance, 999 18th St.- Ste. 00 (8P2-P2), Denver, CO 80202-2466. Phones: (303) 312-6385; FAX (303) 312-6339.

REGION IX—Waste Division, 75 Hawthorne St. (WST-1-1), San Francisco, CA 94105. Phones: (415) 744-2192; FAX (415) 744-1796.

REGION X—Office of Innovation, 1200 6th Ave., Seattle, WA 98101. Phones: (206) 553-4072; FAX (206) 553-6647.

RCRA and Superfund

REGION I—Office of Ecosystem Protection, (MC HHA) and/or Office of Site Remediation and Restoration, One Congress St., Boston, MA 02114-2023. Phones: (617) 918-1501, -1201.

REGION II—Division of Environmental Planning and Protection, 26 Federal Plaza - Rm. 000 (2AWM-SW), New York, NY 10278. Phone: (212) 637-3772.

- Emergency and Remedial Response Division, 290 Broadway, New York, NY 10007. Phones: (212) 637-4390.

REGION III—Waste Chemical Management Division, 841 Chestnut Bldg. (3HWOO), Philadelphia, PA 19107. Phones: (215) 814-2005.

- Hazardous Site Cleanup Division, 1650 Arch St., Philadelphia, PA 19106. Phone: (215) 813-3143.

REGION IV—Waste Management Division, 61 Forsyth St., Atlanta, GA 30303. Phones: (404) 562-8651.

REGION V—Waste, Pesticides and Toxics Division, 77 W. Jackson Blvd., Chicago, IL 60604-3507. Phones: (312) 353-2024.

- Superfund Division, Metcalfe Federal Bldg., 77 W. Jackson Blvd., Chicago, IL 60604. Phone: (312) 353-9773.

REGION VI—Multimedia Planning and Permitting Division and/or Superfund Division, Fountain Place - Ste. 200, 1445 Ross Ave., Dallas, TX 75202-2733. Phones: (214) 665-7200, -6701.

REGION VII—Air/RCRA Toxics Division and/or Superfund Division, 901 N. 5th St., Kansas City, KS 66101. Phones: (913) 551-7020, -7664.

REGION VIII—Hazardous Waste Program, (MC 8P2-SA), Denver Place - Ste. 00, 999 18th St., Denver, CO 80202-2466. Phones: (303) 312-7081.

- Office of Ecosystems Protection and Remediation, 999 18th St. - Ste. 00, Denver, CO 80202. Phone: (303) 312-6598.

REGION IX—Waste Division and/or Hazardous Waste Management Division, 75 Hawthorne St., San Francisco, CA 94105. Phones: (415) 744-2138, -1730.

REGION X—Office of Waste and Chemical Management and/or Office of Environmental Cleanup, 1200 6th Ave., Seattle, WA 98101. Phones: (206) 553-4198, -7151.

Radon Regional Program Office Contacts

REGION I—JFK Federal Bldg. - Ste. 100, One Congress St., (MC CPT), Boston, MA 02114-2023.

REGION II—290 Broadway - 28th fl., (MC R2DEPDIV), New York, NY 10007-1866.

REGION III—1650 Arch St., (MC 3AP23), Philadelphia, PA 19103-2029.

REGION IV—61 Forsyth St. SW, Atlanta, GA 30303-3104..

REGION V—77 W. Jackson Blvd., (MC AE-17J), Chicago, IL 60604-3590.

REGION VI—1445 Ross Ave., Dallas, TX 75202-2733.

REGION VII—901 N. 5th St., (MC ARTD/RALI), Kansas City, KS 66101.

REGION VIII—999 18th St. - Ste. 00, (MC 8P-AR), Denver, CO 80202-2466.

REGION IX—75 Hawthorne St., (MC Air-6), San Francisco, CA 94105.

REGION X—1200 6th Ave., (MC OAQ-107), Seattle, WA 98101-9797.

Beach Monitoring

REGION I *(Connecticut, Maine, Massachusetts, New Hampshire, Rhode Island, Vermont)*—One Congress St. - Ste. 110, (COP), Boston, MA 02114-2023. Phone: (617) 918-1626.

REGION II *(New Jersey, New York, Puerto Rico, U.S. Virgin Islands)*—2890 Woodbridge Ave., (MS 220), Edison, NJ 08837-3679. Phone: (732) 321-6797.

REGION III *(Delaware, District of Columbia, Maryland, Pennsylvania, Virginia, West Virginia)*—1650 Arch St., (3ES10), Philadelphia, PA 19103-2029. Phone: (215) 814-5776.

REGION IV *(Alabama, Florida, Georgia, Kentucky, Mississippi, North Carolina, South Carolina, Tennessee)*—61 Forsyth St. - 15th fl., Atlanta, GA 30303-3415. Phone: (404) 562-9274.

REGION V *(Illinois, Indiana, Michigan, Minnesota, Ohio, Wisconsin)*—77 W. Jackson Blvd., (WT-16J), Chicago, IL 60604-3507. Phone: (312) 353-6704.

REGION VI *(Arkansas, Louisiana, New Mexico, Oklahoma, Texas)*—1445 Ross Ave., (6WQ-EW), Dallas, TX 75202-2733. Phone: (214) 665-7314.

REGION VII *(Iowa, Kansas, Missouri, Nebraska)*—726 Minnesota Ave., Kansas City, KA 66101. Phone: (913) 551-7828.

REGION VIII *(Colorado, Montana, North Dakota, South Dakota, Utah, Wyoming)*—999 18th St. Ste. 500, Denver, CO 80202-2466. Phone: (303) 312-6833.

REGION IX *(American Samoa, Arizona, California, Commonwealth of the Mariana Islands, Guam, Hawaii, Nevada)*—75 Hawthorne St., (WtR-2), San Francisco, CA 94105. Phones: (415) 972-3462, -3452.

REGION X *(Alaska, Idaho, Oregon, Washington)*—120 6th Ave., (OW-134), Seattle, WA 98101. Phone: (206) 553-1597.

GULF OF MEXICO PROGRAM—Gulf of Mexico Program Office, Bldg. 1100 Rm. 02, Stennis Space Cntr., MS 39529-6000. Phone: (228) 688-1576.

National Estuary Program Offices

REGION I—Water Quality Policy Division, Boston, MA 02114-2023. Phone: (617) 918-1511.

REGION II—Environmental Planning and Protection Division, 290 Broadway, New York, NY 10007-1866. Phone: (212) 637-3724.

REGION III—Environmental Services Division, 1650 Arch St., Philadelphia, PA 19103-2029. Phone: (215) 814-2989.

REGION IV—Water Management Division, 61 Forsyth St. SW, Atlanta, GA 30303. Phone: (404) 562-9345.

REGION VI—Water Quality Protection Division, 1445 Ross Ave., Dallas, TX 75202-2733. Phone: (214) 655-7101.

REGION IX—Water Management Division, 75 Hawthorne St., San Francisco, CA 94105. Phone: (415) 744-1860.

REGION X—Office of Ecosystems and Communities, 1200 6th Ave., Seattle, WA 98101. Phone: (206) 553-4181.

Wetland Program Offices

REGION I—One Congress St. - Ste. 00, (MC CSP), Boston, MA 02114. Phone: (617) 918-1669.

66.001 through 66.472 (cont.)

REGION II—290 Broadway, New York, NY 10007. Phone: (212) 637-3817.

REGION III—1650 Arch St., (MC 3EA30), Philadelphia, PA. 19103. Phone: (215) 814-2099.

REGION IV—61 Forsyth St. SW, Atlanta, GA 30303. Phone: (404) 562-9269.

REGION V—77 W. Jackson Blvd., (MC WW16J), Chicago, IL 60604. Phone: (312) 886-0241.

REGION VI—1445 Ross Ave., (MC 6WQ-AT), Dallas, TX 75202. Phone: (214) 665-7275.

REGION VII—901 N 5th St., Kansas City, KS 66101. Phone: (913) 551-7297, -7542.

REGION VIII—999 18th St. - Ste. 00, Denver, CO 80202. Phone: (303) 312-6235.

REGION IX—75 Hawthorne St., San Francisco, CA 94105. Phone: (415) 972-3415, -3468.

REGION X—1200 6th Ave., Seattle, WA 98101. Phone: (206) 553-6219.

66.473   Assistance and Pollution Prevention Office

REGION I—JFK Federal Bldg., One Congress St. - Ste. 100, Boston, MA 02114-2023. Phone: (617) 918-1883; FAX (617) 918-1505.

REGION II—290 Broadway, New York, NY 10007-1866. Phone: (212) 637-3564; FAX (212) 637-3772.

REGION IV—61 Forsyth St., Atlanta, GA 30303. Phone: (404) 562-8632; FAX (404) 562-9961.

REGION V—77 W. Jackson Blvd. (R-21J), Chicago, IL 60604-3590. Phone: (312) 353-2087; FAX (312) 385-5393.

REGION VI—1445 Ross Ave. (6RA-DT), Dallas, TX 75202. Phone: (214) 665-8355; FAX (214) 665-6648.

REGION VII—901 N. 5th St. (PLMG-POIS), Kansas City, KS 66101. Phone: (913) 551-7381; FAX (913) 551-7053, -7267.

REGION VIII— 1595 Wynkoop St. (MC 8P-TA), Denver, CO 80202-1129. Phone: (303) 312-6343; Fax (303) 312-6116.

REGION IX—75 Hawthorne St. (MC CED-3), San Francisco, CA 94105. Phone: (415) 972-3554.

REGION X—1200 6th Ave., Seattle, WA 98101. Phone: (206) 553-2102; FAX (206) 553-0151.

66.474 through 66.600

Listed under **66.001.**

66.604   Environmental Justice

REGION I—One Congress St. - Ste. 100 (RAA), Boston, MA 02203-0001. Phone: (617) 918-1346; FAX (617) 918-0346.

REGION II—290 Broadway Rm. 637, New York, NY 10007. Phone: (212) 637-5027; FAX(212) 637-4943.

REGION III—1650 Arch St. (3ECOO), Philadelphia, PA 19103. Phone: (215) 814-2988; FAX (215) 814-2905.

REGION IV—61 Forsyth St., Atlanta, GA 30303. Phone: (404) 562-9649; (404) 562-9664.

REGION V—77 W. Jackson Blvd. (C14), Chicago, IL 60604-3507. Phone: (312) 353-8894.

REGION VI—Fountain Place - 12th fl., 1445 Ross Ave. (6RA-D), Dallas, TX 75202-2733. Phone: (214) 665-7401; FAX (214) 665-6648.

REGION VII—901 N. 5th St. (ECORA), Kansas City, KS 66101. Phone: (913) 551-7649; FAX (913) 551-9649.

REGION VIII—1595 Wynkoop St., Denver, CO 80202-1129. Phone: (303) 312-0653; FAX (303) 312-6191.

REGION IX—75 Hawthorne St. (CEO-1), San Francisco, CA 94105. Phone: (415) 972-3795; FAX (415) 947-8026.

REGION X—1200 6th Ave. (CRE-164), Seattle, WA 98101. Phone: (206) 553-2899; FAX (206) 553-7176.

**66.605
through
66.701**   Listed under **66.001.**

Pollution Prevention Information Network

**66.707
through
66.717**

REGION I—One Congress St. - Ste. 100, (MC SPN), Boston, MA 02114-2023. Phones: (617) 918-1814; FAX (617) 918-1810.

REGION II—290 Broadway - 25th fl., (MC SPMMB), New York, NY 10007-1866. Phones: (212) 637-3758; FAX (212) 637-3771.

REGION III—1650 Arch St., (MC 3HS32), Philadelphia, PA 19103. Phones: (215) 814-5412, -2074; FAX (215) 814-3274.

REGION IV—Atlanta Federal Center, 61 Forsyth St. SW, Atlanta, GA 30303. Phones: (404) 562-9384; FAX (404) 562-8482.

REGION V—77 W. Jackson Blvd., (MC DW-8J), Chicago, IL 60604-3590. Phones: (312) 866-4669; FAX (312) 353-4788.

REGION VI—1445 Ross Ave. - Ste. 1200, (MC 6EN-XP), Dallas, TX 75202. Phones: (214) 665-6431, -2127; FAX (214) 665-7446.

REGION VII—901 N. 5th St., (MC ARTD/SWPP), Kansas City, KS 66101. Phones: (913) 551-7669; FAX (913) 551-7065.

REGION VIII—999 18th St. - Ste. 00, (MC 8P-P3T). Denver, CO 80202-2466. Phones: (303) 312-6385; FAX (303) 312-6339.

REGION IX—75 Hawthorne St., (MC WST-7), San Francisco, CA 94105. Phones: (415) 972-3283, -3288; FAX (415) 744-1680.

REGION X—1200 6th Ave. Ste. 00, (MC 01-085), Seattle, WA 98101. Phones: (206) 553-4072, -4803; FAX (206) 553-8338.

Pesticide Environmental Stewardship Program

REGION I—One Congress St. - Ste. 100 (CPT), Boston, MA 02114-2023. Phone: (617) 918-1198.

REGION II—2890 Woodbridge Ave., (MS 500), Edison, NJ 08837-3679. Phone: (732) 906-6183.

REGION III—1650 Arch St. (3WC32), Philadelphia, PA 19103-2029. Phone: (215) 814-2129.

REGION IV—61 Forsyth St. SW, Atlanta, GA 30303-8960. Phone: (404) 562-9014.

REGION V—77 W. Jackson Blvd. (DT-8J), Chicago, IL 60604-3507. Phone: (312) 886-3572.

REGION VI—1445 Ross Ave. - Ste. 200 (6PD-P), Dallas, TX 75202-2733. Phone: (214) 665-7562.

REGION VII—901 N. 5th St. (WWPDPEST), Kansas City, KS 66101. Phone: (913) 551-7640.

REGION VIII—999 18th St. - Ste. 00 (8P-P3T), Denver, CO 80202-2466. Phone: (303) 312-6286.

66.707
through
66.717
(cont.)

REGION IX—75 Hawthorne St. (CMD-1), San Francisco, CA 94105. Phone: (415) 947-4240.

REGION X—24106 N.Bunn Rd. (WSU-IAREC), Prosser, WA 99350. Phone: (509) 786-9225.

66.801
through
66.816

Superfund Regional Administrators

REGION I—Office of Site Remediation and Restoration, One Congress St., (MC HBS), Boston, MA 02114-2023. Phones: Toll Free, 1-888-372-7341, (617) 918-1421; FAX (617) 918-1291.

REGION II—Grants and Contracts Management Branch, Office of Policy and Management, 290 Broadway - 27th fl., (MC 2 OPM-GCMB), New York, NY 10007-1866. Phones: (212) 637-3420; FAX (212) 637-3518.

REGION III—1650 Arch St., (MC 3HS52), Philadelphia, PA 19103. Phones: Toll Free, 1-800-553-2509, (215) 814-5522; FAX (215) 814-5518.

REGION IV—Waste Management Division, Program Services Branch, Atlanta Federal Center, 61 Forsyth St., (MC WDCSB), Atlanta, GA 30303. Phones: Toll Free, 1-800-564-7577, (404) 562-8880(DB), -8867(RF); FAX (404) 562-8842.

REGION V—Office of Public Affairs and Community Involvement Section (MC P-19J), Superfund Division and Contracts and Assistance Agreements Section (MC SM-5J), 77 W. Jackson Blvd., Chicago, IL 60604-3507. Phones: Toll Free, 1-800-621-8431, (312) 353-1325, 886-6044; FAX (312) 353-1155, 886-0186.

REGION VI—Wells Fargo Bank, Tower at Fountain Place - Ste. 200, 1445 Ross Ave., (MC 6SF-PO), Dallas, TX 75202-2733. Phones: Toll Free, 1-800-533-3508, (214) 665-8157, -8163; FAX (214) 665-6660.

REGION VII—Office of External Programs, 901 N. 5th St., (MC PBAF), Kansas City, KS 66101. Phones: Toll Free, 1-800-223-0425, (913) 551-7762; FAX (913) 551-7066.

REGION VIII—Office of Communications and Public Involvement, 999 18th St. - Ste. 00, (MC 8EPR-PS), Denver, CO 80202-2466. Phones: Toll Free, 1-800-227-8917, (303) 312-6696; FAX (303) 312-6065.

REGION IX—Office of Community Involvement, 75 Hawthorne St., (MC SFD-3), San Francisco, CA 94105. Phones: Toll Free, 1-800-231-3075, (415) 972-3237; FAX (415) 947-3528.

REGION X—Community Involvement and Outreach Unit, 1200 6th Ave., (MC ECO-081), Seattle, WA 98101. Phones: Toll Free, 1-800-424-4372, (206) 553-0247, -1237; FAX (206) 553-2955.

HEADQUARTERS—Community Involvement and Outreach Branch, Ariel Rios Bldg., 1200 Pennsylvania Ave., NW, (MC 5204G), Washington DC 20460. Phones: (703) 603-8889; FAX (703) 603-9100.

Underground Storage Tank Regional Program Managers

REGION I—One Congress St. - Ste. 100, Boston, MA 02114-2023. Phone: (617) 918-1311.

REGION II—Water Compliance Branch (2DECA-WCB-GWCS), 290 Broadway, New York, NY 10007-1866. Phone: (212) 637-4232.

REGION III—State Programs Branch (3WC21), 1650 Arch St., Philadelphia, PA 19103. Phone: (215) 814-3231.

REGION IV—Atlanta Federal Center, 61 Forsyth St. SW, (MC GW-PB-15), Atlanta, GA 30303-3104. Phone: (404) 562-9441.

REGION V—Underground Storage Tanks (DRU-7J), 77 W. Jackson Blvd., Chicago, IL 60604-3590. Phone: (312) 886-6136.

REGION VI—1st Interstate Bank Tower - Ste. 200. (6PD-U), 1445 Ross Ave., Dallas, TX 75202-2733. Phone: (214) 665-6760.

REGION VII—901 N. 5th St., Kansas City, KS 66101. Phone: (913) 551-7547.

REGION VIII—999 18th St. - Ste. 00 (8P2-W-GW), Denver, CO 80202-2466. Phone: (303) 312-6137.

REGION IX—75 Hawthorne St. - 10th fl. (H-W-4), San Francisco, CA 94105. Phone: (415) 744-2079.

REGION X—1200 6th Ave. (WD-133), Seattle, WA 98101. Phone: (206) 553-1563.

CEPP TECHNICAL ASSISTANCE

REGION I—One Congress St. - Ste. 100, (MC SEP), Boston, MA 02114-2023. Phone: (617) 918-1804.

REGION II—Bldg. 209, 2890 Woodbridge Ave., Edison, NJ 08837-3679. Phone: (732) 906-6194.

REGION III—1650 Arch St., (MC 3HS33), Philadelphia, PA 19103. Phone: (215) 814-3273.

REGION IV—Air Division - 12th fl., 61 Forsyth St. SW, Atlanta, GA 30303. Phone: (404) 562-9085.

REGION V—77 W. Jackson Blvd., (MC SC-6J), Chicago, IL 60604. Phone: (312) 353-9045.

REGION VI—1445 Ross Ave., (MC 6SF-RO), Dallas, TX 75202-2733. Phone: (214) 665-2270.

REGION VII—901 5th St., (MC ATRDCRIB), Kansas City, KS 66101. Phone: (913) 551-7540.

REGION VIII—One Denver Place - Ste. 00, 999 18th St., (MC EPR-SA), Denver, CO 80202-2405. Phone: (303) 312-6760.

REGION IX—75 Hawthorne St., (MC SFD 9-3), San Francisco, CA 94105. Phone: (415) 972-3039.

REGION X—1200 6th Ave., (MC ECL-116), Seattle, WA 98101. Phone: (206) 553-8414.

Hazardous Waste Management for Tribes

REGION I—Phones: (617) 918-1554; FAX (617) 918-1505.

REGION II—Phones: (212) 637-4099; FAX (212) 637-4437.

REGION IV—Phones: (404) 562-8449; FAX (404) 562-8439.

REGION V—Phones: (312) 353-1440; FAX (312) 353-6519.

REGION VI—Phones: (214) 665-7216; FAX (214) 665-6762.

REGION VII—Phones: (913) 551-7669; FAX (913) 551-9669.

REGION VIII—Phones: (303) 312-6149; FAX (303) 312-6064.

REGION IX—Phones: (415) 972-3355; FAX (415) 947-3530.

REGION X—Phones: (206) 553-6502; FAX (206) 553-8509.

66.817 through 66.818 (cont.)

OFFICE OF SOLID WASTE AND EMERGENCY RESPONSE

REGION I—One Congress St. (HBT), Boston, MA 02114-2023. Phone: (617) 918-1424; FAX (617) 918-1291.

REGION II—290 Broadway - 18th fl., New York, NY 10007. Phone: (212) 637-4314; FAX (212) 637-4360.

REGION III—1650 Arch St. (MC 3HS51), Philadelphia, PA 19103. Phone: (215) 814-3129; FAX (215) 814-5518.

REGION IV—Nunn Atlanta Federal Center, 61 Forsyth St., Atlanta, GA 30303. Phone: (404) 562-8792; FAX (404) 562-8628.

REGION V—77 W. Jackson Blvd. (MC SM-7J), Chicago, IL 60604-3507. Phone: (312) 886-7576; FAX (312) 697-2515.

REGION VI—1445 Ross Ave. (6SF-VB), Dallas, TX 75202-2733. Phone: (214) 665-6780; FAX (214) 665-6660.

REGION VII—901 N. 5th St. (SUPR/STAR), Kansas City, KS 66101. Phone: (913) 551-7786; FAX (913) 551-8688.

REGION VIII—1595 Wynkoop St. (SEPR-SA), Denver, CO 80202-1129. Phone: (303) 312-7074; FAX (303) 312-6067.

REGION IX—75 Hawthorne St. (SFD 1-1), San Francisco, CA 94105. Phones: (415) 972-3092; FAX (415) 947-3528.

REGION X—1200 6th Ave. (ECL-112), Seattle, WA 98101. Phones: (206) 553-7299; FAX (206) 553-0124.

66.926 through 66.931

Listed under **66.473.**

66.950 through 66.952

Listed under **66.001.**

COMMODITY FUTURES TRADING COMMISSION

78.004

REGIONAL OFFICES

CENTRAL—300 S. Riverside Plaza. - Ste. 600 N., Chicago, IL 60606. Phone: (312) 353-9000.

- 510 Grain Exchange Bldg., Minneapolis, MN 55415. Phone: (612) 370-3255.

EASTERN—One World Trade Center - Ste. 747, New York, NY 10048. Phone: (212) 466-2071.

SOUTHWESTERN—4900 Main St. - Ste. 21, Kansas City, MO 64112. Phone: (816) 931-7600.

WESTERN—10900 Wilshire Blvd. - Ste. 00, Los Angeles, CA 90024. Phone: (310) 235-6783.

DEPARTMENT OF ENERGY

81.022 through 81.214

FIELD OFFICES - OPERATIONS

California—Oakland Operations Office, 1301 Clay St., Oakland, CA 94612-5208. Phone: (510) 637-1802.

Colorado—Rocky Flats Office, Golden, CO 80402-0928. Phone: (303) 966-7000.

Idaho—Idaho Operations Office, 850 Energy Dr., (MS 1221), Idaho Falls, ID 83401-1563. Phone: (208) 526-0111.

Illinois—Chicago Operations Office, 9800 S. Cass Ave., Argonne, IL 60439-4899. Phone: (630) 252-2001.

New Mexico—Albuquerque Operations Office, Albuquerque, NM 87185-5400. Phone: (505) 845-6049.

Nevada—Nevada Operations Office, P.O. Box 98518, Las Vegas, NV 89193-8518. Phone: (702) 295-1000.

Ohio—Miamisburg, OH 45343-0066. Phone: (937) 865-4020.

Pennsylvania—National Energy Technology Laboratory, 626 Cochrans Mills Rd., P.O. Box 10940, Pittsburgh, PA 15236-0940. Phone: (412) 386-6000.

South Carolina—Savannah River Operations Office, P.O. Box A, Aiken, SC 29801. Phone: (803) 725-6211.

Tennessee—Oak Ridge Operations Office, P.O. Box 2001, Oak Ridge, TN 37831. Phone: (865) 574-1000.

Washington—Richland Operations Office, 825 Jadwin Ave., P.O. Box 550, Richland, WA 99352. Phone: (509) 376-7411.

West Virginia—National Energy Technology Laboratory, 3610 Collins Ferry Rd., Morgantown, WV 26507-0880. Phone: (304) 285-4764.

OFFICE OF ENERGY EFFICIENCY AND RENEWABLE ENERGY

Regional Offices

CENTRAL—1617 Cole Blvd., (MS 1521), Golden, CO 80401. Phone: (303) 275-4785.

MID-ATLANTIC—The Wanamaker Bldg. - Ste. 90 South, 100 Penn Square E., Philadelphia, PA 19107. Phone: (215) 656-6954.

MIDWEST—One S. Whacker Dr. - Ste. 380, Chicago, IL 60606-4616. Phone: (312) 886-8588.

NORTHEAST—JFK Federal Bldg. - Rm. 75, Boston, MA 02203. Phone: (617) 565-9708.

SOUTHEAST—75 Spring St. SW - Ste. 00, Atlanta, GA 30303. Phone: (404) 562-0599.

WESTERN—800 5th Ave. - Ste. 950, Seattle, WA 98104-3122. Phone: (206) 553-2875.

Regional Biomass Energy Program Offices

GREAT LAKES— Council of Great Lakes Governors, 35 E. Wacker Dr. Ste. 1850, Chicago, IL 60601. Phone: (312) 407-0177; FAX (312) 407-0038.

NORTHEAST— CONEG Policy Research Cntr. - Ste. 82, 400 N. Capitol St. NW, Washington, DC 20001. Phone: (202) 624-8450; FAX (202) 624 8463.

NORTHWEST (PACIFIC)— Renewable Resources Specialist, 925 Plum St. SE Bldg. 3, P.O. Box 43165, Olympia, WA 98504-3165. Phone:(360) 956-2004.

81.022
through
81.214
(cont.)

SOUTHEAST—Southern States Energy Board, Norcross, GA 30092. Phone: (770) 242-7711.

WESTERN—Western Governors' Association, 1515 Cleveland Pl. Ste. 200, Denver, CO 80202. Phone: (303) 623-9378.

SUPPORT OFFICES

Colorado—DOE, Denver Regional Support Office, 1617 Cole Blvd. - Bldg.17-2, Golden, CO 80401. Phone: (303) 275-4816.

- DOE, Golden Field Office, 1617 Cole Blvd, Golden, CO 80401. Phones: (303) 275-4737; FAX (303) 275-4788.

Georgia—DOE, 75 Spring St. SW - Ste. 00, Atlanta, GA 30303. Phone: (404) 562-0556.

Illinois—DOE, One S. Wacker Dr. - Ste. 380, Chicago, IL 60606-4616. Phone: (312) 886-8571.

Massachusetts—DOE, JFK Federal Bldg. - Rm. 75, Boston, MA 02203.Phone: (617) 565-9700.

Pennsylvania—DOE, 1880 JFK Blvd. - 5th fl., Philadelphia, PA 19102. Phone: (215) 656-6964.

Washington—DOE, 800 5th Ave. - Ste. 950, Seattle, WA. 98104-3122. Phone: (206) 553-1004.

DEPARTMENT OF EDUCATION

84.007
through
84.033

REGIONAL ADMINISTRATORS/STUDENT FINANCIAL AID

Students should contact their educational institution. Educational institutions should contact:

REGION I—McCormack Post Office and Courthouse - Rm. 02, 5 Post Office Square, (MS 01-0070), Boston, MA 02109. Phone: (617) 223-9328.

REGION II—Institutional Review Branch, 75 Park Place - 12th fl., New York, NY 10007. Phone: (212) 637-6423.

REGION III—3535 Market St. - Rm. 6200, (MS 03-2080), Philadelphia, PA 19104. Phone: (215) 596-1018.

REGION IV—P.O. Box 1692, Atlanta, GA 30301. Phone: (404) 331-0556.

REGION V—401 S. State St. - Rm. 00-D, (MS 05-4080), Chicago, IL 60605. Phone: (312) 353-0375.

REGION VI—1200 Main Tower Bldg. - Rm. 150, (MS 06-5080), Dallas, TX 75202. Phone: (214) 767-3811.

REGION VII—Institutional Review Branch, 10220 N. Executive Hills Blvd. - 9th fl., Kansas City, MO 64153. Phone: (816) 880-4054.

REGION VIII—Institutional Review Branch, 1244 Speer Blvd. - Rm. 22, Denver, CO 80204. Phone: (303) 844-3676.

REGION IX—50 United Nations Plaza - Rm. 27, (MS 09-8080), San Francisco, CA 94102-4987. Phone: (415) 556-8382.

REGION X—1000 2nd Ave. - Rm. 200, Seattle, WA 98174-1099. Phone: (206) 287-1770.

84.044
through
84.047

SECRETARY'S REGIONAL REPRESENTATIVES

REGION I—McCormack Post Office and Courthouse - Rm. 40, Boston, MA 02109. Phone: (617) 223-9317.

REGION II—75 Park Place - 12th fl., New York, NY 10007. Phone: (212) 637-6283.

REGION III—100 Penn Square E. - Ste. 05, Philadelphia, PA 19107. Phone: (215) 656-6010.

REGION IV—61 Forsyth St. SW - Rm. 9T40, Atlanta, GA 30303. Phone: (404) 562-6225.

REGION V—111 N. Canal St. - Rm. 094, Chicago, IL 60606. Phone: (312) 553-8192.

REGION VI—1999 Bryan St. - Ste. 700, Dallas, TX 75201-6817. Phone: (214) 880-3011.

REGION VII—10220 N. Executive Hills Blvd. - Ste. 20, Kansas City, MO 64153-1367. Phone: (816) 880-4000.

REGION VIII—Federal Regional Office Bldg. - Rm. 10, 1244 Speer Blvd., Denver, CO 80204-3582. Phone: (303) 844-3544.

REGION IX—50 United Nations Plaza - Rm. 05, San Francisco, CA 94102-4987. Phone: (415) 437-7520.

REGION X—915 2nd Ave. - Rm. 362, Seattle, WA 98174-1099. Phone: (206) 220-7800.

84.063   Listed under **84.007.**

FEDERAL REAL PROPERTY ASSISTANCE PROGRAM

84.145   ### Regional Offices

EASTERN ZONE (Regions I, II, III, IV, V)—Director, Office of Administrator/Management Services, McCormack Post Office and Courthouse - Rm. 36, Boston, MA 02109-4557. Phone: (617) 223-9321.

WESTERN ZONE (Regions VI, VII, XIII, IX, X)—Director, Office of Administrator/Management Services, 400 Maryland Ave. SW - Rm. C107, Washington, DC 20202. Phone: (202) 401-0506.

84.268
through
84.408

Listed under **84.007.**

PENSION BENEFIT GUARANTY CORPORATION

86.001   *Contact the Employee Benefits Security Administration (Department of Labor) office.*

NATIONAL ARCHIVES AND RECORDS ADMINISTRATION

89.003 **PRESIDENTIAL LIBRARIES**

Arkansas—William J. Clinton Library, 1200 President Clinton Ave., Little Rock, Arkansas 72201. Phone: (501) 374-4242; FAX (501) 244-2883. **Internet:** e-mail, "clinton.library@nara.gov".

California—Richard Nixon Library in Yorba Linda, 18001 Yorba Linda Blvd., Yorba Linda, CA 92886. Phone: (714) 983-9120; FAX (714) 983-9111. **Internet:** e-mail, "nixon@nara.gov".

- Ronald Reagan Library, 40 Presidential Dr., Simi Valley, CA 93065-0600. Phones: Toll Free 1-800-410-8354,(805) 577-4000; FAX (805) 577-4074.

Georgia—Jimmy Carter Library, 441 Freedom Pkwy., Atlanta, GA 30307-1498. Phone: (404) 865-7100; FAX (404) 865-7102. **Internet:** e-mail, "carter.library@nara.gov".

Iowa—Herbert Hoover Library, 210 Parkside Dr., P.O. Box 488, West Branch, IA 52358-0488. Phone: (319) 643-5301; FAX (319) 643-6045. **Internet:** e-mail, "hoov er.library@nara.gov".

Kansas—Dwight D. Eisenhower Library, 200 SE 4th St., Abilene, KS 67410-2900. Phone: (785) 263-6700; FAX (785) 263-6718. **Internet:** e-mail, "eisenhower.libr ary@nara.gov".

Maryland—Office of Presidential Libraries at NARA, 8601 Adelphi Rd. - Rm. 200, College Park, MD 20740-6001. Phone: (301) 837-3250; FAX: (301) 837-3199.

- Richard Nixon Library in College Park, 8601 Adelphi Rd., College Park, MD 20740-6001. Phone: (301) 837-3290; FAX (301) 837-3202. **Internet:** e-mail, "nixon@nara .gov".

Massachusetts—John F. Kennedy Library, Columbia Point, Boston, MA 02125-3398. Phones: Toll Free 1-866-535-1960, (617) 514-1600; FAX (617) 514-1652. **Internet:** e-mail, "kennedy.library@nara.gov".

Michigan—Gerald R. Ford Museum, 303 Pearl St. NW, Grand Rapids, MI 49504-5353. Phone: (616) 254-0400; FAX: (616) 254-0386. **Internet:** e-mail, "ford.museum @nara.gov".

- Gerald R. Ford Library, 1000 Beal Ave., Ann Arbor, MI 48109-2114. Phone: (734) 205-0555; FAX (734) 205-0571. **Internet:** e-mail, "ford.library@nara.gov".

Missouri—Harry S. Truman Library, 500 W. U.S. Hwy. 24, Independence, MO 64050-1798. Phones: Toll Free 1-800-833-1225, (816) 268-8200; FAX (816) 268-8295. **Internet:** e-mail, "truman.library@nara.gov".

New York—Franklin D. Roosevelt Library, 4079 Albany Post Rd., Hyde Park, NY 12538-1999. Phones: Toll Free 1-800-337-8474, (845) 486-7770; FAX (845) 486-1147. **Internet:** e-mail, "roosevelt.library@nara.gov".

Texas—Lyndon B. Johnson Library, 2313 Red River St., Austin, TX 78705-5702. Phone: (512) 721-0200; FAX (512) 721-0169. **Internet:** e-mail, "johnson.library@n ara.gov".

- George H. W. Bush Library, 1000 George Bush Dr. W., College Station, TX 77845. Phone: (979) 691-4000; FAX (979) 691-4050. **Internet:** e-mail, "bush.library@na ra.gov".

- George W. Bush Library, 1725 Lakepointe Dr., Lewisville, TX 75057. Phone: (972) 353-0545; FAX (972) 353-0599. **Internet:** e-mail, "gwbush.library@nara.gov".

OFFICE OF REGIONAL RECORDS SERVICES

CENTRAL PLAINS REGION—200 Space Center Dr., Lee's Summit, MO 64064-1182. Phones: (816) 268-8100; FAX (816) 478-7623.

- 400 W. Pershing Rd., Kansas City, MO 64108. Phones: (816) 268-8000. **Internet:** e-mail, "kansascity.archives@nara.gov".

- (Military Personnel Records) 9700 Page Ave., St. Louis, MO 63132-5100. Phones: (314) 801-0800; FAX (314) 801-9195. **Internet:** e-mail, "MPR.center@nara.gov".

- (Civilian Personnel Records) 111 Winnebago St., St. Louis, MO 63118-4126. Phones: (314) 801-9250; FAX (314) 801-9269. **Internet:** e-mail, "cpr.center@nara.gov".

DISTRICT OF COLUMBIA—Washington National Records Center, Reference Service Branch, Washington, DC 20409-0002. Phone: (301) 457-7000.

- Archives I - Research Room Support Branch, 700 Pennsylvania Ave. NW, Washington, DC 20408. Phones: Toll Free 1-866-325-7208, (202) 357-5000.

GREAT LAKES REGION—7358 S. Pulaski Rd., Chicago, IL 60629-5898. Phones: (773) 948-9000; FAX (773) 948-9050. **Internet:** e-mail, "chicago.archives@nara.gov".

- 3150 Springboro Rd., Dayton, OII 45439-1883. Phones: (937) 425-0600; FAX (937) 425-0604. **Internet:** e-mail, "center@dayton.nara.gov".

MARYLAND—Archives II - Research Room Support Branch, 8601 Adelphi Rd., College Park, MD 20740-6001. Phones: Toll Free 1-866-272-6272, (301) 837-2000.

- The Washington National Records Center (WNRC), 4205 Suitland Rd., Suitland, MD 20746-8001. Phone: 301-778-1600; FAX: (301) 778-1621. **Internet:** e-mail, "suitland.center@nara.gov".

MID ATLANTIC REGION—900 Market St., Philadelphia, PA 19107-4292. Phones: (215) 606-0100; FAX (215) 606-0116. **Internet:** e-mail, "archives@philarch.nara.gov".

- 14700 Townsend Rd., Philadelphia, PA 19154-1025. Phone: (215) 305-2000; FAX (215) 305-2038.

NORTHEAST REGION—10 Conte Dr., Pittsfield, MA 01201-8230. Phones: (413) 236-3600; FAX (413) 236-3609.

- 380 Trapelo Rd., Waltham, MA 02154-6399. Phones: (781) 663-0130; FAX (781) 663-0154. **Internet:** e-mail, "waltham.archives@nara.gov".

- 201 Varick St., New York, NY 10014-4811. Phones: (212) 401-1620; FAX (212) 401-1638. **Internet:** e-mail, "newyork.archives@nara.gov".

PACIFIC REGION—

PACIFIC ALASKA REGION—654 W. 3rd Ave., Anchorage, AK 99501-2145. Phones: (907) 261-7820; FAX (907) 261-7813. **Internet:** e-mail, "alaska.archives@nara.gov".

- 6125 Sand Point Way NE, Seattle, WA 98115-7999. Phone: (206) 336-5115;

- 24000 Avila Rd. - 1st fl. (east entrance), Laguna Niguel, CA 92677-3497. Phones: (949) 360-2640; FAX (949) 360-2624. **Internet:** e-mail, "laguna.archives@nara.gov".

- 1000 Commodore Dr., San Bruno, CA 94066-2350. Phones: (650) 238-3501; FAX (650) 238-3510. **Internet:** e-mail, "sanbruno.archives@nara.gov".

ROCKY MOUNTAIN REGION—Denver Federal Center - Bldg. 48, P.O. Box 25307, Denver, CO 80225. Phones: (303) 407-5740; FAX (303) 407-5709. **Internet:** e-mail, "denver.archives@nara.gov".

SOUTHEAST REGION—5780 Jonesboro Rd., Morrow, Georgia 30260. Phone: (770) 968-2100; Fax: (770) 968-2547. **Internet:** e-mail, "atlanta.archives@nara.gov".

89.003
(cont.)

■ Atlanta Records Center, 4712 Southpark Blvd., Ellenwood, GA 30294. Phone: (404) 736-2820; Fax: (404) 736-2931.

SOUTHWEST REGION—Bldg. 1, 501 W. Felix St., P.O. Box 6216, Ft. Worth, TX 76115. Phone: (817) 831-5620; FAX (817) 334-5621. **Internet:** e-mail, "ftworth.arc hives@nara.gov".

DEPARTMENT OF HEALTH AND HUMAN SERVICES

OFFICE OF THE SECRETARY

93.001
through
93.018

HHS REGIONAL OFFICES

REGION I—JFK Federal Bldg. - Rm. 875, Boston, MA 02203. Phones: (617) 565-1340; TDD (617) 565-1343; FAX (617) 565-3809.

REGION II—Javits Federal Bldg. - Ste. 312, 26 Federal Plaza, New York, NY 10278. Phones: (212) 264-3313; TDD (212) 264-2355; FAX (212) 264-3039.

REGION III—150 S. Independence Mall - Ste. 72, Philadelphia, PA 19106-3499. Phones: (215) 861-4441; TDD (215) 861-4440; FAX (215) 861-4431.

REGION IV—61 Forsyth St. SW - Ste. B70, Atlanta, GA 30323. Phones: (404) 562-7886; TDD (404) 562-7884; FAX (404) 562-7881.

REGION V—233 N. Michigan Ave. - Ste. 40, Chicago, IL 60601. Phones: (312) 886-2359; TDD (312) 353-5693; FAX (312) 886-1807.

REGION VI—1301 Young St. - Ste. 169, Dallas, TX 75202. Phones: (214) 767-4056; TDD (214) 767-8940; FAX (214) 767-0432.

REGION VII—601 E. 12th St. - Rm. 48, Kansas City, MO 64106. Phones: (816) 426-7278; TDD (816) 426-7065; FAX (816) 426-3686.

REGION VIII—1961 Stout St. - Rm. 426, Denver, CO 80294. Phones: (303) 844-2024; TDD (303) 844-3439; FAX (303) 844-2025.

REGION IX—90 7th St. Ste. 4-100, San Francisco, CA 94103. Phones: (415) 437-8310; TDD (415) 437-8311; FAX (415) 437-8329.

REGION X—2201 6th Ave., MS RX-11, Seattle, WA 98121. Phones: (206) 615-2290; TDD (206) 615-2296; FAX (206) 615-2297.

ADMINISTRATION ON AGING

93.041
through
93.054

REGIONAL OFFICES

REGION I *(Connecticut, Maine, Massachusetts, New Hampshire, Rhode Island, Vermont)*—JFK Federal Bldg. - Rm. 075, Government Center, Boston, MA 02203. Phone: (617) 565-1158; FAX: (617) 565-4511.

REGION II *(New York, New Jersey, Puerto Rico, Virgin Islands)*—26 Federal Plaza - Rm. 8-102, New York, NY 10278. Phone: (212) 264-2976. Fax: 212-264-0114

REGION III *(Delaware, District of Columbia, Maryland, Pennsylvania, Virginia, West Virginia)*—Public Ledger Bldg., 150 S. Independence Mall W. Ste. 864,Philadelphia, PA 19106-3499. Phone:(215) 861-4000; FAX (215) 867-4070.

REGION IV *(Alabama, Florida, Georgia, Kentucky, Mississippi, North Carolina, South Carolina, Tennessee)*— Atlanta Federal Cntr., 61 Forsyth St. SW Ste. 5M69, Atlanta, GA 30303-8909. Phone: (404) 562-7600; FAX: (404) 562-7598.

REGION V *(Illinois, Indiana, Michigan, Minnesota, Ohio, Wisconsin)*—233 N. Michigan Ave. Ste. 790, Chicago, IL 60601-5519. Phone: (312) 353-3141; FAX: (312) 886-8533.

REGION VI *(Arkansas, Louisiana, New Mexico, Oklahoma, Texas)*—1301 Young St. - Rm. 36, Dallas, TX 75201. Phone: (214) 767-2971; FAX: (214) 767-2951.

REGION VII *(Iowa, Kansas, Missouri, Nebraska)*—601 E. 12th St., Kansas City, MO 64106. Phone: (312) 353-3141; Fax: (312) 886-8533.

REGION VIII *(Colorado, Montana, North Dakota, South Dakota, Utah, Wyoming)*—1961 Stout St. Rm. 53, Denver, CO 80294. Phone: (303) 844-2951; FAX: (303) 844-2943.

REGION IX *(American Samoa, Arizona, California, Guam, Hawaii, Nevada, Northern Mariana Islands, Trust Territories of the Pacific Islands)*—90 - 7th St. (T-8100), San Francisco, CA 94103. Phone: (415) 437-8780; FAX: (415) 437-8782.

REGION X *(Alaska, Idaho, Oregon, Washington)*— Blanchard Plaza, 2201 Sixth Ave. - Rm. 59, (RX-33), Seattle, WA 98121. Phone: (206) 615-2298; FAX: (206) 615-2305.

CENTERS FOR DISEASE CONTROL AND PREVENTION

93.065 through 93.067   Technical Information Management Section, CDC Procurement and Grants Office, 2920 Brandywine Rd., Atlanta, GA 30341. Phone: (770) 488-2700.

93.071 through 93.072   Listed under **93.041.**

93.083 through 93.084   Listed under **93.065.**

93.085 through 93.089   Listed under **93.001.**

93.090   Regional Administrator, ACF, HHS Regional Office. *Use addresses Listed under* **93.041.**

93.107 through 93.162   Project Officer, Health Careers Pipeline Branch, Division of Health Careers and Financial Support, Bureau of Health Workforce, Health Resources and Services Administration, Department of Health and Human Services, 5600 Fishers Ln., Parklawn Building, Rm. 9C-15, Rockville, MD 20857. Phone: (301) 443-6950.

INDIAN HEALTH SERVICE

93.164   **AREA OFFICES**

Alaska Area *(Alaska)*—4141 Ambassador Dr. Ste. 300, Anchorage, AK 99508-5928. Phone: (907) 729-3686; FAX (907) 729-3689.

Arizona: Navajo Area *(Arizona, Colorado, New Mexico, Utah)*—P.O. Box 9020, Window Rock, AZ 86515. Phone: (520) 871-5811.

■ **Phoenix Area** *(Arizona, Nevada, Utah)*—2 Renaissance Square, 40 North Central Ave., Phoenix, AZ 85004-4424. Phone: (602) 364-5042.

■ **Tucson Area** *(Arizona)*—OHPRD, 7900 S. "J" Stock Rd., Tucson, AZ 85746-7012. Phone: (520) 295-2405; FAX (520) 295-2602.

93.164
(cont.)   **California Area** *(California)*—650 Capitol Mall Ste. 7-100, Sacramento, CA 95814. Phone: (916) 930-3927; FAX (916) 930-3952.

Maryland: Headquarters Office—The Reyes Bldg., 801 Thompson Ave. - Ste. 400, Rockville, MD 20852. Phone: (301) 443-1083.

Minnesota: Bemidji Area *(Michigan, Minnesota, Wisconsin)*—522 Minnesota Ave. NW Rm. 119, Bemidji, MN 56601. Phone: (218) 444-0458; FAX (218) 444-0461.

Montana: Billings Area *(Montana, Wyoming)*—2900 4th Ave. N, Billings, MT 59101. Phone: (406) 247-7107; FAX (406) 247-7232.

New Mexico: Albuquerque Area *(Colorado, New Mexico)*—801 Vassar Dr. NE, Albuquerque, N.M. 87106. Phone: (505) 248-4000; FAX (505) 248-4088.

■ **Headquarters West Office**—5300 Homestead Rd. NE, Albuquerque, NM 87110. Phone: (505) 248-4500; FAX: (505) 248-4115.

Oklahoma: Oklahoma City Area *(Kansas, Oklahoma)*—701 Market Dr., Oklahoma City, OK 73114. Phone: (405) 951-3820; FAX (405) 951-3780.

Oregon: Portland Area *(Idaho, Oregon, Washington)*—1220 SW 3rd Ave. - Rm. 76, Portland, OR 97204. Phone: (503) 326-2020; FAX (503) 326-7280.

South Dakota: Aberdeen Area *(Iowa, Nebraska, North Dakota, South Dakota)*—Office of Professional Services, 115 4th Ave. SE, Aberdeen, SD 57401. Phone: (605) 226-7582; FAX (605) 226-7321.

Tennessee: Nashville Area *(Alabama, Arkansas, Connecticut, Delaware, Florida, Georgia, Illinois, Indiana, Kentucky, Louisiana, Maine, Maryland, Massachusetts, Mississippi, Missouri, New Hampshire, New Jersey, New York, North Carolina, Ohio, Pennsylvania, Rhode Island, South Carolina, Tennessee, Texas, Vermont, Virginia, West Virginia)*—711 Stewarts Ferry Pike, Nashville, TN 37214-2634. Phone: (615) 467-1500; FAX (615) 467-1501.

93.191   Listed under **93.107.**

93.197   Listed under **93.065.**

93.211 through 93.224   Listed under **93.107.**

93.234   Listed under **93.041.**

93.236 through 93.259   Listed under **93.107.**

93.261   Listed under **93.065.**

93.264 through 93.267   Listed under **93.107.**

93.269   Listed under **93.065.**

93.284   Listed under **93.164.**

93.288   Listed under **93.107.**

93.297   Listed under **93.001.**

93.300 through 93.301   Listed under **93.107.**

93.311   Listed under **93.001.**

93.322   Listed under **93.065.**
through
93.339

93.342   Listed under **93.107.**
through
93.403

93.442   Listed under **93.164.**

FOOD AND DRUG ADMINISTRATION

93.448
through
93.449

DISTRICT OFFICES

No field offices. Direct contact with HQ concerning grants. See main entry. However, for general information concerning Food and Drug Administration activities contact the nearest district office, following:

California—1431 Harbor Bay Pkwy., Alameda, CA 94502-7070. Phone: (510) 337-6783.

- 19900 McArthur Blvd. - Ste. 00, Irvine, CA 92715-2445. Phone: (714) 798-7714.

Colorado—Denver Federal Center, 6th and Kipling St., Denver, CO 80225-0087. Phone: (303) 236-3016.

Florida—7200 Lake Ellenor Dr. - Ste. 20, Orlando, FL 32809. Phone: (407) 648-6995.

Georgia—60 8th St. NE, Atlanta, GA 30309. Phone: (404) 347-4344.

Illinois—300 S. Riverside Plaza - Ste. 50 S., Chicago, IL 60606. Phone: (312) 353-7379.

Kansas—11630 W. 80th St., Lenexa, KS 66285-5905. Phone: (913) 752-2144.

Louisiana—4298 Elysian Fields Ave., New Orleans, LA 70122. Phone: (504) 589-2401, ext.124.

Maryland—900 Madison Ave., Baltimore, MD 21201. Phone: (410) 962-4012.

Massachusetts—One Montvale Ave. - 4th fl., Stoneham, MA 02180. Phone: (617) 279-1675, ext.155.

Michigan—1560 E. Jefferson Ave., Detroit, MI 48207. Phone: (313) 226-6260, ext.101.

Minnesota—240 Hennepin Ave., Minneapolis, MN 55401-1912. Phone: (612) 334-4100, ext.121.

New Jersey—Waterview Corporate Center - 3rd fl., 10 Waterview Blvd., Parsippany, NJ 07054. Phone: (973) 331-2901.

New York—850 3rd Ave., Brooklyn, NY 11232-1593. Phone: (718) 340-7000, ext.5301.

- 599 Delaware Ave., Buffalo, NY 14202. Phone: (716) 551-4461.

Ohio—1141 Central Pkwy., Cincinnati, OH 45202-1097. Phone: (513) 684-3504.

Pennsylvania—U.S. Customhouse - Rm. 00, 2nd & Chestnut St., Philadelphia, PA 19106. Phone: (215) 597-4390, ext.4200.

Puerto Rico—466 Fernandez Juncos Ave., San Juan, PR 00901-3223. Phone: (787) 729-6842.

Tennessee—297 Plus Park Blvd., Nashville, TN 37217. Phone: (615) 781-5392, ext.128.

Texas—3310 Live Oak St., Dallas, TX 75204. Phone: (214) 655-5315, ext.302.

Washington—Federal Office Bldg., 22201 23rd Dr. SE, Bothell, WA 98041-3012. Phone: (425) 483-4950.

93.452	Listed under **93.001.**
93.502 through **93.504**	Listed under **93.107.**
93.507	Listed under **93.065.**
93.510 through **93.527**	Listed under **93.107.**
93.533	Listed under **93.065.**
93.549	Listed under **93.107.**

ADMINISTRATION FOR CHILDREN AND FAMILIES

93.550 through **93.623**   Regional Administrator, ACF, HHS Regional Office. *Use addresses Listed under* **93.041.**

ADMINISTRATION FOR COMMUNITY LIVING

93.630 through **93.631**

REGIONAL OFFICES

Region I: *(Connecticut, Delaware, Massachusetts , Maine, Maryland, New Hampshire, Rhode Island, Vermont)*—Regional Administrator, John F. Kennedy Bldg., Rm. 2075, Boston, MA 02203. Phone: (617) 565-1158; Fax: (617) 565-4511.

Region II: *(New York, New Jersey, Puerto Rico, Virgin Islands)*—Regional Administrator, 26 Federal Plaza, Rm. 38-102, New York, NY 10278. Phone: (212) 264-2976; Fax: (212) 264-0114.

Region III: *(District of Columbia, Delaware, Maryland, Pennsylvania, Virginia, West Virginia)*—Regional Administrator, Atlanta Federal Center, 61 Forsyth St., SW, Ste. 5M69, Atlanta, GA 30303-8909. Phone: (215) 356-1683; Fax: (215) 861-4625.

Region IV: *(Alabama, Florida, Georgia, Kentucky, Mississippi, North Carolina, South Carolina, Tennessee)*—Regional Administrator, Atlanta Federal Center, 61 Forsyth St., SW, Ste. 5M69, Atlanta, GA 30303-8909. Phone: (404) 562-7600; Fax: (404) 562-7598.

Region V: *(Illinois, Indiana, Michigan, Ohio, Wisconsin)*—Regional Administrator, 233 N Michigan Ave., Ste. 790, Chicago, IL 60601-5519. Phone: (312) 938-9855; Fax: (312) 886-8533.

Region VI: *(Arkansas, Louisiana, Oklahoma, New Mexico, Texas)*—Regional Administrator, 1301 Young St., Rm. 736, Dallas, TX 75201. Phone: (214) 767-2971; Fax: (214) 767-2951.

Region VII: *(Iowa, Kansas, Missouri, Nebraska)*—Regional Administrator, 233 N Michigan Ave., Ste. 790, Chicago, IL 60601-5519. Phone: (312) 938-9855; Fax: (312) 886-8533.

Region VIII: *(Colorado, Montana, North Dakota, South Dakota, Utah, Wyoming)*— Regional Administrator, 1961 Stout St., Denver, CO 80294-3638. Phone: (303) 844-2951; Fax: (303) 844-2943.

Region IX: *(American Samoa, Arizona, California, Guam, Hawaii, Nevada, Northern Mariana Islands)*—Regional Administrator, 90 7th St., T-8100, San Francisco, CA 94103. Phone: (415) 437-8780; Fax: (415) 437-8782.

Region X: *(Alaska, Idaho, Oregon, Washington)*—Regional Administrator, Blanchard Plaza, RX-33, Rm. 859, 2201 Sixth Ave., Seattle, WA 98121. Phone: (206) 615-2298; Fax: (206) 615-2305.

93.645 through 93.674	Listed under **93.550.**
93.703	Listed under **93.107.**
93.706	Listed under **93.630.**
93.708 through 93.716	Listed under **93.550.**
93.732	Listed under **93.107.**
93.743 through 93.754	Listed under **93.065.**
93.761	Listed under **93.630.**
93.823	Listed under **93.065.**
93.824	Listed under **93.107.**
93.831	Listed under **93.001.**
93.852	Listed under **93.065.**
93.884 through 93.932	Listed under **93.107.**
93.942 through 93.945	Listed under **93.065.**
93.964 through 93.965	Listed under **93.107.**
93.971 through 93.972	Listed under **93.164.**
93.988	Listed under **93.065.**
93.994	Listed under **93.107.**

CORPORATION FOR NATIONAL AND COMMUNITY SERVICE

94.002 through 94.026

ATLANTIC CLUSTER OFFICES

CLUSTER DIRECTOR—801 Arch St. - Ste. 03, Philadelphia, PA 19107-2416. Phones: (215) 597-9972; FAX (215) 597-4933.

Connecticut—One Commercial Plaza - 21st fl., Hartford, CT 06103-3510. Phones: (860) 240-3237; FAX (860) 240-3238.

Delaware—*see* **Maryland**.

Maine—*see* **New Hampshire**.

Maryland—Fallon Federal Bldg. - Ste. 00B, 31 Hopkins Plaza, Baltimore, MD 21201. Phones: (410) 962-4443; FAX (410) 962-3201.

Massachusetts—10 Causeway St. - Rm. 73, Boston, MA 02222-1038. Phones: (617) 565-7000; FAX (617) 565-7011.

New Hampshire—1 Pillsbury St. - Ste. 01, Concord, NH 03301-3556. Phones: (603) 225-1450; FAX (603) 225-1459.

New Jersey—44 S. Clinton Ave. - Ste. 02, Trenton, NJ 08609-1507. Phones: (609) 989-2243; FAX (609) 989-2304.

New York—O'Brien Federal Bldg. - Rm. 18, Clinton Ave. and Pearl St., Albany, NY 12207. Phones: (518) 431-4150: FAX (518) 431-4154.

Pennsylvania—Nix Federal Bldg. - Ste. 29, 900 Market St., Philadelphia, PA 19107. Phones: (215) 597-2806; FAX (215) 597-2807.

Puerto Rico - Virgin Islands—Federal Bldg. - Ste. 62, 150 Carlos Chardon Ave., Hato Rey, PR 00918-1737. Phones: (787) 766-5314; FAX (787) 766-5189.

Rhode Island—400 Westminster St. - Rm. 03, Providence, RI 02903. Phones: (401) 528-5424; FAX (401) 528-5220.

Vermont—*See* **New Hampshire**.

NORTH CENTRAL CLUSTER OFFICES

CLUSTER DIRECTOR—77 W. Jackson Blvd. - Ste. 42, Chicago, IL 60604-3511. Phones: (312) 353-7705; FAX (312) 353-5343.

Illinois—77 W. Jackson Blvd. - Ste. 42, Chicago, IL 60604-3511. Phones: (312) 353-3622; FAX (312) 353-5343.

Indiana—46 E. Ohio St. - Rm. 57, Indianapolis, IN 46204-1922. Phones: (317) 226-6724; FAX (317) 226-5437.

Iowa—Federal Bldg. - Rm. 17, 210 Walnut St., Des Moines, IA 50309-2195. Phones: (515) 284-4816; FAX (515) 284-6640.

Michigan—211 W. Fort St. - Ste. 408, Detroit, MI 48226-2799. Phones: (313) 226-7848; FAX (313) 226-2557.

Minnesota—431 S. 7th St. - Ste. 480, Minneapolis, MN 55415-1854. Phones: (612) 334-4083; FAX (612) 334-4084.

Nebraska—Federal Bldg. - Rm. 56, 100 Centennial Mall N., Lincoln, NE 68508-3896. Phones: (402) 437-5493; FAX (402) 437-5495.

North Dakota - South Dakota—Federal Bldg. - Rm. 25, 225 S. Pierre St., Pierre, SD 57501-2452. Phones: (605) 224-5996; FAX (605) 224-9201.

Ohio—51 N. High St. - Ste. 51, Columbus, OH 43215. Phones: (614) 469-7441; FAX (614) 469-2125.

Wisconsin—Reuss Federal Plaza - Rm. 240, 310 W. Wisconsin Ave., Milwaukee, WI 53203-2211. Phones: (414) 297-1118; FAX (414) 297-1863.

PACIFIC CLUSTER OFFICES

CLUSTER DIRECTOR—P.O. Box 29996, Presidio of San Francisco, CA 94129-0996. Phones: (415) 561-5960; FAX (415) 561-5970.

Alaska—*See* Washington. Phones: (206) 220-7736; FAX (206) 553-4415.

California—11150 W. Olympia Blvd. - Ste. 70, Los Angeles, CA 90064. Phones: (310) 235-7421; FAX (310) 235-7422.

Hawaii, Guam, American Samoa—Federal Bldg. - Rm. 213, 300 Ala Moana Blvd., Honolulu, HI 96850-0001. Phones: (808) 541-2832; FAX (808) 541-3603.

Idaho—304 N. 8th St. - Rm. 44, Boise, ID 83702-5835. Phones: (208) 334-1707; FAX (208) 334-1421.

Montana—Capitol One Center - Ste. 06, 208 N. Montana Ave. Helena, MT 59601-3837. Phones: (406) 449-5404; FAX (406) 449-5412.

Nevada—4600 Kietzke Ln. - Ste. E-141, Reno, NV 89502-5033. Phones: (702) 784-5314; FAX (702) 784-5026.

Oregon—2010 Lloyd Center, Portland, OR 97232. Phones: (503) 231-2103; FAX (503) 231-2106.

Utah—350 S. Main St. - Rm. 04, Salt Lake City, UT 84101-2198. Phones: (801) 524-5411; FAX (801) 524-3599.

Washington—Jackson Federal Bldg. - Ste. 190, 915 2nd Ave., Seattle, WA 98174-1103. Phones: (206) 220-7745; FAX (206) 553-4415.

Wyoming—Federal Bldg. - Rm. 110, 2120 Capitol Ave., Cheyenne, WY 82001-3649. Phones: (307) 772-2385; FAX (307) 772-2389.

SOUTHERN CLUSTER OFFICES

CLUSTER DIRECTOR—60 Forsyth St. SW, - Ste. M40, Atlanta, GA 30323-2301. Phones: (404) 562-4055; FAX (404) 562-4071.

Alabama—Medical Forum - Ste. 28, 950 22nd St. N., Birmingham, AL 35203. Phones: (205) 731-0027; FAX(205) 731-0031.

District of Columbia—*See* Virginia.

Florida—3165 McCrory St. - Ste. 15, Orlando, FL 32803-3750. Phones: (407) 648-6117; FAX (407) 648-6116.

Georgia—75 Piedmont Ave. NE - Ste. 82, Atlanta, GA 30303-2587. Phones: (404) 331-4646; FAX (404) 331-2898.

Kentucky—Federal Bldg. - Rm. 72-D, 600 Martin Luther King Place, Louisville, KY 40202-2230. Phones: (502) 582-6384; FAX (502) 582-6386.

Mississippi—100 W. Capitol St. - Rm. 005A, Jackson, MS 39269-1092. Phones: (601) 965-5664; FAX (601) 965-4617.

North Carolina—300 Fayetteville St. Mall - Rm. 31, Raleigh, NC 27601-1739. Phones: (919) 856-4731; FAX (919) 856-4738.

South Carolina—1835 Assembly St. - Ste. 72, Columbia, SC 29201-2430. Phones: (803) 765-5771; FAX (803) 765-5777.

Tennessee—265 Cumberland Bend Dr., Nashville, TN 37228. Phones: (615) 736-5561; FAX (615) 736-7937.

Virginia—400 N. 8th St. - Ste. 46, P.O. Box 10066, Richmond, VA 23240-1832. Phones: (804) 771-2197; FAX (804) 771-2157.

West Virginia—10 Hale St. - Ste. 03, Charleston, WV 25301-1409. Phones: (304) 347-5246; FAX (304) 347-5464.

94.002 through 94.026 (cont.)

SOUTHWEST CLUSTER OFFICES

CLUSTER DIRECTOR—1999 Bryan St. - Rm. 050, Dallas, TX 75201. Phones: (214) 880-7050; FAX (214) 880-7074.

Arizona—522 N. Central - Rm. 05A, Phoenix, AZ 85004-2190. Phones: (602) 379-4825; FAX (602) 379-4030.

Arkansas—Federal Bldg. - Rm. 506, 700 W. Capitol St., Little Rock, AR 72201. Phones: (501) 324-5234; FAX (501) 324-6949.

Colorado—999 18th St. - Ste. 440 South, Denver, CO 80202. Phones: (303) 312-7950; FAX (303) 312-7954.

Kansas—444 SE Quincy - Rm. 60, Topeka, KS 66683-3572. Phones: (785) 295-2540; FAX (785) 295-2596.

Louisiana—707 Florida St. - Ste. 16, Baton Rouge, LA 70801-1910. Phones: (504) 389-0473; FAX (504) 389-0510.

Missouri—801 Walnut St. - Ste. 04, Kansas City, MO 64106-2009. Phones: (816) 347-6300; FAX (816) 347-6305.

New Mexico—120 S. Federal Place - Rm. 15, Santa Fe, NM 87501-2026. Phones: (505) 988-6577; FAX (505) 988-6661.

Oklahoma—215 Dean A. McGee - Ste. 24, Oklahoma City, OK 73102. Phones: (405) 231-5201; FAX (405) 231-4329.

Texas—903 San Jacinto St. - Ste. 30, Austin, TX 78701-3747. Phones: (512) 916-5671; FAX (512) 916-5806.

SOCIAL SECURITY ADMINISTRATION

96.001 through 96.020

There are 1,296 district and branch SSA offices located in cities and towns throughout the U.S. Consult the local phone directory under "Social Security Administration" or "U.S. Government" or ask for address at local U.S. Post Office.

DEPARTMENT OF HOMELAND SECURITY

IMMIGRATION AND CUSTOMS ENFORCEMENT

DHS,ICE, OIA, PHAB Miami Office, 51 SW 1st Ave. - Rm. 20, Miami, FL 33130. Phone:(305) 536-4261.

97.009 through 97.130

FIELD OFFICES

Alabama—*See* **Atlanta, Georgia** Field Office.

Alaska—Anchorage Field Office, 620 E. 10th Ave. - Ste. 02, Anchorage, AK 99501-3701. Phone: (907) 271-3524.

Arizona—Phoenix Field Office, 2035 N. Central Ave., Phoenix, AZ 85004. Phone: (602) 514-7799.

- Tucson Field Office, 6431 S. Country Club Rd., Tucson, AZ 85706.

Arkansas—

- Fort Smith Field Office, 4977 Old Greenwood Road, Fort Smith, AR 72903. *See also* **Memphis, Tennessee** Field Office.

California—Chula Vista Field Office, 1261 3rd Ave. Ste. A, Chula Vista, CA 91911.

- Fresno Sub-Office, 865 Fulton Mall, Fresno, CA 93721-2816. Phone: (209) 487-5126.

- Imperial Field Office 509 Industry Way Imperial, CA 92251.

- Los Angeles Field Office, 300 N. Los Angeles St., Los Angeles, CA 90012. Phone: (213) 894-4627.

- Sacramento Sub-Office, 650 Capital Mall, Sacramento, CA 95814. Phone: (916) 498-6460.

- San Bernardino Field Office, 655 W. Rialto Ave., San Bernardino, CA 92410.

- San Diego Field Office, 880 Front St. - Ste. 1234, San Diego, CA 92101-8834. Phone: (619) 557-5645.

- San Francisco Field Office, 444 Washington St., San Francisco, CA 94111.

- San Jose Field Office, 1887 Monterey Road San Jose, CA 95112.

- Santa Ana 34 Civic Center Plaza Santa Ana, CA 92701.

Colorado—Denver Field Office, 12484 E. Weaver Pl., Centennial, CO 80111.

Connecticut—Hartford Field Office, 450 Main St. - 1st Fl., Hartford, CT 06103. Phone: (203) 240-3052.

District of Columbia—*See* **Virginia** Washington Field Office.

Florida—Hialeah Field Office, 5880 NW 183rd St., Hialeah, Florida 33015.

- Jacksonville Field Office, 4121 Southpoint Blvd., Jacksonville, FL 32216.

- Kendall Field Office, 14675 SW 120th St., Miami, FL 33186.

- Miami Field Office, 8801 NW 7th Avenue Miami, FL 33150.

- Oakland Park Field Office, 4451 NW 31st Ave., Oakland Park, FL 33309.

- Tampa Field Office, 5524 West Cypress St., Tampa, FL 33607.

- Orlando Field Office. 6680 Corporate Centre Blvd., Orlando, FL 32822.

- West Palm Beach Field Office, 9300 Belvedere Rd., Royal Palm Beach, FL 33411.

Georgia—Atlanta Field Office, 2150 Parklake Dr., Atlanta, GA 30345.

Guam—Agana Field Office, Sirena Plaza - Ste. 100, 108 Hernan Cortez Ave., Hagatna, Guam 96910.

Hawaii—Honolulu District Office, 595 Ala Moana Blvd., Honolulu, HI 96813. Phones: (808) 532-3748, -3746.

Idaho—Boise Field Office, 1185 S. Vinnell Way, Boise, ID 83709. *See also* **Spokane, Washington** Field Office.

Illinois—Chicago Field Office, 101 W. Congress Pkwy., Chicago, IL 60605. *See also* **St. Louis, Missouri** Field Office.

Indiana—Indianapolis Sub-Office, Gateway Plaza - Rm. 400, 950 N. Meridan St., Indianapolis, IN 46204. Phone: (217) 226-6181. *See also* **Chicago, Illinois** Field Office.

Iowa—Des Moines Field Office, Federal Bldg., 210 Walnut St. Rm. 369, Des Moines, IA 50309. *See also* **Omaha, Nebraska** Field Office.

Kansas—Kansas City Field Office, 9747 NW Conant Avenue Kansas City, MO 64153.

- Wichita Field Office, 271 West 3rd St. North - Ste. 1050, Wichita, KS 67202.

**97.009
through
97.130
(cont.)**

Kentucky—Louisville Field Office, Snyder Courthouse - Rm. 04, 601 W. Broadway, Louisville, KY 40202. Phone: (502) 582-6526.

Louisiana—New Orleans Field Office, Metairie Centre, Suite 300 (Third Floor) 2424 Edenborn Avenue Metairie, LA 70001.

Maine—Portland Field Office, 176 Gannett Dr., South Portland, ME 04106.

Maryland—Baltimore Field Office, Fallen Federal Bldg., 31 Hopkins Plaza, Baltimore, MD 21201. Phone: (410) 962-2010.

Massachusetts—Boston Field Office, Kennedy Federal Bldg., Government Cntr. Rm. E-160, Boston, MA 02203. Phone: (617) 565-4214.

■ Lawrence Field Office, 2 Mill St., Lawrence, MA 01840.

Michigan—Detroit Field Office, 11411 East Jefferson Ave., Detroit, MI 48214.

Minnesota—St. Paul Field Office, 2901 Metro Dr. Ste. 100, Bloomington, MN 55425.

Mississippi—Jackson Satellite Office, 100 W. Capitol St. Ste. 727, Jackson MS 39269. *See also* **Memphis, Tennessee** and **New Orleans, Louisiana** Field Offices.

Missouri—Kansas City Field Office, 9747 NW Conant Ave., Kansas City, MO 64153.

■ St. Louis Field Office, Young Federal Bldg. - Rm. 00, 1222 Spruce St., St. Louis, MO 63103-2815. Phone: (314) 539-2516.

Montana—Helena Field Office, 2800 Skyway Dr., Helena, MT 59602.

Nebraska—Omaha Field Office, 1717 Avenue H, Omaha, NE 8110.

Nevada—Las Vegas Filed Office, 3373 Pepper Lane, Las Vegas, NV 89120. Phone: (702) 388-6640.

■ Reno Field Office, 1351 Corporate Blvd., Reno, NV 89502. Phone: (702) 784-5186.

New Hampshire—Manchester Field Office, 803 Canal St., Manchester, NH 03101.

New Jersey—Mount Laurel Field Office, 530 Fellowship Rd., Mount Laurel, NJ 08054.

■ Newark Field Office, Peter Rodino Federal Bldg., 970 Broad St., Newark, NJ 07102.

New Mexico—Albuquerque Field Office, 1720 Randolph Rd. SE, Albuquerque, NM 87106. *See also* **El Paso, Texas** Field Office.

New York—Albany Field Office, 1086 Troy-Schenectady Rd., Latham, NY 12110.

■ Buffalo Field Office, 130 Delaware Ave., Buffalo, NY 14202. Phone: (716) 846-4741.

■ Garden City Field Office, 711 Stewart Ave., Garden City, NY 11530.

■ New York City Field Office, 26 Federal Plaza Rm. 3-310, New York, NY 10278. Phone: (212) 264-3911.

■ Rochester Field Office, 100 State St. Rm. 418, Rochester, NY 14614.

■ Syracuse Field Office, 412 South Warren St., Syracuse, NY 13202.

North Carolina—Charlotte Field Office, 6130 Tyvola Centre Dr., Charlotte, NC 28217. Phone: (704) 344-6313.

■ Raleigh-Durham Field Office, 301 Roycroft Dr., Durham, NC 27703.

North Dakota—*See* **Bloomington, Minnesota** St. Paul Field Office.

Ohio—Cincinnati Field Office, J.W. Peck Federal Bldg., 550 Main St. - Rm. 4001, Cincinnati, OH 45202-5298.

■ Cleveland Field Office, A.J.C. Federal Bldg., 1240 East 9th St. Rm. 501, Cleveland, OH 44199.

■ Columbus Field Office, Leveque Tower, 50 W. Broad St. Ste. 306, Columbus, OH 43215.

Oklahoma—Oklahoma City Field Office, 4400 Southwest 44th St. Ste. A, Oklahoma City, OK 73119.

Oregon—Portland Field Office, 511 NW Broadway, Portland, OR 97209. Phone: (503) 326-3962.

Pennsylvania—Philadelphia Field Office, 1600 Callowhill St., Philadelphia, PA 19130. Phone: (215) 656-7150.

- Pittsburgh Field Office, 3000 Sidney St. Ste. 200, Pittsburgh, PA 15203.

Puerto Rico—San Juan Field Office, San Patricio Office Cntr., 7 Tabonuco St. Ste. 100, Guaynabo, PR 00968.

Rhode Island—Providence Field Office, 1543 Atwood Ave., Johnston, RI 02919.

South Carolina—Charleston Field Office, Park Shore Cntr., 1 Poston Road Ste. 130, Charleston, SC 29407.

- Greer Field Office, 142-D West Phillips Rd., Greer, SC 29650.

South Dakota—*See* **Bloomington, Minnesota** St. Paul Field Office.

Tennessee—Memphis Field Office, 842 Virginia Run Cove, Memphis, TN 38122.

Texas—Dallas Field Office, 6500 Campus Circle Dr. E, Irving, TX 75063.

- El Paso Field Office, 8915 Montana Ave., El Paso, TX 79925. Phone: (915) 225-1941.

- Harlingen Field Office, 1717 Zoy St., Harlingen, TX 78552.

- Houston Field Office, 126 Northpoint Dr., Houston, TX 77060.

- San Antonio Field Office, 8940 Fourwinds Dr., San Antonio, TX 78239.

Utah—Salt Lake City Field Office, 5272 South College Dr. Ste. 100, Salt Lake City, UT 84123.

Vermont—Saint Albans Field Office, 64 Gricebrook Rd., Saint Albans, VT 05478.

Virgin Islands—Charlotte Amalie, St. Thomas, VI Sub-Office, Nisky Center - 1st fl.(Ste. A), Charlotte Amalie, St. Thomas, VI 00802. Phone: (809) 774-1390.

- Christiansted-St. Croix Port of Entry, Sunny Isle Shopping Cntr. Ste. 5A, Christiansted, Saint Croix, USVI 00823.

Virginia—Norfolk Field Office, Norfolk Commerce Park, 5280 Henneman Dr., Norfolk, VA 23513.

- Washington Field Office, 2675 Prosperity Ave., Fairfax, VA 20598.

Washington—Seattle Field Office, 12500 Tukwila International Blvd., Seattle, WA 98168.

- Spokane Field Office, U.S. Courthouse, 920 W. Riverside Rm. 691, Spokane, WA 99201.

- Yakima Field Office, 415 N. Third St., Yakima, WA 98901.

West Virginia—Charleston Field Office, 210 Kanawha Blvd. West, Charleston, WV 25302.

Wisconsin—Milwaukee Field Office, 310 E. Knapp St., Milwaukee, WI 53202. *See also* **Bloomington, Minnesota** St. Paul Field Office.

Wyoming—Casper Field Office, 150 East B St. Rm. 1014, Casper, WY 82601. *See also* **Denver, Colorado** Field Office.

U.S. COAST GUARD

DISTRICT OFFICES

ATLANTIC *(Alabama, Arkansas, Colorado, Connecticut, Delaware, District of Columbia, Florida, Georgia, Illinois, Indiana, Iowa, Kansas, Kentucky, Louisiana, Maine, Maryland, Massachusetts, Michigan, Minnesota, Mississippi, Missouri, Nebraska, New Hampshire, New Jersey, New Mexico, New York, North Carolina, North Dakota, Ohio, Oklahoma, Panama Canal Zone, Pennsylvania, Puerto Rico, Rhode Island, South Carolina, South Dakota, Tennessee, Texas, Vermont, Virgin Islands, Virginia, West Virginia, Wisconsin, Wyoming)*—Commander (md), Maintenance and Logistics Command (Atlantic), 300 E. Main St. - Ste. 00, Norfolk, VA 23510. Phone: (757) 628-4275.

PACIFIC *(Alaska, Arizona, California, Hawaii, Idaho, Montana, Nevada, Oregon, U.S. Pacific Island Possessions, Utah, Washington)*—Commander (md), Maintenance

97.009
through
97.130
(cont.)

and Logistics Command (Pacific), Coast Guard Island, Bldg. 52, Alameda, CA 94501-5100. Phone: (510) 437-3474.

- First Coast Guard District (obr), 408 Atlantic Ave., Boston, MA 02210-2209. Phones: (617) 223-8364; FAX (617) 223-8026.

- Western River Directorate (obr), 1222 Spruce St., St. Louis, MO 63103-2398. Phones: (314) 539-3900; FAX (314) 539-3755.

- Fifth Coast Guard District (Aowb), Federal Bldg., 431 Crawford St., Portsmouth, VA 23704-5004. Phones: (757) 398-6557; FAX (757) 398-6334.

- Seventh Coast District (oan), Brickell Plaza, 909 SE 1st Ave., Miami, FL 33130-3050. Phones: (305) 415-6743; FAX (305) 415-6757.

- Eighth Coast Guard District (obc), Boggs Federal Bldg., 501 Magazine St., New Orleans, LA 70130-3396. Phones: (504) 589-2965; FAX (504) 589-3063.

- Ninth Coast Guard District (obr), 1240 E. 9th St., Cleveland, OH 44199-2060. Phones: (216) 902-6085; FAX (216) 902-6088.

- Eleventh Coast Guard District (oan-2), Bldg. 10 - Rm. 0-6, Alameda, CA 94501-5100. Phones: (510) 437-3514: FAX (510) 437-5836.

- Thirteenth Coast Guard District (ob), Federal Bldg., 915 2nd Ave., Seattle, WA 98174-1067. Phones: (206) 220-7270; FAX (206) 220-7285.

- Fourteenth Coast Guard District (oan), Federal Bldg. - Rm. 139, 300 Ala Moana Blvd., Honolulu, HI 96850-4982. Phones: (808) 541-2315; FAX (808) 541-2318.

- Seventeenth Coast Guard District (oan), Juneau, AK 99802-5517. Phones: (907) 463-2268; FAX (907) 463-2273.

UNITED STATES SECRET SERVICE

Regional or local field offices are located in most state capitals and in some other cities. Consult local phone directory for addresses and phone numbers, or contact headquarters office directly (see main entry).

FEDERAL EMERGENCY MANAGEMENT AGENCY

REGIONAL OFFICES

REGION I—99 High St. - 6th fl., Boston, MA 02110. Phone: (617) 956-7506.

REGION II—26 Federal Plaza - Rm. 307, New York, NY 10278-0002. Phone: (212) 680-3600.

REGION III—1 Independence Mall -6th fl., Philadelphia, PA 19106. Phone: (215) 931-5608.

REGION IV—3003 Chamblee-Tucker Rd., Atlanta, GA 30341. Phone: (770) 220-5200.

REGION V—536 S. Clark St., Chicago, IL 60605. Phone: (312) 408-5500.

REGION VI—Federal Regional Center, 800 N. Loop 288, Denton, TX 76209-3698. Phone: (940) 898-5399.

REGION VII—9221 Ward Pkwy. Ste. 300, Kansas City, MO 64114-3372. Phone: (816) 283-7063.

REGION VIII—Federal Center - Bldg. 710, Denver, CO 80225-0267. Phone: (303) 235-4800.

REGION IX—1111 Broadway - Ste. 200, Oakland, CA 94607. Phone: (510) 627-7006.

REGION X—Federal Regional Center, 130 - 228th St. SW, Bothell, WA 98021-9796. Phone: (425) 487-4600.

AGENCY INDEX

NOTE: Entries cover administrative units and sub-units, referring to program numbers used in Parts II, III, and IV (explained in Part I under "Organization of the Federal Programs").

APPALACHIAN REGIONAL COMMISSION, 23.001-23.011

ARCHITECTURAL AND TRANSPORTATION BARRIERS COM-PLIANCE BOARD, 88.001

COMMISSION ON CIVIL RIGHTS, 29.001

COMMODITY FUTURES TRADING COMMISSION, 78.004

CORPORATION FOR NATIONAL AND COMMUNITY SERVICE, 94.002-94.026

DEPARTMENT OF AGRICULTURE, 10.001-10.999
  Agricultural Marketing Service, 10.153-10.172
  Agricultural Research Service, 10.001, 10.700
  Animal and Plant Health Inspection Service, 10.025-10.030
  Departmental Management, 10.443
  Economic Research Service, 10.250-10.255
  Farm Service Agency, 10.051-10.069, 10.080-10.117, 10.404, 10.406-10.407, 10.421, 10.435, 10.449, 10.451, 10.999
  Food and Nutrition Service, 10.543-10.595
  Food Safety and Inspection Service, 10.475-10.479
  Foreign Agricultural Service, 10.600-10.615, 10.777, 10.960-10.962
  Forest Service, 10.652-10.694
  National Agricultural Statistics Service, 10.950
  National Institute of Food and Agriculture, 10.200-10.228, 10.303-10.331, 10.500
  Natural Resources Conservation Service, 10.072, 10.902-10.933
  Office of the Chief Economist, 10.290
  Risk Management Agency, 10.450, 10.456-10.458
  Rural Business-Cooperative Service, 10.350-10.352, 10.767-10.769, 10.771-10.773, 10.854, 10.866-10.874
  Rural Housing Service, 10.405, 10.410-10.420, 10.427-10.433, 10.438, 10.446-10.448, 10.766
  Rural Utilities Service, 10.759-10.763, 10.770, 10.781-10.851, 10.855-10.864, 10.886

DEPARTMENT OF COMMERCE, 11.001-11.999

Bureau of Economic Analysis, Economics and Statistics Administration, 11.025

Bureau of Industry and Security, 11.150

Census Bureau, 11.001-11.006

Economic Development Administration, 11.300-11.313

Economics and Statistics Administration, 11.026, 11.016

International Trade Administration, 11.106-11.113

Minority Business Development Agency, 11.801

National Institute of Standards and Technology, 11.013, 11.601-11.620

National Oceanic and Atmospheric Administration, 11.008-11.012, 11.400-11.483, 11.999

National Telecommunications and Information Administration, 11.014, 11.549-11.558

Patent and Trademark Office, 11.900

DEPARTMENT OF DEFENSE, 12.002-12.910

Air Force, Materiel Command, 12.800

Army, Materiel Command, 12.431

Army, Medical Research and Material Command, 12.420

Army, Military History, 12.440

Army, National Guard Bureau, 12.400-12.404

Army, Office of the Chief of Engineers, 12.100-12.116

Defense Advanced Research Projects Agency, 12.910

Defense Intelligence Agency, 12.598

Defense Logistics Agency, 12.002

Defense Threat Reduction Agency, 12.351-12.352

Federal Voting Assistance Program, 12.217-12.219

Marine Corps Systems Command, 12.369

National Security Agency, 12.900-12.902

Navy, Office of the Chief of Naval Research, 12.300-12.350

Office of Economic Adjustment, 12.600-12.615

Office of the Secretary of Defense, 12.225, 12.355-12.360, 12.550, 12.560-12.579, 12.630-12.631

Office of the Under Secretary of Defense for Personnel and Readiness, 12.554

Secretaries of Military Departments, 12.700

Uniformed Services University of the Health Sciences, 12.750

DEPARTMENT OF EDUCATION, 84.002-84.421

Institute of Education Sciences, 84.305, 84.324, 84.329, 84.372

Office of Career, Technical, and Adult Education, 84.002, 84.048-84.051, 84.101, 84.191, 84.245, 84.259

Office of Educational Research and Improvement, 84.287

Office of Elementary and Secondary Education, 84.004, 84.010-84.013, 84.040-84.041, 84.060, 84.141-84.144, 84.149, 84.184, 84.196, 84.256, 84.283-84.287, 84.299, 84.330, 84.356-84.362, 84.365-84.369, 84.371, 84.377, 84.403, 84.415

Office of Federal Student Aid, 84.007, 84.033, 84.063, 84.268, 84.379, 84.408

Office of Human Resources and Administration, 84.145

Office of Innovation and Improvement, 84.165, 84.215, 84.282, 84.295, 84.336-84.354, 84.363, 84.370, 84.374, 84.411

Office of Postsecondary Education, 84.015-84.022, 84.031, 84.042-84.047, 84.066, 84.103-84.120, 84.200, 84.217-84.229, 84.274, 84.334-84.335, 84.378, 84.382, 84.407, 84.414

Office of Special Education and Rehabilitative Services, 84.027, 84.126-84.129, 84.160-84.161, 84.173-84.181, 84.187, 84.235-84.240, 84.246-84.250, 84.264, 84.315-84.323, 84.325-84.328, 84.373, 84.380

DEPARTMENT OF ENERGY, 81.003-81.214

DEPARTMENT OF HEALTH AND HUMAN SERVICES, 93.001-93.998

Administration for Children and Families, 93.009, 93.060, 93.075-93.076, 93.086-93.087, 93.090-93.093, 93.235, 93.254, 93.508, 93.550-93.605, 93.612-93.616, 93.623, 93.643-93.948, 93.652-93.676, 93.708-93.716

Administration for Community Living, 93.041-93.054, 93.071-93.072, 93.234, 93.433, 93.464, 93.517, 93.613, 93.617-93.618, 93.630-93.632, 93.706, 93.734, 93.747, 93.761

Agency for Healthcare Research and Quality, 93.225-93.226

Agency for Toxic Substances and Disease Registry, 93.161, 93.240, 93.534

Centers for Disease Control and Prevention, 93.055-93.056, 93.061-93.070, 93.073, 93.079-93.084, 93.097-93.098, 93.116, 93.118, 93.135-93.136, 93.184-93.185, 93.197, 93.261-93.262, 93.268-93.270, 93.283, 93.305, 93.316-93.317, 93.332-93.339, 93.507, 93.521-93.524, 93.531-93.533, 93.535, 93.538-93.542, 93.548,

93.606, 93.649, 93.733, 93.735-93.745, 93.749-93.754, 93.810-93.814, 93.823, 93.832-93.833, 93.845, 93.852, 93.858, 93.860, 93.875, 93.919, 93.938-93.947, 93.977, 93.985-93.988, 93.991, 93.998

Centers for Medicare and Medicaid Services, 93.506, 93.525, 93.529, 93.537, 93.545-93.546, 93.609-93.611, 93.621, 93.624-93.628, 93.634, 93.650-93.651, 93.767-93.791

Food and Drug Administration, 93.103, 93.448-93.449, 93.876

Health Resources and Services Administration, 93.011, 93.059, 93.107-93.110, 93.117, 93.124-93.134, 93.145, 93.153-93.157, 93.162, 93.165, 93.178, 93.186, 93.191, 93.211, 93.223-93.224, 93.236, 93.241, 93.247-93.253, 93.255-93.259, 93.264-93.267, 93.288, 93.300-93.303, 93.342, 93.358-93.359, 93.364-93.365, 93.400-93.409, 93.501-93.504, 93.510-93.516, 93.526-93.528, 93.547, 93.549, 93.622, 93.703, 93.732, 93.822, 93.824, 93.884-93.888, 93.908, 93.912-93.918, 93.923-93.932, 93.964-93.969, 93.994

Indian Health Service, 93.123, 93.164, 93.193, 93.210, 93.228-93.231, 93.237, 93.284, 93.441-93.444, 93.933, 93.970-93.972

National Institutes of Health, 93.077, 93.113, 93.121, 93.140-93.143, 93.172-93.173, 93.187, 93.209, 93.213, 93.220, 93.232-93.233, 93.242, 93.273, 93.279-93.282, 93.285-93.286, 93.307-93.310, 93.313, 93.321, 93.350-93.351, 93.361, 93.389-93.399, 93.701-93.702, 93.704, 93.837-93.879, 93.846-93.847, 93853-93.856, 93.859, 93.865-93.867, 93.839, 93.936, 93.989

Office of Disease Prevention and Health Promotion, 93.990

Office of Minority Health, 93.004-93.006, 93.137, 93.910

Office of Population Affairs, 93.217, 93.260, 93.974, 93.995

Office of the Secretary, 93.001, 93.007-93.008, 93.015-93.019, 93.085, 93.088-93.089, 93.239, 93.290, 93.296-93.297, 93.311, 93.360, 93.452, 93.718-93.728, 93.817, 93.825-93.831, 93.889

President's Council on Fitness, Sports, and Nutrition, 93.289

Program Support Center, 93.291

Substance Abuse and Mental Health Services Administration, 93.104, 93.138, 93.150, 93.243, 93.275-93.276, 93.748, 93.958-93.959, 93.997

DEPARTMENT OF HOMELAND SECURITY, 97.005-97.132

DEPARTMENT OF HOUSING AND URBAN DEVELOPMENT, 14.008-14.914

Office of Community Planning and Development, 14.218-14.278

Office of Disability Employment Policy, 17.720

Office of Federal Contract Compliance Programs, 17.301

Office of Labor-Management Standards, 17.309

Office of the Secretary, Women's Bureau, 17.700

Office of Workers' Compensation Programs, 17.302, 17.307, 17.310

Veteran's Employment and Training Service, 17.801-17.807

Wage and Hour Division, 17.303-17.306, 17.308

DEPARTMENT OF STATE, 19.009-19.901

Bureau of East Asian and Pacific Affairs, 19.124

Bureau of Economic and Business Affairs, 19.322

Bureau of Educational and Cultural Affairs, 19.009-19.012, 19.015, 19.025, 19.400-19.450

Bureau of Intelligence and Research, 19.300

Bureau of International Security and Nonproliferation, 19.033, 19.901

Bureau of Near Eastern Affairs, 19.016, 19.021, 19.221, 19.500, 19.600

Bureau of Personnel, 19.013, 19.020

Bureau of Population, Refugees, and Migration, 19.018, 19.510-19.522

Bureau of Western Hemisphere Affairs, 19.750

Office of Diplomatic Security, 19.030-19.031

Office of Marine Conservation, Bureau of Oceans and International Environmental and Scientific Affairs, 19.204

Office of the Secretary of State, 19.301

DEPARTMENT OF THE INTERIOR, 15.020-15.981

Bureau of Indian Affairs, 15.020-15.025, 15.029-15.041, 15.048-15.057, 15.060-15.113, 15.124, 15.133-15.148

Bureau of Indian Education, 15.026-15.028, 15.042-15.047, 15.058-15.059, 15.114, 15.130, 15.149-15.151, 15.960

Bureau of Land Management, 15.214-15.225, 15.227-15.242

Bureau of Ocean Energy Management, 15.408-15.424, 15.428

Bureau of Reclamation, 15.504-15.534, 15.537-15.565

Bureau of Safety and Environmental Enforcement, 15.441

Fish and Wildlife Service, 15.605-15.677

Indian Arts and Crafts Board, 15.850

National Park Service, 15.406-15.407, 15.904-15.958, 15.962

Office of Insular Affairs, 15.875

Office of the Chief Financial Officer, 66.202-66.203
Office of Water, 66.418-66.472, 66.474-66.481
Region 1, 66.110
Region 4, 66.128
Region 6, 66.124
Region 9, 66.126, 66.600
Region 10, 66.121-66.123

EQUAL EMPLOYMENT OPPORTUNITY COMMISSION, 30.001-30.011

EXECUTIVE OFFICE OF THE PRESIDENT, 95.001-95.006

EXPORT-IMPORT BANK, 31.007

FEDERAL COMMUNICATIONS COMMISSION, 32.001

FEDERAL MARITIME COMMISSION, 33.001

FEDERAL MEDIATION AND CONCILIATION SERVICE, 34.001-34.002

FEDERAL TRADE COMMISSION, 36.001

GENERAL SERVICES ADMINISTRATION, 39.002-39.012

GOVERNMENT PRINTING OFFICE, 40.001-40.002

INDEPENDENT BOARDS AND COMMISSIONS, 90.100-90.500
Broadcasting Board of Governors, 90.500
Delta Regional Authority, 90.200-90.202
Denali Commission, 90.100
Japan-U.S. Friendship Commission, 90.300
U.S. Election Assistance Commission, 90.400-90.403

LIBRARY OF CONGRESS, 42.001-42.009

NATIONAL AERONAUTICS AND SPACE ADMINISTRATION, 43.001-43.010

NATIONAL ARCHIVES AND RECORDS ADMINISTRATION, 89.001-89.003

NATIONAL CREDIT UNION ADMINISTRATION, 44.002

NATIONAL FOUNDATION ON THE ARTS AND HUMANITIES, 45.024-45.313
Federal Council on the Arts and the Humanities, 45.201

MASTER INDEX

- Index entries refer to program numbers used in Part II. The program numbering system is explained on page .

- Italicized program *numbers* indicate programs that provide financial assistance. (Assistance classifications are explained beginning on page 3.) Examples:

  ABANDONED MINE LAND RECLAMATION (AMLR) PROGRAM, *15.252*
  Women, Infants, and Children (WIC) Program, *10.557*

- Subject headings are in bold-face type. Examples:

  Adult education
  Wildlife, waterfowl

- Program titles are in capital letters. Bracketed agency identifiers are inserted when the title inadequately describes program focus. Examples:

  BUSINESS AND INDUSTRY LOANS [USDA], *10.768*

  GENERAL RESEARCH AND TECHNOLOGY ACTIVITY [HUD], *14.506*

- Also provided are (1) popular and abbreviated program titles, (2) government departments and independent agencies, (3) names of Acts, (4) section and title numbers of Acts when in general usage, and (5) entries with general references and cross-references to program activities and governmental sub-entities. Examples:

  (1)   Age Search, 11.006
        VBOP (Veterans Business Outreach Centers), SBA, *59.044*

  (2)   Department of Defense (DOD), 12.002 through 12.910
        Environmental Protection Agency (EPA), 66.001 through 66.952

  (3)   AIDS Housing Opportunity Act, *14.241*

  (4)   Section 22, Water Resources Development Act, 12.110
        Title I, ESEA, migrants, *84.011*

  (5)   Acid precipitation research, NOAA, *11.432, 11.459*
        Brownfield projects, *see* Urban renewal
        National Institute on Drug Abuse (NIDA), NIH, 93.279

- Remarks on using the index are offered on page 13 in the section on "Obtaining Federal Assistance," under "STEP ONE: USE THE MASTER INDEX."

Army Research Office, *12.431*
biomedical imaging research, *93.286*
biomedical research traineeships, international program, *93.989*
biostatistics NRSA, *93.225*
biostatistics, public health graduate traineeships, *93.964*
cancer research, *93.396*
cancer research manpower development, NRSA, *93.398*
carcinogens research, *93.393*
deafness, communicative disorders research, *93.173*
DOD sciences research, fellowships, *12.630*
drug abuse, addiction research, *93.279*
energy-related basic research, *81.049*
environmental health hazards research, *93.113*
EPA environmental sustainability design competition, *66.516*
FDA research, *93.103*
fish, wildlife water, land management, 15.608
fossil energy research, *81.089*
geosciences research, *47.050*
human development research, *93.865*
human genomes research, *93.172*
measurement, engineering research, standards, *11.609*
mental health research training, *93.282*
microbiology, infectious diseases research, *93.856*
military, biological-medical research, *12.420*
minority health, disparities research, researchers education loan repayment, *93.307*
Navy research, education support, *12.300*
neurosciences research, *93.853*
NIEHS Superfund research, hazardous materials, *93.143*
NIH Clinical Research Loan Repayment Program (CR-LRP), *93.280*
NIH intramural research training, *93.140*
NIH Pediatric Research Loan Repayment Program, *93.285*
NIH Undergraduate Scholarship Program, disadvantaged, *93.187*
NOAA unallied projects, *11.452*, *11.472*
NSF biomedical engineering education, research, *47.041*
NSF research, *47.074*
pharmacology, physiology, biorelated chemistry research, training, *93.859*
Polar Programs, *47.078*
research, research infrastructure resources, training, *93.389*
Sea Grant Support, *11.417*
sleep disorders research, *93.233*
stem cell research, *93.839*
transplantation biology research, *93.839*, *93.855*
WMD, domestic preparedness, *97.005*, *97.007*
see also Behavioral sciences, education, services; Cancer control, prevention, research; Chemicals, chemistry; Civil defense; Drug abuse; Drugs, drug research; Environmental sciences; Genetics; Health, medical research; Minority education; National Research Service Awards; Pharmacology, pharmacy; Physical sciences; Science education; Scientific research

BIOLOGICAL SCIENCES, *47.074*
BIOMASS RESEARCH AND DEVELOPMENT INITIATIVE COMPETITIVE GRANTS PROGRAM, *10.312*
Biomass energy, *see* Energy *entries*
BIOMEDICAL ADVANCED RESEARCH AND DEVELOPMENT AUTHORITY (BARDA), BIODEFENSE MEDICAL COUNTERMEASURE DEVELOPMENT, *93.360*
BIOMEDICAL RESEARCH AND RESEARCH TRAINING, *93.859*
BIOMONITORING PROGRAMS FOR STATE PUBLIC HEALTH LABORATORIES, *93.062*
BIOTECHNOLOGY RISK ASSESSMENT RESEARCH, *10.219*
Bioterrorism, *see* Civil defense
Birds, *see* Animal disease control, health, welfare; Poultry, egg products; Recreation*entries*; Wildlife, waterfowl
Birth control, *see* Family planning
BIRTH DEFECTS AND DEVELOPMENTAL DISABILITIES—PREVENTION AND SURVEILLANCE, *93.073*
Black lung, *see* Coal mining; Respiratory diseases
Black Lung Clinics, *93.965*
BLIND REHABILITATION CENTERS, 64.007
Blindness and the blind
   braille, cassettes, talking books, instructional, library services, 42.001
   elderly, independent living services, *84.177*
   federal employment, 27.005
   Food Stamps, *10.551*
   home health services, Medicaid, *93.778*
   income support, Guam, Puerto Rico, Virgin Islands, *93.560*
   income support, Social Security, *96.006*
   interpreter, sign language training, *84.160*
   National Eye Institute research, *93.867*
   preschool education, *84.173*
   rehabilitation personnel training, *84.264*
   veterans, optical aids, 64.013
   veterans rehabilitation centers, 64.007
   vocational rehabilitation personnel training, *84.129*
   see also Audiovisual aids, film, video; Community health services; Disabled, handicapped *entries*; Health, medical *entries*; Veterans, disabled; Vocational rehabilitation; Volunteers
BLM (Bureau of Land Management), DOI, *see* Agency Index
Block grant programs
   Child Care and Development Block Grant Act of 1990, *93.575*, *93.596*
   child care and development, CCDF, *93.575*, *93.596*
   child care/social services, TANF, *93.558*
   community development, entitlement, *14.218*
   community development, Indians, *14.862*
   community development, insular areas, *14.225*
   community development, small cities, *14.228*
   community development, states, *14.228*
   Community Mental Health Services, *93.958*
   community services, CSBG, *93.569*
   community services, discretionary, *93.570*
   energy assistance, low-income, LIHEAP, *93.568*
   Indian housing, *14.867*

voting rights, 16.104

women, 17.700

see also Complaint investigation; Consumers, consumer sciences; Disabled *entries*; Legal services; Mental retardation

CIVIL RIGHTS AND PRIVACY RULE COMPLIANCE ACTIVITIES, 93.001

Civil Rights Division, DOJ, *see* Agency Index

CIVIL RIGHTS OF INSTITUTIONALIZED PERSONS, 16.105

CIVIL RIGHTS PROSECUTION, 16.109

CIVIL RIGHTS TRAINING AND ADVISORY SERVICES [DOED], 84.004

Civil Service employment, *see* Federal employment

CIVIL WAR BATTLEFIELD LAND ACQUISITION GRANTS, 15.928

Claims, *see* Complaint investigation; Insurance; Legal services

Clean Air Act, *see* Air pollution

CLEAN FUELS, 20.519

CLEAN VESSEL ACT PROGRAM, 15.616

Clean Vessel Act Pumpout Grant Program, 15.616

Clean Water Act, *see* Water pollution abatement, prevention

Clean Water State Revolving Fund, wastewater treatment, 66.458

CLEARINGHOUSE SERVICES, CIVIL RIGHTS DISCRIMINATION COMPLAINTS, 29.001

Clearinghouses, *see* Information general, clearinghouses

Climate

air pollution effects studies, demonstrations, 66.034

air quality research, services, 11.459

airport weather reporting equipment, 20.106

Applied Meteorology Research, 11.468

atmospheric research, 47.050

aviation research, 20.108

education, research, facilities, NOAA, 11.469

emergency snowmelt preparations, 12.111

environmental systems research, NOAA, 11.432

Hydrologic Research, 11.462

Hydrometeorological Development, education, training, NOAA, 11.467

National Climate Program Act, 11.431, 11.459

NESDIS environmental sciences education, research, 11.440

National Weather Service and Related Agencies Authorization Act of 1999, 11.460

NOAA Educational Partnerships Program, minority, 11.481

NOAA special projects, 11.460

Polar Programs, 47.078

remote sensing research, 11.440

research, 11.431

research, Coastal Ocean Program, 11.478

snowmelt surveys, 10.907

Weather Service Organic Act, 11.431, 11.459, 11.462, 11.467

wind energy research, 81.087

see also Earth sciences; Flood prevention, control; Hurricanes

CLIMATE AND ATMOSPHERIC RESEARCH, 11.431

Clinic Entrances Act, 16.105

CLINICAL RESEARCH LOAN REPAYMENT PROGRAM FOR INDIVIDUALS FROM DISADVANTAGED BACKGROUNDS, 93.220

Clothing, *see* Home economics

CLPPP (Childhood Lead Poisoning Prevention Program), 93.197

CMH Dissertation Fellowship, 12.440

CMHS (Community Mental Health Services) Block Grant, 93.958

CMHS (Community Mental Health Services) Child Mental Health Service Initiative, 93.104

CMS (Centers for Medicare and Medicaid Services), HHS, *see* Agency Index

CMS (Centers for Medicare and Medicaid Services) Research, 93.779

CNCS (Corporation for National and Community Service), 94.002 through 94.023

COAL MINE WORKERS' COMPENSATION, 17.307

COAL MINERS RESPIRATORY IMPAIRMENT TREATMENT CLINICS AND SERVICES, 93.965

Coal mining

abandoned mine land reclamation, 15.252

Acid Mine Drainage (AMD), 15.253

Black Lung Clinics, 93.965

disabled miners compensation, 17.307

energy production research, 81.089

Federal Mine Safety and Health Amendments Act of 1977, 17.307

mine subsidence, CDBG, 14.225, 14.228

permits, regulation, inspection, 15.250

research, 81.057

subsidence insurance, 15.252

see also Energy research; Mineral resources; Mining, mining industries; Occupational health, safety

Coast and Geodetic Survey Act, *see* Maps, charts

Coast Guard, *see* Agency Index (DOT, U.S. Coast Guard)

COASTAL PROGRAM [DOI], 15.630

COASTAL WETLANDS PLANNING PROTECTION AND RESTORATION ACT, 66.124

COASTAL WETLANDS PLANNING, PROTECTION AND RESTORATION PROGRAM, 15.614

Coastal zone

Atlantic, fisheries management, 11.474

Beach Monitoring and Notification Program, EPA, 66.472

Beaches Environmental Assessment and Coastal Health Act of 2000, 66.472

boundary demarcation, NOAA, 11.400

Clean Vessel Act, pumpout/dump stations, 15.616

Clean Water Act studies, training, 66.436

Coastal Program, FWS, 15.630

Coastal Wetlands Planning, Protection and Restoration Act, 15.614

Coastal Zone Management Act of 1972, 11.419, 11.420

Coral Reef Conservation Act, 11.463

ecological research, NOAA, 11.426

ecosystem management, NOAA, 11.473

emergency rehabilitation, 12.102

environmental systems research, NOAA, 11.432

Conservation, wetlands, *see* Water conservation; Wetlands

Conservation, wildlife, *see* Wildlife, waterfowl

CONSOLIDATED AND TECHNICAL ASSISTANCE GRANT PROGRAM TO ADDRESS CHILDREN AND YOUTH EXPERIENCING DOMESTIC AND SEXUAL VIOLENCE AND ENGAGE MEN AND BOYS AS ALLIES, *16.888*

Consolidated Farm and Rural Development Act (CFRDA), *see* Rural areas

CONSOLIDATED GRANT TO THE OUTLYING AREAS, *84.403*

CONSOLIDATED HEALTH CENTERS (COMMUNITY HEALTH CENTERS, MIGRANT HEALTH CENTERS, HEALTH CARE FOR THE HOMELESS, AND PUBLIC HOUSING PRIMARY CARE), *93.224*

CONSOLIDATED PESTICIDE ENFORCEMENT COOPERATIVE AGREEMENTS, *66.700*

Consolidated Program Support Grants, EPA, *66.600*

CONSOLIDATED TRIBAL GRANT PROGRAM, *15.021*

CONSORTIUM FOR TOBACCO USE CESSATION TECHNICAL ASSISTANCE, *93.751*

Constitutional rights, *see* Civil rights

Construction

armories, *12.400*

Census Bureau data, 11.001

Davis-Bacon Act, 17.201, 17.303

energy conservation, renewable energy outreach, training, *81.117*

federal contracts, wage-hour laws, 17.303

federally assisted contractors, 17.301

flood plain data, services, 12.104

handicapped, accessibility standards, design, research, training, 88.001

industrial, EDA projects, *11.300*

marine, atmospheric sciences projects, *11.469*

National Guard facilities, *12.400*

research, advanced technology, Corps of Engineers, *12.114*

soil surveys, 10.903

standards, research, *11.609*

see also Architecture; Buildings; Community development; Disabled, handicapped *entries*; Education facilities; Energy conservation; Health facilities *entries*; Highways, roads, bridges; Housing *entries*; Public works

CONSTRUCTION & ENVIRONMENTAL COMPLIANCE & REMEDIATION, *43.010*

CONSTRUCTION GRANTS FOR WASTEWATER TREATMENT WORKS, *66.418*

Construction Productivity Advanced Research (CPAR) Program, Corps of Engineers, *12.114*

CONSTRUCTION RESERVE FUND [DOT], *20.812*

CONSULTATION AGREEMENTS [DOL], *17.504*

CONSUMER CREDIT PROTECTION, 17.306

CONSUMER DATA AND NUTRITION RESEARCH, 10.253

Consumer Expenditure Survey (CES), 17.003

CONSUMER OPERATED AND ORIENTED PLAN PROGRAM, *93.545*

Consumer Price Index (CPI), 17.003

Consumer protection, *see* Complaint investigation; Consumers, consumer services

Consumers, consumer services

advertising complaints, 36.001

agricultural marketing, 10.163

agricultural products inspection, 10.162

broadcasting, communications complaints, 32.001

consumer credit reporting, debt collection, 36.001

Consumer Expenditure Survey, 17.003

Consumer Credit Protection Act, 16.103, 17.306

Consumer Price Index, 17.003

credit protection, public assistance recipients, 16.103

Federal Trade Commission Act of 1914, 36.001

fisheries products inspection, 11.413

housing counseling, *14.169*

interstate land sales protection, 14.168

investment, securities market protection, 58.001

manufactured homes safety standards, 14.171

meat, poultry, eggs inspection, 10.477

meat, poultry inspection, *10.475*

packaging complaints, 36.001

perishable foods complaints, 10.165

pollution source reduction information dissemination, outreach, EPA, *66.717*

wage garnishment protection, 17.306

Weights and Measures Service, NIST, 11.606

see also Complaint investigation; Food inspection, grading; Home management; Hotlines; Information, general; Legal services; Volunteers

Contagious diseases, *see* Communicable diseases

Continuing education, *see* Adult education; Higher education

CONTINUUM OF CARE PROGRAM, *14.267*

Contraception, *see* Family planning

CONTRACEPTION AND INFERTILITY RESEARCH LOAN REPAYMENT PROGRAM, *93.209*

Contract Commodity Direct Payments, *10.055*

Contract Support, BIA, *15.024*

Contracts, *see* Government contracts

CONTRIBUTIONS TO INTERNATIONAL ORGANIZATIONS FOR OVERSEAS ASSISTANCE, *19.515*

Controlled substances, *see* Drugs

COOPERATING TECHNICAL PARTNERS [DHS], *97.045*

COOPERATIVE AGREEMENTS FOR PRESCRIPTION DRUG MONITORING PROGRAM, ELECTRONIC HEALTH RECORD (EHR) INTEGRATION, AND INTEROPERABILITY EXPANSION, *93.748*

COOPERATIVE AGREEMENTS FOR STATE-BASED COMPREHENSIVE BREAST AND CERVICAL CANCER EARLY DETECTION PROGRAMS, *93.919*

COOPERATIVE AGREEMENTS FOR STATE-BASED DIABETES CONTROL PROGRAMS AND EVALUATION OF SURVEILLANCE SYSTEMS, *93.988*

COOPERATIVE AGREEMENTS TO IMPROVE THE HEALTH STATUS OF MINORITY POPULATIONS, *93.004*

COOPERATIVE AGREEMENTS TO PROMOTE ADOLESCENT HEALTH THROUGH SCHOOL-BASED HIV/STD PREVENTION AND SCHOOL-BASED SURVEILLANCE, *93.079*

environmental education professionals training, *66.950*

environmental education projects, *66.951*

Global Development Alliance, USAID, *98.011*

highway transportation, *20.215*

library-museum partnerships, *45.312*

Magnet Schools Assistance, *84.165*

Mathematics and Science Partnerships, OESE, *84.366*

model projects, *84.215*

National Health Promotion, *93.990*

native American language preservation, *93.587*

NSF engineering, mathematics, science improvement, *47.076*

pollution source reduction information dissemination, outreach, EPA, *66.717*

postsecondary program improvement, access, FIPSE, *84.116*

project technical assistance, training, *84.283*

rural, Television Demonstration Grants, *10.769*

teacher quality enhancement, recruitment, partnership, *84.336*

see also Adult education; Agricultural education; Aliens, immigrants, refugees; Arts, arts education; Behavioral sciences, education, services; Bilingual education, services; Civil rights; Dental education, training; Disabled, handicapped, education; Disadvantaged, education; Early childhood education; Education *entries*; Elementary and secondary education; English as a second language; Environmental education; Fellowships, scholarships, traineeships; Foreign languages; Health, medical education, training; Higher education; Humanities education, research; Illiteracy; Indian education, training; International programs, studies; Land-grant colleges, universities Law enforcement education, training; Mathematics; Minority education; School, Schools *entries*; Science education; Teacher education, training; Technical training; Tutoring; Veterans education, training; Vocational *entries*

EDUCATION AND HUMAN RESOURCES [NSF], *47.076*

EDUCATION AND OUTREACH INITIATIVES, *14.416*

EDUCATION AND PREVENTION TO REDUCE SEXUAL ABUSE OF RUNAWAY, HOMELESS AND STREET YOUTH, *93.557*

EDUCATION, TRAINING, AND ENHANCED SERVICES TO END VIOLENCE AGAINST AND ABUSE OF WOMEN WITH DISABILITIES, *16.529*

Education and Training Vouchers, ACF, *93.599*

Education counseling

advanced placement test fee payment, DOED, *84.330*

disadvantaged, graduate opportunities, *84.217*

disadvantaged, postsecondary, personal, academic, career guidance, *84.042*

disadvantaged, postsecondary, staff training, *84.103*

disadvantaged youth, higher education preparation, Upward Bound, *84.047*

disadvantaged youth, secondary, postsecondary, Talent Search, *84.044*

Dropout Prevention Programs, *84.360*

Educational Opportunity Centers, adults, *84.066*

Extension Service, *10.500*

health careers programs, *93.107*

Indians, *84.060*

institutionalized neglected, delinquent children, *84.013*

Juvenile Mentoring Program, *16.726*

low-income secondary students, TRIO supportive services, scholarships, *84.334*

Mentoring Children of Prisoners, ACF, *93.616*

migrant children, *84.011*

migrants, college program, *84.149*

migrants, guidance, *84.141*

Services for Trafficking Victims, *16.320*

veterans, service personnel, 64.125

violence prevention, *93.910*

WIA Youth Activities, *17.259*

see also Aliens, immigrants, refugees; Bilingual education, services; Corrections; Disadvantaged, education; Drug abuse; Illiteracy; Juvenile delinquency; Social services; Tutoring; Vocational education; Youth programs

Education, elementary, *see* Elementary and secondary education

Education equipment

Army Research Office, sciences research, *12.431*

Assistance to Schools and Hospitals Abroad, USAID, *98.006*

biological sciences research, *47.074*

agriculture, challenge grants, *10.217*

Community Connect Grants, RUS, *10.863*

DOD engineering, mathematics, sciences research, *12.630*

DOD science, technology projects, *12.910*

1890 institutions, *10.216*

energy-related, used equipment, 81.022

engineering science, higher education, *47.041*

federal surplus personal property donations, 39.003

geosciences research, *47.050*

health research, research infrastructure resources, NIH

impact assistance, DOED-owned schools, *84.040*

library information services, *45.310*

mathematics, science research, NSF program, *47.049*

minority higher education strengthening, *84.031*

minority institutions, engineering, science programs, *84.120*

Native American Library Services, *45.311*

Navy research, *12.300*

NSF engineering, mathematics, science improvement, *47.076*

public radio, television, *11.550*, *93.389*

rural computer networks, RUS, *10.855*

undersea research, *11.430*

vessels, State Marine Schools, *20.806*

see also Agricultural education; Audiovisual aids, film, video; Computer products, sciences, services; Education resources; Technology transfer, utilization

Education exchange programs, *see* International programs, studies

Education facilities

Assistance to Schools and Hospitals Abroad, USAID, *98.006*

atmospheric, marine sciences research, NOAA, *11.469*

campus crime grants, *16.525*

EMERGENCY WATERSHED PROTECTION PROGRAM—FLOODPLAIN EASEMENTS—DISASTER RELIEF APPROPRIATIONS ACT, *10.928*

EMERGING INFECTIONS PROGRAMS, *93.317*

EMERGING INFECTIONS SENTINEL NETWORKS, *93.860*

EMERGING MARKETS PROGRAM [USDA], *10.603*

EMP (Emerging Markets Program), USDA, *10.603*

EMPG (Emergency Management Performance Grants), FEMA, *97.042*

Employee benefits

coal miners, dependents, disability, death compensation, *17.307*

data, compensation, working conditions, *17.005*

domestic violence, stalking victims, *16.736*

Employee Retirement Protection Act, *86.001*

Equal Pay Act, 30.005, 30.010

Family and Medical Leave Act of 1993, 17.303

farm employment, 10.950

Federal Wage Hour Laws, 17.303

longshore, harbor workers, *17.302*

merchant marine, information, 64.115

NHSC, NOAA, PHS, information, 64.115

pension, benefit plans information, standards, 17.150

pension plan insurance, *86.001*

Pension Protection Acts, *86.001*

President's Council on Physical Fitness and Sports, 93.289

public safety officers disability, death benefits, *16.571*

railroad workers, *57.001*

Social Security program research, demonstrations, *96.007*

see also Health insurance; Insurance; Labor *entries*; Occupational health, safety; Social Security Act; Statistics; Unemployment; Veterans *entries*

EMPLOYEE BENEFITS SECURITY ADMINISTRATION, 17.150

Employee Benefits Security Administration (EBSA), DOL, *see* Agency Index

Employee-management relations, *see* Labor-management relations

Employee Retirement Income Security Act (ERISA), 17.150, *86.001*

Employment

college work-study program, *84.033*

discrimination, legal services, 16.101

ETA pilots, demonstrations, research, *17.261*

farm statistics, 10.950

federal employment, 27.001

Job Opportunities for Low-Income Individuals, TANF, *93.593*

minimum wage-hour standards, 17.303

pension, benefit plans information, standards, 17.150

productivity data, 17.004

Senior Community Service Employment Program (SCSEP), *17.235*

senior environmental employment programs, *66.508, 66.518*

statistics, *17.002*

Welfare Reform Research, *93.595*

WIA Incentive Grants, *17.267*

youth, temporary federal employment, 27.003

see also Aging and the aged; Apprenticeship training; Civil rights; Complaint investigation; Disabled, handicapped, employment; Disadvantaged, employment and training; Economic development; Employee benefits; Employment *entries*; Farm workers; Federal employment; Indian education, training; Indian employment; Job creation; Labor *entries*; Statistics; Technical training; Unemployment; Veterans employment; Vocational education; Women; Youth employment

Employment and Training Administration, DOL, *see* Agency Index

Employment development, training

disabled, Job Accommodations Network (JAN), *17.720*

Delta region, *90.200, 90.201, 90.202*

ETA pilots, demonstrations, research, *17.261*

facilities, HUD Dollar Home Sales, 14.313

food stamp program-related, *10.561*

import-caused unemployment, *17.245*

Job Access—Reverse Commute, DOT, *20.516*

Job Opportunities for Low-Income Individuals, TANF, *93.593*

Jobs Training Bill, *93.667*

low-income elderly, *17.235*

National Guard Challenge Program, youth, *12.404*

Native American Employment and Training, *17.265*

Operation Weed and Seed, *16.595*

Presidential management interns, 27.013

refugee training programs, *93.567, 93.584*

research and development, *11.312*

Services for Trafficking Victims, *16.320*

Tribal Work Grants, *93.594*

veterans, DOL projects, *17.802*

WIA Adult Program, *17.258*

WIA Dislocated Workers, *17.260*

WIA Incentive Grants, *17.267*

WIA Youth Activities, *17.259*

Workforce Investment Act of 1998 (WIA), *17.207, 17.258, 17.259, 17.260, 17.261, 17.264, 17.265, 17.267, 17.720, 17.802, 84.002, 96.008, 96.009*

see also Apprenticeship training; Disabled, handicapped, employment; Disadvantaged, employment and training; Economic development; Employment *entries*; Federal employment; Indian education, training; Indian employment; Job creation; Public assistance; Technical training; Unemployment; Veterans education, training; Veterans employment; Vocational *entries*

Employment, disadvantaged, *see* Disadvantaged, employment and training

Employment discrimination, *see* Civil rights

EMPLOYMENT DISCRIMINATION—AGE DISCRIMINATION IN EMPLOYMENT, 30.008

EMPLOYMENT DISCRIMINATION EQUAL PAY ACT, 30.010

EMPLOYMENT DISCRIMINATION—PRIVATE BAR PROGRAM, 30.005

EMPLOYMENT DISCRIMINATION—TITLE I OF THE AMERICANS WITH DISABILITIES ACT, 30.011

EMPLOYMENT DISCRIMINATION—TITLE VII OF THE CIVIL RIGHTS ACT OF 1964, 30.001

highway, bridge construction, *20.215*

historic properties preservation, *15.904*

historic register, 15.914

hydrometeorology development, education, training, NOAA, *11.467*

Mathematics and Science Partnerships, OESE, *84.366*

mass transit, *20.505*

minority institutions, program improvements, *84.120*

National Standard Reference Data System, 11.603

NSF education, *47.041, 47.076*

pollution control, environmental research, EPA, *66.511*

soil survey data, 10.903

Standard Reference Materials, 11.604

standards, *11.609*

standards and certification information center, NCSCI, 11.610

vocational rehabilitation engineering scholarships, *84.129*

Weights and Measures Service, NIST, 11.606

see also Computer products, sciences, services; Energy *entries*; Engineering research; Highways, roads, bridges; Mass transportation; Mathematics; Measurement; Physical sciences; Public works; Science education; Scientific research; Technology transfer, utilization; Transportation

ENGINEERING GRANTS, *47.041*

Engineering research

Air Force Defense Research Sciences Program, *12.800*

Army Research Office, *12.431*

biomedical, hazardous materials, *93.143*

biomedical imaging research, *93.286*

Construction Productivity Advanced Research, Corps of Engineers, *12.114*

deafness, communicative disorders, *93.173*

DOD science, technology projects, *12.910*

DOD sciences research, fellowships, *12.630*

DOE WMD nonproliferation, *81.113*

energy-related, basic sciences, technology, *81.049*

energy-related, conservation technology development, *81.086*

energy-related, used equipment, 81.022

environmental systems, NOAA, *11.432*

EPA environmental sustainability design competition, *66.516*

EPA research fellowships, graduate, undergraduate, *66.513*

forest engineering, *10.652*

homeland security technology development, DHS, *97.077*

Hydrologic Research, *11.462*

injury prevention research, *93.136*

Manufacturing Extension Partnership, NIST, *11.611*

NASA Technology Transfer, 43.002

Navy, education support, *12.300*

NSF computer engineering, *47.070*

NSF education, *47.075*

NSF grants, *47.041*

NSF international, *47.079*

Nuclear Energy Research Initiative, *81.121*

pollution control, environmental research, EPA, *66.511*

standards, projects, *11.609*

STAR (Science to Achieve Results) Program Research, EPA, *66.509*

University-Based Homeland Security Centers, DHS, *97.061*

water desalination development, *15.506*

see also Biological sciences; Computer products, sciences, services; Energy *entries*; Engineering; Mathematics; Measurement; Nuclear sciences, technology; Physical sciences Scientific research; Technology transfer, utilization

English as a second language

adult education demonstrations, *84.191*

BECA English Language Fellow Program, *19.421*

citizenship education, 97.010

language acquisition grants, *84.365*

Low-Income Taxpayer Clinics, *21.008*

Ready-to-Learn TV, early childhood education, *84.295*

refugees, *93.566, 93.567, 93.584*

school civil rights compliance, *84.004*

see also Aliens, immigrants, refugees; Bilingual education, services; Disadvantaged, education

ENGLISH FOR HERITAGE LANGUAGE SPEAKERS GRANTS TO U.S. INSTITUTIONS OF HIGHER EDUCATION, *12.554*

ENGLISH FOR HERITAGE LANGUAGE SPEAKERS SCHOLARSHIPS, *12.555*

English language, *see* Adult education; Bilingual education, services; English as a second language; Illiteracy; Literature

ENGLISH LANGUAGE ACQUISITION STATE GRANTS, *84.365*

English Language Program, BECA, *19.421*

ENHANCE SAFETY OF CHILDREN AFFECTED BY SUBSTANCE ABUSE, *93.087*

ENHANCED HUNTER EDUCATION AND SAFETY PROGRAM, *15.626*

ENHANCED MOBILITY OF SENIORS AND INDIVIDUALS WITH DISABILITIES, *20.513*

ENHANCED SURVEILLANCE FOR NEW VACCINE PREVENTABLE DISEASE, *93.533*

Enterprise Communities, *see* Community development

Environmental education

BLM projects, Cultural Resource Management, *15.224*

brownfield projects job training, *66.815*

Chesapeake Bay Studies, education, training, *11.457*

coastal ecosystem management, NOAA, *11.420, 11.473*

Community Food Projects, USDA, *10.225*

Environmental Education and Training Program, *66.950*

Environmental Education Grants, *66.951*

environmental justice projects, *66.604*

environmental management studies fellowships, EPA, *66.952*

EPA environmental sustainability design competition, *66.516*

EPA New England Regional Office projects, *66.110*

water, wastewater treatment systems, CSBG discretionary, *93.570*

see also Community development; Family farms; Farm workers; Indian housing; Rural *entries*; Veterans housing

Housing site preparation, *see* Housing *entries*; Indian housing; Land acquisition; Subdivisions; Veterans housing

Housing statistics, *see* Census services; Economics, research, statistics; Housing research; Statistics

Housing, subsidized

AIDS-afflicted persons, services, *14.241*

community health centers, *93.224*

counseling, *14.169*

disabled, supportive housing, *14.181*

disaster housing, remote, insular area residents, FEMA, *97.048*

elderly, supportive, *14.157, 14.314*

ETA pilots, demonstrations, research, *17.261*

evaluation, research programs, *14.506*

HOME Program, *14.239*

homeless veterans, DVA provider grants, *64.024*

housing finance agency risk sharing, *14.188*

Officer Next Door Sales Program, 14.198

Project-based Section 8, *14.195*

public housing residents, supportive services, *14.870*

public, modernization, rehabilitation, *14.872*

public, Operation Weed and Seed, *16.595*

public, projects, *14.850*

public, residents, health services, *93.224*

public, residents, literacy programs, *84.002*

Rent Supplement Program, *14.149*

rural, rental, *10.427*

schools, Impact Aid, *84.041*

Section 8 Housing Choice Vouchers, *14.871*

Section 8 Moderate Rehabilitation, *14.856*

Section 236 Interest Reduction Payments, *14.103*

Single Family Property Disposition, 14.311

see also Disabled, handicapped, housing; Group homes; Home management; Homeless persons; Housing, elderly; Housing, low to moderate income; Housing mortgage, loan insurance; Housing, rural; Indian housing

HOUSING TRUST FUND, *14.275*

Housing, veterans, *see* Veterans housing

HPG (Housing Preservation Grants), rural, *10.433*

HPSL (Health Professions Student Loans), *93.342*

HRSA (Health Resources and Services Administration), HHS, *see* Agency Index

HS-STEM Career Development Program, *97.104*

HUD (Department of Housing and Urban Development), 14.103 through 14.914

HUMAN GENOME RESEARCH, *93.172*

Human immunodeficiency virus (HIV), *see* AIDS (Acquired Immunodeficiency Syndrome)

HUMAN IMMUNODEFICIENCY VIRUS (HIV)/ACQUIRED IMMUNODEFICIENCY SYNDROME (AIDS) SURVEILLANCE, *93.944*

Humanities

arts, artifacts indemnity, *45.201*

challenge grants, *45.130*

DHS Scholars and Fellows, *97.062*

Fulbright program, educational exchange, *19.400*

historical collections, preservation, *89.003*

Japan-U.S. Friendship Commission Grants, *90.300*

libraries, collections preservation training, *45.149*

local, state, regional projects, *45.129*

National Gallery of Art exhibits, 68.001

native American language preservation, *93.587*

NEH Public Programs, *45.164*

Save America's Treasures, NPS, *15.929*

see also Arts, arts education; Historic monuments, historic preservation; History; Humanities education, research; International programs, studies; Social sciences

Humanities education, research

BLM projects, Cultural Resource Management, *15.224*

challenge grants, *45.130*

Indian history, tribal heritage, elementary, secondary education, *84.060*

international peace, conflict resolution, *91.001, 91.002*

Japan-U.S. Friendship Commission Grants, *90.300*

Learning Opportunities Grants, IMLS, *45.301*

NEH centers support, *45.161*

NEH curriculum, materials development, *45.162*

NEH fellowships, *45.160, 45.161*

NEH Public Programs, *45.164*

NEH Professional Development, *45.163*

NSF, cultural anthropology, *47.075*

Smithsonian fellowships, *85.601*

teacher training seminars abroad, *84.018*

Woodrow Wilson Center fellowships, *85.300*

see also Arts, arts education; Foreign languages; History; Humanities; International programs, studies; Libraries; Museums, galleries; Social sciences; Teacher education, training

Hunter safety programs, *15.611*

Hunting, *see* Public safety; Wildlife, waterfowl

HURRICANE SANDY COMMUNITY DEVELOPMENT BLOCK GRANT DISASTER RECOVERY GRANTS (CDBG-DR), *14.269*

HURRICANE SANDY DISASTER RELIEF ACTIVITIES-FWS, *15.677*

HURRICANE SANDY DISASTER RELIEF APPROPRIATIONS ACT SUPPLEMENTAL— NATIONAL EMERGENCY GRANTS (NEGs), *17.284*

HURRICANE SANDY DISASTER RELIEF— COASTAL RESILIENCY GRANTS, *15.153*

HURRICANE SANDY PROGRAM, *15.979*

Hurricanes

coastal zone management, *11.419*

coastal zone rehabilitation, 12.102

Emergency Management Performance Grants, *97.042*

emergency rescue, 12.103

farmland rehabilitation, *10.054*

FEMA Community Disaster Loans, *97.030*

Hazard Mitigation Grant, FEMA, *97.039*

Pre-disaster Mitigation, FEMA, *97.047*

search, rescue system, *97.025*

see also Climate; Coastal zone; Disaster assistance; Emergency assistance; Flood prevention, control

HWWS (Household Water Well System) Program, RUS, *10.862*

Hydrographic Center, NOAA, *11.400*

Inmates, *see* Corrections

INNOVATIONS IN APPLIED HEALTH RESEARCH, *93.061*

INS (Immigration and Naturalization Service), DOJ, *see* Agency Index

Inspection and Grading of Fishery Products, 11.413

INSPECTION GRADING AND STANDARDIZATION [USDA], 10.162

Inspection services, *see* Agricultural marketing; Complaint investigation; Consumers, consumer services; Dairy industry; Fisheries industry; Food inspection, grading; Livestock industry; Poultry, egg products

Institute of Education Sciences, DOED, *84.305*

Institute of Museum and Library Services (IMLS), National Foundation on the Arts and the Humanities, *see* Agency Index

Institute of Peace, 91.001 through 91.002

INSTITUTIONAL CAPACITY BUILDING [USAID], *98.005*

Institutions of higher education, *see* Higher education institutions

Insular areas, *see* U.S. possessions, territories

Insular areas community development block grants, *14.225*

Insurance

art works, artifacts, books, manuscripts, motion pictures, photographs, videotapes, *45.201*

brownfields clean-up, *66.817*

Certified Development Company Loans, *59.041*

Crop Insurance in Targeted States, *10.458*

crops, noninsured, disaster assistance, *10.451*

data, Census Bureau, 11.001

Employee Retirement Income Security Act (ERISA), *86.001*

farm crops, *10.450*

farm premium payment loans, *10.406*

FEMA community flood assistance program, *97.023*

fishing vessels, seizure, *19.204*

Flood Mitigation Assistance, *97.029*

flood, mudflow, erosion, NFIP, *97.022*

foreign investments, OPIC, *70.002*, *70.003*

GI insurance, *64.103*

Inspector General Act of 1978, *59.016*

international political risk, *70.003*

longshore, harbor workers compensation, *17.302*

maritime war risk, *20.803*

mine subsidence, *15.252*

National Service Life Insurance Act, *64.103*

pension, welfare benefits information, 17.150

pension plans, *86.001*

railroad workers, death, health, unemployment, *57.001*

relationship verification, Census Bureau, 11.006

Servicemen's Indemnity and Insurance Act, *64.103*

Social Security program research, demonstrations, *96.007*

Social Security, retirement, *96.002*

Social Security survivors, *96.004*

surety bonds, *59.016*

unemployment, *17.225*

U.S. flagships, *20.803*

veterans life, home mortgage protection, *64.103*

War Risk Insurance Act, DVA, *64.103*

World War Veterans Act, *64.103*

see also Agricultural commodities, stabilization; Agricultural loans; Employee benefits; Flood prevention, control; Health insurance; Housing *entries*; Maritime industry; Small business; Social Security Act; Veterans *entries*

INTEGRATED OCEAN OBSERVING SYSTEM, *11.012*

INTEGRATED PROGRAMS [USDA], *10.303*

INTERAGENCY HAZARDOUS MATERIALS PUBLIC SECTOR TRAINING AND PLANNING GRANTS, *20.703*

INTERCITY BUS SECURITY GRANTS [DHS], *97.057*

INTEREST REDUCTION PAYMENTS—RENTAL AND COOPERATIVE HOUSING FOR LOWER INCOME FAMILIES, *14.103*

Intergovernmental personnel, *see* Federal employment; Government

INTERGOVERNMENTAL PERSONNEL ACT (IPA) MOBILITY PROGRAM, 27.011

Intergovernmental Services Program, Census Bureau, 11.004

Interior design, *see* Architecture; Arts, arts education; Buildings; Disabled, handicapped; Disabled, handicapped, housing; Veterans housing

Interjurisdictional Fisheries Act, *see* Fisheries industry

INTERJURISDICTIONAL FISHERIES ACT OF 1986, *11.407*

INTERMEDIARY LOAN PROGRAM, *59.062*

INTERMEDIARY RELENDING PROGRAM [USDA], *10.767*

Intermediate care facilities, *see* Health facilities *entries*; Nursing homes

Internal medicine, *see* Family medicine; Health, medical education, training; Health, medical services; Osteopathy; Pediatrics

Internal Revenue Service (IRS), Department of the Treasury, *see* Agency Index

INTERNATIONAL BROADCASTING INDEPENDENT GRANTEE ORGANIZATIONS, *90.500*

International Collaborative Research and Scientific Exchanges, USDA, *10.961*

International commerce, investment

agricultural, Market Access Program, *10.601*

agricultural marketing, states, *10.156*

agricultural, rural economic research, 10.250

agricultural standards, 10.162

Agricultural Trade Act of 1978, *10.600*, *10.601*

agricultural transportation services, AMS, 10.167

agriculture, export market development, *10.600*

Agriculture, Trade and Development Assistance Act of 1954, *98.007*, *98.009*

antidumping duties, 11.106

BECA English Language Fellow Program, *19.421*

business education centers, *84.220*

Census Bureau data, 11.001

commodity distribution, developing countries, *10.606*

countervailing duties, 11.106

CSREES international agricultural science, education, *10.305*

economic data, analysis, 11.025

Emerging Markets Program, USDA, *10.603*

disclosure, reporting, 17.309

employment discrimination, 16.101, 30.001, 30.010

labor-management committees, FMCS, *34.002*

union members rights, election standards, 17.309

see also Labor *entries*

Laboratory animals

alternative, complementary medicine research, *93.213*

cancer research, *93.393, 93.394, 93.395, 93.396, 93.399*

Lyme Disease, *93.942*

mental health research, *93.242*

microbiology, infectious diseases research, *93.856*

research, research infrastructure resources, training, *93.389*

see also Animal disease control, health, welfare; Veterinary medicine

LABORATORY EQUIPMENT DONATION PROGRAM, 81.022

LABORATORY LEADERSHIP, WORKFORCE TRAINING AND MANAGEMENT DEVELOPMENT, IMPROVING PUBLIC HEALTH LABORATORY INFRASTRUCTURE, *93.065*

LABORATORY TRAINING, EVALUATION, AND QUALITY ASSURANCE PROGRAMS, *93.064*

LAKE CHAMPLAIN BASIN PROGRAM [EPA], *66.481*

LAKE MEAD/LAS VEGAS WASH PROGRAM, *15.540*

LAKE TAHOE EROSION CONTROL GRANT PROGRAM, *10.690*

LAKE TAHOE REGIONAL WETLANDS DEVELOPMENT PROGRAM, *15.543*

Lakes, *see* Great Lakes; Recreation, water; Water resources, supply, management; Wetlands

Land acquisition

airport improvement, *20.106*

business, industrial loans, rural, *10.768*

CDBG, *14.218, 14.225, 14.228, 14.862*

Coastal Program, FWS, *15.630*

coastal wetlands protection, *15.614*

endangered species conservation, *15.615*

estuaries, *11.420*

flood plain data, services, 12.104

health, related facilities, federal surplus property, 93.291

historic sites, *15.904*

Indian lands, Real Estate Programs, *15.040*

Indian reservation land, *10.421*

interstate land sales registration, 14.168

outdoor recreation, *15.916*

public land sale, donation, 39.002

Recreational Trails Program, *20.219*

Self-Help Homeownership Opportunity Program, *14.247*

subdivided land, interstate sales registration, 14.168

Wildlife Restoration, *15.611*

see also Community development; Education facilities; Family farms; Federal property; Federal surplus property; Health facilities *entries*; Homeownership, homebuying; Housing *entries*; Landowners; Mass transportation; Public lands; Subdivisions; Transportation; Urban planning

Land and Water Conservation Fund, *15.639, 15.916*

LAND BUY-BACK PROGRAM FOR TRIBAL NATIONS, *15.152*

Land grant colleges, universities

basic support, *10.205*

competitive research grants, *10.206*

1890 institutions support, *10.216*

Equity in Educational Land-Grant Status Act of 1994, *10.221, 10.222, 10.227*

Extension Service, *10.500*

farmer outreach, socially disadvantaged, *10.443*

1994 Institutions, *10.227*

Small Business Development Centers, *59.037*

sustainable agriculture research, *10.215*

tribal, agriculture, food sciences, *10.221, 10.222*

see also Agricultural education; Agricultural experiment stations; Higher education institutions

Land, public, *see* Public lands

LAND SALES—CERTAIN SUBDIVIDED LAND [HUD], 14.168

LANDOWNER INCENTIVE [DOI], *15.633*

Landowners

dam safety program, FEMA, *97.041*

Environmental Quality Incentives Program, NRCS, *10.912*

Farm and Ranch Lands Protection Program, NRCS, *10.913*

Fire Management Assistance, FEMA, *97.046*

Forest Legacy Program, *10.676*

flood plain data, services, 12.104

forestry assistance, *10.664*

FWS Landowner Incentives, *15.633*

Indian lands, Real Estate Programs, *15.040*

military/community joint land use planning, *12.610*

New Mexico, forest restoration, *10.679*

Religious Land Use and Institutionalized Persons Act of 2000 (RLUIPA), 16.103

soil surveys, 10.903

Wetlands Reserve Program, *10.072*

Wildlife Habitat Incentive Program, *10.914*

see also Agricultural *entries*; Family farms; Homeownership, homebuying; Indian lands; Land acquisition; Subdivisions

Landrum-Griffin Act, *see* Labor-Management Relations

Landscape architecture, *see* Architecture

Landscape Conservation Cooperatives, *15.557*

LANGUAGE FLAGSHIP FELLOWSHIPS, *12.553*

LANGUAGE FLAGSHIP GRANTS TO INSTITUTIONS OF HIGHER EDUCATION, *12.550*

LANGUAGE GRANT PROGRAM [DOD], *12.900*

LANGUAGE RESOURCE CENTERS [DOED], *84.229*

LANGUAGE TRAINING CENTER, *12.579*

Languages, foreign area studies, *see* Bilingual education, services; English as a second language; Foreign languages; Illiteracy; International programs, studies

LATE DISBURSEMENT INTEREST, *15.436*

Law, *see* Civil rights; Complaint investigation; Crime; Criminal justice system; FBI; Law enforcement education, training; Legal services; Legislation; Police; Public safety

LAW ENFORCEMENT ASSISTANCE—FBI ADVANCED POLICE TRAINING, 16.300

dairy products indemnification, *10.053*

Environmental Quality Incentives Program, NRCS, *10.912*

farm operating loans, *10.406*

forage research, *10.202*

Grassland Reserve Program, NRCS, *10.920*

Homeland Security—Agricultural, *10.304*

Indian lands, *10.421*, *15.034*

inspection, grading, 10.162, *10.475*, 10.477

international assistance, *10.960*

international research training, *10.962*

Navajo-Hopi Joint Use Area, *15.057*

noninsurance risk management research partnerships, *10.456*

production data, statistics, 10.950

research, *10.200*

Ruminant Feed Ban Support Project, FDA, *93.449*

sustainable agriculture research, *10.215*

Wetlands Reserve Program, *10.072*

Wild Horse and Burro Management, BLM, *15.229*

wildlife disease control, *10.028*

see also Agricultural *entries*; Animal disease control, health, welfare; Dairy industry; Poultry, egg products; Veterinary medicine

Loan Guarantees for Indian Housing, *14.865*

LOAN GUARANTEES FOR NATIVE HAWAIIAN HOUSING, *14.874*

Loan Guaranty Program, BIA, *15.124*

LOAN REPAYMENT PROGRAM FOR GENERAL RESEARCH [HHS], *93.232*

Loans, *see* Agricultural loans; Banks, banking; Business development; Credit unions; Disadvantaged, business development; Housing *entries*; Minority business enterprise; Small business; Student financial assistance

Loans for Disadvantaged Students (LDS), HRSA, *93.342*

Local Development Districts (LDD), Appalachian region, *23.009*

LOCAL FOOD PROMOTION PROGRAM, *10.172*

Local government, *see* Community development; Government; Indian affairs; Urban planning

LOCAL VETERANS' EMPLOYMENT REPRESENTATIVE PROGRAM, *17.804*

Logging, *see* Farm, nonfarm enterprises; Farm workers; Forestry; Timber industry; Woodlands

LONG ISLAND SOUND PROGRAM, *66.437*

Long Term Resource Monitoring Program (LTRMP), DOI, *15.978*

LONG TERM STANDING AGREEMENTS FOR STORAGE, TRANSPORTATION AND LEASE, *10.999*

LONG-TERM SURVEILLANCE AND MAINTENANCE, *81.136*

LONGSHORE AND HARBOR WORKERS' COMPENSATION, *17.302*

LOUISIANA STATE UNIVERSITY (LSU) COASTAL MARINE INSTITUTE (CMI), *15.422*

Low income, *see* Depressed areas; Disadvantaged *entries*; Housing, low to moderate income; Public assistance; Rural poor; Social services; Volunteers

LOW-INCOME HOME ENERGY ASSISTANCE, *93.568*

LOW-INCOME TAXPAYER CLINICS, *21.008*

LOWER COLORADO RIVER MULTI-SPECIES CONSERVATION PROGRAM, *15.538*

LOWER INCOME HOUSING ASSISTANCE PROGRAM—SECTION 8 MODERATE REHABILITATION, *14.856*

LOWER RIO GRANDE VALLEY WATER RESOURCES CONSERVATION AND IMPROVEMENT, *15.521*

LOWER SNAKE RIVER COMPENSATION PLAN, *15.661*

LSU CMI (Louisiana State University Coastal Marine Institute), *15.422*

LTRMP (Long Term Resource Monitoring Program), DOI, *15.978*

LUNG DISEASES RESEARCH, *93.838*

LUST (Leaking Underground Storage Tanks), EPA, *66.805*

LVER (Local Veterans' Employment Representative) Program, *17.804*

Lyme Disease, *93.942*

MADERA WATER SUPPLY ENHANCEMENT PROJECT, *15.551*

MAGLEV PROJECT SELECTION PROGRAM—SAFETEA—LU, *20.318*

MAGNET SCHOOLS ASSISTANCE, *84.165*

Magnuson-Stevens Fishery Conservation and Management Act, *see* Fisheries industry

Main Street (Affordable Housing Development), *14.878*

MAINSTREAM VOUCHERS, *14.879*

Management, *see* Business development; Disadvantaged, business development; Employment *entries*; Federal employment; Fellowships, scholarships, traineeships; Government; Higher education; Home management; Indian education, training; Labor-management relations; Minority business enterprise; Private sector; Small business; Social sciences; Technical training; Volunteers

MANAGEMENT INITIATIVES, *15.239*

Management-labor relations, *see* Labor-management relations

MANUFACTURED HOME DISPUTE RESOLUTION, 14.171

MANUFACTURED HOME LOAN INSURANCE—FINANCING PURCHASE OF MANUFACTURED HOMES AS PRINCIPAL RESIDENCES OF BORROWERS, *14.110*

Manufactured Home Parks, Section 207, *14.127*

Manufactured housing, *see* Homes, manufactured, mobile

MANUFACTURING AND SERVICES [USDC], 11.110

MANUFACTURING EXTENSION PARTNERSHIP, *11.611*

MAP (Market Access Program), USDA, *10.601*

Maps, charts

census geography, 11.003

census products, services, 11.001

Coast and Geodetic Survey Act, *11.400*, *11.430*

coastal ecosystem, NOAA, *11.473*

flood hazard mapping, FEMA, *97.045*

flood plain data, services, 12.104

geodetic surveys, *11.400*

geologic mapping, *15.810*

geospatial data clearinghouse, *15.809*

metropolitan statistical areas, 11.003

substance abuse, mental health services, PRNS, *93.243*

Substance Abuse Prevention and Treatment Block Grant, *93.959*

Supervised Visitation, Safe Havens for Children, OJP, *16.527*

traumatic brain injury, *93.234*, *93.267*

Unaccompanied Alien Children Program, *93.676*

Vaccines for Children Program, *93.268*

violence, children's exposure, prevention initiative, Safe Start, *16.730*

Welfare Reform Research, *93.595*

WIC Farmers' Market Nutrition Program (FMNP), *10.572*

WIC Grants to States, FNS, *10.578*

women's health, Community Centers of Excellence, *93.290*

youth, independent living education, training, *93.674*

see also Child care services; Community health services; Disabled, handicapped children; Early childhood education; Family planning; Family therapy; Head Start Program; Health, medical *entries*; Indian children; Indian health, social services; Juvenile delinquency; Parenting; Public assistance; Social Security Act; Social services; Victim assistance; Volunteers; Women; Youth *entries*

Maternal Health Research, *93.946*

MATHEMATICAL AND PHYSICAL SCIENCES, *47.049*

MATHEMATICAL SCIENCES GRANTS PROGRAM [DOD], *12.901*

Mathematics

Air Force Defense Research Sciences Program, *12.800*

Army Research Office, *12.431*

Barry M. Goldwater Scholarship Program, *85.200*

DHS Scholars and Fellows, *97.062*

DOD sciences research, fellowships, *12.630*

energy sciences research, *81.049*

mathematical sciences research, *47.049*

mathematical sciences research, education, NSA, *12.901*

Mathematics and Science Partnerships, OESE, *84.366*

measurement, engineering research, standards, *11.609*

mental health research models, *93.242*

NASA education services, 43.001

Navy research, education support, *12.300*

NSF education improvement, research, *47.075*, *47.076*

Upward Bound, *84.047*

see also Adult education; Computer products, sciences, services; Education *entries*; Engineering *entries*; Physical sciences; Science education; Scientific research; Teacher education, training

MATHEMATICS AND SCIENCE PARTNERSHIPS [DOED], *84.366*

MBDA (Minority Business Development Agency), USDC, *see* Agency Index

MCC DOMESTIC ASSISTANCE FOR OVERSEAS PROGRAMS, *85.003*

MCC FOREIGN ASSISTANCE FOR OVERSEAS PROGRAMS, *85.002*

MCH (Maternal and Child Health) Block Grant, *93.994*

MCHEP (Maternal and Child Health Epidemiology Program), *93.946*

McIntire-Stennis Act, forestry, *10.202*

McKinney homeless assistance act, *see* National housing acts (McKinney-Vento Homeless Assistance Act, Stewart B. McKinney Homeless Assistance Act)

MCSAP (Motor Carrier Safety Assistance Program), *20.218*

MDCP (Market Development Cooperation Program), ITA, *11.112*

Measurement

calibration, testing, 11.601

geodetic surveys, *11.400*

National Bureau of Standards Organic Act (NBSOA), 11.601, 11.603, 11.604, 11.606, *11.609*, 11.610

National Standard Reference Data System, 11.603

research, *11.609*

Standard Reference Materials, 11.604

standards and certification information center, NCSCI, 11.610

weights, measures service, 11.606

see also Engineering *entries*; Maps, charts; Physical sciences; Scientific research

MEASUREMENT AND ENGINEERING RESEARCH AND STANDARDS, *11.609*

MEASURES AND ANALYSES OF THE U.S. ECONOMY, 11.025

Meat, *see* Food inspection, grading; Livestock industry; Poultry, egg products

Meat and Poultry Inspection State Programs, *10.475*

MEAT, POULTRY, AND EGG PRODUCTS INSPECTION, 10.477

MECEA (Mutual Educational and Cultural Exchange Act), *see* International programs, studies

Media, *see* Arts, arts education; Audiovisual aids, film, video; Communications, telecommunications; Radio, television

Medicaid, *see* Social Security Act

MEDICAID ADULT QUALITY GRANTS, *93.609*

MEDICAID EMERGENCY PSYCHIATRIC DEMONSTRATION, AFFORDABLE CARE ACT (ACA),*93.537*

Medicaid, Title XIX, *93.778*

MEDICAL ASSISTANCE PROGRAM, *93.778*

Medical education, *see* Health, medical education, training

Medical facilities, *see* Health facilities *entries*

Medical libraries, *see* Libraries

MEDICAL LIBRARY ASSISTANCE, *93.879*

Medical research, *see* Health, medical research

MEDICAL RESERVE CORPS SMALL GRANT PROGRAM, *93.008*

Medical schools, *see* Health facilities; Health, medical education, training; Health professions

Medical services, *see* Community health services; Health, medical services; Indian health, social services; Maternal, child health, welfare; Preventive health services; Public health; Veterans health, medical services

Medical training, *see* Health, medical education, training

Medicare, *see* Social Security

PHMSA PIPELINE SAFETY RESEARCH AND DEVELOPMENT OTHER TRANSACTION AGREEMENTS, *20.723*

Photography, *see* Arts, arts education; Audiovisual aids, film, video

PHS (Public Health Service), HHS, *see* Public health

PHYSICAL DISASTER LOANS, *59.008*

Physical disasters, *see* Disaster assistance; Earthquakes; Flood prevention, control; Hurricanes

Physical fitness, *see* Health, medical services; Occupational health, safety; Recreation

Physical Fitness and Sports, 93.289

Physical sciences

Air Force Defense Research Sciences Program, *12.800*

Army Research Office, *12.431*

atmospheric, marine sciences education, research, facilities, NOAA, *11.469*

Barry M. Goldwater Scholarship Program, *85.200*

calibration, testing, NIST, 11.601

climate, air quality research, services, *11.459*

coal research, *81.057*

coastal ecosystem management, NOAA, *11.473*

DHS Scholars and Fellows, *97.062*

DOD research, fellowships, *12.630*

DOD science, technology projects, *12.910*

DOE used equipment, 81.022

energy-related, renewable resources research, *81.087*

energy sciences research, *81.049*

EPA consolidated research, *66.511*

EPA environmental sustainability design competition, *66.516*

forestry research, *10.652*

geosciences research, *47.050*

hazardous substances, multi-disciplinary research, education, *93.143*

Hydrometeorological Development, NOAA, *11.467*

measurement, engineering research, standards, *11.609*

National Standard Reference Data System, 11.603

Navy research, education support, *12.300*

NESDIS environmental sciences education, research, *11.440*

NOAA special projects, *11.460*

NOAA unallied program, *11.472*

Nuclear Energy Research Initiative, *81.121*

Polar Programs, *47.078*

research support, *47.049*

Smithsonian fellowships, *85.601*

Standard Reference Materials, 11.604

see also Aeronautics, space; Astronomy; Agricultural research, sciences; Biological sciences; Chemicals, chemistry; Climate; Earth sciences; Energy *entries*; Engineering *entries*; Environmental sciences; Forensic sciences; Geology; Marine sciences; Mathematics; Minority education; Nuclear sciences, technology; Science education; Scientific research

Physical therapy, *see* Occupational health, safety; Vocational rehabilitation

Physically handicapped, *see* Disabled, handicapped *entries*; Veterans, disabled

Physicians, *see* Family medicine; Health, medical education, training; Health professions; Osteopathy; Pediatrics

Physics, *see* Engineering *entries*; Nuclear sciences, technology; Physical sciences; Scientific research

Physiology research, *93.859*

PILT (Payments in Lieu of Taxes), BLM, *15.226*

PIMA AGRICULTURE COTTON TRUST FUND, *10.615*

PIPELINE SAFETY PROGRAM STATE BASE GRANT, *20.700*

PIPELINE SAFETY RESEARCH COMPETITIVE ACADEMIC AGREEMENT PROGRAM (CAAP), *20.724*

Pittman-Robertson (P-R) Program, FWS, *15.611*

Planetariums, *see* Museums, galleries

PLANNING AND PROGRAM DEVELOPMENT GRANTS [CNCS], *94.007*

PLANNING ASSISTANCE TO STATES [DOD], 12.110

PLANT AND ANIMAL DISEASE, PEST CONTROL, AND ANIMAL CARE, *10.025*

PLANT MATERIALS FOR CONSERVATION, 10.905

Plant Variety Protection Program, 10.163

Plants

agricultural, inspection 10.162

alternative, complementary medicine research, *93.213*

aquatic plant control, rivers, harbors, 12.100

competitive research grants, *10.206*

conservation use, *10.069*, 10.905

Crop Insurance, *10.450*

disaster assistance, noninsured crops, *10.451*

disease, pest control, *10.025*

endangered species conservation, *10.914*, *15.615*

endangered species, Indian lands, *15.051*

endangered species, pesticides enforcement, *66.700*

Environmental Quality Incentives Program, NRCS, *10.912*

EPA pesticides, toxic chemicals pollution prevention studies, training, outreach, *66.716*

Fish, Wildlife and Plant Conservation Resource Management, BLM, *15.231*

Food Stamp purchases, *10.551*

Forest Health Protection, USFS, *10.680*

FWS Challenge Cost Share, *15.642*

FWS Landowner Incentives, *15.633*

Indian lands, noxious weed eradication, *15.034*

international research exchanges, *10.961*

market promotion, protection, 10.163

plant biology research, *47.074*

Plant Protection Act, *10.025*

research, SBIR, *10.212*

sustainable agriculture research, *10.215*

USGS Gap Analysis Program, *15.811*

vegetation use, Hazard Mitigation Grant, FEMA, *97.039*

wildlife without borders programs, education, research, training, FWS, *15.640*, *15.641*

see also Agricultural *entries*; Biological sciences; Environmental management; Fruit; Pesticides; Seedlings, seeds; Vegetables

PLATTE RIVER RECOVERY IMPLEMENTATION PROGRAM, *15.544*

Playgrounds, *see* Community development; Recreation; Urban parks, playgrounds

PLUS Loans, DOED, *84.268*

Podiatry

education assistance, disadvantaged, *93.342, 93.822, 93.925*

faculty education loan repayments, disadvantaged, *93.923*

veterans, dependents services, 64.009

see also Health, medical education, training; Health professions

Poison, *see* Chemicals, chemistry; Pesticides; Toxic substances, toxicology

Poison Control Centers, *93.253*

POISON CONTROL STABILIZATION AND ENHANCEMENT, *93.253*

POLAR PROGRAMS, *47.078*

Police

Bulletproof Vest Partnership Program, *16.607*

campus crime grants, *16.525*

Community Prosecution Program, *16.609*

Cops Grants, *16.710*

criminal conspiracy, organized crime regional information sharing, *16.610*

domestic violence arrest policies, protection orders enforcement, *16.590*

drug interdiction, motor carriers, *20.218*

FBI Field Police Training, 16.302

highway safety training, vehicles, equipment, *20.600*

housing, Officer Next Door Sales Program, 14.198

Indian Law Enforcement, *15.030*

Interoperable Communications Equipment, DHS, *97.055*

justice personnel, equipment, training, planning grants, *16.738*

misconduct, prosecution, 16.109

officers' dependents educational assistance, *16.615*

officers, disability, death benefits, *16.571*

statistics, 16.305

underage drinking law enforcement, *16.727*

violence, children's exposure, prevention initiative, Safe Start, *16.730*

WMD, domestic preparedness, *97.005, 97.007*

see also Crime; Criminal justice system; FBI; Law enforcement education, training; Public safety; Rescue services

Political Risk Insurance, OPIC, *70.003*

POLICY RESEARCH AND EVALUATION GRANTS [HHS], *93.239*

Pollution, *see* Air pollution; Pollution abatement; Water pollution abatement, prevention

Pollution abatement

agriculture-related research, SBIR, *10.212*

air, prevention, effects studies, demonstrations, *66.034*

coal mining, *15.250*

coal research, *81.057*

coastal, estuarine areas research, *11.426*

Compliance Assistance Centers, EPA, *66.305*

Conservation Security Program, NRCS, *10.921*

control techniques surveys, studies, EPA R&D, *66.510*

DOD sites, reimbursements, *12.113*

DOE industrial, agricultural, (NICE3), *81.105*

Environmental Information Exchange Network Grants, *66.608*

environmental justice projects, *66.604*

Environmental Justice Surveys and Studies, EPA, *66.309*

environmental policy, programs innovation, stewardship, studies, analyses, *66.611*

EPA consolidated program support, *66.600*

EPA consolidated research, *66.511*

EPA environmental sustainability design competition, *66.516*

EPA Performance Partnership Grants, *66.605*

EPA State Information Grants, *66.608*

EPA studies, special purpose assistance, *66.610*

estuary protection, *66.456*

hazardous wastes control, management, *66.801*

Indian lands, environmental management, *66.926*

mine land reclamation, *15.252*

National Ocean Pollution Planning Act of 1978, *11.426*

airports, air, noise, water, *20.106*

Ozone Transport, *66.033*

Pesticide Environmental Stewardship, *66.714*

pesticides control, *66.700*

petroleum underground storage tank program, *66.805*

Pollution Prevention Act of 1990 (PPA), *66.110, 66.708*

prevention information projects, *66.708*

rural business, industrial loans, *10.768*

senior environmental employment programs, *66.508, 66.518*

source reduction information dissemination, outreach, EPA, *66.717*

standards, testing, 11.604

STAR (Science to Achieve Results) Research Program, EPA, *66.509*

Superfund technical assistance to citizen groups, *66.806*

tribal direct implementation agreements, EPA, *66.473*

underground storage tanks, *66.804, 66.816*

POLLUTION PREVENTION GRANTS PROGRAM, *66.708*

Population research

adolescent family life, *93.995*

AIDS/HIV epidemiologic studies, *93.943*

Cancer Centers Support, *93.397*

Cancer Control, *93.399*

Census Bureau data, 11.001

Census Intergovernmental Services, 11.004

census services, 11.005

contraception, infertility research, education loan repayments, *93.209*

family planning services, *93.217, 93.974*

Vital Statistics Reengineering Program, CDCP, *93.066*

see also Alaska, Alaska natives; Census services; Epidemiology; Family planning; Hawaii, Hawaii natives; Indian *entries*; Rural areas; Social sciences; Statistics

Pork, *see* Agricultural marketing; Food inspection, grading; Livestock industry

PORT SECURITY GRANT PROGRAM, *97.056*

Secondary education, *see* Elementary and secondary education

Secretaries of Military Departments, DOD, *see* Agency Index

Section 3 Emergency Dredging Projects, 12.109

SECTION 4 CAPACITY BUILDING FOR COMMUNITY DEVELOPMENT AND AFFORDABLE HOUSING, *14.252*

Section 7, Fishermen's Protective Act, *19.204*

Section 7(a) Loans, SBA, *59.012, 59.054*

Section 7(b) Loans, SBA, *59.008*

Section 7(J) Program, SBA, *59.007*

Section 8 Housing Assistance Payments Program for Very Low Income Families, Moderate Rehabilitation, *14.856*

SECTION 8 HOUSING ASSISTANCE PAYMENTS PROGRAM, *14.195*

SECTION 8 HOUSING ASSISTANCE PAYMENTS PROGRAM SPECIAL ALLOCATIONS, *14.317*

SECTION 8 HOUSING CHOICE VOUCHERS, *14.871*

Section 8(a) Business Development, SBA, 59.006

Section 22, Water Resources Development Act, 12.110

Section 104(b)(3), Clean Water Act, studies, *66.436*

Section 106 Grants, Clean Water Act, *66.419*

Section 106, 111, Clean Air Act, *66.033*

Section 108 Loan Guarantees, HUD, *14.248*

Section 166, WIA Indian Program, *17.265*

Section 184A, native Hawaiian housing loan guarantees, *14.874*

Section 202 Agreements, BLM, *15.222*

SECTION 202 ASSISTED LIVING CONVERSION FOR ELIGIBLE MULTIFAMILY HOUSING PROJECTS, *14.314*

Section 202, supportive housing, *14.157, 14.314*

Section 203 Grants for Planning and Administrative Expenses, EDA, *11.302*

Section 203(b), NHA, home mortgage insurance, *14.117*

Section 203(b), 203(k), 204, HUD single-family property disposition, 14.311

Section 203(h), NHA, disaster victims mortgage insurance, *14.119*

Section 203(k), NHA, housing rehabilitation, *14.108*

Section 203(n), NHA, cooperative housing, *14.163*

Section 205(j)(2), Clean Water Act, *66.454*

Section 207 Manufactured Home Parks, NHA, *14.127*

Section 207, NHA, middle-income rental housing, *14.134*

Section 208, snagging, clearing waterways, 12.108

Section 213 Cooperatives, NHA, *14.126*

Section 220 Multifamily, NHA, urban renewal areas, *14.139*

Section 220 Homes, urban renewal areas, *14.122*

Section 221(d) Single Room Occupancy, NHA, *14.184*

Section 221(d)(3) and (4) Multifamily-Market Rate Housing, NHA, *14.135*

Section 223(e), NHA, declining areas, *14.123*

Section 223(f) and 207, NHA, existing multifamily housing, *14.155*

Section 231, NHA, rental housing, elderly, *14.138*

Section 232 Nursing Homes, NHA, *14.129*

Section 234(c), NHA, condominiums, *14.133*

Section 236 Interest Reduction Payments, NHA, *14.103*

Section 241(a), NHA, multifamily housing, health care facilities, *14.151*

Section 242 Hospitals, NHA, *14.128*

SECTION 245 GRADUATED PAYMENT MORTGAGE PROGRAM, *14.159*

Section 245(a), NHA, Growing Equity Mortgages, *14.172*

Section 251 Adjustable Rate Mortgages, NHA, *14.175*

Section 255, NHA, home equity conversion mortgages, *14.183*

Section 301 and 317, PHSA, *93.268*

Section 306C, RUS, *10.770*

Section 319 Program, Clean Water Act, *66.460*

Section 406, safety belt performance, *20.609*

Section 502 Rural Housing Loans, *10.410*

Section 503 Grants, WIA, *17.267*

Section 504 Loans, SBA, *59.041*

Section 504 Rural Housing Loans and Grants, *10.417*

Section 514 and 516, labor housing, *10.405*

Section 515 and 521, rural rental housing, *10.415*

Section 521, Rural Rental Assistance Payments, *10.427*

Section 523 Technical Assistance, self-help housing, *10.420*

Section 533, rural housing, *10.433*

SECTION 538 RURAL RENTAL HOUSING GUARANTEED LOANS, *10.438*

Section 542(b) Risk Sharing Program, HUD, *14.189*

Section 542(c) Risk Sharing Program, HUD, *14.188*

Section 638 ISDEAA, *93.441*

Section 811, supportive housing, disabled, *14.181*

Section 1110, 1115, SSA, child support enforcement, *93.563*

Section 1442, Safe Drinking Water Act, studies, *66.424*

Section 1906, prohibiting racial profiling, *20.611*

Section 1928, SSA, immunization, *93.268*

Section 2010, motorcyclist safety, *20.612*

Section 2011, child safety, booster seats, *20.613*

Section 5303, Metropolitan Planning, FTA, *20.505*

Section 5307, Urbanized Area Formula Program, FTA, *20.507*

Section 5309, Capital Investment Grants, FTA, *20.500*

Section 5310, Elderly and Disabled, FTA, *20.513*

Section 5311, Nonurbanized Formula Grants, FTA, *20.509*

Section 5314(a), Transit Planning and Research Projects, FTA, *20.514*

Section 8044, Corps of Engineers, 12.116

SECURE RURAL SCHOOLS AND COMMUNITY SELF-DETERMINATION, *15.234*

SECURE WATER ACT—RESEARCH AGREEMENTS, *15.560*

SECURING THE CITIES PROGRAM, *97.106*

Securities Act of 1933, 58.001

Securities and Exchange Commission (SEC), 58.001

SECURITIES—INVESTIGATION OF COMPLAINTS AND SEC INFORMATION, 58.001

SED (Serious Emotional Disturbances), HHS, *93.104*

coastal ecosystem management, NOAA, *11.473*

computer sciences research, *47.070*

Corps of Engineers Construction Productivity Advanced Research, *12.114*

data, trends, 17.004

disabled, educational technology, *84.327*

DOD science, technology projects, *12.910*

DOE Advanced Simulation and Computing Academic Strategic Alliances Program, *81.112*

DOE environmental cleanup, technology development, *81.104*

education project technical assistance, *84.283*

electricity delivery, energy reliability, DOE, *81.122*

energy conservation, research, *81.086*

energy-related, renewable resources, research, development, *81.087*

energy sciences research, *81.049*

foreign language resource centers, *84.229*

forestry assistance, *10.664*

geosciences, research, *47.050*

hazardous waste alternative, innovative treatment research, training, EPA, *66.813*

homeland security technology development, DHS, *97.077*

Information Analysis Infrastructure Protection, DHS, *97.080*

Manufacturing Extension Partnership, NIST, *11.611*

measurement, engineering projects, *11.609*

NASA education services, 43.001

NASA Technology Transfer, 43.002

National Center for Preservation Technology and Training, *15.923*

NSF engineering, *47.041*

NSF research, *47.075*

NSF technology education reform, *47.076*

patent, trademark information, 11.900

Semiconductor Chip Protection Act of 1984, 42.008

Technology Administration Act of 1998, *11.611*

Technology Marketing Unit, small wood species, USFS, *10.674*

University-Based Homeland Security Centers, DHS, *97.061*

see also Business development; Computer products, sciences, services; Engineering *entries*; Information *entries*; Nuclear sciences, technology; Patents, trademarks, inventions; Private sector; Scientific research; Small Business Innovation Research (SBIR)

TEENAGE PREGNANCY PREVENTION PROGRAM, *93.297*

Teenagers, *see* Juvenile delinquency; Maternal, child health, welfare; Youth *entries*

TEFAP (Temporary Emergency Food Assistance Program), *10.557*

Telecommunication, *see* Communications, telecommunications; Computer products, sciences, services

TELEHEALTH PROGRAMS, *93.211*

Telephone service, *see* Communications, telecommunications; Hotlines; Public utilities

Television, *see* Radio, television

Television Demonstration Grants (TDG), rural, *10.769*

TEMPORALLY INTEGRATED MONITORING OF ECOSYSTEMS (TIME) AND LONG-TERM MONITORING (LTM) PROGRAM, *66.042*

TEMPORARY ASSISTANCE FOR NEEDY FAMILIES, *93.558*

TEMPORARY ASSISTANCE FOR NEEDY FAMILIES (TANF) SUPPLEMENTAL GRANTS, *93.716*

Temporary Emergency Food Assistance Program (TEFAP), *10.557*

TEMPORARY LABOR CERTIFICATION FOR FOREIGN WORKERS, *17.273*

Tennis courts, public, *15.916*

TERRITORIES AND FREELY ASSOCIATED STATES EDUCATION GRANT PROGRAM, *84.256*

Terrorism, anti-terrorism, *see* Civil defense

THE MARGIN PROTECTION PROGRAM, *10.116*

THE U.S. PRESIDENT'S EMERGENCY PLAN FOR AIDS RELIEF PROGRAMS, *19.029*

Theater, *see* Arts, arts education; Music

Thermal energy, *see* Energy *entries*

THOMAS R. PICKERING FOREIGN AFFAIRS FELLOWSHIP PROGRAM, *19.013*

TIF (Teacher Incentive Funds), *84.374*

TIFIA Credit Program (Transportation Infrastructure Finance and Innovation Act), *20.223*

TIGER (Topologically Integrated Geographic Encoding and Referencing) system, 11.003

Timber industry

cooperative forestry assistance, *10.664*

Fire Management Assistance, FEMA, *97.046*

forest products utilization research, *10.202*

futures trading information, customer complaints, 78.004

Indian lands, *15.035*

disaster assistance, noninsured crops, *10.451*

research, forestry, *10.652*

see also Farm, nonfarm enterprises; Forestry; Woodlands

Title I, ADA, 30.011

Title I, ESEA, Basic, Concentration, and Targeted Grants, *84.010*

Title I, ESEA, migrants, *84.011*

Title I, ESEA, neglected, delinquent, *84.013*

TITLE I GRANTS TO LOCAL EDUCATIONAL AGENCIES, *84.010*

Title I, Section 2, NHA, manufactured homes, *14.110, 14.162*

Title I, Section 2, NHA, nonresidential, residential improvement, *14.142*

TITLE I STATE AGENCY PROGRAM FOR NEGLECTED AND DELINQUENT CHILDREN AND YOUTH, *84.013*

Title II, Civil Rights Act, public accommodations, 16.103

Title II Grants, Indian Child Welfare Act, *15.144*

Title II, IV, OAA, Discretionary Projects, *93.048*

Title III, HEA, Institutional Aid, *84.031*

Title III, Part B, OAA, supportive services, senior centers, *93.044*

Title III, Part C, OAA, Nutrition Services, *93.045*

Title III, Part F, OAA, preventive health services, *93.043*

Title IV, Civil Rights Act, 16.100

Title IV, Fishermen's Contingency Fund, *11.408*